The
ILLUSTRATED
ENCYCLOPEDIA
of
MUSIC

The
ILLUSTRATED
ENCYCLOPEDIA
of
MUSIC

introduction by RICHARD BAKER

edited by ALAN ISAACS *&* ELIZABETH MARTIN

GALLERY BOOKS
An Imprint of W. H. Smith Publishers Inc.
112 Madison Avenue
New York City 10016

USING THIS ENCYCLOPEDIA

The strictly alphabetical arrangement of the entries and the network of cross references make this encyclopedia very simple to use. Asterisks in the text indicate where further information relevant to the entry being read can be found.

In listing the titles of works we have given the version most commonly used in English-speaking countries, rather than invariably giving the English version. Thus **Magic Flute, The** and not **Zauberflöte, Die** carries the main entry, the German version being simply a cross reference. On the other hand Strauss's *Die Fledermaus* will be found under **Fledermaus, Die,** rather than **Bat, The.**

CONTRIBUTORS

Joan Ashley BA, LRAM
Tony Attwood BA, M Phil
John Burke
James Chater BA, D Phil
Graham Dixon MA, B Mus (Dunelm), BMus (Lond.)
Margaret Gilmore MA
David Harvey
George A. Hooper
D.L. Humphries MA, PhD
Jonathan Hunt MA
Jonathan Katz MA
Christopher Kent M Mus, PhD, FRCO
Alison Latham B Mus
Gordon Lawson MA, Mus B, ARCM
Martin Penney MA
R.D. Taylor B Mus
Andrew Wathey BA
Philip Welch MSc, D Phil
Ewan West BA
Christopher R. Wilson MA

First published in 1990 by The Hamlyn Publishing Group Limited
Michelin House, 81 Fulham Road, London SW3 6RB

This edition published in 1990 by Gallery Books
An imprint of W.H. Smith Publishers Inc.,
112 Madison Avenue, New York, New York 10016

© Copyright The Hamlyn Publishing Group Limited 1982, 1990

ISBN 0 831 74840 0
Printed in Portugal

PREFACE

In a decade that has seen the publication of Stanley Sadie's *The New Grove Dictionary of Music and Musicians* in 20 volumes, one may wonder what justification there could be for producing an entirely new one-volume encyclopedia of music.

While Grove's remains the supreme reference book on music for scholars it will usually be consulted in a library. This volume is designed as a personal handbook for the musician, music student, and music lover; it will not provide critical opinion or detailed analysis of composers and their works. What it will do, however, is to answer many of the questions that we all ask from time to time. How did the western scale develop? From what instrument did the violin evolve? Who wrote *The Violins of St Jacques*? In what year was Busoni born? In what key is Haydn's *Clock Symphony*? Which of the Strauss's wrote the 'Radetsky March'? Who was the cellist of the Amadeus Quartet?

It is this kind of question that we have in mind in compiling this book. While opinions have largely been avoided, the editors take full responsibility for inclusions and omissions, which do represent an implied opinion of relative importance.

Finally, we would like to thank our distinguished team of contributors, who have enabled us to claim the wide scope and accuracy essential to a reference book of this kind.

AL, EAM

Foreword

'Music', wrote the Chinese philosopher Confucius, 'produces a kind of pleasure human nature cannot do without'. He knew what he was talking about, for he was deeply affected by music; so much so that after listening to an orchestra on one occasion he was unable to taste his food for three months. Few music lovers, however passionately addicted they are to the art, experience such drastic after-effects, but the words of Confucius are just as valid today as they were when they were written two and a half thousand years ago.

There is so much music, of so many different kinds, and the effects it produces on the human organism vary widely too. Music can inspire and console us: it can also amuse and entertain. Whatever it seeks to tell us, it goes beyond words. In its direct appeal to the intellect and the emotions, it is the one universal language. Not the least of its merits is that it is capable of addressing the whole of mankind and bringing together people of every race in a shared experience. I certainly can't imagine what my life would have been like without music. When I was young, my father sang and my mother accompanied him on the piano. I started to learn the piano when I was seven and soon my mother and I were playing duets. That kind of music making was, and still is, fun. But my father also took me to the old Queen's Hall in London, to listen to the Proms conducted by Sir Henry Wood, and that was the beginning of a wider acquaintance with the great world of music. From Gilbert and Sullivan I graduated to grand opera and ballet, and night after night I queued patiently with other enthusiasts to get into the gallery at Covent Garden.

My life since then has brought me more musical rewards than I could have dreamed of. My musical talents were never sufficient to make me a professional performer, but they did help to make me a good listener, and listeners are vital to the art of music. What is more, a lifetime of broadcasting, much of it in the musical field, has brought me face to face with many of the world's leading musicians. From them I have learned what it means to cope with one of the most exacting of professions, and how much devoted toil is required to produce the kind of pleasure human beings find so essential.

Now if, as we have said, music is a language which goes beyond words, what need have we of words to describe music? What is the point of a book such as this one? Well, books shouldn't come between us and the music; the message that comes to us direct from the music is what matters most. But once a piece of music has got through to us, it is of the utmost interest to discover who wrote it and why. The circumstances surrounding the creation of music can have real relevance to the nature of that music, and to know a little about it adds depth to our direct musical experience. To me it is the ultimate form of flattery when a professional musician tells me that he's listened to a radio or television programme of mine and found what I've had to say about the music interesting.

Where do I get my information? Of course there are music reference books which are indispensable if you want to go into a certain subject deeply; but here in one volume you have all the essential facts in easily accessible form. It's a down-to-earth presentation of what you really want to know. Just one of the attractive features for me is that you can start by looking up the title of a particular piece that's taken your fancy and go on from there.

However you use it, I am sure you will find the *Illustrated Encyclopaedia of Music* a perfect guide and companion to the art Confucius could not live without.

Richard Baker

A

A The keynote of the scale of A major. It is the note used to tune the instruments of an orchestra. The frequency of A above *middle C is, by international agreement, 440 hertz.

Aaron, Pietro (*c*.1480–*c*.1550) Italian composer and theorist. By 1525 he was maestro of the Order of St John of Jerusalem in Venice. In 1536 he took holy orders and moved to Bergamo. He was associated with Willaert in Venice and claimed to have known Josquin, Obrecht, and Isaac. An important theorist, Aaron discusses modes, counterpoint, and tuning in his most notable work, *Toscanello* (1523).

ab Off. A direction to release a pedal, mute, or organ stop. [German]

Abbado, Claudio (1933–) Italian conductor. He is principal conductor of the Vienna Philharmonic Orchestra (1971–), musical director of La Scala, Milan (1971–), and principal conductor of the London Symphony Orchestra (1979–). Abbado excels in the 19th- and 20th-century repertoire.

Abegg Variations Variations for piano (Op. 1) by Schumann. Composed: 1830. The work is dedicated to 'Countess Abegg,' undoubtedly Schumann's friend Meta von Abegg (although she was not actually a countess). Using German pitch names a theme A–B♭–E–G–G can be derived from her name and this is used by Schumann as the basis for his variations.

Abel, Carl Friedrich (1723–87) German composer and viola da gamba player. He worked in Leipzig and Dresden before going to London in 1759, where he organized the Bach–Abel concerts with J. C. Bach. He wrote many works for the viola da gamba, symphonies, a sinfonia concertante, and other chamber works.

Absil, Jean (**Nicolas Joseph**) (1893–1974) Belgian composer, founder and director of the Etterbeck Academie (1922–64) and professor at the Royal Conservatory of Brussels (1930–59). His works include four symphonies, chamber music, and the opera *Les Voix de la mer* (1951).

absolute music see abstract music.

absolute pitch The ability to recognize or produce a note of a particular *pitch without reference to any other note. In **relative pitch** a note is recognized or produced on the basis of its *interval from another note that is heard. While it is fairly easy to acquire relative pitch with training it is less easy to learn absolute pitch. Many, but not all, musicians possess absolute pitch.

abstract music 1. (*or* **absolute music**) Instrumental music free from romantic or programmatic elements. **2.** In Germany, music that is dry or academic, i.e. lacking in sensitivity. German: **abstrakte Musik**.

Claudio Abbado

Christopher Hogwood at the piano conducting the ensemble of the Academy of Ancient Music

Abt, Franz (Wilhelm) (1819–85) German composer. He was an outstanding choral conductor, holding appointments first in Zürich then as chief kapellmeister at the Brunswick Court Theatre (1855–82). Of his output of over 3000 works, many are songs and part songs in a pleasing simple style.

Abu Hassan Comic opera in one act by Weber with libretto by Heimer, based on an Arabian fairy tale of escaping debtors. First performance: Munich, 1811.

Academic Festival Overture Overture (Op. 80) by Brahms. Composed: 1880; first performance: Breslau, 1881. Brahms wrote the overture, together with its companion work the *Tragic Overture* (1880), in recognition of the honorary doctorate conferred upon him by Breslau University in 1879. German student songs form the basis of the work, the most famous being 'Gaudeamus Igitur.'

academy A society for the study of science and the humanities. Modern academies originated in Italy during the Renaissance and by the 16th century there were many of them, some for specialized musical study. They spread to other European centres and many became concert-promoting organizations (in Germany, *Akademie* often meant concert). The **Academy of Ancient Music** was a society founded in London in 1710; it is also the title of an ensemble founded in 1973 to perform 17th- and 18th-century music. The *Academy of St Martin-in-the-Fields is a London orchestra. During the 19th century teaching institutions became known as academies; an example is the *Royal Academy of Music. See also **Singakademie.**

Academy of St Martin-in-the-Fields British chamber orchestra founded in 1959. It was formed by Neville Marriner, its director until 1978, to give concerts at the church of St Martin-in-the-Fields, Trafalgar Square, London. Consisting mainly of strings, it at first specialized in 18th-century music, but its repertory has expanded to include modern works and it now has an international reputation. Iona Brown became director in 1978.

Accardo, Salvatore (1941–) Italian violinist and conductor. After winning the Paganini Prize at Genoa in 1958 he soon became internationally renowned as a soloist, although he also appears frequently as a chamber-music player and conductor. Accardo teaches at the Accademia Chigiana in Siena.

accelerando Accelerating. Used to indicate a gradually quickening pace. [Italian]

accent The way in which rhythmic stress is applied to the beats in a bar of music. The *rhythm of a piece of music is determined in the notation by the way in which it is divided into bars, the number and kind of beats in the bar, and the way in which the beats are accented. The usual method of achieving a rhythmic quality is for the first beat in the bar to carry the primary accent. If there are more than three beats in the bar there is also usually a secondary accent, less strongly stressed than the primary accent. For example, if there are four beats to the bar, the first beat carries the primary accent and the third beat the secondary accent. However, accents are sometimes changed, transferred (*see* syncopation), or omitted by placing a rest at the beginning of a bar. Unusually placed accents are denoted by the sign > or the letters *sf* (*sforzando*) or *fz* (*forzando*) placed over the note to be stressed.

acciaccatura A musical ornament consisting of one, two (double acciaccatura), or three (triple acciaccatura) notes squeezed in before a regular note, which retains its accent and most of its time value. Sometimes the acciaccatura is played simultaneously with the regular note but almost immediately released. The acciaccatura is written in small type before the regular note and often has a stroke through its tail. Compare **appoggiatura**. [from Italian *acciacciare*, to crush]

accidental 1. A note in a piece of music that departs from the key given by the *key signature. **2.** A sign to denote such a note by raising or lowering its pitch by a semitone (sharp, flat, or natural sign) or a whole tone (double sharp or double flat). The sharp sign (♯) raises the note by a semitone, the flat sign (♭) lowers it by a semitone, and the natural sign (♮) restores a note flattened or sharpened by the key signature, or by a previous sharp or flat sign in the same bar, to the original note. By convention, an accidental sign applies to the note to which it is attached and any subsequent notes of the same pitch in that bar or to any notes to which it is tied in subsequent bars.

accompaniment The provision of a musical background to a solo voice or instrument or to a choir. While the accompaniment may be provided by an orchestra, ensemble, or organ, it is more frequently provided by a piano. Although the pianist in such a role appears to be of lesser importance than the soloist, the art of the accompanist requires great skill, tact, and musical humility; it may also be technically very demanding (as in many 19th-century lieder).

accordatura The tuning of an instrument, especially the pitches to which the strings of a stringed instrument are tuned. [Italian, tuning]

accordion A portable *reed organ containing a set of metal reeds. The reeds are forced to vibrate by air from a bellows operated by the player's arms. The notes are selected by buttons operated by the player's fingers or, in the case of a **piano accordion**, by a piano-type keyboard for the right hand and buttons for the left hand. The accordion was invented in Germany by Friedrich Buschmann in 1822. It is used extensively for playing informal music, but has not found a place in serious music making. See also **concertina**; **melodeon**.

Accursed Huntsman, The see **Chasseur maudit, Le**.

Achtel Quaver. Hence **Achtelpause**, quaver rest. [German, eighth part]

Acis and Galatea Masque by Handel with text by John Gay (with additions by Pope, Hughes, and Dryden). Composed: Canons, about 1718–20 (the date is missing in the autograph), and privately performed there. First public production: Haymarket Theatre, London, 1732. The pastoral theme is centred around the two lovers of the title and a jealous one-eyed giant, Polyphemus.

acoustic bass see **combination tones**.

acoustics 1. The branch of physics concerned with sound and sound waves. In music, the basic acoustic characteristics of a sound are its *pitch, loudness (or intensity), and its *tone colour (*or* timbre). See also **harmonics**. **2.** The characteristics of a building or an *auditorium that enable music and speech to be heard in it without distortion.

action 1. The mechanism between the keyboards and stops of an organ and the pipes. Initially this was mechanical, by **tracker action**, using rods and levers known as trackers to open the pallets from the wind chest to allow air to enter the pipes. The increase in size of organs led to very heavy keys and uneven playing. A variety of solutions were devised of which two survive: from the mid-19th century came **pneumatic action**, using compressed air in tubes to operate the pallets; slightly later **electric action** was used depending on electric relays. These provide fixed playing weight but deny the player any control over the starting and stopping of the pipe's sound. For this reason some modern instruments are now built with tracker action. The *stops controlled by the player operate sliders enabling the player to select a rank of pipes in the organ.

2. The mechanism that initiates the vibration of the strings on depressing a key in a stringed keyboard instrument. In *harpsichord instruments the action consists of sets of jacks, each of which is lifted when a key is depressed. A quill or leather plectrum attached to the jack plucks the string as the jack rises. When the key is released a pivot on the jack enables it to fall back without plucking the string. In the *piano the action is more complicated. When a key is depressed a hammer with a felt or leather head strikes the string or strings, the escapement mechanism enabling the hammer to return, even when the key remains depressed. At the same time the individual string dampers are raised from the string and remain raised until the key is released. The sustaining pedal raises all the dampers and keeps them raised until the pedal is released.

act tune (*or* **curtain music**) Instrumental music played before and between the acts of a play. After the Restoration, composers usually wrote act tunes for particular plays, such as Locke's music for *The Tempest*, printed with *Psyche* (1675), or Purcell's set of tunes for Congreve's comedy *The Double Dealer* (1693). French: **entr'acte**, **divertissement**; German: **Zwischenspiel**.

adagietto 1. (adj.) Slow. Used to indicate a slow pace, but not as slow as adagio. **2.** (n.) A short piece in adagio tempo. [Italian, a little adagio]

adagio 1. (adj.) Slow. Used to indicate a slow pace, generally not as slow as largo. **2.** (n.) A piece or movement in slow tempo. [Italian]

Adam, Adolphe (Charles) (1803–56) French composer and critic. He studied with Benoist, Reicha, and Boieldieu at the Paris Conservatoire, where he became a professor in 1849. He was a prolific composer of stage works but also wrote sacred music and songs. *Le Chalet* (1834), *Le Postillon de Lonjumeau* (1836), and *Si j'étais roi* (1852) are among his most successful opéras comiques but he is best known for his ballet *Giselle* (1841). Adam contributed criticism to Paris journals.

Adam, Theo (1926–) German bass singer. He studied with Dittrich in Dresden before making his debut there in 1949. Outstanding as a Wagner interpreter and oratorio singer, he is one of the leading Wotans of his day.

Adamis, Michael (1929–) Greek composer. His freely serial works emphasize sound textures and include *Anakyklesis* (1964). He heads an electronic music studio and has written mixed-media works, such as *Genesis* (1968).

Adam Zero Ballet in one act with music by Bliss, scenario by Michael Benthall, and choreography by Helpmann. First performance: Covent Garden, London, 1946, by the Sadler's Wells Ballet. It is about the creation of a ballet, symbolizing man's journey through life.

added sixth A chord formed by the addition to the triad of the sixth note from the root; for example in C major it would be CEGA. The added sixth most frequently occurs as an elaboration of the subdominant chord, i.e. FACD.

Addinsell, Richard (Stuart) (1904–77) British composer. After reading law at Oxford, he studied music at the Royal College of Music in London and then in Europe. He composed music for films, theatre, and radio, light music, and songs. Perhaps his greatest success was the Rachmaninov-like *Warsaw Concerto*, from the score of the film *Dangerous Moonlight* (1942).

Addison, John (1920–) British composer. He studied in London at the Royal College of Music under Gordon Jacob and later taught there (1951–58). His stage works include ballets, musicals, and incidental music; concert pieces include *Variations* for piano and orchestra (1948). Since 1958 he has written mainly for films, including scores for *Tom Jones* (1963) and *The Charge of the Light Brigade* (1968).

Adélaïde Concerto Violin concerto attributed to Mozart. In 1934 Marius Casadesus published the concerto, having edited the orchestral accompaniment from a manuscript containing little more than the solo part. The concerto was supposedly written at Versailles in 1766 and dedicated to the French Princess Adélaïde, but although Mozart is known to have written a violin concerto for the princess it is generally considered that this is unlikely to be the work. Stylistically it is unlike Mozart's works of this period and, furthermore, it is not included in the catalogue of his music made by his father in 1768.

Adieux, Les Piano sonata in E♭ (Op. 81) by Beethoven. Composed: 1809. Beethoven himself entitled the sonata *Les Adieux, l'absence et le retour* referring to the departure from Vienna of Archduke Rudolph during the French occupation. The three movements describe in turn the Archduke's farewell, absence, and return to Vienna.

Adler, Larry (1914–) US mouth-organ player, resident in England. He is one of the first exponents of the mouth organ as a concert instrument; Vaughan Williams, Milhaud, Malcolm Arnold, Gordon Jacob, and others have written works for him.

ad lib At will or discretion. Used to indicate that a passage may be played without adhering to strict tempo but at the discretion of the performer or that the inclusion of a passage, part, or instrument so marked is optional. It is also used to indicate that the player may extemporize. Italian: **a piacere**. [from Latin *ad libitum*]

Adriana Lecouvreur Opera by Cilea with libretto by Colautti. First performance: Teatro Lirico, Milan, 1902. The story is based on the play *Adrienne Lecouvreur* by Scribe, about an 18th-century actress at the Comédie Française.

Aegyptische Helena, Die (*The Egyptian Helen*) Opera in two acts by Richard Strauss with libretto by Hofmannsthal. First performance: Dresden, 1928. It is set after the Trojan War and concerns the reinstatement of Helen as wife of Menelaus through the supernatural intervention of the Egyptian sorceress Aithra.

aeolian harp A type of zither in which the strings are sounded by the wind. The strings are all the same length, but being of different thicknesses they sound a chord when placed in a draught. Of great antiquity, there is a legend that the biblical King David slept with such an instrument over his bed. In the 18th and 19th centuries aeolian harps were placed in parks and in the roofs of ruined castles, their ghostly chords adding a gothic element to the tranquil country scene.

Aeolian mode see **modes**.

Aeolian Quartet British string quartet founded in 1927. It was originally called the Stratton Quartet after George Stratton, its first leader. The quartet's personnel has changed frequently but from 1970 the members have been Emanuel Hurwitz and Raymond Keenlyside (violins), Margaret Major (viola), and Derek Simpson (cello). Their performances of Haydn have been particularly praised for the way in which they clarify the individual voices in the quartet texture, a characteristic of all their interpretations.

aerophone A musical *instrument in which the sound is produced by a vibrating column of air. Aerophones include organs, *reed instruments (e.g. harmonium, clarinet, oboe, bassoon), instruments with cup mouthpieces in which the note is made by the player's lips (e.g. horns, trumpets, trombones), instruments with blow holes (e.g. flutes) or whistle mouthpieces (e.g. recorders), and free aerophones, in which the instruments are made to travel through stationary air (e.g. buzzers and bull roarers). See also **wind instruments**. Compare **chordophone; idiophone; membranophone.**

affettuoso Tender; with tender feeling. Hence **affettuosamente**, affectionately. [Italian]

affrettando Hurrying; hastening. Used to indicate an increase in speed. [Italian]

Africaine, L' Opera in five acts by Meyerbeer with libretto by Scribe. First performance (posthumously): Opéra, Paris, 1865. It concerns the explorer Vasco da Gama and the two women who love him: Inez, to whom he is betrothed, and the captive African queen Selika. The opera demands elaborate staging, Act III being set at sea.

Afternoon of a Faun, The see **Après-midi d'un faune, Prélude à l'.**

Agazzari, Agostino (1578–?1640) Italian composer and organist. In 1602 Agazzari was appointed maestro at the German College in Rome and by 1603 he was maestro at the Roman Seminary, but he returned to his birthplace, Siena, in 1607, acting as organist there for a short period. Agazzari's works chiefly comprise motets with basso continuo. *Del Sonare sopra'l basso* (1607) was one of the first treatises on the basso continuo. Other compositions include madrigals and the theatrical work *Eumelio* (1606), which uses recitative.

Age of Anxiety, The Symphony No. 2 for piano and orchestra by Bernstein. First performance: 1949. The title is from W. H. Auden's poem *The Age of Anxiety.* In 1950 the symphony was used as a ballet score.

agitato Agitated; excited. Used to indicate a rapid tempo. [Italian]

Agnus Dei The penultimate section of the Ordinary or Common of the Latin *Mass (in polyphonic settings it usually forms the last part, and in the Requiem Mass it is the fifth section). It has three parts, or prayers, which usually determine its musical structure. [Latin, lamb of God]

Agon Ballet for 12 dancers with music by Stravinsky and choreography by Balanchine. First performance: Paris, October 1957; New York, November 1957. Consisting of 12 short movements, it is modelled on the court dances of Louis XIII and XIV as depicted in a 17th-century French dance manual. The music is composed in a number of styles: diatonic, polytonal, and twelve-tone.

agrément Ornament. Strictly speaking the term applies to the French ornaments of the 17th century, which were also taken up by other countries. [French]

Agricola, Alexander (?1446–1506) Flemish composer. He worked in the Sforza chapel at Milan (1471–74) and was active at Cambrai (1476), Paris (?–1491), and Florence Cathedral (1491–92); from 1500 until his death he served in the chapel of Philip I, Duke of Burgundy. His compositions include masses, motets, and secular chansons.

ai see **al**. [Italian]

Aichinger, Gregor (1564–1628) German composer, a pupil of Lassus at Munich. From 1578 he studied at Ingolstadt University, then went to Venice (1584–87) to study with Giovanni Gabrieli. While in Rome (1599–1600) he took holy orders; he then became vicar and organist at the cathedral of Augsburg. His numerous sacred works, chief among which are the *Sacrae cantiones* (1590, 1595, 1597), reflect the influence of Gabrieli.

Aida Tragic opera in four acts by Verdi with libretto by Ghislanzoni. First performance: Italian Theatre, Cairo, 1871. The opera, commissioned by Ismail Pasha (Khedive of Egypt) to celebrate the opening of the Suez Canal, is based on a story suggested by the French Egyptologist Mariette Bey and drafted in French by Camille du Locle. Set in ancient Egypt, it concerns the warrior Radames (tenor) and the two women who love him: the Egyptian princess Amneris (contralto) and her Ethiopian slave Aida (soprano), who willingly shares his death by entombment.

air 1. A tune or song. **2.** A movement of the baroque *suite, melodious but lacking specific dance characteristics. **3.** A descriptive dance in French baroque opera, whose content reflects either an action or its implications or portrays a character. Such pieces were sometimes given specific titles, e.g. Lully's 'Air pour Jupiter.' See also **aria; ayre.**

Akiyama, Kuniharu (1929–) Japanese composer, a pupil of Cage and Xenakis. His works include film scores and experimental environmental music, such as *Music for Meals* (for the 1964 Olympic athletes' cafeteria).

al (*pl.* **ai**) To the; at the. For example **al fine**, to the place marked *fine* (see **da capo**). [Italian]

Alain, Jehan (Ariste) (1911–40) French composer and organist. A pupil of Dupré, Dukas, and Roger-Ducasse, he was a church organist in Paris (1935–39) and was killed in action in World War II. His large output of organ, piano, and sacred choral music, composed between 1929 and 1939, includes the well-known organ *Litanies*. Other prominent members of his family are his brother **Olivier Alain** (1918–), composer and director of the Ecole César Franck, and his sister **Marie-Claire Alain** (1926–), an organist who specializes in the performance of 17th- and 18th-century music.

Albéniz, Isaac (1860–1909) Spanish composer and pianist. A child prodigy, he went on to study with Gevaert (composition) and Brassin (piano) in Brussels and with Liszt (1880); in Paris he studied with Dukas and d'Indy. From 1890 to 1893 he lived in London under the patronage of Francis Burdett Money-Coutts, whose librettos he set (*Henry Clifford*, *Pepita Jiménez*, and *King Arthur*). Albéniz's opera *The Magic Opal* was produced in London in 1893, the year he moved to Paris. He also wrote orchestral works and songs, but most of his large output is for piano, the best-known work being *Iberia (1906–08), 12 colourful technically demanding pieces. Albéniz is one of the most important figures in Spanish music and created a distinctive national idiom.

Albéniz, Mateo Perez de (*c*.1755–1831) Spanish composer, maestro di cappella at Logroño and San Sebastián. He wrote mainly church music and a tutor, *Instrucción metódica... para enseñar a cantar y tañer la música antigua* (1802).

Albert Hall see **Royal Albert Hall**.

Albert Herring Comic opera in three acts by Britten with libretto by Crozier. First performance: Glyndebourne, 1947. It is adapted from Maupassant's story of a male 'May Queen,' *Le Rosier de Madame Husson*.

Alberti bass A common form of accompaniment in the bass used in much 18th-century keyboard music. It consists of broken or spread chords arranged in a regular rhythmic pattern and is named after Domenico Alberti (1710–40), the first composer to use it extensively.

Albinoni, Tomaso (1671–1751) Italian composer and violinist, who worked primarily in Venice and Mantua. J.S. Bach borrowed his church sonatas. In addition to chamber music and concertos, Albinoni produced many operas and serenades.

alborada A type of Spanish music originally played in the morning, typically an instrumental piece in fairly free rhythm. [Spanish, dawn song]

Albrechtsberger, Johann Georg (1736–1809) Austrian composer, theorist, and organist, teacher of Beethoven, Czerny, Ries, and many others. He was kapellmeister of St Stephen's Cathedral, Vienna (1793–1809). In addition to his tutor, *Grundliche Answeisung zur Composition* (1790),

he produced many organ and chamber works, sinfonias, and oratorios.

Albumblatt A popular though imprecise name for a short 19th-century piece, generally for piano, that might be included in an album. [German, album leaf]

Alceste 1. Opera by Lully with libretto by Quinault. First performance: Opéra, Paris, 1674. **2.** Opera in three acts by Gluck with libretto by Calzabigi. First performance: Burgtheater, Vienna, 1767. It is based on Euripides' tale of the loving wife, Alcestis, who sacrifices her life for that of her husband, Admetus, and is subsequently allowed to return from the underworld as a reward for her nobility. *Alceste* is important in the history of opera in that it is one of the first of Gluck's reform operas, in which he explicitly sought both to free Italian opera from such nondramatic conventions as the da capo aria, excessive coloratura, and artificial breaks between recitative and aria and to compose overtures that set the scene for the ensuing drama.

Alcina Opera by Handel in three acts with libretto by Marchi. First performance: Covent Garden, London, 1735. It is based on the story of Alcina, the enchantress from Ariosto's chivalric poem *Orlando Furioso*.

Alcuin (*c*.732–804) Anglo-Saxon cleric, poet, and educator, who introduced a sung form of the creed from Ireland or Northumberland to the Catholic Church in France.

alcuna licenza, con see **licenza**.

Aldeburgh Festival An annual festival founded in 1948 and based at Aldeburgh, Suffolk, the home of Benjamin Britten and Peter Pears. It presents operas, concerts, and nonmusical events, in which Britten's music plays an

The 1962 Aldeburgh production of Albert Herring

important part. Many operas have had premieres there, including Britten's *A Midsummer Night's Dream* (1960) and *Death in Venice* (1973) and Birtwistle's *Punch and Judy* (1968). Members of Britten's circle perform regularly there, and latterly several Soviet artists (notably Rostropovich) have been associated with the festival. It enlarged its scope when the Maltings at Snape, a fine concert hall, was opened in 1967. Concerts are also given in the church at nearby Orford.

Aldrich, Henry (1647–1710) English composer and theologian Dean of Christ Church (1689). He assembled a large music library, which contains his English settings of Italian works. He composed many services, anthems, and catches, including 'Hark, the bonny Christ Church bells.'

aleatory (*or* **aleatoric**) see **indeterminacy.**

Aleko Opera in one act by Rachmaninov with libretto by Nemirovich-Danchenko, based on Pushkin's poem *The Gypsies*. First performance: Moscow, 1893.

Alexander Nevsky Cantata by Prokofiev. Composed: 1938. The music was originally written for a film about Alexander Nevsky, the Russian prince who defended his country against Teutonic knights in the 13th century, but Prokofiev himself adapted the score for a cantata.

Alexander's Feast Cantata by Handel. First performance: 1736. The words are adapted by Hamilton from an ode by Dryden about Alexander the Great.

Alfano, Franco (1876–1954) Italian composer. He was professor and director of the Bologna conservatory (1916–23), director of the Turin conservatory (1923–39) and Teatro Massimo, Palermo (1940–42), and professor at the Santa Cecilia conservatory, Rome (1942–50). Alfano

composed 12 operas, including *Risurrezione* (1904), and after Puccini's death in 1924 completed the unfinished Act III of *Turandot*.

Alfonso and Estrella Opera by Schubert with libretto by Franz von Schober. Composed: 1821–22; first performance (posthumously): Weimar, 1854. The story concerns two lovers whose fathers are, respectively, a deposed king and a usurping one.

Alfred Masque by Arne with libretto by David Mallet and James Thomson. First performance (private): Cliveden, Bucks. (the residence of the Prince of Wales), 1740. It ends with the famous patriotic song 'Rule Britannia.'

Alfvén, Hugo (1872–1960) Swedish conductor and composer. He studied at the Stockholm conservatory (1887–91), was violinist in the Swedish Royal Orchestra (1890–97), and, after working as a conductor, was Director of Music at Uppsala University (1910–39). His works, romantic and nationalist in character, include five symphonies, three orchestral works (*see* Swedish Rhapsody), much choral music, and the symphonic poem *En Skärgardssägen* (1905).

Aliabiev, Alexander Alexandrovich see **Alyabyev, Alexander Alexandrovich.**

aliquot scaling see **sympathetic strings.**

Alison, Richard (late 16th–early 17th century) English composer. His first known works appeared in East's *Whole Booke of Psalms* (1592) and he later contributed some instrumental variations to Morley's *Consort Lessons* (1599). In 1599 appeared the much admired *Psalmes of David in Meter*, settings of plainchant fitted with English words to be sung a cappella or by a soprano or tenor with

A scene from the Russian film Alexander Nevsky, *for which Prokofiev's music provided the score*

instrumental accompaniment. He also composed a book of *Songs* (1606), settings of poems of a didactic or religious character.

Alkan, Charles Henri Valentin (C. H. V. Morhange; 1813–88) French composer and pianist. He studied the piano with P. J. Zimmermann at the Paris Conservatoire and became a brilliant virtuoso. An enigmatic figure, he rarely played publicly. His compositions are mostly for piano solo or pedal piano but he also wrote vocal, orchestral, and chamber music. The piano pieces, which often have unusual titles (e.g. *Le Chemin de fer*, 1844, and *Le Tambour bat aux champs*, 1859), include many studies: they are complex chromatic pieces of extreme technical difficulty. Alkan's imaginative music has been neglected.

alla To the; at the; in the manner of. For example alla *turca. [Italian]

alla breve A direction to play with the beat as a minim rather than a crotchet, as indicated by the time signature. The effect is that a piece with four crotchets in the bar will be taken on the faster side with two beats per bar. [Italian, originally indicating that the breve in the older timing system was to carry the beat]

allargando Broadening. Used to indicate that the music becomes slower, more dignified, and more powerful. [Italian]

Alldis, John (1929–) English chorus director and conductor. He studied at Cambridge under Boris Ord, afterwards forming the John Alldis Choir, which quickly became successful. The choir has been especially noted for performances of modern works. He formed the London Symphony Orchestra Chorus (1966) and has been associated with the London Philharmonic Choir (1969) and the Danish State Radio Chorus (1972).

allegretto Lively. Indicating a fast pace but not quite as fast as allegro. [Italian, a little allegro]

Allegri, Gregorio (1582–1652) Italian composer and singer. He was a chorister and tenor at S Luigi dei Francesi, Rome, until 1604 and studied under Nanino. He was later active in Fermo and Tivoli and at Santo Spirito in Sassia, Rome. In 1630 he was appointed to the papal choir. Many of his works were written for this choir, including the famous highly ornamented *Miserere*, which is performed to this day. It attracted the attention of Goethe, Mendelssohn, and Mozart but it is not typical of Allegri's output, much of which is in a progressive baroque style.

Allegri Quartet British string quartet founded in 1953. From 1977 the members have been Peter Carter and David Roth (violins), Prunella Pacey (viola), and Bruno Schreker (cello). In addition to playing the standard repertory they have given the first performances of many British works; Britten chose them to record his first two string quartets.

Their performances are characterized by great vitality and reflect the fact that the players are all soloists in their own right.

allegro 1. (adj.) Lively. Used to indicate a lively or brisk speed. It is often used in combination, e.g. **allegro vivace**. **2.** (n.) A movement or piece so marked. [Italian]

Allegro, il Penseroso, ed il Moderato, L' Secular oratorio in three parts by Handel. Composed: 1740. The words of the first two parts are from Milton and those for the third part were written for this work by Jennens.

Alleluia 1. A responsorial chant forming part of the Proper of the Latin *Mass except during Lent, when it is replaced by the Tract. It is absent from the Requiem Mass. **2.** Symphony No. 30 in C major by Haydn. Composed: 1765. See also **Hallelujah**. [from Hebrew, praise the Lord]

allemande 1. A dance in slowish quadruple time that originated in Germany in the 16th century (it became popular in England as the *almain). During the 17th and 18th centuries it became established as the usual opening movement of the baroque *suite, in which it was formalized, bearing little relation to its plain 16th-century forebear, and often coupled to the *courante. The allemande is characterized by concise running melodies, each of its two sections opening with a short upbeat of either a single note or three notes. **2.** (or **deutscher Tanz**) A south German peasant dance, popular after the late 18th century. It has a quick 3/4 or 3/8 time.

Allende, (Pedro) Humberto (1885–1959) Chilean composer and teacher; Professor of Composition at the Santiago conservatory (1928–45). His symphony in B♭ (1910) won the Chilean Centennial Prize; among other instrumental and vocal works are the violin concerto (1942) and the nationalistic *12 Tonadas de carácter popular Chileno* for piano (1918–22).

almain (or **alman, almayne, almond**) An obsolete English form of *allemande. It is often found in 16th-century English music, in which it denotes a heavy dance in four measure. It was slower than the *pavan, although rhythmically similar. During the 17th century it became slower still and was often coupled with a coranto (*see* courante) or with a coranto and *sarabande. Towards the end of the 17th century, like its continental counterpart, it became established as the opening movement of the English *suite, though it was often preceded by a *prelude and sometimes even replaced by another movement.

alphorn (or (German) **alpenhorn**) A wooden trumpet, 8–12 ft (3–4 m) long, used by Swiss mountain farmers to call their cattle. It has a trumpet-like mouthpiece and as it has no valves can only play notes of the harmonic series.

Alpine Symphony, An (German: *Alpensinfonie*) Tone poem (Op. 64) by Richard Strauss. Composed: 1911–15; first performance: Berlin, 1915. This is the last of Strauss's tone poems and describes a day's climbing in the Alps. Although it is entitled a symphony, it is in only one movement and is notable for its extreme length.

Also sprach Zarathustra (*Thus Spake Zarathustra*) Tone poem (Op. 30) by Richard Strauss based on a philosophical text by Nietzsche. First performance: 1896. Each of the work's eight sections attempts to describe in musical terms a particular feature of mankind or its achievements.

alt High. Used to define the notes in the octave rising from G above the treble clef; the notes in this octave are said to be **in alt**, while the notes in the next octave up are **in altissimo**. [from Latin *altus*]

Alt The alto voice. Often used as a prefix to indicate an instrument that is pitched in the alto range of its family, i.e. the second highest; e.g. **Altblockflöte**, treble recorder. [German]

althorn see **saxhorns**.

altissimo see **alt**.

alto 1. (n.) The highest male voice. It is produced by *falsetto to obtain the range from G below middle C to the C an octave and a fourth above, the singer's natural voice being either tenor or bass. (The female equivalent is usually called *contralto.) The alto voice has for many centuries been widely used in liturgical and sacred music sung in English cathedrals and university college and school chapels. In madrigals, glees, and part songs set for three or more male voices, the alto usually takes the highest part. 2. (adj.) Describing instruments whose range is approximately that of the alto voice. [Italian, high]

Alto Rhapsody Rhapsody for contralto solo, male chorus, and orchestra by Brahms. Composed: 1869. The text is taken from Goethe's *Harzreise im Winter* (*Winter Journey in the Harz Mountains*).

Alva, Luigi (1927–) Peruvian tenor. He studied with Ettore Campogalliani at La Scala, Milan, where he made his European debut in *La Traviata* (1953). There he inaugurated, with others, La Piccola Scala in 1955. Particularly successful in light 18th-century and preromantic repertory, he has since specialized in Mozart and Rossini.

Alwyn, William (1905–85) British composer, Professor of Composition at the Royal Academy of Music, London (1926–54). His works include the oratorio (after Blake) *The Marriage of Heaven and Hell* (1936), the *Suite of Scottish Dances* (1946), symphonies, concertos, chamber music, and music for over 50 films.

Alyabyev (*or* **Aliabiev**), **Alexander Alexandrovich** (1787–1851) Russian composer. He wrote much instrumental music and in 1820 began writing for the stage – incidental music, vaudevilles, and operas, some based on Shakespeare. His famous song 'The Nightingale' (1823) was used by several prima donnas in the singing-lesson scene in Rossini's *The Barber of Seville*.

Alypius (*c*.3rd or 4th century) Greek musicologist, who wrote treatise, *Introduction to Music*, on Greek scales and their transpositional system, together with notational tables. This was first published in Italy in 1616.

Amadeus Quartet British string quartet founded in 1947. Its members were Norbert Brainin and Sigmund Nissel (violins), Peter Schidlof (viola), and Martin Lovett (cello). They were among the leading quartets in the world: their polished performances were distinguished by a homogeneous sound and great technical assurance and ensemble. Their repertory was chiefly classical and romantic works (their performances of Mozart and Schubert were much admired), but they also play Bartók, Tippett, and Britten, who wrote his third quartet for them.

Amahl and the Night Visitors Opera in one act by Menotti with libretto by the composer. Originally written for television, it was first performed by the NBC studios, New York, 1951; first stage performance: Indiana University, Bloomington, 1952. It retells the story of the Magi, who visit the crippled boy Amahl.

Amati Family of Italian violin makers. **Andrea Amati** (*c*.1535–*c*.1611) founded a school for instrument makers in Cremona; although he made other instruments, he is best remembered for the construction of the violin in its present-day shape. He had two sons, **Antonio Amati** (1550–1638) and **Girolamo Amati** (1551–1635). The most renowned member of the family was **Nicolo Amati** (1596–1684), son of Girolamo, whose pupils included Stradivari and Guarneri.

Ambrosian chant (*or* **Milanese chant**) One of the four categories of liturgical chant, the others being Gregorian, Gallican, and Mozarabic (*see* plainchant). It was named after St Ambrose, Bishop of Milan from 374, though the form of the chant in use today (for example, in Milan Cathedral) almost certainly dates from a later period, probably the 10th and 11th centuries. It differs little from Gregorian chant; occasionally it incorporates long melismas, especially in the responsories of matins.

Ameling, Elly (1938–) Dutch soprano. Encouraged by Pierre Bernac, she began her concert and recital career with the French repertory and Schubert and has steadily extended it. She won the Edison Prize in 1965 and 1970 for her recordings.

American in Paris, An Descriptive orchestral piece by Gershwin. First performance: 1928. The work describes an American's impressions of Paris and is one of Gershwin's attempts to incorporate jazz idioms into symphonic music. An expanded orchestra is employed, including four taxi horns.

American organ A *reed organ that is similar to a *harmonium, except that air is sucked through the reeds instead of being blown through them as in the harmonium. It has a more mellow tone than the harmonium, but its response time is slower and it is not very effective for playing fast passages. The American organ was developed in 1861 by Mason and Hamlin, a firm of instrument makers, in Boston, USA. US: **cabinet organ**. See also **Mustel organ.**

American Quartet String quartet in F (Op. 96) by Dvořák. Composed: 1893. The quartet was composed while Dvořák was in the USA and the thematic material incorporates some features of Negro song; hence the quartet is also sometimes called the 'Negro' or 'Nigger' Quartet.

Amfiparnaso, L' (*The Slopes of Parnassus*) Madrigal comedy in three acts by Orazio Vecchi. First performed: Modena, 1594; published: 1597. The work comprises a series of 14 madrigals for 5 voices and is among the earliest works in this genre. It has often been claimed that *L'Amfiparnaso* is an early form of opera, but this cannot be substantiated. Although the story told by the madrigals is continuous, Vecchi never intended that the action should be staged, as he intimates in his prologue.

Amico Fritz, L' Opera in three acts by Mascagni with libretto by 'P. Suardon' (anagrammatic pseudonym of the writer N. Daspuro). First performance: Teatro Costanzi, Rome, 1891. Based on Erckmann-Chatrain's novel, it is an idyll relating the awakening of love in a confirmed bachelor, Fritz, for the farmer's daughter Suzel.

Amor brujo, El (*Love, the Magician*) Ballet in one act with music by Falla and scenario by Martinez. First performance: Teatro Lara, Madrid, 1915. Candelas, a Gypsy girl, loves Carmelo but is haunted by the spectre of a dead lover. In the 'Ritual Fire-dance' Carmelo disguises himself as the ghost and cures Candelas of her hallucination.

amore, d' A term used in the names of certain old instruments to indicate a sweeter tone and, sometimes, a lower pitch than normal. See **viola d'amore; oboe d'amore.** French: **d'amour**. [Italian, of love]

amoroso Amorous; loving. Used to indicate that the performance of a piece so marked should have some emotional content. [Italian]

Amy, Gilbert (1936–) French composer and conductor, a pupil of Messiaen, Milhaud, and Boulez. His early works are strictly serial. In *Antiphonies* (1960–63) he experi-mented with spatial factors; in *Diaphonies* (1962) and *Jeux* (1970) he has developed a more impressionistic style, using mobile form.

Anchieta, Juan de (1462–1523) Spanish composer. From 1489 he was employed at the court of Ferdinand and Isabella and by their son, Don Juan. In 1519 he retired to his birthplace, Azpeitia. He composed two masses, several motets, and four polyphonic Spanish songs.

ancora 1. Again; once more. **2.** Still; yet. A direction to repeat a section; e.g. **ancora più**, still more. [Italian]

Anda, Geza (1921–76) Swiss pianist and conductor, born in Hungary. He studied at the Budapest academy under Dohnányi and was particularly noted for his performances of Bartók and Brahms.

andante 1. (adj.) Going; moving. Used to indicate a moderate walking speed. It may indicate a rather quick or a rather slow tempo, but in present-day usage it normally suggests a slowish pace, while in the 18th century it was used more literally to mean 'moving.' **2.** (n.) A piece or movement in andante tempo. [Italian]

andantino 1. (adj.) A direction used to indicate a slightly modified (i.e. faster or slower) andante speed. **2.** (n.) A short piece in andante tempo. [Italian, a little andante]

Anderson, Marian (1902–) US contralto. After studying with Giuseppe Boghetti in New York, she toured as a concert singer. It was not until 1955 that she made her operatic debut, as Ulrica in Verdi's *A Masked Ball* in New York (she was the first Black singer to appear at the Metropolitan Opera). Opera remained secondary for her, however: she was a memorable performer of spirituals.

André, Maurice (1933–) French trumpeter. After a period as an orchestral player, André began his solo career in 1963. Blacher, Jolivet, and Tomasi have written for him and he teaches at the Paris Conservatoire.

Andrea Chénier Opera in four acts by Giordano with libretto by Illica. First performance: La Scala, Milan, 1896. It tells the story of the French Revolutionary poet André Chénier.

Andriessen, Hendrik (**Franciscus**) (1892–1981) Dutch organist and composer. He studied under Jean de Pauw and Bernard Zweers and organist at Utrecht Cathedral before becoming director of the Utrecht conservatory (1937–49). He was also director of The Hague conservatory (1949–57) and professor at Nÿmegen University (1952–63). His works, predominantly late-romantic in style (though he wrote 12-note music in the 1950s), include the operas *Philomela* (1950) and *Spiegel uit Venitië* (1964). His brother **Willem Andriessen** (1887–1964) was a pianist and composer and his sons **Jurriaan Andriessen** (1925–) and **Louis Andriessen** (1939–) are also composers.

Marian Anderson, with Franz Rupp at the piano

Anerio, Felice (*c*.1560–1614) Italian composer, a pupil of Giovanni Maria Nanino. He was maestro di cappella at the English College, Rome (1585), and succeeded Palestrina as composer to the Papal Chapel (from 1594). In his masses and motets, Anerio is a progressive follower of Palestrina; his madrigals, however, resemble Marenzio's in their brilliant sonorities and rhythmic contrasts. His younger brother **Giovanni Francesco Anerio** (*c*.1567–1630), a pupil of Palestrina, was active in Italy (Rome and Verona) and Poland. His works range from masses in a conservative polyphonic style to progressive small-scale motets with basso continuo; the most notable is his collection of spiritual madrigals, the *Teatro armonico* (1619).

Anfossi, Pasquale (1727–97) Italian composer and violinist, a pupil of Piccinni. He worked primarily in Rome and produced many operas buffa, including *La Finta giardiniera* (1774), which was later set by Mozart (1775). He directed the Italian Opera in London (1781–83). After becoming maestro di cappella of S Giovanni in Laterano (1792), Anfossi wrote mainly sacred works and chamber music.

anglaise An 18th-century dance regarded as having an English character. It has a lively duple rhythm and appeared occasionally in the baroque *suite, e.g. Bach's *French Suite III*. [French, English]

Anglican chant A characteristically English method of setting prose *psalms and canticles to music, in which each half of every verse of the psalm is sung to a reciting note and a several-note cadential formula. The earliest Anglican chants, made necessary by the Reformation, consisted merely of harmonizations of various *plainchant tones. Several 16th-century chant melodies contain many of the elements of Anglican chant proper, but none of the great 16th-century composers is known to have written true Anglican chants. Genuine Anglican chant stems from the early 17th century. At first it consisted of single chant, in which the same chant is sung to each verse of the psalm. After the Restoration double chant, which treats two verses alternatively, also became popular, although isolated examples had existed somewhat earlier. The system of indicating where words and notes change, known as *pointing, entered printed editions after 1837.

animato Spirited; animated. Used to indicate a lively, usually fast, performance. [Italian]

Animuccia, Giovanni (*c*.1500–71) Italian composer. Educated in Florence, he was active in Rome by 1550 and in 1555 became maestro of the Cappella Giulia. In Rome he composed laudi for the oratory of St Philip Neri; these pieces are simple homophonic sacred songs in the vernacular, designed to communicate the text with clarity.

Anna Bolena (*Anne Boleyn*) Opera in two acts by Donizetti with libretto by Romani based on the tragedy of Henry VIII's second queen. First performance: Teatro Carcano, Milan, 1830. Revival of interest in the 1950s in this and other bel canto operas is mainly due to powerful interpretations by such singers as Callas and Sutherland.

Années de pèlerinage (*Years of Pilgrimage*) A collection of piano music in three volumes by Liszt. Composed: 1835–77. The first two volumes are entitled 'Switzerland' and 'France' respectively; the third has no title. Each volume consists of a selection of piano pieces, each bearing a descriptive subtitle, referring in the case of the first two volumes to the country concerned. Some of the pieces appear in other volumes of Liszt; the second contains the *Petrarch Sonnets* and the *Dante Sonata*.

Ansermet, Ernest (1883–1969) Swiss conductor. He studied composition with Ernest Bloch and conducting with Artur Nikisch. Ansermet conducted the Ballets Russes (1915–23); in 1918 he founded the Orchestre de la Suisse Romande, which he conducted until his death. He was an outstanding interpreter of Stravinsky.

answer The second entry in a fugal exposition of the traditional type, in which the subject is transposed up a fifth or down a fourth. In a **real answer** the transposition is

Ernest Ansermet

exact; in a **tonal answer** some intervals of the subject are modified and the interval of transposition shifts during the course of the entry. See **fugue**.

Antar Orchestral suite (Op. 9) by Rimsky-Korsakov. Composed: 1868 (revised 1876 and 1897). In four movements, the suite describes the legend of Antar, a 6th-century Arabian hero.

Antheil, George (1900–59) US composer and journalist; pupil of Constantine von Sternberg and Ernest Bloch. He settled in Paris after a concert tour of Europe (1922) but moved back to the USA 1933, going to Hollywood in 1936 to write film music. His early works were often deliberately shocking, such as the *Ballet mécanique* (1926), whose scoring for pianos, xylophones, pianola, electric doorbells, and aircraft propellor caused a sensation. Later he turned to a more conservative neoclassical idiom in the symphonies of 1937 and 1943.

anthem 1. A nonliturgical choral piece forming an optional part of the Anglican service. The 1662 Book of Common Prayer directs that in 'Quires and Places where they sing, here followeth the Anthem' after the collects. The anthem became established after the Reformation, having grown out of the *motet and *antiphon. Early examples, notably by Tye, Tallis, and Sheppard, are mainly simple unaccompanied pieces. During the Elizabethan period the **full anthem** (using the full choir with no solo passages) grew in size and emotional expressiveness. The 17th century saw the introduction of the **verse anthem**, for solo voice or voices, chorus, and independent accompaniment, of which Tomkins and Gibbons were major exponents. Blow and Purcell developed both the full and verse anthems, increasing their length and size. During the 18th century, ceremonial anthems, such as Handel's coronation and funeral anthems, were on a large scale. Small- and large-scale anthems continued to be cultivated thereafter, incorporating the stylistic features of the period in which they were written. In more recent times composers have been content to consolidate what has gone before, writing in a variety of forms that show a continuity of style and tradition from the Elizabethan period. **2.** An occasional hymn, e.g. the National Anthem.

anticipation A device in *harmony in which a note (or notes) of a chord are sounded before the rest of the chord so that dissonance is created with the preceding chord. Compare **suspension**.

Antigone Any of various operas based on Sophocles' tragedy by composers including (1) Honegger, with libretto by Cocteau; first performance: Théâtre de la Monnaie, Brussels, 1927; and (2) Zingarelli, with libretto by Marmontel; first performance: Opéra, Paris, 1790. Zingarelli also set Metastasio's Italian libretto, *Antigono*, as did the composers Hasse, Carfaro, Conforto, Durán, Galuppi, Gluck, Jomelli, Lampugnani, Paisiello, Piccinni, and Traetta. Carl Orff set Hölderlin's German version of *Antigone*, produced in Salzburg in 1949.

antiphon In the Roman Catholic Church, a biblical extract sung before and after a psalm or canticle: on lesser feasts the first singing is restricted to the initial word of the text (*see* plainchant). A **Marian antiphon** is a hymn of praise or supplication to the Virgin Mary. The texts, many of which begin with the characteristic acclamation *Ave!* or *Salve!*, are mostly free compositions by medieval divines. For example *Salve Regina*, attributed to Hermannus Contractus (1013–54), is sung after Compline daily throughout one of the four seasons in the annual cycle. A **processional antiphon** is a relatively lengthy piece of a narrative character sung during processions on certain major feasts (e.g. Palm Sunday and the Purification).

antique cymbals see **cymbals.**

anvil A percussion instrument used in the orchestra for special effects. It may consist of either an imitation of a blacksmith's anvil or a set of steel bars struck by a mallet. It is usually of indefinite pitch but the steel-bar variety can be made to produce notes of a fixed pitch. The instrument is used in Wagner's *Das Rheingold*.

Apollo Musagetes (*Apollo, Chief of the Muses*) Ballet in scenes with music by Stravinsky and choreography by Bolm. First performance: Library of Congress, Washington, DC, April 1928, in concert form; first European performance: Paris, June 1928, with choreography by Balanchine, performed by Diaghilev's Ballets Russes. A ballet of austere dignity, it relates the birth of Apollo to Leto, his education by the Muses, and his ascent of Mount Parnassus. Scored for strings only, it is divided into formal dance movements, as in the suite form.

Apostel, Hans Erich (1901–72) Austrian composer, born in Germany. He was a pupil of both Schoenberg (1921) and Berg (1925–35) and a proofreader for Universal Edition. In the 1950s he adopted 12-note technique. He wrote orchestral music, chamber music, and songs, the *Requiem* (1933), and *Chamber Symphony* Op. 41 (1966).

Apostles, The Oratorio by Elgar, with a text from the Bible arranged by the composer. First performance: Birmingham Festival, 1903. This was the first of a projected trilogy of oratorios; the second was The **Kingdom*, but the third was never written.

Appalachia Variations for choir and orchestra by Delius. First performance: 1904. The title of the work is the ancient name for North America and Delius uses a Negro song as the theme for the variations.

Appalachian Spring Ballet in one act with music by Copland, written for the dancer and choreographer, Martha Graham and commissioned by the Elizabeth Sprague Coolidge Foundation. First performance: Library of Congress, Washington, DC, 1944. The action takes place during the spring celebrations of a newly built pioneer farmstead in Pennsylvania in the early 1800s. Copland won a Pulitzer Prize for his score.

Appassionata Piano sonata in F minor (Op. 57) by Beethoven. Composed: 1804. Beethoven himself never used the title, which was added later by a publisher and refers to the overall mood of the sonata. Although very different in character, this sonata is similar in structure to the *Waldstein Sonata* as both have relatively short middle movements but very long outer movements.

appoggiatura A musical ornament that makes a contribution to the melody of a composition but is written in small type before a regular note. Unlike an **acciaccatura*, which has virtually no time value, the appoggiatura takes half the time value from the note on which it leans. Used with a chord, the appoggiatura leans only on the highest note of the chord, the time values of the other notes remaining unchanged. [from Italian *appoggiare*, to lean]

Après-midi d'un faune, Prélude à l' (*Prelude to 'The Afternoon of a Faun'*) Tone poem by Debussy after a poem by Mallarmé. Composed: 1892–94. One of the first examples of impressionism in music, this work describes a faun dozing in the warm afternoon sun and his erotic dreams about nymphs. As the title 'Prélude' indicates, Debussy originally intended there to be further movements, but these were never composed.

A ballet based on this work, with choreography by Nijinsky, was produced in Paris in 1912.

Arabella Opera in three acts by Richard Strauss with libretto by Hofmannsthal. First performance: Dresden, 1933. It is set in the Vienna of 1860 and relates the tribulations that beset the impecunious parents of two daughters (Arabella and Zdenka), both of marriageable age. Zdenka has been brought up as a boy, Zdenko, to add to the plot's complexity, which finally resolves to the satisfaction of all.

arabesque A piece of music whose melody or accompaniement is highly decorated, as in Schumann's *Arabesque* (Op. 18) for piano. German: **Arabeske**. [the term is borrowed from the visual arts, in which it refers to the delicate tracery characteristic of Arab or Moorish architecture]

Arabian music Before the 7th century and the spread of Islam, Arabian music of the Hijaz, Yemen, and Mesopotamian areas was the legacy of the ancient Semitic tribes— the wandering Bedouins and the town settlers. It was for the most part vocal, with female singers accompanied by a variety of strung, blown, and percussive instruments. Persian influence was strong: the much-favoured **pandore**, a long lute (Arabic: **tunbur**), was of Persian origin.

Mohammed (571–632) founded Islam in 622 and it first developed in the Hijaz region, east of the Red Sea. Understanding the important and basic role of music in the Arabian way of life, he sought to divert it into religious channels. The call to prayer (*adhdan*) was chanted through the streets and from the minaret of the mosque by the muezzin; the sacred book of the Koran (*Qu'ran*) had its own chant, or cantillation (*taghbin*), which at first was of a restrained nature but later developed melodically to the extent that in the 9th century it was including popular ballad tunes. Hymn singing (*nasha'id*) became a social activity, the most obvious changeover being from female to male singers.

From the first spread of Islam until the mid-9th century is the classical period of Arabian music. The Umayyad caliphate (661–750) was interested in the imperial aspects of Islam and established a splendid court at Damascus, in Syria. Secular music flourished and singing, always of prime importance in the history of Arabian music, was accompanied by the **lute* ('ud, literally 'wood,' referring to the wooden belly of the lute, as opposed to the older skin-bellied lute). Songs typically had a single repeated but infinitely varied melody for each verse. Music began to be codified into a theory, which stressed the indigenous nature of Arabian classical music but admitted the influence of Byzantine, Persian, and other cultures. The system of the theorist Ibn Misjah (died *c*.715) postulates eight 'finger modes' (asab') for the lute (similar to the Greek and church **modes*) from which intricate and elaborately embellished melodies were composed; underlying these was a series of rhythmic modes of varying complexity. The golden age of virtuoso singers came in the reign of Harun al-Rashid (of *Arabian Nights* fame) during the late 8th century.

From 847 the political power of Islam was on the wane and music itself declined. New life was infused into it by the Dervish and Sufi sects: the Sufis believed that divine ecstasy was most readily experienced through music. Instrumental music developed; besides the 'ud, popular instruments were the trapezoidal *psaltery (**qanun**), the bowed **rebab** (similar to the European medieval rebec), a spike fiddle (**kamancha**), various kinds of frame drum (**duff**), and a shawm (**surnay**). This was a period of avid translation of Greek works on musical theory; melodic and rhythmic modes became more elaborate and the present-day **maqam** came into being as a melodic type having its own distinctive scale, register, and compass; **iqa** was the rhythmic mode.

The spread of Islam into Spain from 713 to 1492 powerfully influenced southern European music. Later, the distinctive music of the Turkish *janissaries, with its drum, cymbals, and jingles, was fashionable in 18th- and 19th-century European salons and found place in the alla turca movements of Mozart and Beethoven.

Arbeau, Thoinot (Jehan Tabourot; 1519–95) French author. In 1530 he became a priest and in 1574 was appointed a canon at Langres. He is the author of the *Orchésographie* (1588), a treatise on dance with pictorial and musical illustrations.

Arbós, (Enrique) Fernandez (1863–1939) Spanish violinist, conductor, and composer, a pupil of Joachim. After a successful career as a soloist, Arbós was conductor of the Madrid Symphony Orchestra (1904–36). Although his own compositions are neglected, his arrangement of Albéniz's *Ibéria* is frequently performed.

Arcadelt, Jacob (c.1504–after 1567) Flemish composer. From 1539 he was a singer at St Peter's and at the Papal Chapel, Rome, returning to France in about 1553. Arcadelt's works include chansons, masses, and motets; he was one of the first to use the genre of the madrigal, publishing six books between 1539 and 1550. His placid yet gravely expressive *Il Bianco e dolce cigno* was widely disseminated and imitated.

Archduke Trio Piano trio in B♭ (Op. 97) by Beethoven. Composed: 1811. Its nickname comes from Beethoven's friend Archduke Rudolph of Austria, to whom the trio was dedicated.

archlute see **lute**.

arco 1. The bow of a stringed instrument. **2.** (*or* **col arco**) A direction to play with the bow instead of plucking (see **pizzicato**). [Italian]

Arditi, Luigi (1822–1903) Italian conductor and composer. He studied at the Milan conservatory. As a conductor he toured widely – in Havana, the USA, Constantinople, and Russia. In 1858 he settled in London, where he introduced many new operas in various theatres. He wrote operas, orchestral music, songs, and ballads, of which his vocal waltz *Il Bacio* is best known.

Arensky, Anton Stepanovich (1861–1906) Russian composer. He studied composition with Rimsky-Korsakov and counterpoint and fugue with Johannsen at the St Petersburg conservatory (1879–82). He taught at the Moscow conservatory (1882–94) then became director of music at the St Petersburg imperial chapel. Arensky wrote stage music and choral, orchestral, chamber, and keyboard works; among the best known are the piano trio in D minor (1894) and the first suite for two pianos.

Argerich, Martha (1941–) Argentinian pianist. She made her debut in 1946, but it was not until winning the Warsaw Chopin Competition in 1965 that she became widely acclaimed as one of the greatest pianists of her generation.

aria 1. A composition for solo voice or voices and instrumental accompaniment. It is a characteristic feature of *opera, and to a lesser degree of *oratorio and the *cantata, and assumes many diverse forms. In the 16th century the term was applied to the setting of a poem in particular metrical form, e.g. **aria di ottava rima**. Towards the end of the century, strophic songs composed in the new monodic style were called arias, for instance in Caccini's *Le Nuove musiche* (1602), as opposed to through-composed solo *madrigals. 17th-century Italy cultivated beautiful melody with accompaniment in contrast to both the monodic and contrapuntal styles. The aria also became nonstrophic; for example, a typical aria by Luigi Rossi has a smooth melody on a near rhythmically regular bass, fairly consonant harmony, and symmetrical phrases. Poetic form is increasingly disrespected. As the baroque period progressed, the expansion of the aria by modulation rather than by variation resulted in the **da capo aria**. This is characterized by the literal repetition of the opening section after a contrasting middle one, so forming an ABA scheme. Such arias were the most important and commonly used kind after 1650; they played the central role in opera for about a hundred years. The da capo form lost ground in the late 18th century, when Gluck (in particular) attempted, quite successfully, to eliminate it from opera because of its nondramatic qualities. Sonata form increased the scale of the aria, and in classical opera, especially by Mozart, arias were incorporated far more into the drama. Pairs of contrasted slow and fast arias, called respectively *cavatinas and *cabalettas, were an important structural feature of Italian opera in the first part of the 19th century. As the century progressed, Verdi increasingly blurred the demarcations between real aria and ensemble to improve the dramatic flow. Wagner independently went even further in creating a continuous dramatic unity in which arias could no longer be distinguished. In modern opera aria has largely lost its dramatic purpose; instead, songs usually unconnected with the drama are sometimes introduced to provide lyrical interludes. **2.** An instrumental piece characterized by the melodiousness of the vocal aria, e.g. the opening of Bach's *Goldberg Variations*.

Ariadne auf Naxos (*Ariadne on Naxos*) Opera in prologue and one act by Richard Strauss with libretto by Hofmannsthal. The original version (first performance: Stuttgart, 1912) was intended as a divertissement to a shortened version of Molière's Le *Bourgeois Gentilhomme* but the combination of theatrical and operatic companies proved impracticable. Strauss wrote a 35-minute prologue to replace the play and the opera is usually performed in this version (first performance: Vienna, 1916). The setting is the island of Naxos, where Ariadne (soprano), abandoned by her lover Theseus, is wooed by the god Bacchus (tenor).

Ariane et Barbe-bleue (*Ariane and Bluebeard*) Opera in three acts by Dukas with libretto by Maeterlinck after his play of the same name. First performance: Opéra-Comique, Paris, 1907. It tells the story of Bluebeard, contrasting his tyranny with the liberating humanity of Ariane.

arietta A short simple *aria, generally lacking any development or middle section.

ariette 1. An elaborate *aria (often with Italian words) in French baroque opera. **2.** A vocal piece inserted into spoken dialogue in French opéra comique (**comédie mêlée d'ariettes**).

arioso Describing a type of vocal piece that combines the dramatic and declamatory character of the recitative with the more formal structure of the aria or air. The term has now become more widely used to embrace instrumental, keyboard, and orchestral movements cast in a songlike form. [Italian, songlike]

Ariosti, Attilio (1666–c.1740) Italian composer and viola d'amore player. He was organist in Bologna and Mantua and court composer in Berlin (1697–1703). In London (c.1715–c.1728) he participated with G. B. Bononcini in the development of the Royal Academy of Music (1722), for which he wrote operas. His other works include *Lezioni per viola d'amore* (1728), cantatas, oratorios, and serenades.

Ariosto, Ludovico (1474–1533) Italian poet. The first edition of his greatest work, *Orlando Furioso*, appeared in 1516. He worked on this epic throughout his life, making two further editions. Scenes from the work were used by 16th-century Italian opera librettists (*see* Orlando).

Arlésienne, L' (*The Girl from Arles*) Incidental music by Bizet to the play of the same name by Alphonse Daudet. Composed: 1872. Two orchestral suites were drawn from

the original score, one by Bizet himself in 1872 and one by Guiraud after the composer's death.

Armida Any of various operas based on Tasso's poem of the Crusades, *Jerusalem Delivered*, in which the central character is the enchantress Armida (*see also* Rinaldo). The composers of these operas include Lully (*Armide*: Paris, 1686) and Gluck (*Armide*: Paris, 1777), both on libretti by Quinault; Haydn (Esterháza, 1784) on a libretto by Durandi; Rossini (Naples, 1817) with libretto by Schmidt; and Dvořák (Prague, 1904), with libretto by Vrchlitzky.

Armstrong, Sheila (1942–) British soprano. She studied at the Royal Academy in London and made her debut at Sadler's Wells as Despina in Mozart's *Così fan tutte* (1965). This was followed by performances at Glyndebourne (1966) and Covent Garden (1973).

Arne, Thomas Augustine (1710–78) British composer and violinist. He obtained the degree of D.Mus. from Oxford (1759) and made three extended visits to Ireland during his lifetime. Much of Arne's music was composed for plays and masques performed at Drury Lane and Covent Garden; he was appointed composer to Vauxhall Gardens and also wrote songs for Marylebone Gardens and Ranelagh Gardens. Arne's many works include music for Milton's *Comus and the masque *Alfred (1740), which contains the famous 'Rule Britannia.' He produced the opera *Artaserse* (1762) in Italian style, with recitative replacing dialogue, and the ballad opera *Love in a Village* (1762), as well as many oratorios, including *Judith* (1761), and works for vocal and instrumental ensemble.

Arnell, Richard (1917–) British composer. He studied in London at the Royal College of Music under Ireland (1935–38), then worked in the USA before returning to the UK in 1948. His ballets include *The Great Detective* (1953). He has also written symphonies, concertos, and chamber music; the one-act opera *Moon Flowers* (1958); and the multimedia work *Combat Zone* (1969).

Arnold, Malcolm (**Henry**) (1921–) British composer, who studied under Gordon Jacob and Constant Lambert. He was a professional trumpet player until 1948, when he became a full-time composer. His prolific and varied output is tuneful and attractive; it includes the ballet *Homage to the Queen* (1953), the *Tam O'Shanter Overture* (1955), and the music for many films, including *The Bridge on the River Kwai* (1958).

Arnold, Matthew (1822–88) British poet and critic. He studied at Oxford, where later he became Professor of Poetry (1857). Settings of his poetry have been written by Frank Bridge, Charles Stanford, and, most notably, by Vaughan Williams (the *Oxford Elegy*).

Arnold, Samuel (1740–1802) British composer, organist, and editor. He was organist of the Chapel Royal (1783) and

Westminster Abbey (1793) and director of the Academy of Ancient Music (1789). He wrote many oratorios and works for the stage, including *The Maid of the Mill* (1765). He also edited Handel's works and produced a four-volume edition of *English Cathedral Music*.

Aroldo see **Stiffelio.**

arpa Harp. [Italian]

arpeggio (*or* **broken chord**) A chord in which the notes are played in sequence rather than simultaneously. It is usual to play such a broken chord starting from the lowest note although sometimes the highest is played first. [Italian, played in the manner of a harp]

arpeggione (*or* **guitare d'amour**) A six-stringed bowed instrument that has a fretted fingerboard. A cross between a cello and a guitar, it was invented in Vienna in 1823 by G. Staufer; in 1824 Schubert wrote a sonata for it.

arrangement An adaptation of a composition for a different instrument or group of instruments from that intended by the composer. A **transcription** is usually an arrangement in which the transcriber allows himself more freedom in interpreting the composer's intentions (although in the USA a transcription is often the more faithful adaptation). A transcription is also sometimes a simpler version of a piece for the same instrument as the composer intended.

Arrau, Claudio (1903–) Chilean pianist. In 1912 he went Berlin to study with Krause and quickly established himself as one of the leading pianists of his generation, being particularly noted for his performance of Beethoven.

Arriaga (y Balzola), Juan Crisóstomo Antonio (1806–26) Spanish composer. At the Paris Conservatoire he studied the violin with Baillot and harmony and counterpoint with Fétis. His orchestral, chamber, and vocal works use conventional forms but show him to have been a composer of great promise.

Arrigo, Girolamo (1930–) Italian composer, a pupil of Max Deutsch. Strongly influenced by Dante and Marx, his works include the opera *Orden* (1969), chamber music, and incidental music.

Arroyo, Martina (1937–) US soprano. She studied in New York and made her debut in 1958, in Pizzetti's *Murder in the Cathedral*. A European career followed, in which she specialized in Verdi and some French grand opera, with 18th-century classics. In the USA she gives recitals and her rich, warm, and powerful voice is also suited to oratorio. Arroyo's many recordings include Stockhausen's *Momente*.

ars antiqua Medieval music of the 12th and 13th centuries, particularly that associated with the school of Notre Dame in Paris and its two leading composers, *Léonin and *Pérotin. The most important developments of ars antiqua include the introduction of strict measured rhythm and the composition of *organa, clausulae, and the earliest motets. It was succeeded by *ars nova. [Latin, old art]

ars nova Medieval music of the 14th century, particularly that associated with the French composers *Machaut and de *Vitry (the name was taken from de Vitry's treatise *Ars Nova*, c.1325). Ars nova represented a change from the highly organized *ars antiqua with the use of more varied rhythmic patterns, the introduction of *isorhythm, and a gradual increase in the composition of secular music. The Italian ars nova is represented especially by the work of *Landini. [Latin, new art]

Art of Fugue, The (German: *Die Kunst der Fuge*) A collection of contrapuntal music by Bach, begun in 1748 and left unfinished on his death in 1750. For all of the 20 fugues and canons (called 'contrapuncti') Bach used the same theme and all the devices of contrapuntal writing are demonstrated – augmentation, diminution, stretto, etc. There is no indication as to the intended medium; although a keyboard performance would seem most obvious, several arrangements have been made in the 20th century with chamber or orchestral instrumentation. Neither has the proper order of the individual pieces ever been definitively established, due to the inaccuracy of the first publication in 1750. In the last and unfinished fugue Bach uses his own surname as the third subject of a triple fugue (*see* BACH).

Artusi, Giovanni Maria (c.1540–1613) Italian composer and theorist. His life was spent in Bologna and Venice, where he studied under Gioseffo Zarlino. His writings include works on dissonance and counterpoint and celebrated attacks on Monteverdi's use of dissonance.

Asafiev, Boris (Vladimirovich) (1884–1949) Russian composer and writer; music critic under the pseudonym Igor Glebov. He studied under Kalafati and Liadov and pursued an academic career in Leningrad after the Revolution. His compositions include 9 operas and 27 ballets; he also edited the works of Mussorgsky and wrote books on Stravinsky and on musical analysis.

Ashkenazy, Vladimir (1937–) Soviet pianist. After studying at the Moscow conservatory he won the Warsaw Chopin Competition 1955 and the Tchaikovsky Competition in 1962. Ashkenazy is both a solo and a chamber pianist, being particularly famous for performances of Scriabin, Prokofiev, and Rachmaninov. He settled in Iceland in 1973.

Ashley, Robert (1930–) US composer, cofounder (1958) with Gordon Mumma of the Cooperative Studio for Electronic Music in Ann Arbor. He formed the Sonic Arts Union for the performance of electronic theatre pieces, such as *The Wolfman* (1964), and has directed the ONCE multimedia ensemble since 1963.

Plate 1: *Luciano Pavarotti in the rôle of Radames in a scene from*
Aida, *staged at the Royal Opera House, Covent Garden, London,*
in 1984

Plate 2 opposite: *An unauthenticated portrait of Johann Sebastian Bach aged about 30. Museen der Stadt, Erfurt*

Plate 3 right: *One of the costumes designed by Léon Bakst for the ballet based on Rimsky-Korsakov's symphonic suite* Sheherazade

Plate 4: *A scene from the Welsh National Opera's 1986 production of* The Barber of Seville. *Bartolo is played by Donald Adams and Figaro by Gwion Thomas*

assai Very. Often used to qualify other directions; e.g. **allegro assai**, very lively. [Italian]

Assassinio nella cattedrale, L' (*Murder in the Cathedral*) Opera in two acts by Pizzetti based on the composer's Italian version of T. S. Eliot's play about Thomas à Becket. First performance: La Scala, Milan, 1958.

Aston, Hugh (?–1522) English composer. He wrote a *Hornpype* for the virginal and is possibly the author of *My Lady Carey's Dompe*, a set of variations on a ground bass. His bass melodies were used by several later composers, including Byrd.

Atherton, David (1944–) British conductor. Educated at Cambridge and the Royal Academy of Music, he made his debut at the Royal Opera House, Covent Garden, in 1968, since when he has been a resident conductor. He was founder of the London Sinfonietta and its musical director (1968–73). He has made numerous recordings and his publications include editions of Gerhard's works.

Atlantida, La Scenic cantata for solo voices, choir, and orchestra by Falla, with a libretto by Verdaguer. Composed: 1926–41. This work was left unfinished on the composer's death and completed by his pupil Halffter. It describes the myths associated with the New World and its exploration by the Spaniards.

atonality The system of composing music in which no *key is used. *Compare* polytonality. *See also* **twelve-note composition.**

attacca Attack; begin. A direction used to indicate that the player should continue from the end of one section to the beginning of the next without a pause. [Italian]

Attaingnant, Pierre (*c.*1494–*c.*1552) French music publisher. Attaignant was active in Paris and his earliest surviving publication is a breviary of 1525. In 1537 he became royal music printer, a position he retained until his death. His widely circulated publications include many chansons by such composers as Clément Janequin.

Atterburg, Kurt (**Magnus**) (1887–1974) Swedish composer, conductor, and music critic. He was secretary of the Swedish Royal Academy of Music (1940–53) and chairman and founder of the Society of Swedish Composers (1924–47). His works include nine symphonies, five operas, orchestral and chamber music, and the popular rhapsody on Swedish folk tunes, *Varmlandsrhapsodi* (1933).

Attwood, Thomas (1765–1838) British organist and composer, sent by the future George IV to study in Naples and with Mozart in Vienna (1785–87). He was appointed organist at St Paul's Cathedral (1795), the Pavilion Chapel, Brighton (1821), and at the Chapel Royal (1836). He wrote operas and music for the theatre, anthems (including 'I was glad' for the coronation of George IV), and many keyboard works.

aubade A song or piece of music traditionally associated with the morning, i.e. the opposite of a *serenade (evening music). *See also* **alborada.** [French, from *aube*, dawn'

Auber, Daniel-François-Esprit (1782–1871) French composer. He went to London (1802) then studied in Paris with Cherubini; he was director of the Paris Conservatoire (1842–70). Auber's early works were orchestral (including cello concertos), chamber, and vocal. But then he turned to opera, with which he had great success, becoming one of the leading French opéra-comique composers. He collaborated with Scribe, who wrote the librettos for most of his many opéras comiques, including La *Muette de Portici* (1828), *Fra Diavolo* (1830), *Le Cheval de bronze* (1835), and *Manon Lescaut* (1856).

Auden, W(ystan) H(ugh) (1907–73) British poet and critic. He emigrated with Christopher Isherwood to the USA in 1939 and together with Chester Kallmann wrote libretti for Britten's *Paul Bunyan* (1941), Stravinsky's *The Rake's Progress* (1951), and Henz *Elegy for Young Lovers* (1961) and *The Bassarids* (1966). Several of his poems were set by Britten.

auditorium A hall in which people can listen to music being played. In such a concert hall there should be no echoes or *resonance, the music (especially the soft passages) should be clearly audible in all parts of the hall, the reverberation time should be near the optimum for the hall, and the ventilation system should be silent and not permit exterior sounds to enter. Echoes can be reduced by breaking up large plane surfaces (especially high ceilings) and avoiding sweeping curved surfaces, which tend to focus the sound. Resonance of windows, ornaments, etc., must be avoided. Columns and alcoves should not be used if they impede the route of the sound from the performers to the audience. The floor should be raked so that there is a direct path for sound to the audience in the back rows. Reverberation time depends on the size and characteristics of the hall. If it is too long the music sounds badly articulated, i.e. one note does not die away before the next is sounded. On the other hand if it is too short the music sounds dead. Reverberation times are reduced by the presence of an audience and this must be taken into account in the design and the extent to which absorbent materials are used.

augmentation The process of lengthening a musical phrase or melody, usually by doubling the time value of its notes. Compare **diminution.**

augmented interval *see* interval; fourth; fifth; sixth; augmented sixth.

augmented sixth A *chord containing the augmented sixth *interval. The three augmented sixth chords in common use are given the names **French sixth** (in the key of C, A♭CDF♯), **Italian sixth** (A♭CF♯), and **German sixth** (A♭CE♭F♯). Thus all forms include the major third. The origin of the names is not known. See also **Neapolitan sixth.**

aulos A double-reeded pipe of ancient Greece. Often having only three or four finger holes, the aulos was sometimes played in pairs, the melody being played on one and the other providing a drone. The instrument is an early forerunner of the oboe. The Roman equivalent was the **tibia.** See also **Greek music.**

Auric, Georges (1899–1983) French composer, pupil of d'Indy. He was general administrator of the Paris Grand Opéra and Opéra-Comique (1962–68). His prolific output was influenced by Satie and Stravinsky and he was one of the founders of the group of young French composers known as Les *Six. He wrote a number of ballets, of which *Les Matelots* (1925) is perhaps the best known. After the success of his music for René Clair's film *A Nous la Liberté* (1932) he wrote many film scores, including those for *Moulin Rouge* (1952), with its popular hit 'Where is Your Heart,' and *The Lavender Hill Mob* (1951).

Aurora's Wedding see **Sleeping Beauty, The.**

Aus Italien (*From Italy*) Symphony (Op. 16) by Richard Strauss, composed after a visit to Italy in 1886. Each of the four movements bears a subtitle relating to Italian life or scenery: 'The Campagna,' 'The Ruins of Rome,' 'On the Shore of Sorrento,' and 'Neapolitan Folk Life.' The last movement quotes a popular Italian song, 'Funiculi, funicula.'

Austin, Frederic (1872–1952) British baritone and composer. After studying with Charles Lunn, he became an oratorio singer. He arranged the successful modern revival in London of John Gay's *The Beggar's Opera* (1920) and its sequel *Polly* (1923). In 1924, he became artistic director of the British National Opera Company. His compositions include orchestral and incidental music and *Pervigilium Veneris* (1931), for chorus and orchestra.

Austin, Larry (1930–   ) US composer, a pupil of Milhaud. Influenced by jazz improvisation, he has written open-form works, such as *Open Style* (1965), and mixed-media theatre pieces, such as *Agape* (1970).

authentic modes see **modes.**

auxiliary note A type of *passing note that, instead of leading from one chord to another, leads back to the chord or harmony that has just been played.

Ave Maria (*Hail Mary*) A prayer to the Virgin Mary used in the Roman Catholic Church. Also used as an *antiphon, the plainsong associated with the words of the prayer formed the basis for many polyphonic compositions by Renaissance composers, including Josquin and Victoria. Later generations also used the title and words of the prayer; the *Ave Maria* of Gounod superimposes an original melody over the first prelude of Bach's *The Well-Tempered Clavier*, and this is the setting normally associated with the title. Gounod himself called the work *Meditation*; the words of the prayer were added to his melody by somebody else.

Avison, Charles (1709–70) British composer, a pupil of Geminiani. He was organist in Newcastle at the churches of St Nicholas and St John, Westgate Street, from 1736. His *Essay on Musical Expression* (1752), answered by Professor William Hayes of Oxford, aroused much controversy. He wrote many concertos and other chamber works, as well as numerous songs.

Avodath Hakodesh (*Sacred Service*) Setting by Bloch of the Reformed Jewish Sabbath morning service for baritone, choir, and orchestra. Composed: 1930–33. Despite being a liturgical Jewish work, the specifically Jewish qualities of Bloch's music are less apparent in *Avodath Hakodesh* than in much of his earlier music.

ayre A melody-dominated short English song of the late 16th and early 17th centuries. It usually had an accompaniment for lute or other harmony instrument. About one third of the lute ayres published between 1597 and 1622 have extra lower-voice parts. Ayres were usually strophic. The word continued to be used in England throughout the 17th and 18th centuries to denote solo song. Although the spelling is regarded paps obsolete, its retention would help to distinguish the English form from the French *air.

B

B The keynote of the scale of B major. In Germany this note is represented by the letter H, B being used to denote the English B♭. The frequency of B above *middle C is 493.9 hertz (A = 440 hertz).

Baal Shem Suite for violin and piano in three movements by Bloch. Composed: 1923. Subtitled 'Three Poems of Hasidic Life,' the suite is named after Baal Shem Tov (Master of the Good Name), who founded a Jewish pietist sect in the 17th century. The movements are entitled 'Yidui' ('Contrition'), 'Nigun' ('Improvisation') and 'Simchas Torah' ('Rejoicing').

Baba Yaga 1. Orchestral fantasy by Dargomizhsky. Composed: 1862. **2.** Descriptive orchestral piece by Lyadov. Composed: 1904. Called by the composer a 'fairy tale for orchestra,' the work describes the flight of the fairytale witch Baba Yaga, who is also portrayed in one of the movements of Mussorgsky's *Pictures at an Exhibition.*

Babbitt, Milton (1916–) US composer. He studied mathematics before becoming a pupil of Roger Sessions. He is codirector of the Princeton-Columbia Electronic Music Center. From his analytical explorations of serial music, he developed radical new techniques, especially in the field of rhythm, and evolved his own totally serial style. He has written much electronic music, as well as the second (1954) and third (1970) string quartets, *Relata I* (1965) for orchestra, and *Philomel* (1964) for soprano and tape. He has had an immense influence as a teacher and theorist.

Babell, William (*c.*1690–1723) British violinist, harpsichordist, and composer, a pupil of Pepusch. A member of George I's private orchestra and organist of All Hallows, Bread Street, he was one of the first composers to arrange popular operatic airs for the keyboard. He also wrote many sonatas for the violin and other instruments and works for the harpsichord.

Babi Yar Symphony No. 13 by Shostakovitch for bass voice, male choir, and orchestra with words by Yevtushenko. First performance: 1962. Although *Babi Yar* is applied as a nickname to the whole symphony, Shostakovitch himself used it as a subtitle to the first movement only. Babi Yar was the scene of a Jewish massacre by the Nazis in 1941.

baby grand see **piano.**

Bacarisse, Salvador (1898–1963) Spanish composer, resident in Paris from 1939. His works, written in a conservative tonal idiom, include the opera *Charlot* (1933), the ballet *Corrida de Feria* (1930), a piano concerto (1933), a guitar concerto (1953), the cantata *Por la Paz Y Felicidad de Las Naciones* (1950), two string quartets, piano pieces, and songs.

bacchetta see **baguette.**

Bacchus and Ariadne (French: *Bacchus et Ariane*) Ballet in two acts with music by Roussel to a scenario by Abel Hermant. First performance: Opéra, Paris, 1931. The classical ethos of the legend is reflected in music of austere beauty. Ariadne, abandoned by Theseus, is saved from drowning by Bacchus, who bestows the kiss of immortality on her.

BACH A musical theme using the letters of J. S. Bach's name as the notes: B♭–A–C–B♮ (in German nomenclature H = B♮). Bach himself was the first to use this idea, and BACH appears as one of the subjects of the final triple fugue in his *Art of Fugue.* Many later composers have made use of the theme; Schumann wrote a set of six fugues on BACH and Liszt used it in an organ composition. The idea of using one's own name as the basis for a musical composition has been used in more recent times by other composers, including Shostakovitch in his eighth string quartet.

Bach German family of musicians, known since the Reformation (see following entries). The first professional musician was **Johann (Hans) Bach** (?–1626), known as 'der Spielmann' ('the musician'). He was the father of **Christoph Bach** (1613–61), who was the grandfather of Johann Sebastian *Bach and of **Heinrich Bach** (1615–92), whose sons were **Johann Christoph Bach** (1642–1703), organist at Eisenach; and **Johann Michael Bach** (1648–94), organist at Arnstadt and father of J. S. Bach's first wife, **Maria Barbara Bach** (1684–1720).

Bach, Carl Philipp Emanuel (1714–88) German keyboard player and composer, second son of J. S. Bach. He became chamber harpsichordist to Frederick the Great (1740), moving to Hamburg in 1767 as music director of five churches. C. P. E. Bach's compositions emphasize expressive solo writing over counterpoint: he pioneered the use of *sonata form, later developed by Haydn, Mozart, and others. His output includes many keyboard and chamber works, 50 keyboard concertos, 19 symphonies, oratorios and other sacred works, and an important treatise, *Versuch uber di wahre Art das Klavier zu spielen* (1753, 1762).

Bach, Johann Christian (1735–82) German composer, youngest son of J. S. Bach, known as the 'London Bach.' He studied first with his father and brother (C. P. E. Bach) and then with Martini in Italy. In 1762 he moved to London, where he was music master to Queen Charlotte (1763). In London he founded the Bach–Abel concerts (1764); he was also a friend of Mozart, who admired his works. He wrote Italian operas, church music, over 90 symphonies, about 40 concertos and over 30 sonatas for keyboard, and chamber works.

Bach, Johann Christoph Friedrich (1732–95) German organist and composer, second youngest son of J. S. Bach, with whom he studied. Known as the 'Bückeburger Bach,' he was attached to the court of Bückeburg from 1750, becoming leader and director of the chapel there (1758). He set the works of J. G. Herder, writing many cantatas, oratorios, symphonies, and chamber and keyboard works.

Bach, Johann Sebastian (1685–1750) German composer and keyboard player, the most important member of a large and distinguished musical family. Bach was born in Eisenach and may have learnt the basics of music from his father, **Johann Ambrosius Bach** (1645–95), a string player at the Eisenach court. By the age of ten Bach was orphaned and went to live with his brother **Johann Christoph Bach** (1671–1721), who was organist at Ohrdruf and gave Bach his first keyboard lessons. After spending some years as a chorister at Lüneburg, Bach was appointed organist at Arnstadt (1704–07) then moved to a post at Mühlhausen, where he married his cousin Maria Barbara Bach (1684–1720). In 1708 Bach became court organist at Weimar, where he wrote most of his large number of organ works. In 1716 the kapellmeister at Weimar died and was succeeded by his son, an indifferent musician. Disappointed and indignant at being overlooked for this post, in 1717 Bach accepted the appointment of kapellmeister to Prince Leopold of Köthen, where much of his orchestral, chamber, and keyboard music was written. Bach's wife died in 1720 and in 1721 he married Anna Magdelena Wilcken (1701–60); of his 20 children by both marriages several became eminent musicians. In 1723 Bach moved to Leipzig, where as cantor of St Thomas's he wrote the majority of his sacred works and remained for the rest of his life (in his later years he became blind).

During his lifetime Bach was known principally as a superb organist and harpsichordist: the extent of his genius as a composer was not fully recognized until his works were revived in the 19th century, particularly by Mendelssohn and Samuel Wesley. Bach was the last great composer to use counterpoint as a natural means of expression in his music, notably in his fugues. His works also reflect the final development of the chorale and suite.

Bach's organ music includes the *Little Organ Book* (1708–17), over 140 chorale preludes, preludes and fugues, toccatas and fugues, including the *Dorian Toccata and Fugue* (1708–17), and fantasias, sonatas, and trios. His orchestral and chamber works include the 6 *Brandenburg Concertos* (1721), concertos for violin and harpsichord, 4 orchestral suites, A *Musical Offering* (1747), sonatas for various instruments 6 partitas for violin, and 6 unaccompanied cello suites. Of Bach's many fine collections of keyboard music, perhaps the most significant is The *Well-Tempered Clavier* (48 preludes and fugues, 1722–42); among his other keyboard works are the 6 *French Suites* (c.1720), the 6 *English Suites* (c.1725), *Chromatic Fantasia and Fugue* (1730), the *Italian Concerto* (1735) for harpsichord, the *St Anne Fugue* (1739), the *Giant Fugue* (1739), the *Goldberg Variations* (1742), The *Art of Fugue* (possibly for harpsichord), and preludes and fugues, toccatas, and fantasias. His church music – some of his greatest – includes the *St Matthew Passion* (1729) and *St John Passion* (1724), the *B Minor Mass* (1733–38), the *Christmas Oratorio* (1734) and *Easter Oratorio* (1725), over 200 cantatas (among them *Phoebus and Pan*, 1729; and the so-called *Coffee Cantata*, 1732) and 6 motets.

J. S. Bach's works have been catalogued by Wolfgang Schmieder, using *BWV numbers.

Bach, Wilhelm Freidemann (1710–84) German organist and composer, eldest son of J. S. Bach. He was organist in Dresden (1733–46) and in Halle (1746). His father wrote for him the *Clavier-Büchlein* (1720), and his own compositions include several keyboard works, nine symphonies, cantatas, and chamber music.

Bachauer, Gina (1913–76) Greek-born pianist of Austrian and Greek parentage. She studied with Cortot and Rachmaninov and after World War II was based mainly in the USA. She was married to the British conductor Alec Sherman (1907–   ).

Bachianas Brasileiras Set of nine different works for various instrumental groupings by Villa-Lobos. Composed: 1932–45. The instrumentations range from solo piano to full orchestra, sometimes including a part for solo vocalist, and the *bachianas* are organized like a suite. In these compositions Villa-Lobos attempts to apply Bach's contrapuntal techniques to the folk melodies of Brazil.

Bach trumpet see **trumpet.**

Bach-Werke-Verzeichnis see **BWV.**

Backhaus, Wilhelm (1884–1969) German pianist. He studied with Reckendorff at Leipzig and with d'Albert at Frankfurt, subsequently establishing himself as a touring recitalist. Backhaus was particularly noted for his interpretation of Beethoven.

badinerie (or **badinage**) A lively playful piece, e.g. the final movement of Bach's B minor orchestral suite.

Badings, Henk (1907–) Dutch composer. Originally trained in geology, which he taught at Delft until 1934, Badings studied composition with Willem Pijper in 1930–31. From 1934 to 1944 he held academic appointments in music in the Netherlands and Stuttgart. After his conviction as a cultural collaborator he retired from academic life until his appointment as Professor of Acoustics at Utrecht in 1961. His prolific and varied output of operas, symphonies, and instrumental and vocal music includes works written in the 31-note scale of Adriaan Fokker, such as the fourth string quartet (1966), and electronic music, including *Genesis* (1958).

Badura-Skoda, Paul (1927–) Austrian pianist. Badura-Skoda has a particular interest in old keyboard instruments, on which he has recorded all the Beethoven and Schubert sonatas. In addition to his career as a concert pianist, he has produced several books on music; he is married to the musicologist **Eva Badura-Skoda** (1929–).

bagatelle A short piece for piano, which became popular after Beethoven's *Bagatellen* (Op. 33, 119, and 126).

bagpipes Reed instruments in which a bag acts as an air reservoir. Air is either blown into the reservoir by the player or filled with a bellows operated by the player's arm. Air from the bag continuously feeds into the fingered **chanter** (or **chaunter**) pipe on which the melody is played. There are also two to four unfingered drone pipes fed from the bag. The chanter is either cylindrical, usually with a single reed, or conical, in which case it usually has a double reed. Bagpipes have a long and somewhat obscure history, but are still in use in Asia and Africa, as well as in France, Scotland, and Ireland. See also **Union pipes.**

baguette Drumstick or conductor's baton. Italian: **bacchetta.** [French, stick]

Baillie, Dame Isobel (1895–1983) British soprano. She studied in Manchester and Milan. After her London debut in 1923 she became one of England's best-loved sopranos. Her spiritual yet sensuous voice suited oratorio: she excelled in Handel's *Messiah* and Brahms' *A German Requiem.*

Baillot, Pierre (**Marie François de Sales**) (1771–1842) French violinist and composer. He was taught composition by Cherubini and Reicha and quickly gained a reputation as a celebrated virtuoso violinist, touring widely (including a visit to Russia, 1805–08). He was a professor at the Paris Conservatoire, leader of the Paris Opéra orchestra (1821–31) and of the Chapelle Royal orchestra (1825–33), and a noted chamber-music player. Baillot's many violin compositions (including nine concertos and much chamber music) have not been as enduring as his violin method, *L'Art du violon* (1834).

Baird, Tadeusz (1928–81) Polish composer. After early works in a late-Romantic style he adopted serial procedures (c.1956) and the structural use of sound textures, as in *Sinfonia Brevis* (1968). He wrote incidental music and film scores.

Bairstow, Sir Edward Cuthbert (1874–1946) British organist, scholar, and composer of Anglican church music. He studied under Henry Farmer and Sir Frederick Bridge and in 1913 became organist of York Minster. From 1929 until 1946 he was Professor of Music at Durham University and from 1929 to 1930 was President of the Royal College of Organists.

Baker, Dame Janet (1933–) British mezzo-soprano. She studied with Helene Isepp and Meriel St Clair at the Royal College of Music, London. After early roles in Handel, Purcell, and in Cavalli operas she sang in Berlioz's *The Trojans* (in 1969) and more recently in Haydn chamber cantatas. Her warmth of personality is ideally suited to late romantic song cycles, such as Mahler's *Das Lied von der Erde* and Richard Strauss's *Four Last Songs*. She was awarded the DBE in 1976.

Balakirev, Mily Alexeyevich (1837–1910) Russian composer. He spent much of his youth in the country house of the scholar Ulibishev, using his library and working with his orchestra. In 1855 Ulibishev took him to St Petersburg and introduced him to Glinka, who gave him some composition instruction. Balakirev quickly made a reputation as a pianist and teacher. At this time he met Mussorgsky and Cui and later Rimsky-Korsakov (1861) and Borodin (1862), who came to share his nationalist ideas; in 1867 Balakirev's circle became known as The *Five. Balakirev initiated the idea of the Free School of Music at St Petersburg and he organized concerts of works by his circle and by Schumann, Berlioz, and Liszt. He became conductor of the Russian Musical Society (1867–69) and director of the Free School (1868–74). In 1871 he had a nervous breakdown and took a job as an overseer for the railway. In 1874 he returned to music and became director of the Imperial Court Chapel (1883) with Rimsky-Korsakov as his assistant.

Balakirev's uncompromising nationalism led him into conflict with Russian academic musical circles but he was a potent influence on Russian music. In his compositions he fused orientalism and Russian folk elements with a western idiom. His colourful orchestral music includes two symphonies, a piano concerto, two overtures on Russian themes,

Mily Balakirev, a founder member of 'The Five'

and the symphonic poem *Tamara (1867–82). He also wrote much piano music (some of it technically demanding, like the dazzling oriental fantasy *Islamey, 1869), choral and chamber music, and songs. He made many arrangements, editions, and piano transcriptions and published two collections of Russian folk songs (1866, 1898).

balalaika A three-stringed Russian *lute with a fretted fingerboard and a triangular body. It is made in various sizes, from treble to bass. The **dombra** (*or* **domra**) is an earlier version of the balalaika, having a longer neck and an oval body.

Balfe, Michael William (1808–70) Irish composer, singer, and violinist. After playing the violin and singing in London theatres he went to Paris, where he was introduced to Rossini by Cherubini; he sang Figaro in Rossini's *The Barber of Seville* in 1827. He sang in many Italian opera houses, including La Scala, Milan, with Malibran. In 1838 he was Papageno in the first English production of Mozart's *The Magic Flute*. Balfe's operas *The Siege of Rochelle* (1835), *The Maid of Artois* (1836), and *Falstaff* (1838) were all successfully produced in London, but it was *The *Bohemian Girl* (1843) that established him as the leading composer of English operas of the 19th century; it was performed throughout Europe and shows his mastery of the ballad. Balfe was conductor of Her Majesty's Theatre from 1846 to 1852, when he visited St Petersburg and Europe. In addition to many operas he composed choral works, songs, and a little chamber music and wrote three books of singing studies.

ballabile Danceable; to be danced. Used, especially in the 19th century, to denote a dancelike piece. [Italian]

ballad An English narrative poem that is sung, in which words and tune have equal importance. The popular ballad was usually improvised and originally depended for its survival mainly upon an oral tradition. During the 16th century and after, the **broadside ballad**, printed on one side of a sheet of paper, was sold by street singers. During the 19th century a more sophisticated 'drawing-room' ballad arose: these songs were often featured in **ballad concerts**, which were started by the publisher John Boosey in 1867.

ballade 1. One of the standard forms of 14th-century French poetry, often set to music. It developed out of the troubadour–trouvère chanson and normally had three stanzas. Its stanzaic form was usually ababcdE, the last line being the same in all stanzas, so making a refrain. The musical form was AAB (A corresponding to ab and B to the remaining lines). The musical poet Jean de la Mote seems to have been the driving force behind the 14th-century ballade, which Machaut made famous. The form continued to be employed, although less frequently, during the 15th century (for instance by Dufay). **2.** A late German narrative poem, usually romantic and frequently dealing with medieval tales. Such poems were not uncommonly set as longish through-composed songs, e.g. Goethe's 'Erlkönig' set by Schubert. Karl Loewe, who left 17 volumes of *Balladen*, is regarded as the classical master. In the late 19th century large-scale settings with voices and orchestra were written, e.g. Wolf's 'Der Feuerreiter'. **3.** A piano piece distantly related to the romantic heroic song because of its dramatic qualities. Often long, with contrasting lyrical and heroic sections, the form was inspired by Chopin followed especially by Brahms, Liszt, and Grieg.

ballad opera An early 18th-century English type of opera in which ballads set to popular tunes were intermingled with spoken dialogue. One of the earliest and most famous examples is *The Beggar's Opera* (1728), with words by John Gay and music by Pepusch.

ballata One of the three principal forms of 14th-century Italy, the others being the *madrigal and the *caccia. It is the equivalent of the French *virelai, having its origins in the 12th century, and may have any one of five forms depending on the number of lines of the text and the number of syllables in each line. The overall musical form usually comprises two distinct sections, separated by a break (ABBA). The first section is called the **volta** (A), the second the **pedes** (B). Ballate are found in both monodic and polyphonic settings and vary in length. A notable composer was Landini, who exploited the various open and closed cadences at the ends of sections.

ballet 1. The stylized performance of dance and, usually, mime to music. The princely courts of Europe during the 16th and 17th centuries fostered the sort of entertainment from which modern ballet was eventually to emerge. France played a major role, both in courtly and opera ballets, notably by Lully. Performers clad in heavy and elaborate dresses danced daintily. This, together with a stereotyped order and mythological background, was overthrown by Jean-Georges Noverre (1727–1810), who established **ballet d'action** (or **dramatic ballet**). The continuous five-act ballet became more common in the 18th century, the leading centre being Vienna – Gluck's *Don Juan* (1761), Mozart's *Les Petits riens* (1778), and Beethoven's *Prometheus* (1801) are 'Viennese' ballets. By the end of the 18th century the ballet had lost its courtly image and associations and was also featuring a more gymnastic display, although as yet hand movements were mainly omitted. The technique of dancing on the tips of the toes, called **pointe**, came in between 1810 and 1820: Marie Taglioni was one of its first major exponents. Moveover, skin-tight costumes were increasingly preferred, following Maillot's lead. These ingredients were incorporated in the spectacular ballets of the 19th century, e.g. Delibes' *Coppélia* (1870).

Russian ballet increasingly came to the fore during the 19th and early 20th centuries, having been modernized by Hilverding during the latter part of the 18th century. Centred notably at St Petersburg, it produced some marvellous works, especially Tchaikovsky's *Swan Lake* (1877), The *Sleeping Beauty* (1890), and The *Nutcracker* (1892). It made further advances under the direction of the impresario *Diaghilev, who toured with his Ballets Russes throughout Europe. The major composer for his ballets was Stravinsky, whose The *Firebird* (1910), *Petrushka* (1911), and The *Rite of Spring* (1913) were highly acclaimed; notable dancers were Pavlova, Lopokova, Massine, and Nijinsky. During the 1920s many members of the company left and dispersed throughout Europe. One such leading artist, Ninette de Valois, was responsible for the founding of modern English ballet. She started the Sadler's Wells Ballet, which sometimes performed at Covent Garden. Out of this emerged the Royal Ballet of today. Among the earliest productions was Vaughan Williams' *Job* (produced 1931). Another Diaghilev dancer was Marie Rambert, who in 1926 formed her own company in London, the Ballet Rambert. Contemporary ballets in Europe included Ravel's *Bolero* (1928) and La *Valse* (1929) and Bartók's imaginative score for The *Miraculous Mandarin* (1919; altered version 1926).

Present-day ballet incorporates both traditional forms and modern (often nonallegorical) dance, which dispenses with decorative costume and sets. Choreography has progressed, but little original music is now commissioned for the ballet.
2. See ballett.

ballett (or **ballet**) A kind of English *madrigal, distinguished by its regular dance rhythm and 'fa-la' refrain. It originated in 14th-century Europe and in its most primitive form was intended to be sung and danced, although it is most unlikely that the Elizabethans danced their balletts. The 'fa-la' comes at the end of each section. It is a rhythmically florid vocalized refrain, equivalent to an instrumental interlude. Sometimes other syllables are used, e.g. 'no-no' in Weelkes' 'Say, dainty nymphs.' Morley (1595) and Weelkes (1598) each left one complete set of balletts. Many others by various composers are scattered among madrigal collections.

Ballif, Claude (1924–) French composer, a pupil of Messiaen and Boris Blacher. His works include *Spare Parts* (1953) for piano, and *This and That* (1965) for orchestra.

Ballo in maschera, Un (*A Masked Ball*) Opera in three acts by Verdi with libretto by Somma, based on Scribe's libretto for Auber's opera *Gustave III, ou Le Bal masqué*. First performance: Apollo Theatre, Rome, 1859. Censorship demanded that the action be changed from the assassination of Gustav III of Sweden at a masked ball in Stockholm, and it was incongruously reset in Boston, Massachusetts. It is unusual in Verdi that the leading male role, Gustav III (Riccardo in the Boston version), is for tenor rather than baritone.

bamboo pipe A simple form of *recorder, used in schools for teaching music. The instrument is sufficiently rudimentary to be made by the children themselves.

Banchieri, Adriano (1568–1634) Italian composer, organist, and theorist. He was organist of S Michele in Bosco (near Bologna), where he later became abbot (1620). He was also active at Imola (1601–07). He is best known for his madrigal comedies; for instance, *Il Metamorfosi musicale* (1601) consists almost entirely of grotesque musical parodies. In the same humorous vein are *La Pazzia senile* (1598), the *Zabaione musicale* (1603), *La Barca di Venezia* (1605), and the *Festina nella sera di giovedi grasso* (1608). Banchieri also wrote a number of sacred compositions and theoretical works.

band A large group of instrumental players. The word is often applied to a combination of brass (sometimes with woodwind) and percussion, as in the *brass band and *military band. It may be used for sections of the orchestra (e.g. wind band, string band) and it is applied to groups of similar instruments (e.g. accordion band). The term has been widely adopted in the field of jazz and popular music.

bandora see **pandora**.

bandurría A small Spanish 12-stringed fretted *lute used in folk music. It has a waisted body and the strings are tuned in pairs.

Banister, John (*c*.1625–79) English composer, violinist, and flageolet player. At the Restoration he became one of the king's violinists and was later appointed director of the king's band of 12 violins, a group modelled on Lully's 'petit violons.' He lost this post, accused of fraud, but remained in the King's Musick until his death. From 1672 he organized some of the earliest public concerts. His works include songs for plays by Dryden and others and instrumental music. His son, **John Banister** (?–*c*.1725), was also a composer and violinist.

Banks, Don (1923–80) Australian composer, a pupil of Seiber and Dallapiccola and much influenced by Babbitt. He wrote serial works, such as a horn concerto (1965), jazz-based pieces, such as *Settings from Roget* (1966), and film and television music.

Bantock, Sir Granville (1868–1946) British composer and conductor. He trained for the civil service but later entered the Royal Academy of Music. After a spell as director of music at New Brighton (near Liverpool), in 1900 he was appointed principal of the Birmingham and Midland Institute School of Music and from 1908 until 1934 was Professor of Music at Birmingham University. He composed many programmatic works in a conservative early romantic style, including an oratorio setting of Fitzgerald's *Omar Khayyám* (1909) and the *Hebridean Symphony* (1915). He wrote the music for five ballets and the operas *Caedmar*, *Pearl of Iran*, and *The Seal Woman*. He also wrote three choral symphonies, many part songs and song cycles, and a considerable amount of instrumental music, including piano sonatas, sonatas for violin and piano, and pieces for piano and cello.

bar 1. One of the metrical units into which a piece of music is divided. US: **measure. 2.** (*or* **bar line**) Any of the vertical lines drawn through the staves of a piece of music to indicate such units. See also **double bar; rhythm.**

Barber, Samuel (1910–81) US composer. He entered the Curtis Institute, Philadelphia, in 1924 and later taught there (1931–33, 1939–42). He won many awards for his work, including prizes for the violin sonata (1928) and the overture to *The School for Scandal* (1933), the American Prix de Rome (1935), and Pulitzer Prizes (1935, 1936, 1958, 1963). His early music, such as the *Adagio for Strings* from the string quartet (1936), is rich and romantic, but with the violin concerto (1939) his style became more dissonant. He has also written three operas, including **Vanessa* (for which he won the 1958 Pulitzer Prize) and *Anthony and Cleopatra* (1964).

Barber of Baghdad, The see **Barbier von Bagdad, Der.**

Barber of Seville, The (Italian: *Il Barbiere di Siviglia*) **1.** Opera in two acts by Rossini on a text by Sterbini from the play by Beaumarchais. First performance: Teatro Argentina, Rome, 1816. It tells the story of the wooing of Rosina (soprano), ward of Dr Bartolo (bass), by Count Almaviva (tenor) in the guise of an impoverished student, Lindoro, managed by the irrepressible barber-factotum, Figaro (baritone). The plot of Mozart's *The Marriage of Figaro* is a sequel to it. **2.** An opera by Paisiello with libretto by Petrosellini. First performance: St Petersburg, 1782. It, too, is based on Beaumarchais's play.

barber-shop singing A branch of choral singing, particularly associated with men's choirs, originating in the barbers' shops of New York during the last quarter of the 19th century. The style does not easily lend itself to progressive development, and the repertoire is largely based on the popular songs of the period, which were subjected to off-the-cuff close-harmony treatment. The enjoyment and success of this stylized music relies for its impact on attack, perfect intonation, and balance, since chordal progression and the chromatic 'slip' is the distinguishing feature rather than contrapuntal or polyphonic movement. Although there are barber-shop choirs in the UK, the phenomenon has not penetrated very deeply into the ranks of the indigenous male-voice choir tradition.

Barbiere di Siviglia, Il see **Barber of Seville, The.**

Barbieri, Francisco Asenjo (1823–94) Spanish composer and scholar, a pupil at the Madrid conservatory. He composed over 60 *zarzuelas in which he incorporated Spanish folk elements; the best known of them is *El Barberillo de Lavapiés* (*The Little Barber of Lavapies*, 1874). Barbieri assembled the finest collection of music in Spain (now in the Biblioteca Nacional, Madrid); he transcribed many manuscripts and was a prolific writer on music.

Barbier von Bagdad, Der (*The Barber of Baghdad*) Opera in two acts by Peter Cornelius, who wrote his own libretto. First performance (conducted by Liszt, by whom Cornelius was employed as secretary): 1858. It is based on a story from the *Arabian Nights*: the wooing of Margiana (soprano) by Mureddin (tenor), helped and hindered by the outrageous behaviour of the barber, Abul (bass).

Barbirolli, Sir John (1899–1970) British conductor of Franco-Italian parentage. Originally a cellist, he played with the Queen's Hall Orchestra (1915). Subsequently he conducted several major orchestras in the UK and USA, including the New York Philharmonic Symphony Orchestra (1937–43) and the Hallé Orchestra (1943–68). An outstanding conductor of romantic music, Barbirolli was a champion of Elgar and Delius. He was knighted in 1949. The oboist Evelyn *Rothwell was his wife.

barcarolle A Venetian boat song characterized by a lilting 6/8 or 12/8 rhythm, as in Mendelssohn's *Songs Without Words* (Op. 30 No. 6 or Op. 62 No. 5). Italian: **barcarola.**

Daniel Barenboim

Sir John Barbirolli

Bardi, Giovanni de' (1534–1612) Italian music patron, composer, and poet. A member of the Tuscan court, he became lieutenant-general of the pontifical guard to Clement VIII in 1592. In Florence he patronized Giulio Caccini, Vincenzo Galilei, and other musicians, who formed the members of his circle, the so-called *Camerata. This group met to discuss, among other matters, the nature of Greek music and Bardi summarized their findings in his *Discorso*. He was also involved in the production of intermezzi for the Florentine court.

Barenboim, Daniel (1942–) Israeli pianist and conductor. He was taught piano by his parents, then studied at Salzburg, Rome, and Paris, making his debut as a pianist in England (1955) and New York (1957). He made his conducting debut in 1962 (in Israel). Barenboim has held appointments with the English Chamber Orchestra (from 1964) and the Orchestre de Paris (from 1975) and has appeared as guest conductor of many European and US orchestras. He was married to the cellist Jacqueline *du Pré.

baritone 1. The middle voice of the three natural varieties of male voices (compare **bass; tenor**). It is heavier than the tenor but capable of producing a brilliance in the upper register that has been much exploited by opera composers. The upper limit of its range is A♭ above middle C extending downwards for two octaves. **2.** See **saxhorns; saxophone.**

Bärmann, Heinrich (1784–1847) German clarinetist. He was principal clarinetist of the Munich Court Orchestra and Weber wrote many works for him.

Barnby, Sir Joseph (1838–96) British composer and conductor, a pupil at the Royal Academy of Music. From 1871 to 1886 he was organist at St Anne's, Soho, where he gave annual performances of Bach's *St John Passion* and the first performance in England of Dvořák's *Stabat Mater* (1883) and Wagner's *Parsifal* (1884). He was precentor of Eton College from 1875 to 1892, the year he became principal of the Guildhall School of Music and was knighted. Barnby composed an oratorio and much church music, including chants and hymn tunes; his best-known work is the part song *Sweet and Low*.

baroque music Music of the period 1600–1750, named after the corresponding period of German and Austrian architecture, which was characterized by its elaborate and ornate appearance. In the 19th century the term 'baroque' had pejorative connotations, since the music of this period was then regarded as representing no more than a degeneration of Renaissance principles; today the term simply refers to this particular period of composition. Baroque music is characterized by the use of the continuo and its resultant establishment of major and minor tonality, which succeeded the modal system of the Renaissance; hence the former independence and equality of all the individual parts was replaced by two principal lines, the melody and the bass, with the inner parts carrying the harmony and having much less importance. Nevertheless, true polyphony still continued, especially in Germany, and in the late baroque reached the peak of its development. Many new forms came into being during this period, including opera, oratorio, cantata, concerto, and the suite, and the output of instrumental music was greatly increased. The most important baroque composers were Monteverdi, Corelli, and Vivaldi in Italy, Lully and Rameau in France, J. S. Bach in Germany, and Handel and Purcell in England. Compare **rococo music.**

baroque organ An *organ of the type in use during Bach's lifetime.

Barraqué, Jean (1928–73) French composer, a pupil of Messiaen. Rejecting collage and indeterminacy, he evolved his own dramatically expressive serial style in such works as *Séquence* (1950–55), his piano sonata (1952), and *Chant après chant* (1966), part of his unfinished cycle based on Hermann Broch's novel *La Mort de Virgile*.

Barraud, Henry (1900–) French composer. After attending the Paris Conservatoire as a pupil of Caussade (1926–27), he studied privately with Dukas. He was musical director of the 1937 Paris Exhibition (1934–37) then joined French radio and became its musical director (1944–65). He was codirector (with Jean Rivier) of the prewar Triton association. Barraud's works include operas, orchestral and chamber music, and the oratorio *Le Mystère des Saints Innocents* (1946).

barré The laying of the index finger of the left hand across all the strings of a guitar or similar instrument at a particular place on the fingerboard in the course of forming a chord. It is used particularly in playing the wide-necked classical guitar as a way of stopping the bass string (which would be stopped with the thumb in a wire-strung narrow-necked instrument).

barrel organ 1. A pipe organ operated mechanically by a rotating cylinder (barrel) from which pins and studs project to lift tongue-shaped keys, which admit air to the appropriate pipes. The operator turns a handle, which both rotates the barrel and works the bellows. Barrel organs were made in different shapes and sizes; from the end of the 18th century and during much of the 19th century they were used in churches too small or too remote to afford an organist. Hand-cranked barrel organs were also mounted on hand carts and used as street organs by organ-grinders. Fairground **steam organs** operate on the same principle but

A Welsh National Opera production of The Bartered Bride

are larger, more elaborate, and are driven by steam rather than a handle. **2.** (*or* **street piano**) A piano operated by a barrel-and-pin mechanism and used in the streets by buskers and others. The mechanism is operated by turning a handle.

Barrios, Ángel (1882–1964) Spanish guitarist. A pupil of Gédalge, he composed many zarzuelas and instrumental works, particularly guitar music.

Bartered Bride, The (Czech: *Prodaná Nevěsta*) Comic opera in three acts by Smetana, with libretto by Sabina. First performance: National Theatre, Prague, 1866. The tale of the betrothal of Marenka and Jenik is set in a Bohemian village in springtime and complicated by the intrigues of the local marriage broker, Kecal.

Bartholomée, Pierre (1937–) Belgian composer and conductor, a pupil of Pousseur. He has experimented with the use of microtonal intervals, as in *Le Tombeau de Marin Marais* (1967).

Bartók, Béla (1881–1945) Hungarian pianist, ethnomusicologist, and composer; he emigrated to the USA in 1940. A pupil of László Erkel and then of Koessler and Thomas at the Budapest Academy, where he taught the piano (1907–34), Bartók toured as a concert pianist for most of his life. In 1905 with *Kodály he began his lifelong research into East European and Arab folk music, discovering true Magyar folk music to be quite different from the Gypsy style then regarded as authentic. His music, which incorporates the sound of folk music without literal quotation, together with dissonant harmonies, chromaticism, and great contrapuntal and rhythmic vitality, includes six quartets, the trio *Contrasts* (1938), three piano concertos, an opera (*Bluebeard's Castle*, 1911), and other important orchestral works, the best known of which is the *Concerto for Orchestra* (1943). He also wrote a number of piano works, including *Mikrokosmos* (1926–37), a set of pieces for students. He died in poverty in the USA.

Bartolozzi, Bruno (1911–80) Italian composer. He studied at the Cherubini Conservatory, Florence (1926–30), and taught there from 1965; he also studied conducting at the Chiga Academy, Siena (1953). With the *Concerto for Orchestra* (1952) Bartolozzi adopted serial technique. Like his contemporary, Berio, he pioneered the use of advanced instrumental techniques (such as multiphonics) in such works as *Collage* (1967) for oboe, describing these techniques in his book *New Sounds for Woodwind* (1967).

Bartoš, Jan Zdeněk (1908–81) Czech violinist and composer, educated at the Prague School for Music Teachers (1933–35) and the Prague conservatory (1935–43). After World War II he held various Czech government posts in music and education. His works, which include five symphonies and nine string quartets, were in the romantic nationalist style of Vitězslav Novák and Josef Suk.

baryton A type of bass *viol invented towards the end of the 17th century. It had six bowed strings and up to 40 wire strings that ran inside the neck, which was open from the rear so that some of these strings could be plucked by the left thumb; the others acted as drones. Haydn wrote nearly 200 works for the baryton because his patron, Prince Nicolaus Esterházy, was an adept amateur player. Difficult both to tune and to play, the instrument went out of use in the 19th century.

bass 1. The lowest and deepest of men's voices (compare **baritone; tenor**), ranging from middle C down to E one and a half octaves lower. True basses can be classified as either **basso profondo**, with a very low range, or **basso cantante**, more suited to lyrical parts. The Russian basso profondo is capable of producing lower notes than his western counterpart, although in England the Rev John Gostling, the celebrated bass for whom Purcell wrote so many of his songs, had almost the most extensive range in the history of bass singers. **2.** Describing instruments having a low range. **3.** Short for *double bass.

Bassarids, The Opera seria in one act (with intermezzo) by Henze, with libretto by W. H. Auden and Chester Kallman based on Euripides' *The Bacchae*. First performance: Salzburg, 1966. Bassarids is an alternative name for the Bacchae, worshippers of Dionysus. The action symbolizes the revenge taken by the sensual Dionysian side of man's nature if its demands are denied and repressed.

bass clarinet see **clarinet**.

bass clef see **clef**.

bass drum A large drum used in the modern orchestra. It may be double- or single-headed and is normally played with padded drumsticks. It produces a low note but cannot be tuned.

basse Bass. Hence **basse chiffrée** (*or* **basse continue**), figured bass; **basse chantante**, basso cantante (see **bass**). [French]

basset horn see **clarinet**.

basso Bass; bass part or voice. See also **continuo**. [Italian]

bassoon The bass member of the orchestral *woodwind section. It was developed in the 17th century from the *curtal and consists of two parallel tubes joined together at the bottom end. A brass crook containing the double reed and mouthpiece is attached to the upper end of one of the tubes; the other tube terminates in a bell from which the sound issues. Early bassoons had only two to four keys, but the modern instrument has a sophisticated key system devised by Wilhelm Heckel in the 19th century. The range of the instrument is from B♭ below the bass staff to E at the top of the treble staff. The **double-bassoon** (*or* **contrabassoon**) has a range an octave lower. The bassoon is an

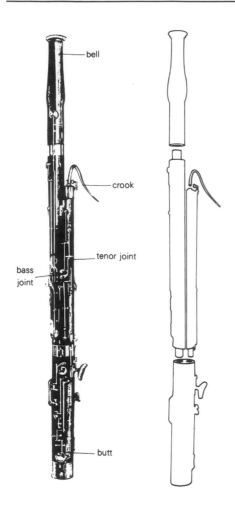

bell

crook

tenor joint

bass joint

butt

The parts of the bassoon and how it is dismantled

important member of the orchestra, its repertoire including concertos by Vivaldi, Mozart, and Weber. Italian: **fagotto**; German: **Fagott**.

bass trumpet see **trumpet**.

Bastien und Bastienne Pastoral operetta by Mozart (aged 12) with libretto by Weiskern. First performance: the garden theatre of Dr Anton Mesmer, Vienna, 1768. It tells the story of the separation and reunion of a pair of lovers.

Bateson, Thomas (*c.*1570–1630) English madrigalist. In 1599 he became organist of Chester Cathedral and by 1609 he had moved to Christ Church Cathedral, Dublin. He composed a madrigal for *The *Triumphs of Oriana* (1601), which arrived too late to be included. Bateson published two collections of madrigals (1604, 1618) in a style reminiscent of Morley and Weelkes; one anthem also survives.

Bath Festival An annual festival of music founded in 1948 as The Bath Assembly and based in Bath. It initially

specialized in 18th-century music under the artistic direction of Ian Hunter. In 1959 Hunter became the festival's manager (until 1968) and was joined by Yehudi Menuhin, who formed the Bath Festival Orchestra (later renamed the Menuhin Festival Orchestra, 1968). Subsequent artistic directors have been Michael Tippett (1969–74), William Glock (1975–84) and Amelia Freedman (1984–   ).

baton The stick with which the conductor of an orchestra, choir, etc., beats time. Originally, in the 15th century, the conductor of an ensemble beat time with a roll of music; in the 17th century the fashion was for the conductor to mark the beat by banging a heavy stick on the floor. The modern baton is thought to have originated in the 18th century in Germany but its use did not become standard practice in England until about 1820.

Battaglia di Legnano, La Lyric tragedy by Verdi to a libretto by Cammarano, based upon the play *La Bataille de Toulouse* by Méry. First performance: 1849. The patriotic nature of the plot is typical of Verdi's early works.

battery The *percussion instruments of the orchestra. French: **batterie**.

Battle of the Huns Tone poem by Liszt based on a painting by Kaulbrach. Composed: 1857.

Battle of Vitoria (*or* **Wellington's Victory**) Symphony by Beethoven. Composed: 1813. Originally written for a mechanical instrument invented by Malzel, this symphony depicts the defeat of Napoleon by the British at the Battle of Vitoria in Spain. It is sometimes called the *Battle Symphony* and quotes 'Rule Britannia' to represent the British army and 'Malbrouck s'en va-t-en guerre' for the French army. This programmatic symphony is not counted as one of Beethoven's nine symphonies.

battuta Beat. The direction **a battuta** is used to indicate a return to strict time after a rhythmically freer episode. [Italian]

Bax, Sir Arnold (Edward Trevor) (1883–1953) British composer. He studied in London at the Royal Academy of Music under Corder and was appointed Master of the King's Music in 1941; he was knighted in 1937. His highly romantic programmatic music was influenced by Celtic folklore, the poetry of Yeats, and northern scenery. He composed seven symphonies, ballets (the best known, *The Truth about the Russian Dancers*, was produced by Diaghilev in 1920), instrumental music, and the four symphonic poems *In the Faëry Hills* (1909), *The *Garden of Fand* (1913), **November Woods* (1917), and *Tintagel* (1917).

Bayle, François (1932–   ) French composer, a pupil of Messiaen. He became a colleague of Schaeffer and later director of the Groupe de Recherches Musical. He has produced musique-concrète works, such as *Murmure des Eaux* (1970), and film scores.

Bayreuth A town in Bavaria, Germany, where Richard *Wagner lived and built his Festival Theatre. The theatre was designed by Wagner with visual and acoustic properties (e.g. a deep hooded orchestra pit) that enabled him to realize his artistic ideals. In 1876 the entire *Ring* cycle was performed there and in 1882 *Parsifal* was staged. Regular Wagner festivals have been held at Bayreuth ever since (apart from interruptions during World War II); they were at first organized by Wagner's widow, Cosima, then by his son Siegfried, and later by other descendants. The Richard Wagner Foundation Bayreuth has administered the festival since 1973.

Bazzini, Antonio (1818–97) Italian violinist, composer, and teacher. Until 1864 Bazzini had a flourishing international career as a virtuoso violinist. He became a composition professor (1873) and director (1882) of the Milan conservatory, where his pupils included Mascagni and Puccini. Bazzini was a leading figure in the revival of nonoperatic composition in Italy; he composed in all genres but is best known for his violin works (among them *La Ronde les lutins*, 1852) and chamber music (six string quartets, two string quintets, etc.).

BBC (*or* **British Broadcasting Corporation**) The BBC has made a great contribution to the increase in knowledge of music this century. Its first broadcast was in 1922 and since then it has had a great influence on British musical life, aiming to reflect interest in music of all kinds. A Music Programme (now Radio 3) was introduced in 1964, taking over from the Third Programme, and it broadcasts a wide range of serious music. Radio 1 broadcasts pop music; Radio 2 light music. The BBC has always recognized its educational role and it broadcasts music programmes for schools; it also publishes books on musical topics and has a well-stocked library.

In addition to administrating the Henry Wood *Promenade Concerts, the BBC has many of its own performing groups: the *BBC Symphony Orchestra, BBC Northern Symphony Orchestra (1934), BBC Scottish Orchestra (1935), BBC Welsh Orchestra (1935), and many smaller groups (the Concert Orchestra, Radio Orchestra, Midland Radio Orchestra, etc.). The BBC Singers is a small professional choir; founded in 1924 as the Wireless Chorus, it became the BBC Chorus in 1935 and took its present name in 1973. The BBC Symphony Chorus sings with the BBC Symphony Orchestra; it was founded in 1928 as the National Chorus and renamed successively the BBC Chorus (1932), the BBC Choral Society (1935), and the BBC Symphony Chorus (1977).

BBC Symphony Orchestra A symphony orchestra founded in London in 1930. It is the chief orchestra of the *BBC and quickly became one of the world's leading orchestras, whose guest conductors have included Richard Strauss, Toscanini, and Weingartner. Among its chief conductors have been Adrian Boult, Malcolm Sargent, Rudolf Schwarz, Anton Dorati, Colin Davis, Pierre Boulez, Gennadi Rozdestvensky, Sir John Pritchard and Andrew Davis. The orchestra is noted for its virtuoso performances of large-scale 20th-century works and has given many premieres, particularly of British works.

Beach, Mrs H. H. A. (Amy Marcy Cheney; 1867–1944) US composer and pianist. In addition to an international career as a concert pianist, Mrs Beach was the leading woman composer of her time: she was the first US woman to write a symphony (the *Gaelic Symphony*, 1896). Though best known for her songs, she also wrote an opera, a piano concerto, and choral, chamber, and piano music, much of it eclectic and complex.

Bear, The 1. (French: *L'Ours*) Symphony No. 82 in C major by Haydn. Composed: 1786. It has been suggested that the last movement is meant to depict a fairground bear dancing to the music of bagpipes, a common spectacle in Haydn's day. This symphony is one of the so-called *Paris Symphonies*. **2.** Opera in one act by Walton with libretto by Paul Dehn, based on Chekhov's short story of the same name. First performance: Aldeburgh Festival, 1967. Commissioned by the Serge Koussevitzky Music Foundation, it tells of a sprightly young widow, Madame Popova (mezzo-soprano), who is debtor to the bearlike landowner Smirnov (baritone).

beating-reed instruments see **reed instruments.**

Béatrice et Bénédict (*Beatrice and Benedick*) Opera in two acts by Berlioz with libretto by the composer based on Shakespeare's *Much Ado About Nothing*. First performance: Baden-Baden, 1862. The plot is simplified by concentrating on the spirited relationship of Béatrice (mezzo-soprano) with Bénédict (tenor) and omitting the intrigue of Don John.

beats A periodic increase and decrease in loudness when two notes of nearly equal pitch are sounded together. The number of beats per second is equal to the difference in the frequencies of the two notes. Beats are useful in tuning two strings to the same pitch; when the beats disappear the strings are in tune. Piano tuners, for example, use beats to assist them in determining when two strings of a particular note are in tune.

According to Helmholtz's theory, beats are the cause of *dissonance. Dissonance is produced either by the beating of two notes a semitone apart (e.g. C and C♯) or by two notes separated by a greater interval (e.g. C and F♯), one of which produces overtones a semitone apart from the other (G and F♯). Consonance, according to the Helmholtz theory, occurs when no such beats are produced, e.g. between fifths. When C and G are played together, for example, no overtones are produced that cause beats.

Beaumarchais, Pierre Augustin Caron de (1732–99) French playwright. His outstanding comedies *Le Barbier de Séville* (1775) and *Le Mariage de Figaro* (1784) were subsequently used as bases for libretti, the former by Rossini (1816) and the latter by Mozart (1786).

Beaux Arts Trio US piano trio founded in 1955. Its members are Menahem Pressler (piano), Isidore Cohen (violin), and Peter Wyley (cello). The trio has recorded many works belonging to the standard repertory and is generally admired for its accurate ensemble and stylish interpretations.

Bebung A *vibrato effect achieved by shaking the finger stopping a string in a bowed instrument or depressing a clavichord key. [German, trembling]

bécarre Natural; the natural sign (♮). See also **accidental**. Italian: **bequadro**. [French]

Bechstein, Karl (1826–1900) German piano maker and founder (in 1853) of the Bechstein company of piano manufacturers in Berlin. In 1901 the Bechstein Hall (renamed Wigmore Hall in 1917) was opened next to the London premises of the Bechstein company. The factory in Berlin was severely damaged during World War II but began to produce pianos again in 1951.

Beck, Franz (*c*.1723–1809) German composer and violinist, a pupil of Johann Stamitz. He fled from Mannheim after a duel and worked in Marseilles (1762) and Bordeaux (1761), where his opera *La Belle jardinière* (1767) was produced. He directed his own *Stabat Mater* in Paris (1783) and wrote many symphonies and divertissements, sacred music, and keyboard works.

Becken Cymbals. [German]

Beckwith, John (1927–) Canadian composer, a pupil of Nadia Boulanger. He has moved from a neoclassical style to the use of serial procedures and collage techniques, as in *Message to Winnipeg* (1960).

Bedford, David (1937–) British composer, a pupil of Lennox Berkeley and Luigi Nono. His works, which often combine advanced techniques with the influence of rock music, include *Music for Albion Moonlight* (1965) and *Star's End* (1974). He has a special interest in music for schoolchildren and has worked in the pop field as an arranger. His brother, **Steuart Bedford** (1939–), is a conductor.

Beecham, Sir Thomas (1879–1961) British conductor. Beecham used his personal fortune (derived from the Beecham pharmaceutical company) to promote his career.

Sir Thomas Beecham rehearsing the London Philharmonic Orchestra

He founded the Beecham Symphony Orchestra (1908), an opera company (1910), the London Philharmonic Orchestra (1932), and the Royal Philharmonic Orchestra (1947). Beecham earned an international reputation by his expressive extrovert style of conducting and his lively wit. He excelled in Haydn and Mozart and championed Richard Strauss and Sibelius. The friend and biographer of Delius, he organized a series of festivals of his music.

Beecroft, Norma (1934–) Canadian composer, a pupil of Copland, Petrassi, and Maderna. She has worked at the Toronto and Princeton electronic studios and written chamber and orchestral music and live-tape pieces.

Beeson, Jack (Hamilton) (1921–) US composer. After studying at the Eastman School of Music he was taught privately by Bartók (1943–44) then worked at Columbia University, where he was appointed Professor of Music in 1967. He has lectured at the Juilliard School (1961–63). His works include a symphony (1959) and six operas, including *Lizzie Borden* (1965).

Beethoven, Ludwig van (1770–1827) German composer and pianist, born in Bonn. Beethoven's father was a court singer who attempted to exploit his son's prodigious musical talent. His first important teacher was Christian Gottlob Neefe, a court organist to whom Beethoven became assistant in 1782. In 1787 he paid a brief visit to Vienna, where he probably met Mozart and may have had lessons from him. In 1789 he returned to Bonn, where he played the viola in the court chapel and theatre and became a close friend of Count Waldstein, whose patronage enabled him to mix in artistic circles. In 1792 Haydn was introduced to Beethoven on a visit to Bonn. He was so impressed with him that he arranged for Beethoven to become his pupil in Vienna. However, the relationship turned out to be unsatisfactory and Beethoven appears to have learnt little from Haydn; his major teachers in this period in Vienna were Albrechtsberger and Salieri. At the same time he was lodging with Prince Lichnowsky, who again introduced him into artistic society, which enabled him to establish a reputation as a virtuoso pianist. In this period (up to 1802), which is known as his early period, Beethoven's compositions were broadly classical and included his first symphony (1800) and his first three piano concertos (1795, 1795–98, 1800) as well as much piano music, including the *Pathetic Sonata* (1798), the *Pastoral Sonata* (1801), and the *Moonlight Sonata* (1801), his first six string quartets (1798–1800), and the ballet suite Die *Geschöpfe des Prometheus* (1801).

In his early thirties Beethoven began to go deaf, experiencing a deep crisis in his life and becoming increasingly isolated and eccentric. However, renewed energy enabled him to enter his 'heroic' period (1803–12) as a composer, producing the second to sixth symphonies

Ludwig van Beethoven

(including the *Eroica Symphony*, 1803–04; and the *Pastoral Symphony*, 1808), his only opera, *Fidelio* (1805–14), the fourth and fifth piano concertos (1805–06, 1809: see **Emperor Concerto**), the violin concerto (1806), five string quartets, the *Choral Fantasia* (1808) and much piano music, including the *Kreutzer* (1803), *Waldstein* (1803–04), and *Appassionata* (1804–05) sonatas and the *Archduke Trio* (1811). Beethoven's deafness increased and his health deteriorated in his later period of composition (1813–27). In this period his music became increasingly more intimate and revealing, culminating with perhaps his greatest achievement, the last five string quartets. To this period, too, belong the seventh and eighth symphonies and the ninth (see **choral symphony**), the *Mass in D* (or *Missa Solemnis*, 1819–23), the *Grosse Fuge* (1825), and yet more piano music and songs.

Beethoven's personal affliction and his independence from patronage enabled him to become the epitomy of the romantic artist, combining the use of classical forms with great depth of personal expression. Not only was Beethoven the dominant figure of the 19th century, his music was (and has remained) more popular than that of any other composer. He is truly the hero of romantic music. Technically, he expanded the concept of the symphony so that from his time onwards it became the normal medium for every composer's profoundest musical ideas. He also stretched the sonata form to its limits, increasing its scale and making the coda an integral part of its continuous development. Beethoven's power of expression and deep spiritual quality rely to a great extent on his use of modulation and dissonance and his mastery of a wide variety of forms.

About 600 of Beethoven's works survive, including his 9 symphonies, 5 piano concertos, 1 violin concerto, 16 string quartets, 10 violin and piano sonatas, 32 piano sonatas, 5 cello sonatas, 2 masses, 1 opera, and some 200 song settings.

Beggar's Opera, The Ballad opera in three acts with words by John Gay set to current popular tunes arranged by Pepusch. First performance: Lincoln's Inn Fields, 1728. It was written as a political and social satire in reaction to the fashionable opera seria. Later arrangements include those of Austin (1920) and Britten (1948). See also **Threepenny Opera, The.**

Begleitung Accompaniment. [German]

bel canto A mellifluous style of singing characterized by smoothness and beauty of tone, shapely phrasing, and delicately graduated dynamics. This style of singing evolved during the development of Italian opera, reaching its peak during the 19th century in the operas of Rossini, Donizetti, Bellini, Verdi, and Puccini. Although traditionally an Italian style of singing, it became the fashionable and accepted norm in most countries where western music was performed and appreciated. [Italian, beautiful singing]

Bell Anthem Verse anthem by Purcell, commencing with the words 'Rejoice in the Lord alway.' Composed: 1684–85. The nickname, which exists in contemporary manuscripts, alludes to the use of a descending scale passage in the bass of the instrumental introduction.

Belle Hélène, La Operetta in three acts by Offenbach with libretto by Meilhac and Halévy, satirizing the story of Helen of Troy. First performance: Théâtre des Variétés, Paris, 1864.

Bellini, Vincenzo (1801–35) Italian composer. He studied at the Naples conservatory (1819–22), where his teachers included Zingarelli, and gained immediate success as an opera composer. *Il Pirata*, first produced at La Scala, Milan, in 1827, earned Bellini an international reputation. To libretti by Felice Romani he composed *La Straniera* (1829), *Zaira* (1829), I **Capuletti ed i Montecchi* (1830), *La *Sonnambula* (1831), **Norma* (1831), and *Beatrice di Tenda* (1833). Bellini visited London (1833) and in 1834 wrote *I *Puritani*, performed in 1835 in Paris, where he died.

Bellini was one of the most important opera composers of the 19th century but for many years his works were unplayed, being regarded as empty vehicles for coloratura singing. Although they do require vocal agility and bel canto singing, the individuality of his (often extended) melodies and careful word setting are now recognized. He also composed some sacred and instrumental music of ephemeral interest.

bells Resonant metal vessels that produce sound when struck. The striking device may be an unattached pellet that is enclosed within the bell (striking the walls of the bell when it is shaken), an internal (or external) clapper that is attached to the bell, or a separate stick with which the bell is struck. **Hand bells** consist of a set of hand-operated clapper bells tuned usually to the notes of the major scale. A team of ringers shake two or four bells each in a prescribed order to play a melody with a simple harmonic accompaniment. **Church bells** have been a feature of Christian churches since the 8th century. Hung in a tower or belfry, the bells are sounded by using a rope to move either the bell (ringing) or the clapper (chiming). In Britain **change-ringing** has been a popular pastime since the 17th century. A ring of church bells consists of 5–12 bells, each of which is swung round in a full circle by a separate ringer according to a prescribed set of 'changes.' On the continent of Europe, church bells consist of a **carillon**, a set of tuned bells operated by wires or levers. The wires or levers are operated by hand in a simple system, by a manual or pedal keyboard in more sophisticated systems, or by a clockwork or electrically

operated rotating barrel (as in a *barrel organ). Clock chimes can also be operated by a carillon.

Struck bells have been used in all parts of the world since earliest times. They are particularly popular in China and Japan. **Chimes of bells** consist of sets of bells tuned to different notes hung in a frame and struck one or two at a time by the player. **Tubular bells** are used in the percussion section of the modern orchestra. They consist of 18 metal tubes of different lengths, which are hung in a frame and struck near the top. A foot-operated damper enables the player to curb the resonance. See also **cowbells.**

belly The top surface of the *body of a stringed instrument, to which the bridge is attached and into which the sound holes are usually cut. The belly may be made of wood, as in a lute, guitar, violin, etc., or of parchment, as in a banjo.

Belshazzar's Feast 1. Cantata for baritone, choir, and orchestra by Walton, with a text from the Old Testament arranged by Osbert Sitwell. First performance: Leeds, 1931. **2.** Orchestral suite by Sibelius, taken from incidental music to the play by Procope. Composed: 1906.

bémol Flat; the flat sign (♭). Italian: **bemolle.** [French]

Benda, Jiří Antonín (Georg B.; 1722–95) Czech composer, oboist, and keyboard player. He was kapellmeister to the Duke of Gotha (*c.*1750–78), studying for six months in Italy (1765–66). Benda composed many works for the stage, including the duodramas *Adriadne auf Naxos* and *Medea* (both 1775), which were admired by Mozart. He also wrote symphonies, cantatas, and keyboard works.

Benedicite 1. One of the more obscure canticles of Morning Prayer of the Anglican liturgy. Its text, the *Song of the Three Holy Children*, comes from the Apocrypha in the early Greek translation of the Old Testament (the Septuagint). **2.** A work by Vaughan Williams for soprano, chorus, and orchestra. First performance: 1929. It uses the Apocryphal text and an extra poem by J. Austin. [Latin, Bless ye]

Benedict, Sir Julius (1804–85) British composer and conductor, born in Germany. He studied with Hummel in Weimar and with Weber, whose protégé he became and who introduced him to Beethoven (1823). Benedict became conductor at the Kärntnertor Theater, Vienna (1824–25), and at the S Carlo and Fondo theatres, Naples (1825–34). In 1835 he settled in London, becoming conductor at the Lyceum Theatre (1836–38), Drury Lane (1838–48), and Her Majesty's (1852). He accompanied Jenny Lind in the USA (1850) and conducted the Norwich Festival (1845–78) and the Liverpool Philharmonic Society (1876–80). He was knighted in 1871. Benedict wrote several operas that were successful in their day, but only *The *Lily of Killarney* (1862) is still heard; he also composed choral music (including the cantata *The Legend of St Cecilia*, 1866), songs, and instrumental works (including two piano

Plate 5: *Béla Bartók. A picture of the composer which was featured on the cover of a Hungarian journal in 1935*

Plate 6: *A view of the Festival Theatre at Bayreuth in Bavaria.
Officially opened in 1882, it was specifically designed for the
performance of Wagner's operas*

Plate 7: *Alexandre Benois' design for the curtain in Act 1 of* Stravinsky's Petrushka, *which received its first performance in Paris in 1911*

Plate 8: *Hector Berlioz. The only truly great French romantic composer, he achieved little recognition during his lifetime*

concertos). His main interest lay in piano music: he composed two sonatas, many fantasias on operatic themes, and a large number of teaching pieces. He also edited the piano works of Beethoven and other piano collections and wrote an important biography of Weber (1881).

Benedictus 1. Part of the Ordinary of the Latin *Mass, beginning 'Benedictus qui venit' ('Blessed is he who comes'). It couples with the Sanctus to form a complete section, although this is frequently ignored in polyphonic settings. **2.** Part of Lauds, beginning 'Benedictus Dominus Deus' ('Blessed be the Lord God'). **3.** The English translation of that section in Lauds, forming an optional part of the Morning Prayer in the Anglican service. [Latin, Blessed]

bene Well; very. [Italian]

Benevoli, Orazio (1605–72) Italian composer. From 1638 to 1644 he was maestro at S Luigi dei Francesi in Rome, and then went to Vienna as kapellmeister to Archduke Leopold Wilhelm. He returned to Rome in 1646 as maestro at S Maria Maggiore, but in the same year moved to the Cappella Giulia. Benevoli's compositions are chiefly of sacred music, including polychoral works for large numbers of choirs.

Ben-Haim, Paul (P. Frankenburger; 1897–) German-born Israeli composer and conductor. He studied in Munich and emigrated to Palestine in 1933. Much influenced by traditional Jewish music, his compositions include two symphonies, a piano concerto, arrangements of traditional melodies, and liturgical works.

Benjamin, Arthur (1893–1960) Australian pianist and composer. After studying in London at the Royal College of Music (RCM) under Cliff and Stanford (1911–14), he became a professor at the Sydney Conservatory (1919–21) and professor at the RCM (1926); he was conductor of the Vancouver Symphony Orchestra (1941–46). In addition to the popular *Jamaican Rumba* (1938), Benjamin wrote five operas (including *A Tale of Two Cities*, 1950) and other vocal, chamber, and orchestral music, including a harmonica concerto (1953).

Bennet, John (late 16th–early 17th century) English composer. He published a set of madrigals (1599), the most famous of which is the melancholic 'Weep, O mine eyes,' based on an Italian poem. Bennet also contributed to *The Triumphs of Oriana* (1601) and Ravenscroft's *Psalmes* (1621).

Bennett, Richard Rodney (1936–) British composer. He studied in London at the Royal Academy of Music (1953–56) under Lennox Berkeley and Howard Ferguson and in Paris (1957–58) with Boulez. His works, in style colourful, fluent, often serial, and rhythmically cogent, include chamber music, orchestral music, and the operas *The *Mines of Sulphur* (1963; produced 1965) and *Victory*

(1970). He has also written many film scores, including *Murder on the Orient Express* (1974).

Bennett, Sir William Sterndale (1816–75) British composer, pianist, and teacher. He was a chorister at King's College, Cambridge (1824–26), then entered the Royal Academy of Music (RAM), where he studied the violin and piano and (with Crotch and Cipriani Potter) composition. Mendelssohn heard him play his first piano concerto (1833) and invited him to Germany. At this time he composed prolifically and became renowned as a concert pianist. In 1836 he again visited Mendelssohn in Leipzig, where he met Schumann (who greatly admired his work) and played his own piano concertos at the Gewandhaus. Back in England (1837) he devoted himself to teaching (privately and at the RAM) and administration: he gave an annual series of Classical Chamber Concerts (1842–56), founded the Bach Society (1849), became conductor of the Philharmonic Society (1855–66), and music professor at Cambridge University (1856–66). In 1866 he became principal of the RAM and in 1871 he was knighted.

Bennett is the leading English composer of the romantic period; in his lifetime his music was highly regarded but most of it is now rarely heard. His four piano concertos, concert overtures (including *Parisina*, 1835, and *The Naiads*, 1836), piano music (including the *Suite de pièces*, 1842), and songs are among his best works; he also composed symphonies, chamber music, and choral works (among them *The May Queen*, 1858, and *The Woman of Samaria*, 1867).

Bentzon, Niels Viggo (1919–) Danish composer. He studied at the Royal Danish Conservatory under Knud Jeppesen and has taught there since 1949. He is a prolific composer in most instrumental and vocal genres and his style is eclectic; works include the opera *Faust III* (1962).

Benvenuto Cellini Opera in three acts by Berlioz with libretto by de Wailly and Barbier, based on Cellini's autobiography (c.1560). First performance: Opéra, Paris, 1838. The story of the Italian goldsmith's completion of his statue, Perseus, failed to please the Parisian public but its overture, under the title Le *Carnaval romain*, became very popular.

bequadro see bécarre.

Béranger, Pierre Jean de (1780–1857) French satirist, poet, and writer of popular songs. His best-known songs satirized the Bourbon monarchy after the downfall of Napoleon.

Berberian, Cathy (1928–) US singer and composer. Her varied education included vocal studies with Giorgina del Vigo in Milan. Her debut in Naples (1957) was followed by associations with John Cage and with Luciano Berio, whom she married (1950–66). Berio and Stravinsky wrote works for her.

berceuse A lullaby, usually in a gently rocking 6/8 rhythm. An example is Chopin's piano piece Op. 57 (1844). [French, literally rocking chair]

Berenice Opera by Handel with libretto by Salvi. First performance: Covent Garden, London, 1737. The story is set in ancient Egypt; the well-known minuet comes from the overture.

Berezovsky, Nicolai (Tichonovich) (1900–53) Russian-born violinist and composer. He was born in St Petersburg (now Leningrad) but emigrated in 1922 to the USA, where he worked as a violinist and conductor. He studied composition at the Juilliard School under Rubin Goldmark; his works include four symphonies, the *Concerto lirico* for cello and orchestra (1934), and the cantata *Gilgamesh* (1947).

Berg, Alban (1885–1935) Austrian composer. Like his close friend Webern, Berg was a pupil of Schoenberg (1904–10). His style progressed from the rich chromatic tonality of early works, such as the piano sonata (1908), to atonality, as in the *Chamber Concerto* (1925). In 1926 he introduced a permutational 12-note technique in passages of the *Lyric Suite*, which led to the completely 12-tone violin concerto (1935). In addition, his works include the important operas *Wozzeck* (1921) and *Lulu*, which was completed in 1979 by Cerha. Berg's music is formally complex and his use of palindromes, permutations, metrical modulation, and rhythmic cells anticipates postwar musical developments.

Berganza, Teresa (1935–) Spanish mezzo-soprano. After studying with Rodrigues Aragon she made her stage debut as Dorabella in *Così fan tutte*. Although she tends to specialize in Mozart and Rossini she also sings Monteverdi and Cesti.

bergerette 1. A piece of 18th-century French music of a simple rustic character. **2.** A standard kind of 15th-century French poetry having the same form as the *virelai, but with only one stanza. [from French *berger*, shepherd]

Berglund, Paavo (1929–) Finnish conductor, a noted champion of Nielsen and Sibelius. From 1973 to 1980 he was principal conductor of the Bournemouth Symphony Orchestra.

Bergonzi, Carlo (1924–) Italian tenor. He studied with Grandini in Parma and at the Boito conservatory. His anti-Nazi activities led to imprisonment during World War II. Bergonzi's debut was in 1948 at Lecce, singing Figaro in Rossini's *The Barber of Seville*. One of the greatest Italian tenors of his time, he has subsequently sung many leading tenor roles in Verdi and more modern Italian opera.

Luciano Berio

Bergsma, William (1921–) US composer, a pupil of Hanson. He has written symphonies and string quartets, an opera (*The Wife of Martin Guerre*, 1956), choral works, and concertos.

Berio, Luciano (1925–) Italian composer, a pupil of Dallapiccola. His earliest works were tonal and romantic but he soon adopted serial procedures, which he has used subsequently with increased freedom. In 1955 Berio formed the Milan Radio Electronic Studio with Maderna and wrote a number of tape pieces; he was one of the first composers to combine the use of tape with live performers. His interest in the voice and word-setting is evident in a long series of vocal works and theatre pieces. In the 1960s Berio developed an eclectic collage-like style, but at the same time he has continued writing pure instrumental pieces. His works include the series *Sequenza (1958–75) for different solo instruments, *Differences* (1959), *Circles* (1960), *Sinfonia* (1969), *Points on a Curve to Find* (1974), and *Coro* (1976).

Bériot, Charles de (1802–70) Belgian violinist and composer. Bériot was one of the most important virtuoso violinists of his generation, playing at the French court and touring widely. As a teacher he had considerable influence and his compositions include violin concertos and tutors for violin.

Berkeley, Sir Lennox (Randal Francis) (1903–) British composer. After studying at Oxford he worked in Paris as a pupil of Nadia Boulanger (1927–33). He was appointed Professor of Composition at the Royal Academy of Music, London (1946–68), and was knighted in 1974. His lyrical Ravel-like style was developed in the *Serenade* for string orchestra (1939) and the first of his four symphonies (1940). In addition, he has written four operas (including *Nelson*, 1953) and vocal and instrumental music.

Berlin Philharmonic Orchestra A symphony orchestra founded in 1882. Its conductors have included Hans Joachim, Hans von Bülow, Arthur Nikisch, Wilhelm Furtwängler, Sergiu Celibidache, and Herbert von Karajan (until 1989); among its guest conductors have been Richard Strauss and Tchaikovsky. Its famous concert hall, the Philharmonie, was destroyed in 1944 and has been replaced by a fine new one. The Berlin Philharmonic Orchestra is one of the leading international orchestras; its repertory is mainly late-18th- to early-20th-century music.

Berlioz, (Louis) Hector (1803–69) French composer, flautist, and conductor. The son of a doctor, Berlioz was forced to study medicine in 1821 but soon abandoned it, against his parents' wishes, for music. He was a pupil of Le Sueur and attended the Paris Conservatoire, winning the Prix de Rome (after several attempts) in 1830. His first successful work, the *Fantastic Symphony* (1830–31), was inspired by his rejection by the Irish Shakespearean actress Harriet Smithson. He became engaged to the pianist Marie Moke shortly before he travelled to Italy to study under the terms of the Prix de Rome. However, during his absence in Rome Marie married Camille Pleyel. On his premature return to Paris, after only 18 months, he was reconciled with Harriet and married her in 1833. In this period he composed the choral work *Lélio, ou Le Retour à la vie*, which was first performed in 1832. His requiem *Grande Messe des Morts* (1837) and the dramatic symphonies *Harold in Italy* (1834) and *Romeo and Juliet* (1839) followed and established his reputation as a great composer of the French romantic movement. Paganini sent him 20,000 francs after hearing the first performance of *Harold in Italy* to enable him to continue composing. However, the opera *Benvenuto Cellini* (1834–38) and the choral work *The Damnation of Faust* (1846) were failures. Berlioz separated from Harriet in 1842 and, after her death in 1854, married Marie Recio, who had been his companion for many years. He suffered from ill health in the 1860s and was further depressed by the deaths of Marie (1862) and his only son Louis (1867).

Berlioz produced two other operas besides *Benvenuto Cellini*: The *Trojans* (two parts; 1855–58) and *Béatrice et Bénédict* (1862), based on Shakespeare's *Much Ado About Nothing*. His other compositions include orchestral works, notably the overtures *Waverley* (1823), Les *Francs juges* (c.1827), *King Lear* (1831), Le *Corsaire* (1831–52), and Le *Carnaval romain* (1844); 25 choral works, including the oratorio *L'Enfance du Christ* (1854; see

Childhood of Christ, The) and the *Te Deum* (1855); various vocal works with orchestra; and many songs. He also wrote the standard treatise on orchestration and an autobiography.

Bernac, Pierre (1899–1979) French baritone. His association with Poulenc, who accompanied him in recitals, began in 1935. He specialized in refined clearly enunciated chansons and satirical songs and was particularly influential as a teacher.

Berners, Gerald Tyrwhitt-Wilson, 14th Baron (1883–1950) British composer, painter, and author. He was educated at Eton and received some musical training in Dresden; from 1909 to 1920 he served as a diplomat. Lord Berners was influenced musically by Satie. Of his five ballets, The *Triumph of Neptune* (1926), written for Diaghilev, is perhaps the most famous. He also wrote orchestral music, piano music, and songs, as well as an autobiography and several novels.

Bernstein, Leonard (1918–) US composer, pianist, and conductor. He was educated at Harvard and the Curtis Institute of Music, Philadelphia, and became a professor at Brandeis University (1951–56). Bernstein was a distinguished conductor of several great orchestras, principally

Leonard Bernstein

the New York Philharmonic (1958–69). A versatile composer, his works include three symphonies (including The *Age of Anxiety, 1949), ballet scores, and the Mass (1971), as well as popular Broadway musicals, such as Candide (1956) and West Side Story (1957).

Béroff, Michel (1950–) French pianist. Béroff has established a reputation as one of the foremost interpreters of contemporary music and is particularly admired for his performance of Messiaen.

Berwald, Franz (Adolf) (1796–1868) Swedish composer and violinist. He was mostly self-taught in music but after an early career as a violinist in Sweden he won a scholarship to study in Berlin (1829). He spent 1841–42 in Vienna, where his music was favourably received, returned to Sweden, then travelled in Europe (1846–49). In 1867 he became composition professor at the Stockholm Academy. Interest in Berwald's music has gradually increased and he is now recognized as Sweden's most individual composer. Of his many compositions, the best are the four symphonies (especially No. 3, Sinfonie singulière, 1845) and the chamber music (including two piano quintets, four piano trios, and three string quartets). He also wrote operas (among them Estrella de Soria, 1841), choral works, a violin concerto, keyboard music, and songs.

Besard, Jean-Baptiste (c.1567–after 1617) French composer and lutenist. Though by profession he practised law and medicine, Besard compiled two large collections of lute music by himself and others in 1603 and 1617. These publications are valuable sources for early baroque music, in which variation form is used extensively. He also wrote a treatise on lute playing that was widely circulated.

Bethlehem Choral drama by Boughton with a libretto from the medieval Coventry nativity play. First performance: 1916.

Betrothal in a Monastery Opera in four acts by Prokofiev with libretto by Mira Mendelson based on Sheridan's The Duenna. First performance (after postponements in 1941 and 1943): Kirov Theatre, Leningrad, 1946. It was performed in New York in 1948 under Sheridan's title, The Duenna.

Bettelstudent, Der (The Beggar Student) Comic opera in three acts by Millöcker with libretto by Zell and Genée. First performance: Theater an der Wien, Vienna, 1882. Set in Cracow in 1704, it is the story of the revengeful intrigues of Colonel Ollendorf (bass) after the Countess Laura (soprano) has struck him across the face with her fan at a state ball.

bian jing see **stone chimes.**

Bibalo, Antonio (1922–) Italian composer. He studied in Trieste and was a pupil of Elisabeth Lutyens (1953–56),

since when he has lived in Norway. Bibalo's works include concertos, symphonic and chamber music, and the opera The Smile at the Foot of the Ladder (1958–62; produced in Hamburg, 1965).

Biber, Heinrich (1644–1704) German composer and violinist. He was choirmaster in Salzburg from 1684. Biber was known for his compositions using scordatura tuning for the violin, especially the 15 Mystery Sonatas. He also wrote for the viola d'amore and composed several masses and serenades.

Biggs, E(dward) Power (1906–77) British-born US organist. He studied in London at the Royal Academy of Music and established nationwide popularity in the USA as a broadcasting recitalist. His repertoire was prodigiously large, reflecting an interest in organ music of all periods.

Billings, William (1746–1800) American composer. He wrote mainly hymns, including 'Chester,' which was sung during the American Revolution. His hymns were published in six collections after 1770.

Billy Budd 1. Opera in four acts by Britten with libretto by E. M. Forster and Eric Crozier based on the story by Melville. First performance: Covent Garden, London, 1951. The tragedy, set aboard HMS Indomitable during the French wars of 1797 and seen in retrospect through the memories of Captain Vere (tenor), concerns the problems of good and evil in a small community. There are no female parts. **2.** Opera by Ghedini using the same source with libretto by Salvatore Quasimodo. First performance: Venice, 1949.

Billy the Kid Ballet in one act with music by Copland and scenario by Kirstein. First performance: Chicago Opera House, 1938. The story of Billy the Kid (the legendary William H. Bonney, who at the age of 21 was reputed to have killed a man for every year of his life) is related in music of rhythmic vitality that evokes a nostalgia and sense of the vastness of the Prairies.

binary form A musical *form cast in two related sections (A and B), which are usually repeated. The structure is commonly designated as AB form. It stemmed from the medieval bar form (AAB), but was used most extensively from the last quarter of the 17th century until the middle of the 18th in instrumental *suites of dances. The phrases are cast symmetrically, in strains of eight bars, and the relationship between the two sections is frequently emphasized by rhyming cadences, i.e. the cadence at the end of the first section (normally in the dominant or relative major) is the same as the one in the tonic key at the end of the second section. The size of the B section gradually increased during the 18th century so that it contained more tonal contrasts and modulations. The keyboard sonatas of Domenico Scarlatti are outstanding in this respect, but in the music of J. S. Bach the form is imbued with contrapuntal ingenuity to serve as the structural foundation of preludes, fugues, sinfonias, and inventions, as well as dances. The expansion of the B section of binary form also led to a *recapitulation of the opening material. This created what is known as **rounded binary form** which, together with the implicit suggestion of a merger with *ternary form, was of considerable importance in the evolution of *sonata form. Pure binary form survived in the themes used for variations in the 19th century, including the arietta of Beethoven's last piano sonata, and in miniatures for piano, such as those from Schumann's *Album für die Jugend*. It is also far from being obsolete in 20th-century music especially in the works of neoclassical composers.

Binchois, Giles (*c*.1400–60) Flemish composer. He was organist at St Waudru, Mons (1419–23), and possibly in the service of William de la Pole, Earl of Suffolk (1424). By 1431 he had entered the service of the Burgundian court, where he remained until retiring to the post of Provost of St Vincent at Soignies in 1453. His works comprise mass movements, antiphons and other liturgical pieces, and chansons, e.g. *Vostre tres douce regars*.

Birds, The (Italian: *Gli Uccelli*) Suite for small orchestra by Respighi. First performance: 1927. Respighi based each of the five movements of this suite on a different baroque harpsichord piece, each of the last four movements being subtitled with the name of a bird. The movements are 'Prelude,' 'The Dove,' 'The Hen,' 'The Nightingale,' and 'The Cuckoo.'

Birmingham Festival A festival held, usually triennially, from 1768 to 1912 in Birmingham; it was revived in 1968. During the 19th century it became the greatest festival in the country, presenting choral works in the Town Hall. Mendelssohn was associated with it (*Elijah* had its first performance at the 1846 festival) and its conductors have included Costa and Richter. Elgar's *Dream of Gerontius* (1900), *The Apostles* (1903), and *The Kingdom* (1906) were written for the Birmingham Festival.

Birmingham Symphony Orchestra, City of A symphony orchestra founded in Birmingham, England, in 1920. Originally called the City of Birmingham Orchestra, it was renamed in 1948. Its first concert was conducted by Elgar; its resident conductors have included Sir Adrian Boult, Rudolf Schwarz, Hugo Rignold, Louis Frémaux, and Simon Rattle (from 1980). The orchestra has commissioned several works from young British composers.

Birtwhistle, Harrison (1934–) British composer, a pupil of Ralph Hall. In 1953 he formed the Manchester New Music Group, which included Goehr and Maxwell Davies. His first characteristic works (e.g. *Tragoedia*, 1965) use simple structures, with an emphasis on ostinati, repetition, and monody. This static style culminated in the opera *Punch*

and *Judy* (1966–67) and *Verses for Ensembles* (1969). Subsequent works, such as *Nenia* (1970) and *The Triumph of Time* (1972), show a greater interest in textures and a concern with larger time spans. Recent works, such as *... agm...* (1979), have explored structures built from fragmentary material. Since 1975 Birtwhistle has been director of music at the National Theatre.

bis 1. The French and Italian call for an *encore. **2.** A direction to repeat the passage or notes so marked. [from Latin, twice]

bisbigliando A direction to produce a special kind of sound, particularly in harp playing, by the rapid and soft repetition of a note or chord. [Italian, whispering]

biscroma Demisemiquaver. [Italian]

Bishop, Sir Henry (Rowley) (1786–1855) British composer and conductor. After studying with Bianchi in London he was musical director at Covent Garden (1810–24) and toured Europe as a conductor. In 1813 he became a founder-member of the Philharmonic Society. He was a professor at the Royal Academy of Music, musical director of Vauxhall Gardens (1825–46), Professor of Music at Edinburgh University (1841–43), principal conductor of the Antient Concerts (1840–48), and Professor of Music at Oxford University (1848–55). In 1842 he was knighted. In his day, Bishop was the leading composer of English opera and songs but his reputation has gradually declined. He wrote many dramatic works, choral and vocal music, and a little instrumental music, but is now only remembered for his songs *Home, Sweet Home* (1823) and *Lo, Hear the Gentle Lark*.

Bishop-Kovacevich, Stephen (1940–) US pianist of Yugoslav parentage, known until 1975 as Stephen Bishop. In 1959 he came to London to study with Myra Hess, making his London debut in 1961. He is widely acclaimed as an interpreter of Beethoven and has also performed much of Rodney Bennett's music.

bitonality see **polytonality.**

biwa see **pipa.**

Bizet, Georges (Alexander César Léopold B.; 1838–75) French composer. Early in life he displayed considerable musical talent and at the age of nine was admitted to the Paris Conservatoire, where his teachers included Gounod and Halévy. His first major work, the symphony in C major, was composed in 1855 (first performed in 1935) and he won the Prix de Rome in 1857, as a result of which he lived in Rome until 1860, when he returned to Paris. He married Halévy's daughter in 1869.

Bizet is best known for his opera *Carmen* (1873–74), first performed in 1875 and initially meeting much criticism. *Carmen's* poor reception may have contributed to Bizet's death just three months later but it went on to become a perennial favourite of generations of operagoers. His incidental music composed for Daudet's play L'*Arlésienne (1872) is also very popular. Bizet's seven other published operas were less successful; they include The *Pearl Fishers (1863), The *Fair Maid of Perth (1867), and Djamileh (1872). He also produced an overture to Sardou's Patrie, piano music, including the suite *Jeux d'enfants (1871), the orchestral suite *Roma (1860–68), and 37 songs, among them 'Chanson d'avril' (?1866) and 'Berceuse' (1868).

Björling, Jussi (1911–60) Swedish tenor. He studied in Stockholm with his father, Joseph Hislop, and John Forsell, making his debut with Swedish Opera as Don Ottavio in Don Giovanni (1930). He specialized in late-19th-century opera.

Blacher, Boris (1903–75) German composer. He studied in Berlin with Koch and Blume and was appointed professor and then director of the Berlin Hochschule (1945–70), where his pupils included von Einem and Klebe. The author of concertos, ballets, operas, and instrumental music, Blacher's reputation was secured by the orchestral Paganini Variations (1947). He began to use 12-note technique in the ballet Lysistrata (1950), and Ornamente (1950) for piano introduces his technique of variable metres. His eclectic style embraced jazz and electronic music.

Blake, David (1936–   ) British composer, a pupil of Hans Eisler. His works, often politically committed, use serial procedures freely. They include Lumina (1969), a choral setting from Pound's Cantos; an opera, Toussaint; and a violin concerto (1978).

Blaník see **Má Vlast.**

Bläser Wind instruments. Often used as a direction in German scores to indicate the wind section of the orchestra. [German, blowers]

Blavet, Michel (1700–68) French composer and flautist. He was a member of the Musique du Roi (1738–68), first flautist of the Paris Opéra (1740), and was possibly in the service of Frederick the Great while he was Crown Prince of Prussia. Blavet wrote many works for two flutes and one of the first opéras comiques, Le Jaloux corrigé (1752).

Blech Brass. Often used as a direction in German scores to indicate the brass section of the orchestra. [German]

Blech, Harry (1910–   ) British conductor, founder (1949) of the London Mozart Players.

Blessed Damozel, The (French: La Damoiselle élue) Cantata for solo voices, choir, and orchestra by Debussy. Composed: 1887–88. The words are a poem by Rossetti, translated into French by Sarrazin.

Sir Arthur Bliss

Blest Pair of Sirens Cantata by Parry, with words taken from Milton's ode 'At a solemn music.' First performance: 1887.

Bliss, Sir Arthur (1891–1975) British composer. He studied at Cambridge and at the Royal College of Music, London (1914), under Stanford and Vaughan Williams. Music director of the BBC (1942–44), Bliss was knighted in 1950 and succeeded Bax as Master of the Queen's Music in 1953. Early works, such as Rout (1919), earned him a reputation as an avant-garde figure, but his style matured in the ballets *Checkmate (1937) and *Miracle in the Gorbals (1944). He also composed vocal, chamber, and orchestral music, including *Colour Symphony (1922), *Morning Heroes (1930), and a cello concerto (1970); an opera, The *Olympians (1949); and some film music, including the score of Alexander Korda's The Shape of Things to Come (1935).

Blitheman, William (?–1591) English composer. He was Master of the Choristers at Christ Church, Oxford (1564), and organist of the Chapel Royal from 1585 until his death. He is the author of 14 organ pieces, which survive in The Mulliner Book. His use of variation technique is reflected in the works of his pupil Bull and of Sweelinck.

Blitzstein, Marc (1905–64) US composer. He studied at the Curtis Institute of Music, Philadelphia, and worked with Nadia Boulanger (1926) and Schoenberg (1927). His musical *The Cradle Will Rock* (1936) was the first of several compositions demonstrating his concern with the social problems of the 1930s.

Bloch, Ernest (1880–1959) US composer, born in Switzerland. His teachers included Jaques-Dalcroze in Geneva and Ysaÿe in Brussels. In 1916 Bloch emigrated to the USA, becoming head of the San Francisco Conservatory in 1925; he lived in Switzerland during the 1930s but returned to California in 1939, remaining in the USA for the rest of his life. His prolific output of orchestral, chamber, instrumental, and vocal music is predominantly neoclassical in style and often inflected with Jewish rhythms and melodies. Many of his works employ Jewish motifs, such as the choral symphony *Israel* (1916) and the Hebrew rhapsody for cello and orchestra *Schelomo* (1915). Other compositions include the quintet (1923), which employs quarter-tones, *Baal Shem* (1923), a violin concerto (1938), and the opera *Macbeth* (1910).

Blockflöte The usual German term for the *recorder. [German, literally block flute]

Blockx, Jan (1851–1912) Belgian composer. He studied with Benoit at the Flemish Music School, Antwerp (1876–79), where he later became a celebrated teacher and succeeded Benoit as director (1901). Blockx composed in a variety of genres but is best known for his Flemish nationalist operas, among them *Thyl Uilenspiegel* (1900).

Blom, Eric (1888–1959) British musicologist. After acting as music critic for various newspapers his rising reputation led him to the editorship of the fifth edition of *Grove's Dictionary of Music and Musicians* (1954). His own works include a book on Mozart (1935) and the *Everyman's Dictionary of Music* (1954).

Blomdahl, Karl-Birger (1916–68) Swedish composer. He studied at Stockholm (under Hilding Rosenberg), Paris, and Rome before becoming a teacher at the Stockholm Royal College of Music (1960–64) and musical director of Swedish radio (1964–68). His early works were influenced by the styles of Bartók and Hindemith, but after World War II he adopted avant-garde vocal, instrumental, and formal techniques in such works as the oratorio *In the Hall of Mirrors* (1952) and operas *Aniara* (1959) and *Herr von Hancken* (1964).

Blow, John (1649–1708) English organist and composer. At the Restoration he became a chorister at the Chapel Royal and in 1668 organist of Westminster Abbey. He was appointed a gentleman of the Chapel Royal (1674) and soon after became Master of the Children, a post he held until his death. He proved very influential in teaching the next generation of English musicians, chief of whom was Henry Purcell. Blow was Master of the Choristers at St Paul's Cathedral (1687–1703), returned as organist of Westminster Abbey on the death of Purcell (1695), and became Composer to the Chapel Royal (1700). Although he concentrated on church music, his only dramatic work, *Venus and Adonis* (1685), is a miniature opera important for showing Italian and French influence. String parts are common in his verse anthems, which were composed for court. His works also include a large number of court odes, secular songs, and catches.

Bluebeard (French: *Barbe-bleue*) Operetta by Offenbach with libretto by Meilhac and Halévy based on the folk tale

A scene from a 1966 production of Bluebeard's Castle

of the tyrant who murders his successive wives. First performance: Théâtre des Variétés, Paris, 1866.

Bluebeard's Castle Opera in one act by Bartók with text by Balázs. First performance: Budapest, 1918. It is a psychological retelling of the Bluebeard legend that may be understood on a number of levels. The two characters are Bluebeard (bass) and Judith, his wife (mezzo-soprano).

Blue Danube, The Waltz by Johann Strauss the Younger. Composed: 1867. This most famous Viennese waltz has been rearranged and parodied many times; originally it included parts for chorus.

Blüthner, Julius (Ferdinand) (1824–1910) German piano maker who founded his own company in 1853. His pianos had a patented aliquot scaling system (see **sympathetic strings**) and acquired an international reputation.

B Minor Mass Setting of the mass for solo voices, choir, and orchestra by Bach. Composed: 1733–38. Bach initially set only the opening Kyrie and Gloria, in the style of a Lutheran 'short mass,' and presented it to the Elector of Saxony with a request to be given the post of court composer. Although he was unsuccessful in his request, Bach subsequently added the remaining three sections using some material from his earlier church cantatas, each of the five sections consisting of a series of arias, choruses, etc. The complete mass is far too long for normal liturgical use and there has been much speculation as to why Bach, who was a Protestant, should have written a Catholic work with a Latin text.

B.Mus. Bachelor of Music.

Boatswain's Mate, The Comic opera in one act, divided into two scenes, with music and libretto (after a tale by W.W. Jacobs) by Ethel Smyth. First performance: Shaftesbury Theatre, London, 1916. It is the story of the abortive wooing of the landlady of 'The Beehive' inn (soprano) by the ex-boatswain, Benn (tenor).

Boccherini, Luigi (1743–1805) Italian composer and cellist. He worked in Lucca and Paris before becoming organist and composer to the Spanish court (1769), where he later lived while in the service of Friedrich Wilhelm II of Prussia (1787). His most important compositions were his quartets (which influenced Haydn), cello quintets, and other chamber works. He also wrote symphonies and church music.

body The part of a stringed instrument to which the *neck is attached. It usually has sound holes in its upper surface (the *belly), which also supports the *bridge. In some instruments, such as the violin, there is a *soundpost below the bridge, inside the body, which transmits vibrations to the back of the instrument.

Boehm, Joseph (1795–1876) Hungarian violinist and teacher. From 1819 to 1848 he was violin professor at the Vienna conservatory – his many eminent pupils included Joachim and Ernst. He was chosen by Beethoven to play in the second performance of the twelfth string quartet and he also played in the premiere of Schubert's B♭ major trio (1827). Boehm left a number of violin compositions.

Boehm, Theobald (1794–1881) German goldsmith and flautist. The mechanism and proportions of the modern flute are modelled on his **Boehm system**, which he developed throughout his life on the flutes made in the factory he founded. This system has also been adapted to the oboe, clarinet, and bassoon.

Boëllmann, Léon (1862–97) French organist and composer. He studied with Lefèvre and Gigout at the Ecole Niedermeyer, Paris, and became organist of St Vincent-de-Paul. He also taught in Gigout's organ school. Boëllmann wrote orchestral works (including the *Variations symphoniques* for cello and orchestra, *c.*1893) and chamber, piano, and vocal music, as well as church and organ music; his best-known organ work is the *Suite gothique* (1895).

Boethius (*c.*480–*c.*524) Roman philosopher, writer, and statesman. His many writings include philosophical and mathematic treatises and theological texts. His treatise on music, *De Institutione musica*, outlined the Greek tetrachord and modal theory, for which he devised a notational system, and Pythagorean musical theory. This treatise was extremely influential in the Middle Ages.

Boguslawski, Eduard (1940–) Polish composer, a pupil of Haubenstock-Ramati. He has written chamber, instrumental, and orchestral works, and choral pieces.

Bohème, La 1. Opera in four acts by Puccini with libretto by Giacosa and Illica. First performance: Teatro Regio, Turin, 1896. It is based on Murger's novel *Scènes de la vie de Bohème*, in which the Parisian bohemian Rodolfo, a poet (tenor), falls in love with Mimi, a seamstress (soprano), who dies in his arms of consumption in the last act. **2.** Opera by Leoncavallo with libretto by the composer based on the same source. First performance: Venice, 1897.

Bohemian Girl, The Opera in three acts by Balfe with libretto by Bunn based on the ballet-pantomime *La Gypsy*, by Saint-Georges. First performance: Drury Lane, London, 1843. It is set in Poland and is a simple story of aristocrats and Gypsies.

Bohm, George (1661–1733) German composer and organist. He worked in Hamburg and was organist at St John's, Lüneburg (1698–1733), where his compositions influenced J. S. Bach. He wrote several choral arrangements for the organ as well as cantatas, motets, and songs.

Böhm, Karl (1894–1981) Austrian conductor, an outstanding interpreter of Haydn, Mozart, Beethoven, and Richard Strauss. Böhm excelled as a conductor of opera: he conducted the Dresden State Opera (1934–43) and the Vienna State Opera (1943–45, 1954–56).

Boieldieu, (François) Adrien (1775–1834) French composer. In 1791 he was appointed organist of St André, Rouen, and soon also appeared as a concert pianist. His first opéra comique was performed in Rouen in 1793. In 1796 he settled in Paris and soon won recognition for his stage works. He taught the piano at the Paris Conservatoire from 1798 to 1803, when he went to St Petersburg and worked in the imperial court. In 1811 Boieldieu returned to Paris; he became court composer and accompanist (1815). In 1825 *La Dame blanche*, based on two novels by Walter Scott, was produced and highly acclaimed. Boieldieu is a leading figure in the opéra-comique tradition; his works are colourful, sensitive, and very lyrical. The best known are *Le Calife de Bagdad* (1800; see **Caliph of Bagdad, The**), *Ma tante Aurore* (1803), and *Jean de Paris* (1812). He also wrote choral music, a piano concerto, a harp concerto, chamber works, piano sonatas, and songs.

Boismortier, Joseph Bodin de (1689–1755) French composer. He lived in Metz and Perpignan before settling in Paris (*c*.1724). Boismortier was a prolific composer of chamber music for woodwind instruments and was known also for his motets and cantatas (including *Actéon*, 1732), opera ballets (including *Don Quichotte chez la duchesse*, 1743), divertimentos, and a dictionary, *Quinque sur l'octave* (1734).

Boito, Arrigo (1842–1918) Italian librettist, composer, poet, and critic. After studying at the Milan conservatory (1853–61) he went to Paris and met Verdi, for whom he wrote a cantata text *Inno dell nazioni* (1862). Back in Milan Boito joined Scapigliatura, an artistic movement that aimed to revitalize the arts in Italy. In 1868 Boito's opera *Mefistofele had a disastrous premiere so he turned his attention to writing libretti (among them *La Gioconda* for Ponchielli, for which he used the pseudonym Tobia Gorrio) and translating operas into Italian. A revised version of *Mefistofele* was acclaimed in Bologna (1875) and at La Scala, Milan (1881). In 1881 Boito revised the libretto of Verdi's *Simon Boccanegra*. He also supplied the librettos for that composer's *Otello* (1887) and *Falstaff* (1893), a collaboration for which he is best remembered. He became director of the Parma conservatory (1889–97) and held several advisory positions. His own output is small: he wrote four acts of a second opera *Nerone* (completed by Tommasini and Toscanini) and some choral works.

Bolcom, William (1938–   ) US composer and pianist, a pupil of Milhaud. His style is eclectic, incorporating serialism, pop, improvisation, microtones, and collage. His works include *Session 2* and *Frescoes*.

Bolden, Buddy (Charles B.; 1868–1931) US Black jazz cornet player. A barber by trade, he was one of the originators of the *New Orleans Style of jazz. He spent the last 24 years of his life in a mental hospital; his legendary improvisations predated the recording of jazz and therefore his playing now exists only in the memories of those who heard him.

bolero A brilliant dance of Spanish origin, in moderate triple rhythm, accompanied by singers and castanets. It was probably first incorporated into classical music by Beethoven. Chopin used the dance in his piano piece Op. 1.

Bolero Ballet in one act with music by Ravel and choreography by Nijinska, written for the dancer Ida Rubinstein. First performance: Paris, 1928, with décor by Benois. Over a sustained crescendo lasting 17 minutes, a Gypsy tavern dancer induces an increasing state of ecstasy in those around her.

Bolshoi Theatre A theatre in Moscow. It opened in 1825 on the site of the Petrovsky Theatre but was burnt down in 1853 and rebuilt in 1856. At the beginning of the 20th century it began to play a leading part in Russia's musical life. Its opera company gave premieres of many new Russian works and its ballet company became established as one of the leading and most influential dance companies in the world.

Bomarzo Opera in two acts (15 scenes) by Ginastera with libretto by Lainez. First performance: Washington, DC, 1967. The opera is based on Lainez's novel about the strange monsters in the gardens of Bomarzo, north of Rome, and their 16th-century creator, Pier Francesco Orsini (tenor).

bombard see **shawm**.

bombarda Euphonium. [Italian]

bombardon see **tuba**.

Bonne chanson, La Song cycle (Op. 61) by Fauré, with poems by Verlaine. Composed: 1892. The cycle comprises nine songs with poems taken from the collection *La bonne chanson*.

Bononcini, Giovanni Maria (1642–78) Italian composer and theorist. He was maestro di cappella of Modena Cathedral (1674–78). His treatise *Musico prattico* (1673) was translated into German (1701). In addition to many works for instrumental ensemble, he also wrote solo cantatas. His son and pupil, **Giovanni Battista Bononcini** (1670–1747), was also a composer. He worked in Bologna, Rome, Vienna, and Berlin, where his opera *Polifemo* was produced (1702). In London (1720–*c*.1735) he rivalled Handel, writing operas and sacred works, including an anthem on the death of his patron, the Duke of Marlborough. He also wrote serenatas and works for vocal ensemble.

Bonporti, Francesco Antonio (1672–1749) Italian composer and violinist. He studied theology at the German college in Rome (1691–94), where he may have become acquainted with Corelli. While a priest at the cathedral in Trent, Bonporti composed solo motets and many works for violin and ensemble. His *Invenzioni a violino solo* (1712) were transcribed by J. S. Bach.

Bonynge, Richard (1930–) Australian conductor, chiefly of opera. He specializes in 19th-century music, revives little-known works, and frequently conducts for his wife, the coloratura soprano Joan *Sutherland.

Boris Godunov Opera by Mussorgsky in prologue and four acts with text by the composer taken from Pushkin's play of the same name and from Karamzin's *History of the Russian State*. First performance: St Petersburg, 1874. It relates scenes from the life of Tsar Boris (d. 1605). There are two versions by Mussorgsky, two edited versions by Rimsky-Korsakov, and one by Shostakovitch.

Borodin, Alexander Porfirevich (1833–87) Russian composer. He studied medicine and became reader in

Alexander Borodin

chemistry at the Medico-Surgical Academy in 1862. The same year he met Balakirev, who encouraged him to compose and study music, and he became a member of the nationalist group The *Five. In 1877 he visited Liszt in Weimar, and gradually gained an international reputation as a composer. Borodin's music uses rich harmonies and is colourfully scored. His greatest achievement, the nationalist opera *Prince Igor*, was unfinished when he died and completed by Rimsky-Korsakov and Glazunov. He composed two symphonies, the tone poem *In the Steppes of Central Asia* (1880), chamber music (including two string quartets and a piano quintet), piano music, and several fine songs.

Bösendorfer Austrian firm of piano makers. **Ignaz Bösendorfer** (1796–1859) founded the firm. The pianos acquired an international reputation when they were found to withstand the dynamic playing of Liszt; in 1830 Ignaz became piano maker to the emperor. His son **Ludwig Bösendorfer** (1835–1919) took over in 1859 and patented an improved action. The firm has consistently produced pianos of the highest quality.

Bossi, (Marco) Enrico (1861–1925) Italian composer, organist, and pianist, a pupil at the Liceo Musicale, Bologna (1871–73), and the Milan conservatory (1873–81). He was organist of Como Cathedral (1881–90), taught at the Naples conservatory (1890–95), and was the director of music schools in Venice (1895–1902), Bologna (1902–11), and Rome (1916–23). Bossi composed operas, orchestral, and chamber music, but is best known for his organ works (including a concerto) and choral music, particularly *Canticum canticorum* (1900), *Il Paradiso perduto* (1902), and *Giovanna d'Arco* (1914). He was a leading figure in the revival of nonoperatic composition in Italy. His son **Renzo Bossi** (1883–1965) was also a composer.

Boston A slow waltz with a sophisticated rhythm, popular especially in Germany after 1918. After 1945 it acquired several jazz elements. It is occasionally found in classical works; for example in Hindemith's first string quartet and Conrad Beck's *Zwei Tanzstücke* (1929).

Boston Symphony Orchestra A symphony orchestra founded in Boston, Massachusetts, in 1881. It was first conducted by Sir George Henschel; other conductors have included Arthur Nikisch, Pierre Monteux, Serge Koussevitzky, Erich Leinsdorf, and Seiji Ozawa (from 1973). Koussevitzky commissioned numerous works from such leading composers as Bartók, Britten, Milhaud, Prokofiev, Ravel, Stravinsky, and Villa-Lobos. He raised the orchestra's standards to a level of excellence it has since maintained, making it among the foremost in the world.

Bottesini, Giovanni (1821–89) Italian double-bass player, conductor, and composer. His virtuosity as a performer earned him the nickname the 'Paganini of the double bass,' and his compositions include many works for double bass. As conductor he directed the first performance of Verdi's *Aida* (1872) and held appointments at several Spanish and Italian opera houses.

Botticelli Triptych see **Trittico Botticelliano.**

bouche fermée, à With closed mouth: a direction to singers to vocalize without words, by keeping the lips closed but with teeth slightly parted. This device has been used extensively by contemporary composers to produce added tonal variety and colourful effects in their choral works, e.g. by using the full chorus instrumentally or by directing a section of the chorus to sing à bouche fermée as an accompaniment to the soloist(s) or semi-chorus who are singing the text. [French]

Boucourechliev, André (1925–) Bulgarian-born composer and music critic, who became a French citizen in 1956. He studied in Sofia (1946–49), at the Paris Ecole Normale (1949–51), and the Darmstadt summer school (1958–62). His works include the tape pieces *Texte I & II* (1959, 1960) and the series of aleatoric instrumental *Archipels.*

boudoir grand see **piano.**

bouffe Comic. See **opéra bouffe.** Compare **buffo.** [French]

Boughton, Rutland (1878–1960) British composer. He studied briefly at the Royal College of Music under Stanford and Walford Davies (1900). After teaching in Birmingham, he founded and organized a series of annual festivals at Glastonbury (1914–27); he then attempted unsuccessfully to establish festivals at Stroud (1934) and Bath (1935). Boughton achieved great success with his opera *The *Immortal Hour* (1914); his choral drama *Bethlehem* (1916) was less well received. His attempt to combine the styles of Wagner and English oratorio began with *The Birth of Arthur* (1909; first performed Glastonbury, 1921), the first of a cycle of five Arthurian music-dramas that concluded with *Avalon* (1946).

Boulanger, Nadia (1887–1979) French teacher, conductor, and composer. She studied at the Paris Conservatoire under Vierne and Fauré and achieved international renown as a teacher of composition; her pupils included Copland, Lennox Berkeley, Carter, and Thea Musgrave. She particularly admired the music of Stravinsky, Debussy, and Ravel and her compositions include orchestral and instrumental works and songs. Her sister, **Lili Boulanger** (1893–1916), was a composer and the first woman to win the Prix de Rome with her cantata *Faust et Hélène* (1913).

Boulevard Solitude Opera in seven scenes by Henze with text by Grete Weil after the play by Walter Jockisch. First performance: Hanover, 1952. It is a modern version of *Manon Lescaut.*

Boulez, Pierre (1925–) French composer and conductor, a pupil of Messiaen and Leibowitz. From 1971 to 1976 he was conductor of the BBC Symphony Orchestra and the New York Philharmonic; in 1977 he became head of the Institut de Recherche et Coordination Acoustique/Musique in Paris. Influenced by Webern's serialism, Boulez developed a totally serial musical language. He has introduced variable elements into some of his pieces and has explored the relationship of poetry and music; in recent works he has extended the range of orchestral textures with some use of electronic music. Boulez's works include *Structures* (1952), *Le *Marteau sans maître* (1955), *Piano Sonata 3* (1957), *Pli selon Pli* (1957–62), *Domaines* (1961–68), and *Eclat/ Multiples* (1971).

Boult, Sir Adrian (Cedric) (1889–1983) British conductor, a pupil of Nikisch. Boult made his debut in 1918 and from 1930 to 1942 was musical director of the BBC. He founded and conducted the BBC Symphony Orchestra (1930–49) and was knighted in 1937; he also conducted the London Philharmonic Orchestra (1949–57). Boult was an outstanding conductor of English music, especially the works of Elgar, Holst, and Vaughan Williams.

bourdon 1. An organ pedal *stop in which the sound is produced by 16-*foot (pitch) stopped diapason *flue pipes. **2.** A drone string on a *hurdy-gurdy or a drone pipe on a bagpipe. **3.** The bass string on a lute or violin. [French, drone]

Bourgeois, Derek (1941–) British composer. His works include symphonies, concertos, and chamber music.

Bourgeois, Louis (*c.*1510–?) French Huguenot composer. Born in Paris, he lived in Geneva (1541–?1557) and then probably returned to Paris. Bourgeois composed a few chansons and three collections of psalms in a French translation by Clément Marot, printed in 1547, 1547, and 1554 respectively. They were for use by the Calvinists in Geneva.

Bourgeois Gentilhomme, Le 1. Incidental music by Lully for the comedy by Molière. Composed: 1670. **2.** Incidental music by Richard Strauss to a shortened translation of Molière's play by Hofmannsthal. First performance: Stuttgart, 1912. This was originally used as a prelude to Strauss's opera *Ariadne auf Naxos* but in 1916 Strauss wrote a new introduction to the opera. He subsequently arranged movements from the incidental music into an orchestral suite, which included a minuet by Lully.

Bournemouth Sinfonietta A chamber orchestra founded in 1968 under the same management as the *Bournemouth Symphony Orchestra.

Bournemouth Symphony Orchestra A symphony orchestra founded in Bournemouth, England, in 1893. It was originally called the Bournemouth Municipal Orchestra; its name was changed in 1954. Its conductors have included Rudolf Schwarz, Charles Groves, Constantin Silvestri, George Hurst, Paavo Berglund, and Uri Segal (from 1980). The orchestra, which performs mostly in western Britain, has given first performances of many British works.

bourrée A French dance similar to the *gavotte, except in its short upbeat beginning. It was popular in the baroque *suite, and in French ballets and operas, notably those of Lully.

Boutique fantasque, La (*The Fantastic Toyshop*) Ballet in one act with music by Rossini arranged and orchestrated by Respighi, décor by André Derain, and choreography by Leonide Massine. First performance: Alhambra Theatre, London, 1919. Commissioned by Diaghilev for the Ballets Russes, it is set in a toyshop in which all the dolls come to life to the entertainment of the customers. It reaches a climax with the *Can-Can*.

bouzouki see **lute.**

bow 1. A stick with horsehairs attached to it at both ends, drawn across the strings of viols, violins, etc., to set them into vibration. The bows used with viols were broader than modern violin bows and were held with the palm of the hand facing outwards. Early fiddles were bowed with a highly curved bow, which gradually became less curved. The first bow specifically for the violin was designed by Arcangelo Corelli at the beginning of the 18th century. It was shorter and less flexible than the modern violin bow, but was still outward curving. Giuseppe Tartini, some 50

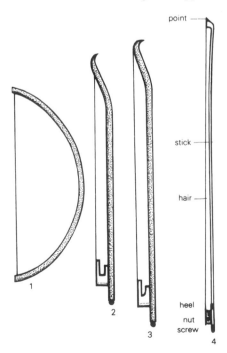

point —

stick —

hair —

heel

nut
screw

1
2
3
4

Types of bow: (1) early fiddle bow; (2) Corelli bow; (3) Tartini bow; and (4) Tourte bow, which is still in use

years later, lengthened the bow, made it more-or-less straight, and improved its flexibility. The **Tourte bow,** currently in use, was designed by François Tourte (1747–1835) in the 19th century and is longer still, with a slight inward curve. **2.** See **musical bow.**

Bowen, (Edwin) York (1884–1962) British composer, pianist, and teacher. He studied in London at the Royal Academy of Music (1898–1905) and taught there after graduating. The author of three symphonies and other orchestral works, he is best known for his viola music and numerous short piano pieces.

Bower, John Dykes (1905–81) British organist. He held cathedral appointments at Truro, Durham, and St Paul's and was organist of New College, Oxford. Bower also undertook editorial work; for example he edited the complete organ music of Bach.

Bowles, Paul (1910–) US composer and writer. A pupil of Copland, Thomson, and Nadia Boulanger, his musical style was influenced by travel in Spain, North Africa, and Latin America. His works include the opera *Yerma* (1958), orchestral music, chamber music, songs, and the novel *The Sheltering Sky* (1949).

Bowman, James (1941–) British countertenor. The finest countertenor since Alfred Deller, he made his debut in 1967 as Oberon in Britten's *A Midsummer Night's Dream*. Britten wrote Voice of Apollo (in *Death in Venice*) for him. Bowman's wide repertory includes much 17th-century music, especially Handel.

Boyce, William (1711–79) British composer and organist, a pupil of Maurice Greene and Pepusch. He was composer to the Chapel Royal (1736), conductor of the Three Choirs Festival (1737), Master of the King's Music (1755), and organist of the Chapel Royal (1758). One of the most notable composers of English church music, Boyce also wrote many works for the stage (his best-known song, 'Heart of Oak,' was written for Garrick's pantomime *Harlequin's Invasion*, 1759), as well as symphonies and chamber music. He also edited the three-volume *Cathedral Music* (1760–78), an important collection of 200 years of church music.

Braga, Gaetano (1829–1907) Italian cellist and composer. After studying at the Naples conservatory (1841–52) he began an international career as a virtuoso cellist. Braga composed operas, two cello concertos, two symphonies, and church and chamber music; his *Leggenda Valacca* (known as *Angel's Serenade*) for voice and cello became extremely popular.

Braham, John (J. Abraham; 1774–1856) British tenor and composer. He was trained by Leoni, who introduced him at Covent Garden in 1787. Thereafter he taught the piano, ran off to Italy with the soprano Nancy Storace (1798), and

Brahms' autograph manuscript of one of his songs

returned to sing in English ballad-opera. Braham is sometimes described as the best and most patriotic tenor of his age; Weber wrote the role of Huon (in *Oberon*) for him in 1826. His own compositions include many popular songs, such as 'The Death of Nelson.'

Brahms, Johannes (1833–97) German composer. The son of a double-bass player living in Hamburg, he displayed music talent early in life. At the age of 11 an offer to tour the USA was turned down and instead Brahms became a pupil of Eduard Marxsen, at the same time supplementing his parents' income by playing in cafés and dance halls. Already an outstanding pianist, he now began to compose. In 1853 he undertook a concert tour with Eduard Reményi, a Hungarian violinist, during which he met Joachim, Liszt, Schumann, and Schumann's wife Clara, with whom he formed a lifelong friendship. Between 1857 and 1860 he was engaged at the court of Lippe-Detmold; in 1863 he settled in Vienna, where he later became musical director of the Gesellschaft der Musikfreunde (Society of Friends of Music; 1872–75). In Vienna Brahms composed some of his most important works: A *German Requiem* (1866–68) was a great success at its first performance in Bremen in 1868 and the *Hungarian Dances* (1869), for piano duet, gained worldwide popularity. His first symphony was not composed until 1876. Thereafter he established himself as a leading romantic composer. He died of cirrhosis of the liver in Vienna.

Brahms composed in traditional forms but in his own lyrical style, abounding with rich harmonies. His works include four symphonies (1876, 1877, 1883, 1885), two piano concertos (1861, 1882), a violin concerto in D (1879), a double concerto for violin and cello in A minor (1888), the *Academic Festival Overture* (1880), the *Tragic Overture* (1880), and the orchestral work *St Anthony Variations* (1873). He also composed a wealth of chamber music, including two string sextets; a piano quintet, clarinet quintet, and two string quintets; three piano quartets and three string quartets; five piano trios and a clarinet trio; and several sonatas for piano and violin and piano and cello. His piano works include five sets of variations and three sonatas, as well as ballades, capriccios, scherzos, waltzes, etc.; he also wrote over 200 songs (including the *Four Serious Songs*, 1896) and other choral works.

Brain, Denis (1921–57) British horn player. His career included both orchestral posts (for example, in the Philharmonia Orchestra) and many solo appearances. Among composers who wrote for him were Britten, Lutyens, Gordon Jacob, Malcolm Arnold, and Hindemith. His father, **Aubrey Brain** (1893–1955), was also a horn player.

Brandenburg Concertos Six concerto grossi by Bach, dedicated to the Margrave of Brandenburg. Composed: 1721. Each of the individual concertos is for a different group of players; only the second, fourth, and fifth are true concerto grossi. Except for the first, which has five movements, the concertos all have three movements, arranged in a fast–slow–fast sequence.

branle (*or* **bransle**) A rustic dance from France, having a duple rhythm and repetitive sections. It was popular with English keyboard composers of the late 16th century, but in the 17th century occurred more frequently in French music.

brass band A type of wind band consisting solely of brass instruments. The constitution varies but in Britain it is usually cornets, flugelhorn, saxhorns, euphoniums, trombones, and tubas (*military bands have added woodwind). In the early 19th century bands were formed in the manufacturing towns of Lancashire and Yorkshire. Among the best known are the Black Dyke Mills, the Grimethorpe Colliery, and the Brighouse and Rastrick bands. Band contests soon started, notably the Belle Vue and the National Brass Band Festival; a feature of these contests is the specially composed test piece (Elgar's *Severn Suite* was one). The high standard of playing has attracted not only light-music composers (such as Gilbert Vinter and Erick Ball) but also such composers as Henze and Birtwistle.

brass instruments Musical *instruments made of brass or a similar metal in which the notes are made by the player's lips blowing into a cup-shaped mouthpiece. Reed instruments made of metal, such as the saxophone, and blow-hole instruments made of metal, such as the flute, are not included in this category. The main brass instruments of the orchestra are the *horn, *trumpet, *trombone, and *tuba. See also **aerophone; wind instruments.**

Bratsche Viola. [German]

bravura Skill. Used particularly in the sense of great technical display; e.g. **aria di bravura**, an aria making great technical demands on the singer. [Italian]

break **1.** A change in the tone quality as voices or wind instruments pass from one register to another. **2.** A change in tone and compass experienced by the voice of a male at puberty. See also **castrato.** **3.** A short solo played by an instrumentalist in a jazz band. It is usually improvised and provides an opportunity for the soloist to demonstrate his technical and musical skill.

Bream, Julian (1933–) British guitarist and lutenist. Taught by his father and encouraged by Segovia, Bream

Julian Bream

Alfred Brendel

was among the first to popularize the classical guitar. Bennett, Britten, Rawsthorne, and Walton have written for him and his collaboration with Peter Pears in Elizabethan music resulted in further compositions from Berkeley and Tippett.

Brecht, Bertolt (1898–1956) German playwright and poet, who collaborated with a number of composers in the production of theatrical and dramatic works. The first collaboration with *Weill (1927–30) produced *The Threepenny Opera* (1928). Brecht worked briefly with Hindemith and then with Dessau and Eisler: the latter association lasted from 1930 until the end of his life. He returned to East Berlin in 1949 and his dramatic company, the Berliner Ensemble, was of the highest international reputation.

Brendel, Alfred (1931–) Austrian pianist, born in Czechoslovakia. A disciple of Feuermann and Fischer, he is noted for his interpretations of Liszt, Mozart, and Schubert.

breve A note, originally a short note having half the time value of a *long. In modern notation it is written as an open square and has the value of two *semibreves. US: **double-whole note.** See **Appendix, Table 1.**

Brian, Havergal (1876–1972) British composer, virtually self-taught. Largely neglected in his lifetime, his works are now promoted by the Havergal Brian Society. These include an oratorio, *The Vision of Cleopatra* (1908); five operas, of which the first, *The Tigers* (1918), requires an elephant on stage; and 32 symphonies (7 written when Brian was over 90), of which No. 1, the huge choral *Gothic* (1922), was first performed in 1961.

bridge 1. A piece of suitably shaped wood that supports the strings in a stringed instrument and transmits their vibration to the belly or soundbox. **2.** (*or* **bridge passage**) A short section in a composition that leads from one main section to another, with or without a change of key. For example, there is usually a bridge passage between the first and second subjects in a piece written in sonata form.

Bridge, Frank (1879–1941) British violist, conductor, and composer. He studied in London at the Royal College of Music under Stanford. His works include the opera *The Christmas Rose* (1919–29), orchestral works (including the suite *The Sea*, 1911), four string quartets and other chamber works, and over 100 songs. Bridge's pupils included Benjamin Britten.

briet Broad. It is often used to mean the same as *largo. [German]

Brigg Fair Orchestral work by Delius, subtitled *An English Rhapsody for Orchestra*. First performance: 1908. The Lincolnshire folk song 'Brigg Fair' is used as the theme for a set of variations; the work is dedicated to Percy Grainger, through whom Delius first heard the folk song.

brillant Brilliant. Used normally as a direction for performance but also sometimes applied to compositions. Italian: **brillante**. [French]

brindisi A drinking song, often found, for instance, in 19th-century operas. [Italian, a toast]

Brindle, Reginald Smith (1917–   ) British composer. A pupil of Pizzetti and Dallapiccola, he worked for Italian radio (1956–61) and since 1970 has been Professor of Music at the University of Surrey. His works, mostly serial in style, include the opera *The Death of Antigone* (1969), *Apocalypse* (1970) for orchestra, guitar music, and percussion music. He has also written textbooks on 20th-century music.

brio Spirit; vigour. Hence **con brio**, vigorously. [Italian]

British Broadcasting Corporation see BBC.

Britten, (Edward) Benjamin, Baron (1913–76) British composer and pianist. A pupil of Benjamin and Ireland at the Royal College of Music in London (1930–34), he also studied privately with Frank Bridge. Britten's fluent diatonic style is inflected with modal, chromatic, and occasionally serial elements. His *Variations on a Theme of Frank Bridge* (1937) brought him international recognition. This was followed by an operetta, *Paul Bunyan* (1941), written in collaboration with W. H. Auden during a three-year stay in the USA (1939–42). With the opera *Peter Grimes* (1945) he began his artistic collaboration with the tenor Peter Pears, his lifelong companion. This was the second of a series of 14 operas that also included The *Rape of Lucretia* (1946), *Billy Budd* (1951), The *Turn of the Screw* (1954), A *Midsummer Night's Dream* (1960), and *Death in Venice* (1973). With these works, the creation of the English Opera Group (1947), and the founding of the annual *Aldeburgh Festival (1948), Britten virtually restored opera to England. His other vocal works include the church pageant opera *Noye's Fludde* (1958); the three church parables *Curlew River* (1964), *The Burning Fiery Furnace* (1966), and *The Prodigal Son* (1968); *Hymn to St Cecilia* (1942); *The Spring Symphony* (1949); A *War Requiem* (1961); the cantata *Phaedra* (1975); and many songs. His instrumental music includes The *Young Person's Guide to the Orchestra* (1945), the *Cello Symphony* (1963), and three string quartets. Britten was awarded the OM in 1965 and was created a life peer in 1976, shortly before his death.

Brixi, František Xaver (1732–71) Czech composer, kapellmeister at Prague Cathedral (1756). In addition to his popular Christmas masses he wrote many instrumental and keyboard works and other church music.

broken chord see **arpeggio**.

broken consort see **consort**.

Brouwer, Leo (1939–   ) Cuban composer and guitarist, a pupil of Persichetti and Wolpe. Influenced by Nono and Henze, he is a committed nationalistic composer who has written much film music and popular mass-media works as well as radical indeterminate scores, such as *Sonograma I* (1963).

Brown, Earle (1926–   ) US composer. From 1952 to 1954 Brown collaborated with John Cage and David Tudor; after a period of strict serialism, he produced his first graphic scores, including *Folio* (1952). Influenced by Pollock and Calder, he experimented with mobile-form works, notably *25 Pages* (1953) and *Available Forms* (1964), in which the performers make creative decisions that determine the ordering of events.

Browne, John (15th century) English composer. Most of his surviving music is in the *Eton Choirbook*. It consists largely of votive antiphons and a setting of the *Stabat Mater*.

browning Any one of several Elizabethan instrumental pieces, the most famous being a *fantasy for five-part strings by Byrd. This piece employs the tune of the first two lines of a popular song, 'The leaves be greene, the nuts be brown,' as a *ground bass upon which 20 melodic variations are built.

Browning, Robert (1812–89) British poet. During his life he composed songs that he later destroyed. In one poem he immortalized Georg Vogler, who was subsequently the teacher of Weber and Meyerbeer. Ives wrote a *Robert Browning Overture* (1908–12).

Bruch, Max (Karl August) (1838–1920) German composer and conductor. He studied composition with Hiller and the piano with Reinecke and Breunung in Cologne. After travelling to various German cities, Paris, and Brussels, he became music director in Koblenz (1865–67) and court kapellmeister in Sondershausen. He conducted the Liverpool Philharmonic Society (1880–83) and the Orchesterverein, Breslau (1883–90). From 1891 to 1910 he taught at the Berlin Academy. Many of Bruch's works are based on folk music of different countries. He is now best remembered for his three violin concertos (G minor, 1868; D minor, 1878; D minor, 1891), the *Schottische Fantasie* (1880) for violin and orchestra, *Kol Nidrei* (1881) for cello and orchestra, and (in Germany) for his many accomplished choral works. He also wrote three operas, songs, three symphonies, and chamber and keyboard music.

Bruckner, (Josef) Anton (1824–96) Austrian composer and organist. Following the death in 1837 of his father, a village schoolmaster and organist, Bruckner became a choirboy at St Florian Abbey, near Linz, where he learnt the organ and later became organist (1851). He began to compose while at St Florian but produced his first major works while cathedral organist at Linz (1855–67). These include the three masses (1864, 1866, 1867–68), his first symphony, and his overture in G minor. He was taught counterpoint by Sechter and was deeply influenced by Wagner, of whom he became an admirer after seeing a performance of *Tristan und Isolde* in 1865. Following Sechter's death (1867), Bruckner unsuccessfully attempted to secure his post as organist at the Hofkapelle in Vienna and was appointed Professor of Harmony and Counterpoint at the Vienna conservatory (1871–91). He spent the remainder of his life in Vienna, except for visits to Nancy, Paris, and London (1869, 1871) as an organ virtuoso. He obtained a lectureship at the University of Vienna in 1875 and was granted a pension in 1891.

Bruckner was at first opposed by the pro-Brahms school in Vienna because of his Wagnerian influence but gradually gained a high reputation, being particularly popular in Austria and Germany. He is best known for his nine symphonies: No. 1 (1866, revised 1891), No. 2 (1872, revised 1876–77), No. 3 (1873, revised 1877–78), No. 4, the *Romantic* (1874, revised 1880), No. 5 (1877, revised 1878), No. 6 (1881), No. 7 (1883), No. 8, the *Apocalyptic* (1887, revised 1890), and No. 9 (1896, with the finale

incomplete). He also wrote sacred vocal music, including a requiem (1848–49, revised 1894), a *Te Deum* (1881, revised 1883–84), and *Psalm CL* (1892) as well as some chamber music and organ music.

Brüggen, Frans (1934–) Dutch recorder player, flautist, and conductor. Brüggen's performances reveal his interest in the authentic performance of a wide range of recorder music and he has also been important as a teacher. Brüggen founded the avant-garde group Sourcream.

Brüll, Ignaz (1846–97) Austrian pianist and composer. After studying with Epstein in Vienna he began a career as a concert pianist. He taught at the Horák piano school, Vienna (1872–78), of which he became a director in 1881. Brüll composed several operas (*Das goldene Kreuz*, 1875, was the most successful), a symphony, two piano concertos, chamber works, and vocal music.

Brumel, Antoine (c.1460–c.1520) French composer. He was master of the choir at Chartres (1483) and at Notre Dame, Paris (1498), receiving a canonry at Laon in the same year; in 1505 he entered the service of the Duke of Ferrara. His works include masses, motets, and French chansons.

Bruneau, (Louis Charles Bonaventure) Alfred (1857–1934) French composer and critic. He studied at the Paris Conservatoire with Franchomme, Savart, and Massenet (1873–81). His second opera, *Le Rêve* (1890), was based on Zola, who from then until his death (1902) collaborated with Bruneau on the librettos for his operas. They include *Messidor* (1894–96), *L'Ouragan* (1897–1900), and *L'Enfant roi* (1902). Bruneau was much influenced by Wagner and used a bold and original harmonic language. In addition to operas, he composed choral works (including a requiem) and vocal, orchestral, and chamber music. He was a music critic for several Paris journals and wrote books on music.

Brustwerk A detachment of organ pipes situated in the middle of the front, typically just above the player in an organ of classical design. The pipes form a group of softer registration than the main set (Hauptwerk) and are played on a different manual. [German]

Brymer, Jack (1915–) British clarinetist. Brymer has combined a career in both orchestral and solo work and has held appointments with many British orchestras and chamber groups. He also teaches at the Royal Academy of Music.

Büchner, Georg (1813–37) German poet, dramatist, and natural scientist. His two most interesting plays, *Dantons Tod* and *Woyzeck*, were the basis of operas by Einem (1944) and Berg (1925) respectively (the latter title was changed to *Wozzeck*).

Plate 9: *A scene from the 1968 production of Harrison Birtwhistle's opera* Punch and Judy *staged at the Royal Opera House, Covent Garden, London*

Plate 10: *A scene from the first act of Mussorgsky's opera* Boris Godunov, *performed at the Bolshoi Theatre in Moscow*

Plate 11: *Georges Bizet. Although he is best known as the composer
of* Carmen, *he also wrote seven other operas*

buffo (*or fem.* **buffa**) Comic: describing a type of comic opera (see **opera buffa**) or comic operatic parts for male or female characters. [Italian]

Buffoon see **Chout.**

bugle A brass valveless *horn used since medieval times as a military signalling instrument and as a hunting horn. It is capable of playing only a few notes of the *harmonic series, but has been is use in military bands since the end of the 18th century. It is still widely used in armies. The **keyed bugle** (*or* **Kent bugle**) was used in some brass bands in the 19th century but has now been replaced by the *cornet and the *flugelhorn.

Bühnenweihfestspiel see **Parsifal.**

Bull, John (1562/63–1628) English organist, virginal player, and composer. After a musical education as a Chapel Royal chorister, Bull became organist and master of the choristers at Hereford Cathedral (1582). In 1586 he became a gentleman of the Chapel Royal and in 1597 was elected public reader in music at Gresham College, London. He contributed to *Parthenia*, the first printed collection of virginal music, but left England in 1613 following serious charges of immorality. He then resided in Brussels and (from 1615) in Antwerp, where he was organist at the cathedral. He is well known for his keyboard music, which demands virtuoso technique and comprises variations, character pieces, and dance movements. He also wrote some anthems and over 100 canons.

Bull, Ole (1810–80) Norwegian violinist and composer. As a violinist of great technical accomplishment his reputation was equalled only by that of Paganini. However, Bull's compositions, with their frequent use of folk melodies, also established him as one of the father figures of Norwegian music.

Bullock, Sir Ernest (1890–1979) British organist and educationalist. After a career as a cathedral organist, with appointments at Exeter and Westminster Abbey, Bullock became Professor of Music at Glasgow University and director of the Scottish Academy of Music and Drama in 1941 and director of the Royal College of Music (1953–60). He also composed music for liturgical use. He was knighted in 1951.

bull-roarer (*or* **thunder stick**) A primitive form of free *aerophone in which an object at the end of a string is whirled through the air while one end of the string is held. Changes of pitch are created by raising or lowering the speed of rotation. It is used by American Indians, Australian Aborigines, and other primitive peoples.

Bülow, Hans von (1830–94) German conductor. He trained as a pianist and from 1850 became an ardent follower of Wagner. He married Liszt's daughter Cosima (1857) and in 1864 became conductor at the court of Ludwig II of Bavaria in Munich. Here Bülow gave the premieres of *Tristan und Isolde* (1865) and *Die Meistersinger* (1868). In 1869 Cosima eloped with Wagner; Bülow continued his career as conductor and pianist, becoming a great champion of Brahms.

Burgmüller, (Johann) Friedrich (1806–74) German composer and pianist. In 1832 he settled in Paris. He composed songs, piano studies, and the ballet *La *Péri* (1843).

Burian, Emil František (1904–59) Czech composer and theatrical manager. He studied at the Prague conservatory (1920–27) and was associated with the Dada theatre in Prague (1933–41, 1945–49); during the period 1929–46 he was intermittently director of the Prague National Theatre. The opera *Marysă* (produced Brno, 1940) is his best-known work. His uncle **Karel Burian** (1870–1924) was an eminent tenor who sang leading roles in *Parsifal* (Bayreuth, 1898) and the premiere of *Salome* (1905).

Burkhard, Willy (1900–55) Swiss composer. He was a pupil of Karg-Elert (1921) and a teacher at the conservatories of Bern (1928–33) and Zürich (1942–55). His polyphonic neoclassical style uses modes; his works include nine cantatas and other liturgical choral music, such as the oratorio *The Vision of Isaiah* (1935). Burkhard also composed orchestral music, chamber music, and an opera, *The Black Spider*, produced in Zürich in 1949.

Burleigh, Henry Thacker (1866–1949) Black US baritone singer and composer. A friend of Dvořák, Burleigh was famous as a singer and arranger of Negro spirituals.

burletta A musical farce. [Italian]

Burney, Charles (1726–1814) British music historian, composer, and man of letters. An organist, he studied under Arne (1744–46). He later travelled extensively on the continent collecting material for his four-volume *History of Music* (1776–89). Burney's compositions, though not of outstanding originality, were frequently performed in his lifetime.

Burrows, Stuart (1933–) Welsh tenor. An Eisteddfod winner in 1959, he appeared with Welsh National Opera in *Nabucco* (1963) and as Beppe in *Pagliacci* (1967). He excels in light tenor roles, such as Ottavio in *Don Giovanni*.

Busch, Fritz (1890–1951) German-born conductor, particularly of opera; he held posts in Russia, Stuttgart, and Glyndebourne. His brother, the violinist **Adolf Busch** (1891–1952), was an outstanding soloist; he played in the Busch String Quartet (founded 1919) and in a duo with his son-in-law, the pianist Rudolf *Serkin. His pupils included Yehudi Menuhin. As anti-Nazis, the brothers renounced their German citizenship in 1933: Fritz settled in Denmark and Adolf took Swiss nationality.

Bush, Alan Dudley (1900–   ) British composer. A pupil of Ireland, he also studied and later taught at the Royal Academy of Music (1925–78). He started the London Workers' Music Association in 1936 and has toured frequently in East Europe as a composer and conductor; several works, such as the opera *Wat Tyler* (Leipzig; 1953), were first performed there. He has written three other operas, three symphonies (including the choral *Byron Symphony*, 1960), the choral piano concerto (1938), chamber music, the string quartet *Dialectic* (1929), song cycles, and solo instrumental music.

Bush, Geoffrey (1920–   ) British composer and teacher. After studying at Oxford, he taught at the university's extramural department (1947–52) and at London University (1952–69); he is musical advisor of the John Ireland Trust. Bush's three operas include *The Equation* (1968); he also composed two symphonies, concertos, choral music, chamber music, and songs.

Busnois, Antoine (c.1430–92) Flemish composer. A contemporary of Ockeghem, he was in the service of Charles the Bold, Count of Charolais (who became Duke of Burgundy in 1467). After Charles' death Busnois remained in Burgundian employ at least until 1482, ending his career as rector cantoriae at St Sauveur, Bruges. His works comprise masses, including those based on L'*Homme armé* and *O crux lignum*; motets, including *In hydraulis*, written in praise of Ockeghem (by 1467); and chansons, including the well-known *Bel acueil.*

Busoni, Ferruccio Benvenuto (1866–1924) Italian pianist and composer. After touring and teaching in Europe and the USA he settled in Berlin in 1894. His eclectic musical style, which he discusses in his *Sketch for a New Aesthetic of Music* (1907), embraces advanced chromaticism, exotic scales, and an intellectual neoclassicism that revived contrapuntal techniques. His works include the choral piano concerto (1904), an immense output of piano music including six sonatinas (1910–24), orchestral music, and four operas including *Turandot* (1917) and the unfinished *Doktor Faust* (1916–   ).

Busser, Paul-Henri (1872–1973) French composer and conductor. A pupil of Gounod, Widor, and Franck, he was a conductor of the Paris Grand Opéra (1902–39, 1946–51) and teacher at the Paris Conservatoire (1921–48). He completed Bizet's unfinished opera *Ivan le Terrible* and his original works include a mass, orchestral music, and several operas, including *Daphnis et Chloé* (1897) and *Les Noces corinthiennes* (1922).

Bussotti, Sylvano (1931–   ) Italian composer, writer, and designer, a pupil of Max Deutsch. Influenced by serialism

and later by John Cage, he has written mainly for solo instruments and voices and for chamber groups; he founded the group L'Opera for his theatre pieces. Bussotti often uses *graphic notation for his works, which are delicate in sound and texture, sensual to the point of eroticism, and full of private references. They include *La Passion selon Sade* (1966), the *Rara Requiem* (1969), and *Bergkristall* (1973).

Butt, Dame Clara (1872–1936). British contralto. She studied with Daniel Rootham and J. H. Blower, making her debut as Ursula in Sullivan's *Golden Legend* (1892). She used her powerful voice effectively in *Orpheus* and in ballad concerts from the platform, often singing in the latter with her husband, the baritone Kennerly Rumford (1870–1957). She was awarded the DBE in 1920.

Butterley, Nigel (1935–   ) Australian composer. He studied in Australia at the New South Wales Conservatory (1952–55) and in London with Priaulx Rainier (1962); he was music advisor to the Australian Broadcasting Company (1955–72). Butterley's works include a violin concerto (1970), *Exploration* (1973) for piano and orchestra, orchestral music, and chamber music.

Butterworth, Arthur (1923–   ) British composer and conductor. He studied at the Royal Manchester College of Music and is conductor of Huddersfield Choral Society. Butterworth has composed numerous works and arrangements for brass band.

Butterworth, George (1885–1916) British composer and folk-song collector. He was educated at Eton, Oxford, and the Royal College of Music. A friend of Vaughan Williams and Cecil Sharp, he shared their interest in folk song and published *11 Folksongs from Sussex* in 1912. Perhaps his best-known works are his settings of Housman in *A Shropshire Lad* (1912) and *Bredon Hill* (1912). Butterworth was killed in action during World War I.

button The pin attached to the body of instruments of the *violin family to which the tailpiece is secured. The button therefore takes the strain of the tension in the instrument's strings. A similar device was used in earlier fiddles and viols.

Buxtehude, Dietrich (Diderik B.; 1637–1707) Danish composer and organist. He was organist in Helsingborg (1657), Helsingør (1660), and at St Mary's Church, Lübeck (from 1668). In Lübeck in 1673 he established the 'Abendmusiken' (evening performances), which were attended by J. S. Bach. Among Buxtehude's distinctive works were his free compositions for organ, which influenced Bach, numerous sacred works, including his cantatas, and sonatas for instrumental ensemble.

BWV Abbreviation for Bach-Werke-Verzeichnis: an index of the works of Bach prepared by Wolfgang *Schmieder in 1950. The works are numbered and prefixed by the initials BWV. See also S.

William Byrd

Byrd, William (1543–1623) English composer, a pupil of Tallis. Although a Roman Catholic, he held various positions in Anglican churches, including organist at Lincoln Cathedral (1563–72) and organist at the Chapel Royal jointly with Tallis (from 1572). His first publication, the *Cantiones sacrae* (1575), comprises 17 motets each by himself and Tallis. In this and two subsequent books of *Cantiones sacrae* (1589, 1591) Byrd developed and expanded the richly complex imitative style of his teacher. However, he could be extremely concise if the liturgy demanded, as in the *Gradualia* (1605 and 1607). His three Latin masses are notable for their independence from liturgical chant and the use of a unifying (or 'head') motive. Byrd's Anglican music includes two settings of the service and a number of verse anthems, a form that he appears to have invented.

He published three song collections – *Psalmes, Sonets, and Songs* (1588), *Songs of Sundrie Natures* (1589), and *Psalmes, Songs, and Sonets* (1611) – a miscellany of psalms, anthems, consort songs (for solo voice and viols), madrigals, and two viol fantasias. Byrd's instrumental music includes 14 fantasias, variations, dances, and 17 cantus firmus settings for keyboard or for viols. He wrote over 120 pieces for keyboard, some of which were contributions to *Parthenia* (*c.*1612) and others in manuscript form (*My Ladye Nevell's Booke* and *Fitzwilliam Virginal Book*). Byrd's style is characterized by a strong sense of tonality and a liking for the sounds of popular melodies; however, his rhythms are often intricate and his free use of dissonance and false relations is highly English.

Byzantine music The music of the liturgical chant of the Eastern Orthodox Church, i.e. the Greek, Russian, Coptic, Armenian, and Syrian churches, as opposed to that of the Western Roman Church. The city of Byzantium itself, rebuilt by Constantine in 330 AD as Constantinople (now Istanbul), was capital of a reunited Roman Empire and a flourishing centre of culture and trade. In 395 division of the empire made it capital of the Eastern Empire (until Turkish conquest in 1453); final schism between the Eastern and Western churches came in 1054. Hellenistic, Jewish, and oriental influences underlie the growth of the Orthodox liturgy, which varied in the different regions of its development (as did the early Western liturgy, in the form of Ambrosian, Mozarabic, Gallican, and Sarum chants).

Before the 8th century, when a rudimentary notation began to develop as an aid to memorizing melodic shapes, the music was handed down in an oral tradition in which the singer based his melodies on a series of eight modes called **echoi**. Each echos was a collection of melodic fragments from which a complete melody could be constructed, there being specific motives for the opening, middle, and closing sections, linking motives, and decorative formulae. These echoi were grouped in four pairs of authentic and plagal modes (as were the western modes) with their final tones respectively on the notes D, E, F, and G. Echoi are not scales in the western sense; they have more in common with the Indian rāga (see **Indian music**).

The most characteristic Byzantine music is the splendid collection of hymns. These evolved from the short responses (**troparia**) sung between the verses of psalms, which gradually grew in importance and eventually acquired an independence of their own. There are two main categories: the **kontakia** of the 6th century and the structurally more elaborate **kanones** of the 8th to 10th centuries. A kontakion was a didactic hymn of some 18 or more stanzas with refrain; a soloist sung the stanzas and the choir answered each with the refrain. The kanon was more of a hymn of praise; it usually consisted of eight divisions (called **odes**), each ode having several stanzas sung to the same melody. Texts were taken from the scriptures or scripture commentaries; the melodies were set syllabically so that the congregation could easily understand them. One of the greatest of these hymns is the *Akathistos*, sung at the Feast of the Annunciation.

The Byzantine liturgy as a whole is more dramatic than the Roman, especially in the presentation of the Mass. Its didactic and devotional texts are set in a widely varied musical language of great splendour and lyrical beauty.

C

C The keynote of the scale of C major. See also **middle C.**

cabaletta 1. A popular song or *aria in rondo form, with a simple and uniform rhythm, as found in Rossini operas. **2.** A short aria characterized by repeats. **3.** A passage within a song that has its own repeats and variations. **4.** The final section of an aria or duet in 19th-century opera (e.g. Verdi), usually involving *stretto and sometimes quicker rhythm.

Caballé, Montserrat (1933–) Spanish soprano. After studying in Barcelona she became a leading Verdi and Donizetti soprano, also singing Wagner and Strauss. She sang at La Scala, Milan, and achieved international recognition in 1965, after replacing the indisposed Marilyn Horne as Lucrezia Borgia in New York, after which she joined the Metropolitan Opera.

Cabezón (*or* **Cabeçón**), **Antonio de** (c.1510–66) Spanish composer, blind from birth. He was employed at the court of Spain. His keyboard music was published posthumously by his son, **Hernando de Cabezón** (1541–1602), as the *Obras* (1578). This collection is one of the first to develop an idiomatic keyboard style, especially in the variations and plainsong settings. Hernando himself and Antonio's brother, **Juan de Cabezón** (?–1566), are also represented in the *Obras*.

cabinet organ see **American organ.**

caccia 1. Hunt; chase. Thus **alla caccia**, in hunting style. Some instruments are labelled **da caccia**, of the hunt, originally because of their distinctive sounds or functions. **2.** One of the three principal forms of 14th-century Italian music, the others being the *ballata and the *madrigal. Two voices sang a lively text in canon, with or without an accompanying instrument. [Italian]

Caccini, Giulio (c.1553–1618) Italian composer and singer. He was a boy singer at St Peter's, Rome (1564–65), and in 1565 entered the service of Cosimo I in Florence, where he learnt singing with Scipione dalle Palle. Later he was associated with the *Camerata, a group of poets and musicians associated with Count Giovanni de' Bardi. In 1579 and 1589 he took part in the musical celebrations of the weddings of the grand dukes Francesco I and Ferdinand I. Although employed almost continually at the Florentine court until his death, Caccini also visited Ferrara, Paris, Genoa, and Turin. Caccini was among the first to write in the recitative style and occupies a crucial place in the history of opera and, especially, of the solo song. His opera *Euridice* (1600) reveals the influence of the Camerata, who regarded monody, not polyphony, as the means of capturing the emotional power of ancient Greek music. *Euridice* was written at the same time as his rival Peri's opera of the same name and based on the same libretto. Also monodic are Caccini's two song collections, *Le Nuove musiche* (1602 and 1614), in which embellishments that would normally be improvised are written out; several new ornaments, such as the gruppo and the trillo, are introduced. Caccini's works are more noted for their lyricism and elegance than for their dramatic power, despite his avowed intention of returning to the spirit of Greek music and 'moving the affect of the soul.' Caccini's two daughters by his second wife, Margherita, were singers: **Francesca Caccini** (La Cecchina; 1587–c.1640), who was also a composer, and **Settimia Caccini** (1591–c.1638).

cachucha A graceful dance in triple time, intended for a solo performer and originating in southern Spain.

cadence A harmonic progression establishing a key or mode at the end of a phrase, section, or composition. The main types of cadence in use in western tonal music are as follows. A **perfect cadence** moves from dominant or dominant seventh to tonic and conveys a sense of completeness; an **imperfect cadence** (*or* **half-close**) moves to the dominant from any one of a variety of other chords and conveys a sense of incompleteness. A **plagal cadence** moves from subdominant to tonic. It often follows a perfect cadence and conveys a sense of confirmation. An **interrupted cadence** (US: **deceptive cadence**) moves from dominant or dominant seventh to a chord other than the tonic (most commonly the submediant). It has the force of an interrupted or frustrated perfect cadence.

The normal 15th-century cadence formula differs from those given above and involves an outward movement from an imperfect consonance to a perfect consonance. The **two-voice cadence** consists of a sixth moving to an octave; in the **three-voice cadence** a six-three chord moves to an eight-five chord. A survival from the late-medieval cadence type found in tonal music is the **Phrygian cadence**, which is occasionally used as a final close as late as the early 18th

The main types of cadence

century. Normally used with a tierce de picardie on the closing chord, it tends to strike present-day ears as a particular type of minor-key imperfect cadence.

cadenza A vocal or instrumental improvisatory passage inserted between the chords of a *cadence. It is used particularly in concertos, the soloist playing a passage that displays his technical skill and virtuosity while the orchestra remains silent. During the classical era a stereotyped formula evolved: the orchestra ends the recapitulation on a second inversion tonic chord and this is followed by the cadenza, which ends with a trill on the dominant chord, leading to the orchestral coda. Originally cadenzas were intended to be improvisations but many composers, perhaps suspicious of the judgment of some soloists, provided their own and it is now customary for the composer's cadenza, or that of a well-known soloist, to be played. An **accompanied cadenza** is one in which there is some orchestral participation during the cadenza. [Italian, cadence]

Cadman, Charles Wakefield (1881–1946) US organist, critic, and composer; he studied in Pittsburgh under Emil Pauer. His works, which include orchestral, choral, and chamber music and about 300 songs, were often influenced by American Indian music, as in *Shanewis* (*The Robin Woman*, 1917), one of seven operas.

Cage, John (1912–   ) US composer, a pupil of Cowell and Schoenberg. During the 1930s, while teaching at Seattle, he experimented with work for percussion orchestra and collaborated with Merce Cunningham in dance works. His interest in exploring new sound sources led to his invention of the *prepared piano, for which he has written a number of pieces. From the 1950s, influenced by Dadaism and non-European philosophies (especially Zen Buddhism), Cage sought to escape the bounds of western music by applying the principle of indeterminism to his work. To encourage audiences to accept the equality of all sound phenomena he has used various devices to ensure randomness in his music, for example by using unspecified instruments and indeterminate duration of performance. He has also devised multimedia events. Cage's works include *Sonatas and Interludes* (1948), for prepared piano; *Imaginary Landscape No. 4* (1951), for 24 radio sets randomly tuned by 12 performers; *4' 33''*(1952), silence for any instrument(s); *Music of Changes* (1957); *Music Circus* (1968); and *Apartment Building 1776* (1976).

John Cage

Caimo, Guiseppe (*c*.1545–84) Italian composer and organist. In 1580 he became organist at Milan Cathedral. Of his output only secular works survive; these range from the conservative first book of madrigals (1564) to the harmonically daring fifth book (1572).

caisse Drum. Thus **caisse sourde** (*or* **caisse roulante**), tenor drum; **grosse caisse**, bass drum; **caisse claire**, side (*or* snare) drum. [French]

Caix d'Hervelois, Louis (*c*.1680–1760) French composer and viola da gamba player, a pupil of Sainte-Colombe. Working mostly in the service of the Duc d'Orléans, he wrote many works for viola da gamba, duets for pardessus de viole, and flute sonatas.

cakewalk A popular dance from 19th-century Black North America. Its name probably comes from the prize – a cake –presented to the best dancers at a gathering. The dance was also incorporated into music-hall burlesque and vaudeville. It has a lively syncopated rhythm. An attractive example in classical piano music is Debussy's 'Golliwog's Cakewalk,' from *Children's Corner* (1906–08).

calando Ebbing; weakening. Used to indicate a lessening of tempo or dynamic power (or both). [Italian]

Caldara, Antonio (*c*.1670–1736) Italian composer and cellist. He was maestro di cappella at the Mantuan court (1700–07), worked for Prince Ruspoli in Rome (1709–16), and became assistant kapellmeister for Emperor Charles VI in Vienna under Fux (1716–36). In addition to over 70 operas and serenatas written for the imperial court, Caldara also wrote about 100 operas, at least 12 of which (including *Dafne*, 1719) were dedicated to the Archbishop of Salzburg; in addition he composed many oratorios and other church music as well as some chamber music, which shows the influence of Corelli.

Calinda, La Short orchestral piece by Delius, originally written for a dance episode in the third act of his opera *Koanga*. Composed: 1895–97. The opera concerns Negro characters and *La Calinda* is the name of a Negro dance brought to America by slaves. Delius used an earlier version of this piece as one movement of his *Florida Suite* (1886).

Caliph of Baghdad, The (French: *Le Calife de Baghdad*) Opera in one act by Boieldieu with libretto by Saint-Just. First performance: Opéra-Comique, Paris, 1800. It is about a caliph who disguises himself in order to find out what people really think of him.

Calisto Opera by Cavalli with libretto by Faustini. First performance: Teatro Sant' Apollinare, Venice, 1651; it was revived at Glyndebourne in 1970. It tells the story from Ovid's *Metamorphoses* of the nymph Calisto, who was turned into a constellation. (*Calisto* is the Italian spelling of the Latin *Callisto*.)

Tito Gobbi and Maria Callas in Puccini's Tosca

Callas, Maria (Maria Anna Kalageropoulos; 1923–77) US-born soprano of Greek parentage. She studied at the Athens conservatory and achieved her first major success at Verona (1947) in *La Gioconda*. After this she was managed by the Italian opera conductor Tullio Serafin (1878–1968) and excelled in classical Italian roles at La Scala, Milan. With her unforgettable coloratura voice she mesmerized audiences in such roles as Medea in Cherubini's opera.

Callisto see **Calisto**.

Calm Sea and a Prosperous Voyage Overture (Op. 27) by Mendelssohn, based on two poems by Goethe. Composed: 1827.

camera, da For the chamber. Used to indicate a type of composition (e.g. **cantata da camera, concerto da camera, sonata da camera**) or performing group originally meant for use other than in church. Compare **chiesa, da**. [Italian]

Camerata 1. A group of intellectuals and musicians who frequented Count Giovanni de' Bardi's salon in Florence (*c*.1573–87). Bardi encouraged Vincenzo Galilei's research into Greek music and Caccini's works were performed. **2.** A similar group, patronized by Jacopo Corsi, that experimented with music drama in the 1590s; from the works of this group the monodic style of opera evolved, of which the first examples are Peri's *Dafne* (1598) and *Euridice* (1600). [Italian, society]

Camidge, Matthew (1764–1844) British organist and composer. He was organist of York Minster (1799–1842) and achieved fame as the director of oratorio concerts in northern England. Camidge composed church and organ music as well as instrumental works.

Camilleri, Charles (Mario) (1931–   ) Maltese composer and conductor, who studied at Toronto University. Influenced by Messiaen and Maltese music and landscape, he has written organ music, piano music, chamber music (including a string quartet, 1973), and a *Missa Brevis* (1975).

campana (*pl.* **campane**) Bell. [Italian]

Campanella, La (*Bell Rondo*) Piano piece by Liszt, the third of his *Etudes d'exécution transcendante d'après Paganini*. Composed: 1838; revised: 1851. The third movement of Paganini's B minor violin concerto (1824) imitates the sound of bells and Liszt based his piano piece on this concerto. See **Paganini Studies.**

campanology The art of bell ringing. See **bells.**

Campion (*or* **Campian**), **Thomas** (1567–1620) English composer, poet, lawyer, and physician. His first works were published in Rosseter's *Ayres* (1601), after which he wrote four books of airs himself (*c*.1513–*c*.1517). His other works include a treatise on quantitative metre (1602), one on counterpoint (1613), and songs for five masques.

Campra, André (1660–1744) French composer. He was choirmaster in Toulon (1679), Arles (1688), Toulouse (1693), and at Notre Dame Cathedral, Paris (1694–1700). In 1723 he succeeded Lalande as choirmaster of the Royal Chapel, where he taught André Philidor. He developed the opera ballet, his first being *L'Europe galante* (1697). In addition he wrote lyric tragedies, divertissements, cantatas, and other church music.

canarie (*or* **canaries**) An old French dance in compound time, in which phrases generally start with a dotted note. It was not uncommon in late-16th-century lute music, from which it was taken over into the French baroque harpsichord repertory, notably the suites of Louis Couperin and Chambonnières. English: **canary.**

cancrizans Denoting a passage in a composition, or the composition itself, in which a theme is repeated backwards (i.e. in retrograde motion). A **canon cancrizans** is a *canon in which the imitating voice proceeds with the notes in reverse order to those of the first voice. [from Latin *cancer*, crab]

Cannabich, Johann Christian (1731–98) German composer. He was a pupil of Stamitz and Jomelli in Rome (*c*.1753). He led the Mannheim orchestra (from about 1758), becoming Director of Instrumental Music in 1774. Mozart taught his daughter Rosina the piano and dedicated sonatas to her. Cannabich wrote symphonies in the style of Stamitz, many ballets, operas, chamber works, and sacred music.

canon A technique or piece in which one melody exactly imitates another at the unison or at different intervals while the first continues. It originated in the 13th century, the earliest and most famous example being the Reading canon, *Sumer is icumen in*. During the 15th and 16th centuries it was a popular device, especially in polyphonic sacred music (such as Ockeghem's *Missa prolationum* and Palestrina's *Missa ad fugam*). During this time the word meant the 'rule' by which the imitative counterpoint proceeded. The present-day meaning of strict imitation was denoted by **fuga.** Among the many kinds are: **mensuration,** in which the parts begin together but continue in strict imitation in different rhythms; **augmentation** and **diminution,** in which the imitation appears in longer or shorter notes; **group,** for many voices, popular in the 16th century (e.g. Byrd's 'Diliges Dominum'); **perpetual,** equivalent to a round with no distinct ending; **mirror,** in which the entire canon is reversed (e.g. the first movement of Bartók's *Music for Strings, Percussion and Celeste*); **double,** two parts against two; **free,** in which intervals are not so precisely reproduced (for instance, a minor third for a major); and **strict,** in which the intervals are exactly repeated. See also **puzzle canon.**

cantabile Singable; in a singing fashion. Used to indicate that a passage should be so played as to bring out its singing melodic character. [Italian]

cantata A sacred or secular vocal piece of moderate length incorporating recitative and aria. The cantata first flourished in Italy in the early 17th century. Luigi *Rossi, for example, wrote many short lyrical pieces generally for solo voice and small instrumental accompaniment. These **chamber cantatas** (*or* **cantate da camera**) typically divide into several sections, often where arias follow each other uninterrupted by recitative. In the 18th century the form developed to include several solo voices, chorus, and orchestra. The German Lutheran **church cantata** (*or* **cantata da chiesa**), made famous by J. S. Bach, used a biblical text and featured arias, recitatives, and chorales. French: **cantate**; German: **Cantate, Kantate.** [Italian, sung]

cantatrice A female singer. [Italian]

Cantelli, Guido (1920–56) Italian conductor. An exceptional musician, he conducted entirely from memory. He died in an air crash.

Canteloube (de Maleret), Marie-Joseph (1879–1967) French pianist, composer, and ethnomusicologist; a pupil of Vincent d'Indy. His main work was the collection and arrangement of French folk songs, on which he lectured and broadcast extensively, publishing four sets of *Chants d'Auvergne* (1923–30) and the four-volume *Anthologie des chants populaires français* (1939–44). Other works include symphonies, chamber music, and two operas, *Le Mas* (1913) and *Vercingetorix* (1933).

canticle A biblical hymn, distinct from a *psalm. In the Roman Catholic liturgy the major canticles, such as *Magnificat and *Nunc Dimittis, come from the New Testament; the minor canticles, for example *Benedicite, are from the Old Testament and form part of Lauds. In the Anglican service canticles occur in Morning and Evening Prayer.

cantilena 1. In medieval music, any of various kinds of secular vocal music. [Latin, song] **2.** Lyrical singing. Used to indicate a flowing vocal or instrumental line. [Italian, sing-song]

cantillation The chanting of Holy Scripture in Jewish worship. The traditional melodies or chants, decorative and florid in style and of a free improvisatory character, are not dissimilar to the modes used in the early Christian Church. Cantillations were often symbolic, vividly expressing a variety of emotions to suit the mood and character of the occasion. The composer Ernest Bloch embodies the spirit of cantillation by using Jewish traditional melodies in those of his works that are rhapsodic in style.

Cantiones Sacrae (*Sacred Songs*) A title used by many Renaissance and early baroque composers for collections of Latin motets. Among others, Tallis, Byrd, and Schütz produced volumes using this title.

canto Song; singing. The direction **col canto** is used, like colla voce, to indicate that the accompaniment should carefully follow the solo line. See also **bel canto.** [Italian]

cantor In Jewish and early Christian churches, the person who led the singing. The cantor in Anglican cathedrals became known as the *precentor. In the Lutheran Church in Germany the cantor (*or* Kantor) was the director of music in a church and usually the person in charge of the educational institution attached to that church. J. S. Bach was cantor of St Thomas's, Leipzig.

cantoris The part of a choir that occupies the stalls on the north side of the aisle of a cathedral or church, i.e. the side on which, by ecclesiastic tradition, the cantor sits. Cantoris and its opposite, **decani**, should if possible be numerically identical, each half having an equal division of parts. True antiphonal singing, as directed by composers in sacred and liturgical music, can then be achieved.

cantus Song; singing; melody. Used in 15th- and 16th-century music to indicate the upper vocal or instrumental line. [Latin]

cantus firmus Fixed melody: a melody taken from an older source and used as the principal line in a contrapuntal composition (see also **counterpoint**). Italian: **canto fermo.** [Latin]

canzona (*or* **canzone**) **1.** A notable Italian verse form set polyphonically during the 16th century. It formed part of the early *madrigal literature; examples are Pisano's settings of Petrarch's canzoni (1520). The form was popular because of its structural and metrical flexibility, and generally only the first stanza was set since the subject matter was complete in each stanza. **2.** An instrumental piece that developed from the vocal canzona. In the early 16th century the Italian canzon alla francese evolved from the French chanson. Because of its sparkling and distinctive rhythms it was apt for lute and other instrumental transcription. Cavazzoni, for instance, published two books containing organ canzoni (1542, 1543), which were arrangements of secular songs. Towards the end of the 16th century, Giovanni Gabrieli moved further away from the vocal prototype and instituted the purely instrumental canzona, allied to the *ricercare. In the 17th century the increased use of the term *sonata displaced the canzona, and the two became assimilated into one. **3.** An 18th-century light song. In opera it denotes the actual song rather than an aria, e.g. 'Voi che sapete' in Mozart's *The Marriage of Figaro*.

canzonet A short polyphonic song of a tuneful nature, popular in Italy and England in the late 16th century. Morley (in 1597) described the form as a simple small-scale *madrigal. The term, however, was applied loosely, and some canzonets are more correctly serious madrigals, e.g. Farnaby's collection (1598). [from Italian *canzonetta*, little *canzona]

canzonetta see **canzonet.**

Caoine see **keen.**

Caplet, André (1878–1925) French composer and conductor. He was a pupil of Leroux at the Paris Conservatoire and won the Prix de Rome (1901). A friend of Debussy, he conducted the premiere of *Le Martyre de Saint Sébastien* in 1911. His own music follows Debussy's style and includes the oratorio *Mirroir de Jésus* (1924).

capo see **capotasto; da capo.**

capotasto (*or* **capo d'astro**) A device attached to the neck of a guitar or similar instrument to shorten the vibrating section of the strings. It enables a player to change key without changing the fingering of chords. Often shortened to **capo.**

cappella Chapel, hence **a cappella** (*or* **alla cappella**), in the church style: describing choral music that is sung unaccompanied. A cappella ecclesiastical music probably dates from the period when organs and instrumental music in churches were the exception rather than the rule. The custom of a cappella singing in the Sistine Chapel in the Vatican has remained unbroken throughout its history, since no instrumentalist has ever played there. See also **maestro (di cappella)**.

Capriccio Opera in one act (of approximately two and a half hours) by Richard Strauss with libretto by Clemens Krauss. First performance: Munich, 1942. Set in the period of Gluck's operatic reforms (see **Alceste**), its subject is the relative importance of music and text in opera itself.

capriccio 1. A 19th-century piano piece of humorous and fanciful nature. An example is Brahms' Op. 116. **2.** A 16th-century instrumental imitative piece, which in the 17th century (like the *ricercare and *canzona) became the precursor of the *fugue. A notable exponent was Frescobaldi. **3.** A late baroque fanciful or free instrumental piece. **4.** An 18th-century *cadenza. English, French: **caprice**. [Italian]

Capriccio espagnol (*Spanish Caprice*) Symphonic suite (Op. 34) by Rimsky-Korsakov. Composed: 1887. Each of the five sections contains rhythmic and melodic features of Spanish music; this work is particularly noted for its fine orchestration.

Capriccio italien (*Italian Caprice*) Orchestral work (Op. 45) by Tchaikovsky. Composed: 1879. This work was written while Tchaikovsky was staying in Italy and much of the thematic material is derived from Italian folk melodies, with which he became acquainted during his visit.

caprice see **capriccio**.

Capriol Suite in six movements for string orchestra by Warlock. Composed: 1926. Capriol is an imaginary figure in Thoinot Arbeau's dance manual *Orchésographie* (1589) and each movement of the suite is based upon a different old French dance melody from this collection. *Capriol* demonstrates Warlock's interest in Renaissance music and he retains the original dance titles for the movements of his suite.

Capuletti ed i Montecchi, I (*The Capulets and Montagues*) Opera in four sections by Bellini with libretto by Romani based on Shakespeare's *Romeo and Juliet*. First performance: Teatro La Fenice, Venice, 1830.

Caractacus Cantata for solo voices and orchestra (Op. 35) by Elgar, with a text by Ackworth. Composed: 1898. The work tells the story of Caractacus, the ancient British chieftain, and his fight against the Romans. Elgar wrote the cantata for the Leeds Festival and dedicated it to Queen Victoria.

Carafa (de Colobrano), Michele Enrico (1787–1872) Italian composer. From 1806 to 1808 he studied with Cherubini and Kalkbrenner in Paris, where he settled and became a professor at the Conservatoire (1840–70). He was closely associated with Rossini, who influenced his operas; they include *Masaniello* (1827) and *Le Nozze di Lammermoor* (1829). Carafa also composed ballets, instrumental music (including pieces for band), and choral works.

Cardew, Cornelius (1936–81) British composer, a pupil of Petrassi and assistant to Stockhausen on *Carré* (1959–60). His early pieces, mostly for piano, are strictly serial. Influenced by Cage, he experimented with graphic scores and indeterminacy, for example in *Treatise* (1963–67). He formed the Scratch Orchestra in 1969 and wrote a great deal for improvisatory ensembles, e.g. *The Great Learning* (1971). Cardew's last works included revolutionary Maoist songs.

Cardillac Opera in three acts by Hindemith with libretto by Ferdinand Lion from E. T. A. Hoffmann's story *Das Fräulein von Scuderi*. First performance: Dresden, 1926. A version with substantially revised text and some musical revision was first performed in Zürich in 1952. Cardillac is the name of the hero, a 17th-century French goldsmith (baritone).

Cardus, Sir Neville (1889–1975) British music critic and cricket writer. He studied singing with Charles Egan in Manchester and in 1913 became music critic there for the *Daily Citizen*, transferring to the *Manchester Guardian* in 1917. He was the paper's chief music critic from 1927 to 1939. From then until 1947 he worked in Australia. He has written books on both music and cricket.

Carey, Henry (1687–1743) English composer and playwright. He wrote many operettas, including *The Contrivances* (1715). The best known of his songs is probably 'Sally in our Alley' from *The Beggar's Opera* (1728) and he also wrote cantatas. The claim that he wrote 'God Save the Queen' is unfounded.

carillon see **bells**.

Carissimi, Giacomo (1605–74) Italian composer. He sang at Tivoli and was later organist there. In 1629 he became maestro di cappella of the German College, Rome, where he remained until his death; in 1637 he became a priest. Carissimi wrote many motets and cantatas, but was most influential in the development of the oratorio; *Jephtha* (before 1650) is the best known of these. There are sharp contrasts between solo and choral sections in his music, which laid the foundation for the 18th-century oratorio.

Carmelites, The see **Dialogues des Carmélites, Les**.

carmen (*pl.* **carmina**) Song; poem. Used in early music to indicate the vocal line of a piece or sometimes the line of the upper voice. [Latin]

Carmen Opera in four acts by Bizet with libretto by Meilhac and Halévy after the novel by Merimée. First performance: Opéra-Comique, Paris, 1875. Carmen (mezzo-soprano) is a Gypsy, working in a cigarette factory, who seduces a corporal, Don José (tenor). Don José kills Carmen in the last scene, because she has flirted with a toreador, Escamillo (baritone). The original spoken dialogue was turned into recitative by Guiraud, in which form it is usually played.

Carmina Burana Cantata by Carl Orff, based on 13th-century Latin poems. First performance: Frankfurt, 1937. The 25 texts, which include some in medieval French and German, are generally profane comments on life, love, and drinking and were written by medieval wandering scholars (goliards). The title (Latin for 'Songs from Beuren') refers to the monastery of Benediktbeuren in Germany, where the manuscripts of the poems are kept.

Carnaval see **Carnival**.

Carnaval romain, Le (*The Roman Carnival*) Concert overture (Op. 9) by Berlioz. Composed: 1844. After the failure of his opera *Benvenuto Cellini* in 1838 Berlioz attempted to salvage some of the musical material by rearranging portions of the score to form this overture.

Carnival 1. (French: *Carnaval*) A collection of 21 piano pieces (Op. 9) by Schumann subtitled 'dainty scenes on four notes' ('scènes mignonnes sur quatre notes'). Composed: 1834–35. Schumann used the letters A–S–C–H (German nomenclature for the notes A–E♭–C–B), the name of the town where his lover was living, together with letters from his own name as the musical material for the pieces, which describe different characters (such as Chopin and Paganini) who are present at an imaginary ball to which Schumann is invited. Some musical ideas from *Carnival* were also used in Schumann's earlier *Papillons*. Glazunov orchestrated some of the pieces for a ballet in 1910. **2.** Overture (Op. 92) by Dvořák. Composed: 1891. *Carnival* was the second of a trilogy of overtures called *Nature, Life and Love*; the other works were *Othello* and *In Nature's Realm*. **3.** Overture by Glazunov. Composed: 1894.

Carnival of the Animals A 'grand zoological fantasy' in 14 movements by Saint-Saëns for two pianos and orchestra. Composed: 1886. Each movement depicts a different animal, which is usually associated with a particular orchestral instrument; for example the 'swan' features a solo cello and the 'elephant' is described by a double bass. One movement is even devoted to 'pianists,' whom Saint-Saëns obviously considered as animals! In the work several well-known melodies are parodied, including ones from Saint-Saëns' own *Danse macabre* and Rossini's *The Barber of Seville*. The composer never allowed a public performance of the work during his lifetime.

Carnival of Venice Theme and variations for violin and piano by Paganini, based on the popular Venetian tune 'O mamma mia.' Composed: 1829. Paganini's example was followed by many other composers, including Schulhoff and Herz, all of whom wrote variations on the tune. It also appears in the opera *Le Carnaval de Venise* (1857) by Thomas.

carol A simple occasional song, most usually associated with Christmas. In its purest form it employs straightforward language and music and is a spontaneous reflection of the occasion it celebrates. It is commonly joyful in spirit. Carols had their origins in the 14th century and became well established by the 15th; the lilting verse and refrain, exemplified in 'This endris night,' is the main innovatory feature of the 15th century. Also popular were **macaronic carols**, in which lines in Latin, taken mainly from the hymns of the Office, were interspersed with lines in the vernacular; a famous example is 'In dulci jubilo.' The earliest printed collection of English carols by Wynkyn de Worde stems from 1521. The form flourished during the 16th and early 17th centuries, only to be suppressed by the Puritans: it never properly recovered. The pure carol was taken over into folk song, to be saved only by collectors and scholars in the late 19th and early 20th centuries. The rediscovery of Christmas in the 19th century saw the carol changed to mean any printed song suitable for Christmas; many carols are simply Christmas hymns. French: **noël**; German: **Weihnachtslieder**.

Carreras, José (1946–) Spanish tenor. He studied under J. F. Puig, making his debut as Ishmaele in Verdi's *Nabucco*. With Montserrat Caballé, who aided him subsequently, he made his London debut in 1971 in a concert version of *Maria Stuarda*. He has since toured widely.

Carrillo, Julian (1875–1965) Mexican composer and conductor. He developed his own microtonal system (Sonido 13) and devised a number of instruments tuned in it. He was a prolific composer of conventional and microtonal works; in some of his pieces microtonal and conventional techniques are combined.

Carter, Elliott (1908–) US composer; a pupil of Piston (at Harvard) and Nadia Boulanger (in Paris), he was later encouraged by Ives. His early works are neoclassical in idiom and rhythmically complex. He pursued his interest in rhythm by exploring nonwestern and unconventional techniques, which led to the development of his metrical modulation (characterized by smooth changes from one tempo to another). His subsequent works are marked by a contrapuntal style of great intricacy, with simultaneous juxtaposition of sound textures and rhythmic patterns. There is often extreme dissociation between instruments or groups, which are treated as dramatic characters. Carter's works include a cello sonata (1948), *Variations for Orchestra* (1955), *String Quartet 2* (1959), *Double Concerto* (1961), *Concerto for Orchestra* (1969), *String Quartet 3* (1973), and *Symphony for Three Orchestras* (1978).

Carulli, Ferdinando (1770–1841) Italian guitarist, composer, and teacher. In 1808 he left Naples and settled in Paris, where he quickly became famous as the leading guitar virtuoso. He composed well over 300 works for the guitar, including concertos, studies, and sonatas, and wrote a guitar method.

Caruso, Enrico (1873–1921) Italian tenor. He made his first stage appearance in Naples (1894) and gained his first success in Milan (1899), where he created the role of Loris in Giordano's opera *Fedora*. Subsequent performances at London's Covent Garden (from 1902) and New York's Metropolitan Opera (from 1903) established his reputation as an outstanding lyric tenor. Caruso's great popularity was

due as much to his many gramophone recordings as to his live performances. Although the recordings were all pre-electric, the quality of his voice can still be heard.

Cary, Tristram (1925–) British composer of electronic music and musique concrète. He has written live tape pieces (e.g. *Narcissus*, 1970), tape and light pieces (e.g. *Music for Light*, 1968), and many scores for film and television.

Casadesus, Robert (1899–1972) French pianist and composer. In addition to establishing a reputation as a solo pianist in Europe and the USA, Casadesus formed a violin and piano duo with Zino *Francescatti and performed duets with his wife **Gaby Casadesus** (1901–). Most of his compositions are unpublished.

Casals, Pablo (Pau C.; 1876–1973) Spanish cellist, conductor, and composer. One of the foremost musicians of his generation, Casals studied under Garcia at Barcelona. His career embraced both solo music, notably Bach's suites for solo cello, and chamber works, including trios with

Pablo Casals

Enrico Caruso

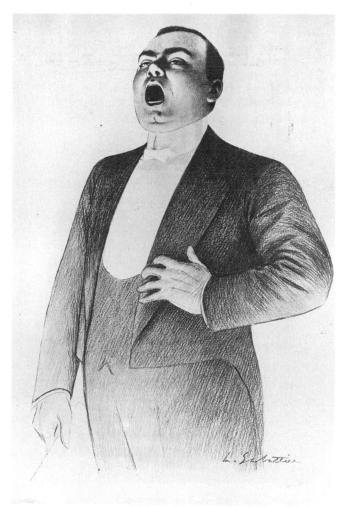

Thibaud and Cortot. As a conductor he founded the Orquestra Pau Casals in Barcelona; he also exercised a wide influence as a teacher. Fauré, Moor, Tovey, and Schoenberg are among the composers who wrote for him. In 1940, as a protest against Franco's government, Casals settled in Prades, France, where he founded an annual festival of chamber music. From 1956 he lived in Puerto Rico.

Casella, Alfredo (1883–1947) Italian composer, pianist, and conductor, a pupil of Fauré. He toured widely in Europe and the USA as a pianist, harpsichordist, and conductor and in 1915 became professor at the Santa Cecilia conservatory, Rome. His works include three operas, four ballets, two symphonies, songs, piano music, and chamber music. The influence of Schoenberg is apparent in his atonal orchestral *Heroic Elegy* (1916), and he developed a Stravinskian neoclassical style in such works as *Scarlattiana* for piano and orchestra (1926). In later works, such as the *Mass* (1944), he used 12-tone technique.

cassa Drum. Thus **cassa rullante**, tenor drum; **gran cassa**, bass drum. [Italian]

Cassadó, Gaspar (1897–1966) Spanish cellist and composer. After studying with his father and Casals, he became known as both a soloist and chamber music player, performing trios with Menuhin and Kentner. Cassado taught at the Accademia Chigiana in Siena.

cassation (*or* **cassazione**) A favourite form of orchestral music devised for open-air presentation during the 18th-century classical period. Similar forms are the serenade, serenata, and divertimento.

Casse-Noisette see **Nutcracker, The.**

Cassuto, Alvaro (Leon) (1938–) Portuguese composer and conductor. He studied at Darmstadt (1960–61), attending classes given by Ligeti, Messiaen, and Stockhausen, and was taught conducting by von Karajan. He has conducted various European and US orchestras, including the Gulbenkian Orchestra, Lisbon (1965–68). The first Portuguese composer to use 12-tone technique, his works include the oratorio *Canticum in Tenebris* (1968) and several orchestral works, including *Circle* (1971).

castanets Concussion instruments consisting of two wooden shells, clicked together in one hand by Spanish flamenco dancers. The castanets occasionally used in orchestras are usually mounted on sticks so that they can be shaken together. [from Spanish *castaña*, chestnut]

Castelnuovo-Tedesco, Mario (1895–1968) Italian composer, resident in the USA since 1939. He studied at the Cherubini Institute under Pizzetti, and after emigrating to the USA (for political reasons) taught at the Los Angeles conservatory and became an active composer for Hollywood. His works include eight operas (including *The Importance of Being Earnest*, 1962), four oratorios, orchestral and chamber works, twelve books of Shakespeare songs (1921–26), and *Noah's Ark*, a contribution to the strange collective work *Genesis* (1947).

Castiglioni, Niccolo (1932–) Italian composer, a pupil of Blacher. In early works, such as *Aprèslude* (1959), he was influenced by Mahler, but later works, such as *Solemn Music II* (1965), show the influence of Boulez. Castiglioni has also written a radio opera, *Through the Looking Glass* (1961), which makes use of electronic music.

castrato A male singer castrated before puberty in order to preserve his soprano or alto voice. Although the voice had a high pitch, its quality was often appreciably different from that of the boy soprano. Castrati were found in Italian church choirs and also became very fashionable in early Italian operas, persisting throughout Europe well into the 18th century. Pressure on humane grounds caused the practice to die out gradually, although recognition of the importance of women in operatic roles from the late 18th century was also a contributory factor in the disappearance of castrati. Characters such as Cherubino (in *The Marriage of Figaro*), originally intended for castrati, are now sung by sopranos.

Catalani, Alfredo (1854–93) Italian composer. He studied in Paris and at the Milan conservatory, where he succeeded Ponchielli as Professor of Composition in 1888. His one-act opera *La Falce* (1875) has a text by Boito, who encouraged his work; of his six operas, *La* *Wally (1892) comes closest to his ideal of Wagnerian Italian opera. Catalani also wrote a symphonic poem, *Ero e Leandro* (1885).

catch A *round, generally for three or more unaccompanied voices. It was particularly popular in 17th-century England, when it often had a humorous or bawdy text.

Cat Duet Duet for two female voices and piano by Rossini. Composed: *c.*1860. This work was described by the composer as the 'Duetto buffo di due gatti' ('Comic duet of two cats') and it is one of the collection of humorous compositions that Rossini called his *Péchés de vieillesse* (*Sins of Old Age*). Both singers vocalize on the word 'miau' and the composition is a satirical allusion to the traditionally malicious character of a prima donna.

Cat's Fugue Harpsichord sonata in G minor by Domenico Scarlatti (No. 30 in the Kirkpatrick catalogue). The nickname, which was not used until after the composer's death, refers to the curiously ascending fugue subject. It has been suggested that the wide intervals of the subject may have been in imitation of the sound produced by a cat walking up the keyboard, but there is no evidence to confirm this.

Cavalieri, Emilio de' (*c.*1550–1602) Italian composer, descended from a noble Roman family. In 1587 he entered the service of Grand Duke Ferdinand in Florence, where he organized and composed part of the music of the *Intermedi* celebrating Ferdinand's marriage (1589); in the 1590s he also wrote the music for at least three dramas by Laura Guidiccioni, none of which survive. In 1600 his *La *Rappresentazione di anima e di corpo* was performed in Rome: it is a morality play set to music throughout and had a decisive influence on the 17th-century oratorio.

Cavalleria rusticana (*Rustic Chivalry*) Opera in one act by Mascagni with text by Menasci and Targioni-Tozzetti based on a story by Verga. First performance: Teatro Costanzi, Rome, 1890. Verga's verismo tale is one of passion and revenge set in a Sicilian village. It is often played in a double bill with *I Pagliacci* (known as *Cav and Pag*).

Cavalli, Pietro Francesco (1602–76) Italian composer, organist, and singer. From 1616 he sang at St Mark's, Venice, under Monteverdi. After a short time as organist of SS Giovanni e Paolo, he became successively second organist (1639), first organist, and maestro di cappella (1668) at St Mark's. He composed for Venice's first opera house, the Teatro S Cassiano, but his most popular opera, *Egisto* (1643), was performed in Paris, where he spent two years (1660–62) at the court of Louis XIV and composed *Ercole amante* (1662). His operas, which include *Ormindo* (1644) and *Calisto* (1651), contain recitative over a slow-moving bass, which contrasts with the simple triple-metre arias. He also wrote sacred music for St Mark's, including the *Messa concertata* and Magnificat settings.

cavatina 1. A short aria lacking development or internal repetition, found in late-18th- and 19th-century opera. **2.** A slow instrumental piece with a dominant and expressive melody, as in Beethoven's quartet Op. 130.

Cavazzoni, Marco Antonio (*c.*1490–after 1569) Italian composer, born in Bologna, active also in Urbino, Rome, Venice, and Mantua. His *Ricercari* (1523) are the first to use points of imitation. His son, **Girolamo Cavazzoni** (*c.*1520–?), was a pupil of Willaert. The ricercari in his *Intavolatura* (1542) explore further his father's innovations. Both composers also cultivated other forms of keyboard music, namely canzoni, and hymn and Magnificat settings.

Cavendish, Michael (*c.*1565–*c.*1628) English composer of lute songs and madrigals, a member of a family known for its patronage of musicians. His only publication (title page missing), in 1598, includes both songs and madrigals. He contributed one madrigal, 'Come gentle swains,' to *The *Triumphs of Oriana* (1601).

cebell A 17th-century English dance in duple rhythm, similar to the *gavotte and generally serious in mood.

Cecilia, St (died *c.*176) Christian martyr and patron saint of music. Early references to Cecilia do not connect her with music and it was not until the late 15th century that she appears in paintings, etc., represented as playing the organ, harp, or other instrument. Feast day: 22 November.

cédez Yield; give way. A direction used to indicate that the speed should be held back. [French]

celeste (*or* **celesta**) A type of *glockenspiel with a keyboard. Invented in 1886 by Auguste Mustel, it looks like a small upright piano and consists of a four-octave piano keyboard, the lowest note of which is middle C. The keyboard operates felt-covered hammers that strike a set of metal bars, each of which has its own wooden resonator. It was first used by Tchaikovsky in his *Nutcracker* ballet and has since been used by a number of composers for special effects. The **dulcitone** is a type of celeste in which the sound is produced by a set of tuning forks rather than by metal bars.

Celibidache, Sergiu (1912–) Romanian conductor. From 1945 until 1951 he conducted the Berlin Philharmonic Orchestra. The vitality and precision of his conducting earned him a legendary reputation.

Cellier, Alfred (1844–91) British organist, conductor, and composer. He held appointments as a church organist and was musical director in several London theatres. From 1877 he worked for Richard D'Oyly Carte at the Savoy Theatre and assisted Sullivan with conducting and orchestration. Cellier's compositions are chiefly stage works in the same style as Sullivan's, his best-known operetta being *Dorothy* (1886).

cello (*or* **violoncello**) A bowed four-stringed instrument that is the bass member of the *violin family. Its strings are tuned at intervals of a fifth, the lowest being C two octaves below middle C (i.e. C, G, D, A). It has a range of over four octaves. Dating from the late 16th century, the cello was used chiefly as an accompanying instrument (see **continuo**) until the 18th century, when it developed a role as a solo instrument and in the *string quartet. The end pin, used to support the instrument in playing, was adopted in the late 19th century. The repertoire includes Bach's six suites for solo cello, concertos by Haydn, Dvořák, and Elgar, and sonatas by Beethoven, Brahms, and Debussy. [from Italian *violone* (see **viol family**) -*cello* (diminutive suffix)]

Celtic harp see **harp**.

cembalo 1. A dulcimer. **2.** (short for **clavicembalo**) A harpsichord. **3.** The *figured bass for a harpsichord accompaniment. **4.** A cymbal. **5.** A Basque tambourine. [Italian]

Cendrillon see Cinderella.

Cenerentola, La see Cinderella.

Cerha, (Friedrich) Paul (1926–   ) Austrian composer and conductor, founder of the ensemble Die Reihe and the journal of the same name. He has written numerous chamber, vocal, and electronic pieces, including *Spiegel* for orchestra and tape. He was responsible for the completion of the unfinished third act of Berg's opera *Lulu*.

Certon, Pierre (*c*.1510–72) French composer. He was a clerk then choirmaster at the Sainte Chapelle from 1542 until his death. He wrote almost 200 chansons, many of them witty and satirical. Certon also wrote metrical psalm settings, motets, and masses.

Cesti, Antonio (1623–69) Italian composer and singer. He joined the Franciscans in 1637 and became organist at Volterra in 1643. While there he enjoyed the patronage of the Medici and composed the opera *Orontea* (1649). Apart from a short period in the papal choir, Cesti worked at the Imperial court in Innsbruck from 1652 to 1665; from 1666 he worked at Vienna. In 1668 he composed the opera *Il Pomo d'oro*, in five acts, using a large orchestra and 24 sets. It is regarded as the most notable baroque court opera.

Chabrier, (Alexis) Emmanuel (1841–94) French composer and pianist. Until 1880 he was a civil servant, but before that he had begun composing and was well

Chabrier, whose work is noted for its verve and humour

acquainted with leading musicians of the day, including Fauré, Duparc, and d'Indy. In 1881 he visited Spain, which made a deep impression and led him to write his best-known work, the colourful rhapsody for orchestra **Espa*na* (1883). Chabrier was an ardent follower of Wagner, whose influence is apparent in his stage works; they include the operas *L'Etoile* (1877), *Gwendoline* (1885), and *Le Roi malgré lui* (1887). He also wrote songs and orchestral music (including the *Marche Joyeuse*, 1888), but was most successful with his influential piano works, among them the *Pièces pittoresques* (1881) and the *Bourrée fantasque* (1891).

chaconne A slow dance in triple time, very often built upon a *ground bass. This bass sometimes migrates to the other parts as the piece progresses. Where there is no such bass the piece is characterized by short sections repeated equally throughout. There appears to be little distinction in practice between chaconne and *passacaglia. Italian: **ciaccona**.

chacony Old English term for *chaconne.

Chadwick, George Whitefield (1854–1931) US composer and teacher. He studied at the Leipzig conservatory and at the Munich Hochschule für Musik. He returned to Boston in 1880, and in 1897 became director of the New England Conservatory of Music. Chadwick's compositions, many of them distinctively American, include operas (the best-known is *Judith*, 1901), choral and orchestral music (including three symphonies and several symphonic poems), chamber works (five string quartets and a piano quintet), and songs.

Chagrin, Francis (Alexander Paucker; 1905–72) Romanian-born composer, resident in England. He studied at the conservatories of Zürich and Bucharest and at the Ecole Normale, Paris, where he was a pupil of Dukas and Nadia Boulanger. He was also taught by Seiber (1944–46). From 1941 to 1944 he was musical director of the BBC French Service and in 1943 he founded the Committee for the Promotion of New Music. His works include three symphonies (the last unfinished), incidental and film music, about 100 songs, and a piano concerto (1948).

Chailly, Luciano (1920–   ) Italian composer. A pupil of Hindemith (1948), he was appointed head of Rome television in 1962. His musical style embraces neoclassicism, 12-note technique, and electronics; his works include incidental music for television and eight operas, including *L'Idiota* (1970) after Dostoyevsky.

Chaliapin, Feodor Ivanovich see **Shaliapin, Feodor Ivanovich**.

chalumeau see **clarinet**.

chamber cantata see **cantata**.

chamber music Intimate ensemble music, as distinct from solo, orchestral, or choral music. One player per part is usual, although music performed in this way (such as much baroque orchestral music) is not necessarily chamber music. In the 17th and 18th centuries, chamber music was generally intended for domestic, private, and very often amateur performance. The existence of highly professional ensembles, whose public concerts are often packed to capacity, has diminished that aspect, and although chamber concerts are now rarely given in large concert halls, they are frequently given in smaller concert halls rather than large salons. The principal form of chamber music is the string quartet, followed by various combinations of strings, wind instruments, and piano.

chamber opera A small-scale opera. Early 17th-century Florentine and Roman operas are in the main chamber works in that they are short and restricted in their musical and theatrical elements, yet because they are intended for a specialist, often aristocratic, audience, they are sophisticated in emotional content. In the early 20th century several chamber operas, such as Stravinsky's *Mavra* and *Renard* (1922), were written partly as a reaction against the grand romantic operas.

chamber orchestra A small orchestra capable of playing in a room (or small hall). The term is loosely applied, but generally refers to a group in which there is more than one player to a part. A string orchestra is not necessarily a chamber orchestra, many string works requiring a large body of performers.

chamber sonata see sonata.

chamber symphony A small-scale symphony, generally for few players. An example is Schoenberg's *Kammer-Symphonie* (Op. 9) for 15 instruments.

Chaminade, Cécile (1857–1944) French pianist and composer. A successful concert pianist, she wrote some 200 pieces of salon music for the piano; her more ambitious works include the choral symphony *Les Amazones* and the ballet *Callirhöe* (both 1888) and other orchestral and stage works.

changed note see nota cambiata.

change-ringing see bells.

chanson 1. Any French strophic song. 2. A French monophonic or polyphonic song using different forms from the 12th century onwards. From this early chanson developed a separately identifiable 16th-century form, inspired by Josquin des Prez. After 1530 the chanson generally had four voices and became specifically French, so losing its Flemish background. Pierre Attaingnant, the famous printer, published many such pieces in the first half of the 16th century.

chant The traditional unison melody of both the Eastern and Western churches. That of the Western Roman Church is known as *plainchant (or Gregorian chant); that of the Anglican Church is *Anglican chant. The chant of the Eastern Orthodox Church is known as *Byzantine music. For the liturgical music of the Jewish Church, see **Jewish music**.

chanter (or **chaunter**) see **bagpipes**.

chanterelle The top (E) string of a violin or the melody string of a lute or banjo.

chapel master A musician in charge of music in a chapel. The term is not used in English, but is a translation of the German *kapellmeister, the Italian *maestro di cappella, and the French maître de chapelle.

Chapel Royal The English court chapel, consisting of a body of musicians, clergy, choirmen, choirboys, and organist associated with the production of sacred music for the court. At the end of the 13th century and the beginning of the 14th, the ad hoc arrangements for music at royal devotions were reorganized and a group of chaplains and choristers was designated the royal chapel. The numbers involved changed during successive reigns and under the patronage of different sovereigns the Chapel had a great influence on the composition of sacred music in England. It flourished particularly under Elizabeth I and most leading English church musicians were associated with it, including Tye, Tallis, Byrd, Gibbons, and Morley. Its influence at that time was profound and it was regarded as one of Europe's foremost musical institutions. During the Commonwealth the Chapel was disbanded; it was reformed under Charles II but never regained its pre-eminence in English musical life. Until 1702 it had no permanent base and its personnel travelled with the royal household to wherever the sovereign was living. Subsequently the Chapel has been based at St James's Palace. It continues to provide music for royal worship in a variety of places.

Chapí (y Lorente), Ruperto (1851–1909) Spanish composer. He studied at the Madrid conservatory (1867–69) then in Rome, Milan, and Paris. He composed over 100 *zarzuelas, which enjoyed great success in Madrid, and orchestral and choral works, as well as four string quartets.

Charpentier, Gustave (1860–1956) French composer. He studied at the Paris Conservatoire under Massenet and won the Prix de Rome (1887). In 1902 he founded the Conservatoire de Mimi Pinson to provide free lessons in music and dancing for working-class girls. He wrote several orchestral and vocal works and is chiefly remembered for his famous picturesque opera *Louise (1900) and its successor, *Julién* (1913).

Charpentier, Marc-Antoine (?1645–1704) French composer. He studied with Giacomo Carissimi in Rome and was then employed in Paris by the Duchess of Guise. He worked in collaboration with Molière's troupe from 1672, writing music for Molière's last play, *Le Malade imaginaire* (1673). In the 1680s he was employed by the grand dauphin and was maître de musique at St Louis; from 1698 he held the same position at the Sainte-Chapelle. Charpentier is remembered for his sacred music, particularly the *Te Deum* and oratorios. His style reflects Italian influence but is essentially French in its use of the récit.

Chasseur maudit, Le (*The Accursed Huntsman*) Symphonic poem by Franck, based upon the ballad *Der wilde Jäger* by Gottfried Bürger. Composed: 1882. The work describes the fate of a huntsman who goes hunting on Sunday rather than going to church and is pursued by demons as a punishment.

Chausson, (Amédée) Ernest (1855–99) French composer. He trained as a lawyer but abandoned that profession for music, becoming Massenet's pupil at the Paris Conservatoire (1879–81); he also attended Franck's classes. He became a leading member of Franck's circle and as a composer preferred to cultivate small forms rather than Wagner-influenced large-scale works. His best-known works are the *Poème de l'amour et de la mer* for solo voice and orchestra (1882–90), the *Poème* for violin and orchestra (1896), the concerto for piano, violin, and string quartet (1889–91), and the piano quartet (1897).

Chávez, Carlos (1899–1978) Mexican conductor and composer. A pupil of Ponce, he founded and directed the Mexican Symphony Orchestra (1928–48), was director of the Mexico conservatory (1928–35), and founded and directed the Mexican Institute of Fine Arts (1947–52). His works include orchestral, chamber, and piano music; seven symphonies, including the choral *Sinfonia proletaria* (1934); the opera *The Visitors* (1957–59); and choral music and songs. Works such as the ballet *Xochipilli* (1940) evoke Aztec myth and ritual.

Checkmate Ballet in one act with music by Bliss and scenario and choreography by the composer and Ninette de Valois. First performance: Théâtre des Champs-Elysées, Paris, 1937, by the Vic-Wells Company. It represents a game of chess between Love and Death.

chef d'attaque Leader of the orchestra. [French, literally leader of the attack]

chef d'orchestre Conductor. [French, literally leader of the orchestra]

Cheltenham International Festival An annual festival founded in 1945 at Cheltenham, Gloucestershire. It presents orchestral and chamber concerts, recitals, and occasionally stage works and has chiefly featured new British music. In the 1960s it widened its scope to include contemporary

Cherubini was both a composer and a theoretician

music of other countries and in 1974 it incorporated the word 'International' in its title.

Cheminée du Roi René, La Wind quintet by Milhaud. Composed: 1939. The title refers to the 15th-century King René, whose name is commemorated in a street in Milhaud's native Aix-en-Provence.

Cherkassky, Shura (1911–) Russian-born US pianist. He was taught by his mother and Josef Hofmann and his reputation was established by a European tour in 1945. Cherkassky is particularly noted for his interpretation of Russian works.

Cherubini, Luigi (Carlo Zanobi Salvadore Maria) (1760–1842) Italian composer, theorist, and teacher, who worked in France. He studied with Sarti in Bologna and Milan and in 1784 went to London. In 1786 he settled in Paris and became musical director of the Italian Opera (1789–92). In 1793 he was appointed inspector of instruction at the Institut National de Musique (from 1795 called the Conservatoire). His operas *Médée (1797) and Les *Deux Journées* (1800) were acclaimed, but subsequent operas were less successful and he turned increasingly to writing church music; in 1816 he and Le Sueur were appointed superintendents of the royal chapel. He became director of the Conservatoire (1822–42), where his policies had a lasting effect on music education; his pupils included Boieldieu, Auber, and Halévy.

Cherubini was a leading figure in French musical life for many years. He transformed opéra comique into a genre

Plate 12: *Bizet's* Carmen *is probably the most popular opera ever composed. This scene is from the 1973 production at the Royal Opera House, Covent Garden. Plácido Domingo,* who plays Don José, *is on the far left*

Plate 13: *A Chinese dignitary seeking inspiration in music for the
writing of poetry. School of Chin Ying. British Museum, London*

Plate 14: *Portrait of Frédéric Chopin by Eugène Delacroix.*
1838. Musée du Louvre, Paris

Plate 15: *Claude Debussy, a portrait by Marcel Baschet, painted
in 1884, the year in which the composer won the Prix de Rome*

capable of expressing powerful dramatic ideas; the best known include *Lodoïska* (1791), *Anacréon* (1803), and *Faniska* (1806). Of his sacred music, the seven masses and two requiems are the most distinguished. He also wrote a little orchestral and chamber music and a treatise on counterpoint (1835).

chest of viols A set of viols of different sizes, usually six in number, that were kept in a specially designed chest. The chest itself became an established piece of 16th-century furniture and the six viols became an established ensemble, for which a considerable amount of music was written.

chest voice The lowest of the three registers of the voice, the others being medium and *head voice. It is so called because the tone appears to come from the area of the chest and is, in fact, intentionally directed downwards from the larynx in order to give substance and sonority to the low notes, which are naturally the weakest ones.

chiesa, da For church. Used to indicate a kind of composition (e.g. **cantata da chiesa, sonata da chiesa**) originally meant for use in the church. Compare **camera, da**. [Italian]

Chilcot, Thomas (?–1766) British composer and organist, teacher of the elder Thomas Linley. He was organist of Bath Abbey (1733) and was best known for his *Twelve English Songs* (1744). Chilcot also wrote keyboard music, concertos, and other chamber works.

Child, William (1606/07–97) English composer and organist. In 1630 he became a clerk at St George's Chapel, Windsor, and in 1632 succeeded John Munday as organist there. A Royalist, he was dismissed from this post during the Protectorate but returned at the Restoration. His only printed collection, *The First Set of [20] Psalmes* (1639), was popular at private meetings during the Protectorate. His prolific output comprises psalms, services, and anthems, mainly composed before 1660.

Child and the Spells, The see **Enfant et les sortilèges, L'**.

Childhood of Christ, The (French: *L'Enfance du Christ*) Oratorio for solo voices, choir, and orchestra (Op. 25) by Berlioz, with words by the composer based on the Bible. First performance: 1854. The work tells the story of Jesus' nativity and the subsequent flight of his family to Egypt. However, the sequence of events as narrated by Berlioz differs slightly from the biblical version.

Child of Our Time, A Oratorio for solo voices, choir, and orchestra by Tippett. First performance: 1944. The oratorio is based upon a true event – the shooting of a German diplomat by a Jew before World War II and the Nazi persecution of the Jews that followed. Musically this work is a kind of modern passion setting, with the traditional chorale replaced by Negro spirituals.

Children's Corner Suite of five piano pieces by Debussy, written for his young daughter Claude-Emma (Chou-chou). Composed: 1906–08. The opening piece is 'Doctor Gradus ad Parnassum,' which jokingly alludes to Clementi's *Gradus ad Parnassum*, a book of studies used by pianists. Then come 'Jimbo's Lullaby,' 'Serenade for the Doll,' 'Snow is Dancing,' 'The Little Shepherd,' and finally 'Golliwog's Cakewalk.' This last piece is one of the earliest examples of jazz idioms influencing 'serious' music and has been orchestrated for several different combinations.

Children's Games see **Jeux d'enfants**.

Children's Overture, A Overture by Quilter, published in 1914. The work is based upon nursery rhymes from Crane's *Baby's Opera*. Quilter originally wrote the overture together with incidental music for the play *Where the Rainbow Ends*, but it was never performed with this play.

Childs, Barney (1926–) US composer. Educated in Nevada, Oxford, and Stanford, he studied under Ratner, Chávez, Carter, and Copland (1952–54); he has been professor and composer-in-residence at the University of Redlands since 1971. His works include two symphonies and other orchestral works. Like Berio and Globokar, Childs has used advanced brass-playing techniques and since 1961 has used chance in such works as *Nonet* (1967).

ch'in see **qin**.

Chinese music From the time of Confucius (554–479 BC), Chinese music has been considered as a means for preparing the mind for philosophical speculation and spiritual enlightenment. From earliest times music was also an essential part of agricultural festivals, of court ceremonial, and of religious ritual, being a means of expressing the cosmic harmony in the balance between heaven and earth and between the male principle, yang, and the female principle, yin.

Chinese music is built on a pentatonic scale extracted from a series of 12 **lü**, somewhat similar to the European chromatic scale (but never used as such). The lü are calculated on the cycle of fifths giving the simple ratio of 3:2 between the intervals; 3 is the Chinese symbolic number for heaven, 2 for earth. The five notes of the pentatonic scale parallel the five elements: earth, metal, wood, fire, and water; a 7-note scale was sometimes in use, using five main and two auxiliary notes. Melody and timbre are the basic constituents of Chinese music; harmony, as understood in European music, is nonexistent, but instead there is a rich sonority of tones and overtones created by the unison playing of the various instruments.

The instruments are classified according to their basic material. They include metal gongs, bells, and chimes; *stone chimes (**bian jing**, *or* **pien ch'ing**); bamboo flutes (**di**, *or* **ti**) and panpipes; wooden and skin percussion instru-

Musicians of the Peking Opera

ments; a clay globular flute; and gourds, such as the **sheng**. This has about 14 small pipes set upwards in a gourd, each with a free metal reed, like a mouth organ, and blown through a substantial mouthpiece. Silk is used for stringing lutes, zithers, and the two-stringed fiddle. Two other important instruments are the *qin (a seven-stringed zither) and the *pipa (a short-necked lute). Both were in use during the Tang dynasty (618–906 AD), a period of great cultural achievement having large orchestras, both male and female, and virtuoso instrumentalists, singers, and dancers, who were trained in the Li Yuan (the Pear-Tree Garden), the imperial academy of music. China has known various forms of pitch notation for over 2000 years.

The Yuan (*or* Mongol) dynasty (1280–1368) introduced a greater variety of instruments and scales and saw the establishment of the southern and the northern schools of Chinese drama. During the Ming dynasty (1368–1644) women were excluded from the drama and men developed the high nasal tone peculiar to Chinese classical drama until 1911.

Chinese pavilion see **jingling johnny**.

Chinese wood block A block of hollowed-out wood used as a percussion instrument. It is struck with a drumstick and gives a resonant note. The **Korean temple block** is another version, consisting of a skull-shaped hollow block. Wood blocks and temple blocks are mainly used in dance bands but are included in some 20th-century orchestral music.

chitarra Guitar. [Italian]

chitarrone see **lute**.

chiuso Closed; stopped. Used in brass instrumental technique to indicate a note stopped by placing the hand in the bell of the instrument. [Italian]

Chocolate Soldier, The (German: *Der tapfere Soldat*) Operetta by Oscar Straus with libretto by Jacobson and Bernauer based on Shaw's *Arms and the Man*. First performance: Theater an der Wien, Vienna, 1908.

choir 1. A group of singers having more than one member to a part, which meets regularly to fulfil a special function. For example a church choir will lead the worship and a nonecclesiastical choir, amateur or professional, gives concerts. Musical and tonal balance is an essential ingredient of a good choir, and the skill of the conductor or trainer is put to the test to achieve this in the face of problems created by numerical imbalance. In cathedrals and some churches it is customary to divide the choir into *cantoris and *decani. **2.** The part of a church to the east of the nave, occupied by the clergy and choir.

choir organ see **organ**.

Chopin, Frédéric François (Fryderyk Franciszek C.; 1810–49) Polish composer and pianist. He had music lessons from Ziwny (1816–22), making his debut as a pianist in 1818, then studied with Elsner (1822–26) and at the Warsaw conservatory (1826–27). In 1828 he went to Berlin and in 1829 to Vienna, where he impressed audiences with his compositions (particularly those in a Polish style) and his fluent improvisations. After returning to Warsaw, where he was soon regarded as a national composer, he set off on a European tour during which he heard that the Russians had captured Warsaw. He thereafter settled in Paris and never returned to Poland. In Paris he became a celebrated virtuoso and mixed with leading musicians of the day (among them Berlioz, Meyerbeer, and Liszt); he was also much sought-after as a teacher in aristocratic circles. He made further tours to Germany (1834–35) and to London (1837). In 1836 Chopin had met Aurore Dupin (George Sand); from 1838 to 1847 they lived together but it was a period marked by Chopin's deteriorating health. The Revolution of 1848 forced him to leave for England and he made his last public appearance in London (1849). Later in the year he returned to Paris, where he died.

The image of Chopin as a consumptive romantic virtuoso for a long time clouded an objective assessment of his achievements as a composer. He devoted himself almost exclusively to the piano, producing not only short pieces (mazurkas, waltzes, etc.) but also showing himself a master of complex large-scale forms (the ballades, *Polonaise-fantaisie*, etc.). Although many of his works demand virtuoso technique, the basic texture is a chromatic ornamented melody in the right hand, with left-hand accompaniment; this is particularly true of the *nocturnes, a form he took over from John Field and transformed with rich thematic material and striking harmony. He exploited the piano's sonority, particularly in his preludes and studies. His Polish pieces influenced nationalist composers later in the century to incorporate folk elements into their music.

For piano solo, Chopin wrote 3 piano sonatas (the well-known funeral march is from No. 2, known as the *Funeral March Sonata, 1839), 27 *studies, such as the *Revolutionary Study (1831) and the *Winter Wind Study (1834), 19 nocturnes, 25 preludes, including the *Raindrop Prelude (1839), 4 scherzos, 4 ballades, 14 waltzes, including the *Minute Waltz (1847), 10 polonaises, over 50 mazurkas, a berceuse, impromptus, etc. He also wrote two piano concertos, the rondo Krakowiak (1828), a cello sonata (1845–46), a piano trio (1828–29), and 17 Polish songs. He contributed a variation to the *Hexameron (1837).

Chopsticks A popular quick waltz melody for the piano. Since it can be played using the sides of the little fingers the resultant 'chopping' motion of the hand provides the nickname (there is no reference to Chinese chopsticks). Many composers have used this anonymous tune as the basis for variations, including Borodin, Liszt, Franck, and Lyadov.

choragus A person who holds a special post at Oxford University subordinate to the Professor of Music.

choral Denoting music that is sung by a choir or chorus. see also **choral symphony**. Compare **chorale**.

chorale 1. Originally, the polyphonic settings of plainsong in the German Roman Catholic liturgy. A few examples of extensive settings are found, e.g. Isaac's *Choralis Constantinus*. 2. A German Protestant hymn, adapted or copied from plainsong or a secular melody and intended for unison congregational singing. It was inspired by Martin Luther, who also wrote many chorales. The earliest ones were often irregular in metre. Harmonization of chorales, made famous by J. S. Bach, stems from the late 16th century, a notable exponent being Scheidt. The chorale has held an important and special position in post-Renaissance German music, since it provided a unique source of native melodies on which German composers could base their compositions; an example of such a work is Michael Praetorius's *Musae sionae* (1605–10). Chorales were nearly always incorporated into oratorios and sacred cantatas. In church an organ piece, the **chorale prelude**, would often precede the singing of a chorale.

Choral Fantasia Fantasia (Op. 80) by Beethoven for piano, solo voices, choir, and orchestra with a text by Kuffner. First performance: 1808. The fantasia is a set of variations upon a modified version of Beethoven's own song 'Gegenliebe'

(1795) and is in many ways a forerunner of his ninth symphony (1823–24) and its setting of Schiller's 'Ode to Joy.' Both the works have texts in praise of music and there is a great similarity between the main theme of the *Choral Fantasia* and the main theme of the finale of the symphony. Beethoven himself mentions this in his correspondence.

choral symphony A symphony that includes parts for a chorus or solo voices. The best known is Beethoven's *Choral Symphony* (No. 9 in D minor, Op. 125), composed: 1823–24; first performance: Vienna, 1824. Its name is derived from the use of a quartet of solo voices and chorus in the last movement, which is a setting of Schiller's 'Ode to Joy' ('An die Freude'). Other choral symphonies include Mahler's *Symphony of a Thousand*.

chord A combination of two or more notes played simultaneously. A **common chord** (*or* **triad**) consists of a keynote and its *third and *fifth played together (e.g. CEG is the common chord of C major and CE♭G is that of C minor). In popular music, especially for guitars, **chord symbols** are used as a simple harmonic *notation. For example G7 C denotes the sequence consisting of the chord of the *dominant seventh in the key of C followed by the chord of C major. Cmin denotes C minor in this notation; Cdim is the diminished *seventh chord on C.

chording 1. The spacing of the notes making up a chord. 2. A measure of the correctness of the intonation of a chord as sung by a choir. 3. The provision of a chord accompaniment on a guitar, banjo, etc.

chordophone A musical *instrument in which the sound is produced by a vibrating string. The five basic families of chordophones are the bows, lyres, harps, lutes, and zithers. The guitar and violin family evolved from the lutes, while the evolution of the simple zither led to the board zithers, harpsichord, dulcimer, and piano. See also **stringed instruments**. Compare **aerophone; idiophone; membranophone**.

chord symbol see **chord**.

choreographic poem (*or* **dance poem**) A tone poem using dance rhythms and reflecting the spirit of the dance it uses; an example is Saint-Saëns' *Danse macabre*.

choro 1. Originally, a Brazilian popular band comprising flutes, brass, guitars, and percussion. The term is now used for a similar ensemble in which one virtuoso instrumentalist is dominant. 2. A triple-time Brazilian dance used very occasionally in classical music, e.g. by Villa-Lobos.

chorus 1. A number of singers all singing the same music (see also **choir**), as opposed to soloists. The chorus forms an important part of the vocal music in opera and oratorio. 2. The refrain of a song, usually sung by a chorus, in which the verse is sung by a soloist.

Chorzempa, Daniel (1944–) US organist. Chorzempa first made his name as a pianist and harpsichordist, but later established a wide reputation as an organist, being particularly noted for his playing of Liszt.

Chou, Wen-Chung (1923–) Chinese composer, a pupil of Varèse and Martinu, who settled in the USA in 1946. His music combines eastern and western elements, strongly influenced by the Chinese Book of Changes (*I Ching*), Chinese calligraphy, and classical music. His works include *And the Fallen Petals* (1954) and *Yu Ko* (1964).

Chout (*Buffoon*; Russian: *Skazka pro shuta*) Ballet in six scenes with music by Prokofiev and choreography by Slavinsky and Larionev. First performance: Théâtre Gaité-Lyrique, Paris, 1921, commissioned by Diaghilev for the Ballets Russes. The plot, cruel and comic, is based on a popular legend of a buffoon who fools seven of his colleagues by pretending to kill his wife and then restore her to life by means of a magic whip.

Christmas Concerto 1. Concerto grosso in G minor (Op. 6 No. 8) by Corelli. Composed: 1712. A subtitle, *Fatto per la Notte di Natale*, indicates that the work was intended for performance on Christmas Night, hence the nickname. Rather unusually for this genre, the last movement is a pastorale. **2.** The title of concerti by several other composers, including Torelli.

Christmas Oratorio (German: *Weihnachtsoratorium*) Oratorio for solo voices, choir, and orchestra by Bach. Composed: 1734; first performance: St Thomas's Church, Leipzig, 1734. The oratorio comprises six individual cantatas, which were intended for performance on six successive Sundays during Christmas and Epiphany. Much of the music is borrowed from earlier cantatas and the oratorio relates the Christmas story. A precedent for this can be found in Schütz's *Historia der Geburth Jesu Christi* (1664).

Christmas Symphony see **Lamentation Symphony.**

Christoff, Boris (1919–) Bulgarian bass singer. He studied in Rome with Stracciari and in Salzburg with Muratti. International debuts in Mussorgsky's *Boris Godunov* followed, and a London performance in 1958 as Philip II in Verdi's *Don Carlos* was unforgettable. His extensive repertory (over 40 roles) includes much Verdi and recital works.

Christ on the Mount of Olives Oratorio (Op. 85) by Beethoven, an English version of which is known as *Engedi*. First performance: Vienna, 1803. The original libretto by Huber is based loosely upon the Gospel accounts of Jesus in the Garden of Gethsemane, but the English adaptation is centred around the Old Testament figure of David; English audiences found the portrayal of Christ too humanist in Beethoven's setting.

Christophe Colomb (*Christopher Colombus*) Opera in two parts (27 scenes) by Milhaud with text by Claudel. First performance (in German): Opera, Berlin, 1930. It is conceived on a vast scale and uses a cinema screen to show pictures of exotic landscapes while Colombus reads *Marco Polo's Travels.*

Christou, Yannis (1926–70) Greek composer, who studied philosophy at Cambridge. His early works were serial. He later founded an electronic studio in Athens and in his final years produced a series of mystical musical 'stage-rites' (*Anaparastasseis*), in which music and actions are all notated.

Christus 1. Oratorio by Liszt with a text compiled from the Bible and the Roman Catholic liturgy. First performance: 1873. **2.** Incomplete oratorio by Mendelssohn. Composed: 1847.

Chromatic Fantasy and Fugue Harpsichord work (BWV 903) by Bach. Completed: 1730. An early work, the fantasy contains much extreme chromaticism in the harmony and the fugue is based on a very chromatic subject.

chromaticism The use of notes in a composition that are not part of the diatonic *scale of the key in which it is written. The use of chromatic notes to add colour (from Greek *chroma*, colour) dates from the 16th century. It was however, not widely practised until Liszt and Wagner in the 19th century made extensive use of the device in order to modulate from one key to another. In some of the early music of Schoenberg so much use was made of chromaticism that it became meaningless to ascribe a key to a particular composition (see also **atonality**).

chromatic scale A form of *scale in which all the *intervals are a semitone. In the melodic notation it is written with sharps ascending (e.g. CC♯DD♯...) and with flats descending (e.g. CBB♭AA♭...). In the harmonic notation it is written with the sharps or flats of the prevailing major scale and the harmonic *minor scale.

Chung Family of Korean musicians. **Kyung-Wha Chung** (1948–), a violinist, studied at the Juilliard School, New York, making her New York debut in 1968 and her London debut in 1970. She frequently performs in a piano trio with her sister, the cellist **Myung-Wha Chung** (1944–), and brother, pianist **Myung-Whun Chung** (1953–), although each member of the family has established a reputation as a soloist.

church bells see **bells.**

church cantata see **cantata.**

church modes see **modes.**

church sonata see **sonata.**

ciaccona see **chaccone**. [Italian]

Ciccolini, Aldo (1925–) Italian-born French pianist. He was the youngest ever professor at the Naples conservatory and also holds a post at the Paris Conservatoire. Ciccolini is particularly noted for his performances of Fauré, Ravel, and Debussy.

Ciconia, Johannes (?–1412) Flemish composer, working at Padua (1401–12). His earlier career is uncertain and two identities for Ciconia have been suggested: (1) born c.1335, serving Eleanor of Comminges (by 1350) and Cardinal Albornoz (1358–67), residing in Liège in 1372; or (2) born c.1370, appearing as a chorister at St Jean L'Evangeliste in Liège in 1385. Ciconia's works, none of which can definitely be dated before about 1395, include mass movements, motets, canons, and secular pieces. He is also the author of two treatises, *Nova musica* and *De tribus generibus*.

Cilea, Francesco (1866–1950) Italian composer and teacher. He studied at the Naples conservatory (1881–89), where in 1894 he became a piano professor. He taught at the Reale Istituto Musicale, Florence (1896–1904), and was director of the Palermo conservatory (1913–16) and the Naples conservatory (1916–36). Cilea is best known for his opera *Adriana Lecouvreur* (1902); he also wrote several other operas, songs, and choral, orchestral, and chamber music.

Cimarosa, Domenico (1749–1801) Italian composer, taught by Piccinni at the Conservatorio de Santa Maria di Loreto, in Naples. His early years were spent in Rome and Naples, where he rivalled Paisiello as the most important operatic composer of the time. He travelled to St Petersburg (1787–90) and was invited by Leopold II to Vienna, where his most famous opera, The *Secret Marriage* (1792), was performed. Besides his many operas buffa, he wrote symphonies and keyboard works.

cimbalom A Hungarian type of *dulcimer in which the wire strings run across the instrument and in some cases are fitted with dampers. The instrument usually has 32 notes, which are divided into three or four sets by bridges. The lower notes have three strings tuned in unison; higher notes have four or five strings tuned in unison. The strings are struck by hand-held hammers. Some concert music (for example by Kodály) has been written for the cimbalom, which was originally a folk instrument much used by Hungarian Gypsies.

Cinderella 1. (Italian: *La Cenerentola*) Opera by Rossini with libretto by Ferretti based on the fairy tale of Perrault. First performance: Teatro Valle, Rome, 1817. **2.** (French: *Cendrillon*) Opera by Massenet with a libretto by Cain based on the same source. First performance: Opéra-Comique, Paris, 1899. **3.** (Italian: *Cenerentola*) Opera by Wolf-Ferrari with libretto by Pezzè-Pescolato. First performance: Teatro La Fenice, Venice, 1900. **4.** (Russian: *Solyushka*) Ballet in three acts with music by Prokofiev and libretto by Volkov. First performance: Moscow, 1945.

cinema organ (or **theatre organ**) An electrically operated pipe organ formerly played in cinemas during the intervals between films. Programmes usually consisted of a selection of popular music, including dance tunes, light opera, and some of the more familiar classics. Rising from the floor in a flood of coloured lights, the organist and his instrument became a symbol of the era in which the cinema was the entertainment centre of almost every town in the westernized world.

cipher An action fault in an organ causing one or more notes to sound continuously.

Cis C sharp. [German]

citole see **cittern**.

cittern (or **cythern** or **cither**) A plucked stringed instrument with a pear-shaped body and a flat back. Citterns usually had nine wire strings and a fretted fingerboard; the tuning varied. They probably originated in southern Europe in the 15th century from the fiddle. In the 16th to 18th centuries they were widely used by amateur musicians, who found them easier to play than the *lute. By the beginning of the 19th century they were being replaced by the guitar. An early version of the cittern was called the **citole**.

Clair de lune Piano piece by Debussy, the third movement of the *Suite bergamasque*. Composed: 1890–95. A very early work, the musical style as yet shows none of the features of impressionism that Debussy later used. Its great popularity has led to many arrangements being made, including some for orchestra.

Clari, or The Maid of Milan see **Home, Sweet Home**.

claribel (or **clarabella**) An organ *stop in which the sound is produced by 8-*foot wooden *flue pipes.

clarinet A *woodwind instrument with a single beating reed. Folk instruments of this type are of great antiquity in Asia, Africa, South America, and Europe. Some were made in pairs with a fingered melody pipe and an unfingered drone pipe. The modern orchestral clarinet evolved from the **chalumeau** at the end of the 16th century. The chalumeau was a one-piece wooden instrument with finger holes and one or two keys. The earliest clarinets, made in Germany by J. C. Denner, had a separate mouthpiece and bell and additional keys. The modern clarinet has a complicated system of keys developed by Boehm in the 1840s. The most widely used clarinet in the orchestra is the B♭ clarinet, a *transposing instrument with its lowest written note D below middle C. It sounds one tone lower and has a range of over three octaves. The clarinet in A is also a transposing instrument and sounds a semitone lower. Other clarinets in use are the **bass clarinets** in B♭ and A, an octave below the standard instruments. The **double-bass clarinet** plays very low notes but is rarely used except in military bands. It is also called a **contrabass clarinet** (or **pedal clarinet**, although it has no pedals). There is also a rarely used high clarinet in E♭, a fourth above the standard B♭ instrument, and a nontransposing instrument in C. The **alto clarinet**, like the bass clarinet, is shaped more like a *saxophone than a standard clarinet. Alto clarinets are made in E♭ and F, the latter being a modern version of the Bavarian **basset horn**, which was invented in 1770. The basset horn had either a sickle-shaped or angled pipe. It appears in scores by Mozart and Richard Strauss but the parts are now usually played by an alto clarinet.

The clarinet plays an important part in orchestral music and as a solo instrument (with concertos by Mozart, Aaron Copland, and others) as well as in much chamber music (for example the Brahms clarinet quintet). It is also used in military bands and very extensively in jazz and dance music.

Orchestral clarinets comprising (1) E♭, (2) B♭, (3) A, (4) alto, (5) bass and (6) contrabass, of which the B♭ and A are the most often used

clarino 1. The highest register of the trumpet, especially as used in florid passages of 17th- and 18th-century music. **2.** The trumpet itself. **3.** A clarinet. The normal Italian name is **clarinetto**, but clarino was sometimes used in 18th-century Italy.

clarionet An obsolete spelling of *clarinet.

Clarke, Jeremiah (c.1674–1707) English composer and organist. He was organist at Winchester College and vicar-choral at St Paul's Cathedral until 1704, when he became organist jointly with William Croft at the Chapel Royal. He shot himself after a disappointment in love. Clarke composed church music, odes, songs, incidental music for the theatre, a choral setting of Dryden's

Alexander's Feast, and harpsichord pieces. His best-known work, the so-called *Trumpet Voluntary*, was once ascribed to Henry Purcell; it appeared as *The Prince of Denmark's March* in a collection of harpsichord pieces of 1700 and in a suite of pieces for wind instruments.

clàrsach see **harp.**

classical music 1. Art music, as opposed to popular music, folk music, music for entertainment, or jazz. **2.** Any music in which the aesthetic attraction lies mainly in the clarity, balance, restraint, and objectivity of the formal structure rather than in the subjectivity, exaggerated emotionalism, or unrestrained nature of the musical language. In this sense classical implies the antithesis of *romantic music. Compare **neoclassicism. 3.** Music of the period c.1750–c.1830, in particular that of Haydn, Mozart, and Beethoven. The music of this era is also frequently referred to as that of the Viennese Classical School, reflecting the importance of Vienna as the musical capital of Europe at this time. The Viennese Classical School was responsible for the development of the symphony, string quartet, and concerto and saw the final triumph of instrumental music over vocal music. Among its most important lasting achievements was the introduction and establishment of *sonata form as one of the guiding principles of musical composition.

Classical Symphony Symphony No. 1 (Op. 25) by Prokofiev. Composed: 1916–17. One of the earliest and most famous examples of neoclassicism, this symphony is scored for an orchestra of a size that Mozart or Haydn would have used. Prokofiev attempts to combine a work of classical style and proportions with a more modern and dissonant 20th-century musical idiom.

Claudel, Paul (1868–1955) French writer. He collaborated with Milhaud, who wrote music for his translation of the first two parts of the *Oresteia* (1913–15) and *Christophe Colomb* (1927) among other plays. He also worked with Honegger on *Joan of Arc at the Stake* (1935) and wrote texts for several biblical cantatas.

clavecin Harpsichord. [French]

claveciniste Player of the clavecin (harpsichord); harpsichordist: often used to indicate a 17th- or 18th-century French composer for the harpsichord, such as Rameau or Couperin. [French]

clavicembalo (or **cembalo**) Harpsichord. [Italian]

clavichord An early form of keyboard instrument used domestically between the 15th and 18th centuries. It developed from the *monochord and was finally displaced as a popular home instrument during the 18th century. The clavichord action depended on a brass blade, called a **tangent**, attached to the end of each key. When the key was depressed the tangent struck the string (or pair of strings) to be sounded, both setting it into vibration and stopping it at the appropriate point in its length to produce the note of the required pitch. The longer section of the string vibrated to produce the note and the shorter section was damped by a felt pad. The tangent remained in contact with the string (or strings) for as long as the key was depressed, thus a variation of finger pressure changed the string tension, enabling a *vibrato effect to be achieved. In the fretted clavichord several tangents struck the same string (or pair of strings) at different points to make different notes. In the later unfretted instrument each tangent struck its own strings. The clavichord strings ran parallel to the keyboard and the instrument was usually in the form of a rectangular box that was played on a table. Some later models had their own legs.

The gentle and ethereal tone of the clavichord made it unsuitable for public performances except on a very small scale. The greater power of both the *harpsichord and the *piano led to its replacement by these instruments, but it has been revived from time to time in the 20th century.

clavicytherium An upright *harpsichord made in the 16th and 17th centuries. The strings were vertical and the instrument saved space, but its jacks did not fall back by gravity and required a special mechanical arrangement for pulling them back. The instrument was therefore never very successful.

clavier Keyboard. The word was borrowed by the Germans and came to be used to indicate any keyboard instrument. See also **Klavier**. [French]

Clavierübung (or **Klavierübung**) (*Clavier Exercise*) A collection of keyboard works in four parts by Bach. Composed: 1731–42. Part 1 (the six partitas, 1731), Part 2 (including the *Italian Concerto*, 1735), and Part 4 (the *Goldberg Variations*, 1742) were all written for harpsichord, whereas Part 3 (including duets, chorales, the *St Anne Fugue*, and the *Giant Fugue*) were written mainly for organ (with the exception of the duets). *Clavierübung* was the only keyboard music of Bach published during his lifetime.

Clay, Frederic (1838–89) British composer. He studied with Molique and in Leipzig with Hauptmann. He composed many successful light operas, incidental music, and two cantatas, but is now best remembered for his tuneful songs, particularly 'I'll sing thee songs of Araby' (from his cantata *Lalla Rookh*) and the ballad *The Sands of Dee*.

clef A sign used to relate notes written on a *staff to the pitch of actual notes. The **treble clef** fixes the G above *middle C on the second line up of the staff. The **bass clef** fixes the F below middle C on the second line down. The **alto clef** fixes middle C on the middle line of the staff and the

A 16th-century Italian clavichord

tenor clef fixes it on the second line down of the staff. The **soprano clef** (now obsolete) fixes middle C on the bottom line of the staff. The clef appears on each new line of music before the key signature and the time signature. It also appears if there is a change in the middle of a line. See **Appendix, Table 2.**

Clemens non Papa (Jacob Clement; *c*.1510–1557/58) Flemish composer. His early years were probably spent in Paris. His nickname probably arose from the necessity of distinguishing him from the poet Jacobus Papa, who, like Clemens, was active in Ypres. Clemens produced over 230 motets, 15 masses, 15 magnificats, 90 chansons, and 159 *souterliedekens* (psalms translated into Dutch verse). Some of his motets are characterized by chromaticism.

Clement, Jacob see **Clemens non Papa.**

Clementi, Aldo (1925–) Italian composer, a pupil of Petrassi. He moved from a neoclassical style to a Webernian miniaturism, demonstrated in *Three Studi* (1957). His later works, such as the chamber-music series *Informels* (1960), incorporate indeterminate elements.

Clementi, Muzio (1752–1832) British composer, keyboard player, teacher, music publisher, and piano manufacturer, born in Italy. As a church organist in Rome, in 1766 he was heard by Peter Beckford, who took him to England for further study. In 1774 he became conductor at the King's Theatre, London. He toured Europe (1780–85) as a virtuoso pianist and back in London made a reputation as an eminent teacher; his pupils included J. B. Cramer and John Field. During the 1790s he ran his music-publishing firm and a flourishing piano-manufacturing business. He made another European tour (1802–10), chiefly for business purposes, and spent most of his remaining years in London. He retired to Evesham, where he died.

Clementi had far-reaching influence as a pianist, piano teacher, and composer. His didactic works, especially the *Introduction to the Art of Playing on the Piano-Forte* (1801) and **Gradus ad Parnassum* (1817), have remained in use. His large output of piano music, which influenced Beethoven, ranges from simple galant pieces to sonatas (he wrote over 100); the sonatinas are among his best-known pieces. Clementi also wrote chamber music and several symphonies.

Clemenza di Tito, La (*The Clemency of Titus*) Opera seria in two acts by Mozart with libretto by Mazzolà adapted from Metastasio. First performance: National Theatre, Prague, 1791 (for the coronation of the Austrian Emperor as King of Bohemia). It extols the clemency of the Roman emperor Titus (tenor) in the face of the intrigues of Vitellia (soprano). Gluck and Hasse both wrote earlier operas with the same name.

Clérambault, Louis-Nicholas (1676–1749) French composer and organist, a pupil of André Raison, whom he succeeded as organist of the Abbaye des Jacobins de la rue Saint-Jacques (1720). He was subsequently organist at various other Paris churches. His finest works were his chamber cantatas, but he also wrote divertissements, including *L'Idylle de Saint-Cyr* (1745), and other sacred and keyboard music.

Cliburn, Van (1934–) US pianist. After gaining many prizes in the USA he won the Tchaikovsky Competition in Moscow in 1958, which established his international reputation.

Cloak, The see Tabarro, Il.

Clock Symphony (German: *Die Uhr*) Symphony No. 101 in D by Haydn. Composed: 1794. One of the **Salomon Symphonies*, the nickname is derived from the accompaniment figure in the slow movement, which sounds like a ticking clock. Further relevance for the title can be found in the minuet, which was originally composed for mechanical clock.

close A **cadence, especially one having some formal importance. A **full close** is a perfect cadence; a **half close** is an imperfect cadence.

close harmony Harmony in which the notes of the chord are close together. In popular close-harmony singing each voice sings the melody, or as near to the melody as possible, keeping a small interval apart. Compare **open harmony.**

Clutsam, George Howard (1866–1957) Australian pianist and composer; music critic of *The Observer* (1908–18). After completing his operas *König Harlekin* and *After a Thousand Years* (both 1912) he composed several musicals, achieving great success with *Lilac Time* (1923), his adaptation of Heinrich Berté's Schubert operetta *Das Dreimäderlhaus*. *The Damask Rose* (1929) is a similar treatment of Chopin.

Coates, Albert (1882–1953) British composer and conductor. He studied at the Leipzig conservatory under Nikisch before starting a career in 1906 as an international conductor in Europe and the USA, specializing in Wagner and Scriabin. He settled in Johannesburg in 1946. His works, chiefly orchestral music and operas, include the symphonic poem *The Eagle* (1925) and the operas *Samuel Pepys* (1929) and *Tafelberg de Kleed* (1952).

Coates, Eric (1886–1957) British violist and composer of light music. After studying at the Royal Academy of Music under Tertis and Corder, he played in various orchestras and the Hamburg Quartet before becoming a full-time composer in 1918. Coates specialized in orchestral suites, such as the *London Suite* (1933), which contains the

Knightsbridge March; his best-known piece is perhaps the march from the film *The Dam Busters* (1955).

Cobbett, Walter (1847–1937) British amateur violinist and editor of *Cobbett's Cyclopaedic Survey of Chamber Music* (1929).

cobza see **lute**.

Cockaigne Concert overture (Op. 40) by Elgar, subtitled *In London Town*. First performance: 1901. In this overture Elgar attempts to capture in music the atmosphere and spirit of Edwardian London, which he describes in all its aspects.

Cocteau, Jean (1889–1963) French poet, dramatist, novelist, and film director. He wrote the text for an early version of *Parade* with music by Satie. He was intimately associated with the musical group Les *Six, whose works he championed and who in turn wrote music for his films and libretti.

coda The final part of a movement that is intended to round off the piece. In a sonata-form movement, for example, it follows the recapitulation and gives a sense of conclusion. Although it is the Italian word for tail, it is regarded as a part of the musical structure rather than an appendage. see also **codetta**.

codetta A small *coda used to conclude a passage or theme in a composition, rather than a whole movement or piece.

Coffee Cantata Secular cantata for solo voices, choir, and orchestra by Bach. Composed: *c.*1732. Sometimes also known by the opening words, 'Schweiget stille, plaudert nicht' ('Be silent, do not chatter'), this cantata is a satire upon the contemporary popularity of coffee. The story concerns a girl who will not give up coffee until her father provides her with a husband and even when this is accomplished she is unable to do so. The *Coffee Cantata* is one of Bach's few comic works.

Cohen, Harriet (1895–1967) British pianist, a pupil of Matthay at the Royal Academy of Music. Her reputation was based mainly upon her playing of Bach's works and English music: both Vaughan Williams and Bax dedicated works to her. In 1960 she retired from playing due to a hand injury.

col (*or* **colla**, **coll'**, **cogli**, **colle**) With the, for example **col arco**, with the bow. The form depends on the number and gender of the word following. See also **col legno**. [Italian]

Cole, Bruce (1947–) British composer, who studied at the Royal Academy of Music (1968–72) under Birtwistle. His works include the music-theatre pieces *Harlequinade* and *Pantomimes* (both 1972) and the orchestral works *Caesura* (1969) and *Fenestrae sanctae* (1973).

Cole, Hugo (1917–) British composer, critic, and writer. His works include the opera *Persephone* (1958), a serenade

for nine wind instruments, and educational and chamber music. His most recent book is *The Changing Face of Music* (1978).

Coleridge-Taylor, Samuel (1875–1912) British composer, whose father was a doctor from Sierra Leone. He entered the Royal College of Music in 1890 and was a pupil of Stanford. His best-known work is the oratorio trilogy *Hiawatha, consisting of *Hiawatha's Wedding Feast* (1898), *The Death of Minnehaha* (1899), and *Hiawatha's Departure* (1900). His remaining 10 oratorios were less successful; his compositions also include a violin concerto (1911) and the orchestral *African Suite* (1898).

Colette (Sidonie-Gabrielle C.; 1873–1954) French novelist. Her many novels were highly regarded and she was much honoured in later life. She wrote the libretto for Ravel's *L'Enfant et les sortilèges* (1925).

Colgrass, Michael (1932–) US composer and percussionist, a pupil of Foss, Milhaud, Riegger, and Weber. His music is in an eclectic style with the frequent use of literary and dramatic elements. His works include *Three Brothers* (1950), *Virgil's Dream* (1967), *The Earth's a Baked Apple* (1968), and *Concert Masters* (1977).

col legno An instruction to players of bowed instruments to strike the strings with the stick of the bow rather than the hair. [Italian, with the wood]

colophony see **rosin**.

coloratura A florid style of singing, particularly in the upper register of the *soprano voice. Coloratura is usually applied to operatic music, especially Italian opera of the mid- and late 17th century, when it was fashionable for singers to ornament the vocal line in order to display their technical prowess. [Italian, coloured]

colour see **tone colour**.

colour music Music visualized in the form of colours, based on whatever relationship exists, or is thought to exist, between sound and colour. Both are vibrations, but beyond that any relationship is difficult to establish. Sound consists of pressure vibrations in the air; light consists of electromagnetic vibrations in space. Sound has a subjective effect on the human mind that enables it to be classified in terms of notes forming part of a scale and the associated concept of key. Light also has a subjective effect on the human mind that enables a spectrum of colours to be defined in terms of precise (or fairly precise) wavelengths. But the relationship between the scale and spectrum is extremely tenuous. Despite this, resourceful inventors have tried to translate one into the other. The **colour organ** (1895) created by A. Wallace Rimington (1854–1918) was probably the first such attempt. It made no sound, but a musical score was 'played' on a conventional keyboard that produced a colour display on a screen. The basis of the analogy was that the 12-semitone sound scale was matched with a 12-colour spectrum, differences in octave being indicated by changes in luminosity. The **clavilux** (1922) was a later invention of Thomas Wilfred (1888–1968). He abandoned the misleading analogy between pitch and colour and developed a scheme in which colour music consisted of shifting combinations of shapes and colours with a rhythmic element of their own. Neither of these experiments was successful, however, although Scriabin and Schoenberg did make attempts to use them in compositions. Perhaps the only successful attempt to establish an effective interpretation between the two stimuli was Walt Disney's *Fantasia* (1940), in which the Bach toccata and fugue in D minor was interpreted in sound in the conventional manner and simultaneously in pure colour patterns on the screen.

Apart from these formal attempts to establish a relationship between music and light some composers have imagined that certain keys are associated with certain colours. Rimsky-Korsakov, for .instance, saw C major as white, D major as yellow, and so on. Others have used colour symbolically, as did Bliss in his *Colour Symphony* (1922). It does seem, however, that the two arts are separate and any attempt to establish a relationship between them is both unnecessary and inappropriate.

Colour Symphony Symphony by Bliss. Composed: 1922. The symphony is in the normal four-movement form, but each movement is subtitled with the name of a colour: Purple, Red, Blue, and Green respectively. The character of each colour is portrayed within its movement, each colour being described in accordance with its heraldic significance.

combination tones (*or* **resultant tones**) The secondary tones produced when two loud notes are sounded simultaneously. There are two kinds of combination tones: a **differential** (*or* **difference**) **tone** of lower pitch than the original notes, with a frequency equal to the difference between their frequencies; and a **summation tone** of higher pitch with a frequency equal to the sum of the frequencies of the two original notes. Tartini, who discovered combination tones, called them **third sounds** (*terzo suono*). Combination tones are usually faint and sometimes inaudible. However, the **acoustic bass** organ stop is produced by the differential tone when the 16-*foot C pedal is depressed bringing in the fifth above it. The result is equivalent to a 32-foot C.

come As; like. [Italian]

Comedy on the Bridge (Czech: *Komedie na moste*) Comic opera by Martinu, who also wrote the text (after Klicpera). First produced on Prague radio in 1937 and afterwards staged, it ridicules frontier restrictions.

comma of Pythagoras see **temperament**.

common chord see **chord**.

common metre The poetic form of a hymn tune, having a four-line stanza comprising alternate lines of eight and six syllables, indicated in most hymn books simply as 8 6. 8 6. It is also known as **ballad metre**, being derived from the usual form of the popular ballad.

common time see **time signature**.

community singing Massed corporate singing, with the aim of expressing in song the emotions of a gathering of people. It is sometimes started spontaneously and therefore has no pretentions to the attainment of musical perfection. Through the medium of television and radio, with the introduction of such series as 'Songs of Praise' and 'Sunday Half-Hour,' this originally informal type of singing has become more sophisticated.

comodo (*or* **commodo**) Comfortable; easy; convenient. Used to indicate moderation, hence **tempo comodo**, at a moderate speed. [Italian]

compass The range of notes that can be produced by any instrument or voice. With instruments of determinate intonation, e.g. the piano, organ, or harp, there are clearly defined limits. With brass, wind, and stringed instruments, although the lowest note is fixed, the upper limit is dependent upon the skill of the performer. For voices the workable compass is approximately two octaves, although this may alter either way under certain circumstances and conditions. The compass of the voice is capable of limited extension in either direction with skilful training.

Compère, Loyset (*c.*1450–1518) Flemish composer, first recorded as working in Milan (1474). He was a member of the chapel of Charles VIII of France in 1486 and ended his career as a canon of Sainte-Quentin. One of his earliest surviving compositions, *Omnium bonorum plena* (*c.*1470), begins as a Latin translation of *De tous biens plaine* and mentions Dufay, Ockeghem, Josquin, Busnois, Regis, and Caron. He also wrote masses, motets, and secular songs in French and Italian.

composition 1. The act of putting together notes to create an original work of music. Although most composers would claim that an initial inspiration is essential before such an act can take place, the process also requires a previous knowledge and study of compositional techniques, which are then applied to the creative process. These include *harmony, *counterpoint, and *instrumentation as well as free composition itself. **2.** A composed piece of music.

composition pedal (*or* **composition piston** *or* **combination pedal**) An *organ pedal that brings into action a predetermined set of *stops. This obviates the need to operate each stop by hand. In some organs the same effect is achieved by operating a small disc situated below a manual and called a **thumb piston**.

compound interval An interval of more than an *octave. Compare **simple interval**.

compound time Any form of musical time in which the beat note is a dotted note (rather than a plain note), i.e. the value of the beat note is divisible by three (e.g. 6/8 or 9/8). Compare **simple time**. See **Appendix, Table 4**.

comprimario A singer having a subordinate or supporting male role in Italian opera. The feminine form, **comprimaria**, is seldom used, the preferred word being servetta (see **soubrette**). [from Italian *con*, with, *primo*, first]

Comte Ory, Le (*Count Ory*) Comic opera in two acts by Rossini with libretto by Scribe and Delestre-Poirson. First performance: Académie Royale, Paris, 1828. Set in the time of the Crusades, it is the story of the dissolute young Comte Ory (tenor) in pursuit of the Comtesse Adèle (soprano).

Comus 1. Masque with music by Henry Lawes to words by Milton. First performance: 1634. **2.** Masque by Thomas Arne to the same text by Milton. Composed: 1738. **3.** Ballet by Lambert using arrangements of music by Purcell. First performance: 1942.

con With. [Italian]

concert A public musical performance by a substantial number of musicians, excluding stage performances or religious services. Performances by soloists or small ensembles are usually called *recitals. During the Commonwealth (1649–60) there was no court patronage, therefore the organization of musical performances – in houses, colleges, and taverns – became the responsibility of the middle classes. The first public concerts in England were arranged by Ben Wallington (1664) and John Banister (1672). Such enterprises began to flourish and concert rooms were built. In Paris André Danican Philidor established a concert organization (1725) that became the influential Concert Spirituel, and Telemann made Frankfurt an important centre for concerts (1723). The Bach–Abel concerts, established by J. C. Bach and C. F. Abel in 1764 and held in the Hanover Square Rooms from 1775, enabled London audiences to hear works by foreign composers, notably Haydn. Concerts flourished throughout the 19th century, encouraged by the formation of philharmonic societies in many European and North American cities, and took many forms (e.g. open-air concerts, *promenade concerts). The 20th-century concert is usually a performance by an orchestra.

concertante 1. (adj.) Having the form of a *concerto, i.e. using contrasting instruments or groups of instruments. see also **sinfonia concertante**. French: **concertant** (*or fem.*

concertante). **2.** (n.) A concerto-like piece: a term used loosely by some non-Italian composers. [Italian]

concertato 1. (adj.) Indicating the style used in earlier pieces of the *concerto type. **2.** (n.) The smaller group of instruments or the solo instrument in such pieces. [Italian, concerted]

concert band (*or* **symphonic band**) A US band of woodwind, brass, and percussion, similar to the British *military band.

concerted Describing or relating to music in which a number of instruments or voices are performing together.

Concertgebouw A concert hall in Amsterdam. In 1882 the Concertgebouw Society decided to build a hall, which was inaugurated in 1888 with a concert by a large orchestra conducted by Willem Kes. The orchestra became known as the **Concertgebouw Orchestra**. Under Willem Mengelberg (its conductor from 1895 to 1941) it developed into an internationally known orchestra and attracted such guest conductors as Strauss, Ravel, Beecham, and Stravinsky. Since World War II it has been independent of the concert hall. Its resident conductors have included Edward van Beinum, Eugen Jochum, and Bernard Haitink (from 1961). [Dutch, concert building]

concert grand see **piano**.

concertina A type of *accordion with hexagonal or octagonal ends and a relatively small number of notes. The concertina never has a piano-type keyboard, notes being selected by depressing buttons. Patented in 1829, a few years before the accordion, it has largely been replaced by the accordion, although it is still used as an inexpensive instrument for informal music making.

concertino 1. The small group of skilled solo instrumentalists contrasting with the larger ripieno (or concerto grosso) in the baroque *concerto. The concertino included the harpsichordist, who very often acted as musical director or conductor. **2.** A short concerto.

concertize To perform in a concert, especially as a soloist.

concertmaster see **leader**.

concerto A composition for one or more solo performers and a larger group of players, usually in three movements. The word was originally used to describe any composition for more than one performer in harmonious combination (the term derives from Italian: harmony; concert). In the late 16th and early 17th centuries it was also applied to choral works; for example Monteverdi's *Marian Vespers* (1610) was labelled 'da concerto.' As the 17th century progressed the term increasingly signified a kind of instrumental (particularly violin) composition often associated with Bologna. The underlying idea of contrast in the concerto arose here, owing to the widely spaced positioning of players and their differing playing abilities. This gave rise to the **concerto grosso**, in which a small group of highly skilled players called the **concertino** was matched against a larger less virtuosic ensemble, the **ripieno** (which was sometimes itself called the concerto grosso). This was also a feature of contemporary dramatic choral music, such as the oratorios of Stradella, a composer who worked in Rome and influenced Corelli and Muffat. The early baroque instrumental concerto simply enlarged the trio sonata texture and followed *ritornello form, alternating the ripieno tutti with the concertino. With Torelli the fast–slow–fast sequence of movements was firmly established. In addition, various instruments other than strings were now employed, especially for the increasingly virtuoso solo and concertino parts. Torelli notably exploited the trumpet and oboe. The most outstanding exponent of the baroque concerto was Vivaldi, who wrote more than 450 works. A fine example of the concerto grosso is his set entitled *L'Estro armonico* (1712). Vivaldi also developed the newer virtuoso solo concerto, in which – in effect – one instrument constitutes the concertino. Like Albinoni, Vivaldi favoured the polythematic ritornello. J. S. Bach brought together the diverse styles and elements of the baroque concerto, notably (for example) in the fifth *Brandenburg Concerto*.

After the baroque period, and until the 20th century, the concerto grosso form lost favour. The virtuoso solo concerto became dominant in the classical and romantic periods. In the classical concerto the newly invented piano played an important part, notably in works by Mozart. Beethoven wrote six piano concertos, of which five are complete. In the classical concerto the distinction between solo and tutti passages is clear cut and the principle of *sonata form is all-pervading. Unlike the *symphony, the concerto kept the baroque three-movement shape. In the romantic period, in addition to the piano, the solo violin concerto was developed supremely, especially by Beethoven, Mendelssohn, Brahms, Tchaikovsky, Bruch, Sibelius, and many others, corresponding with a huge advance in technique (particularly by Joachim and Paganini). The extended *cadenza became a special feature of the form, having been introduced in the classical concerto. The romantic concerto tended to blur the contrast between solo and orchestra as well as extending form and length.

20th-century concertos range from the neoclassical works of Stravinsky and Hindemith to the late romantic and postromantic concertos of Rachmaninov, Elgar, Bartók, Prokofiev, Britten, Schoenberg, Henze, etc. The solo concerto is highly cultivated today as technical dexterity appears to advance.

concerto grosso 1. An early type of *concerto in which a group of solo instruments, called the concertino, is matched against the rest of the orchestra, called the *ripieno. **2.** The ripieno itself.

concert overture An instrumental piece used to open a concert programme. The idea comes from opera and oratorio, and many opera overtures are singled out as concert starters. The concert overture proper is a single-movement independent work, e.g. Mendelssohn's *Roy Blas* and *Hebrides* overtures.

concert pitch see pitch.

concord A chord of two or more notes that appears to the ear to be complete in itself and not to require *resolution by another chord. Octaves provide the simplest and most perfect concords. Fifths and thirds are also concordant. Compare **discord**.

Concord Sonata Piano sonata No. 2 by Ives. Composed: 1909–15; first performance: 1938. As its name indicates, this work attempts to evoke the atmosphere of Concord, Massachusetts, between 1840 and 1860. Each movement is known by the name of a prominent local resident of the time – 'Emerson,' 'Hawthorne,' 'The Alcotts,' and 'Thoreau.' Six essays introduce the sonata, which includes many innovatory techniques of both composition and performance; for this reason it has at last been acclaimed as one of the most pioneering works in 20th-century music.

concrete music see musique concrète.

conducting The art of directing an ensemble, orchestra, choir, ballet, or opera during rehearsal and performance. When conducting an instrumental work, apart from merely beating time to ensure that all the players start together and stay together, the conductor has an interpretive role in which he is responsible for the tempo at which a piece is played, for signalling changes of tempi, for maintaining a balance in the volume of sound produced by the various instrumental groups, for ensuring that the entry of soloists or groups of instruments occurs at exactly the right moment, and for nuances of accent and phrasing. In short, the conductor controls the sound made by an ensemble just as the instrumentalist controls the sound made by his instrument. The methods used by conductors to achieve their interpretation vary from the flamboyant, gymnastic, and exuberant use of gesture and grimace to the reserved and austere nod.

The role of the conductor as the maestro emerged only relatively recently. Playing an instrument in any kind of ensemble requires not only mastery of the instrument itself but also attention to the other musicians in the group. The leader of the group originally performed the functions of conductor as the first amongst equals – a role that usually fell to the first violinist or a keyboard player. As ensembles became larger the problems of coordination increased to such an extent that the functions of conducting precluded the functions of playing. The precursors of the modern *baton with which many player-conductors beat time was a roll of music or a heavy stick banged on the floor. Only in the 19th century did the composer-conductor, armed with nothing more sonorous than a baton, emerge. This tradition has continued with the professional conductor −a talented musician with an authoritative personality −taking total charge of the musical proceedings at public concerts.

conductus A medieval hymnlike piece originally intended to accompany a church procession. The term itself was first used in the 12th century in the *Play of Daniel* for entry music. The conductus, which was strophic, was the least restricted part of the liturgy since it was not governed by a predetermined text and a fixed chant. Its music was often fairly elaborate, especially in the use of long melismas. It was also used to introduce the 'Benedicamus Domino' at the end of Lauds and Vespers. Both monophonic and polyphonic conductus are found during the 12th and 13th centuries. The form was also incorporated into the secular song repertory of the troubadours, in which the music closely followed the poetic rhythm and form. It did not, however, lose its religious connections and was never used, for instance, as a love song.

conjunct motion see **motion**.

Connolly, Justin (1933–) British composer, a pupil of Fricker. His works for instruments (e.g. *Viola Concerto*, 1975, and *Diaphony*, 1978) and voices (e.g. *Prose*, 1967, and *Verse*, 1969) explore the use of contrasts. Some pieces, such as *Triad IV* (1968), combine live and electronic elements.

Conon de Bethun (*c*.1160–*c*.1220) One of the most important early trouvères. He was active in the Third Crusade, which provided inspiration for his song 'Ahi! amours.'

Consecration of the House, The Overture (Op. 124) by Beethoven, from his incidental music to the play of the same name by Meisl. Composed: 1822. The first performance took place at the opening of the Josefstadt Theater in Vienna in 1824.

consecutive intervals A progression of identical intervals in a composition. For example, the chord CF followed by DG produces consecutive *fourths. Consecutive octaves are widely used in instrumental music but are not regarded as acceptable in academic part-writing for voices. See also **fifth**.

conservatory An institution for training musicians. Its origins lie in the conservatorio of 16th- and 17th-century Italy; these were charitable organizations for orphans at which music was part of the curriculum. By the early 18th century they were highly influential, training singers and instrumentalists. Institutions modelled on them began to appear throughout Europe and the USA during the 19th

century. The Paris Conservatoire (1795) is one of the most celebrated. **Conservatoire** is the French form and is sometimes used in English; **conservatorium** is used in German-speaking countries and Australia.

console The desk of an *organ, which contains the stops, manuals, pedals, thumb pistons, and composition pedals under the control of the organist.

consonance The sounding together of two or more notes to produce a *concord. Compare **dissonance**. See also **beats**.

consort A small instrumental ensemble for performing late-16th- and 17th-century music. A mixed ensemble, e.g. of stringed and woodwind instruments, is now often referred to as a **broken consort**. A consort may also be an ensemble of voices, with or without accompaniment.

Constant, Marius (1926–) Romanian-born composer and conductor who has lived in France since the end of World War II. A pupil of Messiaen, Nadia Boulanger, and Honegger, he experimented early in his career with musique concrète; later he adopted serial and aleatoric procedures. His works include the ballet *Paradise Lost* (1967), the 'mimodrama' *Candide* (1970), *Fourteen Stations* (1970), and *Piano Personnage* (1974).

Consul, The Opera in three acts by Menotti, who also wrote the text. First performance: Philadelphia, 1950. Set in a modern totalitarian state, it is the story of an attempted escape frustrated by bureaucracy. The consul himself never appears.

Contes d'Hoffmann, Les see **Tales of Hoffmann**.

continental fingering see **fingering**.

continuo (*or* **thorough bass**) **1.** The bass line and the harmonic accompaniment derived from it found in much music of the 17th and 18th centuries. A keyboard player, supported by a cello, viola da gamba, etc., improvised harmonies from the notes of the bass line, sometimes aided by numbers placed under the notes to indicate chords (*see* figured bass). **2.** The instrument(s) playing the continuo. [from Italian *basso continuo*, continuous bass]

contrabbasso Double bass. [Italian; often incorrectly spelt *contrabasso* in non-Italian contexts]

contralto The lowest of the three varieties of female voice, the other two being *mezzo-soprano and *soprano. For a soloist, the compass ranges approximately from E below middle C to D an octave and a sixth above; in choral writing, the range is smaller for both the contralto and the *alto (the male equivalent). The rich quality of the timbre in the lower register gives the contralto voice its special character. [from Italian *contra*, lower in pitch, alto]

contrary motion see **motion**.

Contrasts Trio for violin, clarinet, and piano by Bartók. Composed: 1938. In this trio Bartók combines elements of the Hungarian verbunkos and oriental rhythms and melodies. It is his only chamber work to include a wind instrument and the violinist is required to use two instruments: one is tuned normally (G–D–A–E), whereas the second is tuned G♯–D–A–E♭.

contredanse The French equivalent of the English *country dance, especially popular during the 18th century. The French imported English tunes but used their own more formal dances (such as the gavotte). Like the Spanish and Italian contradanza and the German contratanz, the name is a false derivation from 'country dance,' the 'contre' possibly suggested by the face-to-face movement of partners in the English dances.

controfagotto Double bassoon (see **bassoon**). [Italian; sometimes incorrectly spelt *contrafagotto* in non-Italian contexts]

Converse, Frederik Shepherd (1871–1940) US composer, a pupil of Rheinberger. His works, in the traditional conservative New England manner, include operas, such as *The Pipe of Desire* (1906); chamber music; six symphonies; and orchestral pieces, including *Flivver 10,000,000* (1927), celebrating the Ford motor company, and *American Sketches* (1935).

Conversi, Girolamo (c.1540–c.1585) Italian composer. Nothing is known about his life except that he was born in Correggio, in northern Italy. His *Canzoni alla napolitana* (1572 and 1573) are important for introducing counterpoint and word painting into the popular form of the canzonetta, thus preparing the way for the lighter madrigal of the 1580s. Conversi also wrote a book of madrigals for six voices (1571) and one for five (now lost).

Cooke, Arnold (1906–) British composer. Cooke studied in Berlin with Hindemith. His music shows the influence of his teacher in its clarity and balance within traditional concepts of tonality and rhythm. Cooke's works include the opera *Mary Barton* (1949–54), a symphony (1948) and other orchestral works, and chamber music.

Cooke, Benjamin (1734–93) English composer and organist, a pupil of Pepusch. He was conductor of the Academy of Ancient Music (1752–89), master of the choristers at Westminster Abbey (1757), and organist there (1762) and at St Martin's-in-the-Fields (1782). He wrote many works for the Academy of Ancient Music, anthems, glees and catches, and odes.

Cooke, Deryck (1919–76) British musicologist. He studied under Hadley and Orr at Cambridge (1938–40, 1946–47) and afterwards worked for the BBC. In 1960 Cooke wrote a performing version of Mahler's tenth symphony reconstructed from the composer's sketches.

Cooke, Henry (c.1615–72) English composer, singer, and choirmaster. At the Restoration (1660) he was appointed master of the boy choristers at the Chapel Royal, whom he trained to a very high standard. He introduced instruments to accompany anthems and in 1656 collaborated on the music for Davenant's *Siege of Rhodes* and *The First Day's Entertainment at Rutland House*. He also wrote songs and anthems.

Cooper, John see Coperario, Giovanni.

Cooper, Joseph (1912–) British pianist, lecturer, and broadcaster. He has made several recordings but is perhaps best known as a contributor to the BBC's 'Record Review' and as chairman of the television programme 'Face The Music.'

Coperario (*or* **Coprario**), **Giovanni** (John Cooper; c.1570–1626) English composer. According to some authorities, he adopted the Italian version of his name during a visit to Italy before about 1605. Coperario taught

Aaron Copland

music to Charles I (when the latter was Prince of Wales) and to the Lawes brothers. He was a prolific composer for viols, writing over 90 fantasies in addition to masques, anthems, suites, and songs (including the collections *Funeral Teares* and *Songs of Mourning*).

coperto Covered. Sometimes used to indicate the muting or muffling of a drum. [Italian]

Copland, Aaron (1900–) US composer, a pupil of Nadia Boulanger. His works of the late 1920s combine jazz and neoclassical styles. These gave way to atonal serial composition, followed some years later by a simpler tonal idiom using American folk melodies. To this period (1936–50) belong Copland's best-known works. Subsequently he returned to using serial techniques. His output includes the ballets *Billy the Kid* (1938), *Rodeo* (1942), and *Appalachian Spring* (1944); El *Salón México* (1936) for orchestra; *Lincoln Portrait* (1942) for narrator and orchestra; three symphonies; the suite *Quiet City* (1941); concertos for piano and clarinet; and chamber and piano music.

Coppélia Ballet in two acts with music by Delibes and scenario by Nuitter and Saint-Léon based on Hoffmann's story *Der Sandmann* (*The Sandman*). First performance: Opéra, Paris, 1870. It is subtitled *The Girl with Enamel Eyes*. Coppélia is a life-sized doll owned by Dr Coppelius, a toy-maker; Franz, betrothed to Swanhilda, falls in love with the doll, which Swanhilda impersonates to win him back.

Coprario, Giovanni see **Coperario, Giovanni**.

Coq d'or, Le see **Golden Cockerel, The**.

cor Horn. [French]

cor anglais see **oboe**.

corda (*pl.* **corde**) String. See also **tre corde**; **una corda**. [Italian]

Corelli, Arcangelo (1653–1713) Italian violinist and composer, teacher of Geminiani, Locatelli, and others. He worked in Bologna (1666–70) and after 1675 was leader and conductor in Rome, where he directed the festivities of the Accademia del Disegno and played for Handel in *Il Trionfo del tempo* (1708). His distinctive writing for violin, including trio sonatas and concerti grossi (such as the *Christmas Concerto*, 1712), were widely imitated throughout Europe.

Corelli, Franco (1921–) Italian tenor. He studied at Pesaro Liceo, making his debut in 1951 at Spoleto in *Carmen*. Subsequently he sang at Covent Garden (1957), Berlin State Opera (1961), Vienna State Opera (1963), and the Metropolitan Opera (1961), excelling in verismo roles.

Coriolanus Overture (Op. 62) by Beethoven to a play of the same name by H. von Collin. First performance: 1822. Apart from sharing the same title, this play has no other connection with the drama of Shakespeare.

Cornelius, (Carl August) Peter (1824–74) German composer. After studying in Berlin he went in 1852 to Weimar and joined Liszt's circle, becoming closely identified with the New German School. It was in Weimar that he wrote his popular comic opera *Der *Barbier von Bagdad* (1855–58). Cornelius lived in Mainz from 1859 to 1865, the year he met Wagner, with whom he became closely associated. He went with Wagner to Munich, where he taught at the Royal School of Music. Cornelius composed two other operas (*Der Cid*, 1860–62, and *Gunlöd*, 1866–74), many fine songs, duets, and choruses, and a few instrumental works. He was a gifted poet, wrote many essays (several defending Liszt and Wagner), and translated the texts of vocal works. 'Die Könige' from his *Weihnachtslieder* (1856) has become well known in English as the Christmas hymn 'Three kings from Persian lands afar.'

cornemuse A French mouth-blown bagpipe with a chanter and one drone.

cornet A brass three-valved *horn that resembles a *trumpet in appearance. It was developed in France in the 1820s by the addition of valves to the *post horn (cornet de poste), becoming known as the **cornet-à-pistons**. In England it was soon called simply a cornet. Being the first brass instrument to be fitted with valves and to be capable of playing a full range of notes, it was widely used in military bands, brass bands, and the orchestra during the 19th century. However, since the advent of the valved trumpet in the mid-19th century it has ceased to be used in the orchestra. It does, however, retain its popularity in brass and military bands. It is a *transposing instrument in B♭ (or A) with a range of two and a half octaves from E (or E♭) in the middle of the bass staff.

cornett A long thin slightly tapered wind instrument made of wood or ivory, but having a cup-shaped mouthpiece similar to that of a trumpet. It has finger holes of the woodwind type. It was used in 16th- and 17th-century orchestras. The curved cornett, with a gentle S-shape, led to the development of the **serpent**, a much longer (up to 2.1m, or 7 ft) sharply curved bass instrument with the appearance of a snake. Originating in the 16th century, it was used by military bands and in churches in the 19th century.

corno Horn. Hence **corno inglese**, cor anglais (see **oboe**). [Italian]

corno di bassetto Basset horn (see **clarinet**). [Italian]

Cornyshe, William (?–1523) English composer, poet, and playwright. A gentleman of the Chapel Royal (?1496–1523), he became Master of the Children there from 1509 until shortly before his death. Cornyshe's compositions include votive antiphons, a setting of the Magnificat, and secular songs in English. Eight of Cornyshe's works were included in the original plan of the *Eton Choirbook*, of which only three, including the well-known *Salve regina* setting, now survive.

Coronation Anthem 1. One of four anthems by Handel, composed specially for the coronation of King George II in Westminster Abbey in 1727. Each anthem occupied a different place in the service and today they are often performed individually. The four anthems are: *Zadok the Priest, The King Shall Rejoice, My Heart is Inditing*, and *Let thy Hand be Strengthened*. **2.** The setting of the words 'My Heart is Inditing' by Purcell for the coronation of James II in 1685.

Coronation Concerto Piano concerto in D (K. 537) by Mozart. Composed: 1788. Mozart played this concerto together with the concerto K. 459 to celebrate the coronation of King Leopold II at Frankfurt-am-Main in 1790, but only this D major concerto bears the nickname.

Coronation Mass 1. Mass in C (K. 317) by Mozart. Composed: 1779. The mass was written for a ceremony performed annually at the Maria Plain near Salzburg, during which a statue of the Madonna was crowned. **2.** See **Nelson Mass.**

Coronation of Poppaea, The see **Incoronazione di Poppea, L'.**

Corregidor, Der (*The Magistrate*) Opera in four acts by Hugo Wolf with text by Rosa Mayreder-Obermayer based on a story by Alarcón, *El Sombrero de tres picos* (*The Three-Cornered Hat*). First performance: Mannheim, 1896. It is the story of a miller, Tio Lucas (baritone), his pretty wife Frasquita (mezzo-soprano), and the susceptible magistrate Don Eugenio de Zuniga (buffo tenor). See also **Three-Cornered Hat, The.**

Corrette, Michel (1709–95) French composer and organist. He was organist at the Jesuit College in Paris (1738) and later (1780) in the service of the Duc d'Angoulême. Corrette wrote many tutors, including *L'Ecole d'Orphée* (1738), and produced masses, motets, concertos, and other chamber works.

Corsaire, Le Overture (Op. 21) by Berlioz. Composed: 1831; revised 1844 and 1855; first performance: Paris, 1845 (as *Tour de Nice*); Paris, 1855 (final version). The title of the overture is taken from the novel *The Red Rover* by Fennimore Cooper. During the first half of the 20th century this work became particularly associated in England with the conductor Sir Thomas Beecham.

Corsaro, Il Opera in three acts by Verdi with libretto by Piave based on Byron's poem *The Corsair*. First performance: Teatro Grande, Trieste, 1848. It concerns the adventures of the pirate Corrado (tenor) when he attacks a Muslim city.

Cortot, Alfred (1877–1962) French pianist and conductor, trained at the Paris Conservatoire. As a pianist he was particularly admired for his performances of Schumann and Chopin; he also founded the famous Cortot–Thibaud–Casals piano trio. Cortot's conducting career included an appointment at Bayreuth as assistant conductor, and in 1919 he founded the Ecole Normale de Musique in Paris.

Così fan tutte (*Thus do all Women*) Opera buffa in two acts by Mozart with libretto by Da Ponte, subtitled *La Scuola degli amanti* (*School for Lovers*). First performance: Burgtheater, Vienna, 1790. Commissioned by Emperor Joseph II, the story, supposedly a real-life incident in contemporary Vienna, concerns two sisters, Fiordiligi and Dorabella (sopranos), their lovers Guglielmo (bass) and Ferrando (tenor), a wager on the girls' faithfulness by Don Alfonso (baritone), and the witty intervention of their maid Despina (soprano).

Costeley, Guillaume (c.1531–1606) French composer. From 1560 or before he was organist to Charles IX. In 1570 he was elected 'prince' of the Confraternity of St Cecilia at Evreux. His *Musique* (1570) consists mainly of chansons, the most famous of which is *Mignonne, allon voir*.

Cotrubas, Ileana (1939–) Romanian soprano. After studying in Budapest with Elinescu and Stroescu, she made her debut at the State Opera as Yniold in *Pelleas* (1964). At Glyndebourne (1969) she sang an ethereal Melisande; since then she has toured Germany and the USA.

counterpoint The technique of combining musical lines. (The term is a 14th-century one, derived from the Latin *punctus contra punctum*; compare **harmony.**) This relationship is a two-fold one, in which vertical and horizontal elements are contrasting yet interdependent. A simple progression, such as:

demonstrates the principle. On a horizontal plane the two lines combine and contrast different melodic and rhythmic shapes, while on a vertical plane the resulting *intervals make them mutually complementary.

The term counterpoint is almost synonymous with *polyphony, except that the latter tends to be applied to a piece of music with a predominately linear texture, and the former is used in relation to the systematic academic study of a particular style (e.g. Bach or Palestrina). From the beginnings of western polyphonic music in the 9th century until around 1300, counterpoint was the main technique of composition. The textures were based on a *cantus firmus against which one or two descant parts were set in perfect intervals of the fourth, fifth, or octave (see also **conductus; organum**). In his treatise *Ars cantus mensurabilis* (*c*.1260) Franco of Cologne explained that in a three-part texture each voice needed only to be consonant with one other, so that the successive layering of all the parts gave rise to dissonances. During the 14th century the pan-consonant discant style of the English and Burgundian composers, with its increasing awareness of *cadences and *harmony, led to the gradual demise of counterpoint as the supreme arbiter of composition. By the end of the 15th century composers had begun to conceive all the voices of a score simultaneously, so that in the integrated polyphony of the 16th century counterpoint was an automatic, rather than a conscious, aspect of composition. In 16th-century treatises, such as Zarlino's *Le Institutione armoniche* (1588), the disciplines of *species counterpoint, *canon, and *fugue are anticipated as academic studies. Zarlino's treatise also reflects the stylistic ideal of Palestrina, with its web of arching lines, refined balance of rhythms, and complex interplay of accents. The contrapuntal textures of Byrd feature more intense rhythms, cross-accents, and sophisticated detail. In the 17th century, with the advent of operatic vocal writing and the violin, counterpoint became more melodically orientated. The basso continuo technique led to a strong contrapuntal relationship between melody and bass. With the growth of the new melodically orientated instrumental counterpoint, the established counterpoint of Palestrina and his contemporaries became the idealized basis of the stile antico. This became the foundation of Italian contrapuntal teaching, and in the 18th century it formed the basis of Fux's *Gradus ad Parnassum* (1725). Bach was the last great composer for whom counterpoint was a natural means of expression. The simpler textures of the later 18th-century music mark a further stage in the divorce between the practical and academic traditions. Both Haydn and Mozart possessed fine contrapuntal techniques in the Italian tradition, Haydn being self-taught from Fux's treatise and Mozart being taught by Padre Martini. Mozart's contrapuntal virtuosity is evident in the finale of his *Jupiter Symphony*. Beethoven's approach to counterpoint was a strongly personal one, especially in the works of his last period (e.g. the finale of the *Hammerklavier Sonata*). Schubert, Mendelssohn, and Schumann all contributed to the tradition of the 'set-piece' a capella fugue. Brahms' muscular sense of line always provided a lively contrapuntal interest to his work. The textures evolved by several composers of the later 19th century, notably Liszt and Wagner, were predominately linear and contrapuntal. 20th-century composers who have contributed to the didactic tradition of counterpoint include Busoni (*Fantasia contrapuntistica*), Hindemith (*Ludus tonalis*), and Shostakovitch (*24 Preludes and Fugues*). Between the wars the neoclassical movement provided an impulse for a high level of contrapuntal writing. This is reflected in the music composed by Stravinsky, Hindemith, Roussel, Martin, and others. In the didactic field, Knud Jepperson and R. O. Morris have successfully campaigned for a more realistic attitude to the teaching of the 16th-century style, while the analytical theories of Heinrich Schenker (*Der freie Satz*, 1935) have given a new insight into the contrapuntal processes latent in the masterpieces of the 18th and 19th centuries. See also **free counterpoint; strict counterpoint.**

countersubject 1. A subsidiary idea accompanying the second and subsequent entries of the subject of a *fugue. A regularly recurring countersubject is normally strongly contrasted with its subject, and in traditional fugue the two form *invertible counterpoint at the octave so that either can form a bass to the other. **2.** Any subsidiary idea heard against a principal theme.

countertenor A male voice higher than the *tenor. The countertenor can either be a low voice, with a tenorlike *tessitura, or a high voice, not unlike the male *alto and sometimes incorrectly classed as such. The countertenor is in fact a natural voice of considerably greater power and range than the alto, having an effective compass of over two octaves. It was much in vogue during the 17th and 18th centuries and has again become fashionable with the revival of the music of this period and its style of performance: Alfred *Deller, a high countertenor, is the soloist preeminently associated with its revival.

country dance A popular English village dance first stylized at the Elizabethan court, the nature of which is known from Playford's *English Dancing Master*. The musical form is variable but usually has a jolly *jig rhythm; for example Locke's 'Country Dance' in *Melothesia* (1673) is in true 6/4 jig rhythm. After having been nearly lost altogether, the dance has been revived by present-day folk-dance societies. French: see **contredanse**; German: **Contratanz**; Italian: **contradanza.**

coup de glotte A method of vocal attack, generally on a note starting with a vowel rather than one that starts with a consonant (which is called **vibrazione**). In fact, the term 'attack' gives a misleading idea of the correct means of effecting this technique: a caress, allowing the sound to be launched and not struck, is likely to produce a more accurate sound. The exercise is intended to place the voice in the larynx and, if executed correctly, can be of great assistance in voice training.

Couperin, François (1668–1733) French composer, harpsichordist, and organist. In 1686 he succeeded his father as organist of St Gervais, Paris. In 1690 he published two organ masses and in 1693 became organist to

Louis XIV and began to write music for court. In 1717 Couperin was appointed king's harpsichordist. Though influenced by Italian music, he sought to combine it with French expressive and melodic qualities. His *Pièces de clavecin* (1713), which consists of suites (*ordres*), contains many pieces with descriptive titles. He wrote a good deal of small-scale sacred music, the most important being *Leçons de ténébres* (1713–17) for two sopranos. His trio sonatas are modelled on Corelli's but include French airs. Couperin's organ music displays his ability to combine contrapuntal devices with melodious lines.

His uncle **Louis Couperin** (1626–61) became organist of St Gervais in 1653 and played the treble viol at court. His compositions, which include instrumental fantasias, are mainly for keyboard: his organ pieces are the earliest written for specific stops and his most remarkable harpsichord compositions are chaconnes and passacailles. **Charles Couperin** (1638–79), father of François, succeeded his brother Louis as organist at St Gervais in 1661.

coupler An organ stop enabling two manuals, or one manual and the pedalboard, to be connected together so that while one is being played the stops controlled by the other are brought into use. There are also **superoctave couplers** that duplicate the notes played an octave higher and **suboctave couplers** that duplicate notes an octave lower.

couplet 1. See **duplet. 2.** A song in which the same music is repeated for each verse. [from French, verse] **3.** The forerunner of the episode in the *rondo form, as used by Couperin, in which the theme is repeated several times.

courante A moderately fast French dance originating in the 16th century. Affected by graceful Italian rhythms, it is characterized by duple/triple time cross rhythms, such as 6/4 against 3/2, or 6/8 against 3/4, and an upbeat beginning. It was often coupled with the *allemande and later had a firm place in the baroque *suite. English: **corant; coranto.** [French, running]

courses Sets of *lute strings arranged in pairs and tuned in unison or in octaves.

Covent Garden (*or* **Royal Opera House**) A theatre in Bow Street, London. The first theatre was built in 1732 on a site that had once been a Catholic convent garden. It was used chiefly for plays and was burnt down in 1808 and replaced the following year. More opera was gradually given, and from 1847 to 1892 the theatre's resident company was known as the **Royal Italian Opera**. In 1856 the theatre was again burnt down and replaced in 1858 with the one that stands today. From 1892, when it became known as the Royal Opera House, it was used by many visiting companies until World War II, when it became a dance hall. After the war the theatre was re-established as a centre for high-quality opera and ballet. Sadler's Wells Ballet became the resident ballet company and was renamed the Royal Ballet in 1956; the opera company became the Royal Opera in 1969. Standards improved and new operas were presented: the company became one of the foremost in the world, attracting international artists. Its principal conductors have included Karl Rankl, Rafael Kubelik, Georg Solti, and Colin Davis.

cowbells 1. Pellet or clapper *bells tied round the necks of cattle, to enable their owners to locate them in mountainous country. **2.** An orchestral percussion instrument based on such a bell and used to create special effects, for example in Richard Strauss's *Alpine Symphony*.

Cowell, Henry (1897–1965) US composer, a pupil of Charles Seeger. He received a Guggenheim Fellowship (1931–32). In pieces composed between 1912 and 1930, Cowell developed innovatory techniques of piano playing, e.g. tone clusters and sounds produced by plucking the piano strings. Later instrumental and choral works show the influence of eastern music and early American hymnody. Major compositions include symphonies and string quartets.

Cowen, Frederic (1852–1935) British conductor, pianist, and composer. He studied the piano with Goss and Benedict in London then with Plaidy, Moscheles, Reinecke, Richter, and Hauptmann in Leipzig and conducting with Tausig and Kiel at the Stern conservatory, Berlin. He began his career as a pianist but became better known as a conductor, holding posts with leading British orchestras and conducting for the Royal Philharmonic Society (1888–92, 1900–07). Cowen composed several operas, six symphonies (including the colourful *Scandinavian Symphony*, 1880), cantatas, oratorios, chamber music, and songs. He is now best remembered for his popular ballads.

cow horn A brass valveless *horn designed to produce the sound of an animal horn. It is occasionally used for special effects in the orchestra.

Cox and Box Operetta by Sullivan with libretto by Burnand, based on the farce *Box and Cox* by Maddison Morton. First performance: Adelphi Theatre, London, 1867. Cox and Box are night and day tenants, respectively, of the same lodging.

cracovienne see **krakowiak.**

Craft, Robert Lawson (1923–) US conductor. He was a close friend of Stravinsky, with whom he published five volumes of conversational essays and memoirs (1958–65). Craft's recordings include the first complete recording of Webern's music.

Cramer, Wilhelm (1745–99) German violinist and composer. He was a member of the Mannheim chapel (1757–72) before going to London (1773), where he led the king's band and the orchestras at the Opera and Pantheon and at the Handel Festival (1784, 1787). He wrote many chamber works, violin sonatas, and concertos. His son, **Johann Baptist Cramer** (1771–1858), was a pianist, composer, and teacher. He studied with Schroter, K. F. Abel, and Clementi. With Addison and Beale, he established the music publishing firm of J. B. Cramer & Co. Ltd. in London (1824). Of Cramer's many studies for solo piano, the collection *Studio per il pianoforte* (1804–10) is still much used. He also wrote 124 keyboard sonatas, 9 piano concertos, 2 quintets, and 2 piano quartets.

Crawford, Ruth Porter (Ruth Crawford Seeger; 1901–53) US composer. She composed a small number of works, highly experimental in style and technique, the best known of which is a string quartet (1931). Her output also includes other chamber works and songs.

Creation, The (German: *Die Schöpfung*) Oratorio by Haydn to a text by Lidley (or Linnell). Composed: 1794–95. First performance: Vienna, 1798 (German version); London, 1800 (English version). The words are based on the Book of Genesis and Milton's *Paradise Lost* and the work was written at the suggestion of Haydn's English concert manager, Salomon, while Haydn was staying in London. Baron von Swieten, the Austrian patron of the arts, translated the text into German.

Création du monde, La (*The Creation of the World*) Ballet in one act with music by Milhaud and scenario by Blaise Cendrars. First performance: Théâtre des Champs-Elysées, Paris, 1923. It is a Black ballet inspired by a visit to the USA in 1922, the score written for 17 soloists in a jazz idiom.

Creation Mass Mass in B major by Haydn. Composed: 1801. The 'Qui tollis' section of the mass quotes part of Adam and Eve's duet from *The Creation*, hence its name.

Creatures of Prometheus, The see **Geschöpfe des Prometheus, Die.**

crescendo Growing. Used to indicate that the music increases in volume. Abbreviation: **cresc.** [Italian]

Crespin, Régine (1927–) French soprano. She studied with Jouatte and Cabanel in Paris, making her debut in 1950 at Mulhouse, as Elsa in *Lohengrin*. Successful above all in Wagner, her elegance of style was also suited to French opera.

Creston, Paul (Joseph Guttoveggio; 1906–) US composer. Creston composes in a tonal idiom enlivened by moderate use of dissonance. Stylistic influences include jazz and Gregorian chant. His output includes symphonies, concertos, chamber music, and piano works.

Cristofori, Bartolommeo (1665–1731) Italian keyboard instrument maker. In Florence in 1711 he invented a *gravicembalo col piano e forte*, generally considered to be the first authentic *piano.

Croce, Giovanni (*c*.1557–1609) Italian composer and priest. He sang in the choir of St Mark's, Venice, under Zarlino and was maestro di cappella there from 1603 until his death. He composed masses, motets, and numerous secular works, notably the *Mascarate piacevoli e ridicolose* (1590).

croche Quaver. The name 'Monsieur Croche' was invented by Debussy as the pseudonym under which he wrote music criticism. [French, hook; not to be confused with *crotchet]

Croft, William (1678–1727) English composer and organist, a pupil of John Blow. He was appointed organist at the Chapel Royal in 1707 and at Westminster Abbey in 1708, when he was also made Master of the Children at the Chapel Royal. Croft is best remembered for his *Musica sacra* (1724) and other church music, but he also wrote songs, sonatas, and several keyboard works.

crook A detachable length of tubing fitted to brass wind instruments, such as horns and trumpets, to change the key of the instrument. From the middle of the 19th century the use of valves in these instruments made it unnecessary to change crooks during the performance of a piece.

Cross, Beverley (1931–) British playwright and author of *The Mines of Sulphur*, a libretto for the opera by Richard Rodney Bennett (1965).

Cross, Joan (1900–) British soprano. She studied music with Holst and singing at Trinity College, London, with Dawson Freer. Principal soprano at Sadler's Wells from 1931 until 1946, she subsequently created many of Britten's operatic roles. She founded the National School of Opera in 1948 and was made CBE in 1951.

Crosse, Gordon (1937–) British composer, a pupil of Wellesz and Petrassi. His early style, as demonstrated in the 'Corpus Christi Carol' (1961), derives from serialism and medieval techniques. He explored a more dramatic manner in the *Concerto da Camera* (1962) and introduced popular elements in the cantata *Changes* (1966). His interest in drama culminated in a series of operas beginning with *Purgatory* (1966). Later works, such as *Ariadne* (1972), the second violin concerto (1970), *World Within* (1977), and *Thel* (1978), show a fusion of these diverse ingredients.

cross fingering An unusual method of fingering a woodwind instrument to produce notes that are difficult or impossible to obtain by the normal fingering.

cross relation see **false relation.**

Crotch, William (1775–1847) British composer and organist. An infant prodigy, he later became music professor at Oxford (1797) and was the first principal of the Royal

Academy of Music (1822–32). He wrote many anthems, oratorios, concertos, and fugues as well as an ode on the accession of George IV.

crotchet A note having half the time value of a *minim and a quarter that of a semibreve. In modern notation it is depicted as a filled-in circle with a tail. US: **quarter note**. See **Appendix, Table 1.**

crowd see **crwth.**

Crown Imperial March by Walton. Composed: 1937 (for the coronation of King George VI). Walton took his title from the text of a cantata called *In Honour of the City of London*, which he composed in the same year to a poem by William Dunbar. This poem contains the line 'In beauty being the crown imperial.'

Crucifixion, The Oratorio by Stainer, with a text by Simpson based on the Bible. First performance: 1887. This oratorio, which is the only work by which Stainer is now remembered, tells the story of the Easter Passion.

Cruft, Eugene (1887–1976) British double-bass player. He played with the BBC Symphony Orchestra (1929–49) and the Royal Opera House Orchestra (1949–52). As a teacher at the Royal College of Music, his pupils included his son, **Adrian Cruft** (1921–87), who made his career as an orchestral player until 1969, after which he devoted himself fully to composition.

Crumb, George (1929–) US composer, a pupil of Finney and Blacher. His style is eclectic, with much quotation and a strong literary element (usually taken from the Spanish poet and dramatist Lorca). His works, mostly for small ensembles, are often theatrical and concerned with the creation of strange fragile sounds from unusual or amplified instruments. They include *Ancient Voices of Children* (1970), *Vox Balaenae* (1971), *Makrokosmos III* (1975), and *Star Child* (1977).

crumhorn A slender hook-shaped wind instrument with a double reed. It was used in Europe in the 16th and 17th centuries, often in consorts of four instruments of different pitches.

Crusell, Bernhard Henrik (1775–1838) Finnish clarinet-ist and composer. He studied the clarinet with Tausch and Lefèvre and composition with Abbé Vogler, Berton, and Gossec. Crusell became a distinguished soloist, mainly working in Stockholm, and wrote three clarinet concertos, two clarinet quartets, operas, and songs.

crwth A Welsh *lyre played with a bow. Of medieval origins, it survived as a folk instrument in Wales. It was called a **crowd** in England.

csárdás (*or* **czardas**) A popular Hungarian national dance in two contrasting sections, a slow **lassú** and a fast accelerating **friss**. English: **tchardache.**

cuckoo A two-note wind instrument that imitates the call of the cuckoo and is used in toy symphonies.

Cuénod, Hugues (1902–) Swiss tenor. He made his operatic debut in 1928, having already spent some time teaching at the Geneva conservatory. Cuénod's repertoire is very wide and embraces opera, oratorio, and lieder.

Cui, César Antonovich (1835–1918) Russian composer and critic of French descent. He had music lessons from Moniuszko, then studied engineering, specializing in fortifi-cations. An ardent nationalist, he became a member of The *Five, whose ideals he championed in his many writings and criticisms. Cui's compositions include several operas, choral, chamber, and orchestral works (including two scherzos), and many songs and miniatures for piano. He completed Dargomizhsky's *The Stone Guest* and made a performing version of Mussorgsky's *Sorochintsy Fair.*

cuivre Brass instrument. The plural, **cuivres,** is used in French scores to indicate the brass section of the orchestra. **Cuivré,** brassy, indicates the forced metallic sound some-times used in horn technique. [French]

cummings, e. e. (1894–1962) US poet whose works have been set by a number of composers, including Cage, Smalley, and Boulez. He wrote an English translation of the narration in Stravinsky's *Oedipus Rex.*

Cunning Little Vixen, The Opera by Janáček, based on a story of Těsnohlídek. Composed: 1921–23; first performance: Brno, 1924. The opera tells of a forest ranger who finds a vixen cub and takes it home, where it amuses his children. A young woman (who never actually appears on stage) infatuates and then disappoints successively the forester, the priest, and the schoolteacher. The moral of the opera is to show how human behaviour in love compares so badly with that of animals. Janáček's handling of the orchestra is particularly notable in this opera.

Cupid and Death Masque by Christopher Gibbons with words by Shirley. Composed: 1653. In 1659 the masque was revived, but although the original words were retained, new music was composed by Gibbons and Matthew Locke. The second version includes more use of music than does the first version, in which dialogue plays a more important part.

Curlew, The Song cycle by Warlock to four poems by Yeats. Composed: 1920–22. The singer is accompanied by flute, cor anglais, and string quartet.

Curlew River Parable for church performance by Benjamin Britten, with a libretto by William Plomer. First perform-ance: Aldeburgh, 1964. This is the first of three such works and is based upon a medieval Japanese Noh play; the other

Carl Czerny

two works of this trilogy are *The Burning Fiery Furnace* and *The Prodigal Son*. For *Curlew River* the setting is transferred from Japan to the East Anglian countryside, with a demented mother searching for her lost son.

curtain music see **act tune.**

curtal (*or* **curtall**) A 16th-century version of a *shawm that had two tubes bored out of one piece of wood. It was blown through a metal crook that contained the double reed and was an early form of the *bassoon.

Curwen, John (1816–80) British Congregationalist minister and teacher. He was an advocate of the tonic sol-fa method of teaching music and founded an association and a publishing company for its propagation.

Curzon, Sir Clifford (1907–82) British pianist. A pupil of Schnabel in Berlin, Curzon established his reputation by tours of Europe and the USA before World War II. His playing of Mozart was particularly acclaimed and both Rawsthorne and Berkeley dedicated works to him. He was knighted in 1977.

cycle A musical series or large-scale sequence of individual pieces unified by a single idea or common theme, as in Schubert's song cycle *Winterreise* (1827).

cyclic form A technique of unifying individual movements of a larger work, complete in themselves, by a recurrent musical theme or motive. The idea was first applied in the 15th century to the composition of masses (e.g. Dufay's *Missa caput*), which were held together by a single *cantus firmus and a two-voice 'head' motive. The technique has been generally used in large-scale works, such as symphonies and sonatas.

cymbals Concussion or percussion instruments consisting of metal plates, either clashed together or struck with a stick or wire brush. **Antique cymbals** produce a note of a definite pitch and are clashed together. Other orchestral cymbals do not produce a note of a definite pitch. In jazz, dance, and popular music, two untuned cymbals are mounted horizontally on a rod and clashed together with a pedal (**Hi-hat cymbals**). Alternatively a single cymbal is mounted horizontally on a rod and struck with a drumstick or wire brush.

cythern see **cittern.**

czardas see **csárdás.**

Czerny, Carl (1791–1857) Austrian piano teacher, composer, pianist, and writer. He was a pupil of Beethoven, of whose works he became a renowned interpreter, and quickly gained a reputation as an outstanding pianist and (from the age of 15) a celebrated teacher. His pupils included Thalberg, Heller, and Liszt. He composed chamber, orchestral, and choral music but is best known for his numerous piano pieces, which include sonatas, sonatinas, potpourris, and groups of systematic exercises progressing to highly virtuoso studies. Czerny made many arrangements and editions and was a prolific writer on music: he wrote on the art of piano playing, treatises on composition, and an autobiography. He contributed a variation to the *Hexameron (1837).

D

D The keynote of the scale of D major. The frequency of D above *middle C is 293.7 hertz (A = 440 hertz).

D. Abbreviation for Deutsch. It is used as a prefix to indicate the number of a piece in Otto Erich Deutsch's catalogue (1951) of Schubert's works.

da 1. From; for example in *da capo. **2.** Of; from: used in such expressions as da *chiesa and da *camera. [Italian]

da capo From the beginning: a direction indicating that the performer should start again from the beginning. **Da capo al fine** and **da capo al segno** indicate that the repeat should continue up to the word *fine* (end) or the sign, respectively, in the score. A **da capo aria** is one in which the third section is a repeat of the first, with a contrasting second section (see **aria**). Abbreviation: **D.C.** [Italian]

Dahl, Ingolf (1912–70) German-born US composer, conductor, and writer, a pupil of Nadia Boulanger. After an early neoclassical period he adopted the use of serial techniques for virtuoso instrumental writing. His works include a piano quartet (1957), the *Cycle of Sonnets* (1968), the *Elegy Concerto* (1970), and much film and radio music.

Dalayrac, Nicolas (1753–1809) French composer. A member of the guards of the Count d'Artois, he produced one of the first French string quartets, *Quatuors concertants* (1777). He also produced many comic operas, including *Nina* (1786), set later by Paesiello, and *La Maison à vendre* (1800). Dalayrac was made a member of the Academy of Stockholm in 1798.

d'Albert, Eugène (Francis Charles) (1864–1932) Pianist and composer, born in Glasgow, of French descent. He was taught in London by Stainer, Prout, and Sullivan and in 1881 won the Mendelssohn Scholarship to study in Vienna under Liszt. Thereafter he regarded himself as a German musician and after a career as a concert pianist became director of the Berlin Hochschule in 1907. He composed numerous instrumental works and 20 operas, including *Der *Tiefland* (1903).

Dalby, Martin (1942–) British composer, a pupil of Howells and head of BBC music, Scotland (since 1972). His works include a symphony (1970), the *Tower of Victory* (1973), a viola concerto (1974), and *The Dancer Eduardova* (1978).

Dalcroze, Emile Jaques- see **Jaques-Dalcroze, Emile.**

Dale, Benjamin (1885–1943) British composer, a pupil of Frederick Corden. Dale's music, of which there is not very much, has a strong romantic influence; in later years he was concerned with educational work for the Royal Academy of Music and Associated Board. His best-known work is the piano sonata (1902); there are also sonatas for violin and viola, songs, and choral and orchestral works.

Dallapiccola, Luigi (1904–75) Italian composer. Dallapiccola studied in Austria as well as Italy; an interest in the music of Schoenberg and Webern led him to adopt serial technique in the late 1930s. The majority of his works are vocal, many being concerned with the theme of spiritual freedom: these include the operas *Il *Prigioniero* (1949) and *Ulisse* (1968) and the choral works *Canti di prigionera* (1938–41) and *Canti di liberazione* (1951–55). Among Dallapiccola's instrumental works are *Piccola musica notturna* (1954) and *Three Questions with Two Answers* (1962).

Luigi Dallapiccola

Damase, Jean-Michel (1928–) French composer and pianist, recipient of the Grand Prix de Rome (1947). His works include operas, ballets, two piano concertos, a violin concerto, and chamber music.

Damnation of Faust, The Cantata by Berlioz with a libretto arranged·by the composer and Gandonnière from Nerval's translation of Goethe's *Faust*. Composed: 1846. This work was originally composed in 1828 as *Eight Scenes from Goethe's Faust* and only later adapted as a cantata. One of the most popular numbers is the *Rákóczi March*, which is often performed separately. Although never intended for stage performance, several attempts have been made to produce this work as an opera.

Damoiselle élue, La see **Blessed Damozel, The**.

Dämpfer *Mute. The application of the term is wide and also includes the soft pedal on the piano. [German]

Damrosch, Walter (1862–1950) US conductor, born in Germany. An early champion of Wagner, he gave the US premieres of many major works. His father, **Leopold Damrosch** (1832–85), was also a conductor.

dance A rhythmic movement of the body, usually to the accompaniment of song or music. The work is believed to originate from the Sanskrit *tanha*, meaning desire for life or movement. Dancing is an activity that has been practised by men and women all over the world from earliest times and is still performed by the peoples of all cultures. Primitive dances usually consist of a ritual of repeated actions that are either designed to evoke a particular emotion or to cajole the gods (or the forces of nature) into providing suitable weather conditions for agriculture or greater fertility among the childbearers of the participants. Dancing has deep and lasting connection with fertility, and through fertility (when it was understood) with sexual activity. However during classical times dancing had a primarily religious function. The Greeks did not dance with each other and the Romans had a low opinion of dancing except for religious purposes. In Europe, and elsewhere, the primitive elements of dancing re-emerged as the basis of **folk dancing** (see also **folk music**), an open-air rustic pastime in which traditional agricultural activities are celebrated. Dancing as a spectacle, rather than an activity, originated largely in the courts of the European monarchs in the 16th and 17th centuries. It derived from the folk dances of the peasantry but in its stylized form went on to become the basis for *ballet. The galliard, allemande, and volta are typical courtly dances that evolved from folk dances. The galliard itself was the basis for the minuet, which dominated European ballrooms until the introduction of the waltz at the beginning of the 19th century. Thereafter the USA set the fashion for social dancing with its Negro-based jazz and the *cakewalk (a cynical Black imitation of an affluent planters' dance).

Modern ballroom dancing derives mainly from these jazz idioms (charleston, foxtrot, jitterbug) and from the Latin-American dances (tango, rumba, samba). Since the advent of pop music, dancing has ceased to rely on formal steps and intimate bodily contact, depending instead on a visual display of rhythmic movements.

Dance of the Hours A piece of ballet music taken from the third act of Ponchielli's opera *La *Gioconda*. First performance: 1876.

dance poem see **choreographic poem**.

Dances of Galánta Orchestral suite by Kodály. Composed: 1934. The title is taken from the Hungarian town of Galánta; Kodály bases his suite upon tunes taken from a collection of Gypsy music compiled in this town.

Dandrieu, Jean-François (1682–1738) French composer and organist. He was organist of the French Chapel Royal (1721) and later at the church of St Barthélemy (1733). In addition to a tutor, *Principes de l'accompagnement du clavecin* (1718), and several works for keyboard, he also wrote violin sonatas, songs, and chamber music.

Danse macabre Tone poem (Op. 40) by Saint-Saëns. Composed: 1874. The work, based on a poem by Henri Cazalis, describes how Death plays the violin at midnight in a graveyard, while the skeletons dance. A quotation of the Dies irae from the Requiem Mass is included.

Dante Alighieri (1265–1321) Italian poet. His greatest work, *The Divine Comedy*, contains some much-quoted remarks about the relationship of music and poetry. Some madrigal settings of his works survive, but only in the 19th century did composers return to him for material. Dante texts were set by Verdi and Donizetti, and Liszt wrote a *Dante Sonata* and a *Dante Symphony* inspired by his work.

Dante Sonata Piano sonata in one movement by Liszt: its full name is *Après une lecture de Dante* (After a Reading of Dante). Composed: 1837–39; revised: 1849. This sonata is included in the second volume of the *Années de pèlerinage* and is also described as a *Sonata quasi fantasia*. In 1940 the work was arranged by Constant Lambert for piano and orchestra as a ballet score.

Dante Symphony Symphony by Liszt for female choir and orchestra, based upon *The Divine Comedy* by Dante. Composed: 1855–56; first performance: Dresden, 1857. The two movements are called 'Inferno' (which quotes the plainsong Dies irae from the Requiem Mass) and 'Purgatorio.' At the end of the work the women's choir sings a setting of the Magnificat.

Danzi, Franz (1763–1826) German composer and cellist, son of the cellist **Innocentz Danzi** (*c*.1730–98). He studied composition with Abbé Vogler. After touring with his wife, the singer Margereth Marchand, Danzi became kapellmeister in Stuttgart (1807) and Karlsruhe (1808). He wrote early romantic operas, church music, and chamber works.

Daphne Opera in one act by Richard Strauss with libretto by Joseph Gregor. First performance: Dresden, 1938. It is the story of Apollo's love for Daphne (tenor and soprano, respectively) and her transformation into a laurel tree.

Daphnis and Chloe (French: *Daphnis et Chloé*) Ballet in three scenes with music by Ravel and choreography by Fokine. First performance: Théâtre du Châtelet, Paris, 1912, conducted by Monteux (décor by Bakst). Commissioned by Diaghilev for the Ballets Russes, it tells the ancient Greek story of pastoral love, based on Longus' text. Ravel uses a large orchestra and chorus; the two orchestral suites drawn from the ballet represent only a part of the score.

Da Ponte, Lorenzo (1749–1838) Italian poet and librettist. While living in Vienna he wrote libretti for Salieri, Mozart, and other composers. For Mozart he wrote *The Marriage of Figaro*, based on Beaumarchais (1786), *Don Giovanni* (1787), and *Così fan tutti* (1790). For a period he lived in London, intermittently as poet to the Italian Opera and librettist at the King's Theatre, but in 1805 he emigrated to the USA.

Daquin, Louis-Claude (1694–1772) French composer and organist, a pupil of Louis Marchand. A child prodigy, he was appointed organist of the church of Saint-Paul (1727) and became court organist in 1739. In addition to his keyboard works, which include *Nouveau livre de noëls pour l'orgue et le clavecin*, he wrote motets, a cantata (*La Rose*), and chamber works.

Dargason An English folk tune, often used for the song 'It was a maid of my country.' Dating back to at least the 16th century, this tune is also used for a country dance and in this connection it appears in the final movement of the *St Paul's Suite* of Holst.

Dargomizhsky, Alexander Sergeyevich (1813–69) Russian composer. A civil servant by profession, he took up serious composition after meeting Glinka (1833–34). In 1843 he resigned his post and travelled through Europe; on his return (1845) he made a study of Russian folk songs, which was to influence his music (particularly his opera the *Rusalka*, 1855). He developed strong nationalist ideals and became associated with (though not a member of) The *Five. Dargomizhsky wrote four operas (including the unfinished The *Stone Guest, completed by Cui and orchestrated by Rimsky-Korsakov), orchestral music (including the fantasy *Baba Yaga*, 1862), and a large number of fine influential songs.

Dart, (Robert) Thurston (1921–71) British harpsichordist and musicologist, trained at the Royal College of Music. As well as appearing frequently as harpsichordist and continuo player, Dart researched widely into keyboard and consort music of the Renaissance and baroque. He was appointed Professor of Music at Cambridge (1962) and London (1964).

Daughter of the Regiment, The see **Fille du régiment, La.**

David, Félicien (César) (1810–76) French composer. He was a chorister and then maître de chapelle at St Sauveur, Aix-en-Provence. In 1830 he went to the Paris Conservatoire and in 1831 joined the St Simonians; as a missionary for the movement he travelled to the Middle East (1832–35), where he collected oriental folk melodies. Back in Paris his first great success as a composer was the symphonic ode *Le Désert* (1844). He wrote several operas, including *La Perle du Brésil* (1851), *Lalla-Roukh* (1862), and *Le Saphir* (1865). David composed many St Simonian choruses, songs, and orchestral, chamber, and piano music, much of it reflecting his interest in the Orient. He greatly influenced the succeeding generation of composers, particularly Bizet, Massenet, and Delibes.

David, Ferdinand (1810–73) German violinist and composer. After studying with Spohr he established a career as soloist and chamber-music player. In 1843 he began teaching at the Leipzig conservatory, where Joachim and Wilhelmj were among his pupils and his friendship with Mendelssohn led to him giving the first performance of the violin concerto in 1845. His many compositions include violin works, chamber music, and an opera.

Davidde penitente Oratorio (K. 469) by Mozart, the words being generally attributed to Lorenzo Da Ponte. Composed: 1785. The music is a mixture of new arias and portions from the unfinished mass in C minor (K. 427) of 1783. The oratorio was composed for a concert in aid of a musicians' pension fund.

Davidsbündler Tänze Set of 18 piano pieces (Op. 6) by Schumann. Composed: 1837; revised: 1850. The Davidsbund (League of David) referred to in the title is the nickname that Schumann gave in his writings on music to those composers of his day who were fighting the musical Philistines and their cheap drawing-room music. Each of these character pieces is initialled either E. or F., standing for Eusebius and Florestan. These two imaginary figures represent the two sides of Schumann's nature – the introverted and the extroverted, respectively.

Davies, Sir Henry Walford (1869–1941) British composer and organist. He was organist at St George's Chapel, Windsor (1924–32), and was made Master of the King's Music in 1934. Davies' output consists mainly of sacred choral works; other compositions include two violin sonatas, orchestral overtures, and music for children.

Davies, Hugh (1943–   ) British composer, a pupil and assistant of Stockhausen. His works often feature parts for live or recorded electronic sound, improvisation also being an important element. Many of the instruments he uses are of his own invention.

Davies, Peter Maxwell (1934–   ) British composer, a pupil of Ralph Hall and Petrassi. His early works, such as the trumpet sonata (1955), show the influence of serialism, which he later combined with medieval techniques, as in *Prolation* (1958). After a period in musical education, Davies began to introduce decorative improvisation into some of his works, e.g. *Sinfonia* (1962). The opera **Taverner* (1969) shows an integration of diverse musical styles, which is also seen in his series of theatrical chamber works, including **Eight Songs for a Mad King* (1963). Other works include two fantasies on Taverner's *In Nomine* (1962, 1964), *Revelation and Fall* (1966), **Vesalii icones* (1969), *Stone Litany* (1973), the operas *The Martyrdom of St Magnus* (1977) and *The Lighthouse* (1980), and the ballet *Salome* (1978).

Davis, Sir Colin (1927–   ) British conductor. Originally a clarinetist, Davis conducted the BBC Symphony Orchestra (1967–71) and in 1971 became musical director of the Royal Opera. Davis is particularly associated with the music

Peter Maxwell Davies

of Berlioz and Tippett, many of whose works he has recorded.

Davy, John (1763–1824) British composer, violinist, and organist. As a member of the orchestra of Covent Garden, he wrote music for light opera and theatre, including the song 'The Bay of Biscay.' His other compositions include *Six Quartets for Voices* (c.1790) and chamber and keyboard works.

Davy, Richard (c.1465–1516) English composer, organist of Magdalen College, Oxford (1490–92), where a book of his music was bound in 1495–96. Davy's compositions include votive antiphons, part songs and carols in English, and a fragmentary setting of the *St Matthew Passion*, which survives in the Eton Choirbook.

dead march A slow ceremonial march. Among the best known are those in Handel's *Saul* (Act III) and *Samson* (Act III).

Death and the Maiden 1. Song (D. 531) by Schubert, to a poem by Claudius. Composed: 1817. **2.** Nickname for the string quartet No. 14 in D minor (D. 810) by Schubert. Composed: 1826. The song 'Death and the Maiden' is used in the second movement for a set of variations; its melodic and rhythmic influences can be traced in the other movements also.

Death and Transfiguration (German: *Tod und Verklärung*) Tone poem (Op. 24) by Richard Strauss. First performance: 1890. According to the composer, the work was intended to represent the final hours of a dying man. This man, probably an artist, recollects his childhood and his past artistic aspirations and achievements. The programme was actually devised by Strauss himself but a poem on the subject was then written by Alexander Ritter as an interpretation of the music.

Death in Venice Opera in two acts by Britten with libretto by Myfanwy Piper, based on the story by Thomas Mann. First performance: The Maltings, Snape (Aldeburgh Festival), 1973. It concerns the love of the novelist Aschenbach (tenor) for the boy Tadzio (dancer) and his subsequent death.

Debussy, Claude Achille (1862–1918) French composer. Debussy studied at the Paris Conservatoire (1872–80). In 1884 he won the Grand Prix de Rome; on his return from Rome he became associated with the symbolist group of poets, led by Mallarmé. Debussy visited Bayreuth for the first time in 1888 and for a short period came under the influence of Wagner's music. At this time also he came into contact with oriental music, presented at the Paris Exposition of 1889. Apart from composing, Debussy spent his later years playing and conducting in European cities; he also worked occasionally as a music critic. The term 'impressionist,' often used to describe Debussy's music, is only partly appropriate to it: Debussy himself always felt closer to the symbolist movement. Nevertheless, certain works do seem to evoke the descriptive image through suggestion of mood that is regarded as the musical equivalent of impressionism in the visual arts. The colouristic use of unresolving harmony and the use of sonority as a structural element in composition are the most striking and influential aspects of Debussy's mature style; his last works, however, show a return to a baroque-like clarity of texture.

Debussy's many works for piano include the *Suite bergamasque* (1890–1905; which contains the popular piece *Clair de lune*, 1890–95), *Estampes* (1903), two sets of *Images* (1905, 1907), the suite *Children's Corner* (1906–08), 24 preludes in two books (1910, 1913), and a set of 12 *Etudes* (1915). His major stage compositions are the opera *Pelléas et Mélisande* (1892–1902), the incidental music The *Martyrdom of St Sebastian* (1911), and the ballet *Jeux* (1912). Debussy's orchestral compositions include the *Prélude à l'*Après-midi d'un faune* (1892–94), three *Nocturnes* (1893–99), La *Mer* (three symphonic sketches; 1903–05), and a further set of *Images* (1902–12). His chamber music includes *Syrinx* (1913) for flute.

decani The part of the choir that occupies the stalls on the south side of the aisle, i.e. the side on which, by ecclesiastic tradition, the dean sits. See **cantoris**.

decrescendo Decreasing. Used to indicate that the music becomes softer. [Italian]

Deering, Richard see **Dering, Richard.**

degree A note of the diatonic *scale relative to other notes. The first degree is called the *tonic, the second the *supertonic, the third the *mediant, the fourth the *subdominant, the fifth the *dominant, the sixth the *submediant, and the seventh the *leading note. The octave above the tonic is also referred to as the first degree.

dehors Outside. Used to indicate that a passage or instrument so marked should be prominent. [French]

De Koven, (Henry Louis) Reginald (1859–1920) US composer, conductor, and critic. He studied in Stuttgart, Oxford, Frankfurt, and Florence, with Suppé in Vienna, and with Delibes in Paris. He returned to the USA in 1882 and in 1902 founded the Philharmonic Orchestra of Washington, DC. De Koven is remembered for his operettas, set in the Far East and Europe, among them *Don Quixote* (1889) and *Robin Hood* (1890, which contains his popular wedding ballad 'Oh promise me'). He composed two grand operas – The *Canterbury Pilgrims* (1917) and *Rip Van Winkle* (1920) – an orchestral suite, piano works, about 400 songs, and ballets.

Delage, Maurice (1879–1961) French composer. After early careers in commerce and the army, Delage studied

with Ravel and became established as a composer. Oriental influences are felt in his music, which follows impressionist principles. His compositions include orchestral and vocal works and a string quartet (1948).

Delibes, (Clément Philibert) Léo (1836–91) French composer and organist, a pupil of Benoist and Adam at the Paris Conservatoire (1847–50). He was a church organist, but in 1853 he was also appointed accompanist at the Théâtre-Lyrique. He was chorus master at the Paris Opéra (1864–71) and composition professor at the Conservatoire (1881). Delibes composed almost entirely for the stage. His ballets include the well-known *Coppélia* (1870) and *Sylvia* (1876). He wrote many witty operettas (including *Le Roi l'a dit*, 1873), incidental music for *Le Roi s'amuse* (1882), and more serious operas, of which the best are *Lakmé* (1883) and *Kassya* (orchestrated after his death by Massenet). He also composed many choruses and several songs.

Delius, Frederick (Fritz D.; 1862–1934) British composer of German parentage, born in Yorkshire. He began to study music in Florida, where he went in 1884 to work as an orange planter, and in 1888 entered the conservatory at

Frederick Delius in old age

Leipzig, where he became friendly with Grieg. From 1890 Delius lived mostly in France; for the last ten years of his life he was blind and paralysed, but continued to compose with the assistance of Eric Fenby, who from 1928 acted as his amanuensis.

Delius's romantic musical style was influenced by Grieg and Scandinavian culture. At first his works received little attention, but after 1910 – largely through the efforts of Sir Thomas Beecham – his music became widely recognized. Delius composed six operas, including *Koanga (1895–97), A *Village Romeo and Juliet (1900–01), and *Fennimore und Gerda (1908–10); orchestral pieces, including La *Calinda (1895–97), *Brigg Fair (1907), North Country Sketches (1913–14), and the tone poems *On Hearing the First Cuckoo in Spring (1912) and Song of Summer (1930); choral works, including *Appalachia (1902), *Sea Drift (1903), A *Mass of Life (1909), and Requiem (1914–16); chamber music; incidental music, including *Hassan (1920); concertos for piano, violin, and cello; and many songs.

Deller, Alfred (1912–79) British countertenor. Taught music by his father, he became an alto at Canterbury Cathedral. In 1950 he founded the Deller Consort, which effectively revived English lute songs and madrigals. Britten, Fricker, Mellers, Ridout, and Rubbra wrote works for him.

Dello Joio, Norman (1913–) US composer, a pupil of Hindemith. His works show neoclassical characteristics absorbed from his teacher; some are based on Gregorian chant. Dello Joio's compositions include two operas, a symphony (The Triumph of Saint Joan, 1951), chamber music, and choral works.

Del Mar, Norman (1919–) British conductor. He was conductor of the BBC Scottish Symphony Orchestra (1960–65) and is particularly associated with 20th-century British music.

Del Monaco, Mario (1915–82) Italian tenor. He studied at the Pesaro conservatory, making his professional debut at Milan (1941) as Pinkerton in Madame Butterfly. He joined the Metropolitan Opera, New York (1951–59), singing an extensive repertory of Italian and French 19th-century operas.

Demessieux, Jeanne-Marie-Madeleine (1921–68) French organist and composer. A pupil of Dupré, she became professor at the Liège conservatory in 1952 and combined a recitalist's career with several ecclesiastical appointments. Her compositions are mainly for organ.

demisemiquaver A note having half the time value of a *semiquaver and a thirty-second that of a semibreve. In modern notation it is depicted as a filled-in circle with a tail to which triple bars (or hooks) are attached. US: **thirty-second note**. See **Appendix, Table 1**.

Demus, Jörg (1928–) Austrian pianist. In addition to his career as a recitalist, Demus also often appears as an accompanist for such artists as Fischer-Dieskau and Suk. He has a keen interest in collecting historical keyboard instruments and also writes on music.

Denisov, Edison (1929–) Soviet composer. Denisov has been influenced by Russian folk music but has also made use of serial techniques, mobile elements, graphic notation, and electronics. His works include the opera Ivan the Soldier (1959), the cantata Solnze Inkov (1964), concertos for cello (1972), piano (1975), and flute (1975), orchestral music, chamber music (often with voice), piano pieces, and songs.

Dent, Edward Joseph (1876–1957) British musicologist, teacher, and writer. He was Professor of Music at Cambridge (1926–41) and President of the International Society for Contemporary Music (1923–37 and 1945 onwards). He was a well-known musical scholar and wrote English translations of operas by Mozart, Beethoven, and Verdi.

déploration see **dump**.

Dering (or **Deering**), **Richard** (c.1580–1630) English composer. He studied in Italy (1612) and worked as an organist in Brussels (1617–25) and at the court of Charles I (1625). Dering absorbed both the older English style and (after 1612) the new more chromatic Italian style with basso continuo. His works include the City Cryes and Country Cryes, fantasies, madrigals and canzonets with Italian words, and Latin motets.

Dernesch, Helga (1939–) Austrian soprano. Her studies at the Vienna conservatory (1957–61) led to a debut as Marianna in Boris Godunov. Subsequently she sang Wagner (at over 1.8 m (6 ft) tall, she was an ideal Valkyrie) and Strauss and recorded Isolde under Karajan. Dernesch was later associated with Scottish Opera.

descant (or **discant**) **1.** A treble part added to a well-known melody, usually a soprano part added to a hymn tune that is sung by tenors in the choir with or without participation by the congregation. The descant part may be written or improvised. **2.** The upper part of any vocal or instrumental polyphonic music. A **descant recorder** is the smallest and highest of the recorder family of instruments. **3.** Any second melody sung or played with an existing melody; usually the second melody is improvised while the existing melody is not. **4.** A style of *organum in which the voices proceed in a strict note-against-note style, as opposed to the melismatic style in which one note is sustained against florid writing in the upper part(s).

Dessau, Paul (1894–1979) German composer and conductor. He is best known for his work in collaboration with Bertolt Brecht from 1942, including incidental music to such plays as Mother Courage and one opera, The Trial of

Lucullus (1949). Other works include the *Lumumba Requiem* (1962), the opera *Lanzelot* (1969), and much chamber, orchestral, and film music.

détaché A bowing technique used to produce detached notes. In **grand détaché** the full bow is used for each note, the separation being produced by the change in direction of the bow. **Petit détaché** is performed at the point of the bow. [French, detached]

Deuteromelia A collection of English catches, rounds, and other popular pieces for voices, published in 1609. This collection is a sequel to *Pammelia, brought out the same year; both volumes were published by Thomas Ravenscroft.

Deutsch, Otto Erich (1883–1967) Austrian musicologist, writer, and art critic, who lived in England from the *Anschluss* in 1938 until 1952. Among his many publications are documentary biographies of Schubert (1913–14), Handel (1955), and Mozart (1961). He also devised a catalogue of Schubert's works (see **D.**).

deutscher Tanz (*or* **deutsche Tänz**) see **allemande.**

Deutsches Requiem, Ein see **German Requiem, A.**

Deutschland über Alles Patriotic German song with words by Hoffmann von Fallersleben. This song was written before the revolutionary troubles in Europe of 1848 and is an inspiration to national unity by the German people. The melody to which it is sung is the same as that of the Austrian national anthem – The *Emperor's Hymn* of Haydn.

Deux journées, Les (*The Two Days:* better known as *The Water Carrier*) Opera in three acts by Cherubini with libretto by Bouilly. First performance: Théâtre Feydeau, Paris, 1800. It is a rescue opera and influenced Beethoven in his choice of text for *Fidelio.*

development (*or* **working out** *or* **free fantasia**) The part of a composition in which the original *subjects are developed and expanded, usually before their restatement. See **sonata form.**

Devienne, François (1759–1803) French composer and bassoonist. He was first bassoonist at the Théâtre de Monsieur (1789) and Professor of Music at the Paris Conservatoire (1795). He wrote many works for wind instruments, including the tutor *La Méthode de flûte théorique et pratique* (1795), overtures and symphonies, and church music. His comic operas include *Le Mariage clandestin* (1790).

Devil's Trill, The Sonata for violin and continuo by Tartini. Composed: 1714. Tartini claimed to have written the sonata after having dreamt that the devil played it to him. The last movement includes the famous trill after which the sonata is named.

Diabelli, Anton (1781–1858) Austrian publisher and composer. In 1803 he went to Vienna, where he taught the piano and guitar. Many of his arrangements were published there, and in 1817 he established his own publishing firm. It soon began producing quantities of fashionable music and became Schubert's principal publisher. Diabelli composed a theme on which he invited 50 composers to write variations: Beethoven wrote 33 (the *Diabelli Variations*). Diabelli's compositions are in various genres but mainly for piano.

diabolus in musica The interval of the augmented fourth, which is difficult to sing and is therefore avoided in vocal music. The interval is also known as a **tritone** as it consists of three full tones (e.g. F–B). [Latin, from the medieval warning *Mi contra fa diabolus est in musica*, mi to fa is the devil in music (see **solmization**)]

Diaghilev, Sergei (1872–1929) Russian impresario. His first production in Paris was Mussorgsky's opera *Boris Godunov* (1908) but in 1909 he inaugurated his immensely successful Ballets Russes company, with whom he managed to associate many leading talents of the day: Nijinsky the dancer, Fokine the choreographer, and Bakst and Picasso, who designed costumes and sets. He commissioned several of Stravinsky's early masterpieces, including *The Firebird* (1910), *Petrushka* (1911), and *The Rite of Spring* (1913), and also commissioned works by Ravel, Debussy, Strauss, and Prokofiev.

Dialectic String quartet (Op. 15) by Alan Bush. Composed: 1929. The music is very much influenced by Bush's Marxist ideals and did much to establish his reputation as a composer.

Dialogues des Carmélites, Les (*The Carmelites*) Opera by Poulenc with libretto by Bernanos based on the novel *Last on the Scaffold*, by Gertrud von Le Fort. First performance (in Italian): La Scala, Milan, 1957. It is the story of nuns guillotined in 1794.

Diamond, David (1915–) US composer. He studied at the Eastman School and other musical institutions in New York and with Nadia Boulanger in France. After his stay in Paris he became a music professor at the University of Rome (1951) and settled in Florence (1963), returning to the USA in 1965. Since then he has taught and has been awarded various prizes for his compositions. Diamond's works, which show the craftsmanship of a 20th-century classicist, include eight symphonies and other orchestral music; chamber pieces, among them six string quartets; vocal music, including over 100 songs; and dramatic works, such as the ballet suite *Tom.*

diapason normal A former standard of *pitch in which A = 435 hertz.

diapasons The principal open *flue pipes of an *organ, which give the instrument its characteristic appearance and sound. [from Greek, through all]

diaphony 1. Two-voice *organum. In this sense the term was common in medieval music theory up to the 13th century; it was also used by the 14th-century theorist Johannes de Muris (c.1320). **2.** In ancient Greek and medieval music theory, dissonance (in this context any interval other than an octave, fifth, or fourth). [from Latin *diaphonia*, dissonance]

diatonic scale see **scales**.

Diaz, Alirio (1923–) Venezuelan guitarist. From 1954 he has taught at the Accademia Chigiana in Siena and has made concert appearances throughout Europe and the USA. Diaz has also edited much early guitar music.

Dibdin, Charles (1745–1814) British composer and dramatist. He wrote the libretti and music for many of his own stage works, the first of which was *The Shepherd's Artifice* (1765). He planned the Royal Circus (later Surrey Theatre) and after 1789 performed in his own table entertainments. In addition to many song collections (including sea songs) and works for the harpsichord, he wrote several novels and other books.

Dichterliebe Song cycle (Op. 48) by Schumann to 16 poems of Heine, taken from his collection *Lyrisches Intermezzo*. Composed: 1840. The cycle, which is essentially a succession of love songs, originally contained 20 songs but 4 were omitted for the first publication.

Dichtung Poem; hence **symphonische Dichtung**, tone (*or* symphonic) poem. [German]

Dickinson, Peter (1934–) British composer. Dickinson studied in the USA; since returning to Britain he has held academic posts. His music uses serial and aleatoric techniques, although Dickinson's style in music for amateur musicians is less complicated. His works include a string quartet (1958) and much other chamber music, choral works, and songs.

diction The means of conveying the words of a song from performer to listener. Indifferent enunciation, speech impediment, and extremes of local dialect can account for poor diction. Good diction, which necessitates the correct use of lips, teeth, tongue, and palate to produce clear consonants and pure vowels, is a prerequisite of a good singer. Good diction also implies the correct pronunciation of vowel sounds not encountered in the singer's native tongue.

didjeridoo (*or* **didgeridoo**) An Australian Aboriginal wooden trumpet made of one hollowed-out piece of wood some 1.5 m (5 ft) long.

Dido and Aeneas Opera in prologue and three acts by Purcell with text by Nahum Tate. First performance: Mr Josias Priest's Boarding School for Girls, Chelsea, London, 1689. The libretto is taken from Virgil's account of Dido's desertion by Aeneas and her subsequent suicide.

Dieren, Bernard van (1884–1936) Dutch composer. Van Dieren lived in London from 1906. His music is individual in its tonally extended polyphony and metrical freedom. Van Dieren's works include two symphonies (one of which is choral), six string quartets, and songs.

Dies irae The second section of the Requiem Mass (see **requiem**), following 'Requiem aeternam' and 'Kyrie eleison.' The chant, a *Sequence, survived the purges of the Council

Janet Baker in Dido and Aeneas *at Aldeburgh in 1962*

of Trent: it appeared later, for instance in 19th-century symphonic works, such as Berlioz's *Fantastic Symphony* and Saint-Saëns' *Danse macabre*. [Latin, day of wrath]

Dies Natalis Song cycle for high voice and strings by Finzi, to words of Traherne. Composed: 1926–39. The overall shape and construction of the cycle, with its setting of both prose and poetry, is very like that of a Bach cantata.

differential tone (*or* **difference tone**) see **combination tones**.

dim. see **diminuendo**.

diminished interval see **interval**; **third**; **fourth**; **fifth**; **seventh**.

diminuendo Diminishing. Used to indicate that the music becomes softer. Abbreviation: **dim.** [Italian]

diminution The shortening of a melody or phrase by reducing the time values of all its component notes by equal proportions, often by half. Compare **augmentation**.

d'Indy, Vincent (1851–1931) French composer, a pupil of Duparc and Franck. In 1894 he founded the Schola Cantorum in Paris: he later taught at the Conservatoire there. D'Indy's music reflects his early contact with the works of German and Russian composers: in spite of this the strongest influence remains that of his teacher Franck. Other features of his style include elements of French folk music, plainchant, and 16th-century polyphony. His works include operas and incidental music, orchestral works such as the **Symphony on a French Mountaineer's Song* (1886), piano and organ music, chamber music, and songs.

Dioclesian Masque by Betterson with music by Purcell, entitled in full *The Prophetess, or The History of Dioclesian*. Composed: 1690. Although called a masque, this work contains so much sung music that it is often described as an opera: in style it varies little from Purcell's only true opera, *Dido and Aeneas*. The scoring of this work is unusual in including a part for tenor oboe.

dirge A slow funeral or memorial lament. It was also used as a stylized instrumental piece; for example Holst's *Dirge for Two Veterans* (1914) and Stravinsky's *Funeral Dirge* (1908) for Rimsky-Korsakov.

discant see **descant**.

discord A chord of two or more notes that appears to the ear to be incomplete and to require to be followed by another chord to achieve *resolution. Compare **concord**.

disjunct motion see **motion**.

dissonance The sounding together of two or more notes to produce a *discord. Compare **consonance**. See also **beats**.

Dissonance Quartet String quartet in C major (K. 465) by Mozart. Composed: 1785. The opening to the first

movement is unusually dissonant, to the extent that the tonality of the work is not established for some time (hence the name). Despite the opening atonal introduction the remainder of the quartet is harmonically of a fairly conventional nature.

Distratto, Il Symphony No. 60 in C major by Haydn. Composed: 1774. Originally it was written as incidental music to an adaptation of Jean François Regnard's play *Le Distrait* (*The Absent-Minded Man*), first performed privately at Esterhazy. Haydn adapted the overture and five entr'actes from the play into a six-movement symphony, which was first performed in 1774 on 22 November (the feast day of St Cecilia, the patron saint of music). Much of the musical material is derived from folk songs, although these have never been positively identified.

Dittersdorf, Karl Ditters von (1739–99) Austrian composer. He travelled to Italy with Gluck (1763), becoming kapellmeister to the Bishop of Grosswardein (1765) and the Bishop of Breslau (1769). His operas were mainly singspiels, including *Doktor und Apotheker* (1786) and a version of *The Marriage of Figaro*. He also wrote church music, symphonies on Ovid's *Metamorphoses* (1785), chamber and keyboard works, and an autobiography, *Lebensbeschreibung* (published posthumously, 1801).

divertimento 1. An 18th-century orchestral piece comprising several short movements. See also **cassation. 2.** A light-hearted fantasia of popular opera arias. [French, amusement]

divertissement 1. A dramatic or allegorical dance scene, sometimes including popular songs or arias, in French baroque opera, notably in those of Lully and Rameau. **2.** Music performed between acts. **3.** A freely composed instrumental piece or fantasia employing popular melodies.

Divine Poem, The Tone poem for choir and orchestra (Op. 43) by Scriabin. Composed: 1902–04; first performance: Paris, 1905. The choir enters for the final movement of this work, which is also known as Scriabin's third symphony. The programmatic idea behind the work is an explanation of the composer's own beliefs about God and man and their interaction.

divisi Divided: an instruction in a score indicating that instruments having parts with double notes so marked should divide into two groups instead of all playing both notes. German: **geteilt** (*or* **getheilt**). [Italian]

divisions Ornamental melodic variations on a theme or *ground, originating in 16th-century Spain and found particularly in 17th-century English viol music. This manner of embellishment was outlined by (among others) Christopher Simpson in *The Division Violist* (1659). The 'division viol' was strictly speaking the bass, and the simplest divisions were made by inserting short notes between the main notes of the ground. Sometimes these would be played by the treble viol.

Djinns, Les (*The Jinns*) Tone poem by Franck, based on *Les Orientales* by Victor Hugo. Composed: 1884. The orchestration includes a prominent part for solo piano.

D.Mus. Doctor of Music.

do see **solmization.**

Doctor Gradus ad Parnassum see **Children's Corner.**

dodecaphony see **serialism; series; twelve-note composition.**

Dodgson, Stephen (1924–) British composer. Dodgson's style is instrumentally sensitive; his compositions include four concertos; music for guitar, harpsichord, and clavichord; vocal works; and chamber music.

doh see **tonic sol-fa.**

Dohnányi, Ernst von (1877–1960) Hungarian composer and pianist. Dohnányi was Professor of Music at the Berlin Hochschule für Musik (1908–19) and subsequently

Dohnányi enjoyed a great reputation as a pianist

director of the Budapest conservatory. After World War II he settled in the USA. Dohnányi's characteristically romantic music shows the last traces of the Hungarian nationalist tradition. His works include two symphonies; concertos and concert pieces for piano and orchestra, including the *Variations on a Nursery Song* (1913); and operas, piano music, and chamber works.

Doktor Faust Opera in six sections by Busoni, who drew his text from the ancient puppet play *Faust*. First performance: Dresden, 1925 (after the composer's death, having been completed by Jarnach).

dolce Sweet: a direction usually indicating a soft and gentle manner of playing or singing. [Italian]

dolente Sorrowful; mournful. [Italian]

Doles, Johann Friedrich (1715–97) German composer and organist, a pupil of J. S. Bach. He was cantor at Freiberg (1744–55) and at St Thomas's, Leipzig (1756–89), where he was visited by Mozart (1789). His cantatas and oratorios show the influence of Italian opera. He also wrote keyboard and other church music and a singing tutor, *Anfangsgründe zum Singen.*

Dolly Suite of six pieces for piano duet (Op. 56) by Fauré. Composed: 1893. Fauré dedicated the work to the daughter of Emma Bardac, who later became Debussy's second wife; in 1896 Rabaud orchestrated *Dolly* for use as a ballet score.

Dolmetsch British family of antique instrument makers and performers of early music. **Arnold Dolmetsch** (1858–1940), of Swiss descent, was a pioneer in the rediscovery and performance of old music. A collector and restorer of old instruments, he founded workshops for the production of recorders, harpsichords, and clavichords in Haslemere, where he also organized festivals of early music. These are now supervised by **Carl Dolmetsch** (1911–), his second son, who worked with **Mabel Dolmetsch** (1874–1963), Arnold's third wife and a player of the bass viol. This latter instrument she studied with **Hélène Dolmetsch** (1878–1924), Arnold's first wife.

dombra (*or* **domra**) see **balalaika.**

Domestic Symphony see **Symphonia domestica.**

dominant The fifth note above the *tonic of the major or minor *scale. For example, G is the dominant in the key of C major or C minor (see **degree**). The **dominant seventh** is the *chord formed on the dominant of the key with the (minor) *seventh included. For example in the key of C it is GBDF. The **dominant ninth** is the chord formed on the dominant of the key with the *ninth added. For example, in the key of F it is CEGB♭D.

The **Wechseldominante** (German, exchange dominant),

Gaetano Donizetti

Plácido Domingo in Verdi's Otello *in 1987*

or **secondary dominant**, is the dominant of the dominant; for example, in the key of F it would be G. See also **modes**.

Domingo, Plácido (1941–) Spanish tenor. After studying in Mexico he made his operatic debut as Alfredo in *La Traviata* (1960). He was a member of the Israeli National Opera (1962–65) before touring the world extensively. His repertory includes more than 40 roles.

Dona nobis pacem Cantata for solo voices, choir, and orchestra by Vaughan Williams with words from the Bible, Whitman, and Bright. First performance: 1936. Like the fourth symphony (1931–34), this cantata is often regarded as a plea for peace in the face of an increasing threat of European war.

Don Carlos Opera in five acts by Verdi with French libretto by Méry and du Locle based on a play by Schiller. First performance: Opéra, Paris, 1867. Set in the Spain of Philip II (bass), it is the story of Don Carlos, heir to the throne (tenor), and his love for Elizabeth de Valois (soprano), who is destined to be his father's bride.

Don Giovanni Opera in two acts by Mozart with libretto by Da Ponte. First performance: National Theatre, Prague, 1787. Based on the Spanish *Don Juan* legend, it is the story of the amorous adventures of Don Giovanni (baritone) with Donna Anna, Donna Elvira, and Zerlina (sopranos), aided by his servant and confidant Leporello (buffo bass). The stone statue of Donna Anna's father the Commendatore (bass), whom he has killed in a duel, finally drags him down to hell.

Donizetti, (Domenico) Gaetano (1797–1848) Italian composer. After studying with Mayr in Bergamo (1806–14) and Padre Mattei in Bologna (1814–17) he began composing operas, which were produced throughout Italy. His first real triumph was **Anna Bolena* (1830), which gained him an international reputation. He became Professor of Counterpoint at the Naples conservatory and in 1838 went to Paris, where *La *Fille du régiment* (1840) and *La *Favorita* (1840) were highly acclaimed. He returned to Italy in 1841, but his last great success, **Don Pasquale*, was given in Paris in 1843.

Donizetti was a prolific opera composer whose works, like Bellini's, characterized Italian romanticism. His operas have greater dramatic power than Bellini's, but demand vocal agility and bel canto singing; like Bellini, he conceived roles in terms of the particular singers for whom they were created. His other well-known operas are L'*Elisir d'amore (1832), *Lucrezia Borgia (1833), and *Lucia di Lammermoor (1835). He also composed orchestral and sacred music, vocal chamber music, 12 string quartets, piano pieces, and songs.

Don Juan Tone poem (Op. 20) by Richard Strauss, based on a dramatic poem by Lenau. Composed: 1881–89; first performance: Weimar, 1889. *Don Juan* was Strauss's first important work in this genre and its vivid orchestration and description of the amorous adventures of its hero created a sensation on its first performance. The score is prefaced by several quotations from Lenau's poem.

Don Pasquale Comic opera in three acts by Donizetti with text by Ruffini and the composer. First performance: Théâtre-Italien, Paris, 1843. Don Pasquale (bass), an old bachelor, has the tables turned on him when his thoughts turn to marriage.

Don Quixote Tone poem (Op. 35) by Richard Strauss, based upon the novel by Cervantes. Composed: 1897; first performance: Cologne, 1898. The work consists of an Introduction, Theme and Variations, and Finale, with Don Quixote portrayed by a solo cello and his companion Sacha Panza by a solo viola. In describing vividly the adventures of the hero a large orchestra is employed, including a wind machine.

Doppel Double. [German]

Doppelschlag A *turn. [German, literally double stroke]

doppio Double. Hence **doppio movimento**, at double the preceding speed. [Italian]

Dorati, Antal (1906–) Hungarian-born conductor and composer, a pupil of Bartók and Kodály. In 1947 Dorati became a US citizen. He conducted the Minneapolis Symphony Orchestra (1949–60), the BBC Symphony Orchestra (1963–67), the National Symphony Orchestra of Washington, and the Royal Philharmonic Orchestra (1975–). His recordings include the complete symphonies of Haydn.

Dorian mode see **modes.**

Dorian Toccata and Fugue Work for organ (BWV 538) by Bach. Composed: 1708–17. Despite the prevailing tonality of D minor, Bach does not write a B♭ in the key signature, giving the appearance that the work is in the Dorian *mode. In writing one fewer accidental in the key signature than necessary the composer followed a common baroque practice.

dot 1. A mark placed after a note in the notation to lengthen its time value. Until about the mid-18th century the dot indicated a lengthening of imprecise extent – usually between half and three-quarters of its value. In 1769 Leopold Mozart introduced the double dot; thereafter a single dot lengthened a note by half its value and a double dot by half its value again. Notes thus lengthened are called **dotted notes. 2.** A mark placed above or below a note to indicate that it should be played staccato.

double A variation: used especially in baroque instrumental music to indicate an ornamented repeat of the main theme. [French]

doublé A *turn. [French]

double bar A pair of bar lines placed close together to signify that a piece of music, or a section of it, has come to an end. It may be preceded or followed by a *repeat sign.

double bass A bowed four-stringed instrument that is the lowest and largest of the *violin family. Its strings are tuned at intervals of a fourth, the lowest being E three octaves below middle E (i.e. E, A, D, G). Its range is about two and a half octaves but this can be extended downwards by tuning down the bottom string or by adding a fifth string tuned to C four octaves below middle C. This can be reduced a semitone to continue the tuning in fourths. Two types of bow are used: the French bow, which is held overhand as a violin bow, and the Simandl bow, which is held with the palm up as in bowing a viol. The instrument was developed in the 16th century from the violone (see **viol family**) and has been a standard orchestral instrument of the string section since the 18th century. Its repertoire includes music by Boccherini, Beethoven, Schubert, and Richard Strauss. It is also used extensively in jazz and popular music, usually being played pizzicato.

double flat A sign (♭♭) placed before a note to reduce its pitch by a whole tone. See also **accidental.**

double-reed instruments see **reed instruments.**

double sharp A sign (𝄪) placed before a note to raise its pitch by a whole tone. See also **accidental.**

double stopping The stopping of two strings on a bowed stringed instrument to produce a chord.

double-whole note see **breve.**

doux (or fem. **douce**) Sweet. Hence **doucement**, sweetly. See also **dolce.** [French]

Dowland, John (1563–1626) English composer, singer, and lutenist. While in Paris in 1580 he was converted to Roman Catholicism but in 1595 he recanted. He served at the courts of Brunswick and Hessen, visited Venice and Florence, and was lutenist to the King of Denmark (1598–1606). He returned to England in 1606 and was musician to James I (1612–26). Dowland's chief importance lies in his songs, published in four books of ayres (1597, 1600, 1603, and 1612). In them he achieved the drama and passion that makes him the greatest of the songwriters of the period. Although Dowland never wrote any madrigals, his songs reveal the influence of that genre, especially in the use of word painting, chromaticism, and declamation. His famous *Flow my teares* (*Lachrimae*), typically melancholy, was frequently adapted as an instrumental pavan. His son, **Robert Dowland** (1591–1641), also a lutenist and composer, compiled the anthology *A Musicall Banquet* (1610), which contains three songs by his father.

downbeat The downward beat of a conductor's baton, which indicates the stressed beats of a bar, especially the first beat. The **upbeat**, the upward movement of the baton, indicates an unstressed beat, especially the last beat of the bar. Thus the note or notes preceding the first bar line of a composition (i.e. before the first stressed beat) are referred to as the upbeat.

down bow The action of bowing a stringed instrument in which the player pulls the bow from the heel towards the point. Compare **up bow.**

Downes, Edward Thomas (1924–) British conductor. He was associate conductor at the Royal Opera (1952–69) and of the Australian Opera (1971–77).

Downes, Ralph (1904–) British organist, trained at the Royal College of Music and Oxford. In addition to his appearances as a recitalist, Downes has also worked as an organ designer, the most notable example of his work being the organ in the Festival Hall.

Down in the Valley American folk opera in one act by Kurt Weill with text by Arnold Sundgaard. First performance: Indiana University, Bloomington, 1948. It incorporates a number of folk songs into a score composed in folk style.

Draghi, Giovanni Battista (1640–1708) Italian composer, harpsichordist, and organist, resident in England. He came to England to further Charles II's plans for establishing opera. He became first organist at the queen's Catholic chapel in 1673 and at James II's private chapel in 1687. His works are mainly instrumental music for plays, including Shadwell's *The Tempest* (1674); he also set Dryden's *Song for St Cecilia's Day* (1687).

Dragonetti, Domenico (1763–1846) Italian double-bass player and composer. He spent much of his life in London: with the cellist Robert Lindley (1777–1855) he became a feature of English concert life. His output includes several concertos for double bass as well as chamber music.

dramma Drama. Hence **dramma per musica**, drama by music – an Italian term used in the 17th and 18th centuries for opera (see **opera seria**). [Italian]

Dream of Gerontius, The Oratorio for solo voices, choir, and orchestra (Op. 38) by Elgar, to words by Cardinal Newman. First performance: Birmingham, 1900. The work concerns man's death and the eventual fate of his soul, as seen in Gerontius himself.

Dreigroschenoper, Die see **Threepenny Opera, The.**

Dresden, Sem (1881–1957) Dutch composer and conductor, a pupil of Pfitzner and principal of The Hague conservatory. From an early impressionist style his work developed through a more contrapuntal manner to encompass large-scale religious works, such as the *Chorus Symphonicus* (1944) and the oratorio *Saint Antoine* (1955). Other works include chamber and orchestral music and the opera *François Villon* (1957).

Dresden Amen A threefold version of 'Amen,' particularly associated with the Royal Chapel of Dresden, from which the name is derived. This setting was composed (*c.*1764) by J. G. Naumann, using a traditional melody; it is quoted by many later composers, including Wagner in his music drama *Parsifal.*

drones The pipes forming part of a set of *bagpipes that provide a continuous bass above which the melody is played on the chanter. There are usually two to four drones and one chanter, but bagpipes from various parts of the world have different numbers. Some stringed instruments have *sympathetic strings (*or* **drone strings**) to produce a drone bass similar to that of the bagpipes.

Druckman, Jacob (1928–) US composer, a pupil of Persichetti, Mennin, and Copland. Druckman has made much use of electronic music, often in dramatic combination with acoustic instruments. His works include a violin concerto (1956), *Dark Upon the Harp* (1962), *The Sound of Time* (1965), the *Animus* series for instruments and tape (1966), *Windows* (1972), *Chiaroscuro* (1976), and chamber music and songs.

Drum Mass Mass in C major by Haydn. Composed: 1796. Haydn himself called the work *Missa in tempore belli* (*Mass in Time of War*), but the important role of the kettledrum in the mass has led to the use of this more common name.

Drum-Roll Symphony Symphony No. 103 in E♭ major by Haydn. Composed: 1795. The name of this symphony, which was written for the English concert manager Salomon (see **Salomon Symphonies**), comes from the prominent kettledrum roll at the opening of the first movement.

drums A family of *percussion instruments of great antiquity and great variety. All rely on the production of sound by striking a stretched skin or membrane. The *kettledrums (*or* timpani) of the orchestra can be tuned to

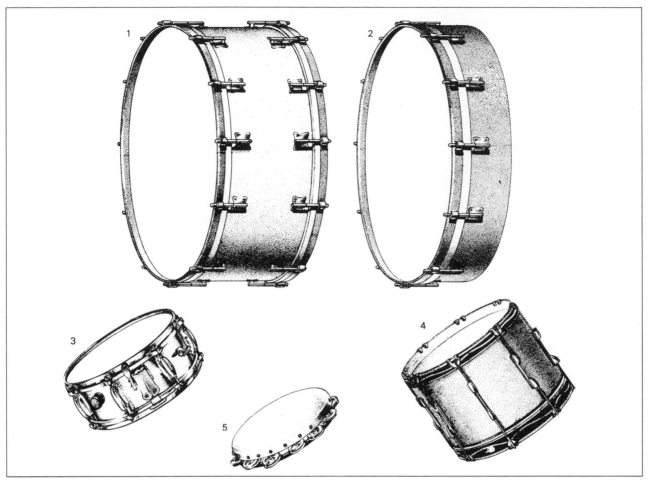

Modern orchestral drums include (1) the double-headed bass drum, (2) the single-headed gong drum, (3) the side drum, (4) the tenor drum and (5) the tambourine

a specific pitch, whereas other orchestral drums (see **bass drum; tenor drum; side drum**) cannot. See also **membranophone; tabor.**

Dryden, John (1631–1700) English dramatist, essayist, and poet. He arranged for Purcell to write music for his plays *King Arthur* (1691) and *Amphytrion*. Various odes of Dryden were set by Clarke, Handel, and Blow. He also wrote an essay on opera.

dry recitative see **recitative.**

Dubois, (François Clément) Théodore (1837–1924) French composer, organist, and teacher. He studied with Marmontel, Benoit, Bazin, and Thomas at the Paris Conservatoire. He held posts at Ste Clotilde and the Madeleine, where he succeeded Saint-Saëns as organist in 1877. In 1896 he became director of the Conservatoire. Dubois wrote stage and instrumental works, but it is for his church music and theoretical writings on harmony and counterpoint that he is best remembered.

Due Foscari, I (*The Two Foscari*) Opera in three acts by Verdi with libretto by Piave based on Byron's play. First performance: Teatro Argentina, Rome, 1844. It is the tragedy of the octogenarian doge Francesco Foscari (baritone) and his son Jacopo (tenor), who are caught in the changing fortunes of Venetian politics of the 15th century.

Duenna, The 1. Comic opera by Thomas Linley, father and son, and other composers with text by the elder Linley's son-in-law, Richard Brinsley Sheridan. First performance: Covent Garden, London, 1775. **2.** Opera by Roberto Gerhard, who wrote his own libretto from Sheridan's *The Duenna* with additional lyrics by Christopher Hassell. First performance: 1948. **3.** See **Betrothal in a Monastery.**

duet A composition for two equally matched voices or instruments with or without accompaniment. The term *duo is often preferred for instrumental works. A **piano duet** is a work for two pianists at one keyboard. French: **duo**; German: **Duett**; Italian: **duo, duetto.**

Paul Dukas

duetto see **duet.**

Dufay, Guillaume (*c*.1400–74) French composer. He was a choirboy and clerk at Cambrai Cathedral from 1409 until 1413 or 1414 and may have been in the service of the Malatesta of Pesaro (*c*.1420–*c*.1426). A member of the papal chapel (1428–33, 1435–37), Dufay was employed at the Savoyard court (1434–35) and in 1438–39 represented Cambrai at the Council of Basle. Apart from two further periods spent at the court of Savoy (1450, 1452–57), Dufay worked at Cambrai from 1439 until his death. His works cover a wide range of styles, from the early chanson *Resveilliés vous* (1423) and the isorhythmic motet *Nuper rosarum flores* (1436) to the later cyclic masses written for Cambrai, including those based on *Ecce ancilla* (1462–63) and *Ave regina celorum* (1472).

Dukas, Paul (1865–1935) French composer. Dukas studied at the Paris Conservatoire (1882–88), where he subsequently became Professor of Composition (1913). Although small, Dukas' output was highly polished and individual in its avoidance of a distinctly impressionistic style. His skilled orchestration and sense of pace and climax is displayed in his most popular work, the orchestral scherzo *L'Apprenti sorcier* (1897; see **Sorcerer's Apprentice, The**). His other works include the opera *Ariane et Barbe-bleue* (1907), the ballet *La *Péri* (1912), a symphony in C (1897) and other orchestral works, and piano music.

Duke, Vernon (Vladimir Dukelsky; 1903–69) Russian-born US composer. An early commission from Diaghilev established Dukelsky's reputation; in the USA his music was promoted by Koussevitsky. As Vernon Duke he became known as a composer of popular songs, his best-known song being 'April in Paris.'

Dukelsky, Vladimir see **Duke, Vernon.**

dulciana An organ *stop in which the soft delicate sound is produced by diapason (in the UK) or string-toned (in the USA) *flue pipes. The **dulciana mixture** is a *mixture stop of soft tone usually found on the swell manual or the echo manual.

dulcimer A board *zither in which the strings are struck with sticks with a flat blade. It originated in Persia and Iraq in the 11th century. The Persian **santir** consists of a box with three sound holes and three courses of metal strings pegged to its opposite sides. The dulcimer became popular in Europe between the 17th and 19th centuries, but was not exported to China until about 1800. The modern *piano is in some respects a dulcimer with a keyboard. The only form of dulcimer still in use is the Hungarian *cimbalom.

dulcitone see **celeste.**

Dumas, Alexandre (Dumas fils; 1824–95) French playwright and novelist. He was author of *La Dame aux camélias* (1848), which he dramatized as *Camille* (1852). Verdi based his opera *La Traviata* (1853) on this play.

Dumbarton Oaks Concerto Concerto for 15 instruments by Stravinsky. Composed: 1938. The title comes from the residence of an important Washington patron, R. W. Bliss, who commissioned the work. In style the concerto, which is in three movements, owes much to the influence of the concerto grosso, in particular the *Brandenburg Concertos* of Bach.

dumka (*pl*. **dumky**) 1. A Slavonic folk ballad usually describing some heroic deed, though contemplative and melancholic in character. 2. An instrumental form invoking various moods from sadness to exuberant happiness. The form was favoured by Dvořák, for example in the piano trio *Dumky* (1891), the elegy *Dumka* (1876), and in *Furiant with Dumka* (1884).

dump (*or* **dompe**) A 16th-century English piece, generally for lute but sometimes for keyboard. It was probably elegiac, equivalent to the French **déploration**; an example is 'The Duke of Somersettes Dompe' (*c*.1560). It usually consisted of variations on a harmonic *ground bass.

Dunhill, Thomas Frederick (1877–1946) British composer, a pupil of Stanford and later a teacher at the Royal College of Music, London. Of his works, Dunhill's educational music, mostly for piano, is most familiar today; his other compositions include a symphony, operas, chamber music, and songs.

Dunstable, John (*c*.1385–1453) English composer, probably in the service of John, Duke of Bedford, and possibly a canon of Hereford Cathedral (from 1419). He was buried at the parish church of St Stephen, Walbrook, in London. Of Dunstable's output, 61 compositions have survived in a total of 41 sources. They include settings of individual mass movements, mass cycles, isorhythmic motets, votive antiphons, and two secular works. The isorhythmic motets are probably among the early works and include *Preco preheminencie* (*c.*1416) and *Albanus roseo rutilat* (?1426); the four-part *Descendi in ortum meum* provides an example of his later work. Dunstable was foremost in the promotion of the English style on the Continent and the smooth consonance of his music influenced that of Dufay, Binchois, and later composers.

duo A composition for two instruments, or the players who perform such a composition. For example, a violinist and a pianist who play sonatas together may be referred to as a duo. Duo pianists play works for two pianos. See also **duet**.

Duparc, Henri (Marie Eugène Henri Fouques D.; 1848–1933) French composer. After piano and composition lessons from Franck he began composing, but severe self-criticism led him to destroy much of his music and in 1885 a nervous disease forced him to abandon composition. Most important in Duparc's slender output are his 16 songs – well-crafted and sensitive miniatures setting carefully selected poetry; they include *Chanson triste* (1868), *L'Invitation au voyage* (1870), *Elégie* (1874), *Extase* (1874), and

Jacqueline du Pré

Testament (1883). He also wrote a few choral, orchestral, and other instrumental works.

duplet (*or* **couplet**) A group of two notes of equal value played in the time of three notes. They are written tied together with a small figure 2 placed on the tie. One of the notes can be replaced by a rest.

duple time A form of musical time in which there are two beats in the bar. For example 2/4 denotes two crotchets (which is *simple time) and 6/8 denotes six quavers in two groups of three (which is *compound time). Compare **triple time**. See **Appendix, Table 4**.

Duplex-Coupler piano A piano designed in the 1920s by Emanuel *Moór, having two keyboards an octave apart.

du Pré, Jacqueline (1945–87) British cellist. She studied with Tortelier and Rostropovich and made her debut in 1961 with Elgar's cello concerto. She married the pianist and conductor Daniel *Barenboim in 1967. When multiple sclerosis put an end to her performing career (1973) she remained active as a cello teacher.

Dupré, Marcel (1886–1971) French organist and composer, a pupil of Vierne and Widor and teacher of Mesiaen. Dupré was the first organist to present the complete cycle of Bach's organ music. His basically tonal compositional idiom is extended by polytonality and chromatic writing. His works include many compositions for organ, works for organ and orchestra, choral music, and songs.

Dur Major (key), e.g. **G dur**, G major. [German, literally hard]

Durante, Francesco (1684–1755) Italian composer and teacher, whose pupils included Jommelli, Piccinni, Pergolesi, and Paisiello. He held teaching positions at various Naples conservatories, including the Conservatorio di Santa Maria di Loreto (1742–55). His compositions include no operas but a great deal of church music in the style of Palestrina and keyboard works.

Durchführung *Development. [German, literally a working through]

durchkomponiert see **through-composed song**.

Durey, Louis (1888–1979) French composer. Durey attended the Schola Cantorum in Paris; he later became a member of Les *Six. Durey's music combines influences of Debussy, Stravinsky, and Satie: his compositions include three string quartets and other chamber works, songs, and choral music. See also **progressist**.

Durkó, Zsolt (1934–) Hungarian composer, a pupil of Petrassi and Farkas. Such works as *Hungarian Rhapsody* (1964) and *Fioriture* (1967) show the influences of folk music and medieval music, respectively. Later works, with an emphasis on melody and sonority, include *Altamira*

(1968), *Turner Illustrations* (1976), and the music drama *Mózes* (1977).

Duruflé, Maurice (1902–) French composer and organist, a pupil of Vièrne and Dukas. He became a professor at the Paris Conservatoire in 1943. The principal influences on Duruflé's small output of compositions are the music of Fauré and plainchant. His works include a requiem (1947) and a mass (1967), organ music, chamber music, and orchestral compositions.

Dušek, Franz Xaver (1731–99) Czech pianist, teacher, and composer. He was a friend of Mozart and taught Kozeluch. He also wrote symphonies, chamber music, and keyboard works.

Dussek (*or* **Dusík**), **Johann Ladislav** (1760–1812) Czech pianist, organist, and composer. He toured widely, studying with C. P. E. Bach in Hamburg (1783) and residing in London (1792–c.1800). He was composer to Count Talleyrand from 1808. Dussek's many keyboard works show the development of the solo piano, for which he wrote a tutor (1796); he also wrote two operas and chamber music.

Dutilleux, Henri (1916–) French composer, a pupil of Gallon and Busser. His works, which show a particular concern for form and structure, include two symphonies (1951, 1959), the ballet *Le Loup* (1953), *Métaboles* (1965), a cello concerto (1970) inspired by Baudelaire, *Timbres, espace, mouvement* (1978) for orchestra, and much incidental and film music.

Dvořák, Antonín (1841–1904) Czech composer. The son of a village innkeeper and butcher, he learnt to play the violin with great skill as a child and was sent to the organ school in Prague. During his early musical career he played the viola and violin in several orchestras, including the orchestra of the National Theatre, Prague, under the direction of Smetana. By 1874 Dvořák had written two symphonies, a considerable amount of chamber music, and numerous songs and his first opera, *King and Collier*, had been given its first performance. During this period of his life he was very poor, although his music had been heard at several successful concerts and his name was becoming known in his native country. In 1875 he was awarded a state grant by the Austrian government, one result of which was that he became a friend of Brahms, who both gave him encouragement and found him an influential publisher. The nationalistic *Moravian Duets* (1876) for soprano and contralto and **Slavonic Dances* (1878, 1886) for piano, which were based on Czech folk music, helped him to gain worldwide recognition. His choral work the *Stabat Mater*

(1877) was especially popular in Britain. In 1892 he was offered the directorship of the newly established National Conservatory of Music in New York. He accepted the post and stayed for three years, during which time he composed his ninth symphony, **From the New World* (1893), which was influenced by both Negro spirituals and his own native Bohemian music. On his return to Prague in 1895 he became head of the city's conservatory.

Dvořák composed a total of nine operas but these have not achieved the same success as his other works. Among his orchestral compositions are nine symphonies (including two published posthumously); these were originally wrongly ordered but since World War II the convention has been to number all the symphonies chronologically. Other orchestral works include the tone poems *The Water Goblin* (1896), *The Noonday Witch* (1896), *The Golden Spinning-Wheel* (1896), *The Wood Dove* (1896), and *Hero's Song* (1871); seven overtures, including **Carnival* (1891), **In Nature's Realm* (1891), and **Othello* (1892); a piano concerto, violin concerto, and cello concerto; and rhapsodies and dances, including the three **Slavonic Rhapsodies* (1878). He also composed a wealth of chamber music, including 13 string quartets, 3 piano trios, a terzetto (1887) for two violins and viola, and the *Dumky Trio* (1891) for piano, violin, and cello. His piano music includes Slavonic dances, humoresques, waltzes, and mazurkas and he also wrote such choral works as the cantata *The *Spectre's Bride* (1884), the oratorio **St Ludmilla* (1885), a mass (1887), and a requiem (1890).

Dykes, John Bacchus (1823–76) British composer. He had lessons with Walmisley at Cambridge and in 1849 became precentor and minor canon at Durham Cathedral. He wrote many hymn tunes, several of which are still used (e.g. *Horbury*: 'Nearer my God to Thee').

dynamics The degree of volume called for in the performance of a piece of music. The **dynamic marks** (*or* **markings**) are the directions and symbols used to indicate loudness and softness.

Dyson, Sir George (1883–1964) British composer. Dyson was director of the Royal College of Music, London 1937–52; he was knighted in 1941. His compositions include a symphony (1937) and other orchestral works, a violin concerto (1943), chamber music, and piano pieces.

Dzerzhinsky, Ivan (1909–) Soviet composer, a pupil of Gnessin. In 1935 he produced the model Soviet folk-song opera, *The Quiet Don*. He followed this with a further eight operas, including *Virgin Soil Upturned* (1937) and *The Fate of Man* (1960). Other works include concertos, orchestral music, and film scores.

E

E The keynote of the scale of E major. The frequency of E above *middle C is 329.6 hertz (A = 440 hertz).

Eagles, Solomon see Eccles, Solomon.

Early Music Consort of London A British ensemble formed in 1967 by David *Munrow (recorder) with James Bowman (countertenor), Oliver Brookes (viols), Christopher Hogwood (harpsichord), and (after 1969) James Tyler (lute). The group performs medieval and Renaissance music on original instruments in an authentic and exuberant way, introducing modern audiences to a large repertory of music previously unperformed. It also gives first performances of British works; for example Peter Maxwell Davies used it in his opera *Taverner* (1972).

East, Michael (*c*.1580–*c*.1648) English composer. He was organist of Lichfield Cathedral and wrote anthems, music for viols, and madrigals, one of which is a contribution to the anthology *The Triumphs of Oriana* (1601).

Easter Oratorio Oratorio by Bach for solo voices, choir, and orchestra. Composed: 1736. The ten sections of the oratorio are based upon an earlier work – the secular cantata *Entfliehet, verschwindet, entweichet ihr Sorgen*, with words by Picander, written for the birthday of the Duke of Saxony in 1725. In its original version the music of the cantata has not survived, but it has been reworked to form the musical basis of the oratorio.

Eberlin, Johann Ernst (1702–62) German composer and organist. He was organist (1729) and kapellmeister (1749) at Salzburg Cathedral and court. His works, which were collected by Mozart, include a large number of sacred compositions as well as some music for the theatre, sinfonias, and toccatas and fugues for organ.

Ebony Concerto Work for solo clarinet and jazz band by Stravinsky. Composed: 1945. This piece was written for the band of the jazz clarinetist Woody Hermann, who gave the first performance in 1946. The introduction of jazz elements into serious music was not new to Stravinsky; in composing this work he was continuing a practice he established over 20 years previously with *Ragtime* (1918) and *Piano Rag-Music* (1919).

Eccles (*or* **Eagles**), **Solomon** (1618–83) English composer. He taught in London (*c*.1646), but after becoming a Quaker (*c*.1660) he publicly burnt his music and instruments; during the Great Plague (1665) he ran about the streets of London naked with a burning brazier on his head, urging people to repent. Later he travelled to the West Indies (1671–80). His works include the treatise *A Musick-Lector* (1667), songs, and instrumental music.

Another **Solomon Eccles**, possibly his son, was a violinist at court (*c*.1685–*c*.1700). His works for violin appear in *The Division Violin* (enlarged second edition, 1685). Another son, **John Eccles** (1668–1735), was also a composer. From 1694 he was a member of the Royal Chapel and in 1700 he was appointed Master of the King's Music. John Eccles wrote much incidental music for the theatre, including settings for Congreve's *Judgment of Paris* (1700); he also wrote music for the coronation of Queen Anne (1702) and instrumental music.

echo manual see **organ**.

eclogue A short poem often with a pastoral theme, sometimes in dialogue form. Musical settings appeared in 16th-century Italian dramatic music and in English madrigals; an example is Kirbye's setting of 'Up then, Melpomene' (1597) from Spenser's 'November Eclogue' in *The Shepheardes Calender* (1579).

écossaise A kind of *contredanse in duple rhythm that appeared in the classical, mainly piano, repertory after 1780; e.g. Schubert's *Zwei Ecossaisen* (1824). [French, Scottish; despite the name the dance seems to have had nothing to do with Scotland]

Edgar Opera in four acts by Puccini with libretto by Fontana based on Musset's melodrama *La Coupe et les lèvres*. First performance: La Scala, Milan, 1889. The unwieldy nature of the libretto has been blamed for the opera's lack of success.

Edinburgh International Festival An annual festival founded in 1947 in Edinburgh. It presents operas, concerts, recitals, dance programmes, and nonmusical events and other unofficial programmes (known as the Fringe). It has always had an international character, featuring foreign opera productions (by the Hamburg, Milan, Prague, Florence, and Stockholm companies among others) and celebrated international orchestras and soloists. Several premieres have been given there.

Egdon Heath Tone poem by Holst, based on *The Return of the Native* by Thomas Hardy. First performance: New York, 1928. Holst's inspiration for this work comes from the description of Egdon Heath in Wessex (Dorset) that is contained in Hardy's novel.

Egk, Werner (W. Mayer; 1901–83) German composer, pupil of Carl Orff in Munich. Egk's music uses dissonance freely as an extension of tonality. His compositions include operas, ballets, chamber and orchestral music, and choral works.

Egmont Incidental music (Op. 84) by Beethoven to the drama by Goethe. First performance: Vienna, 1810. The original score included an overture and eight other pieces (including songs) to accompany the drama; today the overture is frequently performed as a separate concert work.

Eichheim, Henry (1870–1942) US composer. Eichheim's interest in oriental music led him to travel widely in the Far East, collecting music and instruments that he later used in his own compositions. These are mostly orchestral works on oriental subjects, including the suite *Burma* (1927).

Eighteen-Twelve (*or* **1812**) **Overture** Overture (Op. 49) by Tchaikovsky. Composed: 1882. It was written to commemorate the seventieth anniversary of the retreat from Moscow of Napoleon's army (1812). In style this work is rather similar to the *Battle Symphony* of Beethoven and is often reorchestrated with the addition of cannon and mortar effects. Tchaikovsky includes the 'Marseillaise' to represent the French army and the Russian national anthem to represent the Russian army.

eight foot see **foot**.

eighth note see **quaver**.

Eight Songs for a Mad King Work for singer/actor and six instrumentalists by Peter Maxwell Davies, with words by Randolph Stow and King George III. Composed: 1963. The work is a study of King George III and his madness and Maxwell Davies places as much importance on the dramatic as on the musical aspect. Some of the performers sit in cages while they play and the singer, who plays the king, is suitably attired for the part.

Eine kleine Nachtmusik (*A Little Night Music*) Serenade for string quartet and double bass (K. 525) by Mozart. Composed: 1787. Despite its original scoring the great popularity of this work has led to many performances using a full string orchestra rather than the intended quintet.

Einem, Gottfried von (1918–) Austrian composer, best known for his works for the theatre. Although eclectic in his use of avant-garde techniques, Einem's style is distinctive in its dramatic use of dissonance and rhythm. His compositions include operas, such as *Der Prozess* (*The Trial*, 1953) after Kafka, ballet music, and orchestral works.

Einleitung Introduction; prelude. [German]

Einstein, Alfred (1880–1952) German musicologist. He was music critic of the *Berliner Tageblatt* (1927–33) and of *Zeitschrift für Musikwissenschaft* (1918–33). In 1939 he settled in the USA. He wrote many books, including biographies of Schubert (1951) and Mozart (1947) as well as *The Italian Madrigal* (1949).

Eisler, Hanns (1898–1962) German composer, a pupil of Schoenberg in Vienna. Eisler's early works adopt Schoenberg's serial technique; his later style is simpler, his collaboration with the writer Bertolt Brecht inspiring music reminiscent of Weill. His output includes the opera *Johannes Faustus* (1953), incidental music to plays of Brecht, orchestral works, chamber music, and songs.

eisteddfod A competitive festival of music and literature of Welsh origin. Such festivals date back to the Middle Ages (or even earlier), when they were arranged to assess the accomplishments of the bards. Between the Tudor period and the 18th century, the standing of the bards declined and the gatherings ceased. During the 18th century the tradition was revived and the term eisteddfod was first used: by the 19th century the festivals flourished and choral singing became a predominant feature of them. The National Eisteddfod was founded in 1880 and is held in a different town each year; it fosters Welsh traditions and culture and many local eisteddfods are modelled on it. At the International Eisteddfod, held annually at Llangollen since 1947, choirs and dancers from all over the world compete. [Welsh, session]

Ek, Gunnar (1900–) Swedish composer. Ek studied at the Stockholm conservatory and has held positions as cellist and organist. His compositions include three symphonies, a piano concerto, organ music, and songs.

electric action see **action**.

electronic music Music in which various musical ideas are recorded on tape and subsequently reproduced by electroacoustical means, the performance thus being the playback of the tape. Although individual electronic instruments can be used in conjunction with conventional ones, as in the use of the *ondes Martenot in Messiaen's *Turangalîla*, this use of electronic instruments does not constitute electronic music proper. The composition of electronic music began during the early 1950s and was anticipated by the establishment in 1948 of a studio for *musique concrète in Paris by Schaeffer and Henry. Studios for the composition of electronic music were founded in Cologne (used by Stockhausen) and Milan (used by Berio and Maderna), as well as in several other European and US centres.

Originally electronic music referred only to music produced by electronic means, using such instruments as the *synthesizer and *ring modulator, as opposed to musique concrète, in which the sounds are produced either by conventional instruments or by natural noises, such as street cries. In both cases the sounds are then recorded and the tape is manipulated by means of variations of speed, frequency, amplitude, etc. The distinction between musique concrète and electronic music has now disappeared, with the result that both types of music are now known collectively as electronic music. Composers who have employed this style include Ligeti, Boulez, Xenakis, Cage, Varèse, Nono, Reich, and Riley.

electronic organ An organ in which electric signals created by electronic oscillators are amplified and converted into sound by a loudspeaker. Modern instruments offer a wide range of sounds that simulate not only the instruments of the orchestra but also the piano and other instruments used in light music. Internal computers and 'harmonizers' can also provide a harmonized rhythmic accompaniment in a variety of tempi to a melody picked out on the keyboard with one finger. The instrument is thus capable of functioning as a concert organ or theatre organ as well as enabling a beginner to create the impression that he is a competent musician playing as a member of an ensemble.

Electronic Poem Work in electronic medium by Varèse. Composed: 1958. In this piece Varèse employs a wide variety of taped sounds, ranging from pure electronically produced sounds to the use of piano, percussion, and voices. The latter sounds are either reproduced exactly or are modified by manipulation of the tape. The first performance took place at the Brussels Festival of 1958, where over 400 loudspeakers were used to transmit the music.

elegy A slow plaintive song. An example is Berlioz's 'Elégie en prose' from *Neuf mélodies irlandaises* (1830), dedicated to Harriet Smithson, the object of the composer's passions. French: **élégie**.

Elegy for Young Lovers Opera in three acts by Henze with libretto by W. H. Auden and Chester Kallman. First performance (in German): Schwetzingen Festival, 1961. Mittenhofer, a poet (baritone), is writing a poem (*Elegy for Young Lovers*) and the opera is concerned with the vicissitudes of the creative process, from inspiration to the final reading before a fashionable audience.

Elektra Opera in one act by Richard Strauss with libretto by Hofmannsthal, based on Sophocles. First performance: Royal Opera, Dresden, 1909. It is the story of the revenge of Elektra (soprano) for the death of her father, Agamemnon.

Elgar, Edward (1857–1934) British composer and violinist. Elgar received little formal training in music. Recognition as a composer came late, with the oratorio *Caractacus* (1898); the international success of his subsequent works

Elgar (left) at a recording studio with Adrian Boult

revealed Elgar as England's first composer of stature in more than two centuries. He was knighted in 1903 and made Master of the King's Music in 1924. By this time his composing career was virtually over (due to the shock of his wife's death in 1920). Elgar's position in the English musical tradition rests largely on his choral works, the most famous of which is the oratorio *The *Dream of Gerontius* (1900). *The *Apostles* (1903) and *The *Kingdom* (1906) were the first two works in a projected trilogy of oratorios, of which the third part was never written. Although his style owes much to Brahms, his music always retains a peculiarly English atmosphere, even in his two symphonies (1908, 1911). Other works include the *Enigma Variations* (1899) for orchestra; five *Pomp and Circumstance* marches; the overtures *Cockaigne* (1901) and *In the South* (1904); the *Wand of Youth Suite* (1907); a symphonic poem, *Falstaff* (1913); the symphonic prelude *Polonia* (1915); the cantatas *Spirit of England* (1916–17); and concertos for violin (1910) and cello (1919). His chamber music includes a string quartet, piano quintet, and violin sonata, all dating from 1918.

Elias see **Elijah**.

Elijah Oratorio for solo voices, choir, and orchestra (Op. 70) by Mendelssohn. First performance: Birmingham, 1846. The text is taken from the Bible and concerns the story of the Old Testament prophet Elijah. Although originally composed to German words, the first performance took place in England using an English translation. The original German version, *Elias*, was not performed until 1847.

Elisabetta, regina d'Inghilterra (*Elizabeth, Queen of England*) Opera in two acts by Rossini with libretto by Giovanni Schmidt. First performance: San Carlo, Naples, 1815. It is historically important because it is the first of Rossini's operas to be given orchestral accompaniment for all the recitatives and in it Rossini wrote out all the ornamentation fully. The opera relates the downfall of Norfolk (tenor) and the heroism of Leicester (tenor) during the reign of Queen Elizabeth I (soprano).

Elisir d'amore, L' (*The Love Potion*) Opera in two acts by Donizetti with libretto by Romani. First performance: Teatro della Canobbiana, Milan, 1832. Based on Scribe's *Le Philtre*, it tells of the love of Adina (soprano), a wealthy farm owner, and the peasant Nemorino (tenor), who drinks a bottle of wine, thinking it to be a love potion.

Elizalde, Federico (1908–79) Spanish composer. Elizalde studied in Madrid and with Bloch in California. His early music was clearly influenced by Falla; later works showed neoclassical tendencies. His output included the opera *Paul Gauguin* (1948), concertos for piano and violin, and much chamber music.

Ellis, Osian (1928–) British harpist. He has combined a career as an orchestral player, with the London Symphony Orchestra, with that of a recitalist. Both Hoddinott and Matthias have composed concertos for him.

Elman, Mischa (1891–1967) Russian-born US violinist. A pupil of Leopold Auer, he made his debut in 1904 in Berlin and rapidly established himself as one of the greatest violinists of his day. In 1926 he founded the Elman Quartet.

Eloy, Jean-Claude (1938–) French composer, a pupil of Milhaud and Boulez. He has made much use of aleatoric techniques and the application of mathematical permutation procedures, as in *Maches* (1967). Other works include *Equivalences* (1963), *Faisceaux-Diffractions* (1970), and *Shanti* (1975) for tape.

Elsner, Józef Antoni Franciszek (Joseph Anton Franciskus E.; 1769–1854) Polish composer and teacher. He conducted the opera orchestra in Lemberg (now Lvov; 1792–99) and the Warsaw Opera (1799–1824). In 1821 he became rector of the Warsaw conservatory, where he taught Chopin. His works include many operas, sacred music, cantatas, songs, eight symphonies, six string quartets, and piano pieces.

embouchure The position of the lips on the mouthpiece of a wind instrument. [French, mouthpiece]

Emperor Concerto Piano concerto No. 5 in E♭ major (Op. 73) by Beethoven. Composed: 1808. The derivation of the name is not certain; there is no apparent biographical justification for it, except for the grandiose mood of the concerto, and it is likely that the name was added by a later publisher. In structure the work is most unusual for a concerto, with a written-out cadenza for the pianist at the beginning of the first movement; in addition, the second and third movements are linked in the manner of later romantic concertos.

Emperor Jones Opera by Gruenberg with libretto by Kathleen de Jaffa based on Eugene O'Neill's play. First performance: Metropolitan Opera, New York, 1933. It is the story of a Black American railwayman who commits murder and becomes 'emperor' of a Caribbean island.

Emperor Quartet (German: *Kaiserquartett*) String quartet in C major (Op. 79 No. 3) by Haydn. Composed: 1797. In the slow movement Haydn writes a set of variations on *The *Emperor's Hymn*, the setting of the Austrian national anthem that he composed in 1797. During the course of the four variations Haydn places the theme successively in each instrument of the quartet.

Emperor's Hymn, The The Austrian national anthem. The words were written by Haschka in 1797 by request of the Imperial High Chancellor, who wanted Austria to have a national anthem that could compare favourably with the British anthem, 'God Save the King.' In the same year Haydn set the words to music, adapting a childhood folk tune for the melody. This version, with the words 'Gott erhalte Franz den Kaiser' ('May God uphold our Emperor Franz'), was used until the collapse of the Austrian Empire in 1918. When the Republic was established the old setting was retained for the national anthem, but the words were rewritten to begin 'Sei gesegnet ohne Ende' ('Be blessed for evermore'). Haydn himself used the melody for a set of variations in his *Emperor Quartet* and the same setting was also used for the German national anthem, *Deutschland über Alles*.

enchaînez Link together: a direction indicating that movements or sections of a piece should be played without a break in between. [French]

Enchanted Lake, The Tone poem (Op. 62) by Lyadov. Composed: 1909. Originally the musical material was contained in two sketches that Lyadov made for a proposed opera. When he abandoned this idea he collected some of the music into what he described as a 'fairy tale for orchestra.' There is no definite programme to the work; it simply describes a dark lake inhabited by water spirits.

Encina, Juan del (?1468–*c*.1529) Spanish composer, poet, and playwright. He was a chorister at Salamanca Cathedral (1484) and later became a graduate of the university there.

By 1492 he was in the service of the Duke of Alba, becoming Archdeacon of Málaga in 1509 and Prior of León from 1509 until his death. Encina was periodically active at Rome, his creative output including villancicos and several plays, a number of which were published.

encore 1. A call used in English (but the French use *bis) by an appreciative audience to encourage a performer to repeat all or part of a work just performed or to play some other short piece. **2.** A short piece of music played in response to the call for an encore. Most performers have one or two encores prepared, which they play if the response has been sufficiently warm. [French, again]

Enesco, Georges (1881–1955) Romanian composer, conductor, and violinist. Enesco studied the violin from an early age; he later studied composition in Vienna and, with Fauré and Massenet, in Paris. The romantic style of his compositions stems from nationalist traditions. Enesco's works include the opera *Oedipe* (1931); orchestral music, including three completed symphonies and two *Romanian Rhapsodies* (1901–02); chamber music; piano works; and songs. He was also a teacher of the violin, numbering Menuhin among his distinguished pupils.

Enfance du Christ, L' see **Childhood of Christ, The.**

Enfant et les sortilèges, L' (*The Child and the Spells*) Opera in two parts by Ravel with text by Colette. First performance: Monte Carlo, 1925. It is a fantasy in which furniture and toys come to life after a child has ill-treated them.

English Chamber Orchestra British chamber orchestra founded in 1948. Originally called the Goldsbrough Orchestra (after Arnold Goldsbrough, who founded it with Lawrence Leonard), it changed its name in 1960 when its repertory expanded beyond 18th-century music. It is noted for its performances of classical music but it has also been associated with Benjamin Britten and the Aldeburgh Festival and has given many first performances of British works. Raymond Leppard, Colin Davis, Daniel Barenboim, and Pinchas Zukerman have conducted the orchestra regularly; it has no permanent conductor.

English fingering see **fingering.**

English flute see **flute; recorder.**

English horn see **oboe.**

English Music Theatre Company An opera company founded by Benjamin Britten, John Piper, and Eric Crozier in 1947. Originally called the **English Opera Group**, it aimed chiefly to perform new operas and commissioned several works, among them Britten's *Albert Herring*, *The Turn of the Screw*, and *Death in Venice*, Lennox Berkeley's *A Dinner Engagement*, and Harrison Birtwistle's *Punch and Judy*. It was responsible for founding the Aldeburgh Festival (1948).

Georges Enesco

The company also gave performances of earlier operas and toured widely, visiting the Soviet Union among other countries. In 1971 management of the company was taken over by *Covent Garden, with Steuart Bedford as music director and Colin Graham as director of productions. In 1975 it was expanded and renamed the English Music Theatre Company.

English National Opera A British opera company based in London. Until 1974 it was called **Sadler's Wells Opera**. It developed from the Vic-Wells Opera when that company moved permanently to *Sadler's Wells Theatre in 1935. From 1930 to 1935 the Vic-Wells Opera had presented a wide repertory including lesser-known works. In 1935 Lawrance Collingwood became musical director; the newly established Sadler's Wells Opera gave many premieres and leading British artists were attracted to perform with it. During World War II the company mainly toured, but in 1944 Joan Cross became director; a notable event was the first performance of Britten's *Peter Grimes* in 1945 at Sadler's Wells Theatre. In 1948 Norman Tucker began his long association with the company, which expanded and began its policy of presenting adventurous repertory (including many new British operas and the works of Janáček) as well as standard operas (all given in English). In 1968, under Stephen Arlen, the company moved to the Coliseum, St Martin's Lane, where among other important productions was a *Ring* cycle conducted by Reginald Goodall. Its musical directors have included Alexander Gibson, Colin Davis, Charles Mackerras, Charles Groves, and Mark Elder. The company tours the provinces.

The **English National Opera North** (renamed **Opera North** in 1981) is a separate company that was founded in Leeds in 1978.

English Opera Group see **English Music Theatre Company**.

English Suites Six harpsichord suites (BWV 806–11) by Bach. Composed: *c*.1725. Bach himself did not use this title, but there are two explanations for its derivation. Firstly, each suite opens with a prelude, following the pattern of Purcell's suites. Secondly, a manuscript of the work belonging to Johann Christian Bach contains the words 'fait pour les Anglais' ('written for the English').

enharmonic intervals *Intervals that differ only in name. For example, the minor sixth C–A♭ and the augmented fifth C–G♯ are enharmonic on fixed-note instruments. On stringed instruments and in voices, there may be very small differences in pitch between the enharmonic notes, e.g. between G♯ and A♭, as the performer adjusts to a new harmonic structure. An **enharmonic modulation** is one in which a key change is introduced by two enharmonic notes, e.g. from the E♭ of the E♭ chord to the D♯ of the B chord.

Enigma Variations Theme and variations for orchestra (Op. 36) by Elgar. First performance: 1899. All but one of the 14 variations are entitled with the initials of Elgar's friends and in these variations he attempts to capture their personalities in music; the final variation is devoted to himself. The enigma is the melody used for the variations; many attempts have been made to identify it and the most likely explanation is that it is a counterpoint to the Scottish ballad 'Auld lang syne,' a traditional song of parting. The ninth variation, 'Nimrod,' written in memory of Elgar's friend Jaëger, is often performed separately for funerals and occasions of mourning.

En Saga (*A Saga*) Tone poem by Sibelius. Composed: 1892; revised: 1901. Like *Finlandia*, the work is not specifically programmatic; Sibelius attempts to capture in music the general atmosphere of the Scandinavian sagas.

ensemble 1. A small group of players or singers, usually a group in which each part is played or sung by only one performer. **2.** The extent to which such a group performs well (good ensemble) or badly (poor ensemble) as a group rather than as individual players or singers. **3.** A piece in an opera in which two or more soloists sing together.

Entführung aus dem Serail, Die see **Seraglio, The**.

entr'acte Instrumental music played between the acts of plays and operas. See also **act tune; intermezzo**. [French, between acts]

entrée 1. A marchlike instrumental piece used as the dancers' entry music to introduce the ballet in French baroque opera. **2.** Music providing an introduction to any work or part of a work. **3.** A self-contained act within an act of an opera-ballet, as in Rameau's *Les Indes galantes* (1735). [French, entry]

Entremont, Philippe (1934–) French pianist. After studying at the Paris Conservatoire, he established an international reputation with tours of Europe and the USA.

epicedium A solemn funeral ode; for example Blow's *The Queen's Epicedium* (1695) on the death of Queen Mary II, using a poem by George Herbert.

episode 1. A section of a composition, usually of a movement in rondo or ternary form, that occurs between two appearances of the principal theme and contrasts with it in character. In tonal music an episode usually modulates away from the tonic key. **2.** A passage in a *fugue that does not contain a complete entry of the subject (although it may well contain material derived from it).

éponge Sponge. Hence **baguette d'éponge**, a sponge-headed drumstick. [French]

equale A piece for voices or instruments of equal pitch. During the classical period, notably in Austria, the term was specifically used for formal funeral music, of which Beethoven's three *Equali* (1812) for trombone quartet are the most famous. [Italian, equal]

equal-temperament scale see **temperament**.

equal voices Strictly, voices of equal or comparable range; e.g. two sopranos or soprano and tenor. Music written for equal voices has also come to mean, more loosely, music for only female or only male voices.

Erb, Donald (1927–) US composer, a pupil of Gaburo and Nadia Boulanger. Erb, whose style has been influenced by a jazz background, makes much use of tape and has produced mixed-media pieces. His works include *Fallout?* (1964), *In No Strange Land* (1968), *The Seventh Trumpet* (1969), and a cello concerto (1976).

Erkel, Ferenc (1810–93) Hungarian composer, conductor, and pianist. He was conductor of the Hungarian Theatre in Pest (1838–74), where he was also a leading pianist. From 1875 to 1888 he was director of the Academy of Music there. In his compositions Erkel aimed to create a distinctive nationalist style, particularly of opera, and he incorporated folk elements into his music. He wrote ten operas, including *Bátori Mária* (1840), *Hunyadi László* (1844), and *Bánk bán* (1861), and much choral and instrumental music and songs.

Ernani Opera in four acts by Verdi with libretto by Piave based on the drama by Victor Hugo. First performance: Teatro La Fenice, Venice, 1844. It is a story of passion and revenge in 16th-century Spain: Don Carlos, King of Castile (baritone), the aged grandee de Silva (bass), and John of

Aragon (alias Ernani), a bandit chief (tenor), are all in love with Elvira (soprano).

ernst Serious. [German]

Ernst, Heinrich Wilhelm (1814–65) Moravian violinist and composer. He studied at the Vienna conservatory with Joseph Boehm and Seyfried. He was much influenced by Paganini, with whom he played, and his virtuoso technique was as dazzling as Paganini's. He toured widely and settled in London in 1855. Ernst wrote much technically demanding violin music, including concertos.

Eroica Symphony Symphony No. 3 in E♭ major (Op. 55) by Beethoven. Composed: 1803–04. Beethoven originally intended to dedicate the work to Napoleon, but when the latter declared himself Emperor of France Beethoven considered that he had betrayed his principles of freedom and changed the dedication to Prince Lobkowitz. The name is Beethoven's own: he entitled the final score 'Heroic Symphony composed to celebrate the memory of a great man.'

Eroica Variations Variations in E♭ major for piano (Op. 35) by Beethoven. Composed: 1802. The variations are based on a theme from Beethoven's music for *The Creatures of Prometheus* (*Die Geschöpfe von Prometheus*); the same theme was later used for the last movement of the *Eroica Symphony* (hence the name). In 1803 Beethoven also used the melody for the seventh of his 12 *Contredanses*.

Erwartung (*Expectation*) Monodrama for soprano and orchestra (Op. 17) by Schoenberg to a text by Maria Pappenheim. Composed: 1909; first performance: 1924. The plot is in effect a psychological study: a woman is wandering through a forest at night searching for her lover when she discovers his dead body. This provokes a monologue describing their love and her sense of loss, until she is finally reconciled to her lover's death. *Erwartung* is one of Schoenberg's most important expressionist works.

Eschenbach, Christoph (1940–) German pianist and conductor. After winning first prize in the Concours Clara Haskil in Lucerne in 1965 Eschenbach became recognized as a leading pianist of his generation. His repertoire is wide, embracing baroque to 20th-century music; Henze's second piano concerto was written for him. Eschenbach made his conducting debut in 1973.

España Rhapsody for orchestra by Chabrier. First performance: 1883. The melodies in the work are all folk tunes that the composer collected on a visit to Spain in 1882–83.

Esposito, Michele (1855–1929) Italian pianist, composer, conductor, and teacher. He studied with Cesi and Serrao at the Naples conservatory. In 1882 he went to Dublin, where he was piano professor at the Royal Irish Academy of Music, gave many recitals, and founded the Dublin Orchestral Society. His compositions, in many genres, incorporate Irish melodies; they include the opera *The Post-Bag* (1902) and the *Irish Symphony* (1902).

Estampes Set of three descriptive piano pieces by Debussy. Composed: 1903. The three movements are 'Pagodes' ('Pagodas'), 'Soirée dans Grenade' ('Evening in Granada'), and 'Jardins sous la pluie' ('Gardens in the Rain').

estampie (*or* **estampida**) A medieval dance tune, often incorporated into troubadour songs; e.g. Rambaut de Vaquieras' 'Kalenda Maya.' The form involved some internal repetition not unlike the *rondeau.

Esther Oratorio for solo voices, choir, and orchestra by Handel with words by Humphreys based on Racine. First performance: 1732. This is the first of Handel's English oratorios, but the work was originally composed as the masque *Haman and Mordecai* in 1720. It was adapted as an oratorio because the Bishop of London refused to allow a stage production of a religious story.

estinto A direction indicating that a passage should be played extremely softly, almost without tone. [Italian, extinct]

estudiantina 1. A group of student players, generally accustomed to street performance. **2.** A piece of music of the type performed by such wandering students. [Spanish, in the manner of students]

ethnomusicology The comparative study of the music of world cultures in relation to their anthropological and historical development. Originally (in the 1880s) known as comparative musicology, the discipline was renamed ethnomusicology in the 1930s by Jaap Kunst, a specialist in the music of Indonesia. See **Arabian music; Byzantine music; Chinese music; folk music; Greek music; Indian music; Indonesian music; Japanese music; Jewish music; South American music.**

Etler, Alvin Derald (1913–73) US composer, a pupil of Hindemith. He used serial techniques in a strict and free manner and his works often showed the influence of jazz and the composer's interest in new sounds. They include a concerto for brass and string quartets and orchestra (1967) and a concerto for string quartet and orchestra (1968).

Eton Choirbook (*or* **Eton College Manuscript**) A manuscript collection of sacred choral music transcribed between 1490 and 1502 for use at Eton College. Some of the pieces are missing or incomplete but the many composers represented in the manuscript include Cornyshe, Fayrfax, Davy, and Wilkinson. An edition of it has been published (1956–61) and the manuscript itself is in Eton College Library, Windsor (MS 178).

étouffez Stifle: a direction indicating that the tone produced should be immediately dampened or deadened without being first allowed to resonate. [French]

étude see **study**.

Etudes symphoniques (*Symphonic Studies*) Collection of 12 piano pieces (Op. 13) by Schumann. Composed: 1834. The original title was *Études en forme de variations* and the work consists of a set of variations upon a theme by Fricken. The designation 'symphonic' is probably a reference to the orchestral effects of the piano writing.

etwas Somewhat; rather. [German]

Eugene Onegin Opera in three acts by Tchaikovsky with libretto by the composer and Shilovsky based on Pushkin's verse novel. First performance: Imperial College of Music, Moscow, 1879. Tatiana (soprano) falls in love with the proud Onegin (baritone) and writes to tell him in the famous 'Letter Scene.' He rejects her and flirts with Olga, who is engaged to his friend Lenski (tenor), which leads to a duel in which he kills Lenski. Tatiana marries Prince Gremin and Onegin, who learns to love her too late, kills himself.

euphonium see **tuba**.

eurhythmics A system of teaching music by developing the student's response to rhythm in the form of bodily movements. Invented in about 1905 by Emile *Jaques-Dalcroze, Professor of Harmony at the Geneva conservatory, it proved to be of value in physical and mental education generally, as well as in ballet and modern dance training. Institutes of Dalcroze Eurhythmics were set up in various European capitals after the success of the first, established in Dresden in 1910.

Euripides (*c*.485–*c*.406 bc) Greek tragic poet and dramatist who was involved in what is now called the 'new music.' His tragedies have often been used as bases for opera libretti. These include Gluck's *Iphigénie en Aulide* (1774) and *Iphigénie en Tauride* (1779) and more recently *The Bassarids* by Henze (1966, text by Auden and Kallmann).

Euryanthe Opera in three acts by Weber with text by Helmine von Chézy. First performance: Kärntnertor Theatre, Vienna, 1823. The source of the story is medieval: taken from a collection of Schlegel, it relates the ordeal of Euryanthe (soprano), who is required to defend her reputation for chastity.

Eusebius A pseudonym used, together with **Florestan**, by Schumann in his critical writing to illustrate what he saw as the two sides of his character: Florestan the fiery romantic and Eusebius the dreamer.

Evans, Sir Geraint (1922–   ) Welsh baritone. After an amateur career in Cardiff, he studied with Theo Hermann, Fernando Carpi, and Walter Hyde. He made his debut in London (Covent Garden) in 1948, as Beckmesser in *Die Meistersinger*, and in New York (Metropolitan Opera) in 1964, as Falstaff in Verdi's opera. His comic genius is equally apparent as Leporello in *Don Giovanni*. He appeared at Glyndebourne between 1949 and 1961 and was knighted in 1969.

Evening see **Soir, Le**.

Excursions of Mr Broucek, The Opera in two parts by Janácek with libretto based on a satire by Svatopluk Cech. First performance: Prague, 1920. It is a fantasy in which Mr Broucek (tenor) visits first the moon and then 15th-century Bohemia.

exercise 1. A piece, generally lacking aesthetic qualities, intended to develop technique. The form became popular after Clement's *Preludes et exercises* (1790). **2.** An 18th-century keyboard suite. **3.** The composition submitted for a degree, e.g. the Oxford D.Mus.

exposition The part of a composition in which the original *subjects are first stated. See **fugue; rondo; sonata form**.

expressionism A movement in music based mainly in Germany and Austria during the first decades of the 20th century and named after the style of painting evolved by such artists as Ernst and Kokoschka. This style, which aimed at a portrayal of the subjective interpretation of an object rather than a mere visual impression, was characterized by distortion and exaggeration. Expressionism in music was similarly characterized by distortion of typical 19th-century romantic features, as seen in the works of Schoenberg, such as *Erwartung* and *Pierrot lunaire*, and Berg's two operas *Wozzeck* and *Lulu*.

extemporization see **improvisation**.

extension organ see **unit organ**.

extravaganza An exceedingly fanciful composition, such as Gilbert and Sullivan's *Trial by Jury* (1875).

F

F The keynote of the scale of F major. The frequency of F above *middle C is 349.2 hertz (A = 440 hertz).

F. Abbreviation for Fanna. It is used as a prefix to indicate the number of a piece in Antonio Fanna's catalogue (1968) of Vivaldi's works. See also **P.; R.; RV**.

fa see **solmization**.

faburden 1. An English polyphonic method of treating a plainsong *cantus firmus, arising in the late 14th century and used frequently in the early 15th century, notably by Leonel Power and John Dunstable. It was originally an improvisatory technique, but later became part of written compositional structure. In a piece employing faburden the next-to-top voice had the cantus firmus; the top voice added a line a fourth above, and the lower voices accompanied in thirds and fifths below the second voice, so forming first inversion chords. In many early manuscripts the top voice is not written out, but is intended to be improvised. The form should be distinguished from the French **fauxbourdon**, which had the cantus firmus in the top voice, the second voice following a fourth below, and the lowest voice adding a part a third below the second voice. Fauxbourdon was used notably by Dufay in the early 15th century. It is disputed whether faburden or fauxbourdon came earlier.
2. The arbitrary application to any progression of first inversion chords. **3.** 16th-century organ music in which plainsong-derived melodies are set in sixths above a cantus firmus. [Old English, false bass]

Façade 'Entertainment' for narrator and six instruments by Walton to poems by Edith Sitwell. First public performance: 1923. Originally intended for a private entertainment, the poems were recited through a megaphone concealed behind a curtain. The music provided a background to the poetry and many popular melodies are parodied. Walton later arranged two orchestral suites from some of the original music and in 1931 a ballet was produced based on these scores.

facile Easy; fluent. [Italian]

fado A Portuguese melancholic popular song usually with guitar accompaniment. It started in the 1850s as a street song in Lisbon but gradually spread to the provinces. [Portuguese, fate]

Fagott Bassoon. Italian: **fagotto**. [German]

fah see **tonic sol-fa**.

Fair at Sorochintsy, The see **Sorochintsy Fair**.

Fair Maid of Perth, The (French: *La Jolie fille de Perth*) Opera in four acts by Bizet with text by Saint-Georges and Adenis based on Scott's novel of the same name. First performance: Théâtre-Lyrique, Paris, 1867. Set in 15th-century Scotland, it is the love story of the armourer Henry Smith (tenor) and Catherine Glover (soprano), who are aided by Mab, Queen of the Gypsies (mezzo-soprano).

Fair Maid of the Mill, The see **Schöne Müllerin, Die**.

Fairy Queen, The Masque by Purcell to words by Settle. First performance: 1692. The work is an adaptation of Shakespeare's *A Midsummer Night's Dream*.

Falkener, Sir (Donald) Keith (1900–) English bass-baritone. He studied in London, Vienna, and Berlin. Between the wars he toured Europe and the USA, establishing himself as an interpreter of Bach's choral works.

de Falla (centre) with Arthur Honegger on his right

Professor at Cornell University (1950–60) and director of the Royal College of Music (1960–74), he was knighted in 1967.

Falla, Manuel de (1876–1946) Spanish composer, a pupil of Felipe Pedrell. Falla became friendly with Debussy and Ravel in Paris, where he lived from 1907 to 1914. The influence of impressionism, although felt in his harmonic language and orchestral writing, never obscures the Spanish nature of Falla's inspiration. His works possess a clarity of form and progression rare in Spanish music. Falla's compositions include the operas La *Vida breve* (1905–15) and *El Retablo de Maese Pedro* (1923; see **Master Peter's Puppet Show**); the ballets El *Amor brujo* (1915) and *El Sombrero de tres picos* (1919; see **Three-Cornered Hat, The**); the cantata La *Atlantida* (1926–41); *Nights in the Gardens of Spain* (1911–15); a concerto for harpsichord and chamber orchestra (1926); piano music; guitar music, including *Homenaje* (1920); and songs.

false relation (or **cross relation**) A device in harmony in which two different versions of the same note (for example E♮ and E♭) occur simultaneously or in immediate succession in different parts. False relations are produced more by the contours of the individual melodic lines than by any real harmonic theory and although they are not generally acceptable in 'classical' harmony, they are a feature of much Renaissance music.

falsetto The production of an unnaturally high voice by a man once his voice has settled into either a tenor or a bass range. It is the type of voice production used by male *altos.

Falstaff 1. Comic opera in three acts by Verdi with libretto by Boito, based on Shakespeare's *The Merry Wives of Windsor* with additional material from *Henry IV* (parts I and II) and *Henry V*. First performance: La Scala, Milan, 1893. It was Verdi's last opera, written when he was nearly 80, and tells of Falstaff's hapless wooing of Mistress Ford.
2. Symphonic study for orchestra (Op. 68) by Elgar. First performance: Leeds, 1913. The work portrays Falstaff, as seen in Shakespeare's *Henry IV* and *Henry V*, who is a companion of the young Prince Henry but is rejected by the latter upon his ascent to the throne.

familiar style In Renaissance vocal polyphonic music, note-against-note texture, usually in four parts, in which each syllable is sung together by all voices. An example of music in familiar style is Palestrina's *Stabat Mater*.

family of instruments A group of musical *instruments that have a number of features in common. For example, the violin family (violin, viola, cello, and double bass) all have a similar shape, four strings, and are played with a bow. They differ in pitch range and therefore in size. Other features, such as the method of producing sound, may be used as the basis of the grouping in a family.

Fanciulla del West, La see **Girl of the Golden West, The**.

fancy (or **fantasy**) A composition for lute, keyboard, or instrumental ensemble in England in the 16th and 17th centuries. It developed from the 16th-century Italian *ricercare and *fantasia and consisted of a series of themes treated in imitative counterpoint. It also showed some similarity to the English In nomine. The earliest is Newman's 'fansye' in *The Mulliner Book* (c.1550). It is frequently found in the compositions for viol consort of Coperario, Alfonso Ferrabosco, and Orlando Gibbons. In the later 17th century it developed more distinct sections, often interspersed with dance movements, in the works of John Jenkins, Matthew Locke, and Henry Purcell.

fandango An exciting Spanish dance that found its way to Black America. Usually in a quick triple or 6/8 rhythm, it has accelerations and sudden stops. Examples in classical music are the finale of Act III in Mozart's *Figaro* (1786) and Rimsky-Korsakov's *Capriccio espagnol* (1887).

fanfare A flourish played on trumpets or other brass instruments, usually as a ceremonial introduction to some other event or at the head of a procession.

fantasia A freely composed instrumental piece in which one musical idea leads to another without much dependence on form, thus suggesting improvisation. It originated in the 16th century, when such pieces usually ignored established structural procedures. Though instrumental, the fantasia imitated the vocal *motet in employing monothematic sections with imitative four-part writing up to the end of the century. It differed from the *ricercare only in using newly invented thematic material. In the 17th and 18th centuries the two forms became fused into one. The 17th-century keyboard fantasia became gradually less sectionalized; for example in Sweelinck's *Chromatic Fantasia* the chromatic theme is continuously developed. The contrapuntal fantasia for strings, lacking continuo, was the main form of old-fashioned consort music in England after the Restoration (see **fancy**). The 19th- and 20th-century form, generally for piano or strings, continued the multisectional free structure. French: **fantaisie**.

Fantastic Symphony (French: *Symphonie fantastique*) Symphony (Op. 14) by Berlioz. Composed: 1830. Subtitled *Episode from an artist's life*, this work is one of the most important examples of *programme music and was inspired by the composer's passionate love for the actress Harriet Smithson. His programme tells of a young artist who is so distracted by love that he poisons himself with opium and dreams that he is at a witches' sabbath at which his beloved appears. The five movements are entitled 'Dreams-Passions,' 'A Ball,' 'Scene in the Countryside,' 'March to the Scaffold,' and 'Dream of a Witches' Sabbath.' An idée fixe is heard throughout the work to portray the beloved. A sequel to this symphony was composed in 1831 as the monodrama *Lélio, ou Le Retour à la vie*.

Fantastic Toyshop, The see **Boutique fantasque, La**.

fantasy 1. See **fancy**. **2.** The development section of *sonata form. German: **Fantasie**; **Phantasie**.

farandole A Provençal street dance with many steps, led by a pipe and tabor. It has a moderate 6/8 rhythm and is similar to the *branle. Although very ancient, it is still in evidence today. An example in classical music is found in Bizet's *L'Arlésienne* (1872).

Farewell Symphony Symphony No. 45 in F♯ minor by Haydn. Composed: 1772. Haydn wrote the symphony as a hint to his patron, Prince Esterhazy, that the orchestra needed a holiday after a long season's playing. In the last movement, as each player in turn finishes playing, he is instructed to leave, until only two violinists remain.

Farinelli (Carlo Broschi; 1705–82) Italian castrato singer and composer. He made his debut in the serenata *Angelica e Medoro*, with text by Metastasio (Naples, 1720). He toured, sang in London (1734–37), then entered the service of the Spanish kings Philip V (1700–46) and Ferdinand VI (1746–59), becoming very wealthy. He contributed greatly to 18th-century florid styles before retiring to his villa at Bologna.

Farmer, John (late 16th century) English composer. He was organist at Christ Church, Dublin, and lived in London from 1599. Farmer is the author of a set of madrigals for four voices (1599) and contributed to the anthology *The Triumphs of Oriana* (1601).

Farnaby, Giles (*c*.1560–*c*.1640) English composer. Over 50 of his keyboard pieces survive in the *Fitzwilliam Virginal Book*. Some of these have picturesque titles, such as 'Giles Farnaby's Dreame,' 'Farnabye's Conceit,' etc. Farnaby also composed psalms and a book of madrigals (1598).

Farrant, Richard (*c*.1530–1580/81) English composer. He was a gentleman of the Chapel Royal before being appointed organist and choirmaster at St George's Chapel, Windsor (1564); from 1569 he served at both these institutions concurrently. From 1567 he composed music for plays at the court of Elizabeth I; however, only a few of the consort songs written for the stage survive. He also wrote keyboard music, anthems, and a service in A minor (G minor in some manuscripts).

farruca A lively Andalusian dance of Gypsy origins.

Fasch, Johann Friedrich (1688–1758) German composer and organist, a pupil of Kuhnau in Leipzig. After many travels, he became kapellmeister in Zerbst (1722). J. S. Bach arranged five of his orchestral suites. He also wrote a great deal of church music, symphonies, and chamber works.

Faschingsswank aus Wien (*Carnival Pranks in Vienna*) Work for piano (Op. 26) by Schumann. Composed: 1839–40. This piece was described by the composer as a 'grand romantic sonata' and is in five sections. The title alludes to the traditional carnival festivities in Vienna, whose spirit is caught in the music.

Fauré, Gabriel Urbain (1845–1924) French composer, teacher, pianist, and organist. After studying with Niedermeyer and Saint-Saëns he held positions as organist in several Paris churches, including St Sulpice, and was choirmaster of the Madeleine (1877). In 1905 he succeeded Théodore Dubois as director of the Paris Conservatoire, where, until 1920, he introduced many reforms; Ravel was among his pupils. Fauré was the most advanced composer of his generation; his individual approach to harmony and modulation is linked to great melodic invention. He cultivated small forms and is often regarded as the master of French song. His works include operas, among them

Gabriel Fauré

Pénélope (1913); songs, including the cycles *La *Bonne chanson* (1892) and *L'Horizon chimérique* (1921); sacred music (the *Requiem* of 1887–90 is one of Fauré's best-known works); incidental music, such as that for Maeterlincke's **Pelléas et Mélisande* (1898) and Fauchois' **Masques et bergamasques* (1919); secular choral works; orchestral music, including *Pavane* (1887); chamber works, including two violin sonatas, two cello sonatas, two piano quartets, two piano quintets, and other short pieces; and many piano pieces, among them nocturnes, barcarolles, impromptus, and the **Dolly* suite (1893) for piano duet.

Faust Opera in five acts by Gounod with libretto by Barbier and Carré, based on Goethe's *Faust*. First performance: Théâtre-Lyrique, Paris, 1859. With the aid of Mephistopheles (bass), Faust (tenor) wins the love of Marguérite (soprano). To avenge his sister's honour, Valentine (baritone) fights and is killed by Faust in a duel. Unhinged by grief and remorse, Marguérite kills her baby and dies in prison, as Mephistopheles claims the soul of Faust. In Germany the opera is known as *Margarethe*. See also **Damnation of Faust, The; Doktor Faust.**

Faust, Episodes from Lenau's Two orchestral works by Liszt, based upon a poem by Nicholas Lenau concerning Faust. Composed: 1860. The two episodes are entitled *Der nächtliche Zug* (*The Nocturnal Procession*) and *Der Tanz in der Dorfschenke* (*The Dance in the Village Inn*); the latter is also known as the *Mephisto Waltz* No. 1 (see also **Mephisto Waltzes**).

Faust, Scenes from Goethe's Work for solo voices, choir, and orchestra by Schumann. Composed: 1844–53. It seems likely that Schumann originally intended to write an opera based upon Goethe's drama *Faust*, but eventually only set certain portions of the text. The work consists of an overture and six individual sections.

Faust Overture Overture by Wagner. Composed: 1839. It was originally intended that this work should be the first movement of a Faust symphony.

Faust Symphony Symphony for orchestra and chorus by Liszt. Composed: 1857; revised: 1880. The work is based upon Goethe's drama and the three movements describe the three main characters in the play – Faust, Gretchen, and Mephistopheles – and are followed by a choral finale. The first performance of the work was at the unveiling of a memorial to Goethe and Schiller in 1857.

fauxbourdon see **faburden.**

Favola d'Orfeo, La see **Orfeo, La Favola d'.**

Favorita, La (*The Favourite*) Opera in four acts by Donizetti with libretto by Royer and Vaez based on the drama *Le Comte de Commingues* by d'Arnaud. First performance: Opéra, Paris, 1840. It relates the love of the young novice Fernando (tenor) for Leonora (soprano), mistress of King Alfonso of Castile (baritone). They marry, but when Fernando learns of Leonora's past he returns to his monastery, where Leonora follows him and finally dies.

Fayrfax, Robert (1464–1521) English composer. From 1497 a gentleman of the Chapel Royal, by 1502 Fayrfax was master of the choristers at St Albans Abbey, where he was buried and for which he composed his mass *Albanus*. He received the degrees of B.Mus. (1500 or 1501) and D.Mus. (1504) at Cambridge and the degree of D.Mus. (1511) at Oxford. Among his masses are those based on *O quam glorifica* (submitted for his Cambridge doctorate) and *Sponsus amat sponsum*. Fayrfax also wrote settings of votive antiphons, including a *Salve regina* setting in the *Eton Choirbook*; two magnificats, one of which is based on *O bone Jesu*; and some English songs and carols.

Fedora Opera by Giordano with text by Colautti based on a play by Sardou. First performance: Teatro Lirico, Milan, 1898. Princess Fedora (soprano), in avenging the death of her former fiancé, brings love and sorrow into the life of Loris (tenor) before finally taking poison.

Feen, Die (*The Fairies*) Opera by Wagner with libretto by the composer based on Gozzi's *La Donna serpente*. First performance: Munich, 1888 (55 years after its composition).

feierlich Festive or solemn. [German, from *Feier*, holy day or festival]

Feldman, Morton (1926–) US composer, a pupil of Riegger and Wolpe and influenced by John Cage, with whom he was associated in the 1950s. His music is characteristically slow, quiet, and delicate. He used chance and graphic notation to allow freedom of choice to the performers, as in *Projections* (1951). Greater complexity is seen in *Durations* (1961) and *Swallows of Salangan* (1961) and a new use of precise notation is evident in *Structures* (1962). Recent works, such as *Piano and Orchestra* (1975) and *Orchestra* (1976), are more dramatic in style.

Feldpartie (*or* **Feldstücke** *or* **Feldsonate**) 17th- and 18th-century Austrian open-air brass music, e.g. Haydn's *Feldparthie* (1765). It was originally a fanfare for four brass instruments, played by military rather than orchestral players. [German, field suite]

feminine cadence A *cadence in which the final tonic chord occurs on the weak beat of the bar instead of on the more usual strong beat.

Fenby, Eric (1906–) British composer. Largely self-taught, he acted as amanuensis for Delius in France (1928–34) and later became Professor of Composition at the Royal Academy of Music (1964). His compositions include a work for string orchestra and he wrote a book on Delius.

Fennimore und Gerda Opera by Delius in two episodes (11 pictures) with libretto by the composer based on Jens Peter Jacobsen's novel *Niels Lyhne*. Composed: 1908–10; first performance: Frankfurt-am-Main, 1919. It is the story of frustrated love when Niels woos Fennimore, and successful love when he eventually proposes to Gerda; problems of artistic integrity play a large part.

Ferencsik, Janos (1907–84) Hungarian conductor. He conducted the Budapest Opera and the Hungarian State Symphony Orchestra.

Ferguson, Howard (1908–) British composer, a pupil of R. O. Morris. Ferguson taught composition at the Royal College of Music in London (1948–63). His compositions are basically romantic in their expression; his small output includes choral music, orchestral compositions, chamber works, and songs.

fermata *Pause. [Italian, literally a stop]

Fernandez, Oscar Lorenzo (1897–1948) Brazilian composer and teacher. Fernandez's early romantic style gave way in his later works to a nationalistic idiom derived from Brazilian popular music. His compositions include the opera *Malazarte* (1941), two symphonies and other orchestral works, piano pieces, and songs.

Ferneyhough, Brian (1943–) British composer, a pupil of Lennox Berkeley, de Leeuw, and Huber. His early style combines a serial technique with a highly expressive idiom, as in the *Sonatas for String Quartet* (1967), *Prometheus* (1967), and *Firecycle Beta* (1971). Later works are highly complex and make great demands on the performers. They include *Transit* (1975), *Time and Motion Studies I–III* (1971–77), and *La Terre est un homme* (1979). Ferneyhough has been influenced by extramusical ideas from Dürer, Heraclitus, and Renaissance cosmology.

Ferrabosco, Alfonso (1543–88) Italian composer. In about 1560 he entered the service of Elizabeth I of England; in 1578 he returned to Italy permanently and around 1582 he entered the service of the Duke of Savoy. His madrigals were popular in England: 16 of them were printed in *Musica transalpina* (1588, 1597). His father, **Domenico Maria Ferrabosco** (1513–74), was a chorister in the Sistine Chapel, Rome, and a composer of madrigals. Alfonso's son, **Alfonso Ferrabosco** (*c.*1575–1628), was born at Greenwich and became violinist, teacher, and composer at the courts of James I and Charles I. He composed fantasias for viol consort and music for several of Jonson's masques.

Ferretti, Giovanni (*c.*1540–*c.*1609) Italian composer. He was maestro at Ancona, Loreto, and other small cities and

Kathleen Ferrier

apparently lived in Rome for a time. His light madrigals were popular throughout Italy.

Ferrier, Kathleen (1912–53) British contralto. She made her stage debut as Lucretia in the first performance of Britten's opera *The Rape of Lucretia* (1946); her other operatic role was Orpheus. A legend and national institution in Britain, she made famous recordings of *Das Lied von der Erde* with Bruno Walter, and Bliss and Britten both wrote songs for her. Her early death from cancer occurred at the height of her career.

Ferroud, Pierre Octave (1900–36) French composer. The influence of his teacher, Florent Schmitt, is evident in Ferroud's contrapuntal style. His works include an opera, ballet music, a symphony, chamber music, and piano pieces.

Fesch, Willem de (1687–1761) Flemish composer, organist, and violinist. He was maître de chapelle at the cathedral of Notre-Dame, Antwerp (1725). In 1731 he moved to London, where he directed his oratorio *Judith* (1733) and became director of the orchestra of Marylebone Gardens (1748). He also wrote masses and instrumental and vocal chamber works.

Festa, Costanzo (?–1545) Italian composer. From 1517 until his death he was a singer in the Sistine Chapel, Rome.

Festa was one of the first composers to write madrigals (which appeared for the first time in print in 1530) and to experiment with smaller note values and more complex rhythms (from about 1540). He also composed 4 masses, more than 40 motets, 30 hymns, and 13 magnificats.

Festin de l'araignée, Le see **Spider's Banquet, The.**

Festing, Michael Christian (1680–1752) German composer and violinist, who emigrated to England and studied with Richard Jones and Geminiani. He was director of the Italian Opera (1737) and was appointed the first director of music at Ranelagh Gardens (1742). He wrote mainly for the violin but also composed symphonies, odes, and cantatas.

Festival Hall see **Royal Festival Hall.**

Fêtes see **Nocturnes.**

Fêtes d'Hébé, Les, ou Les Talents lyriques (*Hebe's Feasts, or The Lyrical Gifts*) Opera-ballet by Rameau in prologue and three acts with libretto by Gautier de Montdorge. First performance: Opéra, Paris, 1739. The overture is interesting because of its formal originality.

Feuermann, Emmanuel (1902–42) Austrian cellist. He held teaching positions at Cologne and Berlin until 1938, when he emigrated to the USA. Here he performed as a soloist and appeared in piano trios with Schnabel and Hubermann.

Feuersnot (*Fire Famine*) Opera in one act by Richard Strauss with libretto by Ernst von Wolzogen based on a Flemish legend. First performance: Court Opera, Dresden, 1901. Set in medieval Munich, it is a bawdy story of a spurned suitor, aided by a magician, who extinguishes all the fires in the town.

Fibich, Zdeněk (*or* **Zdenko**) (1850–1900) Czech composer. He studied at the Leipzig conservatory (1865–67) under Moscheles and E. F. Richter, then with Jadassohn. He was conductor of the Prague Provisional Theatre (1875–78) and the Russian Orthodox Church (1878–81). After Dvořák and Smetana, Fibich was the leading Czech composer of the time, writing very effective concert and stage *melodramas, among them the trilogy *Hippodamie* (1888–91). His other works, many with a strongly nationalist flavour, include incidental and choral music, songs, seven operas (among them *Šárka*, 1896–97), three symphonies and other orchestral works, and chamber and piano music. His tone poem *At Twilight* (1893) contains the movement 'Poem,' for which he is best known.

fiddle 1. An early form of bowed unfretted stringed instrument. Fiddles have been used in Africa, Asia, and Europe in a variety of shapes and sizes ranging from the primitive single-stringed folk instruments of Ethiopia, the square-bodied **morinchur** of Mongolia, and the *sārangī of India to the medieval European fiddle that evolved into the *lira da braccio and eventually into the modern *violin. The bow used on fiddles has also changed in design from the semicircular to the straight; in some Chinese and Cambodian fiddles it is threaded through the strings. Diverse playing positions have also been used: in early **spike fiddles** the spike was rested on the knee or on the floor, the Bulgarian **gadulka** is held vertically and rested on the knee, while many types of fiddle are held horizontally, rested against the chest or shoulder, and played like the modern violin. See also **rebec. 2.** A violin, especially in the context of folk music. [from Latin *vitulari*, to rejoice, skip like a calf – an allusion perhaps to the motion of the bow. The Italian *viola* is derived from the same Latin word]

Fiddle Fugue Fugue in D minor for organ (BWV 539) by Bach. Composed: after 1720. The name is derived from the fact that Bach arranged the organ version from the fugue of his first violin sonata in G minor (BWV 1001) of 1720.

Fidelio (full title: *Fidelio, oder Die eheliche Liebe*: *Fidelio, or Married Love*) Opera in two acts by Beethoven based on a translation of Bouilly's *Léonore, ou L'Amour conjugal*. The first librettist was Joseph Sonnleithner; a second version was made by Stephan von Breuning; the final version is by Treitschke. Productions of the first two versions in Vienna in 1805 and 1806 were unsuccessful; the definitive version was first performed at the Kärntnertor Theatre, Vienna, in 1814. Beethoven's only opera, it tells the story of the rescue of Florestan, a political prisoner, by his wife Leonora (soprano) disguised as the jailer's assistant, Fidelio. Beethoven wrote four versions of the overture, *Leonora 1, 2,* and *3* being rejected in favour of the fourth, *Fidelio*, which is the one used now; however, the *Leonora* overtures are sometimes played as concert overtures (especially No. 3).

Field, John (1782–1837) Irish composer and pianist. In Dublin he was a pupil of Giordani, and in 1793 he became an apprentice to Clementi in London. By the turn of the century Field had made a reputation as a concert pianist. In 1802 Clementi took him on a tour to Paris, Vienna, and St Petersburg, where Field stayed, quickly becoming much in demand in fashionable circles. He settled in Moscow in 1821 and made a last European tour in 1831–34.

Field's piano playing was sensitive and restrained and represents the beginning of the romantic school of performing. He composed chamber music with piano, seven piano concertos, and works for piano duet. His works for piano solo were strikingly original and influential: he invented the 19th-century *nocturne, which Chopin later developed. The mood and style of Field's pieces greatly influenced composers of romantic piano music. His other solo piano works include rondos, fantasies, sonatas, and studies.

*Neil Howlett (left), Rich-
ard Angas (centre) and
Kathleen Harries (right)
in the English National
Opera's 1988 production
of* Fidelio

Fiery Angel, The Opera in five acts (seven tableaux) by
Prokofiev with libretto by the composer based on a novel
by Briusoff. First concert performance (in French): Théâtre
des Champs Elysées, Paris, 1954; first stage performance:
Venice, 1955. Set in 16th-century Germany, it is a story of
witchcraft and religious hysteria.

fife A small one-piece side-blown *flute that was used in
processions and military bands from the 16th to the 19th
centuries. In modern drum and fife bands the instruments
used are usually piccolos and flutes. The original fife was a
somewhat limited instrument with finger holes and sometimes with one key. Also known as a **whiffle** (the player was
called a **whiffler**), it was used in morris dancing.

fifteenth A diapason organ *stop in which 2-*foot pipes
produce notes two octaves (i.e. 15 notes on the diatonic
scale) above the manual keyboard notes.

fifth An *interval of five notes (counting both the first and
last notes), or seven semitones; e.g. C–G or D–A. This is
called a perfect fifth. An **augmented fifth** has one semitone
more (e.g. D♭–A or D–A♯), while a **diminished fifth** has one
semitone less than the perfect fifth (e.g. D♯–A or D–A♭).
Consecutive fifths consist of a progression of fifths in a
composition. They were regarded as academically unacceptable until the end of the 19th century, except for special
effects. Such rules are now interpreted much less rigidly.
Hidden fifths occur when the movement of two parts in the
same direction implies consecutive fifths but does not strictly
produce them; for example, they may be disguised by the
use of *passing notes.

Fifths Quartet String quartet in D minor (Op. 76 No. 2)
by Haydn. Composed: 1797. The first subject of the first

movement includes many leaps of a fifth, which has led to
the alternative names of the *Bell Quartet* and the *Donkey
Quartet*. In addition the minuet of this quartet is often
referred to as the *Witches' Minuet* because of its mysterious
character.

Figaro see **Marriage of Figaro, The.**

figure 1. An easily identifiable phrase or motif, especially
one that is repeated during the course of a composition. **2.** A
set of movements performed by a number of dancers
following precise rules. A **figure dance** is one in which such
movements are a feature, as opposed to a **step dance**, in
which they are not.

figured bass A musical shorthand indicating the harmony
above a written-out bass part by means of figures. Its
original function was to help players of keyboard and
plucked instruments to play *continuo parts correctly
without a score. The guiding principle is that notes forming
the harmony are indicated by the interval they make with
the bass and are written as an Arabic numeral. However,
some conventional abbreviations save time for the composer
or copyist and make for ease of reading. Common chords
in root position, which would be fully indicated by the
figuring ⅗, are normally left blank unless figuring is
required to avoid ambiguity. With the same qualification,
common chords in the first inversion are usually marked 6
rather than ⁶₃. Second inversion common chords, however,
are always indicated by ⁶₄ since neither of these figures can
be omitted without ambiguity. Seventh chords can usually
be marked simply 7, and their first, second, and third
inversions respectively ⁶₅, ⁴₃, and ⁴₂. Other conventional
figurings are those for dissonant suspensions (23, 43, 76,

78, 98, and combinations of these), while suspensions in the bass can produce a variety of more complex figurings. A note can be inflected with a sharp or flat sign placed next to the figure concerned (the former is sometimes replaced by a short dash struck through the figure itself). A sharp or flat not placed next to the figure applies to the third of the chord, which is assumed to be present unless cancelled by 2 or 4. A line following a figure (or the unfigured third) indicates that the note is held over the succeeding bass notes covered by the line. Rapid passing notes and auxiliary notes are normally left to the player's discretion.

The earliest appearances of figured bass occur in three works published in 1600: the two *Euridice* operas by Peri and Caccini and Cavalieri's *La Rappresentazione di anima e di corpo*. Thereafter it became a regular feature of 17th-and early-18th-century ensemble music. After 1750, when the stylistic evolutions made the continuo player increasingly redundant, the figured bass continued to play a role in keyboard concertos as an aid to the soloist in accompanying the tutti. Later it was used in teaching keyboard harmony, a discipline to which the 20th-century revival of interest in the art of continuo playing has lent a new significance.

Fille du régiment, La (*Daughter of the Regiment*) Opera in two acts by Donizetti with libretto by Saint-Georges and Bayard. First performance: Opéra-Comique, Paris, 1840. Marie (soprano) was found on the battlefield as a baby and has been brought up as the 'daughter of the regiment.' Her love affair with Tonio (tenor), a Tyrolese peasant, undergoes a temporary hitch when it is discovered that she is really the daughter of the Marquise de Birkenfeld (soprano), but the couple are finally united.

Fille mal gardée, La Ballet with music by Hérold (arranged and reorchestrated by John Lanchbery) and choreography by Frederick Ashton. First performance: Covent Garden, London, 1960, by the Royal Ballet (décor by Osbert Lancaster). Based on an earlier ballet by Hérold (1828), it tells how Lise and her lover Colas foil attempts to marry her to the farmer's son, Alain.

film music A 20th-century extension of incidental or *programme music, intended to introduce and highlight the action of a film. Some scores are worthy of concert hall performance, e.g. Walton's *Henry V* (1944), while many others have little or no integral artistic merit. The cinema has inspired some notable compositions, including Koechlin's *Seven Stars Symphony* (1933); Prokofiev's *Alexander Nevsky* (1938) and *Ivan the Terrible* (1942–46) for films by Eisenstein; Vaughan Williams' *Scott of the Antarctic* (1948); and music by Britten, Maxwell Davies, Ligeti, and others. The use in films of music not written specifically for films has sometimes brought great popularity to that music. Anton Karas' zither music in *The Third Man* (1949),

Mahler's music in *Death in Venice* (1970), and Scott Joplin's ragtime in *The Sting* (1973) are examples of different kinds of music that owe some of their popularity to exposure in successful films.

fin End. [French]

final see **modes**.

finale 1. The last movement of a musical work having several movements. **2.** The final scene of large-scale ensemble of an act of an opera or musical show.

fine The end. This word occasionally appears at the end of a score to signify that a composition is complete. It is also used before the end of a score when a portion of the score is repeated as the closing section. It then indicates where the repeat, and the whole composition, finishes. See also **da capo**. [Italian]

Fine, Irving (1914–62) US composer and conductor, a pupil of Piston and Nadia Boulanger. After an early neoclassical period, he adopted serial techniques without rejecting tonality. His works include the partita for wind quintet (1948), the romanza for wind (1958), and a symphony (1962).

Fingal's Cave see **Hebrides, The**.

Finger, Godfrey (*or* **Gottfried**) (*c*.1660–*c*.1723) Moravian composer, who emigrated to England (*c*.1685). There he wrote much influential chamber music and was placed fourth in the competition for the music of Congreve's *Judgment of Paris* (1701). He entered the service of the Queen of Prussia in 1702 and in 1707 became chamber musician to the Elector Palatine in Innsbruck and Mannheim, where he wrote many operas and other stage works.

fingerboard The part of the neck of a stringed instrument on which the strings are stopped by the fingers of the player. In some instruments (such as the violin) the player has to decide by experience where to place his finger in order to shorten a string, while in fretted instruments (such as the guitar) he places his finger between two *frets so that the string touches the fret nearest to the body of the instrument.

finger holes Holes in the tube of a wind instrument that are opened and closed with the fingers. They effectively provide a means of shortening the tube of the instrument, thus reducing the length of the column of vibrating air within it and raising the pitch. Finger holes are used on flutes, clarinets, and oboes in conjunction with keys – a system of levers used to open and close holes by means of leather pads attached to metal cups. They are also used on recorders, bagpipes, and some simple horns.

fingering The technique of using the fingers on an instrument to produce a note. In wind instruments there is usually a standard procedure for operating the *finger holes and keys of the instrument. In stringed instruments the stopping of the strings also usually follows a fixed pattern that the beginner learns during his mastery of the instrument's technique. Music written for beginners will often indicate which finger is to stop which string and in the *tablature notation for lutes and lutelike instruments the fingering forms the basis of the system.

In the playing of keyboard instruments the fingering is more complicated and there has been more variation in the principles with the evolution of the instruments involved. Bach's fingering on the clavichord, for example, would have been substantially different from that of a modern exponent playing his music on the piano. For one thing the clavichord key did not have to be depressed as far as a modern piano key and was less responsive to the actual force of depression. Clavichord players were therefore able to strike the keys with their fingers almost horizontal and they made only restricted use of the thumb and little finger. The modern technique of piano playing, with bent fingers and the use of the thumb as a pivot, largely developed in the 18th century. Now much music is edited to indicate with small figures above or below the notes the most appropriate finger to be used. In the obsolete **English fingering** the thumb was indicated by + and the other fingers 1–4; in the now universally adopted **continental fingering** the thumb is numbered 1 and the other fingers 2–5.

In organ playing the piano technique has largely been followed, but it is often necessary to hold a note for longer and therefore it is quite common to strike a note first with one finger and then to hold it with another.

Finlandia Tone poem (Op. 27 No. 7) by Sibelius. Composed: 1894; first performance: 1900. Although Sibelius does not use actual folk tunes, the main themes of this work are very similar in spirit and shape to patriotic Finnish songs. For this reason *Finlandia* has almost become a national anthem for the Finns and is often performed at important national events.

Finney, Ross Lee (1906–) US composer. Finney studied in Europe with Nadia Boulanger and Berg and in the USA with Sessions. His style, characterized by neoclassical forms, tonal principles, and serial techniques, reflects his wide studies in music. Finney's output includes four symphonies, concertos for piano, violin, and percussion, eight string quartets and other chamber music, and choral works.

Finnissy, Michael (1946–) British composer, a pupil of Stevens and Searle. His music, often complex and violently expressive, has absorbed diverse influences, ranging from the Orient to English folk song. Finnissy's works include *Mr Punch* (1977), *English Country Tunes* (1977), *Goro* (1979), and *Sea and Sky* (1980).

Finta giardiniera, La (*The Girl Disguised as a Gardener*) Opera buffa in three acts by Mozart with libretto probably by Calzabigi. First performance: Residenz-Theater, Munich, 1775. The lovers Violante and Belfiore thread their way through a maze of frustration.

Finta semplice, La (*Just a Pretence*) Early opera buffa by Mozart with libretto by Coltellini after Goldoni. First performance: Salzburg, 1769.

Finzi, Gerald (1901–56) British composer, a pupil of R.O. Morris. Finzi's contemplative style shows the influence of Vaughan Williams and Elgar. Of particular note is his vocal music, which includes settings of Shakespeare and Thomas Hardy for voice and piano, music for unaccompanied chorus, and works for voice and orchestra, the cantata *Dies Natalis* being the best known of these. Finzi also composed a clarinet concerto and a small amount of chamber music.

fioritura The decoration of a melody with *ornaments, especially by the performer. Regarded as the prerogative of 18th-century opera singers, violinists, and pianists, fioriture are now regarded as unnecessary embellishments to good music. [Italian, flowering]

fipple see **recorder**; **flute**.

Firebird, The (Russian: *Zhar Ptitsa*; French: *L'Oiseau de feu*) Ballet with music by Stravinsky and choreography by Fokine. First performance: Opéra, Paris, 1910. Commissioned by Diaghilev for the Ballets Russes in Paris, Stravinsky's first full-length ballet is based on a Russian fairy tale, which gave him scope for a vividly exotic score; Karsavina danced the Firebird and Fokine Prince Ivan.

Fires of London British ensemble founded by Peter Maxwell Davies and Harrison Birtwistle in 1967. It was originally called the **Pierrot Players** (its soprano Mary Thomas and its five instrumentalists frequently performed Schoenberg's *Pierrot lunaire*) but it changed its name in 1970 and Maxwell Davies became sole director. Its repertory is varied and includes mixed-media pieces and electronic music. Many works have been written especially for the Fires of London (including many by Maxwell Davies); it is a versatile and accomplished group that performs regularly in London and tours abroad.

Fire Symphony Symphony No. 59 in A major by Haydn. Composed: 1766–68. In 1774 Grossmann's play *Die Feuersbrunst* (*The Conflagration*) was produced at Esterhazy and this symphony was probably used as an overture, hence the name. Haydn himself wrote a puppet opera called *Die Feuersbrunst* in 1776, but this symphony is in no way connected with that work, as is sometimes mistakenly alleged.

Fireworks Music see **Music for the Royal Fireworks**.

first inversion see **inversion.**

Fischer, Edwin (1886–1960) Swiss pianist. A pupil of Huber and Krause, Fischer's repertoire was centred mainly on the German classics. He also conducted and founded a chamber orchestra in Berlin. His activities as a teacher led to the opening of the Edwin-Fischer-Stiftung and he had many important pupils, including Brendel.

Fischer, Friedrich Ernst (18th century) German composer, active in Leiden (*c*.1741–46) and The Hague. He is possibly identical with F. E. Fisher, the violinist and cellist who led the orchestra of Burney's church (1754) and was active in East Anglia as late as 1773. The works of the latter composer are mainly for instrumental ensemble.

Fischer, Johann Kaspar Ferdinand (*c*.1665–1746) German composer. From 1692 he was kapellmeister to the Margrave of Baden. His output includes preludes and fugues and suites for keyboard and preludes and fugues for organ.

Fischer-Dieskau, Dietrich (1925–   ) German baritone. One of the greatest singers of his time, his concert career began in 1947 with Brahms' *A German Requiem*. He has sung and recorded all Schubert's lieder and is well known for his Schumann interpretations. His operatic roles have included Wozzeck and Kurvenal and he is the author of several books, including *Wagner and Nietzsche* (1976).

Fisher, John Abraham (1744–1806) British composer and violinist, a pupil of G. F. Pinto. He wrote a great deal of theatre music and received the degree of D.Mus. from Oxford (1777) for his oratorio *Providence*. His other compositions include symphonies, preludes, and violin concertos.

Fistoulari, Anatole (1907–   ) Russian-born conductor. A child prodigy, he performed Tchaikovsky's sixth symphony at the age of eight. After 1940 he settled in London. Fistoulari is outstanding as a conductor of ballet.

Fitelberg, Jerzy (1903–51) Polish composer. After enjoying early success in Europe, Fitelberg emigrated to the USA in 1940. His neoclassical style is characterized by a strong sense of rhythm and counterpoint; his compositions include two violin concertos, five string quartets, and other chamber works.

Fitzwilliam Virginal Book A manuscript collection of early 17th-century keyboard music. It contains 297 pieces, mostly by Byrd, Bull, and Farnaby, and was copied by Francis Tregian between 1609 and 1619. An edition of it by J. A. Fuller Maitland and W. B. Squire has been published (1894–99). The manuscript is named after Richard, Viscount Fitzwilliam, who acquired it and bequeathed it to the Fitzwilliam Museum, Cambridge (32.g.29, Mus. MS 168).

Dietrich Fischer-Dieskau, with Gerald Moore at the piano

Five, The A group of five 19th-century Russian composers who aimed to create a consciously nationalist school of Russian music. The members, who were based in St Petersburg, were *Balakirev, *Borodin, *Cui, *Mussorgsky, and *Rimsky-Korsakov. Their approach, drawing on Russian traditions, literature, and folklore, has been contrasted with that of their contemporaries who followed the more academic traditions of western Europe (e.g. Tchaikovsky). The group is often referred to as **The Mighty Handful** (Russian: *moguchaya kuchka*), a term coined by the critic Vladimir Stasov in 1867.

Five Tudor Portraits Choral suite for contralto and baritone soloists, choir, and orchestra by Vaughan Williams to poems by Skelton. Composed: 1936. Each of the poems describes a common Tudor character and Vaughan Williams also sanctioned the separate performance of individual movements. The five movements are 'Elinor Running,' 'Pretty Bess,' 'John Jayberd,' 'Jane Scroop,' and 'Jolly Rutterkin.'

flageolet A type of *recorder in use between the 17th and 19th centuries. The English flageolet had six finger holes and the French version had four finger holes and two thumb holes. The original beaked mouthpiece was replaced in the 18th century by a nozzle mouthpiece. [from French, little flute]

Flagstad, Kirsten (1895–1962) Norwegian soprano. She made her debut in 1913, and after 18 years in Scandinavia

A performance of Die Fledermaus *at Covent Garden in 1983*

became famous at Bayreuth, singing Isolde and Brunnhilde in Wagner's operas. In 1950 she gave the first performance of Richard Strauss's *Four Last Songs* in London. She retired in 1953.

flam A double beat on a side drum consisting of a short note followed by a long note (e.g. a semiquaver followed by a dotted crotchet). In an **open flam** the accented beat is the short note; in the **closed flam** it is the long note.

flamenco An Andalusian song and dance of Gypsy origin and Moorish influence: a form of cante *hondo. Why it is called 'Flemish song' (*cante flamenco*) is not known. It typically consists of a song (**cante**) accompanied by dancing in which the men perform intricate toe and heel tapping steps (**zapateados**) and the women rely on graceful hand and body movements. The predominant styles are **grande** (anguished) and **chico** (gay and amorous) with a variety of intermediate moods. Flamenco guitar playing uses a different style from that of classical guitar playing, including a percussive effect obtained by rhythmically tapping the body of the guitar with the fingers.

flat 1. A sign (♭) placed before a note or in a *key signature to reduce the pitch of that note by one semitone. See **accidental. 2.** Denoting a musical sound that is of lower pitch than it should be.

flat keys Keys that have flats in their *key signatures, i.e. the key of F has one flat, B♭ has two flats, E♭ has three flats, A♭ has four flats, D♭ has five flats, and G♭ has six flats. In each case the relative minor keys have the same signatures as the major keys given. See **Appendix, Table 3.**

Flatterzunge Flutter *tonguing. [German]

flat twenty-first An organ *mixture stop that sounds two octaves and a minor seventh (i.e. 21 notes on the diatonic scale) above the keyboard note.

flautando (or **flautato**) A bowing technique used to produce a thin flutelike tone, in which the bow is drawn lightly across the strings over or near the fingerboard. A similar effect may be obtained by using *harmonics. [Italian, fluting]

flautino (or **flauto piccolo**) **1.** A descant *recorder. **2.** A *flageolet. [Italian, little flute]

flautist (or **flutist**) A flute player. While flautist is more common in the UK, flutist is preferred in the USA.

flauto Flute. The word is used as a generic term for all kinds of flute, though it can be modified to indicate particular instruments, e.g. **flauto piccolo**, little flute, i.e. piccolo. It was also formerly applied to the recorder (see also **flautino**). [Italian]

flebile Tearful; mournful. [Italian]

Fledermaus, Die (*The Bat*) Operetta in three acts by Johann Strauss the Younger, with libretto by Haffner and Genée from the French vaudeville *Le Reveillon* by Meilhac and Halévy. First performance: Theater an der Wien, Vienna, 1874. The title refers to a fancy-dress costume, which plays an important part in the working out of the plot.

Flesch, Carl (1873–1944) Hungarian violinist. Although he had a flourishing career as a performer, both as soloist and chamber-music player, it is as a teacher that Flesch is best remembered: distinguished pupils included Rostal, Szeryng, and Haendel. He also wrote several teaching manuals.

flexatone A type of percussion instrument consisting of a steel blade against which two knobs vibrate when the instrument is shaken. The knobs are attached by spring-steel wires to a frame supporting the blade. Thumb pressure on the blade is used to alter its pitch.

flicorno A family of Italian *brass instruments of the tuba group. A type of saxhorn, the flicorno is made in three sizes: basso, basso grave, and contrabasso.

Fliegende Holländer, Der see **Flying Dutchman, The.**

Flight of the Bumble-Bee, The Orchestral work by Rimsky-Korsakov. Composed: 1900. Although this piece is now usually performed as a concert work in its own right, it was originally an orchestral interlude in the opera The *Legend of Tsar Saltan. This interlude describes how the main character, a prince, turns into a bumble-bee. The moto perpetuo nature of the work has led to many different arrangements made as solo display pieces, most notably for flute.

Flood, The 'Musical play' for solo voices, speakers, and orchestra by Stravinsky. Composed: 1961–62. The work was composed for a US television company, who broadcast the first performance. Robert Craft, Stravinsky's assistant during the last years of his life, prepared the libretto from the Bible and the York and Chester mystery plays. The work tells the story of the great flood sent by God as a punishment to his people, as described in the Book of Genesis.

Florestan see **Eusebius.**

florid Denoting any musical passage that is highly ornamented, especially an elaborate version of a simpler melody or theme.

Flos Campi Suite for solo viola, choir, and small orchestra by Vaughan Williams. Composed: 1925. Although the choir's part is wordless, each movement is prefaced by a quotation from the Song of Solomon in the Bible. Vaughan Williams wrote the work for the great English violist Lionel Tertis, for whom he also wrote another suite in 1934.

Flotow, Friedrich (Adolf Ferdinand) von (1812–83) German composer. After studying with Pixis and Reicha at the Paris Conservatoire (1828–30) he lived for some years in Paris, producing operas. He was intendant of the grand ducal court theatre, Schwerin (1855–63), then moved to Vienna (1863) and Darmstadt (1880). Flotow composed orchestral, chamber, and vocal music and many operas (in French, German, and Italian), of which the two most successful were Stradella (1837) and *Martha (1847).

flourish 1. A fanfare of trumpets. **2.** Any short *florid passage used as an embellishment rather than as a theme.

flue pipe An *organ pipe in which sound is produced by blowing air against a sharp edge in the side of the pipe in a similar manner to a whistle or recorder. The pipe may be open or stopped (closed at the top). Closure lowers the pitch one octave but prevents the development of even harmonics, resulting in a lighter sound. Three categories of *stops use flue pipes: *diapasons, *flute stops, and *string-toned stops. Compare **reed pipe.**

Flügel A grand piano or a harpsichord. [German, wing]

flugelhorn A wind instrument of the brass family with a trumpet-like mouthpiece and a hornlike conical bore. It is used in brass bands, the alto flugelhorn in B♭ being played with the *cornets, with which it has an identical range. The tenor flugelhorn in E♭ is used to play the upper tuba parts in Wagner. See also **saxhorns.** [from German *Flügelhorn*, wing, flank horn, from its use by outside (flank) formations in battle or outside beaters in hunting]

flute 1. (or **end-blown flute**) Originally, a simple pipe with a sharp rim at the upper end and a small number of finger holes along its length. The player blows over the sharp rim into the pipe, changing the pitch of the note by covering and uncovering the finger holes. Instruments of this type are of great antiquity. A **whistle flute** (or **fipple flute**) has a simple mouthpiece through which the player blows onto the sharp edge of a hole cut into the side of the pipe, just below the mouthpiece. Widely used in folk music throughout the world, the whistle flute in Europe developed into the *recorder. Double, triple, and even quadruple end-blown flutes have been used in South America from antiquity and in eastern Europe in more recent times. See also **panpipes.**
2. (or **nose-blown flute**) A simple flute in which the player plugs one nostril and blows with the other. The nose flute may be end-blown, as in Borneo, or side-blown, as in Polynesia. **3.** (or **side-blown** or **transverse flute**) A flute with a blow hole cut into its side, close to a stopped end, through which air is blown by the player, who holds it horizontally, usually to the right side of the face. Originating in Asia in the 9th century BC, it reached Europe in the 12th century AD. Before the 17th century it was mainly used as a military instrument but thereafter it became an important part of the orchestra, developing an intricate system of keys, which was perfected by Theobald Boehm in the 1830s. The modern orchestral flute uses this key system, giving it a range of three octaves from middle C. It is sometimes called a **German flute** to distinguish it from the recorder (or **English flute**). The **piccolo** (from Italian *flauto piccolo*, little flute) is a

Orchestral flutes comprising (1) the standard flute, (2) the piccolo, (3) the bass flute, and (4) the alto flute

smaller version of the flute, sounding an octave higher, and much used in orchestral solos. The **alto flute** (a fourth or a fifth lower than the standard instrument) and the **bass flute** (an octave lower) find limited use in the orchestra. Apart from its place in the woodwind section of the orchestra, the flute has been used for much solo music, including six flute and keyboard sonatas by Bach, a concerto by Mozart, and a sonata for flute and piano by Hindemith. See also **fife.**

flûte-à-bec Recorder. [French, literally beak flute]

flute stops Organ *stops operating open or closed *flue pipes that are made to produce fewer upper harmonics than normal, resulting in a duller sound.

flutist see **flautist.**

flutter tonguing see **tonguing.**

Flying Dutchman, The (German: *Der Fliegende Holländer*) Opera in three acts by Wagner with libretto by the composer based on Heine's *Memoirs of Herr von Schnabelewopski*. First performance: Court Opera, Dresden, 1843. Set in an 18th-century Norwegian fishing village, it relates how the Flying Dutchman (baritone) is redeemed from eternally wandering the seas in his ghostly ship by the love of Senta (soprano). To save him, Senta casts herself into the sea and is finally seen ascending with him into heaven.

Foerster, Josef Bohuslav (1859–1951) Czech composer. Active as a teacher, Foerster taught many 20th-century Czech composers. His nationalist style stems from the romantic tradition of Dvořák and Smetana. Foerster's works include operas, four masses and other choral compositions, five symphonies, concertos for violin and cello, and chamber music.

Foldes, Andor (1913–) US pianist and conductor, born in Hungary. A pupil of Dohnányi, he also studied under Bartók, becoming particularly noted as an interpreter of Bartók's piano works.

Folía, La 1. Dance of Portuguese origin, popular during the 15th century. Although none of the music is extant, it seems likely that this dance was performed using exotic costumes. **2.** A sequence of chords used by many composers in the 17th and 18th centuries as the basis for a set of variations. Over a period of time one particular melody became associated with these harmonies and featured in many of the variation works. The most famous set of variations upon *La Folía* is by Corelli (Op. 15 No. 12) for violin and continuo; composed: 1700. During later periods both Liszt and Rachmaninov used the theme for variation compositions.

folk music Songs, tunes, and dances that have been passed on orally from generation to generation and accepted as part of the tradition of a region, nation, or people. Although originally the works of single composers, they have become anonymous in being altered and shaped by different performers. Another characteristic of folk music is that it originated in rural communities: although it has flourished in industrial areas, and some distinct urban forms have evolved, folk music tends to degenerate with the spread of industrialization and urbanization. The advent of mass communications and the growth of popular music in the 20th century have virtually eliminated it.

Folk music exists in a profusion of forms throughout the world. Its functions include pure self-expression, the transmission of folklore and news of historical events, an accompaniment to dancing, and (in the form of communal singing) an aid in the performance of hard or repetitive work. In primitive societies such music is also used in religious ceremonies, notably during the course of fertility rites.

Folk music usually has a distinct national character, reflecting not only the temperament of a people but also their social conditions, the effects of immigrants, and other historical influences. Most national music has identifiable characteristics, including the use of particular scales or modes, features of style and performance, and a variety of traditional instruments and ensembles. For example, the traditional songs and dances of England (whose folk music has been enriched by prolonged cross-fertilization with that of Scotland and Ireland) include ballads and lighter songs depicting folk legends, children's rhymes and games, songs illustrating the life and social conditions of the people (the agricultural year, the experiences of seamen and (after industrialization) of miners and factory workers), work songs (notably sailors' shanties), drinking and wassailing songs, and a variety of love songs. Instrumental music is almost exclusively dance music, including the ritual *morris dances, sword dances, step and clog dances, and many country dances and *figure dances.

The influence of folk music on the development of art music has been considerable. Not only did art music evolve from folk music, but many composers have returned to it for inspiration – particularly the romantic and nationalist composers of the late 19th and early 20th centuries (Vaughan Williams, Dvořák, and Bartók are notable examples). Popular music also owes much to folk music, several modern genres having developed directly from it. In the USA, for example, the music of White rural communities has evolved bluegrass and the immensely popular country and western styles, whereas jazz and soul music have their roots in the blues and gospel music of Black people. Rock and roll developed from a fusion of Black and White folk-music elements. Because the protest songs of Woody Guthrie, Bob Dylan, and others were styled on folk songs, they (and sometimes almost any songs accompanied by guitars) have been grouped into a loose category called folk music.

In most parts of the developed world genuine folk music, performed in the traditional manner and environment, has all but disappeared. Even in Ireland, where traditional culture has survived for longer than most places, the advance of modernization is taking its toll. In recent years, however, a resurgence of interest in traditional music and dance in most western countries has led to a 'revival' movement. This has been helped greatly by the work of collectors, e.g. Francis Child, Cecil Sharp, and Francis O'Neill, who between them collected many thousands of songs and tunes in Britain, Ireland, and North America in the late 19th and early 20th centuries. This revival cannot be regarded as representing a continuation of the folk tradition since its exponents, its social function, and to some extent the manner of its performance are quite different. Nevertheless, for anyone interested in folk music and dance, a large selection of published material and recorded performances by both traditional and 'revival' artists is available.

Fontane di Roma see **Fountains of Rome.**

foot A measure of the pitch of an organ *stop, based on the nominal length of the lowest pipe. A note of the pitch written is produced by a stop in which the lowest pipe, the C below the bass staff, is approximately 8 ft long. Stopped flue pipes and reed pipes of half this length, which sound the pitch indicated, are also referred to as 8-foot pipes. C an octave higher is produced by a pipe 4 ft long and C an octave lower by one 16 ft long and so on. Thus organ stops are sometimes referred to by what sound will be heard if a note representing an 8-foot C is played. An **8-foot stop** sounds the note itself, a **16-foot stop** sounds an octave lower, and a **4-foot stop** sounds an octave higher, etc. A **2-foot stop** sounds two octaves higher and a **32-foot stop** sounds two octaves lower.

Force of Destiny, The see **Forza del destino, La.**

Ford, Thomas (*c*.1580–1648) English composer. In 1611 he was in the service of Prince Henry (who died in 1613) and in 1626 became a musician at the court of Charles I. His fame rests almost entirely with his lute songs, ten of which were published in his *Musicke of Sundrie Kinds* (1607). Like Dowland's songs, these 'Aries' may be sung by four voices or by a solo voice with instrumental accompaniment. He also composed dances and fantasias.

forlana (*or* **furlano**) An Italian popular dance in 6/8 rhythm, not unlike the gigue (see **jig**). French: **forlane.**

form The element of organization in a piece of music. Schoenberg, in his *Fundamentals of Musical Composition*, wrote: 'form means that a piece is organized: i.e. that it consists of elements functioning like those of a living organism.' More specifically, Riemann explained that the coherence, logic, and unity in diversity that is necessary for a work to become formally comprehensible, stems from 'the consonant chord, the definition of a key, the retention of a beat or rhythm, the recurrence of rhythmic [and] melodic motifs, and the formation and recurrence of pregnant themes: contrast and conflict appear in changes of harmony, dissonances, modulation, alteration of rhythm and motifs, and in the juxtaposition of themes of opposing character.'

This definition accommodates much of the music composed between the 16th century and the early 20th century, but these properties of wholeness, unity, logic, and coherence were first propounded by Aristotle in his *Poetics*. These symmetrical principles are unacceptable to some more recent composers. Writing of Stockhausen's open form (see also **moment**), Roger Smalley expressed a pertinent contemporary view: 'a composer is no longer in the position of beginning from a fixed point in time and moving forwards from it; rather he is moving in all directions within a materially circumscribed world.'

For the principal formal types found in western music, see **binary form; concerto; fugue; minuet; overture; rondo; sonata form; suite; symphony; ternary form; variations.**

formalism A criticism levelled at Soviet composers from time to time by their own government or its organs, implying that their music has abdicated any concern for social values, Marxist belief, and popular appeal in favour of self-indulgent intellectual preoccupation with form and artistic technique. Both Shostakovich and Prokofiev suffered this criticism, which also appeared to denounce modernistic trends in their music. Compare **realism.**

formant see **tone colour.**

Forster, E(dward) M(organ) (1879–1970) British novelist. He collaborated with Eric Crozier on the libretto (based on a story of Herman Melville) of Britten's opera *Billy Budd*, first produced in 1951.

forte Strong; loud. Abbreviation: *f*. Hence **fortissimo**, very loud. Abbreviation: *ff* or *fff*. [Italian]

fortepiano An early Italian name for a pianoforte. See **piano.**

fortissimo see **forte.**

Fortner, Wolfgang (1907–) German composer. Fortner's studies in Leipzig were followed by a successful career as a teacher and composer. His music is characterized by contrapuntal textures: serial procedures are occasionally used. Fortner's works include operas and ballet music, a symphony (1947), concertos for violin, cello, and piano, three string quartets, and other chamber music.

Forty-Eight Preludes and Fugues (*or* **The Forty-Eight**) see **Well-Tempered Clavier, The.**

Forza del destino, La (*The Force of Destiny*) Opera in four acts by Verdi with libretto by Piave based on the Spanish drama by the Duke of Rivas, *Don Alvaro o La Fuerza de sino*. First performance: St Petersburg, 1862. It is a tragedy built on the effect of a curse that is finally expiated by the dying heroine, Leonora (soprano).

Foss, Lukas (1922–) US composer and conductor, a pupil of Hindemith. His early works, such as the *Song of Songs* (1946), show a lyrically contrapuntal style. In 1957 Foss founded the Improvisation Chamber Ensemble, and his works became more experimental, using variable form, electronic music, and new notation. They include *Time Cycle* (1960), *Echoi* (1963), a cello concerto (1966), *Orpheus* (1972), and *Folksong for Orchestra* (1976).

Fountains of Rome (Italian: *Fontane di Roma*) Tone poem by Respighi. First performance: 1917. Although it is in one movement, the work is clearly subdivided into four sections,

each section depicting a different fountain in Rome. *Fountains of Rome* is the first of a trilogy that describes various features of Rome, the other two works being **Pines of Rome* (*Pini di Roma*; 1924) and **Roman Festivals* (*Feste Romane*; 1929).

Four Boors, The see **School for Fathers.**

four foot see **foot.**

Fournier, Pierre (1906–) French cellist, who was trained and later taught at the Paris Conservatoire. One of the leading cellists of his generation, Fournier has had works written for him by Martin, Martinu, and Poulenc. In addition to solo performances, he has appeared frequently in chamber music with Szeryng, Kempff, and others.

fourniture see **furniture.**

Four Saints in Three Acts Opera in four acts by Virgil Thomson with text by Gertrude Stein. First performance: (in concert form) Ann Arbor, Michigan, 1933; (staged) Hartford, Connecticut, 1934. The music has a direct simplicity; the libretto is surrealistic with plenty of saints and scant plot.

Four Seasons, The Set of four concertos for violin and orchestra (Op. 8 Nos. 1–4) by Vivaldi. Published: 1725. The four concertos depict in turn spring, summer, autumn, and winter: each movement describes a different aspect of the particular season and the composer prefaces each concerto with the descriptive sonnet on which it is based. These four concertos are contained within Vivaldi's collection *Il cimento dell' armonia e dell' invenzione* (*The Test of Harmony and Invention*) and are one of the earliest examples of *programme music.

Four Serious Songs (German: *Vier ernste Gesange*) Collection of songs for baritone and piano (Op. 121) by Brahms. Composed: 1896. These songs, which are settings of four biblical texts, were one of Brahms' last compositions. They were later arranged for baritone and orchestra by Sir Malcolm Sargent.

Four Temperaments, The 1. Symphony No. 2 by Nielsen. First performance: 1902. Each movement describes one of the four temperaments thought to be the determining factors in a man's character – choleric, phlegmatic, melancholic, and sanguine. Nielsen's inspiration for this programme came from seeing a collection of pictures at a village inn, which depicted the four temperaments. **2.** Theme and variations for piano and orchestra by Hindemith. Composed: 1940. In this work each of the four variations depicts one of the four temperaments; Hindemith originally intended it for use as a ballet score.

fourth An *interval of four notes (counting both the first and last note), or five semitones; e.g. C–F or D–G. This is called a perfect fourth. An **augmented fourth** has one semitone more, (e.g. D♭–G or D–G♯). The **diminished fourth** is equivalent in equal *temperament to a major third.

Fox, The Dance scene for four male voices and chamber orchestra by Stravinsky, to a libretto by the composer based upon Russian folk tales. Composed: 1915–16; first performance: 1922. The libretto was translated into French as *Le Renard* by Ramuz, with whom Stravinsky also collaborated over *The *Soldier's Tale*. Described as 'a burlesque in song and dance,' the orchestra includes a part for cimbalom.

fractional tone see **microtone**.

Fra Diavolo Comic opera in three acts by Auber with libretto by Scribe, subtitled *L'Hôtellerie de Terracine* (*The Inn at Terracina*). First performance: Opéra-Comique, Paris, 1830. Set in 18th-century Naples, Fra Diavolo (tenor) is a bandit chief of the Robin Hood type.

Françaix, Jean (1912–) French composer, a pupil of Nadia Boulanger. Françaix's music is marked by lightness and grace in an idiom stemming from Ravel. His compositions include operas and ballets, a symphony (1932), concertos for flute, violin, and piano, and chamber works.

Francesca da Rimini 1. Symphonic fantasy (Op. 32) by Tchaikovsky, based upon part of Dante's *Inferno*. First performance: 1877. In this work Tchaikovsky portrays in music the description that Dante gives of Francesca da Rimini's life and fate in hell. Following the tradition of several Russian composers of his day, Tchaikovsky origi-

nally contemplated an opera upon this subject. **2.** Any of several operas based on this theme, including those by (1) Goetz (finished by Ernst Frank), with libretto by the composer (first performance: Mannheim, 1877); (2) Rachmaninov, with libretto by the composer and M. I. Tchaikovsky (first performance: Moscow, 1906); (3) Zandonai, with libretto by Tito Ricordi (first performance: Turin, 1914).

Francescatti, Zino (1902–) French violinist. He has been particularly active in performing contemporary violin music and formed a duo with the pianist Robert *Casadesus.

Francis of Assisi, St Cantata for baritone and orchestra by Claudio Spies (1925–). Composed: 1958. This work tells of the life and work of the nature-loving St Francis.

Franck, César (Auguste Jean Guillaume Hubert) (1822–90) French composer, teacher, and organist, born in Belgium. He studied at the Liège conservatory (1830–35) and then became a pupil of Leborne, Zimmermann, and Benoist at the Paris Conservatoire (1837–42). He began composing (unsuccessfully) and had a short-lived career as a concert pianist. Overwhelmed by the pressure from his ambitious father, in 1845 Franck left home, began teaching, and became organist at Notre-Dame de Lorette. In 1858 he became organist of Ste Clotilde, where he attracted a large following with his fine improvisations and began composing again (his works including the masterful *Six*

César Franck (seated centre) with a group of musicians including (immediately to the composer's left) the violinist Eugène Ysäye

pièces for organ, 1860–62). He had gained a reputation as a teacher and in 1871 was appointed Benoist's successor as organ professor at the Paris Conservatoire (his pupils included d'Indy).

The period from the late 1870s to the end of his life saw the composition of most of his best-known works: the oratorios *Les Béatitudes* (1869–79) and *Rédemption* (1871–72), the tone poems *Le *Chasseur maudit* (1882) and *Les *Djinns* (1884), the *Variations symphoniques* (1885) with piano solo, and the D minor symphony (1886–88). He also wrote his most successful chamber music at this time, the violin sonata (1886) and the string quartet (1889), the *Prélude, choral et fugue* for piano (1884), and the elaborate *Trois chorals* for organ (1890). Franck also composed four operas, secular choral works, songs, and music for harmonium; he made many transcriptions and arrangements. Public recognition came late, but Franck is now acknowledged to have had great influence on later composers. His harmonic language was original, chromatic, and colourful and he developed *cyclic form, in which thematic material is varied and transformed in successive sections or movements of a work (e.g. in the *Variations symphoniques*).

Franck, Melchior (*c*.1579–1639) German composer. In 1602 or 1603 he became kapellmeister to the princes of Coburg and served them during the Thirty Years' War. A prolific composer, he was one of the foremost writers of Protestant music during the first half of the 17th century. His works, conservative in style, include over 40 collections of motets and 13 secular vocal collections, strongly influenced by dance rhythms.

Francoeur, François (1698–1787) French composer and violinist. He became director of the Paris Opéra with Jean-Fery Rebel, with whom he collaborated on several operas. He also wrote many violin sonatas.

Francs juges, Les Overture (Op. 3) by Berlioz. Composed: 1827. Berlioz began work on an opera to a libretto by Ferrand about the secret tribunals held in the Middle Ages in the Black Forest, but only completed the overture and six numbers. Although only the overture is now known by this name, some of the other music was used in later compositions, notably the 'Marche au Supplice' in the **Fantastic Symphony*.

Frankel, Benjamin (1906–73) British composer. After a short period of study in Germany, Frankel worked as an orchestrator and arranger of music for theatre orchestras, subsequently composing music for many films. After World War II his concert works received more attention. Frankel's compositions, often melancholy in mood, include seven symphonies, a violin concerto, five string quartets, and other chamber works.

Franz, Robert (Robert Franz Knauth; 1815–92) German composer. He studied with J. C. F. Schneider in Dessau; at Halle he became conductor of the Singakademie (1842), which he developed into an eminent ensemble, and taught at the university. In 1867 he became deaf and suffered a breakdown, forcing him to abandon composition. Thereafter he devoted himself to arranging and editing the vocal works of Bach and Handel. Franz wrote a few choral works but is best known for over 250 lieder; influenced by Schubert and Schumann, they are in an individual style using a rich harmonic language and reflecting a careful choice of keys and tonality.

Frauenliebe und Leben (*Woman's Love and Life*) Song cycle (Op. 40) by Schumann, to eight poems by Adelbert von Chamisso. Composed: 1840. The poems describe a woman's approach to love, as seen through the eyes of a male poet. It is significant that Schumann composed these songs very shortly after marrying Clara Wieck.

Frau ohne Schatten, Die (*The Woman without a Shadow*) Opera in three acts by Richard Strauss with libretto by Hofmannsthal. First performance: Opera, Vienna, 1919. It is the story of the enlightenment of two couples: the Emperor and Empress (tenor and soprano) and the dyer Barak (bass-baritone) and his wife (soprano). The Empress has no shadow, meaning she cannot bear children; in trying to acquire that of the dyer's wife she comes to a selfless love and acquires a shadow.

Frederick the Great (Friedrich II; 1712–86) King of Prussia (1740–86). An amateur flautist and patron of music, he was taught by Haydn and Quantz. He established a court orchestra (1790) and the Berlin Opera House (1792) and was himself a regular performer.

free counterpoint *Counterpoint that is not dictated by strict consonance and dissonance treatment and control of rhythm (compare **strict counterpoint**). In general, free counterpoint is more closely related to original composition than is strict counterpoint, which is composed in a pastiche idiom.

free fantasia see **development**.

free-reed instruments see **reed instruments**.

Freire, Nelson (1944–) Brazilian pianist, trained in Vienna. A child prodigy, he has since pursued a soloist's career, appearing throughout the world.

Freischütz, Der (*The Free Shot*) Opera in three acts by Weber with libretto by Kind. First performance: Schauspielhaus, Berlin, 1821. The hero, Max (tenor), is persuaded to resort to black magic in order to win the fair Agathe (soprano) in a shooting contest. The scene in the Wolf's Glen, where the magic bullets are forged, is remarkable for its use of *melodrama.

Frémaux, Louis (1921–) French conductor, known especially as an interpreter of French music. He conducted the City of Birmingham Symphony Orchestra (1969–78).

French horn see **horn.**

French overture A form of introductory baroque instrumental music, established by Lully as an introduction to ballets and operas, e.g. *Ballet d'Alcidiane* (1658). It was taken over into the independent keyboard and orchestral repertory. An elaboration of the allemande–courante pairing, it comprised two (sometimes three) contrasted sections. The first was slow, featuring dotted rhythms that were conventionally enlivened or over-dotted. The second was faster and often included fugato. Sometimes the piece would conclude with a slow section. See also **overture; Italian overture.**

French sixth see **augmented sixth.**

French Suites Six suites for harpsichord (BWV 812–17) by Bach. Composed: *c.*1720. The reason for the title is unclear, and Bach himself did not use it. Although there is no opening prelude, as in the *English Suites*, French elements are present to no greater degree than in any of Bach's other suites or those of his contemporaries and thus there is no musical foundation for the name.

Freni, Mirella (1935–) Italian soprano. After studying with Ettore Campogalliani at Bologna she made her debut at Modena in 1955 in Bizet's *Carmen* and subsequently appeared in opera houses worldwide. She sang Violetta in Visconti's 1967 production of Verdi's *La Traviata* and Desdemona in the filmed version of Verdi's *Otello*; since 1970 she has been a member of the Paris Opéra.

frequency A measure of the *pitch of a note equal to the number of vibrations per second of the vibrating string, air column, etc., producing it. Frequency is measured in *hertz (cycles per second).

Frescobaldi, Girolamo (1583–1643) Italian composer and organist. Active in his native Ferrara at the court of Alfonso II d'Este, he was influenced by his teacher, the court organist Luzzaschi, and Gesualdo. When the court moved in 1597, he remained in Ferrara as organist of the Accademia della Morte. Probably in 1601 he went to Rome, becoming organist at S Maria in Trastevere; in 1607 he travelled with his patron, Guido Bentivoglio, to Brussels. In 1608 he became organist of St Peter's, Rome, a post he held until his death apart from a period in Florence (1628–34) as court organist to Ferdinando II.

Frescobaldi wrote a small amount of sacred and secular vocal music, including two masses, but is best known for his keyboard compositions. These include ricercari, canzoni, toccatas, dances, and three organ masses. He contributed to the development of fugal technique and his imaginative improvisatory style represents the high point of Italian

Girolamo Frescobaldi, a contemporary engraving

keyboard music; after his death interest in the keyboard in Italy diminished.

frets A series of strips of metal, wood, or gut running across the *fingerboard of certain stringed instruments to make the stopping of strings easier for the player. Lutes, viols, and guitars are usually fretted whereas fiddles and members of the *violin family are not.

fretta Haste; hurry. See also **affrettando.** [Italian]

Frick, Gottlob (1906–) German bass singer. He studied with Neudorfer-Opitz in Stuttgart, then joined the chorus there at the Opera (1927–31). He has sung in most German state opera houses in Wagnerian bass parts, especially as Hagen in *The Ring*.

Fricker, Peter Racine (1920–) British composer. Fricker's earliest music shows the influence of Bartók, absorbed through his teacher Mátyás Seiber. In his later works this and other influences are developed into a characteristic and personal style. Fricker's compositions include four symphonies, four string quartets, other chamber and orchestral works, and vocal music.

Friedenstag (*Day of Peace*) Opera in one act by Richard Strauss with text by Joseph Gregor. First performance: Munich, 1938. Set in a beleaguered town during the Thirty

Years' War, it poses the problems of deciding between continued strife and surrender.

Friml, Rudolf (1879–1972) Czech composer. Friml settled in the USA, where he became well known as a composer of operettas: his compositions include *The Firefly* (1912), *Rose Marie* (1923), and *The Vagabond King* (1925).

Froberger, Johann Jacob (1616–67) German composer and keyboard player. By 1637 he was an organist at the Viennese court and in the same year travelled to Rome to study with Girolamo Frescobaldi. Vienna remained his base but he travelled extensively in Europe to perform. In 1658 he left the court and eventually died in France. Froberger's works are almost entirely for keyboard and include many pieces in Italianate forms: ricercari, canzonas, and capriccios. His most important works are the harpsichord suites in the French style; their intensity of expression and colourful harmonies became characteristic of German 17th-century keyboard music.

Frog Quartet String quartet in D major (Op. 50 No. 6) by Haydn. Composed: 1787. The main theme of the finale is reminiscent of a frog's croaking, hence the name.

Froissart Concert overture (Op. 19) by Elgar. Composed: 1890. Froissart is a character who appears in Sir Walter Scott's novel *Old Mortality*, in which he talks of the chivalry and patriotism of medieval knights. This overture was intended to reflect these sentiments and the score is prefaced with a quotation from Shelley, 'When Chivalry lifted up her lance on high.'

From Bohemia's Woods and Fields see **Má Vlast**.

From My Life String quartet No. 2 in E minor by Smetana. Composed: 1876. The quartet is an autobiographical description of the composer's life. At the beginning of the work the music reflects his happy existence, but in the finale a high-pitched whistling noise is introduced: this is the sound that Smetana constantly heard before he gradually became deaf during 1874. Smetana also gave this title to the second quartet in D minor (1882), but the name is now usually applied to only the E minor quartet. In 1941 the Hungarian conductor George Szell orchestrated the quartet for full symphony orchestra.

From the House of the Dead Opera in three acts by Janáček with text by the composer taken from Dostoievsky's novel. First performance: Brno, 1930 (posthumously). It is set in a Siberian prison camp with a predominantly male cast.

From the New World (*or* **New World Symphony**) Symphony No. 9 in E minor by Dvořák (formerly known as No. 5). Composed: 1893. This work was composed while Dvořák was staying in the USA and describes his impressions of the New World. The musical material bears both rhythmic and melodic similarities to the songs of both American Blacks and Indians, although some authorities claim that it is equally derived from Bohemian folk songs.

frottola (*pl.* **frottole**) An Italian song of the late 15th and early 16th centuries, characterized by a dominant melody accompanied by two or three lower parts, either vocal or instrumental. The bass, even when vocal, has a distinctive harmonic function. Usually short, the parts start and finish together following the form of the poem set. The frottola was either a specific form – the barzelletta, or generic, encompassing such various forms as strambotto, canzona, oda, etc. The main collection of frottole are contained in 11 books published by Petrucci (1504–41). The form flourished in Mantua, where Tromboncino and Cara worked.

Frühbeck de Burgos, Rafael (1933–   ) Spanish conductor of German descent. He became conductor of the Spanish National Orchestra (1962) and of the Montreal Symphony Orchestra (1975).

Fry, William Henry (1813–64) US composer and critic. He wrote operas, including *Leonora* (1845), which is considered the first large-scale US opera, and *Notre Dame de Paris* (1864), as well as choral, orchestral, and chamber works. Although they contain American elements, they are products of the European tradition. Fry was more influential as a critic: for the *New York Tribune* he was European correspondent in Paris and London (1846–52) and later its music critic; he was an ardent champion of US music.

Frye, Walter (?–1474) English composer, member of the London guild of parish clerks from 1457. His works comprise masses (including those based on *Flos regalis* and *Summe trinitate*), motets, and chansons, some of which survive with alternative texts; for example, the motet *O sacrum convivium* has the English text *Alas alas*.

fuga 1. See **canon**. **2.** See **fugue**.

fugato A passage written in fugal style, although it is not actually a strict *fugue. [Italian, fugued]

fughetta A little *fugue. Compare **fugato**.

fugue A *form of disciplined imitative contrapuntal writing, established in the 17th century, arising out of the Renaissance *ricercare, *canzona, and related forms. In its purest form a fugue has a consistent number of parts or voices (thus 'a fugue in four parts,' etc.) and follows accepted structural principles. The leading, or first, voice of a fugue is the **subject** in the tonic; it is imitated by another voice, the *answer in the dominant. The answer may reply literally, imitating exactly the shape of the subject (see illustration), in a **real fugue**, which is somewhat misleading since the strict imitative scheme may well not apply to the whole piece. When, as more commonly happens, the answer

Real fugue

Tonal fugue

Double fugue with subjects apparently simultaneous (above) or in close succession (below).

Examples of the fugue

alters the intervals of the subject, it is described as a **tonal answer** and the fugue as a **tonal fugue** (see illustration). The leading voice continues its part with a contrapuntal *countersubject against the answer. If there are more than two voices, the remaining voices introduce the subject, countersubject, and answer until all the voices have entered in due order. This need not necessarily be at regular intervals of bars (a feature, for instance, of J. S. Bach's fugues). When all the voices have entered, the fugal **exposition** is complete. There follows a series of **episodes** in free counterpoint joining various developments of the fugal entries in related keys. Towards the end of a fugue, overlapping entries (see **stretto**) often occur. A *codetta may well end a fugue. A more complex kind, the **double fugue**, has two subjects in two voices appearing either simultaneously or in close succession (see illustrations). In vocal fugues, the initial subject sometimes has an instrumental accompaniment, in which case it is called an **accompanied fugue**. Fugues have had a distinctive history and have played a large and consistent part in compositional technique from the baroque to the present day. German: **Fuge**; Italian: **fuga**.

fuguing tune A form of English hymn or psalm tune stemming from the 16th century. It has three sections, the first and last being chordal and the middle section employing imitative counterpoint, hence the name of the form. A good example is Tye's 'Laudate nomen Domini.' The form was taken over and slightly adapted in America in the late 18th century; it was thought to improve singing in church.

full anthem see **anthem**.

full organ A direction to play the *organ at full strength. This usually means using the louder stops on the great organ coupled to the louder stops on the swell organ. French: **plein** (*or* **grand**) **jeu**; Italian: **organo pleno**.

full score see **score**.

fundamental The first *partial of a *harmonic series. It is the note produced when a string or column of air vibrates as a whole. See **harmonics**.

funebre Funereal; of a funeral. Hence **marcia funebre**, funeral march. French: **funèbre**. [Italian]

Funeral March Sonata Piano sonata in B♭ minor by Chopin. Composed: 1839. The third movement is a funeral march, which provides the name of the sonata. This movement is sometimes played separately and has been orchestrated.

fuoco Fire. Hence **con fuoco**, a direction indicating that the playing should be vigorous and powerful. [Italian]

furiant A Bohemian dance having various moods. In quick 3/4 rhythm, it was popular with Dvořák

furlano see **forlano**.

furniture (*or* **fourniture**) A medium-pitched organ *mixture stop consisting of four or five *ranks of pipes.

Furtwängler, Wilhelm (1886–1954) German conductor. He held posts in Berlin, Leipzig, and Bayreuth as well as in the USA (with the New York Philharmonic). Despite clashes with the Nazis, he stayed in Germany during World War II and after 1945 built an outstanding reputation with the Berlin Philharmonic Orchestra. He excelled in the classical repertoire and in Wagner. He was also a composer.

futurism A form of music based on the literary movement founded by the Italian poet Marinetti. First introduced in 1909 in Rome, futurism aimed to combine traditional forms with new sounds more reflective of an industrialized society, such as those produced by thunder-making and whistling instruments. Enjoying the support and encouragement of Mussolini, it continued until World War II, linked in the mind of the public with Marinetti's book *Futurismo e fascismo* (1924). The most fervent musical advocate of futurism was the composer Francesco Pratella (1880–1955).

Fux, Johann Joseph (1660–1741) Austrian composer and theorist, teacher of Gottlieb Muffat. At St Stephen's Cathedral in Vienna he was assistant kapellmeister (1705) and kapellmeister (1712–15) and at court he was composer (1698), assistant kapellmeister (1713), and kapellmeister (1715). His treatise *Gradus ad Parnassum* (1725) was studied by Haydn and Mozart. He wrote mainly sacred and instrumental works and about 18 operas, including *Costanza e Fortezza*, which was produced in Prague in 1723.

G

G The keynote of the scale of G major. The frequency of G above middle C is 392 hertz (A = 440 hertz).

Gabrieli, Andrea (*c.*1520–86) Italian composer. He was second organist at St Mark's, Venice, from 1564 and became first organist in 1585. In both his sacred and secular music Gabrieli broke away from the Netherlandic contrapuntal tradition in favour of homophony, clear but colourful harmonies, and large vocal combinations. Many of his works were written for state ceremonies and religious feasts. The posthumous *Concerti* (1587) contain many such pieces, scored for 6 to 16 voices. Gabrieli also composed vocal music for smaller combinations and was the leading composer of ricercari and canzoni for the organ. In 1585 he wrote the music for a performance of Sophocles' *Oedipus*. His nephew, **Giovanni Gabrieli** (1557–1612), also a composer, became second organist at St Mark's (1585). He developed Andrea's choral style through bolder use of antiphony, more colourful harmonies and word painting, and the addition of basso continuo. He was the editor of the *Concerti* (1587), containing works by both himself and his uncle. Giovanni also composed for the keyboard and for trombones, cornets, and violas: these instruments are used in the *Sacrae symphoniae* (1597, 1615), sometimes to accompany voices. Among Giovanni's pupils were Schutz and Praetorius.

Gabrieli Quartet A British string quartet founded in 1966. Its members are Kenneth Sillitoe and (from 1969) Brendan O'Reilly (violins), Ian Jewel (viola), and Keith Harvey (cello). The quartet's repertory is very wide, embracing works by east European composers. It has given many first performances of British works and is admired for its versatility.

Gabrielli, Domenico (1651–90) Italian composer and virtuoso cellist. He studied in Venice and Bologna, where he became president of the Accademia Filarmonica (1683). In the last seven years of his life he composed 12 operas. Gabrielli is important as the composer of some of the earliest music for cello.

Gaburo, Kenneth (1926–) US composer, a pupil of Petrassi. His style is influenced very much by electronic music and his compositions include improvisation as well as theatrical effects. Gaburo's works include the operas *The Snow Queen* (1952) and *The Widow* (1961); the theatre pieces *Bodies* (1957), *The Dog-King* (1959), and the six-hour-long *Lingua I–IV* (1965–70); a viola concerto (1979); the *Antiphony* series for acoustic instruments with electronic music; and chamber music and many electronic pieces.

Gade, Niels (Wilhelm) (1817–90) Danish composer, conductor, and violinist. In 1843 he went to Leipzig, where he became assistant conductor of the Gewandhaus Orchestra and taught at the Academy of Music. He met Schumann and Mendelssohn, whom he succeeded as chief conductor of the Gewandhaus Orchestra in 1847. In 1848 he returned to Copenhagen and reestablished the Musical Society; he

Niels Gade

was conductor of the Royal Theatre (1862) and director of the Copenhagen Academy of Music (1862). Gade's compositions were strongly influenced by Mendelssohn and Schumann but many have a distinctive Danish character. He was the leading musical figure in 19th-century Denmark. His works include operas, choral music, orchestral works (among them the overture *Echoes from Ossian*, 1840, eight symphonies, and a violin concerto, 1880), chamber and keyboard works, and songs.

gadulka see **fiddle**.

gaillard see **galliard**.

Gál, Hans (1890–) Austrian-born composer and musicologist, who lived in Scotland from 1938. A pupil of Mandyczewski, his style is a development of the romantic tradition. His works include eight German operas written during the 1920s and 1930s, a piano concerto (1947), a triptych for orchestra (1970), a clarinet quintet (1976), and other chamber music. He has also written on Brahms, Wagner, and Schubert.

galanteries Unspecified nonstandard movements of the classical *suite, inserted for light relief. They could be gavottes, bourrées, minuets, etc. German: **Galanterien**.

galant style A style of 18th-century music characterized by elegant superficiality and ornamentation. It is first seen in the keyboard works of Couperin and Telemann and is also found in the music of J. S. Bach and J. C. Bach. Galant style is thus the antithesis of the much more serious and elaborate style of the baroque and it persisted, with some development, into the music of the Viennese Classical School (see **classical music**). [French and German, courtly]

Galilei, Vincenzo (*c.*1520–91) Italian composer and theorist, father of the astronomer Galileo Galilei. He was a pupil of Willaert in Venice; in 1581 he initiated an open dispute with his former teacher in the *Dialogo*, in which he attacks contrapuntal music as inexpressive and advocates a return to the ideals of ancient Greek music. Galilei's ideas were shared by the Florentine *Camerata, of which he was an active member. He is the author of two books of madrigals (1574, 1587) and two of lute music (1563, 1568).

galliard A lively dance originating in the Renaissance. In predominantly triple time, it also alternated or included compound duple time. The galliard was usually coupled with the slower duple-time *pavan. French: **gaillard**; Italian: **gagliarda**.

Galli-Curci, Amelita (1882–1963) Italian soprano. Mainly self-taught, she made her debut as Gilda in Verdi's *Rigoletto* at Rome (1906) and in 1916 at Chicago she sang the same role with sensational effect. She retired through ill health in 1930.

galop (*or* **galopade**) A lively duple-time round dance with a leap or hop at the ends of phrases.

Galuppi, Baldassare (1706–85) Italian composer. After visiting London (1741–43) and St Petersburg (1743), he worked mostly in Venice, becoming assistant maestro di cappella at St Mark's (1748) and maestro di cappella at the Ospedale degl' Incurabili (1762). He wrote over 100 operas, in which his comic settings of Goldoni texts developed the ensemble finale, and much church and keyboard music.

Galway, James (1939–) Irish flautist. After 15 years as an orchestral player, he began to concentrate on solo performances and has a wide and varied repertoire: Schroeder, Musgrave, and Rodrigo have written works for him. Galway teaches in the USA at the Eastman School of Music.

gamba 1. Short for viola da gamba (see **viol family**). **2.** Short for *lira da gamba.

gamelan An Indonesian orchestra. The term is used for different types of orchestra but they are all characterized by gongs, gong-chimes, metallophones, drums, flutes, xylophones, and cymbals. Debussy was impressed by a Javanese gamelan at the 1889 Paris Exposition. See **Indonesian music.**

gamme Scale. [French]

gamut 1. G on the bottom line of the bass clef. [from *gamma* (the lowest note of the *hexachord) plus *ut* (the first note of the scale; see **solmization**)] **2.** The scale starting on this note. **3.** Any entire scale, range, or compass.

Ganzetaktnote Semibreve. [German, literally whole-bar note]

gapped scale Any scale, such as the pentatonic scale, in which intervals of more than a tone are used, i.e. one in which there are less than seven notes.

Gardelli, Lamberto (1915–) Italian-born conductor. He took Swedish nationality and worked in Sweden (1946–55), later building an international reputation.

Garden of Fand, The Tone poem by Bax based on an old Irish legend. First performance: 1920. A magic island emerges out of the sea before some approaching sailors, who see dancing and merrymaking. After the celebrations have reached a climax the island gradually submerges. The Garden of Fand is a poetic name for the sea.

Gardiner, Henry Balfour (1877–1950) British composer. Gardiner studied in Frankfurt and Oxford. He was active in promoting the works of his contemporaries and friends, who included Bax, Holst, Grainger, and Quilter. Gardiner's own compositions include orchestral and chamber works, choral music, and songs.

Gaspard de la Nuit Set of piano pieces by Ravel. Composed: 1908. The work was inspired by a set of poems by Bertrand of the same name, subtitled *Fantasies in the manner of Rembrandt and Callot*. *Gaspard de la Nuit* is a nickname for the Devil; the three movements are entitled *Ondine* (a water nymph who entices sailors to their death), *Le Gibet* (the gallows), and *Scarbo* (a clown).

Gasparini, Francesco (1668–1727) Italian composer, a pupil of Corelli and Pasquini and teacher of Benedetto Marcello. He was maestro del coro at the Ospedale delle Pietà, Venice (1700), where Vivaldi was his leader (1711). His operas include *Il Bajazet* (1711), the libretto of which was reworked by Haym for Handel's *Tamerlano* (1724). He also wrote church music and a tutor, *L'Armonico pratico al cimbalo* (1708).

Gassmann, Florian Leopold (1729–74) Czech composer. He was maestro di cappella at the Conservatorio degl' Incurabili in Venice (1757–62). From 1763 he worked in Vienna, becoming court kapellmeister (1772). He founded the Musikalischen Sozietät der Witwen und Waisen (1771) and wrote many operas (including *L'Amore artigiano*, 1767), ballets, sinfonias, oratorios, and chamber works.

Gastein Symphony Symphony attributed to Schubert. It is presumed that Schubert wrote the work at Gastein in Austria during 1825, but the manuscript is now lost. Despite the efforts of a record company to find the manuscript by offering a reward during the Schubert centenary year of 1928, it has not yet come to light. Some scholars suggest that the *Grand Duo is a piano duet arrangement of the *Gastein Symphony*.

Gastoldi, Giovanni Giacomo (1555–1622) Italian composer. He was employed at the court of Mantua from 1579 or before; in 1592 he was appointed maestro di cappella of S Barbara. He composed sacred music, madrigals, mascherate, and balletts; these last, printed in 1594, were a strong influence on Morley's balletts (1595).

Gaultier, Denis (1603–72) French composer and lutenist, active in Paris. His most important collection, *La Rhétorique des dieux*, contains mostly dances but he also pioneered the *tombeau for lute. Gaultier was closely associated with his cousin **Ennemond Gaultier** (1575–1651), whose compositions appear in his publications.

Gauntlett, Henry John (1805–76) British organist, composer, and critic. He was a lawyer by profession but became recognized as a leading church organist and an expert in organ design. Gauntlett compiled many hymn books and is said to have composed thousands of hymn tunes; among them is *Once in Royal David's City*. A lecturer and critic, he also contributed articles on a wide range of topics to periodicals.

Gaveaux, Pierre (1761–1825) French composer and singer, a pupil of Franz Beck in Bordeaux. He wrote much music for the Théâtre de Feydeau, including *Léonore, ou L'Amour conjugal* (1798; see **Leonora, or Wedded Love**). In addition to several rescue operas, a ballet, and the revolutionary hymn 'Le Réveil du peuple' (1794), he wrote romances, overtures, and works for vocal ensemble.

gavotte A French dance in a gay 4/4 rhythm. Although of country origin, it quickly became stylized as a courtly dance. It was often included in the baroque *suite.

Gay, John (1685–1732) English poet. He was the librettist for The *Beggar's Opera* (1728), a successful satire by Pepusch.

Gayaneh Ballet in four acts with music by Khachaturian and scenario by Derzhavin. First performance: Molotov-Perm, 1942, by the Kirov Ballet. It is set on a collective farm, the heroine, Gayaneh, being unhappily married to the villain of the piece, Giko; later, she is able to marry the man she loves, Kasakov. The 'Sabre Dance' is a popular number from the score, which includes Armenian, Russian, Ukrainian, and Georgian folk music.

Gazza ladra, La see **Thieving Magpie, The**.

Gebrauchsmusik Music intended to be useful to amateurs at home (hence the name, which is German for 'utility music'), as oppposed to purely artistic music – the property of the concert professional. The term was coined in the middle 1920s and reflected aspects of the social and political climate in Germany at the time. Certain composers, notably Hindemith and Krenek, wrote in an ascetic style, in sharp contrast to the overt emotionalism of the romantics. They were, consequently, accused of a journalistic approach; their disciplined simplicity underlies this accusation. The music is simple and clear, of moderate difficulty and average length, and has parts of equal interest to the performer. Hindemith refers to the term in the introduction to his *Plöner Musiktag* (1932) but appears to have disowned it later.

gedackt (*or* **gedact** *or* **lieblich gedac(k)t**) A soft-toned organ *stop in which the sound is produced by a stopped diapason *flue pipe. [from German *gedeckt*, covered, *lieblich*, lovely]

Gedda, Nicolai (1925–) Swedish tenor. After singing in Russian Orthodox choirs he studied with Carl Martin Oehmann and made his operatic debut in 1952 as Chapelon in Adam's *Le Postillon de Longjumeau*. He has toured widely and made many recordings; he also performs lieder.

Geige (*pl.* **Geigen**) Fiddle; violin. [German]

Geisha, The Operetta in two acts by Sidney Jones with libretto by Owen Hall and Harry Greenbank. First performance: Daly's Theatre, London, 1896. The Japanese setting started a fashion for oriental subjects in librettos.

Geister Trio see Ghost Trio.

Geminiani, Francesco (*c*.1680–1762) Italian composer and violinist, a pupil of Corelli, Lonati, and Alessandro Scarlatti. He lived in London after 1714, making three visits to Dublin (1733, 1737, and 1759) and two to Paris (1740, 1749). In addition to his treatises, including his famous violin tutor, *The Art of Playing on the Violin* (1751), he also wrote concerti grossi, sonatas, and keyboard works.

gemshorn A soft-toned organ *stop with a nasal tone produced by a 4-*foot conical open *flue pipe. [German, chamois horn]

Genée, (Franz Friedrich) Richard (1823–95) German conductor, librettist, and composer. From 1847 to 1867 he was a theatre conductor in several German cities, after which he conducted at the Theater an der Wien, Vienna (1868–78). Genée wrote operettas but is better known for his librettos (including that for Strauss's *Die Fledermaus* and several for Suppé) and opera translations.

general pause A rest during which all the performers in an orchestra or ensemble are silent. Abbreviation: **G.P.**

Gentle Shepherd, The *Ballad opera set to traditional tunes by its librettist, Allan Ramsay (1686–1758), adapted from his pastoral comedy of the same name, published in 1725. First performance: Taylor's Hall, Edinburgh, 1729. Patie, the gentle shepherd, is in love with Peggie; Roger, a rich shepherd, is in love with Jenny; it is entirely in Scottish dialect.

Genzmer, Harald (1909–) German composer, a pupil of Hindemith. Genzmer's lyrical and contrapuntal style derives from that of his teacher; like Hindemith, he wrote a large amount of music for amateurs. His works include ballets, concertos (including two for the trautonium – an electronic instrument), chamber music, and piano works.

Gerhard, Roberto (1896–1970) Spanish composer resident in Britain from 1938, a pupil of Granados, Pedrell, and Schoenberg. His early style, in which he used serialism with a Spanish inflection, is demonstrated in the radio opera *The *Duenna* (1947). He later developed his serial language with an emphasis on the use of instrumental colour and contrasts, as in his piano concerto (1951), four symphonies (1953–67), and the concerto for orchestra (1965). Serialism is used in a freer way in his final virtuoso chamber works, *Gemini* (1966), *Libra* (1968), and *Leo* (1969).

German, Sir Edward (E. G. Jones; 1862–1936) British composer and conductor. After studying at the Royal Academy of Music (1880–87), he taught the violin and played in theatre orchestras. In 1888 he became conductor at the Globe Theatre, where his music for a production of *Richard III* won him recognition. He wrote incidental music for *Henry VIII* and soon came to be identified with an 'Old English' style, which he cultivated in his operettas *Merrie England* (1902) and *Tom Jones* (1907). He was knighted in 1928. German is now remembered for his light theatre music and songs, but he also composed tone poems, two symphonies, and chamber, sacred choral, and piano music. He completed Sullivan's score for *The Emerald Isle*.

German flute see flute.

Germani, Fernando (1906–) Italian organist. He held teaching appointments in Siena, Rome, and Philadelphia and was organist of St Peter's, Rome (1948–59). Germani is one of the leading organists of his generation and has achieved international recognition.

German Requiem, A (German: *Ein Deutsches Requiem*) Mass for baritone and soprano soloists, choir, and orchestra (Op. 45) by Brahms. Composed: 1866–68; first complete performance: Leipzig, 1869. Instead of using the customary Latin words of the Requiem Mass, Brahms has taken seven German translations of appropriate passages from the Bible. The Requiem was written after the death of his mother.

German sixth see augmented sixth.

Gershwin, George (1898–1937) US composer. Gershwin's early success as a composer of popular songs did not preclude his study of art music with Goldmark, Cowell, and Schillinger; he also approached Ravel for lessons. His larger compositions use jazz features within an often symphonic context. Gershwin's works include the opera *Porgy and Bess* (1935), *Rhapsody in Blue* (1923–24) originally for piano and jazz band, a piano concerto in F (1925), An *American in Paris* (1928) for orchestra, and piano music. His brother **Ira Gershwin** (1896–) wrote the lyrics for many of his songs.

Ges G flat. [German]

Gesang Song; singing. Hence **geistlicher Gesang**, sacred song; hymn. [German]

Geschöpfe des Prometheus, Die (*The Creatures of Prometheus*) Suite of ballet music by Beethoven. First performance: 1801. This work is important because one theme from it features prominently in some of Beethoven's later music; it is used in both the final movement of the *Eroica Symphony* and in the *Eroica Variations* as the basis for a set of variations. The same melody also appears in the seventh of Beethoven's *Contre-danses*.

gestopft Stopped: used in horn playing to indicate that the fist should be placed in the bell of the instrument in order to dampen the sound. [German]

Gesualdo, Carlo (*c*.1560–1613) Italian composer, Prince of Venosa. Born in Naples, he came from an illustrious

George Gershwin

family (his father, Fabrizio Gesualdo, was an important music patron). In 1590 he murdered his wife, her lover, and a son whose paternity he doubted. He went to Ferrara (1594) and married Leonora d'Este, sister of the reigning duke, returning to Naples in 1597. Gesualdo's six books of madrigals (1594–1616) are characterized by an extremely bold use of chromaticism and textural fragmentation not found in the earlier madrigals. Despite its difficulty and novelty, his music was much admired at the time and more recently attracted the attention of Stravinsky.

geteilt (*or* **getheilt**) see **divisi**.

Ghedini, Giorgio Federico (1892–1965) Italian composer. Ghedini was director of the Milan conservatory (1951–62). An independent figure in modern Italian music, Ghedini shows in his best works a keen sense of instrumental colour. His compositions include operas, such as *Billy Budd* (1949); orchestral works, such as *Architetture* (1940) and the *Concerto dell' Albatro* (1945); choral music; and chamber works.

Ghiaurov, Nicolai (1929–   ) Bulgarian bass. He studied at the Sofia conservatory (with Brambarov) then in Leningrad and Moscow. His debut as Basilio in Rossini's

The Barber of Seville (1955) was followed by extensive European tours.

Ghost Trio (German: *Geister Trio*) Piano trio in D major (Op. 70 No. 1) by Beethoven. Composed: 1808. The slow movement features a haunting melody and the accompanying tremolando string phrases make the name particularly apt.

Gianni Schicchi Comic opera in one act by Puccini with libretto by Forzano. First performance: Metropolitan Opera, New York, 1918. It forms a tryptych (see **Trittico, Il**) with *Il Tabarro* (*The Cloak*) and *Suor Angelica* (*Sister Angelica*). Gianni Schicchi (baritone), a medieval Florentine rogue, dupes a family out of their legacies.

Giant Fugue Choral prelude (BWV 680) by Bach. Composed: 1739. This work is found in the third part of the *Clavierübung* and is based on the chorale 'Wir glauben all an einen Gott.' The chorale is treated fugally and the name derives from the giant striding figure in the pedals.

Giardini, Felice de (1716–96) Italian composer and violinist, a pupil of Paladini and Somis. He worked in Italy, Germany, and France before settling in London, where he became leader of the London Opera (1752) and directed the Three Choirs Festival (1770–76). He collaborated with Avison on the oratorio *Ruth* (1765) and wrote ballad operas, songs, church music, and violin works.

Giazotto, Remo (1910–   ) Italian musicologist, author of a musical history of Genoa and biographies of Albinoni and Vivaldi. In 1967 he became co-editor of *Nuova rivista musicale italiana.*

Gibbons, Orlando (1583–1625) English composer. He sang in the choir of King's College, Cambridge, from 1596 until at least 1598. From 1605 he was organist to the Chapel Royal; later he became a virginalist to James I. From 1623 until his death he was also organist at Westminster Abbey. Gibbons was one of the most versatile and perhaps the most gifted English composer between Byrd and Purcell. All his sacred music is written for the English rite; it includes 16 hymn tunes, 2 sets of preces and psalms, 2 services, 13 full anthems, and 25 verse anthems. The verse anthems foreshadow the baroque in their juxtaposition of soloists and chorus. *The Madrigals and Mottets* (1612) are likewise all set to English words and reveal a melancholy and didactic side of Gibbons' personality. Gibbons also wrote a number of pieces for keyboard and for viol consort, all of which survive in manuscript, and contributed to *Parthenia*. His son, **Christopher Gibbons** (1615–76), was educated at the Chapel Royal. He became organist at Winchester Cathedral (1638) and at the Chapel Royal (1660); in 1660 he also became private organist to Charles II. His viol fantasies and anthems are preserved in manuscript. He collaborated with

The bust of Orlando Gibbons in Canterbury Cathedral

Matthew Locke on the music for Shirley's masque, *Cupid and Death* (1653).

Gibbs, Armstrong (1899–1960) British composer. Gibbs' songs reveal his sensitivity in setting words; his other works include three symphonies, chamber music, and choral works.

Gibson, Sir Alexander (1926–) British conductor. In 1959 he became conductor of the Scottish National Orchestra and he has been chief conductor of Scottish Opera since its inception (1962). He was knighted in 1977.

Gide, André (1869–1951) French novelist, dramatist, and poet. He wrote the text for Stravinsky's *Perséphone* (1933–34); Honegger wrote some incidental music for his *Saül* (1922).

Gielen, Michael (1927–) German-born conductor and composer, conductor since 1973 of the Netherlands Opera and since 1977 of the Frankfurt Opera. As a conductor, Gielen specializes in contemporary music; his own compositions include *Variations* (1959) and *Some Difficulties in Overcoming Anxiety* (1972).

Gieseking, Walter (1895–1965) German pianist. He studied with Leimer at Hanover and after World War I toured Europe extensively. Gieseking was active in promoting contemporary music, by such composers as Schoenberg and Hindemith, and his playing of Debussy was much admired.

giga see **jig.**

Gigli, Beniamino (1890–1957) Italian tenor. He was taught by Agnese Bonucci, Cotogni, and Rosati in Rome and made his debut in *La Gioconda* at Rovigo, Spain

(1914). He became internationally famous as an opera singer, being regarded as Caruso's successor. His popular sentimental style was best suited to Puccini's music.

Gigout, Eugène (1844–1925) French organist, composer, and teacher. He studied with Saint-Saëns and Loret at the Ecole Niedermeyer, where he later taught. From 1863 to his death he was organist of St Augustin and from 1911 organ professor at the Paris Conservatoire. One of the leading French organists of his day, Gigout wrote symphonic pieces for organ and liturgical works incorporating Gregorian chant.

gigue see **jig.**

Gilbert, Sir William Schwenk (1836–1911) British writer and critic, famous for his collaboration (as librettist) with Sir Arthur *Sullivan in the Gilbert and Sullivan comic operas, which began in 1871. See also **Savoy operas.**

Gilels, Emil (1916–) Soviet pianist. Success in the All Union Musicians' Contest in Moscow in 1933 brought him international recognition and after World War II he began to tour Europe and the USA. Gilels has taught at the Moscow conservatory. His sister **Elizaveta Gilels**, a violinist, is married to the violinist Leonid *Kogan.

Giles, Nathaniel (*c.*1558–1634) English composer. He was organist at Worcester Cathedral (1581–85) and from 1585 until his death he was organist and choirmaster of St George's Chapel, Windsor; from 1597 he was also Master of the Children at the Chapel Royal. Giles is the author of 4 services, 32 anthems, 5 motets, and 1 madrigal.

gimel see **gymel.**

Ginastera, Alberto (1916–83) Argentinian composer. Ginastera's early music often drew on melodic and rhythmic patterns found in Argentinian folk music. In his later works these were superseded by serial and avant-garde techniques. His large output includes *Bomarzo* (1967) and two other operas, ballets, concertos, orchestral music, and chamber works.

Gioconda, La (*The Ballad Singer*) Opera in four acts by Ponchielli with libretto by Boito based on Victor Hugo's play *Angelo.* First performance: La Scala, Milan, 1876. Set in 17th-century Venice, it is a tale of intrigue and tragedy concerning the ballad singer, La Gioconda (soprano), who finally kills herself to escape the spy, Barnaba; Act III contains the ballet *Dance of the Hours.*

giocoso Jocose; merry; playful. [Italian]

Gioielli della Madonna, I see **Jewels of the Madonna, The.**

Giordani, Giuseppe (*c.*1753–98) Italian composer, impresario, and singer, a pupil of Fenaroli. He worked mainly as an opera composer, with his first known work, *Epponina,* produced in Florence (1779). He was maestro di cappella in Fermo (1791–98), writing many sacred works. He also wrote ballets, arias, divertimentos, concertos, and keyboard compositions.

Giordani, Tommaso (*c*.1730–1806) Italian composer and singer. He worked in London, where he wrote music for Sheridan's *The Critic* (1779), but was most active in Dublin, where he established the Little Theatre with Leoni (1784) and directed the Spiritual Concerts (1792). He wrote much theatre music, violin concertos, Italian and English canzonettas, and church music.

Giordano, Umberto (1867–1948) Italian opera composer. His works reveal a fine theatrical talent and also a gift for lyrical expression. Giordano's best-known operas are *Andrea Chénier* (1896), *Fedora* (1898), and *Madame Sans-gêne* (1915).

Giorno di Regno, Un (*King for a Day*) Opera buffa in two acts by Verdi with libretto by Romani. First performance: La Scala, Milan, 1840. Set during the Polish wars of succession, it is a story of intrigue concerning the Cavalier di Belfiore (baritone), a French officer impersonating King Stanislao of Poland.

Giovanna d'Arco (*Joan of Arc*) Opera by Verdi in prologue and three acts with libretto by Solera, based on Schiller's play *Die Jungfrau von Orleans*. First performance: La Scala, Milan, 1845.

Giovannelli, Ruggiero (*c*.1560–1625) Italian composer. He was maestro di cappella of three churches in Rome: S Luigi dei Francesi (1583–91), the German College (1591–94), and St Peter's (1594–99). From 1599 to 1624 he was a singer in the papal choir. Giovannelli was a prolific composer of church music; one of his masses is based on Palestrina's own mass parodying *Vestiva i colli*. He is best remembered, however, for his madrigals, which vied in popularity with those of Marenzio. Between 1585 and 1605 he produced three books for five voices, two for four voices, and one for three voices. His early madrigals share with Marenzio's a lightness of touch, clear harmonies, and short memorable rhythmic motives. His most original works are probably the four-voice settings of Sannazaro's *Arcadia* (1585 and 1589), written in a jaunty rhythmic style imitating rustic speech. Many of the later madrigals draw on Guarini's *Il Pastor fido* but lack the profundity of Marenzio's earlier settings.

Giovanni da Cascia (14th century) Italian composer and contemporary of Jacopo da Bologna, working at the court of Mastino della Scala at Verona (1329–1351). His works include madrigals, cacce, and ballate.

Gipps, Ruth (1921–   ) British composer and conductor, a pupil of Vaughan Williams. Her compositions include four symphonies, concertos, songs, and chamber works.

giraffe piano A form of upright *piano made in Germany and elsewhere in the 19th century. It is essentially a grand piano with the case stood vertically on the floor. The long bass strings on the left reach to the full height of the case while the shorter treble strings on the right do not do so. The resulting shape is reminiscent of a giraffe's neck.

Girl from Arles, The see **Arlésienne, L'**.

Girl of the Golden West, The (*La Fanciulla del West*) Opera in three acts by Puccini with libretto by Civinini and Zangarini based on the play by David Belasco. First performance: Metropolitan Opera, New York, 1910. Minnie (soprano), owner of *The Polka* bar, falls in love with Dick Johnson (tenor), a bandit on the run in a Wild West setting.

Gis G sharp. [German]

Giselle Ballet in two acts with music by Adolphe Adam, scenario by Théophile Gautier and de Saint Georges, and choreography by Coralli. First performance: Opéra, Paris, 1841. Subtitled *The Wilis*, it shows how Giselle, a peasant girl betrayed in love by Duke Albrecht, is transformed into one of the Wilis, the spirits of girls who die before their intended marriages.

gittern A medieval form of the *guitar in which the body and neck were carved from the same block of wood, with a hole beneath the fingerboard for the player's thumb. The gittern usually had four pairs of gut strings tuned D, G, B, E (the D being the D below middle C) and was played with a plectrum. It was popular in Europe during the 16th century until it was ousted by the larger five-course guitar.

Giuliani, Mauro (Giuseppe Sergio Pantaleo) (1781–1829) Italian guitarist and composer. From 1806 to 1819 he lived in Vienna, where he quickly made a reputation as the leading guitar virtuoso and composer. He wrote over 200 works for the instrument, including three concertos, chamber works with guitar, and many sets of variations.

Giulini, Carlo Maria (1914–   ) Italian conductor. He was musical director of La Scala (1951–56) and conductor of the Chicago Symphony Orchestra (from 1968) and the Vienna Symphony Orchestra (1973–76). He is particularly associated with Verdi's operas and *Requiem*.

Giulio Cesare see **Julius Caesar**.

giusto Just; proper: used in tempo markings to indicate either moderation or exactness. [Italian]

Glagolithic Mass Mass by Janáček for choir, organ, and orchestra. Composed: 1927. The work has distinct patriotic overtones, Glagolithic being a dead Slavonic language formerly associated with the church. A particularly virtuosic interlude for organ is included in this mass.

Philip Glass

Alexander Glazunov

Glanville-Hicks, Peggy (1912–) Australian composer. She studied in Europe with Vaughan Williams, Nadia Boulanger, and Wellesz before settling in the USA in 1939. Her music shows many nontraditional influences, including ancient Greek and Indian. Her prolific output includes five operas, six ballets, chamber music, and songs.

Glass, Philip (1937–) US composer, a pupil of Persichetti, Nadia Boulanger, and Ravi Shankar. His music has been influenced by oriental modes, serialism, and aleatoricism and in 1967 he organized an ensemble for the performance of his own works. Glass's mature music makes much use of repetition of minimal elements and is increasingly involved with theatre, as in his operatic collaboration with Robert Wilson in *Einstein on the Beach* (1976). Other works include *Music in Fifths* (1970), *Music for Voices* (1972), *Music in Twelve Parts* (1974), and *North Star* (1975).

glass harmonica (*or* **musical glasses**) A simple form of musical instrument in which drinking glasses, partially filled with liquid, are tuned to produce notes when rubbed round the rim with a damp finger. Some serious music has been written for the glass harmonica, for example by Mozart.

Glazunov, Alexander Konstantinovich (1865–1936) Russian composer. At Balakirev's suggestion, he became a pupil of Rimsky-Korsakov and revealed a precocious talent in his first symphony (1882). He was supported by the wealthy patron Mitrofan Belyayev, who took him to Weimar, where he met Liszt. In 1899 he was appointed professor at the St Petersburg conservatory, where in 1905 he became director. In 1928 he went to Vienna, then toured Europe and went to the USA. He settled in Paris. Glazunov is an important figure in Russian music. The fervent nationalism of The *Five had resulted in a distinctive Russian national school of composition, and Glazunov was able to work within that tradition and also to absorb influences from western Europe. He composed nine symphonies (the ninth is unfinished), two piano concertos, a violin concerto (1904, one of his best-known works), a saxophone concerto, overtures, ballets (including *Raymonda*, 1898), incidental music, and choral and chamber works. He completed the third act of Borodin's *Prince Igor* after that composer's death, collaborated in several works, and made many arrangements.

glee A light-hearted unaccompanied vocal piece in sections, each variable according to the mood of the line of poetry set. It was generally homophonic (though with a dominant melody) and was most properly performed by solo male voices. Uniquely English, it was popular from about 1760 to 1840, together with catches and canons in similar vein. The Glee Club was founded in 1787 and lasted until 1857, although by this time the form had been devalued musically and gave way to the part song. Present-day US glee clubs are university singing groups who do not restrict themselves to singing glees.

Glière, Reinhold (1875–1926) Russian composer. After studying at the Moscow conservatory, Glière was active as a teacher, his pupils including Prokofiev. He travelled throughout Russia collecting folk melodies. Glière's nationalism is most evident in his symphonies and symphonic poems. His large output also includes operas, ballet music, incidental music, and songs.

Glinka, Mikhail Ivanovich (1804–57) Russian composer. At school at St Petersburg he had piano lessons from John Field; later he pursued the life of a musical dilettante, associating with leading figures in Russian literature. He spent three years in Italy (1830–33), then went to Vienna and Berlin, where he studied with Dehn and began incorporating Russian folk melodies into his compositions. Back in St Petersburg his nationalist opera *A *Life for the Tsar* was produced in 1836, making Glinka the most celebrated Russian composer. He was appointed kapellmeister of the imperial chapel in 1837. His opera *Russlan and Ludmila* (1842) was less well received, and in 1844 Glinka went to Paris, where he met Berlioz, who admired his work. In 1845 he went to Spain and began a series of Spanish-influenced works, including *Capriccio brillante* (1845), on the jota aragonese, and *Recuerdos de Castilla* (1848). In Warsaw (1848–49) he composed one of his most influential orchestral pieces, *Kamarinskaya*, a colourful inventive work using Russian folk melodies. He returned to St Petersburg and made a few foreign tours before his death.

Glinka is regarded as the founder of 19th-century Russian *nationalism in music and his independence from western musical traditions had a profound influence on later Russian composers, particularly Balakirev and Tchaikovsky. He was the first Russian composer to be recognized outside his country. In addition to stage and orchestral works, he wrote chamber music (including a string quartet, 1824), piano works, and songs.

glissando A sliding scale played on an instrument. On the piano a glissando can only be played in C major, and this is achieved by sliding the finger over the adjacent notes. A similar effect can be produced on a harp. On a bowed instrument a glissando is played on one string by gliding the finger up or down while bowing. A glissando can also be played on a trombone.

Globokar, Vinko (1934–) Yugoslav composer and trombonist, a pupil of Leibowitz and Berio. He has shown a particular interest in the exploration and extension of instrumental techniques in such works as *Fluide* (1967), *Echanges* (1973), and *Discours IV* (1974). He has also written music-theatre pieces, including *Carrousel* (1977).

Glock, Sir William (1908–) British music critic and administrator. He studied at Cambridge and was taught the piano in Berlin by Artur Schnabel (1930–33). He was music critic for *The Observer* (1934–45), musical director of Dartington Hall (1953–79), and controller of music at the BBC (1959–73).

Glocke (*pl.* **Glocken**) Bell. In orchestral scores the word usually refers to the tubular bells in the percussion section. [German]

glockenspiel An orchestral percussion instrument consisting of two rows of steel plates arranged like a piano keyboard, the back row being equivalent to the black notes and the front row to the white notes of a piano. The plates are struck with two hammers, one held in each hand, or with a mechanism operated by a piano keyboard. It has a range of two and a half octaves and a bell-like sound. See also **celeste**. [German, play of bells]

Gloriana Opera in three acts by Britten with text by William Plomer. First performance: Covent Garden, London, 1953 (a gala in connection with the coronation of Queen Elizabeth II). The libretto is concerned with the later years of Elizabeth I's reign and the fall of the Earl of Essex.

Gluck, Christoph Willibald (1714–87) German composer. After studying with Sammartini in Milan he worked in London (*c*.1746) and toured with the Mingotti Troupe, before settling in Vienna (*c*.1750). There he was kapellmeister to the Prince of Sachsen-Hildburghausen (*c*.1754) and wrote his Italian reform operas *Orfeo ed Euridice* (1762), *Alceste* (1767), and *Paride ed Elena* (1770), which used accompanied recitative, chorus, and other methods to emphasize the dramatic effects. From 1773 to 1779 Gluck worked in Paris, where he produced *Iphigénie en Aulide* (1774; see **Iphigenia in Aulis**), *Armide* (1777; see **Armida**), *Iphigénie en Tauride* (1779; see **Iphigenia in Tauris**), and French versions of his Italian operas. His other operas include the Italian *Artaserse* (1741), *Ezio* (1750), and *Il Rè pastore* (1756), and the French *Echo et Narcisse* (1779). He also wrote ballets, symphonies, a *De Profundis* (1787), arias, and chamber and keyboard music.

Glyndebourne An English manor house near Lewes, Sussex, where the Glyndebourne Festival Opera was founded in 1934. John Christie (1882–1962), the owner of the estate, was an opera enthusiast who built an opera house adjoining the manor for his wife, the opera singer Audrey Mildmay (1900–53). It opened in 1934 with a fortnight's performances of *The Marriage of Figaro* and *Così fan tutte*. With Fritz Busch as its musical director, Carl Ebert as producer, and Rudolf Bing as manager, it set high standards and soon attracted internationally acclaimed singers (it has also encouraged many young singers). Mozart has always been central to Glyndebourne's programmes but Strauss's operas have received special attention. Britten's *The Rape of Lucretia* and *Albert Herring* were given their premieres there. The opera company has used the Royal Philharmonic Orchestra and the London Philharmonic Orchestra. Its conductors have included Vittorio Gui, John Pritchard, and Bernard Haitink. The Glyndebourne Touring Opera was formed in 1968.

Gnecchi, Vittorio (1876–1954) Italian composer of operas. His works include *Virtú d'amore* (1896) and *Cassandra* (1905).

Gnessin, Mikhail Fabianovich (1883–1957) Soviet composer, a pupil of Rimsky-Korsakov. Gnessin's music is characteristically romantic in its chromaticism; many of his works are based on Hebrew themes. His compositions include operas and other dramatic works, orchestral music, and chamber works.

Gobbi, Tito (1915–84) Italian baritone. He studied with Giulio Crini and made his debut in Gubbio as Rodolfo in Bellini's *La Sonnambula*. His 100-role repertory (including Rigoletto, Falstaff, and Scarpia in *Tosca*), 26 films, television appearances, and autobiography made him one of the best-known singers of his time.

Godard, Benjamin (**Louis Paul**) (1849–95) French composer. He studied the violin with Hammer and Vieuxtemps and composition at the Paris Conservatoire with Reber. Godard's music is fluent but lightweight. He wrote vocal music, orchestral works (including five symphonies), chamber music (including string quartets and several violin works), piano pieces, and operas; only the 'Berceuse' from his opera **Jocelyn* (1888) is still known.

Godowsky, Leopold (1870–1938) Polish-born US pianist and composer. He had a high European reputation as a performer, although his career was terminated by illness in 1930. Godowsky composed both original works and made several transcriptions, notably of Strauss waltzes.

Tito Gobbi as Almaviva in The Marriage of Figaro

God Save the Queen (*or* **King**) British national anthem. The derivation of both the words and melody is uncertain, although the first appearance of the anthem in anything approaching its present form comes in the *Thesaurus Musicus* of 1744. Neither author nor composer is known, although the melody bears similarities to earlier pieces by Bull and Purcell (among others). During the 1745 rebellion it became very popular as a royalist marching song and from then on was generally adopted as a national anthem. Like **Deutschland über Alles* the setting has been used for different texts; in the USA it is sung to the words 'My Country 'tis of Thee,' written in 1831 by the Rev Samuel Smith.

Goehr, Alexander (1932–) British composer, son of the conductor **Walter Goehr** (1903–60) and a pupil of Hall and Messiaen. His early works, such as *The Deluge* (1958), combine serial techniques with virtuoso instrumental writing. Later, as in the violin concerto (1962) and the *Little Symphony* (1963), he employed repetition and variation form. Goehr's developed style is found in the opera *Arden Must Die* (1966). He formed the Music Theatre Ensemble (1967) for the performance of his theatre works, e.g. *Triptych* (1968–70). Later works include a piano concerto (1972), *Metamorphosis/Dance* (1974), and an oratorio, *Babylon the Great is Fallen* (1979), in a rather traditionalist style.

Goethe, Johann Wolfgang von (1749–1832) German poet and writer. A substantial part of Goethe's poetry was written to be sung and sometimes he devised new words for old popular tunes. Beethoven wrote music for *Egmont* (1809–10). Goethe's greatest writings have inspired many later composers, notably Liszt, who wrote a *Faust Symphony* (1846); Gounod, whose opera *Faust* was first performed in 1859; and Schubert and Mahler.

Goetz, Hermann (**Gustav**) (1840–76) German composer. He studied with Stern, Bülow, and Ulrich at the Stern conservatory, Berlin (1860–62), was organist and choirmaster at Winterthur (1863–72), and finally settled in Zürich because of poor health. Goetz wrote three operas, of which *Der Widerspenstigen Zähmung* (*The Taming of the Shrew*, 1868–72) was very successful; his other compositions include choral works (unaccompanied and with orchestra), songs, orchestral music (including a symphony and two piano concertos), and chamber and piano music.

Goldberg, Szymon (1909–) Polish-born violinist. In addition to a career as both a solo and orchestral player, leading the Berlin Philharmonic Orchestra from 1929 to 1934, Goldberg has made frequent appearances as a conductor. He is the founder and musical director of the Netherlands Chamber Orchestra.

Goldberg Variations Set of variations for harpsichord (BWV 988) by Bach. Composed: 1742. The work comprises 30 variations, arranged so that every third variation is a canonic one, ending with a *quodlibet. Bach was commissioned to write the work by Count Kayserling and it is named after the Count's harpsichordist Johann Goldberg. The *Goldberg Variations* were published as the fourth part of the *Clavierübung*.

Golden Cockerel, The (French: *Le Coq d'or*) Opera in three acts by Rimsky-Korsakov with text, based on a poem of Pushkin, by Bielsky. First performance: Moscow, 1909 (after the composer's death). It is a rich burlesque with the aged, greedy, and lazy King Dodon (bass) as its central character; the cockerel of the title warns of danger to his kingdom.

Golden Sonata Sonata in F major for two violins, viola da gamba, and harpsichord by Purcell. Published: 1697. Purcell himself did not use this name. The *Golden Sonata* is the ninth of the *Sonatas of Four Parts*.

Goldmark, Karl (*or* **Károly**) (1830–1915) Hungarian composer and violinist. After studying at the Vienna conservatory he played in theatre orchestras in Ödenburg and Ofen, returning to Vienna to play at the Theater in der Josefstadt and the Carlstheater. He also taught. He made his reputation as a composer with his string quartet (1860). Goldmark's music, now rarely heard, is coloured by Hungarian folk elements. His most important works were operas (including *Die Königen von Saba*, 1875), but he also wrote orchestral music, such as the overture *Sakuntala* (1865), and the symphony *Rustic Wedding* (1876); choral, chamber, and piano music; and songs. His nephew, the composer **Rubin Goldmark** (1872–1936), worked in the USA. After studying in Vienna he became a pupil of Dvořák in New York. He headed the Juilliard School's composition department from 1924 and taught many US composers, including Copland and Gershwin. His output includes orchestral works, such as *Requiem* (1919) and *A Negro Rhapsody* (1926), chamber music, and songs.

Golliwog's Cakewalk see **Children's Corner**.

Gombert, Nicolas (*c*.1500–after 1556) Flemish composer, possibly a pupil of Josquin. He was employed at the court of Emperor Charles V (1526–*c*.1540) and his last years were probably spent at Tournai. His masses, chansons, and motets display great contrapuntal ingenuity: the texture is densely woven and continuity is obtained through the use of overlapping cadences. Gombert's music is thus a reaction against Josquin's clearcut designs and foreshadows that of Willaert and Palestrina.

Gondoliers, The Operetta by Sullivan with libretto by Gilbert. First performance: Savoy Theatre, London, 1889. Subtitled *The King of Barataria*, it concerns the Duke of

The Golden Cockerel *at the Bolshoi Theatre (1988)*

Plaza Toro and his family and two Venetian gondoliers, who find themselves jointly reigning as king despite their egalitarian principles. The operetta contains a lively dance based on the Spanish *cachucha.

gong A metal (usually bronze) disc that is struck with a stick or hammer. Although they are thought to have originated in SE Asia in the 6th century, gongs were not used in the orchestra until the beginning of the 19th century. They may be either of fixed pitch or of indefinite pitch. The **tamtam** is a gong, or often a pair of gongs, suspended in a frame and struck with a soft padded beater. Tamtams are of indefinite pitch; in the orchestra the word gong is usually reserved for instruments of definite pitch.

Goodall, Sir Reginald (1901–) British conductor. He conducted at Sadlers Wells and Covent Garden, was répetiteur at Covent Garden (1961–71), and has subsequently worked chiefly for English National Opera. A noted Wagnerian, his English *Ring* was used in the first complete English recording of the cycle.

Good-Humoured Ladies, The (French: *Les Femmes de bonne humeur*) Comic ballet in one act with music by Domenico Scarlatti arranged by Tommasini and choreography by Massine. First performance: Teatro Costanzi, Rome, 1917, by Diaghilev's Ballets Russes (décor by Bakst). Based on Goldoni's play *Le Donne di buon umore*, it relates the complicated love affair of Costanza and Rinaldo.

Goodman, Benny (Benjamin David G.; 1909–) US jazz clarinettist. He studied at the Hull House in Chicago and led his first band in 1934. He was prominent in the development of *swing in the mid 1930s. Goodman was also of note as a classical musician: Bartók and Copland wrote works for him.

Goossens, Sir Eugene (1893–1962) British conductor and composer. He has conducted various orchestras, including the Sydney Symphony Orchestra (1947–50), and was knighted in 1955. His compositions include symphonies, operas, ballets, songs, and an oboe concerto written for his brother, the virtuoso oboist **Leon Goossens** (1897–1988). His sisters **Marie Goossens** (1894–) and **Sidonie Goossens** (1899–) are both harpists, Sidonie being involved in many performances of contemporary music.

gopak (*or* **hopak**) A lively Russian dance in duple time, originating in the Ukraine.

Gordon, Gavin (1901–70) British composer, singer, and film actor, a pupil of Vaughan Williams. He composed mostly ballets, including *The *Rake's Progress* (1935).

Gossec, François Joseph (1734–1829) Belgian composer, a pupil of Rameau. He lived in Paris from 1751, directing music for the Prince de Conti (1762) and the Concerts Spirituels (1773–77). He founded L'Ecole Royale de Chant (1784) and was one of the first directors of the Conservatoire (1795). He is best remembered for his large choral and orchestral works, many celebrating the Revolution.

Götterdämmerung see **Ring des Nibelungen, Der.**

Gottschalk, Louis Moreau (1829–69) US composer and pianist. In 1842 he went to Paris to study with Hallé and Stamaty: his debut (1844) in the Salle Pleyel greatly impressed Chopin. Gottschalk's compositions had been well received, but with *Le Bananier* (1850), a Negro song for piano, he became the first composer from the New World to win international acclaim. By this time a celebrated virtuoso, he toured France and Switzerland, spent a year (1851–52) in Spain, then returned to New York, where he found it harder to make his mark. Apart from visits to Havana (1857) and California (1865), he spent the rest of his life in South America, where he gave numerous concerts, some of them involving hundreds of performers.

Gottschalk's works were neglected after his death, but in the 1930s a revival of interest revealed him as an important figure in 19th-century American music. His use of quotations (e.g. in *Le Banjo* for piano, 1854–55) anticipates Ives's technique and his syncopated rhythms were later a feature of ragtime. His surviving output includes operas, two symphonies, a piano concerto and other orchestral music, and songs; his numerous piano pieces include virtuoso fantasias and studies, dances, and caprices, the best-known works being *The Last Hope* (1854) and *The Dying Poet* (1863–64).

Goudimel, Claude (*c.*1520–72) French composer. He studied at Paris University (*c.*1549–57) and from 1553 was a joint publisher with Nicolas du Chemin. He lived in Metz (1557–?1567) and Besançon and in about 1560 he became a Huguenot. He was killed in the St Bartholomew's Day massacre of Protestants in Lyons. Goudimel's most important works are the ten books of psalms translated into French (1552–65), some of which draw on melodies by Franc and Bourgeois. Goudimel also wrote a number of chansons (from 1549).

Gould, Glenn (1932–82) Canadian pianist. After achieving an international reputation, he retired from concert appearances in 1964, devoting his time to writing, recording, and broadcasting.

Gounod, Charles (**François**) (1818–93) French composer, conductor, and organist, who studied with Halévy, Le Sueur, and Zimmermann at the Paris Conservatoire (1836–39). In Rome he won the Prix de Rome and was much impressed with 16th-century polyphony, particularly Palestrina. He travelled to Vienna, Berlin, and Leipzig (where he met Mendelssohn); in Paris he started but did not finish a training for the priesthood. His first really successful opera was *Faust* (1859). From 1870 to 1874 he was in England, where his choral works were well received and he became first conductor of the Royal Albert Hall (now Royal) Choral Society. Gounod's music is melodious, chromatic, and delicate, but although it was acclaimed in his day and influenced the next generation of composers it has not maintained its popularity. He is best remembered for his vocal music; his operas include *La Nonne sanglante* (1854), *Mireille* (1864), and *Roméo et Juliette* (1867; see **Romeo and Juliet**), and his best-known choral works are

Charles Gounod,

the oratorio *La Rédemption* (?1882) and *Mors et vita* (?1885); he also wrote sacred and secular songs and part songs and much liturgical music. His instrumental music includes two symphonies, a *Petite symphonie* for nine wind instruments (1885), and chamber and piano works. He wrote many essays and reviews.

Gow, Nathaniel (1763–1831) Scottish composer and violinist, son of the violinist **Niel Gow** (1727–1807) and a pupil of Robert Mackintosh. He was one of His Majesty's Trumpeters for Scotland (1779–82) and leader of the Edinburgh Assembly Orchestra (1791). He wrote songs and street cries, such as 'Caller Herrin''; collections of dance music, including the *Strathspey Reels* (1797); and chamber music.

Goyescas 1. Two suites of piano pieces by Granados. Composed: 1911. The inspiration for these seven pieces came from a set of etchings of Spanish scenes by Goya.
2. Opera by Granados with libretto by F. Periquet y Zuaznabar. First performance: Metropolitan Opera, New York, 1916. The opera is based on the same source as the suites and Granados incorporated some music from these suites into it.

G.P. 1. See **general pause**. **2.** Abbreviation for Grand-Positif: used in French organ scores to indicate that the great and choir organs should be coupled.

Grabu, Louis (17th century) French composer and violinist. He worked in London as composer to Charles II (1665) and was Master of the King's Music (1666–c.1674). In addition to the music for Dryden's *Albion and Albanius* (1685) and the opera *Ariadne* (1674), he wrote music for other plays and instrumental ensemble.

grace note A note, often printed in small type, that is an ornament to, rather than an essential part of, a melody or harmony.

Gradual 1. The *respond that comes between the Epistle and the Gospel in the *Mass. It is coupled with the Alleluia or Tract. **2.** The liturgical book containing the Concentus of Mass *plainchant, i.e. it is the musical companion to the Missal.

Gradus ad Parnassum 1. A treatise on counterpoint by Johann Joseph Fux, published in Vienna in 1725. It is an important textbook written in dialogue form: the Latin title means 'steps to Parnassus' (the muses' sacred mountain).
2. Collection of 100 keyboard studies by Muzio Clementi. Published: 1817. Debussy parodied one of Clementi's studies in the first piece of his suite *Children's Corner* (1906–08), calling it 'Doctor Gradus ad Parnassum.'

Graener, Paul (1872–1944) German composer. Graener's study in Berlin was followed by a period of travel: he spent some time in London, conducting and teaching. He

subsequently held important academic posts in Germany. His compositions, which combine neoclassical and impressionist features, include *Friedemann Bach* (1931) and other operas, concertos for piano and cello, and chamber works.

Grainger, Percy Aldridge (1882–1961) Australian composer and pianist. Grainger studied with Busoni in Germany and lived in London from 1900 to 1915. In 1906 he met Grieg, who inspired in Grainger an interest in folk music. From 1915 he lived in the USA, eventually taking American citizenship. British folk songs and dances form the basis of much of Grainger's music, such as the orchestral *Mock Morris* (1911), *Shepherds' Hey* (1913), and *Irish Tune from County Derry* (see **Londonderry Air**). Many of these orchestral settings also exist in versions for chamber ensemble or piano. Grainger's other works include songs and choral music.

Granados, Enrique (1867–1916) Spanish composer and pianist, a pupil of Pedrell in Madrid. Granados also studied privately in Paris. His music offers a romantic elaboration of characteristically Spanish musical idioms: this is particularly true of his piano works, which include the suite *Goyescas* (1911), based on paintings by Goya, and a set of 12 *Danzas espa*noles*. His other works include the opera *Goyescas* (1916), which uses music from the piano suite; chamber music; and songs.

gran cassa see **cassa**.

Grand Duke, The Operetta by Sullivan with libretto by Gilbert (their last collaboration), subtitled *The Statutory Duel*. First performance: Savoy Theatre, London, 1896. The Grand Duke loses his title in a duel with playing cards.

Grand Duo Sonata in C major for piano duet (D. 849) by Schubert. Composed: 1824. The grandiose nature of the work, which accounts for its title, has led scholars to suggest that this sonata may possibly be the lost *Gastein Symphony* in an arrangement by the composer for piano duet. A number of orchestral arrangements of the *Grand Duo* have been made, including one by Joachim.

Grandi, Alessandro (c.1575–1630) Italian composer. He worked in Ferrara until 1617, when he joined the choir of St Mark's, Venice, eventually becoming Monteverdi's assistant. In 1627 he became maestro at S Maria Maggiore, Bergamo, and died in the plague. His numerous publications, which include masses, psalms, and motets, ran into many editions. He also wrote some secular music, including four volumes of *Cantade et arie* and madrigals.

grand jeu see **full organ**.

grand opera A large-scale form of *opera established in Paris in the late 1820s to cater for the new and relatively uncultured middle classes. With the librettist Scribe and the composer Meyerbeer the form quickly advanced, notably with *Robert le diable* (1831) and *Les Huguenots* (1836). Grand opera involves spectacle and music to an equally large extent, exploiting ballets, choruses, and big scenes (especially crowd scenes). The musical style is a mixture of Italian and French. The form survived throughout the 19th century, important exponents being Rossini, Auber, and Verdi.

grand piano see **piano.**

Graun, Carl Heinrich (*c.*1704–59) German composer and singer, a pupil of J. C. Schmidt and Pezold. He was kapellmeister for Frederick II (1740), by whom he was sent to Italy (1740–41). He wrote several operas in Italian, including *Montezuma* (1755), as well as many sacred works (such as the cantata *Der Tod Jesu*, 1755), sinfonias, and instrumental works. His elder brother, **Johann Gottlieb Graun** (1702–71), was a composer and violinist, a pupil of Pisendel and Tartini and teacher of Franz Benda. He was concert master in Merseberg (1726) and served Frederick II of Prussia (1732). His works include many violin concertos, symphonies, and chamber music.

grave A direction indicating a slow serious tempo. [Italian, serious; grave]

gravicembalo Harpsichord. [Italian, probably a corruption of the usual word, *clavicembalo*]

grazia Grace. Hence **grazioso**, graceful. [Italian]

Great C-Major Symphony Symphony No. 9 in C major (D. 944) by Schubert. Composed: 1828. This title is used to avoid confusion with the shorter sixth symphony, which is also in C major. However, it is particularly appropriate also because of the grand scale on which this symphony is conceived. Although it is now one of the most frequently performed of all symphonies, Schubert never heard the work performed.

Great Fugue see **Grosse Fuge.**

great organ (*or* **great**) see **organ.**

Great Organ Mass Mass in E♭ major by Haydn. Composed: 1766. This title distinguishes the work from another of Haydn's masses, the *Little Organ Mass* , which is conceived in a similar way. Both works include a prominent part for organ, hence the names.

great service A 16th- and 17th-century specially composed Anglican choir service, distinguished from the **short service** in its size and elaboration. Notable examples are by Byrd, Gibbons, and Weelkes.

great staff see **staff.**

Greek music The tradition of Greek music has its roots in mythology: Hermes was said to have invented the earliest lyre (chelys) using a tortoise shell, and Orpheus reputedly played his lyre to such effect that not only the animals but also the trees and rocks followed him on Mount Olympus.

In historic times, the epic poems of Homer, the *Iliad* and the *Odyssey* (*c.*850 BC), were probably sung by professional bards in recitative fashion accompanied by a kind of lyre (see **kithara**); a smaller lyre, the **lyra**, was used in domestic music making. The typical instrument of the shepherd guarding his flocks was the *panpipes (syrinx), much used in folk music. Choral singing accompanied ritual in paeons (songs dedicated to the gods or battle songs), dithyrambs (songs of the cult of Dionysus), and processions; it was most likely to have been accompanied by kithara. The *aulos, a double-reeded pipe with a nasal tone, was associated with the worship of Dionysus (Bacchus); in the early 6th century BC Sacadas of Argos is reputed to have won the aulos contest at the Pythian Games in honour of Apollo.

Of ancient Greek poetry, only that of the great period of lyric poetry (7th–5th centuries BC) has been preserved. Writing in the 4th century BC, Plato describes the accompaniment of songs on the lyre, which would either play the melody in unison or else embellish it melodically or rhythmically. The Greeks also used a harp (megadis) with 20 strings, on which octaves could be played, and a water organ (see **hydraulis**).

The development of drama during the 6th and 5th centuries BC gave music a new importance. Both tragedies and comedies combined poetry, music, and dance. Choruses were either unaccompanied or accompanied by an instrument (the aulos or the small lyre) that would not obscure the words. Later, parts for solo voice (monodies) were added, especially in tragedy. The dance (**orchesis**) was performed in front of the stage, whence the term 'orchestra' derives. During this classical period melody closely followed the pitch accents of the poetry, being always subservient to the word. Aristophanes (*c.*444–380 BC) describes the decline of this style as due to increasing chromaticism and modulation in an effort to find popular acclaim and theatrical sensation and to a general lowering of standards in instrumental playing.

Greek musical theory is generally biased towards mathematical speculation and connected with number symbolism, astronomy, or mysticism. Pythagoras (*c.*585–*c.*479 BC) is said to have learned the principles of the *Harmony of the Spheres* and seen the apparent cosmic importance of the musical scale during his travels in Egypt; he was particularly concerned with experiments dealing with the numerical ratios of consonant intervals. Aristoxenus, a wandering scholar and musician of the 4th century BC , wrote a work of unique importance on harmonics. As far as theory is applicable to practice, the interval of greatest importance was the perfect fourth, not only the natural leap of the human voice, but the interval of the *tetrachord. Of the four notes of the tetrachord, the two outer ones were considered constant and the two inner ones variable, and the four strings of the lyre were tuned accordingly. The

Plate 16: *A scene from the English National Opera's 1985 production of* Don Giovanni. Don Giovanni *is played by William Shimell*

Plate 17 above: *Plácido Domingo and Carol Neblett in Puccini's opera* The Girl of the Golden West *at the Royal Opera House, Covent Garden, London, in 1982*

Plate 18 opposite: *The National Theatre's 1983 production of John Gay's* The Beggar's Opera. *From the left, Imelda Staunton, Paul Jones and Belinda Sinclair*

Plate 19: Young Woman seated at a Virginal *by Jan Vermeer, 1632.*
The virginal is the simplest and oldest form of harpsichord

intervals within the tetrachord (unlike contemporary practice they were always reckoned in descending order) comprised whole tones or chromatically altered larger or smaller tones, from the ditone (slightly bigger than the major third) to quarter tones; the **leimma** (literally, remnant) refers to what remains of the tetrachord after it has been divided into two equal whole tones. The conjunction of two tetrachords with the octave of the starting note added completes the Greek scale or mode; they are, in fact, more of the nature of the Indian rāga as melodic material. Each is available on the seven notes of the octave; the later church modes were derived from these Greek scales (see **modes**).

Green, Ray (1909–) US composer, a pupil of Bloch. His music, influenced by American hymns, jazz rhythms, and works of the English Renaissance, includes the *Sunday Sing Symphony* (1946), a violin concerto (1952), *The Queen's Obsession* (1959), and many dance scores for Martha Graham and other choreographers. Since 1960 he has made use of electronic music.

Greene, Maurice (1696–1755) English composer and organist. He began his musical education as a chorister at St Paul's Cathedral under Jeremiah Clarke. After a period as organist at two City churches, he became vicar-choral at St Paul's in 1718, teaching William Boyce and John Stanley. On the death of William Croft in 1727, he became organist and composer at the Chapel Royal. By 1735 he was honorary professor at Cambridge and Master of the King's Music. Greene's most important collection is *Forty Select Anthems*, but he is also remembered for large-scale orchestral anthems and organ voluntaries.

Greensleeves English folk melody of uncertain origins. Like many melodies of its kind, it has appeared over the centuries in a number of different forms and with many different sets of words. In more recent times it has become popularized by Vaughan Williams, who used it in his opera *Sir John in Love*. Later he arranged the relevant excerpt into the *Fantasia on Greensleeves*.

Gregorian chant see **plainchant**.

Gregorian tone A *plainchant melody used in the liturgy of the Roman Catholic Church for the recitation of psalms and canticles. There are eight basic melodies (numbered 1–8), one in each of the eight *modes of the Gregorian system. Each of these eight types can be varied by the use of a number of different melodic inflections (flexes). A ninth melody, the *tonus peregrinus, is normally unnumbered.

Gretchaninov, Alexander (1864–1956) Russian composer, a pupil of Rimsky-Korsakov. Gretchaninov was Professor of Composition at the Moscow Institute (1903–22); he subsequently lived in Paris and the USA, becoming an American citizen in 1946. His compositions draw on the

Russian nationalist tradition: they include operas, five symphonies, chamber works, choral music, and songs.

Gretchen am Spinnrade (*Gretchen at the Spinning Wheel*) Song for female voice and piano (D. 118) by Schubert to a poem from Goethe's *Faust*. Composed: 1814. This was the first Goethe lyric that Schubert set to music and this song marks the beginning of a new period in the development of the *lied. To depict the young Gretchen, who is sitting at her spinning wheel, the composer writes an ingeniously descriptive piano accompaniment that imitates the whirring noise of the spinning wheel.

Grétry, André Ernest Modeste (1741–1813) Belgian composer and writer. He studied in Rome (1760–66), where he wrote the intermezzo *La Vendemmiatrice* (1765) and after a year in Geneva settled in Paris (1767). There he wrote many successful operas, the best of which was *Richard Coeur de Lion* (1784). He was named Inspector of the Paris Conservatoire (1795). He also wrote symphonies, sacred and ensemble music, and several essays, including *Memoires ... sur la musique* (1789/97).

Grieg, Edvard (Hagerup) (1843–1907) Norwegian composer and pianist (his great-grandfather was a Scot named Greig). At Ole Bull's suggestion, Grieg studied at the Leipzig conservatory (1858–62), where his teachers included Wenzel, Moscheles, Hauptmann, and Reinecke. In 1863 he went to Copenhagen, where he was encouraged and advised by Gade. A decisive influence was his meeting Rikard *Nordraak, who inspired Grieg with romantic Norwegian nationalism, resulting in the composition of the *Humoresker* (1865) for piano. After a year in Rome (1865–66) he returned to Christiania, where he gave concerts, conducted, taught, and composed. In 1867 he married his cousin, the soprano Nina Hagerup, with whom he gave many song recitals. In Rome in 1870 Grieg met Liszt, who encouraged him and greatly admired his A minor piano concerto (1868), now Grieg's best-known work. A turning point in his career came when Ibsen commissioned him to write incidental music for *Peer Gynt*; the score took a year to write (1874–75) but its first performance in 1876 established Grieg as Norway's most important composer. He spent the rest of his life composing, conducting, and touring Europe.

Grieg's musical language is distinctive and individual: he used rich harmonies and folk-inspired melodies, often over pedal points, creating a deeply poetic effect (his later works are more freely dissonant and impressionistic). He was essentially a miniaturist. His over 120 songs are mostly simple strophic settings of Norwegian poems, often with highly developed accompaniments; they include the song cycle *Haugtussa* (1895). His piano music includes the ballade in G minor (1875–76), the suite *Fra Holbergs tid* (1884), the *Lyric Pieces* (1867–1901), and the *Stimmungen* (1903–05). He composed some large-scale vocal works,

Edvard Grieg (left), shortly before his death, with a group of friends including Percy Grainger (centre)

orchestral music (including the **Holberg Suite*, 1884), and chamber music (three violin sonatas, a cello sonata, and two string quartets).

Griffes, Charles Tomlinson (1884–1920) US composer. Griffes studied composition in Berlin with Humperdink (among others). His style shows influences of Debussy and Indian and oriental music. Of his small output, the piano sonata (1917–18) is his best-known work; he also wrote *The *White Peacock* (1915), orchestral music, and songs.

Grigny, Nicolas de (1672–1703) French organist and composer. He was organist at the abbey of St Denis in Paris and a pupil of Nicolas Lebègue (1693–95). From 1696 until his death he was organist at Rheims. He composed masses and other organ music, much admired by Bach.

Grofé, Ferde (Ferdinand Rudolph von G.; 1892–1972) US composer. Grofé was a leading arranger of jazz in the 1920s; Gershwin's *Rhapsody in Blue* is his best-known orchestration. A combination of jazz and folk influences characterizes his own works, which include the *Grand Canyon Suite* (1931) and other orchestral compositions.

grosse caisse see **caisse**.

Grosse Fuge (*Great Fugue*) Fugue for string quartet (Op. 133) by Beethoven. Composed: 1825. Beethoven's original intention was that this work should form the finale to the Bb major string quartet (Op. 130). However, the fugue was of such length and complexity that Beethoven wrote a new finale to the quartet and issued the fugue separately. Today the quartet is often played in its original version, while the fugue has been arranged for full string orchestra.

grosses Orchester Full orchestra. [German]

grosse Trommel see **Trommel**.

Grossi, Carlo (*c*.1634–88) Italian organist, singer, and composer. He held several posts as maestro in northern Italy and composed sacred and secular works, including four operas.

ground 1. (*or* **ground bass**) A bass line of a musical composition that consists of the same short melodic phrase repeated over and over again. The ground may vary in length from a few notes to several bars, but except for transposition it remains unchanged throughout the composition, while the upper parts proceed in free style. See also **chaconne; passacaglia. 2.** A composition constructed on a ground bass.

Grove, Sir George (1820–1900) British lexicographer. Originally a civil engineer, he became an assistant editor of Smith's *Dictionary of the Bible*, later devoting himself to his *Dictionary of Music and Musicians*, which first appeared in four volumes from 1879 to 1889. It has been greatly expanded in subsequent editions and is now the authoritative English-language musical dictionary. The latest edition (1980) was edited by Stanley *Sadie. Grove was knighted in 1883.

Groves, Sir Charles (1915–) British conductor. He conducted the Bournemouth Symphony Orchestra (1951–

61), the Royal Liverpool Philharmonic Orchestra (1963–78), and was musical director of English National Opera (1978–79). A champion of British music, he was knighted in 1973.

Gruenberg, Louis (1884–1964) US composer. Gruenberg studied in Berlin with Busoni; he was later active in promoting modern music in the USA. Gruenberg's compositions are among the earliest to incorporate jazz elements: his works include *Emperor Jones* (1933) and other operas, five symphonies, concertos, chamber music, and vocal works, including *Daniel Jazz* (1925).

Grumiaux, Arthur (1921–) Belgian violinist. A pupil of Enescu, he established his career after World War II as both a solo and chamber-music player. In 1949 he joined the staff of the Brussels conservatory.

Grümmer, Elizabeth (1911–) German soprano. After a short career as an actress she studied in Aachen, making her debut in 1940 as a Flowermaiden in Wagner's *Parsifal*. She sang in Duisburg (1942–44) and Berlin (1945) and then toured Europe, excelling in Mozart and Strauss.

grupetto see **turn.**

Guarneri Family of 17th- and 18th-century Italian violin makers. **Andrea Guarneri** (1629–98) studied with Stradivari under Nicolo *Amati, whose style he followed. His nephew **Giuseppe Antonio Guarneri** (1687–1745), known as 'del Gesù,' made the most famous Guarneri violins, one of which was owned and played by Paganini.

Guarnieri, Camargo (1907–) Brazilian composer, a pupil of Charles Koechlin in Paris. Guarnieri's compositions often feature rhythmic patterns derived from Brazilian folk music. His works include four symphonies, five piano concertos, other orchestral works, chamber music, and songs.

Gui, Vittorio (1885–1975) Italian conductor and composer. He founded the annual Maggio Musicale festival in Florence and conducted at Glyndebourne.

Guido d'Arezzo (Guido Aretinus; *c*.995–*c*.1050) Italian musical teacher and Benedictine monk. He introduced the staff of four lines and invented the *solmization system for denoting notes by syllables.

Guilain, Jean Adam (18th century) German composer and keyboard player. He is known chiefly as a friend of the organist Louis Marchand, who lived in Paris (*c*.1702). Guilain was organist of the church of St Honore and his compositions are mostly for keyboard.

Guildhall School of Music and Drama A college of music and dramatic art founded in 1880 by the Corporation of London. It moved to Blackfriars in 1887 and to the Barbican Arts Centre in 1977. It was originally for training amateur musicians but after 1935 greater attention was paid to dramatic work. Professional courses are offered to composers, performers, and teachers and in the late 1980s there were about 600 full-time students. Its principals have included Landon Ronald, John Percival, and John Hosier.

Guillaume Tell see **William Tell.**

Guillemain, Louis-Gabriel (1705–70) French violinist and composer. After studying with Somis in Italy, he was appointed leader of the Académie de Musique in Dijon (1729), becoming court musician in Paris in 1737. Guillemain wrote many chamber works, including *Sonates en quatuor* (1738, 1756) in the style of Telemann's *Paris Quartets*; violin sonatas; and divertissements and other theatre music.

Guion, David (1895–) US pianist and composer. He studied for a while under Godowsky and has made many arrangements for piano of traditional American melodies.

Guiraud, Ernest (1837–92) French composer. At the Paris Conservatoire he studied with Marmontel and Halévy, winning the Prix de Rome in 1859. From 1876 until his death he was professor at the Conservatoire, where his pupils included Debussy and Dukas. Guiraud is best known for the recitatives he added to Bizet's *Carmen* and for his arrangement of the second suite from *L'Arlésienne* (he also orchestrated Offenbach's *Tales of Hoffmann*). He also composed music for the stage (mostly light operas, apart from *Frédégonde*, 1895) and vocal and instrumental works and wrote a treatise on instrumentation.

guitar A plucked stringed instrument. The modern **classical** (*or* **Spanish**) **guitar** has six strings, tuned E, A, D, G, B, E; it has a range of three octaves and a fifth from E below middle C. The guitar has a flat back and soundboard and a waisted body shape. The neck supports metal frets. It is played as a classical instrument and is also widespread in folk music, pop music, and jazz. Electronically amplified instruments were developed in the 1940s and 1950s, with bodies of many different shapes.

The guitar was introduced into Europe as a result of the Crusades. Throughout the Renaissance it coexisted with the lute and vihuela, remaining essentially a popular instrument. At this time the guitar was considerably smaller than the modern instrument and was strung with four double courses of strings. It was used to provide a strummed chordal accompaniment to songs and dancing. A fifth course was added at the end of the 16th century, and a sixth in the 17th century. At this time, too, double courses were replaced by single strings. Advances in design and construction in the 19th century gave rise to the modern form of the classical guitar. In the 17th century the strummed style of playing was gradually replaced by a more elaborate plucked style, as in the works of such Spanish composers as Gaspar Sanz and Francisco Guerau. The guitar enjoyed a considerable revival in the early years of the 19th century as a result of the virtuosity of such performers as Fernando Sor and Mauro Giuliani, both of whom wrote a large amount of music for the instrument. The 20th-century popularity of the classical guitar is very largely due to the teaching and playing of the Spanish virtuoso Andrés Segovia. Many 20th-century composers have written music for the guitar, including Falla, Roussel, Frank Martin, and Britten. The repertoire also includes chamber music and a number of concertos, of which Joaquin Rodrigo's *Concierto de Aranjuez* is the best known. See also **flamenco**.

guitare d'amour see **arpeggione**.

Gundry, Inglis (1905–) British composer, a pupil of Vaughan Williams. Gundry wrote many operas, all to his own librettos: these include *Avon* (1949) and *The Prisoner Paul* (1969). He also composed orchestral and chamber music.

Guntram Opera in three acts by Richard Strauss with libretto by the composer. First performance: Court Opera, Weimar, 1894. Set in medieval times, it is Strauss's first opera and was much influenced by Wagner.

Guridi, Jesús (1886–1961) Spanish composer. After studying in Paris and Brussels, Guridi returned to Spain, where he did much to foster interest in Basque folk music, which often features in his compositions. He is best known in Spain for his *zarzuelas, which include the popular *El Caserio* (1929). His other works include orchestral and chamber music and songs.

Gurlitt, Cornelius (1820–1901) German composer and organist. He was an organist in Altona. He composed operas but is now best known for his piano music, much of it educational. His great-nephew, **Manfred Gurlitt** (1890–1973), was a composer, teacher, and conductor. He was musical director at Bremen (1914–27) and later a guest conductor in Germany and Spain. He settled and died in Japan. His works include operas, film and incidental music, and orchestral and chamber pieces.

Gurney, Ivor (1890–1937) British composer and poet. Gurney studied with Stanford and Vaughan Williams. His poetry recalls his experience of World War I: he was badly wounded serving in France and never completely recovered after the war. Most of his songs date from after 1918: in them his feeling for poetry combines with a natural gift for lyrical expression.

Gurrelieder Work for narrator, solo voices, choirs, and orchestra by Schoenberg to a German translation of Danish poems by Jacobsen. Composed: 1901–11; first performance: Vienna, 1913. The work tells of Tove of Gurre Castle, her love for King Waldemar of Denmark, and her eventual death. It is conceived on an unsurpassed scale and requires four soloists, three male voice choirs, and narrator in addition to a large chorus and augmented orchestra. *Gurrelieder* is one of the last great romantic works of Schoenberg and at its first performance created disturbances in the audience.

gusla (*or* **gusle**) A primitive form of one-stringed *fiddle still in use in Yugoslavia. The bow usually consists of a stick with a small branch attached onto which the hair is wound.

gusli An ancient type of Russian *zither used by ballad singers as an accompaniment. It is still in use in parts of the Soviet Union in folk music.

Guy, Barry (1947–) British double-bass player and composer. He started his career as a jazz musician, later studying at the Guildhall School of Music. In addition to playing in leading orchestras and chamber ensembles, Guy has also achieved recognition for his compositions, which combine jazz with other avant-garde techniques.

Guy-Ropartz, Joseph (1864–1955) French composer, a pupil of Massenet and Franck. Ropartz was director of the Paris Conservatoire (1884–1919). The influence of Franck is strongly felt in Ropartz's compositions: his works include the opera *Le Pays* (1912), five symphonies and other orchestral works, six string quartets, songs, and choral music.

gymel (*or* **gimel**) 1. A polyphonic technique in which two voices move in thirds and sixths. In the late 13th and early 14th centuries continental gymel employed almost entirely parallel movement, whereas late-14th- and early-15th-century English gymel also crossed the voices. 2. A direction in 16th-century English choral music to indicate the division of the voice part. The return to unison was indicated by **semel**.

Gypsy Baron, The (*Der Zigeunerbaron*) Operetta in three acts by Johann Strauss the Younger with libretto by Schnitzer, adapted from a story by Jokai. First performance: Theater an der Wien, Vienna, 1885. It is about a young Hungarian farmer who is also a Gypsy chief and eventually becomes a real baron.

Gypsy Princess, The Operetta by Kálmán in the style of Lehár. First performance: Vienna, 1921.

Gyrowetz, Adalbert (1763–1850) Czech composer. He studied in Italy with Paisiello and Sala before travelling in 1789 to London, where he wrote the opera *Semiramide* (1792), which was destroyed in a fire at the Pantheon. In Vienna from 1793, Gyrowetz wrote many operas, including *Die Augenarzt* (1811), and ballets and was composer and kapellmeister of the court theatre (1804–31). He also wrote much chamber music, masses, and an autobiography.

H

H see **B**.

H. Abbreviation for Helm. It is used as a prefix to indicate the number of a piece in Eugene Helm's catalogue of C. P. E. Bach's works.

Haas, Monique (1909–) French pianist. After studying with Casadesus, Serkin, and Enescu she established a formidable European reputation as a recitalist and accompanied Fournier and Enescu, among others. She married the composer Marcel *Mihalovici.

Hába, Alois (1893–1973) Czech composer. An interest in oriental folk music led Hába to experiment in writing microtonal music. In 1927 he published a treatise on chromatic and microtonal harmony, *New Principles of Harmony*. His compositions include a quarter-tone opera *The Mother* (1929), string quartets in quarter-, fifth-, and sixth-tone systems, much other chamber music, and piano works.

habanera A moderately slow old Cuban dance in uneven dotted duple rhythm, which was also imported into Spain and other parts of Europe. It is the forerunner of many modern ballroom dances. Bizet (in *Carmen*) and Ravel wrote famous habaneras. French: **havanaise**.

Hadley, Henry Kimball (1871–1937) US composer. Hadley travelled extensively and did much to promote interest in American music. His own works are traditional in style, although occasional impressionist influences are apparent. Hadley's output includes operas, four symphonies, orchestral and choral works, chamber music, and songs.

Hadley, Patrick (1899–1973) British composer, a pupil of Vaughan Williams. Hadley was Professor of Music at Cambridge University (1946–62). He composed a large number of choral works, including *The Trees So High* (1930) and *Fen and Flood* (1956).

Haebler, Ingrid (1929–) Austrian pianist. After winning prizes at Munich and Geneva she acquired an international reputation, being especially noted for her interpretations of Mozart and Schubert.

Haeflinger, Ernst (1919–) Swiss tenor. He studied in Zürich, Vienna (with Julius Patzak), and Prague (with Carpi). After his concert debut in Bach's *St John Passion* (1942) he sang in the Zürich Opéra (1943–52) and in the Berlin Deutsche Oper.

Haendel, Ida (1924–) Polish-born British violinist. A pupil of Flesch and Enescu, she emigrated from Poland to England in 1937. She has a wide repertoire and has toured in Europe and the USA.

Haffner Serenade Serenade in D major for orchestra (K. 250) by Mozart. Composed: 1776. Mozart wrote the work to celebrate the marriage of Burgomeister Haffner's daughter in Salzburg. Three movements feature a solo violin part – these movements are occasionally detached from the rest of the serenade and played as a concerto.

Haffner Symphony Symphony No. 35 in D major (K. 385) by Mozart. Composed: 1782. This work was arranged from an earlier serenade that Mozart had written for the Haffner family (for whom he had also written the *Haffner Serenade*). To form a four-movement symphony from the serenade, Mozart had to dispense with a march and a second minuet.

Hahn, Reynaldo (1875–1947) French composer. Hahn studied with Massenet at the Paris Conservatoire. He is best known for his many songs (*Chansons Grises*, *Idylles Latines*, etc.) but also wrote extensively for the stage, his output including ballet and incidental music in addition to operas.

Hail Mary see **Ave Maria**.

hairpins (*Colloquial*) The signs used for a crescendo (<) and a diminuendo (>) in music.

Haitink, Bernard (1929–) Dutch conductor. In 1961 he became joint conductor (with Eugen Jochum) of the Amsterdam Concertgebouw Orchestra, with whom he has established an international reputation. In England he has directed the London Philharmonic Orchestra (1967–79) and conducted at Glyndebourne since 1977.

Halb (*or fem.* **Halbe**) Half. Hence **Halbenote**, half note, i.e. minim. [German]

Halévy, (Jacques François) Fromental (1799–1862) French composer, teacher, and writer on music. He studied with Cherubini at the Paris Conservatoire (winning the Prix

Bernard Haitink

de Rome in 1819), where he became a professor of harmony and accompaniment (1827), of counterpoint and fugue (1833), and of composition (1840). His pupils included Gounod and Bizet. He was chef du chant at the Théâtre-Italien (1826–29) and at the Opéra (1829–45). In 1835 two of his most successful works were performed – the opera *La *Juive* and the opéra comique *L'Etoile* – establishing him as a leading stage composer. He wrote over 30 operas, the ballet *Manon Lescaut* (1830), choral works, and songs. His writings are mostly collected in *Souvenirs et portraits* (1861) and *Derniers souvenirs et portraits* (1863).

half-close see **cadence.**

Halffter, Rodolfo (1900–) Spanish-born composer, resident in Mexico. A one-time pupil of Falla, his early music reflects Falla's influence; later he experimented with serialism. In 1940 Halffter founded Mexico's first modern dance company. His works include the opera *Clavileño* (1936); the ballets *Don Lindo de Almeria* (1935) and *Elena la Traicionera* (1930); a violin concerto; *Diferencias* (1970) and *Alborado* (1976); and chamber music, piano pieces, and songs. His brother **Ernesto Halffter** (1905–), a composer, conductor, and writer, was a pupil of Falla and Ravel. In the 1930s he formed a group opposed to nationalism and romanticism in music. His works include the ballet *Sonatina* (1928), the *Portuguese Rhapsody* (1939), a guitar concerto (1969), and several chamber operas. Halffter was responsible for the completion of Falla's *Atlantida.* **Cristóbal Halffter** (1930–), composer

and conductor and nephew of Ernesto and Rodolfo, was a pupil of Tansman. He adopted a freely serial style and has made use of electronic music and spatial and aleatonic elements. His works include *Espejos* (1963), *Fibonaciana* (1969), the cantata *Yes, Speak Out Yes* (1968), *Pinturas negras* (1972), and *Pourquoi* (1975); he has also written chamber, piano, and vocal pieces.

half note see **minim.**

Hälfte, die A direction in orchestral scores to indicate that only half a section should play. [German, the half]

Halka Opera by Moniuszko with libretto by Wolski. First performance: (two-act version) Vilnius, 1848; (four-act version with ballet) Warsaw, 1858. Halka is a peasant girl who drowns herself when her aristocratic lover deserts her because she is expecting a child. Moniuszko uses Wagnerian leitmotiv techniques in the score.

Hallelujah 'Praise Jehovah': used in choruses in Restoration anthems and in oratorios, e.g. Handel's *Messiah*. See also **Alleluia; Hallelujah Chorus.**

Hallelujah Chorus Chorus from the oratorio *Messiah* by Handel. This chorus ends the second part of the oratorio. Upon its first performance in London (1743) the reigning monarch (George II) misunderstood the words 'And he shall reign for ever' as referring to himself and stood up in triumph, initiating a custom that has persisted to the present day.

Hallelujah Concerto Concerto in B♭ major for organ (Op. 7 No. 3) by Handel. Composed: 1751. The name alludes to a quotation in the concerto from the *Hallelujah Chorus.*

Hallé Orchestra British symphony orchestra founded in 1858. Charles Hallé (1819–95) established a series of orchestral concerts in Manchester in 1858 and the orchestra for his concerts became known as the Hallé Orchestra. Hallé promoted many new works, including those of Berlioz, Brahms, and Dvořák. Since his death conductors have included Hans Richter, Thomas Beecham, Hamilton Harty, John Barbirolli, and James Loughran (from 1971). Under Barbirolli, conductor for 27 years, the orchestra's standard reached a very high level. It continues to be one of Britain's leading orchestras, giving notable performances of 19th-century music and introducing new works.

halling A lively popular Norwegian dance, thought to originate in the Hallingdal. Simple duple rhythm music accompanies energetic solo dancing. The dance is used by Grieg in his second volume of *Lyric Pieces* (1883).

Halvorsen, Johan (1864–1935) Norwegian violinist, composer, and conductor. He studied at the Stockholm conservatory and later became conductor of the Christiania National Theatre (1899–1929). His compositions, in many genres and including three symphonies, are in the tradition of Grieg.

Haman and Mordecai see Esther.

Hambraeus, Bengt (1928–) Swedish composer and organist, a pupil of Messiaen and Krenek. He has written numerous organ works and pioneered the use of electronic music in Sweden. His tape works, often based on conventional instrumental sounds, include *Tetragon* (1965) and *Fresque sonore* (1967). Other pieces are *Rencontres* (1971), *Pianissimo in due tempi* (1972), and *Récit de deux* (1973).

Hamerik, Ebbe (1898–1951) Danish composer, also active as a conductor in Copenhagen. His operas include *Stepan* (1924) and *Leonardo da Vinci* (1939); other works include five symphonies, chamber music, and songs.

Hamilton, Iain (1922–) British composer. Hamilton studied in London at the Royal College of Music. His early music is romantic in character; he later adopted serial methods of composition. His works include two symphonies; seven operas, including *The Royal Hunt of the Sun* (1966–68); a piano concerto (1960); chamber music; and vocal works.

Hamlet 1. Fantasy-overture (Op. 67) by Tchaikovsky, based on Shakespeare's tragedy. Composed: 1888. This overture was later shortened and used as the overture in a set of incidental music for a production of the play at St Petersburg in 1891. **2.** Tone poem by Liszt. Composed: 1858. This work was written to be performed as a prelude to Shakespeare's play. **3.** Opera in three acts by Ambroise Thomas with libretto by Jules Barbier and Michel Carré after Shakespeare. First performance: Opéra, Paris, 1868. **4.** Opera by Searle with text from Shakespeare's play. First performance: Hamburg, 1968.

Hammerklavier Sonata Piano sonata in B major (Op. 106) by Beethoven. Although the composer also used the title for his piano sonata in A major (Op. 101), it is to the later work that the name is usually applied. Beethoven preferred to use the term 'Hammerklavier' (piano with hammers) rather than the Italian 'pianoforte.'

Hammond, Dame Joan (1912–) New Zealand soprano. She studied in Sydney, where she made her debut (1929). She then combined a concert and stage career in Vienna (1938), New York (1949), and the Soviet Union (1957) until her retirement in 1965. She has written an autobiography, *A Voice, a Life* (1970), and was made a DBE in 1974.

Hammond organ An electromagnetic organ patented by the Hammond Co. of Chicago in 1935. A forerunner of the *electronic organ, the pipeless Hammond organ has two

Joan Hammond

keyboards and a pedalboard; it produces its notes by a system of rotating discs and electromagnetic pickups.

hand bells see bells.

Handel, George Frideric (Georg Friedrich Händel; 1685–1759) German composer, who settled in England. Handel was born in Halle, where he became a pupil of Zachow. In 1702 he entered Halle University to study law but a year later travelled to Hamburg, where he joined the opera orchestra as a violinist and later a harpsichordist and had his first operas, *Almira* and *Nero* (1705), produced. Handel then toured Italy (1706–09), where he met Alessandro Scarlatti and other leading composers and wrote oratorios (such as *La Resurrezione*, 1708), operas (including the highly successful *Agrippina*, 1709), and church and chamber music. He also established his reputation as a harpsichordist.

Handel's Italian tour made him internationally famous. In 1710 he was appointed kapellmeister to the Elector of Hanover (the future George I of Britain) but, because of the close association between the German and English courts, spent much time in London, settling there permanently in 1712. His opera *Rinaldo* (1711) was enthusiastically received by British audiences and further pieces, for example, *Ode for the Queen's Birthday* (1713) and the *Water Music* (1717), established his popularity in Britain. He received a pension from Queen Anne that was doubled by George I when he succeeded her. In 1718 Handel was appointed musical director to the Duke of Chandos, for whom he wrote the *Chandos Anthems* (1718–20) and the masques *Acis and Galatea* (c.1718–20) and *Haman and Mordecai* (which was later reworked as the oratorio *Esther*, 1732). From 1720, when he was appointed director of the Royal Academy of Music, Handel composed more than 30 Italian operas, including *Julius Caesar* (1724), *Orlando* (1733), *Alcina* (1735), *Berenice* (1737), and *Xerxes* (1738), containing the famous *Largo*. These were successfully produced and Handel triumphed over his rival *Bononcini, but because of problems with the singers in his company and the general unpopularity of Italian opera in England he turned increasingly to English oratorios. His most important works in this genre include *Saul* (1739), *Israel in Egypt* (1739), *Messiah* (1742), *Samson* (1743), *Judas Maccabueus* (1747), *Joshua* (1748), *Solomon* (1749), *Susanna* (1749), and *Theodora* (1750). During his last years Handel became blind, although he continued to compose with the assistance of an amanuensis until the end of his life.

Apart from his oratorios and operas, Handel displayed his mastery of composition in a variety of other genres. Among these works are the *Music for the Royal Fireworks* (1749); harpsichord music, for example The *Harmonious Blacksmith* variations; concerti grossi and organ concertos; cantatas and sacred music, such as *Alexander's Feast* (1736); sonatas and chamber duets; and coronation anthems, including *Zadok the Priest* (1727; see **Coronation Anthem**).

hand horn see **horn**.

Handl, Jacob (Jacobus Gallus; 1550–91) Austrian (Slovenian) composer. He sang at the Abbey of Melk before about 1568 and at the court of Vienna from 1574. From 1579 or 1580 he directed the choir of the Bishop of Olomouc and from 1585 until his death he was cantor of St John's, Prague. Handl employed large forces for his sacred works: 2 of the 445 pieces of the *Opus musicum* (1587) are scored for 24 voices. Some of the more effective texts employ chromaticism. Handl also wrote 20 masses, 3 German songs, 4 secular collections ('Moralia'), and a few motets in anthologies and manuscripts.

Hänsel und Gretel Opera by Humperdinck with libretto by the composer's sister, Adelheid Wette, based on a fairy tale by the brothers Grimm. First performance: Court Opera, Weimar, 1893. The two children of the title get the better of a witch.

Hanslick, Eduard (1825–1904) Austrian critic and writer. From 1861 he was professor of aesthetics and musical history at the University of Vienna. He was an ardent supporter of Brahms and an opponent of Wagner, who later characterized him as Beckmesser in *Die Meistersinger*.

Hanson, Howard (1896–1981) US composer. Hanson's music is romantic in temperament; his four symphonies also show an affinity with Sibelius. His other works include the opera *The Merry Mount* (1925), concertos for organ and piano, symphonic poems, and choral music.

Hanus, Jan (1915–) Czech composer. Hanus's work as an editor of romantic music is reflected in the romantic style of his own compositions. His output includes operas, five symphonies and other orchestral works, chamber music, and songs.

Hardanger fiddle A small highly decorated fiddle used in Norwegian folk music and named after a district in Norway. In addition to its four playing strings it has four *sympathetic strings. Norwegian: **Hardangerfele**.

harmonica see **glass harmonica**; **mouth organ**.

harmonic minor scale see **minor scale**.

harmonics The components of a musical tone having frequencies that are integral multiples of the fundamental frequency. When a string, column of air, etc., vibrates it does so not only as a whole but also in fractions (halves, thirds, quarters, etc.) of its length. The fundamental frequency is the frequency of vibration of the whole string, etc. When it vibrates in two halves, the frequency of vibration of the two halves is double that of the whole length and the note produced is therefore an *octave higher than the fundamental. When the string vibrates in three parts the frequency is trebled, and so on. The first harmonic, or first partial, is called the fundamental; higher harmonics are called *overtones (or upper partials).

The fundamental and higher harmonics are all heard together although they cannot always be distinguished from each other. However, the *tone colour, or quality, of a particular note is a reflection of the way the instrument producing it creates the higher harmonics. While all instruments will produce some **natural harmonics** from their open strings or by normal blowing, some instruments can be made to produce **artificial harmonics** by special techniques. For example, by lightly touching a violin string at its mid-point the silvery tone of its second harmonic can be produced by bowing. See also **harmonic series**.

A harmonic series

harmonic series A series of notes produced by a vibrating string or column of air. The fundamental, or first harmonic (see **harmonics**), is produced by the vibration of the whole string or column, the second harmonic, or partial, by the simultaneous vibration of the string or column in two equal parts, and so on. If the fundamental is the C two octaves below middle C, the first nine members of the series are as shown in the diagram (the numbers indicate the harmonic number and the number of equal divisions of the string or column).

The reciprocal of the harmonic number multiplied by the frequency of the fundamental gives the frequency of that harmonic. In *brass instruments the different notes are produced by blowing techniques that bring out the individual natural notes of the harmonic series. Originally horns and trumpets were restricted to playing the notes of one such series. The use of crooks or shanks added to the tubing enabled notes of a different series to be played, although fitting a crook or shank took an appreciable time. Brass instruments became much more versatile at the beginning of the 19th century, with the introduction of valves: the player could then change from one harmonic series to another merely by depressing a piston.

harmonie 1. Harmony. **2.** A wind band, i.e. a band containing woodwind, brass, and percussion instruments. [French and German]

Harmonie der Welt, Die (*The Harmony of the World*) Opera in five acts by Hindemith with libretto by the composer based on the life of the astronomer Kepler. First performance: Munich, 1957.

Harmoniemesse see **Wind-Band Mass.**

Harmoniemusik Music for wind band. [German]

Harmonious Blacksmith, The Air and variations from Handel's fifth suite for harpsichord. Composed: 1720. It has been suggested that the theme of the work was either a melody that Handel heard a blacksmith whistle or an imitation of a blacksmith's hammering. In fact, the title was added by the publisher Lindern during the 19th century.

harmonium A *reed organ with a keyboard and a small number of stops. It has a set of free reeds, but no pipes; air from the bellows sets the individual reeds in motion when the appropriate keys are depressed. The bellows are either operated by pedals or, in later and more sophisticated models, by an electric motor. Invented in the early 19th century, it has been widely used as a substitute for an organ, especially as an accompaniment to hymn singing. See also **American organ.**

harmony The combination of notes vertically and simultaneously to create *chords, which when sounded successively produce horizontal progressions. Harmony is thus the opposite of *counterpoint, in which vertical relationships

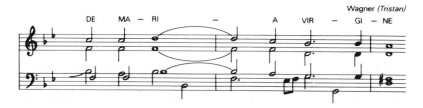

Harmony. Above: Byrd's sharpening of leading notes in harmony led to the emergence of tonality in the 17th century. Below: This example from Wagner displays the development of chromaticism in the 19th century

are created between single lines. Harmony and counterpoint form complementary disciplines of study prior to free composition.

Harmony in western music stemmed from the elaboration of *plainchant during the 10th century with parallel intervals of fourths, fifths, and octaves. On account of their strong acoustic positions in the *harmonic series these were the only consonant intervals permitted by the theorists (*Musica enchiriadis*, c.900). Thirds were used in practice however, notably by English composers of the 13th century (see **gymel**), some time before they were admitted as consonances by theorists.

In French and Italian music of the 14th century (see **ars nova**) harmony ceased to be created by parallel movement, but featured a greater degree of independence and contrary motion between the parts. By the middle of the 16th century composers began to consider harmony as the primary foundation of music. Zarlino's treatise *Le Istitutione harmoniche* (1558) was the first to recognize the significance of full triads and the distinction between major and minor chords. Regular patterns (**progressions**) of chords in their root position or first inversion evolved, together with *cadences. Dissonant intervals were carefully controlled as *suspensions. *Modes remained the theoretical basis of harmony, but in practice the sharpening of *leading notes (see also **musica ficta**) foreshadowed the emergence of *tonality in the 17th century, as in the music of Byrd (see illustration).

The invention of basso continuo and *figured bass in the early 17th century considerably increased the significance of harmony. Chord progressions became strongly sequential, as in the music of Corelli. This established many of the principles of large-scale harmonic organization that were to remain effective for the next two centuries. The controlled and expressive use of *chromaticism was a further aspect of harmony that evolved through the 17th and 18th centuries: it was among the special features of J. S. Bach's style. In 1722 Rameau published his *Traité d'harmonie*, an influential theoretical work that recognized, among other things, the identity between the root position of a chord and its inversions. In the second half of the 18th century the prevailing style of harmony was modified. The rate of harmonic change became considerably slower, with the essential tonic, dominant, and subdominant triads assuming greater importance. Long *pedal points and chords of greater emotive strength, such as the *augmented sixth and diminished *seventh, became more widely employed. These chromatic harmonics were particularly important as means of highlighting the primary diatonic chords. These features are present in the music of Haydn and Mozart, both of whom possessed rich harmonic vocabularies. With Beethoven, who expanded the scale and scope of musical forms, an even greater sense of harmonic drama developed. This is due particularly to the use of keys not immediately related to the tonic. Schubert, too, explored such distant modulations. 19th-century harmony also featured the use of dissonances of even greater intensity, including chords of the ninth, eleventh, and thirteenth. Chromaticism was developed to the extent that it began to significantly disrupt the harmonic stability of the tonal system. Textures became more linear in orientation as cohesion of vertical triadic harmony became weaker. Prolonged chromatic *appoggiaturas, unresolved diminished seventh chords, interrupted cadences, and moments of virtual *atonality are particularly evident in the music of Liszt (e.g. *Bagatelle sans tonalité*) and Wagner (e.g. in *Tristan* (see illustration) and *Parsifal*).

At the beginning of the 20th century many of the disciplines and principles of tonal harmony built on triads were abandoned. This is reflected in the music of Debussy (see **impressionism**), who used parallel chords and unresolved dissonance, and in Scriabin's use of chords built on fourths instead of thirds. Schoenberg and members of the Second Viennese School cultivated atonality and evolved *serialism. Stravinsky, on the other hand, kept some reference to traditional triadic harmony, with the use of bitonality, in many of his works. In his neoclassical works tonal harmony is reinterpreted, with the sense of progression between chords being frozen or dislocated. Some 20th-century composers have evolved personal systems of harmony, including Hindemith, whose method is related to the harmonic series, and Messiaen, with a series of modes. Experiments in quarter-tone harmony have been conducted by Hába and Bartók. In much music composed since 1945 harmony plays a less significant role, but several composers, including Britten and Shostakovich, have successfully maintained a language in which it is vital.

Harnoncourt, Nicolaus (1929–) German conductor and cellist. The founder of the Vienna Concentus Musicus chamber orchestra, he has been a leading figure in the contemporary revival of the authentic performance of baroque music. His recordings include many works by Bach, Handel, and Vivaldi.

Harold in Italy Symphony for viola and orchestra (Op. 16) by Berlioz. Composed: 1834. The work is based on *Childe Harold* by Byron and was composed at the request of Paganini, who wanted a virtuoso work for viola to demonstrate the capabilities of a new viola that he had just acquired. In fact, he never played the work, claiming that it was too easy for him. The four movements are 'Harold in the Mountains,' 'Pilgrims' March and Prayer,' 'Serenade of an Abruzzi Mountaineer,' and 'Orgy of the Brigands.'

harp A plucked stringed instrument in which the strings run diagonally from the soundboard to the neck. The instrument is very ancient and the simplest form, the **bow harp**, is thought to have originated from the *musical bow, with several strings in place of the single string of the bow. The modern three-sided **frame harp**, with a vertical pillar to provide strength, developed from the older **angle harp**, which consists of two members held together at an angle with the strings running between them. Bow harps and angle harps are still found in Africa and were used in ancient Egypt, Greece, and Rome. Frame harps were developed in medieval times; the small frame harp of the 11th-century Irish ruler Brian Boru is still to be seen in Trinity College Museum, Dublin. This typical **Celtic harp** (*or* **clàrsach**) has changed little in the last thousand years. The larger **orchestral harp**, which stands on the floor rather than resting on the knee, was in sporadic orchestral use in the 17th century, but it was severely limited because the strings were tuned to the diatonic scale (the white notes of the piano), which limited it to playing in one key. The **pedal harp**, invented in 1720, enabled all the strings for a particular note in the diatonic scale to be raised by a semitone. This helped but still did not make it possible to modulate freely from key to key or to play in flat keys. Sebastian Erard, in 1820, provided the solution to this problem in the form of the **double-pedal harp**, in which the pedal can be half depressed to raise the pitch of a string by a semitone or fully depressed to raise it by a tone. The modern harp is diatonically tuned to the key of C♭ (B) and has a range of five and a half octaves from C♭ three octaves below middle C. Chromatically tuned harps have also been made, with a string for each semitone. These require no pedals but the diatonic glissando, characteristic of the harp, cannot be played on it. With the invention of Erard's double-pedal harp, 19th-century composers were encouraged to include harp parts in their orchestral music and many composers, including Bizet, Ravel, and Tchaikovsky, have written music featuring the harp. See also **aeolian harp**.

Harper, Heather (1930–) British soprano. Her first operatic appearance was at Oxford (1954), since when she has sung at Covent Garden, Bayreuth, and elsewhere. She is perhaps better known, however, as a concert singer.

Harp Quartet String quartet in E♭ major (Op. 74) by Beethoven. Composed: 1809. This name alludes to the pizzicato arpeggios, a feature of the first movement that was very novel at the time of the quartet's composition.

harpsichord instruments A group of instruments in which strings are plucked using a keyboard-operated mechanism. In all of them, the act of depressing a key raises a wooden jack supported by its far end; a quill or leather plectrum attached to the top of the jack plucks the adjacent string as the jack rises. When the key is released the pivot to which the quill is attached rotates sufficiently for the jack to fall back without the quill touching the string. This mechanism is insensitive to differences of finger pressure, unlike either the clavichord or the piano, and very little expression or accentuation is therefore possible.

There is some confusion as to the names of the various types of harpsichord (French: **clavecin**; Italian: **clavicembalo**). The simplest and oldest form is often called a **virginal** (*or* **pair of virginals**). This consisted of an oblong box, often placed on a table, with one string per note running parallel to the keyboard. It was widely used during the 16th and 17th centuries. Its name probably derives from the Latin *virga* (rod, jack) and not from its supposed popularity with young unmarried ladies. Up to the end of the 17th century, wing-shaped harpsichords were also usually called virginals, but from the 18th century onwards they usually came to be called **spinets** (from the Italian *clavicordo da spinetta*, thorn or quill clavichord). In the spinet there is also one string per note but the strings run into the wing-shaped case at an angle of 45 to the keyboard (see also **clavicytherium**). The spinet was in use from the second half of the 17th century to the end of the 18th century.

The harpsichord itself is a wing-shaped instrument with the strings running at right angles to the keyboard. There are usually two, or sometimes three, strings for each note and stops control the number of strings in use (like the pedals of some pianos). In some of the larger instruments there are two or even three keyboards and on later types a swell pedal is included, which opens and closes slats to control the sound. However, with all these devices the harpsichord's response to the player's attempts to add expression to the music is very limited. The instrument was therefore replaced by the piano at the beginning of the 18th century although it has been revived in the 20th century for playing baroque music and a small amount of modern music written especially for it. Scarlatti, Bach, and Handel wrote extensively for the harpsichord although much of this music is now played on the piano.

harp stop A device on a harpsichord that enables the strings to be damped so that the sound produced resembles that of a harp.

Harris, Roy (1898–) US composer, a pupil of Nadia Boulanger. Harris's style is both romantic and naive in its expression of Americanism. His works include seven symphonies (of which the third (1939), in one movement, is the best known), choral music, and chamber works.

Harrison, Julius (1885–1953) British composer and conductor, a pupil of Granville Bantock. His works often use British folk songs and dances: they include choral, orchestral, and chamber compositions and songs.

Harrison, Lou (1917–) US composer, a pupil of Cowell and Schoenberg. Harrison championed the music of Ives, Cowell, Varese, and Ruggles; his own music, avant-garde in character, shows attempts to find new means of sound production influenced by oriental music. Harrison's works include operas and ballet scores, orchestral works, music for percussion ensemble, and choral music.

Harsányi, Tibor (1898–1954) Hungarian composer, a pupil of Kodály. Harsányi's music often uses themes reminiscent of Hungarian folk music in a polytonal setting enhanced by jazzlike rhythms. His compositions include operas, a symphony (1952) and other orchestral works, chamber music, and piano works.

Hartmann, Johan Peter Emilius (1805–1900) Danish composer and organist. A civil servant from 1827 to 1870, he also had a musical career. He was organist of Copenhagen Cathedral from 1843 to his death and from 1867 was director of the Copenhagen conservatory, where he also taught. In the 1830s and 1840s he toured Germany, meeting leading composers of the day. His compositions are strongly nationalist; he wrote operas (including *The Raven*, 1832), ballets and incidental music, orchestral, chamber, piano, and organ works, and choral music. His son **Emil Hartmann** (1836–98) was also a composer and organist.

Hartmann, Karl Amadeus (1905–63) German composer. Hartmann studied in Munich and later in Vienna with Webern. His music is highly chromatic and atonal, although traditional in formal organization. Hartmann's compositions include eight symphonies, concertos, chamber music, and piano works.

Harty, Sir Hamilton (1879–1941) British conductor and composer, born in Ireland. He conducted the Hallé Orchestra (1920–33) and also in the USA. His compositions include a violin concerto (1909) and the *Irish Symphony* (1924); he made famous arrangements of Handel's *Water Music* and *Music for the Royal Fireworks*.

Harvey, Jonathan (1939–) British composer and writer, a pupil of Babbitt. His early works, such as *Cantata I* (1965) and his symphony (1966), combine serial techniques with tonal references. Later works, which display a broader more eclectic style, include *Persephone Dream* (1972), *Inner Light I–III* (1973–77), the tape piece *Veils and Memories* (1979), and *Concelebration* (1980).

Harwood, Basil (1859–1949) British composer and organist at Christ Church, Oxford (1892–1909). His compositions include psalms, motets, and other church music and works for organ.

Háry János Opera in three acts by Kodály with libretto by Paulini and Harsányi. First performance: Budapest, 1926. Háry János (baritone) tells his companions fantastic tales of adventure; many of the parts are speaking roles, which at times gives the opera the character of a play with incidental music. The *Háry János* orchestral suite is drawn from the opera.

Haskil, Clara (1895–1960) Romanian pianist. She studied with Cortot and Busoni and appeared frequently as an accompanist of such artists as Ysäye and Casals. Haskil's interpretations of Mozart, Beethoven, and Schubert were much acclaimed.

Hassan Incidental music by Delius to the play *Hassan* by Flecker. Composed: 1920. The music that Delius composed for this performance includes the famous *Hassan Serenade*.

Hasse, Johann Adolf (1699–1783) German composer. After studying in Naples with Porpora and Alessandro Scarlatti, he became maestro di cappella in Venice (1727) and kapellmeister in Dresden (1731–63). He lived in Vienna (*c*.1764–73) before returning to Venice, where he died. A prolific composer of operas, he set all Metastasio's plays, including *Ruggiero* (1771). He also wrote oratorios (emphasizing the solo voice) and other church music and works for instrumental ensemble and keyboard.

Hassler, Hans Leo (1564–1612) German composer. After studying with Andrea Gabrieli (1584–85) he was chamber organist to Octavian II Fugger in Augsburg (1586–1600). He was then director of the town music in Nuremberg (1601–04) and employed by the emperor Rudolf II. His last years were spent in Ulm (1604–07), Dresden (from 1608), and Frankfurt, where he died. Hassler's works reveal Italian (especially Venetian) influences in his use of polychoral techniques and warm sonorities. He wrote for both the Protestant and the Roman Catholic rites. Particularly Italianate are his *Madrigali* (1596) and *Canzonette* (1590); Hassler also produced two sets of German songs (1591 and 1601), some of them based on Italian models. His father **Isaak Hassler** (*c*.1530–91) and two brothers **Kaspar Hassler** (1562–1618) and **Jakob Hassler** (1569–*c*.1622) were all musicians.

Haubenstock-Ramati, Roman (1919–) Polish-born composer, resident in Israel (1950–57) and Austria. He is particularly interested in the development of new notations and the use of mobile forms, as in *Tableau for Orchestra* (1971). His chamber works include *Interpolation* (1958) and three string quartets. He has also written theatre pieces, such as *Credentials* (1960), with words by Beckett, and one opera, *Amerika* (1964), based on Kafka.

Hauer, Josef Matthiaus (1883–1959) Austrian composer and theorist. Hauer developed a system of composing using all twelve chromatic pitches, dividing these into six-note 'tropes,' which predates Schoenberg's development of serial technique by some ten years. His compositions include an opera (*Salambo*, 1930), oratorios, orchestral works, and chamber and piano music.

Haussmann, Valentin (1565/70–1614 or before) German composer, editor, and poet, a pupil of Raselius. He appears never to have held a permanent post, preferring to travel from city to city. He was a prolific composer of secular music to German texts and his two collections of intrade, pavans, and galliards (1604) are the first German works in which the violin is used. Between 1606 and 1610 he edited four books by Vecchi and one each by Marenzio, Gastoldi and others, and Morley, fitting the music of these composers to German words.

hautbois see oboe.

hautboy (*or* **hoboy**) Obsolete English name for the *oboe.

havanaise see habanera.

Haydn, (Franz) Joseph (1732–1809) Austrian composer. Born in Rohrau into a poor family, Haydn was sent at the age of eight to Vienna, where for nine years he was a chorister at St Stephen's Cathedral. After leaving the cathedral (*c*.1749) he supported himself by teaching and playing; he also became the pupil and accompanist of Nicola Porpora. During this period he taught himself music theory and composition, mainly through studying the works of C. P. E. Bach. Through some of his pupils he met Baron von Fürnberg, for whose instrumentalists he wrote his earliest string quartets (*c*.1755).

On Fürnberg's recommendation Haydn was appointed musical director to Count von Morzin. It was for the count's small orchestra that Haydn wrote his first symphony (1759). In 1761 Haydn became assistant conductor at the Esterházy court, advancing to musical director in 1766. He considerably enlarged and improved Prince Miklós' ensembles and wrote a number of operas, including *Il *Mondo della luna* (1777) and *Orlando Paladino* (1782), and the **Great Organ Mass* (1766). He also composed symphonies, including the **Fire Symphony* (1766–68), **Mercury Symphony* (*c*.1771), *Il *Distratto* (1774), and *The *Hunt* (1882); string quartets, such as the **Sun Quartets* (1772); and other chamber music, as well as numerous pieces for Prince Miklós to play on the baryton.

In addition he undertook various official commissions, notably the six *Paris Symphonies (1785–86) and The *Seven Last Words of our Saviour on the Cross (1785) for the city of Cádiz.

On visits with Prince Miklós to Vienna, Haydn became friendly with Mozart, who subtly influenced his later works. When Prince Miklós died in 1790 the Esterházy court musicians were dismissed and Haydn, his international reputation firmly established, accepted invitations to London (1791–92, 1794–95) from the impresario J. P. Salomon to write 12 symphonies (the so-called *Salomon Symphonies) and 20 smaller compositions for performance in London.

After his visits to London Haydn settled again in Vienna, where he remained until his death. Inspired by performances of Handel's oratorios in Westminster Abbey, Haydn wrote The *Creation (1794–95). The huge public acclaim this received stimulated him to write a second oratorio, The *Seasons (1801). Among other works composed during this period were six masses (1796–1802), including the *Drum Mass (1796), *Nelson Mass (1798), and *Wind-Band Mass (1802), more string quartets, such as the *Fifths Quartet (1797), and The *Emperor's Hymn (1797), which became the Austrian national anthem.

An enormously prolific composer, Haydn wrote over 100 symphonies, nearly 80 string quartets, over 50 sonatas, and 31 piano trios; in all these he developed the classical forms and style, becoming known as the 'father of the symphony.' His other compositions include about 14 masses and other church music, over 20 operas, and arrangements of English, Scottish, and Welsh folk songs.

His brother, (Johann) Michael Haydn (1737–1806), was also a composer. He was appointed kapellmeister to the Bishop of Grosswardein (1757), konzertmeister to the Archbishop of Salzburg (1762), and cathedral organist at Salzburg (1781), teaching Neukomm, Reicha, and others. His works include the Requiem (1771), the Missa sotto il titulo di Teresia (1801) for Empress Maria Theresia, other sacred works, symphonies, concertos, singspiels, chamber music, and treatises. See also Hob.

hay(e) see hey(e).

head voice The highest of the three registers of the voice, the others being medium and *chest voice, the change from medium to head taking place above E. In sharp contrast to the method of producing tone in the chest register, the singer does not direct the sound into the area of the head: the sound travels there of its own accord by proper positioning of the lower jaw and by raising the soft palate to its fullest extent.

Hebrides, The (or **Fingal's Cave**) Overture (Op. 26) by Mendelssohn. Composed: 1830. Mendelssohn wrote this work after visiting Scotland in 1829, the inspiration coming from a visit to Fingal's Cave in the Hebrides. In its original version the overture was performed at Rome in 1830 as Der einsame Insel (The Lonely Island); it was revised in 1832 for a performance in London.

heckelclarina A type of clarinet with a conical bore, invented by the German firm of Heckel for the first staging (1865) of Wagner's Tristan und Isolde. It was used for the shepherd's pipe that appears in Act III – a part now usually played on the cor anglais.

heckelphone see oboe.

Heifetz, Jascha (1901–87) Russian-born US violinist. A child prodigy, he came to notice after a sensational debut in Berlin in 1912. After a long performing career around the world Heifetz retired to teaching in California. His playing is particularly noted for its technical mastery and he has made many virtuoso transcriptions.

Heiller, Anton (1923–79) Austrian organist and composer. Admired particularly for his interpretations of Bach, Heiller has also appeared as conductor and harpsichordist. His compositions include much church music.

Heine, Heinrich (1797–1856) German romantic poet and prose writer. Many settings of his lyric verse have been written by composers, including Wolf, Brahms, Schubert, and Schumann. Wagner's The Flying Dutchman is derived from his work as perhaps is part of Tannhäuser. Several operas are based on his play William Ratcliff.

Heinichen, Johann David (1683–1729) German composer. He studied in Leipzig, becoming court composer in Zeitz (1709), then lived in Italy (1710–16). From 1717 until his death he worked in Dresden with Antonio Lotti. In addition to his operas, orchestral music, and many sacred and chamber works, he wrote a treatise on figured bass, Neu erfundene und grundliche Anweisung (1711), revised as Der General-Bass in der Composition (1728).

Heldenleben, Ein see Hero's Life, A.

Heldentenor see heroic tenor.

helicon see tuba.

Heller, Stephen (István H., 1813–88) French pianist and composer, born in Hungary. He studied with Czerny and Halm in Vienna, where he met Beethoven and Schubert. He toured east Europe as a pianist (1828–30), lived in Augsburg (1830–38), where he was encouraged by Schumann, then settled in Paris, where he taught and wrote music criticism for the Gazette musicale. Heller wrote over 160 piano pieces: studies (which are still used), variations, atmospheric character pieces, sonatas, sonatinas, short pieces, and many transcriptions and opera fantasias.

Helmholtz, Hermann von (1821–94) German scientist who, in 1863, wrote an influential book on acoustics, the physiology of the ear, and the sensation of hearing, translated as *On the Sensations of Tone* (1875).

Hely-Hutchinson, Victor (1901–47) British composer. He was appointed Director of Music for the BBC in 1944, before which he had held a number of academic posts. Hely-Hutchinson's output includes songs and a small number of orchestral and chamber works.

hemidemisemiquaver A note having half the time value of a *demisemiquaver and a sixty-fourth that of a semibreve. In modern notation it is depicted as a filled-in circle with a tail to which four bars (or hooks) are attached. US: **sixty-fourth note**. See **Appendix, Table 1**.

hemiola (*or* **hemiolia**) A rhythmic change in which three beats replace a more usual two beats, e.g. when three minims replace two dotted minims. [Greek, in the proportion 3:2]

hemitone see **scales**.

Henry Pierre (1927–) French composer, a pupil of Messiaen and Nadia Boulanger. With Schaeffer, he pioneered the development of *musique concrète in the 1950s; their *Symphonie pour un homme seul* (1950) was the first major musique-concrète work. In 1958 Henry founded his own electronic studio. His compositions include ambitious concert works, such as *Le Voyage* (1962); ballet scores for Béjart, such as *Mouvement-rhythme-étude* (1970); mixed-media works, such as *Kyldex* (1973); and numerous pieces of incidental and film music.

Henry VIII (1491–1547) King of England (1509–47). Music played a large part in the life and ceremonies of his court; he employed about 60 musicians and himself played several instruments. His compositions include arrangements of popular melodies, for example, 'Pastyme with good company,' and some original pieces.

Henschel, Sir George (Isidor Georg H.; 1850–1934) German-born British baritone, conductor, pianist, and composer. He studied in the Leipzig conservatory (1867–1870) and sang in the *St Matthew Passion* under Brahms, with whom he became friendly. In 1881 he married the US soprano Lilian Bailey (1860–1901) and for three years was appointed conductor of the Boston Symphony Orchestra (1881–1883). His many works include operas, sacred music, and piano pieces. He settled in England in 1884 and was knighted in 1914.

Hen Symphony (French: *La Poule*) Symphony No. 83 in G minor by Haydn. The name is derived from the second subject of the first movement, which is an oboe theme recalling the clucking of a hen. This symphony is the second of the so-called *Paris Symphonies*.

Henze, Hans Werner (1926–) German composer resident in Italy since 1953, a pupil of Fortner, Leibowitz, and Rufer. After an early neoclassical period, he adopted

Hans Werner Henze

serial procedures. His first operatic success, *Boulevard Solitude* (1952), combines jazz idioms with serial techniques and in subsequent works he sought a more lyrical style, as in his *Elegy for Young Lovers* (1961). He finally rejected serialism in favour of a looser style that allows the coexistence of diverse forms as well as the use of quotation. After The *Bassarids* (1966) Henze disowned the musical establishment and aimed to give his works a Marxist content. For this purpose he has used every available expressive technique or language. His other works include string quartets; six symphonies; the operas *König Hirsch* (1956), *Der *Prinz von Homburg* (1960), *Der *Junge Lord* (1964), and *We Come to the River* (1976); the ballets *Undine* (1958) and *Orpheus* (1978); and the oratorios *Das Floss der Medusa* (1968), *El Cimarron* (1970), *Voices* (1973), and *Tristan* (1973).

heptachord A scale consisting of seven notes.

Herbert, Victor (**August**) (1859–1924) US composer, conductor, and cellist, born in Ireland. He studied at the Stuttgart conservatory and became a member of the Stuttgart court orchestra in 1883. In 1886 he went to the USA, where he became distinguished as a cellist in the Metropolitan Opera orchestra, New York, as a conductor of military bands and the Pittsburgh Symphony Orchestra (1898–1904), and as a teacher. Herbert wrote orchestral music, including two cello concertos, but it is for his successful and attractive operettas that he is best remembered; they include *Babes in Toyland* (1903), *Naughty Marietta* (1910), and *Sweethearts* (1913).

Hérodiade Opera by Massenet to a libretto by Milliet, Grémont, and Zamadin. First performance: Brussels, 1881. The plot is based upon the short story *Hérodias* by Flaubert and is a variation on the biblical tale of Salome. In this version Salome pleads for the life of John the Baptist: when he is beheaded she kills herself.

heroic tenor A tenor voice of agility, brilliance, and power best suited to heroic rather than to lyrical or comic parts. Some Wagnerian roles (e.g. in *Tannhäuser*, *Lohengrin* and *Siegfried*) demand such a voice, and in many German opera houses the heroic tenor is classed as a type as well as a voice. German: **Heldentenor**; Italian: **tenore robusto**.

Hérold, (Louis Joseph) Ferdinand (1791–1833) French composer. In 1806 he entered the Paris Conservatoire, where Méhul was among his teachers, winning the Prix de Rome in 1812. He went to Naples and Vienna, and in 1815 became accompanist at the Théâtre-Italien, Paris; in 1826 he became principal singing coach at the Opéra. Of his many opéras comiques the most successful were **Zampa* (1831) and *Le Pré aux clercs* (1832); he also wrote the ballet *La *Fille mal gardée* (1828), choral works, songs, two symphonies, four piano concertos, and chamber and piano music.

Hero's Life, A (German: *Ein Heldenleben*) Tone poem (Op. 40) by Richard Strauss. First performance: 1899. The work was described by Strauss as a companion piece to **Don Quixote*, but this time showing the struggles of an ordinary man rather than a knight. The work is generally regarded as a musical autobiography of Strauss, although he never specifically indicated this. It tells of Strauss's struggle to become recognized in the face of bitter jibes from critics, although he eventually achieves recognition. The work is in six sections; in one the love of his wife is represented by a solo violin and in another Strauss quotes extensively from his earlier works.

Herrmann, Bernard (1911–75) US composer, best known for his film music. His scores for 61 films, including Welles' *Citizen Kane* (1940) and Hitchcock's *Psycho* (1960), form the largest part of his output; he also composed three operas and a small amount of orchestral and chamber music.

Hertel, Johann Wilhelm (1727–89) German violinist, keyboard player, and composer. He was chamber musician in Strelitz and court kapellmeister in Schwerin (*c*.1770). In addition to his highly esteemed symphonies, keyboard sonatas, and chamber music, he assembled *Musikalischer Schriften aus den Werken der Italiener und Franzosen* (1757–58), a collection of works of Italian and French composers.

hertz The unit of **frequency*. It is equal to 1 cycle per second and is named after Heinrich Hertz (1857–94), the German physicist who discovered radio waves. Abbreviation: **Hz**.

Hervé (Florimond Ronger; 1825–92) French composer, singer, organist, and conductor. After studying with Auber at the Paris Conservatoire, he was organist at the Bicêtre asylum (1839–45) and at St Eustache (1845–53). He had an active career in the Paris theatre (where he used the name Hervé) as a composer, conductor, singer, and producer. In 1854 he opened his own theatre, the Folies Concertantes (later the Folies Nouvelles), and he toured with his company; he performed several times in London. Hervé wrote numerous undistinguished operettas, of which the best known are *Don Quichotte et Sancho Pança* (1848), *L'Oeil crevé* (1867), and *Mam'zelle Nitouche* (1883).

Herz, Henri (Heinrich H.; 1803–88) German pianist, composer, and teacher. He studied with Pradher and Reicha at the Paris Conservatoire, where he later became a professor (1842–74). As a leading piano virtuoso he toured throughout Europe, Russia, the USA, and South America. In 1851 he founded a piano factory and its instruments ranked with those of the best makers. Herz's compositions for piano are mainly virtuoso showpieces; he also contributed variations to **Hexameron* (1837).

Heseltine, Philip see **Warlock, Peter**.

Hess, Dame Myra (1890–1965) British pianist. After studying with Matthay she made her debut in 1907 and toured widely in Britain and the USA. During World War II she established daily lunchtime recitals at the National Gallery in London, for which she was created a DBE in 1941. Her piano transcriptions, such as that of Bach's 'Jesu, Joy of Man's Desiring,' have remained very popular.

heterophony The performance of different versions of the same melody by different voices or instruments at the same time. Usually one is more elaborate than the others.

Heure espagnole, L' (*The Spanish Hour*) Opera in one act by Ravel with text by Franc-Nohain. First performance: Opéra-Comique, Paris, 1911. It is set in the shop of the clock-maker Torquemada (tenor).

hexachord A six-note scale devised by Guido d'Arezzo in the 11th century (see also **solmization**). There were three hexachords: the **hard** (**durum**) **hexachord** beginning on the second G below **middle C* on the modern piano and rising on the white notes to E below middle C; the **natural** (**naturale**) **hexachord** beginning on C below middle C and rising to A; and the **soft** (**molle**) **hexachord** beginning on F below middle C and rising to D above it. This system was in use with modal music until the 17th century but it has now been replaced by the modern **key* system. The German names for major (*dur*) and minor (*mol*) are derived from the Latin names for two of the hexachords.

Hexameron Collection of variations for piano by various composers, based upon a march from Bellini's opera *I Puritani* (*The Puritans*). First performance: 1831. The six composers involved in this project were Chopin, Czerny, Herz, Pixis, Thalberg, and Liszt and each contributed one variation, hence the title (derived from the Greek, six days). Transitory passages from one variation to another were provided by Liszt.

Hexenmenuett see **Fifths Quartet.**

hey(e) (*or* **hay(e)** A late-16th-century round dance, of no clearly established form although similar to the *canarie. Examples are found in J. Playford's *Musick's Handmaid* (1678).

Hiawatha Set of three cantatas for solo voices, choir, and orchestra by Coleridge-Taylor. First performance: 1900. Each cantata is based upon a portion of the poem *Hiawatha* by Longfellow, which tells of the life of the American Indian Hiawatha and his love for Minnehaha. The three cantatas are *Hiawatha's Wedding Feast*, *The Death of Minnehaha*, and *Hiawatha's Departure*.

hidden fifths see **fifth.**

high fidelity Electronic sound reproduction of high quality, i.e. without distortion and hence faithful to the original. Often abbreviated to **hi-fi.**

Highland fling A very vigorous Scottish dance. See **reel.**

Hi-hat cymbals see **cymbals.**

Hildegard of Bingen, St (1098–1179) German composer and mystic, abbess at Disibodenberg and then at Rupertsburg, Bingen. One of the most important medieval composers of chants, she wrote the *Symphonia harmonie celestium revelationum*, comprising over 70 visionary lyric poems with their music, together with the morality play *Ordo virtutum*.

Hill, Alfred (1870–1960) Australian composer. After studying in Germany, Hill lived for a time in New Zealand, where he became interested in Maori music. He later helped found the Sydney conservatory. Hill's compositions include operas and cantatas (some on Maori subjects), symphonies, chamber music, and songs.

Hill, Edward Burlingame (1872–1960) US composer. Hill studied at Harvard and (with Widor) in Paris. His music shows the influence of the French impressionist style and makes occasional use of jazz idioms. Hill's compositions include symphonies, symphonic poems, chamber music, and vocal and piano works.

Hiller, Ferdinand (**von**) (1811–85) German conductor, composer, and teacher. He studied in Weimar with Hummel (1825–27), with whom he visited Beethoven on his deathbed. He lived in Paris (1828–36), where he became a celebrated pianist, then in Italy (1836–42). Hiller succeeded Mendelssohn as conductor of the Leipzig Gewandhaus Orchestra (1843–44) and was appointed city kapellmeister first in Düsseldorf (1847–50) then in Cologne, where he played a leading role in the city's musical development. Hiller wrote six operas, vocal and orchestral music (including three symphonies, two piano concertos, and a violin concerto), choral and piano works, and songs. He was a prolific writer on music.

Hiller, Johann Adam (1728–1804) German composer, conductor, and teacher. In Leipzig he established the Concerts Spirituels (1775), later known as the Gewandhaus-Konzerte (1781), and founded a school of singing. He was made cantor of St Thomas's School in 1789. His works include some of the earliest singspiels (such as *Die Jagd*, 1770), church and chamber music, a singing tutor, and several music textbooks.

Hiller, Lejaren (1924–) US composer, a pupil of Sessions and Babbitt. He pioneered the use of computers in composition: his *Iliac Suite* (1957) was produced by a specially programmed computer. The *Computer Cantata* (1963) shows a more sophisticated approach, while *Machine Music* (1964) combines live instruments with a computer-generated tape. He has also written theatre pieces, including *An Avalanche* (1968).

Hilton, John (?–1608) English composer. Originally a countertenor at Lincoln, he became organist at Trinity College, Cambridge, in 1594. Although his compositions are mainly sacred, he contributed a madrigal to *The Triumphs of Oriana* (1601). His son, **John Hilton** (?1599–1657), took the Cambridge Mus.B. degree in 1626 and in 1628 became organist at St Margaret's, Westminster. He published a collection of rounds and catches in 1652 and was one of the earliest composers of dramatic dialogues.

Himmel, Friedrich Heinrich (1765–1814) German composer, a pupil of Naumann. His first works were sacred compositions, but while studying in Italy (*c*.1793–94) and as court composer in Berlin (from 1795) he wrote mainly Italian operas. After working in Russia (1798–1800) he turned to singspiel, his most famous being *Fanchon* (1804). He also wrote music for ensemble and pianoforte.

Hindemith, Paul (1895–1963) German composer. Hindemith's musical study in Frankfurt was supplemented by his wide experience as an instrumentalist. In 1938 he left Germany as a result of Nazi disfavour; from 1940 until 1951 he worked in the USA, subsequently settling in Switzerland. His earliest music shows influences of expressionism and jazz. In the 1920s Hindemith adopted a neoclassical style, characterized by contrapuntal textures and a return to baroque forms. From this time dates his concept of *Gebrauchsmusik, music written specifically for amateur singers and players. Hindemith's later works

Plate 20: Götterdämmerung, *part of Wagner's Ring Cycle,*
performed by the Welsh National Opera in 1985

Plate 21: *Handel by Philip Mercier. This is the first known portrait
of the composer painted in England*

Plate 22: *Joseph Haydn by Thomas Hardy, 1791. The portrait was painted during Haydn's first stay in London*

Plate 23: *Monteverdi's opera* L'Incoronazione di Poppea, *which had its first performance in Venice in 1642*

extend techniques described in his book *The Craft of Musical Composition* (1934–36), which sets out principles of extended tonal harmony from an acoustic basis.

His principal compositions include the operas *Cardillac* (1926), *Mathis der Maler* (1938), and *Die *Harmonie der Welt* (1956–57); the ballets *Nobilissima visione* (1935) and *The *Four Temperaments* (1940); orchestral works, including a symphony in E♭ (1940) and *Symphonic Metamorphoses on Themes by Weber* (1943); seven *Kammermusik* concertos (1921–27) and other concertos; chamber music, including six string quartets and numerous instrumental sonatas; piano music, including *Ludus Tonalis* (1942); and choral works.

Histoire de soldat, L' see **Soldier's Tale, The.**

HMS Pinafore Operetta by Sullivan with libretto by Gilbert, subtitled *The Lass that Loved a Sailor*. First performance: Opéra Comique, London, 1878, where it ran for 700 consecutive nights. The action takes place aboard a British warship and involves Sir Joseph Porter, First Lord of the Admiralty, who wishes to marry Josephine, the Captain's daughter.

Hob. Abbreviation for Hoboken. It is used as a prefix to indicate the number of a piece in the catalogue (1957–71) of Haydn's works compiled by the Dutch bibliographer Anthony van Hoboken (1887–).

hoboy see **hautboy.**

hocket 1. The use of rests to separate notes, sometimes small groups of notes, so that one part sounds when the other is silent. This technique was popular in the 14th-century *ars nova motet. **2.** A whole piece in which this technique is predominant, e.g. Machaut's *Hoquetus David*. French: **hoquet**; Italian: **ochetto**. [from Latin *hoketus*, hiccup]

Hoddinott, Alun (1929–) British composer. The romantic style of Hoddinott's early music has given way to a modernistic approach, characterized by economical handling of musical material. His works include five symphonies and other orchestral compositions, a piano concerto (1969), chamber music, and keyboard works.

Hodie Cantata for solo voices, boys' choir, mixed choir, and orchestra by Vaughan Williams with a text from the Bible. First performance: 1954. The work was written for performance in celebration of Christmas Day and the words of the traditional Latin Christmas hymn *Hodie* are included in the text.

hoe down Any of various 19th-century Black American folk dances, being imitation jigs, reels, or other lively dances. The term is also applied loosely to popular dances in a vigorous duple rhythm in both England and the USA.

Paul Hindemith

Hoffmann, Ernst Theodor Amadeus (1776–1822) German writer and composer. His fantasy stories influenced Wagner, Schumann (who based *Kreisleriana* on Hoffmann's character Johannes Kreisler the kapellmeister), and Offenbach (who used his stories as the basis for the libretto of *The Tales of Hoffmann*). Hoffmann was a perceptive critic and reviewer of Beethoven. He composed several operas, together with some piano and orchestral works.

Hoffmeister, Franz Anton (1754–1812) German composer and music publisher. In about 1783 he founded the music publishing house in Leipzig and Vienna that brought out the works of Beethoven, Mozart, and others and later became the firm of C. F. Peters (1813). His own compositions include a large number of chamber works, serenades, sacred music, and operas.

Hoffstetter, Roman (1742–1815) German viola player and composer. He was a Benedictine monk at Amorbach and Miltenberg/Main, known primarily as the composer of six quartets formerly attributed to Haydn (Hob. III, 13–18). He also wrote viola concertos and sacred music.

Hofhaimer, Paul (1459–1537) Austrian composer and organist. He was in the service of the Emperor Maximilian I (1480–1519) and organist of Salzburg Cathedral from 1519 until his death. His works include motets, German songs, and organ music.

Hofmann, Josef (1876–1957) Polish-born US pianist and composer. A child prodigy, he was taught by Anton Rubinstein. Hofmann's reputation in the USA led to his appointment as director of the Curtis Institute in 1926. His compositions, some of them written under the pseudonym Michel Dvorsky, include a symphony, five piano concertos, and other works for piano. During his latter years Hofmann became involved with improving piano design and he exercised great influence as a teacher.

Hohlflöte (*or* **Hohl flute**) An organ *stop controlling 8-*foot square *flue pipes, with a sound similar to the *claribel stop. [German, hollow-sounding flute]

Holberg Suite Suite of dance movements for orchestra by Grieg. Composed: 1884. Grieg wrote the work to celebrate the bicentenary of the birth of Ludwig Holberg, the great Norwegian playwright. In its original form the *Holberg Suite* was composed for piano.

Holborne, Antony (?–1602) English composer. He specialized in consort music and in 1599 published a collection, *Pavans, Galliards, Almains in Five Parts*. He was highly regarded in his lifetime and his works appeared in anthologies for some years after his death. His brother **William Holborne** (fl. 1597) was also a composer, but very few of his works survive.

Holbrooke, Joseph (1878–1958) British composer. Holbrooke studied at the Royal Academy of Music. His music is written in an accessible romantic style. His prolific output includes the operatic trilogy *The Cauldron of Anwyn*

(*The Children of Don*, 1912; *Dylan*, 1914; *Bronwen*, 1929), five symphonies, and many songs and piano pieces.

Holliger, Heinz (1939–) Swiss oboist and composer. After a brief period in the Basle Symphony Orchestra he turned to a solo career and founded a chamber group, the Holliger Ensemble. Berio and Henze have written works for him. Holliger's compositions include both instrumental and choral works. He is married to the harpist **Ursula Holliger**.

Hollins, Alfred (1865–1942) British organist and pianist. Blind from birth, he studied in Berlin with Hans von Bülow and toured the USA and Australia.

Holmboe, Vagn (1909–) Danish composer. Holmboe studied in Berlin with Ernst Toch; his interest in folk music stems from his subsequent travels in Romania. Holmboe's style evolved from that of Nielsen and Sibelius: this is most evident in his 18 symphonies. His output also includes an opera, 14 string quartets, and choral music.

Holst, Gustav (Theodore) (G. T. von Holst; 1874–1934) British composer of partly Swedish descent. In 1893 Holst entered the Royal College of Music (RCM) in London to study composition with Stanford, after which he was for a time trombone player in various orchestras. He returned to

Heinz Holliger (right) with the French String Trio

Gustav Holst, best known for his suite The Planets

London to teach, being appointed music master at St Paul's Girls' School (1905), director of music at Morley College for working men and women (1907), and teacher at the RCM (1919).

Holst's output is varied and shows many different influences, including Hindu mysticism, English folk music, and astrology. His most familiar work is the orchestral suite *The *Planets* (1915). Other compositions include the operas *Sāvitri* (1908), *The *Perfect Fool* (1923), and *At the Boar's Head* (1925); *St Paul's Suite* (1913), written for the string orchestra at St Paul's School; the orchestral piece *Egdon Heath* (1928); and many choral works, including *Hymns from the Rig Veda* (1911–13), *The *Hymn of Jesus* (1917), *Ode to Death* (1922), and a *Choral Symphony* (1925). His daughter **Imogen Holst** (1907–84) was a composer and pianist who taught music at various schools and later worked with Britten in organizing the Aldeburgh Festivals. Her compositions include an orchestral overture, piano works, and arrangements of folk music. She has written biographies of her father, Purcell, and Britten.

homage A 20th-century composition dedicated to the name and style of a composer. An example is Falla's *Homenaje*.

Homage March 1. March for brass band by Wagner, written in homage to King Ludwig II of Bavaria, who was a great supporter of Wagner's work. Composed: 1864. Wagner later rearranged the march for orchestra. **2.** March for orchestra by Grieg from the incidental music written for *Sigurd the Crusader* by Bjørson, Composed: 1872.

Homage to the Queen Ballet in one act with music by Malcolm Arnold and choreography by Frederick Ashton. First performance: Covent Garden, London, 1953, by the Sadler's Wells Ballet (décor by Messel). It was devised in honour of the coronation of Queen Elizabeth II.

Home, Sweet Home Popular Victorian parlour song. Composed: 1823. In its original form this song appeared several times throughout Sir Henry Bishop's opera *Clari, or The Maid of Milan*. However, its great popularity and appeal to contemporary sentiment during a time when many Britons were serving the Empire overseas caused it to be performed frequently as an independent piece.

Homenaje Work for guitar by Falla, subtitled *Le Tombeau de Claude Debussy* (*Claude Debussy's Memorial*). Composed: 1920. This work was composed in memory of Debussy and was suggested by his piano piece *Soirée dans la Grenade*. It was later orchestrated.

Homer (8th century BC) Greek poet, whose epic poetry included the legend of Odysseus. Bruch wrote a choral work of the same name (1872). Bliss's *Morning Heroes* (1930) has words by Homer (among others).

Homme armé, L' (*The Armed Man*) Popular 15th-century melody, often attributed to Busnois. The origin of the melody is uncertain (possibly it came from a polyphonic chanson) but it is used as the *cantus firmus for over 30 masses composed during the 15th and 16th centuries. Among the composers who used the melody are Dufay, Palestrina, and Ockeghem; a mass on which this melody is based is usually described as *Missa l'homme armé*. The practice of basing sacred works upon secular melodies was common practice during the Renaissance.

Homme et son desir, L' (*Man and his Desire*) Ballet in three scenes with music by Milhaud, scenario by Claudel, and choreography by Börlin. First performance: Théâtre des Champs-Elysées, Paris, 1921, by the Swedish Ballet. It depicts man's eternal dance of unfulfilled desire.

homophonic Relating to music in which the parts do not have either melodic or rhythmic independence. English hymn tunes are usually homophonic. Compare **polyphonic; heterophony.**

hondo Deep. Hence **cante hondo**, deep song – a Spanish popular song in a melancholic mood. The tuning of some of the intervals and the ornamentation, being derived from folk traditions, are individual and peculiar. [Spanish]

Honegger, Arthur (1892–1955) French composer. Honegger studied with Widor and d'Indy at the Paris

Conservatoire; he later became a member of Les *Six. Classical forms underlie much of Honegger's music: sense of key is often extended through the use of polytonality. His works include the dramatic psalm *Le Roi David* (1921; see **King David**) and other choral works; operas; the musical play **Joan of Arc at the Stake* (1935); orchestral music, including five symphonies and the descriptive **Pacific 231* (1924) and **Rugby* (1928); chamber music; and songs.

Hook, James (1746–1827) British composer and keyboard player. He was organist and composer to Marylebone Gardens (1769–73) and Vauxhall Gardens (1774–1820). He wrote a large number of light songs (including 'The Lass of Richmond Hill'), catches, glees, keyboard and church music, and a treatise, *Guida di musica* (c.1785).

hopak see **gopak**.

Hopkins, Antony (1921–   ) British composer, conductor, and broadcaster, best known for his long-running radio series *Talking About Music*. As a composer he has worked mainly for theatre and film; his compositions also include music for children, an example of which is *John and the Magic Music Man* (1977) for narrator and orchestra.

Hopkinson, Francis (1737–91) US composer, poet, and statesman. A signatory of the Declaration of Independence, Hopkinson is generally considered to be the first US composer. In addition to his collections of sacred and secular songs, which include the early 'My days have been so wondrous free' (1759), he wrote an entertainment and devised improvements to Franklin's harmonica and the method of harpsichord quilling.

Horenstein, Jascha (1898–1973) Russian-born conductor who took Swiss citizenship. He studied with Adolf Busch and Franz Schreker and subsequently held various posts in Europe. He achieved a high reputation, particularly in Bruckner, Mahler, and Nielsen.

horn A reedless wind instrument that has evolved from an animal horn. The basic characteristic of the horn is that it has a conical bore within which the air is made to vibrate by the blower's lips and tongue. The *trumpet is similar in many respects and is blown in the same way but it evolved from a hollowed-out piece of wood with a cylindrical bore, giving it a sharper and harsher tone than the resonant note of the horn. Most primitive horns were end-blown, but some had the blow hole at the side. The primitive horn is limited in the notes it can play to the *harmonic series (an instrument of this type is still in use in the ritual Jewish *shofar). This range can, however, be extended by the use of finger holes – the *cornett (not to be confused with the cornet) is an example of such an instrument.

During the 14th century metal horns, made in imitation of animal horns, began to appear, but were largely restricted in use to hunting horns and military horns. By the 18th century, however, the mouthpiece and the technique of changing the pitch by placing the hand in the bell had developed sufficiently for the horn to be used in the orchestra. The range of these **hand horns**, as they were called, was further increased by the use of detachable crooks (extra lengths of tubing) and by slides. However, it was not until the middle of the 19th century that the horn evolved into its modern form, with the use of valves to replace the detachable crooks. The modern orchestral **French horn** owes its name to the fact that most of this development occurred in France. Until about 50 years ago the standard orchestral horn was a *transposing instrument in F with a range of about three and a half octaves from B below the bass staff. Most orchestras now use the **double horn**, in which the player can change from a horn in F to a horn in B♭ by depressing a thumb valve (an innovation introduced in 1899). Apart from its extensive use in most orchestral music, the horn has been the subject of concertos by Mozart, Haydn, and Richard Strauss. It is also used in military bands. See also **flugelhorn; saxhorns**.

Horn, Karl Friedrich (1762–1850) German-born organist, teacher, and composer. He settled in London in 1782, becoming Queen Caroline's music master in 1789 and organist at St George's Chapel, Windsor, in 1823. Horn was active in the revival of Bach's music, publishing with Samuel Wesley a complete edition of *The Well-Tempered Clavier* (1810–13). His own works include keyboard sonatas and divertimenti for piano and violin. His son, **Charles Edward Horn** (1786–1849), was a composer and singer, beginning his career singing on London stages in 1809. He made several trips to the USA, becoming musical director of the Park Theatre, New York, and taking part in founding the New York Philharmonic Society. Horn composed many dramatically feeble operas and operettas, oratorios, and songs (including the famous *Cherry Ripe*).

Horne, Marilyn (1934–   ) US mezzo-soprano. She studied with Lotte Lehmann at California University and made her debut as Hata in Smetana's *The Bartered Bride* in Los Angeles (1954). She often sang opposite Joan Sutherland in 19th-century Italian operas. In 1960 she married the conductor Henry Lewis.

hornpipe An English dance originally accompanied by an instrument of the same name, which had a wooden tube with a horn 'bell' and was played with a single reed. In the 16th century the dance was among the earliest true English keyboard pieces, e.g. Hugh Aston's 'Hornepype' (c.1560). Similar to the *jig, but in a more moderate triple rhythm, it continued to be used during the 17th century, e.g. by Blow and Purcell. By the end of the 18th century it had changed to a simple duple rhythm and thereafter was associated with sailors.

Horn Signal Symphony Symphony No. 31 in D major by Haydn. Composed: 1765. Instead of the normal two horns Haydn scores for four horns, which feature particularly prominently in the second movement.

Horovitz, Joseph (1926–) Austrian-born British composer, a pupil of Nadia Boulanger. Horovitz is a versatile composer, his works including much music for television and film. His output also includes ballets, vocal music (such as the *Horrortorio*, written for the 1959 Hoffnung Festival), orchestral music, and chamber works.

Horowitz, Vladimir (1904–) Russian-born US pianist. After establishing his reputation in the Soviet Union and western Europe, he settled in the USA in 1940. He has retired on several occasions due to ill health, but still occasionally performs. Horowitz is noted as a performer of Liszt, Prokofiev, Scriabin, and Rachmaninov.

Hotter, Hans (1909–) Austrian bass-baritone. He studied with Matthäus Roemer, making his debut at Troppau as The Speaker in Mozart's *The Magic Flute* (1930). Later he became famous in Wagnerian roles, notably as Wotan in *The Ring*; he produced *The Ring* at Covent Garden (1961–64).

Hotteterre, Jacques Martin ('Le Romain'; *c.*1680–1761) French composer and flautist, member of a famous family of wind-instrument makers. As one of the first players of the transverse flute in France, he established its technique in his tutors, *Principes de la flûte traversière* (1707) and *Méthode pour apprendre à jouer   la flûte traversière* (1728). He also wrote chamber music.

Hovhaness, Alan (1911–) Armenian-born US composer, a pupil of Converse and Martinu. In the 1940s he studied Middle-Eastern musical techniques and his subsequent style blends western and oriental elements. His works include 24 symphonies, the piano concerto *Lousadzak* (1944), a violin concerto (1976), *And God Created Great Whales* (1970) for whale and orchestra, the cantata *Rubaiyat* (1977), and radio and television music.

Howells, Herbert (1892–1983) British composer, a pupil of Stanford at the Royal College of Music, where Howells himself eventually taught composition. His music avoids overt nationalism, nevertheless remaining unmistakably English in its romanticism. Howells' works include much church and organ music, two piano concertos and other orchestral works, chamber music, and songs.

Huber, Klaus (1924–) Swiss composer, a pupil of Blacher. He has used serial procedures and mathematical formal techniques in his music, much of which has a strong mystical-religious element. Huber's works include *Oratio Mechtildis* (1958), *Soliloquia* (1959–62), *Alveare Vernat* (1965), *Tenebrae* (1967), *Tempora* (1970), *Im Paradies oder der Alte van Berge* (1975), and chamber works.

Hucbald (*c.*840–930) Frankish theorist and composer, educated at St Amand, Nevers, and Auxerre, where he founded a school with Remi of Auxerre (*c.*893). Hucbald's treatise *De harmonica institutione* deals with the composition and practice of sacred chant, its main innovation being the improvement of the precision of pitch notation. Hucbald's chant compositions are believed to include the offices for St Peter, St Andrew, and St Theodoric together with the famous Gloria trope *Quem vera pia laus.*

Hudson, George (1615/20–72) English composer. Although appointed court musician before the Civil War, his career really began at the Restoration, when he became composer and violinist in the King's Music. Fourteen suites and one song by him survive. See also **Siege of Rhodes, The.**

Hughes, Arwel (1909–) British composer and conductor, a pupil of Vaughan Williams. As head of music for the BBC in Wales (1965–71), Hughes was responsible for promoting works by many contemporary Welsh composers. His own compositions, strongly influenced by his teacher, include operas, orchestral works, and chamber music.

Hughes, Herbert (1882–1937) Irish composer. Hughes was a founder of the Irish Folksong Society: he spent much time collecting and editing traditional Irish music. His own compositions include incidental music, piano works, and songs.

Hugh the Drover Opera in two acts by Vaughan Williams with text by Harold Child, subtitled *Love in the Stocks.* First performance: Royal College of Music, London, 1924. Set in a Cotswold village during the Napoleonic Wars, it is styled 'a romantic ballad opera' and makes extensive use of English folk songs.

Hugo, Victor (1802–85) French author. Many of his works have been set to music, including *Lucrezia Borgia* (by Donizetti, 1833) and *Rigoletto* (by Verdi, after *Le Roi s'amuse*, 1851). Liszt's symphonic poem *Mazeppa* (1854) is also based on Hugo.

Huguenots, Les Opera in five acts by Meyerbeer with libretto by Scribe and Deschamps. First performance: Opéra, Paris, 1836. The action culminates in the St Bartholomew's Day massacre of French Protestants in 1572.

Hume, Tobias (*c.*1569–1645) English composer and viol player. A mercenary officer in the Swedish and Russian armies, he regarded music as a secondary occupation. *The First Part of Ayres* (1605) and *Captaine Humes Poeticall Ayres* (1607) are his two most important publications; they contain songs and instrumental pieces with fanciful titles for the lyra viol.

Humfrey, Pelham see **Humphrey, Pelham.**

Hummel, Johann Nepomuk (1778–1837) Austrian pianist, composer, teacher, and conductor. A child prodigy, he studied the piano with Mozart (1785–87). With his father he toured Europe, playing in London in 1792. He returned in 1793 to Vienna, where he studied with Albrechtsberger, Salieri, and Haydn. He became orchestral leader to Prince Nikolaus Esterházy at Eisenstadt (1804–11) and kapellmeister at Stuttgart (1816–18) and at Weimar (1818). He undertook several more tours, visiting London in 1831 and 1833. Hummel was one of the most celebrated pianists in Europe and a much sought-after teacher whose pupils included Hiller and Thalberg; his piano method was published in 1828. His compositions, well crafted and melodious, bridge the classical and romantic periods and his piano works influenced later 19th-century composers. He wrote many piano works (including sonatas and variations), much chamber music, piano concertos, a mandolin concerto, orchestral dances, operas, incidental music, choral works, part songs, and songs.

humoresque A joyful and witty instrumental composition. Well-known examples come from Dvořák (1894) and Schumann (1839). German: **Humoreske**. [English and French]

Humperdinck, Engelbert (1854–1921) German composer and teacher. He studied first at the Cologne conservatory (1872–76) then with Rheinberger at the Munich conservatory (1877–79). In Naples in 1880 he met Wagner, who asked him to assist in preparing *Parsifal* for its premiere at Bayreuth. Humperdinck moved to Paris (1882–83) then taught in Barcelona (1885–87), at the Cologne conservatory (1887–89), at the Hoch conservatory, Frankfurt (1890–1900), and in Berlin (1900–20). He was music critic for the *Bonner Zeitung* (1887–88) and the *Frankfurter Zeitung* (1890–96). Humperdinck wrote a little chamber and orchestral music but was most successful with his choral music, songs, and music for the stage; his operas include **Hänsel und Gretel* (1893) and *Königskinder* (1897) and he wrote incidental music for four Shakespeare plays.

Humphrey (*or* **Humfrey**), **Pelham** (1647–74) English composer. He was a chorister at the Chapel Royal under Henry Cooke, leaving in 1664 to travel in France and Italy. On his return he became a gentleman of the Chapel Royal and the music he then wrote shows clearly the influence of foreign styles. In 1672 he succeeded Cooke as Master of the Children and composer to the king – he may have taught Henry Purcell. Humphrey's verse anthems are his most important pieces; they include string parts in the French manner, while their vocal parts owe much to the Italian style. He also wrote secular songs, court odes, and theatre music. His works represent the fruition of the English baroque.

Hungarian Fantasia Work for piano and orchestra by Liszt. Composed: 1852. This work was originally entitled

Engelbert Humperdinck

Fantasia on Hungarian Popular Themes and is the 14th of Liszt's **Hungarian Rhapsodies*.

Hungarian Quartet A string quartet founded in 1935 in Budapest and disbanded in 1970. The original leader was Sándor Végh; at the end of its career the members were Zoltán Székely and Michael Kuttner (violins), Dénes Koromzay (viola), and Gabriel Magyar (cello). The quartet spent some time in the Netherlands then moved to the USA, where it consolidated the reputation it had gained in Europe. It was highly praised for its interpretations of Beethoven but also performed contemporary quartets, particularly Hungarian ones: Székely's close association with Bartók enabled the quartet to give authentic and much-admired performances of Bartók's works.

Hungarian Rhapsodies Collection of 19 piano pieces by Liszt, based on Hungarian Gypsy melodies. Composed: 1851–86. The basic form of each rhapsody is that of a free fantasia, beginning with a slow introduction that leads into a faster section in the nature of a *csárdás. The 14th rhapsody is the so-called **Hungarian Fantasia* and the 15th is an arrangement of a Hungarian national air, the

Rákóczi March. Liszt later orchestrated some of the rhapsodies.

Hunt, The Symphony No. 73 in D major by Haydn. Composed: 1782. This symphony was originally composed as an overture to the opera *La Fedelta premiata* and the finale features horns and oboes in typical hunting motifs; Haydn himself used this title. The second movement is based upon the song 'Gegenliebe.'

Hunter, Rita (1933–) British soprano. She studied at Liverpool with Edwin Francis, in London with Redvers Llewellyn, and with Eva Turner before singing at Sadler's Wells (1960), Covent Garden (1963), and the Coliseum (1970), as Brunnhilde in Wagner's *Die Walküre*. Other roles in Wagner and in Verdi and Weber followed. She became a CBE in 1980.

Hunt Quartet String quartet in B♭ major (K. 458) by Mozart. Composed: 1784. This quartet, which is the fourth in the set of six quartets dedicated to Haydn, has an opening movement that features a motif in imitation of a hunting horn.

hurdy-gurdy (*or* **organistrum**) 1. A form of mechanized violin in which a rosined wheel turned by a handle acts as a bow and sets into vibration the strings, which are stopped by means of tiny piano keys. Drone strings provide a bass. The instrument was popular in France and both Haydn and Mozart wrote music for it. 2. A *barrel organ or street piano (presumably by association with the fact that both the true hurdy-gurdy and the barrel organ are operated by a handle).

Hurlstone, William Yeates (1876–1906) British composer and pianist. He studied composition with Stanford and the piano with Ashton and Dannreuther at the Royal College of Music, where in 1905 he became a professor. He composed orchestral works, including a piano concerto (1896) and the *Fantasie Variations on a Swedish Air* (1904), and chamber, piano, and vocal works.

Husa, Karel (1921–) Czech-born composer resident in the USA, a pupil of Honegger and Nadia Boulanger. His early music makes use of folk-song material but he later adopted a freely serial style. His works include *Evocations of Slovakia* (1951), *Music for Prague* (1968), a trumpet concerto (1973), the ballet *Monodrama* (1976), and much chamber music.

hydraulis (*or* **hydraulus** *or* **water organ**) An ancient type of organ used by the Greeks and Romans. Air was pumped into the wind chest via a water-pressure reservoir, so that if the pumping stopped the wind chest would continue to be supplied with air under pressure for a short time. In operation from the 3rd century BC, the hydraulis was still in use in medieval times.

hymn A song of praise to a god, saint, etc. In the Christian Church it formed part of the very earliest devotional music, formally established by St Ambrose of Milan in the 4th century. The Latin hymn was taken over from the Greek and Byzantine practice into the western Church and gradually became distinguished by its poetic and strophic nature, generally being set syllabically in a tuneful manner. Its subject matter varied considerably, becoming a more individual expression of faith in contrast to the stereotyped formal liturgy. During the 15th and 16th centuries the hymn became an important part of the vernacular in the Roman liturgy. In the German Protestant Church it became the *chorale, the first set being published in 1524. The English hymn emerged principally in the late 16th and early 17th centuries, evolving from the metrical *psalm (although the latter continued alongside the hymn). It received huge impetus with the Nonconformist movement, of which it became the central musical form. In the 19th century it continued to flourish in all branches of the church. Today the words of many old hymns have been given new modern tunes. *Hymns Ancient and Modern* appeared in 1861; it is the precursor of most hymn books in use today.

Hymn of Jesus, The Choral work for two choirs, female semichorus, and orchestra by Holst. Composed: 1917. The text is taken from the Apocryphal Acts of St John and the work is dedicated to Vaughan Williams.

Hymn of Praise (German: *Lobgesang*) Cantata for solo voices, choir, and orchestra (Op. 52) by Mendelssohn. First performance: 1840. As in the ninth symphony of Beethoven, three purely orchestral movements precede a final choral movement, which has a text based upon the Bible. This work is also numbered as Mendelssohn's second symphony.

Hymn to St Cecilia Work for unaccompanied choir by Britten to a poem by W. H. Auden. Composed: 1942. St Cecilia is the patron saint of music and her feast day (22 November) has often been honoured by composers, including Purcell with his *Ode for St Cecilia's Day. As Britten's birthday fell on this day, the work had a particular significance for him.

Hymn to the Sun An aria in praise of the sun from the opera The *Golden Cockerel* by Rimsky-Korsakov. Composed: 1906–07. In the opera this aria is sung by the Queen of Shemakha (soprano).

I

Iberia 1. Four suites of piano pieces by Albéniz, each suite containing three pieces evocative of Spanish scenery. Composed: 1906–08. These pieces were later orchestrated by Arbos. **2.** Symphonic work in three sections by Debussy, forming the second part of *Images*. Composed: 1908. This work attempts to capture in music the atmosphere of Spanish life.

Ibert, Jacques (1890–1962) French composer, a pupil of Gédalge and Fauré. Ibert received the Prix de Rome in 1919 and was director of the French Academy in Rome (1937–55). His compositions show lightness and wit in their predominantly neoclassical inspiration. Ibert's prolific output includes operas, ballet scores, orchestral works (such as the popular *Divertissement*, 1930), chamber music, and songs.

Ibsen, Henrik Johan (1828–1906) Norwegian dramatist and poet. Grieg set some of his songs and wrote incidental music for his play *Peer Gynt* in 1876. Wolf wrote some incidental music for a German production in Vienna in 1891 of *The Feast at Solhang*.

Ice Break, The Opera in three acts by Tippett with libretto by the composer. First performance: Covent Garden, London, 1977. The ice breaking symbolizes the psychological rebirth of the individual to a new depth of self-awareness. It is set forth in visual terms when Yuri (baritone), encased in plaster from injuries received during a riot, is operated on and released by the young doctor Luke (tenor) and is reconciled with his father, Lev (baritone).

idée fixe A *theme or *motto that is repeated, with or without variation, during a composition. Berlioz referred to idées fixes in his *Fantastic Symphony*, which identified specific musical ideas.

idiophone A musical *instrument in which the sound is produced by the vibration of the instrument itself when it is hit, rubbed, scraped, etc. Drums are not included as they are *membranophones. The main categories of idiophones are the *percussion instruments (e.g. xylophones, bells, gongs), the concussion instruments (e.g. some cymbals, clappers), the shaken instruments (e.g. tambourines, rattles), the plucked instruments (e.g. Jew's harp), the friction instruments (e.g. musical saw), and the stamped or stamping instruments (e.g. tubes, poles, stamping boards). Compare **aerophone; chordophone**.

Idomeneo Opera seria in three acts by Mozart with libretto by Abbé Varesco based on a French opera by Campra and Danchet. First performance: Munich, 1781. Idomeneo, King of Crete (tenor), promises Neptune the sacrifice of the first living man he meets in return for deliverance from a storm; unrecognized, it is his son, Idamante (originally a soprano role), who is the victim. But Neptune is finally appeased —Idomeneo abdicates and Idamante, with Ilia (soprano), daughter of King Priam of Troy as his bride, will reign in his place.

idyll A piece with poetic overtones describing blissful rustic life. An example is Wagner's *Siegfried Idyll* (1857).

Iliev, Konstantin Nikolov (1924–) Bulgarian composer and conductor, a pupil of Hába and Talich. His early pieces were influenced by folklore but he later made use of serial procedures. His works include five symphonies, a violin concerto (1971), the opera *Master of Bojana* (1963), and chamber music, including a piano trio (1976).

Illuminations, Les Song cycle for high voice and string orchestra (Op. 18) by Britten to nine poems by Rimbaud. Composed: 1939. This work was written for the British tenor Peter Pears.

illustrative music see **programme music**.

Images 1. Two suites of piano pieces by Debussy, each suite containing three pieces. Composed: 1905–07. **2.** Orchestral work in three parts by Debussy, entitled in full *Images pour l'orchestre* (*Pictures for Orchestra*). Composed: 1902–12. The three parts are *Rondes de printemps* (*Dances of Spring*), *Iberia*, and *Gigues* (Jigs).

imitation A contrapuntal device in which a voice repeats a theme or motive previously stated by another. Imitation is a regular feature of 16th-century polyphonic music and is freely used in the western tradition. Strictly organized types of imitation are *canon and *fugue. In freer types of imitation the imitating voice need not reproduce the idea strictly, a recognizable similarity being all that is required. See also **stretto**.

Mozart's Idomeneo *performed at Glynde-bourne in 1973*

Immortal Hour, The Opera by Rutland Boughton with libretto by the composer. First performance: Glastonbury, Somerset, 1914. The text is Celtic legend taken from the plays and poems of 'Fiona Macleod,' alias William Sharp.

imperfect time see **perfect time.**

Imperial Symphony No. 53 in D major by Haydn. Composed: *c*.1773. The name refers to the grandiose nature of the introduction to the first movement. There are two different versions of the finale to this symphony, both fully authenticated as being the work of Haydn. There are, however, several other finales in existence, whose authorship has never been definitely proven.

Imperial Mass see **Nelson Mass.**

Impresario, The see **Schauspieldirektor, Der.**

impressionism A musical movement of the late 19th and early 20th centuries, named after the style of painting evolved by Monet and Renoir. In music impressionism can be seen to start with Debussy's *Prélude à l'après-midi d'un faune*, which attempts to suggest situations by means of atmospheric effects. To this end a completely new musical vocabulary was developed, making extensive use of *whole-tone scales, parallel motion, modal harmony, and unresolved dissonances. Impressionism was associated chiefly with Debussy, although its influence can also be seen in the work of Ravel, Dukas, Delius, Falla, and others.

impromptu A 19th-century instrumental piece suggesting fairly unrestrained fancy or improvisation. Chopin wrote several fine examples for piano, including Op. 29 (1837) and Op. 36 (1840).

improvisation (*or* **extemporization**) The performance of a piece of music that has been created during the performance itself. Unless a composition is improvised it is either played from memory or read from the music, or a combination of both. However improvisation is not always devoid of these other elements. For example, the interpretation of a *figured bass requires a degree of improvisation, but it is limited by what is written in the music. Similarly the improvisation involved in spontaneously playing a *cadenza will rely heavily on the passages of the movement of the concerto the soloist has just played and which he has retained in his memory. However, pure improvisation, as practised by many of the great composers, may be one of the most important elements in composition.

Inbal, Eliahu (1936–) Israeli conductor. He studied under Sergiu Celibidache in Italy and has conducted the Frankfurt Radio Symphony Orchestra (1974–).

incipit It begins: used to indicate the start of a piece as quoted in an index, catalogue, etc. [Latin]

Incoronazione di Poppea, L' (*The Coronation of Poppaea*) Opera in prologue and three acts by Monteverdi with libretto by Busenello. First performance: Teatro di Santi Giovanni e Paolo, Venice, 1642. Set in ancient Rome, it tells the story of the ambitious love of Poppaea (soprano) for the emperor Nero (soprano; in some modern productions, tenor).

Incredible Flutist, The Ballet with music by Walter Piston, written in collaboration with the dancer Hans Weiner. First performance: Boston, 1938, with the Hans Weiner Dancers. The flute player charms both snakes and humans. A popular concert suite taken from the ballet was first performed in 1940.

Indes galantes, Les (*Love in the Indies*) Opera-ballet in prologue and four entrées by Rameau with libretto by

Fuzelier. First performance: Opéra, Paris, 1735. The four entrées relate love stories of the Turkish, Peruvian, Persian, and Amazonian (noble savage) peoples.

indeterminacy A type of music that emerged in the 1950s, in which certain elements are left undecided by the composer. In **aleatory** (or **aleatoric**) music pure chance is left to determine particular parameters of the composition; for example, John Cage's *Imaginary Landscape* is scored for 12 radio sets. Alternatively, certain decisions may be left to the performer; for example, in Stockhausen's *Zyklus* (*Cycle*) it is the performer who decides on which page of the score he will start the piece.

Indian music The two leading musical cultures of India are shared in part by Sri Lanka, Pakistan, Nepal, and Bangladesh. Despite great areas of ignorance, the history of Indian music from the first millennium BC up to modern times is partly available from literary sources, such as technical treatises in Sanskrit (the classical language of Hindu India) and other languages. At some time around the 13th century AD, after the important arrival of Muslim culture, the classical music began to split into two main traditions – that of the north, called **Hindustani**, and that of southern India, commonly called **Karnatak** (or **Carnatic**) music. These two now quite distinct musical idioms thus have a common origin and share many theoretical and practical features. According to traditional Indian ideas the human voice is the supreme musical instrument; thus the majority of genres of performance have their roots in vocal style.

The melodic basis of all Indian classical music is the **rāga** (or **rāg**), a theoretical arrangement of notes within an octave with certain essential patterns and juxtapositions of notes that give each rāga its individual character. The scale is divided into 12 notes, rather like the semitones of western music, but as there is no such element as western harmony or counterpoint a greater subtlety and flexibility of pitching is possible. Thus in one rāga a note may be almost the same as, but in fact microtonally higher or lower than, an equivalent note in another rāga. Melodic ornamentation is complex and essential and also employs microtonal fluctuations in pitch. There is in theory a very large number of rāgas, but a performing artist possesses a finite repertoire, knowing a number of compositions in the various rāgas he has studied, each composition being confined to a single rāga. There is no real equivalent of western notation, though a rudimentary kind of oral sol-fa system has been used since ancient times to assist the memorizing of melodic patterns and compositions. Written musical notation has never been used much by serious performers and students.

Composition also occupies a rather different place in Indian music. Most types of performance start with the exposition of a short precomposed song or piece (called **chīz** or **bandish** or, for instrumental music, **gat**) and then take various phrases within it as the framework for improvisation, always remaining within the rāga of the composition. A drone is sounded throughout the performance, either by a *tambura, tuned to important notes in the rāga being performed, or by some other instrument that blends more easily with the melodic soloist. The instruments heard most often in Karnatak music are the violin, both as accompaniment to a singer and as a solo, the *vīnā (a plucked fretted lute), the transverse flute, and the double-reed instrument called **nāgasvaram**. The most popular Hindustani instruments are the *sitar, the double-reed **shehnai**, the *sarod (a plucked unfretted lute), and the *sārangī (a kind of bowed fiddle).

In Hindustani vocal music there are two common types of composition. The **khyāl** is a kind of sacred or secular song, which is sung in different styles by artists belonging to different regional schools called **gharānās**. The **thumrī** is a somewhat lighter mode of singing usually employing texts of an amorous content and a more florid and highly ornamented melodic line, which gives more importance to the words of the text than does the khyāl. An older type of singing, the **dhrupad**, is less often heard today and is the preserve of a few distinguished specialists. Karnatak vocal compositions are most often religious texts by saint composers of south India, the most famous being the early-19th-century Tyāgarāja. Instrumental and some vocal forms of performance start with a section called **ālāp**, a rhythmically free improvisation in which the notes of the rāga and its characteristic phrases are elaborated in order to set the mood that the rāga is intended to represent. The ālāp is of indefinite length, and an artist will continue to improvise according to his mood and the responsiveness of his audience. This is followed by the composition and its improvisation, which demands the accompaniment of a rhythm instrument, usually *tabla in Hindustani music and the double-ended drum called the **mrdangam** in Karnatak music. The rhythm of the composition is fixed in a **tāla** (or **tāl**), a repeating unit of definite length and containing a fixed number of beats. The tāla may be in slow, medium, or fast tempo, depending on the composition, but there is no absolute or standard concept of speed. Out of the large variety of possible tālas, Hindustani and Karnatak music each have around a dozen in common use. In addition to the classical music there is an immense variety of folk, theatrical, and devotional music in all parts of the subcontinent, with songs in all the regional languages and an enormous range of instruments. As well as providing the models for developments in other countries, Indian music has absorbed instruments from other cultures, such as the now popular harmonium, which was originally introduced by European missionaries.

Indian Queen, The Incidental music by Purcell to the play by Dryden and Howard. First performance: 1695. This work, which tells a story concerning the rivalry and distrust between Mexican and Peruvian Indians, is often classified as an opera because of the extensive role that music plays throughout. On Purcell's death in 1695 the music had not been fully completed: the masque in the fifth act was composed by Daniel Purcell, the brother of Henry.

Indonesian music Despite successive waves of foreign influence (Chinese, Indian, Islamic, and European) the Indonesian archipelago, especially the islands of Java and Bali, has developed and retained a unique style of music. This is the music of the **gamelan**, an orchestra consisting of a variety of instruments, most of which are of the percussive fixed-note kind and made out of metal or bamboo. The **saron** and **gender** are xylophone-like instruments, with a set of tuned wooden or metal bars supported on a stand and usually having resonators underneath. The **bonang** is a graded chime of gongs and there are also a number of single gongs, various kinds of drum, and untuned cymbals. The **angklung** are bamboo rattle chimes, and there are two flexible melodic instruments – the **suling** (a flute) and the **rebab** (a spike fiddle of Arabic descent; see **rebec**). The orchestras vary in size and magnificence from those employed by noble families to the ubiquitous village band.

Since there are two basic scales in use in Indonesia, with different tunings, and since the instruments are mostly of the fixed-note variety, each gamelan can only play the music of the scale to which it is tuned. The scales are the **pelog** and the **slendro**. The most ancient is the pelog, which divides the octave into seven unequal intervals from which secondary five-note scales are used as the basis of a composition. The slendro is a division of the octave into five approximately equal intervals. The pelog is considered to have a feminine and melancholic character and is used to accompany the cycles of heroic legend; the slendro has a masculine, grave, and noble character and is used in association with the *Wayang kulit*, the shadow puppet theatre. Wealthy establishments have a double gamelan with instruments tuned to both pelog and slendro tonality. A gamelan composition has three main elements: a fundamental melody played in long-drawn notes on the saron, analogous to the cantus firmus of European music; a discreet embroidering of the main theme by a group of higher-pitched chime- and xylophone-type instruments; and an intricate and decorative pattern woven around the central theme by a freer set of instruments, including the suling and rebab. The range of sound is six to seven octaves, creating a dense but constantly changing web of sound, which deeply impressed Debussy when he heard it at the Great Paris Exhibition of 1889.

The Indonesian peoples are unusually sensitive to music in their everyday lives. The rice harvest is beaten out in hollowed wood troughs, raised off the ground so that they resonate to the cross-rhythms of each worker's personal speed, and the terraced paddy fields are irrigated by carefully shaped bamboo water pipes, which are so pivoted that they swing back against stones to give a constant natural accompaniment to the human voice. A popular type of song is the **kronchong**, the 16th-century legacy left by Portuguese sailors, so-called from the narrow five-stringed guitar to which such songs were originally sung.

Inextinguishable, The Symphony No. 4 by Nielsen. First performance: 1916. The title refers to Nielsen's belief that despite struggle and torment all can be eventually resolved by the power of music. This symphony is often seen as an optimistic comment upon World War I.

Ingegneri, Marc' Antonio (1547–92) Italian composer. A choirboy at Verona under Vincenzo Ruffo, he is believed to have studied in Parma under Cipriano de Rore. He was possibly in Cremona by 1570 and was appointed maestro di cappella of the cathedral there in 1581, becoming the teacher of Claudio Monteverdi. Both his sacred and secular music is rather retrospective, but he was a skilled writer of counterpoint. His *Responsories* (1588) are well known since they were once attributed to Palestrina.

inglese English. Thus **corno inglese**, English horn. [Italian]

in modo di In the manner of. [Italian]

In Nature's Realm (*or* **Amid Nature**) Concert overture (Op. 91) by Dvořák. Composed: 1891. This work is one of a trilogy of overtures with the collective title *Nature, Life and Love*, the other two overtures being *Carnival* and *Othello*.

In nomine A type of English 16th-century keyboard composition employing the antiphon melody 'Gloria tibi Trinitas,' first set in the 'Benedictus qui venit in nomine Domine' in a mass by Taverner. It was also used in viol consort music.

instrumentation The art of writing music for particular instruments, taking into account not only their range but also the kinds of sounds they make. Compare **orchestration.**

instruments, musical Any device used to produce musical sounds. The simplest classification is into *percussion, *wind, and *stringed instruments. This classification is somewhat loose in certain cases; for example, a piano is both a percussion instrument and a stringed instrument. In 1914 Erich von Hornbostel and Curt Sachs published a system of classification similar to this system but with the ambiguities avoided. In their system, instruments are classified according to what actually makes the sound, into *aerophones, *chordophones, *idiophones, and *membranophones.

Intendant The administrative director or manager of a German opera house or theatre. [German]

interlude A short piece used to fill in between longer pieces or between the acts of a play, etc. Organ interludes were played between the verses of hymns and metrical psalms in 18th-century England.

intermezzo 1. (*or* **intermedio**) A performance of madrigals and songs between speeches and dialogues in 16th-century Italian courtly entertainments. **2.** A comic episode inserted between scenes in 18th-century opera. These independent sections grew into separate one-act operas, the best-known example of which is Pergolesi's *La Serva padrona* (see **opera buffa**). **3.** An instrumental piece played in the middle of an opera, when the characters are off stage, as in Mascagni's *Cavalleria rusticana.* **4.** A piece by Schumann equivalent to the *trio (with minuet). **5.** A short independent instrumental piece of the 19th century, for example by Brahms and Schumann. French **intermède**. [Italian, in between]

Intermezzo Opera in two acts by Richard Strauss with text by the composer. First performance: Court Opera, Dresden, 1924. The work is based on incidents from the composer's domestic life.

Internationale International socialist anthem. It was originally composed in 1888 by Degeyter to words written in 1872 by a French transport worker, Eugene Pottier. The text was translated into Russian several times, and in 1917 it was adopted as the national anthem of the Soviet Union. In 1943 the USSR adopted a new anthem. However, the *Internationale* had by now become established as a revolutionary anthem of socialism in many countries and is still used as such today.

interrupted cadence see **cadence**.

interval The difference in pitch between two notes. In the scale, intervals of the *octave, the *fifth, and the *fourth are called **perfect intervals**. The **major intervals** are the *second (e.g. C–D), the *third (C–E), the *sixth (C–A), and the *seventh (C–B). When major intervals are reduced by a semitone they become **minor intervals** (e.g. C–E♭ is a minor third). See also **ninth**. When a major interval or a perfect interval is increased by a semitone it becomes an **augmented interval** , while a perfect or minor interval reduced by a semitone is said to be a **diminished interval**. Intervals greater than an octave are known as **compound intervals**. The table gives the names for each interval.

In the South Overture (Op. 50) by Elgar. Composed: 1904. Elgar wrote the work while on a visit to Italy and prefixed the score with the name of the town in which he was staying, Alassio. This overture attempts to describe in musical terms the spirit of Italy, as seen by a foreigner.

In the Steppes of Central Asia Tone poem by Borodin. Composed: 1880. This work, described by the composer as an 'orchestral picture,' depicts the gradual approach of a caravan and its continuation into the distance. It was originally intended that the music should be performed as a background to a tableau vivant.

intonation 1. The act of intoning. **2.** The extent to which a singer, violinist, etc., is in tune (good intonation) or out of tune (bad intonation). **3.** See **temperament**.

intrada A piece of homophonic instrumental music of the 16th and 17th centuries in either duple or triple time, with a festive and martial character. It was frequently the first movement of a German orchestral suite. Subsequently, Beethoven applied the term to the short overture of *Wellington's Victory* (1813) and Sibelius to a solemn prelude for organ.

Introit 1. Part of a psalm chanted antiphonally at the beginning of the *Mass as the priest processes to the altar. It was introduced by Pope Celestine I in the early 5th century. As part of the Proper of the Mass, the text of the Introit is changed seasonally. **2.** The introductory duo of an isorhythmic motet of the 14th or 15th century that preceded the entry of the tenor part. [from Latin *introitus*, entrance]

inventions The term applied by J. S. Bach to a collection of 15 two-part pieces (*inventiones*) for keyboard in 1723. Since they display considerable contrapuntal skill in the development of a single theme it is possible that they stemmed from the *ricercare. Bach's three-part sinfonias are commonly called inventions as they are similar in style. The term was authentically applied to three-part music by Bach's pupil H. N. Gerber in *Six Inventiones for Organ* (1737).

interval in the key of C	number of semitones	name of interval
C–C♯	1	minor second
C–D	2	major second; diminished third
C–D♯ (E♭)	3	minor third
C–E	4	major third; diminished fourth
C–F	5	fourth
C–F♯ (G♭)	6	augmented fourth; diminished fifth
C–G	7	fifth
C–G♯ (A♭)	8	augmented fifth; minor sixth
C–A	9	major sixth; diminished seventh
C–A♯ (B♭)	10	augmented sixth; minor seventh
C–B	11	major seventh
C–C'	12	octave
C–C'♯	13	minor ninth
C–D	14	major ninth

inversion 1. The process of changing the *position of the notes in a chord. For example, the chord of C major is said to be in the **root position** in the form CEG. The form EGC is its **first inversion**; the form GCE its **second inversion**. A four-note chord has a **third inversion**; for example FGBD is the third inversion of the chord GBDF (the dominant seventh of the chord of C major). **2.** The process of changing a melody by performing successive notes in the opposite direction. For example, the sequence C–G (a major fifth) would be inverted by playing C with the F below it (a major fifth inverted). **3.** The process of changing over the upper and lower melodies in *counterpoint.

inverted pedal see **pedal**.

invertible counterpoint Counterpoint in which two or more parts change places (e.g. the highest part becomes the bass). It is based on inversion of intervals; for example, when two parts are inverted at the octave one part remains in its original position while the other moves up or down an octave, the new intervals complementing those of the original setting. Invertible counterpoint involving two, three, and four parts is known respectively as **double**, **triple**, and **quadruple counterpoint**. As a discipline it is part of *strict counterpoint. It was little used in composition until the baroque period, when it became an important technique in the writing of fugues.

Invisible City of Kitezh, The see **Legend of the Invisible City of Kitezh, The**.

Invitation to the Dance Piano piece in waltz style (Op. 65) by Weber. Composed: 1819. This work was later orchestrated by Berlioz and as such used for the ballet *Le Spectre de la rose*.

Iolanta (*or* **Yolande**) Opera in one act by Tchaikovsky with libretto by his brother, Modest. First performance: St Petersburg, 1892. The story, based on a tale by Hans Andersen, concerns the blind princess Iolanta (soprano).

Iolanthe Operetta by Sullivan with libretto by Gilbert. First performance: Savoy Theatre, London, 1882. Subtitled *The Peer and the Peri*, it relates what happens when Strephon, son of the fairy Iolanthe and the Lord Chancellor, wishes to marry Phyllis, a ward of chancery who is also wooed by various peers in the House of Lords.

Ionian mode see **modes**.

Iphigenia in Aulis 1. (French: *Iphigénie en Aulide*) Opera in three acts by Gluck with libretto by du Roullet based on Racine's tragedy, which in its turn is based on Euripides. First performance: Opéra, Paris, 1774. The story relates the sacrifice of Iphigenia, daughter of Agamemnon and Clytemnestra. **2.** (Italian: *Ifigenia in Aulide*) Opera by Cherubini with libretto by Moretti. First performance: Turin, 1788.

Iphigenia in Tauris 1. (French: *Iphigénie en Tauride*) Opera in four acts by Gluck with libretto by Guillard, based on Euripides. First performance: Opéra, Paris, 1779. The story relates Iphigenia's sojourn in Tauris and subsequent rescue by her brother, Orestes. **2.** Opera by Piccinni with libretto by Dubreuil. First performance: Opéra, Paris, 1781.

Ippolitov-Ivanov, Mikhail Mikhaylovich (1859–1935) Russian composer, teacher, and conductor. He studied at the St Petersburg conservatory (1875–82); from 1882 to 1893 he was director of the Tbilisi Academy of Music and from then until his death he taught at the Moscow conservatory, where he was also director (1905–22). He conducted at Moscow opera theatres. Ippolitov-Ivanov's compositions are conventional and some include folk elements (e.g. *Caucasian Sketches* (1894) for orchestra); he wrote several operas (including *The Last Barricade*, 1933), orchestral, choral, chamber, and piano works, and Acts II–IV for Mussorgsky's unfinished opera *The Marriage*.

Iradier (*or* **Yradier**), **Sebastián** (1809–65) Spanish composer. He lived in Madrid (where he may have been a professor at the conservatory), Paris, and for a short time in Cuba. Iradier contributed to *zarzuelas and wrote many popular songs, among them *El Arreglito*, which Bizet adapted as the habanera in the first act of *Carmen*.

Ireland, John (1879–1962) British composer. Ireland was a pupil of Stanford at the Royal College of Music in London:

John Ireland

he later taught there, his pupils including Britten and Moeran. Ireland destroyed many of his earliest works; his mature compositions all show the careful attention to detail insisted upon by his teacher Stanford. The romantic nature of Ireland's style stems from his lyrical approach to instrumental writing. His works include the tone poem *Mai-Dun (1920–21), a piano concerto (1930), A *London Overture (1936), and other orchestral works; three piano trios and other chamber works; sonatas for violin and piano (1918–20); choral works; and songs.

Iris Opera in three acts by Mascagni with libretto by Illica. First performance: Teatro Costanzi, Rome, 1898. Set in Japan, it is the tragedy of the young and beautiful Iris (soprano), who is abducted into a brothel.

Irmelin Opera by Delius, who also wrote the libretto. Composed: 1890–92; first performance: New Theatre, Oxford, 1953, under Sir Thomas Beecham.

Isaac, Heinrich (c.1450–1517) Flemish composer. In 1484 he joined the service of Lorenzo de' Medici in Florence. Isaac became a member of the imperial court chapel of Maximilian I in 1496, returning at regular intervals to Florence from 1499 until 1512, when he re-entered Medici service permanently. His works include the *Choralis Constantinus* (a large collection of office settings) as well as masses, motets, secular works, and a four-part lament on the death of Lorenzo de' Medici in 1492, *Quis dabit capito meo*, based in part on his *Missa salva nos*.

Ishii, Kan (1921–) Japanese composer. Kan studied in Munich with Carl Orff and his music shows the strong influence of his teacher. Kan is best known in Japan for his ballet music; his works also include orchestral, vocal, and chamber music and film scores.

Islamey 'Oriental fantasy' for solo piano by Balakirev. First performance: 1869. Balakirev was inspired to write the work after a visit to the Caucasus, and in it he attempts to imitate the sound of oriental music and evoke the spirit of oriental life. In 1908 *Islamey* was orchestrated by Alfredo Casella.

Isle of the Dead, The Tone poem by Rachmaninov, inspired by a painting with the same title by Böcklin. First performance: 1909. The painting depicts a desolate and uninhabited island and to emphasize the bleak mood Rachmaninov quotes the *Dies irae* from the Requiem Mass.

isorhythm A structural device of medieval polyphony, associated especially with the *ars nova, in which the tenor part is constructed around a repeated scheme of note values. In an isorhythmic tenor part the liturgical *cantus firmus is presented so that a rhythmic pattern several bars long is constantly repeated throughout the composition, with no deviation except for diminution or augmentation. Occasionally isorhythmic technique was used for all parts of a composition, in which case it is described as **panisorhythmic.**

Israel in Egypt Oratorio for solo voices, choir, and orchestra by Handel, with a text arranged from the Bible. First performance: 1739. This oratorio includes music plagiarized from the work of the German composer Johann Kerll. It is particularly noted for the amount and quality of the chorus writing, which is far more extensive than in any other Handel oratorio and includes several sections for double chorus. The first act includes music from Handel's own funeral anthem for Queen Caroline, 'The Ways of Zion do Mourn,' composed in 1739.

istesso tempo, l' The same tempo: a direction indicating that the pulse or beat remains the same though the nature of the time value of the beat may have changed, for example from a crotchet to a dotted crotchet, where the second should assume the same duration as the first. [Italian]

Italian Caprice see Capriccio italien.

Italian Concerto Work for solo harpsichord (BWV 971) by Bach. Composed: 1735. The *Italian Concerto* appears in the second part of the *Clavierübung* and the name reflects its imitation of the form and style of 18th-century Italian composers, such as Vivaldi, and their concertos. By writing for a two-manual instrument Bach is able to achieve the concerto-like effect of contrasting solo and tutti passages, and the melodic figurations are typically Italian.

Italian Girl in Algiers, The (Italian: *L'Italiana in Algeri*) Comic opera in two acts by Rossini with text by Anelli. First performance: Teatro San Benedetto, Venice, 1813. Deriving from the commedia dell' arte tradition, Isabella (contralto) outwits the Bey of Algiers (bass) while searching for her lover, Lindoro (tenor).

Italian overture An instrumental introduction to an opera or oratorio in three short movements – fast–slow–fast –evolved by Alessandro Scarlatti at the end of the 17th century. It was often known as a sinfonia and was an important forerunner of the 18th-century *symphony. The first movement was sometimes imitative but the others were monophonic. See also **concerto.**

Italian Serenade Work for string quartet by Wolf. Composed: 1887. Originally the piece was simply entitled *Serenade*, but Wolf later referred to it as *Italian Serenade* in a letter to a friend and this title was used when he arranged the work for orchestra in 1892. When he orchestrated the *Italian Serenade* Wolf intended there to be two further movements, but these were never composed.

Italian sixth see augmented sixth.

Italian Symphony Symphony No. 4 in A minor by Mendelssohn. First performance: 1833. This symphony was composed while Mendelssohn was visiting Italy and was

The English National Opera's The Italian Girl in Algiers *(1982)*

influenced by Italian scenery and folk music. The second movement is supposed to have been written after the composer saw a procession of pilgrims, and the finale, entitled 'Saltarello,' includes rhythmic and melodic features of this traditional Neapolitan dance.

Italienisches Liederbuch (*Italian Song-Book*) Collection of songs by Wolf to poems by Paul Heyse. Composed: 1890–96. The poems are taken from a collection of German translations by Heyse of Italian *vispetti* (love poems). Wolf

set 46 of the poems, which were published in two parts (1892 and 1896).

Iturbi, José (1895–1980) Spanish pianist, conductor, and composer. As a result of concert tours of Europe and the USA Iturbi became well known as a pianist. His few compositions are written in a light Spanish style.

Ivanhoe Opera by Sullivan with libretto by Julian Sturgis based on Walter Scott's novel. First performance: Royal English Opera House (now the Palace Theatre), London, 1891. It is Sullivan's only opera, whereas he wrote 23 operettas.

Ivan Susanin see **Life for the Tsar, A.**

Ivan the Terrible 1. (French: *Ivan le Terrible*) Opera by Bizet, with a libretto by Leroy and Trianon. Composed: 1865. Ivan the Terrible was a 16th-century Russian tsar who was notorious for his bloody deeds. After the first performance the work was withdrawn and the manuscript was lost; it reappeared in 1944 and a revival was staged in 1946. **2.** See **Maid of Pskov, The.**

Ives, Charles Edward (1874–1954) US composer. Ives' earliest and most significant instruction in music came from his father, a bandmaster with an extraordinary experimental curiosity. As a student at Yale (1894–98) he was a pupil of Horatio Parker; Ives' original style was at considerable odds with the traditional academicism of Parker. Ives' subsequent career in insurance absolved him from the need to earn his living by music, which would have compromised his artistic and philosophical principles. He retired from business in 1930: bad health and political disillusionment had caused him to all but stop composing some ten years previously.

An openness to different styles and techniques characterizes all of Ives' music, from the short experimental works that make up much of his output to the larger more integrated compositions. His music often anticipates compositional techniques, such as serialism, polytonality, and spatial organization of sound, that were only later developed in Europe. American hymn and folk tunes often appear in his works, as do quotations from the classical repertory. Ives' major works include four symphonies; orchestral works, including the 'set' *Three Places in New England* (1905–14); two piano sonatas (the second is the *Concord Sonata, 1909–15); much chamber music; and songs.

J

jack A part of the *action of a *harpsichord or *piano that rises to pluck or strike a string or set of strings. In the harpsichord each key has its own jack resting on it. When the key is depressed by a finger at one end, it makes the jack at the other rise, causing the quill or plectrum attached to the jack to pluck the string. A pivot on the jack enables the plectrum to fall without touching the string. In an upright piano the jack is the part that is lifted by the lever and causes the hammer to strike the string or strings.

Jackson, William (1730–1803) British composer, a pupil of John Travers. From 1777 he was organist, choirmaster, and lay vicar of Exeter Cathedral. He set Milton's *Lycidas* (1767) and General Burgoyne's *The Lord of the Manor* (1780) but his most popular works were his song collections; he also produced services, anthems, keyboard works, and writings on music.

Jacob, Gordon (1895–1984) British composer and teacher. Jacob taught at the Royal College of Music in London (1926–66). His published writings include books on orchestration and score reading; his compositions include four symphonies, concertos, chamber music, and vocal works.

Jacobson, Maurice (1896–1976) British composer, a pupil of Stanford and Holst. Jacobson's association with the theatre led him to compose incidental music for many of Shakespeare's plays; he later became involved in music publishing. Jacobson's works include the ballet *David* (1935) and the cantata *The Hound of Heaven* (1953).

Jacopo da Bologna (14th century) Italian composer. A writer of secular songs, he was in the service of Luchino Visconti at Padua by 1346, moving in 1349 to the court of Mastino della Scala at Verona, where he remained until the latter's death in 1351. His works include ballate, cacce, and madrigals; one madrigal and the motet *Lux purpurata radiis* were composed in honour of Luchino Visconti. He is also the author of a treatise entitled *L'Arte del biscanto misurato*.

Jahreszeiten, Die see Seasons, The.

Jamaican Rumba Work for two pianos by Arthur Benjamin. Composed: 1938. This piece was written after a visit to Jamaica and incorporates rhythmic and melodic features of native Jamaican music. It is the composer's most popular work and has been arranged many times for various instrumental combinations.

Janácek, Leos (1854–1928) Czech composer. Janácek's early experience of music was as a monastery chorister: he subsequently followed family tradition and entered the music-teaching profession. Although respected as a composer and teacher in his native town of Brno, it was not until the Prague performance of his opera *Jenufa* in 1915 that he became nationally and internationally known. The creative upsurge of the last years of his life reflect this recognition and also his pride in a newly independent Czechoslovakia.

Leos Janácek

Janáček's operas are his principal compositional legacy, displaying all the features of his style that permeate his other compositions. Notable is the character of his melodies, based on a close study of speech patterns, his stark orchestration, frequent use of jagged ostinato motifs in his instrumental writing, and a striking folk-based modal harmonic idiom. Janáček's operas include *Jenufa, The *Excursions of Mr Broucek* (1920), *Katya Kabanová* (1919–21), The *Cunning Little Vixen* (1921–23), The *Makropulos Case* (1926), and *From the House of the Dead* (1927–28); his other works include two string quartets and other chamber compositions, orchestral music (such as the *Sinfonietta*, 1926), choral works (such as the *Glagolithic Mass*, 1927), and piano music.

Janequin (*or* **Jannequin**), **Clément** (1485–1558) French composer. He took holy orders and from 1534 to 1537 was maître de chapelle at Angers Cathedral. His whereabouts thereafter is not certain; he may have lived for a short while in Paris. Janequin's works include some 250 chansons and about 150 psalm settings. The chansons follow the natural rhythm of the words and are often programmatic. In *La Bataille* (1515) the writing is harmonically static but very rhythmic in its imitation of fanfares.

janissaries The sultan's bodyguard from the 14th to the early 19th centuries, consisting of Turkish soldiers. Their music was largely percussive, relying on triangles and other jingling instruments. **Janissary music** is thus any music that includes a strong percussive element, such as the third movement of Brahms' fourth symphony, so described by the composer himself.

Janowitz, Gundula (1939–) German soprano. She studied at Graz. In 1960 Karajan engaged her for the Vienna State Opera, where she made her debut (1961). Under Karajan and Böhm she has sung Strauss, Mozart, and Beethoven.

Japanese music The music of Japan has been much influenced by ancient Indian, Manchurian, Chinese, and Korean forms, which came to Japan by way of conquest, tribute, and religion. Japan is also the most vital area in the Far East for the design and manufacture of instruments, the development of instrumental techniques (for example, the Suzuki violin method), and for composition – composers experiment not only in Japanese and in western styles but in a synthesis of both.

The earliest known music of the Japanese themselves is the Shinto temple chant. Sung with a slow trill between the tones, it is accompanied by a bamboo flute (**yamato-bue**) and a six-stringed zither (**yamato-goto**), both indigenous instruments. From the 3rd century AD, Chinese culture (including the Buddhist music from India) spread across the Sea of Japan; today it is possible to hear Japanese instrumentalists playing music from the 6th-century courts of India and China, *Gagaku* ('elegant music'), which has long since died out in its countries of origin. In the 8th century Japan followed the example of China and founded an official academy for the study of practical and theoretical music.

Since the early 17th century, the *koto has been the national instrument of Japan. It is a kind of long zither, related to the Chinese qin and having an aura of esoteric ritual connected with its performance. The Japanese **biwa** (a short-necked lute) and **sho** (a mouth organ) are related to their Chinese equivalents, the *pipa and sheng (see **Chinese music**). The ubiquitous *samisen is a type of lute without frets. During the 9th century, foreign styles of music and dance in Japan were so diverse that they were classified into two types. In left music, of Chinese and Indian origin, the Chinese kakko drum was used in the orchestra and the dancers entered from the left; in right music, of Korean and Manchurian origin, the Korean san-no-tsuzumi drum was used and the dancers entered from the right. Both used the tiny oboe (**hichiriki**) in the melodic sections of their orchestras, which played music composed on the pentatonic scale, in unison and accompanied by a haze of rich harmonics derived from the percussion and drone instruments.

Noh drama developed in the 14th century as a secular version of the Shinto 'monkey dance.' It is a highly formalized art, accompanied by unison chorus, transverse flute, and drums, with which the voice synchronizes in either recitative-like declamation or song. **Kabuki** is the popular drama, less bound in convention, and accompanied by flutes and drums.

Jaques-Dalcroze, Emile (1865–1950) Swiss composer and devisor of *eurhythmics, a system of musical training utilizing rhythmic body movements that he invented at the Geneva conservatory while Professor of Harmony there. He taught his system near Dresden (1910–14) and at the Institute Jaques-Dalcroze in Geneva, which he founded (1915). Jaques-Dalcroze's compositions include operas, chamber music, and songs.

Jarnach, Philipp (1892–1982) French-born composer with a Spanish father and German mother. In 1915 he met Busoni in Zürich: though never a pupil of Busoni, Jarnach was deeply influenced by his music and ideals. After Busoni's death, Jarnach completed his unfinished opera *Doktor Faust*. His own works include orchestral compositions, chamber music, and piano pieces.

Järnfelt, Armas (1869–1958) Finnish-born Swedish composer and conductor, a pupil of Busoni. Järnfelt's conducting career included positions as principal conductor of Finnish National Opera and the Helsinki Philharmonic Orchestra. His works, often nationalistic in inspiration, include two symphonies and other orchestral works (including *Praeludium*, 1909), chamber music, and songs.

Jarre, Maurice (1924–) French composer. After early works, such as *Passacaille* (1956), and *Mobiles* (1961), he turned to writing music for films, including *Dr Zhivago* (1966).

Jeanne d'Arc au bûcher see **Joan of Arc at the Stake.**

Jeans, Susi (S. Hock; 1911–) Austrian-born British organist, keyboard player, and musicologist. By means of performances and academic writing she has encouraged interest in baroque keyboard music and has been active as a restorer of old instruments. She was married to the scientist **Sir James Jeans** (1877–1946), author of *Science and Music* (1937).

Její Pastorkyna see **Jenufa.**

Jelinek, Hanns (1901–69) German composer, a pupil of Schoenberg. Jelinek adopted serial techniques of composition in the 1930s; later he combined serial writing with jazz styles. His works include six symphonies, two string quartets and other chamber works, and songs.

Jena Symphony Symphony by Friedrich Witt; the date of composition is unknown. So called because the manuscript score was discovered in Jena, Germany, in 1909, it was thought for many years that this was an early symphony by Beethoven, because of an inscription on the manuscript 'par Louis van Beethoven.' However, recent scholarship has demonstrated that the symphony was almost certainly the work of Witt, an Austrian composer and contemporary of Beethoven.

Jenkins, John (1592–1678) English composer. Little is known of his early life, but later he enjoyed patronage from several households, notably the Dereham and L'Estrange families in Norfolk. In 1634 he contributed to the court masque *The Triumph of Peace* and in 1660 was appointed as theorbo player in the King's Music. His best-known pupil was Roger North. Jenkins' consort music is of importance, showing the influence of Coperario and his contemporaries as well as anticipating the style of the Italian trio sonata. His music features virtuoso divisions.

Jensen, Adolf (1837–79) German composer and pianist. He worked as a kapellmeister in various German cities and in 1861 became second director of the Königsberg music academy. He had a flourishing career as a pianist and taught at Carl Tausig's piano school in Berlin (1866–68). Jensen composed an opera and choral and instrumental music but was more successful as a miniaturist: his songs and piano pieces are imaginative and romantic.

Jenufa Opera in three acts by Janácek with libretto by the composer based on a story by Preissová. It was originally entitled *Její Pastorkyna* (*Her Foster-Daughter*). First performance: Brno, 1904. Jenufa (soprano) is the mother of an illegitimate baby drowned by Jenufa's foster-mother, Kostelnicka (soprano), to avoid family shame, when Steva (tenor), Jenufa's lover, refuses to marry her. In the end Kostelnicka confesses to her crime and Jenufa marries Steva's stepbrother, Laca (tenor).

Jeptha 1. Oratorio for four solo voices, chorus, and string orchestra by Carissimi, to a text from the Bible. Composed: *c.*1650. The story of this Old Testament figure is related by the Historicus, or narrator, with the other voices representing different characters in the tale. Carissimi's *Jeptha* is one of the earliest oratorios. **2.** Oratorio by Handel to a text by Morell, arranged from the Bible. First performance: 1752. This is the last of Handel's oratorios.

Jeremiás, Jaroslav (1889–1919) Czech composer and pianist. He studied at the Prague conservatory and then with Novák. His compositional output includes operas, the oratorio *Mistr Jan Hus* (1914–15), and choral, vocal, and chamber works. His brother, the composer and conductor **Otakar Jeremiás** (1892–1962), also studied at Prague and succeeded their father, **Bohuslav Jeremiás** (1859–1918), as director of the music school at Budejovice in 1918. His works, chiefly vocal in the late romantic style, include the opera *The Brothers Karamazov* (1922–27), the song cycle *Láska* (1921), two symphonies, and other orchestral works.

Jesu, Joy of Man's Desiring The concluding chorale from the cantata *Herz und Mut und Tat und Leben* (BWV 147) by J. S. Bach. Composed: 1716. The chorale melody is presented against a running quaver accompaniment and an arrangement by the British pianist Dame Myra Hess has made the work extremely popular.

jeté see **ricochet.**

Jeux Ballet (described as a 'poème dansé') in one act with music by Debussy and choreography by Nijinsky. First performance: Théâtre des Champs-Elysées, Paris, 1913, by Diaghilev's Ballets Russes, conducted by Monteux (décor by Bakst). Three tennis players, two girls and a boy, meet in a garden: the game is flirtation rather than tennis.

Jeux d'enfants (*Children's Games*) Collection of 12 pieces for piano duet by Bizet. Composed: 1871. Several of the pieces were later orchestrated, including some by Bizet himself.

Jewels of the Madonna, The (Italian: *I Gioielli della Madonna*) Opera in three acts by Wolf-Ferrari with libretto by Golischiani and Zangarini. First performance: Berlin, 1911. It is a cloak-and-dagger tragedy set in Naples.

Jewess, The see **Juive, La.**

Jewish music The earliest reference to the music of the Jewish people in the Old Testament (which covers Jewish history from *c*.3000 BC to 200 BC) is to the legendary Jubal (Genesis 4: 21), 'the father of all who play the lyre and pipe.' In Exodus, when Moses is leading his people out of Egypt, the prophetess Miriam, beating her timbrel (a small frame drum), leads the dance and the singing; such song-dances are still enacted by Jewish women on the north African Isle of Djerba. From settlement in the Promised Land and the building of the First Temple by Solomon (*c*.970–933 BC), women were excluded from all ritual music. King David, Solomon's father, was reputed to have been a fine musician (composer, player, and inventor of instruments) and soothed Saul's troubled soul by playing his lyre (see **kinnor**). Within the Temple the central feature of worship was the singing of psalms; men of the tribe of Levi were appointed to supervise the music and the Levites gradually came to be regarded as a sacred caste of musicians, holding office between the ages of 30 and 50 after a 5-year apprenticeship. The instruments associated with psalm singing were the kinnor and the **nevel** (a ten-stringed harp), which defined the melody of the chant; pauses were marked by the clash of copper cymbals (**mziltaim**, later **zelzlim**). Paired trumpets (**hazozra**) and the ram's horn *shofar were used in ritual and sacrificial rites. Dancing also had a place in worship: in the second book of Samuel 'David danced before the Lord with all his might.'

In 587 BC Jerusalem fell to the Assyrian Nebuchadnezzar; the Temple was destroyed and the Jewish people scattered. When they returned in 538 BC, worship was on a modest scale until the consecration of the newly built Second Temple in 514 BC. Antiphonal chanting developed: the precentor or Levite intoned the first half-verse of the psalm and the congregation answered with the second. Records from the 1st century AD give a minimum of 12 instrumentalists (nine lyres, two harps, and a pair of cymbals) for Temple services; a pair of **halilim** (a type of double oboe) was added on festal days. In 70 AD the Romans, under the leadership of Titus, captured Jerusalem: they destroyed the Second Temple and the Jews were forced to flee east and west to escape Roman persecution. Synagogues became local centres of worship. The rabbis discouraged any contact with the degenerate Greek secular music of the period to the extent that all instruments except the ritual shofar were forbidden; instead vocal music developed, especially the solo *cantillation of readings and prayers.

Jewish music is essentially based on practice rather than on theory. The often complex scales or modes were built on a series of descending *tetrachords, while prayer chants were based on eight modes (**octoechos**), possibly relating to the calendar. Vocal extemporization (**hazanut**) became increasingly virtuosic in cantillation chanting. Domestic music was much influenced by Arabic and oriental sources and by the culture of wherever exile took the Jewish people.

They, in their turn, have immeasurably enriched the musical culture of their adopted countries.

Jew's harp A simple primitive instrument consisting of a tongue of springy metal or wood supported in a frame. The free end of this tongue is plucked with the finger and the instrument is held in the mouth. Changes of pitch are effected by altering the shape of the mouth cavity. The name may be a corruption of 'jaw's harp' and has no known connection with the Jews.

jig A popular 16th-century English dance in triple time, widely used in the theatre by comedians. Several settings in the form of variations occur in the *Fitzwilliam Virginal Book*, including 'Nobody's Gigge' by Richard Farnaby and 'Doctor Bull's my selfe.' In the 17th century the jig was introduced into Europe, where it evolved into the **gigue** (French), or **giga** (Italian). Of binary form, the second half often an inversion of the first, the gigue became the lively fourth movement of the classical *suite. In England the jig retained a place in keyboard suites. It is sometimes confused with the *country dance and *hornpipe.

jingling johnny (*or* **Chinese pavilion**) A percussion instrument consisting of a tree, pavilion roof, or Turkish crescent hung with bells. It was used in military bands in Britain and Germany in the 18th and 19th centuries.

Jinns, The see **Djinns, Les**.

Joachim, Joseph (1831–1907) Hungarian violinist, composer, and conductor. After studying at the Leipzig conservatory he became leading violinist at Weimar and later taught in Berlin, where he founded the Joachim Quartet (1869). As one of the leading violinists of his day, Joachim gave the first performance of Brahms' violin concerto and offered invaluable advice to Brahms on orchestration and matters of violin technique. Joachim's own compositions include three violin concertos and orchestral music.

Joan of Arc see **Giovanna d'Arco**.

Joan of Arc at the Stake (French: *Jeanne d'Arc au bûcher*) Music by Honegger to a play of the same title by Claudel, concerning the life of Joan of Arc. First performance: 1938. Some of the characters in the play are given speaking parts only, while others also sing. The work was conceived for stage performance, but this has not prevented successful operatic productions of the music.

Job 1. Oratorio by Parry with words from the Bible. First performance: Gloucester Festival, 1892. **2.** Masque for dancing in eight scenes with music by Vaughan Williams, libretto by Geoffrey Keynes, and choreography by Ninette de Valois. First performance: Cambridge Theatre, London, 1931. Based on Blake's illustrations to the Book of Job, it depicts Job's steadfastness in the face of all disasters.

3. Opera by Dallapiccola, based on the Bible. First performance: Rome, 1950.

Jocelyn Opera in four acts by Godard with libretto by Silvestre and Capone based on Lamartine's poem. First performance: Théâtre de la Monnaie, Brussels, 1888. Jocelyn is a monk tempted by sensual love; the famous 'Berceuse' (lullaby) comes from this opera.

Jochum, Eugen (1902–87) German conductor. After holding positions with the Berlin Radio (1932–34), the Hamburg State Opera (1934–45), and the Bavarian Radio Symphony Orchestra (from 1949), he became conductor of the Amsterdam Concertgebouw Orchestra (1961–64), with Haitink.

Jodel see yodel.

Johannes-Passion see St John Passion.

Johnny Strikes Up see Jonny spielt auf.

Johnson, John (?–c.1594) English composer and lutenist. He became a musician in the court of Queen Elizabeth I in 1579. His compositions are mainly for solo lute and he was responsible for the development of the lute duet. His son, **Robert Johnson** (c.1583–1633), was also a composer and lutenist. In 1596 he entered the service of Sir George Carey and from 1604 was lutenist to James I, a post he also held under Charles I. He wrote many theatre songs, the best known being 'Full fathom five' and 'Where the bee sucks' from *The Tempest* (1611). He also wrote for lute and theorbo.

Johnson, John (fl. 1740–62) British publisher and instrument maker. Active in London, Johnson published music by such composers as John Stanley, Thomas Arne, and Domenico Scarlatti from 1740 onwards.

Johnson, Robert (c.1500–c.1560) Scottish composer. He is said to have been a priest who fled to England in around 1535. His compositions are mainly sacred, notably the large-scale votive antiphon *Ave Dei patris* and an early attempt at setting English words in a chordal style, *O eternal God.*

Johnson, Robert Sherlaw (1932–) British composer and pianist, a pupil of Nadia Boulanger and Messiaen. Early pieces, such as the first piano sonata (1963), are serial; *Improvisation V* (1968) uses mobile elements, and the second piano sonata (1967) employs graphic notation. Johnson is particularly interested in new timbres and has made use of tape, as in *Praises of Heaven and Earth* (1969). Other works include *Green Whispers of Gold* (1971), *Jabberwocky* (1975), and an opera, *The Lambton Worm* (1978).

Johnston, Ben(jamin) (1926–) US composer, a pupil of Milhaud, Partch, and Cage. His early background was in jazz. Johnston has a particular interest in just intonation and the use of microtones, as seen in his second string quartet (1964). He has also written theatre pieces, such as *One Man* (1967), and an opera, *Carmilla* (1970).

Jolas, Betsy (1926–) French composer, a pupil of Messiaen and Milhaud. Jolas' style, though remaining faithful to neoclassical principles, is influenced by serial procedures. Her works include orchestral compositions, chamber music, songs, and choral pieces.

Jolie fille de Perth, La see **Fair Maid of Perth, The.**

Jolivet, André (1905–74) French composer, a pupil of Le Flem and Varèse. In 1936 he helped found the Jeune France movement to promote a French style in music. The oriental influence on his work is combined with his use of unusual sounds and serial procedures. His output includes the opera *Dolorès, ou le miracle de la femme laide* (1942); works for voice and orchestra, such as *Songe à nouveau rêve* (1970); three symphonies; concertos and choral works; and chamber music and piano pieces.

Jommelli, Niccolò (1714–74) Italian composer. He studied in Naples, becoming director of the Conservatorio degli Incurabili, Venice (1747), and holding an appointment at the papal chapel, Rome (1749). In 1753 he became court kapellmeister in Stuttgart, where he produced his best operas, including *Olimpiade* (1761). Jommelli's later works were sacred, including a *Miserere* (1774). In addition to his many operas, which developed recitative and orchestration, he also wrote symphonies.

Jones, Daniel (1912–) British composer. Jones studied composition at the Royal Academy of Music in London (1935–38). His music uses characteristically involved rhythmic patterns and a modal system suggested by that of Indian music within an expressive tonal context. It is for his nine symphonies that Jones is best known; his other works include operas, chamber music, and choral compositions.

Jones, Gwyneth (1937–) Welsh soprano. She studied with Ruth Packer in London and made her debut in Siena. After singing with Welsh National Opera (1963) and at Covent Garden (1963–64), she appeared at Vienna and Bayreuth in Wagner, singing Brunnhilde in the centenary production (1976). She was made a CBE in 1976.

Jones, Robert (?–c.1617) English composer. In 1597 he gained a B.Mus. degree at Oxford and his first book of lute songs was published in 1600. The following year he contributed a madrigal to *The Triumphs of Oriana*. He is remembered for his simple ayres.

Jones, (James) Sidney (1861–1946) British composer. He wrote many highly successful operettas, the best known of which is The **Geisha* (1896).

Jongen, Joseph (1873–1953) Belgian composer. Jongen was awarded the Belgian Prix de Rome in 1897, which enabled him to study in various European countries. He was director of the Brussels conservatory (1925–39). Initially influenced by French music of the late 19th century, Jongen's music later became more individual in style. He wrote orchestral compositions, including concertos for violin, cello, piano, and harp; chamber music; and songs. His brother **Léon Jongen** (1885–1969) was a composer and pianist and succeeded Joseph as director of the Brussels conservatory in 1939. He wrote operas, chamber music, piano works, and songs.

jongleur A medieval professional entertainer, actor, or musician. During the Middle Ages, there were three classes of itinerants who entertained in castle, court, and chamber throughout Europe – jongleurs, *minstrels, and *troubadours or *trouvères. From about 1100 to 1300, jongleurs (executants) were often attendant upon troubadours (creative artists) and were frequently called upon to perform, as accompanist and singer, the heroic chivalrous songs written by the troubadour. It was not unknown for the jongleur and troubadour to exchange roles. By the 14th century, when the troubadour class had almost ceased to exist, the jongleur had lost some dignity and status through the introduction of the minstrel, who was a professional musician.

Jonny spielt auf (*Johnny Strikes Up*) Opera in two parts (eleven scenes) with words and music by Krenek. First performance: Leipzig, 1927. Krenek's most successful work, it used all the technical devices of the modern stage, including wireless and a locomotive. Johnny is a Black jazz violinist whose tangles with White women are satirically observed.

Joseph 1. (full title: *Joseph and his Brethren*) Oratorio by Handel with libretto by James Miller. First performance: Covent Garden, London, 1748. **2.** Opera by Méhul with libretto by Duval. First performance: Opéra-Comique, Paris, 1807. It is based on the biblical story.

Josephs, Wilfred (1927–) British composer, best known for his television and film music. Mastery of many different styles and techniques is a feature of Josephs' works, which include eight symphonies, concertos, chamber music, and songs.

Josephslegende (*Legend of Joseph*) Ballet in one act with music by Richard Strauss, libretto by Kessler and Hofmannsthal, and choreography by Fokine. First performance: Opéra, Paris, 1914, conducted by the composer (costumes by Bakst). Commissioned by Diaghilev for the Ballets Russes, it tells the biblical story of Joseph's rejection of the wife of Potiphar in a 16th-century Venetian setting.

Joshua Oratorio for solo voices, choir, and orchestra by Handel, with a text by Morell based on the Bible. First

The figure (right) is thought to be Josquin des Prez

performance: 1748. It tells the story of Joshua, who led the Jews after the death of Moses and succeeded in destroying the walls of the city of Jericho by commanding his people to blow trumpets.

Josquin des Prez (*c*.1445–1521) French composer. He was a singer at the cathedral in Milan (1459–73), in the Sforza chapel in Milan (1473–79), in the papal chapel (1486–94), and in the employ of Hercules I at Ferrara (1503–04). From 1504 until his death, Josquin lived at Condé sur l'Escaut. Josquin's output comprises masses, including two based on *L'Homme armé*, and the *Missa Hercules Dux Ferrariae* (1487), based on a series of solmization syllables derived from its title, *re ut re ut re fa mi re*; motets, including *Illibata dei Virgo*, the text of which contains an acrostic on Josquin's name; and secular works in French and Italian.

Josten, Werner (1885–1963) German-born US composer. Josten's early works show a lyrical and romantic style, tendencies tempered in his later music by a classical approach to form. His works include a symphony in F (1936) and other orchestral compositions, chamber music, and choral works.

jota A fast Spanish dance from the Aragon region in free triple time, performed to the accompaniment of guitars, tambourines, and triangle. It originated in the 12th century.

Jota melodies are featured in Liszt's *Rhapsodie espagnole* No. 16 and in works by Albéniz, Falla, and Saint-Saëns.

Joubert, John (1927–) South African composer, a pupil of Howard Ferguson. He has written much sacred music, including the *Missa Beati Joannis* (1962), the *Pro Pace* motets (1960), and the cantata *The Raising of Lazarus* (1971). Other works include two symphonies, chamber music, and the operas *Silas Marner* (1961) and *Under Western Eyes* (1969).

Joyce, James (1882–1941) Irish writer whose works contain many musical references and allusions and are sometimes partly constructed analogously to musical compositions. His first book was entitled *Chamber Music* (1907), from which songs have been set by Moeran (1929), Berio (1936), and Barber (1953). 18 composers contributed to *The Joyce Book* (1933) with settings of his poetry.

Jubilate A canticle from the Anglican service of Matins sung as an alternative to the *Benedictus. It comprises the text of Psalm 100 ('O be joyful in the Lord'), plus a doxology, and first appeared in the revised *Book of Common Prayer* (1552). It is sung as a choral setting, with or without organ accompaniment or to *Anglican chant. Choral settings were rare during the 16th century but there are examples from the 17th century by Tomkins and Weelkes. Settings for soloists, chorus, and orchestra include Purcell's *Te Deum and Jubilate for St Cecilia's Day* (1694) and Handel's *Utrecht Te Deum and Jubilate* (1713). Since the 18th century the Jubilate has been widely set as an *anthem or canticle reflecting the stylistic trends of the period of composition.

Judas Maccabaeus Oratorio for solo voices, choir, and orchestra by Handel, with a text by Morell based on the Apocrypha. First performance: 1747. Judas Maccabaeus, who appears in the Book of Maccabees in the Apocrypha, was an Israelite warrior who won many victories over the Syrians.

Judith 1. Oratorio for solo voices, choir, and orchestra by Vivaldi, with a Latin text by Cassetti based on the Book of Judith in the Apocrypha. Composed: 1716. Judith, a young Jewish widow, succeeds in driving away the Assyrians who are threatening her town. This story has inspired several other compositions, including the following. **2.** Oratorio by Thomas Arne, with text by Isaac Bickerstaffe. First performance: London, 1761. **3.** Oratorio by Parry with text from the Bible. First performance: Birmingham, 1888. **4.** Opera by Honegger, with libretto by René Morax. First performance: Monte Carlo, 1926.

Juive, La (*The Jewess*) Opera in five acts by Halévy with libretto by Scribe. First performance: Opéra, Paris, 1835. The text (originally written for Rossini) relates the drama of Rachel (soprano), the 'Jewess,' who is put to death by the 15th-century Cardinal de Brogni (bass): he finds out too late that she was his daughter.

Julius Caesar (Italian: *Giulio Cesare*) **1.** Opera seria in three acts by Handel with libretto by Haym. First performance: Haymarket Theatre, London, 1724. The action takes place in Egypt. **2.** Opera by Malipiero with libretto, based on Shakespeare, by the composer. First performance: Genoa, 1936.

Junge Lord, Der (*The Young Lord*) Opera in two acts by Henze with libretto by Ingeborg Bachmann based on a fable by Hauff. First performance: Deutsche Oper, Berlin, 1965. The young English Lord Barrat (tenor) turns out to be a dressed-up ape.

Jungfernquartette see **Russian Quartets.**

Jupiter Symphony Symphony No. 41 in C major (K. 551) by Mozart. Composed: 1788. The name refers to the stately opening to the first movement, although it was never used by Mozart and was actually coined by the English impresario Salomon. This is the final work in a trilogy of symphonies that were all composed within the space of six weeks in the summer of 1788 and represent the pinnacle of Mozart's achievements in the symphonic field.

K

K 1. Abbreviation for Köchel. It is used as a prefix to indicate the number of a piece in Ludwig von Köchel's catalogue (1862) of Mozart's works. In German usage it may be abbreviated to **KV** (Köchel-Verzeichnis).
2. Abbreviation for Kirkpatrick. It is used as a prefix to indicate the number of a piece in Ralph Kirkpatrick's catalogue (1953) of Domenico Scarlatti's works. See also **L**.

Kabalevsky, Dmitri (1904–) Soviet composer. Kabalevsky studied at the Moscow conservatory, where he later taught composition. His music, written in accordance with the dictates of Soviet realism, is characterized by rich tonal harmony and a clear sense of melodic direction. His prolific output includes operas, four symphonies, three piano concertos and other orchestral works, chamber music, piano compositions, and vocal music.

Kabeláč, Miloslav (1908–79) Czech composer. Kabeláč both studied and taught at the Czech conservatory. His style draws on many influences, including eastern music, early Czech music, and serial procedures. His compositions include eight symphonies, chamber music, and choral works.

Kaddish Traditional Jewish prayer, used since the 13th century by mourners, with a text in Aramaic. These words have been employed by several composers with Jewish connections and sympathies, their most famous setting being in Leonard Bernstein's third symphony. [Hebrew, consecration]

Kagel, Mauricio (1932–) Argentinian composer, resident in West Germany since 1957. After early pieces in a strictly serial style, Kagel explored new sounds using unusual (often bizarre) instruments, electronic music, new notation, and indeterminacy. An increasingly visual element in his compositions has led to a series of theatre pieces and films. Central to Kagel's work has been a critical concern with the conventions of musical performance and the European musical tradition. His works include *Sur scène* (1960), *Heterophonie* (1961), *Tremens* (1965), *Der Schall* (1968) for five players with 54 instruments, *Ludwig Van* (1969), *Variations Without a Fugue on Brahms' Variations on a Theme of Handel* (1972), *Kantrimusik* (1975), *Mare Nostrum* (1975), and the 'opera' *Die Erschöpfung der Welt* (1980).

Kaiserquartett see **Emperor Quartet**.

Kajanus, Robert (1856–1933) Finnish conductor. He was an early champion of Sibelius and founded (1882) the Helsinki Orchestral Society, the first permanent orchestra in Finland.

Kalabis, Viktor (1923–) Czech composer. Kalabis' early works are romantic in character, their style deriving from the music of Brahms; in his later works he uses serial techniques. His compositions include three symphonies, concertos, chamber music, and piano works.

Kalevala A group of Finnish epic songs from the Kaleva region of Finland. For centuries they were transmitted orally but in the mid-19th century collections of them were published. Sibelius drew on them for several of his nationalist works, including *Kullervo*, **Pohjola's Daughter*, and *The* *Swan of Tuonela.

Kalinnikov, Vasily Sergeyevich (1866–1901) Russian composer and conductor. In 1893 he was appointed assistant conductor of the Italian Theatre, Moscow, but ill health forced him to retire and he spent the rest of his life in the Crimea. Kalinnikov wrote dramatic, vocal, and piano music, but it is with his two colourful symphonies that he made his reputation.

Kalkbrenner, Frédéric (Friedrich Wilhelm Michael K.; 1785–1849) German-born French pianist, teacher, and composer. He studied with Nicodami, Adam, and Catel at the Paris Conservatoire (1799–1801). In 1814 he settled in England, quickly winning a reputation as a leading pianist. He toured Europe and in 1824 went to live in Paris, joining the piano manufacturing firm of Pleyel. Kalkbrenner published his piano method in 1831 and soon became an influential teacher. His compositions are mainly virtuoso piano works (4 concertos, other pieces with orchestra, 13 sonatas, studies, etc.), but he also wrote chamber music.

Kalliwoda, Johann Wenzel (Jan Krtitel Václav Kalivoda; 1801–66) Bohemian composer and violinist. He studied at the Prague conservatory and in 1822 moved to Donaueschingen, where for nearly 40 years he conducted the court orchestra. His large compositional output includes operas, seven symphonies, 18 overtures, and other orchestral works, and chamber, piano, and vocal music. Kalliwoda's works were frequently performed in his own day but his music has not survived in the repertory.

Kálmán, Emmerich (1882–1953) Hungarian composer, best known for his operettas. His first operetta, *Tatárjáras* (*The Gay Hussars*, 1908) became exceptionally popular in Europe and the USA. His output also includes orchestral works and songs.

Kammer Chamber. Hence **Kammermusik**, chamber music. [German]

Kapelle A chapel. Like the Italian *cappella, Kapelle came to mean the musical staff of a chapel and finally any orchestra or other musical body. See also **kapellmeister**. [German]

kapellmeister Originally, the musician in charge of a German court chapel (see **Kapelle**). Later the kapellmeister was in charge of all the musicians of the court, including those involved with orchestral concerts and opera, and by the 19th century a kapellmeister was the musical director of any instrumental ensemble. **Kapellmeistermusik** became a derogatory term for well-wrought but unimaginative music. [German, chapel master]

Karajan, Herbert von (1908–89) Austrian conductor. He began his career conducting the Berlin Opera (1938–45) and in 1954 succeeded Wilhelm Furtwängler as conductor of the Berlin Philharmonic Orchestra, a post he held until 1989. He also conducted the Vienna State Opera (1957–64) and founded the Salzburg Easter Festival (1967). Karajan's many recordings include almost the entire major symphonic and orchestral repertoire, as well as operas by Mozart, Wagner, Verdi, Puccini, Richard Strauss, and others.

Karelia Overture (Op. 10) and orchestral suite (Op. 11) by Sibelius. Composed: 1893. At the time of their composition Sibelius was residing in Karelia, a province of Finland in the south of the country, and these two works are intended to describe the atmosphere of the region.

Karg-Elert, Sigfrid (1877–1933) German composer and organist, a pupil of Reinecke. Karg-Elert taught theory and composition at the Leipzig conservatory from 1919. Of his prolific output, his compositions for organ and harmonium are most familiar today: in them, strong baroque influences are combined with impressionist and sometimes atonal techniques. His compositions also include piano works, chamber music, and songs.

Katerina Ismailova Opera in four acts by Shostakovich with libretto by the composer and Preis, based on a story by Leskov. First performance: Leningrad, 1934. Katerina (soprano), though sympathetically portrayed, is driven to murdering both her husband (tenor) and father-in-law (high bass); the opera is also known as *Lady Macbeth of the Mtsensk District*. It was banned by Stalin and revised for the Moscow production of 1963.

Katin, Peter (1930–) British pianist. A pupil of Harold Craxton, Katin appears most frequently as a performer of romantic and impressionist music and is particularly admired for his interpretation of Chopin.

Katya Kabanová (Czech: *Kát'a Kabanová*) Opera in three acts by Janáček with text by Cervinka based on Ostrovaky's *The Storm*. First performance: Brno, 1921. Katya (soprano) lives an insufferable life with her weakling husband, Tikhon (tenor), and overbearing mother-in-law, Kabanicha (contralto). Boris (tenor) becomes her lover and finally, unable to bear the shame and contempt, Katya drowns herself.

kazoo see **mirliton**.

Kb. see **Kontrabass**.

keen An Irish funeral song of folk-song origins, accompanied by weeping and wailing. See **lament**. [from Irish Gaelic *Caoine*]

Keiser, Reinhardt (1674–1739) German composer. He succeeded Kusser in Brunswick (*c*.1694) and soon after moved to Hamburg, where he directed the opera (1703); he was made cantor of Hamburg Cathedral in 1728. In Hamburg Keiser wrote about 116 operas, which influenced Handel (who played in his productions) and raised the standard of German opera. He also wrote sacred and chamber works.

Herbert von Karajan

The English National Opera's Katya Kabanová *(1985)*

Kéler Béla (Adalbert von Kéler; 1820–82) Hungarian conductor, bandmaster, and composer. After a period as an orchestral violinist he took his first conducting post in Berlin in 1854. From 1863 to 1870 Kéler Béla worked at Wiesbaden and then made extensive tours of Europe, travelling to England in 1874. As a composer he produced many waltzes and marches.

Kell, Reginald (1906–81) British clarinetist. He started his career as an orchestral player, combining posts in leading orchestras with a teaching appointment at the Royal Academy of Music. From 1948 to 1971 Kell lived in the USA, where he appeared as a soloist and founded his own wind ensemble.

Kelley, Edgar Stillman (1857–1944) US composer. After studying in Europe Kelly returned to the USA, where he worked as a music critic. He later established himself as a teacher. His works, written in a characteristic vein of late romantic American lyricism, include two symphonies and other orchestral compositions, vocal music, and piano pieces.

Kelly, Michael (1762–1826) Irish composer, singer, and actor, a pupil of Michael Arne and Fenaroli. He knew Mozart in Vienna (1784–87), where he sang Count Basilio and Curzio in *The Marriage of Figaro* (1786). From 1787 he sang in London and composed ballets, songs, and theatre music; his *Reminiscences* (1826) are valuable historical documents.

Kempe, Rudolf (1920–76) German conductor. Initially an oboist, Kempe began to conduct in 1936. He was musical director of the Dresden State Orchestra (1949–52) and the Munich State Opera (1952–54). He subsequently conducted the Royal Philharmonic Orchestra (1961–63; 1964–76). He excelled in Wagner and Richard Strauss.

Kempff, Wilhelm (1895–   ) German pianist. A pupil of Kahn and Barth, he began his career in 1916 and has toured extensively. Kempff has had an important influence as a teacher and from 1924 to 1929 was director of the Stuttgart Musikhochschule. He has also composed orchestral and chamber music.

Kennan, Kent (1913–   ) US composer. In 1936 Kennan was awarded the American Prix de Rome, which enabled him to study in Europe. His early works display impressionist and jazz influences; later compositions are marked by neoclassical features. Kennan's output includes orchestral works and chamber music.

Kent bugle see bugle.

Kentner, Louis (1905–   ) Hungarian-born British pianist. Brother-in-law of the violinist Yehudi *Menuhin, with whom he frequently appears, Kentner is particularly admired for his performances of Liszt and Mozart. He gave the first performance of Bartók's second piano concerto and has championed the music of contemporary British composers.

Kerle, Jacobus de (*c.*1531–91) Flemish composer and organist. He became organist at Orvieto soon after 1555. After taking holy orders he returned to his home town of Ypres as director of music at the cathedral, but was excommunicated after a dispute with the chapter and went to Rome to seek pardon. He held posts as organist in a large number of European cities and died in Prague. Kerle's music is in the Franco-Flemish polyphonic style; his *Preces speciales* (1562) were well received by the Council of Trent, by whom they were commissioned.

Kerll, Johann Kaspar (1627–93) German composer and organist. Active as court organist in Vienna from an early age, he studied under Giovanni Valentini and then in Rome under Giacomo Carissimi. By 1650 he was at the court of Archduke Leopold Wilhelm in Brussels and in 1656 became kapellmeister to the Bavarian Elector in Munich. Here he composed 11 operas (none of which survives), but after his appointment as organist at St Stephen's Cathedral, Vienna (1674), he wrote mainly sacred music. In 1677 he became organist at the Imperial court. Kerll's *Modulatio organica* (1686) for keyboard is notable for its imaginative writing and his two most important sacred works are the *Missa pro defunctis* (1669), reminiscent of Palestrina, and the collection *Delectus sacrarum cantionum* (1669).

Kertesz, István (1929–73) Hungarian-born conductor who settled in Germany. He was musical director of the Cologne Opera (1964–73) and principal conductor of the London Symphony Orchestra (1965–68).

Ketèlby, Albert William (1875–1959) British composer. Ketèlby's descriptive works for orchestra, such as *In a Monastery Garden* (1915) and *In a Persian Market* (1920), achieved great popularity: they are marked by lyrical melodiousness and romantic orchestration. His other works include songs, chamber music, and piano pieces.

kettledrums Drums in which a single membrane is stretched across the top of a deep rounded vessel. Of ancient Egyptian origin, they are still used among primitive people in Africa and Asia. The Arabic naqara (see **nakers**), pairs of small kettledrums with bodies of wood or clay, are the predecessors of the modern orchestral **timpani**. These consist of two or three kettledrums that can be tuned to a definite pitch by means of handles around the rim. The type of drumstick used and the place in which the membrane is struck alter the tone of the sound. In some modern orchestral kettledrums the pitch is altered by a pedal-operated tensioning mechanism, with a gauge to indicate the pitch. Such timpani are called **pedal drums**. Kettledrums are also used in military bands, one slung on each side of a horse.

key 1. The *scale that predominates in a piece of music. For example, if a composition begins and ends with notes closely associated with the scale of E♭ major, it will have this *key signature and may have the name of this key in its title (a symphony in E♭ only implies that its first, and possibly its last, movements are in E♭). A composition in a particular key can move to another key during its course by *modulation and some music is not written in keys at all (see **atonality; polytonality**).

In equal *temperament the difference between the keys is only one of pitch. However in the *modes, which led to the *major and *minor scales on which the key system is based, this was not the case and each mode had a different character. See also **transposition**.

2. A lever on a musical instrument that is depressed to produce a note (for example, on a piano).

keyboard An arrangement of levers enabling a player to control the flow of air into *organ pipes or the striking or plucking of strings in a *clavichord, *harpsichord, or *piano. The earliest keyboards were those made for organs; they consisted of broad keys that were struck with the fist. These keyboards were introduced in the 11th century to replace the hand-operated sliders that formerly had to be manipulated to admit air to the pipes. By the 14th century these broad keys were being replaced by narrow ones adapted to finger pressure – a development that coincided with the evolution of the clavichord, which also made use of an organ-type keyboard. The arrangement of the keys themselves was originally diatonic as the music was at that time still modal (see **modes**). But gradually the need for the five semitones became apparent and these were added as the short black keys that are now a familiar feature of the piano keyboard (see also **scales; temperament**). They were not, however, all added at once; in fact some early organ keyboards still exist with B♭ as the only raised key and some have only three raised keys. However, the present layout was well established by the 15th century, although the use of white for naturals and black for sharps was not standard until the end of the 18th century. In England, for example, ebony naturals and ivory sharps were the usual arrangement on stringed keyboard instruments until about the middle of the 18th century, although some Flemish instrument makers were using bone naturals and ebony sharps by the end of the 16th century.

The present keyboard layout is not, of course, either the only one possible or necessarily the best. It has, however, lasted a long time and survived against many competitors. One interesting special arrangement was the **short octave**, in which the lowest octave of the keyboard started on E (tuned to C below it) with F♯ tuned to D and G♯ tuned to E. When, in later music, the bass F♯ and G♯ were required the short octave keyboard was adapted by making these keys in two parts, the front playing D and E and the back part F♯ and G♯.

keyboard instruments Musical *instruments in which the player selects individual notes or combinations of notes by pressing one or more of a series of levers with his fingers or feet. The first manual keyboards were used on organs and consisted only of what are now called the white notes of the piano keyboard; at that time modal music then current did not require the semitone intervals represented by the black notes. However, the introduction of *musica ficta necessitated the addition of a B♭, which was arranged on the keyboard as a shorter key between B and A. Other semitones became necessary as the old modal system evolved into the modern key system; by the middle of the 15th century the modern shape of the keyboard was fixed (see also **keyboard**).

The modern keyboard is used on the *organ, *piano, *harpsichord, and piano *accordion as well as on a number of instruments derived from these. The modern organ may have more than one manual and usually has, in addition, a pedalboard.

The problem of introducing enharmonic notes into the keyboard has been attempted from time to time. For example, some keyboards were made in which the front half of a black note played a different note to the back half. This kind of compromise solution had to be imposed because the distance apart of the notes of an octave is limited by the span of the human hand. However, the whole problem of enharmonic notes, which so taxed 17th-century ingenuity, was solved by the introduction of equal *temperament. 20th-century ingenuity is being similarly taxed by the design of a quarter-tone keyboard or a keyboard that is capable of playing other microtones.

keyed bugle see **bugle**.

keynote see **tonic**.

key signature An indication given at the start of each line in a piece of music of the prevailing key. It is denoted by one or more sharps or flats. If there are no sharps or flats given the key is taken to be C major or A minor. A major key and its relative minor key have the same key signature. See **flat keys**; **sharp keys**. See also **Appendix, Table 3**.

Khachaturian, Aram (Ilich) (1903–78) Soviet composer, a pupil of Miaskovsky at the Moscow conservatory (1929–34). Khachaturian's music is in the tradition of Glinka, Borodin, and Rimsky-Korsakov in its oriental inspirations: although he was one of the composers officially criticized in 1948 for modernistic tendencies, his music was always rooted in the folk styles of the Russian East. His works include the ballets *Gayaneh (1942: this contains the well-known *Sabre Dance*) and *Spartacus* (1953), three symphonies and other orchestral works, concertos, choral works, and chamber music.

Khan, Imrat (1935–) Indian sitar player. Taught by his brother **Vilayat Khan** (1924–), he has established an international reputation.

khorovod An ancient Russian or Slavic round dance performed by a large group of people with dramatic action and song. The French *branle and *farandole and the English round are all later forms of the khorovod. The dance may be fast or slow with a pattern that expresses a particular activity. Stravinsky used the name as the title of a section

The Soviet Armenian composer, Aram Khachaturian

of *The Firebird* (1910) that is based on a Russian folk melody. [from Russian, to lead the choir]

Khovanshchina (*The Khovansky Rising*) Opera in five acts by Mussorgsky with libretto by the composer and Stassov. First performance: St Petersburg, 1886. Set during Peter the Great's rise to power (1682–89), it depicts the struggle between the reactionary nobles and their supporters, including Prince Ivan Khovansky (bass) and his son Andrew (tenor), and the progressive supporters of the new tsar. Incomplete at the time of Mussorgsky's death, it was completed by Rimsky-Korsakov; a version of this opera written by Shostakovitch in the early 1960s is more faithful to the composer's harmonic idiom.

Khrennikov, Tikhon (1913–) Soviet composer. After a successful early career, in which he pursued in his music the aims of Soviet realism, Khrennikov was elected secretary of the Union of Soviet Composers (1948). Other public honours followed. His position as public spokesman for Soviet music has restricted his output, which includes operas, two symphonies, concertos, songs, and piano pieces.

Kikimora Tone poem by Lyadov. Composed: 1909. Described by the composer as a 'legend for orchestra,' this work depicts the fairy-tale goblin Kikimora and his evil character.

Kinderszenen see Scenes from Childhood.

Kindertotenlieder (*Songs on the Death of Children*) Song cycle for voice and orchestra by Mahler to five poems by Rückert. Composed: 1901–04. Rückert wrote these poems after the death of his child and Mahler produced two alternative versions, one for voice and piano and the other for voice and orchestra (the arrangement normally used today).

King, Charles (1687–1748) English singer, organist, and composer. He trained as a chorister at St Paul's Cathedral under Blow and Jeremiah Clarke, becoming, in 1708, almoner and master of the children there and organist at St Benet Finck. He was made vicar-choral of St Paul's in 1730. King's music includes a large number of anthems and services.

King, James (1925–) US tenor. A pupil of Martial Singher and Max Lorenz, he made his debut in Florence (1961). He sang at Berlin and Salzburg (1962), Vienna (1963), Bayreuth (1965), New York (1966), Milan (1968), and Covent Garden (1974). A light clear voice makes him ideal for lyrical Wagnerian roles, e.g. Parsifal.

King, Robert (late 16th–early 17th century) English composer and violinist. His music was first published in 1676. In 1680 he was appointed musician to the king, a position he retained until his death. Robert King was an important concert promoter but his compositions, mainly secular vocal music, are of little value.

King, William (1624–80) English composer and organist. After graduating from Magdalen College, Oxford, in 1649, he became chaplain there and in 1664 was appointed organist of New College. His anthem *The Lord is King* is still performed.

King Arthur Incidental music by Purcell to a spectacular play by Dryden. First performance: 1691. Subtitled *The British Worthy*, this set of music is often erroneously referred to as an opera because of the important part that music plays throughout, despite the fact that many of the leading characters do not sing.

King Christian II Incidental music (Op. 27) by Sibelius to a play by Adolf Paul. Composed: 1898. King Christian II was the ruler of Denmark during part of the 16th century. Sibelius arranged an orchestral suite from the incidental music in 1898.

King David (French: *Le Roi David*) Oratorio for speaker, choir, and orchestra by Honegger to a text by Morax based on the Old Testament of the Bible. First performance: 1921. Described by the composer as a 'dramatic psalm,' this work depicts the life and death of King David. Conventional recitative is replaced by spoken narration and the work was

originally performed in a stage production, although it is usually heard today in a concert version.

Kingdom, The Oratorio for solo voices, choir, and orchestra (Op. 51) by Elgar to a text arranged by the composer from the Bible. First performance: 1906. *The Kingdom* was the second part of a projected trilogy of oratorios, of which *The Apostles* comprises the first part. The third work was never written.

King Lear 1. Overture (Op. 4) by Berlioz, inspired by Shakespeare's play *King Lear*. Composed: 1831. 2. Overture and incidental music by Balakirev to Shakespeare's play. Composed: 1861. 3. Incidental music by Debussy. Composed: 1904. Much of the score is now lost.

King Priam Opera in three acts by Tippett, who also wrote the libretto. First performance: Coventry, 1962. The work is concerned with the problem of choice confronted by characters involved in events of the Trojan War.

King Roger (Polish: *Król Roger*) Opera in three acts by Szymanowski with libretto by Iwaszkiewicz. First performance: Warsaw, 1926. It concerns King Roger II of Sicily (baritone) during the religious upheavals of the 12th century.

King's Singers A British vocal ensemble founded in 1968. It is so called because five of its original members met at King's College, Cambridge. The ensemble consists of two countertenors, tenor, two baritones, and bass. It originally specialized in Renaissance consort music and other part songs but its repertory has expanded to include humorous songs performed in a style derived from the American barber-shop tradition. Its distinctive sound and entertaining manner quickly brought it international fame. Many works have been specially composed for the ensemble.

King Stephen Incidental music by Beethoven for a play by Kotzebue. Composed: 1811. The score consists of an overture and eight numbers, including six choruses. King Stephen was an 11th-century Hungarian ruler who was canonized for his good works towards the poor.

King Thamos Incidental music by Mozart for a play by Baron von Gebler. Composed: 1773. Little is known of the precise circumstances surrounding the production of this play, which tells of Thamos, King of Egypt.

kinnor A form of lyre mentioned in the Bible. It was the instrument played by King David and seems to have been similar to the Greek *kithara, although the detail offered by the biblical chroniclers is sparse. When David played his kinnor to Saul he 'played with his hand,' which may or may not be a comment on the absence of a plectrum. Moreover the instrument seems to have been one on which joyful rather than sad music was played, for the Jews 'suspended their kinnorim on the willows' during the Babylonian exile, being unwilling 'to sing the Lord's song in a strange land.' see also **Jewish music.**

Kinsky, Georg (1882–1951) German musicologist and pioneer of musical iconography. He was author of *A History of Music in Pictures* (1929) and a thematic catalogue of Beethoven's works, which was published posthumously (1955).

Kipnis, Alexander (1891–1978) Ukrainian-born US bass singer. After studying at Warsaw and at Berlin with Ernst Grenzebach he sang Wagner at Bayreuth and Mozart at Salzburg. He joined the Chicago Opera (1923–32) and the Metropolitan Opera (1940–46), becoming a US citizen in 1934; he retired in 1946.

Kirbye, George (?–1634) English composer. He was employed as a musician at Rushbrooke Hall, near Bury St Edmunds. He contributed a madrigal to *The Triumphs of Oriana* and must have known John Wilbye, who worked nearby at Hengrave Hall. Kirbye composed sacred music, but his madrigals display his most inventive writing.

Kirchner, Leon (1919–) US composer, a pupil of Sessions. Kirchner received a Guggenheim fellowship in 1948; a successful teaching career included an appointment as professor of music at Harvard University. His compositions, which show tendencies toward classical formal principles, include the opera *Lily* (1977), orchestral works, and three string quartets and other chamber compositions.

Kirkpatrick, Ralph (1911–84) US harpsichordist and pianist. He toured extensively and had a wide repertoire ranging from Bach and Scarlatti to Mozart, which he played on authentic instruments. In addition to performing he undertook extensive musicological research and produced a catalogue of Domenico Scarlatti's keyboard works that has become universally recognized (see **K.**).

Kirnberger, Johann Philipp (1721–83) German violinist, theorist, and composer, a pupil of J. P. Kellner and possibly of J. S. Bach. He worked in Poland until 1751 and became kapellmeister to Princess Amalia of Prussia in 1758. He wrote many treatises, his most famous being *Die Kunst des reines Satzes* (1771–79). In addition to his distinctive fugues, he also wrote motets and other keyboard and sacred music.

Kiss, The (Czech: *Hubicka*) Opera in two acts by Smetana with libretto by Krasnohorská. First performance: Prague, 1876. Complications follow a bride-to-be's reluctance to let her betrothed kiss her before their marriage.

kit A small violin-type of instrument that was developed from the *rebec in the 16th century and remained in use until the 18th century. It was small enough to be kept in a pocket and was used by dancing masters to provide music for their pupils. It had a long fingerboard attached to a very small body. French: **pochette**, Italian: **sordine.**

Kitezh see **Legend of the Invisible City of Kitezh, The.**

kithara A type of ancient Greek *lyre having 3–12 equal-length strings strung vertically between a large square wooden soundbox and an upper crossbar. It was later used by the Romans. See also **Greek music.**

Kjerulf, Halfdan (1815–68) Norwegian composer and teacher. Initially a journalist with training in law, in 1849 he went to Copenhagen to study with Gade and in 1850 to the Leipzig conservatory, where he was taught by Richter among others. Returning to his native Christiania, he became a respected piano teacher. Kjerulf's compositions were strongly influenced by Norwegian folk music and he is an important figure in the history of music in Norway. He composed in small forms, writing about 130 songs (many to texts by the Norwegian poet Bjørnsterne Bjørnson), short romantic piano pieces, and choruses.

Klavier (*or* **Clavier**) Keyboard or keyboard instrument. Generally the word is applied to any keyboard instrument but in modern times it most often refers to the piano. [German, from French *clavier*]

Klavierauszug The score of a work arranged for piano. [German, piano reduction]

Klavierübung see **Clavierübung.**

Klebe, Giselher (1925–) German composer, a pupil of Rufer and Blacher. His style is basically serial, but Klebe has a particular interest in instrumental colour and has used electronic music. His works include the operas *Alkmene* (1961), *Ein wahrer Held* (1973), and *Das Rendezvous* (1977); *Die Zwittschermaschine* (1950); *Herzschlage* (1969); *Orpheus* (1976); symphonies and concertos; and vocal works, chamber music, and piano pieces.

Klecki, Paul (1900–73) Polish conductor and composer. He conducted the Royal Liverpool Philharmonic Orchestra (1954–55), the Dallas Symphony Orchestra (1960–63), the Berne Symphony Orchestra (1964–66), and the Suisse Romande Orchestra (1967–69).

Kleiber, Erich (1890–1956) Austrian conductor. Kleiber studied in Prague and later conducted in Darmstadt, Düsseldorf, and Mannheim. He was director of the Berlin State Opera (1923–35) and emigrated to South America in 1935. He held a number of positions in Cuba and the USA, returning to the Berlin Opera shortly before his death. His son **Carlos Kleiber** (1930–) is also a well-known conductor.

klein (*or fem.* **kleine**) Small; little. Thus **kleine Flöte**, little flute, i.e. piccolo. [German]

Otto Klemperer

Klemperer, Otto (1885–1973) German-born conductor and composer. His first appointment was at the German National Theatre in Prague (1907). After conducting at the opera houses in Hamburg, Barmen, Strasbourg, and Cologne, in 1927 he became conductor of the State Opera. Expelled from Germany by the Nazis, as a Jew, Klemperer emigrated to the USA in 1933 and took US citizenship. After various appointments there he returned to Europe to conduct the Budapest Opera (1947–50). From 1959 until his death he was the principal conductor of the Philharmonia Orchestra. In 1970 he took Israeli citizenship. Klemperer is remembered especially as a conductor of Beethoven; he was a close friend and distinguished interpreter of Mahler.

Klenovsky, Paul Pseudonym used by Henry *Wood as arranger of his orchestrated version of the toccata and fugue in D minor by Bach.

Klien, Walter (1928–) Austrian pianist. Klien is an eminent exponent of Mozart (all of whose piano sonatas he has recorded) and Schubert.

Kluge, Die (*The Clever Girl*) Opera by Orff with libretto by the composer based on Grimm's fairy tale *Die kluge Bauerntochter* (*The Clever Farmer's Daughter*). First performance: Frankfurt-am-Main, 1943.

Knaben Wunderhorn, Des (*Youth's Magic Horn*) An anthology of German folk poetry edited by Achim von Arnau and Clemens Brentano and published 1805–08.

Poems from it have frequently set to music, by Schubert, Schumann, Wolf, Mahler, and Strauss, among others.

Knot Garden, The Opera in three acts with words and music by Tippett. First performance: Covent Garden, London, 1970. Seven characters in contemporary England come to a deeper knowledge of themselves and their relationships with others in the shifting maze of Tippett's knot garden.

Koanga Opera by Delius with libretto by Keary based on Cable's novel *The Grandissimes*. First performance (in German): Elberfeld, 1904. Koanga is an African chief in slavery in America. The slave dance, *La Calinda*, is frequently played out of context of the opera.

Kochanski, Pawel (1887–1934) Polish violinist. As well as touring Europe and the USA as a soloist, he held teaching appointments at the Warsaw and St Petersburg conservatories and the Juilliard School, New York. Kochanski made many transcriptions for violin and piano, particularly of Szymanowski's music.

Köchel, Ludwig von (1800–77) Austrian naturalist and musical biographer. He published the first classification of the works of Mozart (1862), using the Köchel numbering system that is still in present-day use (see **K.**).

Koczwara, Franz see **Kotzwara, Franz.**

Kodály, Zoltán (1882 1967) Hungarian composer. Kodály was educated in Budapest at the university and the music academy. His interest in folk song led to a close friendship with Bartók: together they collected many melodies in the years before World War I. From 1907 Kodály taught at the Budapest Academy, also working as a music critic. In 1923 he composed *Psalmus Hungaricus* for the half-century celebrations of the union of the towns Buda and Pest: the success of this and subsequent works established Kodály's national and international reputation as a composer. Kodály's music is strongly rooted in Hungarian folk tradition. His idiom remains tonal, his rhythmic experiments never reaching the extremes of Bartók's. Kodály's output includes the opera *Háry János* (1926); orchestral music, including *Dances of Galánta* (1934) and a late symphony in C (1961); choral music; piano works; and much educational music.

Koechlin, Charles (1867–1950) French composer, a pupil of Massenet and Fauré. Koechlin's works demonstrate his mastery of counterpoint and skilful use of instrumental colour. Koechlin was also active as a writer on music and as a teacher. His large output includes orchestral music, three string quartets and other chamber works, choral music, and songs.

Kogan, Leonid (1924–82) Soviet violinist. One of the foremost Soviet musicians of his day, Kogan appeared as a

Zoltán Kodály

soloist throughout the world and taught at the Moscow conservatory. He was married to violinist Elizaveta Gilels and performed in piano trios with Emil *Gilels and Rostropovich. Khachaturian, Karayev, and Bunin wrote works for him.

Köhler, (Christian) Louis (Heinrich) (1820–86) German composer, pianist, and conductor. He composed in various genres but is now best remembered for his educational piano music.

Kokkonen, Joonas (1921–) Finnish composer and pianist, a pupil of Palmgren. His style is chromatically contrapuntal; he experimented with but rejected serial techniques. Kokkonen's works include two string quartets (1959 and 1966), four symphonies, a cello concerto (1969), and the opera *Last Temptations* (1975).

Kolisch, Rudolf (1896–1978) Austrian-born US violinist. He studied in Vienna and in 1922 founded the famous Kolisch Quartet, which was noted for its promotion of contemporary music. A childhood injury caused Kolisch to hold the violin with his right hand.

Kol Nidrei Work for cello and orchestra by Bruch. Composed: 1881. This work is based upon Jewish music and the score includes the designation 'after Hebrew melodies.' *Kol Nidrei* (Aramaic, all vows) is a Jewish prayer, recited on the eve of the Day of Atonement, in which the worshipper abrogates all the personal vows he has made in the previous year.

Kontarsky, Aloys (1931–) German pianist. With his brother **Alfons Kontarsky** (1932–) he formed a piano duo of international reputation. Kontarsky is known as a promoter of contemporary music and has premiered works by Stockhausen and Berio. He also plays with the cellist Siegfried Palm.

Kontrabass Double bass. Abbreviation: **Kb.** [German]

Kontrafagott Double bassoon. [German]

Konzertmeister see **leader.**

Korbay, Francis Alexander (1846–1913) Hungarian tenor and pianist. After singing with the National Theatre in Budapest he concentrated on the piano, touring Europe and America as a pianist. Korbay then settled in London, where he sang and taught singing and also arranged Hungarian songs with English words.

Korean temple block see **Chinese wood block.**

Kornett 1. Cornet. **2.** (*or* **Zink**) Cornett. [German]

Korngold, Eric Wolfgang (1897–1957) Austrian composer. As result of the astonishing success of his earliest works, Korngold became well known as a prodigy. After a successful career in Europe as an opera composer, he emigrated in 1935 to the USA, where he became a leading composer of film music. Korngold's early works are remarkable for their assimilation of the postromantic style of Strauss and Mahler; this idiom remained consistent throughout his life, not responding to further musical developments. His works include the opera *Die Tote Stadt* (*The Dead City*, 1920), orchestral music, and chamber compositions.

Kostelanetz, André (1903–80) Russian-born conductor. In 1922 he emigrated to the USA and made his reputation as a conductor and arranger of light music.

koto A Japanese long *zither with 13 waxed silk strings and movable bridges. About 1.8 m (6 ft) long and 25 cm (9 in) across, it was formerly the national instrument of Japan. It is played on the floor with three plectra worn on the thumb and two fingers of the right hand while the left hand adjusts the position of the bridges to tune the strings to a pentatonic scale or stops the strings to obtain intermediate notes. The instrument is called **kum** in Korean. The Chinese long zither is the *qin.

Kotzwara (*or* **Koczwara**), **Franz** (*c*.1750–91) Czech composer and player of many woodwind and stringed instruments. Known to have been in London and Dublin at the end of the 18th century, he is famous primarily for his piano trio, *The Battle of Prague* (*c*.1788). He also wrote a collection of sonatas (*The Agreeable Surprize*) as well as other keyboard and chamber works.

Koussevitzky, Serge (1876–1951) Russian-born conductor. Initially a virtuoso of the double bass (for which he composed a concerto in 1905) he subsequently took up music publishing in Berlin, commissioning works by Scriabin, Stravinsky, and Prokofiev. He established his own orchestra (1909) in Moscow but in 1920 he left the USSR. In 1924 he became conductor of the Boston Symphony Orchestra. Koussevitzky was one of the leading champions of contemporary music, commissioning and performing works by Copland, Piston, Barber, Hindemith, Honegger, Roussel, Ravel, Gershwin, many others. This work was continued after his death by the Koussevitzky Foundation, which he established in 1943.

Kovacevich, Stephen see **Bishop-Kovacevich, Stephen.**

Koven, Reginald de see **De Koven, Reginald.**

Kozeluch, Leopold Anton (1752–1818) Czech composer. He studied with Duschek in Prague, where he composed ballets for the National Theatre (from 1771). From 1778 he worked in Vienna, refusing to succeed Mozart as court organist in Salzburg (1781). In addition to ballets and operas, he wrote many symphonies, concertos, chamber and keyboard works, and arrangements of Scottish songs.

Kraft, Anton (1749–1820) Czech cellist and composer. He studied under Haydn in Vienna and both Haydn and Beethoven wrote works for him. In 1796 he joined Prince Joseph Lobkowitz's orchestra in Vienna. His son **Nikolaus Kraft** (1778–1853), also a cellist, toured Vienna, Bratislava, Berlin, and Dresden with his father in 1789, aged 10, and performed with Mozart.

Kraft, William (1922–) US composer, a pupil of Cowell. Kraft is eclectic in his works, exploring many different styles and influences. His compositions include orchestral and chamber works, many featuring important percussion parts.

krakowiak A Polish dance of the early 19th century from the district of Krakow. It is in 2/4 time with syncopation and was performed by large groups of dancers with improvised singing and the striking together of the men's metal-heeled shoes. Fanny Eisler popularized it as the **cracovienne** in the theatre around 1840. Chopin composed a *Krakowiak for Piano and Orchestra* and Heinrich Herz produced examples for solo piano.

Krauss, Clemens (1893–1954) Austrian conductor. He made his conducting debut at Brno in 1912. In the 1920s he directed the Vienna Philharmonic Orchestra and formed an association with Richard Strauss, conducting first performances of that composer's *Arabella*, *Friedenstag*, *Capriccio*, and *Die Liebe der Danäe*. He married the singer Viorica Ursuleac.

Krebs, Johann Ludwig (1713–80) German keyboard player and composer, a pupil of J. G. Walther and the star pupil of J. S. Bach. He was organist at Zwickau (1737), Zeitz (1744), and Altenburg (1756–80). In addition to his well-known *Clavierübungen* (*c*.1750), he also wrote sacred and ensemble music.

Krein, Alexander Abramovich (1883–1951) Soviet composer. Krein was an important figure in the National Jewish movement in the Soviet Union; his works often make use of Hebrew melodies. Krein's compositions include operas, orchestral works, and vocal music. His brother **Grigory Abramovich Krein** (1879–1955) was also a composer, whose works include three symphonic episodes, a violin concerto, and chamber music. Grigory's son **Julian Grigorovich Krein** (1913–) studied in Paris with Dukas, returning to the Soviet Union in 1933. He has written a

Fritz Kreisler

symphonic prelude (*Destruction*) and other orchestral and chamber works.

Kreisler, Fritz (1875–1962) Austrian violinist and composer, who eventually settled in the USA. At the age of seven he was the youngest ever pupil at the Vienna conservatory. He toured the USA in 1889 but ceased playing until 1899, during which time he studied medicine. Elgar wrote his violin concerto for him. In 1935 Kreisler admitted that the *Classical Manuscripts*, attributed to classical composers, were his own work.

Kreisleriana Collection of character pieces for piano (Op. 16) by Schumann. Composed: 1838. Kapellmeister Kreisler is a figure who appears in the story *Fantasiestücke in Callots Manier* (*Fantasies in the Style of Callot*) by E. T. A. Hoffmann; each of the eight pieces in the collection describes a different facet of Kreisler's character. Schumann dedicated this work to Chopin.

Krenek, Ernst (1900–) Austrian-born US composer, a pupil of Schrecker and associated with the Second Viennese School. In his early works Krenek experimented with late romantic and neoclassical styles. With *Jonny spielt auf* (1925–26) he wrote the first jazz opera, which was very successful. From 1930 onwards he used serial procedures. Krenek's other works include the operas *Karl V* (1930–33), *Tarquin* (1941), *Pallas Athene Weint* (1955), and *Der Goldene Bock* (1964); five symphonies; and concertos, chamber music, choral works, and piano pieces.

Kreutzer, Conradin (1780–1849) German composer and conductor. In 1804 he went to Vienna, where he may well have studied with Albrechtsberger. He was court kapellmeister in Stuttgart (1812–16) and at Donaueschingen (1818–22), then in Vienna he was kapellmeister at the Kärntnertortheater (1822–27, 1829–32, 1835–40) and the Theater in der Josefstadt (1833–35). He was city music director in Cologne (1840–42), travelled throughout Europe, and in 1848 settled in Riga, where he died. Kreutzer was a prolific stage composer but only his opera *Das Nachtlager in Granada* (1834) and his music for *Der Verschwender* (1834) are still heard. He also composed vocal works, three piano concertos, and chamber and keyboard music.

Kreutzer, Rodolphe (1766–1831) French violinist and composer. He became violin professor at the Paris Conservatoire in 1795. He was a friend of Beethoven, who dedicated his *Kreutzer Sonata* to him. His own compositions include 40 *Etudes ou caprices* for violin (1796) as well as other violin works, operas, and ballets.

Kreutzer Sonata Sonata in A major for violin and piano (Op. 47) by Beethoven. Composed: 1803. This sonata was originally written for the English violinist George Bridgetower, who gave the first performance, but the eventual dedication in the score was to the French violinist Rodolphe Kreutzer. Tolstoy wrote a novel about the *Kreutzer Sonata*, in which he describes its influence on several characters.

Kricka, Jaroslav (1882–1969) Czech composer. Kricka taught at the Prague conservatory (1919–45). His compositions, which show the influence of Dvórak, include operas, orchestral works, chamber music, and songs.

Krieger, Adam (1634–66) German composer. He was organist at St Nicholas's Church in Leipzig (1655–57) then served as organist in the court of the Elector of Saxony in Dresden. He was a popular writer of secular songs, ranging from the bawdy to the lyrical, but also composed sacred cantatas and funeral songs.

Krieger, Johann Philipp (1649–1725) German composer, organist, and clavier player. He studied the organ in Copenhagen and composition in Italy. In 1677 he became court organist at Halle; when the court moved to Weissenfels he went as kapellmeister, a post he held until his death. Krieger wrote sacred and secular music of which only a small proportion survives, including keyboard works, *Lustige Feld-Music* (1704), and 74 cantatas for church use. The latter are noted for their innovatory use of poetic texts, some by Erdmann Neumeister. His brother, **Johann Krieger** (1651–1735), was also an organist and composer. It is thought that he was court organist at Bayreuth (until 1677), then kapellmeister at Greiz (1678) and Eisenberg (1680). His last post was organist of St Johannis, Zittan (1682–1735). Krieger's *Clavierübung* (1699) and cantatas show his contrapuntal skill. Other works include another collection of keyboard music (*Sechs musicalische Partiten*, 1697), sacred vocal pieces, a large collection of songs, and numerous operas. The operas have not survived.

Krips, Josef (1902–74) Austrian conductor. He held appointments at the Vienna State Opera (1933–38; 1945–74) and was conductor of the London Symphony Orchestra (1950–54), the Buffalo Philharmonic Orchestra (1954–63), and the San Francisco Symphony Orchestra (1963–70).

Kubelik, Rafael (1914–) Czech conductor. After working with the Czech Philharmonic Orchestra (1942–48) and at the National Theatre in Brno, he left Czechoslovakia in 1945. He conducted the Chicago Symphony Orchestra (1950–53), the Covent Garden Opera (1955–58), and the Metropolitan Opera (1972–74). His father **Jan Kubelik** (1880–1940) was a virtuoso violinist.

Kubik, Gail (1914–84) US composer. Kubik studied with Piston and Nadia Boulanger. He composed much music for film and television; other compositions include three symphonies, a piano concerto (1976–77), chamber music, and choral works.

Kuhlau, (Daniel) Friedrich (Rudolph) (1786–1832) Danish pianist and composer, born in Germany. In 1810 he went to Copenhagen, becoming court chamber musician (1812–16) and chorus master at the Royal Theatre (1816–17). He became renowned as a pianist and teacher and travelled widely in Europe (he met Beethoven in Vienna in 1825). The leading Danish composer of his day, Kuhlau wrote six operas, incidental music, a piano concerto, and chamber and vocal music. But he is best remembered for his piano works (sonatas, sonatinas, rondos, variations, etc., for solo and duet), which are often used as teaching pieces. He wrote much profitable flute music but was not, as is often stated, a flautist himself.

Kuhnau, Johann (1660–1722) German organist and composer. He was organist of St Thomas's, Leipzig (1684), and was appointed music director at the university and cantor at St Thomas's (1701). Known especially for his keyboard works, for which he adapted trio sonatas, he also wrote motets. A lawyer and linguist, he left several writings on music.

Kullak, Theodor (1818–82) German pianist, teacher, and composer. He studied in Vienna with Czerny, Sechter, and Nicolai and in 1846 was appointed pianist to the Prussian court. With Marx and Stern, Kullak founded the Berlin conservatory, later known as the Stern Conservatory, but he left it to found his own teaching institution, the Neue Akademie der Tonkunst (its pupils included Moszkowski and Scharwenka). Kullak composed many piano works, of which the studies (particularly the *Schule des Oktavenspiels*, 1848) are the most enduring.

kum see **koto.**

Kunst der Fuge, Die see **Art of Fugue, The.**

Kurz, Selma (1874–1933) Austrian soprano. She studied with Johannes Ress and first sang publicly at Hamburg (1895). In 1899 she joined the Vienna Opera, singing under Mahler, and remained there until 1926. Based in Vienna, she toured Europe, singing at Covent Garden (1904–05 and 1907), and soon established a solid reputation as a coloratura stylist.

Kuula, Toiro (1883–1918) Finnish composer, a pupil of Sibelius, who deeply influenced Kuula's orchestral style. Kuula's works include orchestral music and choral compositions.

KV Abbreviation for Köchel-Verzeichnis (see **K.**).

Kvapil, Jaroslav (1892–1958) Czech composer, a pupil of Janácek and Reger. Kvapil's idiom is basically romantic and expressive. His works include four symphonies, five string quartets and other chamber works, and choral music.

L

L. Abbreviation for Longo. It is used as a prefix to indicate the number of a piece in Alessandro Longo's catalogue (1906–08) of Domenico Scarlatti's works. See also **K.**

la see **solmization.**

Lac des cygnes, Le see **Swan Lake.**

Ladye Nevell's Booke see **My Ladye Nevell's Booke.**

Lady Macbeth of the Mtsensk District see **Katerina Ismailova.**

lah see **tonic sol-fa.**

La Halle, Adam de (*c*.1250–88, or after 1307) French trouvère and poet, who after studying at Paris, returned to his native Arras by *c*.1270. He was possibly among the minstrels present at the investiture of the future Edward II as Prince of Wales in 1306. One of the first composers to exploit secular forms of polyphony not based on the motet, his output includes over 30 monophonic chansons, some 17 jeux partis, 5 motets, and 16 polyphonic secular songs given the title *Li Rondel Adan*.

lai see **lay.**

Lajthan, Laszlo (1892–1963) Hungarian composer and authority on folk music. Lajthan's style is more traditionally inclined than those of his contemporaries Bartók and Kodály. His works include nine symphonies and other orchestral compositions, chamber music, and vocal works.

Lakmé Opera in three acts by Delibes with libretto by Gondinet and Gille based on Pierre Loti's *Le Mariage de Loti*. First performance: Opéra-Comique, Paris, 1883. The opera is set in India, where Lakmé (soprano), daughter of a Brahmin priest, falls in love with Gerald (tenor), an English officer, with tragic consequences.

Lalande, Michel-Richard de (1657–1726) French organist and composer. He was organist for several Parisian churches and after 1683, when he was made superintendant of the royal chapel, he obtained many court appointments; he was granted the Order of St Michael (1722). In addition to his famous *Motets de feu* (1729), Lalande also wrote ballets, divertissements, and chamber music.

Lalo, Edouard (Victoire Antoine) (1823–92) French composer. He studied at the Lille conservatory and with Habeneck at the Paris Conservatoire (1839). He earned his living as a violinist and teacher and composed many songs and much chamber music (including a violin sonata, cello sonata, and three piano trios). He was a founder-member of the Armingaud String Quartet (1855). In the 1870s he gained a reputation as a skilful orchestral composer, particularly with his violin concerto in F (1873) and the *Symphonie espagnole* (1874; see **Spanish Symphony**),both given their premieres by Sarasate, the *Concerto russe* (1879), the ballet *Namouna (1882), the symphony (1886), and the piano concerto (1888–89). Lalo's most successful stage work was the opera *Le* **Roi d'Ys* (1875–88).

Eduoard Lalo

Constant Lambert was a noted composer, conductor and critic

Lambert, Constant (1905–51) British composer. Lambert studied in London with R. O. Morris and Vaughan Williams at the Royal College of Music. An early commission from Diaghilev established Lambert's lifelong association with ballet. Jazz influences are apparent in his popular *The *Rio Grande* (1929) for piano, chorus, and orchestra; Lambert's other works include *Horoscope* (1937) and other ballets, a piano concerto (1930–31) and other orchestral compositions, songs, and piano pieces.

lament 1. A Highland Scottish or Irish melody, with free variations, played on the bagpipes at funerals or other sorrowful occasions. The term **keen** is used by the Irish for a death lament. **2.** A piece commemorating the death of a distinguished person. Monophonic laments were composed on the deaths of Charlemagne (814) and Richard I (1199). A lament in the form of a ballade was composed by Andrieu on the death of Machaut (1377) and Byrd's lament on the death of Tallis (1585), *Ye sacred muses*, is a consort song. Examples from the baroque era include François Couperin's two sonata apothéoses for Corelli and Lully and Froberger's laments for keyboard. Recent examples include Ravel's *Le Tombeau de Couperin* and Stravinsky's *Elegy* for J. F. Kennedy.

Lamentations A setting of the Lamentations of Jeremiah for use during Holy Week at the Roman Catholic service of Matins. They were at first sung to simple recitation chants. From the late 15th century until the 17th century simple polyphonic settings were composed, notably by Palestrina, Tallis, and Byrd. François Couperin's *Leçons de tenebre* are in a deeply expressive arioso style for solo voice and continuo. Recent settings include Stravinsky's *Threni* (1958).

Lamentation Symphony Symphony No. 26 in D minor by Haydn. Composed: 1767–68. The name has arisen because some of the thematic material in the symphony is very similar to the plainsong melodies to which the *Lamentations of Jeremiah* are traditionally sung during Holy Week. This symphony is sometimes also called the *Christmas Symphony* (German: *Weihnachtssymphonie*), although there is no explanation for the choice of this name.

Lamoureux, Charles (1834–99) French conductor and violinist. In 1881 he founded the Concerts Lamoureux, at which he conducted his own orchestra and popularized the works of Wagner and other contemporary composers.

lancers A square dance for 8 or 16 couples: its full name is *The Lancers' Quadrille*. Its invention has been attributed to Duval, a Dublin dancing master (*c*.1817), but was also claimed by Joseph Hart in a publication of 1820. The dance comprises five figures: 'La Rose,' 'La Lodoiska,' 'La Dorset,' 'Les Lanciers,' and 'L'Etoile' to tunes by Spagnoletti, Kreutzer, Gay, Janiewicz, and Storace. 'L'Etoile' was subsequently renamed 'Les Vistes' and later replaced by 'Les Lanciers' as the fifth figure. See also **quadrille.**

Landi, Stefano (1586/87–1639) Italian composer and singer. He entered the German College in Rome as a boy soprano, took minor orders in 1599, and studied at the Seminario Romano (1602–07). He was active as an organist and singer in various Roman churches and spent a short time in Padua as maestro di cappella to the bishop (*c*.1618).

He was appointed alto in the papal chapel in 1629. Landi's most important work, *Il Sant' Alessio* (1632), was among the earliest sacred operas. Other compositions range from two conservative polyphonic masses to monodic arias in the form of strophic variations.

Landini (*or* **Landino**), **Francesco** (?1325–97) Blind Italian composer, organist, and instrumentalist. In the 1360s he was active in northern Italy, possibly in Venice, where –according to the chronicler Villani – he was crowned with laurel by Peter, King of Cyprus. He had settled in Florence by 1375. Landini was one of the most important and apparently prolific composers of his generation; his surviving works include madrigals, cacce, and over 140 ballate.

Landini (*or* **Landino**) **sixth** A *cadence used in 14th- and 15th-century music, named after Francesco *Landini, who used it extensively but probably did not invent it. In this form of cadence the sixth degree of the scale is interposed between the seventh and the final eighth, e.g. BAC. It is not therefore a *sixth in the harmonic sense.

Ländler A slow waltzlike dance from Austria. It was popular in the early 19th century before the advent of the *waltz proper. Collections of Ländler were composed by Mozart, Beethoven, and Schubert. Melodies in the Ländler style occur in the symphonies of Bruckner and Mahler and in the violin concerto of Berg.

Land of Hope and Glory Popular name for the first of Elgar's *Pomp and Circumstance* marches. Composed: 1901. Although originally composed for orchestra only, words for the middle section of the march were added later by Benson. With its appeal to patriotism, this march has almost become a second national anthem in Britain.

Landowska, Wanda (1877–1959) Polish-born harpsichordist. She became an authority on harpsichord technique and on 17th- and 18th-century keyboard music. In 1925 she founded the Ecole de Musique Ancienne near Paris and later lived in the USA. Falla wrote a concerto for her.

Landré, Guillaume (1905–68) Dutch composer, a pupil of Pijper. Landré's works combine the influence of his teacher's style with a more lyrical sense of line. His output includes four symphonies, the opera *De Snoek* (*The Pike*, 1934), chamber music, and vocal works.

Langlais, Jean (1907–) French composer and organist, blind from childhood. Langlais studied with Dukas. His compositions include music for organ and other instruments and choral works.

Lanier, Nicholas (1588–1666) English composer, lutenist, and singer. Brought up under the patronage of the Earl of Salisbury, Lanier was appointed lutenist in the King's Music in 1616. He composed for court masques, including Jonson's *Lovers Made Men* (1617) and, probably in 1625,

became Master of the King's Music. He travelled in Italy and the Low Countries. Few of Lanier's compositions survive; they include the recitative *Hero and Leander* and some of the earliest declamatory ayres.

Lanner, Joseph (Franz Karl) (1801–43) Austrian composer and violinist. Self-taught in music, in 1818 he formed his own ensemble, in which Johann Strauss the Elder played the viola. By 1824 the ensemble had expanded into a full orchestra, which was in such demand that Lanner split it into two, with Strauss conducting one of the bands. Lanner and Strauss were the first composers of the classical Viennese waltz; Lanner's are more lyrical and less rhythmic, the best of his large output being *Die Pesther* (1834), *Die Werber* (1835), and *Die Schönbrunner* (1842). He also wrote other dances and marches.

Lara, Isidore de (I. Cohen; 1858–1935) British composer. Lara studied in Milan and Paris; he composed many operas, including *Messalina* (1899) and *Solea* (1907).

largamente A direction used to indicate that the playing should be dignified and at a fairly slow pace. See also **largo**. [Italian, broadly]

large The longest note in the obsolete medieval system. It was divided into two or three *longs.

larghetto A direction indicating that the playing should be on the slow side, but not so slow as largo. [Italian, a little largo]

largo A direction indicating that the playing should be at a slow speed. [Italian, broad]

Largo, Handel's see Xerxes.

larigot An organ *mutation stop that sounds a note a *nineteenth above written pitch on flute *flue pipes. The length of the pipe (compared to an 8-*foot pipe) is 1.33 ft.

Lark Ascending, The Romance for violin and orchestra by Vaughan Williams. Composed: 1914; first performance: 1921. The inspiration for this work came from a poem by Meredith, which describes the flight of the lark as it soars into the sky.

Lark Quartet String quartet in D major (Op. 64 No. 5) by Haydn. Composed: 1790–92. At the beginning of the first movement there is a high exposed violin melody, which has been likened in character to a soaring lark (hence the title of the work).

Larrocha (y de la Calle), Alicia de (1923–) Spanish pianist. She made her debut at the age of 12. In 1959 she became director of the Marshall Academy at Barcelona.

Larsson, Lars-Erik (1908–86) Swedish composer and pianist, a pupil of Berg. His eclectic style was influenced by Nielsen, neoclassicism, and serialism. Larsson's works include a saxophone concerto (1934), *Music for Orchestra*

(1950), *Variations for Orchestra* (1962), the *Barococo* suite (1973), an opera, *The Princess of Cyprus* (1936), a *Missa Brevis* (1954), and much chamber and piano music.

La Rue, Pierre de (*c*.1460–1518) Flemish composer and contemporary of Josquin des Prez. He was in the service of the Emperor Maximilian I (1492–1506) and Margaret of Austria (1506–16), in whose chanson albums he is strongly represented. One of the few major Netherlandish composers who seems never to have visited Italy, La Rue's output includes masses, motets, and a requiem mass in addition to a few secular works.

La Scala An opera house in Milan, the Teatro alla Scala. It is on the site of the church of S Maria della Scala and it opened in 1778 with an opera by Salieri. It soon became one of Italy's leading opera houses: Rossini, Donizetti, Bellini, Verdi, and Puccini all had new operas produced there. Leading Italian singers and conductors worked there, and by the 20th century it was one of the foremost opera houses in the world. The theatre was damaged in World War II but reopened in 1948. Its musical directors have included Arturo Toscanini and Claudio Abbado. The Piccola Scala, a smaller theatre adjacent to La Scala, opened in 1955.

lassú The slow introductory section of the Hungarian dances the *csárdás and the *verbunkos.

Lassus, Roland de (Orlando di Lasso; *c*.1532–94) Flemish composer. At the age of 12 he entered the service of Ferdinand Gonzaga, viceroy of Sicily, travelling with him to Mantua, Palermo, and Milan. Lassus then went to Naples and Rome, where he became maestro di cappella at St John Lateran in 1553. In 1555 he was at Antwerp, where his first works were published. In 1557 he sang at the court of Munich, becoming maestro there from 1563 until his death. During this period he made frequent trips to France, Italy, and various cities in the Empire. Lassus was honoured and sought after by rulers throughout Europe: he was ennobled by Emperor Maximilian II and Pope Gregory XIII made him a Knight of the Golden Spur.

Lassus was the most prolific and versatile composer of his time. Not only did he master all the musical techniques and genres of the period, but he also commanded an extraordinary emotional range, varying from the bawdiest drinking song to the most fervent motet or spiritual madrigal. The most notable feature of his music is the way in which the words are allowed to generate most if not all the details of a composition: it was the expressive and rhetorical elements of his style that attracted the most attention among Lassus' contemporaries. His favourite genre is the motet, of which he wrote over 450 (the largest collection is the posthumous *Magnum opus musicum*, 1604). These are mostly liturgical, but many, with words drawn from the Bible (especially the Psalms), have no specific liturgical function. Others are ceremonial or didactic in function and some are settings of humanistic texts, of which the *Prophetiae Sibyllarum* (*c*.1560) are remarkable for their highly experimental use of chromaticism. Lassus' 101 magnificats and 75 masses make extensive use of parody technique; many of the masses, however, are extremely short and use freely invented material. His other sacred works include 12 settings of the Nunc Dimittis and 2 sets of Psalms. The chansons (about 70, 1555–90) and lieder (about 60, 1567–90) explore a wide range of moods, often mingling comic narratives and religious subjects in the same collection. The madrigals (about 140, 1555–95) are more serious: many are spiritual in character, like the *Lagrime di San Pietro*, (1595); others draw on Petrarch. Though many of the later madrigals exhibit the rhythmic vivacity of younger composers, such as Marenzio, Lassus chose to be conservative in his later works. In this he is comparable to Palestrina; however, Lassus' rugged, majestic, and succinct manner is very different from Palestrina's more flowing, transparent, and graceful style.

lauda (*pl.* **laudi**) A vernacular hymn of praise and devotion widely used in Italy from the 13th century until the middle of the 19th century. In the 13th century St Francis of Assisi was associated with their development as a series of stanzas, each with a short refrain. Early settings were monophonic in a style suggesting the songs of the *troubadours. Polyphonic settings in three or four parts were composed in the 16th century. The use of laudi in plays contributed to the emergence of the *oratorio in the early 17th century.

Lauda Sion The text of a *Sequence sung after the Gradual at Mass on the feast of Corpus Christi. The text was written by St Thomas Aquinas (*c*.1264) in rhymed trochaic dimeters and spondees. The literary structure of the text is reflected in the plainsong melody. Palestrina composed three polyphonic settings: two for double choir in eight parts and one for four voices. Mendelssohn set the text in 1846 as a cantata for soloists, chorus, and orchestra.

Laudon Symphony Symphony No. 69 in C major by Haydn. Composed: 1778–79. This work was written in honour of the great Austrian soldier Field-Marshal Ernst von Laudon.

lavolta A popular leaping dance of around 1600 in which the woman was swept high into the air. It was usually in a fairly fast triple time with dotted patterns and syncopations. Two settings by Byrd are contained in the *Fitzwilliam Virginal Book*. French: **volte**; Italian: **volta**.

Lawes, Henry (1596–1662) English composer and singer. He was employed by the Earl of Bridgewater and from 1631 was one of Charles I's musicians. He took part in court masques in the 1630s and also wrote incidental music himself, notably for his friend Milton's masque *Comus* (1634). *Zadok the Priest* was sung at the coronation of

Charles II (1661), but he is better remembered for over 400 songs, which set the poems of Milton, Herrick, Lovelace, and others. His brother **William Lawes** (1602–45) was also a composer and musician. A chorister at Salisbury, he was a pupil of Coperario and patronized by the Earl of Hertford. He served Charles I as private musician and from 1633 composed for court masques, including *The Triumph of Peace*. During the Civil War he moved with the court to Oxford, enlisted in the Royalist army, and was killed in battle. His works include music for viols, pieces for violin, and much vocal and stage music.

lay (*or* (French) **lai**) A 13th-century French form of poetry and music evolved mainly by the *trouvères and perfected by Machaut. The poetry, in praise of a lady, is arranged flexibly in irregular stanzas of 6–16 lines, with 4–8 syllables per line. The form of the music was influenced by the *Sequence. Each verse of text was set to a varying number of musical phrases or versicles, which might be repeated, with three or four lines in each stanza. The German **leich** of the 14th century is similar to the lay but has a regular structure of double versicles in each stanza (like the Sequence).

Lazarof, Henri (1932–) Bulgarian-born US composer, a pupil of Ben-Haim, Petrassi, and Shapero. His works, which display a broadly serial style with much attention to structure and texture, include *Structures Sonores* (1966), a cello concerto (1968), *Textures* (1970), and *Chamber Concerto 3* (1974).

leader The principal first violinist of an orchestra. He executes the conductor's wishes, plays solo passages, and has administrative responsibilities. The term is also used for the leading member of an ensemble (e.g. a string quartet). In the USA and Germany an orchestral leader is called a **concertmaster** (German: **Konzertmeister**); the term leader in the USA is often used for the conductor.

leading motive see **leitmotiv**.

leading note The seventh note of the major *scale above the *tonic. For example, B is the leading note in the key of C major. In the minor scale the leading note usually features in ascending but not in descending. The chord of the minor seventh based on the leading note of the major scale is called the **leading seventh**. In C major it is BDFA.

Lebègue, Nicolas-Antoine (1631–1702) French composer, organist, and harpsichordist. By 1661 he was an organist in Paris and in 1678 became organist to the French court. He taught Nicolas de Grigny and was also esteemed as an organ builder. Lebègue's publications were popular and comprise harpsichord music and organ music in which the pedal functions independently.

Lechner, Leonhard (*c.*1553–1606) German composer. A chorister at Munich under Lassus, he probably visited Italy in the early 1570s. By 1575 he was teaching in Nuremberg, eventually becoming town composer. In 1584 he was kapellmeister for a while in Catholic Hechingen but, as he was a Lutheran, left to become a tenor at the Stuttgart court. His sacred music shows the influence of Lassus; his largest work is the four-part Passion (1593). Other compositions are German villanellas, lieder, and the first complete German song cycle.

Leclair, Jean-Marie (1697–1764) French violinist and composer, a pupil of Somis. He worked as a ballet master in Turin before settling in Paris in 1728. Here he performed at the Concerts Spirituels and was Premier Symphoniste du Roi until 1736. In addition to his successful opera, *Scylla et Glaucus* (1746), he wrote many fine works for violin and chamber ensemble.

Lecocq, (Alexandre) Charles (1832–1918) French composer. At the Paris Conservatoire (1849–54) he studied harmony with Bazin and composition with Halévy. In 1856 he and Bizet shared first prize in a competition, organized by Offenbach, for their settings of the operetta libretto *Le Docteur miracle*. Lecocq is known as a prolific composer of stylish melodious operettas, the best-known of which are *Fleur-de-thé* (1868), *La Fille de Madame Angot* (1872), and *Giroflé-Girofla* (1874).

ledger line (*or* **leger line**) A short line drawn horizontally through (or above or below) a note that lies above or below the *staff.

Lees, Benjamin (1924–) US composer, a pupil of Dahl and Antheil. After early work mostly in film music, Lees developed an eclectic style with a tendency to variable metres. His later music includes several symphonies and concertos, the cantata *A Vision of Poets* (1961), the opera *The Gilded Cage* (1964), *Labyrinths* (1975), and *Mobiles* (1980) for orchestra.

Leeuw, Ton de (1926–) Dutch composer, pianist, and writer, a pupil of Badings and Messiaen. His works, which show the composer's interest in electronic music, serial techniques, and non-European rhythms, include the cantata *Job* (1956), *Symphonies of Winds* (1963), the opera *The Dream* (1963), *Litany of Our Time* (1970), *Canzone* (1974), and *Gending* (1975).

Lefanu, Nicola (1947–) British composer, daughter of Elizabeth *Maconchy and pupil of Maxwell Davies, Petrassi, and Thea Musgrave. Her works, which display an eclectic style, include *Hidden Landscape* (1973), the music-theatre piece *Antiworld* (1972), the ballet *The Last Laugh* (1973), and the opera *Downpath* (1977).

Franz Lehár

Le Gallienne, Dorian (1915–63) Australian composer, a pupil of Howells. His works show a characteristic dissonant counterpoint. Le Gallienne's small output includes a symphony (1952–53) and a sinfonietta (1951–56), chamber music, and songs.

legato Bound; tied. A direction used to indicate that the notes so marked should run into each other smoothly. It is the opposite of *staccato. [Italian]

Legend of the Invisible City of Kitezh, The Opera by Rimsky-Korsakov with libretto by Belsky, combining the legend of the miraculous rescue of Kitezh from the Tartars with that of St Fevronia. First performance: Maryinsky Theatre, St Petersburg, 1907.

Legend of Tsar Saltan, The Opera by Rimsky-Korsakov with libretto by Belsky based on Pushkin's poem. First performance: Moscow, 1902. The opera relates the stories of Tsar Saltan, of his son, the hero Prince Gvidon Saltanovich, and of the fair Swan Princess.

léger Light. Hence **légèrement**, lightly. [French]

leggero (*or* **leggiero**) Light. Hence **leggeramente** (*or* **leggieramente**), lightly. [Italian]

Legrand, Michel (1932–) French composer, a pupil of Nadia Boulanger at the Paris Conservatoire. Best known for his work in light music and jazz, Legrand has written scores for many films.

Lehár, Franz (Ferencz L.; 1870–1948) Hungarian composer, best known for his operettas. After studying at the Prague conservatory Lehár worked as a military bandmaster (1894–99) before turning to composition. *The *Merry Widow* (1905) is the most familiar of his operettas, which embody the gaiety of early 20th-century Vienna; others include *The Count of Luxembourg* (1909) and *Frederica* (1928).

Lehmann, Hans Ulrich (1937–) Swiss composer, a pupil of Boulez and Stockhausen. He has made use of serial techniques, his works including *Episodi* (1964), *Quanti* (1962), *Instants* (1969), and *Monodie* (1970).

Lehmann, Liza (Elizabeth Nina Mary Frederica L.; 1862–1918) British soprano and composer. Her teachers included Jenny Lind and Hamish MacCunn. She pursued a career as a recitalist from 1885 to 1894, when she retired and devoted herself to composition. Her works include musical comedies and song cycles, among them *In a Persian Garden* (1896), a setting for four soloists and piano of quatrains from Fitzgerald's version of the *Rubayyāt of Omar Khayyām*.

Lehmann, Lotte (1888–1976) German soprano. She studied in Berlin with Erna Tiedke, Eva Reinhold, and Mathilde Mallinger. During her successful career in England (1924–38) and the USA (1934–46), her principal roles, apart from Wagnerian ones, were the Marschallin in Strauss's *Rosenkavalier*, Desdemona in Verdi's *Otello*, and Leonora in Beethoven's *Fidelio*. She sang The Composer in the first performance of Strauss's *Ariadne auf Naxos* (1916).

Leibowitz, René (1913–72) Polish-French composer, a pupil of Schoenberg and Webern. Leibowitz adopted serial techniques as a result of his studies in Vienna. He was active as a writer, conductor, and teacher and his compositions include operas, orchestral works, chamber music (including eight string quartets), and songs.

leicht 1. Light in style. **2.** Easy. [German]

Leigh, Walter (1905–42) British composer, a pupil of Hindemith. Leigh's works include music for amateurs and the stage; he wrote light operas (such as *Jolly Roger*, 1933), a concertino for harpsichord and strings (1936) and other orchestral works, chamber music, and songs. He was killed in action during World War II.

Leighton, Kenneth (1929–88) British composer and conductor, a pupil of Petrassi. His chromatically contrapuntal style exhibits certain serial elements. He composed church music, such as a mass (1964), using modal scales.

Lotte Lehmann at a concert with Arturo Toscanini

Other works include three piano concertos, an organ concerto (1970), *Sinfonia Mistica* (1974), *Laudes Montium* (1975), and chamber and piano music.

Leinsdorf, Erich (1912–) Austrian-born conductor. He studied in Vienna, emigrating to the USA in 1937, where he conducted the Metropolitan Opera (1956–62). From 1962 to 1969 he conducted the Boston Symphony Orchestra.

leitmotiv A musical theme used, particularly by Wagner, to identify a character, object, or idea in an opera. Earlier composers, including Mozart, had used the device but it is with Wagner's operas that it is predominantly associated. [German, leading motive]

Le Jeune, Claude (*c*.1528–1600) French composer. Probably educated in Valenciennes, he was patronized from 1560 by Huguenot nobles. By 1564 he was teaching at the court of the Duke of Anjou in Paris. He fled to La Rochelle during the siege of 1589 because he was a Protestant. By 1596 he was back in Paris, in Henry IV's household. Most of his output comprises psalm settings and airs. In both genres there is a respect for the text and the texture is mainly homophonic. Le Jeune was an exponent of musique

mesurée, based on the rhythms of ancient Greek music. His most interesting works are the madrigals of the *Livre de meslanges* (1585) and the psalms of the *Dodécacorde* (1598).

Lekeu, Guillaume (1870–94) Belgian composer. In Paris he studied with Franck and d'Indy. At his early death (from typhoid fever) his output was considerable and shows him to have been a gifted composer. As well as music for the stage, he wrote vocal, orchestral, chamber, and piano works, among the best known of which are the violin sonata (1892) and the *Fantaisie sur deux airs populaires angevins* (1892). D'Indy completed Lekeu's cello sonata and piano quartet.

Lélio, ou Le Retour à la vie (*Lelio, or The Return to Life*) Lyric monodrama for actor, solo voices, choir, piano, and orchestra by Berlioz. First performance: 1832. *Lélio* is a continuation of the events described in the **Fantastic Symphony* and describes how the drugged artist comes back to his senses. Although it was intended as a companion piece to the symphony, the two works are now rarely performed together.

Lemminkäinen's Homecoming (*or* **The Return of Lemminkäinen**) Tone poem (Op. 22) by Sibelius. Composed: 1893–95. The work describes the journey of the Finnish hero Lemminkäinen from Pohjola and the subject is taken from the saga *Kalevala*. This is the last of a set of four tone poems by Sibelius based upon subjects from this saga. See also **Swan of Tuonela, The**.

Leningrad Symphony Symphony No. 7 by Shostakovitch. Composed: 1941. This symphony was composed during the German siege of Leningrad in World War II and was conceived as a piece of artistic propaganda, glorifying the fighting spirit of the Soviet army.

lento Slow. Hence **lentamente**, slowly. French: **lent** (*or fem.* **lente**) [Italian]

Leo, Leonardo (1694–1744) Italian composer. He held many posts in Naples, including teaching positions at the conservatories of S Onofrio (1739) and Pietà dei Turchini (1741) and maestro di cappella at court (1744). His best-known works are his Neapolitan operas buffa and his oratorios, including *La Morte d'Abele* (1738). He also wrote other sacred and keyboard works and serenatas.

Leoncavallo, Ruggero (1857–1919) Italian composer and librettist. He studied music at the Naples conservatory (1866–76) and literature at Bologna University (1876–78). Influenced by Wagner, he wrote his first opera (*Chatterton*, 1876) and planned a trilogy on the subject of Renaissance Italy. He then composed, to his own libretto, I **Pagliacci* (1892), a highly acclaimed verismo opera and the only work for which he is now remembered. Subsequent operas included La **Bohème* (1897), which was compared unfavourably with Puccini's opera on the same subject, and *Zazà* (1900). Leoncavallo also wrote many operettas, songs, and piano, chamber, choral, and orchestral works.

Leonhardt, Gustav (Maria) (1928–) Dutch harpsichordist, organist, and conductor. He is admired for his interpretations of the 17th-century keyboard composers, including Frescobaldi and Froberger, and founded the Leonhardt Consort (1955) to perform such works.

Léonin (late 12th century) French composer working in Paris, possibly at Notre Dame. He composed organa dupla (see **organum**) and was the author of the *Magnus liber organi* (*c*.1160–*c*.1180). According to the 13th-century theorist Anonymous IV, Leonin was the greatest composer of organa. His work represents the musical practice of the generation preceding that of Pérotin.

Leonora Three overtures written by Beethoven for his opera *Fidelio. The opera was originally called *Leonora*, after its heroine, and therefore the overtures are numbered 1, 2, and 3. *Leonora No. 1* was composed in 1805 but was never performed with the opera; for the premiere in the same year Beethoven wrote *Leonora No. 2*. When he revised the opera in 1806 Beethoven also reworked the overture as *Leonora No. 3*. For the 1814 production of the final version of the opera yet another overture was composed, the *Fidelio* overture, and the three *Leonora* overtures are now performed only as concert overtures. Both *Leonora No. 2* and *Leonora No. 3* feature an offstage trumpet call.

Leonora, or Wedded Love 1. (French: *Léonore, ou L'Amour conjugal*) Opera in two acts by Gaveaux with libretto by Bouilly based on a historical event. First performance: Théâtre Feydeau, Paris, 1798. This 'rescue' opera is important in that the libretto was the source of Beethoven's *Fidelio. **2.** (Italian: *Leonora, ossia L'Amore conjugale*) Opera by Paer based on Bouilly's libretto. First performance: Court Opera, Dresden, 1804.

Leppard, Raymond (1927–) British conductor. A fellow of Trinity College, Cambridge (1957–67), Leppard became prominent in the revival of early opera, publishing and performing his own realizations of Cavalli's *Callisto* and Monteverdi's *Orfeo* and *Ulisse*. He became conductor of the BBC Northern Symphony Orchestra in 1973 but has lived and worked mainly in the USA since 1977.

Leroux, Xavier (Henry Napoléon) (1863–1919) French composer. He studied with Dubois and Massenet at the Paris Conservatoire, where from 1896 until his death he was a professor. He is best known for his operas, among them *La Reine Fiammette* (1903) and *Le Chemineau* (1907), but he also composed choral and vocal music. Leroux edited the periodical *Musica*.

Le Roy, Adrian (*c*.1520–98) French composer, lutenist, and printer. He published music with his cousin Robert Ballard from 1551, becoming royal music printer in 1551. Le Roy was responsible for introducing Lassus at court and counted Arcadelt, Le Jeune, and Goudimel among his friends. Le Roy's firm dominated French music printing until the mid-18th century. Le Roy himself composed odes, chansons, and music for lute, guitar, and cittern.

Leschetizky, Theodor (1830–1915) Polish pianist, teacher, and composer, a pupil of Czerny in Vienna. In 1852 he moved to St Petersburg, where he became head of the piano department at the conservatory. His method influenced many pianists, including Paderewski, and he was a close friend of Anton Rubinstein.

lesson 1. A short piece of music for the harpsichord or organ from the late 16th century until the 18th century. A canonic piece by Byrd in *My Ladye Nevell's Booke* (1591) is entitled 'A Lesson or Voluntarie' and a further canonic piece of the 16th century, headed 'Lesson: Two Parts in One,' is ascribed to both Tallis and Bull. In the 17th century the term was also used to describe a suite of pieces, as in *A Choice Collection of Lessons* (1696) by Purcell. In the 18th century it became applied to single-movement sonatas for solo keyboard as well as to suites. **2.** Any of various other forms of instrumental music, as in Morley's *Firste Booke of Consort Lessons* (1599) and Robert Dowland's *Varietie of Lute Lessons* (1610).

Le Sueur (or Lesueur), Jean-François (1760–1837) French composer and writer on music. He was choirmaster at Dijon, Le Mans, and Tours, then went to Paris to the Holy Innocents (1784–86) and Notre Dame (1786–88); his policy there of using huge orchestras and opera singers to dramatize the liturgy met with strong opposition and he left. He returned to Paris during the Revolution and became celebrated as a composer of grand operas (*La Caverne*, 1793; *Paul et Virginie*, 1794; *Télémaque*, 1796) and patriotic hymns. He became an inspector at the Paris Conservatoire (1795–1802) and was appointed Paisiello's successor as director of Napoleon's Tuileries Chapel (1804–30). During this time he wrote his successful opera *Ossian, ou Les Bardes* (1804). In 1818 Le Sueur was appointed to teach at the Paris Conservatoire, where his pupils included Berlioz and Gounod. He was the leading musician of his day, well known for his simple but powerful sacred music; he also wrote many historical and theoretical works, including *Exposé d'une musique* (1787).

Lesur, Daniel (1908–) French composer. With Messiaen, Jolivet, and Baudrier, Lesur was a founder member in 1936 of the group La Jeune France. Lesur's style is less progressive than that of his contemporaries in the group. His works include the opera *Andrea del Sarto* (1969), orchestral music, chamber music, and songs.

Let's Make an Opera! Entertainment for young people in two parts (three acts) by Britten with text by Eric Crozier. First performance: Aldeburgh Festival, 1949. Set in the nursery of Iken Hall in 1810, it is the story of the rescue of Sammy, the little sweep (treble), who gets stuck in the chimney. The first two acts are a play in preparation for the opera performance, the conductor rehearsing the audience in four songs; Act III is the opera itself, *The Little Sweep.*

Leveridge, Richard (*c.*1670–1758) English bass singer and composer. He sang at Drury Lane, the Haymarket (1708), Lincoln's Inn Fields Theatre (1715–32), and Covent Garden (1732–51). His compositions include the masque *Pyramus and Thisbe* (1716), possibly the music for *Macbeth* (1702), song collections, and ballads, his most famous being 'The Roast Beef of Old England.'

Levine, James (1943–) US conductor and pianist. In 1975 he became musical director of the Metropolitan Opera, New York.

Lewis, Sir Anthony (1915–83) British musicologist and composer. He studied at Cambridge and with Nadia Boulanger (1934). He worked with the BBC from 1935 to 1947, when he was elected music professor at Birmingham University. He was founder editor of *Musical Britannia*. In 1968 he was appointed principal of the Royal Academy of Music.

Lewis, Richard (1914–) British tenor. He studied with Norman Allin and began his concert career in Scandinavia (1946) before making his British debut at Glyndebourne (1947). His concert and stage career has included many modern roles, such as that of Aron in Schoenberg's *Moses und Aron,* which he sang at Covent Garden (1965).

Leygraf, Hans (1920–) Swedish pianist. A child prodigy, he has become particularly noted for his interpretation of Mozart. Leygraf has also appeared as a conductor and has composed many orchestral and chamber works.

l.h. Abbreviation for left hand. It is written above or below the treble staff in piano music when the composer or editor suggests that it would be better to use the left hand than the right hand. Sometimes the initials **M.G.** are used, standing for *main gauche* (French), or **M.S.**, standing for *mano sinistra* (Italian).

Liadov, Anatol Konstantinovich see **Lyadov, Anatol Konstantinovich.**

Liapunov, Sergey Mikhaylovich see **Lyapunov, Sergey Mikhaylovich.**

libretto The text of an opera, oratorio, or cantata. The history of the libretto is a long and complex one: originally the libretto was a small book containing the text of an opera printed separately for the benefit of the audience. The task of the librettist was the adaptation or translation of a play, book, or folk tale to suit the musical requirements of the composer with whom he was to collaborate. Librettists, while not necessarily being dramatists, were often authors or poets in their own right. Among the most successful partnerships were those of Da Ponte and Mozart, Boito and Verdi, Hofmannsthal and Strauss, and Gilbert and Sullivan. Wagner, for his *Ring* cycle, wrote his own libretti.

Libuse Opera in three acts by Smetana with libretto (originally in German) by Wenzig, translated into Czech by Spindler. First performance: Prague, for the opening of the Czech National Theatre, 1881. It is a festival opera written with the intent of making the Czech nation aware of its glorious past and great future.

licenza Licence; freedom. The direction **con alcuna licenza** (with some licence) is used to indicate that the performer may use some freedom in such matters as speed and strict rhythm. [Italian]

Lidholm, Ingmar (1921–) Swedish composer, a pupil of Mátyás Seiber. Lidholm's music makes use of aleatoric procedures. He has shown great skill in adapting advanced serial techniques to a lyrical vocal style evident in his many choral works. Lidholm's output also includes orchestral music and chamber works.

Liebermann, Rolf (1910–) Swiss composer. Liebermann's style has been influenced by serial procedures. His work as an opera administrator, at the Hamburg State Opera (1959–73) and the Paris Opéra (1973–80), has prevented him from composing a large number of works. His compositions include operas and orchestral music.

Liebeslieder-Waltzer (*Love-song Waltzes*ction of pieces for piano duo and vocal quartet (Op. 52) by Brahms. Composed: 1869. The words of these 18 light-hearted love songs are taken mostly from *Polydora* by Daumer and their style and form is that of a waltz. In 1874 a second set of 15 waltzes appeared, entitled *Neue Liebeslieder* (Op. 65).

Liebesträume (*Dreams of Love*) Set of three piano arrangements by Liszt of some of his songs. Composed: 1850. In their original version the songs deal with amorous themes, hence the title. Although Liszt applied this name to the whole collection, it has today become commonly associated with the third piano arrangement of the set.

lieblich gedackt see **gedackt.**

lied (*pl.* **lieder**) A melodic German folk song, often strophic, which first emerged as a monophonic form in the mid-13th century. Many were composed by members of the *Meistersinger and *Minnesinger traditions. By the 15th and 16th centuries the lied had become a polyphonic form, as in Heinrich Isaac's setting of 'Innsbruck ich muss dich lassen.' The melodies of popular lieder were also featured in *quodlibets. During the baroque period the lied re-emerged as a solo song with a basso continuo accompaniment. By the early 18th century its identity had become overshadowed by the more sophisticated *aria. At the end of the 18th century the lied was revitalized with settings of Goethe's lyric poetry with pianoforte accompaniment. With Schubert the lied became transformed from a convivial vernacular song into an art form in which the solo voice and accompaniment played mutually interdependent roles in conveying the emotional content of the poetry. Schubert's lieder are either in *strophic or *through-composed forms or form part of a song cycle. The tradition established by Schubert was continued by several romantic composers, notably Schumann, Brahms, Wolf, and Pfitzner. Some of the lieder by Mahler, Richard Strauss, and members of the Second Viennese School have an orchestral accompaniment. [German, song]

Lieder eines fahrenden Gesellen (*Songs of a Wayfaring Man*) Song cycle for contralto and orchestra by Mahler to poetry by the composer. Composed 1883–85. This cycle of four songs tells how a young man is rejected by his sweetheart: in choosing this theme Mahler was reflecting his own rejection by the actress Johanne Richter. A young apprentice wanders through the countryside thinking of his sweetheart and their unhappy relationship. He finally lies down to sleep and is gently covered with linden blossom.

Liederkreis see **song cycle**.

Lieder ohne Worte see **Songs Without Words**.

Liedertafel A male-voice choir in German-speaking countries and in places where there are large groups of German expatriates. Liedertafeln originated in the early 19th century as societies of men who met regularly to sing four-part music; their meetings were convivial occasions at which they drank and sang round a table. [German, song table]

Lied von der Erde, Das (*Song of the Earth*) Song cycle for mezzo-soprano and tenor solo with orchestra by Mahler to poems by Bethge. Composed: 1908; first performance: 1911. This work reflects Mahler's interest in oriental philosophy and the six movements are all based on German translations of ancient Chinese poems. This song cycle was considered by Mahler to be a symphony: although it is not numbered as such, it is symphonic in proportion and conception. The movements are entitled 'Das Trinklied von Jammer der Erde' ('Drinking Song of the Earth's Sorrow'), 'Der Einsame im Herbst' ('The Lonely Man in Autumn'), 'Von der Jugend' ('Of Youth'), 'Von der Schönheit' ('Of Beauty'), 'Der Trunkene im Frühling' ('The Drunkard in Spring'), and 'Der Abschied' ('Farewell').

Life for the Tsar, A Opera in four acts and epilogue by Glinka with libretto by Rozen. First performance: St Petersburg, 1836. It opened every new season at St Petersburg and Moscow until 1917, when its title was changed to *Ivan Susanin* (Glinka's original title). Ivan Susanin is a historic peasant hero of the 17th century.

ligature 1. An adjustable band used to secure the reed to the mouthpiece in instruments of the clarinet family. **2.** A *slur used in vocal music to indicate that two or more notes are to be sung to the same syllable. **3.** A mark used in plainsong to bind several notes together.

Ligeti, György (1923–) Hungarian composer resident in Vienna and Cologne since 1956, a pupil of Veress and Farkas. His early works show the influence of Bartók and Stravinsky but in the 1950s he rejected total serialism in favour of the exploration of sound masses and textures. He developed micropolyphony, a style in which shape is produced by a complex of submerged details. Ligeti's later music shows an increasing rhythmic, melodic, and harmonic articulation of detail and the deliberate contrast between the precise and the diffuse. The humour in much of his music is made explicit in a number of theatrical works. His works include *Atmosphères* (1961), *Aventures* (1962), a requiem (1965), *Lontano* (1967), *Melodien* (1971), a double concerto (1972); *Clocks and Clouds* (1973), the opera *Le Grand macabre* (1977), and a piano concerto (1980).

light music Music that makes no demands on the listener. It usually has attractive melodies, a cheerful tempo, and a relatively simple structure. The work of Albert Ketelbey is typical light music. **Light opera** is opera based on this kind of music. See also **operetta**.

Lilburn, Douglas (1915–) New Zealand composer, a pupil of Vaughan Williams. Lilburn was the first New Zealand symphonist and established the country's first electronic studio (1966). His works include *Forest* (1937), *Aoteroa* (1940), three symphonies, *Return* (1965) for tape, and chamber and piano music.

Lillibullero Popular melody dating from the 17th century, often associated with political texts. It was very widely sung in Ireland, with vigorously anti-Papist words, after General Talbot was appointed to govern the country in 1687. The derivation of the melody is unknown, although several composers used it in their work, including Purcell in his incidental music for the play *The Gordian Knot Untied* (1691).

lilting 1. (n.) see **mouth music**. **2.** (adj.) Denoting a melody or tune that has a jaunty rhythm.

Lily of Killarney, The Opera in three acts by Julius Benedict with libretto by John Oxenford and Dion Boucicault based on Boucicault's play *Colleen Bawn*. First performance: Covent Garden, London, 1862. Complications arise when the aristocrat Hardress Cregan (tenor), who is expected to marry the heiress Ann Chute (soprano), secretly marries Eily O'Connor, the Colleen Bawn (soprano). Act I contains the famous duet for baritone and tenor: 'The moon has raised her lamp above.'

Lincoln Portrait Work for narrator and orchestra by Copland. Composed: 1942. The subject of the work, Abraham Lincoln, is depicted by means of selections from his letters and speeches, which are narrated to an orchestral accompaniment.

Lind, Jenny (Johanna Maria L.; 1820–87) Swedish soprano. She studied with Isak Berg and (in Paris) with Manuel Garcia. A brief but sensational career in dramatic opera, which included the creation of Amelia in the first performance of Verdi's *I Masnadieri* (1847), was succeeded by oratorio and concert work in the USA. Known as the 'Swedish Nightingale,' she was immensely popular as much for her charitable works as for her singing.

linke Hand Left hand. [German]

Linley, Thomas (1733–95) British singing master and composer. After studying with Chilcot and in Naples with Paradisi, he worked in Bath and became joint manager of oratorios (1774) and later of music (1776) at Drury Lane Theatre, London. His setting (with his son) of Sheridan's play *The *Duenna* (1775) was very popular. He also wrote many works for vocal ensemble, ballads, and anthems. His son, **Thomas Linley** (1756–78), was a violinist and composer. He studied with Boyce and with Nardini in Florence (1770), where he met Mozart. From 1773 he was leader and soloist at concerts in Bath and at the Drury Lane oratorios, composing an anthem, chamber music, and many theatre songs.

Linz Symphony Symphony No. 36 in C major (K. 425) by Mozart. Composed: 1783. This symphony was composed at Linz in Germany and its first performance was given there, hence the name.

Lipatti, Dinu (1917–50) Romanian pianist and composer. A brilliant virtuoso, he was a pupil of Florica Musicescu and later worked with Cortot and Nadia Boulanger in Paris. Following tours of Germany and Italy he returned to Romania but escaped to Geneva during World War II. He died from a rare form of cancer but left many recordings. His compositions included some piano and chamber music.

Lipkin, Malcolm (1932–) British composer, a pupil of Seiber. Lipkin's works, traditional in their attachment to tonality, include the *Sinfonia di Roma* (1965), concertos for violin and piano, chamber music, and songs.

lira da braccio A bowed unfretted stringed instrument that evolved from the *fiddle in the late 15th century. It had five strings that were stopped on the fingerboard and two unstopped drone strings tuned an octave apart. Originally made with only a slight waist and two C-shaped sound holes, it was later made with f-shaped sound holes and was

a forerunner of the modern violin. See also **lira da gamba; rebec.**

lira da gamba (*or* **lirone**) A bowed unfretted stringed instrument that was a bass version of the *lira da braccio. It first appeared at the end of the 16th century and dropped out of use in the middle of the 17th century. It had 9–14 stopped strings and two unstopped drone strings. In addition to two f-shaped sound holes it also had a small central rose hole derived from the lute.

lirone see **lira da gamba.**

Liszt, Franz (Ferencz L.; 1811–86) Hungarian composer, pianist, and teacher. A child prodigy, he studied with Czerny and Salieri in Vienna from 1821, and in 1823 toured Germany and visited Paris, where he had lessons from Reicha and Paer. He went to England in 1824, 1825, and 1827 but was based in Paris (1823–35), becoming a friend of Belioz and Chopin. From 1835 to 1839 he lived with Countess Marie d'Agoult, mainly in Switzerland (he taught at the Geneva conservatory), and in 1837 their second daughter Cosima was born (she married the German conductor Hans Bülow and later eloped with his friend Wagner). The period from 1840 to 1847 marked the height of Liszt's career as an international virtuoso and he toured widely, in 1847 meeting the Princess Carolyne Sayn-Wittgenstein, his mistress for most of the rest of his life.

Liszt became director of music at the Weimar court (1848–60) and made Weimar a musical centre for his avant-garde followers, known as the New German School. He performed many new works there, but the antipathy of the musical establishment obliged him to leave; he spent eight years in Rome, concentrating on religious music and taking minor orders in 1865. He made several more concert tours and spent time in Weimar, Rome, and Budapest; he taught the piano – Lamond, Sauer, and Weingartner being among his pupils.

Liszt was the greatest pianist of his time, and his technique may still be unmatched; he initiated the concept of the modern piano recital. He was a generous and influential mentor to younger composers, but his strong support for Wagner led him into conflict with Brahms and his followers and caused a rift in the German musical world. Liszt's original piano works are unprecedentedly technically demanding, colourful, and imaginative pieces that exploit the whole range of keyboard sonority; the best known are *Transcendental Studies* (1851), *Album d'un voyageur* (three books, 1835–36), *Années de pèlerinage* (three books, 1835–77), *Paganini Studies* (1838), *Consolations* (1849–50), *Liebesträume* (1850), the sonata in B minor (1854), the *Mephisto Waltzes* (1860–86), and the *Hungarian Rhapsodies* (1846–47, 1882–85). He made many piano transcriptions and wrote fantasias, chiefly on operatic themes. Liszt invented the term 'symphonic poem,' which he used for orchestral works of a programmatic nature (see **tone poem**); **his best known are** Les *Préludes* (1854), *Mazeppa* (1851), and *Hamlet* (1858). He wrote the *Faust Symphony* (1854–57) and a *Dante Symphony* (1855–56) and two piano concertos. Of his many choral works, the best known are the oratorios *Die Legende von der heiligen Elisabeth* (1857–62) and *Christus* (1862–67), but he also wrote masses and psalms. He also composed a few chamber and organ works and over 70 songs. His later works use a greatly expanded harmonic language.

litany An extended form of prayer consisting of a series of suppliant verses each followed by a fixed response. The Roman Catholic litany begins with the Kyrie and ends with the Agnus Dei, with the petitions addressed to God, the Virgin Mary, or the saints in between. It can be sung to simple chant or to homophonic settings. The Anglican litany is similar in its structure, with such responses as 'Good Lord, deliver us.' This text has been set polyphonically by Tallis.

lithophone see **stone chimes.**

Litolff, Henry (Charles) (1818–91) French composer and pianist. He was born in London, where he studied with Moscheles (1830–35), and began an international career as a pianist. In 1849 he settled in Brunswick, where he became a leading figure in musical life, organizing concerts and running his publishing house. In 1855 he was appointed court kapellmeister at Saxe-Coburg-Gotha and in 1858 he settled in Paris, where he became a well-known conductor and piano teacher. Litolff composed operas, choral works, songs, and chamber and orchestral music, but is best known for his piano works. The best of them are the five concertos symphoniques for piano and orchestra (the much-played *Scherzo* is from No. 4), which adopted a new approach to concerto writing and influenced romantic piano composers, especially Liszt.

Little Night Music, A see **Eine kleine Nachtmusik.**

Little Organ Book (German: *Orgelbüchlein*) Collection of chorales arranged for organ by J. S. Bach. Composed: 1708–17. The original manuscript contains 45 chorales, but there are indications that the collection was intended to be much larger. The volume was compiled by Bach with the intention of instructing a novice organist in the art of arranging a chorale for performance on the organ as a chorale prelude; for the most part, therefore, the arrangements are relatively uncomplicated.

Little Organ Mass Mass in B♭ major for solo voices, choir, and orchestra by Haydn. Composed: 1778. This work features a prominent solo part for organ but is shorter than the *Great Organ Mass.*

Little Russian Symphony Symphony No. 2 in C minor by Tchaikovsky. First performance: 1873. The first and last movements of this symphony are based upon Ukrainian folk melodies; since the Ukraine was often referred to in the 19th century as 'Little Russia' this work has come to be known as the *Little Russian Symphony.* However, it is also sometimes called the *Ukrainian Symphony.*

Little Sweep, The The title of the opera rehearsed and performed in Britten's *Let's Make an Opera!*

lituus An ancient Roman bronze military trumpet with a hook-shaped bell.

Liverpool Philharmonic Orchestra see **Royal Liverpool Philharmonic Orchestra.**

Lobgesang see **Hymn of Praise.**

Locatelli, Pietro Antonio (1695–1764) Italian violinist and composer, a pupil of Corelli in Rome. From Amsterdam, where he settled in 1721, he toured widely, teaching Leclair, Pothoff, and many others. Locatelli wrote many violin sonatas, a collection of caprices and concerti grossi (*L'Arte del violino*, 1733), and chamber works.

Locke (*or* **Lock**), **Matthew** (*c.*1622–77) English composer. He was a chorister at Exeter and during the Civil War probably fought as a Royalist. By 1651 he was active in London and in 1656 contributed to Davenant's *The *Siege of Rhodes*, the first English opera. At the Restoration he became court composer and supplied music for Charles II's coronation in 1661. He was queen's organist at St James's (1662–71) and at Somerset House (1671–77). Locke's most important compositions are dramatic and chamber music. The *Consort of Fower Parts*, in the tradition of English viol music, is innovatory in its harmonic writing. His most notable masque music is *Cupid and Death* (1653) and *Psyche* (1675), in which there is an inventive use of recitative. Locke composed much incidental music, notably for Davenant's *Macbeth* (1663) and Shadwell's *The Tempest* (1674). His music 'for His Majesty's Sagbutts and Cornetts' is well known.

Lockhart, James (1930–) British conductor and pianist, born in Scotland. Educated at Edinburgh University and the Royal College of Music in London, Lockhart was appointed conductor at Covent Garden in 1962 and remained there until 1968.

loco A direction used to indicate that the notes so marked should be played or sung at the actual pitch written, rather than an octave higher or lower as in a preceding passage. [Italian, place]

Locrian mode see **modes.**

Loder, Edward (James) (1813–65) British composer and conductor. He studied in Frankfurt with Ries (1826–28) then returned to London, where he wrote several operas and many popular songs and part songs (among them 'The Old House at Home'). He was musical director at the Princess's

Theatre (1846–51) and at the Theatre Royal, Manchester, where his best-known opera, *Raymond and Agnes* (1855), was performed. He composed in all genres but, except for his ballads, most of his works are now forgotten; his 'I heard a brooklet' is a setting of an English translation of Schubert's 'Wohin?' Loder's father **John David Loder** (1788–1846) was a violinist and music publisher and his cousin **George Loder** (1816–68) was a conductor and composer.

Loeffler, Charles Martin (1861–1933) Alsatian-born US composer. Extensive travels in Europe with his family when still a child imparted a large number of national influences to Loeffler's style, chief of which was impressionism. His output includes orchestral works, chamber music, and songs.

Loeillet, Jean Baptiste (*c*.1680–1730) Belgian composer, flautist, and harpsichordist, who moved to London in 1705. He was a famous teacher and performer and composed many works for harpsichord, flute, and ensemble. His cousin, **Jean Baptiste Loeillet de Gant** (*c*.1688–?), worked for the Archbishop of Lyons and composed five sets of sonatas (*c*.1710–17) for recorder and transverse flute.

Loewe, (Johann) Carl (Gottfried) (1796–1869) German composer, conductor, singer, and organist. He was a professor and cantor at the gymnasium and seminary at Stettin, where he became music director (1821–66) and organist of St Jacobus's Cathedral. In 1834 his opera *Die drei Wünsche* was staged with great success at the Berlin Hofoper, after which he toured internationally (visiting London in 1847). In 1864 he had a stroke which left him unconscious for six weeks and after another stroke he died. Loewe was a prolific composer, now best remembered for his fine ballads for voice and piano; the best known are *Herr Oluf*, *Erlkönig*, *Tom der Reimer*, and *Edward*. He also wrote five operas, many oratorios and cantatas, part songs, two symphonies, two piano concertos, four string quartets, and piano music.

Logothetis, Anestis (1921–) Austrian composer, of Greek extraction. Logothetis' early serial style gave way in subsequent works to an idiom using graphic notation. His works include many such scores, mostly for unspecified instrumental ensembles, in addition to conventionally notated orchestral and chamber works.

Logroscino, Nicola (1698–*c*.1765) Italian composer. He studied in Naples at the Conservatorio di Santa Maria di Loreto (1714–27), worked for the Archbishop of Conza (1728–31), and settled later in Palermo. Known mainly for his operas buffa with extensive ensemble finales, written after 1738, he also composed sacred music.

Lohengrin Opera in three acts by Wagner with libretto by the composer. First performance: Court Theatre, Weimar, 1850. Lohengrin (tenor), Knight of the Holy Grail and son of *Parsifal, appears in a boat drawn by a swan and promises to protect Elsa (soprano) against Friedrich (baritone), who claims her kingdom, and to marry her provided she will never ask his name. Lohengrin is victorious but Elsa, tempted by Friedrich's wife Ortrud (mezzo-soprano), asks the forbidden question and Lohengrin sadly withdraws in his boat.

Lombardi, I (*The Lombards*) Opera in four acts by Verdi with libretto by Solera. First performance: La Scala, Milan, 1843. The text derived from a poem by Grossi, *The Lombards at the First Crusade*, and the political implications were quickly popularized by the oppressed Italians of 1843. The stage representation of baptism met with opposition from the Archbishop of Milan.

Lombardy rhythm see **Scotch snap.**

Londonderry Air Popular Irish folk melody dating from the middle of the 19th century. It has also been used by several composers and there are many orchestral arrangements, including one by Grainger. Several sets of words have been written to fit with this melody, the most popular being 'Danny Boy.'

London Overture, A Concert overture by Ireland. Composed: 1936. This work seeks to evoke the atmosphere and spirit of the city of London and includes an imitation of a bus conductor's cry.

London Philharmonic Orchestra British symphony orchestra founded in 1932. Under Thomas Beecham, its founder, it became London's leading orchestra. Its conductors have included Eduard van Beinum, Adrian Boult, William Steinberg, John Pritchard, Bernard Haitink, and Georg Solti, and Klaus Tennstedt (from 1981). The orchestra has been resident at *Glyndebourne Opera Festival and has toured widely overseas.

London Sinfonietta British chamber orchestra founded in 1968. It was formed by Nicholas Snowman and David Atherton (its conductor until 1973) as a flexible ensemble for performing contemporary works unsuited to the forces of conventional orchestras. It quickly gained an international reputation for its versatility and many composers have written specially for it. Elgar Howarth became its conductor in 1973.

London Symphony 1. Symphony No. 104 in D major by Haydn. Composed: 1795. There is no apparent explanation for the choice of this name; although the symphony was written while Haydn was staying in London, so were his 11 preceding symphonies and there is no obvious reason why the title should be applied to this work in particular. See also **Salomon Symphonies. 2.** Symphony No. 2 by Vaughan Williams. First performance: 1914; revised: 1920. Like Ireland's *A London Overture*, this work attempts to evoke the atmosphere of London and includes quotations of London street cries and the chimes of Big Ben.

London Symphony Orchestra British symphony orchestra founded in 1904. It was formed when about 50 players left Henry Wood's Queen's Hall Orchestra after a dispute about deputizing. Hans Richter was the first of its distinguished conductors, who have also included Arthur Nikisch, Elgar, Hamilton Harty, Josef Krips, Pierre Monteux, Isvan Kertesz, André Previn, and Claudio Abbado (from 1979). Since the 1950s the orchestra has been considered one of Europe's greatest and it has toured widely. It is the resident orchestra of the Barbican Arts Centre.

long An obsolete note equal to two or three *breves. In the medieval system it was equal to either a half or a third of a *large.

Longo, Alessandro (1864–1945) Italian pianist and composer. Longo edited the first complete edition of Domenico Scarlatti's keyboard sonatas. His own compositions include many piano works and chamber music.

Lopatnikoff, Nikolai Lvovich (1903–76) US composer born in Russia. Lopatnikoff's music shows the influence of Stravinsky and Hindemith in its adherence to neoclassical principles. His compositions include the opera *Danton* (1930), four symphonies, concertos, chamber music, and piano pieces.

Lorca, Federico García (1899–1936) Spanish poet and dramatist, a friend of Falla. Since his death a large number of works have been based on his writings (he was apparently shot by Franco's supporters during the Spanish Civil War). These include *Epitaffio per Federico García Lorca* (1952–53) and the ballet *Il Mantello rossa* (1954), both by Nono, and George Crumb's *Ancient Voices of Children* (1970).

Loriod, Yvonne (1924–   ) French pianist. She studied at the Paris Conservatoire in the early 1940s with Messiaen, whom she later married, and is noted for her performances of his works and of other modern French composers, notably Boulez.

Lortzing, (Gustav) Albert (1801–51) German composer, singer, and librettist. His parents were actors and he spent his youth travelling with them in Germany, taking minor stage parts and playing the violin and cello. In 1823 he married an actress and started composing operas and compiling singspiels. At the Altes Theater, Leipzig, he became a leading tenor (1833–44) and kapellmeister (1844–46). During this time two of his most successful operas, *Zar und Zimmermann* (1837) and *Der Wildschütz* (1842), were staged. He became kapellmeister of the Theater an der Wien, Vienna (1846–49), but his operas met with little success there. In 1850 he became kapellmeister at the Friedrich-Wilhelmstadt Theater in Berlin, where he died, impecunious and nearly deaf.

Lortzing was an accomplished stage composer, particularly of humorous opera: he wrote some of the most original works with spoken dialogue in Germany at the time. His best-known operas include *Ali Pascha von Janina* (1824), *Hans Sachs* (1840), *Undine* (1845), and *Rolands Knappen* (1849). He also wrote incidental music, choral works, and songs.

Los Angeles, Victoria de (1923–   ) Spanish soprano. She studied at the Barcelona conservatory, making her debut at the Teatro Liceo, Barcelona, as the Countess in Mozart's *Don Giovanni* (1945). She appeared regularly at Covent Garden from 1950 to 1961. Her concert repertory includes folk songs of her native Spain.

Lotti, Antonio (1667–1740) Italian composer, a pupil of Legrenzi. Associated with St Mark's, Venice, from 1687, he became first organist (1704) and maestro di cappella (1736) there. He worked in Dresden (1717–19), where he produced many of his operas, including *Teofane* (1719). After returning to Venice, Lotti wrote only sacred choral works. His other works include madrigals and chamber music.

loud pedal see **piano.**

Loughran, James (1931–   ) British conductor, born in Scotland. He has conducted the BBC Scottish Symphony Orchestra (1965–70) and the Hallé Orchestra (1971–   ). He is also active as a conductor of opera.

Louise Opera in four acts by Charpentier with libretto by the composer. First performance: Opéra-Comique, Paris, 1900. Louise (soprano) is a seamstress; the opera realistically depicts low life in Paris and uses a large cast.

loure 1. A rustic bagpipe used in Normandy. **2.** A dance in 6/4 time, similar to a gigue, that was formerly accompanied by the bagpipes of the same name.

louré A method of bowing a stringed instrument based on the technique of playing the *loure bagpipes. A group of notes are played with one stroke of the bow but are somewhat detached from each other. [French]

Lourié, Arthur Vincent (1892–1966) Russian-born composer of French descent. Lourié studied in St Petersburg; in 1921 he left for Paris and later moved to the USA (1941), becoming a US citizen. His early works show modernistic tendencies; later compositions were influenced by the neoclassical movement. Lourié's output includes the *Sinfonia Dialectica* (1930), chamber music, piano pieces, and choral works.

Love, the Magician see **Amor brujo, El.**

Love of Three Oranges, The Opera in prologue and four acts by Prokofiev with libretto (in Russian) based on the play by Gozzi. First performance (in a French translation):

Chicago, 1921. It is a play within a play, the prince who loves the three oranges finding his princess in the third. There is an orchestral suite drawn from the opera, which includes the popular *March*.

Love in a Village Ballad opera by Arne with libretto by Bickerstaffe. First performance: Covent Garden, London, 1762. The tunes of this opera were written by 16 composers, as well as Arne himself (see **pasticcio**).

Love Potion, The see **Elisir d'amore, L'**.

Lualdi, Adriano (1885–1971) Italian composer, a pupil of Wolf-Ferrari. In addition to his work as a composer, Lualdi was active as a conductor, administrator, and critic. His works include operas, tone poems, chamber music, and vocal works.

Lübeck, Vincenz (1654–1755) German organist and composer. He was organist at St Cosmae et Damiani in Stade (1675) and at St Nicolai, Hamburg (1702). He wrote many preludes and other works for organ as well as sacred vocal music.

Lucas, Leighton (1903–82) British conductor, initially a ballet dancer. He was well-known as a conductor of ballet and film music and was also a composer.

Lucia di Lammermoor Opera in three acts by Donizetti with libretto by Cammarano based on Walter Scott's novel *The Bride of Lammermoor*. First performance: Teatro San Carlo, Naples, 1835. Lucia (soprano) loves Edgar (tenor) despite a family feud. Forced by her brother Henry (baritone) to marry Lord Arthur Bucklaw (tenor), she goes mad (the famous 'Mad Scene' in Act III), slays her husband, and dies. In the final scene Edgar stabs himself and dies.

Lucier, Alvin (1931–) US composer, a pupil of Shapero and Foss. He has a particular interest in live electronics and is a performing member of the Sonic Arts Union. Such works as *Vespers* (1968) and *I am Sitting in a Room* (1970) involve the exploration of environments. Other works include *Music* (1965) and *Still and Moving Lines of Silence in Families of Hyperbolas* (1975).

Lucio Silla Opera seria by Mozart with libretto by Giovanni da Gamerra with amendations by Metastasio. First performance: Teatro Regio Ducal, Milan, 1772. This early work is important in that it gave Mozart an interest in opera seria form, which he never lost.

Lucrezia Borgia Opera in prologue and two acts by Donizetti with libretto by Romani based on a play by Victor Hugo. First performance: La Scala, Milan, 1833. Set in early 16th-century Venice and Ferrara, it relates how Lucrezia (soprano) unwittingly causes the death of her own son, Gennaro (tenor), and takes her own life.

Ludus Tonalis Work for piano by Hindemith. Composed: 1942. *Ludus Tonalis* (Latin, the play of notes) was designed as a kind of 20th-century equivalent to *The *Well-Tempered Clavier*, being a collection of 12 fugues linked by modulating interludes. Hindemith explores many fugal devices and techniques and the prelude to the collection appears in retrograde inversion as an epilogue. Unlike Bach, Hindemith makes no attempt to include a work in every key, although the collection is strictly organized according to his theories of harmonic relationships.

Ludwig, Christa (1924–) German mezzo-soprano. After studying with her mother and with Felice Hüni-Mihacek, she developed her interpretations of Octavian, Venus, Kundry, and others and also sang lieder, especially those by Mahler. She sang with the Vienna State Opera (from 1955) and with the Metropolitan Opera, New York (from 1959).

Luisa Miller Opera in three acts by Verdi with text by Cammarano based on Schiller's play *Kabale und Liebe*. First performance: Teatro San Carlo, Naples, 1849. It is an important transitional work in Verdi's output between the operas using 'set pieces' and those with a more continuous action. Luisa (soprano), a village girl, is loved by Rodolfo (tenor), son of Count Walter (bass); court intrigue brings events to a tragic end.

Lully, Jean-Baptiste (Giovanni Battista Lulli; 1632–87) Italian composer and violinist, active in France. He was brought from Florence to enable Mademoiselle de Montpensier, niece of Louis XIII, to practise her Italian and under the influence of French court music he became a remarkable dancer, violinist, and guitarist. In 1653 he was appointed composer of the king's instrumental music and before 1656 began to conduct the 'petits violons.' In the early 1660s he received further posts at court and collaborated with Corneille and Molière in ballets and other musical entertainments. He began composing operas in the 1670s and royal patents in 1672–73 gave him the monopoly of operatic production. He died of an abscess, resulting from accidentally striking his foot with his conducting baton, and left a large fortune.

Lully's works include numerous operas, such as *Psyche* (1671), *Alceste* (1674), and *Armida* (1686); comedy and court ballets; and some church and instrumental music. His importance lies in the development of the court entertainment, the introduction of new dances, the establishment of the *French overture, and the creation of a new French idiom in his music.

Lulu Opera by Alban Berg with libretto by the composer based on Wedekind's two Lulu plays: *Earth Spirit* and *Pandora's Box*. Berg died before its completion: a two-act version was first performed in Zürich in 1937; the unfinished Act III, long kept back by the composer's widow,

The Florentine-born composer Jean-Baptiste Lully

has been completed by Paul Cerha and the full version of the opera was first performed at the Paris Opéra in 1979. Lulu (soprano), representing female sexuality, lures, is exploited by, and eventually causes the destruction of each of her lovers, who include the Artist (tenor), Dr Schön (baritone), and his son Alwa (tenor); she is finally murdered by Jack the Ripper.

Lumbye, Hans Christian (1810–74) Danish conductor and composer. From 1843 to 1872 he was music director of the Tivoli Gardens, Copenhagen. As a composer he is known for his light music, particularly his galops and other dance music, for which he has been compared with Johann Strauss the Younger.

Lumsdaine, David (1931–) Australian-born British composer, a pupil of Seiber. Lumsdaine's idiom is based on an advanced serial technique. His works include *Kelly Ground* (1966) for piano; orchestral music; chamber works, including *Looking-glass Music* (1970) for brass quintet and electronic tape; and vocal works.

Lupo, Thomas (?–1628) Musician and composer, member of an Italian family who served the English court from 1540 to around 1642. Probably a viol player, he composed sacred and secular vocal works. His instrumental fantasias in three to six parts show him to be a pioneer of the broken consort.

Lupu, Radu (1945–) Romanian pianist. He was trained at the Moscow conservatory and in 1969 won an international competition at Leeds, after which he settled in Britain.

lur 1. A Nordic Bronze-Age *horn consisting of a conical S-shaped bronze tube terminating in a flat disc and having a mouthpiece similar to that of a modern trombone. Such instruments appear to have been made in pairs with the S-curve twisted in opposite directions like a pair of mammoth's tusks, which may have been the original material for making them. The pitch of each instrument was the same. **2.** A Scandinavian herdsman's wooden horn, resembling an *alphorn. [Danish]

lusingando Enticing; coaxing; alluring: a direction to perform a piece in such a manner. [Italian]

lustig Cheerful; merry. [German]

Lustigen Weiber von Windsor, Die see **Merry Wives of Windsor, The.**

Lustige Witwe, Die see **Merry Widow, The.**

lute A plucked stringed instrument, the right hand plucking strings stopped on the fingerboard by the left. The lute has a pear-shaped body and a round vaulted back. The neck and fingerboard support seven or more frets of tied gut. The tuning pegs are housed in a pegbox set at an angle to the neck. The strings, again of gut, are arranged in double courses: the tuning of the 16th-century average-sized lute is G, C, F, A, D, G (the lowest string being G below middle C), other sizes maintaining this relative tuning.

The ancient Mesopotamian lute dates back to 2000 BC, the Arabic 'ud (see **Arabian music**) being the form in which it was introduced into Europe during the Crusades. Medieval lutes usually had four courses of strings and were plucked with a quill. In the 16th century the lute was popular as a courtly instrument throughout Europe (except in Spain, where its musical and social positions were filled by the *vihuela). By this time the lute usually had six courses of strings. The **archlute** (*or* **bass lute**), developed in the 16th century, had two sets of pegs, one set to tune the stopped strings and another set to tune a number of unstopped bass strings. The **theorbo** is a 16th-century archlute with 14 stopped strings and 10 unstopped bass strings. It was a popular instrument in Europe until the end of the 18th century. Another 16th-century archlute was the **chitarrone**, which (with its very long neck) could be 7 ft (over 2 m) high; it had eight pairs of stopped strings and eight bass drone strings. At the end of the 16th century and throughout the 17th century the lute acquired more courses, extending the lower range of the instrument; 11- and 13-course instruments were common in France and Germany, respectively.

The necessary complexity of these instruments, and the popularity of the harpsichord led to the lute's decline in the 18th century. Folk lutes of various shapes and sizes have been used in many parts of the world; they are still found in Balkan countries and include the long-necked fretted Greek **bouzouki**, the short-necked unfretted Romanian **cobza**, and the waisted long-necked Turkish **tar**, which has movable gut frets. The Russian *balalaika and the Spanish *bandurría are further examples of folk lutes. Similar instruments have been made in India, Japan, and China.

Solo lute music in the 16th century consisted of dance movements, variations, and contrapuntal ricercari and fantasias. Notable composers for the instrument include the Italian Francesco da Milano, the German Hans Newsidler, and in England John Dowland and Francis Cutting. The lute was also used in consorts and to accompany song, its music being written in the *tablature system rather than the modern staff notation. In the baroque era German and French composers continued writing music for the lute; the repertoire includes four suites and other pieces by J. S. Bach. Lute playing was revived in the 1950s, largely as a result of the work of Julian *Bream, the leading modern exponent of the instrument.

luth Lute. [French]

Luther, Martin (1483–1546) German theologian and founder of the Lutheran Church. Luther's greatest literary achievement was his translation of the Bible into German but he also wrote many hymns for congregational use. Some of the melodies were adapted from plainsong and popular secular songs and some were newly composed. Well known among his hymns are 'Ein feste Burg' ('A Stronghold Sure'), 'Christ lag in Todesbanden,' and 'Nun komm der Heiden Heiland.'

Lutoslawski, Witold (1913–) Polish composer. His early works, such as the concerto for orchestra (1954), are in a style derived from Szymanowski and Bartók and in *Travermusik* (1958) he experimented with serial techniques. Under the influence of Cage he initiated, with *Jeux Vénitiens* (1961), a style of controlled aleatoricism, which allows the players certain freedoms to produce new sounds. This style was further developed in a string quartet (1964), the second symphony (1967), a cello concerto (1970), preludes and fugue (1972), and *Novelette* (1980). Lutoslawski has written a number of song cycles, including *Paroles tissées* (1965) and *Les Espaces du sommeil* (1975).

Lutyens, Elisabeth (1906–83) British composer, daughter of Sir Edwin Lutyens and a pupil of Caussade. From an early chromatically expressive style, she developed her own form of serialism, which reached its maturity in such works as the sixth string quartet (1952) and the motet (1954) to a text from Wittgenstein. Other works include the opera

Witold Lutoslawski

Elisabeth Lutyens

Infidelio (1954), *Symphonies* (1962), *And Suddenly It's Evening* (1967), *Variations* (1979), and much film, radio, and instrumental music.

Luxon, Benjamin (1937–) British baritone. Luxon studied at the Guildhall School of Music. He subsequently sang the title role of Britten's *Owen Wingrave* (1970) and the Jester in Maxwell Davies' *Taverner* (1972). He has also sung at Glyndebourne and with the English National Opera.

Luzzaschi, Luzzasco (?1545–1607) Italian composer and organist. Active at the Este court in Ferrara, he studied with Cipriano Rore. In 1561 he became a singer at court and in 1564 first organist. He was also organist at the cathedral and the Accademia della Morte. By 1570 he was director of Duke Alfonso's chamber music. After 1597 he probably served Cardinal Aldobrandini, the papal governor. His most celebrated pupil was Girolamo Frescobaldi. Luzzaschi's most popular compositions are his five-part madrigals: though not innovatory they are skilfully composed, with an increasing tendency towards homophony.

Lvov, Alexey Fyodorovich (1798–1870) Russian composer and violinist. In 1847, after a career in the army, he succeeded his father as director of the imperial court chapel choir in St Petersburg. He also pursued a career as a virtuoso violinist. His compositional output reflects these interests: he wrote much sacred choral music and several violin works, including 24 caprices (c 1850), a violin concerto (1840), and *Le Duel* (c.1840) for violin and cello; he also wrote three operas.

Lyadov (*or* **Liadov**), **Anatol Konstantinovich** (1855–1914) Russian composer, teacher, and conductor. He studied, with Rimsky-Korsakov among others, at the St Petersburg conservatory, where in 1878 he became a teacher. He frequently conducted in St Petersburg; with Balakirev and Lyapunov he made expeditions to collect folk songs, arrangements of which were later published. Lyadov wrote several colourful orchestral tone poems, among them *Baba Yaga (1904), The *Enchanted Lake* (1909), and *Kikimora* (1909), as well as choral music and many piano pieces. He failed to produce the ballet score Diaghilev

commissioned from him in 1910, the commission going to Stravinsky (who wrote *The Firebird*).

Lyapunov (*or* **Liapunov**), **Sergey Mikhaylovich** (1859–1924) Russian composer, pianist, and conductor. He studied at the Moscow conservatory, where his teachers included Klindworth, Tchaikovsky, and Taneyev, then became a pupil of Balakirev, who influenced him strongly. Among his many appointments, he was assistant director at the imperial chapel (1894–1902) and taught at the St Petersburg conservatory (1910–17). He pursued a career as a pianist, made expeditions to collect folk songs with Balakirev and Lyadov, and edited the correspondence between Balakirev and Tchaikovsky. Lyapunov's most successful compositions are in small forms: he wrote many piano works (some of them virtuoso pieces), songs, and orchestral music (including two piano concertos and two symphonies).

Lydian mode see **modes**.

lyra see **Greek music**.

lyra viol see **viol family**.

lyre A plucked stringed instrument consisting of a soundbox with two projecting arms, which support a crossbar. The strings run over a bridge on the sound box to the crossbar. First depicted in Sumerian art around 3000 bc, it was widely used in ancient Egypt and ancient Greece. Similar instruments were in use in medieval Europe, some of which were played with a bow. Various types of lyre survive in Africa, where they are used to perform ritual music. See also **crwth; kithara; lira da braccio**.

lyric 1. (adj.) In its strict sense, designating vocal performance with the lyre. Hence, **lyric drama** is opera; the **lyric stage** is the opera stage. 2. (adj.) Describing a short poem that is neither narrative nor epic but short and expressive. The term has been adapted for musical use, as in Berg's *Lyric Suite* and Grieg's *Lyric Piece*. 3. (adj.) Describing a vocal weight between light and heavy, e.g. lyric soprano, lyric tenor. 4. **lyrics** (n.) The words of a musical or 20th-century popular song.

M

Maazel, Lorin (1930–) US conductor and violinist, born in France. A child prodigy, he conducted at the 1939 New York World's Fair. His appointments have included chief conductor of the Berlin Radio Orchestra (1965–75) and musical director of the Cleveland Orchestra (1972–).

Macbeth 1. Opera in four acts by Verdi with libretto by Piave. First performance: Teatro della Pergola, Florence, 1847. The text is based on Shakespeare's tragedy, with a dominant role for Lady Macbeth (soprano). **2.** Opera by Bloch with libretto, from the same source, by Fleg. First performance: Opéra-Comique, Paris, 1910. **3.** Tone poem (Op. 23) by Richard Strauss. Composed: 1886–87; first performance: Weimar, 1890.

McCabe, John (1939–) British composer and pianist. His works, composed in a lyrically romantic style, include three symphonies, three piano concertos, a clarinet concerto (1978), two violin concertos, *Notturni ed Alba* (1970), *Time Remembered* (1973), the ballet *Mary Queen of Scots* (1975), and piano and organ music.

McCormack, John (1884–1945) Irish-born tenor. He won the gold medal in the National Irish Festival at Dublin (1903) then studied with Vincent O'Brien, making his Covent Garden debut as Turridu in Mascagni's *Cavalleria rusticana* (1907). His concert performances included popular sentimental ballads as well as more classical material. In 1917 McCormack became a US citizen.

MacCunn, Hamish (1868–1916) British composer, conductor, and teacher, born in Scotland. After studying with Parry and Stanford at the Royal College of Music (1883–86), he taught harmony at the Royal Academy of Music (1888–94) and composition at the Guildhall School of Music (from 1912). He had an active career as a conductor, mainly in opera houses. Many of MacCunn's technically assured compositions have a Scottish atmosphere, making occasional use of Scottish poetry and folk songs, but few are now played regularly. He wrote operas, including *Jeanie Deans* (1894), and *Diarmid* (1897); choral and vocal works, including the cantata *The Moss Rose* (1885); chamber works; and orchestral music, of which the overture *Land of the Mountain and the Flood* (1887) is the best known.

Lorin Maazel

MacDowell, Edward (Alexander) (1860–1908) US composer, pianist, and teacher. He studied at the Paris Conservatoire (1877–78), with Ehlert in Wiesbaden, and with Heymann and Raff at the Hoch Conservatory, Frankfurt (1879–80). After teaching the piano at the Darmstadt conservatory (1881–82) he went to Weimar and played his first piano concerto to Liszt, who praised it highly. In 1888 MacDowell returned to the USA and settled in Boston, where he became well known as a pianist and teacher and composed prolifically. He became the first music professor at Columbia University, New York (1896–1904). His plan of establishing an artists' colony at his home at Peterborough, New Hampshire, was realized after his death (it is known as the MacDowell Colony). MacDowell is regarded as one of the first great US composers although his music is firmly rooted in the European romantic tradition and shows no leanings towards US nationalism. He wrote much piano music, including the *First Modern Suite* (1880–81), *Forest Idyls* (1884), 12 *Studies* (1889–90), *Woodland Sketches* (1896), and four sonatas; he also composed two piano concertos (1882, 1884–86), tone poems (including *Hamlet* and *Ophelia*, 1884–85), and songs and part songs (many to his own texts). He made many arrangements and editions.

McEwen, Sir John Blackwood (1868–1948) British composer. McEwen taught composition at the Royal Academy of Music, London, from 1898, becoming its principal in 1898. He was knighted in 1931. McEwen's output includes a symphony in C♯ minor entitled *Solway* (1911), 15 string quartets, songs, and piano pieces.

Macfarren, Sir George Alexander (1813–87) British composer. He studied with Cipriani Potter at the Royal Academy of Music (1829–36), where he later taught (1837–47). Although by 1860 he was totally blind, in 1875 he became Professor of Music at Cambridge University and principal of the RAM; he was knighted in 1883. Macfarren was a prolific composer who wrote in all genres (in later life he had an amanuensis). His operas include *King Charles II* (1849) and *Robin Hood* (1860); he also wrote orchestral music (including nine symphonies, a piano concerto, and the overture *Chevy Chace*, 1836), as well as choral, chamber, and keyboard works. He was also the author of several textbooks.

Machaut, Guillaume de (*c*.1300–77) French composer and poet. From about 1323 until 1346 he was in the service of John of Luxembourg, King of Bohemia, with whom he travelled in eastern Europe; later he served Charles of Normandy and Pierre, King of Cyprus. Highly esteemed by his contemporaries, his musical works include ballades, rondeaux, virelais, and a cyclic setting of the Ordinary of the Mass, representing a considerable advance over the polyphonic style of about 1300. His poem 'Voir dit' provides many unique insights into his methods of composition and the dissemination of his work.

machete A four-stringed Portuguese *lute with a flat back and a body shaped like a fish. It is used in folk music and its development in Hawaii led to the emergence of the modern *ukulele.

machine head A mechanism for securing and tensioning the strings of a guitar, mandolin, etc. The strings are attached to holes in spindles that pass through the pegbox parallel to the frets on the fingerboard. The spindles have worm gears attached to their ends, which are rotated by matching worm gears at the end of the pegs. The strings are tensioned by turning the pegs.

Mackenzie, Sir Alexander (1847–1935) British composer. Mackenzie was principal of the Royal Academy of Music (1888–1924); he was knighted in 1895. Much of

Elizabeth Maconchy

Mackenzie's music is explicitly programmatic; his large output includes operas, concertos for piano and violin, chamber music, and songs.

Mackerras, Sir Charles (1925–) Australian conductor. He has conducted the Hamburg State Opera (1965–69) and Sadler's Wells Opera (1970–77), which became the English National Opera after 1974. Mackerras has been largely responsible for the popularization of Janáček's operas in Britain; he has also arranged ballet scores from other composers' music, including *Pineapple Poll (1951) from Sullivan.

Maconchy, Elizabeth (1907–) British composer, a pupil of Vaughan Williams. Her style, much influenced by that of Bartók, is freely chromatic although she has avoided serial procedures. Her works include 11 string quartets, *Sirens' Song* (1974), *Eloise and Abelard* (1979), and *Romanza* (1980) for viola and ensemble. See also **Lefanu, Nicola.**

McPhee, Colin (1900–64) US composer. In 1934 McPhee visited Bali; he later spent a number of years on the island making a study of the *gamelan music, the source of the rhythmic and melodic patterns that often feature in his own compositions. McPhee's works include *Tabuh-tabuhan* (1936) for two pianos and orchestra, three symphonies, chamber music, and choral works.

Macque, Giovanni de (*c*.1550–1614) Flemish composer and organist. A chorister at the imperial chapel in Vienna, he studied at the Jesuit college there. By 1574 he was in Rome and in 1581 was organist at S Luigi dei Francesi. In about 1585 he moved to Naples, becoming organist to the Spanish viceroy in 1594 and maestro in 1599. Macque composed sacred vocal and keyboard music but is best remembered for his madrigals. Those composed in Rome are conservative but the Neapolitan ones are more experimental, with daring dissonances and chromaticism.

Madame Butterfly Opera in three acts by Puccini with libretto by Giascosa and Illica based on a play by David Belasco. First performance: La Scala, Milan, 1904. Set overlooking the harbour in Nagasaki, it is the tragedy of Cio-Cio-San, Madame Butterfly (soprano), with whom Lieutenant Pinkerton (tenor) of the US Navy contracts a Japanese marriage: for her it is binding and she bears his child; for him it is not. Pinkerton returns to America, and while awaiting his return Butterfly sings the aria 'One Fine Day.' Finally, when confronted by Pinkerton's American wife, Butterfly kills herself.

Maderna, Bruno (1920–73) Italian composer and conductor, a pupil of Malipiero and Scherchen. He was codirector, with Berio, of the Milan Radio Electronic Studio. He experimented with but later rejected total serialism, being more interested in the possibilities of performer freedom. In his *Musica su due dimensioni* (1952), he was the first composer to combine tape with live instruments. Other works include *Continuo* (1958) for tape, the composite work *Hyperion* (1965), three oboe concertos, a violin concerto (1969), the *Juilliard Serenade* (1971), *Aura* (1972), and the opera *Satyricon* (1973).

madrigal A piece of vocal music that first became established in Italy during the 14th century as a form in two or three voice parts. These moved in similar rhythms like a *conductus and were delicately ornamented. The form of the poetry frequently comprised two strophes of three lines followed by a two-line *ritornello. This is reflected in the musical form, which has the pattern aab. Rustic love was a popular subject. In the early 16th century the **Italian madrigal** re-emerged from the *canzona and the *frottola as a freer musical form in three or four voice parts. The technique of imitation was contrasted with homophonic writing and polyphony. Arcadelt, Festa, and Verdelot were among the Flemish and Italian exponents of the form. During the mid-16th century, in madrigals by Lassus, Palestrina, and Willaert, the number of voices was increased to five or six and the range of emotional expressiveness was widened. By the end of the 16th century the madrigal had become important in the experiments in chromaticism and dramatic declamation that led to monody. This trend is evident in the madrigals of Gesualdo, Marenzio, and Monteverdi. The later madrigals of Monteverdi, written for solo voice(s) and basso continuo, are monodies. Some have ritornello parts for instruments and are extended in a manner that anticipates the *cantata.

In the mid-16th century the Italian form gave rise to the **English madrigal**, with examples by Byrd and Morley. Following the publication of *Musica transalpina*, Weelkes and Wilbye increased the emotional expressiveness of the madrigal with *false relations, word painting, and subtle alternations between joy and sadness. During the middle of the 18th century the singing of the 17th-century madrigals was revived, and in the 19th century there were further additions to the repertoire, notably by Pearsall. Moeran and Warlock are among the 20th-century composers of English madrigals. [from Italian, perhaps from *mandrialis*, a pastoral song]

Maelzel, Johann Nepomuk (1772–1838) German inventor. At one time a friend of Beethoven, he created the panharmonicon, a mechanical orchestra for which Beethoven composed his *Battle Symphony*; however the two later quarrelled over authorship. Maelzel also patented the *metronome (1816).

maestoso Majestic; with great dignity. [Italian]

maestro A title given to various leading musicians – composers, conductors, teachers, virtuosos, etc. The **maestro di cappella** was the music director of a chapel (see also **kapellmeister**); the **maestro al cembalo** led an 18th-century opera orchestra from the harpsichord, and so on. In the USA nowadays the term is used only for conductors. [Italian, master]

Maestro di musica, Il see **Music Master, The.**

maggiore Major (in key). [Italian]

Magic Flute, The (German: *Die Zauberflöte*) Opera in two acts by Mozart with text by Schikaneder. First performance: Theater an der Wien, Vienna, 1791. In a work of humanism and Masonic symbolism, Prince Tamino (tenor) sets out to rescue Pamina (soprano), daughter of the Queen of Night (soprano), from the high priest Sarastro (bass) and is given a magic flute by the Queen for protection. But Sarastro has imprisoned Pamina for her own good and the couple finally achieve enlightenment after facing various ordeals. On a less exalted level the bird catcher Papageno (baritone), who is protected against danger by magic bells, eventually finds his Papagena (soprano).

Magnificat The canticle of the Virgin Mary from Luke 1: 46–55, sung at the Roman Catholic office of Vespers and at the Anglican service of Evensong. The title is taken from the Latin version of the opening words – *Magnificat anima mea Dominum* ('My soul doth magnify the Lord'). The earliest polyphonic settings of the Roman rite are by Dunstable and Dufay. From the middle of the 15th century

The Glyndebourne production of The Magic Flute *in 1978*

Gustav Mahler

it became common to alternate between plainsong and polyphony in the odd- and even-numbered verses respectively, as in settings by Obrecht and Palestrina. In the 16th and 17th centuries settings alternating between organ and plainsong were composed. Complete Magnificat fugues were composed by German organists of the 18th century, including Pachelbel and J. S. Bach. Choral settings for the Anglican rite have been composed continuously from the 16th century until the present. These include settings by Byrd, Gibbons, Purcell, Stanford, Howells, and Tippett. Extended settings in the manner of a cantata have been made by Schütz and J. S. Bach.

Mahagonny see **Rise and Fall of the City of Mahagonny.**

Mahler, Gustav (1860–1911) Austrian composer. The son of a Jewish tradesman, he showed an early musical talent. After studying at the Vienna conservatory Mahler embarked upon a career as a conductor. Appointments at opera houses in a number of towns led to more important positions at the Royal Opera in Budapest (1888) and Hamburg (1891–97). Following this, Mahler was appointed director of the Vienna Court Opera (1897–1907); in 1907 he became conductor of the New York Metropolitan Opera, spending the last years of his life conducting in both Europe and the USA. He died, aged 49, of pneumonia. Mahler's performances of opera and orchestral music were admired for their precision of ensemble and unity of musical purpose.

His compositions fall into two principal genres: song and symphony. Mahler's earliest characteristic work is the cantata *Das Klagende Lied* (1880), in which many elements of his mature style appear – attraction to German folklore, vivid orchestration that approaches tone painting in its portrayal of nature, and melodic lines that are sometimes close to folk tunes. These characteristics permeate his first four symphonies and the songs of this period, including the settings from *Des Knaben Wunderhorn*, a collection of folk-style poetry. The second (see **Resurrection Symphony**), third, and fourth symphonies include choral and solo vocal movements. With the fifth symphony (1901–02) Mahler's style became more abstractly musical; this and the two following symphonies are notable for their contrapuntal writing. The choral eighth symphony, the *Symphony of a Thousand* (1906–07), combines this stricter organization with elements of Mahler's earlier style. His subsequent works – Das *Lied von der Erde* (1908), the ninth symphony (1908–10), and the unfinished tenth – show Mahler's increasing preoccupation with death, expressed in music of considerable harmonic and tonal complexity. Mahler's music had considerable influence on the succeeding generation of composers. Apart from the symphonies and other works mentioned, his output includes the song cycles *Lieder eines fahrenden Gesellen* (1883–85) and *Kindertotenlieder* (1901–04).

Mahomet II see **Siege of Corinth, The**.

Maid as Mistress, The see **Serva padrona, La**.

Maiden Quartets see **Russian Quartets**.

Maid of Orleans, The Opera in four acts by Tchaikovsky with libretto by the composer based on Zhukovský's Russian version of Schiller's tragedy. First performance: St Petersburg, 1881. The incident of Joan of Arc (soprano) in single combat with Lionel (baritone), whose life she spares and with whom she falls in love, brings the story in line with romantic opera.

Maid of Pskov, The (Russian: *Pskovitianka*) Opera in four acts by Rimsky-Korsakov with libretto by the composer based on a play by Mey. First performance: St Petersburg, 1873. Sometimes called *Ivan the Terrible*, since this tsar is a major character, it is Rimsky-Korsakov's first opera; he composed revised versions in 1877, 1891–92, and 1895.

Mai-Dun Tone poem by Ireland. Composed: 1920–21. Described by the composer as a symphonic rhapsody, this tone poem depicts the prehistoric Dorset earthworks Mai-Dun (Maiden Castle).

major interval see **interval**.

major scale A diatonic *scale in which the *intervals between the degrees are each one tone, except for the intervals between the third and the fourth and between the seventh and the eighth, which are each a semitone (see also **modes**). The scale of C major is thus played on the white notes of the piano from, say, *middle C to the C above it. Each subsequent major scale, which starts on the dominant

of the previous scale, has its seventh sharpened to make the interval between the seventh and the eighth a semitone. Thus the scale of G major has F♯ as its seventh degree, and so on up to B major, which has five sharps (F♯, C♯, G♯, D♯, A♯). Thereafter it is more convenient to use flats rather than sharps, as in equal *temperament F♯ and G♭ are *enharmonic. After passing through the six flat scales (G♭, D♭, A♭, E♭, B♭, F) the cycle returns to C.

A **major key** is the *key based on the major scale of the same name and a **major chord** is a *chord based on the scale of the same name. Compare **minor scale**.

Makropulos Case, The (Czech: *Vec Makropulos*) Opera in three acts by Janácek with libretto by the composer based on Karel Capek's play of the same name. First performance: Brno, 1926. It is the story of a woman, Makropulos, who in 1565 was compelled to drink an elixir of life; over 300 years later, as the singer Emilia Marty (dramatic soprano), she must find the recipe to renew life or come to terms with death.

Mal Time; turn. Hence **das erste Mal**, the first time; **das zweite Mal**, the second time; **einmal**, once; **zweimal**, twice. [German]

malagueña Any of three kinds of Spanish folk music from the southern provinces of Málaga and Murcia: (1) a kind of fandango, (2) a free emotive song, (3) a dance built on a descending tetrachord bass from tonic to dominant of a minor scale. Above this a melody was improvised.

Malcolm, George (John) (1917–) British pianist, harpsichordist, and conductor. He was educated at the Royal College of Music, London, and became master of music at Westminster Cathedral (1947–59). Britten composed a *Missa brevis* for him and the cathedral choir.

Malcuzyński, Witold (1914–77) Polish-born pianist. He was a pupil of Paderewski in Switzerland and made his reputation playing Chopin's music. He lived successively in France, Portugal, South America, and Switzerland.

malinconia (n.) Melancholy. Thus **malinconico** (adj.), melancholy; sad. [Italian]

Malipiero, Gian Francesco (1882–1973) Italian composer. Malipiero studied in Venice and Vienna. Living in Paris from 1913, he absorbed the impressionist style of composition. On returning to Italy he held a number of academic posts and edited the first collected edition of Monteverdi's works. Malipiero's mature style is characterized by a polyphonic texture deriving from Renaissance music, extended by chromaticism and false relation. His works include *Venere prigioniera* (1955) and other operas, ballet music, 11 symphonies and other orchestral works, chamber music, and songs.

Mallet, David (*c.*1705–65) British writer. He collaborated with Thomson on the libretto of the masque *Alfred* (1740), publishing his own version in 1751. As well as other masques, he also wrote ballads, including 'William and Margaret.' 'Rule Britannia' (from *Alfred*) has been attributed to him.

Mamelles de Tirésias, Les (*The Breasts of Tiresias*) Comic opera in prologue and two acts by Poulenc with text by Apollinaire. First performance: Opéra-Comique, Paris, 1947. It is a farce on the changing roles of the sexes, complete with a balloon-breasted husband and a bearded wife.

Ma mère l'oye see **Mother Goose.**

Mancinelli, Luigi (1848–1921) Italian conductor and composer. Mancinelli became famous as an opera conductor in Italy and abroad: he conducted at Covent Garden (1888–1906). His own compositions include operas, songs and other vocal works, chamber music, and orchestral works.

mandola (*or* **mandora**) A small *lute with a sickle-shaped pegbox and a rounded back. It originated in Italy in the Middle Ages and was replaced in the 18th century by the *mandolin. The number of strings of the mandola varied according to the period.

mandolin (*or* **mandoline**) A small lutelike instrument that evolved in the 18th century in Italy from the earlier *mandola. It usually has four pairs of wire strings, each string of a pair tuned to the same pitch. The four pairs are tuned in the same way as the violin. The strings are plucked with a plectrum and the instrument is particularly suitable for tremolo playing. Characteristic mandolin music is provided by Neapolitan folk songs, but Beethoven, Mozart, and Mahler all wrote for the instrument.

Manfred 1. Incidental music (Op. 115) by Schumann for the play by Byron. First performance: 1852. This music includes an overture, often performed separately, and 15 individual numbers. **2.** Symphony (Op. 58) by Tchaikovsky, inspired by Byron's play. First performance: 1886. Although composed in the form of a symphony, the descriptive character of this work makes it more like a tone poem.

Manfredini, Francesco Maria (*c.*1688–1748) Italian violinist and composer, a pupil of Torelli and Perti. He worked in Ferrara (*c.*1700) and at San Petronio, Bologna (1704), and became maestro di cappella in Monaco (1711) and at the cathedral San Filippo, Pistoia (1727). Known mostly for his oratorios, he also wrote concerti grossi, sinfonias, and chamber music.

Mannheim School A group of mid-18th-century composers associated with the Electoral court in the German town of Mannheim. Following Bach and preceding Haydn, these composers are notable for their influence on the development of the symphony. The court orchestra, under the direction of Johann *Stamitz, acquired a high reputation not only for its dynamic skill in playing controlled crescendi and diminuendi, but also for a number of innovations in orchestral techniques. The other composers of the school included Richter, Beck, and the Italian Toeschi.

Manon Opera in five acts by Massenet with libretto by Meilhac and Gille based on the novel *L'Histoire du Chevalier des Grieux et de Manon Lescaut* by Abbé Prévost. First performance: Opéra-Comique, Paris, 1884. Manon (soprano) is torn between her love for des Grieux (tenor) and a longing for riches and universal admiration. Tempted by Manon, des Grieux gambles and is accused of cheating, but is released by his father's influence. Manon is condemned to deportation as a prostitute and dies on the road to Le Havre in des Grieux's arms. See also **Manon Lescaut.**

Manon Lescaut 1. Opera in four acts by Puccini with libretto by Praga, Oliva, and Illica based on Abbé Prévost's novel. First performance: Teatro Regio, Turin, 1893. The story is that of Massenet's *Manon*, except that des Grieux (tenor) and Manon (soprano) reach New Orleans, where she dies of exhaustion, imagining the stars are diamonds. **2.** Ballet with music by Halévy and choreography by Jean-Pierre Aumer. First performance: Opéra, Paris, 1830. **3.** Opera by Auber with libretto by Scribe based on Prévost's novel. First performance: Opéra-Comique, Paris, 1856.

manual A keyboard played with the hands, especially one on an organ or harpsichord to distinguish it from the *pedalboard.

Manzoni Requiem Setting of the Requiem Mass for solo voices, choir, and orchestra by Verdi. Composed: 1874. Verdi wrote this mass to honour the first anniversary of the death of Alessandro Manzoni, a famous Italian poet and novelist. In 1868, on the death of Rossini, he had collaborated with other composers in an abortive project to compose a collective mass, and for the 'Libera me' of the *Manzoni Requiem* he revised that of the earlier setting.

Maometto II see **Siege of Corinth, The.**

Marais, Marin (1656–1728) French composer and bass-viol player. A pupil of St Colombe and Lully, he became a member of the court orchestra (1676) and Ordinaire de la Chambre du Roi pour le Viole (1679). In addition to four operas and chamber works, he wrote extensively for the bass viol in *Pièces de violes* (5 vols; 1686–1725).

Marbeck, John see **Merbecke, John.**

marcato Marked; accentuated: a direction used to indicate that a note or a series of notes or chords should be individually accentuated or emphasized. Hence **ben marcato**, well accentuated. [Italian]

Marcello, Benedetto (1686–1739) Italian composer, theorist, and writer on music. A former lawyer, he was admitted to the Accademia Filarmonica, Bologna, in 1712. In addition to his settings of psalms paraphrased by Giustiniani in *Estro poetico-armonico* (1724–26), he also wrote concertos, oratorios, sonatas, a serenata, and a satirical commentary, *Il Teatro alla moda* (c.1720).

march A piece in strongly marked duple or quadruple time with symmetrical phrases designed to stimulate and accompany the orderly marching of soldiers. The main musical material of the march often alternates with a more melodious *trio section. In the 16th century suites of battle pieces were written for keyboard, such as Byrd's *Battell* in *My Ladye Nevells Booke*. Ceremonial marches occur widely in opera, for example in *L'Incoronazione di Poppea* (Monteverdi), *Scipione* (Handel), *The Magic Flute* (Mozart), and *Die Meistersinger* (Wagner). Extended funeral marches are found in symphonies, including Beethoven's *Eroica Symphony* (1803–04). Among 20th-century marches are Elgar's five *Pomp and Circumstance Military Marches* and Walton's coronation march *Crown Imperial*.

Marchal, André (Louis) (1894–1980) French organist, blind from birth. He studied at the Paris Conservatoire under Gigout, whose assistant he became. He was organist at the Germain-des-Prés (1915–45) and St Eustache (1945–63) and made tours of Europe, the USA, and Australia. Of Marchal's vast repertory, his recordings of Couperin and Franck are perhaps the most significant.

Marchand, Louis (1669–1732) French harpsichordist, organist, and composer. He was organist at Nevers Cathedral (1683) and Auxerre Cathedral (1693) before settling in Paris (1698), where he became court organist in 1708. In addition to his works for organ, including the *Grand dialogue* (1696), he also wrote pieces for harpsichord (1702–03), collections of airs, a cantata, and an educational work.

marche March. [French]

marcia March. Hence **alla marcia**, in the style of a march. [Italian]

Marenzio, Luca (1553/54–99) Italian composer. He was born in Coccaglia and was probably active as a singer at Brescia and Mantua before 1574. In that year he moved to Rome, where his most notable employers were Cardinal Luigi d'Este and Virginio Orsini. From 1596 to 1598 Marenzio was maestro di cappella to the King of Poland. Almost alone among his contemporaries, Marenzio was not regularly employed by a church and was not primarily an ecclesiastical composer. He was one of the most outstanding and advanced madrigal composers of his time. His works

display a wide emotional range and a new technical and expressive sophistication; in particular, he was supreme in the invention of musical motives that capture exactly the meaning and mood of the text. His early style (before 1587) was imitated throughout Europe, but his later style was too personal to influence any of his contemporaries except Monteverdi. Marenzio's works include 18 madrigal books for 4–10 voices (1580–99), 5 books of villanelle for 3 voices, and 2 books of motets for 4–7 voices (1585, 1616).

Maria Theresa Symphony Symphony No. 48 in C major by Haydn. Composed: 1772. This symphony was written in honour of Empress Maria Theresa of Austria when she visited Haydn's patron, Prince Esterházy.

Mariés de la Tour Eiffel, Les (*Wedding-Party on the Eiffel Tower*) Comic ballet in one act with music by members of Les *Six (Auric, Durey, Milhaud, Tailleferre, Honegger, and Poulenc) and libretto by Cocteau. First performance: Théâtre des Champs-Elysées, Paris, 1921, by the Swedish Ballet. A hunchbacked photographer is constantly frustrated in his attempts to photograph a wedding party on the first platform of the Eiffel Tower.

marimba A form of Central American *xylophone that originated in Africa. It consists of tuned strips of wood of different lengths laid out in a frame with resonators below each strip. The wooden strips are struck with drumsticks. Some Mexican marimbas are so large that they require four players. The marimba is also used occasionally in the modern orchestra. The orchestral instrument is played by one percussionist and has a range of between three and five octaves. The **marimbaphone** is a similar instrument using metal (instead of wooden) strips.

Marinuzzi, Gino (1882–1945) Italian composer and conductor. Marinuzzi conducted at the Rome Opera (1928–34) and at La Scala (1934–45). His compositions include three operas and orchestral works.

Maritana Opera in three acts by Vincent Wallace with text by Edward Fitzball based on the play *Don César de Bazan*. First performance: Drury Lane, London, 1845. Set in Madrid, it relates how the Gypsy Maritana (soprano) has problems when she is courted by the aristocratic Don César de Bazan (tenor).

Markevich, Igor (1912–83) Russian-born conductor and composer who settled in Paris. His early ballet *L'Envoi d'Icare* (1933) established him as a composer but after World War II he turned chiefly to conducting. He conducted several major US orchestras and also the Lamoureux Orchestra in Paris (1957–61) and the Monte Carlo Opera (1968–73).

The Marriage of Figaro staged at Covent Garden in 1987

Marriage of Figaro, The (Italian: *Le Nozze di Figaro*) Opera buffa in four acts by Mozart with libretto by Da Ponte based on the play of Beaumarchais *Le Mariage de Figaro*. First performance: Burgtheater, Vienna, 1786. The story is a sequel to Rossini's *The *Barber of Seville*: Count Almaviva (baritone), tiring of his passionately wooed countess, Rosina (soprano), pursues Susanna (soprano), who is betrothed to Figaro (baritone). After a series of complicated intrigues, in which the count's page Cherubino (soprano) is also involved, Figaro and Susanna are united and the count receives his wife's forgiveness.

Marriner, Neville (1924–) British conductor and violinist. He founded the *Academy of St Martin-in-the-Fields, which specializes in baroque music, and has made many recordings. Marriner also conducts the Los Angeles Chamber Orchestra (1969–).

Marschner, Heinrich August (1795–1861) German composer and conductor. After studying in Leipzig he became a music teacher in Count Zichy's service in Pressburg in 1816. In 1820 his opera *Heinrich IV und d'Aubigné* was produced at Dresden, where Marschner became co-conductor with Weber of the opera. He was kapellmeister at Leipzig (1827–30) and conductor of the Hanover Hoftheater (1831–59). The leading German opera composer between Weber and Wagner, Marschner was identified strongly with German national opera. He wrote 13 operas, of which the best known are *Der Vampyr* (1827), *Der Templer und die Jüdin* (1829), and *Hans Heiling* (1831–32); he also wrote two singspiels, a ballet and incidental music, two symphonies, much chamber music (including two piano quartets and seven piano trios), piano music (including seven sonatas), over 120 male-voice choruses, and over 420 songs.

Marseillaise, La French national anthem. It dates from the French Revolution and both the words and music were written in 1792 by Rouget de Lisle. It was adopted by an army of volunteers from Marseilles, who sang the anthem as they marched into Paris (hence the title).

Marsh, Roger (1949–) British composer. He has written electro-acoustic pieces for instruments and for voice, including *Serenade* (1974) and *Dum* (1980), and a number of music-theatre pieces, such as *Deadpan's Romance* (1974) and *Bits and Scraps* (1979).

Marteau sans maître, Le Work for contralto and chamber ensemble by Boulez to words by Char. Composed: 1952–54; revised: 1957. The three poems are set in nine movements and the instrumentation calls for alto flute, guitar, vibraphone, xylorimba, percussion, and viola.

martelé A bowing technique used to produce sharply accentuated detached notes. The hammered effect is obtained by the exertion of pressure immediately before and after the note, the sound being produced with a rapid movement in between. Unlike *spiccato, in martelé passages the bow does not leave the string. [French, hammered]

Martenot see **ondes Martenot.**

Martha Opera in five acts by Flotow with libretto by Friedrich based on a ballet-pantomime *Lady Henriette, ou La Servante de Greenwich*, by Saint-Georges. First performance: Kärnthnertor Theater, Vienna, 1847. The aristocratic heroine, Lady Harriet (soprano), hires herself out as a servant, Martha, in jest, at Richmond Fair. The opera includes the song 'The Last Rose of Summer.'

Martin, Frank (1890–1974) Swiss composer. Martin's studies in Geneva, Zürich, and Paris were followed by a career as a teacher in Switzerland and Holland. His earliest compositions show a strong French influence; this gave way in his later works to a highly personal idiom, occasionally using a modified form of serial technique. Martin's works include the opera The *Tempest (1952–54), the oratorio Le Vin herbé (1938–41), and other choral works, orchestral and chamber music, and songs.

Martini, Giovanni Battista ('Padre Martini'; 1706–84) Italian composer, theorist, and teacher of Jommelli, J. C. Bach, Mozart, and others. He was maestro di cappella of S Francesco, Bologna (1725), where he was also priest. In addition to his richly contrapuntal sacred works, he also wrote ensemble works, sinfonias, concertos, intermezzi, keyboard music, and educational works, including Esemplare di contrappunto (1774–75).

Martini, Giovanni Marco (c.1650–1730) Italian composer and organist. He worked in Milan (1680–81) and for the Modenese court (1686–93), collaborating often with the Accademia dei Dissonanti, Rome. He was director of the Conservatorio dei Mendicanti, Venice (1700–06). His works include operas, oratorios, cantatas, and other sacred works.

Martini il Tedesco ('Martini the German': Johann Paul Aegidius Schwartzendorf; 1741–1816) German composer, organist, and teacher. He settled in Nancy (1760) and Paris (1764) – Italianizing his name – and wrote military music, symphonies, and operas, including L'Amoureux de quinze ans (1771). In 1798 he was made an inspector of the conservatory and director of the court orchestra (1814), writing songs with piano accompaniment (including the well-known 'Plaisir d'amour'), a singing treatise, and other tutors.

Martino, Donald (1931–) US composer, a pupil of Babbitt, Sessions, and Dallapiccola. His music is characterized by instrumental virtuosity and texture within a basically serial technique. His works include Fantasy Variations (1962), a piano concerto (1965), Mosaic (1967), Notturno (1974), and a triple concerto (1977).

Martinon, Jean (1910–76) French conductor and composer. His conducting appointments included the Lamoureux Orchestra (1951–57) and the Chicago Symphony Orchestra (1963–69) and he recorded the complete orchestral music of Debussy. His compositions include symphonies and concertos.

Martinu, Bohuslav (1890–1959) Czech composer, a pupil of Suk in Prague (1922) and Roussel in Paris (1923) but otherwise self-taught in composition. Martinu lived mostly in Paris until World War II, when he emigrated to the USA. He was Professor of Composition at the Prague conservatory (1946–48), then taught in the USA. From 1957 he lived in Switzerland. Martinu's works, often neoclassical in style, include operas, among them Julietta (1936–37) and

Bohuslav Martinu

*Comedy on the Bridge (1937); ballets, such as La Revue de cuisine (1927); six symphonies, tone poems, concertos for one and two pianos, violin, cello, and harpsichord, and other orchestral pieces; chamber music, including seven string quartets and a piano quartet; and works for keyboard.

Martín y Soler, Vicente (1754–1806) Spanish composer. In 1785 he moved from the Spanish court to Vienna, where he collaborated with Da Ponte on several operas, including Una Cosa rara (1786). He became court composer in St Petersburg (1792–96), returning there from a brief visit to London to become Imperial privy councillor (1798). He wrote many operas (buffa and seria), ballets, songs, and cantatas.

Martirano, Salvatore (1927–) US composer, a pupil of Dallapiccola with early experience in dance bands. He has constantly changed mediums and techniques; for example his mass (1953) is strictly serial, while Ballad (1966) incorporates a rock-music style. Other works include Underworld (1965); L's GA (1968), a mixed-media setting of the Gettysburg address; and Selections (1970).

Martyrdom of St Sebastian, The Incidental music by Debussy for a French mystery play by d'Annunzio. Composed: 1911. This music is conceived on a broad scale and includes parts for vocal soloists and chorus.

Marx, Joseph (1882–1964) Austrian composer. Marx was rector of the Vienna Hochschule für Musik (1924–27). His songs are his most significant compositions; Marx's other works include orchestral music and chamber music.

marziale Martial; warlike. [Italian]

Masaniello see **Muette de Portici, La.**

A masque performed at Versailles in the 17th century

Mascagni, Pietro (1863–1945) Italian composer. The success of Mascagni's early opera **Cavalleria rusticana* (1888), which took first prize in a publisher's competition and subsequently became popular throughout Europe and the USA, established his reputation as an opera composer. The work is an example of **verismo* opera, which aimed for realism in its portrayal of human passions. Mascagni's later operas did not repeat his earlier success; these works include *L'*Amico Fritz* (1891), **Iris* (1898), *Le Maschere* (1900), and *Nerone* (1935).

Maskarade see **Masquerade.**

Masked Ball, A see **Ballo in maschera, Un.**

Masnadieri, I (*The Bandits*) Opera in four acts by Verdi with libretto by Count Maffei based on Schiller's drama *Die Räuber* (*The Robbers*). First performance: Her Majesty's Theatre, London, 1847, with Jenny Lind as Amalia (soprano). It is a tale of passion and violence.

Mason, Daniel Gregory (1873–1953) US composer. Born into a musical family, Mason studied at Harvard and in Paris with d'Indy. He taught at Columbia University (1910–42). Mason's compositions show a conservative nature in their adherence to romantic ideals. His output includes three symphonies and other orchestral works and chamber music, including a *String Quartet on Negro Themes* (1919).

Mason, Lowell (1792–1872) US composer, educationalist, and conductor, member of an influential family of US music publishers and instrument makers. He studied with Frederick Abel and began composing hymn tunes, which soon became widely used in the USA. He also compiled anthologies of existing tunes and championed reform in church music. Mason was responsible for the introduction of music into the school curriculum. He travelled widely, lecturing on educational methods, and wrote many books.

masque A staged courtly entertainment of the 16th and 17th centuries in which acting, dancing, poetry, and vocal and instrumental music were combined to present allegorical or mythological stories. The masque was first developed in Italy and France. After its introduction to England it remained popular until after the Restoration. The most distinguished writer of texts was Ben Jonson and among the early-17th-century composers who contributed ayres and dances was Thomas Campion. The stile recitativo was introduced by Henry Lawes, who composed the music for Milton's *Comus* (1643).

In this century the term has been applied to *The Crown of India* (1912) by Elgar (an 'imperial masque') and to *Job* (1931) by Vaughan Williams ('A masque for dancing').

Masquerade (Danish: *Maskarade*) Opera in three acts by Carl Nielsen with libretto by Vilhelm Andersen based on Holberg's comedy of 1724. First performance: Copenhagen, 1906. Adventures at a masked ball inevitably bring the moment of truth at the unmasking.

Masques et bergamasques Incidental music by Fauré for an entertainment by Fauchois. First performance: 1919. The title is taken from a phrase in one of the songs, a setting of Verlaine's 'Claire de lune', that Fauré had composed some years earlier and orchestrated for this production. His incidental music also includes the pavane (Op. 50) of 1887 as well as some music specially composed for the occasion.

Mass The main service of the Roman Catholic Church, which commemorates the Last Supper and Christ's death and Resurrection. The sung parts of the service are in two categories: (1) the Ordinary, consisting of the Kyrie, Gloria, Credo, Sanctus with Benedictus, and Agnus Dei (these movements are sung throughout the year except for the omission of the Gloria during Advent and Lent); and (2) the Proper, containing the Introit, Gradual, Alleluia, Offertory, and Communion (the words of these movements change according to the season of the Christian year).

Most settings of the Mass are of the Ordinary. Plainchant settings of the Ordinary survive from the 13th century, but it was not until the 15th and 16th centuries that complete polyphonic settings were made, as cycles of movements. Among the earliest of these are settings by Dunstable and Dufay, which began a tradition that culminated in the Renaissance masterpieces of Ockeghem, Obrecht, Josquin, Palestrina, and Byrd. Several techniques of musical organization were employed: (1) *cantus firmus* – a melody from a liturgical plainchant or a secular source was sung in long note values, normally by the tenor part, in each movement; (2) *plainsong* – each movement was based on the corresponding chant of a plainsong setting of the Ordinary; (3) *head-motif* – the same figure was used to form similar points of *imitation at the beginnings of movements; (4) *parody* – material was borrowed from a chanson, madrigal, or motet and remodelled to the words of the Mass; (5) *alternation* – the verses of the text were set alternatively to plainchant and polyphony. (See also **organ mass.**) Medieval and Renaissance masses were performed with instruments doubling the vocal parts or by voices alone.

During the 17th century developments in the fields of opera, concerto, and sonata were reflected in settings of the Mass, which included writing for solo voices and independent instrumental parts with basso continuo. The longer texts of the Gloria and Credo were broken up into a series of shorter movements in the manner of a *cantata, as in Vivaldi's *Gloria*. J. S. Bach's *Mass in B minor* (1737) marks the beginning of the tradition of expansive settings too long for liturgical use; Beethoven's *Missa solemnis* (1823) is also in this category. The orchestral and structural aspects of the classical *symphony are reflected both in the latter work and in the six late masses by Haydn. Among later 19th-century settings of the Mass are those by Bruckner, Liszt, and Gounod. During the 20th century distinguished settings have been made by Vaughan Williams, Poulenc, and Stravinsky. [from Latin *missa*, from the final sentence of the service: *Ite missa est*, Go, it is the dismissal]

Massenet, Jules (Emile Frédéric) (1842–1912) French composer. He studied with Laurent, Reber, and Ambroise

Jules Massenet

Thomas at the Paris Conservatoire, winning the Prix de Rome in 1863. Three years later in Paris two of his early works were produced at the Opéra-Comique, but by this time he was better known for his sacred dramas (e.g. *Marie-Magdeleine*, 1873; *Eve*, 1875; *La Vierge*, 1880). From 1878 until his death he was a composition professor at the Conservatoire; his pupils included Charpentier, Koechlin, and Schmitt. When his opera *Hérodiade* was produced in 1881 Massenet's name was made, and with *Manon in 1884 he became recognized as the most popular opera composer in France. The best known of his subsequent operas are *Le Cid* (1885), *Esclarmonde* (1889), *Werther* (1892), *Thaïs* (1894), *La Navarraise* (1894), *Cendrillon* (1899; see **Cinderella**), *Le Jongleur de Notre-Dame* (1902), and *Don Quichotte* (1910). Massenet's musical language is characterized by flowing melody and 'singable' lines. He used leitmotivs and was skilful in his use of dramatic effect. For many years his works were rarely heard, being criticized for their sentimentality and superficiality. Massenet's other compositions include ballets and incidental music, some colourfully orchestrated suites (e.g. the *Scènes napolitaines*, ?1876, and *Scènes alsaciennes*, 1881), a piano concerto (1903), part songs and songs, and piano music.

Mass of Life, A Work for solo voices, choir, and orchestra by Delius to words by Nietzsche. First performance: 1909. The text is taken from the philosophical work *Also sprach Zarathustra (Thus Spake Zarathustra)* and it is this

Zoroastrian philosophy that is described in the work. Thus it is not a mass in the strict sense of the word and does not have any conventional religious significance. Part of *A Mass of Life* was performed at the Munich Festival in 1908, before the first complete performance.

Master of the Queen's (*or* **King's**) **Music** The title of the only remaining secular music post in the British royal household. The office is thought to date back to the reign of Charles I, who maintained a private band for which he appointed a Master. Charles II had a substantial musical household, the King's Music, including a string band (24 violins). Until 1700 composition was not part of the Master's duties but from then until 1820 he was expected to provide court odes. Gradually the Master ceased to have any practical duties but became the eminent musician responsible for composing and arranging music (e.g. fanfares, marches) for state and royal functions. In the 20th century this honorary appointment, the musical equivalent of poet laureate, has been held by Walter Parratt (1893–1924), Edward Elgar (1924–34), Walford Davies (1934–41), Arnold Bax (1942–52), Arthur Bliss (1953–75), and Malcolm Williamson (1975–).

Master Peter's Puppet Show (Spanish: *El Retablo de Maese Pedro*) Opera in one act by Falla with libretto by the composer based on the 26th chapter of Part II of Cervantes' *Don Quixote*. First performance: Seville, 1923 (in the drawing room of Princesse Edmond de Polignac, for whom it was written). The opera uses three singers, actors, and puppets.

mastersinger see **Meistersinger**.

Mastersingers of Nuremberg, The see **Meistersinger von Nürnberg, Die.**

Mather, Bruce (1939–) Canadian composer and pianist, a pupil of Milhaud and Messiaen. His style combines elements of neoclassicism, serialism, and microtonality. His works include *Ombres* (1967), a sonata for two pianos (1970), *Music for Organ, Horn and Gongs* (1973), *Eine Kleine Bläser Musik* (1975), and *Clos de Vougeot* (1977).

Mathias, William (1934–) British composer, a pupil of Lennox Berkeley. Mathias has taught in his native Wales. His music is notable for its vitality and brilliance in an idiom influenced by Tippett. Mathias's works include a symphony (1966), concertos for piano, harp, and clarinet, and other orchestral works, choral music, chamber music, and songs.

Mathis der Maler (*Mathias the Painter*) Opera in seven scenes by Hindemith with text by the composer based on the life of the 16th-century painter Mathias Grünewald, best known for his great altar triptych at Isenheim. First performance: Zürich, 1938. The action parallels political oppression in Hitler's Germany. Hindemith's symphony *Mathis der Maler* is taken from orchestral sections of the score.

Matin, Le (*Morning*) Symphony No. 6 in D major by Haydn. Composed: *c*.1761. It is traditionally said that Prince Esterhazy suggested to Haydn that he should write a set of three symphonies to describe morning, midday, and evening. *Le Matin* is the first of the trilogy, the other two works being the Symphony No. 7 in C major, *Le Midi* (*Midday*); and the Symphony No. 8 in G minor, *Le Soir* (*Evening*). These were the first works written by Haydn for Prince Esterházy.

Matrimonio segreto, Il see **Secret Marriage, The.**

Matsudaira, Yoritsune (1907–) Japanese composer, a pupil of Tcherepnin. His style after 1945 combines serial procedures with thematic elements from the Japanese *gagaku* tradition. His works include *Saibora Metamorphoses* (1953), *Umai somi* (1958), a piano concerto (1965), *Portrait B* (1968), and *Mouvements circulatoires* (1972).

Matthaus-Passion see **St Matthew Passion.**

Matthay, Tobias (1858–1945) British composer and pianist. Matthay was well known as a pianist and teacher. His works include much piano music and a number of books on piano playing.

Mattheson, Johann (1681–1764) German composer and theorist. Trained in Hamburg, he wrote operas, often working with Handel (with whom he became friendly in about 1703). He became secretary to the English ambassador (1704), music director of Hamburg Cathedral (1715), kapellmeister (1719), and legation secretary (1741) to the Duke of Holstein. His works include chamber music, oratorios, passions, secular cantatas, and several treatises, including *Der vollkommene Capellmeister* (1739).

Matthews, Denis (**James**) (1919–) British pianist and writer. He studied at the Royal Academy of Music (1935–40), and with the RAF orchestra (1940–46) travelled to the USA and Potsdam. He is noted for his performance of the classics, especially Beethoven. In 1971 he became the first Professor of Music at the University of Newcastle.

mattinata Morning song: a piece of morning music similar to an aubade. [Italian]

Má Vlast (*My Country*) Cycle of tone poems by Smetana. Composed: 1874–79. Each tone poem was inspired by some feature of Czech life or scenery and thus the collection is an artistic tribute to the composer's national heritage. The six works are 'Vysehrad' (the castle in Prague), 'Vltava' (the River Moldau), 'Sárka' (an Amazon of Czech folk history), 'Z ceských luhuv a hájuv' ('From Bohemia's Woods and Fields'), 'Tábor' (an ancient Czech city), and 'Blaník' (a mountain near Prague).

Plate 24: *This Indian Miniature shows a rāga being played to celebrate spring. The artist was a member of the Bundi School of the 1660s*

Plate 25: *Franz Liszt at the keyboard. He was undoubtedly the
greatest piano virtuoso of his time*

Plate 26: *A scene from a Russian production of Prokofiev's opera*
The Love of Three Oranges

Plate 27: *The composer William Mathias (left) in discussion with Roy Massey during a rehearsal at the 1982 Three Choirs Festival*

Maw, Nicholas (1935–) British composer, a pupil of Lennox Berkeley, Nadia Boulanger, and Deutsch. In early works, such as the *Eight Chinese Lyrics* (1956) and the *Nocturne* (1958), he experimented with serial procedures; *Scenes and Arias* (1962) combines tonal and serial elements in a romantically expressive idiom. Other works include a string quartet (1965), the opera *The *Rising of the Moon* (1970), *Life Studies* (1974), *La Vita nuova* (1978), and *The Ruin* (1980).

Mayer, Sir Robert (1879–1985) British musical patron, born in Germany (he took British citizenship in 1902). In 1923 he founded the Robert Mayer Concerts for Children. He was knighted in 1939 and he made a cogent speech at a gala concert held in the Festival Hall to celebrate his 100th birthday.

May Night (Russian: *Maïskaya Notch*) Opera in three acts by Rimsky-Korsakov with libretto by the composer based on a story by Gogol. First performance: St Petersburg, 1880. It tells of the disruptions of village life when tales of witches and water sprites are told.

Mayuzumi, Toshiro (1929–) Japanese composer. For his music, which shows the influence of Buddhist philosophy, Mayuzumi has adapted Japanese instrumental techniques. His works include *Ectoplasme* (1953), *Bunraku* (1960), the cantata *Pratidesana* (1963), *Showa tempyo raku* (1970) for *gagaku* orchestra, the opera *Kinkakuji* (1976), and many film scores.

Mazeppa 1. Tone poem by Liszt based upon the poem by Victor Hugo. Composed: 1851. Mazeppa was a Ukrainian Cossack king and in this work Liszt describes his life and death. The tone poem is based partly upon one of his *Etudes d'exécution transcendente* for piano, also composed in 1851 and known as the 'Mazeppa Etude.' **2.** Opera by Tchaikovsky with libretto by the composer and Burenin based on Pushkin's *Poltava*. First performance: Moscow, 1884.

mazurka A Polish dance originating from the Mazovia region during the 17th century. It is in triple time with offbeat accents and can vary in pace from slow to fast. Groups of 4, 8, or 12 dancers performed the mazurka to improvised music. The accents were accompanied by heel tapping. The varying expressive moods and speeds of the form are reflected in Chopin's 55 mazurkas for piano: these display advanced chromaticism, pianistic virtuosity, and nuances of melody and harmony that suggest the form's folk origins. Szymanowski, Glinka, and Borodin also composed mazurkas for piano.

Mc- For names beginning Mc, see under **Mac.**

M.D. See **r.h.**

me see **tonic sol-fa.**

mean-tone scale see **temperament.**

measure 1. See **bar. 2.** A poetical name for a dance or dance tune.

Médée (*Medea*) Opera in three acts by Cherubini with French libretto by François Benoît Hoffman based on Euripedes. First performance: Théâtre Feydeau, Paris, 1797. Medea (soprano) avenges herself on Jason (tenor), murdering their children and Jason's new wife, Glauce (soprano).

mediant The third note of the major or minor *scale above the *tonic. For example, E is the mediant in the scale of C major. See also **degree.**

Medium, The Opera in two acts by Menotti with text by the composer. First performance: Columbia University, New York, 1946. Monica (soprano) is caught between the world of reality, which she cannot understand, and the world of the supernatural, in which she cannot believe.

Medtner, Nicolai (1880–1951) Russian composer, a pupil of Taniev. Concert tours in Europe (1900–02) established Medtner's reputation as a pianist and composer. He left the Soviet Union in 1921, settling in France and, later, England. In his music, Medtner eschewed nationalist influences in an attempt to create a classically based idiom. His output includes *Thirty-four Fairy-tales* (1905–29), a *Sonata-Triad* (1904–08), and other piano works and three piano concertos.

Mefistofele (*Mephistopheles*) Opera in four acts, prologue, and epilogue by Boito with libretto by the composer based on both parts of Goethe's *Faust*. First performance: La Scala, Milan, 1868. Boito himself was librettist for Verdi's *Otello* and *Falstaff*.

Mehta, Zubin (1936–) Indian conductor. Initially a pianist and double-bass player, Mehta was launched as a conductor by winning an international conducting competition at Liverpool in 1958. He was director of the Los Angeles Philharmonic Orchestra (1961–78), and is Music Director for life to the Israel Philharmonic Orchestra (1968–), and Music Director of the New York Philharmonic Orchestra (1978–).

Méhul, Etienne-Nicolas (1763–1817) French composer. He was taught by the German organist Wilhelm Hanser and in Paris (from about 1778) by Jean-Frédéric Edelmann. He was greatly influenced by Gluck, whom he may have met in Paris, and began to compose operas, his opéras comiques being particularly significant. *Euphrosine* (1790), Méhul's first opera to be performed, made him famous and he became one of the foremost composers of the Revolution. He was appointed one of five inspectors of the newly founded Paris Conservatoire (1795). His most

Etienne-Nicolas Méhul

Zubin Mehta

famous opéra comique, *Joseph* (1807), was also his last important operatic work. He suffered progressively from ill health and died of tuberculosis.

Méhul's other operas include *Cora* (1789), *Adrien* (*c*.1791), *Stratonice* (1792), *Le Jenne sage et le vieux fou* (1793), *Mélidore et Phrosine* (1794), *Adriodant* (1799), and *Les Amazones* (1811). He also composed ballets, cantatas, symphonies, patriotic songs, notably the *Chant du départ* (1794), and piano sonatas.

Meistersinger (*sing.* and *pl.*) A member of a German literary and musical guild of the 14th to the 17th centuries. The Meistersinger were generally artisans who formed themselves into guilds for composing and performing Meisterlieder (monophonic unaccompanied songs in accepted formulae). The guilds themselves were organized according to strict regulations and flourished particularly in the 16th century as a continuation of the *Minnesinger tradition. Hans Sachs (1494–1576) was a celebrated Meistersinger. Wagner's opera *Die Meistersinger von Nürnberg* (1868) conveys a romanticized view of the Meistersinger. [German, mastersinger]

Meistersinger von Nürnberg, Die (*The Mastersingers of Nuremberg*) Opera in three acts by Wagner with text by the composer. First performance: Royal Court Theatre, Munich, 1868. Set in 16th-century Nuremberg, it is the love story of the knight Walther (tenor) and Eva (soprano), whose hand will be awarded by her father, Pogner (bass), to the winner of the Mastersingers' contest. Walther

eventually wins the contest. The opera is Wagner's own protest at the prejudiced critics who for long refused him recognition.

Melba, Dame Nellie (Helen Armstrong; 1861–1931) Australian soprano. After studying in Paris with Mathilde Marchesi she made her debut at Brussels in 1887 and at Covent Garden in 1888. She began her career by singing brilliant coloratura parts; later she excelled as Mimi in Puccini's *La Bohème*. Saint-Saëns wrote for her. Melba became a DBE in 1918.

Melchior, Lauritz (1890–1973) Danish tenor. Considered the greatest heroic tenor of the 20th century, he studied with Paul Bang at Copenhagen, making his debut there as Silvio in Mascagni's *Pagliacci* (1913). His performances as Siegfried and Tristan in Wagner's operas were legendary: he sang Tristan over 200 times.

melisma 1. In plainsong, a group of notes set to a single syllable. Such passages are described as **melismatic. 2.** A melody of a lyrical rather than a declamatory nature; hence, in instrumental music, melodic fragments woven over sustained chords (as in Vaughan Williams' *The Lark Ascending*). [Greek, song]

Mellers, Wilfrid (1914–) British music critic and composer. Educated at Cambridge, he has written books on Couperin and modern US music. Professor of Music at York since 1964, he has composed operas and vocal and instrumental works.

Mellnäs, Arne (1933–) Swedish composer, a pupil of Blomdahl, Blacher, and Ligeti. He is especially interested in textures and has made much use of tape. His works include *Aura* (1964), the television ballet *Kaleidovision* (1969), *Dream* (1970) for chorus, *Fragile* (1973) for any instruments, *Blow* (1974) for wind, and a church opera, *Erik the Holy* (1976).

mellophone (*or* **tenor cor** *or* **tenor horn**) A simplified version of the orchestral *horn, used in marching bands. It resembles the cornet but has a larger flanged bell. It is made in F and in E♭.

melodeon A type of *accordion in which the melody is played with the right hand on buttons arranged to play diatonic scales in one or two keys. In some instruments accidentals are provided by separate buttons. The left hand has a set of accompanying chords and notes, usually produced by four buttons for each key. Each button produces a different note, according to whether the bellows are being closed or opened. The instrument is popular in Germany and central Europe.

melodic minor scale see **minor scale**.

mélodie Melody; song. [French]

melodrama A dramatic performance midway between an opera and a play with spoken words and background music. Such a work for a single character is called a **monodrama**. Possibly originating in ancient Greece, it became established towards the end of the 18th century with Georg Benda's *Ariadne auf Naxos* (1775). Beethoven's *Fidelio* (1805) and Weber's *Der Freischütz* (1821) have monodrama scenes. More recent examples include Schoenberg's monodrama *Erwartung* (1909) and *Pierrot lunaire* (1912), an evolution of melodrama with sprechstimme.

melody A succession of notes that have a recognizable pattern of pitch variation and sometimes a recognizable rhythmic and harmonic pattern. These three components –melody, *rhythm, and *harmony – are the basic characteristics of music. Some melodies are extremely simple, yet remain popular for centuries; others are forgotten as soon as they are heard. It is difficult to say what distinguishes one kind from the other, but all memorable music is melodic. Several famous 19th-century character pieces were named melodies; for example, Anton Rubinstein's *Melody in F*.

membranophone A musical *instrument in which the sound is produced by the vibration of a stretched membrane or skin. Membranophones include all forms of *drums. Compare **aerophone; chordophone; idiophone**.

Mendelssohn, Felix (Jacob Ludwig Felix Mendelssohn-Bartholdy; 1809–47) German composer. Son of a banker and grandson of the Jewish philosopher Moses Men-

Mendelssohn, an engraving after E. Magnus

delssohn, Mendelssohn was a child prodigy, who studied under Zelter in Berlin. The name Bartholdy, belonging to a maternal uncle, was adopted by the family when they considered it expedient to convert to Christianity. The young Mendelssohn gave his first public performance (in a chamber concert) aged 9 and wrote his first symphony at 15. He composed the overture to A *Midsummer Night's Dream* at 17, the rest of the incidental music to Shakespeare's play being completed in 1842.

At an early age he became a passionate advocate of the neglected music of J. S. Bach, conducting the *St Matthew Passion* in 1829. In this year he paid the first of many visits to England, where his music became very popular and was much admired by Queen Victoria. During a holiday in Scotland he formed the impressions that inspired his overture The *Hebrides* (1830) and the *Scottish Symphony* (3rd symphony; first performed 1842), which he dedicated to Queen Victoria. During a visit to Rome he began his *Italian Symphony* (4th symphony; first performed 1833). After a two-year spell as director of music in Düsseldorf, in 1835 Mendelssohn was appointed conductor of the Gewandhaus concerts in Leipzig, where he later founded the conservatory in which, together with Schumann, he taught composition.

Mendelssohn's two oratorios, *St Paul (first performed Düsseldorf, 1836) and *Elijah* (1846), greatly added to the popularity of his music in England; *Elijah* was given its first performance at the Birmingham Festival with the composer conducting. Mendelssohn began his violin concerto (Op.

64, in E minor) in 1838, but although normally a fast worker, this highly lyrical expression of the romantic movement occupied him for some six years. After the death of his sister, Fanny, in 1847 Mendelssohn's own health deteriorated and he died later in the same year.

In addition to his five symphonies (the last was the *Reformation Symphony, 1830), Mendelssohn wrote the overture Die *Schöne Melusine (1833), the cantata *Hymn of Praise (1840), two piano concertos, seven string quartets, a considerable amount of other chamber music, six organ sonatas, and the popular *Songs Without Words (1832–45) for piano.

Mengelberg, Willem (1871–1951) Dutch conductor. He became conductor of the Amsterdam Concertgebouw Orchestra (1895), a position he held until the end of World War II, when he was banned from conducting in the Netherlands because of his wartime Nazi sympathies. He was a great interpreter of Beethoven and Mahler.

Mennin, Peter (1923–83) US composer. Mennin was appointed director of the Juilliard school of music in 1962. His compositions are strongly romantic in their inspiration: they include eight symphonies, concertos for piano and cello, and other orchestral works, chamber music, and songs.

meno mosso A direction indicating that a slower pace is required. Hence **poco meno** (**mosso**), a little slower. [Italian, less moved]

Menotti, Gian-Carlo (1911–) Italian-born US composer. After studying in Milan (1923–27), Menotti emi-grated to the USA. There he established a reputation as an opera composer with such works as Amelia Goes to the Ball (1937), The *Medium (1946), and The *Consul (1950), in which the composer's skill in writing dramatically effective libretti is matched by his communicative music. Menotti's style stems from the Italian operatic tradition, its lyricism tempered by dissonant orchestral writing at the climaxes. Other operas by Menotti include The *Telephone (1947), *Amahl and the Night Visitors (1951; a Christmas opera written for television), The *Unicorn, the Gorgon, and the Manticore (1958), and The Most Important Man (1971).

Menuhin, Sir Yehudi (1916–) US-born British violinist. He began playing the violin at the age of four and made his professional debut in San Francisco at the age of seven, causing a sensation with his performance of Mendelssohn's violin concerto. He later became a pupil of Enescu in Paris. He was coached by Elgar for the 1932 performance of the composer's violin concerto and Bartók, among others, has written for him. His interest in Indian music has been furthered by the sitarist Ravi Shankar, with whom he has performed duets. Menuhin moved to England in 1959 and directed the Bath Festival from then until 1968. In 1962 he opened a boarding school for musically talented children at Stoke d'Abernon, near London. His sister **Hephzibah Menuhin** (1920–80), a pianist, partnered him in recitals and made appearances as a soloist, especially in Australia. His other sister, **Yaltah Menuhin** (1922–), and his son **Jeremy Menuhin** (1951–), who made his debut at Gstaad in 1965, are also pianists.

Gian-Carlo Menotti

Yehudi Menuhin

Mephistopheles see Mefistofele.

Mephisto Waltzes Four waltzes for piano by Liszt, the title alluding to the Faustian character Mephistopheles. Composed: 1860–86. The first Mephisto Waltz originally appeared in an orchestral version as the second movement of the *Episodes from Lenau's *Faust*; the second waltz was similarly composed for orchestra and then transcribed for piano. Neither of the other two waltzes exists in an orchestral arrangement and the final work was left uncompleted at Liszt's death.

Mer, La (*The Sea*) Set of three symphonic sketches for orchestra by Debussy. First performance: 1905. Each movement describes a different mood of the sea and this work is one of the most important products of impressionism. The movements are entitled 'De l'aube à midi sur la mer' ('From Dawn to Midday on the Sea'), 'Jeux de vagues' ('Play of the Waves'), and 'Dialogue du vent et de la mer' ('Dialogue of the Wind and Sea').

Merbecke (*or* **Marbeck**), **John** (*c*.1508–*c*.1585) English composer and writer. In 1531 he was a clerk and organist at St George's Chapel, Windsor. In 1543 he was arrested for his Calvinist views but was reprieved by Henry VIII. He returned to Windsor and compiled his English biblical concordance (1550), the first of its kind. Merbecke wrote a setting for the first *Book of Common Prayer* in 1550; this consists of plainsong adaptations following natural speech rhythms and is still sung. Other works are a polyphonic mass, two motets, and an anthem.

Mercadante, (Giuseppe) Saverio (Raffaele) (1795–1870) Italian composer and teacher, a pupil of Zingarelli at the Naples conservatory (1808–20). From 1820 he concentrated almost exclusively on writing operas (he wrote 60). He visited Spain and Portugal (1826–27), becoming musical director of the Italian Opera in Madrid (1830–31); he was maestro di cappella of Novara Cathedral. His early operas were in the Rossinian mould, but in 1835 he went to Paris, where he was impressed and influenced by Meyerbeer's music; the first of his works to reflect a more cosmopolitan and dramatic approach was *Il Giuramento* (1837). From 1840 to his death he was director of the Naples conservatory. Although Mercadante's operas were popular and influential in his lifetime, they rapidly disappeared from the repertory. The best known are *Elisa e Claudio* (1821), *I Briganti* (1836), and *Orazi e Curiazi* (1846). He also wrote ballets, much church music, orchestral and chamber works, and songs.

Mercury Symphony Symphony No. 43 in E♭ major by Haydn. Composed: *c*.1771. This nickname was coined in the 19th century, although its derivation is not certain. As the work is noticeably one of Haydn's lighter symphonies,

The Merry Widow *by the English National Opera, 1986*

it is probable that the title refers to the mercurial character of all the movements.

Merrie England Opera by Edward German with text by Hood. First performance: Savoy Theatre, London, 1902. It is set in the time of Queen Elizabeth I.

Merry Widow, The (German: *Die Lustige Witwe*) Operetta by Lehár with libretto by Leon and Stein. First performance: Theater an der Wien, Vienna, 1905. It is a light-weight story of romance and diplomatic intrigue.

Merry Wives of Windsor, The (German: *Die Lustigen Weiber von Windsor*) Opera in three acts by Nicolai with libretto by von Mosenthal based on Shakespeare's comedy. First performance: Opera, Berlin, 1849.

Merulo, Claudio (1533–1604) Italian composer, organist, and publisher. In 1556 he became organist at Brescia and then at St Mark's, Venice. In 1586 he moved to Parma as organist to the duke and the company of the Steccata. Merulo's organ compositions present innovatory ideas on ornamentation and his toccatas allow for improvisation. Other works include madrigals and sacred music.

messa Mass. Hence **messa per i defunti**, mass for the dead, i.e. requiem mass. [Italian]

messa di voce A technique of increasing and then decreasing the power of the voice while singing a long-held note. The practice was especially common in Italy in the 18th century. [Italian, placing of the voice]

Messager, André (1853–1929) French composer, a pupil of Saint-Saëns. Messager conducted the Paris Opera (1907–15); from 1908 he directed the Paris Conservatoire

Olivier Messiaen with the score of Turingalila

orchestra. His output consists mostly of operas and operettas; other works include a symphony (1875) and chamber music.

messe Mass. Hence **messe des morts** (French), mass of the dead, i.e. requiem mass. [French and German]

Messiaen, Olivier (1908–) French composer and organist, a pupil of Dukas and Dupré. In his early works he developed a modal harmony directly opposed to atonality and neoclassicism. The rhythmic complexity of his music derives from the techniques of Stravinsky in *The Rite of Spring* and has been influenced by oriental music. Catholic mysticism has always been a strong element in Messiaen's work and is an expression of his religious beliefs. For melodic material he later made much use of bird song, and some works of the late 1950s use this for their entire construction. Messiaen has been immensely influential both as a composer and a teacher. His works include *L'Ascension* (1934), *Quatuor pour le fin de temps* (1941), the symphony *Turangalîla* (1948), *Reveil des oiseaux* (1953), *Chronocromie* (1960), *La Transfiguration* (1969), and *Des Canyons aux etoiles* (1974), in addition to songs and organ and piano music.

Messiah Oratorio for solo voices, choir, and orchestra by Handel to a text arranged from the Bible by Charles Jennens. First performance: 1742. The three parts of this oratorio tell the events of Jesus' life and death and several individual pieces have become famous in their own right, including the *Hallelujah Chorus* and the aria 'I know that my Redeemer liveth.' *Messiah* was Handel's most popular oratorio and today is one of the most frequently performed of all oratorios.

mesto Sad; mournful. [Italian]

metà Half. [Italian]

Metamorphoses Work for 23 solo strings by Richard Strauss. Composed: 1945. Strauss was inspired to write this work after the bombing of many of the German opera houses in which his works had received their first performances. It was never his intention to compose a lament for Nazi Germany, although this claim is often erroneously made. The score is subtitled 'In Memoriam' and includes a quotation from the funeral march of Beethoven's *Eroica Symphony*. The metamorphoses of the title refers to the constant transformations of the principle themes throughout the work.

metamorphosis The technique of transforming the character of a single musical idea by altering its rhythm, meter, mode, or instrumental colouring (or any combination of these) to represent various moods or poetic ideas. Metamorphosis was used by Berlioz (notably in the *Fantastic Symphony*) but was first fully exploited by Liszt, who employed it regularly in his tone poems. It is also prominent in the *leitmotiv technique of Wagner and Richard Strauss and exerted an influence on the *cyclic form employed in the symphonies of Tchaikovsky, Franck, and Mahler.

metre 1. The rhythmic relationship of the syllables in a line of verse or the lines in a stanza. **2.** A similar relationship in music between the beats in a bar and the bars in a *phrase. See **accent; rhythm.**

metronome A device that enables the tempo of a piece of music to be specified accurately. The traditional metronome is a clockwork instrument with an adjustable pendulum, patented in 1814 by J. N. *Maelzel. A composer or editor wishing to indicate the tempo of a piece writes at the head of it the letters MM (to signify 'Maelzel's metronome') followed by a crotchet and a number. The number indicates the number of crotchet beats per minute. Pocket metronomes, resembling a watch, are also in use.

Metropolitan Opera House An opera house in New York, home of the USA's leading opera company. It opened in 1883 with a performance of a Gounod opera. During the 1880s and 1890s many German operas were given there and the house quickly attracted international artists. The world's leading singers, including Caruso, Shalyapin, Melba, Flagstad, and Callas, have performed there. The Metropolitan's repertory is very wide and the US premieres of many European operas have been staged there. In 1966 the company moved to the Lincoln Center, New York. Among its conductors have been Leopold Damrosch,

Gustav Mahler, Arturo Toscanini, Tullio Serafin, and James Levine.

Meyer, Kerstin (1928–) Swedish mezzo-soprano. A pupil of Arne Sunnegarth and Andreyeva von Skoldonz in Stockholm, she later studied in Europe. She gave first performances of roles in modern operas by Goehr, Maw, Schuller, and Searle. Later she sang at Glyndebourne, New York, and Bayreuth.

Meyerbeer, Giacomo (Jakob Liebmann Meyer Beer; 1791–1864) German composer. He was from a musical family and made his first public appearances as a pianist before he was 11. After studying in Darmstadt with Vogler (1810–12) he continued as a pianist and began composing German operas. In 1813 he became court composer to the Duke of Hesse; he travelled to Vienna, Munich, Paris, and London (1815). He went to Italy in 1816 to study and collect folk songs and stayed there for nine years, producing six successful Italian operas, including *Il Crociato in Egitto* (1824), which established Meyerbeer as an international figure. He met Eugène Scribe, with whom he collaborated on almost all his remaining operas, starting with *Robert le diable* (1831) and *Les *Huguenots* (1836), grand operas that were triumphs in Paris. From 1842 to 1848 Meyerbeer was general music director in Berlin; for the reopening of the opera house there he composed *Ein Feldlager in Schlesein* (1844), in which Jenny Lind sang the principal role. His *Le Prophète* (1849) and *L'Etoile du nord* (1854) were successful in Paris; he died while his last and grandest opera, *L'*Africaine*, was being rehearsed. In addition to his operas, Meyerbeer also composed choral, orchestral, and piano music and many songs.

mezzo (*or fem.* **mezza**) Half. Hence **mezzo-forte** (abbreviation: **mf**), half-loud, i.e. midway between loud and soft; **mezza voce**, at half voice, i.e. half power. [Italian]

mezzo-soprano The middle voice of the three varieties of female voices. The timbre of the mezzo-soprano combines some of the rich quality of the *contralto with the brightness of the *soprano. Its range is from A below middle C to F an octave and a sixth above. The vast repertoire of solo songs written for the female voice is more suited to the mezzo-soprano than to either of the other two voices.

mf Abbreviation for mezzo-forte (see **mezzo**).

M.G. See l.h.

mi see **solmization**.

Miaskovsky, Nicolai (1881–1951) Soviet composer, a pupil of Rimsky-Korsakov. From 1921 Miaskovsky taught at the Moscow conservatory. His large output includes 27 symphonies, chamber music (including 13 string quartets), piano pieces, and songs.

Meyerbeer was noted for his romantic operas

Michelangeli, Arturo Benedetti (1920–) Italian pianist. He studied at the Milan conservatory and won the international piano competition at Geneva. Since World War II he has toured widely, establishing a worldwide reputation as an outstanding performer; at the same time he holds appointments at several European teaching centres.

microtonality A system of composing music using a *scale or scales having smaller *intervals than a semitone. See also **microtone**.

microtone (*or* **fractional tone**) An interval that is smaller than a *semitone. Julián Carrillo devised a scale using microtones as well as instruments to play them. *Quarter tones have been used by Bloch, Bartók, and others.

middle C The note C situated approximately at the centre of the piano keyboard. It has a frequency of 261.6 hertz (A = 440 hertz).

Midi, Le see **Matin, Le**.

Midsummer Marriage, The Opera in three acts by Tippett with libretto by the composer. First performance: Covent Garden, London, 1955. Like Mozart's *The Magic Flute*, this opera is concerned with the need for two pairs of lovers – Mark (tenor) and Jenifer (soprano), Bella (soprano) and Jack (tenor) – to undergo a trial to achieve enlightenment before their love can be consummated. King Fisher (baritone), Jenifer's father, provides the necessary

A production of
The Mikado in modern
dress performed by mem-
bers of the English National
Opera in 1986

human sacrifice. The *Ritual Dances* form the musical core of the opera.

Midsummer Night's Dream, A 1. Incidental music by Mendelssohn for the play by Shakespeare. Composed: 1842. The overture was composed as a separate work in 1826 and included in the incidental music, which also contains the well-known *Wedding March*, for a production of the play in Potsdam in 1843. 2. Incidental music by Carl Orff for Shakespeare's play. Composed: 1939. 3. Opera in three acts by Britten with text by the composer and Peter Pears taken from Shakespeare. First performance: Aldeburgh Festival, 1960. The fairies, particularly Oberon (countertenor), are the framework of the opera; the music is sharply differentiated for fairies, mortals (lovers), and rustics.

Mighty Handful, The see **Five, The.**

Mignon Opera in three acts by Ambroise Thomas with libretto by Barbier and Carré based on Goethe's *Wilhelm Meister*. First performance: Opéra-Comique, Paris, 1866. Mignon (mezzo-soprano), stolen by Gypsies in childhood, is loved by the student Wilhelm (tenor), who restores her to her father Lothario (bass) and castle home.

Mihalovici, Marcel (1898–1985) Romanian-born composer who settled in France, a pupil of d'Indy. His style is basically neoclassical, showing the influence of Stravinsky and Bartók. His works include five symphonies; chamber music; operas, including *Krapp* (1960); orchestral music, such as *Prétextes* (1968); *Chant premier* (1974); *Follia* (1977); and much incidental music. He married the pianist Monique *Haas.

Mihály, András (1917–) Hungarian composer, active as a teacher and conductor. Mihály's early works show the influences of Bartók and Kodály; in his later compositions, such as the orchestral *Monodia* (1970), he uses avant-garde techniques.

Mikado, The Operetta by Sullivan with libretto by Gilbert, subtitled *The Town of Titipu*. First performance: Savoy Theatre, London, 1885. With its Japanese setting, *The Mikado* proved one of the most successful of the Gilbert and Sullivan operettas, initially running continuously for 672 nights.

Mikrokosmos Collection of short piano pieces by Bartók. Composed: 1926–37. Each of the 153 pieces is based upon a particular technical problem or feature of piano writing. The title (Greek, microcosm) alludes to the concentrated attention given to individual problems of performance.

Milán, Luis de (*c*.1500–*c*.1561) Spanish composer. He was active at the court in Valencia until at least 1538. His *El Maestro* (1536) is the earliest collection of music for the vihuela and the earliest publication to include tempo indications.

Milanese chant see **Ambrosian chant.**

Milford, Robin (1903–59) British composer, a pupil of Holst and Vaughan Williams. Milford's style was strongly influenced by folk songs; his output includes orchestral and chamber music and songs.

Milhaud, Darius (1892–1974) French composer, a member of Les *Six. Milhaud studied at the Paris Conservatoire with Gédalge and Widor. While still a student he became associated with such figures as Satie, Cocteau, and the poet Claudel; with Claudel he visited Brazil (1917–18). Milhaud continued to travel widely throughout the 1920s and 1930s, often drawing on experiences of different national musics in his own works. He made many visits to the USA as a teacher, pianist, and conductor. Milhaud's compositions explore many stylistic and technical influences, creating a highly personal idiom. Polytonality features in some of his works; other influences include South American music and jazz. His prolific output includes the ballets *Le Boeuf sur le toit* (1919), *L'*Homme et son desir* (1921), and *La *Creation du monde* (1923), the latter particularly influenced by jazz; operas, such as *Christophe Colomb* (1930); 12 symphonies and other orchestral works; chamber music; piano works, including *Saudades do Brasil* (1921–22); and songs.

military band A band of brass, woodwind, and percussion. The term originally referred only to regimental marching bands (e.g. army and navy) but it is now applied to any band of a similar constitution. The instrumentation of military bands varies but in Britain it is generally flute, piccolo, oboe, clarinets, bassoons, saxophones, horns, cornets (or trumpets), trombones, euphoniums, tubas, and percussion. A double bass is often added for performances when the band is not marching.

Military Symphony Symphony No. 100 in G major by Haydn. Composed: 1794. The scoring of the second movement (allegretto) includes parts for triangle, cymbals, and bass drum and the effect created is an imitation of a military band. This symphony is one of the so-called *Salomon Symphonies*.

Millöcker, Carl (1842–99) Austrian composer. He studied at the Vienna conservatory (1855–58), then held conducting posts in several theatres in Graz and Budapest and in Vienna at the Theater an der Wien (1866–67, 1869–83). Millöcker was a very successful composer of operettas: his works in this genre rank with those of Johann Strauss and Suppé. Among the best known are *Der *Bettelstudent* (1882), *Gasparone* (1884), and *Der Arme Jonathan* (1890); he also wrote other works for the stage and vocal music.

Milner, Anthony (1925–) British composer, a pupil of Seiber. Milner teaches at the Royal College of Music and at London University. His music adheres to traditional concepts of melody, often in textures of great contrapuntal ingenuity. Milner's works include a symphony (1972), much choral music, chamber music, and songs.

Milnes, Sherril (1935–) US baritone. He studied with Andrew White and Hermanus Baer in the USA and has since sung and recorded all important Verdi baritone roles. He is married to the soprano Nancy Stokes.

Milstein, Nathan (Mironovich) (1904–) Russian-born pianist, a pupil of Leopold Auer and Eugène Ysaÿe. In 1925 he left the Soviet Union with Vladimir Horowitz on a concert tour; they decided to remain abroad and Milstein

became a US citizen in 1942. He has published a number of violin transcriptions.

Milton, John (1563–1647) English amateur composer. Educated at Christ Church, Oxford, he went to London in 1585 and became a wealthy member of the Scriveners' Company. His music was highly regarded and he contributed to *The Triumphs of Oriana* (1601). His son was the poet **John Milton** (1608–74). Of the many vocal works based on his writings perhaps the best known are *Samson* (1743), an oratorio by Handel based on *Samson Agonistes*, and *The Creation* (1798) by Haydn.

mime A staged work with imitative or mimic action but without speech. It may be accompanied by music. In ancient Greece a mimic actor was accompanied by the *aulos.

min see **chord**.

minacciando Menacing; threatening. [Italian]

Mines of Sulphur, The Opera by Richard Rodney Bennett with libretto by Beverley Cross. First performance: London, 1965. The title of this ghost story is taken from a passage in Shakespeare's *Othello*.

miniature score A full orchestral *score of a work reduced in size (usually to about 185mm by 140mm) to make it suitable for following the score during a performance. Normally only the conductor has a full score, individual orchestral players having only their own parts. The introduction of miniature scores made it possible for students and others to have a full score of manageable size and cost to study the main works of the orchestral repertoire.

minim A note, originally having the shortest time value. In modern notation it is written as an open circle with a tail and has half the value of a *semibreve or twice the value of a crotchet. US: **half note**. See **Appendix, Table 1.** [from Latin *minima*, shortest]

Minkus, Léon (Aloysius Ludwig M.; 1826–1917) Austrian-born composer, violinist, and conductor, of Czech or Polish origin, who worked in Russia. He was conductor of the Bolshoi Theatre orchestra, Moscow (1862–72), and from 1866 taught the violin at the Moscow conservatory. From 1872 to 1891 he was ballet composer to the imperial theatres in St Petersburg. Minkus's many ballets were popular in his day; they include *Don Quixote* (1869) and *Mlada* (1879) and he collaborated with Delibes on *La Source* (1866).

Minnesinger (*sing.* and *pl.*) A member of a German literary and musical courtly circle of the 12th to the 14th centuries. The Minnesinger were aristocratic (unlike the *Meistersinger) and very similar to the *troubadours and *trouvères in France. Their songs (Minnesang) were chiefly concerned with courtly love and were accompanied by instruments.

Among the most famous Minnesinger were Walther von der Vogelweide (d. 1230) and Neidhart von Reuental (*c.*1180–1240). Wagner's opera *Tannhäuser* and Strauss's *Guntram* are about the Minnesinger. [German, love singer]

minor interval see **interval.**

minor scale A diatonic *scale that exists in two forms: the **harmonic minor scale** and the **melodic minor scale**. In the harmonic form the *intervals between the notes are: 1–2 tone, 2–3 semitone, 3–4 tone, 4–5 tone, 5–6 semitone, 6–7 augmented second, 7–8 semitone. The melodic form is the same as the harmonic except that in ascending the intervals 5–6 and 6–7 are each a tone and in descending 8–7 and 7–6 are each a tone and 6–5 is a semitone. The melodic form thus avoids the augmented second interval of the harmonic form.

Each minor scale has a *relative major scale starting three semitones above it, with which it shares the same *key signature. Thus A minor is the relative minor to C major and C minor is the relative minor of E♭ major. A **minor key** is the *key based on the minor scale of the same name, having the same key signature as its relative major key. A **minor chord** is a *chord based on the scale of the same name.

minstrel A professional entertainer from the 12th to the 17th centuries. The term is more particularly applied to professional musicians, usually instrumentalists, of 14th- and 15th-century France. Minstrels usually belonged to a guild and fulfilled various social and court functions. They generally accompanied their own singing and were similar to *jongleurs. See also **Meistersinger; Minnesinger; troubadour; trouvère.**

Minton, Yvonne (1938–) Australian soprano. Her series of male roles began in 1965, as Rinaldo in Handel's opera; it also included Octavian in *Rosenkavalier*, which she described as 'a woman playing a man playing a woman.' She is a celebrated interpreter of Berlioz.

minuet A triple-time rustic dance that originated in France and became extremely popular throughout Europe in the mid-17th century. During the baroque period an instrumental form was frequently used as one of the movements of the *suite. During the classical period it was incorporated into the *sonata. Here it was most usually accompanied by a *trio, also in triple time, which created a recurring musical form, ABA. The **minuet and trio** was the most frequent form of third movement in the classical symphony, offering light relief after a tense slow movement and before an agitated finale. The adoption of a progressively quicker tempo for this movement led to the development of the *scherzo and trio. French: **menuet**; German: **menuett**; Italian: **minuetto.**

Minute Waltz Waltz in D♭ (Op. 64 No. 1) by Chopin. Composed: 1847. If played at an extremely fast tempo the waltz lasts approximately one minute, but it was never the composer's intention that the piece should be performed in this manner.

Miracle, The Symphony No. 96 in D major by Haydn. Composed: 1791. The name is derived from a story (now known to be untrue) according to which, during the first performance of the symphony, a chandelier fell from the ceiling of the concert hall but amazingly harmed no-one. See also **Salomon Symphonies.**

Miracle in the Gorbals Ballet in one act with music by Bliss, scenario by Michael Benthall, and choreography by Helpmann. First performance: Princes Theatre, London, 1944, by the Sadler's Wells Ballet. Set in the slums of Glasgow, it tells how Christ is reborn in contemporary society and again suffers the Passion and death.

Miraculous Mandarin, The (Hungarian: *A csodálatos mandarin*) Pantomime-ballet in one act with music by Bartók and libretto by Lengyel. First performance: Cologne, 1926. It is a melodrama about three pimps who force a prostitute to rob her customers.

Mireille Opera in three acts (originally five) by Gounod with libretto by Carré based on Mistral's poem *Mireio*. First performance: Théâtre-Lyrique, Paris, 1864. Gounod gave his romantic love story alternative endings in which Mireille (soprano) either lives or dies.

mirliton An instrument in which a vibrating membrane is used to modify sounds made by singing, humming, or blowing. The simplest example is the comb and paper used by children or the toy **kazoo**, in which the membrane is placed half-way down a tube, one end of which is hummed into.

mirror writing A strict form of *inversion in which an extended passage or complete piece is inverted in its entirety. Sometimes the inverted form functions as an equally valid alternative to the original (as in 'Contrapunctus XII' and 'Contrapunctus XIII' of Bach's *The Art of Fugue*); more commonly the two are heard simultaneously (as in Peter Racine Fricker's 12 studies for piano). In 'Chromatic Inversion' from Bartók's *Mikrocosmos VI* the two forms can either be played separately or simultaneously on two pianos.

Miserere The words of Psalm 51, which begin *Miserere mei, Deus* ('Have mercy on me, O God') and are sung at the Roman Catholic office of Lauds at Passiontide and at the Office for the Dead. Simple polyphonic settings in fauxbourdon style (see **faburden**) have been made by Josquin and Allegri – the embellishments of the latter have contributed to its fame. Cantus-firmus keyboard settings of the chant were made by English composers of the 16th and 17th centuries.

Mislivecek, Josef see **Myslivecek, Josef.**

missa *Mass. Hence **missa solemnis**, a fully sung celebration of the Mass with elaborate music; **missa brevis**, a concise musical setting of the Mass, with examples by Palestrina and Britten; **Missa pro defunctis**, Requiem Mass. [Latin]

Missa Papae Marcelli Setting of the Mass for six voices by Palestrina. Composed: c.1555. The title is in honour of Pope Marcellus II, who was crowned and reigned for a short time in 1555 (the precise date of composition is disputed –the work may have been written slightly later). The mass is free in form (i.e. not based on any pre-existing material) and follows closely the dictates of the Council of Trent with its exceptionally clear setting of the words.

misura Measure: used to indicate either musical time measurement in general, as in **senza misura**, without keeping strict time; or in the particular sense of a *bar. [Italian]

Mitropoulos, Dimitri (1896–1960) Greek conductor and pianist. He conducted in Berlin and Paris and subsequently the USA, where he directed the Minneapolis Symphony Orchestra (1937–49) and the New York Philharmonic Orchestra (1949–58). He was a renowned interpreter of 20th-century music.

mixed media see **multimedia.**

mixed voices (*or* **mixed chorus**) A group made up of adult male and female singers.

Mixolydian mode see **modes.**

mixture stop An organ *stop used in conjunction with other stops to add brilliance in the bass and power in the treble. It brings into operation a group of pipes producing the higher harmonics of a note of a particular pitch. In general, a mixture introduces three to five *ranks, the number of ranks usually being indicated by roman figures.

MM Abbreviation for Maelzel's *metronome.

M.Mus. Master of Music.

moderato Moderate; at a moderate pace: also used in conjunction with other directions, e.g. **allegro moderato,** at a moderately lively speed. [Italian]

modes Forms of *scales that were originally used by the Greeks (based on the Pythagorean scale) and were later adapted by medieval musicians, especially for ecclesiastical music. The modes were based on what are now the white notes of the piano with certain differences of tuning (*see* **temperament**). By the 2nd century AD the Greeks were using the Pythagorean scale in seven

different ways. These were adapted in the 4th century by St Ambrose, Bishop of Milan, for church use in four modes, later known as the **authentic modes.** In the 6th century St Gregory the Great elaborated the Ambrosian modes and added four more, which became known as the **plagal modes.** These eight modes are known as the **church modes.** Finally, in the 16th century, the Swiss monk Henry of Glarus (Henricus Glareanus) set out 12 modes and assigned Greek names to them, although many of his identifications with the Greek modes were incorrect. Some of the 12 modes were of little practical use but with the development of harmony in music, two of Glareanus' modes (the **Ionian** and the **Aeolian**) were found to be the best suited to harmony and they became known, from the 17th century onwards, as the *major and *minor scales on which most music has since been based. The medieval modes themselves remain in use in plainsong and some folk music.

In the authentic modes (which were given odd numbers by Glareanus) a melody always ended on the last note of the scale, called the **final.** The plagal modes were formed from the same scale as the authentic modes but the compass was changed to put the final in the middle of the scale. They were named by adding the prefix *hypo-* to the corresponding authentic name (and were given even numbers). In each mode a **reciting note** (*or* **dominant**) was also established. This was normally a fifth above the final in the authentic modes and a third below this in the plagal modes (except where the note should be B, in which case C was substituted). The table gives the modes and their names (the **Locrian mode** – from B to B – was never in use).

The basic difference between the modern *key system and the modal system is that in the key system a change of key entails only a change of pitch – the scale itself is unchanged; in the modal system a change of mode involves a change in the position of the semitones in the scale, which means that music played in different modes sounds different.

number	Glareanus' name	Original Greek name	range	final	dominant
I	Dorian	Phrygian	D–D	D	A
II	Hypodorian	—	A–A	D	F
III	Phrygian	Dorian	E–E	E	C
IV	Hypophrygian	—	B–B	E	A
V	Lydian	Syntolydian	F–F	F	C
VI	Hypolydian	—	C–C	F	A
VII	Mixolydian	Ionian	G–G	G	D
VIII	Hypomixolydian	—	D–D	G	C
IX	Aeolian	Aeolian	A–A	A	E
X	Hypoaeolion	—	E–E	A	G
IX	Ionian	Lydian	C–C	C	C
XII	Hypoionian	—	G–G	C	E

modinha A Portuguese and Brazilian song form developed during the 18th and 19th centuries. It was strongly lyrical and combined aspects of Portuguese folk song with Italian opera. In the 18th century two sopranos might be accompanied by harpsichord and during the 19th century a solo voice was accompanied by guitar.

modo Mode; manner. See also **in modo di**. [Italian]

modulation A change of *key during the course of a composition in accordance with the rules of harmony. The most natural modulations are those in which the change is to a *related key (e.g. to a *relative major or minor key), to the key of the dominant and its relative major or minor, or to the key of the subdominant and its relative major or minor.

modulator A diagram in which the note names in the *tonic sol-fa system are arranged one above the other. It is used for instruction in sight reading and modulation, the teacher pointing to a note and the pupil singing it.

Moeran, Ernest John (1894–1950) British composer, a pupil of Ireland. Moeran's mature compositions show a balance between lyrical elements and a strong formal sense. His output includes a symphony in G minor (1934–37), concertos for violin and cello, chamber music, and songs.

Mohaupt, Richard (1904–57) German-born composer, who emigrated to the USA in 1939, where he taught and composed music for films. Mohaupt's music is characterized by simplicity within a progressive idiom; his works include operas and ballets, orchestral music, songs, and piano music.

Moïse see **Moses in Egypt**.

Moiseiwitsch, Benno (1890–1963) Russian-born British pianist. After studying in Vienna with Leschetizky he made his debut in Reading (1908). Moiseiwitsch made a series of worldwide tours and became a British citizen in 1937. He excelled in playing Rachmaninov's music.

Molière (Jean-Baptiste Poquelin; 1622–1673) French dramatist and originator of the comedy-ballet. Among these were *Le Mariage forcé* (1664) and *Le Bourgeois Gentilhomme* (1670), on which he collaborated with Lully. (Richard Strauss wrote incidental music for the latter, to precede his opera *Ariadne auf Naxos*.) Charpentier composed music for Molière's *Le Malade imaginaire* in 1673.

Molinari-Pradelli, Francesco (1911–) Italian conductor of opera. He has conducted at La Scala, San Carlo (Naples), and Covent Garden and in the USA.

Molinaro, Simone (c.1565–1615) Italian composer. By 1602 he was maestro di cappella at S Lorenzo, Genoa. Of his lute compositions, the *Ballo detto Il Conde Orlando* is the best known; it was arranged by Ottorino Respighi.

moll Minor (in key); e.g. **A moll**, A minor. [German]

Molloy, James Lyman (1837–1909) Irish composer. He was a barrister by profession but composed many popular songs, including 'Love's Old Sweet Song.'

Molter, Johann Melchior (1696–1765) German composer and violinist. From about 1717 he was in the service of the Margrave von Baden-Durlach, Karlsruhe; he became kapellmeister there (1722–33) and at the court of Saxe-Eisenach (1734–41), returning to Karlsruhe in 1742. Molter wrote many chamber works, symphonies, and concertos in the Mannheim style, as well as Italian cantatas and keyboard works.

molto Much; very. Hence **molto allegro**, very quickly. [Italian]

moment A formal concept introduced by Stockhausen as an attempt to help the listener overcome some of the difficulties of listening to serial music. It consists of the free use of a series of contrasting phrases, each known as a moment. Each moment is equal in status and equally dispensible. The composer does not move forwards from a fixed point in time but moves in all directions within cyclic limits. The moments may thus be arranged in any order to achieve an indeterminate *open form, as in Stockhausen's *Momente* (1961).

Moments musicals Six short lyrical pieces for piano (Op. 94) by Schubert. Composed: c.1827. The name was later used for works by Paderewski and Rachmaninov.

Monaco, Mario Del see **Del Monaco, Mario**.

Mondo della luna, Il (*The World on the Moon*) Opera by Haydn with libretto by Goldoni. First performance: Esterháza Palace, 1777, during the marriage celebrations of Count Nicholas Esterházy. Ecclitico (tenor), a bogus astrologer, manipulates his fellow humans in a tale of daughters and dowries, servants and masters; the moon itself is omnipresent in the role of *deus ex machina*.

Moniuszko, Stanislaw (1819–72) Polish composer. After studying in Berlin (1837–38) he returned to Poland and became a church organist in Vilnius; he taught the piano, conducted, and began composing. His opera *Halka* was performed in Vilnius in 1848 and in revised form in Warsaw in 1858, making Moniuszko's reputation as Poland's leading nationalist opera composer. In Warsaw he became conductor of the Grand Theatre (1859) and taught at the Music Institute. Moniuszko's operas include *The Raftsman* (1858), *The Countess* (1859), and *Verbum nobile* (1860). He wrote other stage works, choral music, and orchestral and chamber works; he was an important and popular songwriter, composing over 350 songs (267 of them were published in his *Songs for Home Use*).

Monk, William Henry (1823–89) British organist and composer. He was organist of several London churches, then became choirmaster (1847) and organist (1849) of King's College, London, where he was later (1874) appointed Professor of Vocal Music. Monk championed the use of plainchant in Anglican services. He wrote the hymn tune *Eventide* ('Abide with Me') and was musical editor of *Hymns Ancient and Modern* (1861).

Monn, Matthias Georg (1717–50) Austrian composer and organist. He was organist at St Charles, Vienna (*c*.1738), and is known primarily as the composer of the first four-movement symphony (1740), with the minuet in the third movement. As well as symphonies, he wrote concertos, chamber and keyboard works, and church music.

monochord A device consisting of a single stretched string supported above a soundbox by a movable bridge. It has been in use since ancient Egyptian times to demonstrate the relationship between the length of a string and the note it produces. It has also been used to teach singers to recognize intervals and to give the pitch to a player, although the tuning fork is now more usually used for this purpose. See also **tromba marina.**

monodrama see **melodrama.**

monody A style of composition that evolved around the end of the 16th century and was first used extensively by Caccini. Monody consisted of a single recitative-like melody presented over a simple chordal accompaniment and formed the basis of the first operas. The earliest use of monody can be found in Caccini's collection of songs *Le Nuove musiche* (1601). Compare **homophonic; monophony; polyphonic.** [Greek, single song]

monophony A composition having a single melodic part with no harmonic accompaniment. Compare **homophonic; monody; polyphonic.** [Greek, single sound]

monothematic Denoting a composition that is based on a single theme. This may apply not only to a piece that has only one movement but also to a larger composition having several movements.

Monte, Philippe de (1521–1603) Flemish composer. His early years were spent in Naples, the Netherlands, and England. He was maestro di cappella at the imperial court of Vienna from 1568 until the year of his death. He was a prolific composer, the author of 48 masses and 10 books of motets (1572–1600), a few chansons, and 36 books of madrigals (1554–1600). His music is remarkable for its avoidance of cliché; despite his tendency to understate the emotional meaning of the text, he was always a scrupulous observer of verbal rhythms and his madrigals show that he was well read in the latest and most fashionable literature. His madrigals after about 1580 adopt the more florid virtuoso style for higher voices common to Wert, Marenzio, and other Italians.

Montéclair, Michel Pinolet de (1667–1737) French composer, theorist, and violin teacher. A pupil of Moreau, he was maître de musique for the Prince de Vaudémont and one of the first double-bass players in the Paris Opéra orchestra. As well as opera-ballets and sacred and instrumental music, he also wrote important French and Italian cantatas. He was the author of the violin tutor *Méthode facile* (1711–12).

Montemuzzi, Italo (1875–1952) Italian composer. The success of Montemuzzi's early operas established his reputation in Europe and the USA. His style combines traditional Italian lyricism with Wagnerian influences. Montemuzzi's operas include *L'Amore di tre re* (1913), *Giovanni Gallurese* (1905), and *La Nave* (1918).

Monteux, Pierre (1875–1964) French conductor. An outstanding interpreter of 20th-century music, he made his reputation with Diaghilev's Ballets Russes, for which he conducted many premieres, including the uproarious first performance of Stravinsky's *The Rite of Spring* (1913). Monteux subsequently conducted the Boston Symphony Orchestra (1919–24), the Concertgebouw Orchestra (1925–29), the Orchestra Symphonique de Paris (1929–38), which he founded, and the San Francisco Symphony Orchestra (1936–52).

Monteverdi, Claudio (1567–1643) Italian composer. He was born in Cremona and received his earliest musical training from Marc' Antonio Ingegneri, who was maestro di cappella of the cathedral there. He had already published two volumes of madrigals before obtaining a position as an instrumentalist in the Gonzaga court in Mantua in 1592. Here he came under the influence of Giaches de Wert, and when he succeeded Wert as maestro in 1601 he was an established composer. Monteverdi's first opera, *La Favola d'*Orfeo*, was performed in Mantua in 1607 and in the following year his *L'Arianna*, containing the famous lament, was produced. In 1613 he moved to Venice as maestro at St Mark's, a post he held until his death. The compositions of his Venetian period were produced for St Mark's, secular academies, religious confraternities, and the newly opened opera house. Apart from those already mentioned, Monteverdi's works include the operas *Combattimento di Tancredi e Clorinda* (1624), *Il *Ritorno d'Ulisse in patria* (1641), and *L'*Incoronazione di Poppea* (1642); a book of canzonettes; over 200 madrigals contained in eight books, including *Madrigali guerrieri et amorosi* (1638); three masses; and many psalm settings, including the *Vespro della Beata Vergine* (1610).

Monteverdi believed that music should take second place to the words being set, and this led him to make original use of dissonance where the words demanded it. He was among the earliest composers to introduce the basso continuo to the madrigal (Book 5, 1605). His main innovation was the stile concitato, in which he attempted to create a warlike effect by means of repeated notes. One of the greatest figures in musical history, Monteverdi changed opera into a vehicle for dramatic expression, expanded the emotional range of the madrigal, and was at the forefront of the introduction of a progressive church style.

Montsalvage, Bassols Xavier (1911–) Spanish composer. His style has passed through various phases of polytonality, serialism, and postserialism. His works include the opera *Babel* (1948), *Concerto Breve* (1953), *Five Invocations to the Crucified* (1969), songs, and piano music.

Moog, Robert (1934–) US electronics engineer and inventor of the **Moog synthesizer**, an electronic music *synthesizer widely used by composers and pop groups. It is controlled by a keyboard and can play one note at a time.

Moonlight Sonata Sonata in C♯ minor for piano (Op. 27 No. 2) by Beethoven. Composed: 1801. Beethoven himself called the work *Sonata quasi una fantasia* ('sonata in the style of a fantasia') but did not use this title and had no specific programme in mind when writing the sonata. The present name was coined when the German music critic Rellstab likened the first movement to the reflection of moonlight on Lake Lucerne.

Moór, Emanuel (1863–1931) Hungarian composer, pianist, and conductor. In 1921 he invented the Duplex-Coupler piano, which had two keyboards. Moór's large output of compositions includes eight symphonies, concertos, vocal works, and chamber music.

Moore, Douglas (1893–1961) US composer, a pupil of Horatio Parker, d'Indy, and Nadia Boulanger. Moore was appointed head of music at Columbia University in 1940. As a composer Moore is best known for his opera *The Ballad of Baby Doe* (1956), which combines dramatic skill and fluency with an idiom deriving from American folk music. His other works include the opera *The Devil and Daniel Webster* (1938), orchestral music, chamber works, and songs.

Moore, Gerald (1899–1987) British pianist. He became a leading accompanist of such eminent singers as Dietrich Fischer-Dieskau and Elisabeth Schwarzkopf and such intrumentalists as Pablo Casals. He also wrote books on his reminiscences and lectured, especially after retiring from the concert platform in 1967.

Moore, Thomas (1779–1852) Irish poet and composer. He became famous (and highly paid) with his publication *Irish Melodies* (1807) and several sets of *Selection of Popular National Airs* (1818–28), which included 'The Last Rose of Summer' and were translated and read throughout Europe; Berlioz was a fervent admirer of him and set some of his poetry. Moore wrote an opera with C. E. Horn, *M.P., or The Blue Stocking* (1811).

morality A medieval religious play. Vaughan Williams applied the term to his opera *The Pilgrim's Progress* (1951).

morbido Soft; delicate. Hence **morbidezza**, softness; delicacy. [Italian]

morceau A piece (of music). Hence **morceau symphonique**, symphonic piece. [French]

mordent A musical ornament in which three notes replace a single note. In the **upper mordent** (called in German a **Pralltriller**) the second note is the note above the note marked with a mordent; in the **lower mordent** it is the note below. The mordent can be inflected with a flat or sharp sign to make the second note a semitone above or below the first.

Upper mordent

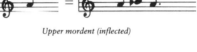

Upper mordent (inflected)

Lower mordent

Lower mordent (inflected)

Various kinds of mordent

Moreau, Jean-Baptiste (1656–1733) French composer and teacher of Montéclair, Clérambault, Dandrieu, and others. Trained at Angers Cathedral, he was choirmaster at Langres Cathedral (1681–82) and at Dijon and received an appointment in Paris at the school of Saint-Cyr (1686). In Paris he wrote music for Racine's plays *Esther* (1689) and *Athalie* (1691); he also composed motets, a requiem, and divertissements.

morendo Dying: a direction used to indicate that the music should fade in tone and sometimes also decrease in speed. [Italian]

moresca A dance of the 15th and 16th centuries, widely used in ballets, in which the performers disguised themselves as Moors with blackened faces and appropriate dress. This included small bells attached to their legs, as in the English *morris dance, which evolved from the moresca.

Mörike, Eduard Friedrich (1804–75) German poet and clergyman. His implicitly musical poetry appealed to Wolff, who set 57 of his poems. Schumann set nine more and Brahms set two poems and a duet.

morinchur see fiddle.

Morley, Thomas (1557–1603) English composer, a pupil of Byrd. After taking the degree of Mus.Bac. at Oxford in 1588, he was active as an organist and (after 1592) as a gentleman of the Chapel Royal. In 1598 he obtained a printing licence. Both as editor and composer, Morley introduced into England the Italian madrigal and related forms. This Italian influence may be seen in his *Triumphs of Oriana* (1601), a collection of madrigals by English composers in praise of Queen Elizabeth I. His own canzonets and ballets are closely modelled on those of Felice Anerio and Gastoldi, respectively. Morley's knowledge of Italian music and culture is also evident in his *Plaine and Easie Introduction to Practicall Musicke* (1597). More typically English are the *Consort Lessons* (1599), which use the broken consort for combined stringed and woodwind instruments. His sacred music comprises Latin motets and English anthems, psalms, and services.

Morning Heroes 'Symphony' for orator, choir, and orchestra by Bliss to words by various poets. First performance: 1930. Each of the five movements sets a passage by a different poet: Homer, Lai-Tai-Po, Whitman, Nichols, and Wilfred Owen respectively. These reflect on the nature of war in general, although the work is dedicated to those killed in World War I, in particular Bliss's brother. At the time of its composition *Morning Heroes* was innovatory in being the first British choral work to use an orator.

Moross, Jerome (1913–83) US composer. Moross's early association with theatre and the dance led to his composing operas and ballets and important scores for films. His works, influenced by jazz and American folk traditions, include the ballet *The Eccentricities of Davy Crockett* (1945), a symphony (1941–42) and other orchestral music, and chamber music.

morris dance An English folk dance for men, derived from the *moresca. The dancers wear white costumes with small bells attached to their legs and perform in two groups of six, with individual performers representing such characters as the Fool and the Queen of the May. The accompaniment is provided by an accordion or pipe and tabor. [from Old English *moreys* (i.e. Moorish) *daunce*]

Morton, Robert (?–?1476) English composer, working at the Burgundian court from 1457 to 1476. Morton was mentioned by Hothby and Tinctoris; the eight works (all chansons) that may be attributed to him include the well-known *Le Souvenir* and *N'aray je jamais*.

Moscheles, Ignaz (1794–1870) German pianist, conductor, and composer, born in Czechoslovakia. In 1808 he went to Vienna, where he studied with Albrechtsberger and Salieri; he was commissioned to make a piano reduction of Beethoven's *Fidelio*, supervised by the composer. He soon gained a reputation as a celebrated and influential virtuoso pianist and travelled throughout Europe (he taught Mendelssohn in Berlin in 1824). In 1825 he settled in London, where he taught at the Royal Academy of Music and conducted the Philharmonic Society. He became principal piano professor at the Leipzig conservatory in 1846. Moscheles composed much ephemeral piano music but his sonatas and studies are of more lasting interest. He also wrote eight piano concertos, a symphony, chamber music, and songs and edited and arranged many works by classical composers.

Moses in Egypt (Italian: *Mosè in Egitto*) Opera in four acts (originally three) by Rossini with libretto by Tottola. First performance: Teatro San Carlo, Naples, 1818. A revised and enlarged version with French libretto by Balochi and de Jouy was prepared for production in Paris in 1827; it was entitled *Moïse*.

Moses und Aron (*Moses and Aaron*) Unfinished opera by Schoenberg, who wrote a complete libretto in three acts and the music of acts I and II. First performance: Hamburg Radio, 1954; first staged performance: Zürich, 1957. The realization of this drama, which concerns the conflict between the thinker, Moses, and the man of action, Aaron, occupied Schoenberg's mind for much of his working life.

mosso Moved; moving; fast. See also **meno mosso**. [Italian]

Mossolov, Alexander Vassilievich (1900–1973) Soviet composer, a pupil of Miaskovsky. Mossolov came under severe official criticism (1927–31) for modernist tendencies in his music; his subsequent works were strongly influenced by the folk music he collected on several expeditions. Mossolov's output includes operas, five symphonies, choral works, chamber music, and songs.

Moszkowski, Moritz (1854–1925) German pianist and composer. He toured Europe as a recitalist and also taught at Kullak's academy in Berlin. Moszkowski's compositions range from popular piano solos and duets to large-scale works, such as the opera *Boabdil* and the symphony *Jeanne d'Arc*. He also appeared frequently as a conductor.

motet A piece of choral music based on a Latin text for use in the services of the Roman Catholic Church. The form has been in existence from the early 13th century, since when it has reflected the styles of successive periods of musical history. The early-13th-century motet evolved from the two-part clausula when the wordless upper part (**duplum**) was given a text (**mots**). The lower part, known as the **tenor**, was a phrase of Gregorian chant. Later in the 13th century a third part (**triplum**) was added with a different text, often secular and in French. In the 14th century the motet became isorhythmic, notably in the works of Machaut and Dunstable. During the early 15th century the singing of different texts simultaneously and the use of a cantus-firmus tenor ceased. Motets were then freely composed with the same text in all the parts.

Between *c*.1450 and *c*.1550 the composers of the Flemish school evolved the style that was to pervade the motets of the Renaissance: four to six voice parts, which contrasted ordered points of imitation with free polyphony or choral homophony and displayed an ever-increasing sensitivity to the expressive content of the words. These features are particularly evident in the motets of Josquin and Gombert, and by the end of the 16th century this style reached full fruition in the motets of Palestrina, Lassus, Victoria, Tallis, and Byrd. (See also **anthem**.) The Venetian polychoral motet also emerged during the second half of the 16th century. In this, eight or more voice parts were divided into two or more choirs, which were contrasted antiphonally. The works of the Gabrielis provide examples of this style.

The new techniques of the baroque era were applied to the motet during the early 17th century, with the use of solo voices, recitative, aria, basso continuo, and obligato parts for instruments. These features appear in the motets of Monteverdi. In Germany, similar developments are evident in the motets of Schütz, but with more emphasis on the chorus. In the 18th century it is often difficult to separate the motet from the *cantata, but the motet proper reached its climax in the six examples by J. S. Bach. Two species of motet flourished in France during the baroque period: the solo motet (one voice and basso continuo) and the grand motet (soloists, chorus, orchestra, and organ), as seen in the works of François Couperin and Charpentier. Among the 19th-century composers of motets are Brahms, Bruckner, Liszt, Gounod, and Franck. Distler, Poulenc, Vaughan Williams, and Stanford have continued the genre in the 20th century.

Mother Goose (French: *Ma mère l'oye*) Suite for orchestra by Ravel based upon a collection of fairy tales by Perrault. Composed: 1908. This work was originally composed for piano duet and the five movements describe *Mother Goose* and various other fairy tales. It was arranged for orchestra in 1915 and performed in that year as a ballet.

Mother of Us All, The Opera by Virgil Thomson with libretto by Gertrude Stein. First performance: Columbia University, New York, 1947. It concerns the life and career of the US feminist leader Susan B. Anthony.

motif see **motive**.

motion The progress of a melodic line in one or more parts. In a single part, **conjunct motion** occurs when the melody moves to adjacent notes and **disjunct motion** occurs when it moves by larger steps. If two parts move together in the same direction they are in **similar motion**; if they move in opposite directions they are in **contrary motion**. If one part holds or repeats a note and the other moves away from it (up or down) there is **oblique motion**. In similar motion in which the parts preserve a constant interval between them there is **parallel motion**.

motive A short melodic or rhythmic figure, several of which may contribute to a *theme. Some composers have used a motive to indicate a recognizable object or idea in programme music or a character in an opera (see **leitmotiv**), while for others a motive constitutes no more than an abstract idea. French: **motif**; German: **Motiv**.

moto Motion. Hence **con moto**, with movement, i.e. briskly; **moto perpetuo**, *perpetuum mobile. [Italian]

Mottl, Felix (1865–1911) Austrian conductor and composer. He was a leading interpreter of Wagner and gave the first complete (two-part) performance of Berlioz's *The Trojans*.

motto (*or* **motto theme**) A *theme that is repeated, with or without transformation, during the course of a composition. In programme music it is used to remind the listener of some idea or object. See also **idée fixe; leitmotiv**.

Motu Proprio A papal decree. In a musical context it usually refers to Pope Pius X's decree of 1902, which advocated limiting the secularization of music in the Roman Catholic Church (the use of women's voices, secular-style works, etc.) and re-establishing the value of plainsong and 16th-century polyphony. [Latin, of his own motion]

Mourning Symphony (German: *Trauersymphonie*) Symphony No. 44 in E minor by Haydn. Composed: *c*.1771. The title reflects the overall mood of this work, which is considerably more serious and mournful than that of most of Haydn's other symphonies. Although it is doubtful whether this title was the idea of the composer, it was Haydn's request that the slow movement should be played at his funeral.

Moussorgsky, Modest Petrovich see **Mussorgsky, Modest Petrovich**.

mouth music Wordless singing used to accompany a song or dance in the absence of a suitable instrument. In the Scottish Highlands it is known as **port á beul** and in Ireland as **lilting**.

mouth organ 1. (*or* **harmonica**) A *reed organ in which a set of small metal reeds are enclosed in slots in a narrow

Plate 28: *A view of the Metropolitan Opera House, New York, seen at night. The new building was opened in 1966*

Plate 29: *Schoenberg's unfin-ished opera* Moses und Aron *— the production staged at the Royal Opera House, Covent Garden, London, in 1967*

Plate 30: *A scene from Benjamin Britten's three-act opera*
A Midsummer Night's Dream, *based on Shakespeare's play*

box. Air is blown into or sucked out of the box by the player's mouth, the note sounded depending on the position of the box in the mouth and the use made of the player's tongue. The instrument in its present form was first made in Germany in 1830. Modern instruments can be quite sophisticated, each blow hole having four reeds – two for natural notes and two for chromatic notes, the latter being brought into action by pushing a button at the side of the instrument. While the instrument is regarded by many as a child's toy, in the hands of a virtuoso it is capable of producing remarkably moving music. The leading exponent, Larry *Adler, has had works written expressly for him by Vaughan Williams and Milhaud, amongst others.

2. An oriental free-reed instrument in which air is supplied by the mouth. It consists of a wind chamber into which the player blows, often through a tube; the wind chamber typically feeds a set of 6, 14, or 16 bamboo pipes, which are sounded by covering the finger holes. When the finger holes are uncovered the air escapes; when the finger holes are covered the air forces the reed within the pipe to vibrate. The instrument is of great antiquity, having been described in China as long ago as 1000 BC. It is still in use in various forms in many Far Eastern countries.

Mouton, Jean (c.1459–1522) French composer and contemporary of Josquin des Prez. He held appointments at the cathedrals of Nesle, Amiens, and Grenoble and (from 1502) at the royal chapel in Paris. Ronsard (1560) mentioned Mouton among those composers he considered 'disciples' of Josquin. His works include masses, motets, psalm settings, and French chansons.

mouvement 1. Motion; speed. Hence **mouvement perpetuel,** *perpetuum mobile. **2.** See **movement.** [French]

movable doh see **tonic sol-fa.**

movement A self-contained part of a large composition, such as a symphony, concerto, or sonata. Such parts are called movements because the French equivalent (**mouvement**) is also used for *tempo or speed, and each movement of a large work usually has a different tempo.

movimento Motion; speed. [Italian]

Mozart, Wolfgang Amadeus (1756–91) Austrian composer. Mozart was born in Salzburg and received his earliest musical training from his father, the violinist and composer Leopold Mozart (see below). An infant prodigy on the harpsichord, Mozart began composing minuets at the age of five. In 1762 Leopold Mozart took Wolfgang and his sister Maria Anna to Munich, Vienna, and Pressburg, where they gave virtuoso performances on the harpsichord. The following year they began their grand European tour, which included visits to Paris, where Mozart had four violin sonatas published, and London, where he met and was influenced by Johann Christian Bach. After a second visit

to Vienna, during which he wrote the opera *Bastien und Bastienne* (1768), Mozart went on an extended tour of Italy: in Bologna he had lessons from Padre Martini and in Rome he produced his opera seria *Mitridate* (1770). In Vienna Mozart had met Haydn, who influenced his early works and was one of the few musicians to fully appreciate Mozart's genius during his lifetime: Mozart later dedicated six string quartets (including the *Hunt Quartet*, 1784) to him. A third visit to Italy saw the composition of the opera *Lucio Silla* (1772) and Il *Sogno di Scipione* (1772).

Between 1773 and 1777, apart from brief visits to Vienna and Munich, where he wrote La *Finta giardiniera* (first performed 1775), Mozart spent most of his time in Salzburg. During a stay in Paris (1777–79) his *Paris Symphony* (1778) was produced, but failing to find an appointment suited to his gifts, Mozart accepted an uncongenial position in the service of the Archbishop of Salzburg (1779–81). In 1781 his opera seria *Idomeneo* was produced in Munich and he settled in Vienna as a freelance teacher, composer, and concert performer. Here he married the singer Constanze Weber (1782) and became a freemason (1784), an influence that was reflected in several of his works. From 1787 he held a nominal position as court composer. Mozart's period in Vienna saw the composition of many fine works: the operas The *Seraglio* (1782), Der *Schauspieldirektor* (1786), The *Marriage of Figaro* (1786), *Don Giovanni* (1787), *Così fan tutti* (1790), The *Magic Flute* (1791), and La *Clemenza di Tito* (1791) and the symphonies nicknamed *Haffner* (1782), *Linz* (1783), *Prague* (1786), and *Jupiter* (1788). Overwork and financial problems probably contributed to his early death, possibly from typhus. His last work, the *Requiem*, was completed after his death by his pupil Süssmayr.

Mozart made outstanding contributions to nearly all musical genres: he played a major role in establishing the classical style of composition, most notably in his piano concertos but also in his symphonies and operas. In addition to his operas he wrote much church music, including 18 masses (among them the *Coronation Mass*), the oratorio *Davidde penitente* (1785), litanies, motets, and the masonic cantata *Mauerische Trauermusik* (1785). His orchestral music includes about 50 symphonies; over 40 concertos, among them 25 for piano (e.g. the *Coronation Concerto*, 1788) and others for horn, violin, and clarinet; serenades, such as the *Haffner Serenade* (1776) and *Eine kleine Nachtmusik* (1787); and divertimenti. His large output of chamber music includes A *Musical Joke* (1787), 7 string quintets, 23 string quartets (among them the *Prussian Quartets*, 1789–90), quintets for piano, clarinet, and horn, quartets for piano, oboe, and flute, piano trios, and sonatas for piano and violin. Mozart's works were catalogued by Ludwig von Köchel (see **K.**).

His father Leopold Mozart (1719–87) was a composer, violinist, and theorist. He was court and chamber composer

(1757) and deputy kapellmeister (1763) in Salzburg, where he wrote school dramas, symphonies, serenades, cantatas, concertos, sacred works, chamber and keyboard music, and the violin tutor *Gründliche Violinschule* (1756).

Mozart and Salieri Opera by Rimsky-Korsakov, a setting of Pushkin's dramatic poem speculating on the (unfounded) possibility that Salieri poisoned Mozart. First performance: Moscow, 1898.

Mozartiana Suite No. 4 for orchestra by Tchaikovsky. Composed: 1887. For each of the four movements of this suite Tchaikovsky orchestrated a work by Mozart, using three piano pieces and the motet 'Ave Verum Corpus.'

M.S. See l.h.

Muck, Karl (1859–1940) German conductor. After conducting all over Europe he directed the Boston Symphony Orchestra (1912–18), a post he had to relinquish when arrested as an enemy alien. After World War I he conducted in Hamburg (1922–33) and Stuttgart. He was an outstanding interpreter of Wagner.

Mudarra, Alonso (*c*.1510–80) Spanish composer and vihuelist. He probably travelled to Italy in 1529 and became a canon at Seville in 1546. His works for vihuela include fantasias, tientos, dances, variations, and intabulations; he also wrote music for the four-course guitar and songs.

Mudge, Richard (1718–63) British composer and clergyman. He was vicar at Great Packington, near Birmingham (1735), and rector of Bedworth, Warwickshire (1756). His only known compositions are his six concertos (1749) and a medley concerto with French horns (*c*.1770).

Muette de Portici, La (*The Dumb Girl of Portici*) Opera in five acts by Auber with libretto by Scribe and Delavigne. First performance: Opéra, Paris, 1828. It is alternatively known as *Masaniello*, the name of the hero (tenor), a revolutionary leader in a story set in Naples in 1647 during the rising against the Spanish. The part of the dumb girl is usually taken by a dancer.

Muffat, Georg (1653–1704) German composer and organist. He studied in Paris with Lully and acted as organist in various German cities; in the 1680s he went to Italy to study with Bernardo Pasquini. From 1690 he was kapellmeister to the Bishop of Passau. Muffat was strongly influenced by Corelli and his later string music shows the adoption of the French overture and dance forms. His son **Gottlieb Muffat** (1690–1770), also a composer and organist, entered the court of Emperor Karl VI in Vienna under Fux, possibly in 1704. In 1717 he became court organist and taught the emperor's children and in 1741 succeeded Fux as first organist, a post he held until his death. Keyboard music constitutes most of his output; his fugues are stylistically conservative while his other pieces

reflect French influence with lavish ornamentation and the use of the refrain.

muffle To reduce the volume of the sound made by a drum, either by laying a cloth on the membrane or by using sponge-headed drumsticks.

Mühlfeld, Richard (1856–1907) German clarinetist. He was principal clarinetist at the Meiningen court orchestra and his playing so impressed Brahms that the composer wrote a clarinet trio, quintet, and two sonatas for him. In later life Mühlfeld toured Europe extensively; Jenner, Marteau, and Reinecke all wrote works for him.

Muldowney, Dominic (1952–) British composer, a pupil of Birtwhistle, with whom he was associated at the National Theatre. Influenced by medieval music, he has developed a style using minimal materials and, often, a theatrical element. His works include a three-part motet (1977), *Five Melodies for Four Saxophones* (1978), and a concerto for four violins (1979).

Mulliner Book A 16th-century manuscript collection of English music, mostly for keyboard but including some pieces for cittern and gittern. Thomas Mulliner compiled the manuscript (*c*.1550–75), which contains 131 pieces by Redford, Blitheman, Tallis, and others. An edition of it was published (1951) by D. Stevens and the manuscript is in the British Library (Add. MS 30513).

multimedia (*or* **mixed media**) Denoting a performance or composition (excluding opera and ballet) that incorporates music, poetry, drama, dancing, etc. Multimedia compositions were a popular form of entertainment in the 1960s.

Mumma, Gordon (1935–) US composer, cofounder with Ashley of the Ann Arbor Electronic Studio. In his work, especially with the Sonic Arts Union, Mumma has shown an interest in the live application of electronic systems; he has also written pieces for movement and dance. His works include *Gestures* (1962), *Hornpipe* (1967), *Ambivex* (1972), and *Cybersonic Cantilevers* (1973).

Munch, Charles (1891–1968) French conductor. Originally a violinist and teacher, he founded the Orchestre de la Société Philharmonique (1935–38), which performed many contemporary French compositions. He made his US debut in 1946 and subsequently conducted the Boston Symphony Orchestra (1949–62). He helped form L'Orchestre de Paris (1967).

Mundy, John (*c*.1555–1630) English composer and organist. He obtained the Oxford degrees of B.Mus. (1586) and D.Mus. (1624) and worked at St George's Chapel, Windsor, for over 40 years. Mundy composed mainly church music, notably *Songs and Psalmes* (1594), but is better known for keyboard pieces contained in the

Fitzwilliam Virginal Book. His father, the composer **William Mundy** (*c.*1529–91), became vicar-choral of St Paul's and in 1564 a gentleman of the Chapel Royal. The works definitely ascribed to him include services, the verse anthem *Ah, Helpless Wretch* (one of the earliest of its kind), and a six-part *Miserere mei Deus*.

Munrow, David (John) (1942–76) British player of early wind instruments, especially the recorder. He was a founder-director of the Early Music Consort of London (1967), which aimed to perform authentic early music. He also composed and arranged music for historical films.

Muradely, Vano (1908–70) Soviet composer, a pupil of Miaskovsky. Muradely's works are influenced by the folk music of his native Georgia, but in 1948 he came under official criticism for modernistic tendencies in his music. Muradely's output includes the opera *October* (1964), orchestral music, and patriotic choral works.

Murder in the Cathedral see **Assassinio nella cattedrale, L'.** [Italian]

Murrill, Herbert (1907–52) British composer, a pupil of Bush. Murrill taught at the London Royal Academy of Music (1933–52) and became head of music for the BBC in 1950. His works are neoclassical in style; they include the opera *Man in a Cage* (1929), two cello concertos, and chamber music.

Musard, Philippe (1793–1859) French composer and conductor, possibly a pupil of Reicha. Known primarily as a composer of fashionable waltzes and quadrilles in Paris and London, where he conducted popular promenade concerts (1840–41), he wrote for large combinations of woodwind, horns, and strings. He also composed three string quartets and a treatise (incomplete).

musette 1. A bellows-blown French bagpipe that was popular at the court of Louis XIV. It had four or five drone pipes enclosed in one cylinder and often an elaborate velvet bag. **2.** A piece of music, similar to a *gavotte, with a persistent drone bass reminiscent of this type of bagpipe.
3. A simple oboe-like instrument with finger holes and a few keys, developed from the chanter of a bagpipe and used as a toy.

Musgrave, Thea (1928–) British composer, a pupil of Gal and Nadia Boulanger. Her early works are in a diatonic style but later she adopted serial procedures. Musgrave has written much for the stage and in recent works has explored dramatic-abstract musical forms. Her orchestral works incorporate solo virtuosity, elements of limited freedom, and sometimes spatial interests. Musgrave's output includes the operas *The Decision* (1964), *Mary, Queen of Scots* (1976), and *A Christmas Carol* (1978–79); *Concerto for Orchestra* (1967); three chamber concertos (1963–66);

concertos for clarinet (1968), horn (1971), and viola (1973); *Space Play* (1974); and chamber music and choral pieces.

music Sound organized in time into rhythmic patterns and according to pitch into melodic and harmonic sequences. The making of music has been a preoccupation of man throughout recorded history and probably in prehistory. It seems that when men and women are stretched – in prayer, in battle, in love – music is capable of evoking something from them that they are unable to find in any other way. What that something is has puzzled philosophers and musicians since the ancient Greeks: for Pythagoras it was mathematical, for Plato and Aristotle ethical, for St Augustine and St Thomas Aquinas devotional, and for Hegel emotional. Kant ranked it as the lowest of the arts because its wordlessness made it incapable of contributing to culture and knowledge, while Schopenhauer regarded it as the highest of the arts because it is not concerned with reflections of other things but is a thing of beauty in itself. More recent analysts have sought to describe music in terms of the specific jargons of their own disciplines. But the results have continued to be consistently unenlightening; the ultimate conclusion has to be restricted to the empirical observation that music is sound organized in such a way that it evokes a number of predictable responses from human beings. The basis of this organization is the musical *scale, various forms of which evolved in many ancient civilizations. The modern western major and minor scales

Thea Musgrave conducting a performance of her own work

and the accompanying concept of *tonality derive from *plainchant, the medieval *modes, and the later polyphonic modal music that preceded the harmonic period in which tonality found its full expression. The medieval modes themselves evolved from the ancient Greek modes, which depended upon Pythagoras's insight into the relationships between frequency, pitch, and interval.

As an adjunct to song and dance, music goes so far back into human history that, like religion, its function is probably too diverse and too complex to be explained in simple rational terms. Indeed, music and religion have had a long-standing relationship; some form of music (if only the beating of a drum) appears as a basic component of every liturgical exercise, however primitive. In Christianity it has been a cornerstone of the whole edifice, in spite of Calvin's warning that its voluptuous and effeminate nature could detract from its piety. Moreover, music's importance to Christianity has been matched by Christianity's importance to music. For western art music has largely developed from the music played in church. Music as a form of entertainment is a relatively recent innovation in the western tradition. The separation of the sonata da camera from the sonata da chiesa (see **sonata**) did not occur until the 17th century, a period during which the first public concerts outside the church were given and the harmonic period, with its tonal music, began. This period, too, saw the growth of musical form, which continued throughout the 18th century; by the 19th century the sonata, concerto, symphony, and string quartet had acquired their modern significance. It is a remarkable fact that the core of western art music was composed in the hundred years following the death of J. S. Bach in 1750. In this century Haydn, Mozart, Beethoven, Schubert, Mendelssohn, Schumann, and Chopin created the basic classical repertoire.

With the advent of broadcasting and the gramophone in the 20th century a new musical dimension was created. The emergence of jazz at about this time and the subsequent development of popular music led to a vast commercial market in music that has little connection either with the art music of the 18th and 19th centuries or traditional European folk music. Vibrant with African rhythms and orchestrated with European harmonies, pop music now provides an idiom of its own that enables young people of many different nations, cultures, and persuasions to communicate with each other.

musica ficta (*or* **musica falsa**) Modal music in which flats or sharps have been inserted in order to avoid awkward intervals (e.g. the tritone) or harmonies. In the Dorian mode the leading note was often sharpened by performers. Edited scores for modern use usually have these changes made. It was the introduction of musica ficta that led to the addition of a B♭ to the organ keyboard. From this innovation the modern *keyboard evolved. [Latin, false music]

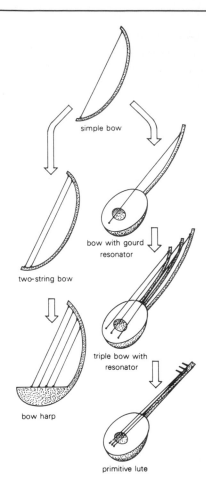

Possible evolution of the harp and the lute from the musical bow

musica figurata 1. Plainsong decorated by auxiliary notes. **2.** Contrapuntal music in which the parts move independently so that shorter notes in one part move against longer notes in other parts. [Latin, decorated or figured music]

musical bow The simplest and most primitive of all stringed instruments and the predecessor of the harp and the lute. Still used in Africa and Asia, the musical bow probably originated with the hunting bow and consisted of a single string attached to the ends of a flexible stick. The note was changed by flexing the bow to alter the tension in the string. Although the string was usually plucked, in some cases it was bowed with a smaller bow. Refinements of the primitive bow include the addition of a resonator at one end of the bow and the use of more than one string, sometimes by joining several bows together. In some cases one end of the bow is held in the mouth, which functions as a resonator. This is called a **mouth bow**.

musical box A device in which a clockwork mechanism rotates a cylinder or disc to which pins are attached; as the cylinder or disc rotates the pins pluck a series of metal tongues, each of which is tuned to a particular pitch. First made in the 18th century by Swiss watchmakers, cylinder-operated boxes, housed in elaborately decorated cabinets, became extremely popular in the 19th century as domestic sources of music. Interchangeable discs largely replaced cylinders in the late 19th century and they, in turn, were replaced by the gramophone in the 20th century. However 18th- and 19th-century musical boxes are now coveted, and very expensive, collectors' items.

Novelty musical boxes in many shapes and sizes have been mass-produced in the 20th century. Working on the same principle, they play a popular melody when picked up, when a lid is opened, or a handle turned.

musical glasses see **glass harmonica.**

Musical Joke, A Work for two horns and strings (K. 522) by Mozart. Composed: 1787. Mozart composed this work as a satire on the work of incompetent provincial composers and deliberately breaks many of the rules of composition by writing dissonant chords and crude progressions.

Musical Offering, The (German: *Das Musikalische Opfer*) Collection of contrapuntal pieces by Bach. Composed: 1747. In this year Bach travelled to Potsdam and played before Frederick the Great of Prussia, extemporizing on the harpsichord upon a theme that the emperor gave him. He later composed 13 contrapuntal pieces based on this theme and presented them to the emperor. *The Musical Offering* includes examples of canon, ricercare, and fugue and is like *The *Art of Fugue* in being a demonstration of contrapuntal skill.

musical saw (*or* **singing saw**) An ordinary wood saw used as a musical instrument. It is held between the seated player's knees and stroked with a violin bow. The player bends the saw to alter the tension of the metal, thus producing different notes. It is more of a music-hall novelty than a serious instrument.

musical switch An ingenious mixture of popular tunes in which a phrase of one tune is rapidly succeeded by a few bars of another. Although of little artistic value, it can prove to be an entertaining part of musical quiz games.

musica reservata The music of Josquin des Prez, so called by contemporary writers to distinguish it from that of the preceding generation. The exact significance and meaning of this description is now disputed, but it is thought to refer either to the more restrained type of figurations in the music or to some 'reserved' secrets within the music governing its performance. An alternative explanation is that it was intended for audiences of a more exclusive nature. [Latin, reserved music]

Musica transalpina Two anthologies of Italian (i.e. transalpine) madrigals with English texts, edited and published by Nicholas *Yonge. The first volume (1588) contains 57 pieces by 18 composers (including Ferrabosco, Marenzio, Palestrina, and Lassus) and the second (1597) contains 24 pieces by 11 composers. The collection reflected current interest in Italian madrigals and greatly influenced English composers.

music drama A development of *opera by Wagner in which music and drama are drawn closer together with unbroken continuity throughout each act. This is achieved through a continuously flowing polyphonic orchestral texture and a free declamatory vocal style without the customary divisions into aria and recitative. Considerable use is made of the *leitmotiv. Wagner expressed his theoretical beliefs for music drama, the *Gesamtkunstwerk*, in *Oper und Drama* (1851). His music dramas include *Der Ring des Nibelungen* (completed 1876), *Tristan und Isolde* (1857–59), *Die Meistersinger von Nürnberg* (1862–67), and *Parsifal* (1877–82).

Music for the Royal Fireworks Suite of music for wind band by Handel. Composed: 1749. This music was written for festivities in celebration of the Peace of Aix-la-Chapelle and at the request of the monarch it was scored only for warlike instruments (i.e. wind and drums). Handel later added parts for string instruments.

Music Makers, The Work for contralto, choir, and orchestra by Elgar to words by O'Shaughnessy. First performance: 1912. In his setting of this ode Elgar includes appropriate quotations from some of his earlier works.

Music Master, The (Italian: *Il Maestro di musica*) Comic opera in one act erroneously attributed to Pergolesi. It is a satire on the profession of the singing master, possibly an altered version of an opera by Auletta with libretto by Palombo entitled *Orazio*, which was produced in Naples in the 1730s.

musicology The scholarly study of music. The term was introduced in the 20th century and covers all aspects of the theoretical study of music (i.e. not performing or composition). The branches of musicology include acoustics, aesthetics, bibliography, history, biography, instruments, harmony, and notation. Musicology and *ethnomusicology are now understood to embrace many different disciplines, among them anthropology, linguistics, sociology, and physics.

music theatre Dramatic works performed on the concert platform with action. Such works are less substantial in scope and structure than opera. The genre has been in existence since the 1960s.

musique concrète The name applied in the late 1940s by a group of Parisian composers to music using prerecorded sounds. Composers, such as Schaeffer and Henry, felt they could establish a 'concrete' composition using natural or real-sound sources fixed in performance by electronic means (such as tape recorders), as opposed to the conventional and somewhat arbitrary notation and interpretation system. A short-lived Groupe de Reserche de Musique Concrète was founded in 1951. See also **electronic music**. [French, concrete music]

Mussorgsky (*or* **Moussorgsky**), **Modest Petrovich** (1839–81) Russian composer. After embarking on a military training in St Petersburg, Mussorgsky abandoned this for a post in the civil service so that he could devote more time to music. His formal music training was rudimentary (he studied briefly under Balakirev) but he developed a highly individual style, strongly influenced by Russian history and folk music. His sympathy with the Russian people was shown particularly in his masterpiece, the opera *Boris Godunov* (1869–72). Mussorgsky was a member of The *Five, but during the latter half of his life he suffered considerable poverty, which led to heavy drinking. This contributed to his early death, leaving many works unfinished.

His compositions include the unfinished operas *The Marriage* (1868), *Khovanshchina* (completed by Rimsky-Korsakov in 1886), and *Sorochintsy Fair* (1874–80); over 60 songs, including the song cycles *The *Nursery* (1868–72), *Sunless* (1874), and *Songs and Dances of Death* (1875–77); the orchestral tone poem *St John's Night on the Bare Mountain* (1860–66); and piano pieces, notably *The Seamstress* (1871) and *Pictures at an Exhibition* (1874).

Mustel organ A *reed organ similar to an *American organ, except that the top and bottom halves of the keyboard can be controlled separately to obtain more expression. It was invented in Paris by Victor Mustel (1815–90).

muta Change: a direction indicating that the player should make some change or adjustment, e.g. to a different tuning or instrument. [Italian]

mutation stop An organ *stop used in conjunction with other stops to produce a variety of tone colours. It does not sound the note played on the keyboard or its octave, but it sounds some other harmonic, such as a *twelfth, *seventeenth, or *nineteenth.

mute A device used to reduce the volume of the sound produced by a musical instrument. On bowed stringed instruments it consists of a three-pronged clip attached to the *bridge of the instrument so that it limits the vibrations of the strings and alters the ability of the bridge to transmit the vibrations through the *soundpost to the body of the instrument. The result is both a reduction in volume and a mellowing of tone. In brass wind instruments a mute consists of variously shaped wood, metal, rubber, or polystyrene objects placed by hand in the bell of the instrument. They also modify the sound in addition to reducing the volume; muted trumpets and trombones are widely used in jazz. See also **muffle; sordino.**

Müthel, Johann Gottfried (1728–88) German composer. He was appointed chamber musician and organist at the court of Mecklenburg-Schwerin in 1747 then settled in Riga, where he directed music for the Russian privy councillor (1753) and became organist (1755). In addition to his concertos, odes, and songs, he wrote keyboard works noted for their virtuoso and expressive passages.

Muti, Riccardo (1941–) Italian conductor. After studying in Naples and Milan he became principal conductor of the Philharmonia Orchestra in 1973 and musical director of the Philadelphia Orchestra in 1981. He also conducts opera and has revived Verdi's *Attila* and *I Masnadieri*.

My Country see **Má Vlast.**

My Ladye Nevell's Booke A manuscript collection of 42 keyboard pieces by William Byrd. John Baldwin transcribed them in 1591 for Lady Nevell (*or* Nevill). An edition of it was published (1926) by H. Andrews and the manuscript is privately owned.

Myslivecek (*or* **Mysliweczek** *or* **Mislivecek**), **Josef** (1737–81) Czech composer. He studied with Pescetti in Venice (1763) and produced his first opera, *Medea* (1764), in Parma. Settling in Naples, he wrote many operas for Italian and German theatres and oratorios, including *Abramo ed Isacco* (1777). His works, which show the influence of Czech folk music, also include sinfonias and chamber music.

N

Nabokov, Nicolas (1903–78) Russian-born US composer, cousin of the novelist Vladimir Nabokov. After study with Busoni in Berlin, Nabokov moved to Paris and (in 1933) to the USA, where he was active as a teacher. His works are lyrical in inspiration; they include three symphonies, ballets, choral music, and chamber works.

Nabucco (*or* **Nabucodnosor**: *Nebuchadnezzar*) Opera in four acts by Verdi with libretto by Solera. First performance: La Scala, Milan, 1842. The opera tells the biblical story of the Israelites' captivity in Babylon and the eventual conversion of Nebuchadnezzar (baritone) to the Jewish faith.

nach After; according to; to. For example, **nach G**, change to G. [German]

Nachez, Tivadar (1859–1930) Hungarian violinist and composer, a pupil of Joachim and Léonard. He attained a high international reputation as a violin player. His compositions include a violin concerto, a string quartet, and violin pieces. From 1889 he lived in London.

Nachschlag 1. The two closing notes that form the end of some kinds of *trill. **2.** A note or notes added in smaller print after a given note. [German, after-stroke]

Nachtanz After-dance: the second of a pair of dances, e.g. the galliard that follows a pavan. [German]

Nacht in Venedig, Eine (*A Night in Venice*) Operetta by Johann Strauss the Younger with libretto by 'Zell' (Camillo Walzel) and Genée. First performance: Friedrich-Wilhelm Städtische Theater, Berlin (for the opening of which it was commissioned), 1883. Set in Italy, it tells of the wooing of Barbara by Enrico and the Duke of Urbino and of Annina by the macaroni maker, Pappacoda, and the duke's barber, Caramello.

Nachtmusik A composition intended for performance in the evening as a serenade to a loved one. Originally intended for open-air performance, works of this character were gradually written for concert performance also, the most famous example being the quartet *Eine kleine Nachtmusik* by Mozart. [German, night music]

nail fiddle (*or* **nail violin**) An instrument, made in the 18th and 19th centuries, consisting of nails of different lengths arranged around the edge of a semicircular resonator. The nails are stroked with a violin bow and produce notes of different pitches, depending on their length.

nakers Two small Arabic *kettledrums from which the modern orchestral timpani evolved. In a miniature of a 14th-century psalter a nakers player is seen playing the two drums with hooked sticks, the drums lying on their sides on the ground with their heads facing away from him. [from Arabic *naqara*]

Name Day see **Namensfeier**.

Namensfeier (*Name Day*) Concert overture (Op. 115) by Beethoven. Composed: 1814. The work was written to be performed on the name day of Emperor Francis II of Austria.

Namouna Ballet in two acts with music by Lalo, libretto by Nuitter and Petipa, and choreography by Petipa. First performance: Opéra, Paris, 1882. Namouna is the favourite slave of Lord Adriani, who stakes her, his ship, and his fortune in a wager and loses; the setting is Corfu.

Nancarrow, Conlon (1912–) US-born Mexican composer, a pupil of Piston, Slonimsky, and Sessions. His music has been much influenced by his experience as a jazz trumpeter in the 1930s and his study of Indian and African music. Nancarrow has experimented with complex rhythms and polyphony in his *Studies for Player Piano* (1949–).

Nanino, Giovanni Maria (*c.*1544–1607) Italian composer. A chorister at Vallerano, he may have studied with Palestrina in Rome during the 1560s. He became maestro at S Maria Maggiore (probably 1567) and at S Luigi dei Francesi (1575). In 1577 he became a tenor in the papal choir, where he taught the choristers. He was a popular composer, but his music has been overshadowed by that of Palestrina. Both his sacred and secular compositions are imaginative and interesting. His brother **Giovanni Bernardino Nanino** (*c.*1560–1618) was also a composer and teacher. He was maestro at S Luigi dei Francesi (1591–1608) and then at S Lorenzo in Damaso. He taught choirboys in the same house as his brother and was a leading figure in the Roman school. His madrigals are not as experimental as those of his brother, but his sacred music from 1610 includes basso continuo parts and uses a progressive vocal style.

naqara see **kettledrums; nakers.**

Nardini, Pietro (1722–93) Italian violinist and composer. He studied for six years with Tartini and became solo violinist and leader in Stuttgart (1762–65). Based in Livorno from 1766, he wrote violin works, concertos, chamber music, and orchestral overtures; from 1770 he directed music at the Florentine court. Nardini's playing was highly esteemed by Leopold Mozart.

Nares, James (1715–83) British organist, teacher, and composer. After studying with Pepusch, he became organist of York Minster (1735) and of the Chapel Royal (1756) and Master of the Children at the Chapel Royal (1757). Nares wrote many anthems, catches, and glees, the dramatic ode *The Royal Pastoral* (c.1769), *Lessons for the Harpsichord* (1747), and harpsichord and singing tutors.

Narváez, Luys de (16th century) Spanish composer and vihuelist. He taught music to the children of Prince Philip (later Philip II) and in the 1540s travelled to Italy and northern Europe. He published a number of pieces for solo vihuela and two of his motets survive.

nasard An organ *mutation stop that sounds a note a *twelfth above the written pitch on flute *flue pipes.

Nasco, Jan (c.1510–61) Flemish composer. In 1547 he was appointed first musical director of the Accademia Filarmonica in Verona and in 1551 became maestro at Treviso. Much influenced by Willaert, he set texts by Petrarch, Ariosto, and Tasso. His madrigals show great care in word setting and both these and his sacred works show a tendency towards homophony, particularly marked in the *St Matthew Passion*.

Nash, Heddle (1896–1961) British tenor. A pupil of Giuseppe Borgatti at Milan, he made his debut there in 1924 as Count Almaviva in Rossini's *The Barber of Seville*. A long career at Covent Garden followed (1924–47), and Nash also sang oratorios.

Nathan, Isaac (1790–1864) Australian composer, born in England. He was closely associated with the court of George IV and a friend of Byron, with whom he collaborated in the *Hebrew Melodies* (1815–19). For financial reasons he settled in Australia in 1841. Nathan made a lasting contribution to Australian musical life: he founded a singing academy in Sydney, was choirmaster of the cathedral, set up a publishing business, gave concerts and opera performances, and taught. He also transcribed much aboriginal music. Nathan composed the first Australian operas and many patriotic songs and odes. Charles *Mackerras is one of his descendants.

nationalism in music A movement in the latter part of the 19th century in which composers of many European nations attempted to make their music more expressive of its country of origin and thus challenge the widespread dominance of German music. Nationalism can be said to have begun with Glinka's opera *A Life for the Tsar* (1836) and its strongest manifestations came in Russia with The *Five, a group of composers including Mussorgsky and Borodin. Other 19th-century composers whose music reflected their national heritage include Smetana (Bohemia), Grieg (Norway), and Albéniz (Spain). Nationalism in music existed in several forms. Composers frequently chose opera plots or titles for tone poems that reflected some feature of their national life, as did Smetana in *Má Vlast*. There was also a wide use both of actual folk music and rhythmic and melodic figurations typical of the composer's national music. Nationalism continued well into the 20th century with the work of such composers as Bartók and Kodály in Hungary, Elgar in England, and Sibelius in Finland.

natural A sign (♮) placed before a note to restore it to its original pitch if it has been flattened or sharpened by the *key signature or by a previous sharp or flat sign in the same bar. See also **accidental.**

naturale Natural: a direction indicating that an instrument or voice should perform in its natural manner rather than using an unusual technique. [Italian]

Naumann, Johann Gottlieb (1741–1801) German composer, a pupil of Padre Martini, Hasse, and Tartini. After producing several operas in Italy he was appointed kapellmeister at Dresden (1776), where he remained for the rest of his life apart from visits to Copenhagen and to Stockholm, where he produced his opera *Gustaf Wasa* (1786). Naumann's works, which exemplify early romanticism, include many operas, sinfonias, songs, sacred works, and music for ensemble and for glass harmonica.

Navarra, André (1911–) French cellist. He performed with the Krettly String Quartet (1929–35) and made his debut as a soloist in Paris (1931). He has taught in France, Austria (Vienna), Germany, and Italy and is particularly noted for his playing of Elgar's cello concerto.

Neapolitan sixth A chord consisting of the notes FA♭ D♭ in the key of C and the corresponding notes in other keys. The origin of the name is not known. Compare **augmented sixth.**

Nebuchadnezzar see **Nabucco.**

neck The part of a stringed instrument, such as a violin or guitar, that carries the *fingerboard. It is attached to the body at one end and terminates in the *pegbox at the other.

Neel, (Louis) Boyd (1905–) British conductor. He founded the Boyd Neel String Orchestra (1933), with whom he toured widely.

Negro spiritual A religious folk song originating in the southern states of the USA with Negro plantation slaves. Usually adapted from the Bible, the story was sung in stanzas by a single voice with a chorus singing the refrain. The element of improvisation in early spirituals is absent in the later harmonized arrangements.

Nelson Mass Mass in D minor for solo voices, choir, and orchestra by Haydn. Composed: 1798. Haydn was very impressed by the character and career of Admiral Lord Nelson and is reputed to have been inspired to write this mass after hearing of Nelson's victory at the Battle of the Nile. His own title was *Missa in Augustis* (*Mass in Time of War*) and the work is also sometimes known as the *Imperial Mass*.

Nenna, Pomponio (*c*.1550–1613) Italian composer. Educated in Bari, he went to Naples in the 1590s and associated with Carlo Gesualdo. By 1608 he was in Rome, where he died. Nenna's madrigals, like Gesualdo's, include chromatic and dissonant passages, though there is less of this in his later Roman madrigals. He also composed two books of responsories.

neoclassicism A musical movement that emphasized the need to return to the classical virtues of formal clarity, balance, and restraint. It was revived in music after World War I. This was a reaction partly to the upheaval of the war and partly to the emotional turbulence of late romantic music. It led to the maintenance of tonal harmony and a revival of 17th-, 18th-, and early-19th-century forms, textures, and styles. The dodecaphonic sonata forms of the Second Viennese School are therefore not neoclassical. The chief neoclassical composer is Stravinsky, from the Pergolesi ballet *Pulchinella* (1920) to *The Rake's Progress* (1951); others include Prokofiev, Hindemith, Roussel, and some US pupils of Nadia Boulanger, including Piston. Neoclassicism has wider implications than is sometimes supposed as it forms part of a more general 20th-century preoccupation with the past.

neoromanticism A musical movement of the 20th century in which such composers as Schoenberg returned to the ideals of *romantic music as a reaction against *neoclassicism.

Neri, St Philip (Filippo N.; 1515–95) Italian mystic. His religious discussions took place in the oratory (prayer hall) of S Girolamo in Rome. He stressed the importance of music in attracting people to church and his circle was officially known the Congregazione dell' Oratorio (Congregation of the Oratory). Victoria and Palestrina probably contributed to its music making and from its name the word *oratorio is derived.

Neumann, Václav (1920–   ) Czech conductor. He studied the violin and conducting at the Prague conserva-

Václav Neumann with the Czech Philharmonic Orchestra

tory. In 1956 he conducted Janáček's opera *The Cunning Little Vixen* in Berlin, Wiesbaden, and Paris with great success. He became chief conductor of the Czech Philharmonic Orchestra in 1968 and was music director of the Stuttgart Opera (1970–73).

neums (*or* **neumes**) Signs used, originally in the 7th century, to give a singer an indication of the general trend of a melody. In its simplest form the neum consisted of a single horizontal line with short sloping lines (like acute and grave accents) set about it. Neums later developed into a more precise notation for indicating changes of pitch for singers of plainsong. The modern five-line staff evolved from this system, the *clef concept being taken directly from the neum notation, together with several signs, such as those for the *trill and the *turn.

Neusidler, Hans (*c*.1508–63) German composer, lutenist, and lute maker. In 1530 he arrived in Nuremberg from Pressburg (now Bratislava) and taught the lute there. His lute books are among the most important early German examples, providing a varied repertory. The first book (1536) gives instructions on lute playing.

Otto Nicolai

Carl Nielsen

Nevin, Ethelbert (Woodbridge) (1862–1901) US composer and pianist. He studied in Boston and (with Klindworth) in Berlin (1884–86). Nearly all his compositions are songs or short piano pieces in a lyrical and sometimes sentimental style, but he also wrote works for violin and piano, choruses, cantatas, and music for the pantomime *Florian's Dream* (1898). His best-known song is 'The Rosary' (1898).

new music 1. See ars nova. **2.** The monodic style of music pioneered by Caccini at the beginning of the 17th century. He called his collection of madrigals and canzonets *Le Nuove musiche* (new music). See also **monody. 3.** The music of Liszt and Wagner and their followers as opposed to the more traditional music of Brahms. **4.** The many new techniques used in musical compositions during the early 20th century, such as serialism and atonality. The term is derived from the German (*neue Musik*).

New Philharmonia Orchestra see **Philharmonia Orchestra.**

New World Symphony see **From the New World.**

New York Philharmonic Orchestra US symphony orchestra found 1842. It was originally the Philharmonic Symphony Society of New York and is the oldest orchestra in continuous existence in the USA. It had many conductors up to 1892, including Theodore Thomas and Leopold Damrosch, and it introduced many European works to the USA. In 1928 it merged with the New York Symphony Orchestra (founded in 1878 by Leopold Damrosch). Its many distinguished conductors have included Emil Paur, Gustav Mahler, Willem Mengelberg, Arturo Toscanini, Bruno Walter, Leopold Stokowski, Dimitri Mitropoulos, Leonard Bernstein, Pierre Boulez, and Zubin Mehta (from 1978). The orchestra has played a leading role in New York's musical life and maintains a high international reputation.

Nibelung's Ring, The see **Ring des Nibelungen, Der.**

Nicolai, (Carl) Otto (Ehrenfried) (1810–49) German composer and conductor. In Berlin he studied with Zelter and at the Royal Institute of Church Music (1828–30) and in 1833 became organist to the Prussian embassy in Rome. He was singing teacher and kapellmeister at the Vienna Hoftheater (1837–38), then returned to Italy, where his operas met with success. In 1841 he became principal conductor of the Court Opera, Vienna, and with its orchestra he inaugurated the concert series that was to become the Philharmonic Concerts. In 1848 he became conductor of the cathedral choir and kapellmeister of the Berlin Opera. The work for which he is best remembered, the opera *Die lustigen Weiber von Windsor* (see **Merry**

Wives of Windsor, The), was produced there two months before his early death. Nicolai composed other operas (in German and Italian), sacred and secular choral music, songs, and orchestral and chamber music.

Nielsen, Carl (1865–1931) Danish composer. Nielsen studied at the Copenhagen conservatory, a pupil of Gade. He was subsequently active as a violinist and conductor, conducting the Copenhagen Royal Opera (1908–14). Nielsen's early style was influenced by the German romantic tradition, but in his later music he evolved a highly personal idiom using dissonantly chromatic harmony with occasional bold experimentation; for example, the improvised side-drum solo in the fifth symphony (1921–22). Nielsen is often cited with Sibelius as a founder of modern Scandinavian music, but his style is essentially different in its avoidance of folk inspiration and its search for new expressive means. Nielsen's output includes the opera *Saul and David* (1902) and *Masquerade* (1904–06); six symphonies, four of them subtitled: The *Four Temperaments* (No. 2, 1901–02), *Sinfonia Espansiva* (No. 3, 1910–11), The *Inextinguishable* (No. 4, 1915–16), and *Sinfonia Semplice* (No. 6, 1924–25); the tone poem *Saga-Drøm* (1907–08); chamber and incidental music; and vocal works.

Nielsen, Riccardo (1908–82) Italian composer, a pupil of Casella. Nielsen's early works were influenced by Stravinsky's neoclassicism; in later compositions he adopted serial methods. Nielsen's output includes a symphony in G (1934), the radio opera *La Via di Colombo* (1953), and other orchestral and chamber works.

niente Nothing. Hence **quasi niente**, almost nothing: a direction indicating extreme softness of tone. [Italian]

Nietzsche, Friedrich Wilhelm (1844–1900) German philosopher. A keen amateur pianist and composer, Nietzsche hailed Wagnerian *music drama as the successor to Greek drama, but later withdrew his support. His powerful writing has influenced several composers: *Also sprach Zarathustra* inspired a tone poem by Richard Strauss of the same name (1896), as well as Delius's *A Mass of Life* (1904–05) and *Requiem* (1914–16) and the fourth movement of Mahler's third symphony (1896).

Nigg, Serge (1924–) French composer, a pupil of Messiaen and Leibowitz. After the exotic tone poems of his early years, such as *Timour* (1944), he adopted serial procedures. In 1959 he formed the Communist progressist movement with Durey and others, which aimed at writing music of mass appeal. His works include two piano concertos, the *Hieronymus Bosch* symphony (1960), *Fulgur* (1969), and *Visages d'Axel* (1967).

nightingale A small whistle-type instrument used to imitate the call of a nightingale. It is used in the *Toy Symphony* attributed to Haydn and in a Scarlatti oratorio.

Birgit Nilsson in Elektra *at Covent Garden*

Night in Venice, A see Nacht in Venedig, Eine.

Night on the Bare Mountain see St John's Night on the Bare Mountain.

Nights in the Gardens of Spain (Spanish: *Noches en los jardines de España*) 'Symphonic impressions' for piano and orchestra by Falla. Composed: 1911–15. Each of the movements was inspired by a different region of Spain, the three movements being 'In the Generalife' ('En el Generalife'), 'Distant Dance' ('Danza lejana'), and 'In the Gardens of the Sierra de Córdoba' ('En los jardines de la Sierra de Córdoba').

Nikisch, Arthur (1855–1922) Hungarian conductor. After conducting in Leipzig, he became director of the Boston Symphony Orchestra (1889–93), the Royal Opera in Budapest (1893–95), and subsequently the Leipzig Gewandhaus and Berlin Philharmonic orchestras. He conducted entirely from memory and was an outstanding interpreter of Brahms.

Nilsson, Birgit (1918–) Swedish soprano. A pupil of Joseph Hislop at the Royal Academy of Music in Stockholm, she made her debut in 1946. One of the finest Wagnerian sopranos of the 20th century, Nilsson was a great and powerful interpreter of Isolde and also a memorable Turandot (in Puccini's opera).

Nilsson, Bo (1937–) Swedish composer. Under the influence of Stockhausen he has made use of serialism, electronic music, phonetic vocal writing, and open form. His works include *Gruppen* (1959), *Entrée* (1963) and *Exit* (1970) for tape and orchestra, *Caprice* (1970), and *NAZM* (1973).

nineteenth An organ *mutation stop that sounds a note a nineteenth (i.e. two octaves and a fifth) above the written pitch on diapason *flue pipes. The length of the pipe (compared to an 8-*foot pipe) is 1.33 ft. See also **larigot**.

ninth An *interval of nine notes (counting both first and last notes), or 14 semitones for a **major ninth**, e.g. C–D', and 13 semitones for a **minor ninth**, e.g. C–D'♭. See also **dominant**.

nobile Noble. Hence **nobilmente**, nobly. [Italian]

Noces, Les see **Wedding, The**.

Noches en los jardines de España see **Nights in the Gardens of Spain**.

nocturne A short composition suggestive of night-time calm. In the 18th century the term was applied to short works in the style of a serenade, as in Mozart's *Serenata notturna*. In the 19th century, beginning with John Field's *18 Nocturnes* for piano the nocturne became a salon form, in which the lyrical aspects of Italian vocal writing were transferred to the keyboard. Chopin expanded the scope of the nocturne with 21 examples expressing a wider range of moods. Other composers to have written nocturnes include Mendelssohn (*A Midsummer Night's Dream*), Debussy (*Nocturnes*), and Britten (*Serenade* for tenor, horn, and strings). Italian: **notturno**.

Nocturnes Set of three pieces for orchestra and female choir by Debussy. Composed: 1893–99. The movements are 'Nuages' ('Clouds'), 'Fêtes,' and 'Sirènes' ('Sirens'). For the last movement the choir joins with the orchestra to imitate the sound of singing sirens luring unwary sailors onto the rocks.

node The point on a vibrating string, or the plane in a column of air, that is stationary and about which the vibrating string or column divides itself into separately vibrating sections. For example, a string that is producing a fourth *harmonic has three nodes.

noël see **carol**.

noire Crotchet. [French, black, i.e. black note]

Nola, Giovanni Domenico del Giovane da (*c*.1515–92) Italian composer. In 1563 he became maestro at the church of Santissima Annunziata, Naples. He is chiefly known as a composer of lively madrigals. These are careful settings of texts by, among others, Petrarch; some, notably *Giunta* *m'ha amor* (1562), are important for their progressive harmonies.

nonet A composition for nine voices or instruments or a group that performs such a composition. The group often includes a mixture of strings and wind instruments, such as a string quartet plus double bass and four woodwind instruments. Two outstanding examples of the composition are Spohr's *Nonet* and Webern's *Concerto for Nine Instruments*.

nonharmonic note A note that is not harmonically associated with the chord that it precedes or follows. See **auxiliary note; passing note**.

Nono, Luigi (1924–) Italian composer, a pupil of Scherchen, Malipiero, and Maderna. His instrumental works of the early 1950s are in a totally serial pointillist style. He then experimented with the introduction of rhythmic continuities and the syllabic setting of texts. Nono grew increasingly committed to the political revolutionary responsibilities of new music, which involved a mistrust of doctrinaire serialism, the treatment of antifascist subjects, and the search for new media and a new proletarian audience. The bulk of his work utilizes electronic music, usually with a strong vocal element. His works include *Incontri* (1955), *Il Canto sospeso* (1956), *Variants* (1957), the opera *Intolleranza* (1961), the cantata *Sul ponte di Hiroshima* (1962), *La Fabbrica illuminata* (1965), *Contrappunto dialettico alla mente* (1968), *Y entonces comprendió* (1970), two piano concertos, and *sofferte onde serene* (1976).

Nordheim, Arne (1931–) Norwegian composer, a pupil of Holmboe. Nordheim studied musique concrète in Paris. He is particularly interested in sound textures and makes much use of tape; his more recent works emphasize tonality. His works include *Epitaffio* (1963), *Lux et Tenebrae* (1970), *Greening* (1973), the ballets *Ariadne* (1977) and *The Tempest* (1979), and the cantata *Tempora Noctis* (1979).

Nordraak, Rikard (1842–66) Norwegian composer. He studied in Berlin with Kullak and Kiel and in 1864 went to Copenhagen, where with his friend Grieg he became a leading figure in the Norwegian nationalist movement. During his short life Nordraak composed incidental music, choral and instrumental works, and songs (many to texts by his cousin the Norwegian poet Bjørnsterne Bjørnson). They use simple musical language but have individuality. Nordraak also wrote the Norwegian national anthem, 'Ja vi elsker.'

Nørgård, Per (1932–) Danish composer, a pupil of Holmboe and Nadia Boulanger. Nørgård's early music shows the influence of Sibelius; his later works explore avant-garde techniques, such as serialism and microtonal writing.

Margaret Price in the title role in Norma

Nørgård's output includes operas and ballets, orchestral works, songs, and chamber music.

Norma Opera in two acts by Bellini with libretto by Romani based on a tragedy by Soumet. First performance: La Scala, Milan, 1831. Norma (soprano) is a Druid priestess torn between duty and her love for Pollione (tenor), Roman pro-consul in Gaul. Pollione turns to a younger priestess, Adalgisa (soprano), and Norma publicly confesses her guilty love and is condemned to death. The contrite Pollione asks to die with her.

Norman, Jessye (1945–) US soprano. A pupil of Carolyn Grant, Elizabeth Mannion, and Pierre Bernac, she made her debut at Berlin in 1969 as Elisabeth in Wagner's *Tannhäuser*. She follows a varied concert career as well as appearing on stage all over the world.

North, Hon. Roger (1651–1734) English music critic and author of the *Memoires of Musick* (written 1728, published 1846). This included the treatise *The Musicall Grammarian* (published 1925), which attempted to give some rules to the art of music.

Northern Sinfonia Orchestra British chamber orchestra founded in 1961. It evolved from a professional orchestra established by Michael Hall in Newcastle-upon-Tyne in 1958. Its conductors have included Rudolf Schwarz,

Christopher Seaman, and Tamás Vásáry and Ivan Fischer (from 1979). The Northern Sinfonia Orchestra tours mainly in north-east England but also further afield and it has commissioned many new works.

nota cambiata A device in strict counterpoint by which a dissonant note occurring on an accented beat is resolved not by falling to the note below, as normal, but by first rising or falling by the interval of a third and only then resolving conventionally. Several different melodic figurations can be described by this term. [Italian, changed note]

notation A method of recording music so that it can be read for performance. The use of letters of the alphabet to identify notes originated with the Greeks and was adopted by the Romans, although these systems do not seem to have been used by performers. The first systematic notation was based on *neums, which were introduced in the 7th century. A **proportional notation**, capable of recording time values, began in the 10th century using notes of different shapes, although bar lines were not introduced until the 15th century. The present **staff notation** gradually evolved over this period and has been in use continuously for over 400 years. It is well adapted for music based on semitone intervals but breaks down where *microtones are used.

A parallel development to the staff notation was *solmization, first introduced in the 11th century and adapted into the *tonic sol-fa system in the 19th century. This system still has limited uses for teaching and in singing.

A different type of notation is based not on the notes produced but on the method of producing them. An example is the *tablature, originally used for lutes and still in use for guitars and other fretted instruments. In popular music a simple harmonic notation is used in which the harmonic sequence is denoted by abbreviations for the names of the *chords.

note 1. A single sound of identifiable *pitch and precise duration (see also **tone**). **2.** A symbol in a particular *notation for such a sound. **3.** A lever on a keyboard that is depressed to make such a sound.

notturno see **nocturne**.

novachord A form of electronic organ patented in 1939 by Lawrence Hammond. It used thermionic-valve oscillators to produce the notes and was capable of playing chords. It had a piano-type keyboard, stops for tone control, and pedals for volume control and sustaining notes.

Novák, Vitézslav (1870–1949) Czech composer, a pupil of Dvořák. Novák was influential as a teacher, his pupils including Hába. While Novák's early works build on the idiom of Dvořák, his later compositions emphasize nationalistic elements. Novák's output includes operas; orchestral music; choral music, including the cantata *The *Spectre's Bride*; and chamber works.

novelette A term introduced by Schumann in 1838 for eight short piano pieces that he described as 'romantic stories in music.'

November Woods Tone poem by Bax. Composed: 1917; first performance: 1920. This was the first of the composer's tone poems to be published; as the title implies, it evokes the atmosphere of an autumnal forest.

Nowowiejski, Feliks (1877–1946) Polish composer. Nowowiejski's early style was influenced by German romanticism; this idiom was extended in his later works to include more diverse elements. His compositions include four symphonies, the oratorio *Quo Vadis* (1903) and other choral works, chamber music, and songs.

Noye's Fludde Operatic setting by Britten of a text based on the Chester miracle play about Noah and the Flood. First performance: Orford Church, during the Aldeburgh Festival, 1958. God is a spoken role and Mr and Mrs Noye are adult parts (bass baritone and contralto); the other parts are written for children, with the audience participating in traditional hymns.

Nozze di Figaro, Le see **Marriage of Figaro, The.**

Nunc Dimittis The canticle of Simeon from Luke 2: 29–32, sung at the Roman Catholic offices of Vespers and Compline and at the Anglican service of Evensong. Unlike the *Magnificat, choral settings of the text for the Roman rite are scarce. In Merbecke's *Book of Common Praier Noted* (1550) it is set to simple recitation tones. Numerous choral settings have been made for Anglican use since the mid-16th century by Tye, Byrd, Gibbons, Tomkins, Purcell, and others. [Latin, from the opening words, '(Lord) now lettest thou (thy servant depart (in peace)']

Nuove musiche, Le see **new music; Caccini, Giulio.**

Nursery, The Song cycle by Mussorgsky to his own words. Composed: 1868–72. Each of the poems reflects upon some aspect of childhood, the seven songs being entitled 'With Nurse,' 'In the Corner,' 'The Cockchafer,' 'With the Doll,' 'Going to Sleep,' 'On the Hobby-Horse,' and 'The Cat Sailor.'

nut 1. The ridge over which the strings of a stringed instrument pass between the pegbox and the fingerboard. An open string vibrates between the nut and the bridge. The nut lifts the strings clear of the fingerboard. **2.** The device attached to the heel of a bow to enable the hairs to be tightened.

Nutcracker, The (French: *Casse-Noisette*; Russian: *Shchelkunchik*) Ballet in two acts with music by Tchaikovsky and choreography by Ivanov, based on a tale by E. T. A. Hoffmann. First performance: Maryinsky Theatre, St Petersburg, 1892. Klara is given a nutcracker for Christmas by her godfather; she falls asleep and dreams that she defends it against the King of the Mice; it turns into a Prince who takes her on a fabulous journey and in the Kingdom of Sweets they are entertained by the Sugar-Plum Fairy. In the 'Dance of the Sugar-Plum Fairy' Tchaikovsky introduced the celesta into Russian music.

The *Nutcracker Suite*, based on music from the ballet, was first performed some months before the ballet.

Nystroem, Gösta (1890–1966) Swedish composer, a pupil of d'Indy. Nystroem's mature works are marked by a combination of baroque and romantic influences. His output includes six symphonies, chamber works, choral music, and songs.

obbligato 1. Not to be omitted in performance; an essential part of a score: an instruction often attached to an instrumental part in a score, meaning that the part cannot be omitted. Thus an **oboe obbligato** is an oboe part that must be played. Compare **ad lib. 2.** May be omitted in performance: this opposite sense is sometimes used as a direction by composers. [Italian, obligatory]

Oberon Opera in three acts by Weber with English libretto by James Robertson Planché. First performance: Covent Garden, London, 1826. Subtitled *The Elf-King's Oath*, it tells how Oberon, king of the fairies (tenor), has quarrelled with his queen, Titania (spoken role), and sworn never to be reconciled until he has found two constant lovers. He eventually finds such a pair in Sir Huon (tenor) and Reiza (soprano). The romance is set in the days of Charlemagne.

Oberto Opera by Verdi (his first), with libretto by Piazza and Solera. First performance: La Scala, Milan, 1839. Set in a castle near Bassano in 1228, it is a tale of the revenge taken by Oberto (bass), exiled Count of San Bonifacio, on behalf of his daughter Leonora (soprano), who has been seduced and abandoned by Riccardo (tenor).

oblique motion see **motion.**

oboe A double-reeded woodwind instrument developed in France during the 17th century from the *shawm. Early oboes had finger holes and two to six keys; during the 19th century, however, a complicated system of keys was added. The modern orchestra uses three different types of oboe. The regular oboe, with a range of two and a half octaves from B♭ below middle C, has been in use for nearly 300 years. The **oboe d'amore** was created in Germany in about 1720 and revived in the 19th century; it is a *transposing instrument sounding a minor third below the regular oboe. The **cor anglais**, the largest of the three, sounds a fifth below the regular instrument. It evolved from the **alto oboe**, a straight instrument with an expanding bell, which was used in hunting at the beginning of the 18th century, when it was called an **oboe da caccia** (hunting oboe). The curved version of the oboe da caccia became known as a cor anglais (English horn), the name being retained even after the oboe da caccia was given a straight form in the 19th century. Two rarely used oboes are the **baritone oboe**, pitched an octave below the regular instrument, and the **heckelphone** (*or* **bass oboe**), a form of baritone oboe with a conical bore and a bulbous bell, invented in 1904 by the German firm of Heckel. Apart from its role in the orchestra, the oboe has a considerable repertoire as a solo instrument, including concertos by Albinoni and Bellini. [from the French *hautbois*, high wood]

Modern orchestral oboes: (1) cor anglais, (2) oboe d'amore and (3) the regular oboe

Obrecht, Jacob (*c*.1450–1505) Flemish composer and contemporary of Josquin des Prez. He was master of the boys at Cambrai (1484–85) and succentor at St Donatian in Bruges (1485–91), after which he moved to posts at Antwerp, Bruges, and Ferrara, where he died of the plague. His works comprise masses, including those based on *L'Homme armé* and *Caput*; motets, including *Salve crux arbor*; and a number of secular songs, some of which are in Dutch.

ocarina A type of whistle *flute with a vessel body containing several finger holes. It was invented in about 1860 by Giuseppe Donati and is used mainly as a toy, although ensembles of ocarinas were formed at the beginning of the 20th century.

Ockeghem, Jean d'(*c*.1420–*c*.1495) Flemish composer. He was a singer in the choir of Antwerp Cathedral (1443) and served in the chapel of the King of France (1452–?1488); he was also the treasurer of St Martin, Tours, from 1459 until his death. Ockeghem's compositions comprise masses (including those based on the *L'Homme armé* and *Caput* melodies), motets, and chansons. He also wrote an early example of the chanson-motet, *Mort tu as navré*,

Jean d'Ockeghem and a group of singers

written in lament of the death of Binchois (1460). Ockeghem's own death was the subject of a similar tribute paid by Josquin des Prez (who was one of his pupils) with his lament *Nymphes des bois*.

octave An interval of eight notes on the diatonic scale, or 12 semitones. The upper note has a frequency exactly double that of the lower note. Notes separated by an octave have the same letter to denote them. See also **consecutive intervals.**

octet A composition for eight voices or instruments or a group that performs such a composition. The scoring may be for strings, as in the octets by Mendelssohn and Gade, or for wind instruments, as in examples by Beethoven and Stravinsky. Schubert's octet is scored for a mixed ensemble of clarinet, horn, bassoon, two violins, viola, cello, and double bass.

octobass A very large and cumbersome double bass invented by Jean-Baptiste Vuillaume of Paris in 1849. The octobass was 12 ft (4 m) high; its strings were stopped by pedals and its bow was supported on blocks. Although octobasses were also made in the USA they were not considered practical instruments.

octuor Octet. [French]

ode A poetic form of ancient Greek origin, with constantly changing metre and rhythm. It is often addressed to a monarch or deity. There are many English musical settings of odes from the 17th and 18th centuries in the form of cantatas. These include Purcell's *Come Ye Sons of Art* composed for Queen Mary's birthday (1694) and Handel's *Ode for St Cecilia's Day* (1739). Examples from the 19th century include Schiller's *Ode to Joy* in the finale of Beethoven's *Choral Symphony* (1824) and Parry's setting of Milton's *Ode at a Solemn Music* (1887).

Ode for St Cecilia's Day 1. Any one of four anthems by Purcell written to celebrate St Cecilia's Day (22 November). The four works are *Laudate Ceciliam* (1683), *Welcome to all Pleasures* (1683), *Hail Bright Cecilia* (1692), and *Raise, Raise the Voice* (the date of composition of this last anthem is unknown, although it is thought that it was written in 1683). **2.** Anthem for choir and orchestra by Handel to words by Dryden. First performance: 1739. This work was also written to honour St Cecilia's Day, following the customary practice of the time.

Ode to Napoleon Work for speaker, strings, and piano by Schoenberg to words by Byron. Composed: 1942. In composing this work Schoenberg made a contemporary political commentary by expressing a fear of dictatorships and drawing parallels between the careers of Napoleon and Hitler. The work is constructed in the manner of an opera, with an overture, arias, and recitatives, although there is no action and the speaking part employs Sprechstimme.

Plate 31: *The English National Ballet in a performance of Tchaikovsky's* The Nutcracker, *given at the Royal Festival Hall, London, in January 1989*

Plate 32 above: *The Elysian Fields scene from the 1982 Glyndebourne production of Gluck's opera* Orfeo ed Euridice, *with Janet Baker as Orfeo, Elisabeth Speiser (in blue) as Euridice and the Glyndebourne Festival Chorus. Produced by Peter Hall, this was Janet Baker's farewell opera performance*

Plate 33 opposite: *The organ at Salamanca Cathedral in Spain with its magnificent case is a fine example of the instrument maker's art*

Plate 34: *Jon Vickers and Heather Harper in Benjamin Britten's*
Peter Grimes *at the Royal Opera House, Covent Garden, London,*
in 1981

Oedipus Rex (*King Oedipus*) *Opera-oratorio in two acts by Stravinsky with text by Cocteau (based on Sophocles), translated into Latin by Daniélou. First performance (in concert form, conducted by the composer): Théâtre Sarah Bernhardt, Paris, 1927; first stage performance: Vienna, 1928. A narrator is used to set the scene for the audience in the vernacular; the Latin text gives a ritualistic ethos to the tragedy.

Offenbach, Jacques (Jacob) (1819–80) French composer, conductor, and cellist, of German origin (his family came from Offenbach am Main, hence the surname). He studied at the Paris Conservatoire (1833–34), then played the cello in the orchestra at the Opéra-Comique (1834–38) and had composition lessons with Halévy. During the 1840s he had an international career as a cello virtuoso. He became conductor of the Théâtre Français (1850–55) and director of the Bouffes Parisiens (1855–62), where he presented short comic operas, including some of his own. He was manager of the Théâtre de la Gaîté (1873–74) and made a conducting tour of the USA (1876). With Johann Strauss the Younger, Offenbach was a leading and influential figure in the composition of popular music in the 19th century. His 90 or so operettas are vigorous and tuneful, satirizing fashionable society; the best known are *Orphée aux enfers* (1858; see **Orpheus in the Underworld**), La *Belle Hélène* (1864), *La Vie parisienne* (1866), *La Grande-Duchesse de Gérolstein* (1867), and *La Périchole* (1868). His only grand opera, *Les Contes d'Hoffmann* (1881; see **Tales of Hoffmann, The**), completed by Guiraud after his death, is in the international repertory. Offenbach also composed ballets and dance music, vocal works, and music for cello.

Offertory Part of the Proper of the *Mass, originally consisting of a psalm with an antiphon sung to plainchant as the bread and wine are placed on the altar. The chants later became more elaborate, with *melismas in the responsorial style. Polyphonic settings of Offertory texts as *motets were made in the 16th century by Lassus and Palestrina. Cantus-firmus organ settings of *Felix namque*, the Offertory for the English Lady Mass, were widely composed in the 15th and 16th centuries. See also **organ mass.**

Ogdon, John (Andrew Howard) (1937–89) British pianist and composer. He was joint winner, with Vladimir Ashkenazy, of the 1962 Tchaikovsky Competition in Moscow and an international career followed. Ogdon, who has had to fight against mental illness for some years, has a wide repertory, with a particular interest in 20th-century works.

Oistrakh, David (1908–74) Soviet violinist. In 1934 Oistrakh became a professor at the Moscow conservatory and combined this with extensive concert appearances;

international recognition came when he won the Violin Competition in Brussels (1937). Oistrakh was one of the leading performers of his day: Prokofiev, Shostakovich, and Khachaturian all dedicated works to him. His son, **Igor Oistrakh** (1931–), has also enjoyed a considerable reputation as a violinist and the two frequently performed together.

Old Hall Manuscript A manuscript collection of late 14th- and early 15th-century English sacred music. It contains Mass movements, antiphons, Sequences, and motets, nearly all by English composers (including Power and Pycard). Compiled *c.*1410–15, it was published in 1933–38. For many years this important manuscript was at St Edmund's College, Old Hall, near Ware; it is now in the British Library (MS Add. 57950).

Oldham, Arthur (1926–) British composer, a pupil of Howells and Britten. His works, which adhere to traditional principles of tonality and harmony, include the ballet *Mr Punch* (1946), orchestral music, choral works, and music for children.

oliphant An end-blown ivory horn, made from an elephant's tusk (hence the name). Oliphants were used as the insignia of African kings and regarded as prized possessions by European noblemen in the 10th to the 12th centuries.

Oliver, Stephen (1950–) British composer, a pupil of Leighton and Sherlaw Johnson. He developed an eclectic

A contemporary caricature of Offenbach

dramatic style in a series of chamber operas culminating in *The Duchess of Malfi* (1971). His other works include a symphony, *Ricercare* (1974), the opera *Tom Jones* (1976), and *Exchange* (1978).

Oliveros, Pauline (1932–) US composer. From an early interest in electronic music and improvisation she turned to multimedia theatre pieces, which demonstrated her use of repetition and extended sounds. Tibetan Buddhism and radical feminism have influenced her works, which include *Night Jar* (1968), *Sonic Meditations* (1970), *Bon-fire* (1977), and *Horse Sings from Cloud* (1977).

Olympians, The Opera in three acts by Arthur Bliss with libretto by J. B. Priestley. First performance: Covent Garden, London, 1949. The Greek gods come down to earth as strolling players and temporarily recapture their ancient powers.

Omphale's Spinning Wheel see **Rouet d'Omphale, Le.**

ondes Martenot (*or* **ondes musicales**) An early form of *synthesizer invented in the 1920s by Maurice Martenot (1898–). Operated by a piano-type keyboard, it was a heterodyne device using thermionic-valve oscillators to produce the sound through a loudspeaker. Used by Honegger in his *Joan of Arc at the Stake*, it has now been superseded by transistor synthesizers.

O'Neill, Norman (1875–1934) British composer. After studying in England and Germany, O'Neill directed the music for a number of London theatres, composing much incidental music. His output also includes orchestral music, chamber works, and songs.

On Hearing the First Cuckoo in Spring Work for small orchestra by Delius. First performance: 1913. For the principal theme Delius employs a popular Norwegian folk song, against which the clarinet imitates the call of a cuckoo with its downward leap of a major third. This work is the first of a set of two descriptive orchestral pieces, the second being *A Summer Night on the River*.

Onslow, (André) Georges (1784–1853) French composer of English descent. He studied the piano in London with Hüllmandel, Dussek, and Cramer and later (1808) in Paris with Reicha. He spent the rest of his life in France. Onslow composed three operas, four symphonies, and a great deal of chamber music (including 34 string quintets, 35 string quartets, and 10 piano trios) of no great distinction.

On Wenlock Edge Song cycle for tenor, string quartet, and piano by Vaughan Williams to six poems by A. E. Housman. Composed: 1909. Wenlock Edge is a beauty spot in Shropshire and in this work Vaughan Williams shows the influence of Ravel, with whom he had been studying.

Op. See **opus.**

open form A composition that can begin or end at any point in the score at the discretion of the performer(s). Stockhausen's *Zyklus* (1959) for solo percussionist is an example. This score is arranged on spiral-bound pages and the percussion instruments are arranged in a circle, so that the player has total freedom of choice over the form and instrumentation of the composer's ideas.

open harmony Harmony in which the notes of the chord are separated by a large interval. Compare **close harmony.**

open string An unstopped string on a plucked or bowed stringed instrument, i.e. a string that is allowed to vibrate over its full length.

Oper Opera; opera house; opera company. [German]

opera A dramatic work that combines music, poetry, action, drama, visual art, and stagecraft. Its western origins have been traced to ancient Greece, where choruses and dances formed an essential part in the productions of tragedies. Music was also allied to action in the liturgical dramas and mystery plays of the medieval church. Two important precursors of opera flourished in 16th-century Italy: the *ballet and the *intermezzo. At the end of the 16th century the poets, musicians, and philosophers of the Florentine *Camerata laid the foundations of opera. The invention of *recitative provided a means of continuously unfolding and amplifying a drama through the medium of music. Peri's *Euridice* (1597) is believed to be the earliest opera. In Monteverdi's *Orfeo* (1607), recitative, combined with considerable musical characterization, was used with several established forms, including ballet, madrigal, ritornello, sinfonia, and toccata. The dramatically appropriate use of a varied ensemble of instruments is a further significant aspect of this opera.

In 1637 opera ceased to be confined to aristocratic court entertainments; with the opening of the San Cassiano theatre in Venice, the world's first public opera house, opera became available to the less privileged. By the middle of the 17th century opera had become more formalized, with established patterns for orchestral *overtures and sinfonias. Most significantly, the *aria emerged as a distinct form. Lavish scenery, spectacular stage effects, and virtuoso vocal writing for *castrato singers became popular attractions.

Opera was established in France by Cambert (*Pomone*, 1671) and Lully (*Cadmus et Hermione*, 1673). A national style grew from a merging of the existing court ballets and tragedies with a skilful adaptation of Italian recitative to the French language. Arias were simple and there was greater use of the chorus. (See also **French overture.**) The style established by Lully was given greater dramatic scope and orchestral brilliance in the operas of Rameau (*Castor et Pollux*, 1737). Attempts to establish opera in 17th-century

England from the existing traditions of the *masque and incidental music to plays were unsuccessful. Blow's *Venus and Adonis* (*c*.1684) and Purcell's *Dido and Aeneas* (*c*.1689) are the only true operas of the period. Italian opera was widely cultivated in German courts in the 17th century, but a national school was established in Hamburg under Keiser. Among the works produced were the first *singspiels. During the 18th century Italian opera was significantly reformed by the librettos of Zeno and Metastasio. These introduced several features that were to become standard in **opera seria**: a plot based on ancient history or legend presented in three acts, the action associated with recitatives, and meditation confined to arias, which were invariably in *da capo form and gave considerable scope for vocal virtuosity. Later baroque opera grew to its climax through the works of Alessandro Scarlatti and Handel. The latter achieved considerable success at dramatic characterization within the tightly defined formal structures. During the final decades of the 18th century the **reform operas** of Gluck (*Orfeo ed Euridice*, 1762; *Alceste*, 1767) drew music and drama closer together; irrelevant vocal virtuosity was curbed and the formal demarcation between recitative and aria became less rigid. Gluck drew the French and Italian styles closer together by introducing ballet and choral scenes into opera seria. Comic and semicomic plots became more common in the later 18th century, as in *The Marriage of Figaro* (1786) and *Don Giovanni* (1787) by Mozart. By virtue of his vivid powers of dramatic and musical characterization Mozart excelled in all forms of opera, including opera seria (*Idomeneo*, 1781) and singspiel (*The Magic Flute*, 1791). Particularly important is his skilful integration of vocal and instrumental forces. **Rescue operas**, in which the hero (or heroine) was saved from desperate situations, were popular at the end of the 18th century and the beginning of the 19th century; a typical example is Beethoven's *Fidelio* (1805–14).

French *grand opera was established in the early 19th century. It featured heroic and historical plots as represented by Rossini's *William Tell* (1829), Meyerbeer's *Les Huguenots* (1836), and Berlioz's *The Trojans* (1863). French **lyric opera** was the result of Italian influence, as in Gounod's *Faust* (1859). After Bellini and Donizetti 19th-century Italian opera was dominated by the achievements of Verdi. His plots feature simple true-to-life situations set to music designed to display the expressive qualities of the human voice, as in *Il Trovatore* and *La Traviata* (both 1853). In *Otello* (1887) and *Falstaff* (1893) Verdi responded to the developments of Wagnerian music drama. 19th-century Russian opera was strongly motivated by nationalism, as reflected in Glinka's *A Life for the Tsar* (1836) and Mussorgsky's *Boris Godunov* (1874). German romantic opera evolved from singspiel and featured plots drawn from national legend and folklore. These reveal a strong affinity with nature and the supernatural, together with nationalistic

sentiments, as displayed in Weber's *Der Freischütz* (1821). This style strongly influenced Wagner (*The Flying Dutchman*, 1843) and was developed by him into a new genre, the *music drama (*Der Ring des Nibelungen*, 1876).

The music drama exerted a significant influence on early-20th-century opera, particularly in Richard Strauss's *Elektra* (1909) and *Salome* (1905). Among the new currents that appeared at this time were verismo opera (Puccini's *La Bohème*, 1896, and *Tosca*, 1900) and *impressionism (Debussy's *Pelléas et Mélisande*, 1902). Among the operas composed by the Second Viennese School are Berg's *Wozzeck* (1925) and Schoenberg's *Moses und Aron*. In *The Rake's Progress* (1951) by Stravinsky there is a neoclassical revival of 18th-century forms, but in Prokofiev's *War and Peace* (1955), opera assumes epic proportions. Since 1945 British opera has flourished through a series of distinguished works by Britten (*Peter Grimes*, 1945, to *Death in Venice*, 1973) and Tippett (*The Midsummer Marriage*, 1955, to *The Ice Break*, 1976).

Opera, particularly grand opera, has during the course of its evolution come to rely on a number of somewhat artificial conventions: complicated and barely intelligible plots, slowed-down action in which the characters express themselves in endlessly repetitive songs, and scenes in which the terminally ill sing with unconvincing vigour. The staging of these melodramatic events requires vast sets and lavish costumes in order to make the entertainment a spectacle that transcends the merely improbable. The vast sets require large choruses to fill them, which, in turn, means large orchestras to enable the music to be heard. These elements have combined with the enormous fees asked by leading operatic singers to make opera a totally uncommercial venture. Most countries therefore now have opera houses financed, or partly financed, by governments or by commercial and industrial concerns. See also **ballad opera; bel canto; libretto; opera ballet; opera buffa; opéra comique; opera-oratorio; operetta.**

opera ballet A French stage work of the 17th and 18th centuries in which opera and ballet are combined with equal importance. The form originated with Campra and Mouret (*Les Fêtes de Thalie*, 1714) and featured three or four acts (entrées), each with different characters but loosely connected through the plot.

opéra bouffe A type of 19th-century French opera, derived from Italian *opera buffa, that is light, witty, and satirical. Examples are Offenbach's operettas *La Belle Hélène* and *Orpheus in the Underworld*.

opera buffa A form of Italian comic opera in the 18th century. These witty two- or three-act operas featured comic characters and ensemble finales, as in Pergolesi's *La Serva padrona* (1733). The form evolved from the humorous *intermezzi performed between the acts of opera seria. See also **opéra bouffe**.

opéra comique A form of French opera with spoken dialogue that is not necessarily humorous. Examples from the 18th century include Rousseau's *Le Devin du village* (1752) and Grétry's *Richard Coeur-de-Lion* (1784); 19th-century examples are Gounod's *Faust* (1859) and Bizet's *Carmen* (1875).

opera-oratorio The term used by Stravinsky to describe his *Oedipus Rex* (1927), in which static action is presented on stage so that the work stands midway between the forms of opera and oratorio.

opera semi-seria An Italian opera that is neither wholly comic nor wholly tragic. The plot might be essentially serious but with strong comic elements provided by servants, as in Mozart's *Don Giovanni* (1787). The term was widely applied to libretti of the 1820s that included spoken dialogue.

opera seria A type of *opera of the 18th and early 19th centuries with a heroic, mythological, or tragic plot. It was not a contemporary term, **dramma per musica** being more usual. Mozart's *Idomeneo* (1781) and Rossini's *Semiramide* (1823) are examples.

operetta A short light opera with spoken dialogue, songs, and dances. It evolved from the *opéra comique and flourished during the second half of the 19th century and the early 20th century. See also **musical comedy**.

ophicleide A large 19th-century keyed *bugle with a U-shaped body similar to a bassoon. It was a baritone instrument made in C or B♭ with 9–12 keys. Although it was used in the orchestra by Mendelssohn and Wagner it has now been replaced by the *tuba. [from Greek *ophis*, serpent *kleides*, keys]

Op. post. See opus.

opus (followed by a number and usually abbreviated to **Op.**) A musical composition by a particular composer. Opus numbers are frequently but not invariably a guide to the chronology of composition: they were usually assigned to works when they were published (by the publisher, not the composer). Opus numbers are more often used to refer to instrumental works. An opus may comprise several pieces, in which case the opus has numbered subdivisions (e.g. Op. 18 No. 3). For posthumously published works the abbreviation **Op. post.**, followed by an appropriate number, is used.

For the works of some composers this number system became very confused and unreliable, in some cases because the composer used more than one publisher, and different systems have been adopted. Composers whose works are now numbered by a different system include J. S. Bach (see

BWV), Mozart (see **K.**), Haydn (see **Hob.**), and Vivaldi (see **RV**).

oratorio A composition for vocal soloists, chorus, and orchestra with a libretto based on a religious or reflective text, performed without action in a concert hall. It evolved in Italy during the mid-16th century, partly from the late medieval liturgical dramas and partly from the *lauda sung at popular services held in oratories. Cavalieri's *Rappresentazione di anima e di corpo* (1600), which employed the new operatic technique of *recitative, is considered to be one of the earliest oratorios, despite it being performed in costume. Later-17th-century oratorios on Old Testament texts include those of Carissimi (e.g. *Jephtha*, 1650) and Stradella. Oratorio was established in Germany by Schütz with *Historia der Auferstehung* (1623) and his *Christmas Oratorio* (1664). With J. S. Bach's *Christmas Oratorio* (1733–34) and Telemann's *Der Tag des Gerichts* German baroque oratorio reached its climax.

With the exception of *Messiah* (1742) English oratorio, as established by Handel, featured a dramatic presentation of Old Testament stories, including *Israel in Egypt* (1737) and *Samson* (1743). Arne (*Judith*, 1764) was foremost among the few English composers who made distinguished contributions to the form after Handel. Oratorios of the late 18th century include Haydn's *Seven Last Words* (1797), *The Creation* (1797), and *The Seasons* (1801), which has a secular text. 19th-century German romantic oratorios include Mendelssohn's *St Paul* (1830) and *Elijah* (1847), Wagner's *Das Liebesmahl der Apostel* (1844), and Liszt's *Christus* (1866). In France, *L'Enfance du Christ* (1854) by Berlioz and *Les Béatitudes* (1879) by Franck represent the only distinguished examples of oratorio since Charpentier's *Le Reniement de St Pierre* (c.1700). At the end of the 19th century English oratorio assumed more distinguished proportions with Parry's *Judith* (1888) and *Job* (1892), Elgar's *The Apostles* (1903) and *The Kingdom* (1906), and Walford Davies' *Everyman* (1904). Among mid-20th-century oratorios are Stravinsky's *Oedipus Rex* (1927; see also **opera-oratorio**) and *Belshazzar's Feast* (1931) by Walton.

Orchésographie A treatise on dancing by Thoinot Arbeau (anagrammatic pen name of Tabourot Jehan; 1520–95). *Orchésographie* was published in 1588 and is an important source of information about contemporary dance music.

orchestra A large mixed group of instrumentalists; more specifically, a body of bowed stringed instruments, with more than one player to each part, plus wind and percussion instruments. An ensemble of wind instruments alone is usually called a *band. There are various types of orchestra in addition to the **symphony orchestra**, including the *chamber orchestra, string orchestra, and theatre orchestra (one used for accompanying musicals).

The constitution of instrumental ensembles up to the end of the 17th century was flexible. By the early 18th century a four-part string ensemble was common; violins replaced viols, wind was added, and harmonic support was provided by a keyboard (see **continuo**). As instruments were developed and improved, more were added to the basic ensemble and they were used more colourfully. In the 19th century further changes were made: string instruments were improved, woodwind was redesigned, and trumpets and horns acquired valves. Harps, trombones, and more percussion were often added to form the modern symphony orchestra. Wagner's requirements necessitated a very large orchestra with a big brass section – a development that has strongly influenced later composers. By the 20th century the symphony orchestra was typically a very large group capable of great sonority and exotic colourful effects.

orchestration The art of scoring music for an orchestra or other large instrumental group or of arranging a piece composed for another medium for an orchestral group. Some composers have had a special interest in writing for the orchestra, using it not simply as a homogeneous group but exploiting the tone colour of individual instruments or groups of instruments.

Orchestre de Paris French symphony orchestra founded in 1967. Its conductors have been Charles Munch, Herbert von Karajan, Georg Solti, and Daniel Barenboim (from 1976).

Ord, Boris (1897–1961) British organist and conductor. Ord was organist and choirmaster at King's College, Cambridge (1929–57), where he did much to establish the choir's international reputation.

ordre The usual French name for *suite in the 17th and 18th centuries.

Orfeo, La Favola d' (*The Story of Orpheus*) Opera in prologue and five acts by Monteverdi with text by Striggio. First performance (private): Accademia degl' Invaghiti, Mantua, 1607. One of the first operas, it is interesting historically in that Monteverdi gives a list of instruments to be used at the beginning of his score. In addition, Orfeo's great aria in his search for the lost Euridice is written out in two forms: one showing the basic melodic line; another giving the expected ornamentation. See also **Orpheus**.

Orfeo ed Euridice (*Orpheus and Eurydice*) Opera in three acts by Gluck with text by Calzabigi based on the classical legend. First performance: Burgtheater, Vienna, 1762. This was the first of Gluck's reform operas; a revised French version (*Orphée et Euridice*), translated by Moline from Calzabigi's libretto, was produced in Paris in 1774. See also **Orpheus**.

Orff, Carl (1895–1982) German composer. Orff's music is marked by a driving rhythm derived from the early works of Stravinsky, his orchestration relying heavily on pianos and percussion instruments. Orff has also been influential in musical education, introducing a large variety of percussion instruments into elementary musical training. His works include the well-known *Carmina Burana* (1937), a setting for chorus, soloists, and orchestra of medieval Latin poems; stage works, including *Der Mond* (1939), Die *Kluge* (1943), and *Antigone* (1949); and choral music.

organ A *keyboard instrument of great antiquity in which sound is produced by blowing air through pipes. The concept originated with the mouth-blown *panpipes, the first mechanically blown instrument being the ancient Greek *hydraulis, invented in the 3rd century BC by Ctesibios of Alexandria. In the earliest organs the air was admitted into the pipes, or stopped from entering them, by means of sliders – wooden slats fitted between the top of the windchest and the bottom of the pipes. In the open position a hole in the slider coincided with a hole in the top of the windchest, enabling air to enter the pipe; in the closed position the holes were not in alignment and the pipe remained silent. By the 11th century these hand-operated sliders were replaced by large cumbersome levers, which

An Italian production of Carl Orff's Carmina Burana

gave way in the 15th century to fist-operated keys. In the 16th century these broad keys evolved into the finger keys of the modern manual.

During the time that the keyboards were developing there was a similar development in the organ's mechanical *action and wind supply. The earliest organs had only a single pipe sounding each note, whereas to obtain a variation in tone colour it is necessary to sound more than one pipe for each note. This was at first achieved by having more than one keyboard; for example, the organ built in 980 in the monastery at Winchester had two keyboards operating two sets of pipes. However, during the 15th century the mechanism of *stops appeared. Thereafter organs had several *ranks of pipes, which could be sounded by depressing a certain key, the pipes to be sounded being selected by the organist drawing a stop (i.e. pulling out a knob). This is the principle of modern organs. Thus, each rank comprises one or more pipes (see **mixture stop**) for each of the (usually) 61 keyboard notes.

In addition to this grouping of the pipes controlled by each stop, several ranks of pipes are grouped into divisions (which are themselves called organs) controlled by separate keyboards. Thus the **great manual** controls the **great organ**, the **swell manual** controls the **swell organ**, and the **choir manual** controls the **choir organ**. Each manual then has its own stops. The great organ is the most powerful division of the whole organ and gives it its characteristic sound. Above the great manual is the swell manual, the pipes of which are enclosed in a **swell box**. This box has Venetian shutters on at least one side, which are operated by the **swell pedal**. Opening and closing the shutters increases and decreases the volume of the sound emerging – one of the few means of introducing expression into organ playing. Below the great manual, in a three-manual organ, is the choir manual, which with its softer stops is used mainly for accompanying choirs. Some organs have a fourth manual –the **solo manual** – above the swell organ, with stops to emulate solo instruments, and a few have a fifth **echo manual,** which is very soft indeed. The pedalboard operates a separate **pedal organ**, the chief stops for which are pitched an octave below the manual stops.

The organ pipes themselves are of two basic types: *flue pipes and *reed pipes. The flue pipes work on the principle of a whistle and may be round or square, wood or metal. The length of the pipe determines its pitch and the width controls the tone quality and volume. The relationship between the length and width is called the **scale** of the pipe. A flue pipe may be open at the top or stopped; a stopped pipe sounds an octave lower than an open pipe of the same length and the even-numbered harmonics are very weak, giving a stopped pipe a light quality. Reed pipes have a metal tongue fixed to the side of a metal tube, which leads to a conical pipe called a **resonator**. This is a beating reed pipe, which differs from the free reed of the *harmonium.

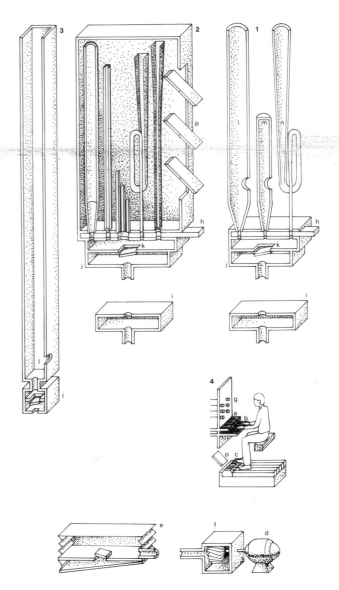

The organist at the console (4) controls the three sections of the organ through the keyboards or manuals - the great manual (a) operates the great organ (1), the swell manual (b) the swell organ (2), and the pedalboard (c) operates the pedal organ (3). An electric generator (d) supplies air to the bellows (e) by means of a fan (f). Through the use of stops (g) on the console that control sliders (h) in the great and swell organs, the organist selects a rank of pipes -open (l), stopped (m), or reed (n). When a key or pedal is pressed, air passes from the reservoir (i) into the wind chest (j), through open pallet holes (k), and then into the selected pipes. Gradual changes of volume are achieved through the swell pedal (o), which opens and closes shutters (p) in the swell box. A complex coupling system enables all sections of the organ to be sounded simultaneously.

The use of the organ has varied considerably over its 2000 years of existence. The Romans used their versions of the hydraulis at many forms of public entertainment, including those in which Christians were torn to pieces by lions. Not surprisingly, therefore, early Christians did not develop a liturgical interest in the instrument for several centuries. However, organs were in common use in Spanish churches by the middle of the 5th century and had appeared in English churches by the 8th century. In addition to these large church organs, however, smaller *portative organs and *positive organs were used for secular purposes during the Middle Ages. Nevertheless from the 16th to the 19th centuries it was on the church organ that most of the organ music composed in this period was intended to be played. By the 19th century improvements to the action and to the wind supply enabled the organ builders to produce instruments that could effectively emulate the orchestra, which led not only to a change in the size and the sound of an organ, but also to a widening of its use and repertoire. By the 20th century the organ had emerged into the concert hall and in the 1920s and 1930s it was a popular instrument in the cinema and theatre (see **cinema organ**). See also **electronic organ.**

organistrum see **hurdy-gurdy.**

organ mass A setting of movements from either the Ordinary of the *Mass, or from both the Ordinary and the Proper, in which verses of the text sung to plainchant alternate with polyphonic settings of the chant as a cantus firmus for organ. Examples from the 15th century occur in the *Buxheim Organ Book*, and a complete setting of the Proper by Thomas Preston survives from the 16th century. The form was widely developed by French and Italian composers during the 17th century. Frescobaldi's three masses in *Fiori musicali* (1635) include toccatas to be played before the Mass, canzonas to follow the Epistle and Communion, ricercari to follow the Credo, and chromatic toccatas for the Elevation. French organ masses of the 17th and 18th centuries include versets for the movements of the Ordinary and an extended piece to be played during the Offertory, as in examples by François Couperin and de Grigny.

organo pleno see **full organ.**

organ point see **pedal.** French: **point d'orgue.**

organum The earliest type of medieval polyphony, current in church music from the 9th century to the 13th century. First described about 900 in *Musica enchiriadis* (authorship disputed), it involves the addition of one or more freely composed voices to a passage of plainchant. There are three basic categories. In **strict organum** the added voice moves mainly in parallel fourths or fifths with the chant, note against note. In **free organum,** current from about 1000, the added voice moves in a free succession of intervals, still note against note. Finally, in the **melismatic organum,** associated with the St Martial and Notre Dame schools (from *c.*1150), several notes in the added voice counterpoint each note of

chant. The most complex forms of melismatic organum are represented in the schools of Léonin and Pérotin as preserved in the so-called *Magnus liber* (*c.*1170). This repertoire introduces measured rhythm in the added voice by means of the rhythmic modes and (in later revisions) the further refinement of three-voice and four-voice organum.

Orgel Organ. [German]

Orlando Opera seria by Handel with Italian libretto by Braccioli based on Ariosto's *Orlando Furioso.* First performance: King's Theatre, London, 1733. Handel vividly characterizes the madness of Orlando in his arias.

Ormandy, Eugene (E. Blau; 1899–1985) Hungarian-born conductor. Originally a violinist, he emigrated to the USA in 1920. He conducted the Minneapolis Symphony Orchestra (1931–36) and the Philadelphia Orchestra (1938–78). He conducted entirely from memory.

Ormindo Opera by Cavalli with libretto by Faustini. First performance: Teatro San Cassiano, Venice, 1644. Ormindo is a prince of Tunis.

ornament A melodic embellishment that is added to vocal or instrumental music either by the composer or by the performer at his own discretion. Ornaments that are written into a score are either denoted by a symbol or by notes written in small type. Common ornaments include the *acciaccatura, *appoggiatura, *mordent, *slide, *trill, and *turn.

Ornstein, Leo (1892–) Russian-born US composer. Ornstein aligned himself with the futurist movement, his early works featuring harsh dissonances and complicated rhythms. His output includes many piano pieces, including *Danse sauvage* (1914) and *Poems of 1917*; a symphony (1934); and chamber music and songs.

Orozco, Rafael (1946–) Spanish pianist, a pupil at the Córdoba and Madrid conservatories. His international career began after he won the 1966 Leeds Piano Competition. An exuberant virtuoso, he specializes in performing Rachmaninov's concertos.

Orphée aux enfers see **Orpheus in the Underworld.**

Orpheus Tone poem by Liszt based upon the mythological figure Orpheus. Composed: 1854. This work was written as the introduction for a production of Gluck's opera *Orfeo ed Euridice* in Weimar in 1854. For other operas dealing with the subject of Orpheus, see **Orfeo, La Favola d';** **Orpheus in the Underworld.**

Orpheus Britannicus Two volumes of songs by Henry Purcell, the 'English Orpheus.' They were published posthumously (1698–1702) by Henry Playford and contain songs for one, two, and three voices. Benjamin Britten and Peter Pears realized and edited 18 of them.

Orpheus in the Underworld (French: *Orphée aux enfers*) Operetta by Offenbach with libretto by Crémieux and Halévy. First performance: Bouffes-Parisiens, Paris, 1858. The classical setting is used to satirize mid-19th-century manners. The aria 'Che farò' from Gluck's *Orfeo ed Euridice* is quoted; the famous *Can-can* comes in the final tableau.

Orr, Robin (1909–) British composer, a pupil of Dent, Casella, and Nadia Boulanger. His works, written in a conservatively tonal idiom, include three symphonies, the song cycle *Journeys and Places* (1971), and the operas *Full Circle* (1968) and *Hermiston* (1975).

Ortiz, Diego (*c*.1510–*c*.1570) Spanish composer and theorist. He was active in Naples as maestro di cappella to the Spanish viceroy from 1556 until at least 1565. His *Trateado de glosas* (1553) is the first treatise on ornamentation for bowed string instruments. Ortiz also wrote a small amount of church music.

O salutaris hostia Hymn of the Roman Catholic Church associated with the service of benediction but occasionally also appearing at other services. The plainsong melody to which *O salutaris hostia* (Latin, 'O saving victim') was traditionally sung is also used for the Ascension hymn *Aeterne Rex Altissime*. Settings of the words were attempted by many Renaissance composers, including Byrd and Palestrina.

ossia An indication that a passage is an alternative to the main text, usually either an editorial correction or an easier version supplied by the composer. [Italian, from *o sia*, or let it be]

ostinato A persistently repeated melodic or rhythmic figure. A **basso ostinato** is a bass that is to be repeated. **Pizzicato ostinato** (used by Tchaikovsky in his fourth symphony) means that the pizzicato is to be applied persistently. [Italian, obstinate]

Ostrcil, Otakar (1879–1935) Czech composer. Ostrcil directed the Prague Opera (1914–19) and was principal conductor at the National Theatre from 1920. His works, which continue the Czech romantic tradition of Dvořák and Smetana, include operas, a symphony (1905), chamber music, and songs.

Otello (*Othello*) **1.** Opera in four acts by Verdi with libretto by Boito based on Shakespeare's tragedy. First performance: La Scala, Milan, 1887. **2.** Opera by Rossini, subtitled *Il Moro di Venezia* (*The Moor of Venice*), with libretto by de Salsa. First performance: Naples, 1816.

ôtez Take away, remove. Hence **ôtez les sourdines**, a direction in organ music to take off the mutes. [French]

Othello Concert overture (Op. 93) by Dvořák based on the play by Shakespeare. Composed: 1892. *Othello* is the

The English National Opera's Orpheus in the Underworld

final work in Dvořák's trilogy of overtures called *Nature, Life and Love*, the other two works being **In Nature's Realm* and **Carnival*. See also **Otello**.

ottava (*or* **8va**) Octave. **All' ottava** (at the 8ve) means that the music written should be played an octave higher. Occasionally **ottava sopra** or **ottava alta** are used in this sense. **Ottava bassa** (low 8ve) and **ottava sotto** mean that the music written should be played an octave lower. [Italian]

ottavino The modern Italian name for the piccolo (see **flute**).

Otterloo, (Jan) Willem van (1907–78) Dutch conductor and composer. He conducted the Utrecht Orchestra (1933–49), the Residentie Orchestra of The Hague (1949–72), and the Düsseldorf Symphony Orchestra (from 1973). He also conducted the Melbourne Symphony Orchestra. His compositions include orchestral and chamber music.

Our Man in Havana Opera by Malcolm Williamson with libretto by Sidney Gilliat based on Graham Greene's novel. First performance: London, 1963. It satirizes colonial espionage and security.

Ours, L' see **Bear, The**.

Ouseley, Sir Frederick Arthur Gore (1825–89) British church musician, clergyman, and composer. He established (1854) the College of St Michael and All Angels at Tenbury, Worcestershire, the first collegiate church founded in England since the Reformation. Using his wealth (he had succeeded to his father's title in 1844) he was able to realize there his ideals of cathedral worship. He was Professor of Music at Oxford University (1855–89) and precentor of

Hereford Cathedral. Ouseley had shown a precocious talent as a composer but his works (mostly sacred choral pieces but also some secular vocal, orchestral, chamber, organ, and piano pieces) are now seldom heard.

overblowing The act of blowing a wind instrument with such force that upper harmonics are produced. Brass instruments produce more harmonics than woodwind instruments. The flute and the oboe produce the octave when overblown but the clarinet family produces the twelfth. Overblowing may also occur in organ pipes if the wind pressure is excessive, but some organs have safety valves to prevent overblowing.

overtones 1. The notes of a *harmonic series excluding the first harmonic (fundamental), i.e. the upper partials. **2.** The sounds produced by a vibrating body that are of higher frequency than the fundamental but are not members of the harmonic series. Many unmusical noises consist of a fundamental note with overtones unrelated to its harmonic series.

overture 1. An instrumental piece serving as the introduction to an opera, oratorio, or play. One of the earliest operatic examples is the toccata that begins Monteverdi's *Orfeo* (1607). The development of the overture in the 17th century was closely connected with the growth of independent instrumental forms, including the sinfonia (Landi's *Il Sant' Alessio*), the canzona, which was used by Venetian operatic composers, and the sonata (Cesti's *Il Pomo d'oro*, 1667). In the later 17th century the *French overture was evolved by Lully and the *Italian overture by Alessandro Scarlatti. The latter were invariably called sinfonias. By the second half of the 18th century the operatic overture more closely reflected the drama that was to follow, as in Haydn's *Creation* (1798) and Mozart's *The Magic Flute* (1791). It also became the practice to incorporate material from the opera into the overture: this began with Rameau's *Castor et Pollux* (1735) and continued in Gluck's *Iphigénie en Tauride* (1778). The process of integrating the overture into the work as a whole was continued in the 19th century by Weber (*Der Freischütz*, 1821) and in the preludes to Wagner's *music dramas. By contrast, the overtures to the comic operas, operettas, and grand operas of the 19th century were built on *potpourris of melodies from the drama. **2.** A concert work that evolved from the dramatically suggestive *Leonora* overtures of Beethoven. Subsequent examples have a literary or programmatic basis (see also **programme music**), as in Mendelssohn's *Hebrides* overture or *In the South* by Elgar. Some concert overtures were originally intended as incidental music to plays, e.g. Mendelssohn's *A Midsummer Night's Dream* overture.

Oxford Elegy, An Work for speaker, chamber choir, and chamber orchestra by Vaughan Williams to words by Arnold. Composed: 1947–49. The text is taken mainly from the poem 'The Scholar Gipsy,' about a wandering Oxford scholar, although some lines from 'Thyrsis' are also used. For many years Vaughan Williams had contemplated writing an opera on this subject, but eventually composed this work instead.

Oxford Symphony Symphony No. 92 in G major by Haydn. Composed: 1788. In 1791 Haydn was conferred with an honorary degree from Oxford University and following the custom of the day he was obliged to provide an 'exercise' – a musical composition to be performed in return for the degree. He composed a symphony especially for the occasion but it was completed too late for adequate rehearsal and thus at the degree ceremony an earlier work was performed instead. It is this earlier work to which the name is now applied.

Ox Minuet Minuet by Ignaz Xaver von Seyfried (1776–1841), appearing in his opera of the same title. Composed: *c.*1805. For this opera Seyfried, who was a pupil of Haydn, assembled various pieces by his teacher but also included some original material. According to a popular story Haydn was rewarded for composing this minuet by being given an ox, although it has now been proved that the work is actually by Seyfried.

Ozawa, Seiji (1935–) Japanese conductor. A pupil of Karajan, he has conducted the Toronto Symphony Orchestra (1965–70), the San Francisco Symphony Orchestra (1969–76), and the Boston Symphony Orchestra (1973–).

Seiji Ozawa

P

p Abbreviation for *piano (soft).

P. Abbreviation for Pincherle. It is used as a prefix to indicate the number of a piece in Marc Pincherle's catalogue (1948) of Vivaldi's works. His catalogue has been superseded by Peter Ryom's (see **R.; RV**).

Pachelbel, Johann (1653–1706) German composer and organist. He became assistant organist at St Stephen's Cathedral in Vienna (1673), court organist in Eisenach (1677), and – after a period in Erfurt – organist at the Württemberg court (1690). His last post was organist of the Sebalduskirche in Nuremberg. A prolific composer, he wrote not only works for organ and harpsichord but also liturgical vocal music. His most important works are organ chorales, which show great variety in the treatment of the melodies, and 95 fugues based on the Magnificat. He proved very influential in the development of German organ music. Three of his children became musically important, the most famous being **Wilhelm Hieronymus Pachelbel** (1686–1764).

Pachmann, Vladimir von (1848–1933) Russian pianist. He studied at Vienna and made his debut in Odessa in 1869. Following this he toured Europe and the USA. His performances were devoted almost exclusively to the works of Chopin.

Pacific 231 Symphonic movement by Honegger. First performance: 1924. The title refers to a famous railway engine in the USA and the tone poem attempts to capture in music an impression of the speed and enjoyment of a journey in a train drawn by this locomotive. Honegger describes the whole journey from start to finish, the speed of the music reflecting the changing speed of the train. See also **Rugby**.

Pacini, Giovanni (1796–1867) Italian composer. After studying singing with Marchesi he turned to composition, becoming a prolific and successful opera composer whose works were produced in many Italian theatres. But Pacini became overshadowed by his contemporaries Bellini and Donizetti and in 1833 he retired to Viareggio, where he established a music school. In 1837 he became director of the ducal chapel at Lucca, where he moved his pupils. He returned to the opera stage, and in 1840 his most admired opera, *Saffo*, was produced. Pacini wrote about 90 operas,

much church music, the *Dante Symphony* (1863), and chamber music.

Paderewski, Ignacy (Jan) (1860–1941) Polish pianist, composer, and statesman. He studied in Warsaw and in Vienna under Leschetizky. Following his first public performances (1887–91) he became known as the finest pianist of his time. His compositions included a piano concerto, many solo pieces, and an opera, *Manru* (1901). In 1909 he became director of the Warsaw conservatory. Paderewski was also the first prime minister of newly independent Poland (1919) but resigned after 10 months to resume his musical career.

Padmâvatî Opera-ballet in two acts by Roussel with libretto by Louis Laloy. First performance: Opéra, Paris, 1923. Padmâvatî (contralto), whose name means 'sacred lotus,' is wife of the just ruler, Prince Ratan-Sen (tenor); their enemies bring death and destruction and the final scene is a ritualistic depiction of his funeral pyre and her immolation.

Paer (*or* **Paër**), **Ferdinando** (1771–1839) Italian composer. Paer was a maestro di cappella in Parma (1792–97), musical director of the Kärntnertor-Theater, Vienna (1797–1801), and court kapellmeister at Dresden (1802–06). In 1807 he was appointed maître de chapelle to Napoleon and settled in Paris, subsequently becoming director of the Opéra-Comique and (in 1812) of the Théâtre Italien (succeeding Spontini); in 1832 he became director of Louis Philippe's private chapel. An important figure in the history of Italian opera, Paer wrote over 50 operas, including *Achille* (1801), *Leonora* (1804; based on the same plot that Beethoven was to use in *Fidelio*), and *Le Maître de chapelle* (1821). He also wrote many choral works (mostly sacred) and much instrumental music.

Paganini, Niccolò (1782–1840) Italian virtuoso violinist and composer. He studied with Giacomo Costa and made his first appearance in 1794. His technical skill and use of such techniques as artificial harmonics, multiple stopping, and pizzicato astonished audiences and made him the most important violinist of the 19th century. Berlioz wrote the symphony *Harold in Italy* for him but Paganini never played it; his own compositions include 24 caprices (1801–07), one of which was a source of variations by Brahms, Rachmaninov, and other composers, *Carnival of Venice

A caricature of Paganini by Edwin Landseer

(1829), 12 concertos for violin and guitar, and 6 violin concertos. Paganini was regarded as a notorious character during his lifetime: he was rumoured to be in league with the Devil and was not buried in consecrated ground until five years after his death.

Paganini Rhapsody Rhapsody for piano and orchestra by Rachmaninov. Composed: 1934. Entitled in full *Rhapsody on a Theme of Paganini*, this work is a set of continuous variations upon the theme from Paganini's 24th caprice in A minor for solò violin. The 18th variation has become particularly popular and is often performed separately.

Paganini Studies 1. Two sets of studies for piano (Op. 3 and Op. 10) by Schumann, based upon themes taken from Paganini's caprices for solo violin. Composed: 1832–33 (the first set appeared in 1832, but the second set was not composed until the following year). Each set contains six studies. **2.** Collection of studies for piano by Liszt. Composed: 1838; revised: 1851. All of the six studies are arrangements of Paganini's violin music; the third is an arrangement of La *Campanella, but the others are based on the caprices for solo violin.

Paganini Variations Two sets of variations for piano (Op. 35) by Brahms. Composed: 1866. Entitled in full *Studies in Piano Technique: Variations on a Theme of Paganini*, these studies are based upon the theme from the 24th caprice in A minor for solo violin by Paganini, on which the violinist had himself written variations. Brahms' work combines the intricacies of virtuoso piano playing with an advanced approach to variation technique. His choice of theme was followed by later composers, such as Rachmaninov (in his *Paganini Rhapsody), Blacher, and Lutoslawski, all of whom used it as the basis for variation treatment.

Pagliacci, I (*The Clowns*) Opera in two acts by Leoncavallo with text by the composer. First performance: Teatro dal Verme, Milan, 1892. Nedda (soprano), wife of Canio (tenor) – leader of a band of travelling players – plans to run away with her lover Silvio (baritone). Tonio (baritone) overhears the plot and tells Canio; the guilty lovers are stabbed to death by Canio during a play in which he is acting Pagliacco (the clown) and Nedda, Columbine. A short opera, it is often played in the same bill as *Cavalleria rusticana* (often known as *Cav and Pag*).

Paik, Nam June (1932–) Korean composer, a pupil of Fortner and an associate of Cage. He is particularly interested in multimedia events, often with a strong element of danger and destruction. Since 1963 he has experimented with video. His works include *Omaggio à John Cage* (1959), *Sinfonie for 20 rooms* (1962), and *Opera Sextronique* (1967).

Paine, John Knowles (1839–1906) US composer, teacher, and organist. He studied at the Berlin Hochschule für Musik and his experience of German musical culture greatly influenced his compositional style when he returned to the USA. He gave lectures and organ recitals and in 1862 was appointed to teach music at Harvard, where he established a music faculty that was later emulated by many other US universities. Paine's compositions include two operas, choral works, songs, two symphonies and other orchestral music, and chamber, organ, and piano pieces.

Paisiello, Giovanni (1740–1816) Italian composer. He was court kapellmeister in St Petersburg (1776–84) and in Naples (1787–99) and served as director of chapel music for Napoleon in Paris (1802) and for Joseph Bonaparte (1806) and Joachim Murat (1808–15) in Naples. He wrote over 80 operas, including The *Barber of Seville* (1782), as well as chamber and keyboard music and – in later life – large sacred works.

Palestrina Opera in three acts by Hans Pfitzner with text by the composer. First performance: Munich, 1917. It is based on an unfounded legend about the composer Palestrina, who saved the art of contrapuntal music for the

Church by his *Missa Papae Marcelli*, supposedly composed by direct angelic influence.

Palestrina, Giovanni Pierluigi da (?1525–94) Italian composer (his surname derives from the town near Rome where he was born). In 1537 he was a singer at S Maria Maggiore, Rome, returning to Palestrina in 1544 to become organist and singer at the cathedral. From 1551 to 1555 he was maestro di cappella at St Peter's, Rome. He then became a papal singer and was appointed maestro at S Maria Maggiore (1561–c.1566). From 1571 until his death he was once again maestro at St Peter's.

Although not a cosmopolitan like Lassus, Palestrina was highly regarded by Italians during his lifetime; since his death he has come to be regarded as one of the most outstanding representatives of the late Renaissance style. While by no means representative of all the stylistic elements of his time, Palestrina's music is nevertheless remarkable for its spiritual qualities and its flawless technique. His melodies have been described by the Danish musicologist Knud Jeppeson as a series of gentle arches in which the 'ascending and descending movements counterbalance each other with almost mathematical exactness.' This sense of balance, together with an avoidance of disruptive disturbing elements, accounts for the calm spiritual quality of his music. The rhythmic flow is also carefully organized and the dissonances are prepared and resolved in an unprecedentedly strict manner.

Palestrina's development may be seen at its clearest in his masses, of which he wrote 104, published in 13 volumes (1554–1601). Many of the earlier ones, such as the **Missa Papae Marcelli* (c.1555), are based on a cantus firmus in the old style, whereas in the later ones the more modern parody-mass technique frequently appears; also, in accordance with the edicts of the Council of Trent, the words become easier to hear through a lighter more transparent polyphonic texture and greater use of declamation. To a lesser extent, Palestrina's emotional reticence may also be seen in his motets, of which he wrote about 400. In these the word painting tends to be restrained and conventional, rising to an unusual degree of intensity in the *Song of Solomon* (1584). Palestrina's other sacred works include 35 magnificats (1591), 79 hymns, and 68 offertories (1593). He composed 94 secular madrigals and 49 spiritual ones: some of the secular madrigals, such as *Vestiva i colli* and *Io son ferito*, attained popularity. In a very few madrigals (such as *A la riva del Tebro*), Palestrina uses dissonance expressively rather than as a purely musical device, as in his sacred music.

palindrome 1. A word or sentence that reads the same backwards as it does forwards. **2.** A piece of music having the same characteristics. See also **cancrizans; recte et retro.**

Giovanni Palestrina

Pallavicino, Benedetto (1551–1601) Italian composer. He was active as an organist in the region around Cremona and in 1584 entered the Mantuan court, becoming maestro there in 1596. A prolific madrigalist, he combined bold dissonance with declamatory rhythms and chromaticism. His other compositions include masses, psalms, and polychoral motets.

Pallavicino, Carlo (?–1688) Italian composer and organist. In 1665 he became organist at S Antonio, Padua, and in 1667 was appointed assistant kapellmeister to the Elector of Saxony in Dresden. He returned to Padua in 1673 and in the following year became maestro di cappella at the Ospedale degli Incurabili in Venice. He returned to Dresden in 1687. Pallavicino composed numerous operas that were popular in Venice; they played an important part in the development of the da capo aria and the orchestral ritornello.

Palmer, Felicity (1944–) British soprano. She studied with her father and then at the Guildhall School, London. Early promise as a concert singer and recitalist led to a stage career beginning at Texas in 1973. She sang Messiaen's *Poemes pour Mi* under Pierre Boulez.

Pammelia The earliest English printed collection of rounds and catches; it contains about 100 anonymous pieces, including songs and ballads, and was published by Thomas

Ravenscroft (1609). A second part, *Deuteromelia*, was also published in 1609. [Greek, all honey]

pandora (*or* **bandora**) A large bass *cittern invented in England in the 16th century. It had a scalloped body, a central rose sound hole, and 14 strings tuned in pairs. From about 1560 to 1670 it was used as a continuo instrument. The **penorcon** was a similar instrument with 18 strings tuned in pairs and a shorter and wider body.

pandore see **Arabian music.**

panpipes (*or* **syrinx**) A set of simple *flutes of different lengths joined together. The lower ends of the pipes are stopped and there are no finger holes, different notes being produced by blowing over different pipes. [according to legend, the Greek god Pan made the first instrument from a reed into which a nymph had been transformed – in love with the nymph, Pan sought consolation from the music it produced]

pantomime A dramatic entertainment with musical accompaniment, originating in ancient Greece. Originally pantomimes had no speech, but instead a miming of the action with gestures and facial expressions. In the late 18th century the pantomime was influenced by characters of the Italian *commedia dell'arte*, including Harlequin, Pantaloon, and Clown. Among the composers to write music were Arne. The modern pantomime, with songs, stems from André Worser's *L'Enfant prodigue* (1890) and Stravinsky's *L'Histoire du soldat* (1917).

pantonality A 20th-century version of tonality in which tonal centres shift, interpenetrate, and mingle without being established in the traditional manner by *cadence. Pantonal harmony is a normal feature of the music of Bartók, Hindemith, Britten, and (until he adopted serialism) Stravinsky. The term was invented by Rudolph Réti and first expounded in his *Tonality, Atonality, Pantonality* (1958).

pantoum The second movement of Ravel's piano trio, in which a *scherzo and trio structure is combined with the musical equivalent of the *pantum*, a Malayan verse form. This consists of a series of four-line stanzas in which the second and fourth lines of the first stanza are repeated as the first and third lines of the next. The last line of the final stanza is the same as the opening line of the first stanza.

Panufnik, Andrzej (1914–   ) Polish composer and conductor resident in Britain since 1954, a pupil of Sikorski and Weingartner. His works, which are mainly orchestral, utilize chromatic tonality within geometric and symmetrical patterning, drawing some elements from Polish musical traditions. They include a piano concerto (1962), the symphonies *Sinfonia sacra* (1966) and *Sinfonia mistica* (1977), the cantatas *Universal Prayer* (1968) and *Winter*

Solstice (1972), a violin concerto (1971), ballet music, and two string quartets.

Papaioannou, Yannis (1911–   ) Greek composer, a pupil of Honegger. Papaioannou's style has been influenced in turn by neoclassicism, serialism, and avant-garde techniques. His output includes orchestral and chamber works, choral music, and songs.

Papillons (*Butterflies*) Collection of 12 short piano pieces (Op. 2) by Schumann. Composed: 1829–31. This work resembles *Carnival in that the description of a ball is suggested, with the final piece including an imitation of a clock striking six o'clock. Much of the musical material in *Papillons*, particularly the themes derived from Schumann's name, reappear prominently in *Carnival*.

Parade Ballet in one act with music by Satie, libretto by Cocteau, and choreography by Massine. First performance: Théâtre du Châtelet, Paris, 1917, by Diaghilev's Ballets Russes. A group of music-hall artists perform in the street outside their theatre as a publicity stunt; Picasso's cubist décor caused a sensation.

Paradies (*or* **Paradisi**), **Domenico** (1707–91) Italian composer, keyboard player, and teacher. He emigrated to

Andrzej Panufnik, seen here with his wife

London (*c*.1746), where he taught – among others – the elder Thomas Linley. He wrote operas and serenatas, concertos, songs, and symphonies, but his best works were for keyboard.

Paradise and the Peri (German: *Das Paradies und die Peri*) Cantata for solo voices, choir, and orchestra (Op. 50) by Schumann to words by Thomas Moore. Composed: 1843. The text is a German translation by the composer of one of the poems from *Lalla Rookh* and tells the Persian mythological tale of the good spirit Peri and his attempt to enter Paradise.

Paradisi, Domenico see **Paradies, Domenico.**

parallel motion see **motion.**

parergon A secondary work that uses the material of another piece, often as an ornamental appendix. An example is Richard Strauss's *Parergon to the Symphonia domestica* for left-handed pianist and orchestra. See also **parody.**

Paris Symphonies Set of six symphonies by Haydn, so called because they were written especially for performance at a series of concerts, the Concerts de la Loge Olympique, in Paris. Composed: 1785–86. These works are catalogued as the symphonies Nos. 82–87, the three most famous being those nicknamed *The *Bear* (*L'Ours*; No. 82), *The *Hen* (*La Poule*; No. 83), and *The *Queen* (*La Reine*; No. 85).

Parker, Horatio (William) (1863–1919) US composer, church musician, and teacher. He studied at the Munich Hochschule für Musik, where his teachers included Rheinberger. In New York (1886–93) he held various posts as organist and teacher and in 1893 was appointed organist and choirmaster of Trinity Church, Boston. From 1894 to his death he was Professor of Music at Yale University. He also conducted the New Haven Symphony Orchestra and Choral Society. Parker's oratorio *Hora novissima* (1893) was the first US work to be performed at the Three Choirs Festival (Worcester): it led to other English festival commissions, including *A Wanderer's Psalm* (1900) and *A Star Song* (1902). He also wrote music for the stage, songs, anthems, services, organ and piano music, a symphony and other orchestral pieces, and chamber works.

parlando Speaking: a direction used to indicate either that a performer should actually speak rather than sing or that while singing the performer should give the impression of speaking. [Italian]

parody 1. The recomposing or modifying of a composition designed for one medium to suit it for another. During the 16th and 17th centuries this was frequently the adaptation of a vocal work for the keyboard or lute. See also **Mass.**
2. The substitution of the original serious text of a work with one that is comic and satirical.

Hubert Parry

Parry, Sir (Charles) Hubert (Hastings) (1848–1918) British composer, teacher, and writer on music. He studied with Pierson at Oxford University. In 1870 he began a business career but abandoned it and took music lessons with Dannreuther, who gave the first performance of his piano concerto in F♯ (1878–79). That and his cantata *Scenes from Prometheus Unbound* (1880) established him as a leading composer. He became a professor at the Royal College of Music (1883), choragus at Oxford University (1883), director of the Royal College of Music (1894), and music professor at Oxford (1900–08). He was knighted in 1898.

Like Stanford, Parry was a key figure in the 19th-century renaissance of English music. He is particularly noted for his choral and vocal music and his sympathetic setting of English poetry. He wrote oratorios (among them **Judith*, 1888, and **Job*, 1892), services, motets (including the masterly *Songs of Farewell*, 1916–18), anthems (one of the best known, 'I was glad,' was for Edward VII's coronation in 1902), secular choral works (including the well-known **Blest Pair of Sirens* (1887) and the unison song *Jerusalem*), and solo songs, most of which were published in 12 sets of *English Lyrics* (*c*.1885–1920). He wrote incidental music for four Aristophanes comedies, four symphonies, three overtures, several orchestral suites (including *Lady Radnor's Suite* for strings, 1894), chamber music (including three string quartets and three piano trios), and piano pieces. Among his books are *The Art of Music* (1893, revised as *The Evolution of the Art of Music*, 1896), and *Style in Musical Art* (1911).

Parry, Joseph (1841–1903) Welsh composer, a pupil at the Royal Academy of Music (1868–71), where his teachers included Sterndale Bennett. He was music professor at the University of Wales, Aberystwyth (1873–79), founded a music school in Swansea (1881–88), and taught at the university in Cardiff (1888–1903). Parry composed operas, choral music, and orchestral works but is best remembered for the hymn tune *Aberystwyth* ('Jesu, Lover of my Soul').

Parsifal Opera in three acts by Wagner with libretto by the composer based on the medieval poem *Parzifal* by Wolfram von Eschenbach. First performance: Bayreuth, 1882. Originally subtitled *Bühnenweihfestspiel* (sacred festival drama), it was Wagner's last opera and exhibits advanced use of the *leitmotiv technique. Parsifal (tenor), the 'pure fool made wise by pity', wins back the magic spear that can heal Amfortas (baritone), ailing ruler of the knights of the Holy Grail, from the magician Klingsor (bass) and his servant Kundry (mezzo-soprano).

part 1. The music written for a particular instrument or voice in an ensemble, orchestra, choir, etc. The **score and parts** includes both the full score for the conductor and the individual parts for the members of the ensemble, etc. **2.** A strand of melody in polyphonic music (see also **fugue**). **Part writing** (US: **voice leading**) is the art of combining these parts together to form a coherent whole. A **part song** is a composition for several voices in which each voice has a separate melodic part. In a part song the principal melody is usually in the highest part, the other voices providing an accompaniment containing some melodic interest. Compare **madrigal. 3.** A section of a large-scale work, such as a cantata or oratorio, corresponding roughly in length to the act of an opera. Handel's *Messiah*, for example, is in three parts.

Partch, Harry (1901–74) US composer (self-taught) and writer. He abandoned conventional composition in 1928 to develop his own musical philosophy, later formulated in *The Genesis of a New Music* (1949). He used a 43-tone scale for which he devised his own instruments and produced exotic music dramas, derived in part from oriental and classical Greek precedents. His works include *The Bewitched* (1957), *Wind Song* (1958), *Water, Water* (1962), and *Delusion of the Fury* (1966).

parte Part. Hence **colla parte**, with the part, i.e. following the solo part: a direction used to indicate that the accompanist should give some freedom to the soloist and follow accordingly. See also **partita**. [Italian]

Parthenia A book of keyboard pieces by Bull, Byrd, Orlando Gibbons, and others, presented to Princess Elizabeth and Prince Frederick at their marriage (1613). The full title of the volume is *Parthenia or the Maydenhead of the First Musicke that ever was printed for the Virginalls*, a pun both on the fact that it was the first keyboard collection to be published in England and on the wedding itself. The pun is continued in the title of the companion volume *Parthenia In-Violata* (c.1614), a collection of anonymous pieces with a part for bass viol.

partials The notes of a *harmonic series produced when a string or column of air vibrates. The lowest note is the fundamental, or **first partial**; the higher notes are the overtones, or **upper partials**. See **harmonics**.

partie 1. Part. **2.** Partita. [French]

partita 1. In the 17th and early 18th centuries, a set of variations, each variation being termed a **parte**. Examples are Frescobaldi's *Partite sopra l'aria della romanesca* and J.S. Bach's chorale partitas for organ. **2.** A *suite of pieces; for example, in Bach's partitas for solo violin. [Italian]

partition Score. [French]

Partitur Score. [German]

Partos, Oedoen (1907–77) Hungarian-born Israeli composer, a pupil of Kodály. Partos' early music shows the influences of both Bartók and Kodály. After his arrival in Palestine (1938) he became interested in Israeli folk music, and his later works use serial techniques. Partos' output includes concertos for violin and viola and other orchestral works, chamber music, and vocal works.

pas Step or pace; hence dance, e.g. **pas de deux**, dance for two; **pas d'action**, ballet scene of a dramatic nature. [French]

pasodoble A one-step Spanish dance in 6/8 time that was popular in the mid-1920s. [Spanish, double step]

passacaglia An instrumental piece consisting of continuous variations in slow triple time above a *ground bass. It derived from a four-bar *ritornello found in early-17th-

Above: an example of a passacaglia bass. Below: J.S. Bach's Passacaglia and Fugue in C minor

century French, Spanish, and Italian songs. A common passacaglia bass is a descending hexachord of a minor key in either a diatonic or chromatic guise (see illustration).

The passacaglia is closely related to the *chaconne but it is not possible to draw any consistently applicable lines of distinction between them. J. S. Bach's passacaglia and fugue in C minor for organ is among the finest examples of the form and is built on an eight-bar theme (see illustration). Webern's *Passacaglia* (1908) and the last movement of Vaughan Williams' fifth symphony (1943) are among recent examples.

passage work A passage in a composition that lacks originality or structural significance and therefore calls for fast and brilliant playing.

Passereau, Pierre (16th century) French composer. Said to have been a priest in Paris, he sang in the chapel of the Duke of Angoulême (later François I) in 1509 and possibly also at Cambrai. Apart from one motet, his output consists of chansons; the most popular of these is *Il est bel et bon*, which imitates the clucking of hens.

passing note An incidental note in a composition that creates a dissonance with the prevailing harmony but is useful in leading from one chord to another. Compare **auxiliary note.**

Passion A setting to music of the account of the Passion of Christ by Matthew, Mark, Luke, or John. During the Middle Ages plainsong settings were made, with appropriate contrasts of vocal compass and speed for the words of the different characters. During the 15th and 16th centuries the words of the crowds (*turba*), and of some individuals were set polyphonically in *faburden style. Examples in this style include settings by Lassus, Victoria, and Schütz. During the baroque period settings made use of operatic innovations, including aria, recitative, and the accompanimental and dramatic use of instruments. In Germany *chorales and other poetic additions were made to the scriptural texts. This led to the evolution of the *oratorio style of Passion from around 1700. A libretto by Brockes was particularly popular, being set by Handel and Telemann. In Italy, a similar text by Metastasio was set by Caldara. In J. S. Bach's *St John Passion* (1723) and *St Matthew Passion* (1729) the scriptural texts are set in recitative, or as short choruses, and the poetic reflections as arias and longer choruses. Their form may be viewed as a series of *cantatas, each ending with a chorale. Subsequent examples include Haydn's *Die sieben Worte am Kreuz* (1785) and Penderecki's *St Luke Passion* (1965).

Passione, La Symphony No. 49 in F minor by Haydn. Composed: 1768. This symphony opens very unusually with a slow movement and for this reason it has been suggested that it may have been composed for performance during Holy Week, possibly to precede a passion play or oratorio.

Pasta, Giuditta (1798–1865) Italian soprano. After studying in Milan and Paris she made her debut in 1815. For the next 35 years she performed as an operatic soprano of great range and dramatic power.

pasticcio A composition formed by the amalgamation of music by two or more composers. The practice was widely applied to opera writing in the 18th century, as in *Il Muzio Scevola* (1721), for which Amadei, G. B. Bonocini, and Handel composed one act each. In the 18th century *potpourris of favourite operatic arias were described as pasticcios. The *F.A.E. Sonata*, composed by Schumann, Brahms, and Dietrich for Joachim, is a 19th-century pasticcio. French: **pastiche.** [Italian, hotch-potch]

pastiche see **pasticcio.**

pastoral 1. (adj.) Denoting music with a rural theme. **2.** (n.) A madrigal with words having a rural theme. **3.** (or (French, Italian) **pastorale**) (n.) A type of early opera, often with dancing, recitatives, choruses, etc., on a pastoral theme. These often allegorical works were popular in the 17th century although less elaborate pastoral dramas with music were common in the 16th century. **4.** (n.) A flowing melodic piece in 6/8 or 12/8 time for instruments or voices, often with a drone bass. It originated in rural Italy, where shepherds played in this style on their shawms on Christmas morning.

Pastoral Sonata Sonata in D major for piano (Op. 28) by Beethoven. Composed: 1801. Beethoven himself did not use this name, which was invented by the composer's publisher, Cranz. It alludes to the character of the finale, which is that of a pastoral dance with modified ground bass that imitates the sound of bagpipes.

Pastoral Symphony 1. Symphony No. 6 in F major by Beethoven. First performance: 1808. Beethoven himself gave the work this title and added descriptions for each of the five movements: 'Awakening of Cheerful Feelings on Arrival in the Country,' 'Scene by the Brook,' 'Merrymaking of the Country Folk,' 'Storm,' and 'Song of the Shepherd's Joy and Gratitude after the Storm.' Despite these programmatic explanations Beethoven claimed that it was his intention more to express his feelings on pastoral life than to depict rural scenes in music. **2.** Symphony No. 3 by Vaughan Williams. First performance: 1922. For the last movement the composer employs a soprano to sing wordlessly.

pastourelle A *chanson of the troubadours or trouvères. The subject matter features rustic love scenes.

Pathetic Sonata (French: *Sonate pathétique*) Sonata in C minor for piano (Op. 13) by Beethoven. Composed: 1798.

Plate 35: *A scene from Trevor Nunn's 1986 production of George Gershwin's opera* Porgy and Bess *at Glyndebourne. Porgy (with sticks), played by Willard White, is singing the 'buzzard song'*

Plate 36 opposite: *Portrait of Henry Purcell by Johann Closter-mann. National Portrait Gallery, London*

Plate 37 above: *A portrait in pastel of the French composer Jean Philippe Rameau*

Plate 38: *A portrait of Camille Saint-Saëns by an unknown artist*

Beethoven himself first used the title in its French version to describe the intense and dramatic nature of the music.

Pathetic Symphony (French: *Symphonie pathétique*) Symphony No. 6 in B minor by Tchaikovsky. Composed: 1893. Tchaikovsky himself chose the name, rejecting his brother's earlier suggestion of the *Tragic Symphony*. This symphony is unusual in that it ends with the slow movement rather than the conventional fast one.

Patience Operetta by Sullivan with libretto by Gilbert. First performance: Opéra Comique, London, 1881. Subtitled *Bunthorne's Bride*, it is a satire on contemporary aestheticism, particularly that of the Oscar Wilde circle; Patience is a dairymaid wooed by the aesthetic Bunthorne.

Patterson, Paul (1947–) British composer. His early works combine Stravinskian rhythm with serial procedures, while his *Kyrie* (1972) shows the influence of the Polish avant-garde. He developed a style of timbre composition with some aleatory elements, as in the clarinet concerto (1976). Later works, such as *Voices of Sleep* (1980), exhibit greater stylistic variety.

patter song A song in which the words are sung as fast as possible. It is a feature of comic operas, especially those of Gilbert and Sullivan. The Chancellor's 'Nightmare Song' from *Iolanthe* is an example.

Patti, Adelina (Adela Juana Maria P.; 1843–1919) Italian soprano. The daughter of singers who settled in the USA, she studied under Ettore Barilli and toured the USA as a child prodigy. Later she sang all over Europe and mesmerized Covent Garden for 30 years, specializing in Italian coloratura roles. Her sister, **Carlotta Patti** (1835–89), was also a soprano.

Patzak, Julius (1898–1974) Austrian tenor. The leading tenor of the 1930s, he was self-taught and made his debut as Radames in Verdi's *Aida* at Liberec (1923). He then sang at Munich (1929–45) and Vienna, excelling in Mozart.

Pauke (*pl.* **Pauken**) Kettledrum. [German]

Paukenmesse see **Drum Mass.**

Paul Bunyan Operetta by Britten with libretto by W. H. Auden about the legendary American lumberjack-hero of the title. First performance: Columbia University, New York, 1941. After the opening performance the operetta was suppressed by the composer and not heard again until 1976, when radio and stage performances were given.

Paulus see **St Paul.**

pausa see **rest.**

Pause see **rest.**

pause A sign used in written music (⌒) to indicate that a note, chord, or rest so marked is to be held longer than its time value would normally allow. The length of time for which it is to be held is determined by the performer. It is also sometimes used at the end of a composition to show that the work is complete.

pavan (*or* (French) **pavane**) A slow court dance of the 16th and 17th centuries, normally in duple time with simple repetitive steps, that originated in the Padua region of Italy. Following Dalza's *Intablatura de lauto* (1508), the pavan spread rapidly throughout Europe. It reached its apotheosis in the works of the English virginalists, who used it for variations and usually paired it with a *galliard. Several 19th- and 20th-century composers have revived the form, including Ravel in his *Pavane pour une infante défunte* (*Pavan for a Dead Infanta*) for piano (1899), later orchestrated.

Pavarotti, Luciano (1935–) Italian tenor. He studied with Pola and Campogalliani and made his debut at Reggio Emilia in 1961 as Rodolfo in Puccini's *La Bohème*, a role he has since sung repeatedly all over the world. Pavarotti specializes in the operas of Puccini and Verdi.

pavillon 1. The bell of a wind instrument, especially that of a horn, trumpet, or trombone. The instruction **pavillon en l'air** in scores indicates that the wind-instrument players should raise their instruments so that they can increase the volume. [French, tent – because the shape of the bell is reminiscent of a bell tent] **2. Pavillon chinois** Chinese pavilion (see **jingling johnny**). [French]

Pearlfishers, The (French: *Les Pêcheurs des perles*) Opera in three acts by Bizet with libretto by Carré and Cormon. First performance: Théâtre-Lyrique, Paris, 1863. Set in ancient Ceylon, it tells how Leila (soprano), priestess of Brahma who has taken a vow of chastity, is loved by both Zurga (baritone), king of the fishermen, and his friend Nadir (tenor). Zurga helps Nadir and Leila to escape when he learns that Leila saved his life when a child but is himself killed.

Pears, Sir Peter (1910–85) British tenor. He studied at the Royal College of Music in London and later with Lucie Manen. Pear's lifelong friendship with Benjamin Britten, whom he met in 1936, resulted in a creative association in which Britten wrote many leading tenor roles for him in operatic and recital works, from *Peter Grimes* (1947) to *Death in Venice* (1973). Pears cofounded the English Opera Group (1946) and the *Aldeburgh Festival (1948). He was knighted in 1978.

Pearsall, Robert Lucas (1795–1856) British composer and antiquarian. A former barrister, he turned to music after 1825, living in Mainz (1825–29), Karlsruhe (1830–42), and Lake Constance (after 1842). A founder member of the British Madrigal Society (1837), he revived interest in Renaissance music, writing both Anglican and Catholic sacred music, vocal ensemble music, and keyboard and chamber works.

Peasant Cantata Secular cantata for solo voices, choir, and orchestra (BWV 212) by Bach to a text by Picander. Composed: 1742. Written to honour the enthronement of a magistrate in Saxony, the words are in local dialect and Bach includes several popular folk melodies. Together with the *Coffee Cantata*, this is one of Bach's few secular cantatas.

Pêcheurs des perles, Les see **Pearlfishers, The**.

ped. Abbreviation for pedal. It occurs in piano music to indicate that the sustaining pedal (see **piano**) should be applied at the point so marked. Compare **una corda**. In organ music it also occurs as an instruction to play the note or section marked on the *pedalboard.

pedal 1. (or **pedal point** or **organ point**) A device in *harmony in which a note is held in the bass, over a passage that includes some chords with which it is dissonant. The note held is usually the tonic or dominant of the prevailing key (termed **tonic pedal** and **dominant pedal**, respectively). An **inverted pedal** is a pedal that is not in the bass. A **double pedal** consists of two notes held in this way, usually the tonic and the dominant. **2.** See **pedals**.

pedalboard An *organ keyboard played by the feet. Compare **manual**; see also **pedal piano**.

pedal clarinet see **clarinet**.

pedal drums see **kettledrums**.

pédalier Pedalboard. [French]

pedal organ see **organ**.

pedal piano A piano fitted with a pedal keyboard to provide organists with an instrument on which to practise. A small amount of music, notably by Schumann, has been written exclusively for this instrument.

pedal point see **pedal**.

pedals 1. Foot-operated levers used in the *organ to produce notes (see **pedalboard**). **2.** Foot-operated levers in a *piano used to sustain notes or to dampen them (see also **ped.**). **3.** Foot-operated levers used on a *harp or kettledrum to alter the tuning of a string or membrane.

Peer Gynt Incidental music by Grieg to the play by Ibsen. First performance: 1876. Peer Gynt is a character from Norwegian folk history and Grieg's incidental music was composed for the first performance of the play. Two orchestral suites were later arranged from the original score.

Peerson, Martin (1571/73–1651) English keyboard player and composer. Although a Roman Catholic who had been convicted of recusancy (refusal to attend Church of England services), he subscribed to the Thirty-Nine Articles to take

his Oxford B.Mus. in 1613. He was probably sacrist at Westminster Abbey (1623–30) and Master of the Choristers at St Paul's Cathedral (from 1624 or 1625). His *Mottects or Grave Chamber Musique* (1630) contains the earliest English printed figured bass. His verse anthems show him to be a progressive composer.

Peeters, Flor (1903–86) Belgian organist, composer, and teacher. He studied the organ with Depuydt, whom he succeeded as organist at the Cathedral of St Rombout, Mechelen. He became noted as a teacher in Europe and the USA and made worldwide tours. His compositions include organ works, chamber music, and choral music.

pegbox The box at the end of the neck of a stringed instrument in which the pegs holding the strings are fitted. Some early lutes had a bent-back pegbox but angled and straight pegboxes were also used. The viols and fiddles had more ornate pegboxes terminating in a carved decoration, such as an animal's head, which has now become standardized in the violin family as the **scroll**. In the modern guitar a *machine head is usually used in place of the traditional pegbox.

Pelléas et Mélisande The title of several works based on Maeterlinck's play of the same name about the tragic medieval lovers. **1.** Incidental music by Fauré (Op. 80; 1898) and Sibelius (Op. 46; 1905). **2.** Opera in five acts by Debussy. First performance: Opéra-Comique, Paris, 1902. In this opera Debussy developed a new and subtle method of setting the French language in *parlando style. **3.** Tone poem by Schoenberg (Op. 5). Composed: 1903; first performance: 1905.

Penderecki, Krzystoff (1933–) Polish composer, a pupil of Malawski. After a brief serialist phase, he developed a style utilizing extreme instrumental effects (clusters, glissandi, etc.) in a dramatic manner, as in the *Threnody for the Victims of Hiroshima* (1960). In the *St Luke Passion* (1965) he combined this style with traditional choral writing. Later works, such as the violin concerto (1976), show a return to conservative romanticism. Other works include two symphonies, *Polymorphia* (1961), *Fluorescences* (1961), the operas *The Devils of Loudun* (1969) and *Paradise Lost* (1978), and a magnificat (1974).

Pénélope Opera in three acts by Fauré with libretto by Fauchois. First performance: Monte Carlo, 1913. It is a retelling of the story of Ulysses' return to Penelope.

penillion An ancient form of Welsh singing that is still practised. It is almost invariably sung to a harp accompaniment. The skill of its performance lies in its use of extemporization and counterpoint: the verses are extemporized by the singer, who also combines an original counterpoint woven against a traditional melody played by the harpist. It is only in the final verses that the singer should

Krzystoff Penderecki

introduce the melody that the harpist has harmonized throughout.

penny whistle see **tin whistle.**

penorcon see **pandora.**

pentatonic scale see **scales.**

Pepping, Ernst (1901–81) German composer. Pepping taught composition at the Berlin Hochschule für Musik (1953–68). His music was influenced by the contrapuntal styles of the 16th and 17th centuries. Choral works form the core of Pepping's output, which also includes orchestral music, chamber works, and music for organ.

Pepusch, Johann Christoph (*or* **John Christopher**) (1667–1752) German-born composer, theorist, and teacher. After an appointment at the Prussian court Pepusch settled in London (*c*.1704), where he wrote much theatre music, including that for The *Beggar's Opera* (1728) and its sequel *Polly* (1729). His other works include church music for the Duke of Chandos (for whom he was music master), chamber music, and a harmony treatise. He was organist of Charterhouse (1737) and elected a Fellow of the Royal Society (1746).

per By; through; in order to; for. [Italian]

percussion instruments Musical *instruments in which the sound is produced when a resonant surface is struck. They include instruments capable of being tuned to a particular pitch, such as the *kettledrums, *glockenspiel, *vibraphone, *xylophone, and tubular *bells, as well as instruments that do not produce sounds with a definite pitch, such as the *side drum, *bass drum, *triangle, and *cymbals. Other special sound effects required by a composer are usually produced by the percussion section of the orchestra; they include castanets, anvil, thunder sticks, chains, etc. See also **membranophone.**

perdendosi Being lost: a direction used to indicate that the music should die away gradually. [Italian]

perfect cadence see **cadence.**

Perfect Fool, The Comic opera with words and music by Holst. First performance: Covent Garden, London, 1923. In this opera Holst parodies the operatic conventions of other composers: the fool of the title (a speaking part) eventually wins the Princess from the Verdian Troubadour and the Wagnerian Traveller. The opera begins with a ballet of the Spirits of Earth, Water, and Fire, which is often played out of context.

perfect intervals *Intervals that are identical in the major and minor keys, i.e. fourths, fifths, and octaves. If they are reduced by a semitone they become **diminished** and if they are raised a semitone they become **augmented.**

perfect time In medieval music, triple time. It was indicated by a full circle. **Imperfect time** (*or* **quadruple time**) was indicated by a broken circle – the origin of the symbol now used for common time (see **time signature**).

Pergolesi, Giovanni Battista (1710–36) Italian composer. In Naples he was appointed maestro di cappella to the Prince of Stigliano (1732) and the Duke of Maddaloni (*c*.1734) and wrote many sacred dramas, cantatas, serenatas, and operas seria and buffa. His comic intermezzo La *Serva padrona* (1733) was highly successful, with important effects on the history of opera buffa. Pergolesi's last works, the *Stabat Mater* and *Salve Regina*, were written in the Franciscan Monastery at Pozzuoli, where he retired because of ill health in 1736.

Peri, Jacopo (1561–1633) Italian composer and singer. A choirboy at the church of Santissima Annunziata in Florence, he was appointed organist at the Badia in 1579. During the 1580s he was probably a member of Giovanni de' Bardi's Camerata and in 1588 he was employed by the Medici. During the 1590s he composed the pastoral *Dafne* and in 1600 *Euridice*, the earliest complete opera to have survived. Its most important feature is the recitative, which closely follows natural speech rhythms and is accompanied by a slow-moving bass line.

Péri, La (*The Peri*) **1.** Ballet in two acts with music by Burgmüller, libretto by Gautier, and choreography by Coralli. First performance: Opéra, Paris, 1843. Sultan Achmet, during an opium dream, is taken by the Queen of the Fairies to her kingdom. **2.** Ballet (described as a 'poème dansée') with music by Dukas and scenario by Clustine. First performance: Paris, 1912. The Peri is found asleep on the steps of the Temple of the god Ormuzd by the oriental King Iskender, who is searching for the Flower of Immortality; she holds it in her hand and when the king steals it she performs an ecstatic dance to win it back.

Perlman, Itzhak (1945–) Israeli violinist. At the age of four he lost the use of his legs through polio and as a result always plays seated. He won a talent competition (1958) to appear on US television and subsequently trained in New York, making his debut in 1963. Since then he has toured in Israel, Europe, and the USA and is noted for his masterly technique and directness of musical expression.

Perosi, Lorenzo (1872–1956) Italian composer, best known for his sacred music. Perosi was musical director of the Sistine Chapel (1898–1915). His works include the oratorio *La Passione di Cristo* (1897), Mass settings, motets, orchestral works, and organ music.

Pérotin (*or* **Perotinus Magnus**) (late 12th–early 13th century) French composer working in Paris, possibly as master of the chapel that occupied the site of the present Notre Dame. According to the theorist Anonymous IV, he was the best composer of *descant, shortening the organa and composing new sections known as clausulae. He also wrote three- and four-part organa, some of which may have been written by 1198, in addition to monophonic and polyphonic conducti.

perpetual canon see **canon**.

perpetuum mobile A piece of music in which there is constant rapid movement through repetitive note values. French: **mouvement perpetuel**; Italian: **moto perpetuo**. [Latin, perpetually moving]

Persephone *Melodrama for speaker, singers, and orchestra by Stravinsky to words by Gide. First performance: 1933. The libretto is based on Greek mythology, and although intended for stage production and first produced as such, *Persephone* is usually given in concert version.

Persicchetti, Vincent (1915–81) US composer and conductor, a pupil of Roy Harris. He employed many styles, ranging from the freely tonal to the quasi-serial. His works include symphonies, concertos, *The Creation* (1970), *Lincoln Address* (1973), ballet music, chamber music, and organ music.

Perti, Giacomo Antonio (1661–1756) Italian composer, teacher of Torelli, Martini, and others. He was composer

Itzhak Perlman

to the Accademia Filarmonica (1681), becoming maestro di cappella at S Pietro, Bologna, in 1690 and at S Petronio in 1696. In addition to his many festive masses, oratorios, and magnificats in distinctive concertato style, Perti also wrote operas and chamber music.

pesante Heavy; heavily: a direction used to indicate that a passage should be played firmly. [Italian]

Peter and the Wolf Work for narrator and orchestra by Prokofiev. First performance: 1936. Intended to appeal to a children's audience, each character in this tale is portrayed by a different instrument in the orchestra – the bird by the flute and the cat by the clarinet, for example – and in this way Prokofiev provides a kind of children's guide to the orchestra. Between the descriptive orchestral passages the narrator relates the events of the story.

Peter Grimes Opera in prologue, three acts, and epilogue by Britten with libretto by Montagu Slater based on a poem by George Crabbe. First performance: Sadler's Wells, London, 1945. Peter Grimes (tenor), a fisherman, is a misfit in the gossiping society of The Borough, an east-coast village in about 1830: his refusal to accept help brings about his tragedy.

Petits Riens, Les Ballet music (K. Anh. 10) by Mozart. First performance: 1778. Mozart composed this music while in Paris and the first production took place there during a performance of Piccinni's opera *Le Finte gemelle*, the choreography being by Noverre. Until 1872 the score of this music was lost.

Petrassi, Goffredo (1904–) Italian composer. The dissonant neoclassical style of his early works evolved into a more lyrical style in the 1940s, and with the *Recreation Concertante* (1953) Petrassi started to use serial procedures. Since writing the string quartet (1957) he has adopted a style that makes much use of discontinuous fragments and nonrepetition. His works include a magnificat (1940), *Coro di morti* (1941), *Noche oscura* (1951), *Orationes Christi* (1975), eight concerti for orchestra, *Estri* (1967), *Grand Septuor* (1979), and chamber and piano music.

Petrovics, Emil (1930–) Hungarian composer. Petrovics' style is rooted in the Hungarian folk tradition but is also influenced by the music of Schoenberg and Berg. His works include the opera *C'est la guerre* (1961), vocal works, chamber music, and incidental music for films, television, and theatre.

Petrucci, Ottaviano (dei) (1466–1539) Italian music printer. Brought up in Urbino at the court of Guidobaldo I, he went to Venice in about 1490. There, in 1498, he was given exclusive permission to print measured music for 20 years. He was the first to print polyphonic music from movable type; the composers represented include Josquin, Obrecht, Tromboncino, and Mouton.

Petrushka Ballet in four scenes with music by Stravinsky and choreography by Fokine. First performance: Théâtre du Châtelet, Paris, 1911, conducted by Monteux, with Karsavina and Nijinsky (décor by Benois). Commissioned by Diaghilev for the Ballets Russes, it is set in Admiralty Square, St Petersburg, during the Butterweek Fair of 1830. The owner of a puppet theatre brings Petrushka, the Ballerina, and the Moor to life; Petrushka loves the Ballerina; she prefers the Moor, who kills Petrushka.

Petzoldt, Johann Christoph see **Pezel, Johann Christoph**.

Peyer, Gervase (Alan) de (1926–) British clarinettist. He studied at the Royal College of Music and was appointed first clarinet of the London Symphony Orchestra in 1955. He is a founder member of the Melos Ensemble and an associate conductor of the Haydn Orchestra.

Pezel (*or* **Petzoldt**), **Johann Christoph** (1639–94) German composer and bandsman. He served in various town bands, including that of Leipzig, and his compositions include two collections (1670 and 1685) of five-part music for cornetts and trombones.

pezzo A musical piece. [Italian]

Pfitzner, Hans (1869–1949) German composer, also active as a teacher and conductor. Pfitzner's early works were hailed by critics as prime examples of music in the true

Margot Fonteyn and Mikhail Baryshnikov in a production of Petrushka

German tradition, his operas in particular receiving great praise. Later his fame declined and he spent his last years in poverty. Pfitzner's works include the musical legend *Palestrina* (1912–15) and other operas, orchestral music, chamber works, and songs.

Phaedra Cantata for mezzo-soprano, solo cello, strings, percussion, and harpsichord by Britten to a translation of Racine by Low. Composed: 1975. This was Britten's last vocal work and is constructed like a short operatic episode, with the recitative passages accompanied by the cello and harpsichord. Phaedra is a character in Greek mythology who falls in love with her stepson while her husband is away fighting. *Phaedra* was composed for the British singer Dame Janet Baker.

Philadelphia Orchestra US symphony orchestra founded in 1900. Its first conductor was Fritz Scheel (who established the orchestra), who was succeeded by Karl Pohlig. Under Leopold Stokowski (conductor 1912–41) it became one of the world's finest orchestras, with its characteristic sonorous virtuoso style. It introduced many new works to the USA, by Mahler, Scriabin, Stravinsky, Schoenberg, and Varèse among others, and made many pioneering recordings. The orchestra's pre-eminence was maintained under Eugene Ormandy (conductor 1938–78). Riccardo Muti was appointed musical director in 1981.

Philharmonia Orchestra British symphony orchestra founded in 1945 by Walter Legge, who intended it chiefly to make recordings. From these it gained an international reputation, also giving concerts in London (where it is based) and abroad. In 1964 the orchestra became self-governing and was renamed the **New Philharmonia Orchestra**; in 1977 it reverted to its original name. Guest conductors have included Richard Strauss and Arturo Toscanini. Otto Klemperer had a long association with the orchestra, among whose other conductors have been Carlo Mario Giulini, Lorin Maazel, and Riccardo Muti.

philharmonic Fond of music: used in the titles of various musical organizations and orchestras. It does not denote a particular type of orchestra but is simply part of the name; e.g. London Philharmonic Orchestra.

Philidor French family of musicians, originally named Danican. **André Danican Philidor** (*c.*1647–1730) was an instrumentalist and composer who assembled the Philidor Collection of court and church music. His son **François André Danican Philidor** (1726–95), the composer and chess player, was the most important member of the family. He studied with Campra and wrote many opéras comiques, including *Tom Jones* (1765). He visited London frequently, producing there his setting of Horace's *Carmen Saeculare* (1779). In addition to his operas and sacred works, he also composed chamber music.

Philips, Peter (*c.*1560–1628) English composer and organist. He sang at St Paul's Cathedral and in 1582 fled to the continent because of his Catholic faith, becoming organist at the English College, Rome. In 1585 he travelled to Genoa, Madrid, France, and the Netherlands, entering the service of Archduke Albert in Brussels in 1597. His keyboard music, written in the English tradition, is most inventive. His madrigals and motets are more Roman in style, containing intricate polyphony and madrigalian word painting.

Philosopher, The Symphony No. 22 in E♭ major by Haydn. Composed: 1764. Like *La *Passione*, this symphony begins with a slow movement rather than the customary fast one and the introspective character of this movement has prompted the name for the symphony.

Phoebus and Pan Secular cantata (BWV 201) for solo voices, choir, and orchestra by Bach to words by Picander. Composed: 1729. The complete title of the work is *The Contest Between Phoebus and Pan* (German: *Streit zwischen Phoebus und Pan*): Phoebus and Pan were two figures in Greek mythology who engage in a musical contest. It is thought that Bach composed *Phoebus and Pan* as a satire on the writings of Scheibe, editor of the musical journal *Der Kritische Musikus*, who appears in the work as the character Midas.

phrase A group of notes or chords that constitutes a section of a melody. A **phrase mark** on music is a line indicating which bars go to make up a phrase. Phrases provide a form of punctuation in music and good phrasing by a performer not only includes observing the composer's phrase marks but also a correct distribution of stresses. In singing and wind instruments this will involve correct breath control, in stringed instruments it requires good bowing, and in keyboard instruments fluent fingering is essential. Two or three phrases may often hang together to make up a **sentence**.

Phrygian cadence see **cadence**.

Phrygian mode see **modes**.

piacere, a see **ad lib.** [Italian]

piacevole Pleasant; agreeable. [Italian]

piangendo Plaintive. [Italian, weeping]

pianissimo see **piano**.

piano 1. (adj., adv.) Soft. Abbreviation: *p.* Hence **pianissimo**, very soft. Abbreviation: *pp.* **2.** (or **pianoforte**) (n.) A versatile instrument with a keyboard derived from the *harpsichord and a hammer action based on that of the dulcimer. The first instrument of this kind was made in Florence in 1709 by Bartolommeo Cristofori. He called it a *gravicembalo col piano e forte* ('harpsichord with soft and loud') because of its ability to play softly or loudly according to the force with which the notes are struck – a facility lacked by the harpsichord with its plucked strings. The idea was copied, with some improvements, by Gottfried Silbermann in about 1726 in Freiberg, Germany; some of Silbermann's pianos were seen by Bach, who suggested several modifications. In the 1760s an ex-apprentice of Silbermann's, called Johannes Zumpe, came to settle in London bringing with him designs for a **square piano**. These square pianos, which gained considerable popularity (especially in continental Europe), had strings running parallel to the keyboard, unlike the earlier wing-shaped pianos based on the harpsichord. Their chief advantage was that they were lighter and cheaper than the wing-shaped pianos and that they took up less space. However, by the beginning of the 19th century they were being replaced as a popular home instrument by the **upright piano**, with vertical strings, which was originally developed by John Hawkins of Philadelphia in 1800. Since the middle of the 19th century both grand pianos, with horizontal strings, and upright pianos have been in use. The modern **grand piano**, with its iron frame and overstrung heavy strings, also emerged in about 1800. In overstringing, the strings are arranged in two different layers, which cross over each other. This has the advantage of saving space and bringing bass and treble strings closer together to enhance *resonance. Grand pianos are made in three sizes: the **baby grand** (5ft 6in–5ft 10in), the **boudoir grand** (6–7ft), and the **concert grand** (7–9ft). All have about 88 keys (starting on G and ending on A) set out in the harpsichord fashion – an arrangement that has survived for some 700 years.

Modern pianos have two or three strings tuned in unison for each note (except for the bass notes, which are single strings); all the strings are made of steel, the bass notes being wound with copper to increase their resonance. Both upright and grand pianos have at least two pedals: the **soft pedal** either moves the action sideways so that the hammer only strikes two of the three strings or brings the action closer to the strings to reduce the impact; the **sustaining** (or **loud**) **pedal** removes the dampers from the strings so that the strings continue to sound after the note has been released. Some pianos, especially those made by the Steinway Co., have a third pedal enabling individual notes to be sustained.

The repertoire of music for the piano in enormous, including solo pieces, chamber music, and concertos. It is also an extremely versatile accompanying instrument. See also **pedal piano; player piano; prepared piano.**

piano accordion see **accordion.**

pianoforte see **piano.**

Pianola (*Trademark*) see **player piano.**

piano quartet see **quartet.**

piano quintet see **quintet.**

piano score see **score.**

piano trio see **trio.**

Piatigorsky, Gregor (1903–76) Russian-born cellist and composer, who settled in the USA. Acclaimed the leading cellist of his generation, he trained at the Moscow conservatory. He was appointed principal cellist of the Bolshoi Theatre orchestra (1919) but left Russia in 1921, making his debut in the USA in 1929. He formed trios with Horowitz and Milstein (1930) and with Heifetz and Artur Rubinstein (1949).

pibroch Scottish Highland music in the form of ornate variations for the bagpipes on a theme known as an **urlar.** This music originally used a system of notation based on syllables that indicated both intervals and motifs.

Picardy third (*or* **tierce de Picardie**) A major third used in the final chord of some compositions in a minor key. This device was extensively used until the middle of the 18th century but not very much thereafter. The origin of the name is uncertain (the French word *tierce* is an obsolete name for a third).

Piccinni (*or* **Piccini**), **Niccolo** (1728–1800) Italian composer. In Naples he studied with Leo and Durante and produced his first operas buffa, including *La Cecchina* (1760), and operas seria: in Rome his *La Buona figliuola* was a great success. In 1776 he went to Paris, where he rivalled Gluck in composing French operas with Italian elements, such as *Didon* (1783) and *Atys* (1780). Returning to Naples in 1791, he wrote oratorios and other sacred works, sinfonias, and keyboard music.

piccolo see **flute.**

piccolo trumpet see **trumpet.**

Pictures at an Exhibition Suite for piano by Mussorgsky. Composed: 1874. After the death of the distinguished Russian painter Hartmann in 1873 an exhibition of his works was arranged, and this suite attempts to describe in music ten of the pictures from the exhibition. They include a depiction of the Russian fairy-tale witch 'Baba Yaga' and the legendary 'Great Gate of Kiev.' Between most of the movements comes an interlude entitled 'Promenade,' which changes in character throughout the work. Several orchestral arrangements have been made, the most famous and most frequently performed being by Ravel.

pien ch'ing see **stone chimes.**

Pierné, Gabriel (1863–1937) French composer, a pupil of Franck and Massenet. Pierné was awarded the Grand Prix de Rome in 1882. He conducted the Concerts Colonne in Paris (1910–32). Pierné's works, which combine a typical French lightness with a more intense element of expression, include operas and ballets, orchestral music, chamber works, and songs.

Pierrot lunaire Song cycle for voice and chamber orchestra by Schoenberg to words by Giraud, translated by Hartleben. First performance: 1912. Described as a cycle of 'three times seven' songs, these 21 pieces make extensive use of speech song and *Pierrot lunaire* is one of the earliest and most important products of expressionism: the weird and macabre plot is typical of expressionist works.

piffaro (*or* **pifa**) An Italian folk *shawm. It has double reeds and is used to accompany bagpipes. A player of this instrument is called a **pifferaro**.

Pijper, Willem (1894–1947) Dutch composer, director of the Rotterdam conservatory (1930–47). Pijper's early works show romantic and impressionist influences. His later compositions explore more modern techniques, such as polytonality and polymetry, and often derive much of their material from a single chord or motif. Pijper's output includes the opera *Halewijn* (1933), five string quartets and other chamber works, and vocal music.

Pilgrim's Progress, The Opera (a 'Morality') in prologue, four acts, and epilogue by Vaughan Williams with libretto by the composer taken from Bunyan. First performance: Covent Garden, London, 1951. It incorporates an earlier one-act opera by the composer: *The Shepherds of the Delectable Mountains* (1922).

Pilkington, Francis (*c*.1570–1638) English composer. He gained the Oxford B.Mus. in 1595, was a lay clerk at Chester by 1602, and took holy orders in 1614. His works comprise lute songs, two volumes of madrigals (1613/14, 1624), and a small number of instrumental pieces.

Pineapple Poll Ballet in three scenes with Sullivan's music arranged by Charles Mackerras and libretto and choreography by Cranko. First performance: Sadler's Wells Theatre, London, 1951, by the Sadler's Wells Ballet (décor by Osbert Lancaster). The scenario is based on one of W. S. Gilbert's *Bab Ballads*, 'The Bumboat Woman's Story,' in which the girls of Portsmouth find Captain Belaye so fascinating that they disguise themselves as sailors and board his ship, HMS *Hot Cross Bun*.

Pines of Rome (Italian: *Pini di Roma*) Tone poem by Respighi. Composed: 1924. It depicts four landscapes near Rome: the Villa Borghese, a catacomb, the Janiculum (which includes a recording of the song of the nightingale), and the Appian Way. See also **Fountains of Rome; Roman Festivals.**

Pinto, George Frederick (1785–1806) British composer, pianist, and violinist. He studied the violin with Salomon and gave concerts from a very early age. In his short career

as a composer he produced many striking and original piano works (including two sonatas and a fantasia and sonata in C minor); he also wrote four violin sonatas, violin duets, and some promising songs.

pipa (*or* **p'i p'a**) A four-stringed Chinese *lute, with frets extending onto the pear-shaped belly of the instrument. It has been in use for over 1500 years, being particularly popular during the Tang dynasty (618–906) for accompanying songs and as a solo instrument (see also **Chinese music**). **The Japanese biwa** is a more recent development with four silken strings. The tuning of the strings of both instruments varies greatly.

pipe 1. Any hollow tube used to produce a musical sound, particularly an end-blown whistle flute or similar instrument. See **organ; panpipes. 2.** A one-handed whistle flute played with a *tabor. The pipe and tabor combination was widely used in rural communities from the 12th to the 18th centuries. **3.** Short for *bagpipes.

Pipkov, Lubomir (1904–74) Bulgarian composer. Pipkov studied in Paris with Dukas (1926–32). His works, influenced by Bulgarian folk traditions, include the opera *Antigona 43* (1961), orchestral compositions, patriotic choral works, and chamber music.

Pique-Dame see **Queen of Spades, The.**

Pirates of Penzance, The Operetta by Sullivan with libretto by Gilbert, subtitled *The Slave of Duty*. First performance: Bijou Theatre, Paignton, England, 1879 (for reasons of copyright, one day before its opening at the Fifth Avenue Theatre, New York). Frederic, an apprentice pirate, is torn between his loyalty to the pirate band and his duty as a law-abiding citizen. All ends happily when the pirates turn out to be noblemen, loyal to the Queen.

Pisador, Diego (*c*.1509–after 1557) Spanish composer and vihuelist. Active in Salamanca, he took minor orders in 1526 but was never ordained a priest. His one collection of vihuela music includes fantasias and intabulations of works by many leading composers.

Pisk, Paul Amadeus (1893–) Austrian composer, a pupil of Schoenberg. Pisk emigrated to the USA in 1936. His music uses serial techniques and includes orchestral and choral works, chamber music, and songs.

piston 1. A valve on a brass wind instrument. When the valve is depressed the effective length of the tube is increased. **2.** Short for **cornet à pistons**, the French name for a *cornet.

Piston, Walter (1894–1976) US composer, a pupil of Nadia Boulanger. Piston taught at Harvard University from 1926: among his pupils were Carter, Bernstein, and Berger. The many awards gained by Piston include a Guggenheim Fellowship and Pulitzer Prizes for his third and seventh symphonies. In Piston's music traditional concepts of tonality and form are combined with jazz-influenced rhythms and a strong contrapuntal sense. His works include eight symphonies, concertos for violin, viola, clarinet, and piano, the ballet The *Incredible Flutist (1938), and chamber music, including five string quartets.

pitch A quality of a musical sound that determines its position in a *scale. It is measured as the *frequency of the pure tone of specified loudness that is judged by a normal ear to occupy the same place in the scale. Thus although pitch is measured in terms of frequency, it also depends to a certain extent on the loudness and quality of a note. As the loudness of a low-frequency note is increased its pitch decreases, while the pitch of a high-frequency note increases with loudness (for example, increasing the loudness of a 200-hertz note from 60 decibels to 120 decibels reduces its pitch by 20%).

Musical instruments have to be tuned to an agreed pitch in order that they can be played together. The frequency of A above middle C is usually taken as the tuning note. This frequency has varied from time to time. For example, Handel's *tuning fork gave a frequency of A = 422.5 hertz. Modern standard pitch, agreed internationally in 1960, gives A = 440 hertz (this was formerly known as **concert pitch**).

Pitfield, Thomas (1903–   ) British composer, poet, and artist. Pitfield's works are characterized by simplicity of style: his output includes a piano concerto and choral music.

più More. Hence **più allegro**, faster; **più lento**, slower. [Italian]

piuttosto Somewhat; rather: used with directions to indicate moderation in their execution. [Italian]

Pixis, Johann Peter (1788–1874) German pianist and composer. From an early age he toured as a pianist, often with his brother, the violinist **Friedrich Wilhelm Pixis** (1786–1842). In 1823 he settled in Paris, where he earned a reputation as a leading virtuoso and eminent piano teacher. In 1840 he moved to Baden-Baden. Pixis' compositions are chiefly brilliant piano pieces (including three sonatas, a piano concerto, and salon pieces); he contributed a variation to the *Hexameron (1837).

pizz. see **pizzicato**.

Pizzetti, Ildebrando (1880–1968) Italian composer. Pizzetti taught at many Italian conservatories. As a composer he is best known for his operas, in which the natural declamation of their arioso vocal style contrasts with the lyrical opulence of Puccini. Pizzetti's operas include Fedra (1909–12), Debora e Jaele (1915–21), and L'*Assassinio nella cattedrale (1958); his output also includes orchestral, choral, and chamber music.

pizzicato (or **pizz.**) Plucked: used as an instruction to pluck the strings of a bowed stringed instrument. [Italian]

plagal cadence see **cadence**.

plagal modes see **modes**.

plainchant (or **plainsong**) The unaccompanied melody to which the texts of the Roman Catholic liturgy are sung. The type traditionally adopted in liturgical practice is **Gregorian chant**, whose connection with Pope Gregory I (reigned 590–604) is probably largely nominal (it seems to have reached its final form under the Frankish monarchs of the 8th and 9th centuries). In its basic form, **cantus planus**, it is rhythmically free, following the prose rhythms of the psalms and prayers set, and has a small melodic range, complying with one of the eight church *modes (see also **Gregorian tone**). There are two categories: chants for the Proper and the Ordinary. The Proper chants, originally a little more ornate than those of the Ordinary, were sung either antiphonally or responsorially. In its original form the *antiphon acted as a refrain between psalm verses, but over the centuries it has contracted into the accompaniment of a single verse. Indeed, most antiphons have become responses, sung by the choir in alternation with the solo. The performance of Ordinary chants is more straightforward and consistent. Gradually the chant repertory has become standardized in such collections as the Kyriale – chants for the Ordinary; the Vesperale – for Vespers and Compline; and the single-volume modern compendium, the Liber Usualis.

The traditional plainchant notation, which developed gradually during the Middle Ages, uses a variety of note shapes (known as *neumes) written on a four-line stave with the C-clef or F-clef in any one of a number of positions.

A less highly organized type of plainchant is *Ambrosian chant, named after St Ambrose.

plainsong see **plainchant**.

Planets, The Orchestral suite by Holst. Composed: 1915; first performance: London, 1918. It consists of seven movements, each portraying the astrological nature of one planet. The orchestra includes an organ and, in the final movement, a female choir. The theme from the middle section of 'Jupiter' is also used as the popular hymn tune for 'I vow to thee my country.'

player piano A piano that plays itself. The best example is the **Pianola**, patented in 1897, in which the keys are depressed by air pressure controlled by holes in a roll of paper. As the roll unwinds over a bar containing holes corresponding to the notes of the piano, a hole in the roll activates a mechanism for depressing the appropriate note. The mechanism and the air pump are supplied with energy by foot pedals or by an electric motor. The perforations in the rolls were originally made mechanically, but later developments included the making of perforations by a device activated by a live performance. In these rolls additional perforations were made to control the dynamics of the piece. Pianolas had a vogue at the end of the 19th century that lasted until about the 1920s, when they were largely replaced by the gramophone. The more sophisticated models were sometimes called **reproducing pianos**.

plectrum Any device for plucking the strings of a chordophone, such as the quill attached to the *jack of a harpsichord or the metal, tortoiseshell, or plastic device held in the hand of the player of a lute, mandolin, electric guitar, zither, or banjo. A plectrum is usually used with wire strings; gut or nylon strings are usually plucked with the fingers.

plein jeu 1. See **full organ. 2.** An organ *mixture stop that includes the note played, its octave, and its twelfth. [French, full play]

Pleyel, Ignaz Joseph (1757–1831) Austrian composer and piano maker. A pupil of Haydn, he became kapellmeister of Strasbourg in 1789. In 1792 he went to London for a year to conduct a series of concerts. He settled in Paris in 1795, opening up a publishing house and in 1807 a piano factory. He was a prolific composer, especially for chamber ensembles, whose work was much admired in his lifetime.

pneuma A melodic phrase sung to a vowel at the close of a word or sentence. Decorative in style, it was in common use in the music of the early church and was said to enhance the devotional atmosphere. Among its most frequent uses were those in connection with the word 'Alleluia' in the Mass, when the final 'a' provided a vowel over which a melody was embellished. [Greek, breath]

pneumatic action see **action**.

pochette see **kit**.

pochettino see **poco**.

pochissimo see **poco**.

poco A little; e.g. **poco lento**, a little slower. Hence **pochissimo** and **pochettino**, a very little; very slightly. [Italian]

poem One of several types of works by various romantic composers, including Liszt (see **tone poem**), Chausson (*Poem for Violin and Orchestra*), and Scriabin (*The *Divine Poem* – his third symphony, 1905).

Poem of Ecstasy, The Tone poem by Scriabin. First performance: 1908. It was the composer's intention to portray in this work the ecstatic feeling of joy experienced by an artist in working creatively.

Poem of Fire, The see **Prometheus**.

Poet and Peasant (German: *Dichter und Bauer*) Overture by Suppé. Composed: 1846. Although heard today almost invariably as a separate concert work this overture was originally part of the incidental music that Suppé composed for the play of the same name by Elmar. Many arrangements have been made for a wide variety of instrumental combinations.

Pohjola's Daughter Tone poem (Op. 49) by Sibelius. Composed: 1906. This work is based upon an incident in the Finnish saga *Kalevala* concerning Louhi, the daughter of Pohjola.

poi Then: used in directions to indicate that a section follows a repetition of the previous section; e.g. **poi la coda**, then play the coda. [Italian]

point 1. The end of the *bow of a stringed instrument opposite to the end that is held. See also **punta. 2.** Short for *pedal point (*or organ point*).

point d'orgue 1. Organ point. See **pedal. 2.** The pause on the second inversion of a chord at which the *cadenza in a concerto is traditionally introduced. **3.** The pause sign ⌢. [French]

pointillism The technique of composing music to give the impression that it consists of sequences of 'dots' of sound rather than flowing melodic lines. Pointillism in music is derived from the school of painting in which dots of colour are applied to the canvas. Some of the music of Stockhausen and Webern is described as pointillist.

pointing In psalmody, the system of dividing up the verses of psalms by signs, each sign corresponding to a bar line in the chant. Until the period of the Oxford Movement (initiated in the 1830s) the regular use of the *Anglican chant was restricted to cathedrals and collegiate churches. In 1837 Robert Janes, organist of Ely Cathedral, produced a method of pointing the psalms. Different methods have subsequently appeared, the most scholarly dating from the early years of the 20th century in *The English Psalter*, *The Oxford Psalter*, and *The Parish Psalter*.

Poisoned Kiss, The Opera in three acts by Vaughan Williams with libretto by Evelyn Sharp based on fairy stories by Richard Garnett and Nathaniel Hawthorne. First performance: Arts Theatre, Cambridge, 1936. The magician Rappaccini has brought up his daughter, Tormentilla, on poisons so that when she kisses the empress's son, Amaryllis, she will kill him. True love defeats the plot.

polacca see **polonaise**.

Polish Symphony Symphony No. 3 in D major by Tchaikovsky. Composed: 1875. The finale of this symphony is in the style of a polonaise, a Polish national dance, hence its name.

polka A Bohemian dance that originated in the early 19th century. It is in brisk duple time with vigorous rhythms.

Examples occur in the music of Smetana (*The Bartered Bride*) and Dvořák. A form of the dance has evolved in Paraguay in which there is a cross-rhythm accompaniment in triplets against the duple rhythm of the melody.

Pollini, Maurizio (1942–) Italian pianist, a pupil of Michelangeli. In 1960 he won the International Chopin Competition in Warsaw. His repertory includes both classical and modern works.

Polly Ballad opera with music arranged by Pepusch and words by John Gay. Published in 1729, it was banned from the London stage as being subversive to authority and not produced until 1777. It is a sequel to The *Beggar's Opera*. Modern arrangements include those by Austin (London; 1922) and Addison (Aldeburgh; 1952).

polo A Spanish dance from the southern region of Andalusia. It is in 3/8 time with *hemiola syncopations and passages of rapid vocal coloratura. Bizet includes a polo by Manuel Garcia (*Cuerpo bueno*) in Act IV of *Carmen*.

polonaise A Polish dance that probably originated in court ceremonies and processions in the 16th century. J. S. Bach included examples in his sixth *French Suite* and second *Orchestral Suite*. There are few immediately recognisable features of the polonaise before the early 19th century, when it began to display a characteristic dotted rhythm in 3/4 time, *feminine cadences, and the repetition of short motifs. These features occur in polonaises for the piano by Beethoven, Schubert, and Liszt as well as in the 16 well-known polonaises by Chopin, which are usually regarded as his most intensely patriotic pieces. Italian: **polacca**.

Polonia Symphonic prelude (Op. 76) by Elgar. Composed: 1915. Elgar wrote the work for a concert to benefit the Polish Relief Fund and dedicated it to Paderewski, who at that time was helping to raise money for the fund. The Polish connection is indicated in the work by a quotation of the Polish national anthem as well as themes by Chopin and Paderewski himself.

Polovtsian Dances Set of dances for choir and orchestra by Borodin, taken from the second act of his opera *Prince Igor*. First performance: 1890. The title refers to Polovtsy, leader of a band of nomads known as the Polovtsians, who captured the Russian soldier-hero Prince Igor.

polymodality Music that is based on more than one *mode. An example is Vaughan Williams' *Pastoral Symphony*. Compare **polytonality**.

polyphonic Relating to music in which there are two or more parts each having independent melodic lines. The music itself is called **polyphony**. In the **polyphonic period** (13th to 16th centuries) harmonic progressions were controlled more by the independent melodies, whereas in the later polyphony of Bach and his contemporaries the polyphony was governed by the harmonic structure of the composition.

polyrhythmic Denoting music in which different parts, based on different rhythms, are played at the same time.

polytonality The system of composing music in which more than one *key is used at the same time. Holst and Milhaud used this system. **Bitonality** refers to compositions in which only two keys are used. Compare **atonality**.

pommer see **shawm**.

Pomp and Circumstance Set of five marches for orchestra (Op. 39) by Elgar. Composed: 1901–30. The title of the collection is taken from a phrase in the third act of Shakespeare's *Othello*: 'pride, pomp and the circumstance of glorious war.' Elgar originally intended there to be six marches but only five were completed, the first four between 1901 and 1907 and the fifth in 1930. The first march is sometimes known as *Land of Hope and Glory* after the words later added to it; the words 'All men must be free' were set to the fourth march.

Ponce, Manuel (1882–1948) Mexican composer, a pupil of Dukas in Paris. Ponce is regarded as the founder of modern music in Mexico. The folk-influenced style of his early works, such as the well-known song 'Estrellita,' gave way in his later compositions to a distinctive contrapuntal idiom. Ponce's works include concertos for violin and guitar and other orchestral music, chamber works, songs, piano pieces, and guitar music.

Ponchielli, Amilcare (1834–86) Italian composer. He studied at the Milan conservatory (1843–54), where he was later (1880–86) Professor of Composition. From 1854 he was an organist and conductor in Cremona (from 1854) and in 1881 became maestro di cappella of S Maria Maggiore, Bergamo. Ponchielli was a leading opera composer in Italy in the second half of the 19th century, but only La *Gioconda* (1876; which includes the well-known ballet music, the *Dance of the Hours*) survives in the repertory (other operas include *I Promessi sposi*, 1856, and *I Lituani*, 1874). He also wrote prolifically in other genres: ballets, cantatas, sacred and other vocal music, and works for orchestra, band, and piano.

ponticello The bridge of a stringed instrument. Hence **sul ponticello**, on the bridge: an instruction to the player of a bowed stringed instrument to draw the bow as close to the bridge as possible. [Italian, little bridge]

Poot, Marcel (1901–) Belgian composer. Poot cofounded the modernist Group des Synthétistes in 1925 and directed the Brussels conservatoire (1949–66). His music, which combines traditional harmonic concepts with an individual rhythmic sense, includes the opera *Moretus* (1943), orchestral works, chamber music, and songs.

Popp, Lucia (1939–) Austrian soprano. After studying at Brno and Prague she made her debut in Vienna (1963) as the Queen of the Night in Mozart's *The Magic Flute*. She has since sung throughout Europe and recorded Mozart and Wagner.

Popper, David (1843–1913) German-Czech cellist. After playing as principal cellist of the Vienna Hofoper and as a member of the Hellmesberger Quartet, he made several European tours and settled in Budapest (1896) as a professor at the royal conservatory, remaining there for the rest of his life. His many compositions include the *Requiem* for three cellos, first performed in London in 1891.

Porgy and Bess Opera in three acts by George Gershwin with text by du Bose Heyward and Ira Gershwin. First performance: Boston, 1935. Set in downtown South Carolina and with a Black cast, it is the story of the crippled Porgy (bass-baritone) and his love for Bess (soprano), who belongs to the stevedore Crown (baritone). The music has borrowings from spirituals and jazz but uses no actual folk songs.

Porpora, Nicola (1686–1768) Italian composer and singing teacher. A pupil of Gaetano Greco and Ottavio Campanile, he taught many famous singers, including Antonio Uberti and Farinelli. He taught in Naples and Venice, visiting London in 1733–36, where he rivalled Handel in opera and oratorio. Porpora was appointed kapellmeister in Dresden (1748) and in Vienna (1752–60), where Joseph Haydn became his pupil and accompanist. His works include over 50 operas, many oratorios, masses, motets, cantatas, and some instrumental music.

port á beul see **mouth music.**

portamento (*or* **portando**) The carrying of a note into the next note without a break in a legato fashion. This is possible with the voice, a bowed instrument, and a trombone. [Italian, carrying]

portative organ A small portable organ with flue pipes in which the player pumped the bellows with the left hand and played the (usually) two-octave keyboard with the right hand. These organs were popular from the 12th to the 17th centuries and, unlike the *positive organs, they could be carried in procession. See also **regal.**

port de voix *Portamento in singing. [French, carrying of the voice]

Porter, Quincy (1897–1966) US composer, a pupil of Horatio Parker, d'Indy, and Bloch. He wrote two symphonies and many concertos, including the *Concerto Concertante* (1954) for two pianos, but is chiefly known for his chamber music, which includes the ten string quartets.

Porter, Walter (*c.*1595–1659) English composer, lutenist, and singer. A chorister at Westminster Abbey, he became a gentleman of the Chapel Royal in 1617, by which time he claimed to have studied under Monteverdi. He took part in the masque *The Triumph of Peace* (1634) at the court of Charles I and in 1639 became Master of the Choristers at Westminster. His *Madrigals and Ayres* (1632, *c.*1639) show Italian influence and are among the few English madrigals in the concertato style.

Portsmouth Point Concert overture by Walton. Composed: 1925. Walton was inspired to write this work after seeing a picture entitled 'Portsmouth Point' by Thomas Rowlandson, in which a busy dockside scene is depicted, and he attempts to convey in musical terms the lively and varied spirit of the drawing.

Posaune (*pl.* **Posaunen**) Trombone. [German]

positif Choir *organ. [French]

position 1. The way in which the notes of a *chord are set out. In the **root position** the lowest note is the keynote; in other positions the chord is said to be an *inversion. **2.** One of several points on the fingerboard of a stringed instrument at which the left hand is placed to enable the fingers to stop the strings. These points are known as the first position, second position, etc. **3.** One of the seven playing positions of the slide of a *trombone. The first position is the one with the slide in its least extended configuration.

positive organ 1. A small flue-pipe organ, designed for use in church or home, that was fixed in position and – unlike a *portative organ – could not be carried in procession. Positive organs were used from the 10th to the 17th centuries. **2.** A single-manual organ without pedals invented by Thomas Carson in 1887. It had many of the attributes of a two-manual organ with pedals and an automatic transposing device.

possibile Possible, usually in the sense (as much as) possible, e.g. **presto possibile**, as fast as possible. [Italian]

post horn A straight or coiled valveless brass *horn that is capable of playing only its fundamental note and the relative harmonic series. It was formerly used by postillions for announcing the arrival of a coach. The *cornet evolved from it by the addition of valves.

postlude An organ *voluntary played at the end of a church service. It may be improvised, so as to provide the exact duration of music to accompany the exit of the choir and congregation.

Poston, Elizabeth (1905–87) British composer. Poston's style recalls the idiom of Tudor composers. Her works include choral music, chamber music, and songs.

potpourri An assemblage of popular melodies drawn from opera or folk song that are played as a series. There may be some introductory or connecting phrases. See also **pasticcio**.

Potter, (Philip) Cipriani (Hambly) (1792–1871) British composer, pianist, and teacher. He studied with Attwood, Crotch, and Woelfl, making his debut as a pianist in 1816 in London. In 1817 he went to Vienna and, at Beethoven's suggestion, studied with Aloys Förster. Back in England, he performed as a pianist and conducted the Royal Philharmonic Society concerts. From 1822 he taught at the Royal Academy of Music, where he succeeded Crotch as principal (1832–59). Potter composed mainly instrumental music; his nine symphonies are the most acclaimed of his works but he also wrote piano concertos, chamber music, piano pieces, and vocal music.

Poule, La see **Hen, The**.

Poulenc, Francis (1899–1963) French composer, a pupil of Koechlin and a member of Les *Six. Poulenc's works were influenced by Satie and Ravel in their classical restraint of expression. His frequent use of a popular melodic idiom earned him a reputation as a musical clown, clearly unjustified when such works as the organ concerto (1941) and the choral *Gloria* (1960) are considered. The apparent simplicity of his musical idiom belies the great subtlety of its harmonic and melodic effect. Poulenc's output includes the operas *Les *Mamelles de Tirésias* (1940) and *Les *Dialogues des Carmélites* (1957); the ballet *Les Biches* (1923); orchestral works, including concertos for piano (1950), two pianos (1932), and organ, the *Concerto champêtre* (1927–28) for harpsichord and orchestra, and *Marches militaires* for piano and orchestra; sacred music, including cantatas and a mass in G minor; chamber music; many piano pieces; and songs, including the song cycle *Le Bestiaire* (1919). He was also a noted pianist, accompanying in particular the tenor Pierre Bernac in concerts in Europe and the USA.

Pousseur, Henri (1929–) Belgian composer, a pupil of Boulez. He adopted serialism in the 1950s, being particularly interested in its relations with harmony. He worked with electronic music, founding the Liège electronic studio. He abandoned strict serialism in the 1960s and subsequent works have demonstrated Pousseur's concern with a progressive musical and social utopianism and the musical past. *Votre Faust* (1960–67), a variable-form opera, integrates different harmonic styles and *Couleurs croisées* (1968) applies the same treatment to the protest song 'We shall overcome.' Other works include *Quintette* (1955), *Symphonies* (1955), *Les Ephemerides d'Icare* (1970), *Invitation à l'Utopie* (1971), *Le Temps des Paroboles* (1972), *Die Erprobung des Petrus Hebraïcus* (1974), and *Songs and Tales from the Bible of Death* (1979).

Powell, Mel (1923–) US composer and writer, a pupil of Schillinger, Toch, and Hindemith. In his early career he arranged music for Benny Goodman and Glenn Miller, and he developed a highly chromatic miniature style in the 1950s. In 1960 Powell founded the Yale electronic studio and he has used tape in many pieces. His works include *Filigree Setting* (1959), *Events* (1963), and *Cantilena* (1970).

Power, Lionel (c.1370–1445) English composer. A contemporary of John Dunstable, he was instructor of the choristers in the household chapel of Thomas, Duke of Clarence (?1413–21), and master of the Lady Chapel choir at Christ Church, Canterbury (?1438–45). Power's creative output, which spans almost 50 years, includes votive antiphons and Mass settings as well as a treatise on descant. His earliest compositions (probably dating from the late 14th century) include a setting of *Beata progenies*; an example of his later works is the cyclic mass based on *Alma redemptoris*.

praeludium see **prelude**.

Praetorius, Michael (c.1570–1621) German composer, organist, and theorist. Educated in Torgau, Anhalt, and Frankfurt an der Oder, he became organist in Frankfurt probably in 1587. In the early 1590s he was appointed court organist in Wolfenbüttel, becoming kapellmeister in 1604; from 1613 he held the same post in a variety of German towns. Praetorius' theoretical work, *Syntagma musicum*, contains important documentation of performance practice. His compositions are mainly sacred and include over a thousand chorale settings for various forces. His only secular collection, *Terpsichore* (1612), contains French instrumental dances.

Prague Symphony Symphony No. 38 in D major (K. 504) by Mozart. Composed: 1786. This work received its first performance in Prague in 1787, when Mozart went to assist with a production of *The Marriage of Figaro* (hence the name). It is unusual in that there is no minuet and thus only three (rather than the customary four) movements.

Pralltriller The German name for an upper *mordent.

precentor A person who leads the singing in church (e.g. the cantor in a synagogue). In Anglican cathedrals the precentor is the clergyman in charge of choral music. In Scottish Presbyterian and English dissenting churches the precentor leads the tune in unaccompanied singing.

Preciosa Incidental music by Weber to the play by Wolff. First performance: 1821. The plot is based upon the Gypsy play *La Gitanella* by Cervantes and the overture is sometimes performed separately.

precipitato (*or* **precipitoso**, **precipitando**, etc.) Hastening; impetuous. [Italian]

preclassical Denoting music that followed the *baroque music of the early 18th century and preceded the *classical music of the late 18th century. The most important composers of preclassical music are C. P. E. Bach and the Mannheim School.

prelude An instrumental piece serving as the introduction to a *fugue, *suite, or a church service. A prelude during the 15th and 16th centuries was a freely composed work for lute or keyboard; it was thus distinguished from works based on a cantus firmus or other borrowed material. Examples occur in *The Buxheim Organ Book* (*c.*1465) and in pieces by John Bull and Basard. From the middle of the 17th century preludes formed the first movements of suites for the lute and harpsichord. These were sometimes of an improvisatory nature, particularly the unmeasured preludes of Louis Couperin.

  The **prelude and fugue** form for organ was also established in the early 17th century and has continued to be cultivated, with examples by Buxtehude, J. S. Bach (see **Well-Tempered Clavier, The**), Mendelssohn, Brahms, etc., until the present day. In the 19th and 20th centuries the term prelude has also been applied to miniatures for piano by Chopin, Scriabin, Debussy, Rachmaninov, and others. Shostakovich continued the prelude and fugue tradition of Bach with three sets for piano. See also **Vorspiel.** [from Latin *praeludium*]

Prélude à l'après-midi d'un faune see **Après-midi d'un faune, Prélude à l'.**

Préludes, Les Tone poem by Liszt after a poem by Lamartine. Composed: 1848; revised: 1854. This work reflects the view of Lamartine's poem that life is a series of preludes to the life after death. It was, however, composed originally as the overture to an unpublished choral work and the programme was only added later by Liszt.

preparation A device in *harmony in which a note is first sounded in a chord with which it is consonant and then again in a chord with which it is dissonant. The resulting dissonance is then said to be **prepared.** An **unprepared dissonance** is one that has not been treated in this way.

prepared piano A piano that has been altered to produce special effects. Such instruments are particularly associated with John *Cage, who prepared his pianos by placing objects on the strings to produce novel sounds. Cage wrote music especially for prepared piano.

pressez Increase speed; accelerate. [French]

prestissimo see presto.

presto Fast: a direction implying a faster speed than *allegro. Hence **prestissimo**, very fast. [Italian]

Preston, Simon (John) (1938–) British organist, harpsichordist, and conductor. He studied at the Royal College of Music, making his debut at the Festival Hall (1962), and has toured Europe and North America. From 1970 he taught at Christ Church, Oxford, and in 1981 he was appointed organist of Westminster Abbey.

Prêtre, Georges (1924–) French conductor. He has conducted at Covent Garden and the Metropolitan Opera, New York, and was musical director of the Paris Opera (1970–71). He made memorable recordings with Callas and has recorded much of Poulenc's orchestral and choral music.

Previn, André (Andreas Ludwig Priwin; 1929–) German-born US conductor, pianist, and composer. After making a reputation in the USA as a jazz pianist and film composer, he became principal conductor of the Houston Symphony Orchestra (1967–70), the London Symphony Orchestra (1969–79), and the Pittsburgh Symphony Orchestra (1976–84). His compositions include concertos for guitar and sitar.

Leontyne Price at a rehearsal

Margaret Price giving a recital

Previtali, Fernando (1907–85) Italian conductor, composer, and writer on music. He conducted the Rome Radio Orchestra (1936–53) and subsequently directed the Academy of St Cecilia.

Prey, Hermann (1929–   ) German baritone. He studied at the Berlin Music Academy with Günther Baum and Harry Gottschalk and made his debut at the Wiesbaden State Theatre in 1952. He has since sung in Germany, at Salzburg, and in London (Covent Garden, 1973).

Price, Leontyne (1927–   ) US Black soprano. She studied in New York at the Juilliard School of Music and with Florence Kimball, making her debut on Broadway in Virgil Thomson's opera *Four Saints in Three Acts* (1951). In the same year she first appeared as Bess in Gershwin's *Porgy and Bess.*

Price, Margaret (1941–   ) Welsh soprano. She made her debut as Cherubino in Mozart's *The Marriage of Figaro* with the Welsh National Opera (1962). Her association with the conductor and pianist James Lockhart began soon afterwards and they gave memorable recitals. She meanwhile continued on stage, particularly in Mozart and Verdi.

prick song A piece of music from England during the 15th and 16th centuries that was written in mensural notation, as distinct from one written in unmeasured plainchant notation. The 'pricking' of music books meant the writing or copying of manuscripts.

Prigioniero, Il (*The Prisoner*) Opera in prologue and one act by Dallapiccola with libretto by the composer based on the story *La Torture par l'espérance* (*Torture by Hope*) by Villiers de l'Isle-Adam, concerning a prisoner of the Inquisition. First performance (in concert on Radio Italiana): Turin, 1949; first stage performance: Florence, 1950.

prima donna The chief female singer in an operatic production. Overuse of the term may lead to more than one singer in a production being called prima donna, in which case the most important singer is known as the **prima donna assoluta**. [Italian, first lady]

primo (*or fem.* **prima**) First. Hence **prima volta**, first time: see **volta**. [Italian]

Primrose, William (1903–82) British violist, born in Scotland. He studied under Ysaÿe in Belgium and was resident in the USA from 1937. He formed the Primrose Quartet (1939) and the Festival Quartet (1955–62). Primrose became the foremost European viola virtuoso and Bartók wrote his viola concerto for him.

Prince Igor Opera in prologue and four acts by Borodin with libretto by the composer based on a play by Stassov. Unfinished at the time of the composer's death in 1887, it was completed by Rimsky-Korsakov and Glazunov. First performance: St Petersburg, 1890. Prince Igor (baritone) is a 12th-century Russian warrior: he is captured by the Polovtsians, whose famous dances come in Act II (see **Polovtsian Dances**), and eventually escapes.

Prince of the Pagodas Ballet in three acts with music by Britten and scenario and choreography by Cranko. First performance: Covent Garden, London, 1957, by the Royal Ballet with Beriosova (décor by Piper). It is a fairy tale of an emperor of China and his two daughters, one good, the other evil.

Princess Ida Operetta by Sullivan with libretto by Gilbert. First performance: Savoy Theatre, London, 1884. Subtitled *Castle Adamant*, it is styled 'a respectful perversion of Tennyson's *The Princess*' and relates what happens when Princess Ida starts a women's university.

principal 1. (adj.) Denoting the leading player of a section of the orchestra, e.g. principal flute. **2.** (adj.) Denoting a singer who takes leading parts in opera. A principal tenor is one who takes principal roles, not the leading tenor of the opera company. **3.** (n.) An open *diapason organ *stop that sounds an octave higher than the note played, i.e. a 4-*foot stop on the manuals and an 8-foot stop on the pedals. **4.** (n.) (*or* **principale**) The great organ. **5.** (n.) (*or* **principale**) The lower trumpet parts in 17th- and 18th-century music.

Prinz von Homburg, Der (*The Prince of Homburg*) Opera in three acts by Henze with text by Ingeborg Bachmann based on the drama by von Kleist. First performance: Hamburg State Opera, 1960. It is the story of a poet, against a background of Prussian militarism in the 17th century.

Pritchard, John (1921–) British conductor. He conducted the Royal Liverpool Philharmonic Orchestra (1957–63) and the London Philharmonic Orchestra (1962–66); he has also conducted at Covent Garden and Glyndebourne (1969–77). In 1979 he became chief guest conductor of the BBC Symphony Orchestra.

Prix de Rome A composition prize awarded annually from 1803 to 1968 by the Académie des Beaux Arts, Paris. It was given to the student from the Paris Conservatoire who was judged to have made the best setting of a given (cantata) text. The winner spent four years at the Villa Medici, Rome, thereby winning some recognition. Winners of the Prix de Rome have included Berlioz (1830), Bizet (1875), and Debussy (1884).

Prodaná Nevěsta see **Bartered Bride, The.**

programme music (*or* **illustrative music**) A work that is inspired or motivated by a nonmusical idea (the term was introduced by Liszt). The beginnings of programme music can be seen in the practice of word painting in Italian vocal music of the 14th century and in Jannequin's descriptive chansons of the 16th century, including *Le Chant des oyseaux* (c.1528) and *La Guerre* (1515). Descriptive keyboard music was widespread during the 17th century, as in Martin Peerson's *The Fall of the Leafe*. Among baroque examples are Froberger's laments, Kuhnau's *Biblical Sonatas*, numerous pieces for harpsichord by Couperin and Rameau, and Marais' musical account of a gallstone operation for viol and harpsichord (1717). Following Beethoven's *Pastoral Symphony* (1807–08), programme music evolved significantly through the programme symphony and the *tone poem. These genres are represented by Berlioz's autobiographical *Fantastic Symphony* (1830–31) and Liszt's *Mazeppa* (1851). 19th-century nationalism found outlets in programme music with Smetana's *Má Vlast* (1874–79) and Sibelius' *En Saga* (1892). The 19th-century tradition of programme music culminated in the tone poems of Richard Strauss, including *Till Eulenspiegel* (1895) and *A Hero's Life* (1899). Impressionism in programme music is represented by Debussy's *Prelude à l'après-midi d'un faune* (1894) and *La Mer* (1903–05). Among other 20th-century orchestral examples are Elgar's symphonic study *Falstaff* (1913) and Honegger's steam-locomotive epic *Pacific 231* (1923).

progression see **harmony.**

progressist Designating the music of a group of French communist composers, active after 1945, which was designed to appeal to 'the masses.' These composers include Durey, who was secretary of the Association Française des Musiciens Progressistes from 1948. His works include *La Longue Marche*, to words by Mao Tse Tung.

progressive tonality A type of music in which a work or movement opens in one key and after progressing through other keys closes in a different key. This system was used by Mahler and was important for the subsequent development of atonality.

Prokofiev, Sergei (1891–1953) Soviet composer. A child prodigy, Prokofiev, who was born in the small village of Sontsovka, first studied with his mother and then took private lessons with Reinhold Glière. He entered the St Petersburg conservatory at the age of 13 to study with Rimsky-Korsakov; by this time he had already composed a number of operas and other works. In the early years of the 20th century he became associated with modernist circles in St Petersburg, where he gave brilliant performances of his own piano works. In 1918 Prokofiev emigrated to the USA, where he lived for four years before moving to Paris and also spending some time in England. However he never broke his ties with the Soviet Union, returning there to live in 1936 and remaining in Moscow for the rest of his life.

The music of Prokofiev's early maturity is marked by a sense of irony and wit, underlined frequently by harsh dissonances and violent rhythms. His later works, composed after his return to the Soviet Union, are written in a less severe idiom notable for its melodic ease. Prokofiev's output includes *The Gambler* (1915–17), *The *Love of Three Oranges* (1919), *Simeon Kotko* (1930) **War and Peace* (1941–43), **Betrothal in a Monastery* (1946), *The*

Sergei Prokofiev

Fiery Angel (1954), and other operas; ballets, including *Ala i Lolli* (1914–15), **Chout* (1915), **Romeo and Juliet* (1935), and *Cinderella* (1945); six symphonies, the first (1916–17) known as the **Classical Symphony*; concertos for piano, violin, and cello; the 'symphonic fairy-tale' **Peter and the Wolf* (1936) and other orchestral works; nine piano sonatas and other piano works; chamber and choral music including **Alexander Nevsky* (1938); and songs.

prolation The division of a semibreve in medieval music into two minims (**minor prolation**) or three minims (**major prolation**).

promenade concert Originally, a *concert at which the audience could walk about (e.g. at the London pleasure-garden concerts of the 18th and 19th centuries). A promenade concert is now usually one in which cheaper tickets are available for members of the audience who are prepared to stand. From 1833 Philippe *Musard gave a series of promenade concerts in Paris on which similar concerts in London were modelled in 1838. In 1895 Robert Newman started a series at the Queen's Hall, London, conducted by Henry *Wood. From 1927 they were organized by the BBC in the Queen's Hall, where they continued until it was bombed during World War II. Since then they have been given almost exclusively in the Royal Albert Hall. Known familiarly as the 'Proms', they are held annually for two months from mid-July and include a wide variety of music, including several specially commissioned works, played by different orchestras. The last night of the Proms is a national television occasion in which the mainly youthful Albert Hall audience participates, with good-humoured vigour, in singing an arrangement of sea shanties and *Land of Hope and Glory*. Other promenade concerts have been given in Britain (e.g. by the Hallé Orchestra and the Scottish National Orchestra) and elsewhere (e.g. the 'Boston Pops' in the USA).

Prometheus 1. Ballet music by Beethoven (see **Geschöpfe des Prometheus, Die**). **2.** Tone poem (Op. 60) by Scriabin. Composed: 1910. The title of the work is derived from its foundation upon the chord that Scriabin referred to as his 'mystic,' or 'Promethean,' chord – a chord based entirely on fourths rather than thirds. Subtitled *The Poem of Fire*, this work is scored for piano, organ, and choir in addition to a large orchestra; Scriabin also wrote a part for colour organ (see **colour music**) although this is almost invariably omitted in performance.

Prophetess, The see **Dioclesian**.

proportional notation see **notation**.

Prout, Ebenezer (1835–1909) British music theorist, teacher, and composer. He was Professor of Composition at the Royal Academy of Music (1879) and music professor at Dublin University (1894). Prout wrote a long series of treatises on harmony, counterpoint, and analysis. His edition of Handel's *Messiah* (1902) is widely known.

Prussian Quartets 1. Set of string quartets by Mozart, dedicated to King Friedrich Wilhelm II of Prussia. Composed: 1789–90. Mozart originally intended to compose six quartets after having been invited to Berlin by the king in 1789, but only three works were completed. These are the quartets in D major (K. 575), B♭ major (K. 589), and F major (K. 590) and are Mozart's last string quartets, their prominent cello parts being in deference to the king's ability on this instrument. The composer himself did not use this title. **2.** Set of string quartets (Op. 50 Nos. 1–6) by Haydn. Composed: 1787. They were so called because the title page of the first edition includes a dedication to Friedrich Wilhelm II of Prussia.

psalm One of the 150 songs from the Book of Psalms in the Old Testament. The psalms have been set to music for religious use in many different styles. In the original Hebrew texts they are divided into verses, with regular accentuation patterns, and sung to recitation tones similar to those of Gregorian chant. In the Christian Church musical settings of psalm texts reflect a considerable number of polyphonic vocal forms from every style and period of Western music.

Metrical psalms are those in which the text has been translated into verse and set to hymn tunes (see **psalter**).

psalmody The singing or composition of psalm settings. In English and American Protestant churches from the 17th century to the early 19th century the term was applied generally to both the chanting of psalms and the singing of metrical psalms (e.g. *The Old Hundredth*). In country districts of England metrical psalms were performed by choirs in the galleries of churches. During the 18th century bands of accompanying instruments became widespread, but they were replaced by organs or harmoniums from the mid-19th century. In urban churches more elaborate settings were sung by choirs or charity children, or a quartet, under the direction of a professional organist. The advent of the tractarian movement in the mid-19th century accelerated the demise of this form of church music.

Psalmus Hungaricus Cantata for tenor solo, choir, and orchestra by Kodály to a text by Végh. Composed: 1923. This work was commissioned by the Hungarian government to be performed in celebration of the 50th anniversary of the linking of the cities Buda and Pest. The words are a translation into Hungarian of Psalm 55 by the 16th-century poet Michael Végh.

psalter An edition of the Book of Psalms paraphrased for singing as part of the liturgy. The singing of metrical psalms was a characteristic of Protestant worship from the Reformation. Miles Coverdale's verse translation *Goostly Psalmes and Spirituall Songes* (*c*.1538) and Robert Crowley's *The Psalter of David Newely Translated into Englyshe Metre* (1549) are the earliest complete surviving psalters in English. Thomas Sternhold's and John Hopkins's psalter (1549–64) was the basis of later English and Scottish psalm books. Other notable English psalters include those by Thomas East and John Playford. The singing of metrical psalms was gradually replaced by hymn singing.

psaltery An early form of plucked board *zither. It was derived from the Arabian **qanun**, which had been in use since the 10th century. The qanun was usually trapezoidal in shape, with strings running from one side of a board to the other. The board itself consisted of the top of a box resonator. The qanun reached Europe in the 11th century and was known as a psaltery from then until the 17th century, when it became a favourite instrument for amateurs. Thereafter it became known as a zither and acquired a fretboard and other refinements. Early psalteries were usually square or triangular, but by the 14th and 15th centuries they were being made in a variety of shapes – a pig's head and a wing being particularly popular. [from Greek *psalterion*, stringed instrument]

Pskovitianka see **Maid of Pskov, The.**

Psyche 1. Opera by Lully to a libretto by Quinault, Molière, and Corneille. Composed: 1671. This work, based on the Greek mythological figure Psyche, was written at the request of King Louis XIV, who wished to see once again the stage machines that had already been used in the earlier opera *Ercole amante*. *Psyche* was one of the most important forerunners of opera in France. **2.** Stage music by Locke for the drama by Shadwell. Composed: 1675. This work was written in imitation of Lully's opera and its extensive music makes it almost an opera in style. Although Locke is usually credited with writing the complete score, the instrumental dances were actually composed by Giovanni Draghi.

Ptolemaic scale see **temperament.**

Puccini, Giacomo (1858–1924) Italian composer. The son of a musician, who died when Puccini was four, he became organist at the church in his native Lucca at the age of 19. His mother's efforts to raise sufficient money enabled him to study at the Milan conservatory with Ponchielli (1880–83); thereafter he enjoyed moderate local success with the operas Le *Villi* (1884) and *Edgar* (1889). The triumph of his subsequent works, *Manon Lescaut* (1893) and La *Bohème* (1896), established Puccini's reputation in Italy and abroad, a reputation maintained with his next operas, *Tosca* (1900) and *Madame Butterfly* (1904). Puccini's outstanding gift as a composer of expressive melody, together with his flexible harmonic idiom, are the keys to his success as an opera composer. He excelled in particular in creating female roles, which dominate many of his works. Other operas by Puccini include The *Girl of the Golden West* (1910), the three one-act operas Il *Tabarro*, *Suor Angelica*, and *Gianni Schicchi* (1918), and *Turandot* (1926); his output also includes choral and orchestral music and chamber works.

Giacomo Puccini

Pugnani, Gaetano (1731–98) Italian composer, violinist, and teacher, a pupil of Somis and Ciampi and teacher of Viotti. Famed for his bowing, he was court violinist in Turin from 1750, becoming leader in 1770; he visited London (1767–69). In addition to operas, symphonies, and sacred works, he also wrote much music for solo violin and ensemble.

Pugno, (Stéphane) Raoul (1852–1914) French pianist, teacher, and composer. He studied at the Paris Conservatoire (1866–69), where he later taught (1891–1901). In 1871 he became director of the Opéra. In 1872 (at the fall of the Commune) he became organist of St Eugène and from 1878 to 1892 he was choirmaster there. Pugno was a renowned pianist and a good chamber music player (he gave recitals with Ysaÿe). His compositions, mostly comic operas, vaudevilles, ballets, and salon music, were of no great consequence.

Pulcinella Ballet music by Stravinsky. First performance: 1920. The score is based on works attributed to Pergolesi, in which the music is subtly rearranged with the addition of dissonances and syncopations to produce a 20th-century flavour. At the time of its composition Stravinsky was severely criticized for what was seen as a desecration of the original music, although *Pulcinella* is today recognized as one of the earliest and most important products of neoclassicism.

Pult An orchestral music stand shared by two players, and hence either of the players themselves. [German, desk]

punta Point, especially the point of a *bow. Hence **a punta d'arco** means that a string should be bowed with the point of the bow. [Italian]

Purcell, Henry (1659–1695) English composer, organist, and singer. Purcell, one of the greatest 17th-century composers, was a chorister in the Chapel Royal. After his voice broke in 1673 he became assistant keeper of instruments and also worked copying music. In 1677 he replaced Matthew Locke as composer for the violins and two years later succeeded John Blow as organist at Westminster Abbey. In 1682 he became one of the organists of the Chapel Royal. His positions at court continued under James II and William III; he wrote music for their coronations and for the funeral of Queen Mary in 1694.

Purcell's output was clearly conditioned by the London of his period: his court connections were responsible for the 24 welcome songs and birthday odes for the royal family, including the *Odes for St Cecilia's Day*; for over 70 verse anthems with string orchestra, including 'Man that is born of a woman' and 'Rejoice in the Lord alway' (see **Bell Anthem**); and for much of his instrumental music. The thriving London theatre called for a stream of incidental music and songs for over 40 plays by Dryden, Congreve, and others, including *The Double Dealer*, The *Indian Queen*, and *Abdelazer*, while a girls' school in Chelsea saw the performance of the first true English opera, *Dido and Aeneas* (1689). Purcell also wrote semi-operas, including *King Arthur* (1691) and The *Fairy Queen* (1692). His instrumental fantasias, which demonstrate his contrapuntal skill and include 13 viol fantasias (1680), were probably written for private performance. Other instrument music includes the G minor chacony and pieces for harpsichord and organ. Purcell's sacred music includes a small amount of Anglican service music and some Latin pieces.

While his early music tends to be conservative, Purcell's later works fall under the influence of Italian and French styles, while preserving some basically English traits. His 22 trio sonatas (1683, 1697) are Italian in conception as is much of his vocal writing, with its recitative and aria styles (he composed over 100 secular songs for one to three voices and 57 catches). French influence emerges in the dances and dance rhythms as well as in some overtures. His premature death was a tragedy affecting the subsequent development of English music.

Puritani, I (*The Puritans*) Opera in three acts by Bellini with libretto by Count Pepoli. First performance: Théâtre des Italiens, Paris, 1835. Inspired by Walter Scott's *Old Mortality*, it is a story of Cavaliers and Roundheads set in a fortress near Plymouth.

Pushkin, Alexander (1799–1837) Russian poet, dramatist, and novelist, whose works have had enormous influence on Russian composers. Glinka's opera *Russlan and Ludmila* (1842) was taken from Pushkin's fairy tale; Mussorgsky's *Boris Godunov* (1874) and Tchaikovsky's *The Queen of Spades* (1890) are among the more widely known of many other operatic settings.

Puyana, Rafael (1931–) Colombian harpsichordist, a pupil of Wanda Landowska. He has toured North and South America and Europe and is now resident in Paris. His wide repertory includes works from the 16th to 18th centuries as well as contemporary music.

puzzle canon (*or* **riddle canon**) A *canon that can be performed only after a literary riddle has been solved. A famous example occurs in the Agnus Dei of Dufay's *Missa L'Homme armé*: 'let the crab proceed full and return half.' This means that the tenor voice should first be read backwards, in full note lengths (a crab walks 'backwards'), and then from the beginning, in halved note lengths.

Pythagoras (*c*.582–*c*.500 BC) Greek mathematician and philosopher, founder of a philosophical and religious community in Croton. He discovered the numerical ratios of the principal intervals of the musical scale.

Q

qanun see psaltery; zithers.

qin (or chin) A Chinese long *zither with seven strings made of silk and no bridges. A row of 13 ivory discs in the soundboard indicates the stopping positions for the strings. In use for over 2000 years, the qin was the solo instrument of the ancient philosophers, demanding ritual preparation in its performance. It was also a favourite instrument for accompanying singers and used in large numbers in orchestras (120 of them are recorded as being in a court orchestra of the Tang dynasty, during the 8th century). See also Chinese music.

quadrille A square dance that made its first appearance in the ballroom of Napoleon's court, having been introduced into ballet in the 18th century from military horse manoeuvres. Brought to England at the beginning of the 19th century, it became formalized as a dance with five different sections. Each section has different music, usually adapted from country dances, operatic melodies, or popular songs. The *lancers, a mid-19th-century variant of the quadrille, makes a notional return to its quasi-military origins.

quadruple counterpoint see invertible counterpoint.

quadruplet A group of four notes of equal value played in the time of three notes. They are written tied together with a small figure 4 placed on the tie. Some of the notes can be replaced by rests.

quail A whistle flute designed to imitate the call of a quail. It is used in the Toy Symphony attributed to Haydn.

Quantz, Johann Joachim (1697–1773) French flautist and composer. He mastered many instruments in addition to the transverse flute, for which he wrote Versuch einer Anweisung die Flöte traversiere zu spielen (1752). After travelling widely, Quantz became flute teacher to the future Frederick the Great (1733) and entered his service in 1741, after the latter became King of Prussia. Here at Dresden he wrote most of his sonatas, chamber and vocal music, and other writings.

quarter note see crotchet.

quarter tone A *microtone consisting of half a *semitone. Quarter tones only occur in western music in the 20th century, having been used occasionally by Hába, Bloch, Bartók, and others. They can, of course, be played on unfretted stringed instruments and some quarter-tone pianos have been constructed.

quartet A composition for four voices or instruments or a group that performs such a composition. When the term is used without further qualification it usually implies a string quartet, i.e. two violins, viola, and cello; the *Amadeus Quartet is an example of such a group. Other types of quartet usually consist of three stringed instruments together with the instrument specified; e.g. piano quartet (piano, violin, viola, and cello).

Quartettsatz (Quartet Movement) First movement of Schubert's unfinished string quartet in C minor. Composed: 1820; first performance: Vienna, 1867.

quasi Almost; nearly; as if: used in directions to indicate approximate manner of performance, e.g. quasi allegro. [Italian]

Quattro rusteghi, I see School for Fathers.

quatuor Quartet. [French]

quaver A note having half the time value of a *crotchet and a quarter that of a minim. In modern notation it is depicted as a filled-in circle with a tail to which a single bar (or hook) is attached. In the United States: eighth note. See Appendix, Table 1.

Queen, The (French: La Reine) Symphony No. 85 in B♭ major by Haydn. Composed: 1785–86. According to a popular story, this was Marie Antoinette's favourite Haydn symphony and the inscription La Reine de France (The Queen of France) was printed on the title page of the first printed edition. It is possible that the monarch was impressed by this work – one of the *Paris Symphonies –on account of its use of a French folk song in the slow movement.

Queen of Spades, The (German: Pique-Dame) Opera in three acts by Tchaikovsky with libretto by his brother, Modest Tchaikovsky. First performance: St Petersburg, 1890. Based on a story by Pushkin, it concerns Herman (tenor), a young officer in love with Lisa (soprano), who is obsessed with discovering the secret of the past gambling success of Lisa's grandmother, the old Countess (mezzo-soprano), nicknamed the Queen of Spades. His obsession leads to his eventual suicide after Lisa drowns herself.

Querflöte Transverse *flute. [German]

Quest, The Ballet in five scenes with music by William Walton, choreography by Frederick Ashton, and libretto by Doris Langley Moore. First performance: New Theatre, London, 1943, by the Sadler's Wells Ballet with Fonteyn and Helpmann (décor by Piper). Based on Spenser's *The Faerie Queene*, it relates St George's victory over the powers of evil.

Roger Quilter

Quiet City Suite for trumpet, cor anglais, and strings by Copland. First performance: 1941. This work was originally part of a score of incidental music composed for a play entitled *Quiet City* (hence its title).

Quilter, Roger (1877–1953) British composer. Quilter's studies in Germany led to his association with the Frankfurt group of composers. He is best known for his many songs, which reveal his sensitivity in setting words. Quilter's output also includes A *Children's Overture* (1914) and other orchestral music and piano pieces.

quint An organ *stop that sounds a fifth above the written pitch. It is used with the acoustic bass (see **combination tones**).

quintadena (*or* **quintatön**) An organ *stop that sounds the note played together with the *twelfth.

quintet A composition for five voices or instruments or a group that performs such a composition. Examples are the **string quintet**, consisting of a string *quartet (two violins, viola, and cello) with an extra viola or cello; **piano quintet**, consisting of piano and a string quartet; and **clarinet quintet** (clarinet with string quartet).

quintuplet A group of five notes of equal value played in the time of three or four notes. They are written tied together with a small figure 5 placed on the tie. Some of the notes can be replaced by rests.

quodlibet A medley of popular tunes ingeniously woven together. At the end of the *Goldberg Variations*, Bach used a quodlibet based on two popular contemporary tunes, no doubt in recognition of the Bach family's annual reunions at which quodlibets were frequently sung. [Latin, what you please]

R

R. Abbreviation for Rinaldi. It is used as a prefix to indicate the number of a piece in Mario Rinaldi's catalogue (1945) of Vivaldi's works. It is sometimes used as an abbreviation for Peter Ryom's catalogue, which supersedes it and which is generally abbreviated to *RV. See also **P.**

Rabaud, Henri (1873–1949) French composer, a pupil of Massenet. Rabaud won the Prix de Rome in 1894. He directed the Paris Conservatoire (1922–41). Much influenced by Wagner, Rabaud wrote *La Fille de Roland* (1904), *Martine* (1947), and other operas, two symphonies and other orchestral works, chamber music, and choral works.

Rachmaninov, Sergei Vassilievich (1873–1943) Russian composer. Rachmaninov studied at both the St Petersburg and Moscow conservatories; his teachers at the latter included Taneyev and Arensky. He graduated in 1892 with the Moscow conservatory's highest award, the Gold Medal. Concert tours quickly established Rachmaninov's reputation as a virtuoso pianist and composer. He also conducted opera in Moscow. After the 1917 revolution Rachmaninov left Russia for Switzerland; in 1936 he emigrated to the USA.

Rachmaninov's idiom stems from the romantic tradition in Russian music and is particularly influenced by the works of Tchaikovsky. His style is characterized by a broad melodic sense, rich tonal harmony, and restrained but fitting orchestration. His virtuosity as a pianist never led to empty technical display in his piano works, which explore the sonorous and expressive capabilities of the instrument. Rachmaninov's output includes four operas; three symphonies; four piano concertos, the second (in C minor, 1901) being the most popular; a *Rhapsody on a Theme of Paganini* (1934; see **Paganini Rhapsody**) for piano and orchestra, the tone poem *The *Isle of the Dead* (1909), and other orchestral works; many piano pieces, including three sonatas, preludes (including the popular prelude in C♯ minor, 1892), and studies; sacred music; and songs, chamber music, and choral works, including *The Bells* (1910) for solo voice, chorus, and orchestra.

Racine, Jean (1639–99) French poet and dramatist. With Lully he wrote *L'Idylle de la paix* (1685) and Moreau contributed the music for his plays *Esther* (1689) and *Athalie* (1691). In later years Gluck wrote *Iphigénie en Anlide* (1774) based on Racine; incidental music was written by Saint-Saëns for *Andromaque* (1903) and by Honegger for *Phèdre* (1926).

racket (*or* **ranket**) A wind instrument with a double reed, consisting of a short fat solid wooden cylinder with a number of interconnecting tubes bored out around its periphery and joined to each other to form a continuous channel, which was connected to a central channel from which the sound emerged. A reeded bassoon crook was fitted into the first of the peripheral tubes. The instrument was made in five sizes, from the 6-inch (15-cm) treble version to 20-inch (50-cm) double bass, and was in use between the 16th and 18th centuries, when it was superseded by the bassoon. The original racket was called a **cervelas** (type of sausage) in French and was sometimes known informally as a **sausage bassoon**. [from Upper German *rank*, to and fro]

Sergei Rachmaninov in London in the 1920s

Radetzky March March by Johann Strauss the Elder. Composed: 1848. Field-Marshal Radetzky was a famous Austrian soldier in whose honour this march was written. It has become popular throughout Europe as a marching tune and is associated particularly with military bands.

Raff, (Joseph) Joachim (1822–82) German composer and teacher. He was self-taught in music but in 1845 in Basle he met Liszt, who took him to Germany. In 1850 he became Liszt's copyist and assistant in Weimar and in 1856 moved to Wiesbaden, where he taught the piano and composed prolifically. He was appointed director of the Hoch conservatory in Frankfurt in 1877; his pupils included MacDowell and Ritter. In his compositions, Raff tried to synthesize early romantic styles with the ideals of Liszt and the New German School. His large output includes operas, choral and vocal works, 11 symphonies (including No. 3, *Im Walde*, 1869), concertos and other orchestral works, chamber music (including the well-known cavatina for violin and piano), and numerous piano solos. He made many arrangements and contributed essays to music periodicals.

rāga see **Indian music.**

Raimondi, Pietro (1786–1853) Italian composer and teacher. In Naples he studied at the conservatory and in 1824 was appointed musical director of the royal theatres. He wrote undistinguished operas, sacred dramatic works, and ballets for Naples. He taught counterpoint at the conservatories in Naples (1825–33) and Palermo and was musical director of the Palermo Opera. Raimondi was a renowned contrapuntist who produced several didactic works and much sacred music. In the 1820s he began experimenting with complex contrapuntal combinations and produced a series of huge works that could be performed simultaneously, among them three oratorios (*Putifar*, *Giuseppe*, and *Giacobbe*, 1847–48). Their performance made Raimondi's name, and in 1852 he became maestro di cappella at St Peter's, Rome.

Raimondi, Ruggero (1941–) Italian bass singer. He studied with Pediconi and Piervenanzi, making his debut at Spoleto in 1964. Considered one of the finest basses in early-19th-century Italian opera, he has also sung the title roles in Mozart's *Don Giovanni* and Mussorgsky's *Boris Godunov*.

Raindrop Prelude Prelude in D♭ major for piano (Op. 28 No. 15) by Chopin. Composed: 1839. It has been suggested that this prelude imitates the sound of raindrops dripping from Chopin's house and that these are portrayed by the repeated note A♭, which continues throughout the work.

Rainier, Priaulx (1903–86) British composer born in South Africa, a pupil of Nadia Boulanger. Rainier's early works extend tonal harmony in an experimental rhythmic setting; more dissonant harmony is characteristic of her later compositions. Rainier's works include orchestral music, a string quartet (1939) and other chamber works, choral music, and songs.

Rake's Progress, The 1. Ballet in six scenes with music by Gavin Gordon and choreography by Ninette de Valois based on Hogarth's series of paintings (1735). First performance: Sadler's Wells Theatre, London 1935, by the Vic-Wells Ballet with Gore and Markova (decor by Rex Whistler). **2.** Opera in three acts and epilogue by Stravinsky with libretto by W. H. Auden and Chester Kallman. First performance: Venice Festival, 1951. The subject is derived from Hogarth's paintings.

Rákóczi March March by János Bihari (1764–1827). Composed: 1809. Named after Prince Rákóczi, a Hungarian nobleman who led his country in a popular revolt to overthrow Austrian domination, this marching tune is quoted by many composers, including Berlioz in *The Damnation of Faust*, Strauss in the opera *The Gypsy Baron*, and Liszt in his 15th *Hungarian Rhapsody*.

rallentando Slowing down. Abbreviation: **rall.** [Italian]

Rameau, Jean Philippe (1683–1764) French composer and theorist. While organist at the cathedrals of Clermont (1702–06, 1715), Dijon (1709), and Lyons (1713), he wrote motets, cantatas, and his treatise *Traité de l'harmonie* (1722). In Paris from about 1723, he collaborated with Voltaire in composing operas, such as *Hippolyte et Aricie* (1733), and opera-ballets, including *Les *Indes galantes* (1735) and *Les *Fêtes d'Hébé* (1739), as well as writing chamber music, keyboard works, and other treatises.

Rampal, Jean-Pierre (1922–) French flautist, a pupil at the Marseilles and Paris conservatoires. He specializes in performing 18th-century music in authentic style. Poulenc, Jolivet, and others have written for him.

Rands, Bernard (1935–) British composer, a pupil of Dallapiccola, Boulez, Maderna, and Berio. Rands' music has revealed his interest in new sounds, use of graphic notation, and preoccupation with Hinduism. His works include *Wildtrack I–III* (1969–75), *Ology* for jazz orchestra (1973), *AUM* (1974), *Scherzi* (1975), and *The Unquestioned Answer* (1977).

Rangström, Türe (1884–1947) Swedish composer, a pupil of Pfitzner. Rangström's early music was influenced by Wagner; in his later works he adopted a largely homophonic style characterized by structural simplicity. Rangström's output includes four symphonies and other orchestral works, operas, chamber music, and songs.

rank (*or* **register**) A set of organ pipes of similar tone colour arranged in an ascending scale, one pipe for each note of the organ keyboard. A rank of pipes is controlled by a *stop, but a rank itself is also sometimes called a stop.

ranket see racket.

Rankl, Karl (1898–1968) Austrian composer, a pupil of Schoenberg and Webern. Rankl conducted in opera houses in Germany until the outbreak of World War II, when he fled to England. After the war he became director of the re-established Covent Garden opera house. His works, all unpublished, include the opera *Deirdre of the Sorrows* (1951), orchestral music, and chamber works.

rant An old English dance, the exact nature of which is no longer known. The *Peterborough Rant*, for example, is a dance tune by John Jenkins.

ranz des vaches A Swiss alphorn melody, often with vocal accompaniment, used in mountainous regions to call cattle. Many versions exist, each locality often having its own. The sound of a ranz des vaches is reputed to be so nostalgic and unnerving to Swiss nationals abroad that in some European armies in the 18th century, to play or sing one was punishable by death. This was for fear that any Swiss mercenaries within earshot might undermine the military efficiency of their units by bursting into tears. A ranz des vaches has been used by various composers, such as Rossini (in the overture to *William Tell*), Strauss (in *Don Quixote*), and Beethoven (in the *Pastoral Symphony*). [French, cow rank]

Rape of Lucretia, The Opera in two acts by Britten with libretto by Ronald Duncan based on Obey's play *Le Viol de Lucrece*. First performance: Glyndebourne, 1946. Set in ancient Rome, the tragedy of Lucretia (contralto) is enacted within the framework of a male and female chorus (tenor and soprano); the opera is scored for chamber orchestra.

Rappresentazione di anima e di corpo, La (*A Representation of the Soul and the Body*) Sacred drama with music by Cavalieri and text by Manni, important in the development of both opera and oratorio. First performance: Oratory of St Philip Neri, Rome, 1600.

rasch Quick. [German]

Rasumovsky Quartets Set of three string quartets (Op. 59 No 1–3) by Beethoven. These works are named after Count Rasumovsky, Russian ambassador to Vienna, who also commissioned them. He requested that Beethoven should include a Russian folk melody in each quartet —Beethoven complied in the first two quartets, labelling the melody 'thème russe' (Russian theme), but in the third quartet he apparently ignored the count's instructions.

Rathaus, Karol (1895–1954) Polish-born composer, a pupil of Schreker. In 1938 Rathaus settled in the USA, teaching from 1940 at Queen's College, New York. His music is romantic in spirit, coloured by influences from

Simon Rattle

Polish and expressionist styles. Rathaus' output includes the opera *Fremde Erde* (1929–30), three symphonies, songs, chamber music, and piano music.

Ratsche Rattle. [German]

rattle A type of shaken idiophone of ancient origin, widely used in primitive music making in all parts of the world. Initially, rattles consisted of dried gourds containing pellets or beads, such as the maracas, which are still in use in Latin-American dance music. Other wooden and metal rattles of many designs, often lavishly carved, have been used throughout the ages. In the modern orchestra a ratchet rattle is occasionally called for by composers.

Rattle, Simon (1955–) British conductor. He won the John Player International Conductors' Competition in 1974 and subsequently became assistant conductor of the Bournemouth Symphony Orchestra. In 1976 he became associate conductor of the Royal Liverpool Philharmonic Orchestra and in 1979 principal conductor of the City of Birmingham Symphony Orchestra. He gave the premiere of Peter Maxwell Davies' first symphony (1978).

Rauzzini, Venanzio (1746–1810) Italian singer and composer. After studying in Rome, he was in the service of Elector Max Joseph III (1766–72). In 1774 he settled in England, where he worked as a singer and teacher in Bath and at the King's Theatre, London, writing operas, ballets, pasticcios, Italian and English songs, cantatas, chamber music, and a singing tutor.

A sketch of Maurice Ravel at the piano

Ravel, (Joseph) Maurice (1875–1937) French composer. Ravel entered the Paris Conservatoire in 1889 and became a pupil of Fauré. Although often considered as a follower of Debussy, Ravel did not limit his style to the influence of the impressionist aesthetic but also drew on aspects of classical and baroque music, dance styles, jazz, and oriental music. The exotic harmonies that characterize some of his works are matched by luxuriant and brilliant orchestration.

Ravel's large output includes the operas *L'*Heure espagnole* (1907–09) and *L'*Enfant et les sortilèges* (1920–25); the ballets **Daphnis et Chloe* (1909–12) and **Bolero* (1928); orchestral works, including *Pavan for a Dead Infanta* (see **pavan**), **Spanish Rhapsody* (1907), **Mother Goose* (1908), *La Valse* (1919–20), and two piano concertos; piano music, including the impressionistic *Jeux d'eaux* (1901), the suites *Miroirs* (1904–05) and **Gaspard de la nuit* (1908), **Valses nobles et sentimentales* (1911), and *Le Tombeau de Couperin* (1914–17); chamber music, including a string quartet (1902–03), *Introduction et allegro* (1905) for harp, flute, clarinet, and string quartet, and a piano trio (1914); and songs, including the cycles **Sheherazade* (1903) and *Histoires naturelles* (1906).

Ravenscroft, Thomas (*c*.1582–*c*.1635) English composer, editor, and theorist. He sang at Chichester and at St Paul's Cathedral and after obtaining the Cambridge B.Mus. degree taught music at Christ's Hospital (1622). Ravenscroft's compositions are not important but he wrote a treatise, *Brief Discourse* (1614), and edited the earliest English collection of rounds and catches (1609; see **Pammelia**) and a psalter (1621).

ravvivando Quickening; gathering momentum: a direction used to indicate return to a faster tempo after slowing down. [Italian, reviving]

Rawsthorne, Alan (1905–71) British composer. After studying in England and abroad and occupying various teaching positions, Rawsthorne devoted himself to composition. His music builds on traditional concepts of tonality in a texture of great rhythmic and contrapuntal flexibility. Rawsthorne's output includes three symphonies, concertos, and other orchestral works, chamber music, and vocal works.

ray see **tonic sol-fa**.

Raymond Opera in three acts by Ambroise Thomas with libretto by de Leuven and Rosier. First performance: Opéra-Comique, Paris, 1851. Subtitled *The Queen's Secret* (French: *Le Secret de la reine*), it is based on *The Man in the Iron Mask* by Dumas (père).

Raymonda Ballet in three acts with music by Glazunov and choreography by Petipa. First performance: Maryinsky Theatre, St Petersburg, 1898, with Legnani and Sergei Legat. Raymonda, betrothed to the Crusader de Brienne, is also loved by the Saracen Abderakhman, who is worsted in a duel before the marriage celebrations get under way.

Razor Quartet String quartet in F minor (Op. 55 No. 2) by Haydn. Composed: 1787. When the English music publisher Bland visited Haydn at Esterhazy the composer is reported to have said in jest that he would 'give his best quartet for a good razor.' When Bland produced the desired article this quartet was composed as payment.

re see **solmization**.

Reading Rota see **Sumer is icumen in**.

real answer see **answer; fugue**.

real fugue see **fugue**.

realism 1. The use of real sounds in music. Examples include birdsong, bells, cannon fire, etc. In some cases recordings of these real sounds may be used, while in others they are imitated on musical instruments with varying degrees of accuracy. 2. See **verismo**. 3. A form of commendation offered to Soviet composers by their own government or its organs, praising their concern for social values, popular appeal, and the optimism of their music. Compare **formalism**.

realization The process of writing out a full version of a composition that was left incomplete by its composer. This often includes completing the harmony of a 17th-century piece from the continuo bass line. It implies more than editing but less than an arrangement.

real sequence see **sequence**.

rebab see **rebec**.

rebec (*or* **ribible**) A medieval bowed unfretted stringed instrument, similar to the *fiddle, that evolved in the 13th century from the north African **rebab**, an 11th century waisted two-stringed fiddle with a short neck. The rebec itself usually had three or four strings, a pear-shaped body, and was made in various sizes: soprano, tenor, and bass were the most common. It was used by troubadours to accompany singing and dancing and eventually was replaced by the violin, of which it was a forerunner. The **lira** of Greece and other Balkan countries is a tenor rebec. See also **kit**.

Rebikov, Vladimir Ivanovich (1866–1920) Russian composer. Rebikov studied in Moscow, Berlin, and Vienna. His music, which anticipates impressionism in its use of whole-tone scales and harmonies, includes the opera *The Christmas Tree* (1903) and many piano pieces.

recapitulation The part of a composition in which the original *subjects are restated after their development. See **sonata form**.

récit 1. An accompanied solo, such as an organ piece in which a solo stop is used. **2.** A swell organ. [French]

recital A performance given by a solo instrumentalist, a singer with piano accompaniment, or duettists. The term was first used in a musical context in the 19th century, particularly by Liszt. A performance by a larger ensemble is usually referred to as a *concert.

recitation A poem, or similar declaratory work, using a musical background. Examples include Prokofiev's *Peter and the Wolf* and Schoenberg's *Ode to Napoleon* (words by Byron).

recitative A form of speech used in opera and oratorio for some dialogue or narrative. The words are declaimed on a fixed note and without rhythm or metre, although it is often written by convention in 4/4 time with bar lines. In **recitativo secco** (*or* **dry recitative**) the only accompaniment is an occasional broken chord from a harpsichord or cello, sometimes with reinforcement of the bass by a double bass. This was used in 18th- and 19th-century opera. **Recitativo accompagnato** *or* **recitativo stromentato** (**accompanied recitative**) is accompanied by the orchestra also used to

modulate to the key of the *aria that follows it. See also **stile rappresentativo**.

reciting note see **modes**.

recorder (*or* **English flute**) An end-blown whistle *flute that was used extensively in European music between the 16th and 18th centuries. After about 1750 it was largely replaced by the more versatile and louder side-blown flute. The mouthpiece of the recorder consists of a curved end to the tube, which is blocked with a piece of wood called a **fipple**. Air is blown through a windway between the fipple and the tube onto a sharp lip cut into a hole on the side of the tube. The recorders most widely used are the **treble recorder** (range two octaves from F above middle C) and the **tenor recorder** (range two octaves from middle C). The **descant recorder** sounds an octave higher than the tenor instrument and the **sopranino recorder** sounds an octave higher than the treble instrument. The **bass recorder** sounds an octave lower than the tenor instrument. The recorder was revived in the 20th century by Arnold Dolmetsch as one of the easiest instruments on which to teach schoolchildren the rudiments of music. See also **flageolet**.

recte et retro (*or* **rectus introversus**) Denoting a canon in which the imitating voice plays or sings the first theme backwards. Italian: **al rovescio**. See also **cancrizans**. [Latin, forwards and backwards]

Redford, John (?–1547) English composer and organist. He was involved with St Paul's Cathedral from at least 1534 but there is no evidence that he was organist there. Most of his music, mainly for organ, is contained in *The Mulliner Book*. It comprises some of the earliest surviving English organ music and much of it is based on plainsong melodies.

reed instruments Musical *instruments in which the sound is made by the vibration of the **reed** (a tongue of cane, metal, etc.). In the **beating-reed instruments**, the reed vibrates against an air slot (as in the clarinet), whereas in the **free-reed instruments** it vibrates through the slot (as in the harmonium and accordion). In the **double-reed instruments** two reeds vibrate against each other (as in the oboe and bassoon). The *woodwind instruments of the orchestra are all reed instruments (except the flute). The organ uses brass beating reeds.

reed organs Musical instruments in which a set of free reeds vibrate to produce individual notes (see **reed instruments**). There are no pipes and the reeds are set in motion by air being blown over them. The main members of the family are the *harmonium and the *American organ. In these instruments the air pressure is produced by pedals (or an electric motor). In the *mouth organ, which works on a similar principle, the player blows air directly over the reeds, and in the *accordion air pressure is produced by pumping bellows with the arms.

reed pipe An *organ pipe in which sound is produced by causing a metal reed to beat regularly against an opening into the pipe in a manner similar to that of the clarinet. **Chorus reeds** are designed to blend with other stops whereas **solo reeds** are made to stand out from the rest of the instrument. **Imitative reeds** are a 19th-century invention that attempt to reproduce the sounds of the orchestra. **Reed stops** are *stops used to control the reed pipes. Compare **flue pipe**.

reel A fast dance for two or more couples, usually in 2/4 or 4/4 time. A national dance of Scotland (the **Highland fling** being a particularly vigorous version), it is also found in Ireland and in Scandinavia. It forms part of some sword dances used in North Yorkshire.

Reformation Symphony Symphony No. 5 in D minor by Mendelssohn. Composed: 1830. Mendelssohn composed this work to honour the tercentenary of Luther's founding of the German Reformed Church in 1530 at Augsburg, but although it was originally intended for performance at Augsburg the symphony was eventually first played in Berlin due to opposition from the Roman Catholic community in Germany. Two liturgical melodies are quoted in the symphony – the Catholic *Dresden Amen* and the Protestant chorale *Ein' feste Burg*.

refrain A recurring part of a song, usually appearing at the end of each verse. Apart from minor variations, the words and music of the refrain are the same each time they occur.

regal A small portable organ with reed pipes that was in use from the 15th to 17th centuries. It was used in churches to regulate the singing. The **Bible-regal** was shaped like a Bible and could be folded shut after use. In later models of the regal, flue pipes were sometimes added.

Reger, (Johann Baptist Joseph) Max(imilian) (1873–1916) German composer, organist, pianist, and teacher. He studied with Riemann in Sondershausen and Wiesbaden. In 1901 he went to Munich, where he soon became a well-known pianist. He was composition professor and director of music at Leipzig University (1907–11), gaining an international reputation as a teacher and touring widely as an organist in Europe and Russia. From 1911 to 1913 he was conductor of the court orchestra at Meiningen and in 1915 moved to Jena.

Reger was opposed to the ideals of the New German School and to *programme music. His music is moulded by a strong harmonic framework but he extended the possibilities of tonality. He was a dedicated contrapuntist, much influenced by Bach, and was a master of fugue and variation techniques (as shown particularly by his many organ works). A prolific composer, Reger wrote orchestral music (including a piano concerto, a violin concerto, and sets of variations and fugues on themes by Beethoven, Hiller, and Mozart), choral works, chamber music (including six string quartets, a clarinet quintet, three clarinet sonatas, and seven violin sonatas), over 250 songs, numerous piano pieces, and organ music (chorale fantasias, sonatas, preludes and fugues, and short pieces). He made many editions and arrangements and contributed to music periodicals.

register 1. (n.) See **rank. 2.** (vb.) To select the *stops to be used in a particular piece of music to be played on the organ. **3.** (n.) Any of the different parts of the range of the human voice, named after the part of the body that was thought to produce it (e.g. head register, chest register).

Reich, Steve (1936–   ) US composer, a pupil of Milhaud and Berio. His style, developed after a study of non-European and oriental musical traditions, explores the phenomenon of 'phase-shifting' within the repetition and gradual change of small motifs. Reich's works include *Drumming* (1971), *Music for Eighteen Musicians* (1976), *Music for Large Ensemble* (1978), *Octet* (1979), and *Variations* (1980).

Reicha, Antoine (*or* **Antonín**) (1770-1836) Czech composer, theorist, teacher, and flautist, later naturalized French. He played the violin and flute in the Bonn Hofkapelle orchestra with Beethoven, who may have given him lessons, then went to Bonn University (1789–94). He lived in Hamburg (1794–99), Paris (1799–1801), and Vienna (1802–08), where he was a close friend of Haydn, then settled in Paris, where he became a professor at the Conservatoire (1818). His pupils included Berlioz, Gounod, Franck, and Liszt. Reicha was a prolific composer of operas, choral works, songs, symphonies, overtures, concertos, wind quintets, string quartets, horn trios, an octet and other chamber music (much of it with flute), and piano and organ works. His treatises were in long and widespread use, the most important being the *Traité de haute composition musicale* (1824–26) and the *Art du compositeur dramatique* (1833).

Reichardt, Johann Friedrich (1752–1814) German composer and writer on music. After travelling widely, he was appointed kapellmeister of the Berlin Opera (1775), writing liederspiele and collaborating with Goethe on the singspiel *Claudine von Villa Bella* (1789). Dismissed for French Revolutionary sympathies, he retired to Giebichenstein (1794) and wrote his travel diaries. In addition to dramatic music, Reichardt also wrote a large number of strophic songs.

Reincken (*or* **Reinken**), **Johann Adam** (*or* **Jan Adams**) (1623–1722) Dutch or German composer and organist. He was organist in Deventer (1657) before becoming assistant to his former teacher in Hamburg, Scheidemann, whom he succeeded as organist of St Catherine's in 1663. Reincken wrote much organ music in the tradition of Sweelinck, the suite *Hortus musicus* (1687), cantatas, and other keyboard works.

Reine, La see **Queen, The.**

Reinecke, Carl (Heinrich Carsten) (1824–1910) German composer, teacher, pianist, and conductor. He studied music with his father and began a career as a pianist. Between 1851 and 1859 he held teaching and conducting posts in Cologne, Barmen, and Breslau. In 1860 he was appointed to teach at the Leipzig conservatory, becoming its director in 1897. He conducted the Leipzig Gewandhaus Orchestra until 1895. Reinecke wrote six operas and vocal, orchestral, and chamber music, but is best known for his piano music. He wrote many books and essays on music.

Reiner, Fritz (1888–1963) Hungarian-born conductor. His early appointments were in Budapest and Dresden. He subsequently took US citizenship and conducted the Cincinnati Symphony Orchestra (1922–31), the Pittsburgh Symphony Orchestra (1938–48), and the Chicago Symphony Orchestra (1953–63).

Reinken, Johann Adam see **Reincken, Johann Adam.**

Reizenstein, Franz (1911–68) German composer and pianist, of Hindemith. Reizenstein also studied with Vaughan Williams and later taught in London at the Royal Academy of Music. His works, which are romantic in character, include two piano concertos and other orchestral compositions, chamber music, and choral works.

Rejoice in the Lord alway see **Bell Anthem.**

related keys Keys that are harmonically close so that *modulation between them is relatively simple. These are the *relative major or minor, the key of the dominant or its relative major or minor, and the key of the subdominant or its relative major or minor.

relative Denoting a relationship between major and minor keys having the same *key signatures. Thus the relative minor key to E♭ major is C minor (both have a key signature of three flats). Similarly the relative major key to E minor is G major (one sharp). See **Appendix, Table 3.**

relative pitch see **absolute pitch.**

repeat An instruction to play or sing a section of a piece of music a second time. To avoid writing the section out twice, repeat signs or marks are used in conjunction with a *double bar. The double bar at the end of the section to be repeated is preceded by two dots, usually placed in the second and third spaces of the staff. The beginning of the section to be repeated is denoted by a double bar followed by two dots. If there is no mark to denote the beginning of a section to be repeated it is played from the start of the composition.

répétiteur The member of an operatic company whose task is to coach the singers and play the piano for rehearsals. In German opera houses the appointment also involves the training of the chorus. German: **Repetitor;** Italian: **repetitore.**

répétition Rehearsal. Hence **répétition générale,** dress rehearsal. [French]

reprise 1. A repeated section of a composition. 2. The restatement of the first subject at the beginning of the recapitulation in *sonata form. 3. The reappearance of a song or dance number in a musical or operetta, often with the full company at the end of an act. [French, repetition]

requiem 1. (*or* Requiem Mass) A musical setting of the Roman Catholic Mass for the dead, the *Missa pro defunctis*. The liturgical structure of this Mass is slightly different from that of the normal Mass in that the Ordinary excludes parts considered too joyful for an occasion of mourning (i.e. the Gloria and Credo) and replaces the Alleluia with a Tract. In addition the *Dies Irae is sung and the Mass is named after its opening Introit 'Requiem aeternum dona eis Domine' ('Give them eternal rest O Lord'). In addition to plainsong and polyphonic Renaissance settings, composers such as Mozart, Berlioz, Verdi, Fauré, and Duruflé have set the words of the Requiem Mass. Unlike normal Mass settings, passages of the Proper are frequently set as well as those of the Ordinary. 2. Any work that commemorates the departed, without specifically setting the Catholic service. Notable examples of this genre include Brahms' *A German Requiem* and Britten's *War Requiem*.

Resnik, Regina (1922–) US soprano. She studied in New York, at Hunter College and later with Rosalie Miller, making her debut there as Santuzza in Mascagni's *Cavalleria rusticana* (1942). After 1957 she became a mezzo-soprano and was particularly successful as Bizet's Carmen.

resolution The passage from *discord to *concord in *harmony. For example, the chord of the *dominant seventh usually resolves on the tonic chord.

resonance The vibration of a system capable of vibrating at a fixed frequency, in sympathy with an outside vibration of the same frequency. For example, a guitar can be tuned to a piano by resonance. If the guitar is laid flat and a tiny slip of paper is placed on (say) the E string, the paper will jump off the string when E is sounded on the piano if the string is in tune. If it is not in tune the tuning peg is turned until the paper jumps off. The paper jumps off when the guitar string resonates with the piano strings. Resonance can cause unwanted effects in concert halls if a window (say) has a resonant frequency in the audible range. It will then vibrate noisily when the pitch of a note played has a frequency equal to its resonant frequency.

Ottorino Respighi (left) with his wife and librettist

Respighi, Ottorino (1879–1936) Italian composer, a pupil of Rimsky-Korsakov. His style is one of great colour, influenced by the vivid orchestration of the Russian school. His works include operas; La *Boutique fantasque and other ballets; the tone poems *Fountains of Rome (1911), *Roman Festivals (1929) *Pines of Rome (1929), the suites The *Birds and *Trittico Botticelliano (1927), and other orchestral works; chamber music; and vocal works.

respond (*or* **responsory**) In church services, a plainsong or choral setting sung by the choir in response to solo passages by the priest. Examples are the *Alleluia and *Gradual in the Mass.

rest A period in a piece of music during which a player makes no sound. In the musical notation rests have time values in the way as notes. See **Appendix, Table 1.**German: Pause; Italian: pausa.

resultant tones see **combination tones.**

Resurrection Symphony Symphony No. 2 for soprano and contralto soloists, choir, and orchestra by Mahler. Composed: 1894. The title of this work refers to Mahler's setting for soprano, choir, and orchestra of Klopstock's poem 'Auferstehung' ('Resurrection') for the final movement. In the second movement Mahler also sets the poem 'Urlicht' ('Primeval Light'), from the collection *Des Knaben Wunderhorn* (*Youth's Magic Horn*), for contralto and orchestra. The symphony is unusual in having five movements rather than the customary four.

Retablo de Maese Pedro, El see **Master Peter's Puppet Show.**

retardation see **suspension.**

retenu Held back; holding back: a direction used to indicate that the speed should be immediately reduced. [French]

Return of Lemminkäinen, The see **Lemminkäinen's Homecoming.**

Reubke, (Friedrich) Julius (1834–58) German composer, and organist, son of the organ builder **Adolf Reubke** (1805–75). From 1851 he studied at the Berlin conservatory, where he later taught the piano. In 1856 he became a pupil of Liszt in Weimar. His two most important compositions are a piano sonata in B♭ minor and an organ sonata in C minor based on Psalm 94, both influenced by Liszt.

Reutter, Hermann (1900–85) German composer and pianist. Reutter taught in Berlin and in Stuttgart, where he directed the Hochschule für Musik from 1956. His compositions, strongly influenced by Hindemith, include operas, orchestral works, chamber music, and songs.

Revolutionary Study Study for piano in C minor (Op. 10 No. 12) by Chopin. Composed: 1831. It is said that the dramatic and passionate nature of this piece is a patriotic outburst inspired by the news that Chopin's native Warsaw had been overrun by the Russian army.

Revueltas, Silvestre (1899–1940) Mexican composer. A career as a conductor preceded Revueltas' work as a composer. His music reflects Mexican folk traditions and includes *Esquinas* (1930) and *Redes* (1938) for orchestra, chamber music, and songs.

Reynolds, Roger (1934–) US composer, a pupil of Finney and Gerhard. After an early serial style Reynolds explored movement and action in multimedia works and recent orchestral works show his interest in sonority and graphic notation. His works include *PING* (1968), *Blind Man* (1966), *Compass* (1973), *Promises of Darkness* (1976), and *Fiery Wind* (1978).

Reznicek, Emil Nikolaus von (1860–1945) Austrian composer and conductor. Reznicek's works include many operas, four symphonies and other orchestral compositions, and vocal works.

rfz. see **rinforzando.**

r.h. Abbreviation for right hand. It is written above or below the bass staff in piano music when the composer or editor suggests that it would be better to use the right hand rather than the left hand. Sometimes the initials **M.D.** are used, standing for *main droite* (French) or *mano destra* (Italian).

rhapsody In the 19th century, a piece that is generally free in form and based on a folk melody, as in Liszt's *Hungarian Rhapsodies* and Dvořák's *Slavonic Rhapsodies*. Brahms applied the term to some ballade-like pieces for piano and to a setting of part of Goethe's *Harzreise im Winter* for contralto, male chorus, and orchestra. 20th-century rhapsodies often feature a solo instrument and orchestra, as in Debussy's *Rapsodie* for clarinet and orchestra and Gershwin's *Rhapsody in Blue. Rachmaninov's *Rhapsody on a Theme of Paganini* (see **Paganini Rhapsody**) follows the form of theme and variations. [From Greek *rhapsōidia*, epic poem (literally, songs stitched together)]

Rhapsody in Blue Work for piano and orchestra by Gershwin. First performance: 1924. Gershwin originally composed this rhapsody for solo piano, but the orchestral parts were arranged shortly afterwards by Grofé and it is this latter version that is normally performed today. *Rhapsody in Blue* is important in being one of the first serious concert works to make extensive use of jazz idioms and features a prominent part for clarinet.

Rheinberger, Joseph (Gabriel) (1839–1901) German composer, organist, conductor, and teacher. He was a church organist in Vaduz from the age of seven. He studied at the Munich conservatory (1851–54), where in 1859 he was appointed to teach the piano and later theory and where from 1867 to his death he was professor. He became organist of St Michael's Church (1859–64), conductor of the Munich Choral Society (1864–77), and court kapellmeister (1877–1901). Most of Rheinberger's many compositions are conservative, and although he wrote in all genres only his sacred vocal music and his striking organ pieces (including 2 concertos and 20 sonatas) are still heard. He was more influential as a teacher, his pupils including Humperdinck, Wolf-Ferrari, Horatio Parker, and Furtwängler.

Rheingold, Das see **Ring des Nibelungen, Der.**

Rhenish Symphony Symphony No. 3 in E♭ major by Schumann. Composed: 1850. Schumann was inspired to compose this work after a journey down the Rhine and according to him the stately fourth movement was written after seeing a grand service in Cologne Cat l. The *Rhenish Symphony* is unusual in having five rather than four movements.

rhythm The arrangement of the notes in a piece of music in relation to *time. In the notation in general use the rhythm is determined by the way in which the notes are grouped into bars, the number and types of beat in the bar (see **time signature**), and the way in which the *accent falls on the beats. Rhythm, like *melody and *harmony, is one of the basic characteristics of music. In some types of music, such as jazz and pop music, the rhythm is the predominant

characteristic; in others, such as plainsong and polyphonic choral music, the rhythm is less obtrusive. A sense of rhythm is, however, a necessary attribute of all performers of music. It is not easy to define as it requires something more than the ability to reproduce accurately and mechanically the instructions expressed in the notation – a Pianola, for example, sounds different from a skilled pianist because the former has no intrinsic sense of rhythm whereas the latter has.

rhythmic modes Six patterns on which the rhythm of medieval music was based. They correspond to poetic rhythms.

ribattuta see **trillo.**

ribible see **rebec.**

Ricci, Ruggiero (1918–   ) US violinist. A noted soloist and performer of concertos specializing in 19th-century works, he has made tours of Europe and the Soviet Union.

ricercare (*or* **ricercar, ricercata, recercada**) An instrumental piece of the 16th and 17th centuries. The most important species of ricercare have contrapuntal textures, with prominent use of imitation. Among the earliest examples are those by Willaert (1540), which are for ensembles of instruments in the style of *motets. Organ ricercari were widely developed in Italy by Cavazzoni, Andrea Gabrieli, and Frescobaldi (see illustration). These frequently display remarkable contrapuntal ingenuity, with augmentation, diminution, and inversion. They may be based on a single subject or on up to as many as four, which might be combined. The contrapuntal ricercare reached its culmination with the two examples, in three and six parts respectively, in J. S. Bach's *Musical Offering* (1747). Noncontrapuntal ricercari of the same period were written for lute, organ, viol, or even voice. These are often freely constructed technical studies, of a suitably idiomatic nature. [Italian, to seek out]

Frescobaldi's Ricercare No. 2 (1615)

Richafort, Jean (*c.*1480–*c.*1547) Franco-Flemish composer. In 1507 he became maître at St Rombaud, Mechelen. As a member of the French royal chapel, he travelled to Italy. From 1542 to 1547 he was maître at St Gilles, Bruges. Richafort's writing shows the influence of his probable teacher, Josquin des Prez, in its proficient use of counterpoint and observance of the text. His best-known motet,

Quem dicunt homines, was used for parody masses by Mouton, Morales, Ruffo, and Palestrina.

Richards, (Henry) Brinley (1819–85) British pianist and composer, born in Wales. He studied in London at the Royal Academy of Music, where he was later a teacher and influential director. He was a distinguished pianist and prolific composer, but the only work which he is now remembered is 'God bless the Prince of Wales' (1862).

Richter, Franz Xaver (1709–89) German composer and singer. In about 1747 he became musician at the Palatine court in Mannheim, for which he wrote many symphonies and concertos. He was appointed kapellmeister of Strasbourg Cathedral in 1769. Richter's other compositions include chamber music, sonatas, oratorios and other sacred works, and a treatise.

Richter, Hans (1843–1916) Hungarian-born conductor. A great interpreter and friend of Wagner, Richter conducted the Vienna Philharmonic Society and the Vienna Opera (1875–97). From 1897 until 1912 he was conductor of the Hallé Orchestra. He continued to conduct at Covent Garden and Bayreuth and was also a champion of Brahms' music.

Richter, Karl (1926–80) German conductor, harpsichordist, and organist. An outstanding interpreter of Bach, he was organist at St Thomas's Church, Leipzig, and founded the Munich Bach Choir.

Richter, Sviatoslav (Teofilovich) (1914–   ) Soviet pianist. He won the Stalin Prize in 1949 and is famous as a concert and recording performer. At his most creative with 19th-century romantic music, he is particularly noted for his performances of Beethoven, Schubert, Schumann, and Prokofiev.

ricochet (*or* **jeté**) A form of staccato bowing in which the third of the bow nearest to the point is thrown onto the string producing between two and six rapidly bouncing notes, all in the same stroke, i.e. without changing the direction in which the bow moves. Compare **spiccato**. [French, rebound (*or* thrown)]

riddle canon see **puzzle canon**.

Riders to the Sea Opera by Vaughan Williams, the libretto being the play of the same name by J. M. Synge. Composed: 1925–32; first performance: 1937. The plot concerns a fishing family in Ireland and the composer set the play almost exactly in its original version.

Ridout, Alan (1934–   ) British composer, a pupil of Howells and Tippett. Since 1960 Ridout has taught composition at the Royal College of Music, London. His works reflect many different stylistic influences; they include the opera *The Rescue* (1963), six symphonies and other orchestral compositions, choral music, chamber works, and music for children.

Riegger, Wallingford (1885–1961) US composer. He developed his own serial technique, which was often combined with the use of clusters; he wrote much music for dance companies, including Martha Graham's. His works include four symphonies, *Study in Sonority* (1927), *Dichotomy* (1932), *Music for Brass Choir* (1949), a piano concerto (1953), and *Variations* (1959) for violin and orchestra.

Rienzi Opera in five acts by Wagner with libretto by the composer based on Bulwer-Lytton's novel of the same name. First performance: Court Opera, Dresden, 1842. Set in Rome in the 14th century, it involves the political and personal preoccupations of the Rienzis and their adversaries, the Colonnas. It incorporates ballet and chorus.

Ries German family of musicians. **Franz Anton Ries** (1755–1846) was a violinist and teacher of Beethoven. His son **Ferdinand Ries** (1784–1838), a composer and pianist, was pupil, copyist, and secretary to Beethoven; he was active in London (1813–24) and Aachen (1834). He wrote piano music, chamber works, symphonies, concertos, operas, and sacred music. Ferdinand's son **Hubert Ries** (1802–86), a composer and violinist, was director (1835) and leader (1836) of the Berlin Philharmonic Society. He wrote a violin tutor, violin concertos, duets, and other chamber works.

Rifkin, Joshua (1944–   ) US musicologist, pianist, and composer. He has researched into Renaissance and baroque music but is best known for his records of Scott Joplin's ragtime music. He joined the staff of Brandeis University in 1970.

rigaudon (*or* **rigadoon**) A dance that originated in southern France in the 17th century. In 2/2 or 2/4 time, it consists of three or four parts.

Rigoletto Opera in three acts by Verdi with libretto by Piave based on Victor Hugo's play *Le Roi s'amuse*. First performance: Teatro la Fenice, Venice, 1851. Rigoletto (baritone) is the tragic hunchback jester at the court of the Duke of Mantua (tenor), who unknowingly assists the Duke in the abduction of his daughter Gilda (soprano). To avenge his daughter, Rigoletto plans to have the Duke killed by the assassin Sparafucile (bass) but in the end Gilda gives her own life to save the Duke. Act III contains the famous aria 'La donna è mobile.'

Riley, Terry (1935–   ) US composer and saxophonist. A pupil of Shiffrin, he also studied North Indian singing with Pandit Pran Nath. His music shows obsessive patterning built from repeated series, ostinati, and tape loops to give a hypnotic meditative effect. Riley's works include *In C* (1965), *Dorian Reeds* (1966), *A Rainbow in Curved Air* (1969), *Persian Surgery Dervishes* (1971), the ballet *Genesis '70* (1970), and *Shri Camel* (1978).

Rilke, Rainer Maria (1875–1926) German poet. The best-known settings of his verse are the cycle *Das Marienleben* for soprano and orchestra by Hindemith (1938–59) and *Two Songs* for voice and chamber orchestra by Webern (1911–12). Kurt Weill based the tone poem *Weise vom Liebe und Tod* (?1920, now lost) and *Das Stundenbuch*, six songs with orchestra (1924), on Rilke.

Rimsky-Korsakov, Nikolai (Andreyevich) (1844–1908) Russian composer and teacher. He spent his early childhood on a country estate where he became acquainted with the Russian folk songs and church music that were to influence his work. The nephew of an admiral, he entered the naval academy at St Petersburg at the age of 12; three years later he started to study seriously the piano and composition. In 1861 he met Balakirev, who encouraged him to write a symphony; this was completed when Rimsky-Korsakov returned from a three-year naval voyage (1862–65) and was successfully performed in St Petersburg in 1865 – the first Russian symphony to be performed. His association with Balakirev and the other nationalist composers led him to become one of the leading members of The *Five. In 1871 he was appointed Professor of Composition and Orchestration at the St Petersburg conservatory, a post he held until his death (except for a brief period during 1905, when he was dismissed for supporting students on strike). His first opera, *The *Maid of Pskov*, was performed in 1873, the year in which he left the navy, and in 1874 he conducted his third symphony. In 1874 he was also appointed director of the Free Music School, St Petersburg. After Mussorgsky's death (1881) he edited his works for publication and made major changes to the opera *Boris Godunov*, which met with some criticism.

Rimsky-Korsakov is regarded as the founder of the Russian school of composition and his works considerably advanced Russian national music. Russian fairy tales, literature, and history provided the subjects for most of his 16 operas, which include *May Night* (1880), *The *Snow Maiden* (1880–81), *Sadko* (1898; containing the well-loved 'Song of India'), *The *Tsar's Bride* (1899), and *The *Golden Cockerel* (1906–07). Among his orchestral works are three symphonies: No. 1 in E♭ minor (1861–65, revised 1884), No. 2, *Antar* (1868, revised 1876 and 1897), and No. 3 in C major (1874, revised 1886); the tone poem *Sheherazade* (1880); the symphonic suite *Capriccio espagnol* (1887); the overture *Russian Easter Festival* (1888); and the famous *The *Flight of the Bumble Bee* (from the opera *The *Legend of Tsar Saltan*, 1900). Other compositions include over 80 songs and some chamber music, including 2 string quartets, a string sextet, and a quintet for piano and wind instruments. He also wrote an autobiography, *Chronicle of My Musical Life* (1909), and two music textbooks.

Rinaldo Opera by Handel with text by Rossi based on Torquato Tasso's poem *Jerusalem Delivered* (see also **Armida**). First performance: Queen's Theatre, London, 1711. This is the first of Handel's Italian operas written in London; Rinaldo is the Crusader hero.

rinforzando A direction used to indicate that notes or chords should be individually accentuated. Abbreviations: **rfz.; rinf.** [Italian, reinforcing]

Ring des Nibelungen, Der (*The Nibelung's Ring*; often shortened to *The Ring*) Cycle of four operas by Wagner with libretto by the composer, ideally to be performed on four consecutive nights. The first performances were as follows: **Das Rheingold** (*The Rhinegold*): Munich, 1869; **Die Walküre** (*The Valkyrie*): Munich, 1870; **Siegfried** and **Götterdämmerung** (*Twilight of the Gods*): Bayreuth, 1876 (the first performance of the complete cycle).

Das Rheingold. Alberich (bass baritone), the Nibelung dwarf, steals the Rhinegold from the Rhine-maidens and with it forges a ring to become master of the world. Wotan (bass baritone), ruler of the gods, steals the ring to pay the giants Fasolt and Fafner, who have built Valhalla.

Die Walküre. Siegmund and Sieglinde (tenor and soprano) begotten by Wotan and Erda (contralto), the earth goddess, find each other; Siegmund is directed to the magic sword, Nothung. Fricka (soprano), Wotan's wife, prevents Brünnhilde (soprano), Wotan's daughter and favourite Valkyrie, from saving Siegmund's life in combat with Hunding (bass), husband of Sieglinde.

Siegfried. Siegfried (tenor), son of Siegmund and Sieglinde, reforges the sword Nothung; he kills the giant Fafner and takes the ring. Led by the Woodbird (soprano), he finds Brünnhilde and claims her as his bride.

Götterdämmerung. The three Norns (contralto, mezzo-soprano, and soprano) prophesy the end of the gods. Siegfried is deceived by a magic potion to forget Brünnhilde and weds Gutrune (soprano). Hagen (bass), son of Alberich, slays Siegfried to gain the ring. But Brünnhilde alone is able to take it from his finger; she throws herself on his funeral pyre and all is engulfed in flames. Valhalla is consumed, the Rhine overflows its banks, and the ring is received back into its depths by the Rhine-maidens.

ring modulator A standard electronic device used in *electronic music studios as a sound modifier. It modifies the frequency components of a given sound from one input in relation to those of another source at the second input (there is a single output). Ring modulators are used to create new complex sounds or transformations. Stockhausen used the device in such works as *Mixtur* and *Mantra*.

Rio Grande, The Work for piano, choir, and orchestra by Constant Lambert to words by Sacheverell Sitwell. First performance: 1929. The orchestration excludes all wood-wind instruments but includes parts for dance-band instruments. Lambert makes extensive use of jazz idioms throughout the work.

ripieno 1. (n.) The main body of instrumentalists in 17th-and 18th-century orchestral music. The term was applied particularly to the tutti group in the *concerto grosso, as opposed to the solo group (called the *concertino). The instruction **senza ripieno** means that the leading orchestral players only should perform. **2.** (adj.) (*or* **ripiano** *or* **repiano**) Describing the supporting cornets in a brass band, who reinforce the 'first' cornets. [Italian, full]

Riquier de Narbonne, Guiraut (1254–84) One of the last troubadours, composer of a substantial number of songs and over 100 poems.

Rise and Fall of the City of Mahagonny (German: *Aufstieg und Fall der Stadt Mahagonny*) Singspiel by Weill to a libretto by Brecht. First performance: Baden-Baden, 1927. Like most of the Brecht/Weill collaborations this work has strong political overtones and is a satire on capitalism and its self-destructive nature. In 1930 it was revised and produced at Leipzig as an opera.

Rising of the Moon, The 1. Orchestral interlude from the one-act opera *In the Well* by the Czech composer Vihém Blo (1834–74), which was first performed in Prague in 1867. **2.** Opera by Maw with libretto by Beverley Cross and the composer. First performance: Glyndebourne, 1970.

ritardando Slowing down; holding back. Abbreviation: **rit.** [Italian]

ritenuto Held back: often used to indicate the same as *ritardando. [Italian]

Rite of Spring, The (French: *Le Sacre du printemps*) Ballet in two parts with music by Stravinsky and choreography by Nijinsky. First performance: Théâtre des Champs-Elysées, Paris, 1913, by the Ballet Russes with Maria Piltz. Commissioned by Diaghilev, it caused an uproar on the first night but was kept going by the imperturbable conducting of Monteux and rhythmic direction by Nijinsky from the wings. It represents ancient Russian fertility rites during which a virgin is sacrificed.

ritmo Rhythm. Hence **ritmo di tre** (*or* **quattro**) **battute**, rhythm based on a three-bar (or four-bar) unit. [Italian]

ritornello Originally a refrain, as in the madrigals of the 14th and 15th centuries. During the early 17th century the term was applied to an instrumental piece that recurred during the course of a musical stage work, and later to the instrumental passages separating the vocal parts of an anthem or aria. In the baroque and classical *concertos the ritornello became the orchestral tutti portion that alternated with the solo concertino part. Hence the term **ritornello form** was used for movements based on this alternation. [Italian, little return]

Ritorno d'Ulisse in patria, Il (*Ulysses' Return Home*) Opera in prologue and five acts by Monteverdi with text by Badoaro. First performance: Teatro San Cassiano, Venice, 1641. It is based on the final sections of the *Odyssey*, in which Ulysses (tenor) returns to his faithful wife Penelope (contralto) after years of wandering.

Ritual Dances Suite for choir and orchestra by Tippett. First performance: 1955. The suite consists of a selection of dance episodes that form an integral part of Tippett's opera The *Midsummer Marriage*.

Roberto Devereux (*Robert Devereux*) Opera in three acts by Donizetti with libretto by Cammarano based on Ancelot's tragedy *Elisabeth d'Angleterre*. First performance: Naples, 1837. Centred around Elizabeth I's favourite the Earl of Essex, the opera bears little relation to historic fact; for its Paris premiere (1838) Donizetti wrote a new overture with a woodwind version of 'God Save the Queen.'

Roberton, Sir Hugh Stevenson (1874–1952) British conductor and composer. Born in Scotland, he founded and conducted the Glasgow Orpheus Choir (1906–51). His works include arrangements of Scottish folk songs.

Rochberg, George (1918–) US composer, a pupil of Menotti. His early works are in a serial idiom, but in the

The Royal Ballet performing The Rite of Spring

1960s he rejected modernism and attempted to resuscitate traditional musical values. He did this first by incorporating quotation, in such works as *Contra Mortem et Tempus* (1965), and then by pursuing his own traditional idiom, as in the third string quartet (1972), the violin concerto (1975), and the piano quintet (1975).

rococo music Music of the early and mid-18th century, particularly of Couperin, Telemann, J. C. Bach, and Mozart (see also **galant style**). The expression derives from the French word *rocaille*, meaning 'fancy rock-work,' and was originally applied to the highly ornamental architecture and interior decoration that evolved in France in the period. Rococo music is characterized by a light and delicate elegance. Compare **baroque music.**

Rodeo Ballet in two scenes with music by Copland and choreography by Agnes de Mille. First performance: Metropolitan Opera House, New York, 1942, by the Monte Carlo Ballet, who commissioned it. Set in pioneer times, it depicts the Saturday afternoon rodeo, the meeting place for men and women of the district. There is a popular concert suite of four episodes from the ballet: 'Buckaroo Holiday,' 'Corral Nocturne,' 'Saturday Night Waltz,' and 'Hoe-Down.' The score contains a number of American folk songs.

Rodrigo, Joaquín (1902–) Spanish composer. Blind from early childhood, Rodrigo studied in Paris with Dukas. Spanish folk traditions have influenced the melodic material of his music, which is often set in classical textures and forms. Rodrigo's output includes the *Concierto de Aranjuez* (1939) for guitar and orchestra, other concertos for guitar, harp, flute, violin, cello, and piano, chamber music, and songs.

Roger-Ducasse, Jean Jules Aimable (1873–1954) French composer. A pupil of Fauré, he later became a teacher of composition at the Paris Conservatoire. Roger-Ducasse's music shows individual traits of melody and harmony in an idiom extending that of his teacher. His works include the opera *Cantegril* (1931), orchestral music, chamber music, and piano pieces.

Rogers, Benjamin (1614–98) English composer and organist. He sang as a chorister at St George's Chapel, Windsor, and after a period in Dublin became a lay clerk there in 1641. In 1653 he became a clerk at Eton and was awarded the Cambridge Mus.B. From 1660 to 1664 he was organist at Eton. In 1665 he became organist and choirmaster at Magdalen College, Oxford, and in 1669 received the D.Mus. Rogers is remembered for his sacred music: his *Hymnus eucharisticus* was performed before Charles II in 1660 and his short service in A minor is still performed.

Rogers, Bernard (1893–1968) US composer, a pupil of Bloch and Nadia Boulanger. Roger's involvement with poetry and the visual arts has influenced his compositions, which include operas and choral works, five symphonies, chamber music, and songs.

Rogg, Lionel (1936–) Swiss organist. After studying at the Geneva conservatory Rogg established an international reputation, based especially on his playing of Bach. In 1960 he became a professor at the Geneva conservatory.

Rohrflöte (*or* **Rohr flute**) An organ *stop controlling 8-*foot stopped diapason metal pipes in which a thin metal tube protrudes through the plug. [German *Rohr*, reed (referring to the metal tube)]

Roi David, Le see **King David.**

Roi d'Ys, Le (*The King of Ys*) Opera in three acts by Lalo with libretto by Edouard Blau. First performance: Opéra-Comique, Paris, 1888. Based on a Breton legend, it is the tale of Margared and Rozenn (sopranos), daughters of the King of Ys (bass), who both love the hero Mylio (tenor).

Roland-Manuel (Roland Alexis Manuel Levy; 1891–1966) French composer and writer on music, a pupil of d'Indy and Ravel. Roland-Manuel taught at the Paris Conservatoire from 1947. His music is classically influenced and avoids romantic emotionality; it includes operas and ballets, a piano concerto (1938), chamber music, and songs.

Roldán, Amadeo (1900–39) Cuban composer and conductor. Roldán's works draw on native musical traditions, combining these with European influences. His output includes ballets and orchestral music, songs, chamber works, and music for percussion ensemble.

roll A rapid succession of drumbeats having an almost continuous sound. It is produced by very rapid alternating strokes from two drumsticks.

Roma (*Rome*) Suite for orchestra by Bizet. Composed: 1860–68; revised: 1871. Bizet's inspiration for this work came in 1860 after a visit to Italy, when he planned to compose a four-movement symphony, each movement representing an Italian city: Rome, Venice, Florence, and Naples, respectively. Although this work was produced as a symphony on several occasions, it was eventually published in 1881 as the 'troisième suite de concert' ('third concert suite').

Roman, Johan Helmich (1694–1758) Swedish composer. In England (1715–21), he served the Duke of Newcastle, studied with Pepusch, Geminiani, and others, and was greatly influenced by Handel. In Stockholm he became court deputy kapellmeister (1721), kapellmeister (1727), and steward (1745). Roman's output includes sinfonias and suites, sacred vocal and chamber works, and sonatas; he also translated theoretical works into Swedish.

romance An instrumental or vocal composition that is typically songlike in character and mood and generally considered to be romantic in nature. Although many character pieces are described as romances, the term is also used for complete concerto movements, as in Mozart's D minor piano concerto. German: **Romanze**; Italian: **romanza**. [French, song]

Roman Festivals (Italian: *Feste Romane*) Tone poem by Respighi. First performance: 1929. The work is divided into four sections, depicting the Circus Maximus, the Jubilee, the October Festival, and Epiphany. See also **Fountains of Rome; Pines of Rome.**

romantic music Music that conforms to the general romantic movement in art and literature of the late 18th century and early 19th century, in which the emphasis was on feeling, the passions, and the exotic rather than the reason, restraint, and aestheticism of classical art (see also **classical music**). The earliest traces of romanticism in music can be seen in the works of Beethoven and Schubert and the movement initially flourished with such composers as Schumann, Mendelssohn, and Weber. A later period of romanticism is represented by Brahms, Wagner, and Liszt and the general principles and musical style of this aesthetic were carried into the 20th century with the music of Mahler, Elgar, and Sibelius. In addition to the 'back to nature' theme of much early romanticism there was also a preoccupation with the supernatural and the exotic. As the movement gradually came to favour the portrayal of extremes of emotion the art song, *tone poem, and character piece were greatly developed during this period. Music also became much more dependent upon other arts for a stimulus, as seen in the choice of literary subjects as the basis for tone poems. The early 20th century saw a definite antiromantic movement, which resulted in the partial decline of this tradition and the rise of such styles as *impressionism and *expressionism. See also **neoromanticism.**

Romberg, Andreas Jakob (1767–1821) German violinist and composer. With his cousin, the cellist and composer **Bernhard Heinrich Romberg** (1767–1841), he made concert tours of Europe. In 1790 they joined the electoral orchestra in Bonn, of which Beethoven was a member, then worked in Hamburg (1793–95, 1797–1800), where Andreas settled. In 1815 Andreas became court kapellmeister in Gotha; he composed eight operas, vocal music, ten symphonies, concertos, chamber music, and songs (of which the *Lied von der Glocke* became well known).

In 1801 Bernhard Romberg became a cello teacher at the Paris Conservatoire and in 1805 joined the royal court orchestra in Berlin, of which he became court kapellmeister in 1816. In 1819 he resumed his career as a solo cellist, living chiefly in Hamburg. He wrote music for the stage, five symphonies, ten cello concertos, and chamber and vocal music.

Romberg, Sigmund (1887–1951) Hungarian-born composer of operettas. Romberg emigrated to the USA in 1909, abandoning a career in engineering to compose. His works include *The Student Prince* (1924) and *The Desert Song* (1926).

Rome see **Roma.**

Romeo and Juliet Shakespeare's tragedy has formed the basis of many musical works, the best known of which are listed below. **1.** Work for solo voices, choir, and orchestra (Op. 17) by Berlioz. Composed: 1839. Although described as a 'dramatic symphony' by the composer, this work does not follow a conventional symphonic structure. **2.** Opera in five acts by Gounod with libretto by Barbier and Carré. First performance: Théâtre-Lyrique, Paris, 1867. **3.** Fantasy-overture by Tchaikovsky. First performance: Moscow, 1870. **4.** Ballet by Prokofiev. First performance: Moscow, 1935. Two orchestral suites were made by the composer from the ballet music.

Ronald, Sir Landon (L. R. Russell; 1873–1938) British conductor, pianist, and composer. He was accompanist to Melba, conducted in London and Europe, and in 1910 became Principal of the Guildhall School of Music.

rondeau (*or* **rondel**) **1.** A medieval poetic and musical structure. In the 13th century it consisted of stanzas with eight short lines. Of these, lines 1, 4, and 7 were the same, as were also lines 2 and 8. Lines 1 and 2 were a refrain and music was composed for them alone, as in the 13th-century monophonic example illustrated. If the refrain lines are designated A and B, the following pattern emerges: ABaAabAB. Polyphonic settings in three parts for voice and two instruments were made during the 14th century by Machaut and his contemporaries. The 15th-century composers of rondeaux include Dufay, Binchois, and Ockeghem.

2. A form used in the 17th century by French clavecin (harpsichord) composers, consisting of a refrain followed by differing couplets in contrasting keys. The pattern is expressed: ABACAD etc. In the 18th century this form evolved into the *rondo and sonata-rondo structures.

An example of a 13th-century monophonic rondeau

Rondine, La (*The Swallow*) Comic opera in three acts by Puccini with libretto by Adami based on a German text written by Willner and Reichert. First performance: Monte Carlo, 1917. Originally commissioned in 1912 as an operetta of the Viennese type, war delayed its fulfilment and Puccini eventually set Adami's libretto as an opera (no spoken text).

rondo A *form widely used in the final movements of concertos, sonatas, symphonies, and chamber works in the second half of the 18th century and during the 19th century. It evolved from the *rondeau movements of 17th-century French harpsichord music with the pattern ABACADA, where A is the rondo, or returning theme, between the contrasting *episodes. The finale of Mozart's piano sonata in B♭ is an example. This simple rondo form was combined with *sonata form as **sonata-rondo form**. This structure can be expressed as ABACABA, where A and B represent the exposition and recapitulation, and the episode, C, the development. The last movement of Beethoven's *Pathetic Sonata* contains an example. Single-movement works in rondo form of the 19th century include Mendelssohn's *Rondo capriccioso* in E for piano and the tone poem *Till Eulenspiegel* by Richard Strauss. The final scenes of the first two acts of Berg's *Wozzeck* (1921) also employ rondo form.

root The lowest note of a major or minor *chord. For example, in the chord CEG, C is the root and in this *position the chord is said to be in the **root position** (see also **inversion**).

Ropariz, Guy see **Guy-Ropartz, Joseph.**

Rore, Cipriano (*c.*1516–65) Flemish composer. He seems to have studied in Venice in the 1540s and by 1547 was maestro di cappella at Ferrara. In 1563 he succeeded Willaert as maestro at St Mark's, Venice. A year later he went to Parma, where he died. Rore's parody masses and motets are in the style of Josquin and Willaert, but it is for his madrigals that he is best known; the early ones are mainly Petrarch settings and in his later madrigals he develops an increasing emphasis on the text. Rore's works are important in the history of the madrigal and were much admired by Monteverdi.

Rorem, Ned (1923–   ) US composer and writer, a pupil of Sowerby, Thomson, Copland, and Honegger. Best known as a song composer, he has also written instrumental music in a modified serial idiom. His works include the song cycle *Ariel* (1971), the *Santa Fé* songs (1980), the operas *Miss Julie* (1965) and *Bertha* (1973), three symphonies, concertos, *Air Music* (1973), and *Assembly and Fall* (1974).

rosalia see **sequence.**

Rosamunde, Princess of Cyprus Incidental music by Schubert for the play *Rosamunde, Prinzessin von Cypern* by Helmina von Chézy. First performance: 1823. Although the most famous part of the score is now the overture, for the first production of the play the overture to Schubert's opera *Alfonso und Estrella* was used; the present (and published) *Rosamunde* overture belonged originally to the melodrama *Die Zauberharfe* (*The Magic Harp*). The original score comprised three entractes, two ballet tunes, a romance for contralto, and several choruses.

Rosbaud, Hans (1895–1962) Austrian conductor. He conducted various German orchestras and was well-known as an interpreter of contemporary music; he directed the premiere of Schoenberg's *Moses und Aaron* (1957).

rose see **sound hole.**

Rose, Leonard (1918–84) US cellist. After following a career as an orchestral player, he concentrated on solo appearances from 1951. As a teacher at both the Juilliard School and the Curtis Institute he exercised a wide influence.

Rosen, Charles (1927–   ) US pianist. Although he has achieved widespread recognition as a performer, Rosen has also written several highly acclaimed books on music. He teaches at the State University of New York.

Rosenberg, Hilding (1892–1985) Swedish composer. Rosenberg was a leading figure in 20th-century Swedish music. His style combines the influences of Schoenberg, Stravinsky, and Hindemith in an individual manner that builds on the romantic tradition in Swedish music. Rosenberg's prolific output includes operas and ballet scores 8 symphonies, concertos, and other orchestral works, 12 string quartets (some of which use serial technique), songs, and piano music.

Rosenkavalier, Der (*The Knight of the Rose*) Opera in three acts by Richard Strauss with libretto by Hofmannsthal. First performance: Royal Opera, Dresden, 1911. The Rosenkavalier is a ceremonial bearer of a silver rose between wooer and beloved: Octavian (soprano – a travesty role), lover of the ageing Marschallin (soprano), eventually wins Sophie (soprano). In this opera Strauss writes for a very large orchestra.

Rosenmüller, Johann (*c.*1619–84) German composer and organist. In 1642 he taught at St Thomas's School in Leipzig and in 1651 became organist of the church of St Nicholas. In Venice from 1658, he was composer at the Pietà (1678–82), returning to Germany in 1782 as kapellmeister at Wolfenbüttel. A popular composer, Rosenmüller played an important part in the transmission of the Italian style to Germany. His instrumental music includes dances and a collection of sonatas (1692) but his sacred music is more important; this comprises the motets of the *Kern-Sprüche* (1648), psalm settings, and funeral songs.

A scene from Der Rosenkavalier, *performed at the Royal Opera House, Covent Garden, in 1985*

Rosenthal, Manuel (1904–   ) French composer, a pupil of Ravel. Rosenthal has been active as a conductor, promoting 20th-century music. His own works, which are neoclassical in spirit, include operas, ballets, a symphony (1949), choral music, and songs.

Rose of Castille, The Opera in three acts by Balfe with libretto by Harris and Falconer. First performance: Lyceum Theatre, London, 1857. It is based on Adolphe Adam's *Le Muletier de Tolède*.

Roses from the South Waltz by Johann Strauss the Younger. Composed: 1880. Although almost invariably heard as a separate piece, this waltz first appeared in the operetta *Das Spitzentuch der Königin* (*The Queen's Lace Handkerchief*). Like all of Strauss's waltzes it exists in many different arrangements.

Rosetti, Antonio (Franz Anton Rösler; 1750–92) Czech-born German composer and bass player, who Italianized his name. In Öttingen-Wallerstein he was court musician (1773), deputy kapellmeister (1780), and kapellmeister (1785); from 1789 he served the Duke of Mecklenburg-Schwerin as kapellmeister. He wrote much music in the style of Haydn, for wind and other ensemble, concertos, symphonies, oratorios, and other vocal works.

rosin (*or* **colophony**) A yellowish resin obtained by distilling turpentine. It is rubbed onto the hair of the bows used on stringed instruments to produce the necessary friction between string and hair.

Rösler, Franz Anton see Rosetti, Antonio.

Rosseter, Philip (*c*.1568–1623) English composer and theatre manager. In 1603 he became lutenist to James I and in 1609 managed a group of boy actors, later known as the Children of the Queen's Revels. He composed lute music, *Lessons for Consort* (1609) for broken consort, and *A Booke of Ayres* (1601), in which the lute accompaniment is largely chordal.

Rossi, Luigi (*c*.1597–1653) Italian composer and singing teacher. Educated at the Neapolitan court, he studied with Giovanni de Macque and moved to Rome in 1621. In 1633 he was organist at S Luigi dei Francesi, a post he held until his death. For 20 years Rossi was patronized by the Borghese family but in 1641 he entered the service of Cardinal Barberini, for whom he produced the opera *Il Palazzo incantato*. In 1646 he went to Paris, where his opera *Orfeo* (1647) was produced and proved most successful. Rossi also composed over 300 chamber cantatas in a bel canto style, which is also evident in his operas.

Rossi, Salamone (?1570–*c*.1630) Italian composer and viol player. Born in Mantua, this Jewish musician spent his entire career there and was connected with the Gonzaga court. He published the earliest madrigals with continuo (1602) and polyphonic settings of the Hebrew psalms, but his most progressive music is found in his contributions to the trio sonata and chamber duet.

Rossini, Gioacchino Antonio (1792–1868) Italian composer. The son of a trumpet player, Rossini was born in Pesaro and studied at the Liceo Musicale in Bologna. In 1810 his first comic opera, *La Cambiale di matrimonio* (*The Marriage Contract*), was performed in Venice and thereafter his operas were highly successful. After **Tancredi* (Venice, 1813) and *The *Italian Girl in Algiers* (1813) came **Elisabetta, regina d'Inghilterra* (1815), *The *Barber of*

Rossini in old age

Seville (1816), which was not immediately successful, and *Semiramide* (1823). He then left Italy and took up residence in Paris, where he became director of the Théâtre Italien. His *Le *Comte Ory* (1828) was first performed there and his *William Tell (1829) was produced at the Paris Opéra. Of his 36 operas *La Cenerentola* (1817; see **Cinderella**), *The *Thieving Magpie* (1817), and *Moses in Egypt (1818) are still part of the international repertoire. At the age of 37 Rossini gave up writing operas and took some 10 years to complete his *Stabat Mater* (1831–41). His **Soirées musicales*, a collection of songs and duets, were published in 1835. In retirement in Florence and Paris his musical output was inconsequential, except for his *Petite Messe solennelle* (1863). Highly regarded as a cook, his dinner parties were renowned; he invented a number of recipes, including the perennial favourite Tournedos Rossini.

Rostal, Max (1905–) Austrian-born British violinist. A pupil of Arnold Rosé and Carl Flesch, he has held appointments at music academies in Berlin, London, Cologne, and Berne. Bush, Frankel, Reizenstein, Stevens, and Seiber have written works for him and, in addition to solo appearances, Rostal has performed with various chamber ensembles.

Rostropovich, Mstislav (Leopoldovich) (1927–) Soviet cellist, pianist, and conductor. He became cello professor at the Moscow conservatory in 1957. Rostropovich is one of the greatest cellists of the 20th-century: Britten, Prokofiev, Shostakovich, Lutoslawski, and others have written works for him. As a pianist Rostropovich accompanies his wife, the soprano Galina Vishnevskaya (1926–). They were forced to leave the Soviet Union in 1975 and Rostropovich became conductor of the National Symphony Orchestra of Washington in 1977.

rota see **round**.

Rota, Nino (1911–79) Italian composer, a pupil of Pizzetti and Casella. He composed operas, symphonies, chamber music, and songs but is best known for his scores for such films as King Vidor's *War and Peace* (1956), Visconti's *The Leopard* (1963), and most of the films of Fellini.

Rothwell, Evelyn (1911–) British oboist. After studying with Leon Goossens she became an orchestral player. In 1939 she married the conductor John *Barbirolli and during her career as a soloist many composers have dedicated works to her, including Rubbra, Jacob, and Maconchy.

Rouet d'Omphale, Le (*Omphale's Spinning Wheel*) Tone poem by Saint-Saëns. Composed: 1871. The composer himself described this work as depicting 'the triumphant struggle of weakness against strength,' here seen in the story of Hercules' enslavement to Omphale. According to Greek mythology, Hercules spent three years spinning wool for Omphale in penance for the killing of his friend Iphitus. The music includes a prominent spinning-wheel motif.

Rouget de Lisle, Claude-Joseph (1760–1836) French poet and composer. He wrote the words and music for the *Chant de guerre pour l'armée du Rhin* (1792), better known as *La *Marseillaise*. He also wrote libretti and musical compositions, including *Hymne à la liberté*, set by Pleyel (1791).

round A short *canon for unaccompanied voices, in which each voice sings a complete melody. All voices sing the same melody at the same pitch or at the octave but each voice enters at a different time. Popular in the 16th century, rounds such as 'London's burning' are still sung. A **rota** is an older name for a round, **Sumer is icumen in* being known as the Reading Rota.

Rousseau, Jean-Jacques (1712–78) Swiss composer, philosopher, and writer, resident in France from 1742. His compositions include the popular comic opera *Le Devin du village* (1752) and the melodrama *Pygmalion* (1770), with speeches and orchestral interludes: in these works he demonstrated his support for Italian opera in the so-called

Rostropovich with Benjamin Britten at the piano

'Guerre des Bouffons' and his preference for greater expressiveness in music. Rousseau proposed a cipher notation system; his other musical works include symphonies, chamber music, and songs.

Roussel, Albert (1869–1937) French composer. Roussel's early training in music was followed by a period in the French navy (1889–94), during which he visited the Far East. He subsequently studied and taught at the Schola Cantorum, his pupils including Satie and Varese. Roussel's early works, influenced by his travels to the East, show impressionist features. These gave way to the neoclassical idiom adopted in his later works. Roussel's prolific output includes the ballets The *Spider's Banquet* (1913) and *Bacchus and Ariadne* (1931), the opera-ballet *Padmâvatî* (1914–18), four symphonies, a string quartet (1932) and other chamber works, piano pieces, and songs.

rovescio, al 1. See **recte et retro. 2.** Denoting a passage or composition that may be played backwards. [Italian, in reverse]

Roxelane, La Symphony No. 63 in C major by Haydn. Composed: 1777. The title is that of an old French song melody used by Haydn as the basis for a set of variations in the second movement of this symphony.

Royal Academy of Music (*or* **RAM**) **1.** A college of music founded in London in 1822 by John Fane, Lord Burghesh, later 11th Earl of Westmorland. In 1830 it was

granted a royal charter. The RAM moved to its present premises in Marylebone Road in 1912; these now include a concert hall, opera theatre, and library. The academy provides courses for performers, composers, and teachers and in the late 1980s there were 500 full-time students. Among its principals have been William Crotch, Cipriani Potter, Sterndale Bennett, G. A. Macfarren, Thomas Armstrong, and Anthony Lewis. **2.** An association to promote Italian opera in London. It was organized by Handel, Bononcini, and Ariosti in 1718–19.

Royal Albert Hall A large hall in Kensington, London, built in 1871 on the site of part of the 1851 Great Exhibition in memory of Prince Albert, who promoted the exhibition. It is used as one of London's main concert halls. The *promenade concerts organized by the BBC are given here.

Royal College of Music (*or* **RCM**) A college of music founded in London in 1883 by royal charter. It succeeded the National Training School for Music and its first director was George *Grove. The college moved to its present premises in Prince Consort Road in 1894 and a concert hall was later added. The college has a fine library and collection of instruments; it provides courses for performers, composers, and teachers, and in the late 1980s there were 520 full-time students. Its principals have included Hubert Parry, George Dyson, Keith Falkner, and David Willcocks.

Royal Festival Hall A concert hall on the South Bank of the River Thames, in London, built in 1951 as a permanent monument to the Festival of Britain. The main concert hall is used for orchestral concerts while the associated Queen Elizabeth Hall is used for chamber music and the Purcell Room is used for recitals.

Royal Liverpool Philharmonic Orchestra British symphony orchestra founded in 1840. The Liverpool Philharmonic Society began promoting its concerts and in 1849 the Philharmonic Hall was opened; until it was burnt down in 1933 it was considered among the best in Europe. It was replaced in 1939. The orchestra was granted the prefix 'Royal' in 1957. Its conductors have included Alfred Mellon, Julius Benedict, Max Bruch, Charles Hallé, Frederic Cowen, Henry Wood, Thomas Beecham, Malcolm Sargent, Hugo Rignold, John Pritchard, Charles Groves, Walter Weller, and David Atherton. During World War II it became the best-known British orchestra. It was the first orchestra to give industrial concerts.

Royal Opera House see **Covent Garden.**

Royal Philharmonic Orchestra British symphony orchestra founded in 1946. Thomas Beecham established it in London and was its conductor until his death (1961). Subsequent conductors have included Rudolf Kempe, Antal Dorati, and Walter Weller. The orchestra has been resident at the *Glyndebourne Opera Festival (1948–63) and has

Gennadi Rozhdestvensky

Rozhdestvensky, Gennadi Nikolayevich (1931–) Soviet conductor. He has conducted at the Bolshoi Theatre (1965–70), the Stockholm Philharmonic Orchestra (1974–77), and the BBC Symphony Orchestra (1978–81). His exceptionally wide repertoire includes British as well as much Soviet music.

Rózsa, Miklós (1907–) Hungarian-born composer. Rózsa emigrated to the USA in 1939 and became an American citizen. He has written music for many films, including the epics *Quo Vadis?* and *Ben-Hur*. His other works, combining neoclassical influences with the folk styles of his native Hungary, include orchestral and chamber music and songs.

rubato (*or* **tempo rubato**) An important method of expressiveness in performance involving a flexibility of timing within a bar or phrase of finite length. This is normally achieved in a 'give-and-take' fashion, in which a note played slightly late in relation to the strict beat is compensated for by another note played slightly early, so

Edmund Rubbra

toured widely. Its repertory is broad and it has given concerts with pop groups. It has no connection with the Royal Philharmonic Society.

Royal Philharmonic Society (*or* **RPS**) A society founded in London in 1813 to cultivate good orchestral music. P. A. Corri, J. B. Cramer, and W. Dance originated the idea, and the inaugural concert was at the Argyll Rooms in 1813. The society continued to promote concert series using a variety of orchestras and conductors, presenting new works and leading virtuosos to London audiences. Its centenary series included specially commissioned works by British composers (Stanford, Parry, and Coleridge-Taylor among others) and the title 'royal' was granted. The RPS has always had a special relationship with Beethoven, commissioning three overtures and the ninth symphony from him. The directors sent Beethoven £100 but the sum was untouched at his death. In 1870 they commemorated his centenary by performing all his symphonies and by striking the Gold Medal; Brahms, Sibelius, Rachmaninov, Stravinsky, and Shostakovich are among foreign winners of the medal. In 1870 Fanny Linzbauer presented the society with a replica of Schaller's bust of Beethoven, which is put on the platform at all RPS concerts. In 1951 the concerts moved from the Royal Albert Hall to the Royal Festival Hall.

Roy Henry Author of two compositions – settings of the Gloria and Sanctus – in the Old Hall Manuscript. He may be identified with either Henry V (reigned 1413–22) or Henry VI (reigned 1422–61, 1470–71). A fragmentary copy of an *Alleluia Henrici Quinti* survives in the Worcestershire County Record Office.

Anton Rubinstein

Artur Rubinstein

that the phrase, taken as a whole, is within time. [Italian, robbed (time)]

Rubbra, Edmund (1901–86) British composer. From a poor Northampton family, he left school at 14 to become a railway clerk. After winning a scholarship to Reading University he later moved to the Royal College of Music, where he became a pupil of Holst and Vaughan Williams. Rubbra himself taught at Oxford University and the Guildhall School of Music. His compositions balance the lyrical elements of his basically romantic idiom with a strong formal sense. Rubbra's large output includes 11 symphonies, concertos for viola, piano, and violin, *Sinfonia concertante* for piano and orchestra, *Festival Overture* for orchestra, a rhapsody for violin and orchestra, four string quartets and other chamber works, two masses (one Anglican and one Roman Catholic after his conversion in 1948), motets, madrigals, and other vocal music.

Rubinstein, Anton Grigorevich (1829–94) Russian pianist and composer. Rubinstein combined his career as a pianist with appointments as a conductor and also held several teaching posts, including the directorship of the St Petersburg conservatory, which he founded in 1862. His reputation as a virtuoso performer was rivalled only by that of Liszt. Rubinstein's compositions include operas, symphonies, concertos, and chamber works as well as many short piano pieces, of which the *Melody in F* (1853) is the best known. His brother **Nikolay Grigorevich Rubinstein** (1835–81) enjoyed widespread popularity as a pianist, and as a conductor was active in promoting the work of Russian nationalist composers, such as Balakirev.

Rubinstein, Artur (1886–1982) Polish-born US pianist. He studied with Barth and Paderewski, making a sensational Berlin debut in 1900. After many tours during which his worldwide reputation was established, Rubinstein settled in the USA in 1946 and finally retired from the concert platform in 1976.

Ruckers Flemish family of harpsichord makers, influential throughout western Europe in the 16th, 17th, and 18th centuries. **Hans Ruckers** (*c*.1550–98) established the manufacturing firm in Antwerp and three of his descendants carried on the business, his sons **Johannes (Hans) Ruckers** (1578–1643) and **Andries Ruckers** (1579–1645) and his grandson **Andries Ruckers** (1607–67).

Ruddigore Operetta by Sullivan with libretto by Gilbert. First performance: Savoy Theatre, London, 1887. Subtitled *The Witch's Curse*, it is a parody of Victorian melodrama, the Ruddigores being a family of 'bad baronets.'

Rugby Symphonic movement by Honegger. Composed: 1928. In this work the composer attempts to capture in music the spirit and excitement of a game of rugby. It is the second of a trilogy of symphonic movements, the other works being **Pacific 231* and *Mouvement symphonique 3*.

Ruggles, Carl (1876–1971) US composer and painter. He developed his own atonal contrapuntal idiom in which the 12 pitches are used as equally as possible. Ruggles composed little and destroyed most of his early pieces; surviving works include *Portals* (1926), *Men and Mountains* (1924), *Suntreader* (1932), *Organum* (1947), and *Affirmations* (1957).

Rührtrommel Tenor drum (see **drums**). [German]

Ruins of Athens, The Incidental music (Op. 113) by Beethoven for a play by Kotzebue. First performance: 1812. This play was produced on the occasion of the opening of the German theatre at Pest in Hungary and the music consists of an overture and eight numbers. One of these, the 'Turkish March,' was composed in 1809 for a set of piano variations (Op. 76).

Rule Britannia Song by Arne, taken from his masque *Alfred* with words by Thomson and Mallet. First performance: 1740. The intense patriotism of 'Rule Britannia,' and 'Land of Hope and Glory,' has made them extremely nostalgic for British nationals.

Rusalka 1. Opera in three acts by Dvořák with libretto by Kvapil. First performance: National Theatre, Prague, 1901. Rusalka (soprano) is a water sprite, daughter of the Spirit of the Lake (bass), who loves a human Prince (tenor). **2.** Opera with words and music by Dargomizhsky based on Pushkin. First performance: St Petersburg, 1856.

Russell, Henry (1812–1900) British singer, composer, and pianist. After a career in children's opera, he studied composition with Rossini and Bellini and toured the USA (1836–44) before returning to England. He wrote about 250 songs, including 'Cheer boys, cheer' and 'A life on the ocean wave.'

Russian Easter Festival Concert overture by Rimsky-Korsakov. Composed: 1888. This overture evokes the spirit of Easter celebrations in Russia and is appropriately based upon religious tunes associated with the Russian Orthodox Church.

Russian Quartets Set of six string quartets (Op. 33) by Haydn. Composed: 1772. Haydn dedicated these works to Grand Duke Paul of Russia (hence the name). However, they are also referred to as both the *Gli Scherzi* quartets and the *Jungfernquartette* (*Maiden Quartets*). Each of the minuet movements is entitled 'scherzo,' suggesting the use of the former name, and the edition of 1782 has a female figure printed on the title page, hence the use of the latter name. Quartets Nos. 2, 3, and 5 are nicknamed 'The Joke,' 'The Bird,' and 'How Do You Do?' respectively.

Russlan and Ludmila Opera in five acts by Glinka with libretto by Shirkov and Bakhturin based on a poem by Pushkin. First performance: St Petersburg, 1842. The lovers of the title (baritone and soprano) eventually overcome magic spells to be united.

Russolo, Luigi (1885–1947) Italian composer. In 1913 Russo published a manifesto advocating futurist music (see **futurism**). He invented many machines to produce the tuned noises required by the futurist aesthetic and demonstrated these in cities around Europe. These instruments, and the music Russolo wrote for them, were destroyed in World War II.

Rust, Friedrich Wilhelm (1739–96) German composer, violinist, and pianist. After studying with W. F. Bach, C. P. E. Bach, Franz Benda, and others, he returned (*c*.1765) to his native Dessau, where he established an opera theatre and was made court kapellmeister (1775). Rust wrote many sonatas and unaccompanied works for violin, chamber music, dramatic works, cantatas, songs, and keyboard music.

Rustic Wedding (German: *Ländliche Hochzeit*) Symphony (Op. 26) by Goldmark. Composed: 1876. This work is in five movements, each one prefixed by a descriptive subtitle and outlining a different aspect of the festivities at a rural wedding.

Rustle of Spring (German: *Frühlingsrauschen*) Piece for piano by Sinding. Composed: 1896. It was published as the third of a collection of six character pieces for piano (Op. 32), although today only *Rustle of Spring* is still performed.

Ruy Blas Overture (Op. 95) and chorus (Op. 77 No. 3) by Mendelssohn. Composed: 1839. These works were composed to accompany a performance of Victor Hugo's play *Ruy Blas* in Leipzig in 1839.

Ruzicková, Zuzana (1928–) Czech harpsichordist. She first came to notice after winning a competition in Munich in 1956, since when she has made solo appearances and performed as a duo with Josef *Suk. She is married to the composer Viktor *Kalabis.

RV Abbreviation for Ryom Verzeichnis. It is used as a prefix to indicate the number of a piece in Peter Ryom's catalogue (1974) of Vivaldi's works. See also **P.; R.**

Rzewski, Frederik (1938–) US composer and pianist. He experimented in group improvisation and composition with Musica Elettronica Viva, for whom he devised *Spacecraft* (1967) and *Sound Pool* (1968). His later works, often overtly political include theatre pieces and much piano music. They include *Attica* (1972), *Coming Together* (1972), the piano variations *No Place to Go but Around* (1975) and *The People United Will Never Be Defeated* (1975), and *The Price of Oil* (1980).

S. Abbreviation for Schmieder. It is used to refer to Wolfgang Schmieder's catalogue (1950) of J. S. Bach's works, but the prefix commonly used to indicate the number of a piece in Schmieder's catalogue is BWV (abbreviation for Bach-Werke-Verzeichnis).

Sabata, Victor de (1892–1967) Italian conductor. He conducted at La Scala, Milan, in Rome, and also in the USA and the UK. He was a renowned interpreter of Verdi.

Sacchini, Antonio (1730–86) Italian composer. He studied in Naples, where he later held various posts and produced his intermezzo *Fra Donato* (1756). After working in Venice, London, and elsewhere he settled in Paris (1781), becoming a rival of Piccinni in writing comic and serious operas, the best of which was *Oedipe* (1787). Sacchini also wrote string quartets and other chamber works, symphonies, songs, and sacred music.

Sacher, Paul (1906–) Swiss conductor. In 1926 he founded the Basle Chamber Orchestra, for which he commissioned a large number of works by such composers as Richard Strauss, Bartók, Honegger, Hindemith, and Martinu.

sackbut see **trombone**.

Sacred Service see **Avodath Hakodesh**.

Sacre du printemps, Le see **Rite of Spring, The**.

Sadie, Stanley (1930–) British musicologist, editor, and critic. After teaching at the Trinity College of Music (1957–65), he became music critic of *The Times* (1964) and editor of *The Musical Times* (1967). In 1970 he became editor of *The New Grove Dictionary of Music and Musicians*.

Sadko Opera in seven scenes by Rimsky-Korsakov with text by the composer and Bielsky. First performance: Moscow, 1898. The opera stems from one of the composer's tone poems of the same name (1867). Set in 10th-century Novgorod and at the bottom of the sea, it retells the exotic legend of the bard Sadko (tenor).

Sadler's Wells A theatre in Rosebery Avenue, London. It stands on land that belonged to a Mr Sadler, who in 1683 discovered a well of water with alleged medicinal properties. He built a music house there to entertain people who had come to take the water, and in 1765 it became known as Sadler's Wells Theatre. It had a chequered history and for a while was derelict, until in the late 1920s Lilian Baylis reopened it as an Old Vic for north London. At first opera and ballet, performed by the Vic-Wells Opera, alternated with Shakespeare, but in 1935 the drama company went to the Old Vic and the opera and ballet companies became Sadler's Wells Opera (renamed *English National Opera in 1974) and Sadler's Wells Ballet (renamed Royal Ballet in 1956; see **Covent Garden**). The theatre is often used for opera and ballet, particularly by visiting companies.

Saga-Drøm Tone poem (Op. 39) by Nielsen. Composed: 1907–08. This work is based upon the Icelandic saga *The Dream of Gunnar*, which relates how Gunnar of Hlidarende dreams during his journey to Norway.

St Anne Fugue Fugue for organ in E♭ major by Bach. Published: 1739. This fugue appears at the end of the third part of the *Clavierübung and the opening notes of its subject bear a coincidental similarity to the melody of Croft to which the hymn 'O God our Help in Ages Past' is normally sung. This tune is known in England as 'St Anne,' hence the nickname of Bach's fugue.

St Anthony Variations Set of variations for orchestra (Op. 56a) by Brahms. Composed: 1873. The theme of these variations, which was taken by Brahms from a work for wind band by Haydn, is the so-called *St Anthony Chorale*, on which Haydn himself also wrote variations. Known also as *Variations on a Theme of Haydn* and called this by the composer, the work also exists in an arrangement for two pianos (Op. 56b).

St John Passion (German: *Johannes-Passion*) Musical setting of the passion story for solo voices, choir, and orchestra (BWV 245) by J. S. Bach. First performance: 1723. The text is taken mainly from the account given in St John's Gospel, but Bach enlarged the story by including some episodes found only in other gospels. An Evangelist (tenor) narrates the events and other solo voices represent Jesus and Simon Peter. The work was composed as a trial piece when Bach applied for the post of cantor of St Thomas's Church, Leipzig – a post he eventually obtained.

St John's Night on the Bare Mountain Work for orchestra by Mussorgsky. Composed: 1860–66. Mussorgsky originally composed this work as a tone poem based upon a passage in *St John's Eve*, a play by Gogol about a witches' sabbath, but in 1872 added parts for choir, incorporating it into his uncompleted opera *Mlada*. In 1875 Mussorgsky completely revised the work for use as the introduction to the third act of his opera *Sorochintsy Fair*: an orchestral arrangement of this version by Rimsky-Korsakov, usually called *Night on the Bare Mountain*, is the form in which the work is best known.

St Ludmilla Oratorio for solo voices, choir, and orchestra (Op. 71) by Dvořák to a text by Vrchlický. Composed: 1885. St Ludmilla was an early Christian missionary, whose life is outlined in this work; although the original text was in Czech, the first performance (at Leeds) used an English translation.

St Matthew Passion (German: *Matthaus-Passion*) Musical setting of the passion story for solo voices, choir, and orchestra (BWV 244) by Bach. First performance: 1729. The text is taken mainly from the account given in St Matthew's Gospel, but Bach also uses nonbiblical material by interspersing settings of verses by Picander. As in the St John Passion, the events are narrated by the Evangelist (tenor), with other solo voices representing the main characters.

St Paul (German: *Paulus*) Oratorio for solo voices, choir, and orchestra by Mendelssohn to a text by Schubring based on the Bible. First performance: 1836. This work tells the story of the Apostle Paul and was composed after Mendelssohn had spent a long period studying the oratorios of Handel. The chorale melody 'wachet auf, uns ruft die Stimme' features prominently in this oratorio.

St Paul's Suite Suite for string orchestra by Holst. Composed: 1913. This work is named after St Paul's Girls' School in London, where the composer was director of music. In the fourth and final movement Holst uses the English folk tunes 'Dargason' and 'Greensleeves.'

Saint-Saëns, (Charles) Camille (1835–1921) French composer, conductor, pianist, and organist. A child prodigy, he began to compose at the age of five. He studied at the Paris Conservatoire, where he was taught by Halévy and was also a pupil of Gounod. His first symphony was performed in 1855. In 1857 he was appointed organist at the Madeleine, Paris, where he remained for 20 years, and in 1861 became piano professor at the Ecole Niedermeyer, where he numbered Messager and Fauré among his pupils. He cofounded Société Nationale de Musique in 1871. A frequent performer in Britain, Saint-Saëns also made extensive tours of Europe, the USA, South America, and the Far East.

Saint-Saëns was a prolific composer and the first Frenchman to make use of the form of the tone poem, examples of which include *Le *Rouet d'Omphale* (*Omphale's Spinning Wheel*, 1871), *Phaëton* (1873), **Danse macabre* (1874), and *The Youth of Hercules* (1877). He wrote 12 operas, including **Samson and Delilah* was first performed in Weimar, 1877, after being rejected by Paris because of its biblical theme) and *Henry the Eighth* (1883); 5 symphonies (the third, 1886, was dedicated to Liszt); 5 piano concertos; 3 violin concertos; 2 cello concertos; chamber music; church music; and choral music. The popular **Carnival of the Animals* (1886) was not performed during his lifetime but has since been widely played by youth orchestras. Saint-Saëns also wrote several books of music criticisms and essays, as well as a number of plays.

salicet (*or* **salicional**) A soft-toned organ *stop with a reedy sound (in the UK) or a string sound (in the USA).

Salieri, Antonio (1750–1825) Italian composer and teacher. A pupil of Gassman (1766), he became court composer and conductor of the Italian opera in Vienna (1774) and court kapellmeister there (1788). He was president of the Tonkünstler Society, teacher of Beethoven, Schubert, and Liszt, and a friend of Gluck. Although he is known to have intrigued against Mozart, the story that he poisoned him is probably false. In addition to his operas, which include *Tarare* (1787), Salieri wrote sinfonias, concertos, chamber music, and sacred works, including the *Requiem* (1804).

Sallinen, Aulis (1935–) Finnish composer, a pupil of Kokkonen. From an early expressionist period he progressed to an economical open-textured style, using simple materials and, occasionally, serial procedures. His works include four string quartets, three symphonies, a violin concerto (1968), a cello concerto (1976), and the operas *The Horseman* (1974) and *The Red Line* (1978).

salmo Psalm. [Italian]

Salome Opera in one act by Richard Strauss based on the play by Oscar Wilde, translated into German by Hedwig Lachmann. First performance: Royal Opera, Dresden, 1905. Set in Galilee about 30 AD, in the palace of Herod (tenor), it tells how Salome (soprano), daughter of Herodias (mezzo-soprano), demands the head of John the Baptist (baritone), imprisoned in the cistern below, as payment for her *Dance of the Seven Veils*.

Salomon, Johann Peter (1745–1815) German composer, violinist, and impresario. After serving as musical director to Prince Heinrich of Prussia (1764–80) he settled in London (1781). Salomon was a founder member and leader of the Philharmonic Society (1813), promoting many concerts, including the visits of Haydn, who dedicated

Robert Tear and Maria Ewing in Salome

several works to him (see **Salomon Symphonies**). He also wrote operas, symphonies, canzonets, and chamber works.

Salomon Symphonies Set of 12 symphonies (Nos. 93–104) by Haydn. Composed: 1791–95. Named after the impresario Johann *Salomon, who commissioned the works, these symphonies were composed during Haydn's two visits to London in 1791–92 and 1794–95. The set includes the *Clock, *Drum-Roll, *London, *Miracle, and *Surprise symphonies.

Salón México, El Orchestral work by Copland. First performance: 1937. The inspiration for this work came during a visit to Mexico in 1932 and the composer quotes traditional Mexican melodies to evoke the atmosphere of a Mexican dance hall.

saltando (*or* **saltato**) A bowing technique that is a form of very rapid detached bowing in which the bow bounces very lightly off the string in one place near the middle of the bow. French: **sautillé**. [Italian, leaping]

saltarello A traditional Italian dance that involves jumps (*salti*). Resembling the *tarantella, it is usually in compound duple time.

Salzburg Festival An annual festival founded in 1877 in Salzburg, Austria, the town where Mozart was born. It presents operas, concerts, and recitals, chiefly of the works of Mozart and Richard Strauss but also including some new music; it uses the Felsenreitschule, the Mozarteum, the Kleines Festspielhaus, and the fine Festspielhaus (opened in 1960). Many guest orchestras have appeared at the festival and its conductors have included Krauss, Strauss, Walter, Toscanini, Furtwängler, Karajan, and Böhm.

Salzedo, Carlos (1885–1961) French-born US composer and harpist. Salzedo studied at the Paris Conservatoire before moving to the USA in 1909. His many compositions for the harp demonstrated the instrument's potential in contemporary music. Salzedo's output includes concertos, solos, duets, chamber music, and songs with harp.

Salzedo, Leonard (1921–) British composer, a pupil of Howells. Salzedo is principally known as a composer of ballet music, his scores including *The Fugitive* (1944) and *Witch Boy* (1956). His other works include orchestral and chamber compositions.

Salzman, Eric (1933–) US composer and writer, a pupil of Luening, Ussachevsky, Sessions, Babbitt, Petrassi, and Stockhausen. In 1970 he founded the ensemble Quog. Salzman has made much use of electronic music and shown a particular interest in multimedia theatrical works and environmental music. His works include *Verses and Cantos* (1967), *Larynx Music* (1968), *The Nude Paper Sermon* (1968–69), *The Conjurer* (1975), the spectacle *Noah* (1978), and the series of improvisatory pieces *The Electric Ear*.

samisen (*or* **shamisen**) **1.** A three-stringed Japanese unfretted *lute with a flat back and a skin belly. It is played with a wide axehead-shaped bone plectrum. It evolved from the Persian *sitar and is known in China as **san hsien**. [Both *sitar* and *san hsien* mean 'three strings'; the Japanese word is a corruption of the Chinese] **2.** A hollow bronze vessel struck with a drumstick that is used in Puccini's *Madame Butterfly*.

Sammartini, Giuseppe (1695–1750) Italian composer and oboist. He was oboist in the orchestra of the Teatro Regio Ducal, Milan (1720), and played in London for Handel and Bononcini (from 1728), serving also as music master to the Prince of Wales' family (1736). His works include concertos, cantatas, arias, and chamber music. His brother **Giovanni Battista Sammartini** (*c*.1700–75) was a composer and teacher of Gluck. He worked mainly in Milan, where he became maestro di cappella of S Ambrogio (1728) and one of the founders of the Philharmonic Society (1758). Composer of the earliest known symphonies, he also wrote some of the earliest string quartets, quintets, and other chamber works, concertos, three operas, and masses and other sacred works.

Sammons, Albert (1886–1957) British violinist. Although he was self-taught Sammons achieved widespread fame as a soloist and also led several major orchestras. In 1907 he founded the London String Quartet.

Samson Oratorio for solo voices, choir, and orchestra by Handel to a text by Hamilton based upon poems by Milton. First performance: 1743. It relates the biblical story of Samson, who loses his great strength when his long hair, the source of his might, is cut off by the treacherous Delilah.

Samson and Delilah (French: *Samson et Dalila*) Opera by Saint-Saëns with libretto by Ferdinand Lemaire. First performance (in German): Court Theatre, Weimar, 1877. It retells the biblical story of the seduction of Samson (tenor) by Delilah (mezzo-soprano) and his eventual destruction of the temple at Gaza.

Sancta civitas (*The Holy City*) Oratorio for baritone and tenor soloists, boys' choir, choir, and orchestra by Vaughan Williams to a text based on the Bible. First performance: 1926. The subject of this work is the fate of man after death, the words being selected mainly from the Book of Revelation.

Sándor, György (1912–) Hungarian-born US pianist. He studied at the Budapest conservatory with Bartók and Kodály, settling in the USA in 1939. Sándor is particularly noted as a performer of Bartók and gave the first performance of his third piano concerto.

san hsien see **samisen**.

santir see **dulcimer**.

Sanz, Gaspar (mid-17th–early-18th century) Spanish composer, guitarist, and priest. A theology graduate from Salamanca, he studied music in Rome under Orazio Benevoli and others. He published a guitar treatise and pieces for instructional purposes.

sarabande A 16th-century Spanish dance, probably of earlier eastern origin. A slow and stately dance in 3/2 time, it became popular throughout Europe in the 17th and 18th centuries. The classical *suite often contained a sarabande as one of its four movements (with allemande, courante, and gigue).

sārangī The popular *fiddle of north Indian folk and classical music. The instrument is carved from a single block of wood and is found in varying sizes and proportions. It is held vertically and the playing strings are stopped by the upper sides of the left-hand fingers. There is usually also a set of *sympathetic strings. See also **Indian music**.

Sarasate (y Navascues), Pablo (Martín Melitón) (1844–1908) Spanish violinist and composer. One of the foremost virtuosos of his day, Sarasate toured Europe and the USA extensively. Saint-Saëns, Lalo, Joachim, Dvořák, Bruch, and Wieniawski dedicated works to him

and Sarasate himself also composed many display pieces, such as *Zigeunerweisen* (1878).

sardana A Catalonian dance, revived in the 19th century and performed to a pipe-and-drum accompaniment.

Sargent, Sir (Harold) Malcolm (Watts) (1895–1967) British conductor. Originally an organist, Sargent conducted the Royal Choral Society (from 1928), the Hallé Orchestra (1939–42), and the Liverpool Philharmonic (1942–47). He also conducted the BBC Symphony Orchestra (1950–57) and many Promenade Concerts.

Sárka see **Má Vlast**.

sarod An Indian short *lute. It usually has four strings and a variable number of drone strings. See also **Indian music**.

sarrusophones A range of eight brass double-reed instruments made by the Frenchman Sarrus in 1856. Sued by Adolphe Sax for infringement of his *saxophone patent, Sarrus won his case in court but was denied a fair trial for his instruments by the French army bands. Only the double bass sarrusophone has had any success; this has been featured in some French orchestral music, although the parts are now usually played by a double bassoon.

Sarti, Giuseppe (1729–1802) Italian composer. He was organist of Faenza Cathedral (1748–52), court kapellmeister and director of Italian opera in Copenhagen (1755, 1768–75), and maestro di cappella of Milan Cathedral (1779). As court chapel director in St Petersburg (1784), he wrote a number of operas, including *The Early Reign of Oleg* (1790), and established Russian pitch (A = 436 hertz). He also wrote sacred works, chamber music, and treatises.

Sarum Use The form of liturgy, not unlike the Roman Missal, that was used at Salisbury Cathedral and throughout much of medieval England until it was superseded by the First Prayer Book of Edward VI in 1549.

Satie, Erik (Alfred Erik Leslie S.; 1866–1925) French composer. Satie's commitment to conventional musical education was sporadic: he had a reputation for laziness during his year at the Paris Conservatoire and he was 39 before enrolling at the Schola Cantorum to study fugue and counterpoint with d'Indy and Roussel (1905–08). In the 1890s he became the composer to the Rosicrucian Society in Paris; work as a café and theatre pianist followed. Satie's association with Cocteau, dating from 1915, brought success, frequent performances of his music, and collaboration with Diaghilev and Picasso in the ballet *Parade* (1917).

Satie's music is notable for its harmonic and textural clarity and melodic poise, features highly influential in Paris at the beginning of the 20th century (see **Six, Les**). His wit often verges on sarcasm in its parody of styles: his works often have bizarre titles, running commentaries sometimes appearing in the printed music. Satie is of particular importance as an influence to many generations of composers, from Debussy and Ravel to the avant-garde of the 1950s. His output includes the ballets *Parade (1917) and *Relâche* (1924); the symphonic drama *Socrate (1918), for voices and orchestra; many piano works, including the famous *Trois Gymnopédies* (1888); and songs.

Satz 1. A movement of a piece. **2.** A musical setting. **3.** A theme, hence **Hauptsatz**, principal theme. [German, setting]

Saudades do Brasil Two suites for piano by Milhaud. Composed: 1921–22. 'Saudades' is a Portuguese word meaning 'reminiscences' and in these pieces Milhaud recalls a visit to Rio de Janeiro.

Sauguet, Henri (Jean Pierre Poupard; 1901–) French composer, a pupil of Koechlin. Sauguet's association with Satie led to the formation of the school at Arcueil in 1923. His works, outwardly simple in style, include the ballet *La Chatte* (1927) and other stage works, orchestral music (including four symphonies), and songs.

Saul Oratorio for solo voices, choir, and orchestra by Handel to a text by Jennens based on the Bible. First performance: 1739. This oratorio tells of Saul's jealousy of David and his plotting against him, as related in the Books of Samuel. The well-known *Dead March* occurs in this work and is often performed separately.

Saul and David Opera in four acts by Carl Nielsen with libretto by E. Christiansen. First performance: Royal Theatre, Copenhagen, 1902. A dramatic retelling of the biblical tale, it contrasts the tragic figure of Saul (baritone) with the adaptable character of David (tenor).

Sauret, Emile (1852–1920) French violinist and composer. He is said to have studied with Bériot and made his debut before he was ten. One of the outstanding violinists of his day, he played in the USA (from 1872), Scandinavia, and the European capitals. He taught in Berlin, in London at the Royal Academy of Music (1890–1903), at the Chicago Musical College (1903–06), and at Trinity College of Music, London. Sauret's compositions are almost all for the violin and he also wrote some teaching works.

sausage bassoon see **racket**.

sautillé see **saltando**.

Savile, Jeremy (fl. 1651–65) English composer of glees and ayres, teacher of singing and the viol. He is best remembered for the song 'Here's a Health unto His Majesty.'

Sāvitri Opera in one act by Holst, who arranged his text from the *Mahā Bhārata*. First performance: Wellington Hall, London, 1916. In this episode from the Hindu scriptures Sāvitri (mezzo-soprano) wrests her husband Satyavān (tenor) from the arms of Death (bass) by her devotion.

Savoy Operas The series of operettas, with music by Sullivan and texts by Gilbert, that were produced by Richard D'Oyly Carte at his newly built Savoy Theatre, London. These Gilbert and Sullivan operettas include *Iolanthe (1882), *Princess Ida (1884), The *Mikado (1885), *Ruddigore (1887), The *Yeoman of the Guard (1888), and The *Gondoliers (1889).

Sawallisch, Wolfgang (1923–) German conductor. He has conducted the Vienna Symphony Orchestra (1960–) and the Bavarian State Opera (1971–) and is a frequent conductor at Bayreuth.

Sax, Adolphe (Antoine-Joseph S.; 1814–1894) Belgian instrument maker. His inventions and improvements to musical instruments were numerous, his most famous creations being the *saxophone (1846) and the *saxhorn (1845). He had a monopoly on the sale of instruments to the French army, which caused bitterness among his rivals.

saxhorns A group of wind instruments of the brass family. Invented by Adolphe Sax in 1840, they consist of valved bugles and are similar to *flugelhorns. There is a set of seven instruments, the three lowest being treated as *tubas. The four higher *transposing instruments are: the **soprano saxhorn** in E♭ (which is almost identical to the E♭ *cornet); the **alto saxhorn** in B♭ (which resembles the B♭ cornet); the **tenor saxhorn** in E♭; and the **baritone saxhorn** in B♭. The tenor and baritone instruments, which are sometimes called **althorns**, are extensively used in brass bands.

saxophone A member of a family of woodwind single-reeded instruments invented by Adolphe Sax in the 1840s. Made with a metal body these instruments are a cross between the clarinet and the oboe, having a clarinet-type mouthpiece and a conical bore like the oboe. Originally the family comprised 14 instruments; the common ones in use today are the **alto saxophone**, which is a transposing instrument in E♭ with a range of two and a half octaves from D♭ below middle C, and the **tenor saxophone** in B♭, a fifth lower. Apart from their occasional use in the orchestra, these saxophones are regularly used in dance bands and military bands. Above the alto are the **sopranino saxophone** in E♭, which is occasionally used in military bands, and the **soprano** in B♭, sometimes used in jazz bands. Below the tenor are the **baritone** in E♭ and the **bass** in B♭, which are rarely used.

Scala, La see **La Scala**.

Scala di seta, La see **Silken Ladder, The**.

scale (of a pipe) see **organ**.

scales Sequences of notes of ascending or descending pitch. In one-part music, the relative pitches of the notes chosen to form a scale are unimportant. However, when two or more people sing or play together it is necessary to choose the notes of the scale so that *dissonance is avoided. Thus all polyphonic music, of whatever origin, uses scales with fixed *intervals.

The origins of the musical scale are obscure but are apparently based on the two most consonant intervals, the *octave and the *fifth. The octave, in which the higher note has twice the pitch of the lower note, is an interval well known to most peoples – indeed the Greeks appear to have used no other form of concord in their harmony. The fifth is also a consonant interval that has been known since ancient times (see **beats**).

A primitive scale might thus consist of FCF (C being the fifth of F). This scale does not, however, provide much scope for either melody or harmony and the obvious additions would be the fifth and octave of C, i.e. FCFGC. If this building of fifths is continued and the notes or their lower octaves are arranged in ascending order one arrives at the scale CDFGA. This is known as the **pentatonic scale**. If all the notes are raised by a *semitone, the scale is that produced by the black notes of the piano. The pentatonic scale is used in much Chinese and ancient Scottish music ('Auld Lang Syne,' for instance, can be played exclusively on the black notes of the piano).

If the sequence of fifths is continued for seven notes instead of five, the **diatonic scale** is produced: CDEFGAB.

Domenico Scarlatti

This scale was understood by Pythagoras both musically and mathematically. The **Pythagorean scale** is based on fifths in which the interval has a frequency ratio of exactly 3/2, i.e. the frequency of the higher note is 1.5 times that of the lower note. Thus the frequency of G is 3/2 times that of C, and the frequency of D is 3/2 times that of G. On this basis the frequency ratio between C and the D above it is $(3/2)^2 \div 2 = 9/8 = 1.125$. This interval, which Pythagoras called a *tone, occurs between C and D, D and E, F and G, G and A, and A and B. However, the intervals EF and BC come out smaller than 9/8: simple arithmetic shows them to be $256/243 = 1.0535$, which Pythagoras called a **hemitone** (for comparison, the interval of the modern equal-temperament semitone is 1.0595). The seven notes of the Pythagorean scale formed the basis of the Greek *modes, which were taken over by medieval music and lasted until the 17th century. Thereafter, only two of the modes were found to be satisfactory and most music since the 17th century has been based on these modes, now known as the *major and *minor scales. In instruments using equal-temperament tuning the semitones of the diatonic scale are all equal so that scales starting on different notes differ only in pitch (see **key**).

If the sequence of the diatonic scale is continued for 12 instead of 7 notes, it will be found that after 7 octaves the sequence repeats itself. Thus the 12 notes can be arranged in a circle like a clockface. These are the twelve notes of the **chromatic scale** and they form the basis of the 12 major and minor keys. See also **temperament; whole-tone scale**.

Scaramouche Suite for two pianos by Milhaud. First performance: 1937. The title refers to the Théâtre Scaramouche in Paris; some earlier incidental music that Milhaud had composed for a play first performed at the theatre was incorporated into this suite.

Scarlatti, (Giuseppe) Domenico (1685–1757) Italian composer, harpsichordist, and organist. Much influenced by his father (see below), by whom he was taught, Scarlatti's early works were mainly vocal: his first operas were produced in Naples, where he was court organist and composer. After a visit to Venice Scarlatti went to Rome, where he became maestro di cappella to the exiled Queen of Poland (1709–14) and maestro at St Peter's (1714–19). During this time he established a reputation as a gifted and artistic harpsichord virtuoso. In 1720 he went to Lisbon, where he worked at the court chapel, and after a brief visit to Italy (1728) left for Spain, where he spent the rest of his life attached to the Spanish court at Seville and later Madrid.

During the years in Spain, Scarlatti produced his best music – the one-movement harpsichord sonatas, which were inspired by Spanish popular music and everyday life. The first pieces were published in the *Essercizi per gravicembalo* (1738) and included the *Cat's Fugue*; later sonatas usually appeared in pairs. The variety and contrast

Plate 39: *Erik Satie, who was to have a considerable influence on the development of French music after World War I*

Plate 40: *Franz Schubert at the piano, with a group of young friends*

Plate 41: *A portrait of Robert Schumann, the German pianist and
composer, and his wife Clara, who gave her first public piano
recitals at the age of nine*

of sound and texture achieved by Scarlatti in his harpsichord pieces have been compared to that of Chopin and Liszt in their piano works. The 550 sonatas of Scarlatti have been catalogued by Ralph *Kirkpatrick. In addition to the sonatas and operas (of which he wrote about 12), Scarlatti composed cantatas and church music, including a *Stabat Mater*.

His father, **Alessandro Scarlatti** (1660–1725), was also a composer, active mainly in Rome and Naples. He was maestro di cappella to Queen Christina of Sweden in Rome (*c.*1680–84) and to the Viceroy of Naples (1684–1702), where he produced his first opera, *Il Pirro e Demetrio* (1694). He worked subsequently in Rome, Florence, and Naples. Alessandro Scarlatti was a great exponent of baroque opera in 18th-century Italy, writing over 100 operas. His other works include about 600 chamber cantatas, 200 masses, oratorios, sinfonias, chamber and keyboard works, and treatises.

scena Originally (in the mid-18th century) an extract from an opera used for concert performance. In the 19th century it developed into a concert work for solo voice in several movements (including recitatives and arias) with orchestral accompaniment. [Italian, scene]

Scenes from Childhood (German: *Kinderszenen*) Collection of character pieces for piano (Op. 15) by Schumann. Composed: 1838. Each of the 13 'scenes' has a title describing some feature of childhood life, such as 'The Wooden Horse' and 'Blind Man's Buff.' The seventh piece, 'Dreaming' ('Träumerei'), is often performed separately.

Scenes from Goethe's Faust see **Faust, Scenes from Goethe's.**

Schaeffer, Pierre (1910–) French composer and writer, who trained as a radio technician. In 1948 he pioneered the concept of musique concrète – taped music using pre-existing naturally produced sound as its raw material. In collaboration with Pierre Henry he produced the first major work in this medium, *Sympho pour un homme seul* (1950), and in 1951 they founded the Groupe de Musique Concrète studio. In 1953 Schaeffer produced the experimental opera *Orphée*. Since the late 1950s, he has devoted himself to theoretical and philosophical speculation.

Schafer, R. Murray (1933–) Canadian composer, a pupil of Weinzweig, Guemerov, and Fricker. In such works as *Son of Heldenleben* (1968) he makes much use of quotation; later works reflect the composer's interest in mixed media and ecology (Schafer initiated the World Soundscape Project to fight noise pollution). His works include *Loving/Toi* (1965), *Requiems for a Party Girl* (1972), *East* (1973), *North/White* (1973), *Waves* (1976), and *Apocalypsis* (1976) for 500 performers.

Schäffer, Boguslav (1929–) Polish composer, a pupil of Nono. In Poland he pioneered serialism and subsequently timbre composition, graphic notation, spatial experiments, electronic music, the use of jazz, and political theatre pieces. His works include *Music for Strings* (1953), *Tertium Datur* (1958), *Collage and Form* (1963), *Quartet* (1966), *Dreams of Schäffer* (1972), and *Missa Elettronica* (1976).

Scharwenka, (Franz) Xaver (1850–1924) German pianist, composer, conductor, and teacher, born in Poland. He studied with Kullak at the Berlin Academy of Music, where he later taught (1870–73). He toured as a concert pianist, and from about 1880 was also active as a conductor in Berlin, where in 1881 he opened his own conservatory. Scharwenka opened a new music school in Berlin in 1914. Meanwhile he had been active in the USA, opening a branch of his conservatory in New York in 1891. Scharwenka was one of the leading pianists of his time. He composed an opera, a symphony, four piano concertos (of which No. 1 in B♭ minor is his best known), chamber music, and piano pieces (including the 'Polish Dances'). His brother, (**Ludwig**) **Philipp Scharwenka** (1847–1917), was also a composer and teacher.

Schat, Peter (1935–) Dutch composer, a pupil of Seiber and Boulez. In his works Schat uses an advanced serial technique: some of his compositions also involve improvisation. His works include the opera *Labyrinth* (1961–62) and a number of compositions based on it, chamber music, and vocal works.

Schauspieldirektor, Der (*The Impresario*) Comic opera in one act by Mozart with libretto by Gottlieb Stephanie (junior). First performance: Schönbrunn Palace, Vienna, 1786. It is a satire on the relationship between an impresario and female singers.

Scheherazade see **Sheherazade.**

Scheidemann, Heinrich (*c.*1595–1663) German composer, organist, and teacher. He studied under Sweelinck and was organist at St Catherine's Church in Hamburg by 1629, a post he held until he died of the plague. Scheidemann was a leading composer of the north German school of organists: his finest extant works are his chorale arrangements, in which he exploits the full capacity of the north German organ. Also notable are his Magnificat settings, chorale fantasias, and the toccata in G.

Scheidt, Samuel (1587–1654) German composer and organist. He studied with Sweelinck and by 1609 was court organist at Halle, where Michael Praetorius was kapellmeister, a post Scheidt himself obtained in about 1619. For a brief period he was director of music for the city of Halle and in 1638 again took up the position of kapellmeister at court. He was a prolific composer, writing madrigals, motets, and settings of German chorales as well as organ music, notably his monumental *Tabulatura nova* (1624). A distinguished teacher, his most famous pupil was Adam Krieger.

Schein, Johann Herman (1586–1630) German composer. As a boy he sang in the court chapel in Dresden, later studying at the University of Leipzig and in Naumberg. In 1615 he became kapellmeister at Weimar and in 1616 took up the post of cantor at St Thomas's School in Leipzig, where he remained until his death. He composed mainly vocal music, transferring an Italian style into a Lutheran context. His *Opella nova* (1618) displays the influence of Viadana, *Israels Brünlein* (1623) contains expressive settings of Old Testament texts, and his *Cantional* (1627) is an important collection of Lutheran hymns with a figured bass part. He also composed secular vocal music, including the first published collection of German continuo madrigals (1624).

Schelomo (*or* **Shelomo**) Rhapsody for cello and orchestra by Bloch. Composed: 1915. Like much of Bloch's music, this work is inspired by a Jewish subject, Schelomo being the Hebrew name for Solomon.

Schemelli Hymnbook A book of hymns, the *Musicalisches Gesangbuch* ('Musical Songbook'), published in 1736 by Georg Christian Schemelli. It contains 954 hymns, 69 of which have tunes with figured bass that Bach is said to have composed or improved. Bach wrote chorale preludes on some of them.

scherzando Joking; playful: a direction used to indicate a light-hearted manner of performance. [Italian]

Scherzi, Gli see **Russian Quartets**.

scherzo 1. A light vocal or instrumental piece of the early 17th century, as in Monteverdi's *Scherzi musicali* (1607). **2.** A movement that evolved from the slower *minuet movement in quartets, sonatas, and symphonies during the late 18th century. In the typical **scherzo and trio** of the symphonies of Beethoven, Schubert, and Bruckner it has a fast tempo in 3/4 time with vigorously percussive rhythms and a sense of humour that can be both genial and menacing; it alternates with the more melodic lightly scored trio in the form ABABA. **3.** A single-movement piano piece. The scherzi composed by Brahms and Chopin express drama, intensity, and lyricism, as well as humour. [Italian, joke]

Schicksalslied see **Song of Destiny**.

Schikaneder, (Johann Josef) Emanuel (1751–1812) German singer, theatre manager, and librettist. He wrote the libretto for Mozart's *The Magic Flute* (1791), in which he himself performed as Papageno. He wrote some 50 plays and other libretti.

Schiller, (Johann Christoph) Friedrich von (1759–1805) German poet, dramatist, and historian whose works inspired many composers. Perhaps the best known of these is the ode *An die Freude*, set in the last movement of Beethoven's *Choral Symphony*. Of the many other works based on Schiller's writings examples are Rossini's *William Tell* (1829) and Verdi's *Luisa Miller* (1849), and *Don Carlos* (1867).

Schippers, Thomas (1930–77) US conductor. He was conductor of the Cincinnati Symphony Orchestra (1970–77).

Schlaginstrumente Percussion instruments. [German, beating instruments]

Schlagobers Ballet in two acts with music and libretto by Richard Strauss and choreography by Kröller. First performance: Vienna State Opera, 1924. A small boy has overeaten at his Confirmation party and has wild dreams (*Schlagobers* is Viennese dialect for 'whipped cream').

schleppend Dragging. Hence **nicht schleppend**, not dragging, i.e. keeping to the correct speed. [German]

Schlick, Arnolt (*c.*1460–*c.*1521) Blind German organist, lutenist, and composer. He was organist at the coronation of the Emperor Maximilian I (1486) and a member of the Heidelberg court chapel by 1511. His output includes a treatise on organ building (1511), music for organ based on chant melodies, music for lute, and music for the coronation of Charles V at Aachen (1520).

Schluss End; conclusion. [German]

Schlüssel Clef. [German, literally doorkey]

Schmelzer, Johann Heinrich (*c.*1623–80) Austrian composer and violinist. Little is known about his early life, but in 1649 he was appointed violinist in the court orchestra in Vienna. In 1671 he became assistant kapellmeister at the imperial court and kapellmeister a year before his death of the plague. His ballet music, written for court, and his *Sonatae unarum fidium* (1664) for violin and continuo are his most important works.

Schmidt, Franz (1874–1939) Austrian composer, a pupil of Bruckner. A distinguished teacher, Schmidt was director of the Vienna Hochschule für Musik (1927–31). His compositions, which are rooted in the Austrian symphonic tradition, include four symphonies, the opera *Notre Dame* (1902–04), chamber works, and organ music.

Schmidt-Isserstedt, Hans (1900–73) German conductor. He founded and directed the Hamburg Radio Symphony Orchestra (1945–71) and also conducted the Stockholm Philharmonic Orchestra (1955–64). He was a memorable interpreter of Mozart and Beethoven.

Schmieder, Wolfgang (1901–   ) German musical bibliographer and librarian. He was custodian of the Breitkopf & Härtel archives (1933–42). His *Bach Werke-Verzeichnis* (1950) is an extensive bibliography of J. S. Bach's manuscripts and sources (see **BWV; S.**).

Schmitt, Florent (1870–1958) French composer, a pupil of Massenet and Fauré. Schmitt won the Prix de Rome in 1900. Both romantic and impressionistic influences are apparent in Schmitt's style, particularly in the tone painting of his early works. His output includes *La Tragédie de Salomé* (1907) and other ballets, two symphonies, chamber music, piano pieces, and songs.

Schnabel, Artur (1882–1951) Austrian pianist and composer. A pupil of Leschetizky, he appeared frequently in solo recitals, as well as partnering artists such as Casals, Szigeti, and Primrose. Schnabel was particularly noted for his playing of Beethoven, Schubert, and Brahms. His compositions include orchestral and chamber works and piano pieces.

Schnebel, Dieter (1930–   ) German composer. In his works Schnebel has experimented with new choral techniques, variable form, and aleatoric music. His output includes *Nostalgia*, for conductor alone; *Drei Klang* (1977), for three simultaneously broadcast ensembles; and the symphonic improvisations *Thanatos-Eros* (1979).

schnell Fast. Hence **schneller**, faster. [German]

Schnittke, Alfred (1934–   ) Soviet composer. He has experimented with serial procedures and unusual instrumental textures, sometimes involving electronic music. His works include two symphonies, three violin concertos, a piano concerto (1960), *Music* (1964), *pianissimo* for orchestra (1969), *Sinfonia* (1972), the oratorio *Nagasaki* (1958), a requiem (1975), the multimedia work *Der gelbe Klang* (1973), *Concerto Grosso* (1977), and the *Hymnus* series of chamber works.

Schobert, Johann (*c*.1735–67) German composer and keyboard player. He is known to have been chamber harpsichordist to the Prince of Conti in Paris (*c*.1760). His development of the keyboard idiom greatly influenced Mozart's early piano sonatas and concertos. As well as keyboard music, he also wrote chamber works, concertos, sinfonias, and opéras comiques.

Schoeck, Othmar (1886–1957) Swiss composer. Schoeck studied in Leipzig with Reger (1907–08), by which time he had already composed a large number of songs. Returning to Switzerland, he was active as a conductor and pianist. Schoeck's song style builds on the romantic lieder tradition: in all his works melody is an important feature. Schoeck's output includes *Penthesilea* (1924–25) and other operas, orchestral music, and songs with both piano and chamber ensemble accompaniment.

Schoenberg, Arnold (1874–1951) Austrian composer. Schoenberg's early musical education was sporadic: financial circumstances forced him to work for a while as a bank clerk, but he later studied in Vienna with Zemlinsky. Schoenberg's earliest employment in music was as an arranger of operettas and popular songs. After a short period of teaching in Berlin Schoenberg returned to Vienna to teach and promote contemporary music. His pupils in Vienna included Berg, Webern, and Wellesz. His teaching continued until the rise of the Nazis forced him (as a Jew) to emigrate to the USA in 1933. He settled in Hollywood, where he held teaching posts at the University of California.

Schoenberg's early music shows the influences of both Brahms and Wagner in its pervasive elaboration of motifs and chromatic harmony. In his subsequent works the idiom of chromatic counterpoint is developed to such an extent that tonality becomes obscured for long stretches; this occurs strikingly in the *Chamber Symphony* (1906), which also uses chords based on fourths. These developments led Schoenberg to abandon tonality during the second decade of the 20th century, the intensity of emotion projected into the works written in this period reflecting the contemporary

Arnold Schoenberg

expressionist movement in the arts. In 1924 Schoenberg perfected a new method of governing tonal relationships in composition, known as *twelve-note composition. Schoenberg's twelve-note works owe more to classical conventions of rhythm, texture, and phrasing than to the harsh tensions of the expressionist idiom. Schoenberg's works include the monodrama *Erwartung* (1909) for soprano and orchestra; the operas *Die Gluckliche Hand* (1910–13), *Von Heute auf Morgen* (1930), and the unfinished *Moses und Aron* (1932–); orchestral works, including the tone poem *Pelleas und Melisande* (1903), *Variations* (1928), and concertos for violin (1936) and piano (1942); *Gurrelieder* (1901–11) for chorus, soloists, and orchestra; *Ode to Napoleon* (1942); chamber music, including four string quartets and the string sextet *Verklärte Nacht* (1899); vocal works, including *Pierrot lunaire* (1912), a cycle of settings for speech song and instruments; and music for piano.

Schönbach, Dieter (1931–) German composer. Schönbach's music often includes visual elements, such as film and dance. His large output includes many such multimedia works, in addition to more conventionally conceived orchestral and chamber works.

Schöne Melusine, Die Concert overture (Op. 32) by Mendelssohn. Composed: 1833. Mendelssohn was inspired to write this overture after attending a performance in Berlin of Conradin Kreutzer's opera *Melusina* (libretto by Grillparzer). His overture is based on the same subject, Melusine being a beautiful woman who is bewitched and turns into a water nymph.

Schöne Müllerin, Die (*The Fair Maid of the Mill*) Song cycle by Schubert to poems by Wilhelm Müller. Composed: 1823. The 20 poems are taken from Müller's collection *Gedichte aus den hinterlassenen Papieren eines reisenden Waldhornisten* (*Poems from the Posthumous Papers of a Travelling Horn Player*) and the sequence outlines the story of a young man's courtship of a miller's beautiful daughter. The man's advances are eventually spurned and the sequel to the story is given in Schubert's song cycle *Die *Winterreise*.

School for Fathers (Italian: *I Quattro rusteghi*, literally *The Four Boors*) Opera in four acts by Wolf-Ferrari with libretto by Pizzolato based on Goldoni's play. First performance (a German version by Teibler): Munich, 1906. In this Venetian comedy (Goldoni wrote it in Venetian dialect) four domestic tyrants are outwitted by their wives and daughters.

Schoolmaster, The Symphony No. 55 in E♭ major by Haydn. Composed: 1774. The slow movement is very grave and serious in character, suggesting the use of the nickname.

Schöpfung, Die see **Creation, The.**

Schottische A ballroom dance in 2/4 time, similar to but slower than a polka, that was popular in the 19th century. It has no known connection with Scotland and is not the same as an *écossaise. [German, Scottish]

Schrammel quartet A type of Viennese instrumental combination for performing light music. In 1878 Josef and Johann Schrammel, both violinists, formed a trio with a guitarist, Anton Strohmayer. About 1886 they joined forces with a clarinetist, Georg Dänzer (later replaced by an accordionist), and the original Schrammel Quartet was established. They popularized a distinctive repertory of old Viennese song tunes and light music that became known as **Schrammelmusik**. Schrammel quartets continue to flourish.

Schrecker, Franz (1878–1934) Austrian composer. Schrecker directed the Berlin Hochschule für Musik (1920–32): his pupils included Křenek and Hába. Schrecker's works, which are characteristic of early 20th-century expressionism, include the opera *Der ferne Klang* (1901–10); orchestral works, including a chamber symphony (1916); and songs.

Schreier, Peter (1935–) German tenor and conductor. He studied with Polster in Leipzig and with Winkler in Dresden, where he made his debut as the First Prisoner in Beethoven's *Fidelio* (1961). He is best remembered as a Mozart interpreter but also has an extensive concert repertory.

Schubert, Franz (Peter) (1797–1828) Austrian composer. The son of a schoolmaster, Schubert was born in a suburb of Vienna and acquired his early musical training from his father and elder brother, later taking his place as the viola player in the family string quartet. A scholarship to the imperial court chapel choristers' school brought him to the notice of several Viennese music teachers, including Salieri, who gave him private lessons after his voice had broken and he had left the school. Schubert was then sent by his father to a teachers' training college and he joined his father's school an assistant master in 1814. He remained a reluctant teacher for four years, during which time his friends the poet Johann Meyrhofer and the baritone Michael Vogl attempted to persuade him to give up teaching. This he finally did, remaining in Vienna (apart from two summer visits to the Esterházy family as domestic musician) and eking out a meagre and somewhat unstable living. In 1822 he contracted syphilis and he died of typhoid in 1828.

Schubert gave only one public concert in his life, in 1828, which was sufficiently successful to enable him to buy a piano of his own. He failed to achieve any success with his nine operas. Yet he worked ceaselessly at his compositions during his short life and left a large corpus of work that has established him as one of the most important Austrian composers of the 19th century. The inventor of the German *lied (and its most prolific exponent), he also composed operas (including *Alfonso and Estrella, 1821–22), *Rosamunde, Princess of Cyprus (1823), 9 symphonies, 7 masses, 22 string quartets, and much other chamber music, including the *Trout Quintet (1819) and the string quintet in C major (1827). His nine symphonies include the *Tragic Symphony (1816), the *Unfinished Symphony (1822), and the *Great C Major Symphony (1828). Of more than 500 songs, many have achieved lasting fame, including the song cycles Die *Schöne Müllerin (1823), Die *Winterreise (1827), and *Schwanengesang (1828).

Schubert's piano works include 21 sonatas, the *Wanderer Fantasy (1822), the fantasy in F minor for piano duet (his first work, completed in 1812), the *Grand Duo (1824), and various moments musicaux (see **Moments musicals**), waltzes, impromptus, and marches.

Schulhoff, Erwin (1894–1942) Czech composer, a pupil of Reger. Schulhoff was active in promoting modern music after World War I; he was a victim of the Nazis after their invasion of Czechoslovakia (1939) and died in a concentration camp. Schulhoff's own works, which show many influences, include six symphonies, chamber works, and piano music.

Schuller, Gunther (1925–) US composer, horn player, and conductor. In the 1950s he played with Miles Davis and coined the term *third stream to denote a style incorporcing elements of jazz improvisation in a classical structure. He frequently worked with the Modern Jazz Quartet. His works include 12 by 11 (1955), the jazz ballet Variants (1961), the opera The Visitation (1966), a double-bass concerto (1968), and a violin concerto (1976).

Schuman, William (1910–) US composer and music administrator, a pupil of Roy Harris. His works, in a romantically rhapsodic style, reflect Schuman's interest in early American music and American themes. They include ten symphonies, concertos, the cantata A Free Song (1943), the ballet Undertow (1945), the opera Mighty Casey (1953), the New England Triptych (1956), and the Concerto on Old English Rounds (1976).

Schumann, Elisabeth (1885–1952) German soprano. She studied with Hänsich in Dresden, Dietrich in Berlin, and Schadow in Hamburg, making her first stage appearance at the Hamburg State Theatre as the Shepherd in Wagner's Tannhäuser (1909). After a period with the Hamburg and Vienna operas she toured the USA (1921) and England (1924), singing superbly in Strauss and Mozart. She also sang and recorded lieder. She settled in the USA in 1938, becoming an American citizen and teaching in her later years.

Schumann, Robert (Alexander) (1810–56) German pianist and composer. The son of a bookseller and

Elisabeth Schumann

publisher, Schumann learnt to play the piano as a young boy, showing considerable talent; he also had considerable literary ability. Following his father's death (1826) he was sent to Leipzig to study law (1828) but devoted more of his time to the study of music. He was taught the piano (1830–32) by Friedrich Wieck but his hopes of becoming a piano virtuoso were dashed when he injured a finger on his right hand. Instead he turned to composition. A love affair with a pupil of Wieck's, Ernestine von Fricken, inspired the early piano works Etudes symphoniques (Symphonic Studies, 1834) and Carnaval (1834–35; see **Carnival**). His engagement to Ernestine was broken off after he fell in love with Wieck's 16-year-old daughter Clara. During the year of his marriage (1840) to Clara, he composed many of his much acclaimed songs, such as Myrthen (Myrtle), the two Liederkreise (song cycles), *Dichterliebe (Poet's Love), and *Frauenliebe und Leben (Women's Love and Life). He suffered a mental breakdown in 1844, after which the Schumanns settled in Dresden. Schumann was appointed municipal director of music at Düsseldorf in 1850 but, unsuited to this office, he was forced to resign in 1854. Increasing mental illness in these years led to his attempted suicide by drowning and he was sent to an asylum in 1854, where he died two years later.

Schumann is known particularly for the songs and for his piano compositions; these include the *Abegg Variations (1830), *Papillons (1829–31), *Paganini Studies (1832–33), *Davidsbündler Tänze (1837), *Kreisleriana (1838), *Scenes from Childhood (1838), and the fantasy in C major (1836). Among his orchestral works are four symphonies: No. 1, the *Spring Symphony (1941), No. 2 (1846), No. 3, the Rhenish Symphony (1850), and No. 4 (1941, rewritten 1851); the overture to Byron's *Manfred (1848–49); the piano concerto in A minor (1841–45); and the cello concerto in A minor (1850). He also composed some chamber music, including three string quartets and three violin sonatas, the opera Genoveva (1847–50), and several choral works, including *Paradise and the Peri (1843) and Scenes from Goethe's *Faust (1844–53). He was a founder of the music journal Die Neue Zeitschcrift für Musik (1834), which he edited (1834–44).

His wife **Clara Schumann** (1819–96), the daughter of Schumann's piano tutor Friedrich Wieck (who had violently opposed the marriage), was a brilliant pianist; her first recitals in public were given at the age of nine. She edited Schumann's compositions and was highly regarded as a teacher.

Schurmann, Gerard (1928–) Dutch composer, a pupil of Rawsthorne. His music, while not quite serial, shows a high degree of large-scale formal integration with much use of repetition. His works include Variants (1970), a piano concerto (1973), a violin concerto (1978), the song cycle Chuench I (1966), the cantata Double Heart (1977), and the 'opera-cantata' Piers Plowman (1980).

Schütz, Heinrich (1585–1672) German composer. After studying law, he was sent in 1609 by his patron, Landgrave Moritz of Hessen-Kassel, to study music in Venice under Giovanni Gabrieli. In 1611 he published a collection of madrigals in Venice and in 1613 returned to Germany as second organist to the Landgrave in Kassel. From 1615 Schütz was active in the Dresden court of the Elector of Saxony, becoming kapellmeister in 1617. His Dafne, the first German opera, was performed in 1627 and in the following year (1628–29) he revisited Venice, coming into contact with Monteverdi. Apart from three visits to Denmark (1633–1645), he spent the rest of his life as kapellmeister in Dresden, though he retired from full-time work in 1657.

Schütz is regarded as the greatest 17th-century German composer: his importance lies in his combination of the Italian style with the German tradition. Surprisingly, he made little use of chorale melodies in his works. He seems to have written no instrumental music and his ballets and stage works have not survived. His extant works, all sacred, include Psalmen Davids (1619, 1628, 1661), magnificent Venetian-style psalms for multiple choirs; Resurrection History (1623); Cantiones sacrae (1625), motets, and sacred

Elisabeth Schwarzkopf as Marschallin in Der Rosenkavalier

symphonies (1629, 1647, 1650); the funeral pieces Musicalische Exequien (1636); Geistliche Concerte (1636, 1639); Geistliche Chor-Music (1648); Geistliche Gesänge (1657); Christmas History (1664); Die sieben Wortte... Jesu Christi; and settings of the Matthew, Luke, and John Passions for unaccompanied voices.

Schwanengesang (*Swan Song*) Song cycle by Schubert to poems by Rellstab, Heine, and Seidl. Composed: 1828. Although categorized as a song cycle, the 14 songs comprising this work do not constitute a genuine cycle (like Die Schöne Müllerin and Die Winterreise) as there is no real connection between them. The title Schwanengesang was given by the publisher Haslinger, who produced the collection after Schubert's death. Of the poems used in the work, seven are by Rellstab, six by Heine, and one by Seidl.

Schwarz, Rudolf (1905–) Austrian-born conductor. He survived concentration camps during World War II and in 1947 became musical director of the Bournemouth Symphony Orchestra, which he greatly improved. He subsequently directed the City of Birmingham Symphony Orchestra (1951–57) and the BBC Symphony Orchestra (1957–62). He has also conducted the Northern Sinfonia (1964–73).

Heinrich Schütz

Schwarzkopf, Elisabeth (1915–) German soprano. She studied with Lula Mysz-Gmeiner and Maria Ivogün, joining the Berlin State Opera in 1938. In 1943 she joined the Vienna State Opera. An artist of great ability, Schwarzkopf possesses one of today's most beautiful voices; as well as opera, notably those of Mozart and Richard Strauss, she is well known for her lieder singing.

Schweigsame Frau, Die (*The Silent Woman*) Opera in three acts by Richard Strauss with libretto by Stefan Zweig based on Ben Jonson's comedy *Epicoene, or The Silent Woman*. First performance: Dresden, 1935. Sir Morosus (bass) is plagued by noise: his barber (baritone) suggests he should marry a young and silent wife.

Schweitzer, Albert (1875–1965) Alsatian theologian, medical missionary, organist, and Bach scholar. He studied the organ under Widor in Paris and became an authority on Bach, writing a biography and editing his complete organ works (the first five volumes with Widor and subsequent volumes with Nies-Bergar, 1912–67). He gave periodic organ recitals of Bach's works and wrote several essays on the art of organ building.

Scipione (*Scipio*) Opera seria by Handel with Italian libretto by Rolli based on Zeno's *Scipione nelle Spagne*. First performance: King's Theatre, London, 1726. Set during Scipio's campaigns in the Spanish provinces, the opera contains the famous *March from Scipio*.

scoop (colloquial) A fault in singing that occurs when a note is approached incorrectly from below its true pitch, rather than being cleanly struck at its centre.

scordatura The tuning of a stringed instrument to unusual intervals, often in order to facilitate the playing of chords, change the tone quality, or to alter the instrument's range. A **scordato** instrument becomes a *transposing instrument, as the music and fingering remain unchanged. The practice is rarely used now except in the cello and double bass, in which the tuning of the lowest string is reduced by a semitone or tone for certain pieces of music. [Italian, mistuning]

score The combined music for all the parts in a vocal or instrumental composition. Normally the players in an orchestra or other ensemble read from music containing only their own parts, while the conductor has a **full score** showing all the parts combined. In a full score the usual arrangement is to have the woodwind at the top of the page, followed by the brass and the timpani. The strings are arranged at the bottom of the page and any solo instrument is fitted in between the violins and the timpani. The treble instruments of each group are placed above the bass instruments. In a **vocal score** the voice parts of operas, oratorios, etc., are given, usually with a piano accompaniment. In a **piano score** the orchestral and vocal parts are reduced to a simple piano transcription, while a **short score** usually refers either to a piano score or to a concise version of a full score prepared by a composer after he has worked out the general principles of the orchestration but before he has worked out the details. See also **miniature score.**

scorrevole Gliding; fluent. [Italian]

Scotch snap (*or* **Scots catch**) A form of rhythm in which a short note on the beat is followed by a longer one that lasts until the next beat. It occurs in many Scottish songs (e.g. 'Coming through the Rye') and in the *strathspey. It was also popular in Italy in the 17th and 18th centuries and was known in Europe as the **Lombardy rhythm.**

Scott, Cyril (1879–1970) British composer. Scott studied in Frankfurt and was a member of the Frankfurt group, which also included Grainger. His music shows great facility within a basically impressionistic idiom and includes the opera *The Alchemist* (1917), three symphonies, chamber music, and songs.

Scott, Francis George (1880–1958) British composer. Scott's music shows a keen nationalistic awareness of his Scottish background. His works include many songs and orchestral compositions.

Scottish National Orchestra A symphony orchestra founded in 1891. Based in Glasgow, it was originally called the Scottish Orchestra, being renamed in 1951. Its conductors have included George Henschel, Frederic Cowen, John Barbirolli, George Szell, Walter Susskind, Karl Rankl, and Alexander Gibson (from 1959). It is the principal professional orchestra in Scotland, giving concerts in many Scottish towns. Under Gibson the orchestra has widened its repertory, given many premieres (particularly of Scottish works), and played for Scottish Opera.

Scottish Symphony Symphony No. 3 in A minor by Mendelssohn. First performance: 1842. According to the composer, the first inspiration for this symphony came during a visit to Holyrood in Edinburgh, while touring Scotland in 1829. Composition began in Italy in 1831 but the score was not completed until 1842, when Mendelssohn dedicated the work to Queen Victoria. In the scherzo Mendelssohn imitates the sound of Scottish bagpipes.

Scotto, Renata (1934–) Italian soprano. She studied in Milan with Ghirardini and Clopart before making her debut there as Violetta in Verdi's *La Traviata* (1953). She then sang all over Europe, specializing in the operas of Verdi and Puccini.

Alexander Scriabin

Scriabin (*or* **Skryabin**), **Alexander** (1877–1915) Russian composer, a pupil of Taneyev. A series of European and American tours established his international reputation as a composer and pianist. Scriabin's early compositions show the influence of Liszt and, particularly, Chopin; in his later works he developed a remarkably individual harmonic idiom, which involved the use of *fourth chords – the 'mystic chord' found in a number of his works is an example. Scriabin's output includes studies, preludes, and many other works for the piano; three symphonies; and orchestral works, including a piano concerto (1897), The *Divine Poem* (1905), The *Poem of Ecstasy* (1908), and *Prometheus: the Poem of Fire* (1911).

scroll see **pegbox**.

Sculthorpe, Peter (1929–) Australian composer, a pupil of Rubbra and Wellesz. He rejected European techniques in the search for an authentically Australian nontonal style and his works show the influence of eastern music, especially from Bali and Tibet. They include nine string quartets, *Music for Japan* (1970), the opera *Rites of Passage* (1973), *Lament for Strings* (1976), and much film and stage music.

Sea, The see **Mer, La**.

Sea Drift Work for baritone, choir, and orchestra by Delius to words by Walt Whitman. Composed: 1903. Delius set an extract from the poem 'Out of the Cradle Endlessly Rocking,' the title *Sea Drift* referring to Whitman's collection from which the poem was taken.

Seaman, Christopher (1942–) British conductor. He is principal conductor of the BBC Scottish Symphony Orchestra (1971–) and the Northern Sinfonia (1974–) and frequently conducts the National Youth Orchestra and the Robert Mayer Concerts for Children.

Sea Pictures Song cycle for contralto and orchestra by Elgar to words by various poets. First performance: 1899. All the poems have a nautical significance; the five movements are 'Sea Slumber Song' (Roden Noel), 'In Haven' (Alice Elgar, the composer's wife), 'Sabbath Morning at Sea' (Elizabeth Barrett Browning), 'Where Corals Lie' (Richard Garnett), and 'The Swimmer' (A. L. Gordon).

Searle, Humphrey (1915–82) British composer, a pupil of Ireland and Webern. After early atonal pieces, such as the *Intermezzo for Eleven Instruments* (1947), he adopted serial procedures; he later experimented within a freely atonal style but finally returned to serialism. His works include five symphonies, concertos, a trilogy (*Gold Coast Customs*, 1949; *Riverrun*, 1951; and *Shadow of Cain*, 1952), *Labyrinth* (1971), *Kubla Khan* (1974), and operas, such as *Diary of a Madman* (1958) and *Hamlet* (1968).

Seasons, The 1. Oratorio for solo voices, choir, and orchestra by Haydn to a libretto by Baron von Swieten based on the poem *The Seasons* by James Thomson. First performance: 1801. The four parts of this oratorio portray in turn spring, summer, autumn, and winter. **2.** Set of four concertos for violin and orchestra by Vivaldi. See **Four Seasons, The.**

Sea Symphony Symphony No. 1 for solo voices, choir, and orchestra by Vaughan Williams. Composed: 1903–09; first performance: 1910. The first three movements of this symphony are settings of words taken from Walt Whitman's *Sea Drift*, which had also been the inspiration for Delius' work of that name. The fourth movement, entitled 'The Explorers,' sets a section of *Passage to India*.

sec A direction used to indicate that a note once played should be immediately released. [French, dry]

secco (*or* **recitativo secco**) see **recitative.**

second An *interval of two notes, or two semitones for a **major second** (e.g. C–D) and one semitone for a **minor second** (e.g. C–D♭).

secondary dominant see **dominant.**

second inversion see **inversion.**

Secret, The (Czech: *Tajemství*) Opera in three acts by Smetana with libretto by Eliska Krasnohorská. First performance: New Czech Theatre, Prague, 1878. Family feuds are overcome in a Czech village allowing the lovers Rose (contralto) and Kalina (baritone) to wed.

Secret Marriage, The (Italian: *Il Matrimonio segreto*) Opera buffa in two acts by Cimarosa with libretto by Bertati based on Colman's play *The Clandestine Marriage*. First performance: Burgtheater, Vienna, 1792, when the entire opera, with its complicated plot based on secrets and misunderstandings, is reputed to have been encored by Emperor Leopold II.

Seefried, Irmgard (1919–88) Austrian soprano. She joined the Aachen Opera under Karajan (1939) and the Vienna State Opera under Bohm (1943); after the war she sang all over the world. Seefried was married to the violinist Wolfgang Schneiderhan (1915–   ), with whom she gave the first performance of Henze's *Ariosi* (for soprano, violin, and orchestra) at Edinburgh (1964). Frank Martin wrote his *Magnificat* for them.

segno Sign. Hence **al segno**, as far as the sign: a direction to repeat a piece from the beginning as far as the sign indicated; **dal segno**, from the sign: a direction to repeat the piece from the sign indicated. In both cases the sign itself is usually :S:. See also **da capo**. [Italian].

Segovia, Andrés (1893–1987) Spanish guitarist. Being self-taught Segovia developed his own playing technique,

Andrés Segovia

which greatly influenced younger generations of guitarists. He made a considerable contribution to the 20th-century revival of the guitar as a concert instrument and many composers have written works for him. Segovia edited much guitar and lute music and held teaching appointments in Siena and California.

Segreto di Susanna, Il see **Susanna's Secret.**

segue Follows: a direction used to indicate that the next section is to be played without pausing after the previous one. [Italian]

seguidilla A Spanish dance in triple time that exists in various forms in different regions. Vocal, guitar, and castanet accompaniments are common; violins and flutes are less common. The vocal accompaniment usually consists of four-line verses followed by three-line refrains. The original form, the seguidilla Manchega, originated in La Mancha in the 16th century, although it may have had an earlier Moorish history.

Seiber, Mátyás (1905–60) Hungarian-born composer and cellist, resident in London from 1935. A pupil of Kodály, he assisted in founding the Society for the Promotion of New Music and was also very influential as a teacher. His own style was eclectic, developing from a Hungarian nationalist mode to incorporate elements of oriental music and jazz and using serial procedures in a lyrical manner. Seiber's works include the opera *Eva spielt mit Puppen* (1934); the cantata *Ulysses* (1947); fragments from Joyce's *Portrait of the Artist as a Young Man* (1956–57); the ballet *The Invitation* (1960); three string quartets and other chamber works; piano music; and film music, including that for the animated *Animal Farm* (1954).

Seixas, (José) Carlos de (1704–42) Portuguese composer and organist. He was organist of Coimbra Cathedral (1718) and of the royal chapel, Lisbon (1720), where he knew Domenico Scarlatti. Remembered mostly for his keyboard sonatas, he also wrote choral works and chamber music.

Semele Dramatic musical work by Handel, which is sometimes staged as opera and sometimes sung as oratorio. The libretto is by Congreve with probable adaptations by Pope. First performance: Covent Garden, London, 1744. Semele, loved by Zeus, dares him to appear to her in his heavenly splendour and is consumed by lightning.

semibreve The longest note used in modern notation, in which it is depicted as an open tailless circle. It has half the time value of the formerly used *breve and twice the value of the *minim. US: **whole note**. See **Appendix, Table 1.**

semichorus A section of a choral body, not necessarily exactly half of it. Some composers have created special antiphonal effects by using a semichorus to contrast with a full chorus; Vaughan Williams used one, for example, in his *Sea Symphony*.

semi-opera A 17th- or 18th-century stage work in which music plays a less dominant part than in a full opera. Some of Purcell's works fall into this category.

semiquaver A note having half the time value of a *quaver and a sixteenth that of a semibreve. In modern notation it is depicted as a filled-in circle with a tail to which two bars (or hooks) are attached. US: **sixteenth note**. See **Appendix, Table 1.**

Semiramide 1. Opera in two acts by Rossini with text by Gaetano Rossi. First performance: Teatro La Fenice, Venice, 1823. The libretto is based on Voltaire's tragedy about Semiramis (Italian: Semiramide), Queen of ancient Nineveh. **2.** Pasticcio with music probably by Vivaldi (recitatives by Handel) on a libretto of Metastasio. First performance: King's Theatre, London, 1733.

semitone The smallest *interval in common use in western music. A semitone is the interval between one note and the next on the piano (whether a white or a black note). In the *chromatic scale all the notes are separated by an interval of a semitone, whereas in the diatonic scale only two of the intervals are semitones (E–F and B–C in the scale of C major). See **scales.**

semplice Simple: a direction to perform a piece in a simple unaffected manner. [Italian]

sempre Always; still. Hence **sempre più**, more and more;

sempre legato, a direction to play smoothly throughout. [Italian]

Senaillé, Jean Baptiste (*c*.1688–1730) French violinist and composer. After playing in the king's orchestra he travelled to Italy (1717–19), where he became a pupil of Vitali. On his return to France he became soloist at the Concerts Spirituels (1728–30). Senaillé was one of the first composers to bring the Italian idiom and sonata form into France, writing five sets of violin sonatas (1710–27).

Senfl, Ludwig (1486–*c*.1542) Swiss composer and a pupil of Heinrich Isaac, whose *Choralis Constantinus* he completed (*c*.1520). He was employed by the Emperor Maximilian I (1496–1519) and worked at the Bavarian court (1523–*c*.1540). His works include masses, motets, settings of the Magnificat, and about 150 German songs.

sentence see **phrase.**

senza Without. [Italian]

septet A composition for seven voices or instruments or a group that performs such a composition.

septuplet (*or* **septimole** *or* **septolet**) A group of seven notes of equal time value played in the time of four or six notes. They are written tied together with a small figure 7 placed on the tie. Some of the notes can be replaced by rests.

sequence The repetition of a phrase in a composition at a higher or lower pitch. In a **melodic sequence** only the melody is repeated, whereas in a **harmonic sequence** a series of chords is repeated. If the intervals between the notes of a melody are changed in order to remain in the same key, the repeated passage is called a **tonal sequence**. If the key is changed and the intervals remain unchanged, it is called a **real sequence**. A real sequence is sometimes called a **rosalia** because this device is used in a popular Italian song beginning 'Rosalia, mia cara '.

Sequence A type of hymn used in the Roman Catholic Mass. Originating in the 9th and 10th centuries, the Sequence follows the Alleluia. At the Council of Trent (1545–63) all previous Sequences were abolished except *Victimae paschali*, *Veni, sancte spiritus*, *Lauda Sion*, and *Dies irae*. The *Stabat Mater* was admitted in the 18th century. The Sequence is sometimes called the **Prose** as originally the hymns were written in prose rather than the rhymed verse of later versions.

Sequenza (*Sequence*) Collection of nine solo works for various instruments by Berio. Composed: 1958–75. The works are for flute (1958), harp (1963), female voice (1966), piano (1966), trombone (1966), viola (1967), oboe (1967), percussion (1975), and violin (1975).

Seraglio, The (full title: *The Abduction from the Seraglio*, from German: *Die Entführung aus dem Serail*) Opera (see singspiel) in three acts by Mozart with libretto by Gottlieb Stephanie after a play by Bretzner. First performance: Burgtheater, Vienna, 1782. Evoking the popular 'Turkish' atmosphere of the day, it tells of the rescue of Constanze (soprano) by her lover Belmonte (tenor) from the court of the Pasha Selim (spoken part). Osmin (bass), the overseer of the harem, is one of Mozart's great dramatic and comic creations.

Serebrier, José (1938–) Uruguayan composer. Serebrier has conducted several orchestras in the USA. His works, which occasionally use serial procedures, include a symphony (1946), *Colores Magicos* (1971) and other multimedia compositions, chamber music, and songs.

serenade By convention, a piece of music intended to be played or sung by a man, in the evening (compare **aubade**), beneath the window of a lady whom he hoped might become his lover. Similarly, the German *Ständchen* is a short song in which it is implied that the singer remained standing. Some compositions having a connection with the evening or its romantic associations are also called serenades. [From Latin *sera*, evening]

Serenade Song cycle for tenor, horn, and strings by Britten to words by various poets. First performance: 1943. The songs are all reflections on some aspect of night or evening, the six poets used being Cotton, Tennyson, Blake, Johnson, Keats and the anonymous author of 'The Lyke-Wake Dirge'. A prologue and epilogue for solo horn frame the vocal settings.

Serenade Quartet String quartet in F major, attributed to Haydn (Op. 3 No. 5) but probably by his contemporary Hoffstetter. Composed: *c.*1768. The name is suggested by the serenade character of the slow movement, with its sustained violin melody against a pizzicato accompaniment.

Serenade to Music Work for 16 solo voices and orchestra by Vaughan Williams to words by Shakespeare. First performance: 1938. Vaughan Williams composed this work to celebrate the 50th anniversary of Sir Henry Wood's career as a conductor and in 1940 he made three arrangements –for four solo voices, choir, and orchestra; for choir and orchestra; and for orchestra alone. *Serenade to Music* is a setting of the passage 'How Sweet the Moonlight Sleeps upon this Bank,' from *The Merchant of Venice*.

serenata 1. A type of dramatic *cantata popular in the 18th century in England. An example is Handel's *Acis and Galatea*. **2.** A composition for small orchestra or ensemble in a fairly light mood. [Italian, serenade]

serialism A method of composition based on the serial ordering of pitches and in some cases other elements also. The classical form of serialism is **dodecaphony** (see **twelve-note composition**), which was first employed systematically by Schoenberg in 1923 and holds a central place in

the later music of Berg and Webern as well as in the works of other disciples of Schoenberg, such as Skalkottas. Since 1945 serial principles have been increasingly applied to rhythm, dynamics, timbre, and other elements (see **total serialism**).

series A repeating cycle of pitches used as material in some types of 20th-century music (see **serialism; twelve-note composition**). A strict **dodecaphonic series** is one in which each pitch class of the chromatic scale appears once only: the example illustrated is taken from Webern's variations for piano (1936). The nondodecaphonic series illustrated appears in 'Ricercar II' from Stravinsky's *Cantata* (1952).

Above: dodecaphonic series. Below: nondodecaphonic series

Serious Songs see **Four Serious Songs.**

Serkin, Rudolf (1903–) US pianist of Russian parentage, who studied in Vienna. His reputation is based especially upon his interpretations of Bach, Mozart, Beethoven, and Schubert and he formed a duo with Adolf *Busch, whose daughter he married. From 1939 Serkin taught at the Curtis Institute in Philadelphia.

Sermissy, Claudin (*c.*1490–1562) French composer. He was a singer at the Sainte-Chapelle in Paris (1508–14) and became a member of the French royal chapel shortly before the death of Louis XII in 1515, succeeding Antoine de Longueval as master of the choristers under Francis I. He was mentioned by Ronsard (1560) as a 'disciple' of Josquin des Prez; his works include masses, motets, and chansons.

Serocki, Kazimerz (1922–81) Polish composer and pianist, a pupil of Sikorski and Nadia Boulanger. After an early neoromantic period he adopted serial procedures, and later works reflect the composer's interest in instrumental sounds, spatial composition, and aleatoric techniques. His works include *Musica Concertante* (1958), *Segmenti* (1961), *Continuum* (1966), *Swinging Music* (1970), *Ad Libitum* (1974), and *Pianophonie* (1978).

serpent see **cornett.**

serré see **stringendo.**

Serva padrona, La (*The Maid as Mistress*) Comic opera in two parts by Pergolesi with text by Federico, designed as an *intermezzo to be played between the acts of an opera seria. First performance: Teatro San Bartolommeo, Naples, 1733. The maid Serpino (soprano) tricks her master Uberto (bass) into marriage by pretending to run away with a soldier (who is actually another servant). This orchestral and vocal miniature achieved enormous popularity and was at the centre of the so-called 'Guerre des Bouffons' in Paris, a 'war' between protagonists of Italian and French opera.

service A setting of the canticles and responses from the Book of Common Prayer for one or more of the offices of the Church of England. These include English translations of the Venite, *Te Deum, *Benedictus, *Benedicite, or *Jubilate at Matins, and of the *Magnificat, *Nunc Dimittis, Cantate Domino, or Deus Misereator at Evensong. For the service of Holy Communion the settings are of the Kyrie, Credo, Sanctus, Benedictus, *Agnus Dei, and Gloria.

During the 16th and 17th centuries the terms **short service** and **great service** were used to indicate the style and scope of the music, the former simple and syllabic, the latter expansive and richly contrapuntal. Short services by Tye and Tallis survive from the 16th century, and there are examples of both kinds by Byrd. In Byrd's short service some verses of the canticles are set for solo voices with organ accompaniment. These are contrasted with sections for full choir. Other pre-Commonwealth composers of services include Gibbons, Morley, Tomkins, and Weelkes. After the Restoration verse settings with solo voices were widespread. It also became common to employ orchestral instruments to accompany festal settings of certain canticles, especially the Te Deum and Jubilate. These display the new operatic technique of *monody and aspects of the French orchestral style. During the 18th century composers preferred to write *anthems but service settings were produced by Battishill, Boyce, Croft, and Greene. The revival of Anglican choral music in the mid-19th century, led by S. S. Wesley and the Oxford Movement, was characterized by the writing of more distinctive organ accompaniments. This can be seen in the service settings of Ouseley, Stainer, Stanford, and S. S. Wesley. 20th-century composers of distinguished service settings include Britten, Walford Davies, Herbert Howells, Rubbra, and Tippett.

sesquialtera An organ *mixture stop containing ranks sounding a twelfth (one octave and a fifth) and a seventeenth (two octaves and a third) above written pitch. The sound was very popular for solos in Germany and England.

Sessions, Roger (1896–1985) US composer, a pupil of Bloch and Horatio Parker. After an early neoclassical period, Sessions' music became progressively more chromatic and expressionistic until he adopted serial procedures in the 1950s. His subsequent music remained densely contrapuntal with a tendency in later works towards great brevity. His works include nine symphonies, *Rhapsody* (1971), a double concerto (1972), *Concertino* (1972), *When Lilacs Last in the Courtyard Bloomed* (1974), the opera *Montezuma* (1963), and chamber and piano music.

Seven Last Words of our Saviour on the Cross, The Orchestral work (Op. 47) by Haydn. Composed: 1785. The work was commissioned by the Chapter of Cádiz Cathedral to be performed on Good Friday 1785 and is in the form of seven slow movements. The seven words of the title are the last utterances of Christ as reported in the Gospels and it was the custom to preach on them during Good Friday. In Haydn's setting each 'word' is performed in recitative, before a sermon on the 'word' preached by the bishop, which is followed by the appropriate orchestral movement: the whole work is thus effectively a series of reflective interludes in the sermon. *The Seven Last Words* were later arranged for string quartet (Op. 48), piano (Op. 49), and as a cantata, although the authenticity of this latter version is disputed.

seventeenth (*or* **tierce**) An organ *mutation stop that sounds a note a seventeenth (i.e. two octaves and a third) above the written pitch on flute *flue pipes. The length of the pipe (compared to an 8-*foot pipe) is 1.6 ft.

seventh An *interval of seven notes (counting both the first and last notes), or eleven semitones for a **major seventh** (e.g. C–B) and ten semitones for a **minor seventh** (e.g. C–B♭). The **diminished seventh** is equivalent to a major sixth (e.g. C–A), but the term **diminished seventh chord** is widely used. The diminished seventh chord on C (written Cdim) is C E♭ G♭ A. See also **dominant**.

Séverac, (Marie-Joseph-Alexandre) Déodat de (1872–1921) French composer. He studied at the Toulouse conservatory (1893–96) and at the Schola Cantorum, Paris (1896–1907), where his teachers included d'Indy and Magnard (composition), Guilmant (organ), and Selva and Albéniz (piano). He became Albéniz's assistant in 1900. A native of southern France, Séverac was greatly influenced by Provençal folk traditions, as seen in his opera *Héliogabale* (1910). Séverac's compositions, many of them impressionistic, include four operas, four tone poems, choral and chamber music, songs, and piano pieces.

sextet A composition for six voices or instruments or a group that performs such a composition.

sextuplet (*or* **sextolet**) A group of six notes of equal time value played in the time of four notes. They are written tied together with a small figure 6 placed on the tie. Some of the notes can be replaced by rests.

sf. see **sforzando**.

sfogato A direction used to indicate an effortless and free manner of performance. [Italian, given free play to]

sforzando Forcing: a direction used to indicate that a note or chord should be strongly emphasized (see **accent**). Abbreviation: **sf.** or **sfz.**; **fz.** (abbreviation for **forzando**) is also sometimes used. [Italian]

sfz. see **sforzando**.

Sgambati, Giovanni (1841–1914) Italian composer, pianist, and conductor. In 1862, as a pianist in Rome, he met Liszt, whose pupil he became. Liszt took him to Germany and the two remained close friends. In 1869 he founded the Liceo Musicale di S Cecilia in Rome and in 1876 met Wagner, who admired his compositions. Sgambati wrote orchestral works (including two symphonies), sacred and chamber music, songs, and many piano pieces. He is an important figure in Italian musical history because he wrote instrumental music at a time when composers favoured opera composition.

shake see **trill.**

Shakespeare, William (1564–1616) English playwright. His plays contain many musical references and interludes, often contributing to the plot's dramatic cohesion and not functioning merely as intermissions. Virtually all of his plays have formed the bases of operas, ballets, or symphonic music: perhaps the greatest of these works are Verdi's operas *Macbeth* (1847), *Otello* (1887), and *Falstaff* (1893) and Prokofiev's ballet *Romeo and Juliet* (1936).

shakuhachi An end-blown Japanese *flute with a wide bore and (usually) four finger holes. It is made of bamboo and the inside of the bore is lacquered. A chromatic scale can be played with some difficulty by half-stopping.

Shaliapin (*or* **Chaliapin**), **Feodor Ivanovich** (1873–1938) Russian bass singer. Considered the greatest dramatic singer of his day, he was largely self-taught. He sang Russian opera (notably Mussorgsky and Rimsky-Korsakov) in Russia (1893–1901) then toured Europe, extending his repertory. After the Russian Revolution (1917) he lived abroad, dying in Paris.

shamisen see **samisen.**

Shankar, Ravi (1920–) Indian sitar player. As well as performing concerts of Indian music he has also appeared with many leading western musicians, notably Yehudi Menuhin. Shankar has founded a school of Indian music in the USA and also composes.

shanty A song with a strong rhythmical element sung by sailors to encourage them to work together in such tasks as hoisting sails, pulling ropes, or working pumps. Traditionally the verse was sung by a nonworking shanty man, with the workers joining in the chorus. [from French *chantez*, sing]

Shapero, Harold (1920–) US composer, a pupil of Křenek, Piston, Hindemith, and Nadia Boulanger. Among his many awards have been the American Prix de Rome (1941) and two Guggenheim fellowships (1946–47). His works adhere to neoclassical principles; they include a *Symphony for Classical Orchestra* (1947) and other

Feodor Shaliapin

orchestral compositions, chamber music, piano works, and electronic compositions.

Shaporin, Yury (1887–1966) Soviet composer. In his studies at St Petersburg Shaporin absorbed the atmosphere of the Russian nationalist tradition. His works include the opera *The Decembrists* (1920–53); orchestral works, including a symphony (1911); chamber music; and incidental music for films and the theatre.

sharp 1. A sign (♯) placed before a note or in a *key signature to raise the pitch of that note by one semitone. See **accidental. 2.** Denoting a musical sound that is of higher pitch than it should be.

Sharp, Cecil James (1859–1924) British musical folklorist and composer. He was director of the Hampstead conservatory (1896–1905) and is remembered for his collection of nearly 5000 English folk songs and dances, which he started in 1899. He founded the English Folk-Dance Society in 1911 and even went to the Appalachian Mountains in the USA to collect examples of English folk songs from the original emigrants' descendants.

sharp keys Keys that have sharps in their *key signatures, i.e. the key of G has one sharp, D has two sharps, A has three sharps, E has four sharps, B has five sharps, and F♯ has six sharps. In each case the relative minor keys have the same signatures as the major keys given. See **Appendix, Table 3.**

Shaw, George Bernard (1859–1950) Irish dramatist and critic. He wrote musical criticism for the *Star* (1888–89) and the *World* (1890–94). In 1898 appeared *The Perfect Wagnerite*, Shaw's analysis of Wagner's *Ring* cycle. The opera *The Chocolate Soldier* (1907) by Oscar Straus is based on his satire *Arms and the Man* (1894).

Shaw, Martin (1875–1958) British composer, a pupil of Stanford. Shaw was organist at a number of London churches. His works include the opera *Mr Pepys* (1926), songs, and choral music.

shawm An early form of double-reeded woodwind instrument with six or seven finger holes that originated in the Middle East. Shawms produce a noisy buzzing sound and were largely played in the open air. By the 13th century they were in use in Europe and during the 17th century, with the addition of keys, evolved into the *oboe. The most usual set of Renaissance shawms consisted of alto, tenor, bass, and great bass instruments. The last two were also known as **bombad** or by the German name, **pommer**.

Shchedrin, Rodion (1932–) Soviet composer, a pupil of Shaporin. Shchedrin's early works incorporate Russian folk tunes; his compositions of the 1960s make tentative use of serial and aleatoric techniques, a sign of a more liberal attitude to the arts in Soviet Russia than hitherto. Shchedrin's output includes an opera, two piano concertos and other orchestral works, chamber music, and piano compositions.

Shebalin, Vissarion Yakovlevich (1902–63) Soviet composer, a pupil of Miaskovsky. Shebalin directed the Moscow conservatory (1942–48). A lyrical, rather than epic, inspiration is evident in the success of Shebalin's chamber music compared to his orchestral works. His compositions include an opera, five symphonies, nine string quartets and other chamber works, songs, and piano works.

Sheherazade (*or* **Scheherazade**) **1.** Symphonic suite (Op. 35) by Rimsky-Korsakov. Composed: 1888. In the *Arabian Nights* Sheherazade is a sultan's wife, who each night tells her husband a new story in order to delay her threatened execution. Each of the four movements is based upon a different story from the collection. **2.** Song cycle with orchestra by Ravel to poems by Klingsor. Composed: 1903. The title is merely an indication of the oriental derivation of the poetry: there is no direct connection with the Sheherazade of the *Arabian Nights*. The three songs are 'Asie' ('Asia'), 'La Flûte enchantée' ('The Enchanted Flute'), and 'L'Indifférent' ('The Indifferent One').

Shelomo see **Schelomo.**

Sheppard, John (*c.*1515–*c.*1560) English composer. In 1543 he became choirmaster at Magdalen College, Oxford, and by 1552 was a gentleman of the Chapel Royal. Most of his early work is lost; what remains seems to date from the reign of Queen Mary (1553–58). His five masses include one based on the *Western Wynde*, a melody also used by Christopher Tye and John Taverner. Other works comprise church music in all the major pre-Reformation forms.

Sherard, James (1666–1738) English composer and violinist. Known primarily as a physician, botanist, and gardener, from 1701 until 1711 he was involved in the musical activities of Wriothesley, second Duke of Bedford, in the company of Nicola Haym. His two sets of trio sonatas, written in the style of Corelli, were published by Roger of Amsterdam (1701, 1711).

Shield, William (1748–1829) British composer and violinist pupil of Avison. He led the violas in the orchestra of the King's Theatre in the Haymarket (1773) and became composer to Covent Garden after the success of his first light opera, *The Flitch of Bacon* (1778). In 1817 he was appointed Master of the King's Music. In addition to his operas and other dramatic works, Shield wrote ballets, songs, chamber music, and arrangements of Scottish songs. He was also the author of treatises on harmony.

Shirley-Quirk, John (1931–) British baritone. After singing in St Paul's Cathedral choir (1961–62) he went to Glyndebourne, where he created various roles in Britten's operas, including *Death in Venice* (1973), which he has sung in New York (1974). His concert repertory is vast.

shofar A ceremonial *horn made from a ram's horn and used for ritual purposes by the ancient Hebrews. Although it is only capable of sounding two notes it was used in biblical times as a prelude to important proclamations and an invocation to the Almighty – more as a source of eschatological noise than a musical instrument. It is still sounded in synagogues to herald the new year and on the Day of Atonement. [Hebrew, ram's horn]

short octave see **keyboard.**

short score see **score.**

Shostakovich, Dmitri (1906–75) Soviet composer. Shostakovich studied at the Petrograd conservatory (1919–25), where he wrote his first symphony as a graduation piece. The impact of this work at its first performance established Shostakovich's place, at the age of 18, among contemporary Soviet composers. Although his subsequent works often won immediate public acclaim, official reaction was unfavourable and culminated in 1936 with an attack in *Pravda* on his opera *Lady Macbeth of Mtzensk* (see **Katerina Ismailova**). As an answer to this and other official rebukes Shostakovich subtitled his fifth symphony 'a Soviet artist's reply to just criticism': the work was hailed as an

Dmitri Shostakovich

Jean Sibelius

epitome of Soviet art. Besieged in Leningrad during the first years of World War II, Shostakovich composed his seventh symphony, which became symbolic of the resistance to the German invasion: it became known as the *Leningrad Symphony* and was played throughout Allied Europe and the USA. After the war Shostakovich's music again came under criticism, this time as part of the decree of 1948 condemning musical modernism. With the death of Stalin in 1953 the cultural atmosphere in the USSR relaxed and Shostakovich was able to pursue a more individual course of musical development.

Shostakovich's musical idiom remained immediately recognizable throughout his career. It is characterized by tonal (although frequently dissonant) harmony, a lucid sense for scoring and orchestration, and adherence to classical forms and genres. In his last works 12-note themes are occasionally used, although not developed in a serial way. Shostakovich's 15 symphonies have established him as the leading symphonist of the mid-20th century. His chamber works include 15 string quartets and sonatas for violin, viola, and cello. His other compositions include ballet, film and theatre scores, vocal music, and music for piano.

Shropshire Lad, A Rhapsody for orchestra by Butterworth. Composed: 1912. Butterworth had earlier composed a song cycle with the same title to poetry by Housman; this

rhapsody is based on a theme from his setting in the cycle of the words 'Loveliest of Trees.'

si see **solmization.**

Sibelius, Jean (1865–1957) Finnish composer. Sibelius showed an interest in music from an early age, his first attempts at composition dating from his tenth year. In 1885 he embarked upon a law course at the University of Helsinki but soon abandoned this in favour of his studies as a violinist and composer. Sibelius' nationalist aspirations revealed themselves in his music of the 1890s, which often drew on the legends of the national epic, the *Kalevala*. The turn of the century marked a move away from the explicit programmatical basis of these earlier works towards a more abstract conception of musical argument as exemplified in his seven symphonies. In 1929 he stopped composing: although an eighth symphony is thought to have existed, it seems that Sibelius destroyed the score. The reasons for this cessation are not clear: self-criticism, dissatisfaction with musical and political developments in postwar Europe, and illness may all have played a part.

Even in the overt nationalism of Sibelius' early works, clear indications of his mature symphonic style are already apparent. His orchestration, often praised for its elemental grandeur, is strongly individual, often featuring long pedal points. Apart from the symphonies, his works include a violin concerto (1904); tone poems based on Finnish legend, such as *En Saga (1892), *Lemminkäinen's Homecoming (1893–95), The *Swan of Tuonela (1893–95), and *Tapiola (1926); incidental music and other orchestral works, including *Karelia (1893), *King Christian II (1898), *Finlandia (1900), *Valse triste (1903), Belshazzar's Feast (1906), and The *Tempest (1926); songs; piano pieces; and a small number of chamber works.

siciliana (*or* **siciliano**) A slow dance or song of Sicilian origin in 6/8 or 12/8 time. Usually in a minor key, it had a swaying rhythm. Arias in this rhythm were written in the 18th century and the instruction **alla siciliana** was used in some suites and slow movements of sonatas.

Sicilian Vespers, The see **Vêpres siciliennes, Les.**

side drum (*or* **snare drum**) A small double-headed drum that is played slightly tilted on its side. The upper head is struck with wooden drumsticks and the lower head is fitted with gut or metal snares that vibrate against the membrane and give brilliance to the drumbeat. They are used in the percussion section of the orchestra, in military bands, and as a standard part of the jazz- or dance-band drum set. For illustration, see **drums.**

Siege of Corinth, The (French: *Le Siège de Corinthe*) Opera by Rossini with libretto by Soumet and Balocchi. First performance: Opéra, Paris, 1826. It is a revision of the earlier *Maometto II* (*Mahomet II*) and tells of the love of the Mohammedan conqueror of Corinth for the daughter of the Christian governor.

Siege of Rhodes, The Opera with music (now lost) by Locke, Henry Lawes, Coleman, Cooke, and Hudson and libretto by William Davenant. First performance: Rutland House, London, 1656. This is believed to be the earliest English opera. Rhodes, the last Christian outpost in the Mediterranean, was besieged by the Turks in 1480 and 1481; the libretto reads like a school lesson on the subject.

Siegfried see **Ring des Nibelungen, Der.**

Siegfried Idyll Work for small orchestra by Wagner. Composed: 1870. On Christmas morning 1870 Wagner organized a group of 15 instrumentalists to perform this work outside his wife Cosima's bedroom to celebrate her 33rd birthday. As they were then living at Triebchen, this work is sometimes called the *Triebschener Idyll.* It is based on themes from his opera *Siegfried,* although the title refers to their son Siegfried, who had been born while Wagner was composing the work. Although it was intended only for private performance, Wagner was later forced to arrange the work for a larger orchestra and publish it to help pay off some debts.

Siepi, Cesare (1923–) Italian bass singer. He made his debut as Sparafucile in Verdi's *Rigoletto* at Schio (1941).

For 24 years (1949–73) he was a member of the New York Metropolitan Opera, where he sang in most of its repertory.

sight reading The art of being able to play an instrument from music seen for the first time. The alternatives are to play from memory or by ear.

signature see **key signature; time signature.**

Silja, Anja (1940–) German soprano. Closely associated with the Bayreuth Festival from 1960, she was the most intense and interesting singer-actress there after the war. Directed by Pierre Boulez, she later sang Marie in Berg's opera *Wozzeck.*

Silken Ladder, The (Italian: *La Scala di seta*) Comic opera in one act by Rossini with libretto by Foppa. First performance: Teatro San Moisè, Venice, 1812. The ladder conveys a lover to the room of his beloved.

Sills, Beverly (1929–) US soprano. She joined the New York City Opera in 1955 and sang radiantly in Handel's *Julius Caesar* as the hero's lover Cleopatra. Her best roles have been in early romantic Italian opera.

silver band A *brass band of instruments coated in a substance to make them look silver.

similar motion see **motion.**

simile Similar: a direction used to indicate that the manner of performance should continue as already indicated. [Italian]

Simon Boccanegra Opera in prologue and three acts by Verdi with libretto by Piave based on a play by Gutiérrez. First performance: Teatro la Fenice, Venice, 1857. Set in 14th-century Genoa, it concerns the election of the doge, Simon Boccanegra (baritone), and his rediscovery of his lost daughter Maria (soprano). Unsuccessful at first, the libretto was recast by Boito for the Milan production of 1881.

simple interval An interval of an *octave or less. Compare **compound interval.**

Simple Symphony Symphony for string orchestra or string quartet by Britten. Composed: 1934. This work was based on music that the composer had written while still a young boy; the four movements are entitled 'Boisterous Bourée,' 'Playful Pizzicato,' 'Sentimental Saraband,' and 'Frolicsome Finale.'

simple time Any form of musical time in which the beat note is a plain note (rather than a dotted note), i.e. the value of the beat note is divisible by two (e.g. 4/4 or 3/4). Compare **compound time.** See **Appendix, Table 4.**

Simpson, Christopher (*c.*1605–69) English composer, theorist, and viol player. A Catholic, he fought with the Royalists in the Civil War. He later lived with the Bolles family at Scampton, Lincolnshire. There he wrote *The*

Plate 42: *The Welsh National Opera's 1986 production of Wagner's* Siegfried

Plate 43 above: *Karlheinz Stockhausen, one of the most important and influential composers of the postwar period*

Plate 44 opposite: *A portrait of Richard Strauss, whose fame rests on his operas and symphonic poems*

Plate 45: *A view of Hereford Cathedral, one of the sites of the annual Three Choirs Festival*

Division-Violist (1659), a viol tutor. By 1663 he had bought an estate in north Yorkshire but he seems to have died in London. His other theoretical work is *A Compendium of Practical Musick* (1667), a musical primer. His compositions are all for the viol and contain many complex divisions.

Simpson, Robert (1921–) British composer and musicologist, a pupil of Howells. His style, influenced by Beethoven, Nielsen, and Sibelius, makes much use of progressive tonality and a rhythmic language built from small units. His works include string quartets, a clarinet trio (1961), a clarinet quintet (1968), a horn quartet (1977), the motet *Media morte in vita sumus* (1975), and six symphonies.

sin' see **sino**.

Sinding, Christian (August) (1856–1941) Norwegian composer and pianist. He studied at the Leipzig conservatory (1874–78) and lived in Germany for about 40 years, later settling in Oslo. He taught at the Eastman School of Music, New York (1921–22). Sinding was a prolific composer, the most important in Norway after Grieg. He wrote operas, orchestral, chamber, and piano music, and songs, most of his works are now rarely played. His best-known pieces are **Rustle of spring* (1896), the variations for two pianos, and the piano sonata.

sinfonia A piece of instrumental music, such as an overture, in an early-18th-century opera. The symphony evolved from this earlier sinfonia. See also **sinfonia concertante**. [Italian, symphony]

Sinfonia Antartica Symphony No. 7 for soprano solo, women's choir, piano, and orchestra by Vaughan Williams. First performance: 1953. This symphony is an arrangement of music that the composer had written for the film score to *Scott of the Antarctic* in 1949. Each of its five movements is prefixed by a literary quotation, taken from Shelley, the Bible (Psalm 104), Coleridge, Donne, and the diary of Captain Scott, respectively. The large orchestra includes parts for wind machine and vibraphone.

sinfonia concertante An orchestral work with solo parts for more than one instrumentalist. Haydn and Mozart both preferred this term to 'concerto' for such works, as seen in Mozart's sinfonia concertante in E♭ major for violin and viola. Various modern composers have also used the term for works with only one solo part, perhaps indicating a greater degree of integration between soloist and orchestra than is normal in a concerto.

Sinfonia da Requiem Symphony (Op. 20) by Britten. First performance: 1941. Britten composed this work shortly after the death of his father and this is reflected in the reference to the Requiem Mass in its title. The three movements are entitled 'Lacrymosa,' 'Dies Irae,' and 'Requiem Aeternam.'

sinfonietta 1. An orchestral work in symphonic form that does not have the weight and importance of a full symphony. **2.** A small symphony orchestra. [Italian, small symphony]

Singakademie A title used by some choirs in German-speaking countries. The first choral organization to use the name was founded in Berlin in 1791 by Carl Friedrich Christian Fasch. It performed many of Bach's works, contributing to the Bach revival; Mendelssohn conducted it in a performance of the *St Matthew Passion*. Many organizations have been modelled on it. [German singing academy]

singing saw see **musical saw**.

singspiel A form of opera popular in Germany and Austria during the 18th century, in which the libretto was in German (rather than the Italian of **opera seria*) and spoken dialogue replaced sung recitative. Singspiel was modelled on the English **ballad opera* and French **opéra comique* and the earliest examples, such as Hiller's *Die Jagd* (1770), had popular and comic plots. The musical style was much simpler than that of opera seria, with frequent use of popular strophic songs replacing elaborate arias. However, by the time of singspiel's artistic peak, as represented in Mozart's two operas *The Seraglio* (1782) and *The Magic Flute* (1791), the score frequently included features of both singspiel proper and opera seria.

Sinigaglia, Leone (1868–1944) Italian composer, a pupil of Dvořák. Sinigaglia was active as a collector of folk songs in his native Piedmont; many of his works are based on these themes. His output includes *Danza piemontesa* (1903) and other orchestral works, chamber music, and songs.

sino (*or* **sin'**) Up to; until. For example, **sin' al fine**, up to the end. [Italian]

Sinopoli, Giuseppe (1946–) Italian composer and conductor, a pupil of Donatoni, Maderna, and Stockhausen. His music rejects experimental modernism and often has a literary poetic inspiration. His works include *Souvenirs à la memoire* (1976), *Tombeau d'Armor I–III* (1975–79), a piano concerto, and choral pieces.

Sir John in Love Opera in four acts by Vaughan Williams with libretto by the composer based on Shakespeare's *The Merry Wives of Windsor*. First performance: Royal College of Music, London, 1929. It includes a setting of *Greensleeves* at the opening of Act III.

Sister Angelica see **Suor Angelica**.

The Royal Ballet in The Sleeping Beauty

sistrum A type of rattle consisting of a frame supporting metal rods threaded through metal discs. When the frame is shaken the discs rattle against each other. Sistra survive from ancient Egypt and from Pompeii; they are still in use in Ethiopian churches.

sitar Originally, a three-stringed Persian lute. The more recent Indian instrument is fretted and has seven metal strings, some of which are used for melody, the others being used as drones; there is also a set of *sympathetic strings. The strings are struck with a plectrum worn on the right thumb. Many variations of this instrument are in use. In recent years the sitar has been popularized in the West by Ravi *Shankar, a leading Indian exponent of the instrument, with the encouragement of Yehudi Menuhin and the Beatles. [Hindi]

Sitwell, Edith (1887–1964) British poet and writer. Walton wrote *Façade* (1923), an entertainment for speakers and chamber orchestra, using her words. Other settings include Tippett's 'The Weeping Babe' (1944) and Searle's *The Shadow of Cain* (1951).

Six, Les A group of French composers: Auric, Durey, Honegger, Milhaud, Poulenc, and Tailleferre. The group met at the Paris Conservatoire between 1910 and 1920 and were inspired by Satie; Jean Cocteau became their spokesman. In their concerts they presented their own compositions, such as Les *Mariés de la Tour Eiffel* (1921), which were characterized at that time by brevity and wit. Their chief common aim was to avoid the lingering element of romanticism and impressionism in French music. By 1925 the group had disbanded.

sixteen foot see **foot**.

sixteenth note see **semiquaver**.

sixth An *interval of six notes (counting both the first and the last notes), or nine semitones for a **major sixth** (e.g. C–A), and eight semitones for a **minor sixth** (e.g. C–A♭). See also **augmented sixth; Landini sixth; Neapolitan sixth**.

sixty-fourth note see **hemidemisemiquaver**.

Skalkottas, Nikos (1904–49) Greek composer, a pupil of Jarnach, Schoenberg, and Weill in Germany. He adopted serial procedures under the influence of Schoenberg, but some of his later works are freely atonal and others are tonal, showing the influence of his collection of Greek folk music in their modalities and meters. Skalkottas's works include three piano concertos; concertos for violin (1938) and double bass (1940); 36 *Greek Dances* for orchestra (1933–36); the symphony *The Return of Ulysses* (1945); and ballet music, chamber works, and piano pieces.

sketch 1. An instrumental composition, often for the piano, that describes some scene in musical terms. It is usually a short piece that is not too demanding on the performer. **2.** A first draft of a composition.

Skilton, Charles Sanford (1869–1941) US composer. After studying in Germany, Skilton made a study of North American Indian music, incorporating themes and folklore into his own works. His compositions include operas, orchestral works, and chamber music.

Skinner, James Scott (1843–1927) Scottish violinist and composer. He worked in Aberdeen as a dancing master and wrote popular dance music based on Scottish reels and other national dances.

Skryabin, Alexander see **Scriabin, Alexander**.

slått A Norwegian folk tune, originally a march played on the fiddle; some Norwegian composers have transcribed them for other instruments.

Slavonic Dances Two sets of dances for piano duet (Op. 46 and Op. 72) by Dvořák. Composed: 1878, 1886. Each set contains eight dances, all influenced in style by the melodic and rhythmic features of Czech folk music, although no actual folk tunes are quoted. Dvořák later orchestrated these dances, and it is in this version that they are best known.

Slavonic Rhapsodies Three orchestral works (Op. 45) by Dvořák. Composed: 1878. As in the *Slavonic Dances no genuine folk melodies are quoted, although the character of these rhapsodies is very much influenced by the style of Czech folk music.

Sleeping Beauty, The (Russian: *Spashaya Krasavitsa*; French: *La Belle au bois dormant*) Ballet in prologue and three acts with music by Tchaikovsky and choreography by Petipa. First performance: Maryinsky Theatre, St Petersburg, 1890. Based on Perrault's fairy tale, it contains some of Petipa's finest dances: the 'Rose Adagio' for Aurora and four princes, various character dances, and the 'Blue Bird' pas de deux; *Aurora's Wedding* is an extract from the ballet. When Diaghilev revived this ballet in London in 1921 he entitled it *The Sleeping Princess* to avoid confusion with pantomime stories.

Sleeping Princess, The see **Sleeping Beauty, The**.

slentando Slowing down. [Italian]

slide 1. The technique of sliding the finger from one position to another on the fingerboard of an unfretted stringed instrument, instead of using a different finger. **2.** A device on a *trombone for changing the length of the tube in order to have available different ranges of harmonics. A slide trumpet, using the same principle, was also formerly used. **3.** An *ornament consisting of two notes leading up to a principal note.

Slonimsky, Nicolas (1894–) Russian-born US composer and music writer. After studying at the St Petersburg conservatory he emigrated to the USA in 1923. As conductor of the Boston Chamber Orchestra (1927–34), he conducted his own *Fragment from Orestes* in 1933. He has edited the *International Cyclopaedia of Music and Musicians* since 1946 and has contributed to other reference works.

Slopes of Parnassus, The see **Amfiparnaso, L'**.

slur A curved line written over two or more notes indicating that they are to be played legato or with one stroke of the bow in bowed instruments. In vocal music it indicates that they are to be sung in one breath to the same syllable.

Smalley, Roger (1943–) British composer and pianist, a pupil of Fricker and Stockhausen. His early works are strictly serial. After a period of experiment with Renaissance material and procedures he followed Stockhausen in adopting *moment form, improvisatory elements, and electronic music. His works include the *Missa brevis* (1967), *Pulses* (1969), *Beat Music* (1971), *Zeitebenen* (1973), *Accord* (1975), and *Echo I–III* (1978).

Smetana, Bedřich (1824–84) Czech composer. The son of a brewer, he played the piano and violin from an early age. After studying music in Prague, he became music teacher to Count Leopold Thun's family. In 1848 he established a piano school in Prague, with Liszt's encouragement; the same year he took part in the revolution against Austria. In 1856 he obtained an appointment as the conductor of the philharmonic society of Göteborg (Sweden). However, the climate suited neither him nor his wife and on his return (1861) he was instrumental in establishing the national opera house in Prague, for which his two most famous operas, *The Brandenburgers in Bohemia* (1862–63) and *The *Bartered Bride* (1863–66), were composed. Smetana, who had suffered from the

Bedřich Smetana

illusion of hearing a continuous high note for most of his life, suddenly became totally deaf in 1874. Nevertheless he continued to compose until insanity overcame him in 1883. He died a year later in an asylum.

Smetana's music is distinctly Czech in character and the strong romantic vein is evident in such works as the symphonic poem cycle *Má Vlast* (1874–79) and the string quartet *From My Life* (1876). His other compositions include the operas *Dalibor* (1868), The *Two Widows* (1874), The *Kiss* (1876), The *Secret* (1878), and *Libuše* (1881), chamber music, piano pieces, choral music, and many songs.

Smit, Leo (1900–43) Dutch composer. From 1927 to 1933 he lived in Paris, which imparted French influence to his style. During World War II he was arrested by the Nazis and died in a concentration camp. Smit's works include orchestral and chamber compositions and piano music.

Smith, John Stafford (1750–1836) British composer, tenor, and organist. He studied with Boyce and in 1761 entered the Chapel Royal as a choirboy, becoming a gentleman (1784), an organist (1802), and Master of the Children (1805–17). Smith composed glees, songs, anthems, and other vocal music, including the song *To Anacreon in Heaven*, from which the tune of *The Star-Spangled Banner*

Dame Ethel Smyth

was adapted. His greatest contribution was as a scholarly collector of priceless music manuscripts, much of which he transcribed and edited in *Musica antiqua* (1812).

Smyth, Dame Ethel (1858–1944) British composer. Ethel Smyth studied in Leipzig and Berlin. On her return to England she played an important role in the women's suffrage movement, for which she was made a Dame of the British Empire in 1922. Her works, which in spite of her strong belief in English musical nationalism are characteristic of her German training, include the operas The *Wreckers* (1906–09) and The *Boatswain's Mate* (1916), orchestral pieces, chamber music, and songs.

snare drum see **side drum**.

Snegurochka see **Snow Maiden, The**.

Snow Maiden, The (Russian: *Snegurochka*) Opera in prologue and four acts by Rimsky-Korsakov with libretto by the composer based on a play by Ostrovsky. First performance: St Petersburg, 1882. The Snow Maiden (soprano) is loved by Misgir (baritone) but she melts in the warmth of the spring sun and he throws himself into the lake in despair.

soave Sweet; gentle. [Italian]

Socrate (*Socrates*) Work for voices and orchestra by Satie to words by Cousin. First performance: 1920. The text is a translation into French of the dialogues of Plato, the three parts being entitled 'Portrait de Socrate' ('Portrait of Socrates'), 'Les Bords de l'Ilussus' ('The Banks of the Ilyssus'), and 'Mort de Socrate' ('The Death of Socrates'). Although described by the composer as a symphonic drama, this work was never intended for stage performance.

Söderström, Elisabeth (1927–) Swedish soprano. She joined the Swedish Opera early in her career but has also appeared at Glyndebourne (from 1957), where her singing of Strauss, Mozart, Henze, and Tchaikovsky was very popular, Covent Garden, and the Metropolitan Opera, New York.

soft pedal see **piano**.

Sogno di Scipione, Il (*The Dream of Scipio*) Dramatic serenade for voices and orchestra (K. 126) by Mozart to a libretto by Metastasio. Composed: 1772. Mozart composed this work to celebrate the installation of Prince Hieronymus von Colloredo as Archbishop of Salzburg, setting a libretto by Metastasio dating from 1735. The serenade presents a 'moral' story with Scipio falling asleep, dreaming that he is being courted by Constancy and Fortune, and having to decide which one to heed.

soh see **tonic sol-fa**.

Sohal, Naresh (1939–) Indian composer, who studied in Britain. His music makes use of quarter tones as an integral part of characteristically brooding textures. His output includes orchestral compositions, vocal works, and chamber music.

Soir, Le see **Matin, Le.**

Soirées musicales Collection of songs and duets by Rossini. Published: 1835. These works are best known in an orchestral arrangement of five of them by Britten that appeared in 1936 under the same title. Some of the *Soirées musicales* were also orchestrated by Respighi for his ballet *La Boutique fantasque.*

sol see **solmization.**

Soldier's Tale, The (French: *L'Histoire de soldat*) Work for actors, dancers, narrator, and chamber ensemble by Stravinsky to a libretto by Ramuz. First performance: 1918. Like *Ragtime* of the same period, this work shows a preoccupation with jazz idioms and is based upon a selection of Russian folk tales featuring a soldier who is ensnared by the Devil. The orchestra consists of six instruments and percussion and provides a series of short character pieces to link the events of the plot, which are acted and narrated.

Soler, Antonio (1729–83) Spanish friar, composer, and organist, a pupil of Domenico Scarlatti. In 1750 he was appointed maestro di cappella at Lérida Cathedral; he then joined the Escorial Jeronymite monks as organist and composer (1752) and maestro di cappella (1757). Soler wrote many keyboard works for royal patrons, organ concertos, sacred vocal works, villancicos, and a treatise, *Llave de la modulación* (1762).

sol-fa see **tonic sol-fa.**

soli see **solo.**

solmization A *notation for designating the notes of the musical scale by syllables. The system was first introduced by Guido d'Arezzo in the 11th century and replaced the early Greek *tetrachords. D'Arezzo's system was based on *hexachords and the syllables were derived from the hymn for the festival of John the Baptist, the first syllable of each line beginning on successive notes of the hexachord:

> **Ut** queant laxis
> **Resonare** fibris
> **Mira** gestorum
> **Famuli** tuorum
> **Solve** polluti
> **Labii** reatum
> **Sancte** Ioannes

The seventh syllable, si, was added later and was taken from the initial letters of the last line. Ut, the first syllable, has largely been replaced by do (except in France). The syllables are not fixed to a particular key and can be transferred by mutation to other keys as long as a semitone always occurs between mi and fa. The *tonic sol-fa is a modern derivative of this system.

solo (*pl.* **solos** (*or* Italian) **soli**) A piece or section of a piece played or sung by one performer alone. [Italian, alone]

Solomon Oratorio for solo voices, choir, and orchestra by Handel to a text by an unknown author based on the Bible. First performance: 1749. The most famous part of the oratorio is the sinfonia in the third part, entitled 'The Arrival of the Queen of Sheba,' which is often performed separately and exists in many arrangements.

Solomon (S. Cutner; 1902–) British pianist. A pupil of Mathilde Verne, he made his debut at the age of eight and rapidly became recognized as a leading pianist of his day. Incapacitated by paralysis, he was forced to retire in 1965.

solo organ see **organ.**

Solti, Sir Georg (1912–) Hungarian-born conductor. A student of Kodály (composition) and Dohnányi (piano), Solti conducted at the Budapest Opera (1933–39) and in Zürich, Munich, and Frankfurt. In the 1950s he emerged as a major conductor; he directed the Covent Garden Opera (1961–71), the Chicago Symphony Orchestra (1969–), the Orchestre de Paris (1971–), and the London Philharmonic Orchestra (1979–). His many recordings include the first complete recording in stereo of Wagner's *Ring* as well as much of the romantic and early 20th-century orchestral repertoire. He became a British citizen and was knighted in 1972.

Sir Georg Solti

Sombrero de tres picos, El see **Three-Cornered Hat, The.**

Somervell, Sir Arthur (1863–1937) British composer, a pupil of Stanford and Parry and later a teacher at the Royal College of Music in London. Somervell was knighted in 1929 for his work in school music. His compositions include choral music, songs, and piano pieces.

sommo (*or fem.* **somma**) Highest; utmost. [Italian]

son Sound. [French]

sonata Originally, a piece of music that was 'sounded,' as opposed to one that was sung (compare **cantata**). Among early examples are Italian instrumental compositions of the late 16th century, such as *canzonas and *ricercari, that are in several short sections contrasting in style and texture. The most famous early sonata is Giovanni Gabrieli's *Sonata pian e forte* (1597), which is scored for violin, cornett, and six trombones. By the middle of the 17th century, partly through the works of Giovanni Legrenzi (1626–90), the two species **sonata da chiesa** (*or* **church sonata**) and **sonata da camera** (*or* **chamber sonata**) had emerged. In the works of Corelli the former became codified as a four-movement piece (slow–fast–slow–fast) and the latter as a *suite with an introduction followed by three or four dances. Both kinds of sonata may be divided into four types according to the forces required: (1) solo, (2) two parts (**a due**), (3) three parts (**a tre**), (4) four or more parts (**a quattro**). The sonata a tre (see also **trio sonata**) is actually performed by four players, since two are required for the basso continuo part. Similarly the sonata a due requires three players. Among the early keyboard sonatas are those of Johann Kuhnau (1692), which are programmatic, and those of Pasquini. These were followed by the 550 single-movement sonatas for harpsichord by Domenico Scarlatti.

The change from the predominantly polyphonic style of the baroque to the mainly homophonic style of the Viennese classical composers that was to culminate in the music of Haydn, Mozart, and Beethoven was concurrent with the evolution of the sonata into its present-day form. This is a three- or four-movement piece (fast–slow–fast, with or without a minuet and trio) either for a solo instrument (with or without keyboard accompaniment) or for an ensemble of instruments. In this latter category the forms trio, string quartet, quintet, and symphony may be included (see also **sonata form**). Among the notable solo keyboard sonatas of this period are those of C. P. E. and J. C. Bach, who respectively influenced Haydn and Mozart. In Beethoven's 32 piano sonatas the established sonata structures were expanded in several directions. These include slow introductions (e.g. in the *Pathetic Sonata*), scherzo and trio movements (as in the second sonata), theme and variation finales (as in the last E major sonata), and the use of fugal textures (as in the *Hammerklavier Sonata*). The composers of piano sonatas of the 19th century also include Schubert,

Schumann, Chopin, and Liszt (see also **cyclic form**). Brahms contributed several sonatas to the repertoire, including three for piano, three for violin and piano, and two for cello and piano. In the 20th century neoclassical composers have been among the writers of sonatas. Some notable 20th-century sonatas include the *Sonata for Two Pianos and Percussion* by Bartók and those of Hindemith and Stravinsky. See also **sonatina.**

sonata form A structure that evolved during the second half of the 18th century in sonatas, symphonies, concertos, overtures, quartets, arias, etc. Its origins are complex, since it was not acknowledged as a standard *form until it was theoretically codified (with very limited terms of definition) by Reicha in 1826 and subsequently by Czerny in his *School of Practical Composition* (1848). Furthermore it was not until 1845 that the actual term 'sonata form' was used by Adolph Marx III. It was not a fixed form in any sense in the late 18th century and evolved from a flexible synthesis of several structures of the earlier part of the 18th century, including *binary form, *ternary form, aria, concerto, and ritornello. Its emergence was associated with most of the changes of musical style and texture that characterized the classical period: the dramatic and often violent opposition of several keys, the contrasting of several different thematic ideas within the same movement, and the articulation of structure through instrumentation. It appears to be a form of the free musical development of ideas that has continued to be of considerable significance well into the 20th century.

Some of the essential features of sonata form, as seen in the first movements of works by Haydn, Mozart, and Beethoven and later codified in the 19th century, are as follows. The musical events and gestures are traditionally explained in terms of three areas: exposition, development, and recapitulation. The **exposition** presents thematic material that articulates the tonal movement from the tonic key to the dominant (or relative major) key. The material in the tonic key may be described as the first group and that in the dominant (or relative major) key as the second group. The **development** is concerned with thematic discussion and transformation. The techniques of thematic development include the fragmentation of material into *motives, the contrapuntal working of themes, and a more rapid rate of harmonic change often allied to a sequential structure. Although thematic development is traditionally associated with the central area of a sonata-form movement it may also be found in the exposition, recapitulation, and *coda. The **recapitulation** reintroduces the material of the exposition, largely in the tonic key area. The dramatic function of this section is to reassert the original key after the shift to the dominant at the end of the exposition and the wider harmonic divergencies and tensions set up in the development.

It is most significant that the writers of the late 18th century described sonata form with reference to its harmonic structures. In lyrical slow movements an abbreviated sonata form, without a development area, is sometimes used. This structure, A'A", is related to both binary form and aria form in which the A section of the latter's ABA' structure is itself in binary form. A variant of the form in miniature occurs in minuets. These bear a clear relationship to binary form, but their dramatic contrasting of keys arguably relate them to the sonata principle. In finales a variant known as **sonata-rondo form** (see also **rondo**), with the scheme ABACABA, is characteristic. This is clearly similar to first-movement form except that the first group (A) is restated before the development (C) and at the end of the recapitulation after the second group (B).

During the 19th century Schubert, Schumann, Bruckner, Brahms, Mahler, and others continued the expansion of sonata forms begun by Beethoven. Some of the most significant factors include the use of mediant, submediant, Neapolitan, and tritone keys as substitutes for the more usual dominant, subdominant, or relative minor relationships. The first movement of Schubert's C major string quintet contains many of these features. At the end of the 19th century, interest in thematic metamorphosis, the merging of movements to create cyclic structures, and the pursuit of intense chromaticism led to sonata form becoming a convenient structure to contain ideas. The opposition of tonalities, which was the life force of classical sonata form, was replaced by a preoccupation with the development of motives and thematic and textural contrasts in many 20th-century works. These features can be seen in the third of Berg's *Three Pieces for Orchestra* and Bartók's fifth string quartet.

sonatina A relatively short and easy-to-play composition in *sonata form, usually one for the piano. [Italian, little sonata]

song A short piece for solo voice with or without accompaniment in a simple style. Songs are common to all cultures throughout the ages. Some fragments of ancient Greek songs have survived but the beginnings of the present western tradition can be found in the unaccompanied songs of the 12th century. These include the music of the *troubadours, *trouvères, *Minnesinger, and *Meistersinger and the *lauda tradition. In the 14th century songs with instrumental accompaniment were of significance in France and Italy. These evolved into the Renaissance *chanson of Dufay, Binchois, and others. The *part song emerged during the second half of the 15th century. Composers of this period include Obrecht and Josquin and in the 16th century, Sermisy and Jannequin. During the early 17th century the lute song flourished in England in the works of Dowland and his contemporaries. In France at this time the air de cour (a courtly song with lute or harpsichord accompani-

ment) evolved. The advent of *monody in the early 17th century transformed the character of song into a freer declamatory style (see also **aria; recitative**). These developments rapidly became absorbed into the new genres of *cantata, *opera, and *oratorio. The 18th-century German song evolved into the romantic *lied of the 19th century. French song became re-established by the end of the 19th century through the works of Duparc and Fauré. The *song cycle was a particularly favoured form, as in Fauré's *La Bonne chanson*. A strong tradition of romantic and nationalistic song in Russia during the 19th century stemmed from the works of Glinka, Tchaikovsky, and The *Five. *Impressionism is projected in the songs of Debussy. English song composers of the 20th century include Bax, Britten, Holst, and Warlock.

song cycle A group of songs arranged, usually by the composer, into a particular order for performance. This order reflects the continuity of the text, which may consist of poems by the same poet or poems by different poets on the same theme.

song form see **ternary form**.

Song of Destiny (German: *Schicksalslied*) Work for choir and orchestra (Op. 54) by Brahms to words by Hölderlin. Composed: 1871. The work is based upon a poem from Hölderlin's collection *Hyperion*.

Song of the Earth see **Lied von der Erde, Das**.

Songs and Dances of Death Song cycle by Mussorgsky to poems by Golenishchev-Gutuzov. Composed: 1875–77. Each of the four songs reflects on a different aspect of death; they are 'Trepak; Death and the Peasant,' 'Cradle Song; the Child Breathes Gently,' 'Death the Serenader; Soft is the Night,' and 'Field Marshal Death; War Rumbles.'

Songs for a Mad King see **Eight Songs for a Mad King**.

Songs of a Wayfaring Man see **Lieder eines fahrenden Gesellen**.

Songs on the Death of Children see **Kindertotenlieder**.

Songs Without Words (German: *Lieder ohne Worte*) Collection of piano pieces by Mendelssohn. Composed: 1832–45. These 48 pieces were published in 8 books (each containing 6 pieces) and some were later given titles, including *The Bees' Wedding* and *Spring Song, although few of these were applied by the composer himself. In style the works are more like vocal compositions than piano pieces, with a lyrical melody presented over a harmonic accompaniment (hence the title).

Sonnambula, La (*The Sleepwalker*) Opera in two acts by Bellini with libretto by Romani. First performance: Teatro Carcano, Milan, 1831. It is set in a Swiss village in the early

19th century: the heroine, Amina (soprano), compromises herself by her habit of sleepwalking but all ends happily.

sonore Sonorous. Italian: **sonoro**. [French]

Sophocles (*c.*496–406 BC) Greek dramatist. Only seven of his hundred or so plays have survived. Of operas based on Sophocles, *Antigone* (1924–27) was written by Honegger and *Oedipus Rex* (1926–27) by Stravinsky (both with libretti by Cocteau). Richard Strauss's opera *Elektra* (1909) was from a libretto by Hoffmanstahl.

sopranino Denoting a musical instrument with a higher pitch than the soprano instrument. Examples are the sopranino *recorder and the sopranino *saxophone.

soprano The highest and most brilliant of the three varieties of female voice, with an effective range of more than two octaves, the lowest note being around middle C. Sopranos can be classified as either dramatic, lyric, or coloratura. The **dramatic soprano** blossomed during the 19th century with the emergence of romantic opera, Wagner's female roles, in particular, calling for a voice of considerable power. The **lyric soprano** is lighter in quality and more suitable in operetta, while the **coloratura** voice is high and agile and has been particularly associated with Italian and Italianate opera throughout its history.

Sor, Fernando (Joseph Ferdinando Macari Sors; 1778–1839) Spanish composer and guitarist. He studied at Montserrat, then lived in Barcelona, Paris (1813–15), London (1815–26), and Paris again (1826–39). He was a celebrated guitarist and teacher who composed many works for his instrument and wrote an influential book on guitar technique (1830). Sor also wrote operas, ballets (including *Cendrillon*, 1822), and vocal and instrumental music.

Sorabji, Kaikhosru Shapurji (Leon Dudley S.; 1892–1988) British composer, son of a Parsee father and a Spanish mother. Largely self-taught, Sorabji developed a musical idiom of unusual complexity deriving from eastern music. In 1940 he banned public performance of his compositions, a ban applying to all but two artists. His compositions include many works for piano, including the cycle *Opus clavicembalisticum* (1929–30); orchestral works; and chamber music.

Sorcerer, The Operetta by Sullivan with libretto by Gilbert. First performance: Opéra Comique, London, 1877. Village life is disrupted when a respectable firm of sorcerers peddle their own brand of love potion to the inhabitants.

Sorcerer's Apprentice, The (French: *L'Apprenti sorcier*) Tone poem by Dukas, based on Goethe's ballad *Der Zauberlehrling*. Composed: 1897. It tells the story of a sorcerer's apprentice who, in his master's absence, casts a spell but is unable to stop it.

sord. see **sordino**.

sordine see **kit**.

sordino Mute. Hence **con sordino**, with mute, a direction indicating a passage to be played with the mute; **senza sordino**, without mute, a direction indicating a passage to be played without the mute. Abbreviation: **sord.** [Italian]

Sorochintsy Fair Opera in three acts by Mussorgsky with libretto by the composer based on an episode from Gogol's *Evenings on a Farm near Dekanka*. Unfinished at the composer's death in 1881, it was first performed in concert form in St Petersburg, 1911. Completed scores have been constructed by Cui, Shebalin, and Tcherepnin, in whose version it is usually performed. The village setting is the scene of the famous *Hopak*, danced by the heroine, Parassia (soprano).

Sors, Ferdinando see **Sor, Fernando**.

sostenuto Sustained: a direction used to indicate either style or tempo of performance. French: **soutenu**. [Italian]

sotto voce A direction used in vocal and instrumental scores to indicate a quiet subdued tone. [Italian, under the voice]

soubrette A stock, but secondary, role in opera given to a maid or serving girl and usually sung by a light soprano. Mozart transformed the type into characters of greater significance with Susanna in *The Marriage of Figaro*, Zerlina in *Don Giovanni*, and Papagena in *The Magic Flute*. Italian: **servetta**. [French]

soundboard A resonant wooden surface that vibrates in sympathy with the strips of a stringed instrument and thereby adds to the volume of sound produced. It is used in the organ, piano, harpsichord, dulcimer, etc. The *belly of many stringed instruments, such as the violin, is also called the soundboard.

sound hole A hole cut in the surface of a soundboard to enhance the resonance of the instrument to which it is fitted. Viols had a pair of C-shaped holes cut in the belly of the instrument, fiddles and violins have S-shaped holes, while lutes and guitars usually have a single decorated round hole, called a **rose**.

soundpost A piece of wood fitted inside the *body of certain stringed instruments, such as the violin, to support the bridge and to transmit vibrations to the back of the instrument. It is usually made of pine and fitted under the right foot of the bridge.

sourdine Mute. [French]

Sousa, John Philip (1854–1932) US composer, conductor, and writer. After conducting the US Marine Band (1880–92) he formed his own band, which quickly achieved immense popularity and gained an international reputation through its tours of Europe and North America. Sousa composed several operettas (including *El Capitan*, 1895) but is best known for his marches, many in a patriotic vein; they include *Semper Fidelis* (*c*.1888), *The Thunderer* (*c*.1889), *The Washington Post* (1889), *King Cotton* (1895), *The Stars and Stripes Forever* (1897), and *Hands Across the Sea* (1899). Sousa also wrote novels, an autobiography, many articles, and a textbook.

sousaphone see tuba.

Souster, Tim (1943–) British composer, a pupil of Stockhausen, Berio, and Rodney Bennett. Greatly influenced by rock music and group improvisation techniques, he founded the ensembles Intermodulation (with Smalley) and OdB (in 1976). His works include *Chinese Whispers* (1970), *Triple Music* (1970), *Spectral* (1972), *Arcane Artifact* (1976), and *Arboreal Antecedents* (1978).

soutenu see sostenuto.

South American music Comparatively little is known about the music of the indigenous Indian tribes of the South American continent: so much of their culture was forcibly absorbed into that of the conquering and colonizing Spanish and Portuguese in the 16th century. The two great Indian civilizations, the Aztecs of what is now Mexico and the Incas of Peru, had an active sacred and secular musical life with court feasts and ceremonies containing songs and dance, trained singing girls, and percussion players. Nevertheless their music seems to have been relatively undeveloped; based on the pentatonic scale, it was of a generally melancholy cast. Instruments they are known to have used include a variety of trumpets (including the gold trumpets of the Chibchas tribe of Colombia), percussion, panpipes, and fipple flutes; the quena flute is said to have been banned by the invading and proselytizing Catholic authorities as having too seductive and nostalgic a tone. One of the last tribes to resist the Spaniards was the Araucanians, who now live in a reserve in southern central Chile; their primitive and monotonous chant ranges only over two or three notes.

South American music is therefore based on imported sacred and secular music from 16th-century Spain and Portugal with a fair leavening of African Negro music devolving from the slave trade. The Jesuits were among the most fearless in penetrating the hinterlands and imposing their creed: Bolivia, in the central Andes, still has some handsome baroque churches of the 17th century where the Mass was sung and European music taught. In Mexico, Spanish musicians were producing church polyphonic music by the last quarter of the 16th century. In the secular field Iberian folk and popular music evolved into a variety of dance and song forms including the rumba, *tonadilla, *habanera, and *jota; the **bambuco** has its roots in Africa. Native Indian dances include the **chokela, yaraví,** and

hayllia. Characteristic of the grasslands of Argentina is the **gaucho** tradition, stemming from the early 19th century, with its epic ballads about the cowboy's lot sung to guitar accompaniment.

Composers who have attempted to preserve the South American tradition in their work include Heitor *Villa-Lobos from Brazil and Carlos *Chávez from Mexico, and as a teacher and folk musicologist, Manual *Ponce was of great importance in the musical life of Mexico. The Chilean pianist Claudio *Arrau is among internationally recognized instrumentalists from South America.

Souzay, Gerard (1920–) French baritone. He studied with Pierre Bernac, whose excellent qualities as a lied interpreter he seems to have inherited; he then expanded his repertory to include other German works and earlier music, such as Monteverdi. Since 1954 Souzay has been accompanied by Dalton Baldwin.

Sowerby, Leo (1895–1968) US composer and organist. His works are composed in an academic European tradition and show some influence from American folk and blues music. They include three symphonies, two cello concertos, an organ concerto (1938), *Canticle of the Sun* (1945), anthems, chamber music, and organ pieces.

Spanisches Liederbuch (*Spanish Song-Book*) Collection of songs by Wolf. Composed: 1889–90. The songs are set to 16th- and 17th-century Spanish poems translated into German by Geibel and Heyse. Of the 44 poems set, 34 have secular subjects and 10 sacred subjects.

Spanish Caprice see Capriccio espagnol.

Spanish Hour, The see Heure espagnole, L'.

Spanish Rhapsody Orchestral suite by Ravel. Composed: 1907. As the title implies, this work was influenced by the spirit of Spanish folk music, the four movements being entitled 'Prélude à la nuit' ('Prelude to the Night'), 'Malagueña,' 'Habanera,' and 'Feria' ('Festival'). The malagueña and habanera are national Spanish dances, whose characteristic melodic and rhythmic figurations are imitated by Ravel.

Spanish Symphony Work for solo violin and orchestra by Lalo. First performance: 1875. Although described by the composer as a symphony, this work is actually more in the form of a concerto with its prominent and virtuosic violin part, written for the celebrated Spanish violinist *Sarasate. The five movements of the work are based on themes that are influenced by the melodic and rhythmic style of Spanish folk music.

species counterpoint A discipline used in the teaching of *counterpoint and composition. The student is given a cantus firmus in semibreves and asked to add a voice of his own that follows each in turn of five rhythmic patterns (**species**) as follows. (1) The added voice moves in semibreves, synchronized with the cantus firmus. (2) The added voice moves in minims, two to each note of the cantus firmus. (3) The added voice moves in crotchets, four to each note of the cantus firmus. (4) As (1), but with the added voice syncopated against the cantus firmus. (5) (known as **contrapunctus floridus**) The added voice freely combines all types of movement found in (1)–(4). In species counterpoint in three or more voices two or more species can be combined (**combined species**).

Spectre's Bride, The Cantata for choir and orchestra (Op. 69) by Dvořák to a Czech text by Erben entitled *Svatebni Kosile* (*The Wedding Shift*). First performance: 1885. The first performance took place at the Birmingham Festival using an English translation.

speech song A word setting on a monotone or dictated by the natural inflexions of speech that preserves metre and rhythmical identity. Schoenberg used this genre of vocal writing to great effect in his *Gurrelieder* (1900), the music drama *Die glückliche Hand* (1909), and *Pierrot lunaire* (1912). Walton's *Façade* (1926) is the most outstanding example of this style of composition by a British composer. German: **Sprechgesang**; **Sprechstimme** is the voice part using Sprechgesang.

Speer, Daniel (1636–1707) German composer, theorist, and author. He was active in Stuttgart, Tübingen, and some small German towns as a teacher and church musician. Speer published church works and quodlibets in a simple style but is best remembered for his theoretical writings; his textbook *Grund-richtiger* (1687) gives some insights into performance practice.

Spelman, Timothy Mather (1891–1970) US composer. Periods of study and residence in Europe enabled Spelman to absorb elements of French and Italian musical style. His compositions include operas, a symphony (1936), ballets, and chamber music.

spianato Smoothed; levelled. [Italian]

spiccato A bowing technique used to perform rapid staccato passages. The bow is dropped onto the string between its mid-point and the nut and consciously lifted from the string between each note. Compare **ricochet**. [Italian, separated]

Spider's Banquet, The (French: *Le Festin de l'araignée*) Ballet in one act with music by Roussel and scenario by Gilbert de Voisins based on Henri Fabre's studies of insect life. First performance: Théâtre des Arts, Paris, 1913. The pictorial delicacy of the score has made it one of Roussel's most popular works, though not typical of his style. A spider catches insects in her web until killed herself by a praying mantis.

spike fiddle see **fiddle**.

spinet 1. See **harpsichord instruments**. **2.** A square *piano.

spirito Spirit; vigour. Hence **con spirito**, spirited. [Italian]

Spirit of England Set of three cantatas for soprano solo, choir, and orchestra by Elgar to words by Binyon. Composed: 1916–17. Each of the texts of these cantatas comments on a different aspect of World War I, which was being fought at the time of their composition. The three cantatas are entitled 'The Fourth of August,' 'To Women,' and 'For the Fallen.'

spiritual see **Negro spiritual**.

Spohr, Louis (Ludwig S.; 1784–1859) German composer, violinist, and conductor. In 1799 he became a court chamber musician to the Duke of Brunswick; he then played as a celebrated violin virtuoso throughout Germany and became orchestral leader in Gotha (1805–12). He soon gained an international reputation as a conductor, using a baton (rare at the time). He became director of the orchestra at the Theater an der Wien, Vienna (1813–15), and directed the Frankfurt Opera (1817–19). After further international tours he became kapellmeister (1821) and general music director (1847) in Kassel. Spohr was a leading early romantic composer of instrumental music; his works are technically assured while showing many individual features. For the violin he wrote 15 concertos (No. 8, 'in modo di scena cantante' (1816), is the only one heard often today) and virtuoso solo works. He wrote nine complete symphonies, overtures, four clarinet concertos, choral music, and over 90 songs. Of his large output of chamber music, the nonet (1813) and octet (1814) are among the best works; he also wrote 34 string quartets, four double string quartets, seven string quintets, piano trios, etc. Of his operas, *Jessonda* (1822) was the most successful. Spohr also wrote a violin method (1831).

Spontini, Gaspare (Luigi Pacifico) (1774–1851) Italian composer and conductor. He studied at the Naples conservatory (1793–95) and his early operas were staged in various Italian cities. In 1803 he went to Paris, where he was patronized by Empress Joséphine and scored a great success with his opera La *Vestale, produced at the Opéra in 1807. He became director of the Théâtre-Italien in 1810 but because of his arrogant personality was dismissed in 1812; he was reinstated from 1814 to 1816. Spontini became musical director of the Berlin Hofoper in 1819, but his own Italian works were eclipsed by the triumphant success of Weber's *Der Freischütz* (1821) and the consequent taste for German opera. After many disputes he was forced to leave in 1842. He spent his final years in Paris and by 1847 was deaf; he died at his Italian birthplace. Spontini was the leading figure in French opera of his day. His operas, many containing bold dramatic strokes, include

La Finta filosofa (1799, revised 1804), *Milton* (1804), *Julie* (1805), *Fernand Cortez* (1809, revised 1817 and 1832), and *Olimpie* (1819). His songs, choral works, and instrumental music are of little consequence.

Sprechgesang and **Sprechstimme** see **speech song**.

springar A popular Norwegian folk dance in 3/4 time.

springer A musical ornament in which an auxiliary note is inserted between two other notes. It robs the preceding note of part of its time value and is thus the opposite of an *appoggiatura.

Spring Sonata Sonata in F major for violin and piano (Op. 24) by Beethoven. Composed: 1801. The name, which was never used by Beethoven himself, refers to the relaxed and happy mood of the work.

Spring Song Piece for piano by Mendelssohn. Composed: 1843. *Spring Song* is the last (No. 30) of a set of six pieces forming the fifth volume (Op. 62) of Mendelssohn's *Songs Without Words*. Although the title is very appropriate to the character of the piece, it was not used by Mendelssohn himself for the first publication but added at a later date.

Spring Symphony 1. Symphony No. 1 in B♭ major by Schumann. First performance: 1841. Schumann himself used this title, originally also giving descriptive subtitles to the individual movements, although these were later removed. **2.** Work for solo voices, boys' choir, choir, and orchestra (Op. 49) by Britten. First performance: 1949. Britten set a variety of texts relating to spring and at the conclusion of the work uses the canon *Sumer is icumen in*.

square piano see **piano**.

Staatsoper State opera or opera house. [German]

Stabat Mater A hymn used in the Roman Catholic Church, attributed to Jacapone da Todi (*c*.1228–1306). From the 15th to the 17th centuries the words of this hymn were set to music by many leading composers, including Josquin, Lassus, and Palestrina, and in 1727 the *Stabat Mater* was officially adopted as a *Sequence by the Roman Catholic Church. The words of the hymn describe the vigil that Mary kept at the Cross after Jesus' crucifixion; more recent settings exist by Rossini, Dvořák, and Poulenc amongst others. The *Stabat Mater* is associated liturgically with the Feast of the Seven Dolors (15 September).

staccato Detached. A direction to indicate that the notes so marked (with dots above them) should be played slightly shorter than their normal time value with a brief pause between notes. This has the effect of making the notes of staccato passages separate from each other. It is the opposite of *legato. [Italian]

Stadler, Anton (1753–1812) Austrian clarinetist and basset-horn player. He was a member of the Vienna Court Orchestra and was a close friend of Mozart, who wrote both his clarinet concerto and quintet for him.

staff (*or* **stave**) The five-line *notation now in use to denote the pitch, time value, and, to a certain extent, the loudness of a musical note. The pitch of a note is determined by the *clef, which locates a note of a particular pitch on the staff. The time values of the notes are indicated by their shapes and whether they are filled or open. The rhythm of a composition is indicated by breaking the staff into bars with bar lines and giving a *time signature at the beginning of a composition. The *key of the music is indicated by the *key signature at the start of each line. A **great staff** is an eleven-line staff in which the treble clef is joined to the bass clef by an eleventh line on which *middle C is situated. It is used only as a diagram to indicate the positions of the other clefs.

Stainer, Sir John (1840–1901) British church musician, composer, and scholar. A chorister at St Paul's Cathedral, he subsequently studied at Oxford University (1859–66) and founded the Oxford Philharmonic Society. He was organist of St Paul's Cathedral from 1872 to 1888, the year he was knighted. From 1876 he was organist, and from 1881 principal, of the National Training School for Music. Stainer composed much sacred choral music, of which the oratorio The *Crucifixion (1887) and the *Sevenfold Amen* (1897) are still often heard. He was a distinguished scholar; among his writings is a book on Dufay (1898).

Stamitz Czech family of musicians. **Johann Wenzel Stamitz** (1717–57), composer, violinist, and teacher, became leader (*c*.1745) and later director (1750) of the Mannheim orchestra, which he made the most important in Europe. He wrote many symphonies, concertos, sacred music, and chamber works and founded the *Mannheim School. His son **Carl Stamitz** (1745–1801) was a composer and virtuoso player of the violin, viola, and viola d'amore. He studied with his father and others and was court composer to Duke Louis of Noailles in Paris (1771–*c*.1777). After touring widely be became musical director to the university at Jena (1794). He wrote many duets and other chamber works, symphonies, concertos, sacred music, and two operas. Carl's brother (**Johann**) **Anton Stamitz** (1754–before 1809) was a violinist and composer of symphonies, concertos, and chamber music.

Ständchen see **serenade**.

Standford, Patric (1939–) British composer, a pupil of Rubbra, Malipiero, and Lutoslawski. His compositions, which occasionally use aleatoric techniques, include orchestral works, chamber music (including two string quartets), songs, and piano works.

Stanford, Sir Charles Villiers (1852–1924) British composer, teacher, conductor, and organist. He studied at

Sir Charles Stanford

Cambridge University (1870–73) and was appointed organist of Trinity College (1873–82). In Leipzig he studied with Reinecke, and in Berlin with Kiel. From 1873 he conducted the Cambridge University Musical Society, for which he composed *The Resurrection* (1875) among other works, winning recognition as a composer and accomplished conductor. His reputation was further enhanced when Tennyson commissioned him to provide incidental music to *Queen Mary* (1876). He became a professor at the Royal College of Music (1883), conductor of the London Bach Choir (1885–1902), and music professor at Cambridge University (1887). He was knighted in 1902.

Stanford was a celebrated composition teacher who had a far-reaching influence: his pupils included Vaughan Williams, Holst, Howells, Ireland, Bridge, Bliss, and Moeran. He was also a prolific composer who played a leading role in the 19th-century renaissance of English music (associated with Parry, Parratt, and Elgar). His church music is of particularly high quality and includes works that are still commonly used, such as the Morning, Communion, and Evening services in B♭ (1879), anthems, and motets. His fine oratorios and cantatas include *The Three Holy Children* (1885), *The Revenge* (1886), *Songs of the Sea* (1904), and the *Stabat Mater* (1907). His best-known operas are *The Canterbury Pilgrims* (1884), *Shamus O'Brien* (1896), *The Critic* (1915), and *The Travelling*

Companion (1919); he also wrote songs and part songs. Stanford's instrumental music is less exceptional; it includes six *Irish Rhapsodies*, seven symphonies, a cello concerto, three piano concertos, two violin concertos, overtures, eight string quartets, two piano quartets, two string quintets, a piano quintet, three piano trios, and two cello sonatas. He edited a collection of Irish folk melodies and wrote books and essays on music.

Stanley, John (1712–86) British composer and organist. Blinded in infancy, he studied with Greene and became organist at All Hallows, Bread Street (*c*.1724) and the Inner Temple (1734) and master of the King's Band (1779). In addition to his famous organ voluntaries, he also wrote concertos, cantatas, odes, the dramatic pastoral *Arcadia* (1761), and keyboard and chamber works.

Starer, Robert (1924–) Austrian-born US composer. Starer studied in Vienna and the Near East. His works, which are notable for their direct expression within a modern idiom, include operas and ballets, three symphonies, concertos, chamber music, and choral works.

stark Strong; loud. [German]

Starker, János (1924–) Hungarian-born US cellist. He studied at the Budapest academy and held appointments in various Hungarian orchestras before settling in the USA in 1948. Starker formed a piano trio with Suk and Katchen in 1967.

Star-Spangled Banner, The National anthem of the USA. The words of the anthem, commencing 'O say, can you see by the dawn's early light,' were written by Francis Scott Key in September 1814 and were inspired by the British bombardment of Fort McHenry near Baltimore. At a later date a melody by John Stafford Smith was set to this poem (the melody was actually composed for another song, beginning 'To Anacreon in Heaven,' and was not originally intended for *The Star-Spangled Banner*). In 1931 the anthem was officially adopted by the US government.

stave see **staff.**

steam organ see **barrel organ.**

Steffani, Agostino (1654–1728) Italian composer, diplomat, and clergyman. In about 1678 he was appointed court and chamber organist in Munich; he then served the Duke of Hanover (1688) and the Elector Palatine (1703) as musical director and diplomat. After various diplomatic missions he was elected Bishop of Spiga (1706) and Apostolic Vicar (1709). Steffani wrote many chamber duets (imitated by Handel, who succeeded him as musical director at the Hanoverian court), operas, overtures, sacred works, and a treatise.

Steg The bridge of a stringed instrument. [German]

Issac Stern

Steinberg, Maximillian (1883–1946) Soviet composer. Steinberg studied with Glazunov and Rimsky-Korsakov; in 1934 he was made director of the Leningrad conservatory. Steinberg's works include four symphonies and other orchestral compositions, chamber music, and songs.

Steinberg, William (1899–1978) German-born conductor. After conducting in German opera houses, he emigrated to the USA in 1937. He conducted the Pittsburgh Symphony Orchestra (1952–76) and the Boston Symphony Orchestra (1969–72) as well as the London Philharmonic (1958–60).

Steinspiel see **stone chimes.**

Steinway and Sons US (New York) firm of piano makers. Heinrich Steinweg (later Henry Steinway, 1797–1871) started building pianos in Brunswick in 1836. He emigrated with his five sons to New York in 1850 and in 1853 established his firm, which rapidly became successful with branches opened in London (1875) and Hamburg (1880).

Stenhammar, (Karl) Wilhelm (Eugen) (1871–1927) Swedish composer, pianist, and conductor. He was largely self-taught but spent a year (1892–93) in Berlin studying the piano with Barth before beginning his career as a pianist. He also had a flourishing career as conductor of the Stockholm Philharmonic Society (1897–1900), the New Philharmonic Society (1904–06), and the Göteborgs

Orkesterförening (1906–22). His compositions, many with a Swedish folk flavour, include operas, incidental music, two piano concertos, two symphonies, two *Sentimental Romances* for violin and orchestra (1910), choral, chamber, and piano music, and many songs.

step dance see **figure.**

Stern, Isaac (1920–) Russian-born US violinist. He studied in San Francisco, where he made his debut in 1935, and quickly achieved widespread acclaim. After his European debut (1948) Stern toured widely, performing both as a soloist and in a successful trio with Istomin and Rose. Stern is recognized as one of the world's leading violinists: his repertory ranges from Bach to Bartók and he has premiered concertos by William Schuman and Leonard Bernstein.

Stevenson, Ronald (1928–) British composer. Stevenson's music draws on influences from many different cultures. His compositions include piano works, such as the extended *Passacaglia on DSCH*; two piano concertos; and chamber music.

Stiffelio Opera in three acts by Verdi with libretto by Piave. First performance: Teatro Grande, Trieste, 1850. It is based on the play *Le Pasteur* by Souvestre and Eugène Bourgeois, and Italian audiences found difficulty in understanding the character of the married priest, the evangelical pastor Stiffelio (tenor), with his forgiving attitude to marital infidelity. The libretto was later recast by Piave in a medieval setting, Stiffelio becoming the crusader Aroldo. This revised version, *Aroldo*, was first performed at the Teatro Nuovo, Rimini, in 1857.

stile rappresentativo A 17th-century form of *recitative used in Italian operas and oratorios. It attempted to represent the spoken inflections of the human voice in order to achieve a natural flow in the musical drama. [Italian, representative style]

Still, Robert (1910–71) British composer. Still's works, traditional in their attachment to tonal principles, include four symphonies, chamber music, and songs.

Still, William Grant (1895–1978) US composer. A short period of study with Varèse inspired avant-garde experiments in Still's music: these subsequently gave way to a romantic idiom deriving from his Black American heritage. Still's *Afro-American Symphony* (1931) attained considerable popularity; his other works include operas, songs, and chamber music.

Stimme 1. The human voice. **2.** A part in a composition. **3.** An organ stop. [German]

Stimmführung Part writing (see **part**). [German]

Stimmung Work for six voices by Stockhausen. Composed: 1968. In this unaccompanied vocal work (the title is German for 'mood' and 'tuning') Stockhausen makes no attempt to set words but experiments instead with the wide range of sounds that the human voice is capable of producing.

stochastic Describing a musical style based on probability theory. A stochastic system produces a random sequence of notes, etc., according to certain probabilities, which at any one point depend on the occurrences of preceding events. Hence, the probability of a particular event occurring is very low in the opening stages but increases towards the end. *Xenakis has used stochastic processes to determine the duration, speed, intensity, etc., of his works, especially when these contain a large number of musical events. An example of his use of stochastic technique is seen in *ST/4* for string quartet (1956–62).

Stockhausen, Karlheinz (1928–   ) German composer, a pupil of Milhaud and Messiaen. From 1953 Stockhausen has worked at the Cologne electronic music studio; during this time he studied phonetics at Bonn, which influenced his composition. During the 1950s he contributed to the development of total serialism, his approach to which broadened with his exploration of electronic sound production. In such works as *Kontrapunkte* (1953), *Zeitmasse* (1956), and *Gruppen* (1957), Stockhausen elaborated group composition and *moment form, in which groups of notes and sound blocks (rather than individual pitches) are the compositional units. In *Kontakte* (1960) he developed techniques of electronic transformation and modulation, which he later applied to live works (e.g. *Momente*, 1962). In the late 1960s, partly influenced by eastern mysticism, he produced 'process' and 'text' pieces, such as *Stimmung* (1968) and *Mantra* (1970), in which much is left to the performers' intuition. His works of the 1970s use a new technique of melody composition and have a pronounced dramatic ritualistic element, which is central to his projected seven-day ceremonial cycle *Licht* (1977–   ). Stockhausen's other works include eleven piano pieces (1952–56), *Gesang der Jünglinge* (1956), *Carré* (1960), *Mikrophonie I and II* (1964–65), *Telemusik* (1966), *Hymnen* (1967), *Aus den sieben Tagen* (1968), *Trans* (1971), *Inori* (1973), and *Sirius* (1977).

Stokowski, Leopold (Antoni Stanislaw Boleslawowich; 1882–1977) British-born conductor of Polish descent, who took US citizenship in 1915. Stokowski conducted the Philadelphia Orchestra (1912–37), introducing many new works and experimenting with the layout of the orchestra. His orchestral transcriptions (e.g. of Bach's toccata and fugue in D minor) and re-orchestrations often attracted criticism. He was one of the first conductors to take a technical interest in recorded and broadcast sound and made experimental stereo records in the 1930s. He also appeared in films and arranged and conducted the score of Walt Disney's *Fantasia* (1940). He subsequently founded the Hollywood Bowl Symphony Orchestra (1945) and the American Symphony Orchestra (1961) and conducted the Houston Symphony Orchestra (1955–60), continuing to conduct in Europe and the USA until his death.

Stolz, Robert (1880–1975) Austrian composer, a pupil of Humperdink. Stolz is best known for his operettas; he also wrote a large number of songs and music for films.

stone chimes An ancient Chinese percussion instrument consisting of 16 L-shaped stone slabs, all the same size but of different thicknesses. The slabs are suspended in two rows in a frame. It was used in Chinese temples; the Chinese name is **bian jing** (or **pien ch'ing**). Prehistoric **lithophones** of a more rudimentary kind have also been discovered in various places in the Far East. Modern stone chimes have been used by Orff in his operas. German: **Steinspiel**.

Stone Guest, The (Russian: *Kamenny Gost*) Opera by Dargomizhsky, a setting of Pushkin's dramatic poem of the same story as Mozart's *Don Giovanni*. Unfinished at the composer's death, it was completed at his dying request by Rimsky-Korsakov and first performed in St Petersburg in 1872.

stop A knob, lever, or switch permitting or preventing the use of all or part of a *rank of pipes on a particular *organ manual or pedalboard. Originally all ranks were used all of the time and this device was introduced to 'stop' a rank from sounding, hence its name.

Storace, Stephen (1762–96) British composer. After studying in Naples, he visited Vienna with his sister, the soprano **Nancy Storace** (1765–1817), and Michael *Kelly and met Mozart. In London (from 1787), he directed Italian operas at Drury Lane (1792–93) and wrote many operas, including *The Haunted Tower* (1789) and *The Pirates* (1792), and other music for vocal and instrumental ensemble.

Stradella, Alessandro (1644–82) Italian composer. In 1658 he became a singer to Queen Christina of Sweden, in whose service he remained for several years. Back in Italy, he composed church music and dramatic works for the first public theatre in Rome. He was forced to leave Rome in 1677 after incurring the anger of Cardinal Cibo and travelled in northern Italy, settling in Genoa where he was murdered (according to legend, because of a love affair). Stradella made significant contributions to major musical genres by using concerto grosso instrumentation and by making a clear distinction between recitative and aria. He wrote a large number of stage works and cantatas but is perhaps best remembered for his oratorios.

Stradivari (or **Stradivarius**) Italian family of violin makers, active at Cremona. **Antonio Stradivari** (?1644–

Vom Walzerkönig.

Zum 50jährigen Kunstjubiläum Johann Strauss.

Von Heinrich Glücksmann.

Johann Strauss' erstes Concert 1844.

Johann Strauss the Younger at his first concert in 1844

1737), a pupil of Nicolo *Amati, is acknowledged as perhaps the maker of the world's finest violins, especially those of the period 1700–25. Two sons, **Francesco Stradivari** (1671–1743) and **Omobono Stradivari** (1679–1742) continued the business.

strascinando A direction used to indicate a heavy slurring in which one note appears to 'drag' the next with it. See **portamento**. [Italian, dragging]

strathspey A slow Scottish folk dance in quadruple time. The dance appears to have originated in the valley (strath) of the River Spey in the 18th century.

Straus, Oscar (1870–1954) Austrian composer. Straus's operettas, such as *A *Waltz Dream* (1907) and *The *Chocolate Soldier* (1908), became immensely popular; his other works include orchestral music and piano pieces.

Strauss, Johann (the Elder; 1804–49) Austrian violinist, conductor, and composer. The son of an innkeeper, Strauss was trained as a bookbinder but learned the violin privately and finally joined Lanner's orchestra, of which he became deputy conductor. In 1825 he formed a rival orchestra of his own, for which he composed 150 waltzes, 28 galops,

19 marches, and 14 polkas in the style that Lanner had made popular in Vienna. The Viennese waltz is thus regarded as the combined invention of Lanner and Strauss. His best-known composition is the *Radetzky March* (1848). His son **Johann** (the Younger; 1825–99), also a violinist, conductor, and composer, was at first discouraged by his father from becoming a musician. However, he studied secretly and when he appeared as a conductor in 1844, his father allowed him to form his own orchestra. When Johann Strauss the Elder died, his son amalgamated the two orchestras. His 16 operettas include *Der Karneval in Rom* (1873), *Die *Fledermaus* (1874), *Eine *Nacht in Venedig* (1883), and *Der Zigeunerbaron* (1885; see **Gypsy Baron, The**). He also wrote the ballet *Aschenbrödel* and a very large number of waltzes, including the famous *The *Blue Danube*, *A Thousand and One Nights*, *Tales from the Vienna Woods*, and *Roses from the South*. Like his father he also wrote many marches and polkas.

Strauss, Richard (1864–1949) German composer. Strauss's father was a principal horn player at the Munich opera house and his musical education began at an early age: his first published composition was written at the age of 12. After studies in philosophy at the University of Munich, Strauss embarked upon a conducting career, holding posts at Menningen, Munich, Weimar, and Berlin. He was director of the Vienna State Opera (1919–24). Strauss's mature compositions fall into three principal genres: tone poems (1886–1903); operas (1900–42); and songs, which he composed throughout his life. His early works include two symphonies and concertos for horn and violin; at the end of his life he returned to writing orchestral music. The main influences on Strauss's early style are the works of Liszt and Wagner. With the operas *Salome* (1904–05) and *Elektra* (1906–08) Strauss approached the atonal idiom of his younger contemporary Schoenberg. He subsequently reverted to a characteristically full romantic style. Strauss's brilliant orchestration is the most immediately striking aspect of his compositions and demands a prodigious technique from all his players and singers. Instrumental solos are prominent in many of his works. In spite of the chromatic harmony often encountered in Strauss's music, his idiom is basically tonal: this feature is reflected by his extension of traditional formal structures in his tone poems and operas.

Strauss's tone poems include *Macbeth* (1886–87), *Tod und Verklärung* (1889; see **Death and Transfiguration**), *Don Juan* (1881–89), *Till Eulenspiegel* (1895), *Also sprach Zarathustra* (1896), *Don Quixote* (1897), and *Ein Heldenleben* (1899; see **Hero's Life, A**). On a larger scale are the *Symphonia domestica* (1902–03) and *An *Alpine Symphony* (1911–15). His most significant operatic collaboration was with the writer Hugo von Hofmanstahl, who supplied libretti for 6 of Strauss's 15 operas. These include, besides *Salome* and *Elektra*, Der *Rosenkavalier* (1911), *Ariadne auf Naxos* (1912), Die *Frau ohne Schatten* (1915), *Intermezzo* (1924), Die *Aegyptische Helena* (1928), *Arabella* (1933), *Daphne* (1938), and *Capriccio* (1942). Other works by Strauss include the ballet *Josephslegende* (1914), two horn concertos (1885 and 1943), *Metamorphoses* (1945), and *Four Last Songs* (1948) for voice and orchestra.

Strauss's relationship with the Nazis has caused some concern. He conducted concerts that Toscanini would not and Bruno Walter (a Jew) could not. He accepted the presidency of Reichsmusikkammer in 1933 but resigned when his collaboration with the Jewish librettist Stefan Zweig incurred Nazi displeasure. Some of his collaboration with the Nazis is said to have been motivated by a desire to protect his Jewish daughter-in-law and he was found not guilty in a postwar denazification trial.

Stravinsky, Igor Feodorovich (1882–1971) Russian-born composer. His father was a singer at the Imperial Opera and in 1907 Stravinsky became a pupil of Rimsky-Korsakov. In 1909 he began his association with Diaghilev's Ballets Russes, which led to his first successful ballet, *The*

Igor Stravinsky

Firebird (1910). Later he also collaborated with Cocteau, Gide, and Auden. In 1914 he left Russia, living in Switzerland (1914–20) and France (1920–39); in 1939 he settled in the USA, becoming a US citizen in 1945. Stravinsky toured extensively as conductor and pianist of his own works. The early Russian ballets are nationalistic in subject and style, but after World War I he developed a detached neoclassical idiom, exemplified in his piano concerto (1924), that lasted until he evolved his own serial technique in the 1950s.

His works, which are remarkable for their striking rhythms and abrupt juxtapositions of material, include the ballets *Petrushka* (1911), The *Rite of Spring* (1913), *Pulcinella* (1920), *Apollo Musagetes* (1928), and *Agon* (1957); the melodrama *Persephone* (1933); the music-theatre pieces The *Soldier's Tale* (1918), The *Wedding* (1923), and The *Flood* (1961–62); a burlesque, The *Fox* (1915–16); symphonies, concertos (among them the *Dumbarton Oaks Concerto*, 1938), and chamber music; jazz music, including the *Ebony Concerto* (1945); the operas *Oedipus Rex* (1927) and The *Rake's Progress* (1951); and much religious music, including the *Symphony of Psalms* (1930), *Threni* (1958), and *Requiem Canticles* (1966).

street piano see **barrel organ**.

stretto 1. The overlapping of entries of a *fugue subject. Stretto entries may be any interval apart, or modified by inversion, augmentation, diminution, or even retrograde motion. The example illustrated shows two stretto entries a fifth apart with a third diminished and inverted. **2.** A direction used to indicate the acceleration or intensification of a passage, especially in the music of Chopin and other romantic composers.

An example of stretto (definition 1)

strict counterpoint The discipline of *counterpoint governed by rigorously applied rules controlling dissonance treatment, rhythm, and melodic contour within an essentially vocal idiom. It comprises *species counterpoint, *invertible counterpoint, 'Palestrina style' (in which additional voices have to be added to a single given part), *canon, and *fugue.

Striggio, Alessandro (*c.*1540–92) Italian composer. During the 1560s he became the leading composer at the Medici court. In 1584 he travelled to Ferrara to compose for Alfonso I d'Este. Striggio was a virtuoso performer on the lira da gamba. His intermezzi for the Medici court were skilfully written and his madrigals were popular abroad. Among his works is a 40-part setting of *Ecce beatam lucem* (1568) for ten four-part choirs.

stringed instruments Musical *instruments in which the sound is produced when a gut, plastic, or wire string under tension is struck, plucked, or bowed. The harp and piano are not normally considered to be stringed instruments, although the sound is produced by vibrating strings. Stringed instruments may be fretted (e.g. lutes, citterns, mandolins, guitars, ukuleles, banjos) or unfretted, as in the strings of the orchestra (violins, violas, cellos, and double basses). Compare **chordophone.**

stringendo Tightening: a direction used to indicate intensification of performance, often involving an increase in speed. French: **serré** (literally, pressed). [Italian]

string quartet see **quartet.**

string quintet see **quintet.**

string-toned stops (*or* **viols**) Organ *stops operating *flue pipes that are similar to the *diapasons but are thinner and thus produce more upper harmonics, giving the sound an edgy tone resembling that from stringed instruments.

string trio see **trio.**

stromentato Instrumented; orchestrated; e.g. **recitativo stromentato** (see **recitative**). [Italian]

strophic song A song in which each verse is set to the same music. Compare **through-composed song.**

strumento Instrument. [Italian]

study (*or* **étude**) A short instrumental composition, designed primarily to aid the student in improving his technical ability. Generally, any one study will concentrate on one particular playing problem; for example, octave playing or trills. Although some collections of studies have little musical value beyond their pedagogical function, works such as the 27 studies for piano by Chopin are also frequently performed as concert works. Other composers who have written studies for concert performance include Liszt, Debussy, and Scriabin. See also **symphonic study.**

subdominant The fourth note of the major or minor *scale above the *tonic. For example, F is the subdominant in the key of C major or C minor. See also **degree.**

subito At once; immediately. [Italian]

subject The principal *theme in a composition. See also **fugue.**

submediant The sixth note of the major or minor *scale above the *tonic. For example, A is the submediant in the key of C major or C minor. See also **degree.**

Subotnick, Morton (1933–) US composer, a pupil of Milhaud and Kirchner. Greatly involved with electronic music, he has produced pure tape works, multimedia and theatre pieces, and also 'sound-environments' for shops and offices. His works include *Silver Apples of the Moon* (1967), *Electric Christmas* (1967), *Ritual Game Room* (1970), *Before the Butterfly* (1976), and *A Sky of Cloudless Sulphur* (1980).

Suggia, Guilhermina (1888–1950) Portuguese cellist. Taught by her father and Julius Klengel, from 1906 to 1912 she lived and worked with Casals, although never married him. Subsequently much of her life was spent in England, where she had a popular following.

suite A sequence of stylized dance movements, all in the same key, that flourished as an important instrumental and keyboard form during the 17th and the first half of the 18th centuries. The normal order of dances was: *allemande, *courante, *sarabande, optional dance(s) (see below), and gigue (see **jig**). The practice of linking dances together began in England and Italy during the 16th century with the pairing of *pavans with *galliards and passamezzos with saltarellos. In the lute books of the French publisher Attaingnant there was a grouping of three or more contrasting dances, but the French keyboard composers of the 17th century preferred to group their dances according to types. The ordering of the dances of the suite as outlined above was largely the work of Froberger, although the gigue did not replace the sarabande as the final movement until the end of the 17th century. The addition of a *prelude and the optional dances between the sarabande and gigue (e.g.

minuet, bourrée, gavotte, passepied, polonaise, anglaise, loure, or air) completed the development of the suite as found in the music of J. S. Bach. In Italy the term sonata da camera described an instrumental suite (as in examples by Corelli) and the French title *Ouverture* was used by J. S. Bach for his four orchestral suites.

In the second half of the 18th century the suite declined, but aspects of the form continued in the *cassation and *divertimento and in the minuet of the symphony. At the end of the 19th century the suite re-emerged in its modern sense as a free selection of excerpts from ballets, operas, or incidental music to plays. Tchaikovsky's *Nutcracker Suite* is a familiar example.

Suk, Josef (1874–1935) Czech composer and violinist, a pupil of Dvořák. Suk was a leading composer in Czechoslovakia at the turn of the century; he was also well known as a member of the Czech String Quartet. In 1922 he was appointed Professor of Composition at the Prague conservatory. Suk's works are romantic in mood and sometimes draw on elements of Bohemian folk music. His output includes two symphonies and other orchestral works, chamber music (including two string quartets), piano pieces, and choral works.

Sullivan, Sir Arthur (Seymour) (1842–1900) British composer and conductor. A chorister at the Chapel Royal, he later studied with Sterndale Bennett and Goss at the Royal Academy of Music (1856–58), then with Hauptmann, Rietz, David, Moscheles, and Plaidy at the Leipzig conservatory (1858–61). In 1862 his incidental music to *The Tempest* was acclaimed and in the mid-1860s he wrote *Cox and Box*, an operetta that showed his talent for the genre; after its production in 1869 he was introduced to W. S. *Gilbert. In 1875 he set Gilbert's libretto *Trial by Jury*, which was so successful that the impresario Richard D'Oyly Carte took the lease of the Opéra Comique Theatre, London, and established a company to perform their operettas. The *Sorcerer* (1877), *HMS Pinafore* (1878), and The *Pirates of Penzance* (1879) followed. During the production of *Patience* (1881) the company moved to the new Savoy Theatre; Gilbert and Sullivan's operettas became known as the Savoy Operas and their performers were called Savoyards. Sullivan was knighted in 1883. He was conductor of the Philharmonic Society concerts from 1885 to 1887. He and Gilbert produced more successful operettas but their relationship suffered when there was a court action in 1890 over production expenses.

Gilbert's polished librettos stimulated Sullivan to write some of his best music. He paid special attention to word-setting, wrote many memorable melodies, and was able to match Gilbert's comic situations with entertaining musical parodies. Their enormously popular comic operas include *Iolanthe* (1882), *Princess Ida* (1884), The *Mikado* (1885), *Ruddigore* (1887), The *Yeomen of the*

Sir Arthur Sullivan (right) with W.S. Gilbert

Guard (1888), The *Gondoliers* (1889), *Utopia Limited* (1893), and The *Grand Duke* (1896).

Sullivan's serious music, now rarely heard, includes the *Irish Symphony* (1866), *Overture di ballo* (1870), the oratorio *The Prodigal Son* (1869), the sacred music drama *The Martyr of Antioch* (1880), the opera *Ivanhoe* (1891), anthems, chamber music, part songs, songs, and hymns (including 'Onward, Christian soldiers').

Sumer is icumen in A musical canon dating from the 13th century. The precise date of composition has long been a subject of controversy amongst musicologists and various dates between 1225 and 1310 have been suggested for this work. *Sumer is icumen in* is a four-voice canon built over a two-voice ground bass that commences with the words 'Sing cucu;' it is unique in being both the oldest canon and the oldest composition for six voices in existence. It is occasionally also referred to as the *Reading Rota*, because a monk of Reading Abbey, John of Fornsete, is reputed to have either composed or made the first copy of this work (c.1240). In addition to this secular text, an alternative Latin text with the words 'Perspice Christicola,' celebrating the Resurrection, exists for church performance.

summation tone see **combination tones.**

Sunless Song cycle by Mussorgsky to poems by Golen-ishchev-Gutuzov. Composed: 1874. The six songs that comprise this cycle are entitled 'Between four walls,' 'Thou didst not know me in the crowd,' 'The idle, noisy day is ended,' 'Boredom,' 'Elegy,' and 'On the river.'

Sun Quartets (German: *Sonnenquartette*) Set of six string quartets (Op. 20) by Haydn. Composed: 1772. The use of this name was suggested by the first printed edition of the quartets, which featured an engraving of the rising sun on the title page.

Suor Angelica (*Sister Angelica*) Opera in one act by Puccini with libretto by Forzano. First performance: Metropolitan Opera, New York, 1918. Sister Angelica (soprano), a nun, longs for the child she once bore and sees it in a vision as she dies after taking a poisonous drink. See also **Trittico, Il.**

supertonic. The second note of the major or minor *scale above the *tonic. For example, D is the supertonic in the key of C major or C minor. See also **degree.**

Suppé, Franz von (Francesco Ezechiele Ermenegildo Cavaliere Suppé Demelli; 1819–95) Austrian composer, born in Dalmatia of Belgian descent. After studying law at Padua, he studied music with Sechter and Seyfried in Vienna, where he became third kapellmeister of the Theater in der Josefstadt in 1840. He conducted in Baden, Ödenburg, and Pressburg and appeared as an opera singer. In Vienna he was kapellmeister of the Theater an der Wien (1845–62), the Kaitheater (1862–65), and the Carltheater (1865–82). Throughout his career Suppé composed prolifically for the theatre – operas, operettas, and incidental music (his well-known overture *Poet and Peasant* is from the music he wrote in 1846 for Elmar's play *Dichter und Bauer*) – as well as choral and orchestral works. He is best known for his fluent and entertaining Viennese operettas, among them *Die Kartenschlägerin* (1862), *Die schöne Galatea* (1865), *Die leichte Kavallerie* (1866), and *Boccaccio* (1879).

Surprise Symphony Symphony No. 94 in G major by Haydn. Composed: 1791. This is the second of the so-called *Salomon Symphonies* and the name refers to the second movement, in which the quiet opening bars are suddenly interrupted by a loud chord. According to a popular story Haydn said of this feature, 'That will make the ladies jump,' and the prominent use of the timpani for this chord has suggested the additional nickname *Sinfonie mit dem Paukenschlag* (*Symphony with the Drumtap*).

Survivor from Warsaw, A Work for speaker, men's choir, and orchestra (Op. 46) by Schoenberg. First performance: 1948. This work was commissioned by the Koussevitzky Foundation and Schoenberg's text tells of the atrocities committed by the Germans against the Jews during World War II. At the end of *A Survivor from Warsaw* Schoenberg sets a traditional Jewish prayer.

Susanna Oratorio for solo voices, choir, and orchestra by Handel to a text by an unknown author based on the Bible. First performance: 1749. Susanna is a figure in the Apocrypha section of the Old Testament.

Susanna's Secret (*Il Segreto di Susanna*) Opera in one act by Wolf-Ferrari with libretto by Golisciani. First performance (in a German version by Kalbeck): Munich, 1909. Susanna's secret is that she smokes.

Susato, Tylman (*or* **Tielman**) (*c*.1500–*c*.1562) Composer and music publisher, active in the Netherlands. His origins were probably in Westphalia, but from 1529 he was a calligrapher at Antwerp Cathedral and in 1531 trumpeter there. From 1532 until 1549 he was town player and from 1543 was one of the first Netherlands music publishers. Most of his publications were anthologies by leading Flemish composers – he was among the first to publish Lassus' music – but he also published his own compositions, including two books of chansons and a book of dances based on popular melodies.

suspension A device in *harmony in which a discord is created by holding over a note from one chord with which it is consonant to another with which it is not, and then resolving the discord by playing the next note down in the scale, this note being part of the second chord. In a **double suspension** two notes are held over. In a **retardation** the resolution is obtained by rising one note in the scale. Compare **anticipation.**

Susskind, Walter (1913–80) Czech conductor, based in Britain from 1939. He conducted the Scottish Orchestra (1946–52), the Toronto Symphony Orchestra (1956–64), and the St Louis Symphony Orchestra (1968–75).

Süssmayr, Franz Xaver (1766–1803) Austrian composer. Trained at Kremsmünster Monastery, he was appointed acting kapellmeister (1792) and kapellmeister (1794) of German opera at the National Theatre, Vienna. A pupil and colleague of Mozart, he wrote many singspiels, ballets, chamber pieces, and sacred works but is best remembered for his completion of Mozart's *Requiem* (1791).

sustaining pedal see **piano.**

Sutermeister, Heinrich (1910–) Swiss composer, a pupil of Carl Orff. Sutermeister's prime consideration has been to create an expressive operatic idiom: to this end he has pursued simplicity and dramatic effect in his music. His works include many operas, orchestral works, incidental music, chamber music, and songs.

Sutherland, Dame Joan (1926–) Australian soprano. Her international success as a coloratura soprano specializing in early-19th-century Italian opera dates from 1959, when she sang the title role of Donizetti's *Lucia di*

Lammermoor at Covent Garden, and she is now regarded as the successor of the great coloratura sopranos of the past. She is married to the conductor Richard Bonynge (1930–) and was made a DBE in 1979.

Švanda the Bagpiper (Czech: *Švanda Dudák*) Opera in two acts by Weinberger with libretto by Kareš. First performance: Prague, 1927. Švanda (baritone) is tempted to leave his cottage and young wife Dorotka (soprano) by tales of the great world; after adventures with the Queen-with-the-Heart-of-Ice (mezzo-soprano) and the Devil (bass) he returns home.

Svendsen, Johan (Severin) (1840–1911) Norwegian conductor, violinist, and composer. He played the violin in Christiania (now Oslo) then studied with Hauptmann, David, Richter, and Reinecke at the Leipzig conservatory (1863–67). In 1868 he met Liszt in Weimar. He became leader of the Euterpe concerts in Leipzig (1871) and in 1872 played at Bayreuth at the inauguration of the Festival Theatre, becoming a close friend and admirer of Wagner. From 1872 to 1877 Svendsen was conductor of the Music Society concerts in Christiania; he toured Europe and returned to Norway as the leading Scandinavian conductor of his day. In 1883 he was appointed conductor of the Royal Opera, Copenhagen. Svendsen was a more cosmopolitan composer than Grieg, though some of his works have a distinctive Norwegian flavour. His orchestral music includes two symphonies (*c*.1865–66, 1877), *Carnival in Paris* (1872), a violin concerto (1869–70), a cello concerto (1870), *Four Norwegian Rhapsodies* (*c*.1876–78), and a romance for violin and orchestra (1881); he also wrote chamber, vocal, and piano music.

swanee whistle A simple whistle flute consisting of a recorder-type mouthpiece attached to a tube with a movable plunger placed in it. It is used primarily as a toy but it has been used in some orchestral music as a special effect.

Swan Lake (French: *Le Lac des cygnes*; Russian: *Lebedinoe ozero*) Ballet in four acts with music by Tchaikovsky and choreography by Reisinger. First performance: Bolshoi Theatre, Moscow, 1877. Princess Odette is turned into a swan by the magician Rotbart and is wooed by Prince Siegfried during the midnight hours, when the swan-maidens are allowed to regain their human form. Only love can break the spell but Rotbart tricks Siegfried by substituting his own daughter, Odile, in Odette's likeness.

Swan of Tuonela, The Tone poem (Op. 22) by Sibelius. Composed: 1893–95. Described by the composer as a symphonic legend, the work was originally intended to form the prelude to an opera but actually became the third of a set of four tone poems based on the Finnish saga *Kalevala* (see also **Lemminkäinen's Homecoming**). Tuonela is the island of death around which a swan swims and sings:

Sibelius characterizes the swan by a very prominent part for cor anglais.

Swan Song see **Schwanengesang**.

Swedish Rhapsody Set of three works for orchestra by Alfvén. Composed: 1903–31. Although all three works were given this title by the composer, it is the first rhapsody, *Midsummer Vigil*, with which the name is usually associated.

Sweelinck, Jan Pieterszoon (1562–1621) Dutch composer, organist, and teacher. From at least 1580 he was organist of the Calvinist Old Church, Amsterdam, where he taught Samuel Scheidt, Heinrich Scheidemann, and others. Vocal works comprise the bulk of his output, none of which is in Dutch; his *Cantiones sacrae* (1619) contains 39 motets on Catholic texts. Sweelinck's keyboard music, published posthumously, is in the English style and includes fantasias, toccatas, and secular and chorale variations.

swell box see **organ**.

swell organ see **organ**.

Sylphides, Les Ballet in one act with music taken from Chopin's piano works and orchestrated by various composers, originally by Glazunov; choreography by Fokine. First performance: Maryinsky Theatre, St Petersburg, 1907. In 1909 it was staged in Paris by Diaghilev with décor by Benois and danced by Pavlova, Karsavina, Baldina, and Nijinsky.

Sylvia (French: *La Nymphe de Diane*) Ballet in three acts with music by Delibes, libretto by Barbier and de Reinach, and choreography by Merante. First performance: Opéra, Paris, 1876. Sylvia, a nymph of Diana, is loved by Amyntas, who has to submit to various tests before winning her.

sympathetic strings A set of unbowed strings used on certain bowed stringed instruments, such as the *viola d'amore. The sympathetic strings vibrate in resonance with those that are bowed although they themselves are not touched by the bow. In **aliquot scaling**, sympathetic strings are provided on some pianos (especially Blüthner pianos) to strengthen the upper notes.

symphonia 1. Any piece of music in which a group of instrumentalists play together. Some modern composers have used the word synonymously with symphony. For example, Richard Strauss's *Symphonia domestica* (1904) is an autobiographical symphony depicting in musical terms his own domestic life. **2.** In medieval music theory, *consonance (compare **diaphony**). [Latin, symphony]

Symphonia domestica (*Domestic Symphony*) Symphony (Op. 53) by Richard Strauss. Composed: 1902–03; first performance: New York, 1904. The *Symphonia domestica* describes Strauss's private home life in the same way as *Ein*

Heldenleben described his public life. Although Strauss removed details of the programme from the score, the work includes obvious musical references to his family and caused an uproar at its first performance. Although it is in one movement it can be subdivided into four distinct sections, corresponding to the movements of a conventional symphony. Strauss's *Parergon zur Symphonia domestica* (1924) for piano left hand and orchestra, written for Paul Wittgenstein, incorporates material from the tone poem.

symphonic band see **concert band**.

symphonic poem see **tone poem**.

symphonic study A major orchestral work that is similar to a *tone poem. The term was first used by Elgar for his *Falstaff* (1913).

Symphonie fantastique see **Fantastic Symphony**.

Symphonie funèbre et triomphale Symphony for choir, military band, and strings (Op. 15) by Berlioz. Composed: 1840. This work was commissioned by the French government to celebrate the tenth anniversary of the 1830 Revolution in Paris; it was intended for open-air performance, hence the use of a large body of musicians.

symphony A *sonata for orchestra. Its history from the mid-18th century to the present day reflects amost every facet of the growth of music. The symphony evolved from several other orchestral forms during the period of stylistic

A scene from the Royal Ballet's 1981 production of Les Sylphides

transition from the baroque to the classical. Most significant among these were the *Italian overture, the *concerto grosso, and the *trio sonata. By the 1740s the familiar four-movement pattern had emerged in the symphony (see below). Among the preclassical composers of symphonies are Sammartini, J. Stamitz (see also **Mannheim School**), J. C. Bach, C. P. E. Bach, and the Viennese composers Monn, Gassmann, and Wagenseil. There was considerable experimentation, which is also evident in the early symphonies of Haydn and Mozart. However, the mature symphonies of both these composers reflect the classical pattern of four movements: an opening allegro (with or without a slow introduction) in *sonata form, a lyrical slow movement, a *minuet and trio, and a fast finale in *rondo or sonata-rondo form. The full classical orchestra consisted of pairs of flutes, oboes, clarinets, bassoons, horns, trumpets, timpani, and strings. This was an enlargement of the ensemble of two oboes, two bassoons, strings, and keyboard continuo. Both Haydn and Mozart made distinctive contributions to the art of developing their materials symphonically. The nine symphonies of Beethoven, which may be seen as standing at the end of the classical period and at the beginning of the romantic era, show an expansion of the form with longer *coda and *development sections in the first movements and the replacing of the minuet by a *scherzo. Beethoven's melodic, rhythmic, and dynamic gestures were more powerful and the development of his material more sharply dramatic and articulate. In the *Choral Symphony* the orchestra is enlarged to include piccolo, double bassoon, trombones, triangle, bass drum, and cymbals, as well as chorus and solo voices. This anticipated the expansion of the symphony in the 19th century as did also the programmatic basis of the five-movement *Pastoral Symphony*.

During the 19th century there were two trends in symphonic composition: (1) a progressive tradition of romanticism, as in the programme symphonies of Berlioz (*Fantastic Symphony*, 1830; *Harold in Italy*, 1834; *Romeo and Juliet*, 1839) and Liszt (*Faust Symphony*, 1857); (2) a conservative tradition, as displayed in the symphonies of Schubert, Mendelssohn (e.g. the *Italian Symphony*), and Schumann (e.g. the *Spring Symphony*). In the second half of the 19th century the four symphonies of Brahms are classical in their articulate structures and abstract expression, but romantic in their melodic and harmonic language. The nine symphonies of Bruckner unite aspects of the Viennese style of Schubert with Wagnerian harmony and orchestration in a grandiose yet inimitably personal lanaguage. In the symphonies of Mahler large orchestral forces are employed, including a considerable use of solo voices and chorus to project sincere and intensely personal feelings and worldly experiences (see **Resurrection Symphony**; **Symphony of a Thousand**). Czech nationalism is expressed in the nine symphonies of Dvořák, despite their structural similarity to Brahms and the Viennese tradition. Russian nationalism is reflected in the symphonies of The *Five. The six symphonies of Tchaikovsky unite aspects of Berlioz's dramatic orchestration, Beethoven's classical clarity, and essentially Russian gestures. Little interest was shown in the symphony by French composers after Berlioz except for single examples by Chausson and Dukas. The symphony by César Franck is in cyclic form.

The early 20th century saw the emergence of an English symphonic tradition, including examples by Elgar, Stanford, Vaughan Williams, Walton, Britten, Tippett, and Maxwell Davies. The symphony has continued to be a pertinent genre in the Soviet Union with examples by Prokofiev and Shostakovich. Stravinsky reinterpreted the term symphony in its literal sense as a 'sounding together' of instruments, as in his *Symphonies for Wind Instruments* (1920) and the *Symphony of Psalms* (1930). His two other symphonies —*Symphony in C* and *Symphony in Three Movements* – are strongly abstract and neoclassical. In addition to his *tone poems are Richard Strauss's *Symphonia domestica* and *Alpine Symphony*. Symphonies by members of the Second Viennese School include two chamber symphonies by Schoenberg and a symphony for chamber orchestra by Webern. Among other German symphonies are five by Hindemith, including *Mathis der Maler*. In 20th-century

France the symphony was revived by Honegger, Milhaud, and Roussel and latterly by Messiaen in his ten-movement *Turangalîla*. US symphonists of the 20th century include Ives, Piston, Barber, and Copland.

Symphony of a Thousand Symphony No. 8 for seven vocal soloists, boys' choir, double choir, and orchestra by Mahler. Composed: 1906–07. In this work the composer abandons the usual four-movement symphonic structure; instead the symphony is in two parts, the first being a setting of the Latin hymn 'Veni creator spiritus' and the second a setting of the closing scene from Goethe's drama *Faust*. The name refers to the enormous forces required to perform this work; although it is possible to perform the symphony with fewer than a thousand musicians, such a large force has occasionally been employed.

Symphony of Psalms Symphony for choir and orchestra by Stravinsky. First performance: 1930. Although commissioned to mark the 50th anniversary of the Boston Symphony Orchestra, the title page of the symphony bears the dedication 'To the Glory of God' and the composer set sections of Psalms 39, 49, and 150 from the Latin Vulgate Bible. For this work Stravinsky used the title 'symphony' in its broadest sense, meaning simply any musical work with two or more parts (rather than implying any strictly defined form): the orchestration is notable for its exclusion of both violins and violas.

Symphony on a French Mountaineer's Song Work for piano and orchestra by d'Indy. Composed: 1886. With its prominent solo piano part, this work combines elements of both concerto and symphony, the title referring to the use of folk-song material collected by the composer in the Ardèche region of France.

syncopation The displacement of the normal rhythmic *accent from the strong beat of a bar to one that usually carries a weak beat. This can be achieved by marking weak notes with a stress mark, by replacing normally stressed notes by rests, or by holding over a note that first occurs on a weak beat to an accented position. Syncopation is a device widely used in all kinds of music. Its occurrence in jazz derives directly from its frequent use in African music.

synthesizer An electronic device that creates musical sounds by electronic means and produces them through loudspeakers. The oscillations themselves are produced by electronic oscillators, usually on the heterodyne principle (i.e. producing an audio-frequency signal from the difference between two radio-frequency signals). The first devices of this kind were made in the 1920s using thermionic valves (see **ondes Martenot**) but more recent synthesizers have been based on the much smaller transistor and microchip. By blending and mixing harmonics and controlling the 'attack' and 'decay' of sounds the operator can produce tone colours that simulate the sounds of conventional instruments or that are characteristic of nothing other than synthesizers. The synthesizer may also contain programs to control the rhythm and volume of the output as well as the harmony. Most modern synthesizers are controlled by a piano-type keyboard, like the **Moog synthesizer** (invented by Robert *Moog).

syrinx see **panpipes**.

Syrinx Piece for solo flute by Debussy. Composed: 1913. Debussy originally entitled this piece *Flûte de Pan*, composing it as incidental music for Gabriel Mourey's drama *Psyché*. In the play this piece is performed to accompany the death of Pan, 'syrinx' being the Latin name for panpipes.

Szeligowski, Tadeusz (1896–1963) Polish composer, a pupil of Nadia Boulanger. Szeligowski was eclectic in his use of different stylistic influences. His works include operas, ballet scores, orchestral compositions, chamber works, and piano pieces.

Szell, George (1897–1970) Hungarian-born conductor. He gained his early experience in German opera houses, subsequently conducting the German Opera and Philharmonic Orchestra in Prague (1929–37), the Scottish Orchestra (1937–39), the Metropolitan Opera, New York (1942–46), and the Cleveland Orchestra (1946–70), which he built up into one of the finest orchestras in the world.

Szeryng, Henrik (1918–) Polish-born Mexican violinist. He studied with Flesch in Berlin and established his European reputation before World War II, emigrating to Mexico in 1946. Szeryng has been active in performing contemporary Mexican music.

Szigeti, Joseph (1892–1973) Hungarian-born US violinist. A pupil of Hubay in Budapest, he made his debut in 1902 and soon began undertaking extensive European tours. Szigeti was active in performing Bartók's music and Bloch, Rawsthorne, and Prokofiev also dedicated works to him.

Szokolay, Sándor (1931–) Hungarian composer, a pupil of Farkas. His music, which is mostly vocal and choral, is influenced by primitive and folk music and makes free use of serial procedures. His works include concertos for violin (1956), piano (1958), and trumpet (1968); the oratorios *Ishtar's Descent into Hell* (1960), *The Power of Music* (1969), and *Hommage à Kodály* (1975); and the operas *Blood Wedding* (1964), *Hamlet* (1968), and *Samson* (1973).

Szymanowski, Karol (1882–1927) Polish pianist and composer. He studied in Warsaw under Noskowski and later in Berlin. His early works were heavily influenced by Straussian romanticism, but from 1914 to 1917 he experimented with chromaticism, atonality, polytonality, and new rhythmic ideas within a basically impressionistic style. In subsequent works Szymanowski developed a simpler harmonic approach, which owed a great deal to his discovery of native Polish folk traditions. His compositions include the operas *Hagith* (1913) and *King Roger* (1924), the ballet *Harnasie* (1926), four symphonies, two violin concertos, the *Symphonie concertante* (1932), the cantatas *Demeter* and *Agawa* (both 1917), the *Stabat Mater* (1928), chamber music, including two string quartets and the *Mythes* (1915) for violin, and piano pieces and songs.

T

Tabarro, Il (*The Cloak*) Opera in one act by Puccini with libretto by Adami based on a play by Didier Gold, *La Houppelande*. First performance: Metropolitan Opera, New York, 1918. The cloak of the title covers the body of a woman's lover, whom her husband has killed. See **Trittico, Il.**

tabla The pair of drums used in most forms of north Indian (Hindustani) music (the word applies strictly to the right-hand higher-pitched drum but is commonly used for the two together). The right-hand drum can be finely tuned and is usually played on the tonic or the fifth of the scale in performance. See also **Indian music.**

tablature A form of *notation in which the note or chord to be played is indicated by the position of the performer's fingers on the instrument. Originally used for the lute, tablature is still in use for popular music for guitars and other fretted instruments. The diagram used, in the case of a guitar, has six vertical lines representing the strings and a number of horizontal lines representing the frets. The position of the fingers for a particular note or chord is indicated by black circles.

tabor A small medieval military drum with two heads, the upper of which is fitted with snares. It is still used in folk music, often with one person playing both the tabor and the *pipe; in this situation the tabor is struck either with the fingers of one hand or with a single drumstick, leaving the other hand free to play the one-handed pipe. The **tambourin de Provence** is a similar instrument used occasionally in the orchestra.

Tábor see **Má Vlast.**

tacet A direction used to indicate that an instrument is silent for some time. [Latin, is silent]

Tafelmusik Music that is suitable for performance during or after dinner. The best-known composer of such music was Georg Telemann. French: **musique de table.** [German, table music]

Tailleferre, Germaine (1892–1983) French composer, a pupil of Ravel and member of Les *Six. Her music is lightweight in style, occasionally using polytonal and serial procedures. Tailleferre's works include the ballets *Marchand d'oiseaux* (1923) and *Parisiana* (1955), *Il était un petit navire* (1951) and other operas and operettas, concertos, chamber pieces, and many songs.

tailpiece The fan-shaped piece to which the strings of a fiddle, viol, or violin are attached at the opposite end to the *pegbox. The tailpiece is attached to the instrument's body by the *button.

Takemitsu, Toru (1930–) Japanese composer, a pupil of Kiyose. During the 1950s he produced musique concrète pieces and chamber music, in which he aimed to combine serialism and traditional Japanese techniques. Subsequent orchestral works emphasize timbre and the use of Japanese instruments. His mature style often uses graphic notation, carefully organized silences, and recently a new emphasis on harmony. His works include *Coral Island* (1962), *November Steps* (1967), *Seasons* (1970), *Gemeaux* (1972), *Quatrain* (1975), *A Flock Descends into a Pentagonal Garden* (1977), piano works, tape pieces, and film scores.

Tal, Josef (1910–) Polish-born Israeli composer. In his works he has made some use of serial procedures and has used combinations of live instruments and electronic music. Tal is director of the Israeli Center for Electronic Music. His works include symphonies, concertos, choral music, the operas *Ammon and Tomar* (1961) *Ashmedai* (1971), and the ballets *Ranges of Energy* (1963) and *Variations* (1970).

Tales from the Vienna Woods (German: *Geschichten aus dem Wienerwald*) Waltz by Johann Strauss the Younger. Composed: 1868. This waltz is one of the most popular of the Strauss waltzes and the orchestration features a prominent part for the zither.

Tales of Hoffmann, The (French: *Les Contes d'Hoffmann*) Opera in three acts by Offenbach with text by Barbier and Carré, based on stories by E. T. A. Hoffmann. First performance: Opéra-Comique, Paris, 1881 (after the composer's death). The score was completed by Guiraud, who also supplied recitatives in place of the original spoken dialogue. It tells of the loves of the poet Hoffmann (tenor) for three women – Olympia, Antonia, and Giulietta – who may be sung by the same soprano.

Talich, Václav (1883–1961) Czech conductor. He studied with Reger and Nikisch and conducted the Czech Philharmonic Orchestra (1919–41) and the National Opera

An Italian engraving of Thomas Tallis

in Prague (1935–45). In 1949 he formed the Slovak Philharmonic Orchestra in Bratislava.

Tallis, Thomas (*c.*1505–85) English composer. Tallis was organist at Waltham Abbey before its dissolution in 1540 and a gentleman of the Chapel Royal until his death. In 1575 he was granted a 21-year monopoly to print music jointly with his pupil Byrd. Tallis's Latin church music includes 3 masses, 42 motets (17 of them in the *Cantiones sacrae*, published with Byrd in 1575), and 2 sets of *Lamentations*; for the Anglican Church his works include 24 anthems and 3 services. He also wrote 12 liturgical keyboard works and 4 part songs and 5 keyboard pieces for secular use. The wide variety of styles in which he wrote were to a great extent dictated by the religious upheavals of the time. In his earlier motets, written for the Sarum rite, Tallis continues the tradition of florid counterpoint found in Fayrfax and other composers of the previous generation. The most complex of these is the 40-voice motet *Spem in alium*, probably written for an important state occasion. His anthems for the Anglican rite, on the contrary, are strictly syllabic and tend towards homophony, in accordance with the principles laid down by Archbishop Cranmer. Tallis's music exhibits many typically English characteristics: false relations (often sounded simultaneously just before a cadence) and freedom in the use of accidentals. The second set of *Lamentations* is remarkable for its freedom in modulating. His two keyboard settings of *Felix namque* (1562 and 1564) are the oldest dateable English plainsong settings.

talon The heel of the bow of a stringed instrument. [French]

Talvela, Martti (1935–) Finnish bass singer. He studied in Stockholm, making his debut there as Sparafucile in Verdi's *Rigoletto* (1961). His powerful voice is well suited to the immense roles in Verdi, Wagner, and Mussorgsky; he also performs Sibelius in smaller-scale recitals.

Tamara Tone poem by Balakirev. Composed: 1867–82. The work is based on Lermontov's poem *Thamar*, about a demon queen.

tambour Drum. Italian: **tamburo**. [French]

tambourin de Provence see **tabor**.

tambourine A shallow frame drum with a single head and metal discs fitted into the walls of the frame. The drum is struck with the knuckles and the instrument is shaken to obtain a jingling sound from the metal discs. Of Middle Eastern origin, the jingling frame drum came to Europe during the Crusades. It was then known as a **timbrel** in English, the French **tambourin** not being adopted until much later. It is sometimes used in the orchestra to impart a Turkish flavour to music, but is mostly used by Gypsy dancers. For illustration, see **drums**.

tambura A long-necked plucked lute with a gourd or wood resonator, used to give the accompanying drone in Indian classical music. The instrument is played on open strings, of which there are usually four, two tuned to the upper tonic, one to the lower tonic, and one to the fifth, fourth, or another important note. See also **Indian music**.

tamburo see **tambour**.

tamtam see **gong**.

Tancredi (*Tancred*) Opera in two acts by Rossini with libretto by Gaetano Rossi based on Tasso's *Gerusalemme liberata* (*Jerusalem Liberated*) and Voltaire's tragedy, *Tancrède*. First performance: Teatro la Fenice, Venice, 1813. It is a heroic tale of the Crusades.

Taneyev, Sergey Ivanovich (1856–1915) Russian composer and pianist. He studied at the Moscow conservatory (1866–67, 1869–75), where his teachers included Tchaikovsky (composition) and Nikolay Rubinstein (piano). In 1875 he gave the first performance of Tchaikovsky's first piano concerto, after which he toured Russia with the violinist Leopold Auer and visited Paris. At the Moscow conservatory he began teaching harmony and orchestration in 1878, the piano in 1880, and composition in 1883; he became director in 1885 but resigned in 1889 to devote himself to composition, his career as a pianist, and writing a book on counterpoint (published 1909). Taneyev was a conservative and academic composer who did not sympathize with the nationalist ideals of Glinka and The *Five. He composed the opera *Oresteia* (1887–94), four symphonies, a piano concerto, six string quartets and other chamber music, and piano, choral, and vocal music. He also completed and arranged several of Tchaikovsky's works. He was an influential teacher whose pupils included Scriabin, Rachmaninov, Lyapunov, and Glier.

Gwynneth Jones as Elizabeth in the 1984 production of Tannhauser *at the Royal Opera House, Covent Garden*

His uncle, **Alexander Sergeyevich Taneyev** (1850–1918), was also a composer. He studied music with Rimsky-Korsakov and was a member of Balakirev's circle. His compositions (operas, orchestral suites, three symphonies, chamber and vocal music) reflect his interest in musical nationalism.

tangent see **clavichord**.

Tannhäuser (full title: *Tannhäuser und der Sänger-krieg auf dem Wartburg*: *Tannhauser and the Song Contest at the Wartburg*) Opera in three acts by Wagner with libretto by the composer. First performance: Dresden, 1845; the so-called 'Paris version' is a revision made for the Paris production of 1861. Tannhäuser (tenor), a knightly minstrel, is torn between his profane love for Venus (soprano) and his ideal love for Elizabeth (soprano). At a song contest he extols the love of Venus; Elizabeth finally dies of grief and Tannhäuser, his sin forgiven, dies also.

Tansman, Alexandre (1897–1986) Polish-born French composer, pianist, and conductor. Tansman's style was eclectic, influenced by folk music, serialism, atonality, and polytonality. His works include seven symphonies, eight string quartets, concertos, the ballets *La Grand ville* (1932) and *Résurrection* (1961), the operas *Le Serment* (1954), *Il Usignolo de Baboli* (1962), and *Georges Dandin* (1974), the oratorio *Isaïe le prophète* (1951), *Psaumes* (1961), *Stèle* (1972), songs, piano pieces, and film music.

tanto So much; as much. Hence **non tanto**, not too much. [Italian]

Tantum ergo sacramentum The first words of the last section of Aquinas's Corpus Christi hymn, *Pange lingua*. It has its own plainsong and has also been set by several composers. [Latin, Therefore (we before him bending,) this great sacrament (revere)]

Tanz Dance. [German]

tape Prerecorded magnetic tape used in performance, either alone or in combination with musical instruments. For example, in a piece for tape and violin, the violinist would play an accompaniment to the prerecorded tape.

Tapiola Tone poem (Op. 112) by Sibelius. First performance: 1926. This work is the last of Sibelius' tone poems based on the great Finnish saga *Kalevala*, the other works including **Lemminkäinen's Homecoming, The *Swan of Tuonela*, and **Pohjola's Daughter*. The subject of this work is Tapio, the god of the forest.

tar see **lute**.

tarantella (*or* (French) **tarantelle**) A rapid 18th-century Italian dance in 6/8 time. It is danced by one or more couples and becomes increasingly fast as it progresses. The dance is named after the southern Italian town of Taranto, the poisonous spider (tarantula) associated with it, and tarantism (the hysterical dancing disease once popularly believed to result from the spider's bite). Two superstitions survive: in one the tarantella is seen as a manifestation of the madness induced by the spider's bite; in the other it is recommended as an antidote to the poisonous effects of the bite.

tárogató An ancient form of Hungarian military oboe with a wide bore. In 1900 W. J. Schunda of Budapest fitted a single-reeded saxophone mouthpiece to the instrument and it is sometimes used for the shepherd's call in Wagner's *Tristan und Isolde*. It is also in use as a folk instrument in Hungary and Romania.

Tárrega (y Eixea), Francisco (1852–1909) Spanish guitarist and composer. He studied at the Madrid conservatory and by the late 1870s was established as a guitar virtuoso and teacher. He toured widely. Tárrega composed numerous works for guitar and made many transcriptions. His pupils included Pujol and Robledo.

Tartini, Giuseppe (1692–1770) Italian composer, violinist, and theorist. In 1721 he became a violinist at St Anthony's Basilica, Padua, where in about 1727 he founded a famous school of violin instruction: his pupils included Nardini, Naumann, and Pugnani. Tartini wrote sonatas, including The **Devil's Trill* (1714), concertos, and treatises for violin, including *L'Arte dell' arco* (*c*.1750), as well as sinfonias, sacred works, and other treatises.

Tasso, Torquato (1544–95) Italian poet and lyricist. His epic *Gerusalemme liberata* was a popular source of texts for composers. Operas based on the poem include Monteverdi's *Combattimento di Tancredi e Clorinda* (1624), Lully's *Armide* (1686), and Handel's *Rinaldo* (1711).

tasto 1. The key of an instrument. Hence **tasto solo**, a direction in continuo playing used to indicate that a note should be played alone without a chord. **2.** The fingerboard of a stringed instrument. Hence **sul tasto**, play on (or near) the fingerboard. [Italian]

Tate, Nahum (1652–1715) English dramatist and poet. He wrote the libretto for Purcell's *Dido and Aeneas* (1689) based on play *Brutus of Alba* (1678). He was appointed poet laureate in 1692.

Tate, Phyllis (1911–87) British composer, a pupil of Farjeon. Her works include many songs and works for solo voice, such as *Nocturne* (1945); *A Secular Requiem* (1967); the television operas *The Lodger* (1960) and *Dark Pilgrimage* (1963); a saxophone concerto (1944); *Songs Without Words* (1976) and other orchestral music; and pieces for children.

Tauber, Richard (1892–1948) Austrian-born British tenor. After specializing in Mozart operas he turned to operettas and light popular music in the 1920s. After 1931 he settled in England, becoming a British citizen in 1940. Tauber also composed light operas.

Tausig, Carl (1841–71) Polish pianist and composer. He studied with Liszt in Weimar, making his debut as a pianist in 1858 and touring Germany. In 1862 he moved to Vienna and in 1865 settled in Berlin, where he founded a short-lived piano school. Tausig was a celebrated virtuoso with a prodigious technique. He composed several works for piano and made many transcriptions (of Wagner, Beethoven, and Scarlatti, among others).

Tavener, John (1944–) British composer, a pupil of Lennox Berkeley and Lumsdaine. His music, which is mostly on religious themes, draws on sources ranging from Renaissance polyphony to Messiaen and Stravinsky. It uses elaborately textured blocks of sound, often incorporating quotation and simultaneous levels of events. Tavener has also explored the use of spatial distribution. His works include *The Whale* (1966), *In Alium* (1968), *Ultimos Ritus* (1972), and the opera *Thérèse* (1976).

Taverner Opera in two acts with words and music by Peter Maxwell Davies. First performance: Covent Garden, London, 1972. The subject is the 16th-century composer John *Taverner and the opera is the culmination of a series of works inspired by and based on Taverner's music, including two orchestral *Fantasias* (1962 and 1964) and *Seven In Nomine* (1963–65).

Taverner, John (c.1490–1545) English composer. In 1524 he was a lay clerk at the collegiate choir of Tattershall,

Richard Tauber

Lincolnshire, and in 1526 he was appointed by Cardinal Wolsey as the first instructor of the choristers at Cardinal College, Oxford (now Christ Church). In 1530 he became a lay clerk at St Botolph's Church, Boston; by 1537 he had left the choir but remained in Boston as a member of the Guild of Corpus Christi. Taverner is chiefly known as a composer of sacred music and many of his works were written during his time at Oxford; they are very often based on the cantus firmus and, rather archaically, feature long melismas and mathematical structures. His best-known mass is the *Western Wynde*, based on a popular melody. The 'In nomine Domini' section of his *Missa Gloria tibi Trinitas* was the basis of the instrumental *In nomine*. Other works include votive antiphons and magnificats.

Taylor, Deems (1885–1966) US composer and music writer. His own music is in the tradition of US romanticism. Taylor's works include the operas *The King's Henchman* (1926), *Peter Ibbetson* (1931), *Ramuntcho* (1942), and *The Dragon* (1958); choral works, such as *The Chambered Nautilus* (1914); orchestral pieces, including the suite *Through the Looking Glass* (1922); and various orchestral arrangements.

Tchaikovsky, Boris (1925–) Soviet composer, a pupil of Myaskovsky and Shostakovich. In the 1950s he made some use of folk material. Later works have ranged from the academic to attempts at a more adventurous idiom. His

Peter Ilyich Tchaikovsky

works include symphonies, concertos, the opera *The Star* (1949), chamber music, piano pieces, and film scores.

Tchaikovsky, Peter Ilyich (1840–93) Russian composer. The son of an inspector of mines, he began his career as a civil servant although he had been a keen amateur musician since the age of 6. In 1862 he gave up his job and enrolled at the St Petersburg conservatory, where he studied under Anton Rubinstein, whose brother Nikolay offered him the professorship of harmony (1866) at the newly opened Moscow conservatory (which he had founded in 1864). In Moscow, Tchaikovsky met the musical nationalists, notably Balakirev and Rimsky-Korsakov, and while he was influenced by them he was never in full sympathy with The *Five. After the success of his first piano concerto (first performance in Russia, 1875) he began a correspondence with Nadezhda von Meck, a wealthy widow, whose financial support enabled him to devote himself to composition. They remained correspondents until a misunderstanding in 1890 ended their relationship, but they never actually met. Tchaikovsky made a disastrous marriage in 1877, possibly in an attempt to conceal his homosexuality; a separation followed an attempted suicide after 11 weeks of marriage. Despite his subsequent depressions he managed to produce his most successful opera, *Eugene Onegin* (1877–78), his fourth symphony (1878), and his violin concerto (1878) during this period. In 1881 he gave up

teaching at the conservatory and for the next seven years was deeply involved in composition. In 1888 he made his first international tour as a conductor, during which he visited Berlin, Paris, and London. This was followed by further tours to the USA (1892) and to London (1893), where his lyrical use of broad melodic figures and flair for orchestration made him immensely popular. His death from cholera in St Petersburg, after imprudently drinking unboiled water, occurred soon after the first performance of his *Pathetic Symphony (No. 6, 1893), which had an indifferent reception.

Tchaikovsky is acknowledged as one of the greatest masters of the ballet: his three ballets *Swan Lake (1876), The *Sleeping Beauty (1889), and The *Nutcracker (1891–92) are the basis of the classical repertoire. He wrote 10 operas, including *Voyevoda (1869), The *Maid of Orleans (1881), The *Queen of Spades (1890) and *Iolanta (1891). His 6 symphonies include No. 2, 1873 (see **Little Russian Symphony**) and No. 3, 1875 (see **Polish Symphony**); his *Manfred symphony (1886) bears more the form of a tone poem. Tchaikovsky's other works include four orchestral suites; the tone poems *Romeo and Juliet (1870) and *Francesca da Rimini (1876); orchestral works, such as the *Capriccio italien (1880) and *Eighteen-Twelve Overture (1882); three piano concertos (the third incomplete); music for solo instruments and orchestra; and many songs.

Tcherepnin, Nikolay Nikolayevich (1873–1945) Russian-born composer and conductor resident in Paris from 1921, a pupil of Rimsky-Korsakov. From 1908 to 1914 he was conductor of Diaghilev's Ballets Russes in Paris. His own works, in a conservative Russian style, include the operas *Swat* (1930) and *Vanka* (1932); the ballets *Le Pavillon d'Armide* (1908), *Le Masque de la mort rouge* (1922), and *Romance of the Mummy* (1924); orchestral works; choral pieces, including the oratorio *La Descente de la Sainte Vierge à l'enfer* (1938); and numerous songs. His son **Alexander Nikolayevich Tcherepnin** (1899–), also a composer, settled with his father in Paris, where he studied and taught. He then worked in the Far East and from 1949 taught in Chicago. His compositions include operas, ballets, four symphonies, five piano concertos, and much chamber music.

te see **tonic sol-fa.**

Tear, Robert (1939–) British tenor. Starting his career with the choir at St Paul's Cathedral, he went on to sing in Britten's operas. Tear has recently toured the Netherlands, and his earlier vocal resemblance to Peter Pears has given way to a more pronounced individuality.

Tebaldi, Renata (1922–) Italian soprano. She made her debut as Elena in Boito's *Mefistofele* at Rovigo (1944). As a lyric soprano she then sang at the Teatro San Carlo,

Kiri Te Kanawa

Naples, and at La Scala, Milan; in 1950 she made her first appearance at Covent Garden. Tebaldi excels in the operas of Verdi and Puccini.

tedesco (*or fem.* **tedesca**) German. Hence **alla tedesca**, in the German style, particularly the style of a waltz. [Italian]

Te Deum laudamus The Latin hymn that is used by many Christian churches to express a supreme moment of rejoicing. The Latin text has a traditional plainsong setting as well as settings with orchestral accompaniment by Haydn, Berlioz, Bruchner, and others. It has also been set in English by Handel and Walton. [Latin, We praise thee, O God]

Teil (*or* **Theil**) Part; section. [German]

Te Kanawa, Dame Kiri (1944–) New Zealand soprano. After winning various prizes in Australia and New Zealand she studied at the London Opera Centre and joined the Royal Opera Company, making her Covent Garden debut in 1970. Her first major role was the Countess in Mozart's *The Marriage of Figaro*, a part she has since become particularly associated with. In 1974 she made her New York debut as Desdemona in Verdi's *Otello* and is now internationally recognized as a fine lyric soprano.

Telemann, Georg Philipp (1681–1767) German composer and teacher. While studying law at Leipzig University

he taught himself to compose and to play various instruments and was appointed organist at the New Church in 1704. He became kapellmeister at Sorau (1705), Eisenach (1708), and Frankfurt (1712) and in Hamburg was cantor of five churches (1721). A friend of Bach, he wrote many chamber works, including *Musique de table* (1733), many cantatas and oratorios, over 40 settings of the Passion, over 40 operas, about 600 French overtures, keyboard music, and treatises, including *Singe-Spiel-und Generalbass-Ubungen* (1733).

Telephone, The Comic opera in one act by Menotti with text by the composer. First performance: Heckscher Theatre, New York, 1947. Lucy (soprano) is so addicted to the telephone that the only possibility for Ben (baritone), who is trying to propose to her, is to ring her up.

tema Theme. [Italian]

temperament The way in which the *intervals between notes are distributed throughout the *scale to enable music in all keys to sound in tune. The necessity arises because of the way scales are constructed in western music. Systems of temperament sharpen or flatten certain notes to compensate for the slight discrepancy that arises in the interval between C and the C seven octaves higher. This interval should be (on the basis of seven octaves) $2^7 = 128$. However, in passing through the cycle of 12 keys, each using as its fundamental the fifth of its predecessor, the interval between Cs becomes $(3/2)^{12} = 129.75$. This difference, known as the **comma of Pythagoras**, can be compensated for in several ways.

The **Pythagorean scale** was built on a series of five perfect fifths (whole tones) and two equal hemitones with intervals that were less than half each whole tone. The tuning of this scale became the basis of the Greek and later the medieval *modes. Modulation between modes was, however, impossible. In the **Ptolemaic scale** (*or* **just intonation**) the intervals between all fifths but one are perfect; the one exception is that the fifth D–A is taken as $40:27 = 1.4815$ instead of 1.5. Just intonation is usable for a melodic line, but produces bad dissonances in harmony, particularly with the chord DFA. The **mean-tone scale** was introduced in the 16th century; by reducing the pitch of each of the fifths C–G, G–D, D–A, and A–E to $\sqrt[4]{5} = 1.495$ a scale was produced in which music sounded acceptable in certain keys (those with few or no sharps and flats). Intervals in more remote keys were badly affected by this compromise and certain organs possessed two separate notes for E♭ and D♯ (see **enharmonic intervals**).

The **equal-temperament scale** was introduced during the lifetime of J. S. Bach, who with his son C. P. E. Bach became its chief supporter. In equal temperament the comma of Pythagoras is distributed equally between the 12 intervals of the scale over seven octaves. Thus each fifth becomes

$^{12}\sqrt{128} = 1.4983$ and the intervals between each semitone are all equal. Notes such as B/C♭ and D♯/E♭ also become identical. This system permits modulation between any two keys and the performance of works in all 12 keys, as demonstrated in J. S. Bach's famous collection of preludes and fugues *The Well-Tempered Clavier*. All forms of temperament are compromises and none is perfect. Modern keyboard and fretted instruments all use equal temperament.

Tempest, The 1. Symphonic fantasy by Tchaikovsky, based on the play by Shakespeare. First performance: 1873. **2.** Set of incidental music (Op. 109) by Sibelius to Shakespeare's play. First performance: 1926. **3.** (German: *Die Zauberinsel*) Opera by Sutermeister, who based his libretto on Shakespeare's play. First performance: Dresden, 1942. **4.** (German: *Der Sturm*) Opera by Frank Martin using Schlegel's German translation of Shakespeare's play. First performance: Vienna State Opera, 1956.

temple block see **Chinese wood block.**

Templeton, Alec (1909–63) British pianist and composer, blind from birth, resident for many years in the USA. He is best known for his jazz arrangements and recompositions of classical pieces, such as *Bach Goes to Town*. He also wrote a number of original piano pieces and light orchestral works.

tempo The speed of a musical composition or section of it. Tempo is indicated either by written instructions known as **tempo marks** (for example, adagio, allegro) or by *metronome markings, which give a much more accurate indication of the correct pace. The word tempo is also used in conjunction with other words to indicate more precise speed markings; for example **tempo primo** (at the original pace), **tempo giusto** (in strict time), and **tempo di minuetto** (at the speed of a minuet). Despite all indications, tempo always remains a matter for the interpretation of the performer and there is really no 'correct' tempo for any one piece of music, since acoustics and other external influences have a great effect upon the speed at which a composition becomes most effective. [Italian, pace; time]

tempo rubato see **rubato.**

ten. see **tenuto.**

tenero Tender. Hence **teneramente**, tenderly; **tenerezza**, tenderness. [Italian]

tenor 1. The highest and most brilliant of the three varieties of male voices (compare **baritone; bass**). Its range is an octave either side of middle C. Tenors can be classified as either lyric or dramatic (see **heroic tenor**), these qualities corresponding to the similar classes of *soprano. The melody or cantus firmus in plainchant and in much early choral music was frequently held by the tenor part. See also

countertenor. 2. Describing instruments with a range comparable to that of the tenor voice. [from Latin *tenere*, to hold]

tenor clef see **clef.**

tenor cor (*or* **tenor horn**) see **mellophone.**

tenor drum A military drum intermediate in size and pitch between the *side drum and the *bass drum. It is double-headed, has no snares, and is played with two wooden sticks. It is also used in the orchestra and in some jazz drum sets. It resembles the side drum in being played with the membranes horizontal but has a considerably deeper body. For illustration, see **drums.**

tenor tuba (*or* **euphonium**) see **tuba.**

tenuto Held: a direction used to indicate that a note or chord should be sustained for its full length and sometimes slightly longer than its strict time value. Abbreviation: **ten.** [Italian]

ternary form A musical *form in three sections, commonly designated as ABA. Generally each section is self-contained (unlike *binary form). The return of A as the third section is often ornamented, as in the *da capo aria, in which case the form is symbolized as ABA'. Ternary form was first regularly employed in German songs, Minnesang, and chorale melodies between the 12th and 16th centuries and in Italian *lauda of the 13th century. Beginning with Monteverdi, 17th-century opera composers used the form with increasing regularity in arias and duets. As the structure evolved, composers sometimes used binary form for the A section and some of the material again for the B section. Alternatively, the B section was in dramatic contrast, with a different texture and accompaniment as well as a different key. In instrumental music ternary form (sometimes called **song form**, because of its vocal background) is most commonly found in the *minuet and trio movements of *suites and, in the later 18th century, in symphonies, where it was also used for slow movements. Ternary form continued to be widely used in the 19th century, especially for piano music. Many examples, sometimes with short introductions and codas, occur in Mendelssohn's *Songs Without Words*, Chopin's waltzes, and Brahms' intermezzi. As **arch form**, the basic shape of ternary form continued to be used in the 20th century, notably by Bartók and Berg.

Tertis, Lionel (1876–1975) British violist. He was one of the first to popularize the viola as a solo instrument and works were written for him by Bax, Bridge, Walton, and Vaughan Williams among others. Tertis made numerous transcriptions for viola.

tessitura The prevailing range of a composition or part. If there is a preponderance of high notes, the tessitura is said to be high; the converse applies. The term is more frequently applied to vocal music than to instrumental music. [Italian, texture]

tetrachord 1. An ancient Greek four-stringed instrument. **2.** A scale consisting of four notes, the interval between the first and last being a fourth.

Tetrazzini, Luisa (1871–1940) Italian soprano. After making her debut as Ines in Meyerbeer's *L'Africaine* at Florence (1890), she toured widely, winning international acclaim as a brilliant operatic coloratura soprano. Her sister, **Eva Tetrazzini** (1862–1938) was also an operatic soprano.

Teyte, Dame Maggie (Margaret Tate; 1888–1976) British soprano. She studied in London at the Royal College of Music and in Paris, where Debussy selected her in 1908 to succeed Mary Garden as Mélisande in his opera *Pelléas et Mélisande* and instructed and accompanied her. She introduced French impressionist vocal music to Britain and the USA, recorded *French Song from Berlioz to Debussy*, and became a DBE in 1958.

Thaïs Opera in three acts by Massenet with libretto by Gallet based on the novel by Anatole France. First performance: Opéra, Paris, 1894. Set in and near Alexandria during the 4th century, it is the story of the courtesan Thaïs (soprano), who becomes a nun. The popular *Meditation* occurs as an orchestral interlude between the second and third acts.

Thalben-Ball, George (1896–1987) Australian organist, who was resident in Britain. He held appointments at the City Temple, London, and at Birmingham University and Town Hall, in addition to performing as a recitalist.

Thalberg, Sigismond (Fortuné François) (1812–71) German or Austrian pianist and composer. He studied music theory with Sechter and the piano with Hummel in Vienna, with Pixis in Paris, and with Moscheles in London. He soon became a celebrated international virtuoso, rivalling Liszt in Paris. He lived for several years in the USA and settled in Italy. Thalberg's dazzling technique is reflected in his many compositions for piano, which include many fantasias on opera arias; he also wrote operas, chamber music, and a piano concerto. He contributed a variation to the **Hexameron* (1837).

theatre organ see **cinema organ**.

theme A musical idea that forms an essential structural part of a composition. Any theme can usually be broken down into several *motives, such as the melodic or rhythmic pattern, and it is by repetition and development of these elements that the theme assumes its structural importance. In certain types of composition, e.g. fugue, the theme is also known as the **subject**. However these distinctions between motive, theme, and subject are not always accepted and

Maggie Teyte

some writers use the terms interchangeably. See also **motto**; **theme song**; **variations**.

theme song A song or other musical theme that occurs from time to time during the performance of a musical, operetta, film, etc. It sometimes has the same title as the whole work (e.g. in *The Sound of Music*) but often does not (e.g. 'As Time Goes By' in the film *Casablanca*). See also **leitmotiv**.

Theodora Oratorio for solo voices, choir, and orchestra by Handel to a text by Morrell. First performance: 1750. Unlike the majority of Handel's oratorios, this work is not based on a biblical subject; Theodora is a 4th-century Christian noblewoman who refuses to celebrate the birthday of a pagan god and is eventually executed as a punishment.

theorbo see **lute**.

theremin An electronic instrument invented by Lev Theremin (*or* Termin; 1896–   ) in the 1920s. It consists of a set of oscillators mounted in a box with a loudspeaker attached. A metal hoop is fitted to the left side of the box and a metal rod protrudes from its top. The pitch of the note produced is controlled by the proximity of the player's right hand to the rod and the volume is controlled by the proximity of his left hand to the hoop. It has been used in some ensembles.

Thibaud, Jacques (1880–1953) French violinist. After studying at the Paris Conservatoire he became known as a soloist in the Colonne in Paris (1898–99). Thibaud then began touring Europe and the USA and formed a very successful trio with Cortot and Casals.

Thibaut IV (1201–53) King of Navarre (1234–53) and one of the most prolific of the late trouvères. He was the author of some 60 songs, mainly love songs.

Thieving Magpie, The (Italian: *La Gazza ladra*) Opera in three acts by Rossini with libretto by Gherardini. First performance: La Scala, Milan, 1817. The serving maid Ninetta (soprano) is sentenced to death for a theft that, in the nick of time, is found to be the work of a magpie.

Thiman, Eric (1900–75) British organist and composer, also teacher at the Royal Academy of Music (from 1930). His works include many pieces for organ and piano, liturgical music and choral works, such as *The Last Supper* (1930), *High Tide on the Coast of Lincolnshire* (1932), and *The Temptations of Christ* (1952), as well as light orchestral pieces.

third An *interval of three notes (counting both the first and last notes), or four semitones for a **major third** (e.g. C–E), and three semitones for a **minor third** (e.g. C–E♭). A **diminished third** is equivalent to a major second.

third inversion see **inversion**.

third sounds see **combination tones**.

third stream A form of music that incorporates the virtues of both jazz and classical styles. The concept was introduced by the US composer Gunther Schuller (who coined the term) with such works as *Conversations for Jazz Quartet and String Quartet* (1959). The discovery of jazz by classical musicians in the 1920s resulted in the incorporation of some jazz motifs into their works by such composers as Milhaud, Stravinsky, and Copland. However any extensive merging of the two forms of music always met the same two barriers – the inability of classical musicians to improvise and the inability of jazz musicians to read music. Encouraged by Schuller, John Lewis (1920–) and his Modern Jazz Quartet, and Howard Brubeck (brother of Dave Brubeck), the idea of a third stream has stimulated gifted musicians from both disciplines to attempt to formulate an idiom that incorporates the best of both worlds.

thirty-second note see **demisemiquaver**.

thirty-two foot see **foot**.

Thomas, (Charles Louis) Ambroise (1811–96) French composer. He studied at the Paris Conservatoire (1828–32), where his teachers included Le Sueur, and won the Prix de Rome in 1832. He returned to Paris in 1835 and began composing successful opéras comiques. In 1856 he became composition professor at the Conservatoire and in 1871 director. Thomas's opéras comiques are in the tradition of Auber and Halévy but more lyrical; the best known are *Raymond (1851), Le Carnaval de Venise (1857), *Mignon (1866), and *Hamlet (1868). His ballets and vocal and instrumental music are now largely forgotten.

Thomé, Francis (François Luc Joseph T.; 1850–1909) French composer and teacher. He studied at the Paris Conservatoire with Marmontel, Duprato, and Ambroise Thomas and soon became well known as a composer and teacher. Thomé's undistinguished compositions include operas, ballets, and choral, vocal, chamber, and piano works (including *Simple aveu*).

Thomson, Virgil (1896–) US composer, writer, and critic, a pupil of Nadia Boulanger. Inspired by the example of Satie and Les Six, he rejected postromanticism and his own dissonant neoclassicism to forge an individual but deeply American lyrical style. It proved particularly suited to word setting, as evidenced by his two operatic collaborations with Gertrude Stein: *Four Saints in Three Acts* (1928) and *The *Mother of Us All* (1947). He also pioneered a new American approach to the composition of film music with such film scores as *The Plow that Broke the Plains* (1936), *The River* (1937), and *Louisiana Story* (1948). His other works include the opera *Lord Byron* (1968), the ballet *The Filling Station* (1937), *Capital Capitals* (1927), *Symphony on a Hymn Tune* (1928), chamber music and piano pieces, including three string quartets and the *Portraits* series, and choral works and songs.

Three Choirs Festival An annual festival, chiefly of choral music, probably founded in 1715 and based in rotation on the cathedrals of Gloucester, Worcester, and Hereford. It originally consisted of performances of liturgical music and anthems at which the (still surviving) practice of making a collection for dependants of the clergy was established. Later in the 18th century Handel's works were often heard; *Messiah* was performed at Hereford in 1759. During the 19th century its scope was extended and larger-scale works were given, particularly those of Mendelssohn. The festival encouraged the performance of new English works, for example by Sullivan, Parry, and Elgar (who became a leading figure of the festival). Vaughan Williams' *Fantasia on a Theme of Thomas Tallis* (1910), Bliss's *A Colour Symphony*, Holst's *Choral Fantasia* (1931), and Howells' *Hymnus Paradisi* (1950) are among works to receive their first performances there. Since 1945 festival programmes have become more varied and include more works of a less devotional character. The cathedral organists have served as festival conductors; they include S. S. Wesley, Herbert Brewer, Ivor Atkins, H. W. Sumsion, P. C. Hull, David Willcocks, Meredith Davies, Douglas Guest, and Richard Lloyd.

thorough bass see **continuo**.

Three Botticelli Pictures see **Trittico Botticelliano**.

Three-Cornered Hat, The (Spanish: *El Sombrero de tres picos*; French: *Le Tricorne*) Ballet in one act with music by Falla, libretto by Sierra, and choreography by Massine. First

A still from the film of The Threepenny Opera

performance: Alhambra Theatre, London, 1919, by Diaghilev's Ballets Russes with Massine and Karsavina (décor by Picasso). Based on a story by de Alarcón, it relates an eternal triangle involving the attractive miller's wife, her jealous husband, and the elderly Corregidor.

Threepenny Opera, The (German: *Die Dreigroschen-oper*) Opera by Weill with libretto by Brecht based on the story of *The* *Beggar's Opera. First performance: Berlin, 1928.

Threni Work for six solo voices, choir, and orchestra by Stravinsky to words from the Bible. Composed: 1958. The title is Greek, meaning lamentations, and the three movements of this work are settings of portions of the Lamentations of Jeremiah, a text traditionally chosen by leading composers, including Palestrina, Lassus, and Tallis. This is the first completely serialist work that Stravinsky composed, and the orchestration is extremely unusual in that trumpets and bassoons are replaced by alto clarinet, bugle, and sarrusophone.

through-composed song A song in which each verse is set to different music. Compare **strophic song**. [from German *durchkomponiert*, through-composed]

thumb piston see **composition pedal**.

thundersheet A large flexible metal sheet suspended from a wooden pole and struck with a soft drumstick. It is used to simulate thunder in certain compositions.

thunder stick see **bull-roarer**.

Thus Spake Zarathustra see **Also sprach Zarathustra**.

tibia see **aulos**.

tie A curved line written over two adjacent notes of the same pitch in a piece of music to indicate that the second note is not to be sounded separately but the sound of the first is to be prolonged so that it continues for the time value of both notes. The tie is also used for chords in the same way. A **tied note** is the second of such a pair of notes.

tief Deep; low. Hence **tiefe Stimme**, low voice. [German]

Tiefland, Der (*The Lowlands*) Opera in prologue and two acts by Eugène d'Albert with libretto by Rudolph Lothar based on the Catalonian play *Tierra Baixa* by Guimerà. First performance: Prague, 1903. It is a verismo story of peasant life.

tierce 1. See **seventeenth**. 2. An obsolete name for a *third.

tierce de Picardie see **Picardy third**.

Till Eulenspiegel Tone poem (Op. 28) by Richard Strauss, based on a medieval German folk tale and entitled in full *Till Eulenspiegels lustige Streiche* (*Till Eulenspiegel's Merry Pranks*). Composed: 1895. Having seen an opera by Kistler about Till Eulenspiegel in 1889, Strauss was initially inspired to compose a one-act operetta on this subject, which he actually sketched but never completed. Instead he later reworked the material into this tone poem, in which he attempts to capture in music the life and spirit of this famous rogue, whose various pranks cause a trail of disaster that ends with his arrest and execution.

Tilson-Thomas, Michael (1944–) US conductor. He specializes in 20th-century and avant-garde music and became associate conductor of the Boston Symphony Orchestra (1970).

timbale Kettledrum. [French]

timbre see **tone colour**.

timbrel see **tambourine**.

time A measure of the rhythmic pattern of a piece of music indicated by its *time signature. Music is broken down into bars, which form the basic structure of its *rhythm. The rhythm within the bars depends on the number of beats to the bar and the value of each beat as well as on the way in which the *accents fall on the beats. Compare **tempo**.

time signature A sign at the beginning of a composition to indicate the kind and number of beats in the bar. If this changes during the course of a composition a new time signature will be required. New time signatures are also given at the beginning of a new movement. The time signature consists of two figures, one written above the other like a fraction. The lower figure indicates the kind of notes into which the bar is divided; for example, as 2 indicates minims (half notes) and a 4 indicates crotchets (quarter notes). The upper figure indicates the number of these notes in the bar. Thus 4/4, called **common time**, indicates that there will be four crotchets in the bar. The time signature used for this is a broken circle resembling a C. See **Appendix, Table 4**. See also **compound time; simple time.**

timpani see **kettledrums.**

Tinctoris, Johannes (*c.*1435–?1511) Franco-Flemish composer and theorist. He may have sung in the choir at Cambrai and was later instructor of the cathedral choirboys in Orléans. In 1472 he entered the service of King Ferdinand I of Naples. Tinctoris wrote few compositions but he is well known for his treatises. The most important is *Terminorum musicae diffinitorium* (1495), which gives 299 definitions of musical terms; others discuss the aesthetic value of music, composition, and improvisation. These writings give an invaluable insight into Renaissance music.

tin whistle (*or* **penny whistle**) A simple whistle flute, usually with six finger holes, made of metal. It is a low-priced *recorder used as a toy.

Tippett, Sir Michael Kemp (1905–   ) British composer. His early music is shaped by a variety of sources – the English madrigal tradition, blues and spirituals, jazz rhythms, and modal harmony. In the 1940s he developed a more complex dynamic, lyrical, and contrapuntal manner. From the 1960s his music became more disjointed: ideas are juxtaposed and contrasted in a mosaic-like structure with an emphasis on texture and sounds. Recent works, however, show a new lyricism and more continuous writing. Tippett's works, particularly his operas, have always expressed social and philosophical ideas. They include four string quartets, three piano sonatas, four symphonies, a concerto for double string orchestra (1939), the oratorio A *Child of Our Time* (1941), a piano concerto (1955), the cantata *The Vision of St Augustine* (1965), a triple concerto (1979), and the operas *The *Midsummer Marriage* (1955), *King Priam* (1961), *The *Knot Garden* (1970), and *The *Ice Break* (1977).

Tjeknavorian, Loris (1937–   ) Iranian conductor and composer of Armenian descent. His works include ballets, film music, and the *Requiem for the Massacred.*

toccata A single-movement keyboard piece in free style, designed mainly to demonstrate the skill of the performer. Originating with Andrea Gabrieli, the toccata was a favourite form in the baroque era and its distinguishing characteristic was the constant use of rapid scale and arpeggio figurations. The term gradually came to have a less precise meaning and was applied to works in several movements (for example, the harpsichord toccatas of J. S. Bach) and also to works with contrapuntal interest (for

Sir Michael Tippett

example, the toccatas of Merulo). Modern toccatas are works in an essentially rhapsodic style. [Italian, touched]

toccatina (*or* **toccatino**) A short toccata.

Toch, Ernst (1887–1964) Austrian-born US composer and pianist, largely self-taught. His style was basically neoclassical, although his works became increasingly dissonant. Toch composed much chamber music, including 13 string quartets. He also wrote seven symphonies, the orchestral pieces *Pinocchio* (1935) and *Peter Pan* (1956), four operas, including *Der Prinzessin auf der Erbse* (1927) and *The Last Tale* (1962), many piano pieces, and film scores.

Tod und Verklärung see **Death and Transfiguration.**

Toeschi, Carlo Giuseppe (1722–88) Italian composer and violinist. A pupil of Johann Stamitz, he was appointed leader of the Mannheim orchestra (1759) and, after the court moved to Munich, its musical director (1780). His works include symphonies, ballets, and chamber music.

Tomasi, Henri (1901–71) French composer and conductor, a pupil of d'Indy. His orchestral music includes 16 concertos for various instruments and several tone poems. He also wrote the operas *L'Atlantide* (1952), *Le Silence de la mer* (1959), and *L'Elixir du Révérend Père Gaucher*

(1962); *L'Eloge de la folie* (1964) and other ballets; choral music, including *Tam-tam* (1931); and chamber works, piano pieces, and songs.

Tomášek, Václav Jan Křtitel (1774–1850) Czech composer and teacher. Although largely self-taught in music, he made a reputation as a teacher in Prague, where in 1824 he established music school. Tomášek became eminent in Prague musical life and travelled throughout Europe: he was a leading figure in the transition from classical to romantic ideals in Czech music. He composed stage works, choral music, and songs (most to German texts), but is better known for his orchestral music (including three symphonies and two piano concertos), chamber music, and works for piano (among them 42 eclogues).

Tomasi, Henri (1901–71) French composer and conductor, a pupil of d'Indy. His orchestral music includes 16 concertos for various instruments and several tone poems. He also wrote the operas *L'Atlantide* (1952), *Le Silence de la mer* (1959), and *L'Elixir du Révérend Père Gaucher* (1962); *L'Eloge de la folie* (1964) and other ballets; choral music, including *Tam-tam* (1931); and chamber works, piano pieces, and songs.

tombeau A composition written to commemorate the death of a famous person (see **lament**). The earliest work of this kind is the ballade 'Armes, amours,' composed by Andrieu in 1377 to commemorate the death of Machaut; the lament 'Mort tu as navré' by Ockeghem to honour Binchois is equally famous. Ravel's *Tombeau de Couperin* (1920), a suite of keyboard pieces in baroque forms in honour of François Couperin, is the best-known example from a later period. [French, tombstone]

Tom Jones 1. Opera in three acts by Philidor with libretto by Poinsinet based on Fielding's novel. First performance: Comédie-Italienne, Paris, 1765. **2.** Operetta by Edward German with libretto from the same source by Thompson, Courtneidge, and Taylor. First performance: Manchester, 1907. **3.** Opera by Stephen Oliver, who adapted his own text. First performance: Newcastle-upon-Tyne, 1976.

Tomkins, Thomas (1572–1656) English composer. Born in St Davids, he was appointed master of the choristers at Worcester in 1596; he had apparently previously studied in London with William Byrd. He contributed a madrigal to *The Triumphs of Oriana* (1601). By 1620 he was Gentleman in Ordinary at the Chapel Royal and became one of the organists there in 1621. Tomkins wrote some of the coronation music for Charles I and seems to have returned to Worcester after 1628. His music is rather anachronistic: his *Songs* (1622), for example, show none of the chromaticism of Weelkes or the harmonic construction of Wilbye. However his church music, including services and numerous verse anthems, was greatly admired.

His keyboard pieces include variations, fantasias, In nomines, and preludes.

Tommasini, Vicenzo (1878–1950) Italian composer and writer. His early works, such as *Chiari di luna* (1915), were influenced by impressionism, whereas his later style was more neoclassical. Tommasini's output includes the operas *Medea* (1904) and *Uguale fortuna* (1911); the ballets *Le Donne di buon umore* (1916; arranged from Scarlatti) and *Tiepolesco* (1940); orchestral music, such as *Paesaggi Toscani* (1922) and *La Tempesta* (1941); and chamber and choral music.

tomtom A double-headed barrel drum native to India that is now used in dance bands and occasionally in the orchestra. It can be tuned by moving rings up and down the lacing to alter the tension of the head.

tonada A Spanish ballad consisting of a setting of a poem to music. Originating in the 16th century, the name has been revived by the Chilean composer Allende, who composed 12 tonadas for piano, some of which have been orchestrated. [Spanish]

tonadilla An intermezzo with vocal solos used in the theatre. Derived from the *tonada, the tonadilla was introduced in Spain in the 18th century.

tonal 1. Denoting a composition that relies on tonality. **2.** Denoting a note or sequence of notes.

tonal answer see **answer.**

tonal fugue see **fugue.**

tonality The use of a major or minor key in a musical composition. Compare **atonality; polytonality.**

tonal sequence see **sequence.**

Tondichtung Tone poem. [German]

tone 1. The interval between the first and second notes of the diatonic scale. See **scales; temperament. 2.** A *note. This usage is largely restricted to the USA. **3.** A pure note from which overtones have been excluded. **4.** The quality of a musical sound, especially in respect of a musical instrument, record player, etc. **5.** A melody used in plainsong.

tone colour (*or* **timbre**) The quality of a sound characteristic of a particular instrument or voice. It is determined by the number and intensity of the *overtones present in the sound in addition to the *fundamental. For example, a trumpet, oboe, and violin make different sounds even when they are playing the same note. This is because none of the instruments produces a pure tone consisting only of the fundamental. If they did the sounds would be the same. Because each instrument produces a different set of overtones of different intensities the sounds have characteristic tone colours. The set of upper *partials associated with a particular instrument is known as its **formant.**

tone poem (*or* **symphonic poem**) A large-scale orchestral work, usually in one movement, distinguished from the *symphony by being based on a nonmusical subject. The term 'symphonic poem' was first used in 1854, referring to Liszt's *Tasso*; other notable contributors to the genre include Strauss, Smetana, Saint-Saëns, and Franck. Tone poems were based upon a wide variety of sources including literary ones (Liszt, *Les Préludes*), paintings (Liszt, *Die Hunnenschlacht*), and plays (Tchaikovsky, *Hamlet*). With Strauss the range of stimuli enlarged to include philosophical ideology, as seen in *Also sprach Zarathustra* and *Tod und Verklärung*. In structure tone poems frequently follow the sonata-form of symphonic first movements, and with its subjective nature the tone poem became a particularly favoured medium for such movements as *nationalism and *impressionism.

tonguing The use of the tongue to interrupt the flow of breath in playing a wind instrument so that certain passages and repeated notes can be articulated more rapidly. In **single tonguing** the tongue is moved as it is in enunciating the letter *t*, in **double tonguing** it is moved as in *tk*, and in **triple tonguing** as in *tkt*. In **flutter tonguing** the letter *r* is trilled to give a birdlike sound on the flute. Tonguing is used on both woodwind and brass instruments.

tonic (*or* **keynote**) The first note of a scale, from which a key takes its name. Thus the tonic of the key of G major or G minor is G.

tonic sol-fa A musical notation devised by John Curwen in the 1840s on the basis of *solmization. It simplifies sight reading for choral singers and obviates complications arising from transpositions of keys. The eight notes of the scale are **doh, ray, me, fah, soh, lah, te, doh**; these are usually represented in music by their initial letters. Accidentals are indicated by changing the vowel sounds for flats (*ra, ma*, etc.) and sharps (*de, re, my*, etc.). The system is now used with a movable doh: thus in the key of E♭ major, doh is E♭ and soh (the dominant) is B♭, whereas in the key of C doh is C and soh is G. In minor keys lah will be the tonic and me the dominant. Time values are indicated by the way in which the letters fill the spaces between the bar lines.

Tonkunst Music; musical skill. Hence **Tonkünstler**, musician. [German, sound-art]

tonus 1. Tone. **2.** Mode. [Italian]

tonus peregrinus 1. A form of *mode I that is similar to the present minor scale. **2.** The plainsong for psalm 114 (*In exitu Israel*), which uses this scale with two reciting notes. It was also used by Bach as a chorale. See also **Gregorian tone**. [Latin, foreign mode]

Torelli, Giuseppe (1658–1709) Italian composer and violinist. From 1686 to 1695 he played in the chapel orchestra at S Petronio, Bologna; he then travelled to Germany and in 1698 was concert master for the Margrave of Brandenburg in Ansbach and spent time in Vienna. By 1701 he was again a violinist at S Petronio. Torelli contributed to the development of the concerto in his *Concerti musicali* (1698) and in the *Concerti grossi con una pastorale* (1709); he also wrote music for trumpet and strings.

Tórroba, Federico (1891–1982) Spanish composer. His output consists mainly of pieces for guitar. He also wrote orchestral works, including a guitar concerto, and contributed pieces to the *zarzuela repertory, including *Luisa Fernanda* (1932), *La Mesonera de Tordesillas*, and *La Chulapona*.

Tortelier, Paul (1914–   ) French cellist. He studied at the Paris Conservatoire, where he became a professor in 1957, and has achieved international acclaim for his performances. Tortelier frequently appears in chamber-music recitals with his wife, the cellist **Maud Martin Tortelier** (1926–   ), his son, the violinist **Jan Pascal Tortelier** (1947–   ), and his daughter **Maria de la Pau** (1950–   ), a pianist. He also composes and conducts.

Tosca Opera in three acts by Puccini with libretto by Giacosa and Illica based on the play *La Tosca* by Sardou. First performance: Teatro Constanzi, Rome, 1900. Tosca (soprano), a prima donna, promises to yield to the chief of police, Scarpia (baritone), in return for his sparing the life of her lover Cavaradossi (tenor), a painter. Tosca stabs Scarpia as he claims his reward but he has double-crossed her and Cavaradossi is shot; Tosca leaps to her death from the battlements.

Toscanini, Arturo (1867–1957) Italian conductor. Originally a cellist, Toscanini began his conducting career in 1886, when he was unexpectedly called upon to conduct a performance of *Aida* in Rio de Janeiro. He subsequently conducted at various Italian opera houses, directing the premieres of *I Pagliacci* (1892) and *La Bohème* (1896). He became conductor at La Scala, Milan (1898–1903; 1906–08) and at the Metropolitan Opera, New York (1908–21). After a further period at La Scala (1921–29) he returned to the USA to conduct the New York Philharmonic Orchestra (1929–36). In 1936 he became director of the NBC Symphony Orchestra, a post he held until his death. Being myopic, Toscanini conducted from memory; the energy, authority, and perfection of his performances became legendary.

Toselli, Enrico (1883–1926) Italian composer and pianist. He achieved notoriety through his elopement with and short-lived marriage to Archduchess Luise Antoinette Marie of Austria-Tuscany. His works include many light songs, such as the well-known 'Serenata' (1900); operettas, including *La Cattiva Francesca* (1912) and *La Principessa*

Arturo Toscanini

bizarra (1913); orchestral and chamber music; and pieces for piano.

Tosti, Sir (Francesco) Paolo (1846–1916) Italian composer and singing teacher. He studied in Naples, where he became singing teacher to Princess Margherita of Savoy (later Queen of Italy). He visited London each year from 1875 to 1880, when he was appointed singing teacher to the royal family. He was knighted in 1908 and returned to Italy in 1912. He wrote many popular songs to English, French, and Italian texts, among the best known being 'Forever' and 'Goodbye.'

Tost Quartets Set of 12 string quartets by Haydn. Composed: 1789–90. These quartets are numbered Op. 54 Nos. 1–3, Op. 55 Nos. 1–3, and Op. 64 Nos. 1–6; they were dedicated to Johann Tost, a wealthy businessman in Vienna and also a good violinist.

total serialism The application of the principles of *serialism to all the elements of a musical composition (pitch, rhythm, tempi, dynamics, methods of attack, etc.). Total serialism has been employed in a strict form by Boulez in *Structures I* (1952) and with more freedom by Stockhausen and Nono.

touch 1. The resistance of a piano key to the fingers of the pianist. This will depend on the design and condition of the *action. If the touch of a piano is too heavy it slows the pianist down in fast passages, whereas a piano with too light a touch is disconcerting for many pianists. **2.** The manner in which a pianist strikes the keys of a piano. While the force of fingers can only alter the loudness or softness of a note, and not its timbre, there is no doubt that different pianists make different sounds on the same piano, largely as a result of differences of touch.

touche The fingerboard of a stringed instrument. Hence **sur la touche**, a direction indicating that the bowing should be near or over the fingerboard. [French]

Tournemire, Charles Arnould (1870–1939) French organist and composer, a pupil of Franck, Widor, and d'Indy. He is best known for his numerous organ pieces, including the vast cycle *L'Orgue mystique* (1927–32). He also wrote eight orchestral symphonies, *La Légende de Tristan* (1926) for orchestra, *Les Dieux sont morts* (1924) and other operas, and chamber music.

Tourte bow see **bow**.

Tovey, Sir Donald Francis (1875–1940) British musical scholar and composer. After a brilliant early career as a pianist, he was appointed Professor of Music at Edinburgh University (1914). He wrote most of the musical entries for the 14th edition of the *Encyclopaedia Britannica* as well as a six-volume *Essays on Musical Analysis* (1935–39). He composed several works, mostly chamber music, and a conjectured completion of Bach's *The Art of Fugue* (1931).

toye (*or* **toy**) A slight playful composition for the virginals that originated in the 16th century.

toy symphony A simple symphony in which strings, and sometimes a piano, are augmented with toy instruments (e.g. quail, cuckoo, etc.). The best-known example, formerly attributed to Haydn, was probably written by Leopold Mozart. Other toy symphonies have been written by Mendelssohn, Romberg, and Malcolm Arnold.

tr. Abbreviation for trill or trumpet.

tracker action see **action**.

Traetta, Tommaso (1727–79) Italian composer. After studying in Naples with Porpora and Durante, he was appointed maestro di cappella at the Spanish court in Parma (1758) and director at the Conservatorio dell' Ospedalatto,

Venice (1765). His best works, including the opera *Antigone* (1772), were composed while he was maestro di cappella in St Petersburg (1768–75). He also wrote about 40 other operas, ballets, sacred works, sinfonias, and divertimenti.

Tragic Overture Overture (Op. 81) by Brahms. Composed: 1880; first performance: Breslau, 1881. Brahms composed this overture, together with its companion work the *Academic Festival Overture* (1880), in recognition of the honorary doctorate conferred upon him by Breslau University in 1879.

Tragic Symphony Symphony No. 4 in C minor by Schubert. Composed: 1816. Schubert himself used this title and the mood of the work is considerably more serious than that of any of his preceding symphonies.

transcription see **arrangement**.

Transfigured Night see **Verklärte Nacht**.

transition 1. (*or* **bridge passage**) A passage in a composition that joins together, with or without a change of key, two other passages. An example is the passage that connects the first and second subjects in sonata form. **2.** An abrupt change of key without *modulation.

transposing instrument A musical instrument pitched in a key other than C major, for which music is written down as if its basic scale were C major. For example, a player of a B♭ clarinet reading music in C major (no flats) will actually be playing in the key of B♭ (two flats). Music written in the key of F major (one flat) will actually sound in the key of E♭ major (three flats). The clarinetist thus has to cope with fewer sharps and flats. The music for the B♭ clarinet is therefore written one tone higher than it sounds, while for the A clarinet it is a minor third (one and a half tones) higher than it sounds. The transposing instruments in the orchestra are the cor anglais, clarinet, horn, and trumpet. The saxophone and bass flute are also transposing instruments.

transposition The process of changing the overall pitch of a piece of music. For example, a composition in C major can be transposed a semitone down by playing it in the key of B major.

transverse flute see **flute**.

trascinando Holding back the speed. [Italian, dragging]

Traubel, Helen (1899–1972) US soprano. After studying at St Louis she made her New York debut in 1939 at the Metropolitan Opera, where she remained until 1953 singing all the principal soprano roles in Wagner's operas.

Trauersymphonie see **Mourning Symphony**.

traverso Transverse. In old scores, short for **flauto traverso**, transverse flute. [Italian]

Traviata, La Opera in three acts by Verdi with libretto by Piave based on Dumas' play *La Dame aux camélias*. First performance: Teatro la Fenice, Venice, 1853. Violetta (soprano), a consumptive courtesan, discovers true love with Alfredo (tenor) but nobly sacrifices it at the request of his father (baritone). Alfredo insults her in front of her new protector, Baron Douphol (baritone), but receives her forgiveness as she lies dying.

Travis, Roy (1922–) US composer, a pupil of Luening and Milhaud. His style has been greatly influenced by Greek drama and African tribal music; he has also made much use of electronic music. Travis's works include the opera *The Passion of Oedipus* (1965), *Collage* (1968) for orchestra, a piano concerto (1969), a concerto for flute, prerecorded African instruments, and synthesizer (1971), and piano music, such as the *African Sonata* (1966).

treble 1. (n.) The voice of a boy who has not reached puberty. The trained voice is capable of producing a penetrating and resonant sound at the top of its range, B♭–C, having more purity of tone and fewer upper partials than the soprano. The characteristic British treble sound is less bright and more mellow than its continental counterpart. Many cathedrals and university colleges support choir schools where the choristers are trained to a high standard of singing and general musical proficiency. **2.** (n.) The highest part in a choir of mixed voices. Descants are sung by the treble (or soprano) voice while the remainder sing the melody in unison. **3.** (adj.) Describing members of families of instruments that are high-pitched.

treble clef see **clef**.

tre corde (*or* **tutte le corde**) A direction in piano playing used to indicate that the soft pedal should be released at the point so marked on the score. Compare **una corda**. [Italian, three (or all the) strings – because the normal action of a piano involves the hammer striking two or three strings]

tremolando Trembling; using a *tremolo effect. [Italian]

tremolo 1. A rapid repetition of a single note, especially as produced on a bowed stringed instrument by quickly moving the bow back and forth or on a mandolin by vibrating the plectrum between pairs of strings. A tremolo effect can also be produced on a wind instrument by control of the breath and on an organ by a *tremulant. **2.** A rapid alternation between two notes performed on any of a number of instruments. Compare **vibrato**. [Italian, trembling]

tremulant A device on an *organ that introduces a regular pulse into the wind supply that causes the sound to fluctuate in pitch and power, thus producing both *tremolo and *vibrato effects.

trepak A vigorous Cossack dance in 2/4 time.

triad see **chord.**

Trial by Jury Operetta by Sullivan with libretto by Gilbert. First performance: Royalty Theatre, London, 1875. It is a burlesque of an action for breach of promise, the only Gilbert and Sullivan operetta to be sung throughout.

triangle A steel rod bent into the shape of a triangle, usually with a small gap at one corner. It is struck with a metal beater and gives a tinkling sound of indefinite pitch. It was introduced into military bands in the mid-18th century, with the cymbals, tambourine, and other special percussion instruments, to give a Turkish effect. It also appeared in the orchestra at about this time and has been used intermittently ever since. It may either be struck from the outside to produce single notes or played tremolo by moving the beater back and forth inside the triangle.

trill (*or* **shake**) A musical ornament in which the note marked with the letters *tr.* is rapidly alternated with the note a semitone or a whole tone above it. The trill has several forms. Italian: **trillo.**

trillo 1. See **trill. 2.** A vocal ornament used in medieval times and in Italian music of the 17th century that involved the repetition of a note, each repetition becoming progressively diminished in value. In the **ribattuta**, a variation of the trillo in which there are alterations of pitch, the seeds of the modern trill can be discerned.

trio 1. A chamber work for three voices or instruments or a group that performs such a composition. For example, a **piano trio** is a work for piano and (usually) violin and cello; Haydn composed 31 piano trios and Mozart, Beethoven, Schubert, Schumann, and Brahms also contributed to this repertoire. A **string trio** is a work for three string players, usually violin, viola, and cello. Haydn wrote 20 examples. **2.** In the 17th century, the middle section of a *march or *minuet, which was scored for three instrumental parts. This established the 18th-century tradition, when a central trio section was included in the minuet movements of suites, sonatas, and symphonies. Such trios were frequently scored for wind instruments, as in Bach's *Brandenburg Concerto No. 1.* **3.** See **trio sonata.**

trio sonata A type of composition commonly played by an ensemble of two violins and one cello (or bass viol) with a background accompaniment supplied by a harpsichord working from a figured bass. Trio sonatas were popular from the late 17th century to the early 18th century.

triple concerto A concerto for three solo instruments, such as Beethoven's concerto for violin, cello, and piano.

triple counterpoint see **invertible counterpoint.**

triplet A group of three notes of equal time value played in the time of two notes. They are written tied together with a small figure 3 placed on the tie. One or two of the notes can be replaced by rests.

triple time A form of musical time in which there are three beats in the bar, e.g. 3/4 denotes three crotchets (which is *simple time) and 9/8 denotes nine quavers in three groups of three (which is *compound time). Compare **duple time.**

Triptych see **Trittico, Il.**

Tristan und Isolde Opera in three acts with music and libretto by Wagner, based on Gottfried von Strassburg's account of the legend. First performance: Munich, 1865. Tristan (tenor) is escorting the Irish princess Isolde (soprano), who is to be the bride of his uncle, King Mark of Cornwall (bass). They fall in love and drink what they think is poison but is actually a love potion. In Cornwall the lovers are denounced to the king by Melot (tenor), who mortally wounds Tristan in a fight, and Isolde dies of grief.

tritone see **diabolus in musica.**

Trittico, Il (*Triptych*) Three one-act operas by Puccini intended to be performed in one evening: *Gianni Schicchi, *Suor Angelica, and Il *Tabarro. First performance: Metropolitan Opera, New York, 1918.

Trittico Botticelliano (*Botticelli Triptych* or *Three Botticelli Pictures*) Suite for small orchestra by Respighi. Composed: 1927. This work attempts to capture in music the spirit of three of Botticelli's paintings with which Respighi was very impressed. The three movements are entitled 'Spring,' 'The Adoration of the Magi,' and 'The Birth of Venus.'

Triumph of Neptune, The Ballet in 12 scenes with music by Lord Berners, libretto by Sacheverell Sitwell, and choreography by Balanchine. First performance: Lyceum Theatre, London, 1926, by Diaghilev's Ballets Russes. This comic piece parodies mythological opera in the setting of a toy theatre.

Triumphs of Oriana, The A collection of English madrigals edited by Thomas Morley (1601). As the madrigals, for five and six voices, all end with the words 'Long live fair Oriana,' it is assumed that they were intended to be a tribute to Queen Elizabeth I. Composers represented include Benet, Tomkins, Morley, Weelkes, Wilbye, and Croce (whose Italian madrigal is translated into English). The volume went into later revised editions.

Troilus and Cressida Opera in three acts by Walton with libretto by Christopher Hassall. First performance: Covent Garden, London, 1954. Set in ancient Troy, it is based on Chaucer's version of the story of the ill-fated love of Troilus (tenor), Prince of Troy, for Cressida (soprano), niece of Pandarus (buffo tenor).

Trojans, The (French: *Les Troyens*) Opera by Berlioz with libretto by the composer based on Virgil's *Aeneid*; it is in two parts: *The Taking of Troy* (*La Prise de Troie*) and *The Trojans at Carthage* (*Les Troyens à Carthage*). First performance (Part I only): Théâtre-Lyrique, Paris, 1863; the complete opera (in German) was first performed at Karlsruhe, in 1890.

tromba 1. A trumpet. [Italian] **2.** (*or* **tromba da tirarsi**) A slide trumpet that was used briefly in the 17th century in Germany. **3.** See **tromba marina**.

tromba marina (*or* **trumpet marine**) A bowed *monochord formerly in use as a performing instrument. Over 6ft (2m) long, it had a single gut string passing over a bridge that was supported by one foot, allowing the other to vibrate against the body to produce a brassy drumming note. The harmonics were produced by lightly touching the string with the thumb. The instrument was in use in Europe from the 12th to the 18th centuries.

Known as a **Trumscheit** (German, drum log) until 1600, the instrument then acquired a number of names, the most popular of which is tromba marina. The trumpet element in this name is perhaps a reference to its brassy tone and the fact that it plays a harmonic series like a trumpet. The nautical element is more enigmatic. The absurd suggestion that such a cumbersome instrument should be used for signalling at sea can probably be discarded (a sailor sitting on the bridge bowing a 6-ft monochord in a high sea seems particularly unlikely). A more plausible explanation is to be found in its other names, **Nonnentrompete** and **Marientrompete**, from its use in convents to replace the masculine, and perhaps rather phallic, brass trumpet.

Tromboncino, Bartolomeo (*c*.1470–*c*.1535) Italian composer. He was active in Mantua as a musician under the patronage of several families. In 1499 he killed his wife for adultery and two years later he fled the city. From 1502 to 1508 he served Lucrezia Borgia at Ferrara and, from 1520, lived in Venice. Tromboncino's most interesting sacred work is the *Lamentations* but he is better known for his secular music. One of the most important frottola writers, he chose texts of a more serious nature than was customary.

trombone A brass wind instrument that is similar to the *trumpet but has a telescopic slide for lengthening and shortening the tube and a larger and deeper mouthpiece than the trumpet. There are seven positions of the slide in each of which the player can produce a harmonic series a semitone apart by varying his breath pressure; this enables a chromatic scale to be played. The two most commonly used trombones are the **tenor trombone**, with a range of about two and a half octaves from E below the bass staff, and the **bass trombone**, with a similar range from the B below the tenor's E. An **alto trombone** and a **double-bass trombone** have also been used. In the **valve trombone**, valves are added to give the player greater flexibility, enabling him to produce more notes without using the slide.

The trombone originated in the 15th century, when it was known as the **sackbut**. By the end of the century it had evolved into its present form. The instrument is now an important member of the orchestral brass section, which usually consists of two tenor trombones and one bass instrument. Little solo music has been written for it but it is also extensively used in jazz and dance bands as well as in military and brass bands.

Trommel Drum. Hence **grosse Trommel**, bass drum. [German]

tronco Broken off; truncated: a direction used to indicate that a note or chord should be broken off abruptly. [Italian]

trope An interpolation in a pre-existent unit in the Roman liturgy. The interpolation may include both new text and new chant or it may involve fitting a new portion of text against a passage of chant originally sung to one syllable. Troping was widespread in the medieval church and was applied to many different liturgical categories. Best known today are the Kyrie tropes, in which additional text was fitted to the chant between the two words *Kyrie* and *eleison*. See also **plainchant.**

troppo Too much: usually used in the form of the negative, **non troppo**, not too much; e.g. **allegro ma non troppo**, lively, but not too much so. [Italian]

troubadour An itinerant lyric poet or poet-musician who worked in southern France in the 12th and 13th centuries. Troubadour poetry is in Provençal; it is generally concerned with courtly love and is often ingenious and complex. It was brought to life in musical performances to specially written melodies. Troubadours were well educated and sophisticated; among the best known were Bernart de Ventadorn (*c*.1130–90) and Arnaut Daniel (*c*.1150–*c*.1200). *Trouvères were active at the same time, in northern France.

Trout Quintet Piano quintet in A minor (Op. 114) by Schubert. Composed: 1819. Although classified as a piano quintet, the instrumentation is slightly unusual in that the second violin is replaced by a double bass and there are five (rather than the customary four) movements. The name refers to the fourth movement, for which Schubert composed a set of variations upon his song 'Die Forelle' ('The Trout').

trouvère An itinerant lyric poet or poet-musician who worked in northern France in the 12th and 13th centuries. Trouvère poetry is in several regional languages; it and its melodies resemble those of the *troubadours but are often less elaborate. Trouvères were of noble birth; among the best known were Blondel de Nesle (fl. 1180–1200) and Adam de La Halle (*c*.1250–88).

Trovatore, Il (*The Troubadour*) Opera in four acts by Verdi with libretto by Cammarano based on a Spanish drama by Gutiérrez. First performance: Teatro Apollo, Rome, 1853. Set in 15th-century Spain, it tells how the troubadour Manrico (tenor), supposed son of the Gypsy Azucena (mezzo-soprano), loves Leonora (soprano), who is also wooed by Manrico's enemy, the Count di Luna (baritone). The Count's prisoner, Manrico is condemned to death and Leonora drinks poison; just after Manrico's execution Azucena reveals that the Count has killed his own brother. The famous 'Anvil Chorus' comes from Act II, set in the Gypsy encampment.

Troyens, Les see **Trojans, The.**

trumpet A reedless brass wind instrument that has evolved from a hollowed-out piece of wood. Its basic characteristic is that it has a more-or-less cylindrical bore, unlike the *horn, which has a conical bore. However, like the horn, the air in the trumpet is made to vibrate by the player's lips and tongue. Although the modern trumpet is a *brass instrument, primitive trumpets were made of wood, bamboo, or clay and were used in all parts of the world. Metal trumpets were used by the Romans, but they were not used in orchestras until the 17th century. The instrument then used, called a **natural trumpet,** had no means of producing notes other than the harmonics of its fundamental note. However, slide trumpets, keyed trumpets, and crooked trumpets were used between the 17th and 19th centuries with varying degrees of success. The modern trumpet, with its three (or four) piston valves, did not evolve until the mid-19th century. It is now widely used in orchestral music, jazz, and dance music.

The standard modern trumpet is a *transposing instrument in B♭ with a range of three octaves from E in the middle of the bass staff. Concertos for trumpet have been written by Haydn and Shostakovitch and the trumpet is featured in many orchestral works. The **bass trumpet** sounds an octave lower than the standard instrument and the **piccolo trumpet** plays an octave higher. Both have some use in military bands but not in the orchestra. The **fanfare** (*or* **herald**) **trumpet** is a Renaissance instrument with a long straight tube from which banners can be hung. The **Bach trumpet** is a 19th-century valved trumpet specially made to play the high-pitched parts written by Bach for a natural trumpet.

trumpet marine see **tromba marina.**

trumpet voluntary A composition for organ in which the use of a trumpet stop is featured, the *voluntary being a musical interlude occurring at some unspecified point in a church service. The most famous *Trumpet Voluntary* was popularized in an instrumental arrangement by Sir Henry Wood and for many years was considered to be the work of Purcell, although it has now been established as having been composed by Jeremiah Clarke and originally entitled *The Prince of Denmark's March.* Despite the many pieces for trumpet bearing this title, there was originally no connection with the instrument itself.

Trumscheit see **tromba marina.**

Tsar and Carpenter see **Zar und Zimmermann.**

Tsar's Bride, The Opera in three acts by Rimsky-Korsakov with libretto based on a drama by Mey with an additional scene by Tumenev. First performance: Moscow, 1899. Marfa (soprano), chosen bride of Ivan the Terrible, is loved by Lykov (bass) and Gryaznoy (baritone), whose mistress, Lyubasha (mezzo-soprano), poisons her.

tuba A bass valved brass instrument with a wide conical bore. First made in Germany in 1830, bass brass instruments of various types have since been called tubas. The standard orchestral tuba, with an upward-pointing flanged bell, is in F with a range of three octaves from F an octave below the bass staff. There is also an E♭ instrument (called the **bombardon**) and a **double-bass** (*or* **contrabass**) **tuba** in B♭ or C. When these tubas are constructed in a circular form, with a very large forward facing flange, they are called **helicons.** The **sousaphone** is such an instrument, developed by John Sousa in the 19th century but still in use today in brass and military bands. Some models are made in fibreglass to reduce their weight for marching bands.

The **euphonium** is a tenor tuba used in brass bands, mostly the USA. It is essentially a large valved bugle and is a *transposing instrument in B♭. It was invented in Germany in 1843.

The tuba is an important member of the orchestral brass section with little solo music in its repertoire except the concerto for tuba by Vaughan Williams. See also **Wagner tubas.**

tubular bells see **bells.**

tucket A fanfare of trumpets: a word used in Elizabethan stage directions. [from French *toquer,* to sound on a drum]

Tuckwell, Barry (1931–) British horn player. He held various posts as an orchestral player before concentrating on a solo career after 1968. Tuckwell plays with various chamber ensembles, including the Tuckwell Wind Quintet, and Thea Musgrave and Iain Hamilton have both written works for him.

Tudor, David (1926–) US pianist and composer. He is particularly associated with the performance of contemporary music – Stockhausen, Cage, and Feldman have all written for him. Tudor's own compositions frequently include the use of electronic devices.

Tudway, Thomas (*c.*1650–1726) English composer and organist. He was a chorister in the Chapel Royal and in 1670 became organist of King's College, Cambridge, where he remained until his death, holding simultaneously the position of organist to Pembroke College. In 1700 he became Professor of Music at Cambridge. Tudway's contribution to church music is an anthology (1714–20) of pieces by composers from Tye to Handel, and he is remembered for his evening service in B♭.

Tunder, Franz (1614–67) German composer and organist, a pupil of Johann Heikelauer, whom he succeeded as court organist at Gottorf (1632). In 1641 Tunder became organist at St Mary's Church, Lübeck, a post he held until his death. In this capacity he organized evening concerts of organ music and Italian vocal music. The small quantity of Tunder's music that survives is in the Italian style. He set Latin and German texts and employed chorale melodies in his choral cantatas. His organ music displays the influence he exerted over his son-in-law, Dietrich Buxtehude.

tune 1. A melody. **2.** Pitch, hence **in tune** means having the correct pitch; **out of tune** means not having the correct pitch.

tuning fork A two-pronged metal fork that when struck produces a more-or-less pure tone (i.e. at the fundamental frequency with practically no upper harmonics) at a constant specified pitch. It is used for tuning musical instruments and giving the pitch in singing. Tuning forks usually sound an A of 440 hertz or a C of 261.6 hertz.

Turandot 1. Opera in three acts by Puccini (completed by Alfano) with libretto by Adami and Simoni based on the play by Gozzi. First performance: La Scala, Milan, 1926. Turandot (soprano) is an icy-hearted Chinese princess who compels her suitors to answer three riddles: the penalty for failure is death. She is finally won by Prince Calaf (tenor).
2. Opera by Busoni with libretto in German by the composer, based on Gozzi's play. First performance: Zürich, 1917. **3.** Incidental music (Op. 37) by Weber for Schiller's German version of Gozzi's play. Composed: 1809.

Turangalîla Symphony by Messiaen. Composed: 1948. First performance: 1950. Messiaen was commissioned to compose this work by the Koussevitzky Foundation and in it employs a large orchestra, including piano, ondes Martenot, and a much expanded percussion section. *Turangalîla* is a compound Sanskrit word embracing a wide variety of meanings relating to life and love: the composer himself described this work as a love song and makes extensive use of the musical languages of eastern cultures.

turca, alla In the Turkish style: an indication used by both Mozart (in his piano sonata in A, K. 331) and Beethoven (in the *Ruins of Athens*) to indicate a sound reminiscent of *janissary music. [Italian]

Turina, Joaquin (1882–1949) Spanish composer, pianist, conductor, and critic, a pupil of d'Indy and Moszkowski. The majority of his works have Spanish subjects and are nationalist in style. They include the religious opera

Navidad (1916), *La Procesión del Rocío* (1912), *Sinfonía sevillana* (1920), *Canto a Sevilla* (1927), *La Oración del torero* (1925) for string quartet, and other chamber pieces, piano works, and songs.

Turn (*or* **grupetto**) A musical ornament consisting of a group of four notes, which are played instead of a single note if the turn sign is placed above the single note; if the sign follows the single note the group is played after it. In the **inverted turn**, the group is played in the reverse order.

Above: turns. Below: inverted turn

Turn of the Screw, The Opera in prologue and two acts by Britten with libretto by Myfanwy Piper based on the story by Henry James. First performance: Venice Festival, 1954. The Governess (soprano) finds that the children in her charge, Miles and Flora (treble and soprano), are visited by the ghosts of two former servants, Miss Jessel (soprano) and Peter Quint (tenor). The opera is written for a chamber group of instruments.

tutte le corde see **tre corde.**

tutti 1. All (the players): a direction used to indicate those passages (e.g. in a concerto) played by the whole orchestra. In choral music it indicates passages for the chorus. **2.** A passage in which all performers play. [Italian]

twelfth An organ *mutation stop that sounds a note a twelfth (i.e. an octave and a fifth) above the written pitch on flute *flue pipes. The length of the pipe (compared to an 8-*foot pipe) is 2.66 ft. See also **nasard.**

twelve-note composition The original and, for a generation after its inception, standard form of *serialism. In classical dodecaphonic serialism the 12 notes of the chromatic scale (each in any octave the composer wishes) recur in a predetermined order known as a *series. In addition to its original form (the **basic set**) the composer has at his disposal its inversion and retrograde inversion. Finally, each form of the series at any occurrence can begin on any degree of the chromatic scale, producing a total of 48 versions, which form the basis of the composition. In the strictest form of serialism no one note of the series may be repeated until all the other 11 notes have been heard, although any number of notes from the series may be combined to form chords as long as its order is not disrupted. The three classical figures in twelve-note composition are *Schoenberg (whose *Serenade* (completed 1923) was the first work to employ it throughout), *Berg, and *Webern. Since 1945 the traditional form of dodecaphony has been employed by Dallapiccola, Stravinsky, Lutyens, Searle, and others. See also **atonality**.

Twilight of the Gods, The (German: *Götterdämmerung*) see **Ring des Nibelungen, Der.**

two foot see **foot.**

Two Widows, The (Czech: *Dvě vdovy*) Opera in two acts by Smetana with libretto by Züngel based on the comedy *Les Deux veuves* by Mallefille. First performance: Prague, 1874; a new version with recitatives instead of spoken dialogue was first performed in 1878. The plot involves the widows Karolina and Anežka (sopranos), their gamekeeper Mumlal (bass), and a neighbouring landowner, Ladislav (tenor), who is mistaken for a poacher.

Tye, Christopher (*c.*1505–72) English composer. In 1536 he took the Cambridge B.Mus. degree and in the following year became a lay clerk at King's College. In 1543 he was appointed master of the choristers at Ely and took his D.Mus. degree two years later. Tye was introduced at court in the late 1540s and was active in King Edward's Chapel. In 1560 he was ordained; he resigned his post at Ely and was appointed to a living at nearby Doddington. Tye was a prolific composer of consort music: many of his In nomines survive. Only 22 sacred works are known, among which are the *Western Wynde* mass, votive antiphons, magnificats, and *The Actes of the Apostles* (1553), which reflects the taste for setting metrical versions of biblical texts.

Tzigane (*Gypsy*) Concert rhapsody for violin and piano by Ravel. Composed: 1924. Ravel composed this piece for the violinist Jelly d'Aranyi and in recognition of her Hungarian nationality included many melodic and rhythmic features of Gypsy music.

U

u.c. See **una corda**.

Uccelli, Gli see **Birds, The**.

Uhr, Die see **Clock Symphony**.

Uillean pipes see **Union pipes**.

Ukrainian Symphony see **Little Russian Symphony**.

Ulisse (*Ulysses*) Opera in prologue and two acts by Dallapiccola with libretto by the composer based on Homer's account of the return of Odysseus after the Trojan wars. First performance: Berlin, 1968, under the title *Odysseus*. The adventures of Ulysses are told in a series of flashbacks.

una corda (*or* **u.c.**) An instruction marked on piano music to indicate that the soft pedal should be applied at the point so marked. Compare **tre corde**. [Italian, one string – because the application of the soft pedal in some pianos shifts the action so that only one string is struck by the hammers instead of two or three]

unda maris An organ stop similar to the *voix céleste stop. [Latin, wave of the sea]

undulating stop An organ *stop controlling a rank of pipes deliberately tuned slightly sharp or flat to produce a regular beating when used in conjunction with another stop.

Unfinished Symphony Symphony No. 8 in B minor by Schubert. Composed: 1822; first performance: 1865. So called because only two movements were completed, this work was dedicated to the Graz Music Society and the two completed movements were sent by Schubert to his friend Hüttenbrenner in Graz. Several explanations have been offered as to why Schubert never proceeded any further than sketching out the beginning of the scherzo, the most likely being that he was too occupied with other compositions and eventually forgot about this symphony entirely. This was not the composer's only uncompleted symphony – the seventh symphony in E minor was also unfinished at Schubert's death, although it is never referred to by this title.

Unicorn, the Gorgon, and the Manticore, The Madrigal opera by Menotti, sometimes called *The Three Sundays of a Poet*, with text by the composer. First performance: Washington, DC, 1958. It is an exploration of new ways of combining orchestral and choral music, mime, and ballet, partly inspired by Vecchi's *L'*Amfiparnaso* and based on tales from a bestiary.

Union pipes (*or* **Uillean pipes**) Irish bellows-blown *bagpipes consisting of a chanter and three drone pipes. [*Uillean* is Gaelic for elbow]

unison 1. (*adj.*) Denoting music played or sung at the same pitch. 2. (*n.*) Singing an octave apart; for example in a choir consisting of men and women. In this sense the term is usually used in the phrase **in unison**.

unit organ (*or* **extension organ**) A compact and relatively inexpensive pipe organ in which the number of pipes required is reduced by the process of borrowing, in which, for example, a four-foot stop borrows the pipes of the eight-foot stop over the appropriate range. *Cinema organs use this principle.

unprepared dissonance see **preparation**.

upbeat see **downbeat**.

up bow The action of bowing a stringed instrument in which the player pushes the bow from the point towards the heel. Compare **down bow**.

upper partials see **partials**.

upright piano see **piano**.

ut see **solmization**.

utility music see **Gebrauchsmusik**.

Utopia Limited Operetta by Sullivan with libretto by Gilbert, subtitled *The Flowers of Progress*. First performance: Savoy Theatre, London, 1893. An ideal Utopia is set up as a British limited liability company.

V

Vactor, David van (1906–) US composer, flautist, and conductor, a pupil of Dukas. Much of Vactor's music features the flute as a solo instrument. He has also written orchestral music, such as the *Sinfonia breve* (1964) and other symphonies; concertos, including one for violin (1950); ballet music, such as the *Suite on Chilean Folk Tunes* (1963); works for chorus, such as *Walden* (1969); and pieces for brass.

Valen, Fartein (1887–1952) Norwegian composer born in Madagascar, a pupil of Bruch. He developed his own techniques of atonal counterpoint, similar in some ways to the serialism of Schoenberg, which he often applied within traditional musical forms. Valen's works include five symphonies, a violin concerto (1940), a piano concerto (1951), the orchestral pieces *Pastorale* (1930) and *Sonnetto di Michelangelo* (1932), two string quartets, choral works, piano and organ pieces, and songs.

Valkyrie, The (German: *Die Walküre*) see **Ring des Nibelungen, Der.**

valse see **waltz.**

Valse, La Orchestral work by Ravel. First performance: 1920. Around 1910 Ravel planned to compose a tone poem entitled *Wien*, in which he would reflect in music his impressions of Vienna and its characteristic waltz music. In fact, he never completed the tone poem but adapted it into this 'poème chorégraphique' (choreographic poem), which was first used as a ballet score in 1928.

Valses nobles et sentimentales Set of waltzes for piano by Ravel. Composed: 1911. The title is borrowed from two sets of waltzes by Schubert, the *Valses nobles* (Op. 77) and the *Valses sentimentales* (Op. 55), which demonstrate two different characters of this dance. In 1912 Ravel orchestrated his waltzes to serve as a ballet score for *Adélaïde, ou Le Langage des fleurs.*

Valse triste 1. Waltz for piano (Op. 9 No. 2) by Schubert. Composed: 1821. 2. Orchestral waltz by Sibelius, originally part of his incidental music for Järnefelt's play *Kuolema* (1903). A version for full orchestra was first performed in 1904; the piece has also been arranged for piano.

valve A mechanical device on a brass instrument that is depressed by the player to increase the length of the tube. With three valves, used alone or in combination, a trumpet can play a chromatic scale as each arrangement enables a different *harmonic series to be produced. This arrangement is now used on all brass instruments except the *trombone, in which the tube length is varied by a *slide. In some modern trombones valves are also used, giving the player greater flexibility and enabling him to produce more notes without using the slide.

vamp To improvise an accompaniment in jazz, dance music, or music, especially an accompaniment consisting of chords to a song.

Vanessa Opera in four acts by Samuel Barber with libretto by Menotti. First performance: Metropolitan Opera, New York, 1958. It is set in a Scandinavian country house about 1905: Vanessa (soprano), after a 20-year wait for her lover's return, is visited by his son, Anatol (tenor).

Vanhal (*or* **Wanhall**), **Johann Baptist** (1739–1813) Czech composer, violinist, and teacher, active in Vienna. After serving as organist in Opocno (1757) and choirmaster at Hnevceves (1759), he studied with Dittersdorf in Vienna (*c.*1761), settling there in 1780. His works, which were performed by Haydn and Mozart, include early classical symphonies, quartets and other chamber works, songs, keyboard music, and treatises.

Varèse, Edgard (1883–1965) French-born composer who settled in the USA (1915), a pupil of d'Indy, Roussel, and Busoni. He described his music as 'organized sound' and his works show little evidence of conventional notions of melody and harmony. Instead they are constructed by the juxtaposition, repetition, and variation of ideas based on timbre, intervallic and rhythmic shape, volume, etc. Varèse explored new orchestral timbres and looked forward to extending the range of compositional techniques by the use of new technology: he made early use of taped sound in *Déserts* (1949–54) and *Poème électronique* (1958; see **Electronic Poem**). His other works include *Offrandes* (1921), *Amériques* (1921), *Octandre* (1923), *Intégrales* (1925), *Arcana* (1927), *Ionisation* (1933), and *Equatorial* (1934).

variations One of the most established *forms of composition, consisting of a number of modified restatements of a *theme. The theme may retain some features of its original version, while others are discarded, developed, or replaced. The variations may be built on the unaltered harmonies of the original theme (as in the passacaglia), on its melody or rhythm, or on a combination of these. Some of the earliest examples of variations are for keyboard or lute (vihuela) and date from early-16th-century England and Spain. The composers include Hugh Aston and Cabezon. Idiomatic keyboard variations were an important part of late-16th- and early-17th-century music, especially in the works of the English virginalists and their Dutch contemporary Sweelinck. In Italy the variations of Frescobaldi and his Austrian pupil Froberger frequently suggest the differing characteristics of the dances of the *suite. J. S. Bach's contributions to the form are considerable and include the *Goldberg Variations* (1742) and several sets of chorale variations for organ, notably the canonic variations on 'Vom Himmel Hoch.' Later in the 18th century sonata forms partially eclipsed variation forms but several outstanding examples can be found in works of the period, especially in the slow movement of Haydn's *Emperor Quartet* and the finale of Mozart's C minor piano concerto. Other examples of variations from the classical period feature fashionable opera arias or popular tunes. Beethoven's *Diabelli Variations* are a highly personal reflection of this tradition. The finale of his *Eroica Symphony* is a further example.

The 19th century saw the development of large-scale concert works in theme and variation form as in Brahms' *Variations on a Theme of Haydn* (1873) and Dvořák's *Symphonic Variations* (1877). Elgar's *Enigma Variations* of 1899 present a series of musical portraits of personalities. Variation form was used by Richard Strauss in his tone poem *Don Quixote*, which is subtitled *Variations on a Theme of Knightly Character*. Variations of the 20th century include those by members of the Second Viennese School, notably Webern (in his symphony and variations for orchestra). Britten, Dallapiccola, and Henze have also used the form.

Variations and Fugue on a Theme of Purcell see **Young Person's Guide to the Orchestra, The.**

Variations on a Theme of Haydn see **St Anthony Variations.**

Varviso, Silvio (1924–) Swiss conductor. Eminent in opera, he has conducted at Covent Garden, Glyndebourne, and the Metropolitan Opera, New York.

Vásáry, Tamás (1933–) Hungarian-born Swiss pianist. He studied at the Budapest academy and launched his career by winning the Liszt Competition in 1948. He played in London and New York and became musical director of the Northern Sinfonia Orchestra.

vaudeville Originally, a satirical French song that is thought to have flourished in the vau de Vire (valley of Vire) in Normandy. It later became a song sung at the end of a spoken drama, each character singing a verse and each verse alternating with a refrain. Mozart used this device at the end of *The Seraglio*. In the 19th century, stage performances with songs and dances became known as vaudeville in France and the word was adopted in the USA for the form of entertainment known as music hall in the UK.

Vaughan Williams, Ralph (1872–1958) British composer, a pupil of Parry and Stanford (at the Royal College of Music, London), Bruch (in Berlin), and Ravel (in Paris). Aiming to free English music from the weight of the prevalent German academic tradition, Vaughan Williams collected English folk tunes and edited English church music. From these sources and using the contrapuntal devices of Elizabethan madrigals, he developed his own modal style.

Vaughan Williams wrote nine symphonies, including the choral *Sea Symphony* (1903–09), A *London Symphony*

Ralph Vaughan Williams

(1913), *A *Pastoral Symphony* (1922), and **Sinfonia Antartica* (1952), based on his score for the film *Scott of the Antarctic*. His other works include the *Fantasia on a Theme by Tallis* (1910); *Flos Campi (1925) and *The *Lark Ascending* (1914), both for solo instruments and orchestra; the operas *Hugh the Drover (1924), *Sir John in Love (1929), *The *Poisoned Kiss* (1936), **Riders to the Sea* (1937), and *The *Pilgrim's Progress* (1951); the ballets *Old King Cole* (1923) and *Job (1931); choral works, such as the mass in G minor (1922), *Sancta civitas (1926), the *Magnificat* (1932), *Dona nobis pacem (1936), and *Hodie (1954); **Five Tudor Portraits* (1936) and **Serenade to Music* (1938), both for solo voices, chorus, and orchestra; an orchestral fantasy on *Greensleeves*; chamber music; and many songs, including *Linden Lea* and other folk-song arrangements and the cycle *On Wenlock Edge (1909).

Vautor, Thomas (early 17th century) English madrigalist. In the service of the Duke of Buckingham, he took the Oxford B.Mus. degree in 1616. Only one of his madrigal collections survives (1619–20); it is dedicated to his patron.

Vecchi, Orazio (1550–1605) Italian composer. Educated in Modena, he had taken holy orders by 1577 and travelled to Brescia and Bergamo. From 1581 he was active as maestro di cappella in some minor north Italian centres, returning to Modena as maestro in 1593; five years later he became court composer to the d'Este family. He is remembered for his *Canzonette* and the madrigal-comedy *L'*Amfiparnaso* (1594).

Vegh, Sándor (1905–) Hungarian violinist. A pupil of Hubay and Kodály, he played with the Hungarian Quartet and in 1940 founded the Vegh Quartet. Vegh has been active as a teacher, holding posts in Basle and Salzburg, and also appears frequently as a soloist.

veloce Rapid; swift: a direction used to indicate uninterrupted smoothness of performance rather than increase in speed. [Italian]

vent Wind. Hence **instruments à vent**, wind instruments. [French]

Ventadorn, Bernart de (*c*.1130–*c*.1190) One of the most important troubadours of the classic period. The son of one of the Count of Ventadorn's servants, Bernart was in the service of Eleanor of Aquitaine (later wife of Henry II of England) between 1152 and 1154. His work was held in high contemporary regard and some 45 poems survive, including the well-known *Can vei la lauzeta mover*.

Venus and Adonis Masque by John Blow to words by an unknown author. First performance: 1685. Although described as a masque, the form and style of this work make it an opera in all but name and the score includes several instrumental and ballet numbers. The plot concerns the love of Venus for Adonis, the interference of Cupid, and the eventual death of Adonis.

Vêpres siciliennes, Les (*The Sicilian Vespers*) Opera in five acts by Verdi with French libretto by Scribe and Duveyrier, commissioned for the Paris Exhibition. First performance: Opéra, Paris, 1855. Set in Palermo in 1282, it is concerned with the occupation of Sicily by French troops. The convention of including a ballet in French grand opera makes Act III exceptionally lengthy if the opera is staged uncut.

Veracini, Francesco Maria (1690–1768) Italian composer and violinist. After serving at the Dresden court (1717–22), he performed as soloist in Venice, Dusseldorf, Florence, and London, where he played a concerto between the acts of Handel's *Acis and Galatea* (1741). Veracini wrote many sonatas for violin, operas, oratorios and other sacred works, and a treatise.

verbunkos A Hungarian soldiers' dance used from about 1780 to 1849 to entice recruits into the army. It has a slow introductory section (the **lassú**) followed by a fast section known as a **friss**. Examples of later music in which these dances were used include Liszt's second *Hungarian Rhapsody*, Bartók's *Rhapsodies for Violin and Orchestra*, and the intermezzo from Kodály's *Háry János*.

Verdelot, Philippe (*c*.1475–before 1552) French composer. He was a singer to Pope Clement VII in Rome (1523–24) then maestro di cappella at the cathedral and baptistry in Florence. His masses and motets were influential and used as the basis for parody masses. *Si bona suscepimus* was parodied by Lassus and Morales and included in several anthologies and intabulations. Some of his madrigals were treated in the same manner by later composers.

Verdi, Giuseppe (1813–1901) Italian composer. Born in the village of Le Roncole to an innkeeper and grocer, Verdi received only a rudimentary education but showed an early musical talent. A wealthy merchant, Antonio Barezzi, became his patron, paying for his musical education in Milan, and later his father-in-law, when Verdi married his daughter Margherita in 1839. After two years as musical director of Busseto, near his native village, he returned to Milan in 1836 when he was given an opportunity to write his first opera, *Oberto. This was produced in 1839 at La Scala; it was sufficiently successful to earn him a commission to write a further three operas. The first of these, *Un *Giorno di regno* (1840), was a failure. Verdi, now widowed and having also lost his two children, declared that he could write no more operas. However, he was persuaded to write his third opera, *Nabucco, for production at La Scala in 1842. This established his reputation and provided him with his second wife, Giuseppina Strepponi, a singer in the cast.

In all, Verdi wrote 27 operas, including *I *Lombardi* (1843), *I *Due Foscari* (1844), *Macbeth* (1847), *Il *Corsaro* (1848), *Luisa Miller* (1849), *Stiffelio* (1850), *Rigoletto* (1851), *Il *Trovatore and *La *Traviata* (1853), *Les *Vêpres siciliennes* (1855), *Simon Boccanegra* (1857), *Un *Ballo in maschera* (1859), *La *Forza del destino* (1862), and *Don Carlos* (1867). In 1871 he produced his opera *Aida* on an Egyptian theme to celebrate the opening of the Suez Canal (1869). His last two operas returned to Shakespeare's plays for their inspiration, *Otello* (1887) and *Falstaff* (1893). Apart from operas, in his later years Verdi wrote several pieces of church choral music, including his *Requiem Mass* (1874), *Ave Maria* (1889), *Te Deum* (1896), and *Stabat Mater* (1897). In 1897 Giuseppina died and the composer's own health declined thereafter: he died of a stroke.

Verdi transformed Italian opera, just as Wagner had done in Germany, integrating the dramatic and musical elements into a single work of art. From humble origins, he became the leading Italian composer of the 19th century.

Veress, Sándor (1907–) Hungarian pianist and composer resident in Switzerland, a pupil of Bartók and Kodály. He assisted Bartók in the collection and editing of Hungarian folk music. His own music shows some use of modal harmonies and, in later works, of serial techniques. Veress's output includes concertos for violin (1939) and piano (1952), *Hommage à Paul Klee* (1952), *Passacaglia concertante* (1961), symphonies, *Songs of the Seasons* (1967) and other choral music, folk-song arrangements, chamber music, and songs.

verismo Denoting an *opera with a libretto based on realistic contemporary events and characters rather than a formal, mythological, or frankly absurd plot. Operas of this type include those by the Italian composers Puccini, Mascagni, and Leoncavallo. [Italian, realism]

Verklärte Nacht (*Transfigured Night*) String sextet (Op. 4) by Schoenberg. Composed: 1899. This is one of the first and most important of Schoenberg's expressionist works and the inspiration for it came from Dehmel's poem 'Weib und Welt' ('Woman and World'). The title refers to the view expressed in the poem that true love between two people can transform even a cold and bleak night into an experience of great beauty. Schoenberg later arranged this work for string orchestra, in which version it is often heard.

Verschiebung Displacing: a direction in piano playing indicating use of the soft pedal, which displaces the action in order to play only one of the three strings for each note. [German]

verse In church music, a passage sung by a solo voice in contrast to those sung by all the voices. The verse *anthem features such passages.

Giuseppe Verdi

verset Originally, a verse of a psalm in which the choir and congregation were silent and the organ played a piece based on plainsong of the psalm. This arrangement was used in Roman Catholic churches, partly to rest the choir and partly to avoid the monotony of the plainsong. Later a verset became a short organ piece, sometimes fugal, played during a church service.

Vesalii icones (*Images from Vesalius*) Dramatic work for male dancer, solo cello, and chamber ensemble by Peter Maxwell Davies. Composed: 1969. The title refers to a treatise on anatomy by Vesalius, which includes several drawings of the human body. To a musical background the naked male dancer demonstrates some of the illustrations, combining them with a portrayal of the various Stations of the Cross; thus the work has both a humanist and religious aspect.

Vestale, La (*The Vestal*) Opera in three acts by Spontini with libretto by de Jouy. First performance: Opéra, Paris, 1807. Set in ancient Rome, it is about the heroine's conflicting passions of sensual love and religious avowal.

via Away! Hence **via sordini**, remove the mutes. [Italian]

Viadana, Lodovico (*c*.1560–1627) Italian composer. He entered the Franciscan order in Viadana before 1588 and was maestro di cappella at Mantua, Cremona, Concordia, and Fano. Viadana made an important contribution to sacred music: his *Concerti ecclesiastici* (1602) is the earliest sacred vocal collection to include a basso continuo. His music became increasingly monodic with ornamental passages and his *Salmi a 4 cori* (1612) effectively exploits the concertato style.

vibraphone (*or* **vibraharp**) A form of *xylophone invented in the 1920s in which light-metal alloy bars are struck with soft-headed beaters. Below each bar is a hollow metal tube-resonator the upper openings of which are alternately closed and opened by electrically operated fans. This gives the sound a vibrato effect, which continues after the note has been struck. It is used by some composers (e.g. Berg) for the orchestra and in some dance music and jazz (in which case it is familiarly known as the 'vibes').

vibrato A rapid and regular variation in the pitch of a note produced by the voice or by an instrument. In a bowed stringed instrument it is produced by shaking the finger stopping a string, on wind instruments it is produced by breath control, and on a *clavichord it is produced by shaking the finger on a depressed key (see also **Bebung**). On an *organ a vibrato effect is produced by a *tremulant. In vocal music, a vibrato effect can either be acclaimed as a mark of good taste and control or, especially if it is involuntary, criticized for its vulgarity. Compare **tremolo**. [Italian, vibrated]

vibrazione see **coup de glotte**.

Vicentino, Nicola (1511–*c*.1576) Italian composer and theorist. He claimed to have studied under Adrian Willaert in Venice and was active in Ferrara, probably in the service of Cardinal Ippolito II d'Este. By 1563 he had left to become maestro at Vicenza, but remained there only a year. His subsequent movements are unclear but he may have worked in Milan, where he died of the plague. Vicentino's surviving collections are of madrigals but he is best known for the treatise *L'Antica musica ridotta alla moderna prattica* (1555). In this he expounds his modal theory and includes a description of the arcicembalo, an instrument on which microtones could be played. His theories encouraged composers away from the church modes and towards the adoption of equal temperament.

Vickers, Jon (1926–   ) Canadian tenor. He studied with George Lambert at Toronto. In 1957 he sang Aeneas in Berlioz's *The Trojans* at Covent Garden and in 1958 appeared opposite Callas in Cherubini's *Médée*. Vickers is considered one of the best heroic tenors of his day.

Victoria (*or* **Vittoria**), **Tomás Luis de** (*c*.1548–1611) Spanish composer. In 1565 he studied at the German College in Rome; he was possibly a pupil of Palestrina at the nearby Roman seminary. Later he became maestro di cappella at the German College (1573–78). In 1575 he

became a priest. From 1587 until 1603 he was in the service of Empress Maria, widow of Maximilian II, at Madrid. All Victoria's works are sacred: he is the author of about 20 masses, 52 motets, and numerous liturgical works published in 11 collections between 1572 and 1605. Victoria's music combines Palestrina's sophisticated technique with a feeling of intense piety and a direct emotional impact. These qualities may be seen in the joyful *O quam gloriosum* as well as in the sombre *O vos omnes*, with its bold dissonances. The same devout attitude is found in his masses, nearly all of which are based on sacred rather than secular models.

Victory, Gerard (Alan Loraine; 1921–   ) Irish conductor and composer. His style is eclectic, drawing on traditional tonal procedures as well as serial and postserial techniques. Victory has written the operas *Chatterton* (1970) and *Eloise and Abelard* (1972); orchestral works, such as *Homage to Petrarch* (1969), *Jonathan Swift* (1971), and *Spirit of Molière* (1972); vocal works, such as *Kriegslieder* (1966); and chamber music.

Vida breve, La (*Brief Life*) Opera in two acts by Falla with libretto by Carlos Fernandez Shaw. First performance: Nice, 1913 (in a French version by Milliet). Salud (soprano), a Gypsy, loves Paco (tenor), who is betrothed to Carmela (mezzo-soprano); at their wedding Salud appears and dies broken-hearted at Paco's feet.

vielle 1. A medieval *fiddle. **2.** A *hurdy-gurdy. [French]

Vienna Blood see **Wiener Blut**.

Vienna Boys' Choir (German: *Wiener Sängerknaben*) An Austrian choir founded in 1498. It was originally part of the chapel of the Austrian imperial court but is now internationally known for its secular performances. It has a wide repertory, sometimes includes adult male voices, and performs with the Vienna State Opera.

Vienna Philharmonic Orchestra Austrian symphony orchestra founded in 1842. Among its conductors have been Otto Nicolai (who conducted its first concert), Hans Richter, Gustav Mahler, Joseph Weingartner, Wilhelm Furtwängler, Bruno Walter, Herbert von Karajan, and Claudio Abbado (from 1971). In the 19th century the orchestra gave many first performances of works by Brahms and Bruckner (among others). Throughout its history it has been one of the finest ensembles in the world and it is renowned for its beauty and range of tone. The orchestra plays for the Vienna State Opera.

Vier ernste Gesänge see **Four Serious Songs**.

Vierne, Louis (1870–1937) French organist and composer, a pupil of Franck and Widor. Blind from birth, he was for many years organist of Notre Dame in Paris and organ professor at the Schola Cantorum. Vierne is best known for

Heitor Villa-Lobos

his five symphonies for organ. Among his other works are a string quartet and other chamber pieces, the *Messe Solenelle* (1900), and various orchestral works. He died at the keyboard of his organ.

Viertel Crotchet. [German, quarter, i.e. quarter note]

Vieuxtemps, Henry (1820–81) Belgian violinist and composer. He studied in Paris with Bériot (1829–31), toured Germany, then studied counterpoint with Sechter in Vienna (1833–34) and composition with Reicha in Paris (1835–36). He played throughout Europe, including St Petersburg and London, and toured the USA. In St Petersburg from 1846 to 1851, Vieuxtemps was solo violinist to the tsar and taught at the conservatory. In 1871 he became a violin professor at the Brussels conservatory. Vieuxtemps was one of the great violin virtuosos of the 19th century. He composed chamber and orchestral music as well as many violin pieces, the best of which are the six violin concertos, in which he made formal innovations. He also wrote cadenzas for Beethoven's violin concerto. One of his brothers, **Lucien Vieuxtemps** (1828–1901), was a pianist and teacher; the other, **Ernest Vieuxtemps** (1832–96), was a cellist.

vif Lively. Hence **vivement**, in a lively way. [French]

vihuela A Spanish plucked stringed instrument much used during the Renaissance. Its body was shaped like a guitar, of which it was the predecessor, but its strings were arranged like those of a *lute.

Village Romeo and Juliet, A (German: *Romeo und Julia auf dem Dorf*) Opera in prologue and three acts by Delius with libretto by the composer based on Gottfried Keller's story *Leute von Seldwyla* (*Seldwyla People*). First performance (in German): Komische Oper, Berlin, 1907. The two lovers, Sali and Vreli (tenor and soprano), are the children of feuding landowners and eventually commit suicide together. The orchestral interlude *The Walk to the Paradise Garden*, containing themes from the opera, was composed and inserted five years later.

Villa-Lobos, Heitor (1887–1959) Brazilian pianist and composer, largely self-taught. After his first visit to Paris he turned to the folk and popular music of Brazil for inspiration. An early work is the *Chôros* series, improvisatory pieces for unorthodox instrumental combinations. In the 1930s, with the *Bachianas Brasileiras*, he attempted to combine Brazilian music with classical traditions. In his later years he turned increasingly to the use of traditional musical forms. Villa-Lobos' enormous output includes 12 symphonies; 5 piano concertos; the operas *Izaht* (1914), *Madalena* (1947), and *Yerma* (1955); the ballets *Uirapúrú* (1917), *Amazonas* (1917), *Mandu-Çarara* (1940), and *Genesis* (1954); 17 string quartets and other chamber music; choral works; piano pieces; and works for guitar.

villancico 1. A 16th-century Spanish song consisting of several verses with refrains between them. **2.** A 17th-century cantata for voices, strings, and organ, often sung at Christmas.

villanella An Italian 16th-century rustic part song. Often featuring consecutive fifths, the music is repeated for each verse. [Italian, country girl]

villanelle A French vocal setting of a poem consisting of three-line stanzas. It is similar, but not identical, to an Italian *villanella. [French, country girl]

Villi, Le (*The Wilis*) Opera by Puccini with libretto by Fontana. Originally in one act, it was first performed at the Teatro dal Verme, Milan, in May 1884; a two-act version was first performed at the Teatro Regio, Turin, in December 1884. Based on a folk story, it has a close parallel in Adam's *ballet *Giselle*. Robert (tenor) returns home from seeking his fortune to find his sweetheart Anna (soprano) dead; her ghost and a pack of wilis dance round him until he falls dead.

vínā Any one of a wide range of Indian stringed instruments, especially a kind of lute or stick zither. The south Indian vínā, which differs from that found in the north, is one of the most popular instruments used there; it is fretted and held horizontally over the knee by the player. See also **Indian music.**

Vinci, Leonardo (*c.*1690–1730) Italian composer, a pupil of Gaetano Greco. Remaining in Naples, he was appointed maestro di cappella for the Prince of Sansevero (1719), acting maestro di cappella of the royal chapel (1725), and maestro at the Conservatorio dei Poveri (1728). His works include many comic and serious operas, oratorios and sacred works, a serenata, songs, and chamber music.

viola A bowed four-stringed instrument that is the alto member of the *violin family. Its strings are tuned at intervals of a fifth, the lowest being C below middle C (i.e. C, G, D, A). It has a range of over three octaves. The viola has a lower pitch than the violin and is some 7.5 cm (3 in) longer; it is more unwieldy to play than the violin but has a mellower tone. Violas came into prominence with the string quartets of Haydn and Mozart and have since featured as orchestral instruments and in much chamber music. The repertoire of the viola includes music by Haydn, Mozart, Berlioz, Glinka, Richard Strauss, and Hindemith.

viola bastarda see viol family.

viola da braccio see viol family.

viola da gamba see viol family.

viola d'amore An unfretted viol played like a violin. It had seven bowed strings and seven *sympathetic strings below them. Its name probably comes from the Cupid-like decorative carving replacing the scroll at the end of the pegbox. It was popular in the 18th century. The **violetta** was an alto viola d'amore with two sets of sympathetic strings. Both instruments were replaced by the violin. [Italian, viol of love]

violetta see viola d'amore.

viol family A family of bowed fretted stringed instruments that evolved before the *violin family and was eventually replaced by it in the 17th century. It owed to the *lute the tuning of its six strings and its use of gut frets. The lowest string of the **treble viol** was tuned to D below middle C, the other strings being tuned a fourth or a third (i.e. D, G, C, E, A, D); the **tenor viol** was tuned a fourth below the treble instrument (i.e. A, D, G, B, E, A); the **bass viol** was tuned an octave below the treble viol. The treble viol was played vertically, resting on the player's knee; the tenor and bass viols were held between the knees. The bass viol was also known as the **viola da gamba** (leg viola), but this name was also applied to all three instruments to distinguish them from the **viola da braccio** (arm viola), i.e. a violin or viola. The **double-bass viol** (or **violone**) was a later addition to the family; it was tuned an octave below the bass viol. The **lyra viol** (or **viola bastarda**) was an intermediate instrument between the tenor and bass viols and was tuned as the *lira da braccio. In the 16th century a considerable repertoire of music was written for ensembles of viols (see **chest of viols**) as well as for the lyra viol as a solo instrument. The emphasis, during the 17th century, on music with a full lyrical sound in the treble led to a preference for the tone of the violin and the treble and tenor viols fell from favour.

The bass viol, however, continued to provide the continuo for baroque music and the **division viol** (a smaller version of the bass viol) had a fashionable period in the 16th and 17th centuries as a solo instrument. Viols have been revived in the 20th century for playing music of their period. See also **viola d'amore**.

violin A bowed four-stringed instrument that is the smallest and highest member of the *violin family. The strings are tuned at intervals of a fifth, the lowest being tuned to G below middle C (i.e. G, D, A, E). It has a range of four octaves. The first violins were made in Italy in the middle of the 16th century, having evolved from the *fiddle and the *lira da braccio. The art of making violins of the highest calibre was for 200 years the preserve of three families from Cremona – the Amati, Guarneri, and Stradivari families. While the violin itself has remained virtually unchanged for 400 years (except for the introduction of thinner strings and a higher bridge in the 19th century), the present form of the *bow did not emerge until the 19th century. Originally convex in relation to the violin, it is now concave.

The violin has a long history in playing folk music that dates back to its origins in the fiddle. During the 17th century it came to replace the treble viol in chamber music and also became the backbone of the orchestra. In the modern orchestra the violins are divided into two sections, the first and the second violins, distinguished to some extent by the former playing the higher parts and the latter the lower parts. The repertoire of music written for the violin is enormous and includes concertos by Bach, Vivaldi, Beethoven, Brahms, Tchaikovsky, Mendelssohn, Bruch, and Berg. It also features in almost all chamber ensembles.

violin family A family of four-stringed unfretted bowed instruments that includes the *violin itself, the *viola, the *cello, and the *double bass. There is some confusion over the evolution of this family, especially concerning the extent that there has been cross-fertilization with the viola da gamba (see **viol family**). The earliest instruments of this type were the *fiddles and *rebecs used by medieval troubadours to accompany song and dance. The *lira da braccio evolved from these instruments at the end of the 15th century, the violin itself emerging in the middle of the 16th century. Members of this family characteristically have round shoulders, four strings, f-shaped sound holes, and no frets (compared to their cousins, the viols, which have sloping shoulders, six or seven strings, C- or flame-shaped sound holes, and fretted fingerboards).

Violins of St Jacques, The Opera in three acts by Malcolm Williamson with libretto by William Chappell based on the novel by Patrick Leigh Fermor. First performance: Sadler's Wells, London, 1966. Set on a Caribbean island that is devastated by volcanic eruption in Act III (depicted in an orchestral interlude), it is a story of a decadent society and its downfall.

violoncello see **cello.**

violone see **viol family.**

viols see **string-toned stops.**

Viotti, Giovanni Battista (1755–1824) Italian violinist and composer. In 1770 he began studying with Pugnani and from 1775 to 1780 played in the royal chapel orchestra in Turin. In 1780 he and Pugnani embarked on a concert tour of Switzerland, Germany, Poland, and Russia. Viotti made his Paris debut in 1782, immediately becoming recognized as one of the leading virtuosos of the day; he entered Marie Antoinette's service and was patronized in aristocratic circles. In 1788 he established his own opera house, the Théâtre de Monsieur (later the Théâtre Feydeau), which presented many new works. In 1792 the Revolution forced him to leave Paris; in London he played in Salomon's concerts, became musical director of the Opera Concerts (1795), managed the Italian Opera (1794–95), and directed the King's Theatre orchestra (1797). In 1801 he started a wine business, which ruined him financially. In Paris again he became director of the Opéra (1819–21) and of the Italian Theatre (1821–22). He died in London.

Viotti was the most influential violinist of the generation before Paganini and the last representative of the classical tradition of Corelli. He composed some conventional chamber music (string quartets, string trios, etc.), arias, and piano music but his best works were for the violin: he wrote solos and duos and 29 important and imaginative violin concertos, containing features of early romantic music (the best known is No. 22 in A minor, c.1792–97).

virelai (or **virelay**) A medieval French song consisting of several verses with a refrain before and after each verse. [French]

Virgil (Publius Vergilius Maro; 70–19 BC) Roman poet. Tate's libretto for Purcell's opera *Dido and Aeneas* (1689) and Berlioz's *The Trojans* (1856–59) are based on Virgil's *Aeneid*.

virginal see **harpsichord instruments.**

virtuoso A player whose mastery of the technique of playing his instrument is so complete that he can play music of any complexity at any speed. While some players regard their virtuosity as no more than a means of enhancing their interpretive skills, others have been accused of treating it as an end in itself. However, virtuosity is not an attribute with which musicians are born; it cannot be attained without a prodigious native talent but even with this talent it requires an obsessive devotion to practice.

Vitali, Giovanni Battista (?1632–92) Italian composer and violinist. A string player at S Petronio, Bologna, he became maestro di cappella of Santissimo Rosario (1673) and master of the ducal chapel in Modena (1674). He composed sonatas for strings and other instruments, dances, psalm settings, and oratorios. His eldest son, **Tommaso Antonio Vitali** (1663–1745), was also a composer and violinist. He studied with his father and with Pacchioni in Modena, where he was court violinist from 1674. He wrote many sonatas, concertos, and chamber works in the style of his father, but did not compose the *Chaconne* attributed to him by Ferdinand David.

Vitry, Philippe de (1291–1361) French composer, poet, and musical theorist, in the service of the French kings (1322–51). A canon from 1323, Vitry was appointed Bishop of Meaux in 1351 by Clement VI, to whom his motet *Petre Clemens/Lugentium* is dedicated; he also corresponded with Petrarch. Vitry wrote a treatise, *Ars nova* (1322–23), the main innovation of which is the extension of Petronian principles to achieve a more comprehensive rhythmic notation. He also composed a number of motets, many of which date from before 1317.

vivace Lively; vivacious. [Italian]

Vivaldi, Antonio (1678–1741) Italian composer and violinist. In 1703 he was ordained – he was known as 'il

Antonio Vivaldi

prete rosso' ('the red priest') because of his red hair – and appointed violin master at the Ospedale della Pietà, Venice. He became maestro di cappella there in 1735 and wrote many of his works for the Ospedale's orchestra and choir, but at the same time travelled extensively throughout his career. In 1740 he moved to Vienna: his music had declined in popularity and he died in relative poverty.

A prolific composer, Vivaldi is best known for his development of the three-movement concerto, which was widely imitated by composers of his generation, including J. S. Bach, who transcribed some of his works. Interest in Vivaldi's music was revived in the mid-19th century and he is now recognized as one of the most influential composers of the baroque period. He wrote about 450 concertos, over 200 of which were for violin (including the set *L'Estro armonico*, 1711; and The *Four Seasons*, 1725). His other works include over 70 sonatas, nearly 50 operas, and oratorios (such as *Judith*, 1716), motets, cantatas, and other sacred music.

vivo Lively; fast. [Italian]

Vladigerov, Pancho (1899–1978) Bulgarian composer and pianist, who studied in Berlin. His style was predominantly conservative although some of his later works incorporated elements from folk music. His works include the opera *Tsar Kaloyan* (1936), the ballet *The Legend of the Lake* (1946), two symphonies, two violin concertos, five piano concertos, chamber works, and piano pieces.

Vltava see **Má Vlast**.

vocalise A wordless vocal exercise in which a vowel sound is sung. Concert pieces, usually for voice and piano, have also been written on this basis. Italian: **vocalizzo**. [French]

vocal score see **score**.

voce Voice. Hence **colla voce**, with the voice: a direction used to indicate that the accompaniment should allow the vocal part some freedom and follow accordingly. [Italian]

Vogel, Vladimir (1896–1984) Russian-born composer, resident in Switzerland after 1939. A pupil of Busoni, he explored serial procedures and his music possesses an important mystical-religious dimension, especially in the large works for speaking chorus and speech song. Vogel's works include the oratorios *Till Eulenspiegel* (1938–45), *Die Flucht* (1963–64), and other choral works; concertos for violin (1937) and cello (1954); *Gli Spaziali* (1969–71), *Abschied* (1973), and other orchestral works; and chamber music.

Vogelweide, Walther von der (*c*.1170–*c*.1230) Minnesinger from the Austro-Bavarian area, working for some time in the Viennese court. His work, held in high contemporary esteem, includes *Unter den Linden* and the Palestine song, *Nu alerst leb' ich* (1228).

Vogler, Georg Joseph (1749–1814) German priest, composer, organist, theorist, and teacher. Known as Abbé Vogler, he was court chaplain to the Mannheim court from 1772 and appointed kapellmeister there in 1784. He was kapellmeister to the Swedish court (1786–99) and toured extensively, giving organ recitals. His many pupils included Meyerbeer and Weber. In addition to his famous theoretical works and his innovations in organ building, Vogler composed operas, ballets, sacred works, and chamber and keyboard music.

voice The sounds of the human voice, produced when air from the lungs passes through the larynx and causes the vocal cords to vibrate: the area of the mouth and nose acts as a resonating chamber. Men's voices fall into three main categories – *bass, *baritone, and *tenor; the female voices are *contralto, *mezzo-soprano, and *soprano. The average human voice has a range of approximately two octaves, the pitch of the male voice being an octave lower than the corresponding female voice. Boys' voices (see **treble**) correspond in range to the soprano and the range of a man's falsetto voice (see **alto**) lies between that of a female voice and his natural voice. The six varieties of voices, however, are reduced to four to conform to the customary habit of disposing vocal music into four parts – soprano, contralto (or alto), tenor, and bass – and the middle voice in each group must join the lower or higher voice.

voice leading US name for part writing (see **part**). [direct translation of the German *Stimmführung*]

voix céleste An 8-*foot organ stop in which each note is produced by two pipes, one tuned slightly higher than the other, so that the sound has an ethereal wavering quality. [French, heavenly voice]

volante Fast and light. [Italian, flying]

Volkmann, (Friedrich) Robert (1815–83) German composer, a pupil of Becker at Leipzig. In 1841 he moved to Budapest, where, apart from a period in Vienna (1854–58), he spent the rest of his life. In 1875 he was appointed to teach at the Hungarian National Music Academy. Volkmann composed sacred and secular choral works and songs but is better known for his instrumental music, which includes two symphonies, four overtures, a cello concerto, and six string quartets.

Volkonsky, Andrei (1933–) Soviet composer and pianist, a pupil of Nadia Boulanger in Paris. His style has been influenced by central Asian folk music and early music and he has utilized serial techniques and electronic music. Volkonsky's works, which are disowned as avant-garde by the Soviet establishment, include the cantata *Dead Souls* (1952), *Serenade for an Insect* (1958), *The Laments of Shchaza* (1962), the *Wanderer Concerto* (1968), *Replica* (1970), chamber music, piano pieces, and film scores.

Volkslied A German popular song or folk song. [German, folk song]

volles Werk Full *organ. [German]

volta 1. Time. Hence **prima volta**, first time: a direction indicating the ending of a passage to be repeated when it is different from the ending of the repeated passage, which is marked **seconda volta** (second time). **2.** See **lavolta**. **3.** See **ballata**.

volti Turn, i.e. turn the page. Hence **volti subito**, turn the page quickly. Abbreviation: **V.S.** [Italian]

voluntary 1. (from the 16th century) An instrumental composition in which the composer is not limited to adding parts to a basic plainsong, as was common until that time. **2.** (until the 19th century) An improvisation on any instrument, especially as a prelude to a written piece. **3.** A piece played on an organ, either improvised or written, before or after a church service and sometimes during the course of the service. See also **trumpet voluntary.**

Von Heute auf Morgen (*From One Day to the Next*) Opera in one act by Schoenberg with libretto by the composer's second wife, Gertrud Kolisch, under the pseudonym 'Max Blonda.' First performance: Frankfurt, 1930. It is a comic opera based on an episode from the life of the composer Franz Schreker.

Voříšek, Jan Václav (1791–1825) Czech composer. He was a precocious child who toured Bohemia giving concerts on the organ and piano. After having composition lessons in Prague with Tomášek he moved to Vienna, where he met leading musicians of the day (including Beethoven). He was conductor of the Gesellschaft der Musikfreunde (1818–25) and assistant court organist (1822–25). Voříšek's compositions, much influenced by Beethoven, include a symphony and other orchestral works, many pieces for piano solo (including impromptus), chamber music, masses and other sacred choral works, and vocal music.

Vorspiel Prelude or overture. [German, literally pre-play]

vox humana An organ *stop controlling an 8-*foot reed pipe of wide bore that is intended to sound like the human voice. [Latin, human voice]

Voyevoda Opera in four acts by Tchaikovsky (his first) with libretto by Ostrovsky based on one of his plays. First performance: Moscow, 1869. It ran for only five nights, after which the composer destroyed most of the music. In 1935 a copy of the score was reported to have been found in a Moscow library.

Vranický, Pavel see **Wranitzky, Paul.**

V.S. see **volti.**

vuoto (*or fem.* **vuota**) Empty. Hence **corda vuota**, open string: a direction to play a note (or notes) on an open string. [Italian]

W

Waart, Edo de (1941–   ) Dutch conductor. Originally an oboist, he has conducted the Netherlands Wind Ensemble and the Rotterdam Philharmonic Orchestra (1973–   ).

Wagenseil, Georg Christoph (1715–77) Austrian composer and keyboard player. He was a pupil of Fux in Vienna (1735–38), where he later became court composer and organist. He also taught Dussek, Schenk, and others. Wagenseil wrote *Ariodante* (1745) and other operas, symphonies, sacred music, and keyboard music.

Wagner (Wilhelm) Richard (1813–83) German composer and conductor. The son of a police clerk, Wagner was born in Leipzig but the family moved to Dresden in 1815 after Wagner's father died and his mother remarried. Interested in opera from an early age, Wagner studied at St Thomas's School and for a short time at the University of Leipzig. In 1833 he was appointed conductor at the Würzberg opera house, subsequently holding similar posts in Magdeburg, Königsberg, and Riga. After marrying the actress Minna Planer in 1836, he went with her to Paris in 1839. The Wagners remained there in some poverty for three years, Wagner unsuccessfully attempting to obtain performances of his operas *Rienzi and The *Flying Dutchman.* The former was finally accepted by the Dresden opera house and performed there in 1842; the latter also appeared there a year later. The success of *Rienzi* led to Wagner's appointment as conductor at the Dresden opera house and his opera *Tannhaüser* received its first performance there in 1845. In 1848, however, Wagner was forced to leave Germany on account of his participation in the Dresden uprising in the wake of the French Revolution. Settling in Zürich, he then began work on his epic cycle of operas based on German mythology, *Der *Ring des Nibelungen.* This mammoth task (which was not completed for some 25 years) was interrupted by the composer's affair with Mathilde Wesendank (the wife of a friend and benefactor), who inspired his great love tragedy *Tristan und Isolde.* However in 1858, after a matrimonial showdown, Mathilde decided to remain with her husband and the Wagners moved out of Zürich, first going to Vienna and then to Lucerne, where *Tristan* was completed (1859). Although it was accepted by the Vienna opera, they later abandoned it as unperformable. In the meantime, Wagner's opera *Lohengrin* had received its first performance (conducted by Liszt) in Weimar in 1850.

In 1862 the Wagners settled on the Rhine at Biebrich, where the composer began work on his opera *Die *Meistersinger von Nürnberg* before moving on to Vienna. However, Wagner was now deeply in debt and only rescued from ignominious imprisonment by an invitation from the 'mad king' Ludwig II of Bavaria to settle in Munich as his artistic adviser. Arranging for his friend Hans von Bülow to be appointed conductor, Wagner accepted the invitation and with financial backing from the king, *Tristan* was first performed there in 1865. Again matrimonial complications arose, as a result of the composer's affair with Cosima, Bülow's wife (and Liszt's daughter). The ensuing scandal, exploited by Wagner's creditors, forced him to leave Munich and he set up home on Lake Lucerne. After Minna's death

Richard Wagner aged 70 with his wife Cosima

in 1866, Cosima joined him and they were married in 1870 (after Cosima had obtained her divorce from Bülow). In this period Wagner completed the *Die Meistersinger* (1868).

In 1872 the Bavarian city of *Bayreuth offered him a site for an opera house of his own. Subscriptions from many parts of the world enabled the theatre to open in 1876, with the first complete performance of the *Ring*. *Parsifal, Wagner's last opera, was given its first performance there in 1882. Wagner, now plagued by ill-health, died while spending the winter in Venice.

Wagner's introduction of leitmotivs and the concept of *music dramas, with words and music welded together into an integrated work of great emotional intensity, make him the chief exponent of German romantic music and one of the most important innovators in the art of opera. Apart from his operas he wrote some piano music, the *Siegfried Idyll* (1870) for small orchestra, a number of songs and choral works, and some 10 volumes of musical criticism and theory. His son **Siegfried (Richard) Wagner** (1869–1930), who trained as an architect, assisted Cosima (his mother) in running the Bayreuth theatre after Wagner's death. **Wieland Wagner** (1917–66), the grandson of the composer, after studying stage design was in charge of production at Bayreuth from its reopening in 1951 until his death.

Wagner tubas Two bass brass instruments designed to Wagner's specification for use in *The Ring*. They are in B♭ and F, with the same range as the *horns in these pitches. The B♭ instrument (called a **tenor tuba**) and the F instrument (called a **bass tuba**) are more akin to horns than to *tubas (the mistaken terminology may have arisen from Wagner's original name for them, *Wagner-Tuben*). Wagner used two each of these instruments together with two double-bass tubas, which are normal tubas. Later composers, such as Richard Strauss, have also used this combination of instruments.

wait 1. Originally in the early Middle Ages, a nightwatchman who sounded a horn at the gates of a town or castle if someone approached. Later, waits were musicians who played the shawm and sounded the hours and other signals. By the late 15th century they had developed into town bands that played distinctive tunes and later included singers. Today waits are Christmas singers who perform hymns and carols in the streets. **2.** (*or* **wayte-pipe**) An Old English instrument of the shawm family, used by the waits.

Walcha, Helmut (1907–) German organist. After his debut in 1924 he quickly established an international reputation, being noted especially for his interpretation of Bach. Walcha teaches at the Frankfurt Music Institute and also composes.

Waldflöte (*or* **woodland flute**) An organ *stop controlling 8-*foot or 4-foot pipes with inverted mouths producing a sound similar to the *claribel stop. [German]

Waldhorn A valveless German hunting *horn. [German, woodland horn]

Waldstein Sonata Piano sonata in C major (Op. 53) by Beethoven. Composed: 1803–04. The work was dedicated to Count Ferdinand von Waldstein and in form this sonata is very similar to the *Appassionata: both have lengthy outer movements, while the middle movement, which is very improvisatory in character, is relatively brief and serves only as a link into the finale.

Waldteufel, (Charles) Emile (1837–1915) French composer, pianist, and conductor. He studied with Marmontel and Laurent at the Paris Conservatoire and was appointed court pianist (1865) and conductor (1866) of the state balls. Waldteufel is the best-known waltz composer after Johann Strauss. He wrote about 300 dances, among them the waltzes *Manolo* (1873), *Les Patineurs* ('Skaters' Waltz,' 1882), and *España* (1886).

Walküre, Die (*The Valkyrie*) see **Ring des Nibelungen, Der.**

Wallace, (William) Vincent (1812–65) Irish composer. He played the violin at the Theatre Royal, Dublin, and was organist of Thurles Cathedral. In 1835 he emigrated to Tasmania and in 1836 settled in Sydney, where he was acclaimed as a violinist and pianist. He travelled throughout the world and toured South America and the USA. Wallace arrived in London in 1845, the year his highly successful opera *Maritana* was produced. He returned to the Americas for long tour then retired to France, where he died. Wallace wrote several less successful operas, including *Lurline* (1847) and *The Amber Witch* (1861); songs and part songs; and many piano pieces, some very technically demanding.

Wallace, William (1860–1940) British composer, writer, and ophthalmologist, born in Scotland. He was strongly influenced by Liszt, particularly in his tone poems. He composed six tone poems, including *The Passing of Beatrice* (1892) and *François Villon* (1909), the overture *In Praise of Scottish Poesie* (1894), the cantata *Massacre of the Macphersons*, and numerous songs.

Wally, La Opera in four acts by Catalani with libretto by Luigi Illica. First performance: La Scala, Milan, 1892. It is based on Wilhelmine von Hillern's novel *Die Geyer-Wally* and set in the Austrian Tyrol about 1800. Wally (soprano) and her lover Hagenbach (tenor) eventually die in an avalanche.

Walond, William (*c.*1725–70) British composer and organist. Known primarily for two sets of voluntaries for organ or harpsichord (*c.*1752, 1758), he also set Pope's *Ode on St Cecilia's Day* (*c.*1760). Another **William Walond** (*c.*1755–1836), possibly his son, was deputy organist (1775) and organist (1776–1801) of Chichester Cathedral.

Bruno Walter

Walter, Bruno (B. W. Schlesinger; 1876–1962) German-born conductor. He became a friend and champion of Mahler while working with him in Hamburg (1894) and Vienna (1901). Walter became conductor of the Leipzig Gewandhaus Orchestra in 1929, but suffered antisemitic persecution from the Nazis and left Germany. After the outbreak of World War II he went to France and then to the USA, where he conducted the Metropolitan Opera and the New York Philharmonic (1947–49). He was a follower of the Austrian anthroposophist, Rudolf Steiner.

Walther, Johann Gottfried (1684–1748) German composer, organist, and writer. Educated in Erfurt, he was appointed organist at St Peter and St Paul, Weimar, in 1707. He taught Prince Johann Ernst at the Imperial court while his cousin J. S. Bach was in the orchestra there. Walther's greatest achievement was his *Musicalisches Lexicon* (1732), the first music dictionary to include musicians' biographies as well as musical terms. His most important compositions were chorale preludes; these are similar to those of J. S. Bach in their contrapuntal brilliance and rich harmonies.

Walton, Sir William (1902–83) British composer. He was trained as a chorister at Christ Church, Oxford, but was largely self-taught as a composer. As a protégé of the Sitwells, he produced a number of works, including the entertainment *Façade* (1923), which was influenced by Les *Six and jazz. Most of his later works, however, are written in a romantically lyrical manner, with the occasional touch of sardonic humour. Walton's output includes two symphonies; concertos for viola (1929), violin (1939), and cello (1957); the concert overture *Portsmouth Point* (1925); the coronation march *Crown Imperial* (1937); *Partita* (1957); *Variations on a Theme by Hindemith* (1963); *Improvisations on an Impromptu by Benjamin Britten* (1970); the operas *Troilus and Cressida* (1954) and The *Bear (1967); the ballets The *Wise Virgins* (1940) and The *Quest* (1943); the oratorio *Belshazzar's Feast* (1931) and other choral works; chamber music; and the scores for a number of films, including Olivier's *Hamlet*, *Henry V*, and *Richard III*.

Walton was knighted in 1951 and lived in Italy.

waltz (*or* **valse**) A dance in triple time that evolved in Germany and Austria late in the 18th century from the earlier *Ländler, a popular folk dance. It spread to France and England at the beginning of the 19th century as a decorous and graceful ballroom dance, the compositions of Lanner and the Strauss family, its principal exponents, becoming immensely popular. Typically, the flowing melody of a waltz is accompanied by a single harmony in each bar, the bass note of the chord being sounded on the accented first beat, with two-, three-, or four-note chords on the second and third beats. Waltzes not intended merely for the ballroom have been written by many composers, including Mozart, Beethoven, Schubert, Brahms, and Chopin. The 14 piano waltzes of Chopin, for example, confine within the basic structure of the waltz instrumental music of great pathos, vitality, and poetry.

Waltz Dream, A (German: *Ein Waltzertraum*) Operetta by Oscar Straus with libretto by Dörmann and Jacobson. First performance: Vienna, 1907. A waltz symbolizes nostalgic longing for Vienna.

Wanderer Fantasy Work for piano (Op. 15) by Schubert. Composed: 1822. The second movement of this four-movement work is a set of variations upon Schubert's song 'Der Wanderer,' composed in 1816. However, each of the other movements is also constructed around a motif derived from this song and thus the *Wanderer Fantasy* is effectively a cyclic sonata, in which all the movements are thematically interrelated. In the last movement Schubert constructs a fugue upon this motif.

Wand of Youth Suite Two suites for orchestra (Op. 1a and Op. 1b) by Elgar. Composed: 1907. When Elgar was ten he composed some incidental music for a family play and in later life decided to re-use the ideas in an orchestral work. The result was the two *Wand of Youth Suites*, and his childhood sketches also provided material for the incidental music to Pearn's play *The Starlight Express* in 1915.

Wanhall, Johann Baptist see **Vanhal, Johann Baptist**.

War and Peace (Russian: *Voina y Mir*) Opera in 13 scenes by Prokofiev with libretto by the composer and his wife, Mira Mendelson, based on Tolstoy's novel. First performance: Moscow, 1945 (concert version); Maly Theatre, Leningrad, 1946 (scenes 1 to 8); Leningrad, 1955 (all scenes except 7 and 11). The scenes are taken from key moments in Tolstoy's novel: the first seven concentrate on peace; the last six on war.

Ward, John (1571–before 1638) English composer. He probably sang at Canterbury and in London was patronized by Sir Henry Fanshawe, for whom he composed music. His works include sacred music, madrigals, and viol pieces.

Warlock, Peter (Philip Heseltine; 1894–1930) British composer. Warlock's style was inspired by the music of Elizabethan England and was also influenced by the works of Delius. His output includes the suite *Capriol* (1926), the song cycle The *Curlew* (1920–22) and other songs, and arrangements of Elizabethan music.

War Requiem, A Work for solo voices, boys' choir, choir, organ, chamber orchestra, and orchestra by Britten. First performance: 1962. This work was commissioned for the consecration of the new Coventry Cathedral, the old building having been virtually completely destroyed by bombing in World War II. Between settings of the various sections of the Requiem Mass, Britten intersperses settings of some of Wilfred Owen's poems, which reflect on the nature of war.

Wasps, The Incidental music by Vaughan Williams to the comedy of the same name by Aristophanes. Composed: 1909. The overture from this music is frequently performed as a separate concert work.

Water Carrier, The see **Deux journées, Les.**

Water Music Two suites for orchestra in F major and D major by Handel. Composed: 1717. It is assumed that these two collections comprise various instrumental pieces that Handel wrote to be played during a royal barge procession on the River Thames on 17 July, 1717, although some of the music may have been composed at a later date.

water organ see **hydraulis.**

Watkins, Michael Blake (1948–) British composer, a pupil of Elisabeth Lutyens and Rodney Bennett. He studied and has written several works for the guitar. Watkins' output includes a double concerto (1972); *Clouds and Eclipses* (1973); a violin concerto (1978); vocal music, such as *Invocation* (1972) and *The Bird of Time* (1979); and chamber pieces, including a guitar quartet (1972) and a clarinet quintet (1980).

Watts, Helen (1927–) British contralto. After studying with Caroline Hatchard and Frederick Jackson in London, she began singing in oratorio. Later she included the operas of Handel, Britten, and Wagner in her repertory and her lieder and recital work ranges from Berlioz to Schoenberg.

Wat Tyler Opera by Alan Bush with libretto by his wife, Nancy Bush. First performance: Leipzig, 1953. It relates the story of the Peasants' Revolt in England in 1381.

Wayenberg, Daniel (1929–) Dutch pianist, born in France. A pupil of Marguerite Long, he has an international reputation based on his wide and varied repertoire. Wayenberg has also composed several orchestral works, including a triple piano concerto.

Webbe, Samuel (1740–1816) British composer and organist. He was organist of the Portuguese and Sardinian chapels (1776–c.1813), writing much Catholic and Anglican church music, but is remembered primarily for his glees and catches. He was librarian of the Glee Club (1787), secretary of the Catch Club and also wrote chamber works and singing tutors.

Weber, Ben (1916–79) US composer. Self-taught as a musician, he was among the first Americans to develop a 12-note idiom while maintaining traditional forms and a strong tonal feeling. His works include a violin concerto (1954), a piano concerto (1961), *Sinfonia Clarion* (1974) for orchestra, the ballet *Pool of Darkness* (1950), two string quartets, chamber music, and piano pieces.

Weber, Carl Maria (Friedrich Ernst) von (1786–1826) German composer, pianist, and conductor; the founder of the romantic school in opera. Weber was the son of a travelling theatre musician and after initial music training from his father he became a pupil of Michael Haydn in Salzburg at the age of 10. He also studied under Vogler in Vienna, during which period he composed his first surviving opera, *Peter Schmoll und seine Nachbarn* (1803). In 1804 he became kapellmeister at Breslau (now Wrocław) and in 1807 was appointed secretary in the court of King Frederick I of Württemberg. However, in 1810 he was banished from the country because of his dissolute lifestyle. His first romantic opera, *Silvana* (1810), was composed during this period. Travelling first to Mannheim and then to Darmstadt, Munich, and Prague, where he was appointed conductor of the opera (1813), Weber now began to formulate his theories on the romantic movement. In 1817 he settled in Dresden as director of the German opera; here he began work on Der *Freischütz*, the first opera in the German romantic tradition, which was acclaimed at its first performance in Berlin in 1821. The opera *Euryanthe* followed in 1823; less successful this nevertheless is a more ambitious work, which to some extent anticipates Wagner. Weber's last opera, *Oberon* (1826), was written in English to be performed in England; although suffering from tuberculosis he travelled to London to conduct its first performances. There he died shortly before he was due to return to Germany.

Weber composed four other operas, among them *Abu Hassan* (1811). His other compositions include orchestral music, notably *Concertstück* in F minor (Op. 79; 1821); piano, church, and chamber music; and many songs.

Webern, Anton von (1883–1945) Austrian composer, a pupil of Adler and Schoenberg. He formed, with his teacher Schoenberg and fellow student Alban Berg, the group known as the Second Viennese School, which moved from the use of postromantic extended tonality through an atonal period and finally to serialism. Webern's works are characterized by dissonant counterpoint, great brevity of utterance, and strict adherence to serial principles. His final works are marked by a classical formal transparency and simplicity of texture. Webern's influence on the postwar developments of serial language was profound. His output includes a passacaglia (1908), *Six Pieces for Orchestra* (1910), a symphony (1928), *Varia for Orchestra* (1940), *Das Augenlicht* (1935) and two cantatas (1940 and 1943), chamber music, and many songs, often with unusual instrumental accompaniments.

Wechseldominante see **dominant**.

We Come to the River Opera by Henze described by the composer as 'Actions for Music' in 2 parts and 11 scenes, with libretto by Edward Bond. First performance: Covent Garden, London, 1976. It is an indictment against war and social injustice; the stage is divided into three areas so that different actions can be shown in progress at the same time.

Wedding, The (French: *Les Noces*; Russian: *Svadebka*) Ballet in four scenes with music by Stravinsky, choreography by Nijinsky, and décor by Gontcharova. First performance: Théâtre Gaité-Lyrique, Paris, 1923, conducted by Ansermet. Commissioned by Diaghilev for the Ballets Russes, the four scenes of a Russian wedding ritual are 'The Blessing of the Bride,' 'The Blessing of the Bridegroom,' 'The Bride's Departure from her Parent's House,' and 'The Wedding Feast.' The music is for four pianos, percussion, and chorus.

Wedge Fugue Fugue for organ in E minor (BWV 548) by Bach. Composed: 1727–31. This work is so named because the intervals between the notes of the subject become progressively wider, hence giving the impression of a wedge.

Weelkes, Thomas (*c*.1576–1623) English composer. He became organist at Winchester College in 1598 and contributed a madrigal to *The Triumphs of Oriana* (1601). In 1602 he took the Oxford B.Mus. degree and, probably in the same year, went to Chichester as organist and choirmaster. In 1617 he was dismissed from this post for drunkenness. Weelkes was an important composer of madrigals and church music; his madrigals are particularly fine and show a good deal of imagination, while his church music is generally more restrained.

Weigl, Joseph (1766–1846) Austrian composer and conductor. After studying in Vienna with Albrechtsberger and later Salieri, he was appointed deputy kapellmeister (1790) and kapellmeister and composer (1792) at the court theatre, with which he was associated throughout his life. Weigl composed over 30 operas (in German and Italian), ballets, and incidental music, as well as sacred and secular choral music and instrumental works. His father, **Joseph Weigl** (1740–1820), was a cellist in Prince Paul Esterházy's orchestra at Eisenstadt, which Haydn conducted.

Weigl, Karl (1881–1949) Austrian-born US composer, a pupil of Adler and Zemlinsky. Weigl was an associate of Mahler at the Vienna Opera and his own music is in a conservative Viennese idiom. His works include six symphonies; concertos for violin (1928), cello (1934), and piano (1937); eight string quartets and other chamber pieces; choral works, such as the *Weltfeier* cantata (1912); and numerous lieder.

Weihnachtsoratorium see **Christmas Oratorio**.

Weihnachtssymphonie see **Lamentation Symphony**.

Weill, Kurt (1900–50) German composer, a pupil of Humperdinck, Busoni, and Jarnach. He is best known for his stage works: in collaboration with Bertolt Brecht he developed a new genre of opera dealing with topical subjects

Kurt Weill

in a satirical manner, incorporating parody elements and jazz influences in the music. After settling in the USA in 1935, Weill successfully adapted this style to the Broadway stage, notably in conjunction with the librettist Maxwell Anderson. He was married to the singer Lotte Lenya (1898–1981), who often performed in his works.

Weill's operas include The *Threepenny Opera (1928), *Rise and Fall of the City of Mahagonny (1929), and Die sieben Todsünden der Kleinbürger (1933), all with Brecht; Der Protagonist (1926) and Der Silbersee (1932) with Georg Kaiser; and *Down in the Valley (1948). He also wrote various chamber, orchestral, and choral works and, in the USA, the musicals Johnny Johnson (1935), Knickerbocker Holiday (1938), Lady in the Dark (1941), Street Scene (1947), and Lost in the Stars (1949).

Weinberger, Jaromir (1896–1967) Czech composer, a pupil of Reger and from 1938 resident in the USA. His music, which makes much use of folk tunes and rhythms, had an early popular success with the opera *Švanda the Bagpiper (1927). Subsequent works include the opera Valdštejn (1937); orchestral works, such as Under the Spreading Chestnut Tree (1939), The Legend of Sleepy Hollow (1940), and Prelude and Fugue on Dixie (1940); and vocal and chamber pieces.

Weiner, Leó (1885–1960) Hungarian composer and writer. His style is in the tradition of 19th-century classicism and romanticism and opposed to modernist trends, although he made some use of folk material. Weiner's works include the Divertimenti (1934–49) for orchestra, the tone poem Toldi (1952), two violin concertos, Passacaglia (1955), chamber music, piano pieces, and many orchestral transcriptions.

Weir, Gillian (1941–) British organist. She launched her career by winning the St Alban's Competition in 1964, following this by extensive international tours. Weir is particularly admired for her playing of Messiaen and also occasionally performs as a harpsichordist.

Weiss, Sylvius Leopold (1686–1750) German composer and lutenist, member of a family of lutenists. He worked with both Scarlattis in Italy (1708–14), becoming court musician in Dresden in 1717. He toured widely, often performing with Quantz and Pisendel. Weiss's works, all for lute, include sonatas, partitas, and concertos.

Weissenberg, Alexis (1929–) Bulgarian-born French pianist. He studied in Israel and at the Juilliard School, New York, making his debut in 1947. His subsequent career as a virtuoso pianist with a wide repertory was interrupted in 1956 by a 10-year period of teaching and study.

Weldon, John (1676–1736) British composer and organist, a pupil of Purcell. He was organist of New College, Oxford (1694), the Chapel Royal (1708), and St Martin's-in-the-Fields (1714), and became second composer at the Chapel Royal in 1715. He wrote the prize-winning setting of Congreve's masque The Judgment of Paris (1701), anthems, including Divine Harmony (1716), songs, and other dramatic and instrumental works.

Weller, Walter (1939–) Austrian conductor. Originally a violinist, he has conducted the Royal Liverpool Philharmonic Orchestra (1977–80) and the Royal Philharmonic Orchestra (1980–85).

Wellesz, Egon (1885–1974) Austrian composer and writer on music, a pupil of Adler, Schoenberg, and Bruno Walter and resident in England from 1939. Although he made occasional use of serial techniques he never entirely dispensed with traditional tonality. His most significant compositions were the stage works written in the 1920s and the postwar series of symphonies. As a musicologist he devoted himself in particular to the study of Byzantine chant and baroque opera, becoming reader in Byzantine music at Oxford. Wellesz's works include the operas Alkestis (1924), Der Opferung des Gefangenen (1926), Die Bakchantinen (1931), and Incognita (1952); ballets, such as Akhilles auf Skyros (1927); nine symphonies (1945–61); a violin concerto (1961); choral and vocal works, including the mass in F minor (1934) and The Leaden Echo and the Golden Echo (1944); and nine string quartets and other chamber music.

Wellington's Victory see **Battle of Vitoria.**

Well-Tempered Clavier, The (German: Das wohltempierte Clavier) Collection of preludes and fugues for keyboard (BWV 846–893) by Bach. Composed: 1722–42. The 48 works that comprise this collection were published in two books of 24 works each, in 1722 and 1744 respectively; the two sets together are often known simply as **The Forty-Eight.** Bach's aim in composing them was to demonstrate that with the new system of tuning by equal *temperament it was possible to play equally well in any key: the collection thus includes a prelude and fugue in every major and minor key. Although Bach himself applied the title to the first book only, it is also used for the second volume.

Werke see **opus.** [German, work]

Werle, Lars Johan (1926–) Swedish composer. His early works make use of serial techniques but Werle abandoned these to develop a lyrically expressive style that often incorporates electronic music. His works include the operas Dreaming about Thérèse (1964) to be performed 'in the round,' The Journey (1969), and Tintomara (1973); the ballet Zodiac (1966); Summer Music (1965); vocal pieces, including Flower Power (1974); and film music.

Werner, Gregor Joseph (1693–1766) Austrian composer. From 1728 he was kapellmeister to the Esterházy court, being succeeded by Haydn, whose superior he was from 1761 to 1766. In addition to chamber works, symphonies, masses, and cantatas, Werner wrote many oratorios and six introductions and fugues for string quartet (arranged by Haydn, 1804).

Wert, Giaches de (1535–96) Flemish composer. Most of his life was spent in Italy; from 1565 until his death he directed the music at the court of Mantua and had close contact with the musical and literary circles at nearby Ferrara. In 1591 or 1592 he wrote the music for a projected performance of Guarini's *Il Pastor fido*. Wert's compositions comprise numerous motets, masses, and magnificats for the chapel of S Barbara, Mantua, and 12 books of madrigals published between 1558 and 1595. The latter, especially, reveal the influence of Rore in their use of unusual harmonies and dissonance for dramatic effect. His later madrigals are less complex polyphonically than the earlier ones; many of them were written for professional female singers and are therefore extremely florid in the upper voices.

Werther Opera in four acts by Massenet with libretto by Blau, Milliet, and Hartmann based on Goethe's novel *Die Leiden des jungen Werthers*. First performance (in German): Vienna Opera, 1892. Werther (tenor) loves Charlotte (soprano), who is betrothed to Albert (baritone); overwhelmed by his sentimental passion, Werther shoots himself.

Wesley, Charles (1757–1834) British composer and organist, nephew of John Wesley, the founder of Methodism. He was a pupil of Boyce and later organist of many churches, including that of St Marylebone. His compositions include many chamber works, anthems, and organ and keyboard music. His brother **Samuel Wesley** (1766–1837) was also a composer and organist. As a child he showed precocious musical gifts, composing an oratorio (*Ruth*) at the age of eight. Samuel Wesley was active in the revival of J. S. Bach's music and edited many of his works. He wrote many hymns, anthems, Latin church music, symphonies, concertos, secular part songs, and keyboard and organ works. Samuel's illegitimate son, **Samuel Sebastian Wesley** (1810–76), an organist and composer, was taught by his father and held posts as organist at the cathedrals of Hereford (1832), Exeter (1835), Winchester (1849), and Gloucester (1865). He became organ professor of the Royal Academy of Music in 1850. His works include services, anthems, hymn tunes, and other church music, many organ pieces, and songs.

Westrup, Sir Jack (1904–75) British musicologist and conductor. He was a music critic of *The Daily Telegraph* (1934–40) and subsequently music professor at Birmingham University (1944–46) and at Oxford University (1947–71). He wrote many books on music (notably on Purcell), contributed to Grove's *Dictionary* and other dictionaries of music, and was editor of the *New Oxford History of Music*.

Wexford Festival An annual festival founded in 1951 in Wexford, Eire, by T. J. Walsh. Using a small 18th-century theatre, it presents three (often rarely heard) operas at each festival, as well as recitals and other entertainments.

whiffle see **fife**.

whip A percussion instrument consisting of two hinged pieces of wood that can be snapped together to simulate the sound of a cracking whip.

whistle 1. The sound produced by blowing through a small gap in the lips. The pitch is changed by altering the shape of the lips and the position of the tongue. **2.** A simple end-blown pipe or vessel producing a sound similar to the human whistle. The sound is produced by blowing across the edge of a blow hole (see **flute**) or into a mouthpiece that feeds a blow hole. See also **tin whistle**.

White Peacock, The Work for piano by Griffes. Composed: 1915. In its original version this piece was one of the collection of character pieces (Op. 7) entitled *Four Roman Sketches* and was inspired by Fiona Macleod's poem *The White Peacock*. In 1919 Griffes orchestrated this work for use as a ballet, in which version it is normally heard today.

White (*or* **Whyte**) **Robert** (*c.*1538–74) English composer. He sang at Trinity College, Cambridge, and took the B.Mus. degree in 1560. Two years later he became master of the choristers at Ely and in 1566 he moved to Chester. He subsequently went to Westminster Abbey (probably in 1569). White's church music, notably the *Lamentations*, marks the highpoint of Elizabethan church music; these and his Latin motets are highly inventive; his anthems are less interesting.

Whithorne, Thomas see **Whythorne, Thomas**.

Whitlock, Percy (1903–46) British organist. He held appointments at Rochester Cathedral and in Brighton, where he was borough organist. Whitlock also composed organ and choral works.

whole note see **semibreve**.

whole-tone scale A *scale in which all the intervals between notes are whole tones, rather than semitones (as in the chromatic scale) or whole tones and semitones (as in the diatonic scale). Only two such scales are possible, one beginning on C and the other on Db, but each can begin at any point as there is no keynote. The whole-tone scale has six different notes, the one beginning on C being CDEF♯G♯A♯C.

Whyte, Robert see **White, Robert.**

Whythorne (*or* **Whithorne**), **Thomas** (1528–96) English composer and lutenist. After studying at Magdalen College, Oxford, he entered the service of various noble families and made a trip to Naples. In 1571 he published his *Songes for Three, Fower and Five Voyces*, the earliest of its kind in England. A second publication (1590) was intended for two voices or instruments; both show Italian influence.

Widor, Charles Marie (**Jean Albert**) (1844–1937) French organist, composer, and teacher, a pupil of Lemmens and Fétis in Brussels. He became organist of St Sulpice, Paris (1870–1934), and in 1890 succeeded Franck as organ professor at the Paris Conservatoire, where he later (1896) became Professor of Composition. His pupils included Tournemire, Schweitzer, Dupré, Honegger, and Milhaud. Widor composed stage works, orchestral music (including three symphonies, two piano concertos, and a cello concerto), and chamber and piano music but is best known for his organ works, particularly the ten organ symphonies (the famous toccata is from the fifth). He wrote much music criticism and a book on orchestration and with Albert Schweitzer he edited Bach's organ works.

Wiegenlied A cradle-song, or lullaby. Such pieces are short, restful, and usually in 6/8 time, with an accompaniment that imitates the rocking of a cradle. The best-known examples are by Brahms and Wolf. See also **berceuse.** [German]

Charles Widor

Wiener Blut (*Vienna Blood*) Operetta compiled from the music of Johann Strauss the Younger by Adolf Müller at the dying composer's request, with libretto by Leon and Stein. First performance: Carltheater, Vienna, 1899. A tale of romantic intrigue set in Vienna in 1815, it is named after the Strauss waltz incorporated in it.

Wiener Sängerknaben see **Vienna Boys' Choir.**

Wieniawski, Henryk (1835–80) Polish violinist and composer, a pupil at the Paris Conservatoire (1843–46, 1849–50). With his brother, the pianist **Józef Wieniawski** (1837–1912), he toured Russia (1851–53). He became internationally famous for his virtuoso playing and brilliant compositions. From 1860 to 1872 Wieniawski lived in St Petersburg, where he was solo violinist to the tsar and taught at the conservatory (1862–68). He then toured the USA with Rubinstein and became violin professor at the Brussels conservatory (1875–77). One of the leading violinists of his day, Wieniawski composed many works for his instrument, including two violin concertos, mazurkas, caprices, and some very demanding studies (*L'Ecole moderne*, 1854; *Etudes-caprices*, 1863).

Wilbye, John (1574–1638) English composer, in the service of the Kytson family of Hengrave Hall, near Bury St Edmunds, from about 1595. His fame rests entirely on his two madrigal books of 1597 and 1609, in which the expressive devices of the Italian madrigalists (especially Marenzio) are used with unprecedented subtlety and concern for musical form. Two particular hallmarks of his style are thematic reminiscence and major–minor contrasts. Both techniques are used in the typically melancholy *Adieu, sweet Amarillis* and *Draw on sweet Night.*

Wild, Earl (*c*.1930–) US pianist. His reputation is based on his performance of 19th-century and contemporary piano music and he has premiered several 20th-century concertos. Wild is noted for his interpretation of Gershwin and also composes.

Wilde, David (1935–) British pianist. A pupil of Reizenstein and Nadia Boulanger, he specializes in the performance of Bartók and Liszt. Wilde has held teaching appointments in Manchester and in London at the Royal Academy of Music.

Wilhelmj, August (1845–1908) German violinist. He studied in Liepzig with David and Raff and made his debut in 1854. After touring Europe and the USA as a recitalist he moved to London in 1894 to teach at the Guildhall School of Music. Wilhelmj made several transcriptions for violin and wrote a teaching manual.

Wilkinson, Marc (1929–) French-born Australian composer, a pupil of Messiaen and Varèse. The majority of his music has been for the theatre and for films. From 1964 to 1967 he composed incidental music for productions at the Old Vic in London. His other works include the cantata *Voices* to texts by Beckett.

Willaert, Adrian (*c*.1490–1562) Flemish composer, a pupil of Mouton. He studied law in Paris before travelling to Rome in 1515 or before. He was then employed at Ferrara (?1520–25) and perhaps Milan (1525–27), before being elected maestro di cappella at St Mark's, Venice, where he remained until his death. Willaert was perhaps the most revered and influential composer of his generation. In Venice he was active in a wide circle of poets and musicians and his pupils included such composers as Rore, Vicentino, Parabosco, Zarlino, and Andrea Gabrieli. He was hailed as the composer of a new kind of music more closely associated with the meaning of the words than to the external form of the poetry. In his more mature music, strict imitative polyphony is modified in favour of such features as homophony and soloistic writing in each of the voices. Willaert's most important work is the *Musica nova* (printed in 1559 but probably composed *c*.1530–*c*.1545), a collection of 33 motets and 25 madrigals. He is also the author of a few chansons and masses, three books of motets (1539), a book of psalms for double chorus (1550), and nine instrumental ricercari (1551).

Willcocks, Sir David (1919–) British conductor and organist. Although he held cathedral appointments at Salisbury and Worcester, it was as choirmaster of King's College, Cambridge, that Willcocks became best known. From 1974–84 he was director of the Royal College of Music. He is also conductor of the London Bach Choir. He was knighted in 1977.

Williams, Grace (1906–77) Welsh composer, a pupil of Vaughan Williams and Wellesz. Her style is basically lyrical and makes much use of folk elements, culminating in a marked Welsh nationalism in her later works. Her output includes *Penillion* (1955), the opera *The Parlour* (1961), a trumpet concerto (1963), *Ballads for Orchestra* (1968), *Castell Caernarfon* (1969), *Missa Cambrensis* (1971), and many songs and folk-song arrangements.

Williams, John (1942–) Australian guitarist, resident in Britain. He was a pupil of Segovia and has taught at the Royal College of Music. In addition to solo appearances throughout the world, Williams frequently performs guitar duos with Julian Bream and has also formed the pop group Sky. Dodgson, Previn, and Torroba have all written for him.

Williams, John Tower (1932–) US composer and pianist, a pupil of Castelnuovo-Tedesco. He has written a number of concert works that make use of jazz techniques and modified serial procedures. They include the *Essay for Strings* (1966); a sinfonietta, concertos, and chamber pieces. He is best known, however, for his music for such films as *Jaws, Star Wars*, and *Close Encounters of the Third Kind*.

Williamson, Malcolm (1931–) Australian composer, pianist, and organist, resident in England, a pupil of Eugene Goosens, Elisabeth Lutyens, and Erwin Stein. In 1975 he became Master of the Queen's Music. His style is eclectic, deriving many elements from jazz and popular music. He has written many pieces for children. His works include the operas *Our Man in Havana* (1963), *The Violins of St Jacques* (1966); chamber operas; concertos for piano, organ (1961), and violin (1965); symphonies; *Ode to Music* (1973); *Hammerskjold Portrait* (1974); *Mass of Christ the King* (1977–78); and chamber music, piano pieces, and songs.

William Tell (French: *Guillaume Tell*) Opera in four acts by Rossini with libretto by de Louy and Bis based on Schiller's drama. First performance (in four acts): Opéra, Paris, 1829 (it was reduced to three acts in 1831). Set in 13th-century Switzerland, the story of William Tell (baritone), who rallies the Swiss against the Austrians, is combined with the love story of the Swiss patriot Arnold (tenor) and the Austrian Mathilde (soprano).

Wilson, John (1595–1674) English composer, lutenist, and singer. Active at court and London theatres from 1614, he became a city wait in 1622 and a member of the King's Musick in 1635. He was appointed Professor of Music at Oxford University in 1656 but resigned in 1661 to become a gentleman of the Chapel Royal. His most important works are songs for plays by Middleton, Fletcher, and others and music for theorbo.

wind band A band of mixed wind instruments, usually with percussion. In Britain the term *military band is preferred, which is distinct from a *brass band (made up only of brass instruments). In the Middle Ages a wind band was a group of pipers who provided music at civic occasions.

Wind-Band Mass (German: *Harmoniemesse*) Mass in B♭ by Haydn. Composed: 1802. The name derives from the use of a larger than usual wind section in the orchestra.

Windgassen, Wolfgang (1914–74) German tenor and producer. He made his debut at Pforzheim as Alvaro in Verdi's *La Forza del destino* (1941) and then worked with the Stuttgart Opera (1945–72). From 1951 until 1970 he was the leading Wagnerian heroic tenor at Bayreuth and from 1970 he produced many operas in Stuttgart.

wind instruments Musical *instruments in which the sound is produced by a vibrating column of air. Organs and accordions are not usually included in this family of instruments, which is normally restricted to instruments blown by the player. The usual orchestral division is into *brass instruments (horns, trumpets, trombones, etc.) and *woodwind instruments (flutes, clarinets, oboes, and bassoons). See also **aerophone**.

Winter Journey, The see Winterreise, Die.

Winterreise, Die (*The Winter Journey*) Song cycle by Schubert to poems by Wilhelm Müller. Composed: 1827. The 24 songs that comprise this work form a sequel to Schubert's earlier cycle, *Die *Schöne Müllerin*. After being rejected by his lover, as the earlier work relates, the young man leaves his home to wander through the bleak winter countryside, reflecting on his misfortune, his lost love, and his future. The last song relates how he eventually meets an old organ grinder whom he decides to join.

Winter Wind Study Study for piano in A minor (Op. 25 No. 11) by Chopin. Composed: 1834. The name is an allusion to the rapid character of the piece.

wire brush A form of drumstick used on side drums and symbols by drummers in dance music and pop music. It consists of a fan-shaped collection of stiff metal wires held together at their apex by a handle. It produces a characteristic brushing sound.

Wirén, Dag (1905–86) Swedish composer and music critic, who studied in Paris. His early work is mostly light music in a style to which he later occasionally returned. After 1944, however, he developed his metamorphosis variation technique, which he applied in more substantial works. His output includes the *Serenade for Strings* (1937), five symphonies, concertos for violin (1946), piano (1950), and cello (1936), *Music for Strings* (1966), five string quartets, and stage and film music.

Wise, Michael (*c.*1647–87) English composer. Following appointments as chorister at the Chapel Royal and lay clerk at St George's Chapel, Windsor, and Eton College, Wise became organist at Salisbury (1668). In 1687 he took up the position of master of the choristers at St Paul's Cathedral, but was killed in that year during an argument with the night watch. He wrote services and anthems, of which *The Ways of Sion* is notable.

Wise Virgins, The Ballet with music arranged by William Walton from compositions of Bach and choreography by Frederick Ashton. First performance: Sadler's Wells Ballet, London, 1940, with décor by Rex Whistler. It consists of nine numbers, mainly from Bach's cantatas and including the Passion chorale from the *St Matthew Passion*; there is an orchestral suite of six of the movements.

Wishart, Peter (1921–84) British composer, a pupil of Hely-Hutchinson and Nadia Boulanger. His works include the operas *The Captive* (1960), *Two in a Bush* (1959), *The Clandestine Marriage* (1971), and *Clytaemnestra* (1973), two symphonies, two violin concertos, pieces for organ and piano, and vocal and choral works.

Witches' Minuet see Fifths Quartet.

Wittgenstein, Paul (1887–1961) Austrian pianist. He made his debut in 1913, but shortly afterwards lost his right arm in World War I. Wittgenstein appeared after the war playing one-handed works written specially for him by such composers as Ravel, Strauss, Britten, and Prokofiev.

Wohltempierte Clavier, Das see Well-Tempered Clavier, The.

wolf (*or* **wolf note**) An unpleasant sound produced by a member of the violin family as a result of an unwanted body resonance or by a keyboard instrument tuned to mean-tone *temperament when playing in an extreme key.

Wolf, Hugo (Philipp Jakob) (1860–1903) Austrian composer. He entered the Vienna conservatory in 1875 but was dismissed the following year and subsequently made a living as a teacher, often in poverty. From about 1888 Wolf began composing lieder and was to bring this form of song to its highest point of development. He composed 53 songs to words by Mörike, 20 to words by Eichendorff, and 51 to words by Goethe. In 1891 the *Spanisches Liederbuch (Spanish Song-Book)*, based on the poems of Heyse and Geibel, appeared and was followed by *Italienisches Liederbuch (Italian Song-Book*: Part 1, 1892; Part 2, 1896). Wolf also produced songs based on the poems of Ibsen and Michelangelo. In 1897 he became mentally ill and was admitted to a sanatorium; although discharged as cured in 1898 he suffered a relapse and was confined in a mental asylum, where he remained until his death.

Wolf's other compositions include two operas (*Der *Corregidor*, which was a failure when first performed in 1896, and the unfinished *Manuel Venegas*), the tone poem *Penthesilea* (begun 1883) based on a tragedy by Kleist, the *Italian Serenade* (1887) for string quartet, choral music, and some other orchestral pieces.

Wolff, Christian (1934–) French-born US composer, who became Professor of Classics at Harvard University. He was a colleague of John Cage in the 1950s. Wolff's music is generally static, using a restricted set of pitches; he uses chance and performer freedom to encourage spontaneity and invention. His works, many of which show a radical political involvement, include *Nine* (1951), *Summer* (1961), *In Between Pieces* (1963), *Snowdrop* (1970), *You Blew It* (1971), and *Accompaniments* (1972).

Wolf-Ferrari, Ermanno (1876–1948) Italian composer of German-Italian parentage, a pupil of Rheinberger. Wolf-Ferrari's style is straightforwardly lyrical. His comic operas, for which he is best known, make much use of parody and pastiche. His works include the operas *La Cenerentola* (1900; see **Cinderella**), *I Quattro rusteghi* (1906; see **School for Fathers**), *Il Segreto di Susanna* (1909; see **Susanna's Secret**), *I Gioielli della Madonna* (1911; see **Jewels of the Madonna, The**), *Gli Amanti sposi* (1916), *Sly*

(1927), and *Il Campiello* (1936); *La Vita nuova* (1901) and other cantatas; and chamber music.

Wolpe, Stefan (1902–72) German-born composer who settled in the USA (1938), a protégé of Busoni, Scherchen, and Webern and associated with the Bauhaus. Apart from a short-lived attempt in the 1920s to adopt a more populist style, his music is concerned with developing variation and formal organization, especially in the mature serially organized pieces. Wolpe's works include a symphony (1955), the ballet *Man from Midion* (1942), a string quartet (1969), and much chamber music and incidental music.

Wolstenholme, William (1865–1931) British organist, violinist, pianist, and composer. Blind from birth, he was taught for a time by Edward Elgar and his career included a successful tour of the USA. Wolstenholme's compositions are mainly pieces for organ and piano but also include choral works, such as *Lord Ullin's Daughter* and *Sir Humphrey Gilbert*, chamber music, and songs.

WoO Abbreviation for Werke ohne Opuszahl (works without opus number). It is used as a prefix to indicate the number given to such pieces by Georg Kinsky in his catalogue (1955; completed by Hans Halm) of Beethoven's works.

Wood, Haydn (1882–1959) British violinist and composer, a pupil of Stanford. His works include concertos for piano and violin, orchestral pieces, choral music, and works for chamber ensembles. He is best known, however, for his popular sentimental songs, such as 'Roses of Picardy' (1916). He also wrote the musical *Cash on Delivery* (1917).

Wood, Sir Henry (Joseph) (1869–1944) British conductor, organist, and composer. After a period as a theatre conductor, he became conductor of the newly founded Queen's Hall Orchestra in 1895. With this orchestra he inaugurated the famous *Promenade Concerts, which he conducted for the rest of his life. Wood was a champion of contemporary music, including the works of Debussy, Scriabin, and Bartók. He was knighted in 1911. See also **Klenovsky, Paul.**

Wood, Hugh (1932–) British composer, a pupil of Antony Milner, Iain Hamilton, and Seiber. Wood's style derives from the serialism of Schoenberg. His works include three string quartets, concertos for violin (1972) and cello (1969), a chamber concerto (1971), *Scenes from Comus* (1965), and song cycles, such as the *Neruda-Logue* song cycle (1974).

Wood, Thomas (1892–1950) British composer and writer, a pupil of Stanford. His output consists chiefly of vocal music; he wrote a number of songs with orchestra, such as *Master Mariners* (1927) and *The Ballad of Hampstead Heath* (1927). His other works include the cantata *Chanticleer* (1947), *The Rainbow* (1950), *Over the Hills and Far Away* (1949), chamber music, and pieces for piano and organ.

wood block see **Chinese wood block.**

woodland flute see **Waldflöte.**

woodwind instruments Musical *instruments, usually made of wood, in which a column of air is made to vibrate by one or two reeds (see **reed instruments**) or by a blow hole. The notes are made by opening and closing holes in the tube of which the instrument consists to shorten or lengthen the vibrating column of air. The main woodwind instruments of the orchestra are the *flute, *clarinet, *oboe, and *bassoon; others include the piccolo, cor anglais, and *saxophone. See also **aerophone; wind instruments.**

Wordsworth, William (1908–88) British composer, a pupil of Tovey. His music stays within the bounds of traditional tonality and includes five symphonies; the orchestral pieces *Conflict* (1968) and *Confluence* (1975); chamber music, including six string quartets; and songs, such as *Four Sacred Sonnets* (1944), *Ariel Songs* (1968), and *The Solitary Reaper* (1973).

working out see **development.**

World of the Moon, The see **Mondo della luna, Il.**

Wotquenne, Alfred (Camille) (1867–1939) Belgian music bibliographer. As librarian, he extensively enlarged the manuscript collection of the Royal Conservatory in Brussels. He published bibliographies of Gluck (1905) and C. P. E. Bach (1906) among others.

Wozzeck Opera in 3 acts (15 scenes) by Alban Berg with libretto by the composer based on Büchner's drama *Woyzech*. First performance: Berlin Staatsoper, 1925. Wozzeck (baritone), a private soldier, is persecuted by the Captain (tenor); his mistress Marie (soprano) takes a new lover, the Drum-Major (tenor). In his anguish Wozzeck stabs her and later drowns himself, searching for the knife.

Wq. Abbreviation for Wotquenne. It is used as a prefix to indicate the number of a piece in Alfred Wotquenne's catalogue (1905) of C. P. E. Bach's works.

Wranitzky, Paul (Pavel Vranický; 1756–1808) Czech composer and violinist. He was a violinist at the Esterházy court and in 1790 appointed director of the court opera in Vienna. His works include *Oberon* (1789) and other singspiels and operas, symphonies, concertos, and sacred and keyboard music. His brother **Anton Wranitzky** (Antonín Vranický; 1761–1820), also a composer and violinist, was a pupil of Mozart, Haydn, and Albrectsberger. In Vienna he was kapellmeister to Prince Lobowitz (1790) and director of several court theatres. He wrote early romantic chamber music, symphonies, concertos, sacred works, and the tutor *Violin fondament* (1804).

Wreckers, The Opera in three acts by Ethel Smyth with libretto by Brewster based on his Cornish drama. First performance: Leipzig, 1906. It is set on the Cornish coast in the late 18th century, during the Wesleyan revival: the villagers believe every ship wrecked to be a direct gift from Providence.

Wuorinen, Charles (1938–) US composer and pianist, a pupil of Luening and Ussachevsky. His music combines a basically serial organization with a feeling for dramatic gesture and virtuosity. His works include three symphonies, three chamber concertos, two piano concertos, *Time's Encomium* (1969), *Arabia Felix* (1974), the *Percussion Symphony* (1976), and an opera, *The Whore of Babylon* (1975).

Xenakis, Iannis (1922–) Romanian-born Greek composer, resident in Paris. Trained as an architect and engineer, he was a colleague of Le Corbusier and a pupil of Milhaud, Messiaen, and Scherchen. Xenakis rejected total serialism and aleatoricism in favour of the application of statistical principles to the composition of sound blocks, a style he termed *stochastic. He has also used game theory, as in *Stratégie* (1962), and elements of set theory and symbolic logic, as in *Nomos Alpha* (1965). The *Polytopes* series reflects Xenakis' interest in electronic music and the organization of spatial and light elements into music. His other works include *Orient-Occident* (1960), *Eonta* (1964), *Aroura* (1971), *Cendrées* (1974), *Erikthon* (1974), *Persepolis* (1971), and *Bonn* (1979).

Xerxes (Italian: *Serse*) Opera in three acts by Handel with libretto by Minato, which was written for Cavalli's earlier

opera in 1654 and revised by Bononcini in 1694. First performance: King's Theatre, London, 1738. Set in ancient Persia, it includes the aria *Ombra mai fù* (*Forever Shade*), commonly known as *Handel's Largo*.

xylophone A percussion instrument consisting of two rows of wooden bars arranged like the black and white notes of the piano, with a range of three or four octaves. Each bar is suspended over a metal tube resonator and the bars are struck with various types of beaters. Its first major use in the modern orchestra was by Saint-Saëns in his *Danse macabre* (1874) and it has since been a regular feature of the percussion section. The instrument has a long history, probably originating in SE Asia, but similar instruments are still in use in many parts of the world (see also **marimba**). The **xylorimba** is a composite instrument consisting essentially of a large marimba with a five-octave range.

Yamash'ta, Stomu (Tsutomo Yamashita; 1947–) Japanese percussionist. After a period as an orchestral player, Yamash'ta concentrated on freelance work and also appeared in jazz concerts. He founded the Red Buddha Theatre and has also composed several much acclaimed dramatic works.

Yeoman of the Guard, The Operetta by Sullivan with libretto by Gilbert, subtitled *The Merryman and his Maid*. First performance: Savoy Theatre, London, 1888. Its setting

is the Tower of London in the 16th century. The strolling jester Jack Point and his companion Elsie become involved in a plot to free Colonel Fairfax, under sentence of death on a false charge of sorcery.

Yepes, Narcisso (1927–) Spanish guitarist. He made his debut in 1947 and subsequently continued studies with Enescu and Gieseking. In addition to an international performing career, Yepes has edited much early music for guitar and also composed several film scores.

yodel (*or* (German) **Jodel**) A type of singing without words (see **vocalise**) that is practised in alpine countries. Both the natural and falsetto voices are used, and the melodic pattern can be simple and diatonic (as in the 'Yodelling Song' in Walton' *Façade*), ornate, resembling a tremolando, or a combination of both.

Yolande see **Iolanta**.

Yonge, Nicholas (?–1619) English singer and editor of music. He edited two anthologies of Italian music with texts in English (see **Musica transalpina**).

Young, Alexander (1920–) British tenor. After studying with Steffan Pollmann in London, he sang with the BBC and at Glyndebourne and made his solo debut as Scaramuccio in Strauss's *Ariadne auf Naxos* at Edinburgh (1950). Berkeley and Searle have written works for him, apart from which he specializes in Handel.

Young, France (1927–) US composer of extreme minimalist tendencies. He has also extended John Cage's ideas on silence into the realm of opera, and many of his shorter pieces dispense entirely with performers and audience. Young's works include *It's Golden!* (1957) for any or no instruments, *Tacet* for large orchestra (1959), *Messe pour la trappe* (1963), and the theatre piece... *the rest is...* (1969).

Young, La Monte (1935–) US composer, a pupil of Pandit Pran Nath and Stockhausen. His influences range from his early experiences of jazz to eastern philosophy. Much of Young's music is based on minimal material – a single note or a few sine waves. In 1962 he founded the Theatre of Eternal Music. His works include the *Composition* series (instructions for actions) and *The Tortoise is Dreams and Journeys* (1964   ).

Young, William (?–1662) English composer and viol player. Active in the court of Archduke Ferdinand Karl, he was renowned throughout Europe as a viol player. His output includes viol compositions (which show the influence of a visit to Italy in 1652) and sonatas – in 1653 he became the first English composer to use the term.

Young Lord, The see **Junge Lord, Der.**

Young Person's Guide to the Orchestra, The Orchestral work (Op. 35) by Britten. Composed: 1945. Britten was asked in 1945 by the Ministry of Education to compose the background music for a film entitled *The Instruments of the Orchestra*, designed to help children differentiate between the sounds of the various orchestral instruments. To achieve this Britten composed a set of variations on a theme taken from Purcell's incidental music to the play *Abdelazar* (1695), each variation featuring a different instrument. The instruments are then all combined in a fugue of Britten's own composition. This music, which is also occasionally known as the *Variations and Fugue on a Theme of Purcell*, was later produced as a concert work.

Yradier, Sebastián see **Iradier, Sebastián.**

Ysäye, Eugène (1858–1931) Belgian violinist and conductor. A pupil of Vieuxtemps, he toured Europe and the USA as a recitalist, chamber-music player, and conductor. Franck, Chausson, and Debussy dedicated works to him and Ysäye himself composed various concert pieces and six sonatas for solo violin.

Yun, Isang (1917–) Korean-born composer, resident in Germany. He adopted serialism, combining it with decorative oriental elements; in later works he has continued to explore oriental sounds and vocal and instrumental techniques. Yun's output includes a string quartet (1960), *Bara* (1960), *Reak* (1966), a cello concerto (1976), *Muak* (1978), the choral works *Om Mani Padme Hum* (1964) and *Der Weise Mann* (1977), and the operas *The Dream of Liu-Tung* (1965) and *Sim Tjong* (1972).

Z

Z. Abbreviation for Zimmerman. It is used as a prefix to indicate the number of a piece in Franklin Zimmerman's catalogue (1963) of Purcell's works.

Zabaleta, Nicanor (1907–) Spanish harpist. He has been active in promoting the harp as a solo instrument, presenting both newly discovered pieces and many contemporary works. Křenek, Milhaud, and Villa-Lobos among others have written for him.

Zachau, Friedrich Wilhelm see **Zachow, Friedrich Wilhelm.**

Zacher, Gerd (1929–) German organist. He has held various posts as church organist, including that of the Lutherkirche, Hamburg. Zacher has done much to promote contemporary organ music and Bussotti, Cage, and Křenek have written works for him.

Zachow (*or* **Zachau**), **Friedrich Wilhelm** (1663–1712) German composer, organist, and teacher. He was organist at the St Mary's Church, Halle (1684), where he is remembered primarily as the teacher of Handel and many others, including Krieger, Kirchoff, and Ziegler. He wrote cantatas and other sacred works and chorales for organ.

Zadok the Priest see **Coronation Anthem.**

Zampa Opera in three acts by Hérold with libretto by Mélesville. First performance: Opéra-Comique, Paris, 1831. Subtitled *La Fiancée de marbre* (*The Marble Betrothed*), it tells how Zampa, a 16th-century pirate, is dragged under the sea by the marble statue of the girl he has betrayed.

zapateado A Spanish dance in 3/4 time in which the rhythm is marked by stamping of the heels, rather than with castanets.

Zarlino, Gioseffo (?1517–90) Italian priest, composer, and theorist. He studied at Chioggia and by 1540 was organist at the cathedral there. In 1541 he went to Venice and studied with Adrian Willaert and in 1565 was appointed maestro at St Mark's. Zarlino's pupils included Claudio Merulo, Girolamo Diruta, and Giovanni Artusi. His *Le Istitutioni harmoniche* (1558) is one of the most important works of musical theory; in it he discusses the sonorous numbers and the Greek tonal system and sets out the rules of counterpoint, which are modelled on Willaert.

Zar und Zimmermann (*Tsar and Carpenter*) Opera in three acts by Lortzing with libretto by the composer based on the play by Mélesville, Merle, and de Boirie. First performance: Leipzig, 1837. Tsar Peter the Great (baritone) is working in the Saardem shipyards under the assumed name of Peter Michaelov.

zarzuela A type of Spanish comic opera, usually with music based on Spanish folk tunes and a satirical libretto some of which is spoken. Some improvisation is a feature of a zarzuela, in which the audience sometimes participates.

Zauberflöte, Die see **Magic Flute, The.**

Zauberharfe, Die (*The Magic Harp*) Incidental music for choir and orchestra by Schubert to the play of the same name by Hofmann. First performance: 1820. The overture is better known today as the *Rosamunde* overture (see **Rosamunde, Princess of Cyprus**).

Zelenka, Jan Dismas (1679–1745) Czech composer, a pupil of and Lotti. In 1710 he became a court musician in Dresden, returning there after two years in Vienna (from 1719) to work with Heinichen, whom he succeeded as director of church music in 1729. His works include many oratorios and other sacred music, chamber works, and concertos.

Zelter, Carl Friedrich (1758–1832) German composer, conductor, and teacher. In Berlin he was a pupil (1784–86) of Fasch, to whom he became assistant conductor at the Singakademie. In 1800 he succeeded Fasch and in 1807 founded the Ripienschule, an instrumental group to accompany the choir. He took an active part in the Bach revival. Zelter founded the *Liedertafel in 1809, when he also became music professor at the newly established University of Berlin. His compositions are chiefly choral works written for the Singakademie or the Liedertafel, but he also wrote some noteworthy songs as well as orchestral and keyboard music.

Zemlinsky, Alexander von (1871–1942) Austrian conductor and composer, in later life resident in the USA. He was the teacher and brother-in-law of Schoenberg, with whom he was associated in the promotion of new music in

Vienna. With Mahler's encouragement he enjoyed a successful career as a conductor and composer of operas. Zemlinsky's own works explored post-Wagnerian harmony but he never followed his composer-friends into atonality and later adopted a more conservative neoclassical manner. His output includes the operas *Sarema* (1897), *Es war einmal* (1900), *Eine florentinische Tragödie* (1917), *Der Zwerg* (1922), and *Der Kriederkreis* (1932), the *Maeterlinck Lieder* (1910), *Lyric Symphony* (1923), three symphonies, four string quartets, and numerous songs and piano pieces.

Ziehharmonika Accordion. [German]

Zigeunerbaron, Der see **Gypsy Baron, The.**

Zigeunerweisen (*Gypsy Airs*) Work for violin and piano (Op. 20) by Sarasate. Composed: 1878. The name refers to the imitation of Gypsy folk music in this work, which was later arranged for violin and orchestra.

Zimbalist, Efrem (1890–1985) US violinist. In addition to his international performing career, Zimbalist was director of the Curtis Institute (1941–68). Menotti dedicated his violin concerto to him.

Zimmerman, Franklin Bershir (1923–) US musicologist. In 1968 he became Professor of Music at the University of Pennsylvania. He is a noted scholar of the English baroque and of Purcell in particular: he has published a thematic catalogue of Purcell's works (see **Z.**) and a biography (1967) of the composer himself.

Zimmermann, Bernd-Alois (1918–70) German composer, a pupil of Jarnach, Fortner, and Leibowitz. After an early expressionist period he adopted total serialism. In the 1960s he developed a pluralist style, drawing on diverse elements (often quotations) in a collage technique that demonstrated his ideas on the spherical nature of time. The opera *Die Soldaten* (1960–65) applies these ideas in its treatment of time and use of quotation within a serial framework. Other works include an oboe concerto (1952), *Perspectives* (1955), *Présence* (1961), *Phototopsis* (1968), *Requiem für einen jungen Dichter* (1969), and *Stille und Umkehr* (1970).

Zingarelli, Niccolò Antonio (1752–1837) Italian composer and teacher. After studying in Naples he began composing operas for Italian theatres. He was musical director of Milan Cathedral (1793–94), of the Santa Casa, Loreto (1794–1804), and of St Peter's, Rome (1804–11). In 1813 he became principal of the Naples conservatory and in 1816 musical director of Naples Cathedral too. Zingarelli wrote over 40 operas (among them *Antigone, 1790; and Giulietta e Romeo*, 1796) but after 1811 he turned his attention to choral music, writing many functional liturgical works; he also wrote secular choral music and some instrumental works.

Zipoli, Domenico (1688–1726) Italian composer and organist, a pupil of Alessandro Scarlatti. He was appointed organist of the Jesuit church in Rome (1715), subsequently becoming a Jesuit priest (1716) and travelling to South America (1717), where he studied in Córdoba, Argentina. In addition to his famous book of keyboard music, *Sonate d'intavolatura* (1716), he wrote many masses, oratorios, and other sacred works.

zithers A group of stringed instruments of ancient origin in which the strings run the whole length of the instrument body. Primitive zithers exist in a variety of forms. In the **trough zither** the strings run above a trough in a hollowed-out piece of wood; in a **stick zither** they run along the top of a stick, to the base of which one or more resonators may be attached. The Indian *vīnā* is a sophisticated stick zither. The long zithers of China and Japan (see **koto; qin**) have a long board as a resonator. The Arabian **qanun** derives from these instruments and evolved into the European **board zithers**, in which the strings are stretched across the top of a board that forms the top of a box resonator. An early European board zither is the *psaltery. The qanun reached Europe in the 11th century and the psaltery remained popular until the end of the 17th century.

The modern zither is a popular European folk instrument and has five wire melody strings that run over a fretted fingerboard. These are stopped with the fingers of the left hand and plucked with a plectrum worn on the right thumb. The gut accompanying strings are plucked with the fingers of the right hand. The European zither was featured in Carol Reed's film *The Third Man* (1949) with music written and played by Anton Karas. Both the zither and Karas thereafter acquired world-wide popularity. The *dulcimer is a board zither struck with hammers and the piano is a board zither in which the hammers are operated by a keyboard.

zoppa, alla In a syncopated rhythm. [Italian, from *zoppo*, lame]

Zukerman, Pinchas (1948–) Israeli violinist. A pupil of Galamian, he launched his international career after his New York debut in 1969. He also plays the viola and conducts.

TABLE 1: NAMES OF NOTES AND RESTS

Note	Rest	British	American
𝄶	𝄺	breve	double-whole note
𝅝	𝄻	semibreve	whole note
𝅗𝅥	𝄼	minim	half note
𝅘𝅥	𝄽 or 𝄼	crotchet	quarter note
𝅘𝅥𝅮	𝄾	quaver	eighth note
𝅘𝅥𝅯	𝄿	semiquaver	sixteenth note
𝅘𝅥𝅰	𝅀	demisemiquaver	thirty-second note
𝅘𝅥𝅱	𝅁	hemidemisemiquaver	sixty-fourth note

TABLE 2: THE CLEFS

Clef	Fixed note	Position of Middle C
G *or* treble clef		
F or bass clef		
C (soprano) clef		
C (alto) clef		
C (tenor) clef		

TABLE 3: KEYS AND KEY SIGNATURES

Major Key	Relative Minor Key	Key Signature (sharp keys)	Key Signature (flat keys)
C	A		
G	E		
D	B		
A	F♯		
E	C♯		
B = C♭	G♯		
F♯ = G♭	E♭		
C♯ = D♭	B♭		
A♭	F		
E♭	C		
B♭	G		
F	D		

TABLE 4: TIME SIGNATURES

Simple Time

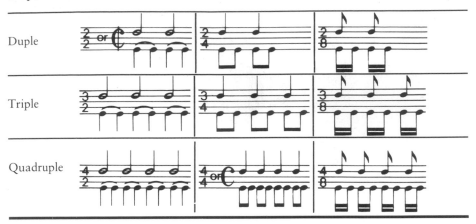

Duple			
Triple			
Quadruple			

Compound Time

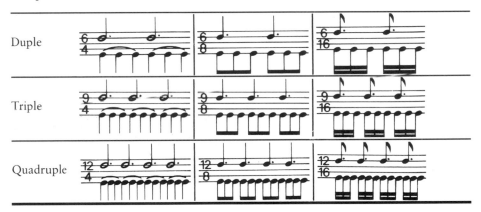

Duple			
Triple			
Quadruple			

ACKNOWLEDGEMENTS

The colour illustrations are reproduced by kind permission of the following collections: Catherine Ashmore 4, 16, 18, 20, 31, 34, 42; Clive Barda/London 43; Zoë Dominic 1, 9, 12, 17; Éditions Albert Skira 24; E.T. Archive 3, 7, 13; Mary Evans/Explorer 5, 8, 11, 14, 25, 38, 39; Mary Evans Picture Library 15, 40, 41, 44; Guy Gravett 23, 30, 32, 35; John Harris 27, 45; Museen der Stadt Erfurt 2; National Gallery, London 19; National Portrait Gallery 36; Novosti Press Agency 10, 26; Octopus Group Picture Library 21, 33; Photographie Giraudon 37; Royal College of Music 22; Reg Wilson 29; ZEFA 6, 28.

The black and white photographs were kindly supplied by: F Arborio Mella 94; Catherine Ashmore 129, 183, 193, 237, 317, 346; Erich Auerbach 9, 19, 20, 33 left, 33 right, 61, 67 left, 97, 128, 148, 158, 170, 192, 198, 219 bottom, 236 right, 238, 257, 295, 319, 320 bottom, 335, 337, 357, 360, 378, 390, 394, 401; Clive Barda/London 10, 42, 54 left, 54 right, 109, 146 left, 166, 219 top, 221, 222, 234 right, 251, 261, 273, 283, 284, 294, 304, 321 right, 349, Bassano Studios 356; Bildarchiv der Oster-reichische Nationalbibliothek 39, 224 bottom;Éts J.E. Bulloz 189; Camera Press 86; Jean-Loup Charmet 199; Zoë Dominic 14, 47, 62, 101, 104 right, 125, 228, 240, 259, 285, 313, 325, 365, 370, 373; Mary Evans Explorer 396; Mary Evans Picture Library 30, 72, 103, 136, 139, 154, 171, 181, 200, 234 left, 278, 301, 305, 309, 318, 321 left, 334, 336, 343 right, 348, 362, 372, 281, 392, 399; Guy Gravett 177, 224 top; Harlingue-Viollet 406; Hulton-Deutsch 28, 46, 70, 93, 113, 123, 143, 231, 236 left, 258 left, 276, 302, 328; Kobal Collection 15; Larousse 53, 115, 134, 174, 203, 258 right, 264; Lipnitzki-Viollet 108, 229; Mansell Collection 59, 67 right, 98, 104 left, 144, 146 right, 150, 169, 208, 209, 218, 230, 235, 239, 265, 275, 298, 341, 347, 359, 369; Musée Instrumental du Conservatoire de Paris 79; Novosti Press Agency 149, 195, 320 top, 343 left; Philips Classics Productions/Werner Neumeister 43; Photo-Pic 74; Popperfoto 159, 277, 333, 371, 375, 403; Roger-Viollet 119, 121, 184, 297; Royal College of Music 204; Sylvia Salmi 331; Richard H Smith 272; Teatro alla Scala 269; © 1989 Taurus/Klan 377; Welsh National Opera 34.